International
Human Rights Law

International Human Rights Law

Second Edition

Professor Javaid Rehman
Brunel University

Longman
is an imprint of

PEARSON

Harlow, England • London • New York • Boston • San Francisco • Toronto
Sydney • Tokyo • Singapore • Hong Kong • Seoul • Taipei • New Delhi
Cape Town • Madrid • Mexico City • Amsterdam • Munich • Paris • Milan

Pearson Education Limited

Edinburgh Gate
Harlow
Essex CM20 2JE
England

and Associated Companies throughout the world

Visit us on the World Wide Web at:
www.pearsoned.co.uk

———————————

First published 2003
Second edition published 2010

© Pearson Education Limited 2003, 2010

ISBN: 978-1-4058-1181-1

British Library Cataloguing-in-Publication Data
A catalogue record for this book is available from the British Library

Library of Congress Cataloging-in-Publication Data
Rehman, Javaid.
  International human rights law : a practical approach / Javaid Rehman. – 2nd ed.
     p. cm.
  ISBN 978-1-4058-1181-1 (pbk.)
  1. Human rights.   I. Title.
  K3240.R44 2009
  341.4′8—dc22

                                                                    2009031602

10 9 8 7 6 5 4 3 2 1
13 12 11 10 09

Typeset in 10/12 pt Minion by 35
Printed and bound in Great Britain by Henry Ling Ltd, Dorchester, Dorset

The publisher's policy is to use paper manufactured from sustainable forests.

Contents

Part IV
Group rights

Part V
Issues arising in international human rights law   713

20 International criminal law and international human rights law   715

21 International human rights law and international humanitarian law   764

Acknowledgements

Author's acknowledgements

The first edition of this book was published in 2002 and in this intervening period a lot of things have happened both to the world of human rights and to myself personally. There have been monumental changes in the entire frame of international human rights law: most of the previously written 16 chapters of the first edition therefore had to be thoroughly revised and re-written. The United Nations Human Rights Commission and its Sub-Commission – hitherto focal points of the practices and procedures of human rights activities within the United Nations – have been dismantled. This edition examines in detail the institutional changes brought about within the United Nations human rights machinery including the role, procedures and processes of the Human Rights Council and the Council's Advisory Committee. The jurisprudence of the Human Rights Committee as well as the Committee of International Covenant on Economic, Social and Cultural Rights (ICESCR) has expanded enormously: the adoption of the Optional Protocol to ICESCR in 2008 has heightened the interest and significance of economic, social and cultural rights. This volume takes account of the significant changes in the regional machinery, at the European, Inter-American and African level. Uniquely, this edition also examines the position of human rights within the other regions of the world in Chapter 11. This edition contains additional chapters on refugees and internally displaced person, rights of persons with disabilities and the rights of migrant workers and their families. The growing significance and interaction of international criminal law and international humanitarian law with human rights law has been captured in two further chapters. This edition also dedicates a full complete chapter to the crime of enforced disappearances and rights of the victims of such disappearances. The period between 2002–09 also witnessed innumerable assaults on human rights and minority rights under the banner of 'war on terror': the Iraq invasion and the Guantánamo Bay and Belmarsh detentions provide horrid memories of this era. The implications of the 'war on terror' on human rights law are examined in various chapters of this book.

At a more personal level, my youthful exuberance towards life has, I believe, given way to a more matured understanding of life and its issues. I have a greater appreciation of human values, as well as human rights and human dignity. My father was an inspirational figure in that he always campaigned for deprived and underprivileged communities: his death in 2007 remains an irrecoverable loss, and yet his vision continues to inspire me. The tragedy of my father's death was mitigated by the unstinting care, love and dedication from Maleeha and chatu jani – they remain my biggest joy in life. Without Maleeha's understanding, patience and support, this book would not have been possible. I also thank my mother, my sisters, their children and the wider family based in Pakistan for their considerable support at a time of considerable upheavals.

Many people have helped and supported me in writing this edition – too numerous to mention. Several of these colleagues read individual chapters and their critical observations improved the quality of the work. Others were always available to address any of my queries and questions. I would like to thank Professor Kaiyan Homi Kaikobad, Professor Ben Chigara,

Dr Alexandra Xanthaki, Dr Manisuli Ssenyonjo and Dr Mohamed Elewa Badar (all from Brunel Law School) for their very useful comments. I am also very grateful to Professor Rebecca Wallace (UHI Centre for Rural Childhood at Perth College), Dr Nazila Ghanea (Oxford University), Annapurna Waughray and Paul Okojie (Manchester Metropolitan University), Professor Sandy Ghandhi (Reading University), Peter Cumper (Leicester University), Dr George Letsas (UCL), Colm O'Cinneide (UCL and Vice President European Committee of Social Rights), Sonia Morano-Foadi (Oxford Brookes University), Dr Siobhán Mullally and Dr Siobhan Wills (University College Cork, Ireland), Dr Ayesha Shahid (Hull University), Dr Hélène Lambert (University of Westminster), Dr David Keane (Middlesex University), Dr Helen Stalford (Liverpool Law School), Dr Sylvie Langlaude (QUB), Anna Lawson and Dr Amrita Mukherjee (Leeds University) for their encouragement as well as their critical comments and observations on various chapters of this book. Amongst the United Nations Special Rapporteur and members of working groups and various committees, I would particularly like to thank Professor Shaheen Sardar Ali, Professor Patrick Thornberry, Sir Nigel Rodley, Professor Surya Subedi and Asma Jahangir for their advice and consistent encouragement on various human rights issues. My friend Kamran Arif has been a great source of strengthen and friendship and I remain grateful to him.

I would like to thank most sincerely my assistant Stephanie Berry for her hard work, support and dedication in completing this book. I would also like to thank Edward Guntrip and Alka Sood for his editorial assistant. I thank Harriet Hoffler for her overall support and assistance in the EURASIA-NET project. My special thanks to Owen Knight and to Anita Atkinson at Pearson Education for their kindness, support and encouragement throughout the duration of this project. The final product owes much to the careful editing of Linda Dhondy and I remain extremely thankful to her. I have tried to make the book current to 30 March 2009 although it has been possible to provide brief updates to subsequent legal developments.

Javaid Rehman
Uxbridge
April 2009

Publisher's acknowledgements

We are grateful to the following for permission to reproduce copyright material:

Extract on pages 62–5 from OHCHR Thematic Mandates, Rules of Procedure, reproduced with permission; Extract on page 611 from Fundamental Principles, *The UN Convention on the Rights of Persons with Disabilities* (United Nations 2006), http://www.un.org/disabilities/convention/conventionfull.shtml, reproduced with permission; Extract on page 615 from Article 2: Definitions, *The UN Convention on the Rights of Persons with Disabilities* (United Nations 2006), http://www.un.org/disabilities/convention/conventionfull.shtml, reproduced with permission; Extract on pages 613–4 from Article 24, *The UN Convention on the Rights of Persons with Disabilities* (United Nations 2006), http://www.un.org/disabilities/convention/conventionfull.shtml, reproduced with permission; Extract on page 791 from Legality of the threat or use of Nuclear Weapons, *Dissenting Opinion of Judge Higgins. Advisory Opinion of 8 July 1996* (United Nations), reproduced with permission.

In some instances we have been unable to trace the owners of copyright material, and we would appreciate any information that would enable us to do so.

Table of cases

International Courts and Tribunals

Permanent Court of International Justice

International Court of Justice

Contentious cases

United Nations Committee Against Torture (CAT)

Committee on the Elimination of Discrimination Against Women (CEDAW)

Committee on the Elimination of Racial Discrimination (CERD)

International Tribunals

International arbitration

Regional

European Committee of Social Rights

European Court of Justice

Inter-American Commission on Human Rights

Table of treaties

Treaties

International

Regional

African Union (previously the Organisation of African Unity)

Table of other documents

OSCE/CSCE

Abbreviations

AALR	Anglo-American Law Review
ACHR	American Convention on Human Rights
ACRWC	African Charter on the Rights and Welfare of the Child
ADHR	American Declaration of the Rights and Duties of Man
AFCHPR	African Charter on Human and Peoples' Rights
AJIL	American Journal of International Law
ALJ	Australian Law Journal
American ULR	American University Law Review
APJEL	Asia Pacific Journal of Environmental Law
ASEAN	Association of South-East Asian Nations
AU	African Union
AUJILP	American University Journal of International Law and Policy
AYBIL/AYIL	Australian Yearbook of International Law
Buff LR	Buffalo Law Review
BYIL	British Year Book of International Law
CalWestILJ	California Western International Law Journal
CAT	Committee against Torture
CDHRI	Cairo Declaration on Human Rights in Islam
CEDAW	Committee on the Elimination of Discrimination against Women
CERD	The Committee on the Elimination of Racial Discrimination
CHRLR	Columbia Human Rights Law Review
CJIL	Chinese Journal of International Law
CLF	Criminal Law Forum
CLJ	Cambridge Law Journal
CLP	Current Legal Problems
COE	Council of Europe
Col.JTL	Columbia Journal of Transnational Law
Conn. J. Int'l L.	Connecticut Journal of International Law
CRC	Convention on the Rights of the Child
CRPD	The UN Convention on the Rights of Persons with Disabilities
CSW	Commission on the Status of Women
CYBIL	Canadian Year Book of International Law
Denver JIP	Denver Journal of International Law and Policy
Duke J. Comp. & Int'l L.	Duke Journal of Comparative and International Law
Duke LJ	Duke Law Journal
ESC	European Social Charter
E.T.S	European Treaty Series
ECHR	The Convention for the Protection of Human Rights and Fundamental Freedoms (European Convention on Human Rights)

ECJ	European Court of Justice
ECOSOC	Economic and Social Council
EHRLR	*European Human Rights Law Review*
EJIL	*European Journal of International Law*
EL Rev	*European Law Review*
ESC	European Social Charter
EU	European Union
Eur. J. Migrat. Law	*European Journal of Migration and Law*
GA.JICL	*Georgia Journal of International and Comparative Law*
GAOR	General Assembly Official Records
Geo. Imm. L. J.	*Georgetown Immigration Law Journal*
GYIL	*German Year Book of International Law*
Harv. Hum. Rts. J.	*Harvard Human Rights Journal*
Harv. Int'l L.J./	
Harvard Int. L.J	*Harvard International Law Journal*
HCNM	High Commissioner on National Minorities
HRC	Human Rights Committee
HRCP	Human Rights Commission of Pakistan
HRLJ	*Human Rights Law Journal*
HRLR	*Human Rights Law Review*
HRQ	*Human Rights Quarterly*
I.L.M.	International Legal Materials
ICC	International Criminal Court
ICCPR	International Covenant on Civil and Political Rights
ICESCR	International Covenant on Economic, Social and Cultural Rights
ICJ	International Court of Justice
ICL	International Criminal Law
ICLQ	*International and Comparative Law Quarterly*
ICRMW	International Convention on the Protection of the Rights of All Migrant Workers and Members of Their Families
ICTR	International Criminal Tribunal for Rwanda
ICTY	International Criminal Tribunal for the Former Yugoslavia
IDPs	Internally Displaced Persons
IHHR	*International Human Rights Reports*
IHL	*International Humanitarian Law*
IJCL	*International Journal of Constitutional Law*
IJIL	*Indian Journal of International Law*
IJLF	*International Journal of Law and Family*
IJMGR	*International Journal on Minority and Group Rights*
IJRL	*International Journal of Refugee Law*
ILA	International Law Association
ILC	International Law Commission
ILO	International Labour Organization
ILR	*International Law Reports*
Iowa LR	*Iowa Law Review*
Israel L.R.	*Israel Law Review*

IRO	International Refugee Organization
IYHR/IYBHR	*Israel Year Book on Human Rights*
JAL	*Journal of African Law*
JILP	*Journal of International Law and Policy*
JOLS	*Journal of Law and Society*
LJIL	*Leiden Journal of International Law*
LQR	*Law Quarterly Review*
McGill L.R.	*McGill Law Review*
Melbourne JIL/MJIL	*Melbourne Journal of International Law*
MLR	*Modern Law Review*
MRG	Minority Rights Group
NGOs	Non-Governmental Organisations
NILR	*Netherlands International Law Review*
NILR	*Netherlands International Law Review*
NJHR	*Nordic Journal of Human Rights*
NLMs	National Liberation Movements
Nordic JIL	*Nordic Journal of International Law*
Northern Ireland Legal Q.	*Northern Ireland Legal Quarterly*
NQHR	*Netherlands Quarterly of Human Rights*
NYIL	*Netherlands Year Book of International Law*
NYUJILP	*New York University Journal of International Law and Politics*
O.A.S.T.S	Organization of American States Treaty Series
OAS	Organization of American States
OAU	Organization of African Unity
ODIHR	The Office for Democratic Institutions and Human Rights
OHCHR	Office of the High Commissioner for Human Rights
OIC	Organization of the Islamic Conference
OP–CRC–AC	Optional Protocol to the Convention on the Rights of the Child on the Involvement of Children in Armed Conflict
OP–CRC–SC	Optional Protocol to the Convention on the Rights of the Child on the Sale of Children, Child Prostitution, and Child Pornography
OSCE	The Organization for Security and Co-operation in Europe
PASIL	*Proceedings of the American Society of International Law*
Penn. St. L. Rev.	*Penn State Law Review*
Race Convention	International Convention on the Elimination of All Forms of Racial Discrimination
Rec. des Cours	*Recueil des Cours de l'Académie de Droit International*
SAARC	South Asian Association for Regional Co-operation
Stan. J.Int. Law	*Stanford Journal of International Law*
Tex.ILJ/Texas ILJ	*Texas International Law Journal*
Transnat'l L. & Contemp. Probs.	*Transnational. Law & Contemporary Problems*
U Tas LR	*University of Tasmania Law Review*
U.K.T.S	United Kingdom Treaty Series
U.N.T.S	United Nations Treaty Series
UDHR	The Universal Declaration of Human Rights

UN	The United Nations
UNESCO	United Nations Educational, Scientific and Cultural Organization
UNHCR	The Office of UN High Commissioner for Refugees
Va.JIL/VJIL	*Virginia Journal of International Law*
Valparaiso Univ. L.Rev	*Valparaiso University Law Review*
Vand.JTL	*Vanderbilt Journal of Transnational Law*
VCLT	Vienna Convention on the Law of Treaties
W.L.R	*Weekly Law Reports*
WGAD	Working Group on Arbitrary Detention
WGEID	Working Group on Enforced and Involuntary Disappearances
WHO	World Health Organization
Yale LJ	*Yale Law Journal*
YBIHL	*Year Book of International Humanitarian Law*
YBILC	*Year Book of the International Law Commission*
YBUN	*Year Book of the United Nations*
YEL	*Year Book of European Law*
YJIL	*Yale Journal of International Law*
Y.B. World Aff.	*Year Book of World Affairs*

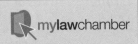

Part I

International legal systems and the
development of human rights law

1   Introduction

Just as the French Revolution ended the divine rights of kings, the human rights revolution that began at the 1945 San Francisco Conference of the United Nations has deprived the sovereign states of the lordly privilege of being the sole possessors of rights under international law. States have had to concede to ordinary human beings the status of subjects of international law, to concede that individuals are no longer mere objects, mere pawns in the hands of states.[1]

1   HUMAN RIGHTS OF THE INDIVIDUAL IN INTERNATIONAL LAW[2]

The emergence of human rights law in the international sphere is one of the most significant developments to have taken place since the end of the Second World War.[3] International human rights law has challenged and jettisoned the traditional rules relating to State sovereignty. These traditional rules perceived international law as a law primarily related to sovereign States in which non-State actors, in particular individuals, had very little role to play. A key aspect of the traditional legal order was the reliance of States upon the principle of non-interference in their domestic affairs, which meant that violations of human rights were not a matter of international concern.[4]

---

[1] Sohn, 'The New International Law: Protection of the Rights of Individuals Rather than States' 32 *American ULR* (1982) 1 at p. 1.

[2] See Cassese, *Human Rights in a Changing World* (Temple University Press, 1990); Feldman, *Civil Liberties and Human Rights in England and Wales* (Oxford University Press, 2001) pp. 34–112; Harris, *Cases and Materials on International Law* (Sweet & Maxwell, 2004) pp. 654–785; Henkin (ed.), *The International Bill of Rights* (Columbia University Press, 1981); Mahoney and Mahoney (eds), *Human Rights in the Twenty-First Century, A Global Challenge* (Martinus Nijhoff Publishers, 1993); McDougal, Lasswell, Chen, *Human Rights and World Public Order: The Basic Policies of an International Law of Human Dignity* (Yale University Press, 1980); Meron (ed.), *Human Rights in International Law: Legal and Policy Issues* (Clarendon Press, 1984); Robertson and Merrills, *Human Rights in the World: An Introduction to the Study of the International Protection of Human Rights* (Manchester University Press, 1996); Tomuschat, *Human Rights: Between Idealism and Realism* (Oxford University Press, 2008); and Weissbrodt and de la Vega, *International Human Rights Law, An Introduction* (University of Pennsylvania Press, 2007) pp. 251–270.

[3] Lauterpacht, *International Law and Human Rights* (F.A. Praeger, 1950); Oda, 'The Individual in International Law' in Sørensen (ed.), *Manual of Public International Law* (MacMillan, 1968) pp. 469–530; Robertson and Merrills, above n.2; these developments are considered in detail in subsequent chapters of this book.

[4] See Bilder, 'An Overview of International Human Rights Law' in Hannum (ed.), *Guide to International Human Rights Practice* (Transnational Publishers, 2004) pp. 3–18 at p. 4.

In historical terms, the rights of individuals (with the limited exceptions of treatment of aliens and arguably that of humanitarian intervention) was a subject that was not addressed by international law.[5] Even in relation to the aforementioned exceptions, the international legal order represented the dominance of States without according individuals any specific rights. Thus, in the absence of an independent legal personality for individuals, if their rights were violated by a foreign State, it was the State of the victim that was authorised to bring a claim for violation of their rights. In the case of humanitarian intervention, while force was sometimes used to intervene militarily to protect (primarily religious) minorities, such actions were often accompanied (if not dictated) by selfish motives, e.g. territorial gains.[6] Individuals themselves were unable to claim the right of humanitarian intervention nor was there a wholesale recognition of any such right at the global level.[7]

The growth and expansion of human rights law has brought about a radical change to the ideological bases of international law. Such a change is evident through a variety of ways. Firstly, it is now well established that investigations into human rights abuses can not be prevented by arguments based upon the principle of State sovereignty and domestic jurisdiction.[8] These are concerns for the international community as a whole, with the growing recognition that the protection of fundamental human rights is an obligation *erga omnes*.[9] Secondly, as we shall consider in this book, since the last quarter of the twentieth century there have been monumental changes in the bodies dealing with human rights issues, as well as a mushrooming of international human rights instruments. Specific treaties focusing *inter alia* upon the prohibition of racial discrimination, torture, enforced disappearances and those defining and promoting children's and women's rights have been adopted.

Further significant modifications have taken place in field of human rights during the opening years of the new millennium. The United Nations Human Rights Council was established in 2006, abolishing the Human Rights Commission.[10] New procedures of review of State practices have been brought into operation, and human rights is now fortunately beginning to engage with highly significant (although previously ignored)

---

[5] See McGoldrick, *The Human Rights Committee: Its Role in the Development of the International Covenant on Civil and Political Rights* (Clarendon Press, 1991) p. 3.

[6] For a survey of the literature on the subject see Tesón, *Humanitarian Intervention: An Inquiry into Law and Morality* (Transnational Publishers, 1998); Ronzitti, *Rescuing Nationals Abroad through Military Coercion and Intervention on Grounds of Humanity* (Martinus Nijhoff Publishers, 1985); Franck and Rodley, 'After Bangladesh: The Law of Humanitarian Intervention by Military Force' 67 *AJIL* (1973) 275; Lillich (ed.), *Humanitarian Intervention and the United Nations* (University Press of Virginia, 1973); Lillich, 'Intervention to Protect Human Rights' 15 *McGill LR* (1969) 205; Behuniak, 'The Law of Unilateral Humanitarian Intervention by Armed Force: A Legal Survey' 79 *Military Law Review* (1978) 157; Fonteyne, 'The Customary International Law Doctrine of Humanitarian Intervention: Its Current Validity under the UN Charter' 4 *Cal.WestILJ* (1974) 203; Kritsiotis, 'Reappraising Policy Objections to Humanitarian Intervention' 19 *Michigan Journal of International Law* (1998) p. 1005.

[7] Since the ending of the cold war, the Security Council under Chapter VII of the United Nations has on occasion authorised collective armed intervention in response to gross violations of human rights. See Chesterman, *Just War or Just Peace* (Clarendon Press, 2001); Alston, 'The Security Council and Human Rights: Lessons to be Learned from the Iraq-Kuwait Crisis and its Aftermath' 13 *AYBIL* (1990–91) 107; Adelman, 'Humanitarian Intervention: The Case of Kurds' 4 *IJRL* (1992) 4; Malanczuk, 'The Kurdish Crises and Allied Intervention in the Aftermath of the Second Gulf War' 2 *EJIL* (1991) 114; see further chapter 3 below.

[8] Sands and Klein, *Bowett's Law of International Institutions* (Sweet & Maxwell, 2001) p. 24.

[9] See *Barcelona Traction, Light and Power Company, Limited Case (Belgium v. Spain)*, Judgment 5 February 1970, (1970) ICJ Reports 3, 32; Jennings and Watts, *Oppenheim's International Law* (Longman, 1992) vol. 1, at p. 5.

[10] See GA Res. 60/251 (3 April 2006) www2.ohchr.org/english/bodies/hrcouncil/docs/A.RES.60.251_En.pdf <last visited 1 January 2009>.

areas such as the human rights of disabled persons.[11] Thirdly, the setting up of various mechanisms to publicise, promote and protect human rights has heightened human rights awareness which has had a significant impact on other areas of international law such as international criminal law, international refugee law and international humanitarian law. Fourthly, the procedural advancement of international human rights law has meant that individuals, groups and other non-State actors are more directly involved in challenging violations of their rights and have a more recognised role within international courts, committees and tribunals.

Notwithstanding these advances, in practice human rights law continues to be constrained and limited. Subsequent chapters establish that not only are there substantive weaknesses in existing rights, the application of these rights is impaired by the absences, weaknesses and limitations of implementation mechanisms and procedures. Our analysis will elaborate upon many of these weaknesses and limitations. The lack of enforcement machinery impinges upon all areas of international law, although its impact is felt most vividly and fully in human rights law.

2 STRUCTURE OF THE BOOK

This book has been divided into five parts and consists of 24 chapters. These introductory comments represent the first chapter within Part I of the book, which is entitled 'International Legal System and the Development of Human Rights Law'. This introductory chapter also provides a brief consideration to a number of themes and concepts which consistently recur in this book; a proper understanding of these forms an essential prerequisite to a comprehensive understanding of the subject. The overall objective of Part I is to provide an overview of the essential jurisprudential background to the subject, the nature of modern international law, the United Nations System and its relationship with modern human rights law. Chapter 2 elaborates upon the nature, characteristics and sources of public international law and in so doing relates these issues to the development and operation of international human rights law. In the light of the *sui generis* character of international law and in recognition of the fact that international human rights law is a branch of public international law such an analysis appears necessary. Chapter 3 – also contained in Part I – deals with the United Nations system and its relationship with the modern human rights regime. This chapter provides consideration of the principal organs of the United Nations with particular reference to their role in protecting human rights.

Part II of the Study is entitled 'The International Bill of Rights'. It consists of three chapters and examines in depth the Universal Declaration of Human Rights (UDHR),[12] the International Covenant on Civil and Political Rights (ICCPR)[13] and the International Covenant on Economic, Social, and Cultural Rights (ICESCR).[14] Part III of the book analyses the regional protection of human rights. The oldest and by far the most advanced system of regional protection of human rights is the Council of Europe's European

---

[11] International Convention of the Rights of Persons with Disabilities and its Optional Protocol, UN GAOR, 61st Sess., Item 67(b), UN Doc. A/61/611 (6 Dec. 2006).

[12] GA Res. 217A (III), UN Doc. A/810 at 71 (1948).

[13] New York, 16 December 1966 United Nations, 999 U.N.T.S. 171; 6 I.L.M. (1967) 368.

[14] New York, 16 December 1966, 993 U.N.T.S. 3; 6 I.L.M. (1967) 360.

Convention on Human Rights (ECHR):[15] the jurisprudence of the Convention is examined in considerable detail in Chapter 7. Chapter 7 also considers the implementation mechanisms of ECHR and the difficulties arising out of the huge case-load now confronting the European Court of Human Rights. The work of the Council of Europe in the context of protecting social and economic rights is also of great value and is examined in Chapter 8. Chapter 8 also considers the role of two other regional organisations, the European Union (EU) and Organisation for Security and Co-operation in Europe (OSCE). As this chapter establishes, both these inter-governmental organisations are increasingly involved in promoting various strands of human rights. Chapter 9 analyses the interesting though complex protection afforded to the Americas by the Inter-American System of Human Rights. Chapter 10 examines the African Charter on Human and Peoples' Rights (AFCHPR).[16] The AFCHPR is potentially the most innovative of all human rights treaties. A detailed study of this Charter reveals a number of interesting features, which also represents a distinctly African character of rights and approach towards human rights protection. The final chapter of Part III, Chapter 11, examines regional systems and institutions which are rather less well-established and are less known. Despite their current limitations, this consideration is justified on the premise that these mechanisms have the potential to positively impact various regions across the globe. Such an exercise also aims to cover an important lacuna in the study of international human rights – whilst there is considerable jurisprudence built on European, Inter-American and African system of human rights, there is a dearth of materials on other potentially significant regional schemes operating in the Middle-East, the Islamic world and South-Asia. The chapter presents brief overviews of the developments in the context of the Arab League, the Organisation of Islamic Conference (OIC) and the South Asian Association for Regional Cooperation (SAARC).

Part IV of the book analyses the position of individuals *qua* group members. Although distinctions based on group rights are not simplistic, the chapters in this part of the study focus on racial and religious discrimination, minorities, indigenous peoples, women, children, the disabled, refugees and internally displaced persons and migrant workers and members of their families. Chapter 12 of the book explores the issue of equality and non-discrimination. Although recognised as the linchpin of modern human rights, the discussion underlines the complexities in generating *de facto* equality within societies which have historically been burdened with inequities. Chapter 13 of the study examines another controversial subject – the rights of minorities in international law. Chapter 14 engages with the concept of 'Peoples' in international law. The relevance of 'Peoples' is highlighted in the context of the controversial right of self-determination – a right which has acquired a *jus cogens* character within international law.[17] 'Peoples' right to self-determination has impacted numerous areas of international law, although controversy continues to surround the meaning and content of this right, particularly in the post-colonial context. The application of self-determination insofar as indigenous peoples are concerned has also been a matter of considerable conjuncture and is assessed in Chapter 14. The interest in the position of indigenous peoples has been heightened not only by the increasing

---

[15] ETS No. 005 213 U.N.T.S. 222, entered into force 3 September 1953, as amended by Protocols Nos 3, 5, and 8 which entered into force on 21 September 1970, 20 December 1971 and 1 January 1990 respectively.

[16] African [Banjul] Charter on Human and Peoples' Rights, adopted 27 June 1981, OAU Doc. CAB/LEG/67/3 rev. 5, 21 I.L.M. 58 (1982), entered into force 21 October 1986.

[17] For an elaboration of the meaning of *jus cogens* see below chapter 2.

acknowledgment of the rights of indigenous peoples within international law, but also due to the adoption of the Declaration of Indigenous Peoples by the General Assembly in 2007.[18]

Women and children have both in historic and contemporary terms suffered from various forms of discrimination. International human rights law has attempted to overcome this discrimination through the adoption a number of treaties, the primary ones being the Convention on the Elimination of All Forms of Discrimination against Women (1979)[19] and the Convention on the Rights of the Child (1989).[20] Both these conventions have had considerable support from the international community of States with overwhelming ratifications and accessions, and yet as Chapters 15 and 16 elaborate, there are serious difficulties in respect of application and implementation. Disability and the human rights of disabled persons within international law has until recently remained an unexplored area. In the light of the adoption of the International Convention on the Rights of Persons with Disabilities and its rapid acceptance by the international community, Chapter 17 examines the rights of disabled person and the impact of this treaty.[21] Chapter 18 examines in detail the issues confronting refugees and internally displaced persons. Chapter 19, the final chapter in Part IV, assesses another less examined although highly significant area of international human rights – the rights of migrant workers and their families.

The final part of the book – Part V – deals with specific issues concerning international human rights law. Chapter 20 examines issues arising from international criminal law whereas Chapter 21 explores the relationship of international humanitarian law with international human rights law. The final three chapters of Part V are concerned with specific crimes against the dignity of mankind. Chapter 22 analyses the unfortunate (although widely practised) crime of torture against individuals. This chapter presents a detailed survey of efforts on the part of the international community to condemn torture, cruel, inhuman and degrading treatment or punishment. Chapter 23 examines the tragic practice of enforced disappearances and explores the international community's efforts to curb this scourge. On 20 December 2006, the United Nations General Assembly adopted the International Convention for the Protection of All Persons from Enforced Disappearance.[22] Although the UN Convention has yet to come into force, as the chapter argues the Convention could prove to be a useful tool in the armoury of international human rights law in combating arbitrary and enforced disappearances. The concluding chapter of Part V and the entire book, considers the subject of terrorism and its role in violating fundamental human rights. The evil of terrorism has been confronted by a number of States, and in some cases for very long and sustained periods. As we shall consider, although several instruments have been adopted to combat terrorism, recent political events have highlighted the inadequacies of the existing regime to protect individuals from international and national terrorism. On the other hand, the initiation of the so-called 'war on terror' has led to a serious erosion of human rights and civil liberties.

---

[18] United Nations Declaration on the Rights of the Indigenous Peoples, UN Doc. A/RES/61/295.

[19] International Convention on the Elimination of All Forms of Discrimination against Women, New York, 18 December 1979 United Nations, *Treaty Series*, vol. 1249, p. 13.

[20] Convention on the Rights of the Child, New York, 20 November 1989 United Nations, *Treaty Series*, vol. 1577, p. 3.

[21] Convention on the Rights of Persons with Disabilities, New York, 13 December 2006 UN Doc. A/61/611.

[22] International Convention for the Protection of All Persons from Enforced Disappearance, New York, 20 December 2006, UN Doc. A/61/488.

3 THEMES IN INTERNATIONAL HUMAN RIGHTS LAW

(i) Universalism and regionalism[23]

There has been a long-standing philosophical debate over the nature, categorisation and prioritisation of rights. There is also a debate about the universality of human rights norms. Is the content and scope of rights variable according to regional, religious and political backgrounds or is there is a single set of human rights applicable to every individual? The debate upon the issue of universality has been a divisive one with challenges being presented on the basis of regional, cultural and religious distinctions.[24] Advocates of universalism take the position that human rights are global in nature and belong to every human being, regardless of gender, colour, race, ethnicity, religion or regional and geographical background. Proponents of regionalism, for example, those purporting Asian or African regionalism, have advocated the establishment of distinct systems.[25] The Islamic States – as represented by the Organisation of the Islamic Conference – which form a significant block, have advanced their standards of human rights. The Islamic States claim that primacy should be accorded to the *Sharia*, even if it were to be in conflict with modern norms of human rights law.[26]

The consideration of this debate, its reasoning and outcome is not purely academic but has contributed to a varying set of standards. Furthermore, localised breaches of human rights standards in respect of, for example, minorities, refugees or the prohibition of terrorism can have a global impact. Yet at the same time, regional diversities, outlook and methods in dealing with these issues has resulted in a differing or sometimes varying set of standards.[27] This book considers these standards and their effectiveness is analysed in the context of international and regional mechanisms for the protection of human rights. At the international level, views differ on such fundamental issues as the rights of women, children and religious minorities. Another lively although inconclusive debate centres around criminal process and the compatibility of certain punishments with modern human

---

[23] See Brems, *Human Rights: Universality and Diversity* (Kluwer Law International, 2001); Donnelly, 'Cultural Relativism and Universal Human Rights' 6 *HRQ* (1984) 400; Donoho, 'Relativism Versus Universalism in Human Rights: The Search for Meaningful Standards' 27 *Stanford Law Journal* (1991) 345; Eide, 'Making Human Rights Universal: Unfinished Business' 6 *NJHR* (1988) 51; Espiell, 'The Evolving Concept of Human Rights: Western, Socialist and Third World Approaches' in Ramcharan (ed.), *Human Rights: Thirty Years after the Universal Declaration: Commemorative Volume on the Occasion of the Thirtieth Anniversary of the Universal Declaration of Human Rights* (Brill, 1979) pp. 41–65; Renteln, 'The Unanswered Challenge of Relativism and Consequences of Human Rights' 7 *HRQ* (1985) 514; Renteln, *International Human Rights: Universalism versus Relativism* (Sage Publications, 1990).

[24] See Arzt, 'The Application of International Human Rights Law in Islamic States' 12 *HRQ* (1990) 202; Sullivan, 'Advancing the Freedom of Religion or Belief through the UN Declaration on the Elimination of Religious Intolerance and Discrimination' 82 *AJIL* (1988) 487; An-Na'im, 'Religious Minorities under Islamic Law and the Limits of Cultural Relativism' 9 *HRQ* (1987) 1.

[25] See Nguema, 'Human Rights Perspective in Africa: the Roots of a Constant Challenge' 11 *HRLJ* (1990) 261; Ibhawoh, 'Cultural Relativism and Human Rights: Reconsidering the Africanist Discourse' 19 *NQHR* (2001) 43; Subedi, 'Are the Principles of Human Rights "Western" Ideas? An Analysis of the Claim of the "Asian" Concept of Human Rights from the Perspectives of Hinduism' 30 *Cal.WILJ* (1999) 45.

[26] See Report on the Human Rights Situation in the Islamic Republic of Iran by the Special Representatives of the Commission, UN Doc. E/CN.4/1987/23 (1987). Also see the Reservations made by Islamic States to the Convention on the Elimination of All forms of Discrimination Against Women (1979) and the Convention on the Rights of the Child (1989). Discussed below chapters 15 and 16. Schabas, 'Reservations to the Convention on the Rights of the Child' 18 *HRQ* (1996) 472.

[27] See Claude, *Swords into Plowshares* (Random House, 1984) at p. 102.

rights values. In some instances (e.g. minority rights or rights of indigenous peoples) significant differences have led to a failure in formulating comprehensive legally binding instruments. In some others (e.g. the rights of women and children) the strength of international consensus has been diluted through large-scale reservations placed by States parties to the relevant treaties. Subsequent chapters will consider the controversies that exist amongst States on such issues as the prohibition of capital and corporal punishments.[28] In the light of these dissensions and disagreements, Waldron's point has credence that 'the idea [that] there might be such things as *human rights*, valid for all peoples in all times and places, has often seemed implausible in the face of wide variety of what we would call "oppressive" and "inhuman" practices that are taken for granted – even expected – in different parts of the world'.[29]

The existing variations in approach towards human rights (both in terms of substantive rights and implementation mechanisms) are considered through a study of the European, American and African systems. In addition to the aforementioned regional systems, the study briefly examines other human rights systems including those established under the auspices of the Arab League and the South Asian Association of Regional Cooperation (SAARC), which adopt a relativist approach.[30] As this book discusses, it is important to note that in recent years, with the rise of the pan-Islamic movement, Islamic States have propagated a distinct human rights code.[31] There is no single, simple answer to the complex subject of prioritising regionalism over universalism. Having examined and assessed these divergencies, it can be contended that cultural relativism and universalism are not incompatible with each other. Universal human rights values have now matured to such an extent to defy the justification or rationalisation of such practices as genocide, torture, female genital mutilation or physical amputations; cultural or religious relativism is no longer a shield for protecting theocracies or dictatorial regimes and for the denial of the rule of law. This book recommends that while legitimate variations exist between various versions of human rights, there is a central core of all human rights values. This central core represents the most fundamental of human rights from which no derogations are permissible.

(ii) Interdependence of human rights[32]

The varied perceptions of human rights have also led to claims that there are 'three generations' of human rights. The so-called 'first generation' of human rights is represented by civil and political rights and can be found in treaties such as the ICCPR and ECHR. These rights have traditionally been associated with, and have been given priority by, Western

---

[28] See in particular below chapters 5, 7, 10 and 11.

[29] Waldron, 'Introduction' in Waldron (ed.), *Theories of Rights* (Oxford University Press, 1984) pp. 1–20, at p. 3 (emphasis provided).

[30] Ahsan, *SAARC: A Perspective* (University of California Press, 1992) An-Na'im, 'Human Rights in the Arab World: A Regional Perspective' 23 *HRQ* (2001) 701.

[31] See the Islamic Universal Declaration of Human Rights (1981). For further analysis see Mayer, *Islam and Human Rights: Tradition and Politics* (Westview Press, 1999); Rehman, 'Accommodating Religious Identities in an Islamic State: International Law, Freedom of Religion and the Rights of Religious Minorities' 7 *IJMGR* (2000) 139.

[32] See below Part II and Part III. Steiner, Alston and Goodman (eds), *International Human Rights in Context* (Oxford University Press, 2008) pp. 263–374; Scott, 'Reaching Beyond (without Abandoning) the Category of "Economic, Social and Cultural Rights"' 21 *HRQ* (1999) 633; Leckie, 'Another Step Towards Indivisibility: Identifying the Key Features of Violations of Economic, Social and Cultural Rights' 20 *HRQ* (1998) 81.

States. The social, economic and cultural rights are equated with the 'second generation' of human rights. These rights have been canvassed very strongly by the socialist countries and by the developing world. Views on the value and application of the two generations of rights differ markedly. The first generation of rights has often been given priority over second-generation rights. It is generally viewed that civil and political rights could be implemented immediately, whereas economic social and cultural rights can be introduced only progressively. It is also argued that the application of civil and political rights is less costly (as the State is required to abstain from certain activities, e.g. not to engage in torture) and that civil and political rights are justiciable whereas economic, social and cultural rights are not. As this study examines, the assumption that economic, social and cultural rights are of a lesser value, lack the properties of justiciability or are devoid of legal validity have been challenged vociferously by human rights bodies. The arguments supporting the lack of justiciablity and impracticability of the implementation of economic, social and cultural rights have been weakened by the recent adoption of the Optional Protocol to the International Covenant on Economic, Social and Cultural Rights.[33] Furthermore, the claim that economic, social and cultural rights (*vis-à-vis* civil and political obligations) are much more difficult to implement since they require considerably greater resources represents a grossly oversimplified assessment – many civil and political rights, such as the provision of the right to a fair trial to all communities in a State are incredibly financially demanding.[34]

In the last quarter of the twentieth century, another generation of human rights, the 'third generation' of rights emerged. The idea of the 'third generation' of rights was supported largely by the developing world. This set of rights includes collective group rights and such rights as the right to self-determination, the right to environment and more controversially a possible right to development.[35] In our analysis of the subject, whilst appreciating the various viewpoints on the nature and scope of human rights, it is important to adopt a holistic approach. This approach follows the principles established by UDHR, which affords recognition to all generations of rights. Modern human rights instruments increasingly recognise and incorporate all three generations of rights. This book argues that it is important to accord equal protection and importance to all sets of rights and to acknowledge that 'all human rights are universal, indivisible and inter-dependent and interrelated'.[36]

(iii) The scope of human rights law – individual and group rights[37]

For much of the period since 1945, the focus of modern international human rights law has been upon the rights of the individual. The issue of minority rights has remained

---

[33] Protocol to the International Covenant on Economic, Social and Cultural Rights, 10 December 2008, UN Doc. A/RES/63/117. See below chapter 6.

[34] Eide, 'Economic, Social and Cultural Rights as Human Rights' in Eide, Krause and Rosas (eds), *Economic, Social and Cultural Rights* (Brill, 2001) at p. 24.

[35] As this book shall examine in greater detail, the idea of 'third generation' of rights has now been further additions and innovations of 'fourth generation' and 'fifth generation' of rights. See Kayess and French, 'Out of Darkness into Light? Introducing the Convention on the Rights of Persons with Disabilities' 8 *HRLR* 1, pp. 32–33; discussed further in chapter 19 below.

[36] United Nations World Conference on Human Rights, *Vienna Declaration and Programme of Action* (1993) para 5 (pt 1). Adopted 25 June 1993.

[37] See below Chapter 12–14; see Thornberry, *International Law and the Rights of Minorities* (Clarendon Press, 1991); Rehman, *The Weaknesses in the International Protection of Minority Rights* (Kluwer Law International, 2000).

peripheral to human rights notwithstanding the fact that often individuals are victimised or discriminated against because they belong to a particular ethnic, racial, religious, social or political group. It is therefore not surprising to note that only a limited discussion of the subject of minority rights can be found in classical international human rights textbooks. The events of the past three decades have (alongside significant changes in global political geography) brought a shift in the approach of international community. The tragedies of Rwanda and the former Yugoslavia prompted the United Nations to establish *ad hoc* tribunals to try and punish those involved in, *inter alia*, crimes against humanity and genocide.[38] In 1998, the Statute of the International Criminal Court was adopted and came into force on 1 July 2002.[39] The International Criminal Court has the jurisdiction to try individuals for serious violations of human rights including genocide and crimes against humanity. While the International Criminal Court has thus far proved disappointing in its failure to conduct any successful prosecutions, there are nevertheless discernable signs that perpetrators of crimes against humanity and genocide may not always escape justice.[40]

International and regional organisations have also been active in further standard setting for the promotion of the rights of minorities and indigenous peoples. In 1989 the International Labour Organisation (ILO) adopted the Convention Concerning Indigenous and Tribal Peoples in Independent Countries, ILO No. 169[41] and in December 1992 the United Nations General Assembly approved a resolution on the Rights of Persons belonging to National or Ethnic, Religious and Linguistic Minorities.[42] Further important developments have taken place through the appointment of Ms Gay McDougall appointed as the first Independent Expert on Minority Issues in 2005 and the establishment of the Forum on Minority Issues on 28 September 2007.[43] As we have already noted a giant leap towards global standard-setting for indigenous peoples was undertaken through the General Assembly's adoption of a Declaration on Indigenous Peoples in 2007.[44]

The Council of Europe, and other regional organisations have also adopted a number of instruments, which aim to protect minorities. The Council of Europe's Framework Convention for the Protection of National Minorities (1994) is of particular importance in this regard.[45] Within the changing global environment, claims from minority and indigenous groups are having a substantial impact on the theory and practice of human rights law. Minorities as well as indigenous groups differ in their approaches, some claiming group identity or constitutional autonomy while some others, more radical in their demands, may resort to violence, destruction and terrorism. In specifically addressing the position of minorities and indigenous peoples, it is submitted that this book is taking an approach befitting the legal and political realities of the 21st century.

---

[38] See chapters 13 and 20 below.
[39] Rome Statute of the International Criminal Court, 2187 U.N.T.S. 90, entered into force 1 July 2002.
[40] 'On 4 March 2009 the judges of Pre-Trial Chamber I issued an arrest warrant for Sudanese President Omar Hassan Ahmad al-Bashir named by the Prosecutor of the International Criminal Court (ICC) Luis Moreno-Ocampo in his July 2008 filing in the Darfur situation. The Chamber held that there are reasonable grounds to believe that President al-Bashir bears criminal responsibility for crimes against humanity and war crimes allegedly committed in Darfur in the past five years. Omar Hassan Ahmad al-Bashir has been the president of Sudan since 1993' www.iccnow.org/?mod=darfur <last visited 5 March 2009>.
[41] 72 ILO Official Bull. 59, entered into force 5 September 1991, 28 I.L.M. (1989) 1382.
[42] Declaration on the Rights of Persons Belonging to National or Ethnic, Religious and Linguistic Minorities, UN Doc. A/Res/47/135.
[43] For further details see below chapter 13.
[44] United Nations Declaration on the Rights of the Indigenous Peoples UN Doc. A/RES/61/295.
[45] Framework Convention on the Protection of National Minorities, ETS No. 157, 34 I.L.M. (1995) 351.

(iv) The public/private divide in human rights law[46]

The progression of human rights law has generally been in the direction of according protection to the individuals against their States with the 'anti-State' stance flowing 'from the assumption that individual persons must be protected from the abuse of power of parliaments, governments and public authorities'.[47] As this book will consider in detail, human rights instruments, in targeting the State, direct their attention towards governments and other public bodies. In this paradigm, one legitimate criticism has been that international law has failed to focus directly on violations conducted by non-State actors, e.g. individuals, terrorist organisations or torture gangs. As shall be examined, certain international treaty agreements aim to limit State responsibility to a point where the offending actions are undertaken 'at the instigation of or with the consent or acquiescence of a public official or other person acting in an official capacity'.[48] Does this means that violations of human rights conducted by private individuals against each other cannot be the subject of scrutiny of international human rights mechanisms?

It is noticeable that many of the violations of individual and group rights are regularly conducted by private individuals themselves against vulnerable groups such as refugees, minorities, women and children.[49] It would clearly be absurd if these non-State actors were under no obligation to protect human rights in the same way as governments and public officials. The *sui generis* nature of human rights undertakings on the part of States are broad and represent an obligation not only *not* to violate human rights themselves, but also establish an undertaking to 'ensure'[50] or 'secure'[51] the rights of individuals. This position is reaffirmed by the provisions of both the International Covenant on Civil and Political Rights (1966) and the International Covenant on Economic, Social and Cultural Rights (1966). Article 2(1) of the International Covenant on Civil and Political Rights (1966) provides that 'Each State Party to the present Covenant undertakes to respect and to ensure to all individuals within its territory and subject to its jurisdiction the rights recognised in the present Covenant.'[52] Similarly according to Article 2(1) of the International Covenant on

---

[46] See Clapham, *Human Rights in the Private Sphere* (Clarendon Press, 1993); Forde, 'Non-Governmental Interferences with Human Rights' 56 *BYIL* (1985) 253. These issues are of particular relevance to the protection of such groups as women, children, minorities, refugees and persons with disabilities; see below Part IV.

[47] von Prondzynski, *Freedom of Association and Industrial Relations: A Comparative Study* (Mansell Publishing, 1987) at p. 1.

[48] See Article 1(1) Convention against Torture (1984), which defines torture as 'any act by which severe pain or suffering, whether physical or mental, is intentionally inflicted on a person for such purposes as obtaining from him or a third person information or a confession, punishing him for an act he or a third person has committed or is suspected of having committed, or intimidating or coercing him or a third person, or for any reason based on discrimination of any kind, *when such pain or suffering is inflicted by or at the instigation of or with the consent or acquiescence of a public official or other person acting in an official capacity*. It does not include pain or suffering arising only from, inherent in or incidental to lawful sanctions' (emphasis added) discussed below chapter 22. Also note the definition of 'enforced disappearances' as provided in Article 2 International Convention for the Protection of All Persons from Enforced Disappearance (2006).

[49] See the terminology of the ECHR, discussed below.

[50] See ICCPR Article 2(1); ACHPR Article 1.

[51] See ECHR Article 1; according to Article 1 AFCHPR the 'undertaking is to give effect to [the rights]'.

[52] General Comment 31 [No. 80] *Nature of the General Legal Obligation Imposed on States Parties to the Covenant: 26/05/2004. CCPR/C/21/Rev.1/Add.13* (General Comments) where the Human Rights Committee notes: 'positive obligations on States Parties to ensure Covenant rights will only be fully discharged if individuals are protected by the State, not just against violations of Covenant rights by its agents, but also against acts committed by private persons or entities that would impair the enjoyment of Covenant rights in so far as they are amenable to application between private persons or entities. There may be circumstances in which a failure to ensure Covenant rights as required by article 2 would give rise to violations by States Parties of those

Economic, Social and Cultural Rights, State parties commit themselves to undertaking steps 'with a view to achieving' rights recognised in International Covenant on Economic Social and Cultural Rights.

The process, by which human rights are to be protected from violations conducted by private individuals – sometimes referred to as the horizontal or positive application of law – has been approved and applied by human rights courts and tribunals. This horizontal or positive application of law aims to provide a comprehensive protection of human rights.[53] State liability will be incurred in circumstances where the State has control over the actions of the non-State actor. It will extend to situations, where the State condoned, tolerated or even allowed unlawful actions conducted by private actors. Furthermore, and most importantly, within the context of an international and regional human rights treaty-based regime, State liability would also extend to instances where the State has failed in its obligations to 'secure' or to 'ensure' the right contained in the instruments by not rendering unlawful actions by private persons that violated them.[54] Thus, the European Court of human rights jurisprudence has established State liability where criminal law failed to provide a means whereby a sexual attack upon a mentally disabled women could be the subject a criminal prosecution,[55] or instances where the law permitted an employer to dismiss his employee for refusal to join a trade union as required under the 'closed shop agreement'[56] or where the State had failed in providing effective protection to a nine-year-old child from beatings from his stepfather within a family setting.[57] Such views have been consolidated through the case-law that has emerged from both the Inter-American and African human rights systems. In the *Velasquez* case, the Inter-American Court made the following important observations:

> An illegal act which violates human rights and which is directly not imputable to a State (for example, because it is the act of a private person or because the person involved has not been identified) can lead to international responsibility of the State, not because of the act itself, but because of lack of the diligence to prevent the violation or to respond to it as required by the Convention.[58]

rights, as a result of States Parties' permitting or failing to take appropriate measures or to exercise due diligence to prevent, punish, investigate or redress the harm caused by such acts by private persons or entities. States are reminded of the interrelationship between the positive obligations imposed under article 2 and the need to provide effective remedies in the event of breach under article 2, paragraph 3. The Covenant itself envisages in some articles certain areas where there are positive obligations on States Parties to address the activities of private persons or entities. For example, the privacy-related guarantees of article 17 must be protected by law. It is also implicit in article 7 that States Parties have to take positive measures to ensure that private persons or entities do not inflict torture or cruel, inhuman or degrading treatment or punishment on others within their power. In fields affecting basic aspects of ordinary life such as work or housing, individuals are to be protected from discrimination within the meaning of article 26'. Ibid. para 8.

[53] See the Inter-American Court of Human Rights in *Velasquez Rodriguez Case*, Judgment of 29 July 1988, Inter-Am.Ct.H.R. (Ser. C) No. 4 (1988), para 170. In the African Human Rights system *Commission Nationale des Droits de l'Homme et des Libertés* v. *Chad*, Communication No. 74/92.

[54] Harris, O'Boyle, Bates and Buckley, *Harris, O'Boyle and Warbrick Law of the European Convention on Human Rights* (Oxford University Press, 2009) at pp. 18–21.

[55] *X and Y* v. *The Netherlands*, Application No. 8975/80 (Judgment of 26 March 1985), para 22.

[56] *Young, James and Webster* v. *the United Kingdom* (1982) 4 E.H.R.R. 38.

[57] *A* v. *United Kingdom*, Application No. 25599/94 (Judgment of 23 September 1998). In the context of the Human Rights Act see Cooper, 'Horizonality: The Application of Human Rights Standards in Private Disputes' in English and Havers (eds), *An Introduction to Human Rights and the Common Law* (Hart, 2000), at pp. 53–69; Hunt, 'The "Horizontal Effect" of the Human Rights Act' *Public Law* (1998) 423.

[58] *Velasquez Rodriguez Case*, Judgment of 29 July 1988, Inter-Am.Ct.H.R. (Ser. C) No. 4 (1988), para 172. The Inter-American Court found Honduras in Breach of Velasquez's right to life, liberty and humane treatment.

1

Introduction

The African Commission in pursuance of the African Charter on Human and Peoples' Rights (1981) has held that where a State neglects to ensure rights provided under the Charter, it violates the provisions of the Charter 'even if the State or its agents are not the immediate cause of violation [on the basis that] the government had a responsibility to secure the safety and liberty of its citizens, and to conduct investigations into murders'.[59] It is thus established that States must undertake positive steps to ensure protection from human rights violations that take place in the confines of private or personal life. A further extension of the breakdown of the private/public dichotomy is the recognition by international human rights instruments of the duties upon individuals or other non-State actors. The International Covenants, for example, in their respective preambles recognise that individuals have duties. UDHR in Article 29(1) refers to the obligations of the individuals *vis-à-vis* the community. The American Declaration on the Rights and Duties of Man,[60] as well as the African Charter on Human and Peoples' Rights are explicit in placing obligations upon individuals in addition to providing human rights. The concept of duties upon individuals and their obligations are more fully stated within International Criminal Law, and particularly in relation to accountability for crimes against humanity and genocide.[61]

(v) The *sui generis* character of international human rights law

As we shall consider shortly, States continue to be the principal subjects of international law and have developed a large network of human rights law by entering into a range of agreements. While these agreements bind States in treaty law, in customary law or within general principles of law, international human rights law is of a *sui generis* character. In emphasising this particular issue, the Inter-American Court of Human Rights made the observation that human rights treaties

> are not multilateral treaties of the traditional type concluded to accomplish the reciprocal exchange of rights for the mutual benefit of concluding States. Their object and purpose is the protection of the basic rights of individual human beings, irrespective of their nationality, both against the State of their nationality and all other contracting States. In concluding these human rights treaties, the States can be deemed to submit themselves to a legal order within which they, for the common good, assume various obligations, not in relation to other States, but towards all individuals within their jurisdiction.[62]

Human rights treaties and instruments increasingly do not represent a State-centric model of treaty negotiation in which instruments are negotiated behind closed doors away from the very people they are intended to benefit. These instruments are moving toward a participatory approach that involves non-governmental actors and takes the views and life

---

[59] *Commission Nationale des Droits de l'Homme et des Libertés* v. *Chad*, Communication No. 74/92. See also, African [Banjul] Charter on Human and Peoples' Rights, adopted 27 June 1981, OAU Doc. CAB/LEG/67/3 rev. 5, 21 I.L.M. 58 (1982), entered into force 21 October 1986.

[60] OAS Res. XXX, OAS Doc. OEA/Ser.L.V/II.82 doc.6 rev.1 at 17 (1992).

[61] See Provost, *International Human Rights and Humanitarian Law* (Cambridge University Press, 2002) at pp. 68–73.

[62] *Effects of Reservation on the Entry into force of the American Convention on Human Rights (Articles 74 and 75)* Inter-American Court of Human Rights Advisory Opinon OC-2/82 of 24 September 1982, Ser. A, No. 2, para 29.

experiences of the affected as the principal point of departure. This is clearly witnessed in some of more recent international treaties such as the International Convention of the Rights of Persons with Disabilities and its Optional Protocol.[63] This was also the case in relation to the United Nations Declaration on the Rights of the Indigenous Peoples (2007).[64] As this study will examine, textual provisions or procedural regulations are increasingly acknowledging the role (and affording greater participation) to non-State actors such as non-governmental organisations and the victims of violations themselves.

A further, highly striking feature of international human rights law is its relationship with international humanitarian law. Two key points need to be introduced at this juncture. Firstly, that international human rights law is applicable equally in times of peace and conflict. While human rights treaties provide for the derogation of certain provisions during times of public emergencies including armed conflict, there are other articles which are non-derogable at all times. Secondly, the *sui generis* nature of humanitarian law treaties, such as the four Geneva Conventions (1949), is confirmed by the fact that these treaties (unlike political and economic agreements) are not exhausted by an outbreak of conflict between States. In fact, as espoused by Professor Leslie Green, an armed conflict is a trigger for the commencement of humanitarian law treaties. Professor Green makes the useful observation that

[a]lthough political and economic treaties between the belligerents are terminated or suspended, this is not the case with regard to treaties of a humanitarian character, such as the Genocide Convention, 1948, while treaties relating to armed conflict, such as the Geneva and Hague Conventions, come into operation immediately upon the outbreak of hostilities. While this is not specifically provided for in any of the Conventions, Article 3 of Protocol 1, 1977, expressly states that 'the Conventions and this Protocol shall apply from the beginning of any situation referred to in Article 1' of the Protocol, which itself refers back to Article 2 common to all four 1949 Geneva Conventions.[65]

Having said that, as this study examines, the implementation of fundamental human rights during armed conflict has raised substantial issues. International or regional implementation mechanisms, for example, the Human Rights Committee or European Court of Human Rights, are restricted in regulating human rights provisions to the extent that are covered in their treaties. This, therefore, leaves a considerable lacunae in the effective protection of fundamental rights during times of armed conflicts.

---

[63] See below chapter 17.

[64] Luís Chávez (Peru), when introducing the text of Declaration before the General Assembly noted that 'I must say that for the first time in the history of the United Nations representatives of indigenous peoples, those who were to enjoy the rights contained in the Draft, took part actively in the work on the text, attributing to it unquestionable legitimacy.' Cited in Oldham and Frank, '"We the peoples . . .": The United Nations Declaration on the Rights of Indigenous Peoples' 24 *Anthropology Today* (2008) 4 at p. 5. For further discussion see below chapter 14.

[65] Green, *The Contemporary Law of Armed Conflict* (Manchester University Press, 2000) at p. 76.

2 International law and human rights

1 INTRODUCTION[1]

In order properly to comprehend the structure of international human rights law, a basic understanding of the nature and operation of international law is required. International law is in itself divided into public international law and private international law (also known as 'conflicts of laws'). Private international law represents a distinct system wherein domestic courts operating within a legal system are required to deal with cases containing a foreign element, thereby raising issues as regards the application of foreign law or the role of courts in a foreign jurisdiction.[2] This book deals with public international law and *not* with private international law, and therefore all references to international law are to be understood as meaning and referring to public international law. International human rights law is a branch of public international law and shares the characteristics and sources of public international law. These introductory comments on the nature of international law should be particularly useful for those students who have no previous experience of international law. This chapter considers the nature and definition of international law. As will be established by our discussion international law has a character distinct from national laws. International law, unlike national systems, does not base itself on a single unified legislature which passes legislation, an executive organ which enforces it and a judiciary with jurisdiction to decide upon any disputes. This *sui generis* character has led international law to develop through a range of sources. Treaty law and custom are well established and classed as recognised sources of international law. There are also other, less conventional

---

[1] See Brownlie, *Principles of Public International Law* (Oxford University Press, 2008) pp. 3–30; Cassese, *Human Rights in a Changing World* (Temple University Press, 1990); Forsythe, *Human Rights in International Relations* (Cambridge University Press, 2006); Harris, *Cases and Materials on International Law* (Sweet & Maxwell, 2004) pp. 654–785; Lauterpacht, *International Law and Human Rights* (F.A. Praeger, 1950); Robertson and Merrills, *Human Rights in the World: An Introduction to the Study of the International Protection of Human Rights* (Manchester University Press, 1996); Shaw, *International Law* (Cambridge University Press, 2008) pp. 265–396; Wallace, *International Law* (Sweet & Maxwell, 2005) pp. 1–35; and Weissbrodt, Fitzpatrick and Newman, *International Human Rights: Law, Policy, and Process* (LexisNexis, 2001).

[2] English Private international law defines the nature of the subject as '[t]hat part of English law known as private international law comes into operation whenever the court is faced with a claim that contains a foreign element. It is only when this element is present that private international law has a function to perform. It has three main objects. First, to prescribe the conditions under which the court is competent to entertain such a claim. Secondly, to determine for each class of case the particular municipal system of law by reference to which the rights of the parties must be ascertained. Thirdly, to specify the circumstances in which (*a*) a foreign judgment can be recognised as decisive of the question in dispute; and (*b*) the right vested in the judgment creditor by a foreign judgment can be enforced by action in England'. North and Fawcett, *Cheshire and North's Private International Law* (Oxford University Press, 1987) at p. 3.

and traditionally regarded as subsidiary, sources. As this chapter elaborates, the role of General Assembly Resolutions has been significant in developing international law. The chapter concludes with a consideration of those norms of international law from which no derogation is permissible.

2 NATURE AND DEFINITION OF INTERNATIONAL LAW

The issues related to the nature and definition of international law are of significant value in establishing the sphere of modern human rights law. As noted in the previous introductory chapter, international law has traditionally been seen as a law that regulates relations between independent and sovereign States, and while the impact of individual human rights has been significant, international law continues to be primarily concerned with the relationship amongst States. States are the principal subjects of international law, and not only do they play a key role in the creation of international law, they also remain pivotal in its execution and enforcement. International law has been defined by Sir Robert Jennings and Sir Arthur Watts as

the body of rules which are legally binding on states in their intercourse with each other. These rules are primarily those which govern the relations of states, but states are not the only subjects of international law. International organisations and, to some extent, also individuals may be subjects of rights conferred and duties imposed by international law.[3]

Notwithstanding the recognition of the limited role which international organisations and individuals play in the international legal system, the dominant position of States remains firmly established. States retain an exclusive position in the creation of norms of international law. Their exclusive membership of the United Nations ensures their absolute control of the principal organs such as the General Assembly, the Security Council and the Economic and Social Council. It is only States which can appear before the International Court of Justice in contentious proceedings.[4] As subsequent chapters elaborate, the recognition of international human rights and the enhanced procedural standing of individuals has been a product of international treaty agreements. These obligations have been undertaken by States themselves to allow the individual the *locus standi* to make claims before international bodies. In the light of these observations, Professor Cassese's analogy to 'puny Davids confronted by overwhelming Goliaths holding all the instruments of power', when describing the relationship between individuals and States, is an accurate one.[5]

3 FUNDAMENTAL CHARACTERISTICS OF INTERNATIONAL LAW

International law is distinct from national legal systems. Unlike domestic legal systems, there is, as such, no legislature (making laws for the entire international community) nor

[3] Jennings and Watts (eds), *Oppenheim's International Law* (Longman, 1992) pp. 3–4.
[4] Article 34(1) Statute of the International Court of Justice.
[5] Cassese, *International Law* (Oxford University Press, 2005) p. 4.

is there an executive which enforces the decisions made by the legislature.[6] There are also no comparable judicial institutions which can try violations of law and award a judgment against the offender.[7] Our analysis of the position of the United Nations will establish that none of the principal organs are comparable to those that are found within the national legal system. Thus, the United Nations General Assembly whilst representing all Member States is not the equivalent of a national legislature. The General Assembly Resolutions, save for limited exceptions, are of a recommendatory nature and as such cannot bind Member States. The executive functions of the Security Council are circumscribed both 'legally and politically'.[8] The powers of enforcement actions are triggered not by any breach of international law, but only through a determination of a 'threat to the peace, breach of the peace, or act of aggression'.[9] The consent of State Parties remains the critical element in invoking the contentious jurisdiction of the International Court of Justice.

The absence of a legislature, an executive body and a judiciary with compulsory jurisdiction over all its members, makes international law very different from national legal systems. The absence of a sovereign authority has led critics to doubt whether international law could be termed as 'law'; some would treat it more as an aspect of 'positive morality' than law.[10] The essence of a proper understanding of the nature of law, it is submitted, is to acknowledge its differences from national law and its *sui generis* characteristics. Commenting on these characteristics, Professor Shaw notes

[w]hile the legal structure within all but the most primitive societies is hierarchical and authority is vertical, the international system is horizontal, consisting of over 190 independent states, all equal in legal theory (in that they all possess the characteristics of sovereignty) and recognising no one in authority over them. The law is above individuals in domestic systems, but international law only exists as between the states. Individuals only have the choice as to whether to obey the law or not. They do not create the law. That is done by specific institutions. In international law, on the other hand, it is the states themselves that create the law and obey or disobey it. This, of course, has profound repercussions as regards the sources of law as well as the means for enforcing accepted legal rules.[11]

4 SOURCES OF INTERNATIONAL LAW

The *sui generis* character of international law is not only evident in the organisation of the system but is also reflected through the manner in which international laws are created. Within domestic legal systems, sources of law can be readily identified. In the case of the United Kingdom, the Acts of Parliament are regarded as the primary sources of law. As noted earlier within international law, there are no institutions comparable to a domestic

---

[6] Shaw, above n.1, at p. 3; Wallace, above n.1, at pp. 2–5.
[7] Ibid.
[8] Malanczuk, *Akehurst's Modern Introduction to International Law* (Routledge, 1997) p. 3.
[9] Article 39 United Nations Charter (1945) discussed further in chapter 3 below.
[10] See Hart's introduction and commentary in Hart (ed.), *Austin: The province of jurisprudence determined, and, The uses of the study of jurisprudence* (Weidenfeld & Nicolson, 1954) pp. 134–142; Rona, 'Interesting Times for International Humanitarian Law: Challenges from the War on Terror' 27 *Fletcher F. World Aff.* (2003) 55 at p. 55.
[11] Shaw, above n.1, at p. 6.

legislative body. The absence of any single identifiable legislature, however, is substituted by a range of means, all of which essentially emanate from the consent of States. Concomitant to the absence of a legislative organ, is the consensus regarding the list of sources of international law. Article 38(1) of the Statute of the International Court of Justice[12] is often invoked as providing sources of international law. It provides as follows:

> The Court, whose function is to decide in accordance with international law such disputes as are submitted to it, shall apply:
> (a) international conventions, whether general or particular, establishing rules expressly recognized by the contesting states;
> (b) international custom, as evidence of a general practice accepted as law;
> (c) the general principles of law recognized by civilized nations;
> (d) subject to the provisions of Article 59, judicial decisions and the teachings of the most highly qualified publicists of the various nations, as subsidiary means for the determination of rules of law.

(i) International conventions

The reference in Article 38(1)(a) is directed to international treaties, which are also varyingly described as covenants, charters, pacts, protocols and conventions. In our study we will come across various examples of treaties, which include the United Nations Charter,[13] the International Covenant on Civil and Political Rights[14] and the International Covenant on Economic, Social and Cultural Rights,[15] the International Convention on the Elimination of All Forms of Racial Discrimination,[16] and the Convention on the Elimination of All Forms of Discrimination against Women.[17] As Shaw has observed, treaties represent legally binding obligations undertaken by States parties and represent 'a more modern and more deliberate method' of creating laws.[18] The most widely recognised definition of a treaty can be found in the Vienna Convention on the Law of Treaties (1969).[19] According to Article 2, a treaty for the purposes of the Vienna Convention is

> an international agreement concluded between States in written form and governed by international law, whether embodied in a single instrument or in two or more related instruments and whatever its particular designation.[20]

---

[12] Adopted at San Francisco, 26 June 1945. Entered into force 24 October 1945, 59 Stat. 1055, 3 Bevans 1179.
[13] 26 June 1945, 59 Stat. 1031, T.S. 993, 3 Bevans 1153.
[14] New York, 16 December 1966 United Nations, 999 U.N.T.S. 171; 6 I.L.M. (1967) 368.
[15] New York, 16 December 1966, 993 U.N.T.S. 3; 6 I.L.M. (1967) 360.
[16] New York, 7 March 1966 United Nations, *Treaty Series*, vol. 660, p. 195.
[17] New York, 18 December 1979 United Nations, *Treaty Series*, vol. 1249, p. 13.
[18] Shaw, above n.1, at p. 93.
[19] Concluded at Vienna 23 May 1969. 1155 U.N.T.S. 331, 8 I.L.M. 679 entered into force 27 January 1980.
[20] Ibid. Article 2(1)(a). This definition excludes a number of agreements (e.g. unwritten agreements between States and those between States and international organisations). Such an exclusion however does not mean that these agreements can not be characterised as binding or as treaties. An agreement would be established so long as the parties intend to create binding legal relationship amongst themselves. See Shaw, above n.1, at p. 904. Treaties between States and international organisations are regulated by the Vienna Convention on the Law of Treaties Between States and International Organisations (1986) I.L.M. p. 543; See Shaw, above n.1 at pp. 953–955.

The binding nature of treaties can be likened to contractual agreements in domestic law, although such an analogy is most suited for the so-called treaty-contracts. Treaty-contracts are those treaties which are entered into by two or a few States and deal with a particular matter. By contrast, the 'law-making treaties' create legal obligations, the observance of which does not dissolve treaty obligations. A vital characteristic of law-making treaties is the laying down of general or universal application.[21] It is in this context that the role of treaties as a source of international law is of great significance. Examples of law-making treaties include the United Nations Charter,[22] the Convention on the Prevention and Punishment of the Crime of Genocide,[23] and the four Geneva Conventions (1949).[24]

An essential feature of treaty law is that a treaty does not bind non-States parties. However, law-making treaties can in fact bind non-parties, not as a treaty obligation, but as part of customary international law. We shall consider the elements which constitute customary law in the next section. Suffice to mention here, that a treaty provision could possess customary force if it fulfils the basic criterion of the establishment of custom – it could reflect customary law if its text declares or its *travaux préparatoires* state, with the requisite *opinio juris*, that its substance is declaratory of existing law. This position is recognised in the Vienna Convention on the Law of the Treaties itself, whereby Article 38 provides that '[n]othing in [convention] articles . . . precludes a rule set forth in a treaty from becoming binding upon a third State as a customary rule of international law, recognized as such'.[25]

Another significant feature of treaty law is the freedom which it provides to States in their decisions to commit themselves to international legal obligations. In the case of multilateral treaties, while a State may be prepared to accept most of the provisions contained in the treaty, it may object to some articles. In these circumstances, it may decide to make a reservation to those provisions it does not wish to be bound by. The effect of a reservation made by a State party is to exclude or modify the obligations of a treaty provision in its application to that State. Article 2(1)(d) of the Vienna Convention on the Law of Treaties defines a reservation as

a unilateral statement, however phrased or named, made by a State, when signing, ratifying, accepting, approving or acceding to a treaty, whereby it purports to exclude or to modify the legal effect of certain provisions of the treaty in their application to that State.

---

[21] In highlighting the features of law-making treaties, Sunkin *et al.*, identify the following: 'whether [the treaty] was concluded for the purpose of laying down general rules of conduct among a large number of States; the subject matter it addresses; the large number of States participating in its negotiations; the number of States participating in its negotiations; the number signing it or becoming parties to it; the commitments it establishes; and State practice prior to and following its entry into force' Sunkin, Ong and Wight, *Source Book on Environmental Law* (Cavendish Publishing Ltd, 2002) at pp. 3–4.

[22] 26 June 1945, 59 Stat. 1031, T.S. 993, 3 Bevans 1153.

[23] 9 December 1948, United Nations, *Treaty Series*, vol. 78, p. 277. Considered above chapter 20.

[24] See Geneva Convention (No. I) for the Amelioration of the Condition of the Wounded and Sick in Armed Forces in the Field. Concluded at Geneva, 12 August 1949. Entered into force 21 October 1950. 75 U.N.T.S. 31; Geneva Convention (No. II) for the Amelioration of the Condition of Wounded and Sick and Shipwrecked Members of Armed Forces at Sea Concluded at Geneva, 12 August 1949. Entered into force 21 October 1950. 75 U.N.T.S. 85; Geneva Convention (No. III) Relative to the treatment of Prisoners of War (without Annexes) Concluded at Geneva 12 August 1949. Entered into force, 21 October 1950. 75 U.N.T.S. 135. Geneva Convention (No. IV) Relative to the Protection of Civilian Persons in Time of War (without annexes) Concluded at Geneva 12 August 1949. Entered into force 21 October 1950, 75 U.N.T.S. 287.

[25] Article 38, Vienna Convention on the Law of the Treaties (1969).

According to traditional practice, reservations to multi-lateral treaties were only accepted as valid if the treaty allowed such a reservation and all the other parties consented to it.[26] However, significant flexibility was added to this practice by the International Court of Justice in its ruling in the *Reservations to the Genocide Convention Case*.[27] In the light of the special characteristics of the Genocide Convention, the Court refused to follow the earlier rigid practice. The Court, relying upon the so-called 'object and purpose' test, stated that it was 'the compatibility of a reservation with the object and purpose of the [Genocide] Convention that must furnish the criterion for the attitude of a State in making the reservation on accession as well as for the appraisal by a State in objecting to the reservation'.[28] This position has been confirmed by the Vienna Convention on the Law of the Treaties, which entitles a State to enter a reservation unless it is contrary to the 'object and purpose' of the treaty.[29] The induction of the element of subjective judgment has led to disagreements over the compatibility of a reservation, and consequently the status of a State as a party to a convention. As our subsequent discussion will confirm, the issue of reservations has raised substantial difficulties in determining not only the nature of the obligations undertaken by reserving States, but also the effect such reservations have upon those States which have objected to these reservations. Amidst this lack of a consensus as to what constitutes the 'object and purpose' of a convention, the Human Rights Committee (which operates as the monitoring and implementing body for the ICCPR) has observed *inter alia* that non-derogable rights, judicial guarantees, the peremptory norms of human rights law as well as rules of customary international law should not be made the subject of reservations.[30] The extensive usage of reservations, and at times the deployment of vague expressions to restrict legal obligations are particularly evident in the cases of conventions that relate to the rights of women and children.[31] Notwithstanding the difficulties that have been generated by reservations, treaties have played a leading role in developing the modern human rights regime. In particular, multilateral human rights treaties, as law-making treaties have established rules of universal application. These fundamental rules emanating from human rights treaties (e.g. rules dealing with the prohibition of torture, genocide and racial

---

[26] Redgwell, 'Universality or Integrity: Some Reflections on Reservations to General Multilateral Treaties' 64 *BYIL* (1993) 245, at p. 236; See also the General Comments by the Human Rights Committee, General Comment No. 24 on Reservations to ICCPR, 15 *HRLJ* (1995) 464; 2 *IHRR* (1995) 10.

[27] *Reservations to the Convention on the Prevention and Punishment of the Crime of Genocide*, Advisory Opinion 28 May 1951, (1951 ICJ Reports, 15).

[28] Ibid. p. 24.

[29] Article 19(c).

[30] Human Rights Committee, General Comment 24(52), UN Doc. CCPR/C/21/Rev.1/Add.6 (1994). The Committee notes: 'Reservations that offend peremptory norms would not be compatible with the object and purpose of the Covenant. Although treaties that are mere exchanges of obligations between States allow them to reserve *inter se* application of rules of general international law, it is otherwise in human rights treaties, which are for the benefit of persons within their jurisdiction. Accordingly, provisions in the Covenant that represent customary international law (and *a fortiori* when they have the character of peremptory norms) may not be the subject of reservations. Accordingly, a State may not reserve the right to engage in slavery, to torture, to subject persons to cruel, inhuman or degrading treatment or punishment, to arbitrarily deprive persons of their lives, to arbitrarily arrest and detain persons, to deny freedom of thought, conscience and religion, to presume a person guilty unless he proves his innocence, to execute pregnant women or children, to permit the advocacy of national, racial or religious hatred, to deny to persons of marriageable age the right to marry, or to deny to minorities the right to enjoy their own culture, profess their own religion, or use their own language. And while reservations to particular clauses of article 14 may be acceptable, a general reservation to the right to a fair trial would not be', ibid. para 8. Also see Pasqualucci, *The Practice and Procedure of the Inter-American Court of Human Rights* (Cambridge University Press, 2003) at pp. 96–97.

[31] See below chapters 13 and 14.

equality) are so firmly grounded, as to bind all States (parties and non-parties alike) in customary international law.

(ii) International customary law

Article 38(1)(b) refers to this source of international law as 'international custom, as evidence of a general practice accepted as law'. International customary law represents a combination of two elements: firstly, State practice and secondly, the acceptance of such practice as law (*opinio juris*). State practice is a term which incorporates not only actions by States but also omissions and abstentions from taking part in certain activities. The evidence of State practices could be found, *inter alia*, through a survey of statements and declarations made by governmental spokesmen to their Parliaments, to foreign governments, and in inter-governmental conferences. Useful sources of ascertaining State practice include governmental and administrative actions, State laws and judicial decisions, since the executive, legislature and judiciary form part of the State apparatus. The approach adopted by representatives in the United Nations organs such as the General Assembly and the Security Council is a strong indicator of State practices.[32]

In order to establish customary law, State practice, in general, needs to be uniform and consistent. The International Court of Justice (ICJ) in the *Asylum Case (Colombia v. Peru)*[33] noted that a rule of customary law must be 'in accordance with a constant and uniform usage practised by States in question'.[34] The requirements of uniformity and the extensive nature of State practice have been emphasised by the Court in its subsequent case law.[35] There is as such no requirement of excessive repetition 'or an absolutely rigorous conformity'[36] of a particular practice by States, although an exercise of this kind strengthens the material evidence in confirming its consistency and uniformity. Furthermore, as pointed out by Professor Dinstein, it is not necessary that all States must have participated in a certain practice: the requirement is one of 'general' practice not universal practice and the practice of the most influential or powerful States would carry the greatest weight.[37] A certain practice by itself remains insufficient: in order to distinguish customary law from habits or codes of morality, States need to feel convinced that a certain action (or omission) is required of them by law. This psychological element in the formation of customary law is termed as *opinio juris*.[38] Once a practice is established as forming part of the plethora of customary international law, all States, even those which initially failed to contribute to the practice are regarded as being bound by this practice.[39] While there is consensus that once

---

[32] See the International Court of Justice's Advisory Opinion in the Legal Consequences of the *Construction of a Wall in the Occupied Palestinian Territory* (2004) ICJ Reports 136, p. 171.

[33] *Asylum Case (Columbia v. Peru)*, Judgment 20 November 1950, (1950) ICJ Reports 266.

[34] Ibid. pp. 276–277.

[35] *The Fisheries Case (United Kingdom v. Norway)*, Judgment 18 December 1951, (1951) ICJ Reports 116, 131, 138. *North Sea Continental Shelf Cases (Federal Republic of Germany v. Denmark; Federal Republic of Germany v. Netherlands)*, Judgment 20 February 1969, (1969) ICJ Reports 3.

[36] *Military and Paramilitary Activities in and Against Nicaragua (Nicaragua v. United States of America)*, (Merits) Judgment 27 June 1986, (1986) ICJ Reports 14, at para 186.

[37] Dinstein, *The Conduct of Hostilities under the Law of International Armed Conflict* (Cambridge University Press, 2004) at p. 6. Professor Dinstein correctly points out to the possibility of establishment of regional and even bilateral custom between two States.

[38] D'Amato, *The Concept of Custom in International Law* (Cornell University Press, 1971) pp. 66–72; Elias, 'The Nature of the Subjective Element in Customary International Law' 44 *ICLQ* (1995) 501.

[39] Dinstein, above n.37, at p. 6.

crystallised, customary international law attains a binding nature on all States, there nevertheless, remains some controversy as regards the position of those States which have persistently objected to the application of a rule of law during in its formative phases. A possibility of 'opt out' for the 'persistent objectors' provides, in the words of Thirlway, 'an attractive option', which also prevents the imposition of a particular rule by the majority over a minority.[40] On the other hand, as Thirlway himself acknowledges, 'there is little State practice to support [this proposition] and its very existence has been questioned by commentators'.[41] This study is inclined to support the latter proposition and argues that once established customary law becomes binding on all States regardless of their previous stance: such proposition might also rationalise the binding character of customary law on new States.

Although not as visible as treaty law, customary law represents the essential basis upon which modern human regime is grounded. General Assembly Resolutions, if accompanied by the requisite *opinio juris*, can lead to the formation of customary international law. Many of the General Assembly Resolutions have established fundamental principles of human rights. Amongst the most notable Resolutions are the Universal Declaration of Human Rights,[42] the Declaration on the Granting of Independence to Colonial Countries and Peoples (1960)[43] and the Declaration on Principles of International Law Concerning Friendly Relations and Co-operation Amongst States in Accordance with the Charter of the United Nations (1970).[44] Treaties, as *de facto* evidence of State practice, aid in the creation of customary law. A treaty provision could possess customary force if it fulfils the basic criteria relative to the establishment of custom; it could reflect customary law if its text declares or its *travaux préparatoires* state, with the requisite *opinio juris*, that its substance is as such declaratory of existing customary international law.[45]

(iii) General principles of law

Inserted originally in the Statute of the Permanent Court of International Justice[46] for the purpose of providing guidance to the Court in cases of gaps within treaty and customary law, the contemporary position and stature of general principles as a source of international law is a matter of some debate. It is also not clear whether these principles are taken

---

[40] Thirlway, 'The Sources of International Law', in Evans (ed.), *International Law* (Oxford University Press, 2006) pp. 115–140, at p. 127.

[41] Ibid. On the 'persistent objector debate see further Charney, 'The Persistent Objector Rule and the Development of Customary International Law', 56 *BYIL* (1985) 1; Stein, 'The Approach of the Different Drummer: The Principle of the Persistent Objector in International Law', 26 *Harv. Int'l L.J.* (1985) 457; Holning, 'Rethinking the Persistent Objector Doctrine in International Human Rights Law' 6 *Chicago Journal of International Law* (2005) 495.

[42] Adopted on 10 December 1948, UN GA Res. 217 A(III), UN Doc. A/810 at 71 (1948).

[43] Adopted on 14 December 1960, UN GA Res. 1514 (XV); UN GAOR 15th Session, Supp. 16, at 66, UN Doc. A/4684 (1961).

[44] Adopted on 24 October, 1970, UN GA Res. 2625 (XXV), 25 UN GAOR, Supp. 28 at 121, UN Doc. A/8028 (1971); 9 I.L.M. (1971) 1292. On the value of General Assembly Resolutions in general international law see Sloan, 'General Assembly Resolutions Revisited: (Forty Years Later)' 58 *BYIL* (1987) 39; Bleicher, 'The Legal Significance of Re-Citation of General Assembly Resolutions' 63 *AJIL* (1969) 444; Cheng, 'United Nations Resolutions on Outer Space: "Instant" International Customary Law?' 5 *IJIL* (1965) 23.

[45] Akehurst, *A Modern Introduction to International Law* (Harper Collins, 1987) pp. 26–27; Baxter, 'Multilateral Treaties as Evidence of Customary International Law' 41 *BYIL* (1965–66) 275; Akehurst, 'Custom as a Source of International Law' 47 *BYIL* (1974–5) 1 at pp. 42–52.

[46] 16 December 1920, 6 L.N.T.S. 379. Predecessor to the Statute of the International Court of Justice.

from the corpus of international law or are extracted from national legal systems. Akehurst has suggested that there is no reason why principles from both the national and international system should not be extrapolated to strengthen this source.[47] The approach adopted by international tribunals supports this assertion. Thus, obligations in international law to make reparations have been regarded as part of the corpus of general principles,[48] so have such features taken from national law on procedure and evidence.[49] General principles have made a notable contribution to human rights law. Many principles, particularly those in the criminal justice system (e.g. presumption of innocence and right to free trial), can be identified as general principles of law.

(iv) Subsidiary sources of international law

The subsidiary sources of international law include 'judicial decisions and the teachings of the most highly qualified publicists'.[50] Despite this subsidiary position, as we shall consider in this book, judicial decisions have been of great value in developing human rights law. In this regard, judicial decisions made by domestic courts and international courts are worthy of consideration. It is the case that the decisions of the International Court of Justice have no binding force except between the parties and in respect of the particular case.[51] It is also the case that the International Court of Justice lacks a compulsory jurisdiction and does not have formal power to establish precedents. Despite this, the work of the International Court of Justice has been of great significance in developing many areas of international law.[52] The International Court of Justice has played an instrumental rule in the development of fundamental principles such as the right to self-determination. The regional human rights bodies, notably the European Court of Human Rights, have dispensed judgments which have added to jurisprudence of human rights law. Similarly to international and regional court decisions, domestic courts have, for example, provided important ruling on key concerns such as torture, see for example, *Filártiga* v. *Peña-Irala*[53] and the *Pinochet* cases.[54] As this study will examine in considerable detail, additional, *ad hoc* international criminal tribunals have played a large part in interpreting existing principles of international law, and in expanding the jurisprudence of international human rights law and international criminal law.[55]

---

[47] Akehurst, above n.45, at p. 34.
[48] *Chorzow Factory Case (Germany* v. *Poland)*, PCIJ [1928] Series A, No. 17, p. 29.
[49] *Corfu Channel (United Kingdom* v. *Albania)*, (Merits) Judgment 9 April 1949, (1949) ICJ Reports 18.
[50] Article 38(1) Statute of the International Court of Justice.
[51] Article 59 Statute of the International Court of Justice.
[52] See Rosenne, *The World Court: What It Is and How it Works* (Brill, 1995); Fitzmaurice, *The Law and Procedure of the International Court of Justice* (Cambridge University Press, 1986); for a detailed survey see Thirlway, 'The Law and Procedure of the International Court of Justice: 1960–1989' 60 *BYIL* (1989) 1, and its following 10 volumes at p. 1; Schwelb, 'The International Court of Justice and the Human Rights Clauses of the Charter' 66 *AJIL* (1972) 337; Rodley, 'Human Rights and Humanitarian Intervention: The Case Law of the World Court' 38 *ICLQ* (1989) 321; Rehman, 'The Role and Contribution of the World Court in the Progressive Development of International Environmental Law' 5 *APJEL* (2000) 387.
[53] 630 F. 2d 876 (1980); 19 ILM 966. US. Circuit Court of Appeals, 2nd Circuit.
[54] *R.* v. *Evans Ex p. Pinochet Ugarte (No. 1)*, (HL) 25 November 1998, [1998] 3 WLR 1456; *R.* v. *Bow Street Metropolitan Stipendiary Magistrate Ex p. Pinochet Ugarte (No. 2)*, (HL) 15 January 1999, [1999] 2 WLR 272; *R.* v. *Bow Street Metropolitan Stipendiary Magistrate Ex p. Pinochet Ugarte (No. 3)*, (HL) 24 March 1999, [1999] 2 WLR 827
[55] See below chapter 20.

The writing and teachings of commentators such as Hugo Grotius had astronomical influence during the formative stages of the modern law of nations. With the rapid growth of treaties and growing recognition of customary international law, the influence of jurists in developing international law has declined. Having said that, as this study establishes, the teachings of jurists remains of value in many areas of international human rights. During the course of this study we shall consistently rely upon authorities such as Sir Hersch Lauterpacht, Lassa Francis Lawrence Oppenheim, Michael Akehurst and David Harris.

(v) Additional sources of international law

A notable omission from the list of sources provided by Article 38(1) is the reference to the actions of inter-governmental organisations, such as the United Nations (UN), International Labour Organization (ILO), Council of Europe (COE) and The Organization for Security and Co-operation in Europe (OSCE). We have already considered the significance of the United Nations General Assembly Resolutions as sources of international law; the influence of the Assembly's Resolutions in developing and re-shaping principles of international law is a recurring theme throughout this book. For example, declarations such as the UN Universal Declaration of Human Right and the Inter-American Declaration of the Rights and Duties of Man are not binding sources of law but have been extremely influential in the development of international human rights standards. Other organs of the United Nations (e.g. the Security Council and the Economic and Social Council) represent important vehicles for advancing norms of international law and international human rights law. The OSCE has adopted a number of instruments which although not legally binding *per se* (and recognised as 'soft-law') are important expressions of State practice. Instruments, such the Helsinki Final Act, have in the case of the former Soviet Union been of greater significance than binding human rights treaties.[56] Another example of 'soft-law' is the Standard Minimum Rules for the Treatment of Prisoners which, as we shall see, have established important standards in the treatment of prisoners and young offenders.[57]

5 *JUS COGENS* AND HUMAN RIGHTS LAW

As noticed in our earlier discussion, States through treaties or customary law establish or develop international law. At the same time, the discretion to formulate new laws is not unlimited and there remain certain rules of international law from which no derogation or reservation is permissible. In strict legal terms these rules have attained the status of norms of *jus cogens*. The elaboration of the doctrine of *jus cogens*, or peremptory norms as they are also known, is provided by the 1969 Vienna Convention on the Law of Treaties.[58] According to Article 53 of the Convention:

---

[56] See below chapter 7.

[57] Standard Minimum Rules for the Treatment of Prisoners, adopted by the First United Nations Congress on the Prevention of Crime and the Treatment of Offenders, held at Geneva 1955, and approved by UN ECOSOC Resolution 663 C (XXIV) 31 July 1957 (Amended – New Rule 95 added – by ECOSOC Resolution 2076 (LXII) 13 May 1977).

[58] For a consideration of the meaning of *jus cogens* see Article 53 and 64 of the Vienna Convention on the Law of Treaties; see Schwelb, 'Some Aspects of International *Jus Cogens* as Formulated by the International Law Commission' 61 *AJIL* (1967) 946; Whiteman, '*Jus Cogens* in International Law, with a Projected List' 7 *GA.JICL* (1977) 609.

A treaty is void if, at the time of its conclusion, it conflicts with a peremptory norm of general international law. For the purposes of the present Convention, a peremptory norm of general international law is a norm accepted and recognized by the international community of States as a whole as a norm from which no derogation is permitted and which can be modified only by a subsequent norm of general international law having the same character.

Furthermore by virtue of Article 64 newly emergent peremptory norms of general international law, terminate or render void any existing conflicting treaty provisions.[59] Two important features of Articles 53 and 64 need to be noted. Firstly, the provisions of Article 53 and 64 are now subsumed into customary law, thereby binding all States, parties and non-parties to the Vienna Convention. Secondly, the restrictions contained within Articles 53 and 64 apply as much to other sources such as customary law or general principles of international law as they do to treaties. Although there is no specification as to what constitutes such a norm, fundamental rights such as the right of all peoples to self-determination, and the prohibition of slavery, genocide, torture and racial discrimination represent settled examples of *jus cogens*. This point is well established by various commentaries on the subject. According to the Commentary of the International Law Commission's analysis of 'best and settled rules' of *jus cogens* prohibition include

(a) a treaty contemplating the performance of any other act criminal under international law and

(b) a treaty contemplating or conniving at the commission of acts, such as trade in slaves, piracy or genocide . . .".[60]

In Professor Brownlie's categorisation, the 'least controversial examples of the class are the prohibition of the use of force, the law of genocide, the principle of racial non-discrimination, crimes against humanity and the rules prohibiting trades in slaves and piracy'.[61] To this, we can add the prohibition on torture,[62] the right to life[63] and liberty and security of the person.[64]

6 | CONCLUSIONS

As a recognised branch of international law, human rights law partakes the sources and characteristics of international law. In elaborating upon the definition and scope of international law, this chapter has highlighted its *sui generis* character. Unlike national legal systems, international law does not have readily ascertainable judicial, executive, administrative structure. Despite its obvious deficiencies, limitations and unique characteristics, the international legal system is operative and remains visible through multifarious

---

[59] Article 64 of the Vienna Convention on the Law of Treaties (1969).
[60] See YBILC (1966) vol. II. pp. 247–248; Brownlie, above n.1, at pp. 510–512.
[61] Ibid. pp. 510–511.
[62] *Prosecutor* v. *Anto Furundzija*, Case No. IT-95-17/1-T. 10 December 1998. Judgment Judicial Supplement 1.
[63] Gormley, 'The Right to Life and the Rule of Non-Derogability: Peremptory Norms of *Jus Cogens*' in Ramcharan (ed.), *The Right to Life in International Law* (Brill, 1985) at p. 120.
[64] *Michael Domingues* v. *U.S.*, Report No. 62/02, Merits, Case 12.285.

manifestations. This chapter has also identified and briefly discussed the sources of international law (as well as international human rights law). Both treaty law and customary law retain considerable significance as sources of international human rights law although, as our examination disclosed, many aspects of treaty law as well as customary law remain controversial and unsettled. The effect of reservations upon human rights treaties remains a contested aspect. Although binding on all States in general international law, the formation and evolution of a customary rule often has been a point of much contestation: as our study will examine, there are many principles whose customary value remains subject to serious debates and disagreements. The study has also considered the *jus cogens* characteristics of certain norms of international law – the *jus cogens* or peremptory norms are of particular significance for international human rights law. The elevated status of peremptory norms signals the impossibility of any derogations or deviations. The chapter has also briefly considered the relevance of general principles of law and subsidiary sources of international human rights. Amongst additional sources of international law, General Assembly resolutions have a particular relevance. As our next chapter will demonstrate, the Universal Declaration of Human Rights – a resolution of the United Nations General Assembly – *per se* a non-binding instrument, has been the catalyst in reshaping human thought and developing the international law of human rights.

2

International law and human rights

3 The United Nations system and the modern human rights regime (1945–)[1]

1 INTRODUCTION

> If we fail to use the Charter and the organization we have created with it, we shall betray all of those who died in order that we might live in freedom and in safety . . . This Charter is no more perfect than our own Constitution, but like that Constitution it must be made to live.[2]

The inception of international human rights law is generally related to the developments that took place at the end of the Second World War. After that war, the United Nations was established to 'save succeeding generations from the scourge of war . . . and to reaffirm faith in fundamental human rights'.[3] The United Nations Charter,[4] which represents the constitution of the organisation, is also an international treaty, the provisions of which bind all States that are parties to the treaty.[5] The Charter assigns a range of functions to the United Nations, and although there are references to human rights, there has been considerable debate over the priorities which dictate the role and performance of this organisation. As noted above, the UN Charter contains a number of references to human rights. According to the preamble of the Charter:

---

[1] See Alston (ed.), *The United Nations and Human Rights: A Critical Appraisal* (Clarendon Press, 1992); Alston and Crawford (ed.), *The Future of UN Human Rights Treaty Monitoring* (Cambridge University Press, 2000); Harris, *Cases and Materials on International Law* (Sweet & Maxwell, 2004) pp. 654–785; Humphrey, *Human Rights and the United Nations* (Baxter Publishing Co., 1963); Khare, *Human Rights and United Nations* (Metropolitan Book Co., 1977); Meron, *Human Rights Law-Making in the United Nations* (Oxford University Press, 1986); Shaw, *International Law* (Cambridge University Press, 2008) pp. 265–395; Steiner 'International Protection of Human Rights' in Evans (ed.), *International Law* (Oxford University Press, 2006) pp. 753–782; Steiner, Alston, and Goodman (eds), *International Human Rights in Context* (Oxford University Press, 2008) pp. 735–843; Tomuschat, *Human Rights: Between Idealism and Realism* (Oxford University Press, 2008) pp. 133–166; and Weissbrodt and de la Vega, *International Human Rights Law, An Introduction* (University of Pennsylvania Press, 2007) pp. 251–270.

[2] President Harry S. Truman, Address to the Delegates in San Francisco at the adoption of the United Nations Charter (1948), cited in Hottelet, 'Ups and Down in UN History' 5 *Washington University Journal of Law and Policy* (2001) 17 at p. 17.

[3] Preamble of the United Nations Charter (1945).

[4] 26 June 1945, 59 Stat. 1031, T.S. 993, 3 Bevans 1153.

[5] The substantive provisions of the Charter also binds non-State parties in general international law. See Sands and Klein, *Bowett's Law of International Institutions* (Sweet & Maxwell, 2001) p. 24. Professor White regards the Charter as not simply an inter-State agreement but representing transcendental public law, with the laws produced by the organisation having 'applicability [and binding] both institutions and states, depending upon the nature of the activities undertaken'. White, 'The Applicability of Economic and Social Rights to the UN Security Council' in Baderin and McCorquodale (eds), *Economic, Social and Cultural Rights in Action* (Oxford University Press, 2007) pp. 89–107, at p. 94.

We the peoples of the United Nations, determined . . . to reaffirm faith in fundamental human rights, in the dignity and worth of the human person, in the equal rights of men and women and of nations large and small . . . have resolved to combine our efforts to accomplish these aims.[6]

Article 1(3) states that one of the purposes of the United Nations is the promotion and encouragement of respect for human rights and fundamental freedoms for all 'without distinction as to race, sex, language or religion'. According to Article 8, '[t]he United Nations shall place no restrictions on the eligibility of men and women to participate in any capacity and under conditions of equality in its principal and subsidiary organs'. According to Article 55 the United Nations shall 'promote . . . universal respect for, and the observance of, human rights and fundamental freedoms for all without distinction as to race, sex, language or religion'. In accordance with Article 56 '[a]ll members of the United Nations pledge themselves to take joint and separate action in co-operation with the Organization for the achievement of the purposes set forth in Article 55'. Articles 56 and 55 should be read together to formulate what one learned commentator has termed as '[probably] the only clear legal obligations in the Charter on members to promote respect for human rights'.[7]

The Charter also devolves authority to the Economic and Social Council (ECOSOC) to initiate studies and reports in relation to 'international economic, social, cultural, educational, health, and related matters and may make recommendations with respect to any such matters to the General Assembly, to the Members of the United Nations, and to the specialized agencies concerned'.[8] According to Article 62(2) the ECOSOC 'may make recommendations for the purpose of promoting respect for, and observance of, human rights and fundamental freedoms for all'. The trusteeship system incorporated in the United Nations Charter also carries with it the notion of equality and human rights for all.[9] One of the objectives of the trusteeship system has been 'to encourage respect for human rights and for fundamental freedoms for all without distinction as to race, sex, language, or religion, and to encourage recognition of the interdependence of the peoples of the world'.[10]

In addition to these explicit references to human rights, there is a more implicit recognition of the role which the UN organs can play in promoting human rights. Thus, in accordance with Article 10, the General Assembly may discuss (and has discussed on a number of occasions) matters within the scope of the Charter including human rights issues. Article 66(2), which grants authority to ECOSOC with the approval of the General Assembly to 'perform services', *inter alia* with respect to human rights, has been used as the basis of various UN human rights initiatives including awards and fellowship programmes and human rights seminars.[11]

---

[6] Preamble of the United Nations Charter (1945).

[7] Humphrey, 'The UN Charter and the Universal Declaration of Human Rights' in Laurd (ed.), *The International Protection of Human Rights* (Thames & Hudson, 1967) pp. 39–56 at p. 42. For further analysis of the human rights obligations see Schwelb, 'The International Court of Justice and the Human Rights Clauses of the Charter' 66 *AJIL* (1972) 337.

[8] Article 62(1).

[9] For further consideration of trusteeship see below.

[10] Article 76(c).

[11] Humphrey, above n.7, at p. 46.

2   LIMITATIONS OF THE CHARTER

Notwithstanding these references to human rights, it must not be assumed that human rights, equality and self-determination were the primary concerns of the politicians who had engaged themselves in the drafting of the United Nations Charter.[12] The Dumbarton Oaks proposals of 1944 (representing the blueprint for the establishment of a world organisation) had made only one general reference to human rights.[13] The major powers, prominently the United States and Great Britain, had been reluctant to uphold the cause of complete equality and non-discrimination.[14] They were also not fully committed to an international regime of human rights. A Chinese proposal to uphold the principle of 'equality of all States and races'[15] proved unacceptable to the United States, Great Britain and Soviet delegates at Dumbarton Oaks and hence was eliminated.[16] It was eventually the pressure from various NGOs and lobbying from a number of States that highlighted the necessity for greater recognition of human rights provisions in the Charter. At the time of its drafting several proposals were put forward including one from Panama for the incorporation of a bill of rights within the Charter.[17] None of these proposals materialised. The one proposal which, however, was accepted and has proved significant was the inclusion in Article 68 of the Charter which provided authorisation for ECOSOC to establish a Commission on Human Rights.[18] The Commission, which was formed in 1946, held its first meeting in January 1947. After its establishment, ECOSOC entrusted the Commission with the task of submitting proposals, recommendations and reports with a view to formulating an International Bill of Rights.[19]

The Charter does not establish any particular regime of human rights protection, and the emphasis is upon non-intervention in the affairs of Member States of the United Nations.[20] The main focus of the Charter is directed towards the promotion of international peace and security. Professor Nigel White correctly observes that

[12] See Henkin, 'International Law: Politics, values and Functions' 216 (IV) *Rec. des Cours* (1989) 9, at p. 215.

[13] See Ch. 9 Sect. A(I) Dumbarton Oaks Proposals UNCIO iv, 13; Text in Goodrich, Hambro and Simons, *Charter of the United Nations: Commentary and Documents* (Columbia University Press, 1969) 664–672; Robertson and Merrills, *Human Rights in the World: An Introduction to the Study of the International Protection of Human Rights* (Manchester University Press, 1996) p. 26.

[14] Renteln, *International Human Rights: Universalism versus Relativism* (Sage Publications, 1990) p. 21.

[15] 'Tentative Chinese Proposals for a General International Organization' 23 August 1944, in U.S. State Department., FRUS, 1944, 1: 718.

[16] Lauren, 'First Principles of Racial Equality: History and the Politics and Diplomacy of Human Rights Provisions in the United Nations Charter' 5 *HRQ* (1983) 1 at p. 10.

[17] See Huston, 'Human Rights Enforcement Issues of the United Nations Conference on International Organization' 53 *Iowa LR* (1967) 272 at p. 276; Alston, 'The Commission on Human Rights' in Alston (ed.), above n.1, 126–210, at p. 127; Document of the United Nations Conference on International Organisation (1945) vi 545–9; Robertson and Merrills, above n.13, at p. 26; Alfredsson and Eide, 'Introduction' in Alfredsson and Eide (eds), *The Universal Declaration of Human Rights: A Common Standard of Achievement* (Kluwer Law International, 1999) pp. xxv–xxxv at p. xxvii.

[18] Humphrey, 'The Universal Declaration of Human Rights: Its History, Impact and Juridical Character' in Ramcharan (ed.), *Human Rights: Thirty Years after the Universal Declaration* (Brill, 1979) pp. 21–37 at p. 21.

[19] See ECOSOC Res. 5(I) and 9(II). ECOSOC OR 1st Year, 2nd. Session, pp. 400–402.

[20] See Article 2(7) of the United Nations Charter which provides that 'Nothing contained in the present Charter shall authorize the United Nations to intervene in matters which are essentially within the domestic jurisdiction of any state or shall require the Members to submit such matters to settlement under the present Charter; but this principle shall not prejudice the application of enforcement measures under Chapter VII'. Article 2(7) has been given great prominence by States. According to one commentator 'the discussions of the San Francisco Conference on the Charter indicates that there was a general agreement that the general prohibition of intervention in domestic affairs is an overriding principle or limitation, and controls each and every organ of the U.N'. Boulesbaa, *The UN Convention on Torture and the Prospects for Enforcement* (Brill, 1999) pp. 92–93.

although human rights and human rights issues did seem to receive (almost) equal billing with peace and security concerns in the preamble and article 1, their equal status is eroded by the remainder of the Charter. While Chapter IX of the Charter on International and Economic Co-operation is the foundation of a relatively weak system for the supervision of the protection and promotion of human rights by member states, the Economic and Social Council (ECOSOC) and a number of the Specialized Agencies, Chapter VII of the UN Charter, in combination with the 'hard' treaty obligations in articles 2 and 25, underpin the value of peace and security with significant institutional powers.[21]

With regard to the right to equality and non-discrimination, it must be emphasised that at the time when the Charter came into operation in October 1945, there were serious impediments towards establishing a regime based on equality and non-discrimination; colonialism persisted in large measure, racial, religious and sex-based apartheid was widely in practice and the right to self-determination of all peoples, although inscribed in the text of the Charter was considered by many a *desideratum* rather than a firmly established legal right.[22]

Notwithstanding these shortcomings, over the years the United Nations (as an organisation of almost universal membership) has confirmed its influence in international legal and political developments. Since the establishment of the organisation in 1945 the role of the United Nations has been critical to the global promotion and protection of human rights. The role has been performed through a wide range of mechanisms and methods – some proving more effective than the others. The UN consists of the following principal organs: the General Assembly, the Security Council, the Economic and Social and Council (ECOSOC), International Court of Justice, the Trusteeship Council and the Secretariat. In order to have an adequate understanding of the United Nations, involvement with international human rights law it is important to consider each of its principal organs.

3 PRINCIPAL ORGANS OF THE UNITED NATIONS

(i) The General Assembly[23]

The General Assembly is the plenary organ of the United Nations currently representing all 192 States.[24] The UN Charter establishes the General Assembly as a platform where all

---

[21] White, above n.5, at p. 90.

[22] See Gearty, 'The Internal and External "Other" in the Union Legal Order: Racism, Religious Intolerance and Xenophobia in Europe' in Alston (ed.) *The EU and Human Rights* (Oxford University Press, 1999) pp. 327–358 at p. 328; '[the principle of self-determination] was regarded as a goal to be attained at some indeterminate date in the future; it was one of the *desiderata* of the Charter rather than a legal right that could be invoked as such' Blum, 'Reflections on the Changing Concept of Self-Determination' 10 *Israel Law Review* (1975) 509 at p. 511; Emerson, 'Self-Determination' 65 *AJIL* (1971) 459 at p. 471. See below chapter 14.

[23] See Sands and Klein, above n.5, at pp. 27–39; Bailey, *The General Assembly of the United Nations: A Study of Procedure and Practice* (Praeger, 1964); Peterson, *The General Assembly in World Politics* (Harper Collins, 1986); Sloan, *United Nations General Assembly Resolutions in Our Changing World* (Transnational Publishers, 1991); Andrassy, 'Uniting for Peace' 50 *AJIL* (1956) 563; Rowe, 'Human Rights Issues in the UN General Assembly 1946–1966' 14 *Journal of Conflict Resolution* (1970) 425; Johnson, 'The Effect of Resolutions of the General Assembly of the United Nations' 32 *BYIL* (1955–56) 97; Cassese, 'The General Assembly: Historical Perspective 1945–1989' in Alston (ed.), above n.1, pp. 25–54; Quinn, 'The General Assembly in the 1990s' ibid. pp. 55–106.

[24] For a list of the UN member States and the dates of their membership see www.un.org/members/list.shtml <last visited 2 January 2009>.

States can debate any relevant matter, with the Assembly having a broad competence to consider human rights issues. All members of the UN are represented in the General Assembly. Each member may have up to five representatives but only one vote. Decisions on important questions require a two thirds majority vote, others a simple majority. A non-exhaustive definition of 'important question' is given in Article 18(2). These include election, suspension or expulsion of members, election of the non-permanent members of the Security Council and recommendations in relation to the maintenance of international peace. The single vote for each State means no account is taken of size, economic strength or world influence, so, for example, the vote of the USA has the same value as that of Bangladesh. This may be seen as unrealistic but on the other hand it does mean that the decisions of the General Assembly are genuinely representative of world opinion.[25]

The rules relating to the membership of the General Assembly are contained in Article 4 of the Charter. Article 4 provides

1. Membership in the United Nations is open to all other peace-loving states which accept the obligations contained in the present Charter and, in the judgment of the Organization, are able and willing to carry out these obligations.

2. The admission of any such state to membership in the United Nations will be effected by a decision of the General Assembly upon the recommendation of the Security Council.

In practice, however, the issue of admission and expulsion has been surrounded by political rivalries particularly during the Cold-War years.[26] According to Article 5 of the UN Charter a member of the United Nations may be suspended on the recommendation of the Security Council. Article 6 allows for the expulsion of a member from the UN where that member has persistently violated the principles of the UN. According to the provisions of the Charter, the powers of the General Assembly are (with one exception) of deliberative or recommendatory nature. The exception concerns the internal budgetary obligations of Member States.[27] The authority to discuss and make recommendations derives largely from Articles 10–14 of the UN Charter, although, as we shall see, the scope of its authority has been enhanced considerably through subsequent developments of international law.

Articles 10 and 11 authorise the General Assembly to discuss 'any questions or any matters'[28] within the scope of the UN Charter (except where the Security Council is dealing with the same subject)[29] and make appropriate recommendations to the State(s) concerned and the Security Council.[30] In accordance with the mandate provided under Article 13 of the UN Charter, the General Assembly has commissioned a number of studies for the purpose of promoting international co-operation in various fields and 'assisting in the realization of human rights and fundamental freedoms'.[31]

---

[25] Ibid.
[26] See Article 4 UN Charter; Abi-Saab, 'Membership and Voting in the United Nations' in Fox (ed.), *The Changing Constitution of the United Nations* (British Institute of International and Comparative Law, 1997) pp. 19–39.
[27] See Article 17 UN Charter.
[28] Article 10 UN Charter.
[29] Article 12 UN Charter.
[30] Article 11(2) UN Charter.
[31] Article 13(1)(b).

In strict interpretation of the provisions of the Charter, the General Assembly is not a legislative body. It is not to be treated as a substitute for the Security Council nor has it been accorded a primary role in the promotion and protection of international human rights. A number of factors, however, led the General Assembly to become a forum of enormous significance.[32] During the 'Cold War', the inability of the Security Council to attain consensus on areas affecting peace and security, provided the General Assembly with the opportunity to exert some political authority. A step towards establishing such authority was taken by the Assembly when it adopted the *Uniting for Peace* Resolution on 3 November, 1950.[33] The Resolution provides that

> if the Security Council, because of lack of unanimity of the permanent members, fails to exercise its primary responsibility for the maintenance of international peace and security in any case where there appears to be a threat to the peace, breach of the peace, or act of aggression, the General Assembly shall consider the matter immediately with a view to making appropriate recommendations to Members for collective measures, including in the case of a breach of the peace or act of aggression the use of armed force when necessary, to maintain or restore international peace and security.[34]

Through the adoption of this Resolution, the Assembly assumed a role in the determination of threats to peace and security, including making recommendations on the use of armed force. Whilst invoked sparingly, the Resolution nevertheless enhanced the position of the Assembly *vis-à-vis* the Security Council. A second factor in enhancing the power of the General Assembly was a direct consequence of the enlarged membership of the UN due to the new States from Asia and Africa. These new States (which came to represent the majority of UN membership) have influenced not only the role and proceedings of the General Assembly but also international law more generally. While the General Assembly Resolutions are recommendatory and cannot as such establish binding legal obligations, they present evidence of State practice. State practice provides an essential ingredient in the development of binding customary law.[35] The developing world has also used the Resolutions to advance their agenda of international law. In this context it is important to note the highly authoritative General Assembly Resolutions such as the Declaration on the Granting of Independence to Colonial Countries and Peoples (1960)[36] and the Declaration on Principles of International Law Concerning Friendly Relations and Co-operation Amongst States in Accordance with the Charter of the United Nations (1970).[37] Reference can also be made to other General Assembly Resolutions which have been used to advance

---

[32] Cassese, 'The General Assembly: Historical Perspectives 1945–1989' in Alston (ed.), above n.1, pp. 25–54, at p. 29.

[33] Adopted 3 November 1950, UN GA Res. 377(V), GAOR, 5th Sess. Supp. 20, at 10.

[34] Ibid. A(1).

[35] For the elements required to establish customary international law, see above chapter 2.

[36] Adopted 14 December 1960, UN GA Res. 1514 (XV); UN GAOR 15th Session, Supp. 16, at 66, UN Doc. A/4684 (1961).

[37] GA Res. 2625 (XXV) (1970). On the value of General Assembly Resolutions in general international law see Sloan, 'General Assembly Resolutions Revisited: (Forty Years Later)' 58 *BYIL* (1987) 39; Bleicher, 'The Legal Significance of Re-Citation of General Assembly Resolutions' 63 *AJIL* (1969) 444; Cheng, 'United Nations Resolutions on Outer Space: "Instant" International Customary Law?' 5 *IJIL* (1965) 23.

The United Nations system and the modern human rights regime (1945–)

3

the political aspirations of the developing world. These would include, *inter alia*, the Charter of Economic Rights and Duties of States,[38] the Declaration on the Establishment of a New Economic Order[39] and the Declaration on the Right to Development[40] which contain claims of economic self-determination and sovereignty over national resources.[41]

A distinct, though important role, is played by the General Assembly in preparing, drafting and adopting international treaties. While annexed to General Assembly Resolutions, these treaties are opened for accession by Member States and upon coming into force, as legal obligations bind States parties to them. The normal Assembly voting procedures are used to adopt these treaties.[42] Examples of such annexations include the International Covenants[43] and the International Convention on the Elimination of All Forms of Racial Discrimination.[44] When considering the implementation mechanism of the various UN sponsored treaties, we shall notice that the General Assembly plays a vital role in receiving and reviewing States Parties' compliance with international obligations.[45]

(ii) The Security Council[46]

The Security Council, like the General Assembly, is one of the principal organs of the United Nations. The Security Council acts as the executive body of the United Nations with its primary responsibility being the maintenance of international peace and security.[47] The Security Council has 15 members, five of which are permanent. The permanent members of the Council are China, France, the Russian Federation, the United Kingdom and the United States. The other 10 members are elected by the Assembly for two years. They are elected by a two-thirds majority vote of the General Assembly. The UN Charter Article 23(1) refers to equitable geographical distribution and there is an informal agreement that there should be five members from Afro-Asian States, one from Eastern Europe, two from Latin America and one from Western Europe and one from other States (e.g. Canada, Australia).[48] The justification for the five permanent members has been that any action in

---

[38] GA Res. 3281 (XXIX) 14 I.L.M. (1974) 251.

[39] GA Res. 3201 (S-VI) 13 I.L.M. (1974) 715.

[40] GA Res. 128, UN GAOR, 41 Sess., Supp. 53 at 186, UN Doc. A/Res/41/128 (4 December 1986).

[41] See Harris, above n.1, pp. 767–772.

[42] Shaw, above n.1, at p. 909.

[43] International Covenant on Civil and Political Rights, New York, 7 March 1966 United Nations, *Treaty Series*, vol. 660, p. 195, International Covenant on Economic, Social and Cultural Rights, New York, 16 December 1966, 993 U.N.T.S. 3; 6 I.L.M. (1967) 360.

[44] New York, 7 March 1966 United Nations, *Treaty Series*, vol. 660, p. 195.

[45] See Davidson, *Human Rights* (Open University Press, 1993) p. 67.

[46] See Sands and Klein, above n.5, at pp. 39–55; Bailey, 'The Security Council' in Alston (ed.), above n.1, pp. 304–336; Bailey, *Voting in the Security Council* (Indiana University Press, 1969); Bailey, *The Procedure of the UN Security Council* (Clarendon Press, 1988); Higgins, 'The Place of International Law in the Settlement of Disputes by the Security Council' 64 *AJIL* (1970) 1; Brand, 'Security Council Resolutions: When do they Give Rise to Enforceable Legal Rights? The United Nations Charter, the Byrd Amendment and a Self Executing Treaty Analysis' 9 *Cornell International Law Journal* (1976) 298; Woods, 'Security Council Working Methods and Procedures: Recent Developments' 45 *ICLQ* (1996) 150; Fassbender, *UN Security Council Reform and the Right of Veto: A Constitutional Perspective* (Brill, 1998); Sarooshi, *The United Nations and the Development of Collective Security* (Oxford University Press, 2000).

[47] See Article 24(1) UN Charter.

[48] The 10 non-permanent members of the Council during 2009 are as follows: Austria (2010), Burkina Faso (2009), Costa Rica (2009), Croatia (2009), Japan (2010), Libyan Arab Jamahiriya (2009); Mexico (2010), Turkey (2010), Uganda (2010) and Vietnam (2009): www.un.org/sc/members.asp <last visited 1 February 2009>.

the face of opposition from one or more of these major powers would be unrealistic. At the time of the establishment of the United Nations, the five in question could all be described as major powers. Although it is fully recognised that over the past 60 years the global power has shifted to include a number of other States, amendments to the Charter to remove one of these five powers would require the consent of the five concerned[49] and agreement on who should be included instead would be very hard to obtain. The tacit acceptance that Russia could succeed to the seat that the Charter allocated to the former Soviet Union illustrates a reluctance to open up discussion on the general issue of who are appropriate permanent members. In 2005, the then Secretary-General, Kofi Annan, in his report 'In Larger Freedom' proposed two models for reforming the Security Council. The first model, 'Model A' provided for six new permanent seats though with no veto powers attached to these permanent seats. At the same time this model established three new two-year term non-permanent seats. The second model, called 'Model B', provided that there would be no new permanent seats. However, it created a new category of eight four-year renewable-term seats and one new two-year non-permanent (and non-renewable) seat, divided among the major regional areas.[50]

The Security Council, in addition to the periodic meetings provided for by Article 28(2) of the UN Charter, may hold meetings at any time at short notice.[51] However, the period of time between such meetings should not exceed 14 days. Any country (member or non-member) or the Secretary-General may bring to the Security Council's attention a dispute or threat to peace and security.[52] There is a difference in voting in the Security Council as compared to the General Assembly. To pass a resolution, an affirmative vote of nine members is required. However, a negative vote by any of the permanent members on a resolution that relates to a non-procedural matter would veto the resolution.[53] The power to veto resolutions was incorporated into the Charter to prevent the Council taking any substantial decision detrimental to the interests of any of the permanent members. The power of veto was used extensively at the height of the Cold War, leading to an inability on the part of the Security Council to take any effective steps to maintain peace and security or to prevent extensive violations of human rights. Strong disagreements between permanent members and the threat of veto may lead States not to advance a Resolution under Chapter VII.

---

[49] See Article 108 of the UN Charter, which states that '[a]mendments to the present Charter shall come into force for all Members of the United Nations when they have been adopted by a vote of two thirds of the members of the General Assembly and ratified in accordance with their respective constitutional processes by two thirds of the Members of the United Nations, including all the permanent members of the Security Council'.

[50] 'In Larger Freedom: Towards Security Development and Human Rights for All' Report by the Secretary-General of the United Nations for Decisions of Heads of State and Government in September 2005 A/59/2005 (21 March 2005) daccessdds.un.org/doc/UNDOC/GEN/N05/270/78/PDF/N0527078.pdf?OpenElement <last visited 1 January 2009>.

[51] Rule 1, Rules of Procedure of the Security Council, S/96/Rev.7.

[52] Article 35 UN Charter.

[53] See Article 27 the UN Charter: Abstention should be distinguished from absence. In 1950 the Soviet Union boycotted meetings because the government of China had not been permitted to take its country's place on the Security Council. At this point the Korean War broke out and the Security Council authorised military action by UN members, action which the Soviet Union would certainly have vetoed if it had been present. It subsequently argued that the action was illegal, as being present and abstaining was very different from not being present at all. On the other hand, Article 28 of the Charter imposes a duty on members to be represented at all times and if the Soviet argument was correct a state could prevent the Council from acting at all by absenting itself. The situation has never been repeated.

In view of the strong opposition from France and Russia, the United States decided not to present a Resolution sanctioning using of force against Iraq during the 2003 crisis.

As a political organ the Security Council does not as such establish international law. That said, Security Council Resolutions have also had a direct role in developing international law, in that these Resolutions may provide useful assistance in the interpretation of the Charter, establish evidence of general principles of law, or reflect *opinio juris* provided the subject matter in question does not relate to specific cases or circumstances.[54] More significantly and as shall be considered in this book, Security Council Resolutions passed under Chapter VII represent normative obligations with binding and overriding legal consequences. According to Article 24 of the UN Charter, Member States agree to confer primary responsibility upon the Security Council for the maintenance of international peace and security. By virtue of Article 25, Member States undertake to accept and carry out the decisions of the Council. The powers conferred upon the Security Council are elaborated upon in subsequent chapters of the Charter. Chapter VI (Articles 33–38) assigns recommendatory powers to the Security Council in relation to the peaceful settlement of disputes, whereas Chapter VII (Articles 39–51) confers upon the Council the authority to deal with threats to the peace, breaches of the peace and acts of aggression. Acting under Chapter VII, the Security Council has an absolute discretion in the determination of whether there exists a threat to peace and security under Chapter VII[55] and in respect of enforcement powers such as economic sanctions or military action.

The role played by the Security Council under Chapter VI and VIII has important implications for human rights. After the collapse of the Soviet Union in 1991 and the thaw in East–West relations there had been expectations that the Security Council would work as a more effective body to promote and protect human rights. With the authorisation of the Security Council – through its Resolution 678 (1990) and passed under Chapter VII of the United Nations Charter[56] – the allied forces were successful in expelling Iraqi forces from Kuwait in 1991. Subsequently, the Security Council passed Resolution 688 (1991) against Iraqi repression of the Kurdish people which was relied upon by the allied powers to establish a 'safe-haven' and maintain a 'no-fly zone' in Northern Iraq.[57] Despite expressing grave

---

[54] Saul, 'Definition of "Terrorism" in the UN Security Council: 1985–2004' 4 *Chinese Journal of International Law* (2005) 141 at p. 142; de Brichambaut, 'The Role of the United Nations Security Council in the International Legal System' in Byers (ed.) *The Role of International Law in International Politics: Essays in International Politics and International Law* (Oxford University Press, 2000) pp. 269–276 at p. 273.

[55] See *Prosecutor* v. *Tadic* – Case No. IT-94-I-AR72, 15 July 1999, Decision on the Defence Motion for Interlocutory Appeal on Jurisdiction, 2 October 1995, paras. 29–30 www.un.org/icty/tadic/appeal/decision-e/51002.htm <last visited 4 January 2009>; Gowlland-Debbas, 'The Relationship Between the International Court of Justice and Security Council in the Light of the *Lockerbie* Case' 88 *AJIL* (1994) 643 at p. 662. A more recent example of the use of such discretion by the Security Council has been evidenced through the adoption of Resolution 1422 (2002). SC Res 1422 (2002) 12 July 2002, UN Doc. S/RES/1422 (2002) available at www.un.org <last visited 5 January 2009>. This Resolution which was passed unanimously by the Security Council provides exemptions for peacekeeper from International Criminal Court's Jurisdiction for a (renewable) period of 12 months. The adoption of a Resolution under Chapter VII mandate has been the object of criticism. See Stahn, 'The Ambiguities of Security Council Resolution 1422 (2002) 14 *EJIL* (2003) 85 at p. 86; MacPherson, 'Authority of the Security Council to Exempt Peace Keepers from International Criminal Court Proceedings' ASIL Insight July 2002 www.asil.org/insigh89.cfm <last visited 5 January 2009>. On the International Criminal Court, see below chapter 20.

[56] See SC Res. 678 (29 November 1990).

[57] In this regard note the absence of a specific authorisation by the Security Council to establish the safe-havens. See Franck, 'When, If Ever, May States Deploy Military Force without Prior Security Council Authorization' 5 *Washington University Journal of Law and Policy* (2001) 51 at pp. 62–63; also see Shaw, above n.1, at pp. 1254–1255.

concern, Resolution 688 (1991) was not adopted under Chapter VII.[58] The Security Council has, however, made extensive use of its resolutions and enforcement powers under Chapter VII in the territories of the former Yugoslavia,[59] Somalia,[60] Haiti[61] and more recently in East Timor.[62] During 1994 (and prior to the creation of the International Criminal Court) the Security Council also undertook the unprecedented step of establishing *ad hoc* tribunals for the trials of those accused of gross violations of human rights in the former Yugoslavia (ICTY) and Rwanda (ICTR).[63] In the case of ICTR, this was the first time that an international criminal tribunal was established essentially for a non-international situation.[64] The role and prestige of the Security Council was severely dented in the events post 11 September 2001 and particularly in relation to actions undertaken by individual Member States, in particular the United State in its pursuit of the so-called 'war on terror'. The bombing campaign of Afghanistan initiated in October 2001 has remained controversial. The Security Council was bitterly divided on the subject of Iraq and failed to authorise the armed intervention of the country in 2003.[65]

A recurring debate relates to the obligations of the Security Council in promoting and protecting human rights. The Council (in common with organs of the UN) is under an obligation to promote and protect human rights, although unlike the General Assembly and ECOSOC, the Charter is restrictive in that Article 24(2) states that '[i]n discharging these duties the Security Council shall act in accordance with the Purposes and Principles of the United Nations'. Furthermore, a cumulative effect of Article 25 (which provides that UN Member States agree to accept and carry out the decisions made by the Security Council) and Article 103 (which provides that obligations under the Charter shall prevail over inconsistent treaty obligations) have led the Council to impinge upon individual and collective human rights in a variety of manners. Various examples of such actions and decisions can be found in this rejuvenated body since the collapse of the Soviet Union. Targeting of individuals – as happened in the case of the Lockerbie suspects or those suspected of international terrorism[66] – and (economic or military) sanctions against those States adjudged to have been a threat to peace and security under Chapter VII provide recent examples.[67] The Security Council has, in common with other international actors, a well established role in ensuring the right of self-determination to people, a right to democratic governance and the more fundamental right to life and the prohibition from torture, cruel inhuman or degrading treatment. Therefore, it would be unacceptable, if the Security Council was exempted from

---

[58] Goodwin-Gill and McAdam, *The Refugee in International Law* (Oxford University Press, 2007) p. 4; Shaw, above n.1, at pp. 1254–1255.

[59] See SC Res. 757 (30 May 1992); SC Res. 770 (13 August 1992); SC Res. 787 (16 November 1992); SC Res. 815 (30 March 1993); SC Res. 819 (16 April 1993); SC Res. 824 (1993); SC Res. 1199 (23 September 1998).

[60] See SC Res. 733 (23 June 1992) adopted at the 3039th mtg; and SC Res. 794 (3 December 1992) adopted at 3145 mtg.

[61] See SC Res. 841 (16 June 1993); SC Res. 940 (31 July 1994).

[62] See SC Res. 1272 (25 October 1999); SC Res. 1410 (2002); Roberts, 'The Laws of War: Problems of Implementation in Contemporary Conflicts' 6 *Duke Journal of Comparative and International Law* (1995) 11.

[63] The ICTR was created by SC Res. 955 (8 November 1994) and the ICTY by SC Res. 827 (25 May 1993).

[64] See Roberts, above n.62, at p. 65.

[65] For the controversy over the legality of the use of force in Iraq in March 2004 see chapter 24 below.

[66] For a critical assessment, see 'The European Convention on Human Rights, Due Process and United Nations Security Council Counter-Terrorism Sanctions' Report prepared by Professor Iain Cameron 06/02/2006 www.coe.int/t/e/legal_affairs/legal_co-operation/public_international_law/Texts_&_Documents/2006/I.%20Cameron%20Report%2006.pdf <last visited 5 January 2009>.

[67] On the impact of sanctions see below.

decisions and actions even in instances where these constitute violations of *jus cogens* norms of human rights law. The impact of sanctions, as witnessed in cases of Libya and Iraq, can have a crippling effect on the enjoyment of fundamental human rights.[68] As the ICESCR Committee noted in its General Comment:

> While the impact of sanctions varies from one case to another, the Committee is aware that they almost always have a dramatic impact on the rights recognized in the Covenant. Thus, for example, they often cause significant disruption in the distribution of food, pharmaceuticals and sanitation supplies, jeopardize the quality of food and the availability of clean drinking water, severely interfere with the functioning of basic health and education systems, and undermine the right to work. In addition, their unintended consequences can include reinforcement of the power of oppressive élites, the emergence, almost invariably, of a black market and the generation of huge windfall profits for the privileged élites which manage it, enhancement of the control of the governing élites over the population at large, and restriction of opportunities to seek asylum or to manifest political opposition. While the phenomena mentioned in the preceding sentence are essentially political in nature, they also have a major additional impact on the enjoyment of economic, social and cultural rights.[69]

In addition to the imposition of sanctions, the Security Council has on occasions demanded reparations and compensation from individual States. Thus, in the aftermath, of the Iraqi invasion and the subsequent liberation of Kuwait in 1991, the Security Council under its Resolution 692 of May 1991 established a compensation Commission. Compensation was demanded on the principle of wrongful actions on the part of the Iraqi regime.[70] While such a coercive approach on the part of the Security Council did have the obvious advantage of swift resolution and monetary compensation, jurists such as Adam Roberts are critical in that

> holding an entire country liable for the entire costs of a war is intensely problematic. It is likely to force a whole population to pay for the offenses committed by a minority among them. The process of payment may drag out for decades and cause dangerous political resentment against those imposing the penalties.[71]

The continuing misadventures by the Security Council in the field of maintaining peace and security and its usurpation of judicial and legislative roles raises the question of reviewing and challenging the actions of the Council, especially in cases which result in gross violations of human rights. Attempts have been made by individuals and States to hold international organisations including the UN Security Council judicially accountable

---

[68] Professor Cassese regards these economic sanctions as frequently 'unfair and counterproductive'. Cassese, *International Criminal Law* (Oxford University Press, 2003) p. 4.

[69] See *The Relationship Between Economic Sanctions and Respect for Economic, Social and Cultural Rights*: 12/12/97. E/C.12/1997/8, CESCR General Comment 8. (*General Comments*), para 3.

[70] See S/RES/692 (1991) 20 May 1991, Resolution 692 (1991) Adopted by the Security Council at its 2987th meeting on 20 May 1991. Adopted by a vote of 14 in favour, none against, and one abstention (Cuba) www.kuwaitmission.com/SC-RES_692.htm <last visited 8 April 2009>.

[71] Roberts, above n.62, at p. 54.

for its actions; all these endeavours have thus far failed with domestic and international courts refusing to review Security Council decisions.[72]

However in the recent exceptional decision of the European Court of Justice in *Yassin Abdullah Kadi and Al Barakaat International Foundation* v. *Council and Commission*, the Court set aside the judgments of the Court of First Instance.[73] It ruled that the Community judicature had the jurisdiction to review measures undertaken and adopted by the European Community giving effect to the United Nations Security Council Resolution. In the exercise of its jurisdiction, the Court held that Council Regulation (EC) No. 881/2002 of 27 May 2002 which was aimed at implementing the United Nations Security Council Resolution infringed the rights of Mr. Kadi and Al Barakaat International Foundation. The Court, however, was careful in not challenging the overall supremacy of international law or the United Nations Security Council. Hence, notwithstanding this apparently revolutionary stance, in reality the prospects of judicial review of the Security Council Resolutions, especially those passed under Chapter VII, remains remote and unlikely. White's comments are reflective of the *real politic* that 'while the primary rules of international law . . . are applicable to the activities of the Security Council, the UN system is woefully inadequate in ensuring the accountability of the Security Council in this, or in any other regard'.[74] Such lack of accountability and failure to provide remedies against an injudicious Security Council in itself poses a threat to international peace and security.

(iii) The Economic and Social Council (ECOSOC)[75]

ECOSOC is concerned with a number of economic and general welfare issues. These include trade, developmental and social matters including population, children, housing and racial discrimination. While the mandate of ECOSOC covers wide-ranging issues, its actual powers are limited to recommendations which are not binding upon States. ECOSOC consists of 54 members, who are elected by the General Assembly for a three year term in office. Up until 1991, ECOSOC used to have two annual sessions each lasting for four weeks. However, the General Assembly in May 1991 decided that from 1992 ECOSOC would hold an organisational session of up to four days in New York in early

---

[72] *Ahmed Ali Yusuf and Al Barakaat International Foundation and Yassin Abdullah Kadi v. Council of the European Union and Commission of the European Communities* (Judgments of the Court of First Instance in Case T-306/01 and Case T-315/01). (The European community is competent to order the freezing of individuals' funds as part of the 'war against terrorism' and as required by UN Security Council. These measures fall for the most part outside the scope of judicial review and do not infringe the universally recognised fundamental human rights.) Wessel, 'The UN, the EU and Jus Cogens', 3 *International Organizations Law Review* (2006) 1. *Bosphorus Hava Yollari Turizm v. Ireland* (2006) 42 E.H.R.R. 1; Costello 'The *Bosphorus* Ruling of the European Court of Human Rights: Fundamental Rights and Blurred Boundaries in Europe' 6 *Human Rights Law Review* (2006) 87.

[73] Judgment of the Court of Justice in Joined Cases C-402/05 P and C-415/05 P. *Yassin Abdullah Kadi and Al Barakaat International Foundation* v. *Council and Commission* (3 September 2008).

[74] White, above n.5, at p. 106.

[75] See O'Donovan, 'The Economic and Social Council' in Alston (ed.), above n.1, pp. 107–125; Mangone, *UN Administration of Economic and Social Programs* (Columbia University Press, 1966); Stinebower, *The Economic and Social Council: An Instrument of International Cooperation* (Commission to Study the Organization of Peace, 1946); Loveday, 'Suggestions for the Reform of the United Nations Economic and Social Machinery' 7 *International Organization* (1953) 325; Malinowski, 'Centralization and Decentralization in the United Nations Economic and Social Activities' 16 *International Organization* (1962) 521.

February of each year and one substantive session of four weeks to take place in alternate years in New York and Geneva in July.[76] Unlike the position within the Security Council, no provisions are made for the permanent membership of ECOSOC, although in practice the permanent members (within the Security Council) are repeatedly elected to ECOSOC.[77] It is also the case that the issue of being elected to ECOSOC is not as politically volatile as compared to such organs such as the new Human Rights Council, which has replaced the previous Human Rights Commission. In ECOSOC sessions it is the usual practice that a State is represented by its permanent representative stationed either in New York or Geneva. In the light of the rapidly declining prestige of ECOSOC, the most articulate political and governmental representatives prefer to be part of the Human Rights Council with its more public profile as opposed to the publically less-known ECOSOC.

According to Article 62 of the UN Charter, ECOSOC may initiate or make studies on a range of subjects and may make recommendations to the General Assembly, members of the UN and to relevant specialist agencies. The UN Charter makes provisions for ECOSOC to consult NGOs in its work.[78] ECOSOC may also prepare draft conventions and call international conferences.[79] The functional commissions of ECOSOC include the Commission on the Status of Women.[80] ECOSOC also has a number of regional commissions[81] and several standing committees and expert bodies.[82] It also runs a number of programmes such as the UN Environment Programme[83] and has played a role in the work of the UN High Commissioner for Refugees.[84] During the 2005 World Summit, it was decided by the Heads of State and Government that ECOSOC should hold Annual Ministerial Reviews (AMR) and a biennial Development Cooperation Forum (DCF). The AMR is created to examine the progress that is being made in achieving internationally agreed development goals (IADGs) drawn up at major conferences and summits. The AMR consists of an annual thematic review as well as presentations made voluntarily on progress and challenges in reaching the IADGs. The launch of the AMR was conducted in 2007. The 2007 AMR examined eradication of poverty, while the theme for the 2008 AMR was hunger and sustainable development.[85] 'Implementing the internationally agreed goals and commitment in regard

---

[76] Rule 2, Rules of Procedure, E/5715/Rev.2.

[77] O'Donovan, above n.75, at p. 108.

[78] Article 71, UN Charter.

[79] Article 62(3) and (4), UN Charter.

[80] In all there were nine functional commissions. Apart from the now defunct Commission on Human Rights and the existing Commission on the Status of Women, there are the following: Statistical Commission, Commission on Population and Development, Commission for Social Development, Commission on Narcotic Drugs, Commission on Crime Prevention and Criminal Justice, Commission on Science and Technology for Development, Commission on Sustainable Development and United Nations Forum on Forests.

[81] The five Regional Commissions are: Economic Commission for Africa (Addis Ababa, Ethiopia), Economic and Social Commission for Asia and the Pacific (Bangkok, Thailand), Economic Commission for Europe (Geneva, Switzerland), Economic Commission for Latin America and the Caribbean (Santiago, Chile) and Economic and Social Commission for Western Asia (Beirut, Lebanon).

[82] The three standing committees are: Committee for Programme and Coordination, Committee on Non-Governmental Organizations and Committee on Negotiations with Intergovernmental Agencies. In addition the Council has a number of expert bodies on subjects including development planning, indigenous issues, public administration, international cooperation in tax matters and economic, social and cultural rights. There are also *ad hoc* bodies on energy and sustainable development and informatics.

[83] Under the Department of Economic and Social Affairs.

[84] Statute of the Office of the United Nations High Commissioner for Refugees, GA Res. 428 (V), annex, 5 UN GAOR Supp. (No. 20) at 46, UN Doc. A/1775 (1950), paras 3 and 4.

[85] See Annual Ministerial Review, www.un.org/ecosoc/newfunct/amr.shtml <last visited 5 January 2009>.

to global public health' has been assigned the theme for the 2009 AMR.[86] The principal objective of DCF is the enhancement of coherent and effective activities of different development partners. The Forum reviews the trends and progress that is being made in international development cooperation, and also provides policy guidance and recommendations for improving the quality and impact of development co-operation. Launched in Geneva in July 2007, the first biennial forum was held on 30 June and 1 July 2008 in New York.[87] The UN work on human rights has focused around ECOSOC. The primary human rights monitoring task has now been transferred to the Human Rights Council, to which we will turn our attention later on in this chapter.

(a) The Commission on the Status of Women[88]

The Commission on the Status of Women (CSW) is one of the functional commissions of the ECOSOC. The CSW currently consists of 45 members who are elected by the Human Rights Council for a four-year term. The CSW comprises of one representative from each of the 45 Member States on the basis of equitable geographical distribution: thirteen representative members from Africa; nine from Latin America and the Caribbean; eleven from Asia; eight from Western Europe and other States and four from Eastern Europe. The meetings of the Commission are held annually at the UN Headquarters in New York for 10 working days (late February to early March). The CSW was a product of ECOSOC Resolution 11(II) of June 1946 to prepare reports and recommendations for the Council to advance and promote women's rights.[89] In practice the most prominent achievement of the CSW has been in the field of standard-setting. While it has played a pivotal role in the drafting of a number of instruments including the Convention on the Political Rights of Women,[90] the Convention on the Nationality of Married Women[91] etc. its single most significant achievement is the work on the drafting of the Convention on the Elimination of All Forms of Discrimination against Women.[92] The CSW has a continuing involvement with the Convention as it receives reports from the Committee on CEDAW under the 1979 Convention.[93] The CSW has been involved in information gathering, cooperation with other international agencies and preparing recommendations and reports on the rights of women in political, economic, civil, social and educational fields. It is also possible for this Commission to appoint a sessional working group to review confidential communications 'which appear to reveal a consistent pattern of reliably attested injustice and discriminatory practice against women',[94] and to prepare a report which will indicate the categories in which communications are most frequently submitted to the Commission.[95]

[86] Ibid.
[87] For further information on DCF see Development Cooperation Forum, www.un.org/ecosoc/newfunct/develop.shtml <last visited 5 January 2009>.
[88] See Reanda, 'The Commission on the Status of Women' in Alston (ed.), above n.1, pp. 265–303.
[89] The CSW has procedures analogous to ECOSOC Resolution 728F and 1503 – these, however, remain obscure through a lack of utilisation.
[90] 1952, 193 U.N.T.S. 135, entered into force 7 July 1954.
[91] 1957, 309 U.N.T.S. 65, entered into force 11 August 1958.
[92] See below chapter 15.
[93] New York, 18 December 1979 United Nations, *Treaty Series*, vol. 1249, p. 13, Article 21(2) CEDAW.
[94] For further details of this mechanism see Commission on the Status of Women, www.right-to-education.org/node/173 <last visited 1 April 2009>.
[95] Reanda, above n.88, at pp. 265–303, at p. 274.

(iv) International Court of Justice[96]

The International Court of Justice (ICJ) is 'the principal judicial organ of the United Nations'.[97] The ICJ was established in 1945 and began work in 1946 as the successor to the Permanent Court of International Justice. The Statute of the ICJ forms an integral part of the UN Charter and all UN members are automatically parties to the Statute of the ICJ.[98] The Court consists of 15 judges elected by concurrent votes of the Security Council and the General Assembly.[99] The jurisdiction of the ICJ is either contentious or advisory. Only States can be parties to the Court's contentious jurisdiction, a jurisdiction that is based upon the consent of the parties in dispute.[100] In contentious cases, the judgment of the Court is final and binds only States which are parties to the case.[101] The ICJ has the power to award provisional measures – a power which derives from Article 41 of the Statute of the ICJ, as well as from the general principles of International Law.[102] The ICJ is also authorised to deliver advisory opinions. A request for such an opinion could be brought forth by a number of organs including the General Assembly or the Security Council, although the advisory jurisdiction is not open to States.[103] In effecting the advisory jurisdiction, the objective of the Court is to 'offer legal advice to the organ and institutions requesting the opinion'.[104] The Court, however, has adopted a restrictive approach towards the competence of organs and institutions forwarding demands for advisory opinions. The WHO (World Health Organisation) asked the ICJ for an advisory opinion as to whether the dangerous environmental effect and negative consequences on health resulting from the deployment of nuclear weapons by States would breach States international obligations, including those established in the WHO constitution. The ICJ adopted a very restrictive view and rejected the request, and in so doing held that the question was beyond the remit of WHO's responsibilities.[105]

---

[96] See Chapter XIV UN Charter. See Higgins, 'Human Rights in the International Court of Justice' 20 *LJIL* (2007) 745; Rosenne, *The World Court: What It Is and How it Works* (Brill, 1995); Fitzmaurice, *The Law and Procedure of the International Court of Justice* (Cambridge University Press, 1986); for a detailed survey see Thirlway, 'The Law and Procedure of the International Court of Justice: 1960–1989' 60 *BYIL* (1989) 1, and its following ten volumes at p. 1; Schwelb, 'The International Court of Justice and the Human Rights Clauses of the Charter' 66 *AJIL* (1972) 337; Rodley, 'Human Rights and Humanitarian Intervention: The Case Law of the World Court' 38 *ICLQ* (1989) 321; Rehman, 'The Role and Contribution of the World Court in the Progressive Development of International Environmental Law' 5 *APJEL* (2000) 3; Thirlway, 'The International Court of Justice' in Evans (ed.), above n.1, at pp. 561–588.

[97] Article 92, UN Charter.

[98] According to Article 93(1) 'All Members of the United Nations are *ipso facto* parties to the Statute of the International Court of Justice' and Article 94(1) provides that 'Each member of the United Nations undertakes to comply with the decisions of the International Court of Justice in any case to which it is a party'.

[99] Judges hold nine-year terms, ending on 5 February of the year indicated in parentheses next to their name. As at 31 March 2009, the composition of the Court is as follows: Ronny Abraham (France) (2018), Awn Shawkat Al-Khasawneh (Jordan) (2018), Mohamed Bennouna (Morocco) (2015), Thomas Buergenthal (United States) (2015), Antônio Augusto Cançado Trindade (Brazil) (2018), Christopher Greenwood (United Kingdom) (2018), Shi Jiuyong (China) (2012), Kenneth Keith (New Zealand) (2015), Abdul G. Koroma (Sierra Leone) (2012), Hisashi Owada (Japan) (2012), Bernardo Sepulveda Amor (Mexico) (2015), Bruno Simma (Germany) (2012), Leonid Skotnikov (Russian Federation) (2015), Peter Tomka (Slovakia) (2012), Abdulqawi Ahmed Yusuf (Somalia) (2018) www0.un.org/geninfo/faq/factsheets/fs25membership.pdf <last visited 31 March 2009>.

[100] See Articles 34(1) and 36 *Statute of the International Court of Justice*, 26 June 1945, 59 Stat. 1055, 3 Bevans 1179.

[101] Article 59 Statute of the ICJ.

[102] Elkind, *Interim Protection: a Functional Approach* (Brill, 1981) p. 162.

[103] Article 65, Statute of the ICJ. States are however allowed participation in proceedings before the Court. Individuals do not have any *Lows Standi* before the Court. See Harris above n.1, at p. 1077.

[104] *Legality of the Use by a State of Nuclear Weapons in Armed Conflict*, Advisory Opinion 8 July 1996, (1996) ICJ Reports 66, paras 15 and 35.

[105] Ibid.

As the principal judicial organ of the UN, the ICJ's task is to decide upon matters involving judicial disputes. It is neither the Court's role to create new law nor to decide upon matters without a legal basis. Having said that, in reality it is often difficult to isolate legal from political matters, a situation that becomes apparent in cases involving allegations of human rights violations. Furthermore, the limitation of adjudication rather than the development of law is also unrealistic. The decisions and advisory opinions of the Court are of great value and have in a number of instances been highly significant in the advancement of international law. Indeed, so significant has been the Court that its principal provision for adjudication of a dispute is regarded as providing the catalogue of primary sources of international law.[106] Since its establishment, the Court has not been used as extensively as one might have envisaged, especially in relation to human rights matters.

The contributions of the ICJ towards the development of international law have nevertheless been significant.[107] One only has to look at such cases as the *North Sea Continental Shelf Cases*,[108] the Anglo-Norwegian *Fisheries Case*,[109] the *Asylum Case*,[110] and the advisory opinions of the Court in the *Reparations for Injuries Suffered in the Service of the United Nations Case*,[111] *Namibia Case*[112] and the *Western Sahara Case*[113] to appreciate this point. Furthermore, an enormous body of jurisprudence has been accumulated by the Court including a rich case-law in human rights and related areas of international humanitarian law and environmental protection.[114] Amongst the innumerable judgments and advisory opinions where the Court has expanded on the jurisprudence of international human rights norms, reference could be made to the *Reservations to the Genocide Convention Case*,[115] the *Barcelona Traction case*,[116] the *Namibia case*,[117] the *Tehran Hostages case*,[118] the *East Timor Case*[119] and *Legal Consequences of the Construction of a Wall in the Occupied Palestinian Territory*.[120] Notwithstanding the limitations in respect of both jurisdiction and the actual enforcement of the Court's judgments, the ICJ has played a valuable role in the implementation of international laws. Roberts made the valid point that 'the International Court of Justice (ICJ) at The Hague has long had certain limited roles in respect of

---

[106] Article 38(1) Statute of the International Court of Justice. see above chapter 2.

[107] Gross, 'Some Observations on International Court of Justice' 56 *AJIL* (1962) 33; Shearer, *Starke's International Law* (LexisNexis UK, 1994) pp. 33–62. For an excellent survey of the contribution of the Court to various areas of international law as well as other related issues see Lowe and Fitzmaurice (eds), *Fifty Years of the International Court of Justice: Essays in Honour of Sir Robert Jennings* (Cambridge University Press, 1996).

[108] *North Sea Continental Shelf Cases (Federal Republic of Germany v. Denmark; Federal Republic of Germany v. Netherlands)*, Judgment 20 February 1969, (1969) ICJ Reports 3; Friedman, 'The North Sea Continental Shelf Cases: A Critique' 64 *AJIL* (1970) 229.

[109] *The Fisheries Case (United Kingdom v. Norway)*, Judgment 18 December 1951, (1951) ICJ Reports 116.

[110] *Asylum Case (Columbia v. Peru)*, Judgment 20 November 1950, (1950) ICJ Reports 266.

[111] Advisory Opinion 11 April 1949 (1949) ICJ Reports 174.

[112] Advisory Opinion 21 June 1971 (1971) ICJ Reports 16.

[113] Advisory Opinion 16 October 1975 (1975) ICJ Reports 12.

[114] See Roberts, above n.62, at pp. 43–45.

[115] *Reservations to the Convention on the Prevention and Punishment of the Crime of Genocide*, Advisory Opinion 28 May 1951, (1951) ICJ Reports 15.

[116] See *Barcelona Traction, Light and Power Company Limited (Belgium v. Spain)*, Preliminary Objection, Judgment 24 July 1964, (1964) ICJ Reports 6.

[117] *Legal Consequences for States of the Continued Presence of South Africa in Namibia (South West Africa) notwithstanding Security Council Resolution 276 (1970)*, Advisory Opinion 21 June 1971, (1971) ICJ Reports 16.

[118] See *United States Diplomatic and Consular Staff in Tehran (United States of America v. Iran)*, Judgment 24 May 1980, (1980) ICJ Reports 3.

[119] *East Timor Case (Portugal v. Australia)*, Judgment 30 June 1995, (1995) ICJ Reports 90.

[120] Advisory Opinions of 9 July 2004, (2004) ICJ Reports 136.

implementation of the laws of war. There are specific references to the ICJ in the 1948 Convention and the 1954 Hague Cultural Property Convention.'[121]

(v) The Trusteeship Council[122]

The work of the Trusteeship Council is predominantly of historical interest, although with significant contemporary implications in modern developments of international human rights law. The objectives of the trusteeship system included, *inter alia,*

> to encourage respect for human rights and for fundamental freedoms for all without distinction as to race, sex, language, or religion, and to encourage recognition of the interdependence of the peoples of the world.[123]

After the formation of the UN, former mandated territories under the Covenant of the League of Nations were placed under the protection of the UN trusteeship system, with a council in charge of supervising the system. The only mandated territory not placed under the trusteeship system or granted independence was South West Africa. The issue became a subject of contention, in the process creating substantial human rights jurisprudence in the areas of racial non-discrimination and the right to self-determination. The International Court of Justice provided four advisory opinions and one judgment.[124] The matter was also the subject of a series of General Assembly Resolutions. The main aim of the Council was to supervise the social advancement of the people of trust territories, with the aim ultimately of preparing them for self-government and independence. Originally there were 11 trust territories, mostly in Africa and the Pacific Ocean, but with the independence of Palau in 1994 there remains no such territory. Consequently, on 1 November, 1994 the Council suspended its operations. The Trusteeship Council thereafter also amended its Rules of Procedure: the obligation to meet on an annual basis was removed. According to the amended rules, the Council continues to exist and can be convened by its President at the request of the Security Council or the General Assembly.[125] Although currently suspended, the system may have a future role to play for those territories where the State and government have collapsed leading to a situation of complete anarchy. It might be worth considering whether a State, for example, Somalia, Afghanistan and Iraq (ravaged by civil war and terrorism), should be placed under trust to an international organisation or to a willing State. A broader mandate has been suggested by a former

---

[121] See Roberts, above n.62, at p. 43.

[122] See Sands and Klein, above n.5, at pp. 63–68; Kunz, 'Chapter XI of the United Nations Charter in Action' 48 *AJIL* (1954) 103; Reisman, 'Reflections on State Responsibility for Violations of Explicit Protectorate, Mandate and Trusteeship Obligations' 10 *Michigan Journal of International Law* (1989) 231; Gordon, 'Some Legal Problems with Trusteeship' 28 *Cornell Journal of International Law* (1995) 301.

[123] Article 76(c) UN Charter.

[124] *International Status of South West Africa,* Advisory Opinion 11 July 1950 (1950) ICJ Reports 128, *Voting Procedure on Questions relating to Reports and Petitions concerning the Territory of South West Africa,* Advisory Opinion 7 July 1955 (1955) ICJ Report 67, *Admissibility of Hearings of Petitioners by the Committee on South West Africa,* Advisory Opinion 1 June 1956 (1956) ICJ Reports 23, *Legal Consequences for States of the Continued Presence of South Africa in Namibia (South West Africa) notwithstanding Security Council Resolution 276 (1970),* Advisory Opinion 21 June 1971 (1971) ICJ Reports 16, *South West Africa (Ethiopia* v. *South Africa) (Liberia* v. *South Africa)* Judgment 21 December 1962 (1962) ICJ Reports 319.

[125] See www.un.org/geninfo/faq/factsheets/fs25membership.pdf <last visited 5 January 2009>.

President of the United Nations General Assembly according to whom, 'in addition to its role under the Charter, the Trusteeship Council should hold in trust for humanity its common heritage and its common concerns: the environment; the protection of extra-territorial zones and resources of the sea and the seabed; the climate and the right of future generations'.[126] A firmer decision on the future of the Trusteeship Council or the assignment of a revised role remains pending.[127]

(vi) The Secretariat[128]

Headed by the Secretary-General, the Secretariat provides staff for the day-to-day functioning of the UN. The Secretary-General is appointed by the General Assembly on the unanimous recommendation of the Security Council.[129] The UN Charter does not specify a term of office but by convention he (or she) serves for five years and may then be re-appointed for a further five years. Article 98 provides that he (or she) shall carry out such functions as may be assigned to him by the General Assembly, the Security Council, Economic and Social Council or the Trusteeship Council and Article 99 gives him (or her) an independent role; he (or she) 'may bring to the attention of the Security Council any matter which in his opinion may threaten the maintenance of international peace and security'. He (or she) may propose issues to be discussed by the General Assembly or any other organ of the United Nations. The Secretary-General often acts as a 'referee' in disputes between Member States and on a number of occasions his (or her) 'good offices' have been used to mediate in international disputes. Since the creation of the UN, a total of eight Secretary-Generals have been appointed, the present incumbent being Ban Ki-moon from the Republic of Korea. The Secretary-General is assisted by a Deputy Secretary-General and by a group of advisors called the 'Senior Management Group'. The current deputy Secretary-General is Dr. Asha-Rose Migiro from Tanzania who took office 1 February 2007. The Secretary-General can play a notable part in the future developments of international law. One recent example is that of the publication of *Agenda for Peace* by a former Secretary-General, Dr. Boutros Boutros-Ghali, which has encouraged States to re-evaluate their practices in respect of securing peace and human rights.[130]

The role of Secretary-General in respect of human rights, although variable and dependent on the individual personalities, can be potentially very significant. Successive Secretary-Generals have maintained that it is within their mandate to use their offices to raise and resolve human rights concerns. Many examples of the involvement of the Secretary-General could be found in his intervention to prevent serious violations of human rights, the recent examples being the initiatives of Kofi Annan to condemn the terrorist attacks of September 11, 2001 and to the usage of his offices to avert the US led invasion in Iraq during 2003. Other notable examples could be found in the Secretary-General's involvement during the invasion of Kuwait (1990–91), attempts during 1998 to enforce the compliance of Iraq with the Security Council's Resolutions, the 1999 agreement with Libya leading to the Lockerbie

---

[126] Concluding Statement of the General Assembly President, UN Doc. A/45/PV.82 at 21 (1991).

[127] See Wilson, 'Changing the Charter: The United Nations Prepares for the Twenty-First Century' 90 *AJIL* (1996) 115 at p. 122.

[128] See Ramcharan, *Humanitarian Good Offices in International Law: The Good Offices of the United Nations Secretary-General in the field of Human Rights* (Brill, 1983); Van Boven, 'The Role of the United Nations Secretariat' in Alston (ed.), above n.1, pp. 549–579.

[129] See Article 97 of the UN Charter.

[130] Shaw, above n.1, at p. 834.

bombing trials and the efforts to resolve the East Timor conflict (2000). At the same time, it can not be stated with certainty in which human rights situations the Secretary-General would exercise his good offices. There is also no definitive and specific procedure invoking the good offices of the Secretary-General.[131] Applications should be made to him via the High Commission on Human Rights in Geneva or in New York.[132] In practice, in terms of petitioning it would perhaps be more useful to approach the United Nations High Commissioner for Human Rights. The High Commissioner has a specific mandate in this regard significant information is available about the activities of the High Commissioner on the website which includes a 'hotline' for reporting urgent situations.[133]

4 THE HUMAN RIGHTS COUNCIL[134]

The formation of the United Nations Human Rights Council in March 2006 by the General Assembly, and consequently its replacement of the Human Rights Commission, represents one of the most profound changes to the United Nations human rights system since 1945.[135] In order to have a comprehensive understanding of the current process operational within the United Nations it is important to consider, albeit briefly, the developments since the establishment of the organisation in 1945.

(i) Historical background – the Human Rights Commission and the Sub-Commission

The formation of the United Nations Human Rights Council in 2006 and its replacement of the Human Rights Commission present one of the most significant changes since 1945. Notwithstanding its demise, the Human Rights Commission has left a considerable imprint on the 'story' of human rights law as it has developed over time within the United Nations. An appreciation of the Commission's role is important not only to comprehend this 'story' but also to predict the future directions and institutional developments within the UN System.

---

[131] Rodley and Weissbrodt, 'United Nations Non-Treaty Procedures for Dealing with Human Rights Violations' in Hannum (ed.) *Guide to International Human Rights Practice* (Transnational Publishers, 2004) pp. 65–88, at p. 85.

[132] Ibid.

[133] For details of the website see Appendix I.

[134] See Alston, 'The Commission on Human Rights' in Alston (ed.), above n.1, at pp. 126–210; Eide, 'The Sub-Commission on Prevention of Discrimination and Protection of Minorities' ibid. pp. 211–264; Ghanea, 'From UN Commission on Human Rights to UN Human Rights Council: One Step Forwards or Two Steps Sideways' 55 *ICLQ* (2006) 695; Hannum, 'Reforming the Special Procedures and Mechanisms of the Commission on Human Rights' 7 *Human Rights Law Review* (2007) 73; Schrijver, 'The UN Human Rights Council: A New "Society of the Committed" or Just Old Wine in New Bottles?' 20 *LJIL* (2007) 809; Alston, 'Reconceiving the UN Human Rights Regime: Challenges Confronting the New UN Human Rights Council' 7 *Melbourne JIL* (2006) 185.

[135] The proposal to replace the Human Rights Commission with a Human Rights Council was made public by the UN Secretary-General in March 2005. He repeated his previous criticisms of the Commission's credibility deficit and declining professionalism to argue that 'If the United Nations is to meet the expectations of men and women everywhere – and indeed, if the Organization is to take the cause of human rights as seriously as those of security and development – then Member States should agree to replace the Commission on Human Rights with a smaller standing Human Rights Council', *Report of the Secretary-General, In Larger Freedom: Towards Development, Security and Human Rights for All*, 21 March 2005, A/59/2005 at para 183. In December 2004, the High-Level Panel on Threats, Challenges and Change had concluded that 'the Commission on Human Rights suffers from a legitimacy deficit that casts doubts on the overall reputation of the United Nations', Report of the High-Level Panel on Threats, Challenges and Change, A More Secure World: Our

In its initial incarnation, the UN Charter required that ECOSOC 'set up commissions in the economic and social fields and for the promotion of human rights'.[136] In its first meeting in 1946, the ECOSOC established two functional commissions; the Commission on Human Rights and the Commission on the Status of Women. Over the years the representation of the Commission on Human Rights grew and at the time of its abolition consisted of 53 individuals sitting in their capacity as governmental representatives.[137] Other States used to send representatives to the proceedings as observers but they did not have the right to vote.[138] The Commission met for an annual session of six weeks in Geneva during March and April and its proceedings were reported to the General Assembly via ECOSOC.[139]

The initial terms of reference of the Human Rights Commission were that the Commission should submit proposals, recommendations and reports to ECOSOC concerning:

(a) An international bill of rights

(b) International Declarations or Conventions on Civil Liberties, the Status of women, freedom of information and similar matters

(c) The Protection of Minorities

(d) The Prevention of discrimination on grounds of race, sex, language or religion

(e) Any other matter concerning human rights not covered by items (a), (b), (c), (d).[140]

For the first 20 years, the Human Rights Commission confined itself to standard-setting mechanisms. In 1947 the Commission adopted the statement (which was subsequently heavily criticised) that it had 'no power to take any action in regard to any complaints concerning human rights'.[141] Substantial issues confronted the domestic polices of even major Western liberal democracies such as the United States, United Kingdom and France. These included the existence of colonialism and difficult race relations. Up until 1967 the Commission refused to consider complaints of human rights violations in Member States of the United Nations. In addition, up until that time it was anticipated that the Commission would focus on standard-setting and that the effective implementation of the International Covenants would redress this situation. The limitations of review led one critic to note that by the mid 1960s the system had become 'the world's most elaborate waste-paper basket.'[142] However, in the 1960s there was also a discernible change in the political environment. A number of States had emerged who were anxious to promote international action against colonialism and racial discrimination. The increased membership of the UN also allowed them to have greater representation in the Commission. In 1966, ECOSOC decided almost to double the size of the original membership of the Commission to 32 members, 20 of

---

[136] Article 68 UN Charter (Chapter X).
[137] The allocation of these seats were on a geographical basis. The membership was based on the following: 15 African States, 13 Asian States, 11 Latin American States, five Eastern European States and 10 Western European and other States.
[138] Rodley and Weissbrodt, 'United Nations Non-Treaty Procedures for Dealing with Human Rights Violations' in Hannum (ed.), above n.131, at p. 66.
[139] Rule 37 of Rules of Procedure of the Human Rights Commission E/5975/Rev.1
[140] ECOSOC Res. 5(1) of 16 February 1946 and Resolution 5(11) of 21 June 1946.
[141] E/259 (1947) paras 21–22; See Zuijdwijk, *Petitioning the United Nations: A Study in Human Rights* (Palgrave MacMillan, 1982) pp. 1–14; Moller, 'The Right to Petition: General Assembly Resolution 217B' in Alfredsson and Eide (eds), above n.17, at p. 653.
[142] Humphrey, 'The Right of Petition in the United Nations' 4 *Human Rights Journal* (1971) 463.

3

The United Nations system and the modern human rights regime (1945–)

whom came from the developing world.[143] While perceiving racial oppression and apartheid as the great threat to world peace, these State representatives were strong advocates of an international petitioning system for receiving and acting upon complaints of racial discrimination and apartheid. The successful and rapid adoption of the Convention on the Elimination of All forms of Racial Discrimination provided a major encouragement.

Further extensions to the mandate of the Human Rights Commission took place.[144] Amongst the Commission's significant achievements were its standard-setting through the preparation of human rights instruments. The list of accomplishments in this regard is extensive. The jewel in the crown was the Commission's work in the drafting of the Universal Declaration of Human Rights[145] and the two International Covenants.[146] There were other human rights instruments including the International Convention on the Elimination of All Forms of Racial Discrimination (1966),[147] the Convention on the Rights of the Child (1989)[148] and the Convention on the Elimination of All Forms of Discrimination Against Women.[149] The Commission engaged itself in the preparation *inter alia* of the Declaration on the Elimination of All Forms of Intolerance and of Discrimination Based on Religion or Belief,[150] and the Declaration on the Rights of Persons Belonging to National or Ethnic, Religious and Linguistic Minorities.[151] In addition, it authorised the setting up of various working-groups and Special Rapporteurs, known collectively as non-conventional mechanisms.

The Commission also had a subsidiary organ, the Sub-Commission on the Promotion and Protection of Human Rights. At the time of its establishment in 1947, it was known as the Sub-Commission on Prevention of Discrimination and Protection of Minorities. The Sub-Commission originally consisted of 12 members but this was subsequently increased to 26 members who served in their individual capacity independently of their governments. The terms of reference under which the Sub-Commission worked were:

(a) To undertake studies, particularly in the light of the Universal Declaration of Human Rights, and to make recommendations to the Commission concerning the prevention of discrimination of any kind relating to human rights and fundamental freedoms and the protection of racial, national, religious and linguistic minorities; and

(b) To perform any other functions which may be entrusted to it by [ECOSOC] or the Commission.[152]

The Sub-Commission members were elected by the Human Rights Commission on the basis of regional distribution from amongst individuals nominated by governments but

---

[143] Alston, 'The Commission on Human Rights' in Alston (ed.), above n.1, 126–210 at p. 143.

[144] ECOSOC Res. E/1979/36.

[145] GA Res. 217A (III), UN Doc. A/810 at 71 (1948).

[146] International Covenant on Civil and Political Rights, New York, 7 March 1966 United Nations, *Treaty Series*, vol. 660, p. 195, International Covenant on Economic, Social and Cultural Rights, New York, 16 December 1966, 993 U.N.T.S. 3; 6 I.L.M. (1967) 360.

[147] New York, 7 March 1966 United Nations, *Treaty Series*, vol. 660, p. 195.

[148] New York, 20 November 1989 United Nations, *Treaty Series*, vol. 1577, p. 3.

[149] 18 December 1979 United Nations, *Treaty Series*, vol. 1249, p. 13.

[150] Adopted on 25 November 1981. GA Res. 55, UN GAOR, 36 Sess., Supp. 51 at 171, UN Doc. A/36/684. See below chapter 12.

[151] UN Doc. A/Res/47/135. See below chapter 13.

[152] Sub-Commission on the Promotion and Protection of Human Rights, www.unhchr.ch/html/menu2/2/sc.htm <last visited 31 March 2009>.

acting in an independent and expert capacity. During its tenure, the Sub-Commission had one annual session of three weeks (during late July–early August) in Geneva proceeded by working groups lasting for one or two weeks, which were attended by non-governmental organisations and by governmental observers.[153]

The Human Rights Commission envisioned to be the mouthpiece and champion of human rights of all individuals regardless of race, religion or nationality but in effect turned out to be a politically biased and bloc based body devoid of objectivity in its approaches towards human rights. Candidates for the Commission were first nominated by the regional groups with the nominees being submitted for elections by ECOSOC members. As a matter of practice regional groups frequently forwarded the same number of nominees as there were seats which in a number of instances forced ECOSOC members to elect States with dubious human rights record. Thus, the Sudan – a country heavily criticised for its human rights record generally, particularly in the Darfur region – was elected and re-elected in 2001 and 2004. Matters came to a head with the failure of the United States to have its candidacy renewed in 2001 – a seat which it had consistently maintained since 1946.[154] As we shall consider, under the revised procedures, the Human Rights Council members are directly elected by the UN General Assembly through an absolute majority – each candidate, therefore, requiring the majority support of the Assembly to be successful. This, in practice should provide greater latitude in electing States that are more committed to human rights issues.

Prior to their demise, the activities of the Commission and the Sub-Commission represented the focal point in terms of the UN human rights practices and procedures. The Commission made a significant contribution to the standard-setting and more recently to the monitoring and implementation of human rights obligations. In addition, the Commission engaged itself in such activities as studies and seminars, fellowship programmes and providing advisory services. The Commission, nevertheless, had serious limitations and weaknesses, foremost amongst these were the political biases that impinged upon an objective upholding of human rights standards. The Commission's members were nominated by their respective governments and their political positions were dictated closely by their governments. The Commission had been rightly described as 'a highly political animal, with its initiatives and priorities reflecting bloc interests'.[155] The Commission was disgraced for consistently approaching human rights issues based on political bloc interests and apathy towards dealing with violations objectively; these weaknesses contributed to the ultimate demise of the Commission.

(ii) Structure and functions of the Human Rights Council

(a) Mandate and responsibilities

The agenda for reforming the United Nations human rights system has a considerable history although the immediate impetus for the establishment of the Human Rights Council

[153] The Promotion and Protection of Human Rights 2005 www2.ohchr.org/english/bodies/subcom/docs/leaflet2005-En.pdf <last visited 31 March 2009>.
[154] See Alston, above n.134, at p. 192; Ghanea, above n.134, at p. 699.
[155] Harris, above n.1, at p. 658; according to Higgins, the Commission 'is a body in body in which supporting one's friends' record often assumes priority along with attacking the human rights of those who are not one's friends' Higgins, 'United Nations Human Rights Committee' in Blackburn and Taylor, *Human Rights for the 1990s: Legal, Political and Ethical Issues* (Continuum International, 1991) pp. 67–74 at p. 67.

was derived from the former Secretary General Kofi Annan's report – *In Larger Freedom: Towards Development, Security and Human Rights for All* in March 2005.[156] The report was further discussed and approved by Heads of States and other high level UN officials who convened in September 2005 to address and examine issues of security, human rights and development. The Human Rights Council was established by the UN General Assembly through its Resolution passed on 15 March 2006, which also outlined the mandate, responsibilities and functions of the Council.[157] According to the General Assembly Resolution, the Council has the responsibility for 'promoting universal respect for the protection of all human rights and fundamental freedoms for all, without distinction of any kind and in a fair and equal manner'.[158] The Council will 'address situations of violations of human rights, including gross and systematic violations, and make recommendations thereon'.[159] The Council will also promote and co-ordinate the mainstreaming of human rights within the UN system. To achieve these targets, the Council will undertake a universal periodic review of each UN Member States.[160] The resolution provides for the adequate transition of responsibilities from the Human Rights Commission to the new Human Rights Council.[161] Similarly to the Commission, the Human Rights Council is to continue to collaborate with the OHCHR.[162] It will work to maintain and improve the system of special mandates, expert advice, and complaint procedures instituted by the Commission.[163] The Council shall promote human rights education, advisory services, technical assistance, and capacity building with the relevant Member States.[164] The Council is to serve as a forum for dialogue on thematic human rights issues and recommend opportunities for the development of international human rights law to the UN General Assembly;[165] and promote the full implementation of human rights obligations by Member States, and follow-up on human rights commitments from other conferences.[166]

The Human Rights Council, in its Resolution adopted on 18 June 2007,[167] dealt with a number of institutional issues including further elaboration on mechanisms, procedures and Universal Periodic Review. It is towards these developments that we will now turn our attention.

(b) Status within the UN Framework

The Council has an enhanced position within the United Nations human rights institutional hierarchy. The Council is designated as a subsidiary body of the UN General Assembly, a substantial improvement from the standing of the Commission, which as noted above was the subsidiary body of ECOSOC.[168] The Human Rights Council reports directly to the UN General Assembly's 192 Member States as opposed to the ECOSOC's 54

---

[156] *In Larger Freedom: Towards Development, Security and Human Rights for All*, Report of the Secretary General www.un.org/largerfreedom/contents.htm <last visited 31 March 2009>.

[157] GA Res. 60/251 Human Rights Council www2.ohchr.org/english/bodies/hrcouncil/docs/A.RES.60.251_En.pdf <last visited 31 March 2009>.

[158] Ibid. para 2

[159] Ibid. para 3.

[160] Ibid. para 5(e).

[161] Ibid. para 5(g).

[162] Ibid. para 5(g).

[163] Ibid. para 6.

[164] Ibid. para 5(a).

[165] Ibid. para 5(b) and (c).

[166] Ibid. para 5(d).

[167] Human Rights Council Resolution 5/1. Institution-building of the United Nations Human Rights Council.

[168] See GA Res. 60/251.

members. Kofi Annan, the former UN Secretary-General, predicted that the stature of the Council might be elevated to that of a principal organ of the United Nations, similar in nature to the Security Council or the General Assembly.[169] The Council consists of 47 members with seats being distributed in the following UN regional groupings: 13 each from African and Asian States; six from Eastern Europe States; eight from Latin America and the Caribbean States; and seven from Western European and other States.[170] Council Members are elected for a period of three years and are ineligible for re-election after holding a Council seat for more than two consecutive terms.[171] In cases where a Council member commits 'gross and systematic violations of human rights' the General Assembly has the mandate to suspend membership with a two-thirds vote of members present.[172]

Eligibility of membership of the Council is open to all UN Member States. Elections to the Council are conducted through a secret ballot by the General Assembly with absolute majority (97/192). Whilst voting for elections, States are required to consider 'the contribution of candidates to the promotion and protection of human rights and their voluntary pledges and commitments'.[173] States wishing to be elected must advance a firm written commitment towards the promotion and protection of human rights. In order to create transparency and remove political blocs, procedural changes have been made to the system of elections. The direct election of States to Council membership is intended to allow States all possible opportunity to elect States based on their human rights credentials. The Council's headquarters are based in Geneva, Switzerland. It meets for three or more sessions every year for ten weeks or more, including in having a high-level session.[174] The Council is entitled to hold special sessions – and has already had a number of special sessions – at the request of any Council member with the support of one-third of the Council membership.[175] The Council is required to submit annual reports directly to the General Assembly. A global report on its work and functions should be provided by the Council for the General Assembly after five years of the Council's operation (i.e. 2011).[176]

(iii) Universal Periodic Review (UPR) – specific details

The Human Rights Council, Resolution 5/1 of 18 June 2007, establishes the essential framework for the various activities to be conducted including the UPRs.[177] According to the Resolution, the UPR mechanism is to be conducted on the basis of the UN Charter, the Universal Declaration of Human Rights and human rights treaties to which the State is a party.[178] An additional basis is the voluntary commitments and pledges undertaken by the

---

[169] As discussed earlier in this chapter the Principal Organs of the United Nations are designated by Article 7 of the UN Charter; 'a General Assembly, a Security Council, an Economic and Social Council, a Trusteeship Council, an International Court of Justice, and a Secretariat'.

[170] GA Res. 60/251, para 7.

[171] Ibid.

[172] Ibid. para 8.

[173] Ibid. para 8.

[174] Ibid. para 10.

[175] Ibid. para 10. As of 31 March 2009, the Council has had ten Special Sessions: www2.ohchr.org/english/bodies/hrcouncil/specialsession/10/index.htm <last visited 31 March 2009>.

[176] Blanchfield, *CRS Report for Congress, The United Nations Human Rights Council: Issues for Congress* (2008) http://ncseonline.org/NLE/CRSreports/07Oct/RL33608.pdf <last visited 21 May 2009>.

[177] Human Rights Council, 5/1. Institution-building of the United Nations Human Rights Council (18 June 2007).

[178] United Nations Human Rights Council Resolution 5/1. Institution-Building, 1. Universal Periodic Review Mechanism A, para 1.

State when submitting a candidate for election to the Council.[179] The UPR takes into account the overlapping and applicable areas of international humanitarian law.[180]

The review is based on the principles of 'the universality, interdependence and inter-relatedness of all human rights', and is aimed to '[b]e a cooperative mechanism based on objective and reliable information and on interactive dialogue'.[181] As noted above, the UPR is designed to provide 'universal coverage and equal treatment of all States',[182] which would involve the participation of the State in question and would complement rather than duplicate existing monitoring systems.[183] It aims to ensure the involvement of all stakeholders including NGOs and human rights institutions.[184] The objectives of the UPR include the improvement of the human rights situation in the country along with the fulfilment of its human rights commitments.[185] UPR also seeks to establish best practices amongst States, enhance mutual co-operation amongst States and amongst all stakeholders including the UN and the Office of the United Nations High Commissioner for Human Rights.[186]

According to the established rules, Member States of the Council are reviewed in the course of their term of membership.[187] UPRs are to be conducted on the basis of equitable geographic distribution.[188] The first cycle of UPR is to be completed within four years, which would mean reviewing 48 States every year within three sessions of the Working Group, each of two weeks duration.[189] As per the guidelines, the UPR is based on the following documentation:

(a) Information prepared by the State concerned, which can take the form of a national report, on the basis of general guidelines to be adopted by the Council at its sixth session . . . and any other information considered relevant by the State concerned, which could be presented either orally or in writing, provided that the written presentation summarizing the information will not exceed 20 pages, to guarantee equal treatment to all States and not to overburden the mechanism;

(b) Additionally a compilation prepared by the Office of the High Commissioner for Human Rights of the information contained in the reports of treaty bodies, special procedures, including observations and comments by the State concerned, and other relevant official United Nations documents, which shall not exceed 10 pages;

(c) Additional, credible and reliable information provided by other relevant stakeholders to the universal periodic review, which should also be taken into consideration by the Council in the review. The Office of the High Commissioner for Human Rights will prepare a summary of such information which shall not exceed 10 pages.[190]

---

[179] Ibid. para 1(d).
[180] Ibid. para 2.
[181] Ibid. B.1, para 3(a) and (b).
[182] Ibid. B.1, para 3(c).
[183] Ibid. B.1, para 3(e) and (f).
[184] Ibid. B.1, para 3(m).
[185] Ibid. B.2, para 4(b).
[186] Ibid. B.2, para 4(d)(e) and (f).
[187] Ibid. C, para 8.
[188] Ibid. C, para 11.
[189] Ibid. C, para 14.
[190] Ibid. D, 1, para 15.

The State's written submission and other summaries as prepared by the High Commissioner's Office are made ready six weeks in advance of the UPR by the Working Group.[191] The review is conducted in one Working Group, which is chaired by the President of the Council and consists of all 47 members of the Council.[192] Observer States and other stakeholders are allowed to attend the review within the Working Group.[193] A group of three rapporteurs, which is selected by the drawing of lots amongst Council members from different Regional Groups – known as a *troika* – is established to facilitate each review, which also includes the preparation of the report of the Working Group.[194] An interactive dialogue between the Council and the State under review takes place within the Working Group.[195] The Rapporteurs are able to collate questions or other relevant issues which are to be transmitted to the State under review in order to assist its preparation and focus the interactive dialogue, while at the same time guaranteeing fairness and transparency.[196] Each review of a country takes up to three hours, with an additional one hour for the consideration of the outcome by the Council acting in its plenary session.[197] Half an hour is provided for the adoption of the report of each country under review in the working group. A reasonable timeframe is allocated between the review and the adoption of the report on each State in the working group.[198] The final outcome is adopted by the plenary of the Council.[199] 'The format of the outcome of the review [is] a report consisting of a summary of the proceedings of the review process; conclusions and/or recommendations, and the voluntary commitments of the State concerned.'[200] States are required to assess the outcome of the UPR with sincerity and to implement the recommendations emergent from the UPR.[201] There are, however, no sanctions attached to the non-implementation of recommendations save that failure would lead the Council to address 'cases of persistent non-cooperation with the mechanism'.[202] The first session of the Working Group on the UPR took place in 2008 with the first cycle being completed in four years.[203]

(iv) Complaint procedure

(a) The Human Rights Commission and Resolutions 1235 and 1503

In 1967, ECOSOC passed Resolution 1235 (XLII) which has proved to be of enormous significance.[204] In this Resolution ECOSOC authorised the Human Rights Commission and its Sub-Commission on the Prevention of Discrimination and the Protection of

---

[191] Ibid. D.1, para 17.
[192] Ibid. D.2, para 18(a).
[193] Ibid. D.2, para 18(b) and (c).
[194] Ibid. D.2, para 18(d).
[195] Ibid. D.2, para 21.
[196] Ibid.
[197] Ibid. D.2, paras 22 and 23.
[198] Ibid. D.2, para 24.
[199] Ibid. D.2, para 25.
[200] Ibid. E.1, para 26.
[201] Ibid. F, para 33.
[202] Ibid. F, para 38.
[203] Fact Sheet: Human Rights Council – Universal Periodic Review www.ohchr.org/EN/HRBodies/UPR/Documents/UPRFactSheetFinal.pdf <last visited 31 March 2009>.
[204] Economic and Social Council Resolution 1235 (XLII), 42 UN ESCOR Supp. (No. 1) at 17, UN Doc. E/4393 (1967).

Minorities to 'examine information relevant to gross violations of human rights and fundamental freedoms, as exemplified by the policy of apartheid as practised in the Republic of South Africa . . . and [] racial discrimination as practised notably in Southern Rhodesia, contained in the communications listed by the Secretary-General pursuant to [ECOSOC] Resolution 728 F (XXVIII) of 30 July 1959'[205] and 'to make a thorough study of situations which reveal a consistent pattern of violations of human rights . . . and report, with recommendations thereon, to the Economic and Social Council'.[206] The procedures adopted under Resolution 1235 (unlike Resolution 1503) were non-confidential and were of a public nature. They could be commenced by the Sub-Commission or by States themselves and operated in variety of manners. These could be country-specific mandates, consider States with similar pattern of violations or target gross violations of human rights. The Commission made the ultimate decisions as to the action on these resolutions and also retained the authority (subject to the approval of the ECOSOC) for the appointment of a Rapporteur or any other mechanism for studying a given country situation or acting on a thematic basis. In reliance upon Resolution 1235, the Commission established a number of public procedures.[207] These included investigations into alleged violations of human rights in various States. The Commission also created various Working-Groups, Special Rapporteurs and expert bodies to monitor human rights situations. These Special Procedures are now a prominent part of the Human Rights Council and will be discussed later on. Significantly, under Resolution 1235, NGOs were not authorised to make representations and submissions regarding violations taking place in any Member State of the United Nations.[208] However in 1967, the Sub-Commission recommended to the Commission that it should establish a special committee of experts to consider, in addition to the South African situation, situations in Haiti (under Francois Duvalier) and in Greece (under the Colonels). This submission encouraged the Commission to develop a confidential procedure to consider information from a variety of sources. Resolution 1503 (XLVIII) was adopted as an ECOSOC Resolution on 27 May 1970.[209] The procedure allowed the Commission and its Sub-Commission to consider in private, communications which 'appear to reveal a consistent pattern of gross and reliably attested violations of human rights'.[210]

Resolution 1503 was a 'petition-information' system because the objective was to use complaints as a means to assist the Commission in identifying situations involving a 'consistent pattern of gross and reliably attested violations of human rights and fundamental freedoms'.[211] An individual complaint was a piece of evidence which, in combination with other related cases, would be of sufficient importance to spur the United Nations into some form of action. After the demise of the Commission, the procedures of the Commission have also been revised.

---

[205] Ibid. para 2.
[206] Ibid. para 3.
[207] 'Adoption of Resolution 1235 is now generally considered as the basis for the establishment of special thematic and country procedures' Gutter, 'Special Procedures and the Human Rights Council: Achievements and Challenges Ahead' 7 *Human Rights Law Review* (2007) 93 at p. 97; Harris, above n.1, at p. 659.
[208] See Rodley and Weissbrodt, 'United Nations Non-Treaty Procedures for Dealing with Human Rights Violations' in Hannum (ed.), above n.131, at p. 67.
[209] Resolution 1503 (XLVIII) 27 May 1970, ECOSOC; Procedure for dealing with communications relating to violations of human rights and fundamental freedoms.
[210] Ibid. para 1.
[211] Ibid.

(b) The Human Rights Council Complaints Procedure[212]

The 1503 Procedure, after the abolition of the Human Rights Commission has been replaced by the Complaint Procedure provided for in Resolution 5/1 of the Human Rights Council. The Council operates a complaint procedure which allows individuals and groups to report human rights abuses in a confidential setting.[213] The objective of the procedure is to encourage and facilitate dialogue and cooperation among the accused State, Council members, and the complainant(s). Retaining the feature of confidentiality from the Resolution 1503 procedure, the new complaints procedure is established to 'address consistent patterns of gross and reliably attested violations of all human rights and all fundamental freedoms occurring in any part of the world and under any circumstances'.[214] The new procedure establishes two Working Groups – the Working Group on Communications (WGC) and a Working Group on Situations (WGS). The Working Groups work on the basis of consensus, failing which decisions are taken by a majority.[215] The Working Groups operate through their own rules of procedure. Both WGC and WGS evaluate the complaints and bring these to the attention of the Council.[216] The groups hold two five-day meetings per year to consider complaints and replies from concerned states.[217] The full Council determines whether to take action on the reports based on complaints arising from the recommendation of the Working Groups.[218]

WGC is appointed by the Human Rights Council's Advisory Committee from amongst its own members for a three-year period, which is renewable once.[219] WGC comprises five independent experts and takes cognisance of appropriate geographical representation.[220] The primary purpose of the Working Group is to examine the admissibility and merits of communications received and to make an assessment as to whether a particular communication in itself or in combination with other communications received reveals a consistent pattern of gross and reliably attested violations of human rights.[221] WGC's Chairperson conducts the initial screening and scrutiny, which is based on admissibility under the following criteria.[222]

---

[212] Human Rights Council Resolution 5/1. Institution-building of the United Nations Human Rights Council, IV. Complaint Procedure.
[213] Ibid. IV. A, para 86.
[214] Ibid. IV. A, para 85.
[215] Ibid. IV. C, para 90.
[216] Ibid. IV. C, para 89.
[217] Ibid. IV. D, para 100.
[218] Ibid. IV. D, paras 103 and 104.
[219] Ibid. IV. C.1, paras 91 and 93.
[220] Ibid. IV. C.1, para 91.
[221] Ibid. IV. C.1, para 95.
[222] Ibid. IV. C.1, para 94.

The United Nations system and the modern human rights regime (1945–)

3

A communication related to a violation of human rights and fundamental freedoms is admissible, so long as:

(a) It is not manifestly politically motivated and its object is consistent with the Charter of the United Nations, the Universal Declaration of Human Rights and other applicable instruments in the field of human rights law;

(b) It gives a factual description of the alleged violations, including the rights which are alleged to be violated;

(c) Its language is not abusive. However, such a communication may be considered if it meets the other criteria for admissibility after deletion of the abusive language;

(d) It is submitted by a person or a group of persons claiming to be the victims of violations of human rights and fundamental freedoms, or by any person or group of persons, including non-governmental organizations, acting in good faith in accordance with the principles of human rights, not resorting to politically motivated stands contrary to the provisions of the Charter of the United Nations and claiming to have direct and reliable knowledge of the violations concerned. Nonetheless, reliably attested communications shall not be inadmissible solely because the knowledge of the individual authors is second-hand, provided that they are accompanied by clear evidence;

(e) It is not exclusively based on reports disseminated by mass media;

(f) It does not refer to a case that appears to reveal a consistent pattern of gross and reliably attested violations of human rights already being dealt with by a special procedure, a treaty body or other United Nations or similar regional complaints procedure in the field of human rights;

(g) Domestic remedies have been exhausted, unless it appears that such remedies would be ineffective or unreasonably prolonged.[223]

Those communications which are manifestly ill-founded or are anonymous are screened and are not transmitted to the State parties concerned.[224] However, the Chairperson provides members with lists of all communications that have been rejected after the initial review.[225] Rejected communications also include brief reasons for such a decision. The remaining communications which have not been rejected are transmitted to State parties concerned with a view to obtaining the views of the State parties on alleged violations.[226] WGC makes the decision on the admissibility as well as assessing the merits of allegations of violations, including the decision as to whether the communication, on its own or in conjunction with other related communications, reveals a consistent pattern of gross and reliably attested violations of human rights and fundamental freedoms.[227] WGC provides its sister Working Group, WGS, with a file of all the communications containing admissible communications and the recommendations that are made by the WGC.[228] It is possible for the WGC to keep a case under review in instances where, for example, there is outstanding information.[229]

---

[223] Ibid. IV. B, para 87.
[224] Ibid. IV. C.1, para 94.
[225] Ibid. IV. C.1, para 94.
[226] Ibid. IV. C.1, para 94.
[227] Ibid. IV. C.1, para 95.
[228] Ibid. IV. C.1, para 95.
[229] Ibid. IV. C.1, para 95.

Like the WGC, WGS also consists of five members with each regional group appointing a representative of a member State of the Council to serve on this Working Group.[230] Due and appropriate consideration is to be accorded towards ensuring a gender balance within the WGS.[231] WGS members work in a personal capacity.[232] Members of WGS are appointed for a period of one year and their mandate is renewable once, if the State concerned is a member of the Human Rights Council.[233] WGS's main task is to review the communications received from the WGC, in the light of any responses received from concerned States and other relevant information.[234] In the light of the information it has, WGS presents the Human Rights Council with its reports 'on consistent patterns of gross and reliably attested violations of human rights and fundamental freedoms'.[235] WGS makes recommendations to the Human Rights Council as regards the future action to be undertaken. This is normally in the form of a draft resolution or decision.[236] Similar to the WGC, the WGS may also defer a particular communication until the next session if further or additional information is pending. Furthermore, the WGS may also dismiss cases or cease to consider situations, although reasons need to be provided for reaching such decisions.[237]

The Council considers the communications which are brought to its attention by WGS on a confidential basis, as frequently as possible but provides consideration at least once every year.[238] In order to ensure a timely and effective response, the time between the transmission of the complaint to the State and consideration of the complaint is not to exceed 24 months.[239] The Complaint Procedure Rules allow for the participation and involvement of the complainant in the following significant manner:

(a) When a communication is deemed inadmissible by the Working Group on Communications or when it is taken up for consideration by the Working Group on Situations; or when a communication is kept pending by one of the Working Groups or by the Council;

(b) At the final outcome.[240]

The complainant is also to be informed of the registration of his communication at the registration stage.[241] Furthermore, if the complainant requests confidentiality in respect of their identity, this request is respected.[242] All States undertake to co-operate with the Working Groups and to make all possible efforts to provide a reply within three months of the requests made by the Working Groups.[243]

---

[230] Ibid. IV. C.2, para 96.
[231] Ibid.
[232] Ibid. IV. C.2, para 97.
[233] Ibid. IV. C.2, para 96.
[234] Ibid. IV. C.2, para 98.
[235] Ibid. IV. C.2, para 98.
[236] Ibid. IV. C.2, para 98.
[237] Ibid. IV. C.2, para 99.
[238] Ibid. IV. D, para 103.
[239] Ibid. IV. D, para 105.
[240] Ibid. IV. E, para 106.
[241] Ibid. IV. E, para 107.
[242] Ibid. IV. E, para 108.
[243] Ibid. IV. D, para 101.

The Rules of the Complaint Procedure provide for the following possible measures to be taken:

(a) To discontinue considering the situation when further consideration or action is not warranted;

(b) To keep the situation under review and request the State concerned to provide further information within a reasonable period of time;

(c) To keep the situation under review and appoint an independent and highly qualified expert to monitor the situation and report back to the Council;

(d) To discontinue reviewing the matter under the confidential complaint procedure in order to take up public consideration of the same;

(e) To recommend to OHCHR to provide technical cooperation, capacity-building assistance or advisory services to the State concerned.[244]

(v) Special procedures

(a) Under the Human Rights Commission[245]

One of the earliest activities in respect of Special Procedures (and indeed the first of the thematic mechanisms) was the establishment of the Working Group on Enforced and Involuntary Disappearances (WGEID) in 1980 by the Human Rights Commission.[246] In its Resolution 20 (XXXVI) 29 February 1980, the Human Rights Commission made the decision to establish the Working Group (WGEID) consisting of five members, who would serve in an individual and independent capacity 'to examine questions relevant to enforced or involuntary disappearances of persons'.[247] Since 1980, the mandate has been extended by the Commission and now the Human Rights Council. Since 1986, this has been done biennially and from 1992 on a three-year basis. In 2004, the mandate of WGEID was extended for three years.[248] A further three-year extension of the mandate was provided by the Human Rights Council in March 2008.[249]

Since its establishment, the Working Group has considered in excess of 50,000 cases from over 70 countries. The WGEID is mandated to examine questions concerning enforced or involuntary disappearances. Its primary role is to provide assistance to families of the disappeared and detained persons in order to ascertain the fate of their family members.[250] WGEID meets three times a year for five to eight working days. WGEID works

---

[244] Ibid. IV. F, para 109.

[245] See Weissbrodt, 'The Three "Theme" Special Rapporteurs of the UN Commission on Human Rights' 80 *AJIL* (1986) 685; Kramer and Weissbrodt, 'The 1980 UN Commission on Human Rights and the Disappeared' 3 *HRQ* (1981) 18; Rodley, 'United Nations Action Procedures against "Disappearances," Summary or Arbitrary Executions, and Torture' 8 *HRQ* (1986) 700.

[246] Commission on Human Rights, Question of Missing and Disappeared Persons, Resolution 20 (XXXVI) 29 February 1980, Adopted at 1563rd meeting, on 29 February 1980, without a vote. See Rodley, *The Treatment of Prisoners in International Law* (Clarendon Press, 1999) pp. 270–276.

[247] Ibid. para 1.

[248] Human Right Commission Resolution 2004/40.

[249] See A/HRC/7/L.30 (25 March 2008). The current members of WGEID are: Mr. Santiago Corcuera, Chairperson (Mexico), appointed in 2004; Mr. Stephen Toope (Canada), appointed in 2002; Mr. Jeremy J. Sarkin (South Africa), appointed in 2008; Mr. Saied Rajaie Khorasani (Islamic Republic of Iran), appointed in 2003; Mr. Darko Göttlicher (Croatia), appointed in 2004.

[250] See United Nations, *Enforced or Involuntary Disappearances: Fact Sheet No. 6* (Rev. 2) pp. 5–6.

on individual cases, country reports and the general phenomenon of disappearances, including the question of impunity. Members of the group have also conducted visits to various countries including Mexico, Bolivia, Peru, the Philippines and Somalia.[251] The Working Group has called for investigation, prosecution and punishment of those responsible for disappearances. The contributions and role of the Working Group encouraged the General Assembly to adopt the Declaration on the Protection of All Persons from Enforced Disappearances.[252] The Declaration expanded the Working Group's mandate to monitor compliance with duties under the Declaration, including the obligation to establish civil liability as well as criminal responsibility for disappearances. The Declaration also provided the inspiration for the drafting and ultimate adoption of the International Convention on Enforced Disappearances in 2006. Another valuable thematic mechanism established under Resolution 1235 procedure was the Working Group on Arbitrary Detention (WGAD). WGAD was set up by the Commission in 1991[253] and operates under the following mandate:

(a) To investigate cases of detention imposed arbitrarily or otherwise inconsistently with relevant international standards set forth in the Universal Declaration of Human Rights or in the relevant international legal instruments accepted by the States concerned provided that no final decision has been taken in such cases by domestic courts in conformity with domestic law;

(b) To seek and receive information from Governments and intergovernmental and non-governmental organisations, and receive information from the individuals concerned, their families or their representatives;

(c) To present a comprehensive report to the Commission at its annual session.

WGAD may investigate cases of arbitrary deprivation of liberty, accepts communications from detained individuals or their families as well as governments and inter-governmental and non-governmental organisations. It was for a period of time the only non-treaty based mechanism whose mandate expressly provided for consideration of individual complaints – therefore, allowing for a right to individual petition from any person across the globe, without any treaty-based or jurisdictional limitations. If WGAD decides after its investigation that arbitrary detention is established then it makes recommendations to the government concerned.[254] It transmits this recommendation to the complainant three weeks after sending these to the government. The opinions and recommendations of the Working Group are published in an annex to the report presented by the group to the Human Rights Council at each of its annual sessions. In addition to the investigation of cases of arbitrary detentions and taking relevant action on these cases, WGAD also conducts field-missions (country visits) upon the invitation of governments, in order to have a better

---

[251] See Rodley, above n.246, at p. 274.
[252] Adopted 16 December 1992, GA Res. 133, UN GAOR, 47 Sess., Supp. 49 at 207; UN Doc. A/Res/47/133. 32 I.L.M. (1993) 903.
[253] Human Rights Commission Resolution 1991/42.
[254] For an exhaustive list of Special Procedures Mandate Holders now dealing with Communications see: Special Procedures of the Human Rights Council. Urgent appeals and letters of allegation on human rights violations. www2.ohchr.org/english/bodies/chr/special/docs/communicationsbrochure_en.pdf <last visited 31 March 2009>.

understanding of cases of arbitrary detentions in a particular country. The WGAD reports these visits to the Human Rights Council in its annual report. The WGAD's annual reports are very substantial consisting *inter alia* of observations on a country's judicial practices, legislative and administrative institutions and policies pertaining to detentions.[255]

In addition to the thematic mandates accorded to WGEID and WGAD, a number of other mandates were established by the Human Rights Commission that have been continued by the Human Rights Council, although the tasks are entrusted to individual experts described varyingly as Special Rapporteurs, Independent Experts or Special Representatives of the Secretary-General.

(b) Under the Human Rights Council

The Council, like its predecessor, continues with a system of Special Procedures which includes country and thematic mandates. However, the Council, in accordance with Resolution 5/1 has undertaken a review of all mandates within the system of Special Procedures.[256] At the time of writing, all thematic mandates which had been reviewed had been extended (albeit with some changes to the scope of particular mandates) with the additional establishment of some new mandates. In respect of Country mandates, the majority had been extended with the exception of the Democratic Republic of the Congo and Liberia. Country mandates, which last for one year and can be renewed, allow for Special Rapporteurs to examine and advise on human rights situations in specific countries.[257] The number of country mandates has steadily fallen since the late 1990s, triggering concern that they are proving politically unattractive though no less critical for the defence of human rights. Thematic mandates, which last for three years and can also be renewed, allow Special Rapporteurs to analyse major human rights phenomena globally.[258] As was the position under the Commission, the Special Rapporteurs serve in an independent, personal capacity and conduct in-depth research and onsite visits pertaining to their issue or country. They can be nominated by UN Member States, regional groups within the UN human rights system, international organisations, NGOs, or individuals.[259] A newly established 'consultative group' nominates Rapporteurs for country and thematic mandates.[260] Based on the consultative group's input, the Council President submits a list of possible candidates to Council members, who then consider each appointment.[261]

Special Procedures were established by the former Human Rights Commission and have now been adopted by the Human Rights Council. The Special Procedures deal with either thematic issues related to human rights violations or specific country situations. At present there are eight country specific mandates and 30 thematic mandates.

---

[255] The current members of the WGAD are: Mr. Aslan Abashidze (Russian Federation), since 2008; Ms. Manuela Carmena Castrillo (Spain), since 2003 (Chairperson-Rapporteur); Roberto Garretón (Chile), since 2008; Mr. Malick El Hadji Sow (Senegal), since 2008 (Vice-Chairperson); Ms. Shaheen Sardar Ali (Pakistan), since 2008.

[256] Human Rights Council Resolution 5/1, II.B.

[257] Ibid. para 60.

[258] Ibid.

[259] Human Rights Council Resolution 5/1, II.A, para 42.

[260] Human Rights Council Resolution 5/1, II.A, para 47.

[261] Human Rights Council Resolution 5/1, II.A, para 47.

COUNTRY MANDATES

Independent Expert on the situation of human rights in Burundi (2004)[262]

Special Representative of the Secretary General for human rights in Cambodia (1993)[263]

Special Rapporteur on the situation of human rights in Democratic Peoples Republic of Korea (2004)[264]

Independent Expert on the situation of human rights in Haiti (1995)[265]

Special Rapporteur on the situation in Myanmar (1992)[266]

Special Rapporteur on the situation of human rights in the Palestinian territories occupied since 1967 (1993)[267]

Independent Expert on the situation of human rights in Somalia (1993)[268]

Special Rapporteur on the situation in Sudan (2005)[269]

[262] The mandate was established by the Human Rights Commission Resolution 2004/82 in 2004. The duration of the mandate was not specified. The mandate was extended by the Human Rights Council in its Resolution 9/19 in 2007. The current mandate holder is Mr. Akich Okola from Kenya. For further information see www.ohchr.org/EN/countries/AfricaRegion/Pages/BIIndex.aspx <last visited 31 March 2009>.

[263] The mandate was established by the Human Rights Commission Resolution 1993/6 in 1993. The mandate was extended by the Human Rights Council in its Resolution 9/15 in 2008 for a period of one year. The current mandate holder is Mr. Yash Ghai from Kenya. In April 2009 Professor Surya Subedi (Nepal) was appointed by the Human Rights Council as the successor to Mr. Ghai as the next mandate holder. For further information see www.ohchr.org/EN/countries/AsiaRegion/Pages/KHIndex.aspx <last visited 31 March 2009>.

[264] The mandate established by the Human Rights Commission Resolution 2004/13 in 2004. The duration of the mandate was not specified. The mandate was extended by the Human Rights Council in its Resolution 7/15, in 2008 for a period of one year. The current mandate holder is Mr. Vitit Muntarbhorn from Thailand. For further information see www.ohchr.org/EN/countries/AsiaRegion/Pages/KPIndex.aspx <last visited 31 March 2009>.

[265] The mandate was established by the Human Rights Commission Resolution 1995/70 in 1995. The duration of the mandate was not specified. The mandate was extended by the Human Rights Council in 2007 for one year. The current mandate holder is Mr. Michel Forst from France. For further information see www.ohchr.org/EN/countries/LACRegion/Pages/HTIIndex.aspx <last visited 31 March 2009>.

[266] The mandate was established by the Human Rights Commission Resolution 1992/58 in 1992. The mandate was extended by the Human Rights Council in its Resolution 7/32 in 2008 for a period of one year. The current mandate holder is Mr. Tomas Ojea Quintana from Argentina. For further information see www.ohchr.org/EN/countries/AsiaRegion/Pages/MMIndex.aspx <last visited 31 March 2009>.

[267] The mandate established by the Human Rights Commission Resolution 1993/2 A with an open-ended mandate 'until the end of the Israeli occupation'. The current mandate holder is Mr. Richard Falk from the United States of America. For further information see www.ohchr.org/EN/countries/MENARegion/Pages/PSIndex.aspx <last visited 31 March 2009>.

[268] The mandate was established by the Human Rights Commission Resolution 1993/86 in 1993. The mandate was extended by the Human Rights Council Resolution in its Resolution 7/35 for a period of one year in 2008. The current mandate holder is Ms. Shamsul Bari from Bangladesh. For further information see www.ohchr.org/EN/countries/AfricaRegion/Pages/SDIndex.aspx <last visited 31 March 2009>.

[269] The mandate was established by the Human Rights Commission Resolution 2005/82 in 2005. The mandate was extended by the Human Rights Council Resolution in its Resolution 9/17 for a period of one year in 2007. The current mandate holder is Ms. Sima Samar from Afghanistan. For further information see www.ohchr.org/EN/countries/AfricaRegion/Pages/SDIndex.aspx <last visited 31 March 2009>. On the violations of human rights in Sudan see in particular chapters 13 and 20 below.

THEMATIC MANDATES

Special Rapporteur on Extrajudicial, Summary or Arbitrary Executions (1982)[270]

Special Rapporteur on the independence of judges and lawyers (1994)[271]

Special Rapporteur on torture and other cruel, inhuman or degrading treatment or punishment (1985)[272]

Representative of the Secretary-General on the human rights of Internally Displaced Persons (2004)[273]

Special Rapporteur on Freedom of Religion or Belief (1986)[274]

Working Group on the use of mercenaries as a means of impeding the exercise of the right of peoples to self-determination (2005)[275]

Special Rapporteur on the Promotion and Protection of the Right to Freedom of Opinion and Expression (1993)[276]

Special Rapporteur on Contemporary Forms of Racism, Racial Discrimination, Xenophobia and Related Intolerance (1993)[277]

---

[270] The mandate was established by the Human Rights Commission Resolution 1982/35 in 1982. The duration of the mandate was extended most recently by the Human Rights Council in its Resolution 8/3 in 2008, for a period of three years. The current mandate holder is Mr. Philip Alston from Australia. For further details see www2.ohchr.org/english/issues/executions/index.htm <last visited 31 March 2009>.

[271] The mandate was established by the Human Rights Commission Resolution 1994/41 in 1994. The duration of the mandate was extended most recently by the Human Rights Council in its Resolution 8/6 in 2008, for a period of three years. The current mandate holder is Mr. Leandro Despouy from Argentina. For further details see www2.ohchr.org/english/issues/judiciary/index.htm <last visited 31 March 2009>.

[272] The mandate was established by the Human Rights Commission Resolution 1985/33 in 1985. The duration of the mandate was extended most recently by the Human Rights Council in its Resolution 8/8 in 2008, for a period of three years. The current mandate holder is Mr. Manfred Nowak from Austria. The role and contributions of the Special Rapportuer on torture and other cruel, inhuman or degrading treatment or punishment are discussed further in chapter 22 below. See also www2.ohchr.org/english/issues/torture/rapporteur/index.htm <last visited 31 March 2009>.

[273] The mandate was established by the Human Rights Commission Resolution 2004/55 in 2004 for an initial duration of two years. The duration of the mandate was extended most recently by the Human Rights Council in its Resolution 6/32 in 2007, for a period of three years. The current mandate holder is Mr. Walter Kälin from Switzerland. For further analysis on the rights of internally displaced persons see chapter 18 below. See also www2.ohchr.org/english/issues/idp/index.htm <last visited 31 March 2009>.

[274] The mandate was established by the Human Rights Commission Resolution 1986/20 in 1986. The duration of the mandate was extended most recently by the Human Rights Council in its Resolution 6/37 in 2007, for a period of three years. The current mandate holder is Ms. Asma Jahangir from Pakistan. For a consideration of the role and contributions of the Special Rapportuer on Freedom of Religion or Belief see chapter 12 below. See also www2.ohchr.org/english/issues/religion/index.htm <last visited 31 March 2009>.

[275] The mandate was established by the Human Rights Commission Resolution 2005/2 in 2005 for an initial duration of three years. The duration of the mandate was extended most recently by the Human Rights Council in its Resolution 7/21 in 2008, for a period of three years. The current mandate holders are as follows: Mr. Alexander Ivanovich Nikitin (Chairperson; Rapporteur) (Russian Federation); Mr. José Gómez del prado (Spain); Ms. Najat Al-hajjaji (Libyan Arab Jumurhiya); Ms. Amada Benavides de Pérez (Columbia); Ms. Shaista Shameem (Fiji). See further www2.ohchr.org/english/issues/mercenaries/index.htm <last visited 31 March 2009>.

[276] The mandate was established by the Human Rights Commission Resolution 1993/45 in 1993. The duration of the mandate was extended most recently by the Human Rights Council in its Resolution 7/36 in 2008, for a period of three years. The current mandate holder is Mr. Frank La Rue Lewy from Guatemala. See further www2.ohchr.org/english/issues/opinion/index.htm <last visited 31 March 2009>.

[277] The mandate was established by the Human Rights Commission Resolution 1993/45 in 1993. The duration of the mandate was extended most recently by the Human Rights Council in its Resolution 7/34 in 2008, for a period of three years. The current mandate holder is Githu Muigai from Kenya. For an analysis of the issues see below chapter 12 below. See also www2.ohchr.org/english/issues/racism/rapporteur/index.htm <last visited 31 March 2009>.

Special Rapporteur on the Sale of Children, Child Prostitution and Child Pornography (1990)[278]

Special Rapporteur on Violence against Women, its Causes and Consequences (1994)[279]

Special Rapporteur on contemporary forms of slavery, including its causes and consequences (2007)[280]

Special Rapporteur on the Situation of Human Rights Defenders (2000)[281]

Special Rapporteur on the Adverse Effects of the Movement and Dumping of Toxic and Dangerous Products and Wastes on the enjoyment of human rights(1995)[282]

Special Rapporteur on the Human Rights of Migrants (1999)[283]

Independent Expert on the Effects of Foreign Debt and Other Related International Financial Obligations of States on the Full Enjoyment of Human Rights, Particularly Economic, Social and Cultural Rights (2000)[284]

Special Rapporteur on the Right to Education (1998)[285]

Special Rapporteur on the Right to Adequate Housing as a component of the right to an adequate standard of living, and on the Right to Non-Discrimination in this Context (2000)[286]

---

[278] The mandate was established by the Human Rights Commission Resolution 1990/68 in 1990. The duration of the mandate was extended most recently by the Human Rights Council in its Resolution 7/13 in 2008, for a period of three years. The current mandate holder is Ms. Najat M'jid Maala from Morocco. For a further analysis see chapter 16 below. See also www2.ohchr.org/english/issues/children/rapporteur/index.htm <last visited 31 March 2009>.

[279] The mandate was established by the Human Rights Commission Resolution 1994/45 in 1994. The duration of the mandate was extended most recently by the Human Rights Council in its Resolution 7/24 in 2008, for a period of three years. The current mandate holder is Ms. Yakin Ertürk from Turkey. For a consideration of the role and contributions of the Special Rapportuer see chapter 15 below. See also www2.ohchr.org/english/issues/women/rapporteur/index.htm <last visited 31 March 2009>.

[280] The mandate was established by the Human Rights Council in its Resolution 6/14 in 2007. The current mandate holder is Ms. Gulnara Shahinian from Armenia. For further information see www2.ohchr.org/english/issues/slavery/rapporteur/index.htm <last visited 31 March 2009>.

[281] The mandate was established by the Human Rights Commission Resolution 2000/61 in 2000. The duration of the mandate was extended most recently by the Human Rights Council in its Resolution 8/6 in 2008, for a period of three years. The current mandate holder is Ms. Margaret Sekaggya from Uganda. For further information see www2.ohchr.org/english/issues/defenders/index.htm <last visited 31 March 2009>.

[282] The mandate was established by the Human Rights Commission Resolution 1995/81 in 1995. The duration of the mandate was extended most recently by the Human Rights Council in its Resolution 9/1 in 2008, for a period of three years. The current mandate holder is Mr. Okechukwu Ibeanu from Nigeria. For further information see www2.ohchr.org/english/issues/environment/waste/ <last visited 31 March 2009>.

[283] The mandate was established by the Human Rights Commission Resolution 1999/44 in 1999. The duration of the mandate was extended most recently by the Human Rights Council in its Resolution 8/10 in 2008, for a period of three years. The current mandate holder is Mr. Jorge A. Bustamante from Mexico. For further information see www2.ohchr.org/english/issues/migration/rapporteur/index.htm <last visited 31 March 2009>. See also chapter 19 below.

[284] The mandate was established by the Human Rights Commission Resolution 2000/82 in 2008. The duration of the mandate was extended most recently by the Human Rights Council in its Resolution 7/4 in 2008, for a period of three years. The current mandate holder is Mr. Cephas Lumina from Zambia. For further information see www2.ohchr.org/english/issues/development/debt/index.htm <last visited 31 March 2009>.

[285] The mandate was established by the Human Rights Commission Resolution 1998/33 in 1998. The duration of the mandate was extended most recently by the Human Rights Council in its Resolution 8/4 in 2008, for a period of three years. The current mandate holder is Mr. Vernor Muñoz Villalobos from Costa Rica. For an examination and analysis of the role of the Special Rapporteur on the right to education see below chapter 6. See also www2.ohchr.org/english/issues/education/rapporteur/index.htm <last visited 31 March 2009>.

[286] The mandate was established by the Human Rights Commission Resolution 2000/9 in 2000. The duration of the mandate was extended most recently by the Human Rights Council in its Resolution 6/27 in 2007, for a period of three years. The current mandate holder is Ms. Raquel Rolnik from Brazil; see below chapter 6. For further information see www2.ohchr.org/english/issues/housing/index.htm <last visited 31 March 2009>.

3

The United Nations system and the modern human rights regime (1945–)

Working Group on People of African Descent (2002)[287]

Special Rapporteur on the Right to Food (2000)[288]

Special Rapporteur on the Situation of Human Rights and Fundamental Freedoms of Indigenous People (2001)[289]

Special Rapporteur on the promotion and protection of human rights while countering terrorism (2005)[290]

Special Rapporteur on trafficking in persons, especially in women and children (2004)[291]

Special Rapporteur on the Right of everyone to the enjoyment of the highest attainable standard of physical and mental health (2002)[292]

Independent Expert on the question of Human Rights and Extreme Poverty (1998)[293]

Independent Expert on the issue of human rights obligations related to access to safe drinking water and sanitation (2008)[294]

---

[287] The mandate was established by the Human Rights Commission Resolution 2002/68 in 2002. The duration of the mandate was extended most recently by the Human Rights Council in its Resolution 9/14 in 2007, for a period of three years. The current mandate holders are: Mr. Joe Frans (Chairperson and Rapportuer) (Sweden); Ms. Maya Sahli (Algeria); Ms. Monorama Biswa (Bangladesh); Ms. Mirjana Najcevska (Former Yugoslav Republic of Macedonia) and Mr. Ralston Milton Nettleford (Jamaica). See www2.ohchr.org/english/issues/racism/groups/african/4african.htm <last visited 31 March 2009>.

[288] The mandate was established by the Human Rights Commission Resolution 2000/10 in 2000. The duration of the mandate was extended most recently by the Human Rights Council in its Resolution 6/2 in 2007, for a period of three years. The current mandate holders is Mr. Olivier de Schutter (Belgium). For an examination and analysis of the role of the Special Rapporteur on the Right to Food see below chapter 6. See also www2.ohchr.org/english/issues/food/index.htm <last visited 31 March 2009>.

[289] The mandate was established by the Human Rights Commission Resolution 2001/57 in 2001. The duration of the mandate was extended most recently by the Human Rights Council in its Resolution 6/12 in 2007, for a period of three years. The current mandate holder is Mr. James Anaya from the United States of America. For an examination and analysis of the role of the Special Rapporteur on the situation of human rights and fundamental freedoms of indigenous people see below chapter 14. See also www2.ohchr.org/english/issues/indigenous/rapporteur/ <last visited 31 March 2009>.

[290] The mandate was established by the Human Rights Commission Resolution 2005/80 in 2005. The duration of the mandate was extended most recently by the Human Rights Council in its Resolution 6/28 in 2007, for a period of three years. The current mandate holder is Mr. Martin Scheinin from Finland. For an examination and analysis of the role of the Special Rapporteur on the promotion and protection of human rights while countering terrorism see below chapter 24. See also www2.ohchr.org/english/issues/terrorism/rapporteur/srchr.htm <last visited 31 March 2009>.

[291] The mandate was established by the Human Rights Commission Resolution 2004/110 in 2004. The duration of the mandate was extended most recently by the Human Rights Council in its Resolution 8/12 in 2008, for a period of three years. The current mandate holder is Ms. Joy Ngozi Ezeilo from Nigeria. For further information see www2.ohchr.org/english/issues/trafficking/index.htm <last visited 31 March 2009>.

[292] The mandate was established by the Human Rights Commission Resolution 2002/31 in 2002. The duration of the mandate was extended most recently by the Human Rights Council in its Resolution 6/29 in 2007, for a period of three years. The current mandate holder is Mr. Anand Grover from India. For an examination and analysis of the role of the Special Rapporteur on the right of everyone to the enjoyment of the highest attainable standard of physical and mental health see below chapter 6. See also www2.ohchr.org/english/issues/health/right/index.htm <last visited 31 March 2009>.

[293] The mandate was established by the Human Rights Commission Resolution 1998/25 in 1998. The duration of the mandate was extended most recently by the Human Rights Council in its Resolution 8/11 in 2008, for a period of three years. The current mandate holder is Ms. Maria Magdalena Sepúlveda Carmona from Chile. For further information see www2.ohchr.org/english/issues/poverty/expert/index.htm <last visited 31 March 2009>.

[294] The mandate was established by the Human Rights Council Resolution 7/22 in 2008 for a period of three years. The current mandate holder is Ms. Catarina de Albuquerque from Portugal. For further information see www2.ohchr.org/english/issues/water/iexpert/index.htm <last visited 31 March 2009>.

Working Group on Arbitrary Detention (1991)[295]
Working Group on Enforced on Involuntary Disappearance (1980)[296]
Independent Expert on Minority Issues (2005)[297]
Independent Expert on human rights and international solidarity (2005)[298]
Special Representative of the Secretary General on human rights and transnational corporations and other business enterprises (2005)[299]

Source: The United Nations is the author of the original material.

The Office of the High Commission for Human Rights has the responsibility for providing support to the mandate holders and these mechanisms through research, logistical and personal assistance in discharging their functions.[300] The mandate accorded by the Procedures call on the mandate holders to examine, monitor and advise and report on human rights violations and situations within specific countries or situations.[301] Special Rapporteurs have a wide range of possible activities including taking action in respect of complaints, visits and investigations, research studies, advising on technical issues to countries or issues and dealing with human rights issues.[302] The Special Procedures are considered the most effective, flexible and responsive mechanisms within the UN human rights system. The Council's review of these procedures aims to strengthen the system and to ensure greater synergy with other human rights mechanisms within the UN system. Special procedures are either in the form of an individual (called 'Special Rapporteur', 'Special Representative of the Secretary-General', 'Representative of the Secretary-General', or 'Independent Expert')

[295] The mandate was established by the Human Rights Commission Resolution 1991/42 in 1991. The duration of the mandate was extended most recently by the Human Rights Council in its Resolution 6/4 in 2007, for a period of three years. The current mandate holders are: Ms. Manuela Carmena Castrillo (Chairperson and Rapportuer) (Spain); Ms. Shaheen Sardar Ali (Pakistan); Mr. Malick El Hadji Sow (Senegal); Mr. Aslan Abashidze (Russia) and Mr. Roberto Garreton (Chile). For further information see www2.ohchr.org/english/issues/detention/index.htm <last visited 31 March 2009>.

[296] The mandate was established by the Human Rights Commission Resolution 20 (XXXVI) in 1980. The duration of the mandate was extended most recently by the Human Rights Council in its Resolution 7/12 in 2007, for a period of three years. The current mandate holders are: Mr. Santiago Corcuera Cabezut (Chairperson and Rapportuer) (Mexico); Mr. Jeremy Sarkin (South Africa); Darko Göttlicher (*Croatia*); Mr. Saeed Rajaee Khorasani (Islamic Republic of Iran) and Mr. Olivier de Frouville from France. For an examination of the role and contribution of Working Group on Enforced on Involuntary Disappearance see below chapter 23. See also www2.ohchr.org/english/issues/disappear/index.htm <last visited 31 March 2009>.

[297] The mandate was established by the Human Rights Commission in its Resolution 2005/79 in 2005. The duration of the mandate was extended most recently by the Human Rights Council in its Resolution 7/6 in 2008, for a period of three years. The current mandate holder is Ms. Gay McDougall from the United States of America. For an examination of the role and contribution of Independent Expert on minority Issues see below chapter 13. See also www2.ohchr.org/english/issues/minorities/expert/index.htm <last visited 31 March 2009>.

[298] The mandate was established by the Human Rights Commission in its Resolution 2005/55 in 2005. The duration of the mandate was extended most recently by the Human Rights Council in its Resolution 7/5 in 2008, for a period of three years. The current mandate holder is Mr. Rudi Muhammad Rizki from Indonesia. For further information see www2.ohchr.org/english/issues/isolidarity/index.htm <last visited 31 March 2009>.

[299] The mandate was established by the Human Rights Commission in its Resolution 2005/69 in 2005. The duration of the mandate was extended most recently by the Human Rights Council in its Resolution 8/7 in 2008, for a period of three years. The current mandate holder is Mr. John Ruggie from the United States of America. For further information see www2.ohchr.org/english/issues/trans_corporations/index.htm <last visited 31 March 2009>.

[300] Manual of Operations of the Special Procedures of the Human Rights Council, August 2008, para 21 www2.ohchr.org/english/bodies/chr/special/docs/Manual_August_2008.doc <last visited 31 March 2009>.

[301] Ibid. para 5.

[302] Ibid. paras 5, 23–27, 75, 77 and 78.

or a working group usually composed of five members (one from each region).[303] The Special Rapporteurs, as well as other mandate holders, are recognised figures in the field of human rights; they serve in an impartial and personal capacity.[304]

The Special Rapporteurs and Independent Experts have performed valuable tasks in promoting the practice of human rights. At the same time they are ultimately reliant upon the co-operation of the States and governments themselves. Their mandates were limited to reporting to the Commission (and now the Council) and do not have any means to enforce their views. Commenting on some of the contributions and limitation of the work of Rapporteurs, a United Nations document notes:

> Through their reports to the [Council], the experts highlight situations of concern. Their reports often provide an invaluable analysis of the human rights situation in a specific country or on a specific theme. Some reports bring to the attention of the international community issues that are not adequately on the international agenda. Many reports name victims and describe the allegations of violations of their human rights. Throughout the year, many experts intervene on behalf of victims. While the work of experts is often a major driving force contribution to change, it is difficult to attribute concrete results in the field of human rights to one factor. Much depends on how Governments, the civil society in a particular country and the international community to react to the violations and to the findings, conclusions and recommendations of experts.
>
> The continuous examination of a particular situation, however, signals to victims that their plight is not forgotten by the international community and provide them with the opportunity to voice their grievances. The perpetrators of human rights violations know that they are being watched. The authorities concerned know that the assessment of their human rights record will have an impact on political, developmental and humanitarian considerations. This sometimes brings improved accountability and therefore change for the better.[305]

(vi) Human Rights Council's Advisory Committee

The Sub-Commission on the Promotion and Protection of Human Rights has been replaced by an Advisory Committee of the Human Rights Council. The underlying objective of the Advisory Committee is to support the Council's work. Functioning as a think-tank, the Advisory Committee provides expertise and advice as well as conducting substantive research and studies on thematic issues of human rights.[306] The experts are elected by Council members through a secret ballot, although nomination is initiated by UN Member States.[307] The Advisory Committee consists of 18 experts serving in their personal capacity.[308] The candidature of the Committee is established and approved by the Council on the basis of recognition, competence and experience in the field of human rights, high moral standing as well as independence and impartiality.[309] Those holding governmental positions and those with decision-making powers which are likely

---

[303] Ibid. para 6
[304] Ibid. para 9. Human Rights Council Resolution 5/1 para 39.
[305] www.ohchr.org/Documents/Publications/FactSheet27en.pdf. Ibid. pp. 12–13.
[306] Human Rights Council Resolution 5/1 para 65.
[307] Ibid. paras 66 and 70.
[308] Ibid. para 65.
[309] Ibid. para 67.

to lead to a conflict of interest are to be excluded from the membership of the Advisory Committee.[310] The geographic distribution of the Advisory Committee membership is: African and Asian States: five members each; Latin American and Caribbean States three members; Western European and other States: three members; and East European States with two members.[311] The Committee members serve for three years and they are eligible for re-election once.[312]

In the performance of its mandate, the Advisory Committee is urged to establish inter-action with States, national human rights institutions, NGOs and other civil society entities.[313] The Committee meets up in two sessions, for a maximum of 10 working days, per year with the possibility of additional sessions to be held on an *ad hoc* basis as approved by the Council.[314] The Advisory Committee has a highly restrictive authority; it is implementation-oriented with an operation sphere limited to thematic issues related to the Council's mandate of promotion and protection of all human rights.[315] The focus of the Advisory Committee is primarily on studies and research-based advice.[316] The Advisory Committee does not have the power to adopt resolutions or decisions although it may, whilst acting under its mandate, make suggestions to the Council for increasing its procedural efficiency and suggest further research proposals within the scope of the Council's work.[317]

The Council, in accordance with paragraph 84 of Resolution 5/1, decided at its sixth session on the most appropriate mechanisms to continue the work of the Working Groups on Indigenous Populations; Contemporary Forms of Slavery; Minorities and the Social Forum. The Social Forum in accordance with Resolution 6/13 of the Human Rights Council has continued to discharge its duties,[318] appointed a Special Rapporteur to replace the Working Group on Contemporary Forms of Slavery under Resolution 6/14,[319] established a Forum on Minorities to replace the Working Group under Resolution 6/15[320] and the Expert Mechanism on the Rights of Indigenous Peoples to replace the Working Group following an informal meeting convened by the UN High Commissioner for Human Rights.[321] Since it was established in March 2006, the Council has held several regular sessions and special sessions. The regular sessions dealt with a mixture of procedural and substantive issues, with a focus on improving the working methods of the Council. The special sessions included three sessions on human rights violations in the Occupied Palestinian Territories and in Lebanon, one session addressing the human rights situation in Darfur, Sudan, and one session addressing human rights in Myanmar. During its first year the Council faced considerable criticism from governments, NGOs, and other observers: Political blocs have continued with certain States, for example, Israel being a focus of

---

[310] Ibid. para 68.
[311] Ibid. para 73.
[312] Ibid. para 74.
[313] Ibid. para 82.
[314] Ibid. para 79.
[315] Ibid. para 76.
[316] Ibid. para 75.
[317] Ibid. para 77.
[318] Human Rights Council Resolution 6/13, The Social Forum (Adopted without a vote 21st meeting 28 September 2007).
[319] Human Rights Council Resolution 6/14, Special Rapporteur on Contemporary Forms of Slavery (Adopted without a vote 21st meeting 28 September 2007).
[320] Human Rights Council Resolution 6/15, Forum on Minority Issues (Adopted without a vote 21st meeting 28 September 2007).
[321] Human Rights Council Resolution 6/36, Expert Mechanism on the Rights of Indigenous Peoples (Adopted without a vote 34th meeting 14 December 2007).

criticism. In its fifth regular session, the Council also terminated the mandates of the Special Rapporteurs for Belarus and Cuba – an action which received considerable criticism as the States were perceived widely as abusers of human rights.[322] Another limitation of the Council is the lack of leadership from democratic, powerful States. The United States was one of the four States which voted against General Assembly Resolution 60/251 establishing the Human Rights Council. This contrasts with the overwhelming majority of 170 States that voted in favour of the resolution establishing the Council.

During its sixth session, from 10–28 September and 10–14 December, 2007, the Council continued to review its process for Special Procedures. It passed resolutions expanding the mandates of the Special Rapporteurs on (1) the human rights of internally displaced persons,[323] (2) adequate housing,[324] (3) the protection and promotion of human rights and fundamental freedoms while countering terrorism,[325] and (4) the freedom of religion or belief.[326] The Council also agreed to extend the mandates of the Special Rapporteur on human rights in Sudan[327] and the Independent Expert on human rights in Liberia for one year.[328] Council members requested that the Special Rapporteur on the human rights situation in Myanmar conduct follow-up visits before the seventh regular Council session During its Special Sessions the Human Rights Council has focused on issues of particular concern including, the human rights situation in Darfur,[329] Myanmar,[330] human rights violations emanating from Israeli military incursions in the Occupied Palestinian Territory,[331] and 'the negative impact on the realization of the right to food of the worsening of the world food crisis, caused inter alia by the soaring food prices'.[332] During its eighth session (2–18 June 2008) the Council extended the mandates of the Special Rapporteurs on extrajudicial, summary or arbitrary executions[333] and Torture,[334] amongst others and at its ninth session (8–26 September 2008) extended the mandate of the Working Group of Experts on People of African Descent.[335]

(vii) The Office of the High Commissioner for Human Rights[336]

On 25 June 1993, delegates representing 171 States adopted the Vienna Declaration and Programme of Action of the World Conference on Human Rights.[337] The Vienna

---

[322] Country mandate were preserved for Burma, Democratic Republic of Congo, Haiti, North Korea, Somalia and Sudan. See UN Doc. A/HRC/5/L.11 18 June 2007, p. 38.
[323] Human Rights Council Resolution 6/32.
[324] Human Rights Council Resolution 6/27.
[325] Human Rights Council Resolution 6/28.
[326] Human Rights Council Resolution 6/37.
[327] Human Rights Council Resolution 6/34.
[328] Human Rights Council Resolution 6/31. Note that the Independent Expert on Liberia has subsequently not had its mandate renewed, Human Rights Council Resolution 9/16.
[329] Human Rights Council 4th Special Session.
[330] Human Rights Council 5th Special Session.
[331] Human Rights Council 6th Special Session.
[332] Human Rights Council 7th Special Session.
[333] Human Rights Council Resolution 8/3.
[334] Human Rights Council Resolution 8/8.
[335] Human Rights Council Resolution 9/14.
[336] Clapham, 'Creating the High Commissioner for Human Rights: The Outside Story' 5 *EJIL* (1994) 556; Alston, 'Neither Fish nor Fowl: The Quest to Define the Role of the UN High Commissioner for Human Rights' 8 *EJIL* (1997) 321.
[337] Adopted by the World Conference on Human Rights, UN Doc. A/CONF.157/23 12 July 1993.

Declaration – to which this study consistently refers – reaffirmed the foundational principles of the international human rights regime. In addition to highlighting the inter-dependence of the 'three-generations of human rights', the Declaration reiterated the world communities concern for vulnerable groups *inter alia* children, minorities, indigenous peoples and women. It also provided concrete recommendations for consolidating, streng-thening and harmonising the monitoring capabilities of the United Nations. One sub-stantial proposal in this regard was for the establishment of the position of a High Commissioner for Human Rights by the General Assembly.[338] The General Assembly duly complied with this recommendation and the Office of the High Commissioner for Human Rights (OHCHR) was established pursuant to the General Assembly's Declaration adopted on 20 December 1993.[339] In this Resolution, the Assembly decided that the Human Commissioner is to be a person of high moral standing and personal integrity,[340] and is to have expert knowledge in the field of human rights as well as an overall understanding of cultures and issues of cultural diversities and sensitivities.[341] The High Commissioner is appointed by the UN Secretary General and approved by the General Assembly which takes into account a geographical rotation in such nomination.[342] The post is for a fixed tenure of four years, although with a possibility of renewal for another four years.[343] The desig-nated High Commissioner carries the rank of Under-Secretary General.[344]

In accordance with the provisions of the General Assembly Resolution, the High Com-missioner is the principal UN officer with primary responsibility for the human rights activities conducted by the organisation.[345] The High Commissioner functions within the framework of United Nations mechanism established for the promotion of human rights, most notably the International Bill of Rights.[346] The High Commissioner remains guided by the fundamental principle of the universality and indivisibility of all human rights, including a recognition and realisation of the right to development of all peoples.[347] The mandate accorded to the High Commissioner includes undertaking steps to promote and to ensure realisation of human rights as contained within international human rights standards.[348]

In order to fulfil his or her duties, the High Commissioner conducts a range of duties, including co-ordinating and strategising human rights promotion and protection schemes within the framework of the United Nations.[349] One of the significant assignments therefore is to make recommendations to various UN bodies in order to enhance the pro-tection of human rights.[350] He or she has conducted various visits to UN Member States and has engaged actively in dialogue with governments on a wide range of issues.[351] The High Commissioner has also campaigned actively in instances of clear violations of human

---

[338] Vienna Declaration, para 18 (Section II).
[339] General Assembly Resolution 48/141 (20 December 1993) A/RES/48/41.
[340] Ibid. para 2(a).
[341] Ibid.
[342] Ibid. para 2(b).
[343] Ibid.
[344] Ibid. para 2(c).
[345] Ibid. para 4.
[346] Ibid. para 3(a).
[347] Ibid. para 3(c).
[348] Ibid. para 4(a).
[349] Ibid. para 4(a)–(k).
[350] Ibid. para 4(b).
[351] Ibid. para 4(g).

rights: one noticeable example was the criticisms and campaign by Mrs. Mary Robinson in relation to the US detention in Guantánamo Bay. Mrs. Robinson demanded that the Guantánamo detainees were entitled to fundamental rights as provided by international humanitarian and human rights laws.[352] The Office of the High Commissioner also provides public information, as well as technical and financial assistance in supporting human rights activities. In order to generate greater cohesiveness, the Office of the High Commissioner and the Centre for Human Rights were merged together in 1997 under the overall supervision and responsibility of the UN High Commissioner for Human Rights.

The High Commissioner reports on an annual basis as regards his/her activities to the United Nations Human Rights Council and through the Economic and Social Council to the General Assembly.[353] The Office of the High Commissioner for Human Rights is located in Geneva although it has a liaison office in New York.[354] The High Commissioner's office has been provided staff and resources to carry out these functions. The Office of High Commissioner has placed extensive information concerning the Office as well as the human rights issues on its official web-page.[355] The wealth of information, comments and news of current human rights issues provided through the internet by the Office is remarkable; its global reach means that access is guaranteed to members of all communities in every part of the world.

The first United Nations High Commissioner for Human Rights was José Ayala-Lasso. He was appointed on 5 April 1994 and remained in office until his resignation from this office on 15 March 1997. José Ayala-Lasso was succeeded by Mrs. Mary Robinson, a former Irish President. Mrs. Robinson took office 12 September 1997 and remained the High Commissioner until the expiry of her term in 2002. During her tenure, the Office saw considerable elevation and strengthening of the position of the High Commissioner. Sergio Vieira de Mello was appointed United Nations High Commissioner for Human Rights on 12 September 2002, although his position became vacant through his tragic assassination in Iraq in August 2003. Sergio Vieira de Mello's replacement was Louise Arbour, who kept post of the High Commissioner between 1 July 2004 and July 2008. The current UN High Commissioner for Human Rights is Dr. Navanethem Pillay, whose appointment was approved by the General Assembly on 28 July 2008, and she took office on 1 September 2008.

5 CONCLUSIONS

The present chapter has presented an overview of the modern human rights regime within the operational sphere of the United Nations. Chastened by the unfortunate failure of the League of Nations to prevent conflict or war, the United Nations as an organisation was

---

[352] See the statement made by High Commissioner for Human Rights on the Detention of Taliban and Al-Qaeda prisoners at the US Base in Guantánamo Bay, Cuba, 16 January 2002: www.unhchr.ch/huricane/huricane.nsf/view01/C537C6D4657C7928C1256B43003E7D0B <last visited 31 March 2009>. 'All persons detained in this context are entitled to the protection of international human rights law and humanitarian law, in particular the relevant provisions of the International Covenant on Civil and Political Rights (ICCPR) and the Geneva Conventions of 1949 . . . All detainees must at all times be treated humanely, consistent with the provisions of the ICCPR and the Third Geneva Convention.' Ibid.

[353] General Assembly Resolution 48/141 (20 December 1993) A/RES/48/41. para 5.

[354] Ibid. para 6.

[355] Office of the High Commissioner for Human Rights, www.ohchr.org/EN/Pages/WelcomePage.aspx <last visited 31 March 2009>.

primarily targeted to ensure peace, security and stability within global affairs. The Security Council, as we examined, remains the body principally in charge of maintaining and enforcing international peace and security. A designation of permanent membership and veto power was introduced to ensure that law or policies could not adopt a course detrimental to specific interests. This, however, was an arbitrary and undemocratic step. A further limitation of the United Nations Charter was its emphasis on the notion of State Sovereignty – an ideal promoted and relied excessively by the Communist States. The United Nations Charter does contain several references to the promotion and protection of human rights, although attempts to incorporate a bill of rights within the Charter proved unsuccessful. Notwithstanding these initial limitations, the United Nations organs have made considerable strides towards both human rights standard-setting as well as the implementation of international human rights standards. In our analysis we considered that all of the United Nations principal organs, also including the Security Council, have come to associate themselves more closely to human rights law. For decades, the more focused standard-setting operations were conducted by the Commission on Human Rights and its Sub-Commission. The Human Rights Commission, undoubtedly made a significant contribution towards the establishment of international instruments concerning key aspects of human rights – the jewel in the crown of the achievement remains the drafting and adoption of the Universal Declaration of Human Rights (1948). The Human Rights Commission nevertheless suffered from serious limitations and weaknesses, foremost amongst these were the political jockeying and biases upon which it so fervently relished its operations. The replacement of the Commission with the Human Rights Council in 2006 has removed some of the criticisms although the Council itself has not been immune from political and ideological neutrality. The Council's procedures such as the Universal Periodic Review as well as the revamping of the Complaints Procedures and other mechanisms represent an improvement over previous schemes. The long-term advances which the Human Rights Council would make in the effective protection of individual and collective rights remain a matter of conjecture.[356] As discussed in the previous section, the Office of the High Commissioner on Human Rights has proved to be a useful mechanism for streamlining and strengthening the United Nations human rights machinery.

---

[356] See Ghanea, above n.134, at pp. 704–705.

Part II

The International Bill of Rights

4 The Universal Declaration of Human Rights[1]

1 INTRODUCTION

> We stand today at the threshold of a great event both in the life of the United Nations and in the life of mankind. This Universal Declaration of Human Rights may well become the international Magna Carta of all men everywhere. We hope its proclamation by the General Assembly will be an event comparable to the proclamation of the Declaration of the Rights of Man by the French people in 1789, the adoption of the Bill of Rights by the people of the United States, and the adoption of comparable declarations at different times in other countries.[2]

We have noted that the United Nations Charter contains a number of references to 'human rights', though no elaboration is provided to the meaning of the concept within the Charter itself. It has also been noted that efforts by certain States, notably Panama, to have a 'Bill of Rights' included within the United Nations Charter proved unsuccessful.[3] After the coming into operation of the United Nations Charter, there was a move to spell out the meaning of the concept of 'human rights' in greater detail. In 1945, the preparatory commission recommended that ECOSOC should establish a Commission on Human Rights which would then prepare a Bill of Rights. The recommendation was approved by the General Assembly and a Human Rights Commission was established in 1946. The first regular sessions of the

---

[1] See Alfredsson and Eide (eds), *The Universal Declaration of Human Rights: A Common Standard of Achievement* (Kluwer Law International, 1999), Dachi, Flinterman and Senders (eds), *Innovation and Inspiration: Fifty Years of the Universal Declaration of Human Rights* (Edita KNAW, 1999); Glendon, *A World Made New: Eleanor Roosevelt and the Universal Declaration of Human Rights* (Random House, 2002); Hannum, 'The Status of the Universal Declaration of Human Rights in National and International Law' 25 *Georgia Journal of International and Comparative Law* (1995–1996) 287; Humphrey, 'The Universal Declaration of Human Rights: Its History, Impact and Juridical Character' in Ramcharan (ed.), *Human Rights: Thirty Years after the Universal Declaration* (Brill, 1979) pp. 21–37; Johnson and Symonides, *The Universal Declaration of Human Rights: A History of its Creation and Implementation, 1948–1998* (UNESCO, 1998); Schwelb, 'The Influence of the Universal Declaration of Human Rights on International and National Law' PASIL (1959) 217; Steiner, Alston and Goodman (eds), *International Human Rights in Context: Law, Politics, Morals* (Oxford University Press, 2008) pp. 151–160; and Van der Heijden and Tahzib-Lie (eds), *Reflections on the Universal Declaration of Human Rights: A Fiftieth Anniversary Anthology* (Brill, 1998); Morsink, *The Universal Declaration of Human Rights: Origins, Drafting and Intent* (University of Pennsylvania Press, 2000).

[2] Eleanor Roosevelt, *Address to the United Nations General Assembly*, On the Adoption of the Universal Declaration of Human Rights (Paris, 9 December 1948).

[3] See above chapter 3; also see Humphrey, 'The UN Charter and the Universal Declaration of Human Rights' in Laurd (ed.), *The International Protection of Human Rights* (Thames & Hudson, 1967) pp. 39–56 at p. 47.

Human Rights Commission began on 27 January 1947. The Human Rights Commission immediately got down to its first task, i.e. that of drafting the International Bill of Rights. A consideration of the proceedings of the Human Rights Commission (amongst a specifically established Drafting Committee) represents divisions as to the form that the International Bill of Rights should take. The primary divisions were amongst those who wanted a declaration and those who were in favour of a binding convention or treaty.[4] In the second session of the Human Rights Commission late in 1947, it was decided that the International Bill of Rights should have three parts: a declaration; a Convention; and 'measures of implementation', i.e. a system of international supervision.[5] It was subsequently decided to split the Covenant into two separate Covenants.

The Declaration was adopted on 10 December 1948 with 48 votes in favour, none against and eight abstentions.[6] The UDHR was adopted by Resolution 217(III) which consisted of five parts. Part A consisted of the UDHR whereas Part B was entitled the Right of Petition.[7] In Part C of the Resolution, the General Assembly called upon the Economic and Social Council to request the United Nations Commission on Human Rights and United Nations Sub-Commission on the Prevention of Discrimination and the Protection of Minorities 'to make a thorough study of the problem of minorities, in order that the United Nations may be able to take effective measures for the protection of racial, national, religious or linguistic minorities'.[8] Part D related to the publicity to be given to the UDHR and Part E was entitled 'Preparation of a Draft Covenant on Human Rights and Draft measures of Implementation'. The Declaration has 30 articles covering the most important fundamental human rights. The General Assembly adopted the Declaration as a 'common standard of achievement for all peoples and all nations'. The catalogue of rights contained within the Declaration, provides for both civil and political rights as well as economic, social and cultural rights. These rights are contained in the following Articles:

Article 1	Recognition of being born free and equal in dignity and rights
Article 2	Right to equality
Article 3	Right to life, liberty and security of person
Article 4	Freedom from slavery or servitude
Article 5	Freedom from torture or cruel, inhuman or degrading treatment or punishment
Article 6	Right to recognition everywhere as a person before the law.
Article 7	Right to equality before the law
Article 8	Right to an effective remedy by the competent national tribunals
Article 9	Right not to be subjected to arbitrary arrest detention or exile
Article 10	Right to fair trial

---

[4] Steiner, Alston and Goodman, above n.1, at p. 138.

[5] Humphrey, above n.1, at pp. 22–23.

[6] 10 December, 1948, UN GA Res. 217 A(III), UN Doc. A/810 at 71 (1948). Byelorussia, Czechoslovakia, Poland, Ukraine, USSR, Yugoslavia, Saudi Arabia and South Africa. For the text of the Resolution see http://daccessdds.un.org/doc/RESOLUTION/GEN/NR0/043/88/IMG/NR004388.pdf?OpenElement <last visited 10 December 2008>.

[7] See Zuijdwijk, *Petitioning the United Nations: A Study in Human Rights* (Palgrave MacMillan, 1982) pp. 90–93.

[8] GA Resolution 217 C(III) (1948). See Eide, 'The Sub-Commission on Prevention of Discrimination and Protection of Minorities' in Alston (ed.), *United Nations and Human Rights: A Critical Appraisal* (Clarendon Press, 1992) pp. 211–264, at p. 220; Eide, 'The Non-inclusion of Minority Rights: Resolution 217C (III)' in Alfredsson and Eide (eds), above n.1, at pp. 701–723.

Article 11 Presumption of innocence and prohibition of retroactive criminal law
Article 12 Prohibition of arbitrary interference with privacy, family, home or correspondence
Article 13 Right to freedom of movement
Article 14 Right to seek asylum
Article 15 Right to a nationality
Article 16 Right to marry and found a family
Article 17 Right to own property
Article 18 Right to freedom of thought, conscience and religion
Article 19 Right to freedom opinion and expression
Article 20 Right to freedom of peaceful assembly
Article 21 Right to participate in the governance of the State, and the right to democracy
Article 22 Right to social security
Article 23 Right to work
Article 24 Right to rest and leisure
Article 25 Right to a decent standard of living
Article 26 Right to education
Article 27 Right to cultural life
Article 28 Right to social and international order suitable for the realisation of human rights

2 RANGE OF RIGHTS CONTAINED AND THE RATIONALE FOR INTERNATIONAL CONSENSUS

The Declaration contains a remarkable range of rights. It includes classical civil and political rights,[9] social, economic and cultural rights[10] and group or peoples rights.[11] The civil and political rights bear resemblance to those rights contained in the 18th- and 19th century classical human rights documents; much like the French Declaration of the Rights of Man, the Universal Declaration thrives on the rights to liberty, equality and fraternity.[12] The Declaration provides a comprehensive set of civil and political rights. These rights also known as first-generation rights, include, for example, the right to equality, to life, to an effective remedy by national tribunals, to fair trial, to freedom of assembly, opinion and expression and thought, conscience and religion. A characteristic feature of such rights as the right to equality and non-discrimination is the 'all-embracing language'[13] with references to race, colour, sex, language, religion, political or other opinion, national or social origin, property, birth or other status as one of a non-exhaustive nature.[14]

[9] Also known as first generation rights. See above chapter 1.
[10] Also referred to as second generation rights. See above chapter 1.
[11] Also known as third generation rights, or solidarity rights. See above chapter 1. Also see Alston, 'The Commission on Human Rights' in P. Alston (ed.), above n.8, pp. 126–210, at p. 188.
[12] See Marks, 'From the "Single Confused Page" to the Decalogue for Six Billion Persons: The Roots of the Universal Declaration of Human Rights in the French Revolution' 20 *HRQ* (1998) 459.
[13] Cholewinski, *Migrant Workers in International Human Rights Law: Their Protection in Countries of Employment* (Clarendon Press, 1997) at p. 48.
[14] Ibid.

The Declaration condemns torture and slavery and prohibits arbitrary interference with privacy, family, home or correspondence. The Declaration also contains certain civil and political rights which have retained a controversial standing. One example is the right to property. The right to property, although included in Article 17 of the UDHR, could not be provided for either in the ICCPR (1966) or in the ICESCR (1966).[15] Another interesting example is that of the right to seek asylum as provided in Article 14 of the UDHR.[16] The UDHR proclaims 'the right to seek and enjoy in other countries asylum from persecution' – the initial terminology of 'the right to seek and be granted, in other countries, asylum' being replaced as a consequence of objections within the United Nations Human Rights Commission from States to remove a sense of obligation on United Nation members to grant asylum to individuals.[17] Article 12 of the ICCPR (1966) goes further than the provisions of the UDHR. It provides freedom for everyone to be free to leave any country, including his or her own country. Yet at the same time it is restrictive in that it does not allow the right of entry to another country for the purpose of seeking asylum. Such an omission from Article 12 of the ICCPR, it is contended, was intentional.[18] Even more interestingly, as we shall consider in more detail, the UN Convention Relating to the Status of Refugees does not provide for the *right* to seek asylum; the obligation on States to admit those seeking asylum is restricted to a recommendation attached to the Final Act of the Conference adopting the Refugee Convention.[19]

In addition to the aforementioned civil and political rights, the Declaration contains a number of social, economic and cultural rights. These rights, also referred to as second-generation rights, include the right to social security, to work, to rest and leisure and the right to education. The right to cultural life is accorded by Article 27. Article 28 takes a broad approach and provides for the third-generation rights of a suitable international order and the right to peace. According to this Article, everyone is entitled to a social and international order in which the rights and freedoms set forth in this Declaration can be fully realised.

This cataloguing of rights in a single document appears even more remarkable when considered in light of the great consensus shown in adopting the document. Various reasons for such a consensus can be put forward, some more obvious than the others. Firstly and most importantly, it was relatively easy to find acceptance amongst UN States because of

---

[15] Krause and Alfredsson, 'Article 17' in Alfredsson and Eide (eds), above n.1, pp. 359–378.

[16] Lillich, 'Civil Rights' in Meron (ed.), *Human Rights in International Law: Legal and Policy Issues* (Clarendon Press, 1984) pp. 115–170 at p. 152; Kjærum, 'Article 14' in Alfredsson and Eide (eds), above n.1, pp. 279–295 at p. 285.

[17] See Goodwin-Gill and McAdam, *The Refugee in International Law* (Oxford University Press, 2007) at pp. 359–360. See UNGAOR Part 1 (3rd Session, 1948), 'Summary Records of Meetings' 121nd Meeting (4 November 1948).

[18] Fitzpatrick, 'Revitalizing the 1951 Refugee Convention' 9 *Harvard Human Rights Journal* (1996) 229, at p. 246. Some regional human rights instruments do provide for this right. The African Charter on Human and Peoples' Rights (1981) provides that 'Every individual shall have the right, when persecuted, to seek and obtain asylum in other countries in accordance with laws of those countries and international conventions', Article 12(3). According to Article 22(7) of the American Convention on Human Rights (1969) 'Every person has the right to seek and be granted asylum in a foreign territory, in accordance with the legislation of the state and international conventions, in the event he is being pursued for political offenses or related common crimes'. See below chapter 11 and chapter 10 respectively.

[19] Fitzpatrick makes the following comment 'when the "soft law" of the Universal Declaration was succeeded by the Refugee Convention, no mention was made of the right to seek and to enjoy asylum. The Convention's key obligatory provisions (Articles 31, 32 and 33) assume a situation in which refugees, possibly by irregular means, have somehow managed to arrive at or in the territory of the contracting State. The obligations of States to admit asylum seekers is referenced only in a recommendation attached to the Final Act of the Conference adopting the Convention', Fitzpatrick, above n.18, at p. 245. See further chapter 19 below; note, however, the provisions of the UN General Assembly Declaration on Territorial Asylum (1967).

the belief that the Declaration, as a General Assembly Resolution, was a non-binding instrument.[20] International consensus would have been much harder, had State representatives been faced with the prospect of accepting legally binding obligations. Secondly, it was also a fact that at the time of adoption of the Declaration, there were far fewer States, making it relatively easier to find a common ground. As we shall consider, soon after the adoption of the Declaration, rapid changes to the global political geography took place. The former colonies emerged as new States and did not have the same priorities and claims. Finally, a range of strategies was adopted by the drafters to achieve consensus and have the Declaration adopted by the international community. Pointing to these strategies, Samnøy mentions the exclusion of controversial issues and usage of generalised and vague terminology.[21]

3 NATURE OF OBLIGATIONS AND RELEVANCE FOR HUMAN RIGHTS PRACTITIONER

As already indicated, the Declaration was adopted by General Assembly Resolution 217 (III) and was not intended to be legally binding. The intention of those who drafted the Declaration was to provide guidelines which States would aim to achieve. Thus according to Mrs. Eleanor Roosevelt, the Chairperson of the Human Rights Commission, 'it [the Declaration] is not, and does not purport to be a statement of law or of legal obligation';[22] it is instead 'a common standard of achievement for all peoples of all nations'.[23] Given the *prima facie* non-binding character of the Declaration, the immediate question arises as to the practical relevance of the consideration of this instrument. The most direct answer to this question is that notwithstanding the hortatory character of the Declaration over a period of time, its substantive provisions have become binding on all States. The binding authority derives from the following sources.

(i) UDHR as an authoritative interpretation of the Charter

The United Nations Charter, while making references to human rights, does not itself provide a catalogue of human rights. After the enforcement of the Charter, it was intended that a detailed Bill of Rights would provide explanation to the content of human rights. As the first part of such a bill, the Declaration is arguably an authoritative interpretation of the meaning of human rights as prescribed within the United Nations Charter. This argument is substantiated both by the *travaux préparatoires* of the Declaration and from its text. The preamble to the Declaration makes reference to Articles 55 and 56 of the United Nations Charter. As one leading authority has pointed out such references can lead to the argument that 'each right contained in the Universal Declaration is effectively incorporated into [the] Charter articles 55 and 56'.[24]

During the drafting stages of the Declaration, a number of State's representatives treated the Declaration as a document interpreting the human rights provisions of the Charter.

[20] Schwelb, above n.1, at p. 218.
[21] Samnøy, 'The Origins of the Universal Declaration of Human Rights' in Alfredsson and Eide (eds), above n.1, pp. 3–22 at pp. 14–15.
[22] Quoted in Whiteman, 1 *Digest of International Law* (1963) 55.
[23] See Preamble to UDHR.
[24] See Rodley, *The Treatment of Prisoners in International Law* (Clarendon Press, 1999) p. 63.

The Chinese representative was of the view that, while the United Nations Charter placed Member States under an obligation to observe human rights, the Universal Declaration 'stated these rights explicitly'.[25] According to Professor Réne Cassin of France, a member of the Commission and the Drafting Committee, the Universal Declaration 'could be considered as an authoritative interpretation of the Charter'.[26] Similarly, the Chilean representative remarked that 'violations by any State of the rights enumerated in the Declaration would mean violation of the principles of the United Nations'.[27] Amongst the Islamic States, the Egyptian representative took the view that the Declaration was an 'authoritative interpretation of the [UN] Charter'[28] supported by the Syrian and Pakistan delegates. Ironically, it was the concern that the non-binding General Assembly Resolution might in fact come to have binding effect (through its recognition as an authoritative interpretation of the UN Charter's human rights provisions) that produced substantial disquiet on the part of South Africa, leading ultimately to its abstention from the vote.[29]

(ii) UDHR as part of customary international law

A significant proportion of this book deals with human rights treaties, such as the ICCPR,[30] the ICESCR,[31] the ECHR[32] and the AFCHPR.[33] As we have seen in Chapter 2, treaties are legally binding obligations undertaken by States parties.[34] However, treaty law represents one aspect, albeit a significant one, of the international law-making process. We have also noted that other sources of international law include international customary law and general principles of law. International customary law, which binds all States, consists of two key ingredients: State practice and the belief that such a practice amounts to law (*opinio juris*).[35]

In the light of existing State practice it can be argued that a majority of the provisions of the Declaration now represent customary international law.[36] There is overwhelming evidence of State practice with the requisite *opinio juris* to confirm the customary binding nature of many of the provisions of the Declaration.[37] Such evidence can be derived from

---

[25] Cited in Humphrey, above n.3, at p. 50.
[26] Ibid. p. 51.
[27] A/C.3/S.R 91 at 97.
[28] UN Doc. A/C.3/SR 92 at 12. See Arzt, 'The Application of International Human Rights Law in Islamic States' 12 *HRQ* (1990) 202 at pp. 215–216.
[29] See Humphrey, above n.1, at pp. 32–33.
[30] New York, 16 December 1966 United Nations, 999 U.N.T.S. 171; 6 I.L.M. (1967) 368.
[31] New York, 16 December 1966, 993 U.N.T.S. 3; 6 I.L.M. (1967) 360.
[32] Convention for the Protection of Human Rights and Fundamental Freedoms ETS No. 005 213 U.N.T.S. 222, entered into force 3 September 1953.
[33] African [Banjul] Charter on Human and Peoples' Rights, adopted 27 June 1981, OAU Doc. CAB/LEG/67/3 rev. 5, 21 I.L.M. 58 (1982), entered into force 21 October 1986.
[34] See above chapter 2.
[35] Ibid.
[36] According to one authority 'the Universal Declaration is the ius constituendum of the United Nations Charter to the term "human rights" and most of the international lawyers support the opinion that its principles are customary international law'. Heintze, 'The UN Convention and the Network of International Human Rights Protection by the United Nations' in Freeman and Veerman (eds), *Ideologies of Children's Rights* (Martinus Nijhoff, 1992) pp. 71–78, at p. 72; Joseph, *Corporations and Transnational Human Rights Litigation* (Hart, 2004) at p. 26; Sohn, 'The New International Law: Protection of the Rights of Individuals rather than States' 32 *American University Law Review* (1982–1983) 1, at p. 17.
[37] See e.g. the Preambles to the European Convention on Human Rights (1950) and the African Charter on Human and People's Rights (1981).

its constant reaffirmation by the General Assembly.[38] According to one source, in the first 21 years after its adoption, the Declaration was cited no fewer than 75 times by the General Assembly, an exercise that has remained prevalent in the subsequent human rights activities of the Assembly.[39] There is also a consistent referral to the Universal Declaration in international instruments, in bi-lateral agreements[40] and multilateral human rights treaties.[41] In the context of multilateral human rights treaties it is important to note that the International Covenants and three regional human rights treaties make specific reference to the Declaration. In his consideration, Professor Brownlie points to the Final Act of the Conference on Security and Co-operation in Europe,[42] and the Proclamation of Tehran[43] whereby States express their intention to follow the principles of the Universal Declaration on Human Rights.[44] To this one could add the Vienna Declaration and Programme of Action, which was adopted by a consensus of representatives from 171 States.[45] In addition to containing numerous references to the Universal Declaration, it emphasises

> that the Universal Declaration of Human Rights, which constitutes a common standard of achievement for all peoples and all nations, is the source of inspiration and has been the basis for the United Nations in making advances in standard setting as contained in the existing international human rights instruments, in particular the International Covenant on Civil and Political Rights and the International Covenant of Economic, Social and Cultural Rights.[46]

A further recognition of the binding nature of the UDHR by States is either by replication of its provisions in their national constitutions or by reference in their constitutional documents.[47] National and international tribunals have also relied upon the Declaration, treating it as a binding document.[48]

---

[38] See the Declaration on Granting of Independence to Colonial Countries, which provides 'All States shall observe faithfully and strictly the provisions of the Charter of the United Nations, the Universal Declaration of Human Rights and the present Declaration'. GA Res. 1514 (XV) 1960, para 7.

[39] Bleicher, 'The Legal Significance of Recitation of General Assembly Resolutions' 63 *AJIL* (1969) 444 at p. 456; Zuijdwijk, above n.7, at p. 101.

[40] See e.g. the Franco-Tunisian Convention (1955) *UNYBH* (1955) 340, at p. 342.

[41] See Robertson and Merrills, *Human Rights in the World: An Introduction to the Study of the International Protection of Human Rights* (Manchester University Press, 1996) p. 29; Humphrey, 'The International Bill of Rights: Scope and Implementation' 17 *William and Mary Law Review* (1975–1976) 527; Humphrey, above n.1, at pp. 28–29.

[42] See the Final Act of the Conference on Security and Co-operation in Europe, Adopted by the Conference on Security and Co-operation in Europe at Helsinki, 1 August 1975. Reprinted in 14 I.L.M. (1975) 1292. Discussed below.

[43] See the Proclamation of Tehran, *The Final Act of the United Nations Conference on Human Rights*, Tehran, 22 April–13 May 1968, UN Doc. A/CONF. 32/41 (New York) E. 68, XIV. 2.

[44] Brownlie (ed.), *Basic Documents on Human Rights* (Clarendon Press, 1981) p. 21.

[45] *Vienna Declaration and Programme of Action* adopted by the World Conference on Human Rights, UN Doc. A/CONF.157/23 12 July 1993.

[46] Ibid. Preamble to the Vienna Declaration and Programme of Action.

[47] See e.g. the Constitution of Bosnia and Herzegovina (1995).

[48] See e.g. *United States Diplomatic and Consular Staff in Tehran (United States of America v. Iran), Judgment 24 May 1980, (1980) ICJ Reports 3*, where the International Court notes 'Wrongfully to deprive human beings of their freedom and to subject them to physical constraint in conditions of hardship is in itself manifestly incompatible with . . . the fundamental principles enunciated in the Universal Declaration of Human Rights' ibid. para 91. Commenting on the Tehran case, Professor Rodley, makes the valid point that '[a] more natural interpretation is that the Court was simply stating that the Declaration as a whole propounds fundamental principles recognised by general international law' Rodley, 'Human Rights and Humanitarian Intervention: The Case Law of the World Court' 38 *ICLQ* (1989) 321 at p. 326. See also *Filártiga* v. *Peña-Irala* 630 F. 2d 876 (1980); 19 ILM 966. US Circuit Court of Appeals, 2nd Circuit.

While endorsing the customary value of many of the rights contained in the Declaration, at the same time some caution is recommended. As we shall see during the course of this study, not all rights contained in the Universal Declaration have generated a sufficient degree of consensus to be recognised as binding in customary law. There is debate about the legal value and content of a number of rights, in particular of economic, social and cultural rights.[49] Thus, questions have been raised about the legal and juridical value of such rights as the right to rest and leisure, the right to a decent standard of living, and the right to participate in the cultural life of the community. In the light of divisions it is sensible to take account of the views of one leading authority when he writes 'it must not be assumed without more that any and every human right referred to [in UDHR] is part of customary international law'.[50]

(iii) UDHR binding States with its *jus cogens* character

The chapters in this book will confirm that a number of the rights contained in the UDHR have become so firmly established in international law that they are now treated as having a *jus cogens* character. We have already noted that no specification has been provided on the norms forming *jus cogens*. At the same time, several of the fundamental rights enunciated in the Declaration such as the right to equality (Article 2), right to life, liberty and security (Article 3) freedom from slavery or servitude (Article 4), freedom from torture or cruel, inhuman or degrading treatment or punishment (Article 5), right to a fair trial (Article 10) the presumption of innocence and the prohibition of retroactive criminal law (Article 11) partake of the norm of *jus cogens*.

The existence of such substantial affirmation of the rights has led many commentators to take the position that the normative provisions of the Declaration form part of *jus cogens*, thereby binding all States.[51] As this book analyses in detail, the aforementioned fundamental rights of the Declaration now form part and parcel of every human rights instrument. It is well established that it is not possible to derogate from these rights. At the same time, a number of rights are arguably not even part of customary law and categorising those, as part of the body of *jus cogens*, would be inaccurate. There is significant debate about the customary position not only of economic, social and cultural rights such as the right to social security (Article 22), right to rest and leisure (Article 24), right to a decent standard of living (Article 25) and right to participate in cultural life (Article 27), but also of civil and political rights which includes the right to seek asylum (Article 14) and the various facets of the right to freedom of thought, conscience and religion (Article 18).[52]

4 CONCLUSIONS

10 December 2008 marked the 60th anniversary of the adoption of the Universal Declaration of Human Rights. Notwithstanding its age the Declaration remains a remarkable instrument. It contains a remarkable array of rights, covering not only civil and political

---

[49] See below.
[50] Thornberry, *International Law and the Rights of Minorities* (Clarendon Press, 1991) p. 322.
[51] See McDougal, Lasswell and Chen, *Human Rights and World Public Order* (Yale University Press, 1980) p. 64.
[52] See below chapters 5 and 6.

rights, but also economic, social and cultural rights as well as the so-called third generation of rights. Our earlier discussion has analysed the metamorphosis of this instrument – from a declaration intended to have moral persuasion and representing a common standard to one where many of the provisions are binding upon all States as customary law. Some provisions, such as the freedom from torture, have *jus cogens* character. On the whole, the Universal Declaration continues to command respect from political figures, diplomats and all those engaged in the struggle for the protection of universal human rights. The impact of the Declaration in the transformation of human rights values has also been no less spectacular, possibly exceeding its 'authors' most sanguine expectations'.[53] The comments made by Professor Steiner are an accurate reflection of the respect and command which the Declaration invokes. He notes that the Declaration

has retained its place of honor in the human-rights movement. No other document has so caught the historical moment, achieved the same moral and rhetorical force, or exerted as much influence on the movement as a whole. Parent to the two major covenants that followed it and grandparent to the many specialized treaties in the field, the Declaration expressed in lean, eloquent language the hopes and idealism of a world released from the grip of World War II. However self-evident it may appear today, the Declaration bore a more radical message than many of its framers perhaps recognized. It proceeded to work its subversive path through many rooted doctrines of international law, forever changing the discourse of international relations on issues vital to human decency and peace. It underscored the need for international human-rights institutions that could exercise novel jurisdictions over states. It animated peoples in many countries to rethink their plight and to demand of their leaders an unprecedented recognition of their human rights. This remarkable Declaration has become the constitution of the universal human-rights movement.[54]

---

53 See Robertson and Merrills, above n.41, at p. 29.
54 Steiner, 'Securing Human Rights: The First Half-Century of the Universal Declaration and Beyond' *Harvard Magazine* (September–October 1998) http://harvardmagazine.com/1998/09/world3.html <last visited 31 December 2008>.

5 International Covenant on Civil and Political Rights[1]

1 INTRODUCTION

After the adoption of the Universal Declaration of Human Rights (UDHR),[2] the next stage was to establish legally binding principles on international human rights. In its Resolution 217B and E(III) of 10 December 1948 the General Assembly, through the ECOSOC, requested the Human Right Commission to continue to accord priority to the drafting of the International Covenant and measures of implementation.[3] Originally it had been intended to draft a single Covenant covering all the fundamental rights. However, with the emergence of the Cold War and the rise of new nation States (with their own priorities) it became impossible to incorporate all the rights within one document.[4] The Western States put the emphasis on civil and political rights whereas the focus of the socialist and newly independent States was upon economic, social and cultural rights and the right to self-determination. There were divisions as regards having civil and political rights, alongside the economic, social and cultural rights within the text of a single treaty. Those in favour of a single Covenant argued that

---

[1] Bair, *The International Covenant on Civil and Political Rights and its (First) Optional Protocol: A Short Commentary Based on Views, General Comments and Concluding Observations by the Human Rights Committee* (Peter Lang, 2005); Bayefsky, *The UN Human Rights Treaty System: Universality at the Crossroads* (Brill, 2001); Buergenthal, 'The UN Human Rights Committee' 5 *Max Planck UNYB* (2001) 341; Bossuyt, *Guide to the 'Travaux préparatoires' of the International Covenant on Civil and Political Rights* (1987); Boerefijn, *The Reporting Procedure under the Covenant on Civil and Political Rights: Practice and Procedures of the Human Rights Committee* (Intersentia, 1999); Conte, Davidson and Burchill, *Defining Civil and Political Rights: The Jurisprudence of the United Nations Human Rights Committee* (Ashgate, 2004); Ghandhi, *The Human Rights Committee and the Right of Individual Communication: Law and Practice* (Ashgate Publishing Co, 1998); Harris, *Cases and Materials on International Law* (Sweet & Maxwell, 2004) pp. 624–764; Harris and Joseph (eds), *The International Covenant on Civil and Political Rights and United Kingdom Law* (Clarendon Press, 1995); Joseph, Schultz and Castan, *The International Covenant on Civil and Political Rights: Cases, Materials, and Commentary* (Oxford University Press, 2004); McGoldrick, *The Human Rights Committee: Its Role in the Development of the International Covenant on Civil and Political Rights* (Clarendon Press, 1991); Nowak, *UN Covenant on Civil and Political Rights: CCPR Commentary* (N.P. Engel, 2005); Steiner, Alston and Goodman (eds), *International Human Rights in Context: Law, Politics, Morals: Text and Materials* (Oxford University Press, 2008) pp. 151–262; Tomuschat, *Human Rights: Between Idealism and Realism* (Oxford University Press, 2008); Young, *The Law and Process of the UN Human Rights Committee* (Transnational Publishers, 2002).

[2] 10 December 1948, UN GA Res. 217 A(III), UN Doc. A/810 at 71 (1948).

[3] Ghandhi, above n.1, at p. 3.

[4] See Steiner, Alston and Goodman (eds), above n.1, at p. 136.

human rights could not be clearly divided into different categories, nor could they be so classified as to represent a hierarchy of values. All rights should be promoted and protected at the same time. Without economic, social and cultural rights, civil and political rights might be purely nominal in character; without civil and political rights, economic, social and cultural rights could not be long ensured.[5]

However the opposing camp prioritised civil and political rights as more significant.[6] They also pointed to the progressive nature of the social and economic rights, some even doubting that they were rights in the real sense. A critical issue related to the implementation mechanism. While it was possible to install a scheme of implementing civil and political rights (through legislation), the same was not thought to be feasible for social and economic rights.[7]

It was ultimately decided to have two different treaties, one covering primarily civil and political rights (i.e. ICCPR)[8] and the other economic, social and cultural rights (i.e. ICESCR)[9] As we shall analyse in detail, although some rights contained within these treaties overlap, there are, nevertheless, substantial differences in the content, nature of obligations and the implementation mechanisms. The ICCPR and the ICESCR were approved by the Third Committee of the General Assembly in December, 1966. Each Covenant required 35 ratifications and both came into force in 1976. The Optional Protocol was approved in 1966 and required 10 ratifications. As of 8 April 2009, there are 163 States parties to the ICCPR. In addition, 112 States have made declarations pursuant to the First Optional Protocol to the ICCPR.[10] The Second Optional Protocol aimed at the Abolition of Death Penalty was adopted and opened for signature, accession or ratification on 15 December 1989.[11] It came into operation on 11 July 1991. There are currently 71 States parties to this Protocol. The ICCPR consists of a preamble and 53 articles, which are divided into eight parts. The ICCPR consists of the following rights:

Article 1	The right to self-determination
Article 6	The right to life
Article 7	Freedom from torture or cruel, inhuman or degrading treatment or punishment
Article 8	Freedom from slavery and slave trade
Article 9	The right to liberty and security

---

[5] Annotations on the Text of the Draft International Covenants on Human Rights, UN Doc. A/2929 (1955), 7 para 8.

[6] For a useful analysis of the debates and the ultimate decision to draft two separate covenants see Baderin and McCorquodale, 'The International Covenant on Economic, Social and Cultural Rights: Forty Years of Development' in Baderin and McCorquodale (eds) *Economic, Social and Cultural Rights in Action* (Oxford University Press, 2007) pp. 4–24, at 6.

[7] McGoldrick, above n.1, at pp. 11–13; Feldman, *Civil Liberties and Human Rights in England and Wales* (Oxford University Press, 2002) at pp. 39–40; for a consideration of implementation mechanism in the Covenants see Moller, 'The Right to Petition: General Assembly Resolution 217B' and 'Introduction' both in Alfredsson and Eide (eds), *The Universal Declaration of Human Rights* (Kluwer Law International, 1999) pp. 653–659.

[8] Adopted at New York, 16 December 1966. Entered into force 23 March 1976. GA Res. 2200A (XXI) UN Doc. A/6316 (1966) 999 U.N.T.S. 171; 6 I.L.M. (1967) 368.

[9] Adopted at New York, 16 December 1966. Entered into force 3 January 1976. GA Res. 2200A (XXI) UN Doc. A/6316 (1966) 993 U.N.T.S. 3; 6 I.L.M. (1967) 360.

[10] New York, 16 December 1966 United Nations, 999 U.N.T.S. 302.

[11] Annex to GA Res. 44/128. Reprinted in 29 I.L.M (1990) 1464. See generally Schabas, *The Abolition of Death Penalty in International Law* (Cambridge University Press, 1997).

Article 10 The right of detained persons to be treated with humanity
Article 11 Freedom from imprisonment for debt
Article 12 Freedom of movement and choice of residence
Article 13 Freedom of aliens from arbitrary expulsion
Article 14 Right to a fair trial
Article 15 Prohibition against retroactivity of criminal law
Article 16 Right to recognition everywhere as a person before the law
Article 17 Right to privacy for every individual
Article 18 Right of freedom of thought, conscience and religion
Article 19 Right of opinion and expression
Article 20 Prohibition of propaganda for war and of incitement to national, racial or religious hatred
Article 21 Right of peaceful assembly
Article 22 Freedom of association
Article 23 Right to marry and found a family
Article 24 Rights of the child
Article 25 Political rights
Article 26 Equality before the law
Article 27 Rights of persons belonging to minorities

The ICCPR has many rights which are covered by UDHR or other international and regional human rights treaties. However, unlike the UDHR, the ICCPR does not accord protection to the right to property (covered by Article 17 UDHR and ECHR first protocol).[12] For the most part the ICCPR grants rights to all individuals who are within States parties' territories and are subject to their jurisdiction, regardless of their constitutional or political status. Thus, the protection covers nationals, aliens, refugees and illegal immigrants.[13] The reference in the ICCPR to 'everyone' or 'all persons' in relation to a majority of rights confirms this view.[14] In order to ensure the rights within the Covenant, States parties undertake to provide for an effective remedy, by competent and judicial authorities, and to ensure the enforcement of these remedies by competent authorities.[15]

2 THE INTERNATIONAL COVENANTS AND THE RIGHT TO SELF-DETERMINATION[16]

Both the ICCPR and the ICESCR begin with identical provisions on the right to self-determination. Article 1 of the Covenants provides that

---

[12] See chapters 3 and 5 respectively. ECHR, First Protocol (adopted 20 March 1952) entered into force 18 May 1954, ETS 9.
[13] The Position of Aliens under the Covenant 11/04/86. CCPR General Comment 15 (General Comments) para 2.
[14] McGoldrick, above n.1, at pp. 20–21.
[15] Article 2(3).
[16] See Cassese, *Self-Determination of Peoples* (Cambridge University Press, 1995); Hannum, *Autonomy, Sovereignty and Self-Determination: The Accommodation of Conflicting Rights* (University of Pennsylvania Press, 1990);

1. All peoples have the right of self-determination. By virtue of that right they freely determine their political status and freely pursue their economic, social and cultural development.

2. All peoples may, for their own ends, freely dispose of their natural wealth and resources without prejudice to any obligations arising out of international economic co-operation, based upon the principle of mutual benefit, and international law. In no case may a people be deprived of its own means of subsistence.

3. The States Parties to the present Covenant, including those having responsibility for the administration of Non-Self-Governing and Trust Territories, shall promote the realisation of the right of self-determination, and shall respect that right, in conformity with the provisions of the Charter of the United Nations.

Self-determination is a difficult right to define in international law and there is a significant amount of controversy as to the exact parameters of this right. The implementation of the right to self-determination has also raised controversy and debate. In the drafting process, several States questioned the value of this right in the post-colonial world. Many States were particularly concerned that minority groups within independent States may use this right as a basis of their claim to secession. In its General Comment, the Human Rights Committee (HRC) – the committee in charge of implementing the Covenant – has been assertive and has advocated a continuing obligation to advance the right to self-determination.[17] In this General Comment, HRC notes that the article imposes specific obligations, not only confined to their own peoples but in relation to all peoples who have not been able to exercise their right to self-determination or are deprived from exercising this right. HRC, however, has shown dissatisfaction at the lack of coverage of this right in State reports. The Committee notes:

Although the reporting obligations of all States parties include article 1, only some reports give detailed explanations regarding each of its paragraphs. The Committee has noted that many of them completely ignore article 1, provide inadequate information in regard to it or confine themselves to a reference to election laws. The Committee considers it highly desirable that States parties' reports should contain information on each paragraph of article 1.[18]

Hannum, 'Rethinking Self-Determination' 34 *Va.JIL* (1993) 1; Klabbers, 'The Right to be Taken Seriously: Self-Determination in International Law' 28 *HRQ* (2006) 186; Koskenniemi, 'National Self-Determination Today: Problems of Legal Theory and Practice' 43 *ICLQ* (1994) 241; McCorquodale, 'The Right of Self-Determination' in Harris and Joseph (eds), above n.1, pp. 91–119; McCorquodale (ed.), *Self-Determination in International Law* (Dartmouth Publishing Co., 2000); McCorquodale, 'Self-Determination: A Human Rights Approach' 43 *ICLQ* (1994) 857; Musgrave, *Self-Determination and National Minorities* (Oxford University Press, 2000); Nanda, 'Self-Determination in International Law' 66 *AJIL* (1972) 321; Suzuki, 'Self-Determination and World Public Order: Community Response to Territorial Separation' 16 *Va.JIL* (1976) 779; Thornberry, 'Self-Determination, Minorities, Human Rights: A Review of International Instruments' 38 *ICLQ* (1989) 867; Tomuschat (ed.), *Modern Law of Self-Determination* (Martinus Nijhoff, 1993); White, 'Self-Determination: Time for a Re-Assessment?' 28 *NILR* (1981) 147; for further analysis see below chapter 14.

[17] The Right to Self-determination of peoples (Art. 1) 13/03/84. CCPR General Comment 12. (General Comments) para 3.

[18] Ibid.

It has urged States parties to present their constitutional and political processes which allow for the exercise of the right to self-determination.[19] On the other hand, it seems certain that violations of Article 1 cannot be the subject of a complaint under the first Optional Protocol.[20] In a number of cases HRC has taken the position that as a right belonging to peoples, it is not open to individuals to claim to be victims of the violation of the right to self-determination.[21] A group of individuals cannot make claims to be victims under this article. However, it is possible that Article 1 can be used in the interpretation of other rights, specifically Articles 25, 26 and 27.[22] Equally, reservations have been entered upon the Article. India, at the time of its ratification, entered a reservation to Article 1 according to which:

> The Government of the Republic of India declares that the words 'the right of self-determination' appearing in [that article] apply only to the peoples under the foreign domination and that these words do not apply to sovereign independent States or to a section of a people or nation – which is the essence of national integrity.[23]

3 GENERAL NATURE OF OBLIGATIONS[24]

Articles 2–5 of both the Covenants constitute Part II, containing in each instance an undertaking to 'respect and to ensure'[25] or to 'to take steps . . . with a view to achieving progressively'[26] the substantive rights which follow in Part III together with certain other provisions. According to Article 2(1) of the ICCPR 'Each State Party . . . undertakes to respect and to ensure to all individuals within its territory and subject to its jurisdiction the rights recognized in the present Covenant . . .'.[27] These provisions have been described as 'fundamental', with a positive obligation directing States parties to immediately implement

---

[19] Ibid. para 4.

[20] Lewis-Anthony and Scheinin, 'Treaty-Based Procedures for Making Human Rights Complaints within the UN System' in Hannum (ed.), *Guide to International Human Rights Practice* (Transnational Publishers, 2004) pp. 43–63, at p. 46.

[21] See *Lubicon Lake Band* v. *Canada*, Communication No. 167/1984 (26 March 1990), UN Doc. Supp. No. 40 (A/45/40) at 1 (1990) paras 13.3 and 32.1; *Ivan Kitok* v. *Sweden*, (197/1985) para 6.3. *Wilson* v. *Australia* (1239/2004), Communication No. 1239/2004, UN Doc. CCPR/C/80/D/1239/2004 (2004), para 4.3; *Antonio Hom* v. *Philippines*, Communication No. 1169/2003, UN Doc. CCPR/C/78/D/1169/2003 (2003), para 4.2; See also General Comment 23(50), The rights of minorities Article 27, 08/04/94, UN Doc. CCPR/C/21/Rev. 1/Add.5 (1994) at para 3.1.

[22] Nowak, above n.1, at p. 19.

[23] UN Centre for Human Rights, Human Rights: Status of International Instruments (1987) 9 UN Sales No. E.87.XIV.2; HRC has urged India to review its reservations, 'with a view to withdrawing them': *Concluding observations of the Human Rights Committee: India. 04/08/97 (CCPR/C/79/Add.81)* CCPR/C/79/Add.81; 4 August 1997, para 14; for analysis see, *Submission of Committee on Human Rights (COHR) Manipur, on Human Rights Situation in Manipur (India) to OHCHR concerning the universal periodic review of the government of India at the UN Human Rights Council in April 2008* lib.ohchr.org/HRBodies/UPR/Documents/Session1/IN/COHR_IND_UPR_S1_2008_CommitteeOnHumanRights_uprsubmission.pdf <last visited 10 June 2008>.

[24] See Joseph, Schultz and Castan, above n.1, at pp. 3–52; McGoldrick, above n.1, at pp. 3–43; Harris, 'The International Covenant on Civil and Political Rights in the United Kingdom Law' in Harris and Joseph (eds), above n.1, pp. 1–67.

[25] ICCPR Article 2(1).

[26] ICESCR Article 2(1). See below chapter 6.

[27] General Comment 31 [No. 80] Nature of the General Legal Obligation Imposed on States Parties to the Covenant: 26/05/2004. CCPR/C/21/Rev.1/Add.13 (General Comments) para 10 discussed below.

the substantive rights guaranteed by the Covenant at domestic level.[28] It is also important to note that the obligations are incurred on a 'territorial' as well as a 'jurisdictional' basis by the States parties: Article 2(1) provides for 'within its territory and subject to its jurisdiction'.[29]

While there is an obligation undertaken by States to 'respect and to ensure' the rights recognised in the Covenant, there is no obligation to incorporate the treaty into domestic law.[30] HRC has tried to investigate the exact status which the Covenant has in relation to the constitutional regimes of States parties. In elaborating upon the provisions of this article, HRC has noted that in order to ensure the rights, States are under obligations of both a positive and negative nature. In its General Comment, No: 31 [80] Nature of General Legal Obligations Imposed on States Parties to the Covenant adopted in 2004, the Committee considered that

> The legal obligation under article 2, paragraph 1, is both negative and positive in nature. States Parties must refrain from violation of the rights recognized by the Covenant, and any restrictions on any of those rights must be permissible under the relevant provisions of the Covenant. Where such restrictions are made, States must demonstrate their necessity and only take such measures as are proportionate to the pursuance of legitimate aims in order to ensure continuous and effective protection of Covenant rights. In no case may the restrictions be applied or invoked in a manner that would impair the essence of a Covenant right.[31]

HRC, in its General Comment also reiterates the binding nature of the Covenant on all organs of the State, with an overall obligation on the State party as whole. It notes:

> The obligations of the Covenant in general and article 2 in particular are binding on every State Party as a whole. All branches of government (executive, legislative and judicial), and other public or governmental authorities, at whatever level – national, regional or local – are in a position to engage the responsibility of the State Party. The executive branch that usually represents the State Party internationally, including before the Committee, may not point to the fact that an action incompatible with the provisions of the Covenant was carried out by another branch of government as a means of seeking to relieve the State Party from responsibility for the action and consequent incompatibility. This understanding flows directly from the principle contained in article 27 of the Vienna Convention on the Law of Treaties, according to which a State Party 'may not invoke the provisions of its internal law as justification for its failure to perform a treaty'. Although article 2, paragraph 2, allows States Parties to give effect to Covenant rights in accordance with domestic

---

[28] See Joseph, Schultz and Castan, above n.1, at p. 9; also see Harris, 'The ICCPR and the UK: An Introduction' in Harris and Joseph (eds), above n.1, at p. 3.

[29] Ibid.

[30] Several States parties, including the United Kingdom have not incorporated the ICCPR in their domestic laws. For United Kingdom's position see Higgins, 'The Role of Domestic Courts in the enforcement of International Human Rights: The United Kingdom' in Conforti and Francioni (eds), *Enforcing International Human Rights in Domestic Courts* (Brill, 1997) pp. 37–58. HRC's preference is however that 'Covenant guarantees may receive enhanced protection in those States where Covenant is automatically or through specific incorporation part of domestic legal order'. See General Comment 31, above n.27, para 13.

[31] Ibid. para 6.

constitutional processes, the same principle operates so as to prevent States parties from invoking provisions of the constitutional law or other aspects of domestic law to justify a failure to perform or give effect to obligations under the treaty. In this respect, the Committee reminds States Parties with a federal structure of the terms of article 50, according to which the Covenant's provisions 'shall extend to all parts of federal states without any limitations or exceptions'.[32]

Article 2(1) provides that the States parties undertake to guarantee that the rights enunciated in the present Covenant will be exercised without distinction of any kind as to race, colour, sex, language, religion, political or other opinion, national or social origin, property, birth or other status.[33] According to the provisions of Article 2(3), States parties undertake to 'ensure' that individuals whose rights are violated, 'shall have an effective remedy, notwithstanding that the violation has been committed by persons acting in an official capacity[34] . . . to ensure that any person claiming such a remedy shall have his right thereto determined by competent judicial, administrative or legislative authorities, or by any other competent authority provided for by the legal system of the State, and to develop the possibilities of judicial remedy'[35] and to make sure that competent authorities enforce these remedies.[36] Equality upon the basis of gender is also an issue addressed in Article 3, according to which States parties undertake to ensure the equal rights of men and women to the enjoyment of all civil and political rights set forth in the present Covenant.[37]

(i) Derogations in times of public emergency[38]

Article 4 provisions permit States parties to make derogations from the ICCPR 'in time of public emergency which threatens the life of the nation'. Article 4(1) provides as follows:

---

[32] Ibid. para 4.
[33] For further elaboration of the Committee on the Article see Equality of Rights between men and women (Article 3) 29/03/2000 General Comment No. 28 CCPR/C/21/Rev.1/Add.10. Equality of treatment does not however mean identical treatment in every instance, see e.g. Article 6(5) prohibition of death penalty for children (under 18) and pregnant women Article 10(3); segregation of juveniles; Article 25 (differences based on nationality) General Comment No. 18; Article 13 (Application Limited to Aliens) General Comment No. 15, the Position of Aliens under the Covenant 11/04/86 (37th session, 1986); General Comment No. 18, Non-Discrimination CCPR (37th session, 1989).
[34] Article 2(3)(a).
[35] Article 2(3)(b).
[36] Article 2(3)(c).
[37] In its revised General Comment No. 28, HRC has called upon all States parties to ensure gender-based equality in the enjoyment of all the rights provided in the Covenant, in particular by removing discriminatory legislation and tradition, rooted in traditions, culture or history. Such discriminatory practices could never be justified. HRC has invited all States to report on these matters; see above n.33.
[38] *General Comment No. 05: Derogation of rights (Art. 4). 31/07/81. CCPR General Comment No. 5; Replaced by General Comment 29: States of Emergency (Article 4)* CCPR/C/21/Rev.1/Add.11 31/08/2001; Buergenthal, 'To Respect and to Ensure: State Obligations and Permissible Derogations' in Henkin (ed.) *International Bill of Rights: The Covenant on Civil and Political Rights* (Columbia University Press, 1981) pp. 78–66; Ghandhi, 'The Human Rights Committee and Derogation in Public Emergencies' 32 *GYIL* (1989) 323; McGoldrick, 'The Interface Between Public Emergency Powers and International Law' 2 *International Journal of Constitutional Law* (2004) 380; Oraa, *Human Rights in States of Emergency in International Law* (Clarendon Press, 1992).

In time of public emergency which threatens the life of the nation and the existence of which is officially proclaimed, the States Parties to the present Covenant may take measures derogating from their obligations under the present Covenant to the extent strictly required by the exigencies of the situation, provided that such measures are not inconsistent with their other obligations under international law and do not involve discrimination solely on the ground of race, colour, sex, language, religion or social origin.

Article 4 authorises a State party to derogate from many of the international obligations as provided in the Covenant. There are, however, limitations placed upon the actions of the State in question. First, the capacity to make derogations is limited to times of 'public emergency which threaten the life of the nation'.[39] Second, such a state of public emergency must have been 'officially proclaimed' both at the national level as well as information being transmitted internationally through the office of the UN Secretary-General.[40] Third, even in circumstances where States are allowed to derogate from their obligations these measures must only be to the extent 'strictly required by exigencies of the situation'.[41] The restoration of normalcy with the full respect of rights contained in the Covenant is, according to the Committee, the predominant objective for States making derogations and any derogatory measures are of an exceptional and temporary nature.[42] Fourth, since derogation provisions are likely to affect rights other than those covered under a derogation provision, HRC has frequently required an explanation of the exercise of substantive rights, including those rights from which derogations have been made.[43] Fifth, any measures of derogation are only permissible if they are not inconsistent with the State's obligations under international law and do not involve discrimination solely on the ground of race, colour, sex, language, religion or social origin.[44] Sixth, and most importantly, no derogations are permissible from Article 6, 7, 8 (paras 1 and 2) 11, 15, 16 and 18.[45] Seventh, the scope of derogation has also been narrowly construed by HRC which retains the ultimate discretion in deciding whether a particular derogation satisfies the enumerated

---

[39] The argument of allowing the State discretion in determining the legitimacy of a declaration of emergency or derogation of fundamental rights has been rejected. The Siracusa Principle 63 provides that 'the provisions of the Covenant allowing for certain derogations in a public emergency are to be interpreted restrictively'. The intention of the Principle is to discard the concept of 'margin or appreciation' in its deployment of emergency or derogation from fundamental rights. See 'The Siracusa Principles on the Limitation and Derogation Provisions in the International Covenant on Civil and Political Rights' 7 *HRQ* (1985) 3 at p. 10; also see Provost, *International Human Rights and Humanitarian Law* (Cambridge University Press, 2002) at pp. 288–289.

[40] See Article 4(3) ICCPR. UN Doc. A/56/40, vol. I, Annex III (as amended at the seventieth session, October–November 2000) (CCPR/C/GUI/Rev.2); see also 'Report of the Human Rights Committee on the Work of its 48th Session' UN Doc. A/51/40 (1996) para 349 (in relation to Peru); Reviewing the Periodic Report of Nigeria, UN Doc. CCPR/C/SR/1505 (1996) paras 66 (Lallah) and 71 (Aguilar Urbina); Committee's comments on the Report of the Russian Federation, UN Doc. CCPR/C/79/Add.54 (1995) para 27. Discussed by Provost, above n.39, at p. 285.

[41] *Jorge Landinelli Silva* et al. v. *Uruguay*, Communication No. 34/1978, UN Doc. CCPR/C/OP/1 at 65 (1984) (inability to provide evidence that steps were strictly necessary renders the derogation provisions inapplicable); Harris, 'The ICCPR and the UK: An Introduction' in Harris and Joseph (eds) above n.1, 1–67, at p. 8.

[42] See General Comment No. 29, above n.38, para 1.

[43] UN Doc. CCPR/C/SR.224, para 47 (Suriname); UN Doc. CCPR/C/SR.442, para 15.

[44] When making a derogation under Article 4(1), States are under an obligation to provide sufficient detailed account of the relevant facts justifying the presence of a situation necessitating derogation *Consuelo Salgar de Montejo* v. *Colombia*, Communication No. 64/1979, UN Doc. CCPR/C/OP/1 at 127 (1985).

[45] Article 4(2) General Comment 29, above n.38, at para 7.

requirements.[46] Eighth, it is the case that in accordance with human rights law, it is not permissible to derogate from norms of a *jus cogens* or customary international legal standing.[47] The derogation provisions have become of increasing significance during the course of the so-called 'war on terror' led by the United States and the United Kingdom.[48]

4 ANALYSIS OF SUBSTANTIVE RIGHTS

(i) The right to life, prohibition of torture and the issues concerning capital punishment[49]

The right to life, contained in Article 6, represents the most fundamental of all human rights.[50] It has been protected by all international and regional human rights instruments.[51] According to Article 6(1): 'Every human being has the inherent right to life. This right shall be protected by law. No one shall be arbitrarily deprived of his life.' The Committee has pronounced it as the supreme right and the provisions of the treaty establish firmly that no

---

[46] General Comment No. 29, above n.38, at para 2. The Committee has taken the view that '[m]easures derogating from the provisions of the Covenant must be of an exceptional and temporary nature. Before a State moves to invoke article 4, two fundamental conditions must be met: the situation must amount to a public emergency which threatens the life of the nation, and the State party must have officially proclaimed a state of emergency. The latter requirement is essential for the maintenance of the principles of legality and rule of law at times when they are most needed. When proclaiming a state of emergency with consequences that could entail derogation from any provision of the Covenant, States must act within their constitutional and other provisions of law that govern such proclamation and the exercise of emergency powers; it is the task of the Committee to monitor the laws in question with respect to whether they enable and secure compliance with article 4. In order that the Committee can perform its task, States parties to the Covenant should include in their reports submitted under article 40 sufficient and precise information about their law and practice in the field of emergency powers.' See also Higgins, 'Derogations under Human Rights Treaties' 48 *BYIL* (1976–77) 281 at p. 281; Kiss, 'Permissible Limitations on Rights' in Henkin (ed.), above n.38 at pp. 290–310.

[47] McGoldrick, above n.1, at p. 389.

[48] *A v. Secretary of State for the Home Department*, [2004] UKHL 56 paras 11, 44; In this high profile case decided by the House of Lords on 16 December 2004, in an unprecedented sitting of nine Judges, the Appellate Committee of the House of Lords, held that the derogation made by the United Kingdom to Article 9 of the ICCPR and Article 5 of the ECHR (right to liberty and detention without trial) were incompatible with the Article 15 Derogation provision contained in the European Convention as it was a disproportionate response. For commentaries on the case see Dickson, 'Law Versus Terrorism, Can Law Win?' 1 *EHRLR* (2005) 11 at p. 19; Walker, 'Prisoners of "War all the Time"' 1 *EHRLR* (2005) 50; Shah, 'The UK's Anti-Terror Legislation and the House of Lords: The First Skirmish' 5 *HRLR* (2005) 403; Arden, 'Human Rights in the Age of Terrorism' 121 *LQR* (2005) 604; Elliott, 'United Kingdom: Detention without Trial and the "War on Terror"' 4 *International Journal of Constitutional Law* (2006) 553.

[49] See Gormley, 'The Right to Life and the Rule of Non-Derogability: Peremptory Norms and *Jus Cogens*' in Ramcharan (ed.), *The Right to Life in International Law* (Brill, 1985) pp. 120–159; Joseph, 'The Right to Life' in Harris and Joseph (eds), above n.1, pp. 155–184; Rodley, *The Treatment of Prisoners under International Law* (Clarendon Press, 1999); Joseph, Schultz and Castan, above n.1, at pp. 154–293; Martin, Schnably, Wilson, Simon and Tushnet *International Human Rights and Humanitarian Law: Treaties, Cases, and Analysis* (Cambridge University Press, 2006) at p. 35; *Stewart v. United Kingdom* (1985) 7 E.H.R.R. 453; Van Boven describes this as 'the most fundamental of all human rights' Van Boven, 'The Need to Stop Deliberate Violations of the Right to Life', in Premont (ed.), *Essais sur le concept de 'droit de vivre' en memoire de Yougindra Khushalani* (Bruylant, 1988) 285–292, at p. 285.

[50] Dinstein, 'The Right to Life, Physical Integrity and Liberty' in Henkin (ed.), above n.38, pp. 114–137; Sieghart, *The Lawful Rights of Mankind: An Introduction to the International Legal Code of Human Rights* (Oxford University Press, 1985) p. 107; also see Ghandhi, 'The Human Rights Committee and Article 6 of the International Covenant on Civil and Political Rights' 29 *Indian Journal of International Law* (1989) 326.

[51] See Article 3 UDHR; Article 2 ECHR; Article I ADHR; Article 4 ACHR; Article 4 AFCHPR.

derogations are permissible from this right, even in times of public emergency.[52] The term 'inherent' as used in Article 6(1) connotes a positive and broad obligation including, for example prevention of wars and reduction in infant mortality.[53] War, armed conflict and internal disturbances result in an uncountable number of deaths.[54] In its commentary, HRC has expressed concern over the proliferation of weapons of mass destruction. Special concern is reserved for nuclear weapons, which the Committee regards as amongst the greatest threats to the right to life. It, therefore, asserts that the production, testing, possession as well as the use of nuclear weapons should be prohibited with activities being recognised as a crime against humanity.[55]

Article 6 does not provide an absolute prohibition of taking life but only 'arbitrary' deprivation of life which raises questions about the nature and scope of the right to life. According to Professor Shestack:

> Surely the right to life guaranteed by Article 6(1) of [ICCPR] would seem to be so basic as to be considered absolute. Yet Article 6(1) only offers protection against 'arbitrary' deprivation of life. What is the effect of this qualification on the nature of the rights involved?[56]

Some elaboration has been provided by HRC on the meaning of 'arbitrary'. In *Guerrero* v. *Columbia*[57] (also referred to as the *Camargo* case), the Colombian police had raided a house in which they believed a kidnapped person was being detained. The kidnapped person was not found in the house. However, the police waited for the suspected kidnappers, and seven persons who were not proved to be connected with the kidnap were shot without warning at their arrival in the house. The forensic evidence repudiated initial police claims that the deceased persons had died whilst resisting arrest. To the contrary, forensic evidence was produced confirming that the individuals concerned had been shot from point-blank range and without any warning. They had also been shot down at varying intervals. Guerrero, the victim herself, had been shot several times after she had died of a heart attack.[58] The police action was justified by the State because of a Legislative Decree No. 0070. This decree provided police with a defence to any criminal charge 'in the course of operations planned with the object of preventing and curbing kidnapping'[59] for so long as the national

---

[52] See Article 4(2) ICCPR; General Comment No. 6 The right to life (Article 6) 30/04/82; also see General Comment No. 14, *Nuclear Weapons and the Right to Life* (Article 6) (23rd Session) 1984, 09/11/84, para 1.

[53] Ibid. para 2.

[54] Ibid. para 4.

[55] Ibid. para 4, cf. Legality of the Threat or Use of Nuclear Weapons, Advisory Opinion, I.C.J. Reports 1996, p. 226, The ICJ found 'that it does not have sufficient elements to enable it to conclude with certainty that the use of the nuclear weapons would necessarily be at variance with the principles and rules of law applicable in armed conflict in any circumstance' (para 95) particularly 'by a State in an extreme circumstance of self-defence, in which its very survival would be at stake' (para 97). However, it also recognised that attention should be paid to international humanitarian law, 'at the heart of which is the overriding consideration of humanity' and that 'methods and means of warfare, which would preclude any distinction between civilian and military targets, or which would result in unnecessary suffering to combatants, are prohibited' (para 95).

[56] Shestack, 'The Jurisprudence of Human Rights' in Meron (ed.), *Human Rights in International Law: Legal and Policy Issues* (Clarendon Press, 1984) pp. 69–113 at p. 71.

[57] *Husband of Maria Fanny Suarez de Guerrero* v. *Colombia*, Communication No. R.11/45 (5 February 1979), UN Doc. Supp. No. 40 (A/37/40) at 137 (1982).

[58] The Committee's decision on the issue of causing Guerrero's death remains unclear. See McGoldrick, above n.1, at p. 341.

[59] The Decree Doc. A/37/40, 137, paras 1.4, 7.1, 7.2.

territory remained 'in a state of siege'.[60] HRC found that the Colombian police could not justify its action on the basis of the national legislation. The Committee found 'no evidence that the action of the police was necessary in their own defence or that of others, or that it was necessary to effect the arrest or prevent the escape of the prisoners concerned'.[61] According to the Committee, the police action had resulted in arbitrary deprivation of life violating Article 6 of the ICCPR. In the *Guerrero* case, HRC, while expanding on the concept of 'arbitrary', noted that the mere fact that the taking of life is lawful under national law does not by itself prevent it from being 'arbitrary'.[62] The prohibition of 'arbitrary' taking of life connotes that an individual must not be deprived of his life in unreasonable or disproportionate circumstances.[63] In its views, HRC implies that there are limited exceptions to taking of life (that is self-defence, arrest and the prevention of escape) applicable in national and international law.[64] According to HRC, targeted killings or the practice of assassinating suspected terrorists cannot be justified.[65]

In *Baboeram-Adhin and Others* v. *Suriname*,[66] the State attempted to justify the execution of 15 individuals on the basis that the men were killed while trying to escape after an unsuccessful coup attempt. HRC, in the absence of adequate evidence provided by the State found a violation of Article 6. The Committee took the view that

> it is evident from the fact that fifteen prominent persons lost their lives as a result of the deliberate action of the military police that the deprivation of life was intentional. The State party has failed to submit any evidence proving that these persons were shot while trying to escape.[67]

HRC has also found violations of Article 6 where capital punishment has been awarded in absentia,[68] or has been awarded in a discriminatory or arbitrary manner in conjunction with a breach of the right to fair trial[69] or there has been a failure by the State to inform the

---

[60] Ibid. para 1.5.

[61] *Husband of Maria Fanny Suarez de Guerrero* v. *Colombia*, Communication No. R.11/45 (5 February 1979), UN Doc. Supp. No. 40 (A/37/40) at 137 (1982), at para 13.2. Discussed by Rodley, above, n.49 at p. 184.

[62] *Husband of Maria Fanny Suarez de Guerrero* v. *Colombia*, Communication No. R.11/45 (5 February 1979), UN Doc. Supp. No. 40 (A/37/40) at 137 (1982). At para 13.3.

[63] Joseph, Shuiltz and Castan, above n.1, at p. 156.

[64] The same exceptions to right to life are provided in other instruments see e.g. ECHR Article 2(2); see Rodley, above n.49, at pp. 181–184; also see Harris, above n.1, at p. 654. For exposition of the meaning of 'Arbitrary' as used in Article 4(1) see the Inter-American Commission on Human Rights report in Case 10.559 (Peru) 136 at pp. 147–148. The case is discussed by Davidson, 'The Civil and Political Rights Protected in the Inter-American Human Rights System' in Harris and Livingstone (eds), *The Inter-American System of Human Rights* (Clarendon Press, 1998) pp. 213–288, at p. 218.

[65] Concluding observations on Israel (2003) UN Doc. CCPR/C8/78/ISR. Furthermore, 'arbitrary' taking of life also incorporates the duty not to allow unlawful or negligent deprivation of life; *Rickly Burrell* v. *Jamaica*, Communication No. 546/1993, UN Doc. CCPR/C/53/D/546/1993 (1996) or attempted assassinations; *Rodger Chongwe* v. *Zambia*, Communication No. 821/1998, UN Doc. CCPR/C/70/D/821/1998 (2000).

[66] *K. Baboeram-Adhin, and J. Kamperveen* et al. v. *Suriname*, Communication Nos. 146/1983 and 148–54/1983, UN Doc. CCPR/C/21/D/146/1983 (1984), UN Doc. CCPR/C/OP/2 AT 5 (1990), para 6.3.

[67] Ibid., para 14.3.

[68] *Daniel Monguya Mbenge* v. *Zaire*, Communication No. 16/1977 (8 September 1977), UN Doc. Supp. No. 40 (A/38/40) at 134 (1983).

[69] *Lloydell Richards* v. *Jamaica*, Communication No. 535/1993, UN Doc. CCPR/C/59/D/535/1993 (31 March 1997), paras 7.2, 7.5; *Earl Pratt and Ivan Morgan* v. *Jamaica*, Communication No. 210/1986 and 225/1987 (6 April 1989), UN Doc. Supp. No. 40 (A/44/40) at 222 (1989); *Little* v. *Jamaica*, Communication No. 283/1988

victim of an appeal hearing until after it had been conducted[70] or the manner of execution is inhuman or degrading.[71] Where a violation of the right to life takes place, States parties are under an obligation to establish procedures for a thorough investigation by an impartial body.[72]

Article 6 does not abolish capital punishment but provides that:

> [i]n Countries which have not abolished the death penalty, sentence of death may be imposed only for the most serious crimes in accordance with the law in force at the time of the commission of the crime . . . This penalty can only be carried out pursuant to a final judgement rendered by a competent court.

In respect of abolitionist States, deporting persons to retentionist States where they are under sentence of death, in *Judge* v. *Canada*,[73] HRC amended its previous views in *Kindler* v. *Canada*.[74] While in *Kindler* it was decided that:

> While States must be mindful of the possibilities for the protection of life when exercising their discretion in the application of extradition treaties, the Committee does not find that the terms of article 6 of the Covenant necessarily require Canada to refuse to extradite or to seek assurances. The Committee notes that the extradition of Mr. Kindler would have violated Canada's obligations under article 6 of the Covenant, if the decision to extradite without assurances would have been taken arbitrarily or summarily.[75]

In *Judge* it was emphasised that the ICCPR is a 'living instrument' and in interpreting it the HRC should bear in mind

---

(19 November 1991), UN Doc. CCPR/C/43/D/283/1988 (1991), paras 8.4 and 8.6; *Pinto* v. *Trinidad and Tobago*, Communication No. 232/1987 (20 July 1990), Report of the HRC, Vol. II, (A/45/40), 1990, at 69, paras 12.5–12.6 and *Robinson* v. *Jamaica*, Communication No. 223/1987, UN Doc. Supp. No. 40 (A/44/40) at 241 (1989). In *Jiménez Vaca* v. *Colombia*, Communication No. 859/1999 UN Doc. CCPR/C/74/D/859/1999 (2002) HRC stressed the right to impose an obligation on the State to investigate State killings, see also *Herrera Rubio* v. *Colombia*, Communication No. 161/1983, UN Doc. Supp. No. 40 (A/41/40) at 190 (1988). Duty to punish offenders involved in State killings; *Bautista Bautista de Arellana* v. *Colombia*, Communication No. 563/1993, UN Doc. CCPR/C/55/D/563/1993 (1993) an unsuccessful assassination attempt can also breach article 6(1) provisions; *Rodger Chongwe* v. *Zambia*, Communication No. 821/1998, UN Doc. CCPR/C/70/D/821/1998 (2000).

[70] *Lumley* v. *Jamaica*, Communication No. 662/1995, UN Doc. CCPR/C/65/D/662/1995 (30 April 1999), para 7.4.

[71] McGoldrick, above n.1, at p. 346; with in the ECHR see *Soering* v. *United Kingdom*, (1989) 11 E.H.R.R. 439.

[72] *Basilio Laureano Atachahua* v. *Peru*, Communication No. 540/1993, UN Doc. CCPR/C/56/D/540/1993 (1996); *Mojica* v. *Dominican Republic*, Communication No. 449/1991, UN Doc. CCPR/C/51/D/449/1991 (1994); *Alfredo Rafael and Samuel Humberto Sanjuán Arévalo* v. *Colombia*, Communication No. 181/1984 (3 November 1989), UN Doc. Supp. No. 40 (A/45/40) at 31 (1990); *Herrera Rubio* v. *Colombia*, Communication No. 161/1983, UN Doc. Supp. No. 40 (A/43/40) at 190 (1988).

[73] *Roger Judge* v. *Canada*, Communication No. 829/1998, UN Doc. CCPR/C/78/D/829/1998 (2003).

[74] *Kindler* v. *Canada*, Communication No. 470/1991, UN Doc. CCPR/C/48/D/470/1991 (1993).

[75] *Kindler* v. *Canada* para 14.6. For HRC's views on extradition amounting to Article 7 violation see paras 15.1–16. Specifically, '[in] determining whether, in a particular case, the imposition of capital punishment could constitute a violation of article 7, the Committee will have regard to the relevant personal factors regarding the author, the specific conditions of detention on death row, and whether the proposed method of execution is particularly abhorrent', para 15.3.

that there may be exceptional situations in which a review of the scope of application of the rights protected in the Covenant is required, such as where an alleged violation involves that most fundamental of rights – the right to life – and in particular if there have been notable factual and legal developments and changes in international opinion in respect of the issue raised.[76]

In cases of extradition to face the death penalty this means:

For countries that *have* abolished the death penalty, there is an obligation not to expose a person to the real risk of its application. Thus, they may not remove, either by deportation or extradition, individuals from their jurisdiction if it may be reasonably anticipated that they will be sentenced to death, without ensuring that the death sentence would not be carried out.[77]

Issues surrounding capital punishment have been complex and will be addressed shortly. Insofar as other aspects of the right to life are concerned, no specific guidelines are provided as to the point in time at which life terminates or commences. Abortion *per se* is not contrary to the provisions of the ICCPR and attempts to incorporate a prohibition on abortion proved unsuccessful.[78] Similarly, from the jurisprudence of HRC it would appear that voluntary euthanasia is also not unlawful.[79]

Article 7 is a very significant article, the provisions of which are non-derogable,[80] and have been addressed by the Committee in State reports, in its General Comment and in the Optional Protocol.[81] The fundamental objective of Article 7 is the protection of the dignity as well as the mental and physical integrity of an individual. Article 7 involves a duty upon the States parties to accord protection through legislative and administrative mechanisms to prevent acts contrary to Article 7, regardless of whether these actions are conducted by people in an official or private capacity.[82] There is also an obligation to investigate all violations of Article 7.[83] Article 7 does not provide for the principle of *non-refoulement*,

---

[76] *Judge* v. *Canada*, para 10.3.

[77] *Judge* v. *Canada*, para 10.4.

[78] Rehof, 'Article 3' in Alfredsson and Eide (eds), above n.7, 89–101, at p. 96. In its jurisprudence the HRC has been criticised the criminalisation of abortion laws (Concluding Observations: Mauritius, 27 April 2005, CCPR/CO/83.MUS at para 9) and has expressed concern at the restrictive nature of abortion laws even where the woman's life is in danger (Concluding Observations: Chile, 18 May 2007, CCPR/C/CHL/CO/5 at para 8) or where the pregnancy has resulted from rape (Concluding Observations of the HRC regarding Gambia, 12 August 2004, CCPR/CO/75/GMB at para 17) with the confirmation that such restrictions contravene women's right to life under Article 6 of the ICCPR. (Concluding Observations: Peru, 15 November 2000, CCPR/CO/70/PER at para 20). For a review and criticism of restrictive abortion laws in Peru see the Committee's findings in *Karen Noelia Llantoy Huamán* v. *Peru*, Communication No. 1153/2003, UN Doc. CCPR/C/85/D/1153/2003 (2005), denial of therapeutic abortion is a violation of Article 7 para 6.3. See further Zampas and Gher 'Abortion as a Human Right – International and Regional Standards' 8 *HRLR* (2008) 249.

[79] Nowak, above n.1, at p. 155 *cf. Pretty* v. *the United Kingdom*, (2002) 35 E.H.R.R. 1 – the right to life does not incorporate a right to die.

[80] Article 4 ICCPR. Rodley, above n.49, at p. 83.

[81] *General Comment No. 20: Replaces General Comment 7 Concerning Prohibition of Torture and Cruel Treatment or Punishment (Art. 7):. 10/03/92 CCPR General Comment No. 20. (General Comments)*. Also see Ghandhi, 'The Human Rights Committee and Articles 7 and 10(1) of the International Covenant on Civil and Political Rights, 1966' 13 *Dalhousie Law Journal* (1990) 758.

[82] Concluding Observations on Yemen (2002) UN Doc. CCPR/CO/75/YEM.

[83] Bair, above n.1, at p. 24.

nor does it explicitly prohibit *refoulement* in cases where the individual is likely to face torture, inhuman or degrading treatment or punishment. The HRC has, however, interpreted the provisions of Article 7 so as to preclude removal of individuals to States where they would face a 'real risk' of the violations of the rights contained therein.[84] According to the HRC, 'real risk' is determined by considering 'the intent of the country to which the person concerned is to be deported, as well as from the pattern of conduct shown by the country in similar cases'.[85]

A useful example of the Committee's jurisprudence on Article 7, under the Optional Protocol, is provided through the *Conteris* v. *Uruguay case.*[86] Mr. Conteris was a Methodist pastor, a journalist and a university professor who had been arrested and detained by the Uruguayan police because of his previous connections with the Tupamaros movement. He was held incommunicado for three months and subjected to various forms of physical torture including hanging by wrists and burning. After having been forced to sign a confession he was sentenced by a military court to 15 years' imprisonment. After a change in government he was subsequently released. HRC found violations of several articles of ICCPR. These were Article 7, Articles 9(1), 9(2), 9(3), 9(4), 10(1), 14(1) and 14(3).

Whilst reporting on this Article, HRC requires States parties not only to describe the steps undertaken for the general protection of Article 7 but, in addition,

provide detailed information on safeguards for the special protection of particularly vulnerable persons. It should be noted that keeping under systematic review interrogation rules, instructions, methods and practices as well as arrangements for the custody and treatment of persons subjected to any form of arrest, detention or imprisonment is an effective means of preventing cases of torture and ill-treatment. To guarantee the effective protection of detained persons, provisions should be made for detainees to be held in places officially recognized as places of detention and for their names and places of detention, as well as for the names of persons responsible for their detention, to be kept in registers readily available and accessible to those concerned, including relatives and friends. To the same effect, the time and place of all interrogations should be recorded, together with the names of all those present and this information should also be available for purposes of judicial or administrative proceedings. Provisions should also be made against incommunicado detention. In that connection, States parties should ensure that any places of detention be free from any equipment liable to be used for inflicting torture or ill-treatment. The protection of the detainee also requires that prompt and regular access be given to doctors and lawyers and, under appropriate supervision when the investigation so requires, to family members.[87]

---

[84] *GT* v. *Australia*, Communication No. 706/1996 (4 November 1997); UN Doc. CCPR/C/61/0/706/1996; para 8.4; see below chapter 19.

[85] *GT* v. *Australia*, Communication No. 706/1996 (4 November 1997); UN Doc. CCPR/C/61/0/706/1996; para 8.1; also note General Comment No. 20, above n.81, where the Committee notes 'States parties must not expose individuals to the danger of torture or cruel, inhuman or degrading treatment or punishment upon return to another country by way of their extradition, expulsion or refoulement' at para 9. See Goodwin-Gill and McAdam, *The Refugee in International Law* (Oxford University Press, 2007), at p. 302.

[86] *Hiber Conteris* v. *Uruguay*, Communication No. 139/1983 (17 July 1985), UN Doc. Supp. No. 40 (A/40/40) at 196 (1985), arbitrary prison practices aimed at humiliating prisoners constituted a violation of Article 7, such as subjection to cold, repeated solitary confinement and relocation to a different cell, para 9.2.

[87] General Comment No. 20, above n.81, para 11.

In its consideration of periodic reports, HRC has requested States parties to provide detailed information on the measures taken to implement this Article. States have been asked to ensure compliance with international standards such as the UN Minimum Standard Rules for the Treatment of Prisoners,[88] the UN Code of Conduct for Law Enforcement Officials[89] or Standard Minimum Rules for the Administration of Juvenile Justice.[90] The Committee has questioned various forms of punishments and practices such as interrogation techniques,[91] the use of illegally obtained information,[92] flogging,[93] collective punishment for those found guilty,[94] and loss of nationality.[95] HRC has held acts of enforced disappearances,[96] (and the stress related to such disappearances to immediate family),[97] physical acts of arm twisting and putting a pistol in the mouth,[98] electric shocks,[99] blows,[100] kicking and strangulation,[101] and breaking of the jaw[102] as amounting to torture, cruel, inhuman or degrading treatment or punishment.

At the same time it needs to be conceded that the Committee has tended to avoid (or be consistent in dealing with) the problematic issue of distinguishing between the various facets of Article 7, i.e. 'torture', 'cruel', 'inhuman' or 'degrading treatment or punishment'. Instead it has relied generally on the broad prohibitions contained in the Article.[103]

---

[88] Adopted by the First United Nations Congress on the Prevention of Crime and the Treatment of Offenders, held at Geneva in 1955, and approved by the Economic and Social Council by its resolution 663 C (XXIV) of 31 July 1957 and 2076 (LXII) of 13 May 1977 www.unhchr.ch/html/menu3/b/h_comp34.htm <last visited 14 December 2008>.

[89] Code of Conduct for Law Enforcement Officials Adopted by General Assembly resolution 34/169 of 17 December 1979 www.unhchr.ch/html/menu3/b/h_comp42.htm <last visited 14 December 2008>.

[90] United Nations Standard Minimum Rules for the Administration of Juvenile Justice 'The Beijing Rules' Adopted by General Assembly Resolution 40/33 of 29 November 1985 www.unhchr.ch/html/menu3/b/h_comp48.htm <last visited 13 December 2008>.

[91] SR 65 para 3 (Tomuschat on Czechoslovakia) SR 69 para 18 (Graefrath) SR 148 paras 3–6 (Lallah on UK).

[92] SR 69 para 32 (Tarnopolsky on UK) SR 98 para 64 (Tomuschat on Yugoslavia) SR 143 para 28 (Tomuschat on Austria).

[93] See Human Rights Committee, Sixty fourth session, *Concluding observations of the Human Rights Committee: Libyan Arab Jamahiriya.* 06/11/98. CCPR/C/79/Add.101. (Concluding Observations/Comments), para 11. HRC has criticised floggings and amputations as inhuman and degrading within Sudan. HRC was also critical of the practice of Blood money. See Concluding Observations of HRC for Sudan (Ninetieth Session, 9–27 July 2007) 29 August 2007 CCPR/C/SDN/C03.

[94] Ibid. para 12.

[95] SR 129 para 5 (Bouziri on Chile).

[96] *S. Jegatheeswara Sarma* v. *Sri Lanka*, Communication No. 950/2000, UN Doc. CCPR/C/78/D/950/2000 (2003); *Bautista de Arellana* v. *Colombia*, Communication No. 563/1993, UN Doc. CCPR/C/55/D/563/1993 (1995); *El-Megreisi* v. *Libyan Arab Jamahiriya*, Communication No. 440/1990, UN Doc. CCPR/C/50/D/440/1990 (1994).

[97] *María del Carmen Almeida de Quinteros* et al. v. *Uruguay*, Communication No. 107/1981, UN Doc. CCPR/C/OP/2 at 138 (1990); *S. Jegatheeswara Sarma* v. *Sri Lanka*, Communication No. 950/2000, UN Doc. CCPR/C/78/D/950/2000 (2003).

[98] *Teofila Casafranca de Gomez* v. *Peru*, Communication No. 981/2001, UN Doc. CCPR/C/78/D/981/2001 (2003).

[99] *Isidore Kanana Tshiongo a Minanga* v. *Zaire*, Communication No. 366/1989, UN Doc. CCPR/C/49/D/366/1989 (1993).

[100] *Rawle Kennedy* v. *Trinidad and Tobago*, Communication No. 845/1999, UN Doc. CCPR/C/67/D/845/1999 (31 December 1999); *Wilfred Pennant* v. *Jamaica*, Communication No. 647/1995, UN Doc. CCPR/C/64/D/647/1995 (3 December 1998).

[101] *Abduali Ismatovich Kurbanov* v. *Tajikistan*, Communication No. 1096/2002, UN Doc. CCPR/C/79/D/1096/2002 (2003).

[102] *Sergio Euben Lopez Burgos* v. *Uruguay*, Communication No. R.12/52, UN Doc. Supp. No. 40 (A/36/40) at 176 (1981). *Delia Saldias de Lopez* v. *Uruguay*, Communication No. 52/1979 (29 July 1981), UN Doc. CCPR/C/OP/1 at 88 (1984).

[103] According to the Committee, it is unnecessary 'to draw up a list of prohibited acts or to establish sharp distinctions between the different kinds of punishment or treatment; the distinctions depend on the nature, purpose and severity of the treatment applied' General Comment No. 20, above n.81, para 4; *cf.* the position in ECHR, below chapter 7; Rodley, above n.49, at p. 96.

There also remain the difficult issues in relation to the nature of punishment and what constitutes inhuman and degrading treatment.[104] While issues of cultural relativism have been considered regarding such subjects as corporal punishment, this has not prevented HRC from classifying it as a violation of Article 7.[105] Further controversial issues are raised in debates surrounding capital punishment and extradition to States where the convicted person may be awarded a death penalty. The position in international law is not established and State practice is inconsistent. As noted earlier, in 1989 the United Nations adopted the second optional protocol to the ICCPR, Aiming at the Abolition of Death Penalty,[106] a treaty that has not yet been widely ratified. Nearly a third of the world's States retain capital punishment as a sentence for a range of offences, some of which may not (in objective terms) be regarded as the 'most serious crimes'. Arguably there are traces of evidence whereby international practice is taking an abolishonist approach. The *ad hoc* Tribunal for former Yugoslavia (ICTY) or Rwanda (ICTR) proscribe capital punishment. Similarly, the Rome Statute for International Criminal Court (ICC) does not sanction such a sentence.[107] Having said that, the death sentence as a punishment continues to be awarded in many parts of the world.[108] In view of the numbers and influence of the retentionist States, one leading authority on the subject has noted that 'it is hardly surprising that general international law does not expressly require the abolition of the death penalty'.[109]

As regards the issue of whether a significant delay in execution of a convicted person (the so-called death row phenomenon) *per se* constitutes inhuman, cruel and degrading treatment and violates Article 7, there exists substantial disagreement even amongst international tribunals.[110] The European Court of Human Rights has held that extradition of an individual in circumstances where he is likely to spend long periods awaiting execution

---

[104] In *Antti Vuolanne* v. *Finland*, Communication No. 265/1987, UN Doc. Supp. No. 40 (A/44/40) at 311 (1989). The HRC made the following observations: 'It observes that the assessment of what constitutes inhuman or degrading treatment falling within the meaning of article 7 depends on all the circumstances of the case, such as the duration and manner of the treatment, its physical or mental effects as well as the sex, age and state of health of the victim. A thorough examination of the present communication has not disclosed any facts in support of the author's allegations that he is a victim of a violation of his rights set forth in article 7. In no case was severe pain or suffering, whether physical or mental, inflicted upon Antti Vuolanne by or at the instigation of a public official; nor does it appear that the solitary confinement to which the author was subjected, having regard to its strictness, duration and the end pursued, produced any adverse physical or mental effect on him. Furthermore, it has not been established that Mr. Vuolanne suffered any humiliation or that his dignity was interfered with apart from the embarrassment inherent in the disciplinary measure to which he was subjected. In this connection, the Committee expresses the view that for punishment to be degrading, the humiliation or debasement involved must exceed a particular level and must, in any event, entail other elements beyond the mere fact of deprivation of liberty.' Ibid. para 9.2.

[105] See General Comment 7(16) para 2. In *George Osbourne* v. *Jamaica*, Communication No. 759/1997, UN Doc. CCPR/C/68/D/759/1997 (2000), HRC stated that '[irrespective] of the nature of the crime that is to be punished, however brutal it may be, it is the firm opinion of the Committee that corporal punishment constitutes cruel, inhuman and degrading treatment or punishment contrary to article 7 of the Covenant.' *cf. Tyrer* v. *UK* (1978) 2 E.H.R.R. 1.

[106] Annex to GA Res. 44/128. Reprinted in 29 I.L.M (1990) 1464.

[107] See Schabas, *An Introduction to the International Criminal Court* (Cambridge University Press, 2001) pp. 164–166.

[108] Note the trial and the circumstances of the award of capital punishment to the former Iraqi President, Saddam Hussein. Also consider the findings of the Working Group on Arbitrary Detentions, Opinion No. 31/2006 (Iraq and United States of America) 1 September 2006 UN Doc. A/HRC/4/40/Add.1 (2007) p. 103.

[109] Rodley, above n.49, at p. 96.

[110] See Ghandhi, 'The Human Rights Committee and the Death Row Phenomenon' 43 *Indian Journal of International Law* (2003) 1.

would amount to cruel, inhuman or degrading treatment.[111] A similar position was adopted by the United Kingdom's Privy Council in *Pratt and Morgan* v. *Jamaica*.[112] However, HRC has taken a different approach on the subject in *Pratt and Morgan* v. *Jamaica*[113] and *NG* v. *Canada*.[114] In the absence of additional compelling circumstances, HRC does not regard prolonged periods of detention under a severe custodial regime on death row *per se* a violation of Article 7.[115] However executions must not be held in public and as confirmed by the case of *NG*, the manner of the execution could have significant bearing as to whether it is in contravention of the provisions of Article 7. The case of *NG* is a striking one in that the Committee relied on the manner of execution (gas asphyxiation) rather than the fact of execution as a ground for finding a violation of Article 7. In 1985, Mr. NG, the author, a resident of the United States, was convicted in Canada of shooting a security guard. In 1990, the Canadian courts ordered his extradition to the United States (California) to stand trial for kidnapping and 12 other murders. The Canadian government, after a substantial review of the case took the decision not to exercise their power to obtain assurances that the death penalty would not be imposed as a condition of extradition. In 1991, the author appealed to the Committee claiming that his extradition was in violation of Articles 6 and 7 of the ICCPR. HRC took the view that Canada's decision to extradite Mr. NG in the present circumstances did not violate Article 6. The Committee endorsed the Canadian Minister of Justice's position that there was 'the absence of exceptional circumstances, the availability (in California) of due process and of appeal against conviction and the importance of not providing a safe haven for those accused of murder'.[116] However, in finding a violation of Article 7, HRC did take the position that

> the author has provided detailed information that execution by gas asphyxiation may cause prolonged suffering and agony and does not result in death as swiftly as possible, as asphyxiation by cyanide gas may take over 10 minutes. The State party had the opportunity to refute these allegations on the facts; it has failed to do so. Rather, the State party has confined itself to arguing that in the absence of a norm of international law which expressly prohibits asphyxiation by cyanide gas, 'it would be interfering to an unwarranted degree with the internal laws and practices of the United States to refuse to extradite a fugitive to face the possible imposition of the death penalty by cyanide gas asphyxiation' . . . [T]he Committee

---

[111] See *Soering* v. *United Kingdom*, (1989) 11 E.H.R.R. 439; see below chapter 7.

[112] *Pratt* v. *Attorney General of Jamaica* (PC (Jam)) Privy Council (Jamaica), 2 November 1993, [1994] AC 1 at 35.

[113] *Earl Pratt and Ivan Morgan* v. *Jamaica*, Communication No. 210/1986 and 225/1987 (6 April 1989), UN Doc. Supp. No. 40 (A/44/40) at 222 (1989).

[114] *Chitat Ng* v. *Canada*, Communication No. 469/1991 (7 January 1994), UN Doc. CCPR/C/49/D/469/1991 (1994). See McGoldrick, 'Extraterritorial Application of the International Covenant on Civil and Political Rights' in Coomans and Kamminga (eds), *Extraterritorial Application of Human Rights Treaties* (Intersentia, 2004) pp. 41–72 at p. 41.

[115] Seven years on death row as such does not constitute cruel, inhuman degrading treatment or punishment: *Franklyn Gonzales (represented by Barlow Lyde & Gilbert, a law firm in London)* v. *Trinidad and Tobago*, Communication No 673/1995, UN Doc. CCPR/C/65/D/673/1995 (30 April 1999) para 5.3. In the absence of additional procedural irregularities, a delay between issuing of a warrant for an execution and its stay during which time a person is detained in a special cell does not constitute violation of Article 7. *Cf.* the notification of the authors, 45 minutes before their execution and a delay of approximate 20 hours from the time a stay of execution is granted, to the time a person is notified and removed from his death cell, constitutes cruel and inhuman treatment under Article 7, *Pratt* v. *Jamaica* (210/1986) para 13.7.

[116] Ibid. para 15.6.

concludes that execution by gas asphyxiation, should the death penalty be imposed on the author, would not meet the test of 'least possible physical and mental suffering', and constitutes cruel and inhuman treatment, in violation of article 7 of the Covenant.[117]

(ii) Rights to liberty and security of person, prohibitions of arbitrary detentions and unfair trials[118]

Denials of liberty and security of person and arbitrary detentions have been a source of substantial concern. A United Nations document correctly expresses this concern in that '[a]ll countries are confronted by the practice of arbitrary detention. It knows no boundaries, and thousands of persons are subjected to arbitrary detention each year.'[119] We have noticed earlier that the continued practices of arbitrary and unlawful detentions led the Human Rights Commission to establish a working group on Arbitrary Detention.[120] The progress of the Working Group ultimately led to the drafting and adoption of the United Nations Convention on Enforced Disappearances in 2006.[121]

Article 9 protects the valuable right of liberty and security of person. The Article confirms that in pursuance of this right:

No one shall be subjected to arbitrary arrest or detention. No one shall be deprived of his liberty except on such grounds and in accordance with such procedure as are established by law.[122]

In its General Comment No. 8, HRC has confirmed that Article 9(1) applies to all forms of deprivation of liberty, not only in criminal cases but also in other instances *inter alia* mental illness, vagrancy, drug addiction, educational purposes, immigration control, etc.'[123] The Article goes on to provide procedural guarantees for the detained person.[124] The reasons for arrest must be given at the time of arrest and the arrested person needs to be promptly informed of the charges against him.[125] Persons arrested or detained for criminal

---

[117] Ibid. paras 16.3 and 16.4; see Schabas, 'Soering's Legacy: The Human Rights Committee and the Judicial Committee of the Privy Council take a Walk Down Death Row' 43 *ICLQ* (1994) 913

[118] See Dinstein, 'The Right to Life, Physical Integrity and Liberty' in Henkin above n.38, pp. 114–137; Harris, above n.1, pp. 637–680; Joseph, Schultz and Castan, above n.1, at pp. 303–376; Lillich, 'Civil Rights' in Meron (ed.), above n.56, pp. 115–170; McGoldrick, above n.1, at pp. 362–458; Rehof, 'Article 3' in Alfredsson and Eide (eds), above n.7, at p. 89; Steiner, Alston and Goodman (eds), above n.1, at pp. 136–237.

[119] United Nations, *The Working Group on Arbitrary Detention: Fact Sheet No: 26* www.unhchr.ch/html/menu6/2/fs26.htm <last visited 22 December 2008> p. 2.

[120] See above chapter 3.

[121] See below chapter 24.

[122] Article 9(1).

[123] General Comment No. 8: *Right to liberty and security of persons (Art. 9)*: 30/06/82. CCPR General Comment No. 8 (General Comments), para 1.

[124] Article 9(2)–(5).

[125] Article 9(2). In its General Comment, the Committee makes the point that 'if so-called preventive detention is used, for reasons of public security, it must be controlled by these same provisions, i.e. it must not be arbitrary, and must be based on grounds and procedures established by law (para 1), information of the reasons must be given (para 2) and court control of the detention must be available (para 4) as well as compensation in the case of a breach (para 5). And if, in addition, criminal charges are brought in such cases, the full protection of Article 9(2) and (3), as well as Article 14, must also be granted.' General Comment No. 8: above n.123, para 4.

International Covenant on Civil and Political Rights

5

offences are to be brought promptly before a judge and must be tried within a reasonable period or released.[126] Persons deprived of their liberty are entitled to challenge the legality of their detention and in case of unlawful detention are entitled to the right of compensation.[127]

A useful example of the State violation of rights contained in Article 9 and the Human Rights Committee's analysis is provided by the case of *Mukong* v. *Cameroon*.[128] M was a journalist and long-standing critic of the government. He had been campaigning for multiparty democracy in Cameroon for a long time. In 1988 he was arrested and detained after a BBC broadcast in which he had criticised the Cameroonian government. The reasons given for his arrest were that he had made subversive comments contrary to a State Ordinance. He was subsequently charged with offences under the Ordinance. He was released only to be rearrested in 1990 for his campaign for the installation of multi-party democracy. M appealed to the Committee claiming violations of various provisions of the Covenant. In its response the Committee found violations of Articles 7, 9 and 14 and it took the view that M's detention for the period 1988–90 and subsequently in 1990 was in violation of Article 9.

In another case, *Carballal* v. *Uruguay*,[129] Carballal was arrested on 4 January 1976 and held incommunicado for more than five months. During his detention, for long periods he was tied and blindfolded and kept in secret places. Attempts to have recourse to *habeas corpus* proved unsuccessful. He was brought before a military judge on 5 May 1976 and again on 28 June but detained for over a year. HRC found, *inter alia*, violations of Article 9(1), 9(2), 9(3) and 9(4).

Article 10 provides for the right of detained persons to be treated with humanity. In relation to this Article, the Committee has given this Article a broad ambit, noting its application to anyone who has been deprived of his liberty including such people who are detained in prisons, hospitals, and in particular psychiatric or mental hospitals.[130] It has insisted that:

> [t]reating all persons deprived of their liberty with humanity and with respect for their dignity is a fundamental and universally applicable rule. Consequently, the application of this rule, as a minimum, cannot be dependent on the material resources available in the State party. This rule must be applied without distinction of any kind, such as race, colour, sex, language, religion, political or other opinion, national or social origin, property, birth or other status.[131]

---

[126] Article 9(3). In its General Comment, the Committee notes that 'in criminal cases any person arrested or detained has to be brought "promptly" before a judge or other officer authorized by law to exercise judicial power. . . . in the view of the Committee, delays must not exceed a few days'. Ibid. para 2.

[127] Article 9(4) and 9(5).

[128] *Womah Mukong* v. *Cameroon*, Communication No. 458/1991 (10 August 1994), UN Doc. CCPR/C/51/D/458/1991 (1994). See Starmer and Christou (eds) *Human Rights Manual and Sourcebook for Africa* (British Institute of International & Comparative Law, 2005) at p. 94.

[129] *Leopoldo Buffo Carballal* v. *Uruguay*, Communication No. 33/1978 (8 April 1981), UN Doc. CCPR/C/OP/1 at 63 (1984).

[130] General Comment No. 21: Replaces General Comment No. 9 concerning humane treatment of persons deprived of liberty (Art. 10): 10/04/92. CCPR General Comment No. 21. (General Comments) para 4.

[131] Ibid. para 4.

Article 14 represents the core of the criminal justice system within international law.[132] Compliance with the provisions of Article 14 is an essential prerequisite to ensuring fairness in criminal proceedings. The Committee has elaborated on the right to fair trial through its General Comment, State reports and decisions from individual communications.[133] The Article ordains that all persons be equal before courts and tribunals.[134] The Article encapsulates the common law principle of rule of law and equality of all before the law.[135] The concept of equality of arms is applicable not only in the courts and judicial tribunals but there also needs to be 'equality of the citizen *vis-à-vis* the executive'.[136]

The earlier edition of this book had been critical of HRC for not elaborating sufficiently the meaning of 'criminal charge' or 'rights and obligation in a suit at law'. This weakness appears to have been overcome in the revised General Comment of HRC, General Comment No. 32.[137] In this Comment, HRC notes in paragraphs 15 and 16 respectively:

> Criminal charges relate in principle to acts declared to be punishable under domestic criminal law. The notion may also extend to acts that are criminal in nature with sanctions that, regardless of their qualification in domestic law, must be regarded as penal because of their purpose, character or severity.[138]

> The concept of determination of rights and obligations 'in a suit at law' (*de caractère civil/de carácter civil*) is more complex. It is formulated differently in the various languages of the Covenant that, according to article 53 of the Covenant, are equally authentic, and the *travaux préparatoires* do not resolve the discrepancies in the various language texts. The Committee notes that the concept of a 'suit at law' or its equivalents in other language texts is based on the nature of the right in question rather than on the status of one of the parties or the particular forum provided by domestic legal systems for the determination of particular rights.[139] The concept encompasses (a) judicial procedures aimed at determining rights and obligations pertaining to the areas of contract, property and torts in the area of private law,

5

International Covenant on Civil and Political Rights

---

[132] See Weissbrodt, *The Right to a Fair Trial under the Universal Declaration of Human Rights and the International Covenant on Civil and Political Rights* (Brill, 2001).

[133] General Comment No. 32 Right to Equality before Courts and Tribunals and to a Fair Trial (Ninetieth Session, 9–27 July) CCPR/C/GC/32, 23 August 2007.

[134] Article 14(1).

[135] Equality before the law also enshrines the right to have access to courts. A law which is applicable only to husbands to represent matrimonial property violates Article 14 since it denies the women equality before the courts, *Avellanal v. Peru*, Communication No. 202/1986, UN Doc. Supp. No. 40 (A/44/40) at 196 (1988) para 10.2; the absence of provisions for legal aid constitutes violation of Article 14, *Rawle Kennedy v. Trinidad and Tobago*, Communication No. 845/1998, UN Doc. CCPR/C/74/D/845/1998 (2002) para 7.10.

[136] SR 187 para 26 (Tomuschat on Poland), *Mariam Sankara et al. v. Burkina Faso*, Communication No. 1159/2003, UN Doc. CCPR/C/86/D/1159/2003 (2006) para 12.4, a registrar's failure to inform the author of the requirement of security and the court's knowledge of this failure amounted to a violation of equality of arms. See also *Weiss v. Austria*, Communication No. 1086/2002, UN Doc. CCPR/C/77/D/1086/2002 (2002), para 9.6. and *Frank Robinson v. Jamaica*, Communication No. 223/1987, UN Doc. Supp. No. 40 (A/44/40) at 241 (1989), para 10.4.

[137] See General Comment No. 32, above n.133. For further consideration see *Y. L. v. Canada*, Communication No. 112/1981 (8 April 1986), UN Doc. Supp. No. 40 (A/41/40) at 145 (1986); also see *Larry James Pinkney v. Canada*, Communication No. 27/1978 (2 April 1980), UN Doc. CCPR/C/OP/1 at 12 (1984). On the European Court of Human Rights see below chapter 7.

[138] General Comment No. 32, above n.133, Article 14 para 15, see also *Paul Perterer v. Austria*, Communication No. 1015/2001, UN Doc. CCPR/C/81/D/1015/2001 (2004), para 9.2.

[139] Ibid. para 16, see also *Y.L. v. Canada*, Communication No. 112/1981, paras 9.1 and 9.2.

as well as (b) equivalent notions in the area of administrative law such as the termination of employment of civil servants for other than disciplinary reasons,[140] the determination of social security benefits[141] or the pension rights of soldiers,[142] or procedures regarding the use of public land[143] or the taking of private property. In addition, it may (c) cover other procedures which, however, must be assessed on a case by case basis in the light of the nature of the right in question.

HRC has formulated substantial jurisprudence on fair and public hearings by a competent, independent and impartial tribunal. The Committee has viewed with concern the setting-up of special or military courts,[144] *Sharia* courts,[145] State security courts,[146] temporary appointments of judges,[147] and the use of faceless judges[148] upon the independence of the judiciary and the liberty of advocates freely to exercise their profession.[149]

The Committee has also put emphasis on the independence of the judiciary and the separation of State organs, in particular the executive from the judiciary.[150] Whilst jury trials (in criminal trials) or specific procedural requirements are not mandated by the provisions of the Article, the right to fair trail encapsulates the presumption of innocence in criminal trials and in order to secure a conviction the prosecution has an obligation to establish its case beyond reasonable doubt.[151] In order to ensure a fair trial, Article 14(3) provides for a set of minimum guarantees. These consist of being informed promptly and in detail in a language which the accused understands;[152] of having adequate time and facilities for the

---

[140] *Casanovas* v. *France*, Communication No. 441/1990, UN Doc. CCPR/C/51/D/441/1990 (1994) para 5.2.

[141] *García Pons* v. *Spain*, Communication No. 454/1991, UN Doc. CCPR/C/55/D/454/1991 (1995), para 9.3.

[142] *Y. L.* v. *Canada*, Communication No. 112/1981, UN Doc. CCPR/C/OP/2 at 28 (1990), para 9.3.

[143] *Anni Äärelä and Jouni Näkkäläjärvi* v. *Finland*, Communication No. 779/1997 (4 February 1997), CCPR/C/73/D/779/1997, paras 7.2–7.4.

[144] See Concluding observations by the Human Rights Committee: Peru. 15/11/2000. CCPR/CO/70/PER. (Concluding Observations/Comments) Seventieth session, para 12.

[145] See SR 200 para 8 (Graefrath on Iraq).

[146] SR 282 para 22 (Opsahl on Mali).

[147] See the Concluding Observations/Comments of the Human Rights Committee: Syrian Arab Republic CCPR/CO/71/SYR, para 15.

[148] *Polay Campos* v. *Peru*, Communication No. 577/1994, UN Doc. CCPR/C/61/D/577/1994 (1997), para 9. *José Luis Gutiérrez Vivanco* v. *Peru*, Communication No. 678/1996, UN Doc. CCPR/C/74/D/678/1996 (2002). para 7.1.

[149] See Human Rights Committee, Sixty-fourth session, *Concluding observations of the Human Rights Committee: Libyan Arab Jamahiriya.* 06/11/98. CCPR/C/79/Add.101. (Concluding Observations/Comments), para 14.; Concluding Observations of the Human Rights Committee: Democratic People's Republic of Korea. 27/07/2001. CCPR/CO/72/PRK. (Concluding Observations/Comments) Seventy-second session, para 8.

[150] Political repercussions or consequences cannot be allowed to affect the impartiality of the trial: *González del Río* v. *Peru*, Communication No. 263/1987, UN Doc. CCPR/C/46/D/263/1987 (1992), para 5.1. Powers given to the President of appointment and removal of judges subject only to ratification of National Assembly without safeguards or inquiry by an independent judicial tribunal are not compatible with Article 14; Concluding Observations on Zambia UN Doc. CCPR/C/79/Add.95.

[151] See General Comment No. 13: *Equality before the courts and the right to a fair and public hearing by an independent court established by law* (Art. 14): 13/04/84, para 7.

[152] Article 14(3)(a). Provided that the information discloses the relevant law and the facts on which the charge is based, the requirements can be met by stating either or orally – if later confirmed in writing or in writing; General Comment No. 32 above n.133, para 31. The obligation to provide information to the accused under Article 14(3) needs to be more precise that under Article 9(2).

preparation of a defence;[153] of being tried without undue delay;[154] of being tried in person and being able to adequately defend his case,[155] to have free assistance of an interpreter if he cannot understand or speak the language of the court, [156] and of not being forced into making a guilty plea,[157] and having the right to have his conviction and sentence being reviewed by a higher tribunal according to the law.[158] The Committee acting under the First Optional Protocol has on a number of occasions elaborated on the meaning and content of this right. In *Pratt and Morgan* v. *Jamaica*, the Committee found a breach of Article 14 when it took 20 hours (thereby meaning waiting for the accused until 45 minutes before scheduled execution) before a communication of reprieve.[159] In another case involving appeal against conviction of death penalty in Jamaica, the Committee found a violation of Article 14(3)(d). In this case, the victim claimed that his lawyer had, without consulting him, withdrawn his appeal against conviction. The victim contended that had he foreseen the likely action of his lawyer, he would have sought another counsel. In finding violations of the Article, the Committee took the view that

> while article 14, paragraph 3(d) does not entitle the accused to choose counsel provided to him free of charge, measures must be taken to ensure that counsel, once assigned, provides effective representation in the interests of justice. This includes consulting with, and informing, the accused if he intends to withdraw an appeal or to argue before the appeals court that the appeal has no merit.[160]

---

[153] Article 14(3)(b). Adequate time depends on the nature of each case although if the counsel for the accused feels inadequately prepared it is incumbent on the counsel to seek an adjournment: *Nicholas Henry* v. *Jamaica*, Communication No. 610/1995, UN Doc. CCPR/C/64/D/610/1995 (21 October 1998) para 7.5 'Facilities' includes having access to all relevant documentation and other evidence required for the preparation of the case.

[154] Article 14(3)(c). The guarantees provided in Article 14(3)(c) are related not only to the commencement of the trial, but also include the time by which the trial should end and a judgment is provided. General Comment No. 13: above n.151. There is an overlap between Article 14(3)(c) and Article 9(3) which provides guarantees of a trial within reasonable time, or release of anyone arrested or detained on a criminal charge. Article 9(3) is related to the length of time between arrest and trial, whereas Article 14(3) relates to the determination of a criminal charge without regard to arrest or detention. Exceptional circumstances (e.g. fraud cases) can justify delay in bringing charges.

[155] Article 14(3)(d)(e). The right to oral hearing, and the right to appear in person or be represented by a counsel must be provided: *Orejuela* v. *Colombia*, Communication No. 848/1999, UN Doc. A/57/40 at 172 (2002), para 7.3.

[156] Article 14(3)(f). In territories where a language other than the official language is spoken, it is incumbent upon the State party to ensure that the official charge forms and charge sheets as well as court documents have to be made available in a language which is spoken and comprehended by the majority of the population. Concluding Comments on United Kingdom of Great Britain and Northern Ireland (Hong Kong) (1995) CCPR/C/79/Add.57 para 12.

[157] Article 14(3)(g). It is incumbent upon State parties to ensure that legislation exists to place the burden of proof on the prosecution, that any statements or confessions by the accused person have been made through his own free will and that any statements obtained in violation of Article 7 are excluded from the evidence. Concluding Comment on Romania (1999) UN Doc. CCPR/C/79/Add.111 para 13. Legislative or administrative provisions that adverse inferences may be drawn from silence of the accused person for crimes are contrary to Article 14. Concluding Comments on United Kingdom of Great Britain and Northern Ireland (1995) UN Doc. CCPR/C/79Add.55, para 17. Similar provisions of juries drawing negative inferences are also contrary to Article 14. Concluding Comments on United Kingdom of Great Britain and Northern Ireland (1995) UN Doc. CCPR/CO/73/UK, para 17.

[158] Article 14(5).

[159] *Earl Pratt and Ivan Morgan* v. *Jamaica*, Communication No. 210/1986 and 225/1987 (6 April 1989), UN Doc. Supp. No. 40 (A/44/40) at 222 (1989), para 137; Rodley, above n.49, at p. 235.

[160] *Paul Kelly* v. *Jamaica*, Communication No. 253/1987, UN Doc. CCPR/C/41/D/253/1987 at 60 (1991), para 5.10. Annual Report 1991 (A/46/40), Annex XI.D.

(iii) Rights to privacy, freedom of expression, conscience, opinion, assembly and association[161]

Amongst the essential ingredients of modern human rights law are rights to privacy, and freedom of expression, opinion, assembly and association. These rights are protected by all international and regional human rights instruments. Within the ICCPR, these rights can be found in Article 17–20. Article 17 protects the important right to privacy, family, home and correspondence. The article has been elaborated further by the Committee's General Comment No. 16 and its case-law under the optional protocol.[162] In the *Aumeerudy-Cziffra case*,[163] a number of Mauritian women claimed violations of their rights *inter alia* under Article 17(1), 2(1), 3 and 26 of ICCPR. They claimed that the laws were being applied discriminatorily by the Mauritan immigration authorities discriminating between Mauritian men on the one hand and Mauritian women who had married foreign men on the other hand. The claim in relation to Article 17(1) arose because of the interference with their right to family life. The Committee reviewed the existing laws and found a violation of the right to family life. It also found that the existing distinction in Mauritius breached the non-discrimination provisions contained in the ICCPR. In *Toonen* v. *Australia*,[164] a claim that the Tasmanian Criminal Code making private homosexual conduct a criminal offence, was upheld to be in breach of Article 17.[165]

---

[161] Alexander, *Is There a Right to Freedom of Expression?* (Cambridge University Press, 2005); Cumper, 'Freedom of thought, Conscience and Religion' in Harris and Joseph (eds), above n.1, pp. 355–389; Ewing, 'Freedom of Association and Trade Union Rights' in Harris and Joseph (eds), above n.1, pp. 465–489; Feldman, 'Freedom of Expression' in Harris and Joseph (eds), above n.1, pp. 391–437; Humphrey, 'Political and Related Rights' in Meron (ed.), above n.56, pp. 171–203; Joseph, Schultz and Castan, above n.1, at pp. 476–584; McGoldrick, above n.1, at pp. 459–497; Michael, 'Privacy' in Harris and Joseph (eds), above n.1, pp. 333–353; Murphy, 'Freedom of Assembly' in Harris and Joseph (eds), above n.1, pp. 439–464.

[162] In its General Comment on this Article the Committee notes 'Article 17 provides for the right of every person to be protected against arbitrary or unlawful interference with his privacy, family, home or correspondence as well as against unlawful attacks on his honour and reputation. In the view of the Committee this right is required to be guaranteed against all such interferences and attacks whether they emanate from State authorities or from natural or legal persons. The obligations imposed by this article require the State to adopt legislative and other measures to give effect to the prohibition against such interferences and attacks as well as to the protection of this right'. It goes on to provide that 'relevant legislation must specify in detail the precise circumstances in which such interferences may be permitted. A decision to make use of such authorized interference must be made only by the authority designated under the law, and on a case-by-case basis. Compliance with article 17 requires that the integrity and confidentiality of correspondence should be guaranteed *de jure* and *de facto*. Correspondence should be delivered to the addressee without interception and without being opened or otherwise read. Surveillance, whether electronic or otherwise, interceptions of telephonic, telegraphic and other forms of communication, wire-tapping and recording of conversations should be prohibited. Searches of a person's home should be restricted to a search for necessary evidence and should not be allowed to amount to harassment. So far as personal and body search is concerned, effective measures should ensure that such searches are carried out in a manner consistent with the dignity of the person who is being searched. Persons being subjected to body search by State officials, or medical personnel acting at the request of the State, should only be examined by persons of the same sex.' Human Rights Committee, General Comment No. 16 The Right to Respect of Privacy, Family, Home and Correspondence, and Protection of Honour and Reputation (Art. 17): 08/04/88 (thirty-second session, 1988), paras 1 and 8.

[163] *Shirin Aumeeruddy-Cziffra and 19 other Mauritian women* v. *Mauritius*, Communication No. 35/1978 (9 April 1981), UN Doc. CCPR/C/OP/1 at 67 (1984).

[164] *Toonen* v. *Australia*, Communication No. 488/1992 (4 April 1994), UN Doc. CCPR/C/50/D/488/1992 (1994).

[165] Ibid. para 8.6. See Joseph, 'Gay Rights under the ICCPR – Commentary on *Toonen* v. *Australia*' 13 *U Tas LR* (1994) 392; Helfer, 'Will the UN Human Rights Committee Require Recognition of Same-Sex Marriages?' in Wintemute and Andenas (eds) *Legal Recognition of Same-Sex Partnerships: A Study of National, European and International Law* (Hart, 2001) pp. 733–742; for ECHR jurisprudence see *Dudgeon* v. *United Kingdom* (Application no. 7525/76) 22 October 1981; *Norris* v. *Ireland* (Application no. 10581/83) 26 October 1988 and *Modinos* v. *Cyprus* (Application No. 15070/89) 22 April 1993.

As a subsequent chapter will analyse in detail, the right to freedom of thought, conscience and religion is one of most significant, yet highly controversial human rights.[166] A measure of its importance within the Covenant can be ascertained from the fact that no derogations are permissible from Article 18, even in times of public emergency.[167] The right covers freedom of thought on all matters pertaining to thought, conscience and religion and includes theistic, non-theistic and atheistic beliefs as well as the right not to profess a religion or belief.[168] Freedom to manifest religion or belief may be exhibited either individually or in a community and in private and in public. This encompasses worship, observance, practice and teaching. The concepts of worship includes ritual and ceremonial acts giving direct expression to belief as well as various practices integral to such acts, including the building of places of worship and observance of holidays and rest. The observance and practice of religion or belief includes not only ceremonial acts but also includes customs and traditions in the nature of observance of dietary regulations, the wearing of distinctive clothing or head coverings, participation in rituals associated with certain stages of life and the use of a particular language customarily spoken by a group.[169] The practice and teaching of religion or belief includes the religious groups' basic affairs, e.g. the freedom to choose their religious schools and the freedom to prepare and distribute religious texts or publications. Military duties do not violate the right of conscientious objectors although the obligation to use lethal force might;[170] refusal to pay taxes on the grounds of conscientious objection falls outside the scope of protection of Article 18.[171]

The freedom to have or adopt a religion or belief necessarily entails, according to the HRC, acts integral to the conduct by religious groups of their basic affairs including the freedom to choose their religious leaders, priests and teachers, the freedom to establish seminaries or religious schools and the freedom to prepare and distribute religious texts or publications. However such activities cannot be in contravention of the provisions of Article 20. The freedom to have or adopt a religion or belief contains the freedom to choose a religion or belief, including *inter alia* the right to replace one's current religion or belief with another or to adopt atheistic views, as well as the right to retain one's religion or belief. No one can be compelled or coerced to change or recant their belief or religion, and State

---

[166] See chapter 12 below.

[167] General Comment No. 29, above n.38, para 7.

[168] General Comment No. 22: *The right to freedom of thought, conscience and religion (Art 18)*: 30/07/93, CCPR/C/21/Rev.1/Add.4, para 2.

[169] Article 18(1) ICCPR; also see General Comment No. 22, above n.168, para 4.

[170] *Paul Westerman (represented by E. Th. Hummels, legal counsel) v. The Netherlands*, Communication No. 682/1996, UN Doc. CCPR/C/67/D/682/1996 (13 December 1999) para 9.3. General Comment No. 22, above n.168, para 11. However, HRC has more recently moved further towards military conscription being a violation of Article 18. In *Yeo-Bum Yoon and Myung-Jin Choi v. Republic of Korea*, Communication Nos. 1321/2004 and 1322/2004, UN Doc. CCPR/C/88/D/1321-1322/2004 (2006) it was held that as 'an increasing number of those States parties to the Covenant which have retained compulsory military service have introduced alternatives to compulsory military service, and considers that the State party has failed to show what special disadvantage would be involved for it if the rights of the author's under article 18 would be fully respected . . . It likewise observes that it is in principle possible, and in practice common, to conceive alternatives to compulsory military service that do not erode the basis of the principle of universal conscription but render equivalent social good and make equivalent demands on the individual, eliminating unfair disparities between those engaged in compulsory military service and those in alternative service. The Committee, therefore, considers that the State party has not demonstrated that in the present case the restriction in question is necessary, within the meaning of article 18, paragraph 3, of the Covenant.' para 8.4.

[171] *J.v.K. and C.M.G.v.K.-S. v. The Netherlands*, Communication No. 483/1991, UN Doc. CCPR/C/45/D/483/1991 (1992), para 4.2; *J.P. v. Canada*, Communication No. 446/1991, UN Doc. CCPR/C/43/D/446/1991 (1991), para 4.2.

parties must ensure that their laws are in compliance with the obligations provided in Article 18.[172] The fact that a religion is recognised as a State religion, or that it is established as the official or traditional religion, or that its followers comprise the majority of the population, is compatible with Article 18 as long as this does not result in any impairment of the freedom under Article 18.[173]

Article 18(3) permits restrictions on freedom to manifest religion or belief only if law prescribes limitations and these restrictions are necessary to protect public safety, order, health or morals, or the fundamental rights and freedoms of others. Limitations imposed must be established by law and must not be applied in a manner that would violate the rights guaranteed in Article 18. Article 18 is not violated if an action by State authorities taken against a person is 'not aimed at his thoughts or beliefs as such, but rather at the manifestation of those beliefs within a particular context'.[174] Restrictions are permissible under Article 18(3), e.g. where the issue is one of public safety, health or morals (e.g. Sikhs having to wear hard hats).[175] Restrictions allowed are narrowly and strictly construed and cannot be used by States for purposes not stated in the provisions, e.g. national security.

Article 19, represents the right of opinion and expression. It is an important right, parallel rights can be found in Article 19 UDHR, Article 10 ECHR and Article 9 ACHR. Article 19(1) provides that 'everyone shall have the right to hold opinions without interference'.[176] Thus, the right to hold opinion is an absolute right and no interference from any source is permissible. By contrast, the provisions relating to freedom of expression are subject to restrictions. According to Article 19(2):

> Everyone shall have the right to freedom of expression; this right shall include freedom to seek, receive and impart information and ideas of all kinds, regardless of frontiers, either orally, in writing or in print, in the form of art, or through any other media of his choice.

However, restrictions are provided by Article 19(3) which states:

> The exercise of the rights provided for in paragraph 2 of this article carries with it special duties and responsibilities. It may therefore be subject to certain restrictions, but these shall only be such as are provided by law and are necessary:
>
> (a) For respect of the rights or reputations of others;
>
> (b) For the protection of national security or of public order (ordre public), or of public health or morals.

---

[172] General Comment No. 22, above n.168, paragraph 5; Concluding Comments on Morocco (1999), UN Doc. CCPR/C/79/Add.113, para 22. Constitutional provisions requiring judges to make a declaration with religious references are incompatible with Article 18 provision; Concluding Comments on Ireland (2000), UN Doc. CCPR/CO/69/IRL. Joining religious organisation cannot provide lawful grounds for disqualification from the Public Service, Concluding Comments on Germany (2004), UN Doc. CCPR/CO/80/DEU, para 19.

[173] General Comment No. 22, above n.168, para 9.

[174] *Malcolm Ross* v. *Canada*, Communication No. 736/1997, UN Doc. CCPR/C/70/D/736/1997 (2000), para 11.8.

[175] *Singh Bhinder* v. *Canada*, Communication Nos. 208/1986, UN Doc. CCPR/C/37/D/208/1986 (1989) it was argued that this provision was not necessary to protect public safety as the only risk would be confined to Singh Bhinder himself. However, the Committee found that the legislation to be 'reasonable and directed towards objective purposes that are compatible with the Covenant', Nowak, above n.1, p. 52.

[176] General Comment No. 10: *Freedom of expression* (Art. 19): 29/06/83.

In its survey of reports the Committee has examined and raised concerns over, e.g. banning or censorship,[177] governmental controls of various forms,[178] limitations on certain groups such as civil servants and armed forces,[179] and penal responsibility for publications.[180] HRC has also been unhappy over the applicable limitations embodied in criminal laws for offences including blasphemy or blasphemous libel,[181] sedition,[182] subversive propaganda,[183] etc. In *Hertzberg and others v. Finland*,[184] the authors of the communication alleged violation of their rights of freedom of expression and opinion by the State-controlled broadcasting company (FBC). Their claim was that Article 19 rights were breached in relation to the sanctions imposed on expression and information through censorship of radio and TV programmes on homosexuality. In its defence, Finland relied *inter alia* upon protection of public morals and claimed that these actions were fully supported by public opinion. Furthermore, the State also argued that the decision on sanctions represented the internal ruling of the autonomous broadcasting company. The Committee took account of the Finnish argument pertaining to the defence of public morals. It came to the conclusion that 'since a certain "margin of discretion" must be accorded to the responsible national authorities'[185] in issues concerning public morals, the application of Article 19(3) meant that no violation had taken place of the freedom of opinion and expression. The Committee's view is in line with other international bodies such as the European Court of Human Rights.[186]

Another related concern for human rights law has been the advocacy of religious and racial hatred and propaganda for war.[187] The prohibition on such forms of expression are provided for by Article 20. Elaborating on the provisions of this Article, the Committee in its General Comment has noted that:

> Not all reports submitted by States parties have provided sufficient information as to the implementation of Article 20 of the Covenant . . . State parties are obliged to adopt the necessary legislative measures prohibiting the actions referred to therein. However, the reports have shown that in some States such actions are neither prohibited by law nor are appropriate efforts intended or made to prohibit them. Furthermore, many reports failed to give sufficient information concerning the relevant national legislation and practice.[188]

---

[177] SR 26 para 10 (Vincent-Evans on Syria).

[178] SR 89 para 41 (Esperson on Iran).

[179] SR 321 para 27 (Movchan on Netherlands).

[180] SR 54 para 36 (Tarnopolsky on Denmark).

[181] SR 161 para 23 (Bouziri on Belize, then UK Dependency).

[182] See e.g. SR 402 para 6 (Tarnopolsky on Australia).

[183] See e.g. SR 222 para 32 (Tomuschat on Columbia).

[184] *Leo R-Hertzberg, Uit Mansson, Astrid Nikula and Marko and Tuovi Putkonen, represented by SETA (Organization for Sexual Equality) v. Finland*, Communication No. R.14/61 (7 August 1979), UN Doc. Supp. No. 40 (A/37/40) at 161 (1982).

[185] Ibid. para 10.3.

[186] See *Handyside v. United Kingdom* (1976) 1 E.H.R.R. 737; below chapter 7.

[187] See generally Kretzmer, 'Freedom of Speech and Racism' 8 *Cardozo Law Review* (1987) 445; Caitlin, 'A Proposal for Regulating Hate Speech in the United States: Balancing Rights Under the International Covenant on Civil and Political Rights' 69 *Notre Dame Law Review* (1993–1994) 771; McGoldrick and O'Donnell, 'Hate-Speech Laws: Consistency with National and International Human Rights Law' 18 *Legal Studies* (1998) 453; Ghanea, 'Articles 19 and 20 of the ICCPR' prepared for the UN Office of the High Commissioner for Human Rights Expert Seminar: Freedom of Expression and Advocacy of Religious Hatred that Constitutes Incitement to Discrimination, Hostility or Violence, 2–3 October 2008, Geneva www2.ohchr.org/english/issues/opinion/articles1920_iccpr/docs/experts_papers/Ghanea.doc <last visited 15 December 2008>.

[188] Human Rights Committee, *General Comment No. 11: Prohibition of Propaganda for War and Inciting National, Racial or Religious Hatred* (Art. 20) 29/07/83 (Nineteenth session, 1983), para 1.

A number of States have entered reservations to this Article pointing to the vagueness of the provisions and the lack of definition of the terms of 'propaganda' and 'war'. These States include France, Australia, Finland, Denmark, the Netherlands, Luxembourg, Iceland, New Zealand, Norway and Sweden.[189] Article 20(2) prohibits by law any advocacy of national, racial or religious hatred that constitutes incitement to discrimination, hostility or violence. While in itself a worthy aspiration, there nevertheless remains the potential of conflict with Article 19, freedom of opinion and expression, and in this regard a careful balance needs to be established.[190]

(iv) The interaction between principles of equality and non-discrimination with minority rights[191]

The strong focus of modern human rights law on principles of equality and non-discrimination necessitate constant referrals and analysis. In their application to ICCPR, equality and non-discrimination represent the most dominant subjects; a subsequent chapter, in presenting a detailed analysis, considers the value of Articles 2, 3, 25 and 26 of the Covenant.[192] For the present purposes a number of points need to be made. Firstly, the principles of equality and non-discrimination as utilised in the Covenant incorporate *de facto* equality, thereby sanctioning affirmative action policies.[193] Secondly, equality and non-discrimination represent independent rights and do not need to be linked to violations of substantive rights.[194] Thus, in the cases of *Broeks* v. *the Netherlands*[195] and *Zwaan De Vries* v. *Netherlands*[196] the Committee found that social security legislation discriminated against women and thereby contravened Article 26. This view was taken notwithstanding the absence of a substantive right to social security in the Covenant. Accordingly, Article 26 constitutes a 'free-standing' right to equality. There is, thus, as Tomuschat makes the point, no limitations *ratione materiae* for HRC so long as the complaint made alleges a form of discrimination.[197] Thirdly, the enjoyment of rights on equal footing does not necessarily

[189] McGoldrick, above n.1, at p. 494.

[190] McGoldrick, above n.1, at pp. 486–490. *Cf.* discussion in *Malcolm Ross* v. *Canada*, Communication No. 736/1997, UN Doc. CCPR/C/70/D/736/1997 (2000) para 11.5

[191] Joseph, Schultz and Castan, above n.1, at pp. 679–793; Lester and Joseph, 'Obligations of Non-Discrimination' in Harris and Joseph (eds) above n.1, pp. 563–595; Ramcharan, 'Equality and Non-Discrimination' in Henkin (ed.), above n.38, at pp. 246–269; Thornberry, *International Law and the Rights of Minorities* (Clarendon Press, 1991) pp. 141–319; Weller, *Universal Minority Rights: A Commentary on the Jurisprudence of International Courts and Treaty Bodies* (Oxford University Press, 2007). For detailed consideration of the issues in international law see below chapters 12–14.

[192] See below chapter 13.

[193] See e.g. the Human Rights Committee, General Comment No. 25, *The Right to Participate in Public Affairs, Voting Rights and the Right of Equal Access to Public Service* (Art. 25) (12/07/96), CCPR/C/21/Rev.1/Add.7. para 23. Reservations of Seats, Quota system is permissible; Concluding Comments on India (1997), UN Doc. CCPR/C/79/Add.81.

[194] Consider comparable provisions in the ECHR; note however the developments since the adoption of Protocol 12 to the ECHR. See below chapter 7.

[195] *S.W. M. Broeks* v. *The Netherlands*, Communication No. 172/1984 (9 April 1987), UN Doc. Supp. No. 40 (A/42/40) at 139 (1987).

[196] *F. H. Zwaan-de Vries* v. *The Netherlands*, Communication No. 182/1984 (9 April 1987), UN Doc. Supp. No. 40 (A/42/40) at 160 (1987).

[197] Tomuschat, above n.1, at p. 205. Such an approach has led some States notably Liechtenstein and Switzerland to reserve 'the right to guarantee the rights contained in article 26 of the Covenant concerning the equality of all persons before the law and their entitlement without any discrimination to the equal protection of the law only in connection with other rights contained in the present Covenant'. Liechtenstein's reservation concerning article 26 as cited in Nowak, above n.1 at p. 951. See also, Switzerland's reservation, p. 958.

mean identical treatment. The Covenant itself prescribes variation of treatment, e.g. the prohibition on the death penalty for persons below 18 and pregnant women (Article 6(5)); segregation of juvenile offenders from adults (Article 10(3)), and political rights guaranteed only on the basis of citizenship under Article 25. Fourthly, even in circumstances where a State is allowed derogation from certain provisions of the Convention, discrimination solely on the grounds of race, colour, sex, language, religion or social origin is impermissible.[198] Fifthly, in its jurisprudence on non-discrimination, the HRC has utilised the definition of discrimination used in the Race Convention, of course with the caveat that additional grounds of sex, language, religion, political or other opinion are relied upon. Sixthly, States parties are under an obligation to prevent discrimination in the public sector, quasi-public sector and amongst private parties.[199] The inclusion of the terminology 'such as' in Article 26 indicates a non-exhaustive list of grounds of non-discrimination: reference to sex in the article also includes sexual orientation.[200]

While the emphasis on the individual's right to equal treatment and non-discrimination is overwhelming, modern international law has remained reluctant in according collective rights to minority groups.[201] The dominant themes of non-discrimination, were for a long time regarded as a substitute for minority rights, an approach confirmed by the non-incorporation of minority rights articles in the United Nations Charter, UDHR and the ECHR. This point is reiterated by the United Nations Special Rapporteur Francesco Capotorti who, while preparing his study pursuant to Article 27 of ICCPR, commented that the prevention of discrimination and the implementation of special measures to protect minorities 'are merely two aspects of the same problem; that of fully ensuring equal rights to all persons'.[202] Article 27 itself is structurally incoherent and does not accord minorities collective rights. Having said that, the ICCPR is unique amongst international law treaties for its inclusion of an article which provides rights on the basis of an individual's minority characteristic. Article 27 provides that:

> In those States in which ethnic, religious or linguistic minorities exist, persons belonging to such minorities shall not be denied the right, in community with the other members of their group, to enjoy their own culture, to profess and practise their own religion, or to use their own language.

HRC's jurisprudence has established a number of principles in relation to Article 27 and minorities. Firstly, the rights contained in Article 27 cannot be treated as akin to the right of self-determination. Self-determination – the right belonging to all peoples – is as such not cognisable under the optional protocol procedure.[203] Article 27 as an individual right can

---

[198] General Comment No. 29, above n.38, para 8.

[199] Concluding Comments on Mauritius (1997), UN Doc. CCPR/C/79/Add.60; Concluding Comments on Chile (1999) CCPR/C//79/Add.104; *Nahlik v. Austria* (608/95).

[200] *Toonen v. Australia*, Communication No. 488/1992, UN Doc. CCPR/C/50/D/488/1992 (1994).

[201] See below chapter 12.

[202] Capotorti, *Special Rapporteur, Study on the Rights of Persons Belonging to Ethnic, Religious and Linguistic Minorities*, UN Doc. E/CN.4/Sub.2/384/Rev.1, UN Sales No E.78.XIV.I (1978) Reprinted in 1991 by the United Nations Centre for Human Rights, UN Sales No E.91.XIV.2, 26 para 585.

[203] *Lubicon Lake Band v. Canada*, Communication No. 167/1984 (26 March 1990), UN Doc. Supp. No. 40 (A/45/40) at 1 (1990) paras 13.3 and 32.1; *Ivan Kitok v. Sweden* (197/1985) para 6.3; Thornberry above n.191, at p. 211.

be invoked by individuals.[204] Secondly, the existence of ethnic, religious or linguistic minorities in a State is not dependent on any criterion drawn by the State party, with HRC deploying an objective criterion.[205] Thus, '[a] group may constitute a majority in a province but still be a minority in a state and thus be entitled to the benefits of article 27'.[206] However, the reverse is not true, a minority in a province, that constitutes a majority in a State is not entitled to protection regarding minority rights. Thirdly, the rights provided in this Article are guaranteed to persons belonging to minorities who *exist* in a State party; it is not relevant to the Committee, given the nature and scope of the right provided under Article 27, to determine the degree of permanence that the term '*exist*' connotes. Thus, persons belonging to minorities would include those with a less than permanent standing, e.g. migrant workers, visitors and those seeking asylum.[207] It is, therefore, incumbent upon States parties to ensure mechanisms to protect the rights of all persons belonging to minorities.[208] Fourthly, the case-law and the jurisprudence on Article 27 confirm that minorities include indigenous peoples. A number of communications have involved a discussion of the provisions of Article 27,[209] though the case that has attracted significant attention is that of *Lovelace* v. *Canada*.[210] Mrs. Lovelace had lost her status as a Maliseet Indian after her marriage to a non-Indian according to the Indian Act of Canada.[211] She claimed that an Indian man who married a non-Indian woman would not have lost his status and that the law was discriminatory. The essence of the original communication filed by her had been that this loss of status and deprivation of the right to return to her original reserve lands had been in breach of Articles 2(1), 3, 23(1), 23(4), 26 and 27 of the Covenant.

In relation to admissibility she had argued that she was not obliged to exhaust the domestic remedies that are provided in Article 5(2)(a) of the Optional Protocol since the Canadian Supreme Court had already declared that regardless of any inconsistencies with the Canadian Bill of Rights and Legislation Prohibiting Discrimination, the relevant provisions[212] remained operative.[213] The Communication was declared admissible in August 1979 and the Committee provided its interim decision in July 1980. In giving its decision the Committee took the view that the denial of opportunity to Sandra Lovelace to return to her reserve was essentially a breach of Article 27. After having found a violation of Article 27, the Committee considered it unnecessary to examine general provisions of discrimination

---

[204] See General Comment No. 23: *The Rights of Minorities* (Art. 27): 08/04/94, *CCPR/C/21/Rev.1/Add.5, General Comment No. 23.* at para 3.1.

[205] *Cf.* the approach taken in *Greco-Bulgarian Communities Case* [1930] PCIJ, Ser B, No. 17 p. 22: 'the existence of communities is a question of fact; it is not a question of law'.

[206] *Ballantyne, Davidson, McIntyre* v. *Canada*, Communications Nos. 359/1989 and 385/1989, UN Doc. CCPR/C/47/D/359/1989 and 385/1989/Rev.1 (1993), para 11.2.

[207] General Comment No. 23, above n.204, para 5.2; On migrant workers see chapter 19 below; on refugees see chapter 18 below.

[208] Concluding Comments on Ukraine (2001). UN Doc. CCPR/CO/73/UKR.

[209] See e.g. *Ivan Kitok* v. *Sweden*, Communication No. 197/1985 (27 July 1988), UN Doc. Supp. No. 40 (A/43/40) at 221 (1988); *Lubicon Lake Band* v. *Canada*, Communication No. 167/1984 (26 March 1990), UN Doc. Supp. No. 40 (A/45/40) at 1 (1990).

[210] *Sandra Lovelace* v. *Canada*, Communication No. 24/1977 (30 July 1981), UN Doc. CCPR/C/OP/1 at 83 (1984). For commentaries see Bayefsky, 'The Human Rights Committee and the Case of Sandra Lovelace' 20 *CYBIL* (1982) 244; McGoldrick, 'Canadian Indians, Cultural Rights and the Human Rights Committee' 40 *ICLQ* (1991) 658.

[211] S.12(1)(b); Can. Rev. Stat., C.1–6.

[212] Ibid.

[213] *A-G of Canada* v. *Jeanette Lavelle, Richard Isaac* et al. v. *Yvonne Bedard* (1974), SCR 1349.

contained in Articles 2, 3 and 26.[214] However in an individual opinion Mr. Bouziri was of the view that there had also been violations of Articles 2(1), 3, 23(1) and (4) and 26 since the provisions of the Indian Act were discriminatory, especially on the basis of gender.[215]

Kitok v. Sweden[216] is another example of issues arising out of minority and indigenous rights. In this case, the petitioner alleged that he had inherited rights to breed reindeers, land and water in Sorkaitum Sami village, but through the operation of a Swedish law, he was denied the power to exercise those rights resulting from the loss of his membership from the Sami village. The communication alleged violations of Articles 1 and 27 of the ICCPR. The Committee declared his claim inadmissible under Article 1 viewing that the

> author, as an individual, could not claim to be the victim of a violation of the right to self-determination ... Whereas the Optional Protocol provides recourse to individuals claiming that their rights have been violated, Article 1 deals with rights conferred upon people, as such.[217]

As far as the provisions of Article 27 were concerned, the Committee decided to consider the communication on its merits. However, it observed that the overall provisions of Swedish law were consistent with the spirit of Article 27 and that there was no violation of Article 27.

5 THE HUMAN RIGHTS COMMITTEE (HRC)[218]

The Human Rights Committee (HRC) is a body of experts in charge of the implementation of the ICCPR. It works on a part-time basis. The functions of HRC are detailed in ICCPR, the First Optional Protocol and rules of procedure.[219] Part IV of the ICCPR provides for the setting up of the Committee and elaborates on its role and activities. HRC consists of 18 members elected from amongst nationals of States Parties to the ICCPR.[220] These

---

[214] Paras 13.2–13.19.

[215] Ibid. p. 175.

[216] *Ivan Kitok v. Sweden*, Communication No. 197/1985 (27 July 1988), UN Doc. Supp. No. 40 (A/43/40) at 221 (1900), Prior decisions CCPR/C/WG/27/D/197 1985; CCPR/C/29D/197 1985 (admissibility 25 March 1987).

[217] Ibid. para 6.3.

[218] See De Zayas, Möller and Opsahl, 'Application of the International Covenant on Civil and Political Rights under the Optional Protocol by the Human Rights Committee' 28 *GYBIL* (1985) 9; Gandhi, above n.1; Gandhi, 'The Human Rights Committee and the Right of Individual Communication' 57 *BYIL* (1986) 201; Gandhi, 'The Human Rights Committee: Developments in its Jurisprudence, Practice and Procedures' 40 *Indian Journal of International Law* (2000) 405; Gandhi, 'The Human Rights Committee and Reservations to the Optional Protocol' 8 *Canterbury Law Review* (2001) 13; Heffernan, 'A Comparative View of Individual Petition Procedures under the European Convention on Human Rights and the International Covenant on Civil and Political Rights' 19 *HRQ* (1997) 78; McGoldrick, above n.1; Opsahl, 'The Human Rights Committee' in Alston (ed.), *The United Nations and Human Rights: A Critical Appraisal* (Clarendon Press, 1992) pp. 369–443; Ramcharan, 'Implementing the International Covenants on Human Rights' in Ramcharan (ed.), *Human Rights: Thirty Years after the Universal Declaration Commemorative Volume on the Occasion of the Thirtieth Anniversary of the Universal Declaration of Human Rights* (Brill, 1979) pp. 159–195; Rehman, 'The Role of the International Community in Dealing with Individual Petitions under the Optional Protocol' 9 *Journal of Law and Society* (1992) 13; Steiner, Alston and Goodman, above n.1, pp. 844–924.

[219] For the Revised and amended Rules of Procedure see International Covenant on Civil and Political Rights, UN Doc. HRI/GEN/3/Rev.2/Add.1, (9 May 2006).

[220] Article 28(1) Rule 11 of Rules of Procedure provided that the 'members of the Committee shall be the 18 persons appointed in accordance with articles 28 to 34 of the Covenant'.

members are anticipated to be of a high moral character with established competence in the field of human rights.[221] The members of HRC are elected to serve in their personal capacity for four-year terms.[222] They are eligible for re-election if re-nominated. The elections to HRC take place by secret ballot by State parties to the Covenant at meetings that are convened by the United Nations Secretary-General. In the elections

consideration shall be given to equitable geographic distribution of membership and to the representation of the different forms of civilization and of the principal legal systems.[223]

Each State party is entitled to nominate a maximum of two persons who should also be its nationals.[224] HRC may not include more than one national from the same State.[225] The persons elected are those nominees who obtain the largest majority of votes and an absolute majority of votes of the representatives of States parties present and voting.[226] HRC meets three times a year, in spring[227] summer and autumn[228] for three weeks sessions.[229] As noted earlier, HRC members serve in their personal capacity and not as representatives of their States. This independent stance is reinforced by the requirement that each member must, on appointment, make a solemn declaration that they will perform their functions impartially and conscientiously.[230] While it is important for members of the HRC to be independent, the Covenant itself does not provide a condition to have complete independence from the government. HRC members have included individuals in various governmental positions including ministers and members of Parliament, though the changing composition of the Committee is revealing a greater move towards a lack of any connections with the governments. As part-time workers, HRC members receive emoluments.[231] The meetings of the Committee and any subsidiary body are in public unless the HRC decides otherwise.[232] The adoption of Concluding Comments under Article 40 however take place in closed meetings.[233] Twelve members of HRC constitute a quorum for the conduct of business.[234]

There are four main mechanisms of implementation performed by the HRC. Firstly, there is the compulsory reporting procedure whereby all States Parties are obliged to present reports showing compliance with the ICCPR. Secondly, the Committee produces General Comments interpreting and explaining ICCPR provisions. Thirdly, there exists an inter-State complaints procedure and finally there is an individual complaints procedure. We shall be dealing with each of these mechanisms in greater detail in the remainder of this chapter.

---

[221] Article 28(2).
[222] Article 32(1). Half of the Human Rights Committee are elected every two years, Article 32(1). The Committee is required to elect from its members a chairperson, three vice-chairpersons and a Rapporteur (Rule 17, Rules of Procedure of the Human Rights Committee).
[223] Article 31(2).
[224] Article 29(2).
[225] Article 31(1).
[226] Article 30(4).
[227] In New York.
[228] In Geneva.
[229] See Rule 2(1), Rules of Procedure.
[230] Note the existence of certain other safeguards from participation in discussion concerning his/her State. Article 38.
[231] Article 35.
[232] Rule 33, Rules of Procedure.
[233] Ibid.
[234] Rule 37, Rules of Procedure.

6 THE REPORTING PROCEDURE

There are three types of reports: initial, supplementary and periodic reports. Initial reports are required after one year of the entry into force of the Covenant for the State Party concerned. From 1981–99, HRC required periodic reports to be submitted every five years. During its 66th session held in 1999, HRC decided that 'the submission of a State party's subsequent periodic report is set on a case-by-case basis at the end of the Committee's concluding observations on any report under article 40'.[235] In further developing the procedure, as from November 2000, HRC has requested that each State party, while considering its report, produce a more focused report within a short time and if that is submitted satisfactorily, a date is then provided for the next report. In case of non-submission of the follow-up report, the time-frame set for the next report is the one which was considered during the consideration of the previous report.[236]

As we shall consider shortly, the Committee has provided guidelines for initial and periodic reports.[237] Notwithstanding these guidelines, the reports are often incomplete. Additional guidelines have been provided for periodic reports. Article 40(3) deals with the provision of information by specialised agencies, which is further supplemented by Rule 67 of the Rule of Procedure.[238] NGOs are invited to provide both written and oral submissions to the Committee.[239] Furthermore, the Committee itself has reserved the right to extend NGO participation in the State reporting process.[240] However, the HRC has decided not to allow specialised agencies and NGOs to comment on the State's reports.[241] It has nevertheless been possible to acquire information from various non-governmental sources. NGOs are allowed to submit information to individual members of the HRC in their individual capacity – this information, often provided in the form of 'counter-reports' or other forms of written evidence, has proved increasingly beneficial to the Committee in its assessment of a State's compliance or non-compliance with the provisions of the Covenant.

The reporting procedure, it needs to be emphasised, is the principal mechanism of implementation and is the only compulsory procedure to which all States parties must comply. The obligation entails that each State report upon the 'measures [it] has adopted'

---

[235] UN Doc. A/55/40 (Vol. I) para 55. See further Joseph, Shultz and Castan, above n.1, at p. 18; Report of the Human Rights Committee, UN Doc. A/55/40 Vol I (hereafter 2000 Annual Report of the HRC), Annex III, 113, para B.1. See Rule 66(2), Rules of Procedure. 'The general rule . . . is that State parties should present their periodic report to the Committee every four years. However, the Bureau can add or subtract one year to this four-year period depending on the level of compliance with the Covenant's provisions by the State party.' www2.ohchr.org/english/bodies/hrc/workingmethods.htm <last visited 24 January 2009>.

[236] See Rule 72 of the Rules of Procedure, 'Where the Committee has specified, under rule 71, paragraph 5, of these rules, that priority should be given to certain aspects of its concluding observations on a State party's report, it shall establish a procedure for considering replies by the State party on those aspects and deciding what consequent action, including the date set for the next periodic report, may be appropriate'; O'Flaherty, *Human Rights and the UN: Practice before the Treaty Bodies* (Brill, 2002) at p. 30.

[237] See Guidelines Regarding the Form and Content of Reports from States Parties under Article 40 of the Covenant. UN Doc. CCPR/C/66/GUI/Rev.2, UN Doc. CCPR/C/5/Rev.2; UN Doc. A/32/44.

[238] Rule 67 provides '(1) The Secretary-General may, after consultation with the Committee, transmit to the specialized agencies concerned copies of such parts of the reports of States members of those agencies as may fall within their field of competence. (2) The Committee may invite the specialized agencies to which the Secretary-General has transmitted parts of the reports to submit comments on those parts within such time limits as it may specify.'

[239] See www2.ohchr.org/english/bodies/hrc/workingmethods.htm <last visited 24 January 2009>.

[240] UN Doc. A/57/40 (Vol. I) *Annual Report of the Human Rights Committee*, Annex III, Section B para 12.

[241] Harris, above n.1, at p. 648.

to give effect to the provisions of the ICCPR and also indicate under Article 40(2) to 'the factors and difficulties, if any, affecting the implementation of the Covenant'.[242] Initial reports are made within one year of entry of the Covenant into force for that State. These reports are to be considered by the Committee. The role of the Committee is to 'study' the reports and to transmit its reports, and such general comments as it may consider appropriate, to the States parties.[243] The Committee may also submit to ECOSOC those comments, in addition to the State reports received from States parties.

A few months ahead of submission of their report, the States are provided with a list of issues to prepare themselves for meeting with Committee members. Periodic reports require a response to be made to the issues raised in the previous concluding comments. Prior to the consideration of the State report, HRC establishes a country report task force (CRTFs).[244] A CRTF is made up of four to six members of HRC, and also includes at least one person from the region of the State concerned. In the consideration of the State report, CRTF also typically reviews the 'country profile' which is devised by the Secretariat and based on previous concluding observations and previous reports submitted to HRC. One member of CRTF is designated as the Country Rapporteur who is authorised to take the lead role in preparing a list of questions arising from the analysis of the report, which is then put to the State representative. The questions typically involve omissions from the report, follow-up from the previous report and any other issues arising from the report. The list of questions may be made public once the session has started. The consideration of a report takes place over two or three public meetings. A representative of the reporting State is invited to introduce the report and answer questions as contained in the list prepared by the Country Rapporteur. The HRC also receives information from other informal sources. It may seek additional information from the State party concerned through supplementary reports.[245] At the completion of the session, the Committee proceeds to draft and adopt its Concluding Observations. The observations represent the HRC's view on a State party's report. The standard pattern of observations comprises: A. Introduction B. Positive Aspects of the Report and C. Principal subjects of concern and Recommendations. Periodic reports follow a similar pattern in the consideration of which the HRC continually emphasises the elaboration on the follow-up procedures in the light of the comments made by the HRC.[246] According to Article 45 the HRC is to 'submit to the General Assembly of the United Nations through ECOSOC annual reports of its activities'. Within the United Nations, the third committee considers the Annual Reports of the Committee. A procedure was devised in 1985 to deal with supplementary reports.[247]

(i) Reporting guidelines[248]

While the reporting procedure appears an attractive mechanism of monitoring progress, in practice there are substantial difficulties and hurdles. The States reports are frequently

---

[242] See Rule 66(1), Rules of Procedure.
[243] Cited in McGoldrick, above n.1, at p. 9.
[244] Tomuschat, above n.1, at pp. 182–183.
[245] While seeking addition information from the State party, the Committee has used a method of asking questions on a topic-by-topic basis.
[246] Ghandhi, above n.1, at p. 24.
[247] UN Doc. A/41/40, para 45.
[248] Human Rights Committee, General Comment 30, *Reporting obligations of States parties under article 40 of the Covenant*, UN Doc. CCPR/C/21/Rev.2/Add.12 (2002).

delayed and are often incomplete, failing to provide the required information.[249] In the light of these hurdles, the HRC has also made a significant concession to those States which submit supplementary reports. Thus, if a State party submits additional or supplementary information within a year of its initial or periodic report, the HRC makes the provision for deferring the periodicity of report.[250]

In order to facilitate States regarding the content of the reports, in February 2001 the HRC set out general guidelines.[251] According to these guidelines, the provisions of Articles in Parts I, II and III of the ICCPR alongside the General Comments on any Articles should be taken into account when preparing the report. The reports should describe measures adopted giving effect to the rights in the Convention. Reports should also refer to the difficulties and other factors affecting the implementation of the rights.[252] The guidelines require States to outline the legislative, administrative or other mechanisms within the initial report, in regard to the rights contained in the ICCPR and to demonstrate progress that has been made in ensuring the rights contained within the Convention.[253] Such an obligation may entail affirmative action policies and may relate to situations within the private sphere. Guidelines have also been provided for periodic reports under Article 40(1)(b). According to HRC, subsequent periodic reports need to take account of the concluding observations on previous reports and summary records of the Committee's considerations.[254]

The effect of these efforts has, however, been limited and various examples could be found of incomplete or inadequate compliance with the reporting procedures. Since there are no sanctions attached to non-compliance, the powers of the HRC remain limited, though it has more recently instituted procedures whereby it could consider State reports in the absence of a representative or even in the absence of a report submission.[255]

In order to provide strength to its concluding observations, in 2002, HRC decided to appoint a 'Special Rapporteur for follow-up on Concluding Observations'.[256] The Special Rapporteur was assigned the task of examining all follow-up information from the relevant State party as a consequence of the Concluding Observations. Furthermore, the Rapporteur also seeks 'such other relevant information as may be provided to him'[257] and makes recommendations to the Committee. Upon receipt of the information, HRC examines the same and adopts any appropriate recommendations. At that stage it could

---

[249] Tomuschat makes reference to the one-page report submitted by Syria and half-page report by Cyprus as examples of the inadequacies in submission. Tomuschat, above n.1, at p. 178. In order to deal with the subject of inordinate delays, the Committee has amended its Rules of Procedure allowing review of the case of a State party even in the absence of a report, or in the absence of a delegation sent to introduce or defend such a report that has been submitted. See Rule 68 (Rules of Procedure).

[250] UN Doc. A/37/40, Ax IV; adopted by Human Rights Committee at its 380th meeting 28 July 1982.

[251] See General Guidelines Regarding the form and Content of Reports from State Parties under Article 40 of the Covenant GAOR 56th Session No. 40 (UN Doc. A/56/40). Report of the Human Rights Committee vol. 1, 162–167.

[252] Ibid. C.4.

[253] Ibid. D.1.

[254] Ibid. E.1.

[255] For an excellent analysis of the procedure see Ghandhi, 'The Human Rights Committee of the International Covenant on Civil and Political Rights: Practice and Procedure in the New Millennium' 48 *Indian Journal of International Law* (2008) 208, at p. 213.

[256] See Report of the Human Rights Committee, 30 October 2002, A/57/40 (vol. I) at para 54 and Annex III A, paras 3–5. Mr. Maxwell Yalden was appointed by the Committee as the Special Rapporteur; See O'Flaherty, 'The Concluding Observations of United Nations Human Rights Treaty Bodies' 6 *Human Rights Law Review* (2006) 27 at p. 47. The Current Special Rapporteur for follow-up on Concluding Observations is Sir Nigel Rodley.

[257] Report of the Human Rights Committee 1 November 2003, A/58/40, vol. 1, para 263 (HRC).

also determine the date when the next report from the State party is to be required. Informal contacts are made with the State party in addition to reminders being sent for any follow-up information. In case of the failure of the State party to provide any follow-up information, the Special Rapporteur sets up a meeting with the State representative. If all efforts to receive information fail, the HRC records this in its Annual Report.

NGOs – a vital source of information have no official position within the reporting mechanism – are in strict procedural terms not authorised to intervene during the examination of a State report. The contribution and influence of NGOs nonetheless has been enormous. This, as we shall examine, is particularly strong in the reporting procedure of ICESCR. NGOs have developed personal contacts with members of the HRC, providing them within invaluable information. Over the years, NGOs have engaged in providing 'alternative' or 'Counter' reports to the official State reports.

Since 1991, HRC has also deployed a procedure in order to deal with emergency situations. The procedure is based on Article 40 in conjunction with Rule 66(2) of the Rules of Procedure.[258] Under this procedure urgent reports have been required from a number of States.[259] Under Rule 68(1) the HRC through the Secretary-General is required to notify those States parties expecting consideration of reports as early as possible of the date, duration and place of the relevant submission.

7 GENERAL COMMENTS[260]

The Human Rights Committee is also entitled to provide General Comments, comments which relate to various rights within the Covenant and are non-country specific.[261] The practice of producing General Comments began in 1981. The overall purpose behind these General Comments is to

> make the Committee's experience available for the benefit of all States Parties, so as to promote more effective implementation of the Covenant; to draw the attention of States parties to insufficiencies disclosed by a large number of reports; to suggest improvements in the reporting procedure; to clarify the requirements of the Covenant; and to stimulate the activities of States Parties and International Organisations in the promotion and protection of human rights. General Comments are intended also to be of interest to other States, especially those preparing to become parties to the Covenant. They are intended, in addition, to strengthen co-operation amongst States in the universal protection and promotion of human rights.[262]

[258] Joseph, 'New Procedures Concerning the Human Rights Committee's Examination of State Reports' 13 *NQHR* (1995) 5; O'Flaherty, 'Treaty Bodies Responding to State of Emergency: The Case of Bosnia and Herzegovnia' in Alston and Crawford (eds), *The Future of UN Human Rights Treaty Monitoring* (Cambridge University Press, 2000) pp. 439–460.

[259] In 1992 special reports were asked for by the Committee from Bosnia-Herzegovina, Croatia and the Federal Republic of Yugoslavia; in 1993 from Angola and Burundi and in 1994 from Haiti and Rwanda.

[260] See Opsahl, 'The General Comments of the Human Rights Committee' in J. Jekewitz *et al.* (eds), *Des Menschen Recht Zwischen Freiheit Und Verantwortung, Festschrift für Karl Josef Partsch zum 75. Geburstag* (Duncker and Humbolt, 1989) at pp. 273–286; Tomuschat, above n.1, at pp. 189–191.

[261] ICCPR Article 40(4).

[262] Ghandhi, above n.1, at p. 25.

In its initial set of General Comments, the HRC considered aspects of reporting obligations of States and procedures and the obligations on States parties under Article 2 to undertake specific activities to enable individuals to enjoy their rights. General Comments have been made on Articles 1–4, 6, 7, 9, 10, 12, 14, 17–20, 23–25, 27, 40 and 41, as well as on the position of aliens under the Covenant, non-discrimination, the continuity of obligations and the nature of the general legal obligations imposed upon States parties. In its most recent General Comment, the HRC has elaborated upon the obligations of States parties under the first Optional Protocol to the ICCPR.[263]

The General Comments delivered have been addressed to all States parties, and in its consideration of State reports the Committee has increasingly referred to these General Comments. The General Comments not only act as an invaluable guide to the interpretation of particular articles, but have added considerably to the existing jurisprudence of civil and political rights. We have already considered the value of the General Comments in our analysis of the substantive rights of the Covenant, although the significance of these Comments upon controversial subjects such as the rights of the child,[264] minorities[265] and freedom of religion[266] cannot be overstated. Although originally designed as a mechanism to provide guidance for States in the interpretation of substantive articles of the Covenant, HRC has also been able to take into account its experiences with individual communications in providing General Comments.[267]

8 INTER-STATE APPLICATIONS[268]

The second mode of implementation is the inter-State complaints procedure as authorised under Articles 41 and 42 of the ICCPR. Although part of the same treaty, the procedure is optional, with States that are interested in using this mechanism being required to make an additional declaration.[269] Both of the parties, the complainant and the State against whom the complaint is made must have made a declaration under Article 41.[270] According to this procedure, a State (A) that considers another State (B) as violating the provisions of the Covenant can bring that fact to the attention of the State party concerned. State (B) must respond to the allegations within three months.[271] If, however, within six months the matter has not been resolved since the receipt of the initial communication either State may bring the matter to the attention of the HRC.[272] The HRC must decide whether all local remedies

---

[263] 5 November 2008.

[264] Human Rights Committee, *General Comment No. 17, Rights of the Child (Art. 24)*: Thirty-fifth session, 1989, 07/04/89; see also Ghandhi, 'Family and Child Rights' in Harris and Joseph (eds) above n.1, pp. 490–534.

[265] Human Rights Committee, *General Comment No. 23, The Rights of Minorities (Art. 27)* Fiftieth Session, 1994, 08/04/94.

[266] Human Rights Committee, *General Comment No. 22*, above n.168.

[267] Tomuschat, above n.1, at p. 190.

[268] See Leckie, 'The Inter-State Complaint Procedure in International Human Rights Law: Hopeful Prospects or Wishful Thinking?' 10 *HRQ* (1988) 249.

[269] Article 41(1).

[270] Rule 78(a) Rules of Procedure.

[271] Article 41(1)(a).

[272] Article 41(1)(b) Rule 74(1), 78(b) Rules of Procedure.

have been exhausted before considering the case in closed sessions.[273] The HRC's task is to make an attempt to resolve the dispute through its good offices.[274] The HRC is obliged to produce a written report within 12 months of the date of receipt of notice of complaint. If a solution is reached then the HRC's report will be brief and confined to facts and the solution reached.[275] If a friendly solution has not been reached then the HRC is required to confine its report to a brief statement of facts. '[The] written submissions and a record of the oral submissions made by the States Parties concerned are to be attached to the report.'[276]

According to Article 42 (if the matter is not resolved amicably) the HRC may, with the consent of States parties concerned, appoint a five member *ad hoc* Conciliation Commission.[277] The Commission is required to report to the Chairman of the Committee its findings within 12 months of having been seized of the matter.[278] If no solution has been reached then the Commission report must state the facts and indicate 'its views on the possibilities of an amicable solution'.[279] The Conciliation Commission has the power to make recommendations, although these recommendations are not binding upon States. In each case the matter will be referred to the General Assembly by the Committee in its annual report. Like other international procedures of a similar nature, the inter-State complaints procedure has not proved to be of any major significance. Inter-State proceedings, in the words of one commentator, 'are undeniably complex, cumbersome and elongated'.[280] States often feel reluctant to challenge other States for political and diplomatic reasons. As yet the inter-State Complaints procedure has not been used.[281] In its General Comment 31, the HRC reminded States parties of the desirability of using this procedure. It reminded

> States Parties of the desirability of making the declaration contemplated in article 41. It further remind[ed] those States Parties already having made the declaration of the potential value of availing themselves of the procedure under that article. However, the mere fact that a formal interstate mechanism for complaints to the Human Rights Committee exists in respect of States Parties that have made the declaration under article 41 does not mean that this procedure is the only method by which States Parties can assert their interest in the performance of other States Parties. On the contrary, the article 41 procedure should be seen as supplementary to, not diminishing of, States Parties' interest in each others' discharge of their obligations. Accordingly, the Committee commends to States Parties the view that violations of Covenant rights by any State Party deserve their attention. To draw attention to possible breaches of Covenant obligations by other States Parties and to call on them to comply with their Covenant obligations should, far from being regarded as an unfriendly act, be considered as a reflection of legitimate community interest.[282]

---

[273] Article 41(1)(c)(d); Rule 74(2) provides 'The notice referred to in [74(1)] of this rule shall contain or be accompanied by information regarding: (a) Steps taken to seek adjustment of the matter in accordance with Article 41 paragraphs 1(a) and (b), of the Covenant, including the text of the initial communication and of any subsequent written explanation or statements by States parties concerned which are pertinent to the matter; (b) Steps taken to exhaust domestic remedies; (c) Any other procedure of international investigation or settlement resorted to by the States parties concerned.'

[274] Article 41(1)(e).

[275] Article 41(1)(h)(i).

[276] Article 41(1)(h)(ii).

[277] Article 42(1)(a)(b).

[278] Article 42(7).

[279] Article 42(7)(c).

[280] Ghandhi, above n.1, at p. 26.

[281] Ibid. at p. 27.

[282] See HRC, General Comment No. 31, above n.27, para 2.

9 THE INDIVIDUAL COMPLAINTS PROCEDURE[283]

A third mechanism, and by far the most significant, insofar as individuals are concerned, is the Individual Complaints Procedure under the first optional protocol to the ICCPR. At the time of drafting of the ICCPR it had been proposed to incorporate a mechanism of individual complaints within the Covenant itself, an effort which proved abortive in the light of widely differing views and disagreements. The Protocol, which emerged as a separate treaty came into operation on 23 March 1976, and as of 1 July 2009 there are 112 States parties to it, a population that covers well over a billion people from all continents of the world. Under this Protocol, the Committee has provided consideration to more than 1400 cases emerging from 82 States parties.

According to Article 1 of the Protocol, a State party to the Covenant that also becomes a party to the Protocol

> recognizes the competence of the Committee to receive and consider communications from individuals subject to its jurisdiction who claim to be victims of violation by that State Party of any of the right set forth in the Covenant. No communication shall be received by the Committee if it concerns a State Party to the Covenant which is not a party to the present Protocol.[284]

The Communication should be sent to the Secretariat of the Office of the High Commissioner for Human Rights. Communications must be in written form. There is no restriction of language, and unlike the European system there is not the requirement of a time limit of submission after the exhaustion of domestic remedies.[285] The Committee has produced a model communication with the objective of assisting complaints.[286] However, prior to submission, and in accordance with Article 2, the individual who claims to be the victim of violations of his or her rights must have exhausted all available domestic remedies.[287]

The communication must provide essential prerequisite information. This consists of the name, address and nationality of the victim and the author. The State against which the complaint is being made needs to be identified clearly. When a State is not party to the Optional Protocol, the Secretary General returns the communication with the notification that the State concerned is not a party. There should also be identification of the breach,

---

[283] For a detailed consideration see Ghandhi, above n.1; Lewis-Anthony and Scheinin, 'Treaty-Based Procedures for Making Human Rights Complaints within the UN System' in Hannum (ed.), above n.20, at pp. 44–53.

[284] Article 1, 1st Optional Protocol.

[285] *Víctor Villamón Ventura* v. *Spain*, Communication No. 1305/2004, UN Doc. CCPR/C/88/D/1305/2004 (2006), para 6.4. *Cf. Armand Anton* v. *Algeria*, Communication No. 1424/2005, UN Doc. CCPR/C/88/D/1424/2005 (2006), Concurring opinion of Committee members Ms. Elisabeth Palm, Sir Nigel Rodley and Mr. Nisuke Ando, 'The Committee notes the delay of 15 years in this case between the ratification of the Optional Protocol by the State party in 1989 and the submission of the communication in 2004. It observes that there are no explicit time limits for submission of communications under the Optional Protocol. However, in certain circumstances, the Committee is entitled to expect a reasonable explanation justifying such a delay.' *Ernst Zundel* v. *Canada*, Communication No. 1341/2005, UN Doc. CCPR/C/89/D/1341/2005 (2007), para 6.5.

[286] Model Communication, www2.ohchr.org/english/bodies/docs/annex1.pdf <last visited 25 July 2008>.

[287] Article 5(2)(b) 1st Optional Protocol.

the articles which are alleged to have been breached and substantiation of alleged violation through relevant facts and dates. There also needs to be a statement to the effect of having satisfied the admissibility requirements, i.e. exhaustion of domestic remedies, the same matter not being considered by another international procedure, etc.[288] The communication must be signed and dated. Article 3 of the Protocol provides that '[the] Committee shall consider inadmissible any communication which is anonymous, or which it considers to be an abuse of the right of submission or to be incompatible with the provisions of the Covenant'.[289]

Consideration of the communication under Optional Protocol is confidential at the merit and admissibility stage; this remains the case (unless otherwise decided by HRC) until the HRC adopts its views or the case is concluded. On receipt of the communication, it is screened by a member of the office of the High Commissioner for Human Rights. The 'petition team' prepares a summary of the communication and passes it to a member of the Human Rights Committee, authorised to deal with communications received between sessions. The Committee member is known as the Special Rapporteur on New Communications.[290] The Special Rapporteur, a member of the Committee, provides the initial scrutiny and ensures that the necessary information is provided or contained in the communication. A communication may be registered if the Special Rapporteur feels satisfied with the compliance with preliminary admissibility requirements. The revision introduced through Rule 97 means that HRC considers issues of admissibility and merit at a single stage, unless the Special Rapporteur on New Communications decides otherwise.[291] After registration the Special Rapporteur instructs the 'petition team' to transmit the communication to the State concerned, seeking information on the admissibility and merits.[292] The Special Rapporteur also requests States to undertake interim measures where these are warranted.[293] Unless the petition is patently inadmissible, the State concerned is provided

---

[288] Article 5(2)(a)(b). *Luis Bertelli Gálvez* v. *Spain*, Communication No. 1389/2005, UN Doc. CCPR/C/84/D/1389/2005 (2005) as the case was only considered on procedural grounds by the European Commission and not on its merits, this did not preclude HRC from considering the Communication, para 4.3, *Yuri Bandajevsky* v. *Belarus*, Communication No. 1100/2002, UN Doc. CCPR/C/86/D/1100/2002 (2006), 'the complaints procedure before the Executive Board's Committee on Conventions and Recommendations of UNESCO is extra-conventional, without any obligation of the State party concerned to cooperate with it; that no conclusion of violation or non-violation of specific rights by a given State is made in the examination of individual cases; and that such an examination ultimately does not lead to any authoritative determination of the merits of a particular case. The Committee concluded that the UNESCO complaints procedure does not constitute another "procedure of international investigation or settlement" in the sense of article 5, paragraph 2(a), of the Optional Protocol', para 5. *Duilio Fanali* v. *Italy*, Communication No. 75/1980, UN Doc. Supp. No. 40 (A/38/40) at 160 (1983), 'The Committee held that the concept of "the same matter" within the meaning of article 5(2)(a) of the Optional Protocol had to be understood as including the same claim concerning the same individual, submitted by him or someone else who has the standing to act on his behalf before the other international body', para 7.2. *Teun Sanders* v. *Netherlands*, Communication No. 1193/2003, UN Doc. CCPR/C/84/D/1193/2003 (2005), '[t]he Committee notes that this matter was already considered by the European Court of Human Rights on 29 May 2002. However, it recalls its jurisprudence that it is only where the same matter is being examined under another procedure of international investigation or settlement that the Committee has no competence to deal with a communication under article 5, paragraph 2(a), of the Optional Protocol', para 6.2.

[289] See also Rule 96(c)(d) of the Rules of Procedure.

[290] For the terms of reference for the Special Rapporteur on New Communications, see GAOR, 46th Session, Supplement No. 40 (A/45/40) Report of the Human Rights Committee, p. 218.

[291] Rule 97(2) Rules of Procedure.

[292] O'Flaherty, above n.236, at p. 42.

[293] Rule 92 Rules of Procedure.

six months to respond to the communication,[294] after which the author has a two-month period to respond to the State's reply.[295] After the initial exchanges between the State and the author the Communication is passed to a five-member Working Group on Communications. The Working Group consists of five members of the Human Rights Committee and meets for one week before the session. A communication can be declared admissible by a unanimous decision of the Working Group.[296] Otherwise the issue of admissibility is considered by the whole Committee.[297] The general practice is that the recommendations of the Working Group are followed by the Committee,[298] and without formal discussion.[299] Cases found to be admissible are considered on their merits after further consultation with the State party and the author of the Communication. As indicated earlier, HRC holds closed meetings when examining individual communications and the pleadings are treated as confidential.[300] HRC formulates its views in the light of all the written information made available to it by the individual and by the State party concerned. There are no apparent mechanisms for oral or onsite investigations.[301] HRC, its Working Group or designated Special Rapporteur may request the State party to undertake interim measures to ensure the alleged victim's security.[302] This authority, of requesting interim measures is however a limited one. HRC can, according to its Rules of Procedure, inform a State party of its views 'as to whether interim measures may be desirable to avoid irreparable damage to the victim of the alleged violation'.[303]

HRC presents its views through consensus, though individual members can write concurring or dissenting opinions.[304] HRC is not bound by the doctrine of precedent.[305] The HRC forwards its formulated views to the State party and to the individual. According to Article 6, the HRC includes in its annual report under Article 45 of the Covenant a summary of its activities under the Optional Protocol. The HRC's views are not legally binding but carry only moral and political obligations.[306] The terminology, i.e. using 'communications' rather than 'complaints' and 'views' as opposed to 'decisions', confirms the limited nature of the mandate of the HRC. Having said that, the HRC interprets the provisions of

---

[294] If the State party wishes to contest the admissibility, its arguments must be presented in writing within two months. O'Flaherty, above n.236, at p. 42. Article 4(2) of the Optional Protocol and Rule 97(2) and 99(2) of the Rules of Procedure.

[295] Rule 99(3) Rules of Procedure CCPR/C/3/Rev.8 22 September 2005 <last visited 28 January 2009>.

[296] Rule 95(2) Rules of Procedure.

[297] See Lewis-Anthony and Scheinin, 'Treaty-Based Procedures for Making Human Rights Complaints within the UN System' in Hannum (ed.), above n.20, at pp. 47–49.

[298] Ghandhi, above n.1, at p. 75.

[299] Rule 93(3) Rules of Procedure.

[300] See Rules concerning Confidentiality; Rule 102, Rules of Procedure.

[301] Lewis-Anthony and Scheinin, 'Treaty-Based Procedures for Making Human Rights Complaints within the UN System' in Hannum (ed.), above n.20, at pp. 48–50.

[302] Rule 92 Rules of Procedure. See *Anthony B. Mansaraj* et al.; *Gborie Tamba* et al.; *Abdul Karim Sesay* et al. v. *Sierra Leone*, Communication No. 839/1998, UN Doc. CCPR/C/72/D/839/1998 (2001) paras 5.1–5.3.

[303] Rule 92 Rules of Procedure; See Ghandhi, 'The Human Rights Committee and Interim Measures of Relief' 13 *Canterbury Law Review* (2007) 203.

[304] For the difficulties surrounding decision-making by consensus see Ghandhi, above n.1, at pp. 32–35.

[305] See Joseph, Schultz and Castan, above n.1, at pp. 17–18. *Roger Judge* v. *Canada*, Communication No. 829/1998, UN Doc. CCPR/C/78/D/829/1998 (2003), '[t]he Committee considers that the Covenant should be interpreted as a living instrument and the rights protected under it should be applied in context and in the light of present–day conditions', para 10.3.

[306] De Zayas, Möller and Opsahl, above n.218, at p. 11.

a legally binding instrument and its findings have a judicial flavour[307] – decisions on merits resemble findings of breach or non-breaches, and its views contain recommendations suggested, e.g. repeal of impugned legislation,[308] payment of damages,[309] release of prisoners[310] or the commutation of the death penalty.[311]

The HRC's views have not been readily endorsed by States parties and the lack of compliance with the views of the HRC has been a source of some concern.[312] Between 1982 and 1990, HRC sent out letters to the States parties concerned with requests to take action in response to its views. This process has not proved to be satisfactory. From 1990 onwards the Committee has undertaken greater efforts to ensure compliance. A Committee member is now designated as a 'Special Rapporteur for the Follow-Up of Views' to oversee and monitor the implementation process.[313] The Committee's practices in cases of violation are to require the State concerned to inform the Committee of any actions undertaken in espousal of the Committee's findings. In order to ensure monitoring of State compliance, the Special Rapporteur has the wide mandate of making 'such contacts and take such action as appropriate for the due performance of the follow-up mandate'.[314] In pursuit of this mandate the Special Rapportuer has contacted a number of permanent representatives or missions of States parties to discuss the actions undertaken by the State.[315] The HRC regards dialogue between the Special Rapporteur and the non-compliant State party as a vital key to the implementation of its views. The Special Rapporteur, as noted above, is assigned with the task of retaining contact and dialogue, and reports to the HRC on the progress of such dialogue on a regular basis.[316]

A further initiative to ensure compliance has been through onsite visits.[317] In August 1995, the Special Rapporteur conducted his first onsite investigation mission to monitor the compliance of Jamaica with the Committee's view on administration of justice in cases

---

[307] The Committee notes 'while the function of the Human Rights Committee in considering individual communications is not, as such, that of a judicial body, the views issued by the Committee under the Optional Protocol exhibit some important characteristics of a judicial decision. They are arrived at in a judicial spirit, including the impartiality and independence of committee members, the considered interpretation of the language of the Covenant, and the determinative character of the decisions' para 11. HRC, General Comment No. 33 The Obligation of States Parties under the Optional Protocol to the International Covenant on Civil and Political Rights CCPR/C/GC/33 (5 November 2008), para 11.

[308] *Toonen* v. *Australia*, Communication No. 488/1992, UN Doc. CCPR/C/50/D/488/1992 (1994), para 11.

[309] *A* v. *Australia*, Communication No. 560/1993, UN Doc. CCPR/C/59/D/560/1993 (30 April 1997), para 11.

[310] *Paul Kelly* v. *Jamaica*, Communication No. 253/1987, UN Doc. CCPR/C/41/D/253/1987 at 60 (1991), para 7.

[311] *Lawrence Chan* v. *Guyana*, Communication No. 913/2000, UN Doc. CCPR/C/85/D/913/2000 (2006), para 8. *Raymond Persaud and Rampersaud* v. *Guyana*, Communication No. 812/1998, UN Doc. CCPR/C/86/D/812/1998 (2006), para 9.

[312] See Evatt, 'Reflecting on the Role of International Communications in Implementing Human Rights' 5 *Australian Journal of Human Rights* (1999) 20.

[313] According to Rules of Procedure, Rule 101(1), 'The Committee shall designate a Special Rapporteur for follow-up on Views adopted under article 5, paragraph 4, of the Optional Protocol, for the purpose of ascertaining the measures taken by States parties to give effect to the Committee's views'. Rule 101(2) provides that 'The Special Rapporteur may make such contacts and take such action as appropriate for the due performance of the follow-up mandate. The Special Rapporteur shall make such recommendations for further action by the Committee as may be necessary'. See also Schmidt, 'Follow-up Mechanisms Before UN Human Rights Treaty Bodies and the UN Mechanisms Beyond' in Bayefsky (ed.), *The UN Human Rights System in the 21st Century* (Brill, 2000) pp. 233–249.

[314] Rule 101(2) Rules of Procedure.

[315] Lewis-Anthony and Scheinin, 'Treaty-Based Procedures for Making Human Rights Complaints within the UN System' in Hannum (ed.), above n.20, at p. 49.

[316] HRC, General Comment No. 33, above n.307. para 11.

[317] Ibid.

involving the death penalty and death row phenomenon. It needs to be noted that lack of funding for such visits can be a discouraging factor for planning future initiatives. The HRC's annual report submitted to the General Assembly includes not only reference to those States which have not complied with the Committee's views but also information on the follow-up activities. The Committee has also tended to assert within its final views a requirement that State parties inform the Committee of the measures in pursuance of its pronouncement within 90 days.[318] States are also required to provide information on action undertaken in response to the Committee's view in their periodic reports submitted under Article 40 of the Covenant.

(i) Admissibility requirements under the Optional Protocol

(a) Who may submit a petition?

According to Article 1 of the OP, the Committee may receive communications from

> individuals subject to [the State Party's] jurisdiction who claim to be victims of a violation by that State Party of any of the rights set forth in the Covenant.

HRC may only receive communications from individuals. There is no requirement of nationality, provided that the victim has been within the jurisdiction of the State. The Committee, therefore, is competent to receive communication from nationals, aliens, refugees or anyone else so long as the individuals concerned is subject to jurisdiction.[319] As noted above, only natural as opposed to artificial persons can claim to be victims. Therefore, organisations (e.g. non-governmental organisations) associations, or companies are as such not entitled to submit communications.[320] Insofar as individuals are concerned

---

[318] Tomuschat, above n.1, at p. 221.

[319] See *Miguel Angel Estrella* v. *Uruguay*, Communication No. 74/1980 (17 July 1980), UN Doc. Supp. No. 40 (A/38/40) at 150 (1983) para 4.1.

[320] *Disabled and handicapped persons in Italy* v. *Italy*, Communication No. 163/1984 (10 April 1984), UN Doc. CCPR/C/OP/1 at 47(1984), para 5; *J. R. T. and the W. G. Party* v. *Canada*, Communication No. 104/1981 (6 April 1983), UN Doc. CCPR/C/OP/1 at 25 (1984) regarding an unincorporated political party, para 8(a). On the position relating companies see *S.M.* v. *Barbados*, Communication No. 502/1992, UN Doc. CCPR/C/50/D/502/1992 (4 April 1994), paras 6.2–6.3. *Erkki Hartikainen* v. *Finland*, Communication No. 40/1978, UN Doc. CCPR/C/OP/1 at 74 (1984) – the Communication was inadmissible insofar as it was submitted by author in his capacity as Secretary-General of the Union of Free thinkers in Finland on behalf of the organisation, para 3(b). On the admissibility of corporations see *A Newspaper Publishing Company* v. *Trinidad and Tobago*, Communication No. 360/1989, UN Doc. CCPR/C/36/D/360/1989 (1989), para 3.2. and *A Publication and Printing Company* v. *Trinidad and Tobago*, Communication No. 361/1989 UN Doc. CCPR/C/36/D/361/1989 (1989), para 3.2. Also see the General Comment No. 31, above n.26, para 9. Contrast the position adopted by the Human Rights Committee to that of jurisprudence of the European Convention on Human Rights which authorises individuals, Non-governmental organisations as well as corporate bodies to invoke Article 34 of the Convention. In the case of ICCPR, NGOs may nevertheless represent an author. There is no established procedure for NGOs to present *amicus curiae* briefs. See Harris, above n.1, 'Introduction' at p. 34 (footnote 200). The fact that a claim refers to both the rights of an individual as well as an organisation does not lead the individuals rights to be inadmissible, *Singer* v. *Canada*, Communication No. 455/1991, UN Doc. CCPR/C/51/D/455/1991 (1994), para 11.2; similarly the number of petitioners does not render the communication *actio popularis* so long as each of the authors can claim to be the victim of violation of the rights, *E.W.* et al. v. *The Netherlands*, Communication No. 429/1990, UN Doc. CCPR/C/47/D/429/1990 (1993), para 6.3.

there is 'no objection to a group of individuals, who claim to be similarly affected, collectively to submit a communication about alleged breaches of their rights'[321] and yet the claim to the right of self-determination contained in the Article is not justiciable under the Optional Protocol. The person submitting the communication is identified as the 'author'.[322] Only one or several 'individuals' (acting either himself/themselves or through his/their representatives) may submit a communication under Article 1 of the Protocol. By representative, the Committee has taken the meaning of a 'duly appointed representative', for example, the alleged victim's lawyer.[323]

The HRC, however, has adopted a flexible approach in circumstances where it has not been possible for the victim to submit the communication because of arbitrary detention, being held *incommunicado*, strict mail censorship, an incapacitating illness consequent upon detention or death occurring as a result of State actions or omissions.[324] In these circumstances the Committee has allowed others to petition on behalf of the victim provided there is a sufficient link between the individual and the complainant and that the victim has (would have) consented him or herself to such an action. This position is reconfirmed by Rule 96(b) of the Committee's Rules of Procedure, according to which a 'communication should normally be submitted by the individual personally or by that individual's representative'[325] although it may be submitted on behalf of the alleged victim 'when it appears the individual in question is unable to submit [it] personally'.[326] The petitioner must, nevertheless, have authorisation from the victim, which cannot simply be presumed.[327]

In *Massera* v. *Uruguay* the author's communication on behalf of her husband, her stepfather, and her mother was held admissible,[328] and so have communications on behalf of daughter,[329] uncle and aunt[330] and father-in-law[331] by reason only of close family connections. The onus is upon the authors to establish a sufficient linkage with the victim and that

---

[321] *Lubicon Lake Band* v. *Canada* (167/1984) para 32.1.

[322] McGoldrick, above n.1, at p. 170.

[323] UN Doc. A/33/40 para 580. *Cf. Humanitarian Law Center* v. *Serbia*, Communication No. 1355/2005, UN Doc. CCPR/C/89/D/1355/2005 (2007) – lawyer but must have the consent of the alleged victim even if they have previously acted on their behalf paras 6.3–6.7.

[324] See *Joaquín David Herrera Rubio* et al. v. *Colombia*, Communication No. 161/1983, UN Doc. CCPR/C/OP/2 at 192 (1990), para 10.2–11.; *Jean Miango Muiyo* v. *Zaire*, Communication No. 194/1985, UN Doc. CCPR/C/OP/2 at 219 (1990), paras 8.2–9. See Ghandhi, above n.1, at p. 85.

[325] Rule 96(b) Rules of Procedure.

[326] Ibid. See *Pereira* v. *Panama*, Communication No. 436/1990, UN Doc. CCPR/C/51/D/436/1990 (1994). The Communication was held inadmissible in the absence of documentary proof of authorisation, paras 5.2–5.3; also see *the Mikmaq Tribal Society* v. *Canada*, Communication No. 78/1980 (30 September 1980), UN Doc. Supp. No. 40 (A/39/40) at 200 (1984) para 8.2 and *Holzer* v. *Italy*, Communication No. 565/1993, UN Doc. CCPR/C/50/D/565/1993 (1994), para 4.2. This rule has met with widespread approval and similar rules of procedures have been devised by Committee against Torture Rule 107(a) CAT Rules of Procedure, UN Doc. CAT/C/3/Rev.4 and, Rule 91(b) of CERD Rules of Procedure, and Article 2 of the OP-CEDAW.

[327] *Y (Name deleted)* v. *Australia*, Communication No. 772/1997, UN Doc. CCPR/C/69/D/772/1997 (2000). Solicitor submitting a communication while not acting in a representative capacity for an asylum seeker, paras 6.2–6.3. *P.S.* v. *Denmark*, Communication No. 397/1990, UN Doc. CCPR/C/45/D/397/1990 (1992). Non-custodial parent making a communication on son's behalf without consent, para 5.2.

[328] *Moriana Hernandez Valentini de Bazzano* v. *Uruguay*, Communication No. 5/1977, UN Doc. CCPR/C/OP/1 at 40 (1984), para 5.

[329] *Maria del Carmen Almeida de Quinteros, on behalf of her daughter, Elena Quinteros Almeida, and on her own behalf* v. *Uruguay*, Communication No. 107/1981 (17 September 1981), UN Doc. Supp. No. 40 (A/38/40) at 216 (1983).

[330] *Beatriz Weismann Lanza and Alcides Lanza Perdomo* v. *Uruguay*, Communication No. R. 2/8 (20 February 1977), UN Doc. Supp. No. 40 (A/35/40) at 111 (1980) paras 4–5.

[331] *Daniel Monguya Mbenge* v. *Zaire*, Communication No. 16/1977 (8 September 1977), UN Doc. Supp. No. 40 (A/38/40) at 134 (1983) para 5.

he or she has or would have authorised submission before the HRC. The Committee has not limited the acceptance of communications from close family members.[332] At present NGOs are not authorised to present communications on behalf of the alleged victim, and organisations in general may not act as authors of communications since Articles 1 and 2 of the Protocol explicitly refer to 'individuals'. However, class actions have been held admissible, although all of the prospective author's must have given express, written consent, otherwise the communication is held inadmissible in respect of those who have not given such consent.[333]

(b) Are *actio popularis* communications permissible?

Under the provisions of the Protocol a person can only claim to be the 'victim' if his or her rights are actually being affected[334] or such an effect is imminent.[335] It is undeniably a matter of degree how concretely this requirement should be taken. However it is clear that no individual could in the abstract, by way of *actio popularis*, challenge a law or practice by claiming it to be contrary to the Covenant.[336] If the law has not already been concretely applied to the detriment of the individual it must in any event be applicable in such a way that the alleged victim's risk of being affected is more than a theoretical possibility.[337]

[332] *Natalya Tcholatch v. Canada*, Communication No. 1052/2002, UN Doc. CCPR/C/89/D/1052/2002 (2007). HRC has accepted communications regarding the rights of the author's children even in the case of no access, para 7.4. *Darmon Sultanova v. Uzbekistan*, Communication No. 915/2000, UN Doc. CCPR/C/86/D/915/2000 (2006). Communication on behalf of husband, where able to consent has been held inadmissible, para 6.2.

[333] See, *E.W. et al. v. The Netherlands*, Communication No. 429/1990, UN Doc. CCPR/C/47/D/429/1990 (1993), para 6.3. *Cf. In E. H. P. v. Canada*, Communication No. 67/1980, UN Doc. CCPR/C/OP/1 at 20 (1984), the individual made a complaint on behalf of herself and on behalf of 'present and future generations'. 'Present and future generations', were not admissible as authors but were rather taken by the Committee as to highlight the gravity of the situation, para 8. *Peter Michael Queenan v. Canada*, Communication No. 1379/2005, UN Doc. CCPR/C/84/D/1379/2005 (2005). In the case of unborn children, the author cannot said to be personally a victim of a violation, para 4.2.

[334] *Shirin Aumeeruddy-Cziffra and 19 other Mauritian women v. Mauritius*, Communication No. 35/1978 (9 April 1981), UN Doc. CCPR/C/OP/1 at 67 (1984), para 9.2, *André Brun v. France*, Communication No. 1453/2006, UN Doc. CCPR/C/88/D/1453/2006 (2006) – regarding GMO crops, para 6.3. *Aalbersberg and 2084 other Dutch citizens v. The Netherlands*, Communication No. 1440/2005, UN Doc. CCPR/C/87/D/1440/2005 (2006), regarding nuclear weapons, the authors cannot prove that they are victims and that their rights have been violated, para 6.3.

[335] *E.W. et al. v. The Netherlands*, Communication No. 429/1990, UN Doc. CCPR/C/47/D/429/1990 (1993), regarding the deployment of cruise missiles between 1 June 1984–8 June 1987 and the continuing deployment of other nuclear weapons in Netherlands. This did not place authors in the position of victims as '[for] a person to claim to be a victim of a violation of a right protected by the Covenant, he or she must show either that an act or an omission of a State party has already adversely affected his or her enjoyment of such right, or that such an effect is imminent, for example on the basis of existing law and/or judicial or administrative decision or practice', para 6.4. *Vaihere Bordes and John Temeharo v. France*, Communication No. 645/1995, UN Doc. CCPR/C/57/D/645/1995 (1996) – underground nuclear tests by France on Mururoa and Fangatuga, paras 5.5–5.7.

[336] *Shirin Aumeeruddy-Cziffra and 19 other Mauritian women v. Mauritius*, Communication No. 35/1978 (9 April 1981), UN Doc. CCPR/C/OP/1 at 67 (1984), para 9.2. The Committee pointed that '. . . A person can only claim to be a victim in the sense of article 1 of the Optional Protocol if he or she is actually affected. It is a matter of degree how concretely this requirement should be taken. However no individual can in the abstract, by way of *actio popularis*, challenge a law or practice claimed to be contrary to the covenant . . .' Ibid. para 9.2.

[337] See *A. R. S. v. Canada*, Communication No. 91/1981 (28 October 1981), UN Doc. CCPR/C/OP/1 at 29, 30 (1984), para 5.2. Contrast with the requirement laid down in ACHR (Article 44). Below chapter 9. *Cf. Ballantyne, Davidson, McIntyre v. Canada*, Communications Nos. 359/1989 and 385/1989, UN Doc. CCPR/C/47/D/359/1989 and 385/1989/Rev.1 (1993) where the Communication was held admissible although the law restricting usage of French language in bill posting and in commercial advertising outdoors was not enforced against two of the three authors. 'However, it is the position of the Committee that where an individual is in a category of persons whose activities are, by virtue of the relevant legislation, regarded as contrary to law, they may have a claim as "victims" within the meaning of article 1 of the Optional Protocol', para 10.4.

Furthermore, the alleged victim needs to establish that a violation of the Covenant has prejudiced the enjoyment of his rights.[338] However, the author does not have to be victim throughout the period under consideration.[339] Nor is the requirement invalidated, where the victim's own behaviour has been tainted.[340]

In *Shirin Aumeeruddy-Cziffra and Nineteen Other Mauritian Women* v. *Mauritius*,[341] the authors of the communication complained that two pieces of legislation on immigration and deportation resulted in gender discrimination violating the right to found a family and home and removed the protection of courts of law, breaching Articles 2–4, 17, 23, 25 and 26 of the Covenant. To further their complaints, the authors argued that under the new laws

alien husbands of Mauritian women lost their residence status in Mauritius and must now apply for a 'residence permit' which may be refused or removed at any time by the Minister of Interior. The new laws, however, do not affect the status of alien women married to Mauritian husbands who retain their legal right to residence in the country. The authors further contend that under the new laws alien husbands of Mauritian women may be deported under a ministerial order which is not subject to judicial review.[342]

At the time of the communication, 17 authors were unmarried and only three co-authors were married to foreign husbands. The HRC applying the test of 'alleged victim's risk being more than a theoretical possibility' held that only those women directly affected by Mauritian legislation could claim to be victims. This excluded the 17 unmarried Mauritian women. The HRC, however, held the three married women to be 'victims'. Despite this apparently narrow view taken in the Mauritian women's case, the existence of a risk will suffice and the petitioner need not show that the law has in fact been applied to his or her detriment.

The existence of risk was used as a criterion in *Toonen* v. *Australia*,[343] where a practising homosexual was regarded as a 'victim' when he challenged a law criminalising homosexual acts, a law that not been enforced for 10 years. Justifying its views, the Committee noted that 'the threat of enforcement and the pervasive impact of the continued existence of these

---

[338] See *Ponsamy Poongavanam* v. *Mauritius*, Communication No. 567/1993, UN Doc. CCPR/C/51/D/567/1993 (1994), the author's claim was held inadmissible since the author had failed to establish, how, the absence of a jury in fact prejudiced the enjoyment of his rights in the covenant, para 4.4.; *Morrison* v. *Jamaica*, Communication No. 663/1995, UN Doc. CCPR/C/64/D/663/1995 (25 November 1998), para 6.4.

[339] *A* v. *Australia*, Communication No. 560/1993 HRC noted 'that several of the events complained of by the author had occurred prior to the entry into force of the Optional Protocol for Australia; however, as the State party had not wished to contest the admissibility of the communication on this ground, and as the author had remained in custody after the entry into force of the Optional Protocol for Australia, the Committee was satisfied that the complaint was admissible ratione temporis. It further acknowledged that the State party had conceded the admissibility of the author's claim under article 9, paragraph 1' para 6.1.

[340] *Michael and Brian Hill* v. *Spain*, Communication No. 526/1993, UN Doc. CCPR/C/59/D/526/1993 (2 April 1997), para 9.1.

[341] *Aumeeruddy-Cziffra and 19 other Mauritian women* v. *Mauritius*, Communication No. 35/1978 (9 April 1981), UN Doc. CCPR/C/OP/1 at 67 (1984).

[342] Ibid., para 1.2; for commentary on the case see Ghandhi and MacNamee, 'The Family in the UK and the International Covenant on Civil and Political Rights 1966' 5 *International Journal of Law, Policy and the Family* (1991) 104, at p. 109.

[343] *Toonen* v. *Australia*, Communication No. 488/1992 (4 April 1994), UN Doc. CCPR/C/50/D/488/1992 (1994).

provisions on administrative practices and public opinion had affected [the author] and continued to affect him personally'.[344] The existence of risk is also a critical factor in cases where the victim faces being extradited to a non-State party with a strong possibility of facing torture or risk capital punishment. In *Kindler* v. *Canada*, the Committee noted:

> A State party would . . . be in violation of the Covenant if it handed over a person to another State in circumstances in which it was foreseeable that torture would take place. The foreseeablity of the consequence would mean that there was present a violation by the State party, even though the consequence would not occur until later on.[345]

(c) Communications *ratione materiae*

The HRC's competence to examine communications is limited to violations of rights contained within the ICCPR. Other alleged violations (not contained in the Convention) are inadmissible.[346] Thus, allegations of being over-taxed (based on racial discrimination),[347] right to property[348] and the right to asylum[349] or the right to conscientious objection are outside the remit of the HRC's consideration.[350] However, an overlap with rights contained in other international instruments does not render the alleged violation inadmissible.[351] As a general principle complaints must be submitted against a State party, which has violated the victim's rights and not against any other State party.[352] That said, the victim may justifiably argue a violation of his ICCPR rights in case of extradition, deportation or removal to a third State.[353]

---

[344] Ibid. para 5.1.

[345] *Kindler* v. *Canada*, Communication No. 470/1991 (11 November 1993), UN Doc. CCPR/C/48/D/470/1991 (1993), para 6.2; *Roger Judge* v. *Canada*, Communication No. 829/1998, UN Doc. CCPR/C/78/D/829/1998 (2003), para 10.6, *Cox* v. *Canada*, Communication No. 539/1993, UN Doc. CCPR/C/52/D/539/19930 (1994), para 16.1.

[346] *K. L.* v. *Denmark*, Communication No. 59/1979 (26 March 1980), UN Doc. CCPR/C/OP/1 at 24 (1984); *C. E.* v. *Canada*, Communication No. 13/1977 (25 August 1977), UN Doc. CCPR/C/OP/1 at 16 (1984); *H.* v. *The Netherlands*, Communication No. 217/1986, UN Doc. CCPR/C/OP/2 at 70 (1990), Complaints against International Organisations held inadmissible, para 3.2.

[347] *I. M.* v. *Norway*, Communication No. 129/1982 (6 April 1983), UN Doc. CCPR/C/OP/1 at 41 (1984), para 5.

[348] *Armand Anton* v. *Algeria*, Communication No. 1424/2005, UN Doc. CCPR/C/88/D/1424/2005 (2006), para 8.2.

[349] *V. M. R. B.* v. *Canada*, Communication No. 236/1987 (18 July 1988), UN Doc. Supp. No. 40 (A/43/40) at 258 (1988), para 6.3.

[350] *L. T. K.* v. *Finland*, Communication No. 185/1984 (9 July 1985), UN Doc. Supp. No. 40 (A/40/40) at 240 (1985), para 5.2.

[351] See *S. W. M. Broeks* v. *The Netherlands*, Communication No. 172/1984, UN Doc. CCPR/C/OP/2 at 196 (1990), para 12.4; *F. H. Zwaan-de Vries* v. *The Netherlands*, Communication No. 182/1984, UN Doc. Supp. No. 40 (A/42/40) at 160 (1987), paras 12.4–12.5. *Josef Frank Adam* v. *The Czech Republic*, Communication No. 586/1994, UN Doc. CCPR/C/57/D/586/1994 (1996), para 6.2. McGoldrick, above n.1, pp. 163–165.

[352] *Carmen Améndola and Graciela Baritussio* v. *Uruguay*, Communication No. 25/1978, UN Doc. CCPR/C/OP/1 at 136 (1985), para 7.2.

[353] *Kindler* v. *Canada*, Communication No. 470/1991, UN Doc. CCPR/C/48/D/470/1991 (30 July 1993); planned extradition by Canada to the US where the victim risked death penalty potentially constituted a violation of Article 6(2) or Article 7, para 13(2). In this instance no violation. *Roger Judge* v. *Canada*, Communication No. 829/1998, UN Doc. CCPR/C/78/D/829/1998 (2003). HRC held that States parties which have abolished the death penalty have an obligation under Article 6(1) to protect this right and 'may not remove, either by deportation or extradition, individuals from jurisdiction if it may be reasonably anticipated that they will be sentenced to death, without ensuring that that death sentence would not be carried out', para 10.4.

(d) Against whom?

It is only possible to bring an action against a State party and not against an international or regional organisation.[354] It is also important to verify that the concerned State is a party to both the ICCPR and the Optional Protocol. That said, as has been discussed, the individual does not need to be a citizen or a resident of the State party against whom an action is being brought. The material question is whether the individual was subject to the State party's jurisdiction at the time of the alleged violation.[355] Once a State is identified as having accepted obligations under the ICCPR and the Protocol, there are two additional issues which have generated complexities. First, sometimes it can be difficult to identify whether a particular organ is part of the State or a private body, and in this regard the comments in Chapter 1 need to be recalled.[356] State responsibility extends to officially or semi-officially controlled agencies (e.g. an industrial board[357] or a broadcasting corporation).[358] Secondly, since the undertaking on the part of the State is 'to respect and to ensure all individuals . . . the rights' it is also possible to hold the State accountable in situations where although the breach was conducted by a private party, the State had nevertheless the duty to prevent that breach.[359]

(e) Communications *ratione temporis*

In accordance with the general rules of international law, consideration of alleged breaches of the Covenant which occurred before the Covenant and the Protocol had entered into force,[360] with regard to the State party concerned, are beyond the scope of consideration.[361] If, however, the alleged violations have continued after the relevant date,[362] or violations have continued effects,[363] or the alleged offences began and continued even though the initial arrest took place before the entry into force for the relevant State of the Covenant

---

[354] *H.* v. *The Netherlands*, Communication No. 217/1986 (24 March 1988), UN Doc. CCPR/C/OP/1 at 70 (1984), Where the Communication against the author's employer European Patent Office was held inadmissible, para 3.2. Similar to ECHR decision *CFDT* v. *European Communities/their Members* Application No. 8030/77, 13 D & R 231 (European Commission). As a general principle complaints must be submitted against a State party, which has violated or risk violating the victim's rights and not against any other State. That said the victims may justifiably argue a violation of his ICCPR rights in case of extradition, deportation or removal to a third State, *Kindler* v. *Canada*, Communication No. 470/1991 (11 November 1993), UN Doc. CCPR/C/48/D/470/1991 (1993).

[355] Lewis-Anthony and Scheinin, 'Treaty-Based Procedures for Making Human Rights Complaints within the UN System' in Hannum (ed.), above n.20, at p. 49. *Carmen Améndola and Graciela Baritussio* v. *Uruguay*, Communication No. 25/1978, UN Doc. CCPR/C/OP/1 at 136 (1985), para 7.2.

[356] See above chapter 1.

[357] *B. d. B.* et al. v. *The Netherlands*, Communication No. 273/1989 (30 March 1989), UN Doc. Supp. No. 40 (A/44/40) at 286 (1989), para 6.5.

[358] *Leo R- Hertzberg, Uit Mansson, Astrid Nikula and Marko and Tuovi Putkonen, represented by SETA (Organization for Sexual Equality)* v. *Finland*, Communication No. R.14/61 (7 August 1979), UN Doc. Supp. No. 40 (A/37/40) at 161 (1982), para 9.1.

[359] See the Committee's approach in *Herrera Rubio* v. *Colombia*, Communication No. 161/1983 (2 November 1987), UN Doc. Supp. No. 40 (A/43/40) at 190 (1988), para 11. *Elcida Arévalo Perez* et al. v. *Colombia*, Communication No. 181/1984, UN Doc. CCPR/C/37/D/181/1984 (1989), para 10.

[360] *Lucia Sala de Touron* v. *Uruguay*, Communication No. 32/1978 (31 March 1981), UN Doc. CCPR/C/OP/1 at 61 (1984), para 7.

[361] *A. R. S.* v. *Canada*, Communication No. 91/1981 (28 October 1981), UN Doc. CCPR/C/OP/1 at 29 (1984), para 5.1. See also *Könye* v. *Hungary*, Communication No. 520/1992, UN Doc. CCPR/C/50/D/520/1992 (1994). Examining of alleged violation after the entry into force of ICCPR but prior to the entry of OP would also be inadmissible *Ratione Temporis*, para 6.4.

[362] *William Torres Ramirez* v. *Uruguay*, Communication No. 4/1977 (26 August 1977), UN Doc. CCPR/C/OP/1 at 3 (1984), para (c).

[363] *J.L.* v. *Australia*, Communication No. 491/1992, UN Doc. CCPR/C/45/D/491/1992 (1994), para 4.2.

and the Protocol,[364] or the alleged offences have produced effects which within themselves constitute violations after the date where the Covenant to the Protocol became operational,[365] as in *Kulomin* v. *Hungary*[366] and *Gueye* et al. v. *France*,[367] the communication could be declared admissible. If the alleged violation is the nature of wrongful conviction, the critical date is that of the conviction, rather than prior events giving rise to the conviction.[368] However, an independent legal action to obtain remedies for an alleged violation prior to ratification and entry of the Optional Protocol cannot be regarded as part of continuing violation.[369]

(f) Communications between petitioner and the State complained against

Interpretation of Article 1 of the Protocol in relation to Article 2(1) of the Covenant – meaning of 'within its territory and subject to its jurisdiction'

According to Article 2(1) of the Covenant, 'each State Party undertakes to respect and ensure to all individuals within its territory and subject to its jurisdiction the rights recognised in the present Covenant without distinction of any kind'. By contrast Article 1 of the Protocol refers only to the requirement of 'jurisdiction' but not that of territory. The Committee has adopted a broad approach to the meaning of jurisdiction.[370] Thus, in a number of circumstances, complaints have been held admissible for individuals not physically within the territory of the State concerned.[371] In *Samuel Lichtensztejn* v. *Uruguay*[372] the Committee held a petition admissible by a Uruguayan citizen who was resident in Canada, in relation to the non-renewal of his passport. According to the Committee the words, 'subject to its jurisdiction', in Article 1 of the Protocol refer to 'the relationship between the individual and the State in relation to a violation of any of the rights set forth in the Covenant, wherever they occurred'.[373]

---

[364] *Luciano Weinberger Weisz* v. *Uruguay*, Communication No. 28/1978 (29 October 1980), UN Doc. CCPR/C/OP/1 at 57 (1984), para 6(b); *Leopoldo Buffo Carballal* v. *Uruguay*, Communication No. 33/1978 (8 April 1981), UN Doc. CCPR/C/OP/1 at 63 (1984), para 5(a).

[365] *Sandra Lovelace* v. *Canada*, Communication No. R.6/24, UN Doc. Supp. No. 40 (A/36/40) at 166 (1981), para 11.

[366] *Vladimir Kulomin* v. *Hungary*, Communication No. 521/1992, UN Doc. CCPR/C/50/D/521/1992 (1996), para 6.2.

[367] *Ibrahima Gueye* et al. v. *France*, Communication No. 196/1985, UN Doc. CCPR/C/35/D/196/1985 (1989), para 5.3.

[368] *Keun-Tae Kim* v. *Republic of Korea*, Communication No. 574/1994, UN Doc. CCPR/C/64/D/574/1994 (4 January 1999), para 6.2.

[369] *Mr. Eugeniusz Kurowski* v. *Poland*, Communication No. 872/1999, UN Doc. CCPR/C/77/D/872/1999 (2003), para 6.3–6.5.

[370] According to the Human Rights Committee in its General Comment No. 31: 'States Parties are required by article 2, paragraph 1, to respect and to ensure the Covenant rights to all persons who may be within their territory and to all persons subject to their jurisdiction. This means that a State party must respect and ensure the rights laid down in the Covenant to anyone within the power or effective control of that State Party, even if not situated within the territory of the State Party.' See HRC, General Comment No. 31 see above n.26, para 10. *Carmen Améndola and Graciela Baritussio* v. *Uruguay*, Communication No. 25/1978, UN Doc. CCPR/C/OP/1 at 136 (1985), para 7.2.

[371] *Massiotti and Baristussio* v. *Uruguay (25/1978)* – authors resident in Netherlands and Denmark at the time of submitting petition, paras 7.1–7.2. *Mbenge* v. *Zaire*, Communication No. 16/1977 (8 September 1977), UN Doc. Supp. No. 40 (A/38/40) at 134 (1983) M tried *in absentia* in contravention of Article 14(3)(d) even though M was at the time of the trial in Belgium.

[372] *Samuel Lichtensztejn* v. *Uruguay*, Communication No. 77/1980 (30 September 1980), UN Doc. Supp. No. 40 (A/38/40) at 166 (1983), para 6.1.

[373] *Delia Saldias de Lopez* v. *Uruguay*, Communication No. 52/1979 (29 July 1981), UN Doc. CCPR/C/OP/1 at 88 (1984), paras 12.2 – the author's husband kidnapped in Argentina by Urugayan Security forces and subsequently transported to Uruguay. Communication held admissible in both jurisdictions since each of the actions was undertaken by Uruguayan agents; also see a similar decision in *Lilian Celiberti de Casariego* v. *Uruguay*, Communication No. 56/1979, UN Doc. CCPR/C/OP/1 at 92 (1984), para 10.2–3.

Thus, depending on the nature of the alleged complaint it is possible for the victim to be outside the territory of the State party. Therefore, refusal to renew a passport in another State would result in the denial of the right to freedom of movement. Abduction in the territory of another State,[374] violations committed within a territory over which the State has effective control[375] or atrocities committed after occupation of foreign land[376] or having control of a (disputed) territory such as Israel has over Southern Lebanon or West Bank also provide examples.[377] Furthermore, the victim does not have to be in the territory or jurisdiction of the concerned State at the time of the filing of the communication. In *Massiotti and Baristussio* v. *Uruguay*,[378] notwithstanding the fact that the authors were residents in the Netherlands and Sweden at the time of lodging applications, they were acknowledged as victims; according to the Human Rights Committee the jurisdictional criterion was confirmed since at the material time of the alleged violation the authors were within the jurisdiction of Uruguay.[379] The decision in the *Lilian Celiberti de Casariego case*[380] confirms that the Committee sees no problem in declaring a communication from refugees admissible.[381] It would also appear that a communication would be held admissible on the basis that at the relevant time the individual concerned was under the 'effective control' of the respondent State regardless of the theoretical territorial boundaries.[382] This position has been affirmed both by General Comment No. 31,[383] as well as the HRC's jurisprudence.[384] In the absence of a declaration, the provisions in the ICCPR and Optional Protocol

---

[374] Ibid. *Attorney-General of the Government of Israel* v. *Eichmann* 36 ILR (1961) 5; Fawcett, 'The Eichmann Case' 38 *BYIL* (1962) 181; Green, 'The Eichmann Case' 23 *MLR* (1960) 507.

[375] E.g. Israel bears responsibility for implementing the provisions of ICCPR in Israel and occupied territories of West Bank and Gaza. See Concluding Observations of the Human Rights Committee: Israel. 21/08/2003 CCPR/CO/78/ISR (Concluding Observations/Comments). HRC notes: 'the State party's position that the Covenant does not apply beyond its own territory, notably in the West Bank and in Gaza, especially as long as there is a situation of armed conflict in these areas. The Committee reiterates the view, previously spelled out in paragraph 10 of its concluding observations on Israel's initial report (CCPR/C/79/Add.93 of 18 August 1998), that the applicability of the regime of international humanitarian law during an armed conflict does not preclude the application of the Covenant, including article 4 which covers situations of public emergency which threaten the life of the nation. Nor does the applicability of the regime of international humanitarian law preclude accountability of States parties under article 2, paragraph 1, of the Covenant for the actions of their authorities outside their own territories, including in occupied territories. The Committee therefore reiterates that, in the current circumstances, the provisions of the Covenant apply to the benefit of the population of the Occupied Territories, for all conduct by the State party's authorities or agents in those territories that affect the enjoyment of rights enshrined in the Covenant and fall within the ambit of State responsibility of Israel under the principles of public international law.' para 11.

[376] See Committee Against Torture, *Initial Reports of States parties Due in 1997*: Kuwait. 15/10/97. CAT/C/37/Add.1. (State Party Report) paras 53, 54.

[377] See Concluding Comments on Israel, UN Doc. CCPR/C/79 Add. 93 para 10; see generally, Dennis and Surena 'Application of the International Covenant on Civil and Political Rights in Times of Armed Conflict and Military Occupation: The Gap between Legal Theory and State Practice' 6 (2008) *EHRLR* 714.

[378] *Carmen Améndola and Graciela Baritussio* v. *Uruguay*, Communication No. 25/1978, UN Doc. CCPR/C/OP/1 at 136 (1985).

[379] Ibid. para 7.2.

[380] *Lilian Celiberti de Casariego* v. *Uruguay*, Communication No. R.13/56 (17 July 1979), UN Doc. Supp. No. 40 (A/36/40) at 185 (1981).

[381] In fact many communications seem to be presented by individuals in similar situations.

[382] For controversies around 'effective control' in the context of the European Convention on Human Rights see below chapter 7.

[383] General Comment No. 31, above n.27, para 10.

[384] See *Sergio Euben Lopez Burgos* v. *Uruguay*, Communication No. R.12/52, UN Doc. Supp. No. 40 (A/36/40) at 176 (1981), *Delia Saldias de Lopez* v. *Uruguay*, Communication No. 52/1979 (29 July 1981), UN Doc. CCPR/C/OP/1 at 88 (1984), *Celiberti de Casariego* v. *Uruguay* (56/1979); *Mabel Pereira Montero* v. *Uruguay*, Communication No. 106/1981, UN Doc. Supp. No. 40 (A/38/40) at 186 (1983), paras 5, 9.3.

extend to the State itself and its Colonies.[385] Although the obligations to ensure the rights contained in ICCPR are upon States parties alone, a State party may nevertheless incur liability in instances where a State 'takes a decision relating to a person within its jurisdiction and the necessary and foreseeable consequence is that that person's right under the covenant will be violated in another jurisdiction'.[386]

(ii) Admissibility and procedural requirements connected with the content of the petition

(a) Effect on admissibility of the existence of international procedures (Article 5(2)(a))

According to this article, a communication cannot be considered if it contains the same matter as that which is being examined by another international procedure, e.g. by the European Court of Human Rights[387] or by Inter-American Commission on Human Rights.[388] This limitation does not apply to the State reporting system such as those prescribed by Article 16 of the ICESCR[389] or considerations under the previous ECOSOC Resolution 1503 procedure,[390] the ILO freedom of Association Committee,[391] those pending before the United Nations Working Group on Enforced or Involuntary Disappearance established by the Commission on Human Rights in its Resolution 20(XXXVI) February, 1980,[392] or the Country-Studies by the Inter-American Commission on Human Rights.[393] Furthermore, only procedures implemented by inter-State or inter-governmental organisations fall under this provision. NGOs petitioning conducted by, for example, the inter-parliamentary council, Amnesty International or International Commission of Jurists does not constitute a 'procedure of international investigation or settlement' for the purpose of Article 5(2)(a). Similarly, procedures, such as the petition system of the General Assembly Special Committee against Apartheid, and of several *ad hoc* fact-finding bodies on human rights in certain countries do not constitute a 'procedure of international investigation or settlement'.[394] The examination of State reports under the ICESCR does not come within

---

[385] *Wan Kuok Koi* v. *Portugal*, Communication No. 925/2000 (15 December 1999), CCPR/C/73/D/925/2000, para 6.3.

[386] *Kindler* v. *Canada* (470/1991) para 6.2.

[38/] See *D.F.* et al. v. *Sweden*, Communication No. 183/1984, UN Doc. CCPR/C/OP/1 at 55 (1984), para 3. Hence it is irrelevant if the matter had been previously examined by the European Commission on Human Rights *L.E.S.K.* v. *The Netherlands*, Communication No. 381/1989, UN Doc. CCPR/C/45/D/381/1989 (1992) para 5.2 or had been previously considered inadmissible by another body: *H.* v. *The Netherlands*, Communication No. 217/1986, UN Doc. CCPR/C/OP/2 at 70 (1990), para 3.2; *R. L. A. W.* v. *The Netherlands*, Communication No. 372/1989, UN Doc. CCPR/C/40/D/372/1989 (1990), para 6.2. Or the complaint had been withdrawn or the decision had been made on the merits of the case, *Wright* v. *Jamaica*, Communication No. 349/1989, UN Doc. CCPR/C/45/D/349/1989 (1992), para 5.2.

[388] See *Miguel A. Millan Sequeira* v. *Uruguay*, Communication No. 6/1977 (29 July 1980), UN Doc. CCPR/C/OP/1 at 52 (1984) para 9.

[389] *S. W. M. Broeks* v. *the Netherlands*, Communication No. 172/1984 (9 April 1987), UN Doc. Supp. No. 40 (A/42/40) at 139 (1987), para 6.2.

[390] *A et al.* v. *S*, Communication No. 1/1976 (26 January 1978), UN Doc. CCPR/C/OP/1 at 17 (1984).

[391] *John Khemraadi Baboeram* et al. v. *Suriname*, Communication No. 146/1983 and 148 to 154/1983 (4 April 1985), UN Doc. Supp. No. 40 (A/40/40) at 187 (1985), para 9.1.

[392] *Basilio Laureano Atachahua* v. *Peru*, Communication No. 540/1993 (16 April 1996), CCPR/C/56/D/540/1993, para 7.1.

[393] Harris, above n.1, at p. 650.

[394] See Doc. A/33/40 para 582.

the terms of Article 5(2)(a).[395] Note that the admissibility is barred in instances only of complaints under the Optional Protocol being concurrently considered by an international procedure. A matter previously considered, therefore, is not precluded from consideration.[396] Equally, there is nothing to prevent an applicant exhausting another international procedure and then submitting a communication to the HRC.[397] Similarly, the HRC is not precluded from the consideration of a communication which has been withdrawn from another international procedure[398] or submitted by an unrelated third party.

As regards the content or substance of 'the same matter' the HRC has adopted generous rulings. In one case, the Committee determined that a two-line reference to the author in a list of over 100 persons detained did not breach the provisions of Article 5(2)(a).[399] In *Miguel A. Millan Sequeira v. Uruguay* the Committee also decided that a communication submitted to the Inter-American Commission on Human Rights prior to the entry into force of the ICCPR and Optional Protocol could not relate to the event alleged to have taken place after that date.[400] Similarly, the rule was not breached by a subsequent opening of the case by an unrelated third party,[401] or where one of the authors was earlier a co-defendant in proceedings concerning different allegations before the European Commission of Human Rights.[402] A case which has already been examined under another procedure of international investigation could not concern the same matter if it was submitted to that particular procedure prior to the entry into force of the Protocol and the Covenant for that particular State.[403] Nor had the same matter been decided where the author's co-defendant had raised similar issues arising from the same incident before the European Commission on Human Rights.[404]

(b) Effect on admissibility by non-exhaustion of domestic remedies (Article 5(2)(b))

One of the most significant admissibility requirements is that the victim must have exhausted all domestic remedies before attempting to have recourse to the Committee.[405]

---

[395] McGoldrick, above n.1, at p. 183.

[396] *L.E.S.K.* v. *The Netherlands*, Communication No. 381/1989, UN Doc. CCPR/C/45/D/381/1989 (1992) para 5.2.

[397] This formula has allowed communications to be the Human Rights Committee subsequent to a decision being made by the European Human Rights institutions. In order to prevent the Committee acting as an appeal body to the European Court of Human Rights, the Council of Europe made recommendations to its members to enter reservations to the Protocol. Several States have made such a reservation, although quite a few have not. A number of cases have been taken where the dissatisfied applicant has used the Optional Protocol procedure subsequently to a failed application to the European Commission. See *Corriel and Aurik*, where the European Commission had held the case to be 'manifestly ill-founded'. However the communication to the Human Rights Committee was successful. See *Final views of 31 October 1994 [1995] Report of the HRC vol. II*, UN Doc. CCPR/C/57/1, 23. Several European States have made reservations to Article 5(2)(a) construction.

[398] *Raul Sendic Antonaccio* v. *Uruguay*, Communication No. R.14/63 (28 November 1979), UN Doc. Supp. No. 40 (A/37/40) at 114 (1982), paras 7–8. According to the Human Rights Committee 'same matter refers to having 'identical parties to the complaints advanced and facts adduced in support of them', *V. O.* v. *Norway*, Communication No. 168/1984 (17 July 1985), UN Doc. CCPR/C/OP/1 at 48 (1984), para 4.4.

[399] *Miguel A. Millan Sequeira* v. *Uruguay*, Communication No. 6/1977 (29 July 1980), UN Doc. CCPR/C/OP/1 at 52 (1984), para 9(a).

[400] Ibid. para 6(a).

[401] *Lilian Celiberti de Casariego* v. *Uruguay*, Communication No. 56/1979 (29 July 1981), UN Doc. CCPR/C/OP/1 at 92 (1984), para 5(b).

[402] *Duilio Fanali* v. *Italy*, Communication No. 75/1980, UN Doc. Supp. No. 40 (A/38/40) at 160 (1983), para 11.1.

[403] *Alberto Grille Motta* v. *Uruguay*, Communication No. 11/1977 (29 July 1980), UN Doc. CCPR/C/OP/1 at 54 (1984), para 5(a).

[404] *Duilio Fanali* v. *Italy*, Communication No. 75/1980, UN Doc. Supp. No. 40 (A/38/40) at 160 (1983), para 7.2.

[405] *N. S.* v. *Canada*, Communication No. 26/1978 (28 July 1978), UN Doc. CCPR/C/OP/1 at 19 (1984).

Thus, in the event of available (and not unreasonably prolonged) domestic remedies the Committee is barred from considering the communication. While not stated explicitly, HRC has considered both the reasoning and the nature of the provision in the light of existing principles of general international law. Explaining the rationale HRC noted:

> The purpose of article 5, paragraph 2(b), of the Optional Protocol is, inter alia, to direct possible victims of violations of the provisions of the Covenant to seek, in the first place, satisfaction from the competent State party authorities and, at the same time, to enable State parties to examine, on the basis of individual complaints, the implementation, within their territory and by their organs, of the provisions of the Covenant and, if necessary, remedy the violations occurring, before the Committee is seized of the matter.[406]

Domestic remedies mean all judicial and administrative remedies have to be exhausted once a final judgment is rendered from which no appeal is available.[407] However, unlike ECHR, there are no time limits and the approach of the Committee has been flexible and generous. The applicant has the initial burden of proof to show that he has exhausted domestic remedies. After having established the *prima facie* case, the burden of proof shifts to the State to refute the alleged violations. If the domestic remedies are ineffective,[408] unreasonable in nature or excessively onerous,[409] unduly prolonged[410] or are no longer open or are in fact unavailable[411] to the victim then he is not under obligation to exhaust these remedies. However, doubts regarding the effectiveness of remedies and financial burden do not absolve the author of the obligation to exhaust them.[412] Similarly, there is no obligation on the victim to resort to extraordinary or executive (e.g. mercy petition to the Governor-General death row) remedies,[413] or to appeal on points of law in instances where there is already contrary Supreme Court ruling, or to contest where an action is authorised by domestic legislation or constitutional provision. The domestic remedies are also applicable to other comparable international and regional admissibility procedures,

---

[406] *H. K [name deleted]* v. *France*, Communication No. 222/1987, UN Doc. CCPR /C/37/D/222/1987 (1989), para 8.3; also see Ghandhi, 'Some Aspects of the Exhaustion of Domestic Remedies Rule Under the Jurisprudence of the Human Rights Committee' 44 *German Yearbook of International Law* (2001) 485.

[407] *R. T.* v. *France*, Communication No. 262/1987, UN Doc. CCPR/C/35/D/262/1987 (1989), para 7.4.

[408] *Guillermo Ignacio Dermit Barbato and Hugo Haroldo Dermit Barbato* v. *Uruguay*, Communication No. 84/1981, 27 February 1981, UN Doc. Supp. No. 10 (A/30/10) at 124 (1983), para 9.4. HRC has taken the position that where the alleged offence is particularly serious, purely administrative or disciplinary measures are unlikely to constitute effective remedy, in *Josi Vicente and Amado Villafaqe Chaparro, Lums Napolesn Torres Crespo, Angel Marma Torres Arroyo and Antonio Hugues Chaparro Torres* v. *Colombia*, Communication No. 612/1995 (14 June 1994), CCPR/C/60/D/612/1995, para 5.2.

[409] See *T.K.* v. *France*, Communication No. 220/1987 (08 December 1989), UN Doc. CCPR/C/37/D/220/1987, para 8.2. *H.K.* v. *France*, Communication No. 222/1987 08 December 1989, CCPR/C/37/D/222/1987, para 8.2.

[410] *Alba Pietraroia* v. *Uruguay*, Communication No. 44/1979 (27 March 1981), UN Doc. CCPR/C/OP/1 at 65 (1984), para 12.

[411] *Eduardo Bleier* v. *Uruguay*, Communication No. R.7/30 (23 May 1978), UN Doc. Supp. No. 40 (A/37/40) at 130 (1982), para 2.5. The failure to pay court fees because authors were dispersed at different detention centres allowed HRC to consider communication admissible, see *Nqalula Mpandanjila* et al. v. *Zaire*, Communication No. 138/1983, UN Doc. Supp. No. 40 (A/41/40) at 121 (1986), para 5.2.

[412] *Azem Kurbogaj and Ghevdet Kurbogaj* v. *Spain*, Communication No. 1374/2005, UN Doc. CCPR/C/87/D/1374/2005 (2006), para 6.3.

[413] *Earl Pratt and Ivan Morgan* v. *Jamaica*, Communication No. 210/1986 and 225/1987 (6 April 1989), UN Doc. Supp. No. 40 (A/44/40) at 222 (1989) 12.3–12.7. *Paavo Muhonen* v. *Finland*, Communication No. 89/1981, UN Doc. Supp. No. 40 (A/40/40) at 164 (1985), para 11.2.

e.g. International Convention on the Elimination of All forms of Racial Discrimination, CAT and its Optional Protocol.

In the absence of evidence suggesting the existence of ineffective and unreasonably prolonged remedies, the Committee has declined to accept general statements from the State party concerned regarding the non-exhaustion of domestic remedies. The Committee has noted on a number of occasions that the State is required to show that remedies are available and effective.[414]

Whilst the author is required to establish a *prima facie* case of exhaustion of domestic remedies, the HRC has also placed the burden of proof on the State party to rebut the allegations made by the individual because it is the State which is in a stronger position and has access to pertinent information. In *Eduardo Bleier* v. *Uruguay*, the Committee said, in relation to burden of proof, this cannot rest on the author of the communication, especially considering that the author and the State do not always have equal access to the evidence and that frequently the State party alone has access to the information.[415] It is implicit in Article 4(2) of the Optional Protocol that the State party has the duty to investigate in good faith that all the allegations are corroborated by evidence submitted by the author. In cases where the author has submitted allegations supported by substantial witness testimony, and where clarification of the case depends on information exclusively in the hands of the State party, the HRC may consider allegations as substantiated in the absence of satisfactory evidence and explanation by the State party.[416] Similarly, in *William Torres Ramirez* v. *Uruguay*, a general denial by Uruguay of non-exhaustion of domestic remedies was declared as totally insufficient.[417] The author's allegations, where they have been either uncontested or the details are of a general character, have often been accepted unconditionally. This approach of the Committee in relation to burden of proof issues is commendable, commenting on which, Davidson notes, that the Human Rights Committee has signalled

quite clearly in its jurisprudence that it is the State which must show which remedies are specifically available to a complainant when it denies that local remedies have not been exhausted.[418]

(iii) Other admissibility requirements

In general, the victim needs to establish a *prima facie* case. In other words, the communication must not be 'entirely without foundation or merit in legal principle'.[419] Thus, where

---

[414] 'It is incumbent on the State party to prove the effectiveness of remedies the non-exhaustion of which it claims' and the availability of the alleged remedy must be 'reasonably evident', para 6.2. In *C. F.* et al. v. *Canada*, Communication No. 113/1981, 25 July 1983 (nineteenth session), 12 April 1985 (twenty-fourth session), UN Doc. CCPR/C/OP/1 at 13 (1984).

[415] *Eduardo Bleier* v. *Uruguay*, Communication No. R.7/30 (23 May 1978), UN Doc. Supp. No. 40 (A/37/40) at 130 (1982), para 13.1.

[416] *Eduardo Bleier* v. *Uruguay*, Communication No. R.7/30 (23 May 1978), UN Doc. Supp. No. 40 (A/37/40) at 130 (1982), para 11.2.

[417] *William Torres Ramirez* v. *Uruguay*, Communication No. 4/1977 (26 January 1978), UN Doc. CCPR/C/OP/1 at 4 (1984), para (b).

[418] Davidson, *The Inter-American Court of Human Rights* (Dartmouth, 1992) at pp. 71–72.

[419] Ghandhi, above n.1, at p. 181.

a petitioner is complaining, e.g. of breach of the right to fair trial and racial discrimination, he or she needs to substantiate his claims with some evidence.[420] According to Article 3 of the Optional Protocol, the Committee is barred from considering any communication that is anonymous. The author of the communication is required to identify him or herself though the Committee may agree (depending on the circumstances) not to reveal his or her identity to the State. The communication must also not abuse the right of submission, or be incompatible with the provisions of the Covenant.[421] Communications have rarely been held inadmissible because of abuse of the right to petition.[422]

10 CONCLUSIONS

The ICCPR has had considerable influence in shaping modern human rights law: with its universal reach, the Covenant has been rightly described as 'probably the most important human rights treaty in the world'.[423] As at the end of April 2009, 163 States had ratified the Covenant – over three-quarters of the States. These include States from all continents, with varying constitutional, political and religious affiliations and developmental stages. For these States, the ICCPR presents a binding document requiring implementation of the rights as established in the text of the treaty.[424] Even for those States which have refused to become parties to this treaty, it is no longer possible to evade the provisions – the Covenant is frequently used as evidence of customary international law or general principles of international law. The standards set out in the treaty provide a barometer for measuring State records.

Since the First Optional Protocol procedure came into effect in March 1979, as of 9 January 2009 the HRC had found 489 violations of various rights contained in the ICCPR. An analysis of the jurisprudence of HRC provides an impressive exhibition of the manner in which a body with limited resources and powers could nevertheless exert influence to protect the rights of individuals. The Committee has over the past two decades emerged as the most important organ striving for the universal enforcement of human rights within the framework of the United Nations. Imaginative and ambitious ideas have been taken up. Reference could be made to the provisions for informing the respondent State of desirable

[420] *C. L. D.* v. *France*, Communication No. 228/1987 (18 July 1988), UN Doc. Supp. No. 40 (A/43/40) at 252 (1988).
[421] Article 3 Optional Protocol.
[422] See *K. L.* v. *Denmark*, Communication No. 59/1979 (26 March 1980), UN Doc. CCPR/C/OP/1 at 24 (1984). The Committee found that the author's submission an abuse of the right to petition. K.L.'s communication related to the author's taxable income with the author claiming violation of Articles 14 and 26 of ICCPR. He had previously submitted a similar communication, which had been held inadmissible because of lack of factual evidence and substantiation of the actual violation of the rights. In the present instance there was a similar lack of substantiation. It was held inadmissible and an abuse of the right to petition. Although this is becoming increasingly so, regarding communications submitted a significant period of time after the violation with little or no justification for such a delay. *Ernst Zundel* v. *Canada*, Communication No. 1341/2005, UN Doc. CCPR/C/89/D/1341/2005 (2007), para 6.5, *Armand Anton* v. *Algeria*, Communication No. 1424/2005, UN Doc. CCPR/C/88/D/1424/2005 (2006), Concurring opinion of Committee members Ms. Elisabeth Palm, Sir Nigel Rodley and Mr. Nisuke Ando.
[423] Joseph, Schultz and Castan, above n.1, at p. 4.
[424] McGoldrick, above n.1, at p. 381.

interim measures 'to avoid irreparable damage to the victim'[425] (which is especially important in death penalty cases) and the publication of its final decisions without abridgement in spite of Article 6 of the Protocol providing merely for a 'summary of its activities'.[426] In contrast to the ECHR, the grounds for rejecting individual communications are restrictively applied. There is no time limit as compared to the ECHR's six-month rule. While the Committee has utilised concepts of other human rights systems such as the ECHR's doctrine of 'margin of appreciation',[427] it has been very restrictive in granting discretionary powers which are likely to be misused.[428] In addition to finding violations, HRC has reiterated calls for providing an effective remedy as required under Article 2(3) of the ICCPR. Significantly, there is an elaboration of what constitutes an effective remedy, e.g. the release of victims, commutation of death sentence and provisions for compensation. HRC has used imaginative policies to enhance consultative processes. In March 2003, HRC was briefed by a member of UN Security Council Counter Terrorism Committee. In 2003, the vice-chairperson of HRC briefed the Security Council on issues relating to the significance of human rights law.[429] For the purpose of submitting communications, costs to be spent on petitioning are relatively small and there are no specific requirements relating to the language in which communications ought to be made. Despite these positive features, there are significant difficulties faced by the Committee.

The Committee is not a court of law and its views are not binding upon relevant parties.[430] There is no possibility of sanctions (comparable to ECHR) attached to the Committee's decisions nor are any provisions made for the appointment of an *ad hoc* investigation committee (as in ECOSOC Resolution 1503 procedure)[431] nor for the appointment of an *ad hoc* conciliation commission as in its own inter-State procedure.[432] Nevertheless, as

---

[425] Rule 92 [formerly Rule 86] of the Rules of Procedure provides authority to the Committee before forwarding its [final] views on the communication to the relevant State party to inform that State 'of its views as to whether interim measures may be desirable to avoid irreparable damage to the victim of the alleged violation'. See *O. E.* v. *S*, Communication No. 22/1977 (25 January 1978), UN Doc. CCPR/C/OP/1 at 5 (1984), para (c); *Alberto Altesor* v. *Uruguay*, Communication No. R.2/10, UN Doc. Supp. No. 40 (A/37/40) at 122 (1982), para 2. In recent years, the Committee has emphasised that States are bound to comply with its views on interim measures and has expressed regret where in disregard to Rule 92, the relevant party has executed an individual whose application was still pending before the Committee. See *Piandiong* et al. v. *The Philippines*, Communication No. 869/1999, UN Doc. CCPR/C/70/D/869/1999 (2000), paras 5.1–5.4; *Anthony B. Mansaraj* et al.; *Gborie Tamba* et al.; *Abdul Karim Sesay* et al. v. *Sierra Leone*, Communication No. 839/1998, UN Doc. CCPR/C/72/D/839/1998 (2001), para 5.2; *Barno Saidova* v. *Tajikistan*, Communication No. 964/2001, UN Doc. CCPR/C/81/D/964/2001 (2004), paras 1.2, 4.1–4.4; *Glenn Ashby* v. *Trinidad and Tobago*, Communication No. 580/1994, UN Doc. CCPR/C/74/D/580/1994 (2002), paras 7.5, 10.8–10.10.

[426] Article 6 Optional Protocol.

[427] *Leo R- Hertzberg, Uit Mansson, Astrid Nikula and Marko and Tuovi Putkonen, represented by SETA (Organization for Sexual Equality)* v. *Finland*, Communication No. R.14/61 (7 August 1979), UN Doc. Supp. No. 40 (A/37/40) at 161 (1982), para 10.3. See below chapter 6.

[428] According to Professor Harris: 'No margin of appreciation doctrine is applied under the International Covenant on Civil and Political Rights either, largely for fear of State abuse.' See Harris, 'Regional Protection of Human Rights: The Inter-American Achievement' in Harris and Livingstone (eds), above n.64, pp. 1–29 at p. 10.

[429] Farrior, 'International Reporting Procedures' in Hannum (ed.) above n.20, pp. 189–215 at p. 200.

[430] Crawford, 'The UN Human Rights Treaty System: A System in Crisis' in Alston and Crawford (eds), above n.258, at p. 2. Nor does examination of individual communications under the Optional Protocol takes the form of judicial proceedings. Article 5(1) of the Protocol provides that the Committee is to consider communications it has received 'in the light of all written information made available to it'. Cf. Article 22(4) CAT and Article 7(1) OP-CEDAW, where there is no such requirement of 'written information'.

[431] See above chapter 3.

[432] See above inter-State procedure.

noted earlier, interpreting a legally binding instrument, the HRC views are issued 'in a judicial spirit'[433] which has influenced States to changes their legislative and administrative practices. On a more holistic level, the essential spirit of the First Optional Protocol and the purpose for which the Committee was established must not be overlooked. The Committee was never perceived to be a Supreme Court for international protection of human rights. The Protocol and any international human rights system can only work effectively in co-operation with States parties' involvement and co-operation. Although limited to those States that are parties to the Protocol, the procedure presents the only attempt within the UN system to deal with cases from individuals covering a broad range of civil and political rights in a quasi-judicial procedure and to render an opinion upon the merits of the case.

Before concluding, a number of concerns and limitations faced by the Committee under the Optional Protocol need to be mentioned. Firstly, the absence of sanctions attached to the Committee's views does, in fact, mean that the full potential of the international system of human rights protection is not realised. While the Committee has persuaded many States to change their laws and administrative practices, the overall position has appropriately been described as 'disappointing'.[434] The Committee's initiative of establishing 'Special Rapporteur for Follow-up on Concluding Observations', as considered earlier has only brought limited results. This situation is certainly unsatisfactory when compared to the European human rights system. Secondly, attached to this lack of sanctions is the concern for non-co-operation or even non-recognition of the Committee's decisions. We have already considered the Committee's efforts to ensure compliance and co-operation. These efforts are only partially successful. Thirdly, no system of legal aid exists for those seeking to invoke the (Optional Protocol) jurisdiction of the Committee.[435] Last, but not least, the Committee, like other UN bodies, is facing a substantial crisis of personnel and funding. In its work it is facing a huge backlog of at least three years.[436] There is an urgent need to support the Committee with additional funds, and it would be useful to hold a number of extraordinary sessions to overcome the existing backlog.

---

[433] Selected Decisions of the Human Rights Committee under the Optional Protocol, CCPR/C/OP/2 (1988), 1.

[434] McGoldrick, above n.1, at p. 202.

[435] Butler, 'Legal Aid Before Human Rights Treaty Monitoring Bodies' 49 *ICLQ* (2000) 360.

[436] Steiner, 'Individual Claims in a World of Massive Violations: What Role for the Human Rights Committee?' in Alston and Crawford (eds), above n.258, pp. 15–53 at p. 33.

6 The International Covenant on Economic, Social and Cultural Rights[1]

1 INTRODUCTION

> All human rights are universal, indivisible and interdependent and interrelated. The international community must treat human rights globally in a fair and equal manner, on the same footing, and with the same emphasis.[2]

The Vienna Declaration and Programme of Action (1993) clearly recognises the inter-relationship and interdependence of civil and political rights, and economic, social and cultural rights. This recognition is present in varying degrees in all the major human rights instruments. As we have already noted, the UDHR[3] affirms the interdependence and interrelatedness of all human rights.[4] The ICCPR also retains as its primary article the right to self-determination, which is a collective right, the right of peoples.[5] It also contains Articles on equal protection of the law (Article 26), right to freedom of association (Article 22(1)), right to life (Article 6(1)) and rights of minorities including their cultural rights (Article 27). Issue or group specific treaties such as the Race Convention,[6] Women's

---

[1] Baderin and McCorquodale (eds) *Economic, Social and Cultural Rights in Action* (Oxford University Press, 2007); Beetham, 'What Future for Economic and Social Rights?' 43 *Political Studies* (1995) 41; Craven, *The International Covenant on Economic, Social and Cultural Rights: A Perspective on its Development* (Clarendon Press, 1995); Eide, Krause and Rosas (eds), *Economic, Social and Cultural Rights: A Textbook* (Martinus Nijhoff Publishers, 2001); Eide, 'Realization of Social and Economic Rights and the Minimum Threshold Approach' 10 *HRLJ* (1989) 35; Harris, *Cases and Materials on International Law* (Sweet & Maxwell, 2004) pp. 735–758; Peces-Barba, 'Reflections on Economic, Social and Cultural Rights' 2 *HRLJ* (1981) 281; Steiner, Alston and Goodman (eds), *International Human Rights in Context* (Oxford University Press, 2008) pp. 263–374; Ssenyonjo, *Economic, Social and Cultural Rights in International Law* (Hart Publishing, 2009); Trubek, 'Economic, Social and Cultural Rights in the Third World' in Meron (ed.), *Human Rights in International Law* (Clarendon Press, 1984) pp. 205–271; Tomuschat, *Human Rights: Between Idealism and Realism* (Oxford University Press, 2008); Sepúlveda, *The Nature of the Obligations under the International Covenant on Economic, Social and Cultural Rights* (Intersentia, 2003); Waldron, 'A Rights-Based Critique of Constitutional Rights' 13 *Oxford Journal of Legal Studies* (1993) 18.
[2] *Vienna Declaration and Programme of Action* (1993) para 5 (pt 1). Adopted by the United Nations World Conference on Human Rights, UN Doc. A/CONF.157/23 12 July 1993. Scott, 'Reaching Beyond (without Abandoning) the Category of "Economic, Social and Cultural Rights"', 21 *HRQ* (1999) 633.
[3] 10 December 1948, UN GA Res. 217 A(III), UN Doc. A/810 at 71 (1948).
[4] See above chapter 4.
[5] Adopted at New York, 16 December 1966. Entered into force 23 March 1976. GA Res. 2200A (XXI) UN Doc. A/6316 (1966) 999 U.N.T.S. 171; 6 I.L.M. (1967) 368. See above chapter 5.
[6] Convention on the Elimination of All Forms of Racial Discrimination. (CERD), Adopted and opened for signature and ratification by General Assembly resolution 2106 (XX) of 21 December 1965, entry into force 4 January 1969, in accordance with Article 19. UN *Treaty Series*, vol. 660, p. 195. See also Amendment to Article 8, adopted 15 January 1992, not yet in force, UN GA Res. 47/111.

Convention,[7] Child Rights Convention,[8] Migrant Workers Convention[9] and the Convention on the Rights of the Disabled[10] cover both civil and political rights as well as economic, social and cultural rights, with their implementation mechanisms targeting comprehensively the rights contained in these treaties. Similarly, other international and regional human rights instruments reiterate the overlap between economic, social and cultural rights, and civil and political rights. Regional human rights treaties, primarily represented by the ECHR,[11] the American Convention on Human Rights (ACHR)[12] and the AFCHPR,[13] indulge in various ways to protect economic, social and cultural rights, while retaining a focus on civil and political rights.

This chapter begins by presenting an examination of the argument of superiority of civil and political rights *vis-à-vis* economic, social and cultural rights. It then focuses on the ICESCR and provides a consideration of the rights contained in the International Covenant on Economic, Social and Cultural Rights (ICESCR). It goes on to consider the implementation mechanisms and the machinery that has been deployed to monitor the application of economic, social and cultural rights. There is a brief consideration of innovative though highly useful practices such as the day for general discussion on a specific issue or issues. The chapter, then briefly discusses the Optional Protocol to ICESCR and concludes with some critical observations regarding the limitations within international human rights with respect to the attainment of economic, social and cultural rights.

2 ARGUMENTS OVER THE SUPERIORITY OF RIGHTS

Notwithstanding the above noted interaction, there have been divisions over the status of economic, social and cultural rights. A variety of arguments continue to be put forward asserting the superiority of civil and political rights. Civil and political rights are advocated as being more important since they arguably form a critical basis for protecting human rights.[14]

---

[7] Convention on the Elimination of All Forms of Discrimination Against Women (CEDAW), adopted and opened for signature and ratification on 19 December 1979 by a General Assembly Resolution, entry into force 3 September 1981, in accordance with Article 27(1). UN *Treaty Series*, vol. 1249, p. 13. Optional Protocol to CEDAW, Adopted 6 October 1999, entry into force 22 December 2000, in accordance with Article 16(1), UN Doc. A/RES/54/4. See also Amendment to Article 20(1) CEDAW, adopted 22 November 1995, not yet in force, UN Doc. CEDAW/SP/1995/2.

[8] Convention on the Rights of the Child (CRC), adopted and opened for signature, ratification and accession by General Assembly Resolution 44/25 of 20 November 1989, entry into force 2 September 1990, in accordance with Article 49. UN *Treaty Series*, vol. 1577, p. 3. Amendment to Article 43(2) CRC, adopted 12 December 1995, entry into force 18 November 2002.

[9] International Convention on the Protection of the Rights of All Migrant Workers and Members of Their Families. Adopted by General Assembly resolution 45/158 of 18 December 1990, entry into force 1 July 2003 in accordance with Article 87(1), UN Doc. A/RES/45/158.

[10] Convention on the Rights of Persons with Disabilities, Adopted 13 December 2006, entry into force 3 May 2008, in accordance with Article 45, UN Doc. A/61/61. Optional Protocol to the Convention on the Rights of Persons with Disabilities, adopted 13 December 2006, entry into force 3 May 2008 in accordance with Article 13. UN Doc. A/61/611. See in particular Article 24 (education), Article 27 (work/employment) and Article 28 (adequate standard of living and social protection).

[11] Signed at Rome, 4 November 1950. Entered into force 3 September 1953. 213 U.N.T.S. 221; E.T.S. 5.

[12] Signed at San Jose, 22 November 1969. Entered into force 18 July 1978. 1144 U.N.T.S. 123; O.A.S. *Treaty Series* No. 36, O.A.S. Off. Rec. OEA/Ser.L.V/II.82 doc.6 rev.1 at 25 (1992).

[13] Adopted on 27 June 1981. Entered into force 21 October, 1986, OAU Doc. CAB/LEG/67/3 Rev. 5, 21 I.L.M. (1982) 58.

[14] Leckie, 'Another Step Towards Indivisibility: Identifying the Key Features of Violations of Economic, Social and Cultural Rights' 20 *HRQ* (1998) 81 at p. 82.

This assumption of the superiority of civil and political rights has, as Leckie notes, led to gross violations and neglect of economic and social rights. He notes:

> when people die of hunger or thirst, or when thousands of urban poor and rural dwellers are evicted from their homes, the world still tends to blame nameless economic or 'developmental' forces, or the simple inevitability of human deprivation, before placing liability at the doorstep of the state. Worse yet, societies increasingly blame victims of such violations for creating their own dismal fates, and in some countries, they are even characterized as criminals on this basis alone.[15]

Attached to the assumption of the superiority of civil and political rights is the claim that these rights establish immediately binding obligations, whereas the language of economic, social and cultural rights largely represents undertakings of a progressive nature.[16] 'Progressive achievement' is thus described as the linchpin of ICESCR.[17]

A view very commonly held by commentators and State representatives is that, in order to ensure civil and political rights, governments are required to abstain from certain activities (e.g. not to conduct torture or to deprive people of their liberties). In comparison, economic, social and cultural rights are believed to require States' intervention and are, therefore, seen as positive rights. While in some instances this distinction can be made out, in other cases of protecting civil and political rights, active State action is equally required.[18] Associated with this point is the claim that civil and political rights are easier to enforce and implement since the cost implications are not so significant – the 'liberal [civil and political] rights directed against undue interference, it was argued were "directly enforceable before courts"'.[19]

Furthermore, it is argued that economic, social and cultural rights obligations are much more difficult to implement since they remain dependent on the economic strength of the State in question. Such assumptions and cost-based analyses have been termed as a 'gross oversimplification'[20] and are in actual fact proven to be incorrect. While it is true that some economic and social obligations (e.g. to provide everyone with a decent standard of living, to ensure that no one is hungry or unemployed) represent substantial commitments, fulfilling many of the civil and political rights can be equally onerous. Thus, for example,

---

[15] Ibid. p. 82.

[16] See Harris, above n.1, at p. 741; Trubek, 'Economic, Social and Cultural Rights in the third World' in Meron (ed.), above n.1, at pp. 210–212.

[17] Alston and Quinn, 'The Nature and Scope of State Parties' Obligations under the International Covenant on Economic, Social and Cultural Rights' 9 *HRQ* (1987) 156 at p. 172; according to Robertson and Merrills, 'It is thus quite clear that this is what is known as a promotional convention, that is to say, it does not set out rights which the parties are required to implement immediately, but rather lists standards which they undertake to promote and which they pledge to secure progressively, to the greatest extent possible, having regard to their resources': Robertson and Merrills, *Human Rights in the World: An Introduction to the Study of the International Protection of Human Rights* (Manchester University Press, 1996) at p. 276; McGoldrick, *The Human Rights Committee: Its Role in the Development of the International Covenant on Civil and Political Rights* (Clarendon Press, 1991) pp. 11–13; Van Bueren, 'Combatting Child Poverty – Human Rights Approaches' 21 *HRQ* (1999) 680 at p. 684.

[18] Beetham, above n.1, at p. 51.

[19] Nowak, *UN Covenant on Civil and Political Rights: CCPR Commentary* (N.P. Engel) 2005, paras 1–16.

[20] Eide, 'Economic, Social and Cultural Rights as Human Rights' in Eide, Krause and Rosas (eds), above n.1, pp. 9–28 at p. 24.

satisfying all the segments of the right to fair trial can be a financially demanding obligation.[21] Liebenberg mentions the right to vote and equality rights as having considerable budgetary and financial commitments.[22]

Those advocating the superiority of civil and political rights point to the differences in approach within the substantive provisions, as well as in the measures of implementation.[23] We have already noted the approach adopted in ICCPR while dealing with civil and political rights. Contrast these provisions with those of ICESCR. Whereas the ICCPR relies on an authoritative terminology such as 'everyone has the right', 'no one shall be', and has provided definitive rights, the ICESCR relies on imprecise terminology; usage of such terms as 'recognition' arguably makes it difficult to regard them as legally enforceable rights. The ICESCR has also been criticised for advancing relatively novel claims as 'rights'. Commentators have doubted the existence of such economic 'rights' as the 'right to food'.[24]

The apparent weak and vague nature of the provisions contained within the ICESCR has led some critics to question whether the treaty provides legally binding and enforceable rights. Although not entirely accurate, there is a measure of truth in the views of these critics. As we shall analyse in the course of this chapter (before the adoption of the Optional Protocol to the ICESCR), the implementation mechanisms applicable for ICESCR were much weaker when compared to ICCPR and the system, unlike the ICCPR, did not have an inter-State procedure or an individual communications procedure. However, On 18 June 2008, the Human Rights Council adopted an Optional Protocol on Economic, Social and Cultural Rights, which provides both for an inter-State communications procedure as well as an individual complaints procedure.[25] As shall be examined in due course, on 10 December 2008, the United Nations General Assembly unanimously adopted the Optional Protocol to the International Covenant on Economic, Social and Cultural Rights.

3 GENERAL NATURE OF OBLIGATIONS: PROGRESSIVE REALISATION OF RIGHTS

In Article 2 of the Covenant, the nature of the obligations undertaken by States parties is spelled out. According to Article 2(1):

> Each State Party to the present Covenant undertakes to take steps, individually and through international assistance and co-operation, especially economic and technical, to the maximum of its available resources, with a view to achieving progressively the full realization of the rights recognized in the present Covenant by all appropriate means, including particularly the adoption of legislative measures.

---

[21] See the Human Rights Committee's General Comment No. 32 *Article 14: Right to Equality before Courts and Tribunals and to a Fair Trial* (Nineteenth Session, 9–27 July 2007) CCPR/C/32, 23 August 2007.

[22] Liebenberg, 'The Protection of Economic and Social Rights in Domestic Legal Systems' in Eide, Krause and Rosas (eds), above n.1, pp. 55–84, at p. 60.

[23] For a rebuttal of these claims see Foster, *International Refugee Law and Socio-Economic Rights: Refugee from Deprivation* (Cambridge University Press, 2007) pp. 162–163.

[24] See Bard, 'The Right to Food' 70 *Iowa Law Review* (1985) 1279. *Cf.* Van Hoof, 'The Legal Nature of Economic, Social and Cultural Rights: A Rebuttal of Some Traditional Views' in Alston and Tomaševski (eds), *The Right to Food* (Martinus Nijhoff Publishers, 1984) pp. 97–110.

[25] See below for more details on the Optional Protocol. See Tomuschat, above n.1, at pp. 197–199.

Some commentators doubt whether the Covenant imposes obligations carrying immediate legal affect. The matter has been controversial, although the correct view appears to be that the Article imposes legal obligations that are required to be given immediate legal affect by the State party concerned. Thus, according to the Limburg Principles:[26]

> [t]he obligation 'to achieve progressively the full realization of the rights' requires States parties to move as expeditiously as possible towards the realization of the rights. Under no circumstances shall this be interpreted as implying for States the right to defer indefinitely efforts to ensure full realization. On the contrary all States parties have the obligation to begin immediately to take steps to fulfil their obligations under the Covenant.[27]

These obligations however are limited to 'taking steps' with a view to 'achieving progressively the full realization of the rights' that are recognised in the treaty. It is interesting to note that the contrasting provisions of the ICCPR provide an obligation on States to 'respect and to ensure'. The provisions of Article 2(1) have been further explored by the Committee's General Comment on the Nature of State Parties Obligation (Article 2, para 1), where the Committee notes 'while the Covenant provides for progressive realization and acknowledges the constraints due to the limits of available resources, it also imposes various obligations which are of immediate effect'.[28] The Committee has emphasised that even in situations where there are inadequate resources, the obligation remains on the State party to try and ensure the enjoyment of rights.[29]

While legislative means are required, they do not represent the entire scheme of ensuring implementation and it is a matter for the State concerned to determine whatever means (legislative or otherwise) would be required to respect, protect and fulfil the rights recognised within the Covenant. In its third General Comment, the Committee observed that the phrase

> 'by all appropriate means' must be given its full and natural meaning while each State party must decide for itself which means are the most appropriate under the circumstances with respect to each of the rights, the 'appropriateness' of the means chosen will not always be self-evident. It is therefore desirable that States parties' reports should indicate not only the measures that have been taken but also the basis on which they are considered to be most 'appropriate' under the circumstances. However, the ultimate determination as to whether all appropriate measures have been taken remains one for the Committee to make.[30]

---

[26] These principles represent guidelines on the implementation of the Covenant. *The Limburg Principles on the Implementation of the International Covenant on Economic, Social and Cultural Rights*, UN ECCOR. Res. Commission on Human Rights, 43rd, Sess. Agenda Item 8, UN Doc. E/CN.4/1987/17Annex (1987), reprinted as 'The Limburg Principles on the Implementation of the International Covenant on Economic, Social and Cultural Rights' 9 *HRQ* (1987) 122.

[27] Limburg Principles, principle 21. See also *the Statement to the Committee on Economic, Social and Cultural Rights* by B.G. Ramcharan, Deputy High Commissioner, ICESCR, 25th. Session, 23 April 2001.

[28] CESCR General Comment 3, *The Nature of States Parties Obligations (Art 2 para 1)* General Comment No. 3 (14/12/90). E/1991/23, Annex III UN ESCOR, Supp. (No. 3), 84, para 1.

[29] Ibid. UN Doc. E/1991/23, para 11. On the question of whether ICESCR provides for transnational obligations on the part States parties, Skogly and Gibney note that 'a preliminary conclusion can be drawn that the drafters of the ICESCR have envisioned that the fulfilment of these rights has transnational dimensions as well as domestic ones' Skogly and Gibney, 'Transnational Human Rights Obligations' 24 *HRQ* (2002), 781, at p. 791.

[30] CESCR General Comment 3, above n.28, para 4.

Article 2(2) represents the crucial non-discrimination provision within the Covenant. According to this provision the rights contained within the treaty are to be exercised without 'discrimination of any kind as to race, colour, sex, language, religion, political or other opinion, national or social origin, property, birth or other status'. As we shall analyse in the course of this study, the norm of non-discrimination informs the entirety of human rights law. The effective application of a regime of equality and non-discrimination is particularly important in the context of ensuring economic, social and cultural rights. The significance of this principle is underlined by Craven when he notes:

> [i]t is very much apparent that a notion of equality runs through the heart of the Covenant. The Covenant assumes the creation or maintenance of State welfare institutions and social safety nets (for example the provision of housing, food, clothing and social security), and as such is openly redistributionist.[31]

States are required not only to provide *de jure* equality, but are allowed to introduce distinctions amongst various sections of the community in order to ensure *de facto* equality. According to one commentator the policy of affirmative action has been sanctioned by the terminology of Article 2(1) itself.[32]

(i) Gender equality

The equal rights of men and women to the enjoyment of all human rights is one of the fundamental principles recognised under international law and is enshrined in international human rights instruments. Gender equality is a theme which runs across the human rights regime. As we have examined, the International Bill of Rights places emphasis on the equal rights of men and women. Gender equality is also established in numerous other instruments and, as we shall consider, the Convention on the Elimination of All Forms of Discrimination Against Women and its Protocol have attracted considerable attention. Equality between men and women in the context of economic, social and cultural rights invokes particular sensitivities. Despite some recognition of women's rights, human development has not attained a stage whereby gender-based equality is universally acknowledged, let alone applied within the domestic constitutional apparatus – frequently set against deep rooted traditional, cultural and religious patterns.[33] In aiming to eradicate discrimination based on sex and providing for genuine gender equality, Article 3 of ICESCR provides for the equal right of men and women to the enjoyment of the rights articulated in the Covenant. This provision is founded on Article 1, para 3, of the United Nations Charter and Article 2 of the Universal Declaration of Human Rights. Except for the reference to ICESCR, it is identical to Article 3 of the International Covenant on Civil and Political Rights (ICCPR), which was drafted at the same time.[34] Article 3, restates the fundamental position in relation to ensuring equality between men and

---

[31] Craven, above n.1, at pp. 157–158.
[32] Ibid. pp. 157–158.
[33] For further discussion see below chapter 15.
[34] CESCR, *Substantive Issues Arising in the Implementation of the International Covenant on Economic, Social and Cultural Rights: General comment No. 16 (2005) The Equal Right of Men and Women to the Enjoyment of all Economic, Social and Cultural Rights* (Article 3 of the International Covenant on Economic, Social and Cultural Rights) E/C.12/2005/4 11 August 2005, para 1.

women in the usage of the rights contained in the Covenant. The principle of establishing *de facto* equality through policies of affirmative action is evident in the ICESCR Committee's approach towards Article 3. The ICESCR Committee in its General Comment notes as follows:

> The enjoyment of human rights on the basis of equality between men and women must be understood comprehensively. Guarantees of non-discrimination and equality in international human rights treaties mandate both *de facto* and *de jure* equality. *De jure* (or formal) equality and *de facto* (or substantive) equality are different but interconnected concepts. Formal equality assumes that equality is achieved if a law or policy treats men and women in a neutral manner. Substantive equality is concerned, in addition, with the effects of laws, policies and practices and with ensuring that they do not maintain, but rather alleviate, the inherent disadvantage that particular groups experience.[35]

The Committee goes on to make the point that:

> The principles of equality and non-discrimination, by themselves, are not always sufficient to guarantee true equality. Temporary special measures may sometimes be needed in order to bring disadvantaged or marginalized persons or groups of persons to the same substantive level as others. Temporary special measures aim at realizing not only *de jure* or formal equality, but also *de facto* or substantive equality for men and women. However, the application of the principle of equality will sometimes require that States parties take measures in favour of women in order to attenuate or suppress conditions that perpetuate discrimination. As long as these measures are necessary to redress *de facto* discrimination and are terminated when *de facto* equality is achieved, such differentiation is legitimate.[36]

Article 3 has also attracted similar observations from bodies engaged in economic, social and cultural rights, and support is invoked through an examination of international instruments that focus on gender equality. Commenting on this article, Principle 45 of the Limburg Principles observes that '[i]n the application of article 3 due regard should be paid to the Declaration and Convention on the Elimination of All Forms of Discrimination against Women and other relevant instruments and the activities of the supervisory committee (CEDAW) under the said Convention'.[37] As we shall examine in this book, the economic, social and cultural dynamics of gender-based equality remain a significant though challenging aspect of the human rights paradigm.[38]

Article 4 provides for a general limitation clause which is applicable to the substantive rights contained in Part III of the treaty. Article 5 contains what can be termed as a saving clause which creates the effect that treaty provisions cannot be used as a justification either for the violation of the rights contained therein or already established rights elsewhere.[39]

---

[35] Ibid. para 7.
[36] Ibid. para 15.
[37] Limburg Principles, principle 45.
[38] See below chapter 15.
[39] Alston and Quinn, above n.17, at p. 192.

4 SELF-DETERMINATION AND ECONOMIC, SOCIAL AND CULTURAL RIGHTS

Article 1 of the Covenant deals with the important right of self-determination. As noted earlier, the provisions within the article are identical to those of Article 1 in the ICCPR. Our earlier discussion regarding this needs to be recalled,[40] as the present analysis will focus on those aspects of self-determination which are directly relevant to economic, social and cultural rights. The right to self-determination, which includes economic self-determination, has been clearly established as a right in international law, and forms a part of the norms of *jus cogens*.[41] The inspiration to incorporate within the Covenant, the right to freely dispose of their natural wealth and resources was drawn from the 1962 General Assembly Resolution on 'Permanent Sovereignty over Natural Resources'.[42] In conceptualising the economic, social and cultural dimensions of this right to self-determination, it is important to mention that the impetus for the development of a legally binding right of self-determination came from the developing and socialist world.[43] The *travaux préparatoires* of the human rights covenants confirm that a number of developing States were at the forefront of incorporating the right to economic self-determination. For these States, a cardinal aspect of self-determination was the right to permanent sovereignty over natural wealth and resources along with a right to nationalisation of property.[44]

In so far as economic self-determination is concerned, this position is established within Article 1 of the Covenant. According to Article 1:

> (1.) All Peoples have the right of self-determination. By virtue of that right they freely . . . pursue their economic, social and cultural development. (2.) All peoples may, for their own ends, freely dispose of their natural wealth and resources without prejudice to any obligations arising out of international economic co-operation, based upon the principle of mutual benefit, and international law. In no case may a people be deprived of its own means of subsistence.

Article 2(3) goes on to assert the point that:

> Developing countries, with due regard to human rights and their national economy, may determine to what extent they would guarantee the economic rights recognised in the present Covenant to non-nationals.

---

[40] See above chapter 5.

[41] On *jus cogens* see above chapter 2. For further discussion on the relationship of self-determination with *jus cogens* see below chapter 14.

[42] GA Res. 1803 (XVII) 14 December 1962. See Rosas, 'The Right to Self-Determination' in Eide, Krause and Rosas (eds), 111–118, at p. 114.

[43] Thus, e.g. the Saudi delegate made the following observations' [t]he Committee must adopt some text recognizing the right of peoples freely to dispose their natural resources. If it were not to do so immediately it would have to do so later when the will of the peoples compelled the community of States to embody that essential right in an international instrument. The right of self-determination was of the utmost importance in the modern world . . .' 672 meeting; see also the Afghan delegate UN GAOR, third committee (638th mtg) 70 UN Doc. A/C.3/SR.638 at 70–71; also see Banerjee, 'The Concept of Permanent Sovereignty over Natural Resources–An Analysis' 8 *Indian Journal of International Law* (1968) 515; Kofele-Kale, *The International Law of Responsibility for Economic Crimes: Holding State Officials Individually Liable for Acts of Fraudulent Enrichment* (Ashgate, 2006) pp. 86–90.

[44] See Shaw, *International Law* (Cambridge University Press, 2008) p. 40.

6

The International Covenant on Economic, Social and Cultural Rights

References within Article 1 to 'economic, social and cultural development' were to be the driving force of instigating a right to development in international law. The ideal of permanent sovereignty and the right to exploit nationally-based resources has led to substantial controversies over the issue of expropriation and nationalisation of foreign property. Developed States have insisted that any expropriation of foreign property needs to comply with 'minimum international standards'[45] and be based on compensation that is 'prompt, adequate and effective'.[46] By contrast, the developing countries advanced the so-called 'New International Economic Order', which authorised an unfettered discretion over natural resources including a right to nationalisation.[47] This vision of permanent sovereignty over natural resources was evidenced in the Charter of Economic Rights and Duties of States[48] and the Declaration on the Establishment of a New Economic Order.[49] The Declaration on the Establishment of a New Economic Order contains provisions asserting permanent sovereignty over natural resources. Paragraph 4(e) asserts the right to

[f]ull permanent sovereignty of every State over its natural resources and all economic activities. In order to safeguard these resources, each State is entitled to exercise effective control over them and their exploitation with means suitable to its own situation, including the right to nationalization or transfer of ownership to its nationals, this right being an expression of the full permanent sovereignty of the State. No State may be subjected to economic, political or any other type of coercion to prevent the free and full exercise of this inalienable right.

Article 25 of ICESCR, alongside the above-mentioned provisions of Article 1, was deployed by the developing world to advance claims of economic sovereignty and self-determination. According to Article 25, nothing in the ICESCR shall be interpreted to impair 'the inherent right of all people to enjoy and utilize fully and freely their natural wealth and resources'.[50] While substantial differences exist in relation to a suitable agenda for economic reform, insofar as the issues of expropriation are concerned, over the past two decades the traditional distinctions appear to have blurred. The developing States have become more conscious of the value of foreign investment, and have come round to the idea of providing guarantees of adequate compensation, so as to attract foreign investors. This eagerness to attract foreign investments has also been influenced by the collapse of socialist planned economies, accompanied by a growing recognition that expropriation and nationalisation of foreign property is damaging for a continuing flow of foreign capital investments. Having said that, the exact position on expropriation within *lex lata* is not fully established[51] and the modern jurisprudence on arbitration

---

[45] See Harris, above n.1 at p. 595.

[46] Derived from a formula devised by a former United States Secretary of State, Cordell Hull, and known generally as the 'Hull formula' (1938). According to which 'no government is entitled to expropriate private property, for whatever purpose, without provision for prompt, adequate and effective payment thereof.' Text in 32 *AJIL* (1938), Supp., 192.

[47] See Jennings and Watts, *Oppenheim's International Law* (Longman, 1992) vol. II, pp. 921–925.

[48] GA Res. 3281(XXIX) 14 I.L.M. (1975) 251.

[49] GA Res. 3201 (S-VI) 13 I.L.M. (1974) 715.

[50] See Article 25.

[51] See Qureshi, *International Economic Law* (Sweet & Maxwell, 1999), at p. 376; *cf.* Malanczuk, *Akehurst's Modern Introduction to International Law* (Routledge, 1997) p. 237. Also see Rehman, 'Islamic Perspectives on International Economic Law' in Qureshi (ed.), *Perspectives in International Economic Law* (Kluwer Law International, 2002) pp. 235–258.

awards for the nationalisation and expropriation of foreign property does not eradicate the existing uncertainties.[52]

5 ANALYSIS OF THE STRUCTURE AND SUBSTANTIVE RIGHTS

The ICESCR was adopted at the same time as the ICCPR and entered into force on 3 January, 1976.[53] Attempts to establish a complaints procedure based on an optional protocol (Similar to ICCPR's First Optional Protocol) have recently taken shape, though the actual success of an individual complaints mechanism as yet remains speculative.[54] The ICESCR is divided into five parts: Part I (Article 1) deals with the right to self-determination; Part II (Articles 2–5) provides, *inter alia*, for the general nature of States parties' obligations; Part III (Articles 6–15) provides for specific substantive rights; and Part IV provides for implementation; and Part V provides general provisions of a legal nature. As we shall see, the Covenant is supplied with an implementation mechanism. The body in charge of implementation is called the Committee on Economic, Social and Cultural Rights (the Committee). In addition to the work of the Committee, the jurisprudence on the subject has been enhanced by a number of sources including the Limburg Principles on the Implementation of International Covenant on Economic, Social and Cultural Rights[55] and the Maastricht Guidelines on Violations of Economic, Social and Cultural Rights.[56] As their respective titles indicate, these documents articulate principles and guidelines on the Convention rights and violations of these rights.

The Covenant sets out the following substantive rights:

Article 1	The right to self-determination
Article 6	The right to work
Article 7	The right to just and favourable conditions of work
Article 8	The right to form trade unions and the right to strike
Article 9	The right to social security, including social insurance
Article 10	The right to protection and assistance to the family, including special assistance for mothers and children
Article 11	The right to an adequate standard of living including adequate food, clothing and housing, and continuous improvement of living conditions
Article 12	The right to the enjoyment of the highest attainable standard of physical and mental health

6

The International Covenant on Economic, Social and Cultural Rights

---

[52] See in particular the jurisprudence of the Iran-United States Tribunal: Fitzmaurice and Pellonpää, 'Taking property in the Practice of the Iran-United States Claim Tribunal' 19 *NYIL* (1988) 53; Mouri, *The International Law of Expropriation as Reflected in the work of the Iran-U.S. Claims Tribunal* (Martinus Nijhoff Publishers, 1994).

[53] Adopted at New York, 16 December 1966. Entered into force 3 January 1976. GA Res. 2200A (XXI) UN Doc. A/6316 (1966) 993 U.N.T.S. 3; 6 I.L.M. (1967) 360.

[54] See below for recent developments.

[55] The text of Limburg Principles published in UN Doc. E/CN.4/1987/17, Annex. Reprinted in 9 *HRQ* (1987) 122.

[56] See 20 *HRQ* (1998) 691; Dankwa, Flinterman and Leckie, 'Commentary to the Maastricht Guidelines on Violations of Economic, Social and Cultural Rights' 20 *HRQ* (1998) 705.

> **Article 13** The right to education, primary education being compulsory and available to all, and secondary and higher education being generally available. Adult education to be encouraged and improvements to be made to the system of schooling
>
> **Article 14** Compulsory (free of charge) primary education to be introduced within two years of acceptance of the treaty
>
> **Article 15** The right to take part in cultural life and to enjoy the benefits of scientific progress

(i) The right to work and rights of workers

Article 6 provides for the right to work which includes 'the right of everyone to the opportunity to gain his living by work which he freely chooses or accepts, with an undertaking on States parties to take appropriate steps to safeguard this right'.[57] This right is a very significant one as, in the words of Seighart, work represents 'an essential part of the human condition'.[58] It is also protected by other international human rights instruments including the UDHR,[59] the American Declaration on the Rights and Duties of Man (ADHR)[60] and the European Social Charter (ESC).[61] The value of the right to work as well as its relationship with other human rights was highlighted by the Committee in its General Comment No. 18.[62]

Craven rightly observes that

> not only is [work] crucial to the enjoyment of 'survival rights' such as food, clothing or housing, it affects the level of satisfaction of many other human rights such as the right to education, culture and health.[63]

In establishing a normative content of this right, the Committee in its General Comment has noted:

> The right to work is an individual right that belongs to each person and is at the same time a collective right. It encompasses all forms of work, whether independent work or dependent wage-paid work. The right to work should not be understood as an absolute and unconditional right to obtain employment. Article 6, paragraph 1, contains a definition of the right to work and paragraph 2 cites, by way of illustration and in a non-exhaustive manner, examples of obligations incumbent upon States parties. It includes the right of every human being to decide freely to accept or choose work. This implies not being forced in any way whatsoever to exercise or engage in employment and the right of access to a system of protection guaranteeing each worker access to employment. It also implies the right not to be unfairly deprived of employment.

---

[57] Article 6(1).

[58] Sieghart, *The Lawful Rights of Mankind: An Introduction to the International Legal Code of Human Rights* (Oxford University Press, 1986) p. 123.

[59] 10 December, 1948, UN GA Res. 217 A(III), UN Doc. A/810 at 71 (1948). Article 23.

[60] OAS Res. XXX, OAS Doc. OEA/Ser.L.V/II.82 doc.6 rev.1 at 17 (1992). Article XIV. See below chapter 9.

[61] Adopted at Turin 18 October 1961. Entered into force, 26 February 1965. 529 U.N.T.S. 89; ETS 35 and 163. Article 1. See below chapter 8.

[62] See CESCR General Comment, *The Right to Work*, General Comment No. 18: *06/02/2006* E/C.12/GC/18 (6 February 2006).

[63] Craven, above n.1, at p. 194.

Work as specified in article 6 of the Covenant must be *decent work*. This is work that respects the fundamental rights of the human person as well as the rights of workers in terms of conditions of work safety and remuneration. It also provides an income allowing workers to support themselves and their families as highlighted in article 7 of the Covenant. These fundamental rights also include respect for the physical and mental integrity of the worker in the exercise of his/her employment.

Articles 6, 7 and 8 of the Covenant are interdependent. The characterization of work as decent presupposes that it respects the fundamental rights of the worker . . .[64]

The phenomenon of arbitrary discrimination and denial of the right to work has been deployed to victimise individuals and groups in many parts of the world. Ethnic minorities and women in a number of States are deprived of equal opportunities or free choices in employment.[65] The Committee has criticised violations of the Covenant provisions whereby, for example, women require permission from their husbands before being able to work outside their homes,[66] or 'persistent gender inequalities [remain] particularly in the fields of vocational training, employment, and low representation of women in public life and managerial posts, both in the public and private sectors',[67] or there are racial, ethnic or gender-based motivations behind discrimination in granting employment.[68] In its General Comment No. 5, the Committee has also emphasised the integration of persons with disabilities into the workforce. According to the Committee, States parties need to remove any physical barriers from within the workplace which place restrictions upon persons with disabilities. Furthermore, the Committee emphasises upon transportation, which 'is crucial to the realization by persons with disabilities of virtually all rights recognized in the Covenant'.[69]

According to Article 6(2), steps are to be taken by State parties to the present Covenant to achieve the full realisation of this right. The steps shall include technical and vocational guidance and training programmes, policies and techniques to achieve steady economic, social and cultural development, and full and productive employment under conditions safeguarding the fundamental political and economic freedoms of the individual. Article 7 expands on the subject of working conditions and remuneration and provides for recognition of the right to:

[64] See CESCR General Comment, *The Right to Work*, General Comment No. 18, above n.62, paras 6, 7 and 8.

[65] See e.g. Discrimination against religious and ethnic groups in States. Minority Rights Group (ed.), *World Directory of Minorities and Indigenous Peoples* (2007) www.minorityrights.org/directory <last visited 20 May 2009>. Sieghart makes the valuable point that the issue of work and working environment 'gives rise to much conflict, for it also continues to be one of the most persistent occasions for the exploitation of human beings by their own kind' Sieghart, above n.58, at p. 123.

[66] See the Concluding Observations on report of Iran E/C.12/1993/7 at 3, para 6.

[67] See the Concluding Observations on report of Uzbekistan E/C.12/UZB/CO/1 (24 January 2006) para 15.

[68] See the Summary Records on the Part of the 30th meeting on Report by Dominican Republic (06/03/1996) E/C.12/1996/SR.30 (Summary Record) para 17; *Concluding observations of the Committee on Economic, Social and Cultural Rights: Kuwait. 07/06/2004.* E/C.12/1Add.98, para 13.

[69] See CESCR General Comment No. 5. (General Comments): *Persons with Disabilities:. 09/12/94,* Eleventh Session, 1994, E/1995/22, para 23.

enjoyment of just and favourable conditions of work which ensure, in particular:

(a) Remuneration which provides all workers, as a minimum, with:

    (i) Fair wages and equal remuneration for work of equal value without distinction of any kind, in particular women being guaranteed conditions of work not inferior to those enjoyed by men, with equal pay for equal work;

    (ii) A decent living for themselves and their families in accordance with the provisions of the present Covenant

Article 7 emphasises fairness in remuneration for work which is of equal value. In order to satisfy the requirement of fair wages, the Committee has advocated a system of minimum wages conforming largely to the ILO Minimum Wage-Fixing Convention 1970.[70] It lays stress upon an equitable system based on fairness in remuneration between men and women.[71] Article 7(a) is also concerned with the adequacy of rights to allow a decent living for individuals and their families.[72] The various elements of the right to just and favourable conditions of work include equal remuneration between men and women,[73] a decent living for the workers and their families,[74] safe and healthy conditions of work,[75] equal opportunities in employment including merit-based opportunities for promotion,[76] rest, leisure and reasonable limitation of hours of work along with paid periodic holidays.[77]

The review of these rights by the Committee has raised a number of concerns. A significant and problematic area has been the treatment of migrant workers in labour markets as well as in societies in general. Every one in 10 workers operates in a migratory capacity across the globe, a situation which has not only raised serious issues but has also prompted the United Nations to adopt international standards on the rights of migrant workers.

We shall in due course be analysing the legal position under the International Convention on the Protection of the Rights of All Migrant Workers and Members of Their Families (1990).[78] Within general human rights law, the role of the International Bill of Rights, in particular that of the ICESCR, continues to remain of great significance. For its part, the ICESCR Committee has played a significant role in highlighting the issues confronted by various abuses suffered by migrant workers. For instance, in its analysis of State reports, the Committee has expressed unhappiness and dissatisfaction over the employment of what it has termed as 'irregular workers'. These are workers who perform the same tasks as other employees, but their employment is not officially recognised, they are on a lower wage, and they do not have any health or unemployment benefits.[79]

---

[70] ILO Minimum Wage-Fixing Convention 1970 (No. 131) 825 U.N.T.S. 77, entered into force 29 April 1972.

[71] Article 7(a)(i).

[72] Article 7(a)(ii).

[73] Ibid.

[74] Ibid.

[75] Article 7(b)

[76] Article 7(c).

[77] Article 7(d).

[78] See below chapter 19; see generally Cholewinski, *Migrant Workers in International Human Rights Law: Their Protection in Countries of Employment* (Clarendon Press, 1997); Berg, 'At the Border and Between the Cracks: The Precarious Position of Irregular Migrant Workers under International Human Rights Law' 8 *MJIL* (2007) 1; Keane and McGeehan, 'Enforcing Migrant Workers' Rights in the United Arab Emirates' 15 *IJMGR* (2008) 81.

[79] See Concluding Observations of the Committee on Economic, Social and Cultural Rights: Japan. 24/09/2001. E/C.12/1/Add.67, 24 September 2001(Concluding Observations/Comments), para 61.

In a report prepared by the Secretary-General several States acknowledged the maltreatment of migrants and particularly the migrant women. Thus, for example,

> Mexico noted that women migrant workers were vulnerable to physical and/or psychological violence, racism, xenophobia and other forms of discrimination . . . Mexico also reported that women migrant workers were subject to violations of their rights by border-patrol officials, including battering, rape and kidnapping . . . Costa Rica indicated that the fact that many women migrant workers were undocumented made them vulnerable to abuse, including sexual harassment and sexual violence. Kuwait acknowledged that there might be rare cases of violence against women migrant workers . . .[80]

Article 8 affords the right to form and join trade unions to everyone. The Article also states that no restrictions should be placed on the exercise of this right other than those that are necessary for national security, public order or for protecting the rights of others.[81] The right to strike, although controversial, was incorporated by the Third Committee as the majority then considered that it was indispensable for the protection of the interests and rights of workers, up to a point whereby the absence of this right would render meaningless any guarantee of trade union rights.[82] This right to strike is subject to being in conformity with laws of the particular country.[83] The right to strike provisions stand out in human rights treaties, as only the European Social Charter has similarly explicit provisions.[84] The Committee has suggested that the right to strike should be incorporated as part of the contract of employment.[85]

Article 8 can be regarded as an extension of the right to freedom of association and it also overlaps with civil and political rights; the terminology of the article is reminiscent of the obligations within civil and political rights. The wording of the article emphasises that the right needs to be given immediate effect. According to Article 8(2) this article shall not prevent the imposition of lawful restrictions on the exercise of these rights by members of the armed forces, the police or the administration of the State. Article 8(2) restricts members of armed forces, following the lead by the ECHR which also has similar restrictions.[86]

(ii) Social security and family rights

According to Article 9, the States parties recognise the right of everyone to security which includes social insurance. This article has more recently been the subject of a General Comment where the Committee makes the following pertinent observations.[87] It notes:

---

[80] See Report of the Secretary-General, *Violence against Women Migrant Workers*, A/56/329, Fifty-Sixth session (4 September 2001), para 11.

[81] Article 8(1)(a).

[82] See Morosov (USSR) E/CN.4/SR.298 at p. 8 (1952); Bracco (Uruguay) E/CN.4/SR.229 at 3 (1952); Brena (Uruguay) A/C.3/SR. 719, at 191, para 25 (1956).

[83] Article 8(1)(d).

[84] ESC, Article 6(4). See below Chapter 8.

[85] See Konate on the Report from Jamaica E/C.12/1990/SR.15 at p. 6, para 25.

[86] ECHR Article 11(2).

[87] See CESCR General Comment No. 19. (General Comments): *The Right to Social Security (Art. 9)* Thirty-ninth session (5–23 November 2007) E/C.12/GC/19, 4 February 2008.

The International Covenant on Economic, Social and Cultural Rights

6

The right to social security requires, for its implementation, that a system, whether composed of a single scheme or variety of schemes, is available and in place to ensure that benefits are provided for the relevant social risks and contingencies. The system should be established under domestic law, and public authorities must take responsibility for the effective administration or supervision of the system. The schemes should also be sustainable, including those concerning provision of pensions, in order to ensure that the right can be realized for present and future generations.[88]

It goes on to note that an acceptable system needs to ensure nine main branches of the social security system, which are healthcare, sickness, old age, unemployment, employment injury, family and child support, maternity, disability, survivors and orphans.[89] Article 10 deals with the important subject of promoting and protecting the family. In encouraging States parties to provide all possible assistance to families, the article treats family as 'the natural and fundamental group unit of society', a terminology applied in other international and regional human rights treaties.[90] The article notes the value of family in the education and upbringing of children. A corollary to the family unit is the institution of marriage, which according to the article must be entered into with the free consent of the intending spouses.[91]

Article 10(2) states that special protection should be accorded to mothers for a reasonable period before and after childbirth. During such a period, working mothers should be given paid leave or leave with adequate social security benefits. According to Article 10(3) special measures of protection and assistance need to be taken on behalf of all children and young persons without any discrimination for reasons of parentage or other conditions. Children and young persons are to be protected from economic and social exploitation. Their employment in work harmful to their morals or health, dangerous to life or likely to hamper their normal development should be punishable by law. States are also required to set age limits below which the paid employment of child labour should be prohibited and punishable by law.

In the light of the frequent abuse from which women and children suffer, the protection of their rights has become a special concern for human rights law. In contemporary societies the exploitation of children is conducted through such abominable practices as prostitution, sexual slavery, labour and servitude. Child labour and exploitation is an institutionalised practice in many parts of the world. According to conservative estimates there are approximately 165 million 5–14 year olds who are forced into child labour, with over 100 million who are hired into the full-time labour market.[92] The actual figures are likely to be much higher.[93] The prostitution and sale of children (especially young girls) and their sexual abuse is also an unfortunate, although not uncommon, occurrence. The provisions of Article 10(3) have been further reinforced by a number of recent initiatives.

---

[88] Ibid. para 11.

[89] Ibid. paras 12–21.

[90] See Article 23(1) ICCPR; Article 18 AFCHPR; Article 17 ACHR.

[91] Article 10(1).

[92] Scouts, 'World Day Against Child Labour – 12 June: Creating a Better World' (2008) www.scout.org/en/information_events/news/2008/world_day_against_child_labour_12_june <last visited 12 May 2009>. Van Bueren, *The International Law on the Rights of the Child* (Martinus Nijhoff Publishers, 1998) p. 263; also see Ehrenberg, 'The Labor Link: Applying the International Trading System to Enforce Violations of Forced and Child Labor' 20 *YJIL* (1995) 361.

[93] See further below chapter 16.

Notably amongst these are the enforcement of the Convention on the Rights of the Child,[94] and the more recent Protocol on the Sale of Children, Child Pornography and Child Prostitution.[95]

(iii) Adequate standard of living and mental and physical health

Article 11 provides for the right to an adequate standard of living. According to Article 11(1) States parties recognise the

> right of everyone to an adequate standard of living for himself and his family, including adequate food, clothing and housing, and to the continuous improvement of living conditions.

The important provisions of this Article have been the subject of General Comments as well as a thorough investigation by the Committee.[96] In its General Comment No. 4, the Committee, in emphasising the importance of the Article, treats it as the most important provision contained in the Covenant. The Committee notes with disquiet the gaps between the provisions of Article 11(1) and actual realities in many parts of the world.[97] According to the General Comment the reference to 'himself and his family' represents assumptions about gender roles and economic activity patterns commonly accepted in 1966 when the Covenant was adopted, and that the concept of 'family' must be understood in the wider sense, and in particular in the context of Article 2(2).[98]

In its General Comment No. 4, the Committee notes that the right to housing needs to be given a wider construction and should be perceived as the right to live somewhere in security, peace and dignity. The right to housing also incorporates such key features as legal security of tenure, availability of services, materials, facilities and infrastructure, affordability, habitability, health principles of housing, accessibility, location and cultural adequacy. In its observations the Committee points to the importance of adequate housing as a fundamental human right and has treated forced eviction as a violation of the Article. In reviewing the report from the Dominican Republic the Committee asserted:

> [t]he information that had reached members of the Committee concerning the massive expulsion of nearly 15,000 families in the course of the last five years, the deplorable conditions in which the families had to live, and the conditions in which the expulsions had taken place were deemed sufficiently serious for it to be considered that the guarantees in Article 11 of the Covenant had not been respected.[99]

---

94 See above n.8. For further analysis and discussion below chapter 16.

95 New York, 25 May 2000 UN Doc. A/RES/54/263. See Dennis, 'Newly Adopted Protocols to the Convention on the Rights of the Child' 94 *AJIL* (2000) 789. See below chapter 16.

96 CESCR General Comment 4, *The Right to Adequate Housing* (Art. 11(1)) (13/12/91). (Sixth Session, 1991, E/1992/23); CESCR General Comment 7, *The Right to Adequate Housing: Forced Evictions* (Article 11(1)) (20/05/97). (Sixteenth Session, 1997, E/1998/22, annex IV).

97 CESCR General Comment 4, *The Right to Adequate Housing* (Art. 11(1)) (13/12/91) para 4.

98 Ibid. para 6.

99 UN ESCOR, Supp. (No. 3) at 64, para 249, UN Doc. E/C.12/1990/8, (1991). Joseph regards 'mass evictions . . . especially if inflicted with violence [to] constitute as a clear breach of the right to adequate shelter under Article 11 of the ICESCR' Joseph, *Corporations and Transnational Human Rights Litigation* (Hart Publishing, 2004) at p. 32.

In its sixth session, the Committee found that evictions of large numbers of people had led Panama 'not only [to infringe] upon the right to adequate housing but also on the inhabitants' right to privacy and security of the home'.[100] The Committee members have criticised States for reduction in low-cost housing, for shortage of low-income housing[101] and for the ghettoisation of minorities and migrant workers in poor neighbourhoods.[102] The recognition on the part of States of the 'right of everyone to . . . adequate food', it appears, has only been piecemeal and disjointed. As is common knowledge, violations of the right to food regularly take place and have not been the subject of international condemnation, nor has the conjoined right to be free from hunger formed the primordial principle of human rights law.[103] In an investigation into State practice, many contemporary States find themselves failing in their commitment. According to recent studies over 850 million people – 85 per cent of those from the States in the developing world – suffer from hunger and malnutrition.[104] Nearly 60 per cent of annual deaths, over 36 million, are a consequence of lack of adequate food and nutritional deficiencies.[105] Jean Ziegler, UN Special Rapporteur on the Right to Food (2001–08) was nominated to the Membership of the Advisory Committee of the United Nations' Human Rights Council. Jean Ziegler completed his mandate in April 2008 and was succeeded by Olivier De Schutter on 1 May 2008. With this mandate, Olivier De Schutter is in charge of the promotion and protection of the Right to Food. Both Ziegler and De Schutter have produced a number of useful country reports, which highlight the difficulties amongst State practices of recognition of the right to food, *strictu sensu*, but also of the effective implementation of any such right.[106]

---

[100] UN Doc. E/C.12/1991/4, para 135.
[101] See e.g. Romero E/C.12/1988/SR.12 at 10–11, para 52 and Concluding Observations on report of Italy E/1993/22 at 50, para 192.
[102] In its concluding observation on France's third periodic report, the Committee in expressing concern notes that 'persons belonging to racial, ethnic and national minorities, especially migrant workers and persons of immigrant origin, are disproportionately concentrated in poor residential areas characterized by low-quality and poorly maintained housing complexes, limited employment opportunities, inadequate access to health care facilities and public transport, under-resourced schools and high exposure to crime and violence'. Committee on Economic, Social and Cultural Rights, Fortieth Session, 28 April–16 May 2008) E/C.12/FRA/CO/3, para 21.
[103] See the documentation from the Former UN Commission on Human Rights Resolution 2000/12 on Human Rights and Extreme Poverty, E/CN.4/RES/2000/12; Resolution 1999/26 on Human Rights and Extreme Poverty, E/CN.4/RES/1999/26; Resolution 1999/26 on Human Rights and Extreme Poverty, E/CN.4/RES/1998/25; Report of Ms. M. Lizin, Independent Expert on Human Rights and Extreme Poverty E/CN.4.2000/52 (25 February 2000); Report of the Workshop on Human Rights and Extreme Poverty E/CN.4/2000/52/Add.1 (17 November 1999); Final Report on Human Rights and Extreme Poverty submitted by Special Rapporteur Mr. Leandro Despouy, E/CN.4/Sub.2/1996/13 (28 June 1996); UN General Assembly Resolution, Human Rights and Extreme Poverty (A/RES/47/134) 18 December 1992; Skogly 'Is There a Right not to be Poor?', 2 *HRLR* (2002), 59; Skogly, Crimes Against Humanity–Revisited: Is There a Role for Economic and Social Rights?' 5 *International Journal of Human Rights* (2001) 58.
[104] The Right to Food, Report of the Special Rapporteur on the right to food, Jean Ziegler (E/CN.4/2006/44) 16 March 2006. 'The Special Rapporteur is gravely concerned to report to the Commission that global hunger is continuing to increase. At least 852 million children, women, and men are gravely and permanently undernourished. Millions of people die every year for lack of food. Every five seconds, one child under the age of 5 will die from malnutrition and related diseases' Ibid. at 2.
[105] Ibid. at 2.
[106] For further information, and a review of reports and the contributions made by the Special Rapporteur see www.righttofood.org/spip.php?article6 <last visited 30 May 2009>.

Article 11(2) of ICESCR details certain provisions to advance the right of individuals to freedom from hunger. The article has been the subject of a General Comment where the Committee notes:[107]

> The right to adequate food, like any other human right, imposes three types or levels of obligations on States parties: the obligations to *respect*, to *protect* and to *fulfil*. In turn, the obligation to *fulfil* incorporates both an obligation to *facilitate* and an obligation to *provide*. The obligation to *respect* existing access to adequate food requires States parties not to take any measures that result in preventing such access. The obligation to *protect* requires measures by the State to ensure that enterprises or individuals do not deprive individuals of their access to adequate food. The obligation to *fulfil* (*facilitate*) means the State must pro-actively engage in activities intended to strengthen people's access to and utilization of resources and means to ensure their livelihood, including food security. Finally, whenever an individual or group is unable, for reasons beyond their control, to enjoy the right to adequate food by the means at their disposal, States have the obligation to *fulfil* (*provide*) that right directly. This obligation also applies for persons who are victims of natural or other disasters.[108]

Whilst there is academic debate surrounding the exact nature of the right to food in international law, human rights scholars, such as Narula, increasingly assert the 'absolute' nature of the right to be free from hunger (as provided in Article 11(2) of ICESCR) and have elevated the right to the status of customary international law.[109] Narula connects this right to fundamental rights such as the right to life, and the right to self-determination. Provisions of treaty law, as well as customary international law, can be advanced, leading to the binding nature of this right in international law.[110]

Article 12 provides for the right to the highest attainable standard of physical and mental health. The steps required for the realisation of the right include formulating adequate provisions for the reduction of the stillbirth rate and of infant mortality, for the healthy development of children,[111] the improvement of industrial and environmental hygiene for everyone,[112] preventative measures and treatment of epidemic, endemic and other diseases,[113] and making available the required medical care to everyone.[114]

---

[107] CESCR General Comment 12, *The Right to Adequate Food* (Article 11) General Comment No. 12 E/C.12/1999/5 (12/05/99).

[108] Ibid. (emphasis provided), para 15, See also Bard, above n 24

[109] Narula, 'The Right to Food: Holding Global Actors Accountable Under International Law' *Centre for Human Rights and Global Justice Working Paper* (No. 7, 2006) at p. 11.

[110] Article 12(2) of the Convention on the Elimination of All Forms of Discrimination against Women (1979) provides that 'States Parties shall ensure to women appropriate services in connection with pregnancy, confinement and the post-natal period, granting free services where necessary, as well as adequate nutrition during pregnancy and lactation'. Similarly Article 24(2)(c) of the Convention on the Rights of the Child (1989) places an obligation on States parties to 'combat disease and malnutrition, including within the framework of primary healthcare, through inter alia, the application of readily available technology and through the provision of adequate nutritious foods and clean drinking water, . . .'. Also see Geneva Convention 1949 (Geneva Convention III) Articles 20, 26; Can the violation of the 'right to be free from hunger' be regarded cruel, inhuman or degrading treatment as provided in the United Nations Convention against Torture and Other Cruel, Inhuman or Degrading Treatment or Punishment? See Boulesbaa, *The UN Convention on Torture and Prospects for Enforcement* (Martinus Nijhoff Publishers, 1999) pp. 9–15.

[111] Article 12(2)(a).

[112] Article 12(2)(b).

[113] Article 12(2)(c).

[114] Article 12(2)(d).

The Right to Health has been the object of a General Comment by the Committee on Economic, Social and Cultural Rights.[115] The Committee's views are extremely pertinent when it notes:

[h]ealth is a fundamental human right indispensable for the exercise of other human rights. Every human being is entitled to the enjoyment of the highest attainable standard of health conducive to living a life in dignity. The realization of the right to health may be pursued through numerous, complementary approaches, such as the formulation of health policies, or the implementation of health programmes developed by the World Health Organization (WHO), or the adoption of specific legal instruments. Moreover, the right to health includes certain components which are legally enforceable.[116]

Elaborating on Article 12(1) which provides a definition of the right to health the Committee observes that:

[t]he right to health is not to be understood as a right to be *healthy*. The right to health contains both freedoms and entitlements. The freedoms include the right to control one's health and body, including sexual and reproductive freedom, and the right to be free from interference, such as the right to be free from torture, non-consensual medical treatment and experimentation. By contrast, the entitlements include the right to a system of health protection which provides equality of opportunity for people to enjoy the highest attainable level of health.[117]

In its General Comment the Committee emphasises the requirements of availability and accessibility of healthcare for all individuals, a provision which should also be sensitive to medical ethics and distinct cultures.[118] The Committee then considers specialist topics relating to the healthcare of groups such as women, children, the disabled, elderly and indigenous peoples.[119] The now defunct Commission on Human Rights established a Special Rapporteur on the right of everyone to the enjoyment of the highest attainable standard of physical and mental health in 2002[120] and Professor Paul Hunt took office as the first such Special Rapporteur in September 2002.[121] The term of the Rapporteur was renewed for a further three years during the 61st session of the Commission.[122] The newly formed Human Rights Council on 30 June 2006, extended all mandates of the Commission on Human Rights including those of the Special Rapporteur.[123] The mandate of the Special

---

[115] CESCR General Comment No. 14, *The Right to Highest Attainable Standard of Health* (Article 12) (11/08/00). (E/C.12/2000/4), (Twenty-Second Session) 25 April–12 May 2000.

[116] Ibid. para 1.

[117] Ibid. para 8.

[118] Ibid. para 12.

[119] Ibid. para 21–27; also see Graham, 'The Child's Right to Health' in Freeman and Veerman (eds), *Ideologies of Children's Rights* (Martinus Nijhoff Publishers, 1992), pp. 203–211.

[120] See Commission on Human Rights Resolution 2002/31, E/2002/23–E/CN.4/2002/200 (Adopted without a vote) 22 April 2002.

[121] See www2.ohchr.org/english/issues/health/right/visits.htm <last visited 30 May 2009>.

[122] The Right of Everyone to the Enjoyment of the Highest Attainable Standard of Physical and Mental Health E/CN.4/RES/2005/24 Human Rights Resolution 2005/24 15 April 2005; www2.essex.ac.uk/human_rights_centre/rth/docs/3pagerupdatemay2007.doc

[123] Human Rights Council, Decision 1/102 Extension by the Human Rights Council of all mandates, mechanisms, functions and responsibilities of the Commission on Human Rights (1st Session) A/HRC/DEC/1/102 (30 June 2006).

Rapporteur on health was extended for a further three years by the Human Rights Council in 2007.[124] At the expiry of the two-term tenure of Professor Hunt, Mr. Anand Grover, Head of the HIV/AIDS Unit of Lawyer's Collective (India) and a member of the UNAIDS Reference Group on HIV and Human Rights, was appointed by the Human Rights Council in July 2008 as the Special Rapporteur on the right of everyone to the enjoyment of the highest attainable standard of physical and mental health.[125] In accordance with his mandate the Special Rapporteur performs a number of significant assignments. Under the overall umbrella of the right to health he examines several related and interconnected themes such as the health dimensions of HIV/AIDs, mental health, sexual and reproductive health and poverty elevation.[126] During the course of his tenure, the Special Rapporteur has not only served as an ambassador for projecting and promoting the right to health but has also through his reports and exchanges enhanced considerably the jurisprudence on the right to health.[127] He has undertaken missions and transmitted communications where violations of the right to health have been alleged.[128]

(iv) Right to education

Education, as one the most significant human rights, is provided for by all international human rights instruments. Article 26 of the Universal Declaration on Human Rights (1948), in according this right, notes that:

1. Everyone has the right to education. Education shall be free, at least in the elementary and fundamental stages. Elementary education shall be compulsory. Technical and professional education shall be made generally available and higher education shall be equally accessible to all on the basis of merit.
2. Education shall be directed to the full development of the human personality and to the strengthening of respect for human rights and fundamental freedoms. It shall promote understanding, tolerance and friendship among all nations, racial or religious groups, and shall further the activities of the United Nations for the maintenance of peace.
3. Parents have a prior right to choose the kind of education that shall be given to their children.

---

[124] Human Rights Council, Resolution 6/29, Right of everyone to the enjoyment of the highest attainable standard of physical and mental health (6th Session) A/HRC/RES/6/29 14 December 2007; see www2.ohchr.org/english/bodies/chr/special/themes.htm <last visited 30 May 2009>. Human Rights Council Res. 6/29.

[125] See Strong HIV and Human Rights Activist appointed new UN Special Rapporteur (11 July 2008) www.unaids.org/en/KnowledgeCentre/Resources/FeatureStories/archive/2008/20080711_Special_Rapporteur .asp <last visited 30 May 2009>.

[126] Ibid. See Hunt and MacNaughton 'Impact Assessment, Poverty and Human Rights: A Case Study Using The Right to the Highest Attainable Standard of Health Submitted to UNESCO 31 May 2006' available at www2.essex.ac.uk/human_rights_centre/rth/docs/Impact%20Assessments%209Dec06[1].doc. <last visited 30 May 2009>.

[127] See The Report by the Special Rapporteur, 'Implementation of General Assembly Resolution 60/251 of 15 March 2006 Entitled 'Human Rights Council–Report of the Special Rapporteur on the Right of Everyone to the Enjoyment of the Highest Attainable Standard of Physical and Mental Health: Paul Hunt' A/HRC/4/28 (17 January 2007).

[128] Amongst the Special Rapporteur's recent visit include India (November–December 2007) A/HRC/7/11Add.4, Uganda (17–25 March 2005) E/CN.4/2006/48/Add.2, Mozambique (15–19 December 2005) E/CN.4/2005/ 51/Add.2 and Peru (6–15 June 2004) E/CN.4/2005/51/Add.3.

The International Covenant on Economic, Social and Cultural Rights

6

Article 13 of the ICESCR affirms this right and establishes that:

1. The States Parties to the present Covenant recognize the right of everyone to education. They agree that education shall be directed to the full development of the human personality and the sense of its dignity, and shall strengthen the respect for human rights and fundamental freedoms. They further agree that education shall enable all persons to participate effectively in a free society, promote understanding, tolerance and friendship among all nations and all racial, ethnic or religious groups, and further the activities of the United Nations for the maintenance of peace.

2. The States Parties to the present Covenant recognize that, with a view to achieving the full realization of this right:
   (a) Primary education shall be compulsory and available free to all;
   (b) Secondary education in its different forms, including technical and vocational secondary education, shall be made generally available and accessible to all by every appropriate means, and in particular by the progressive introduction of free education;
   (c) Higher education shall be made equally accessible to all, on the basis of capacity, by every appropriate means, and in particular by the progressive introduction of free education;
   (d) Fundamental education shall be encouraged or intensified as far as possible for those persons who have not received or completed the whole period of their primary education;
   (e) The development of a system of schools at all levels shall be actively pursued, an adequate fellowship system shall be established, and the material conditions of teaching staff shall be continuously improved.

3. The States Parties to the present Covenant undertake to have respect for the liberty of parents and, when applicable, legal guardians to choose for their children schools, other than those established by the public authorities, which conform to such minimum educational standards as may be laid down or approved by the State and to ensure the religious and moral education of their children in conformity with their own convictions.

4. No part of this article shall be construed so as to interfere with the liberty of individuals and bodies to establish and direct educational institutions, subject always to the observance of the principles set forth in paragraph I of this article and to the requirement that the education given in such institutions shall conform to such minimum standards as may be laid down by the State.

Education provides a human being not only with essential tools for civilised behaviour but is also the gateway to a rewarding, intellectually stimulating and an economically successful life. It is a right which encompasses elements of both civil and political rights as well as economic, social and cultural rights, and as our subsequent discussion confirms is established in major international human rights instruments.[129] The accomplishment of the right to education is likely to further the ideals of 'understanding, tolerance, peace and friendly relations between the nations and all racial or religious groups'.[130] Education can

[129] For a useful discussion see Smith, *Textbook on International Human Rights* (Oxford University Press, 2007) at pp. 290–302.
[130] Vienna Declaration of the World Conference on Human Rights (1993) Part I, para 33.

form the basis of properly constituting a right to identity for minority ethnic, linguistic and religious groups.[131] Notwithstanding an appreciation of the value of this right, there are deep divisions not only in the recipients of this right but also in the nature and quality of education that is to be provided. The Universal Declaration on Human Rights provides for free and compulsory education at elementary levels, provisions which are reaffirmed by Article 13 of the ICESCR. In practice, however, education is denied at all levels with many States unwilling even to make a commitment to providing free and compulsory education at elementary levels. Education is also used as tool for establishing further divisions and schisms, a particular feature of societies embedded in religious, ethnic and political conflicts.

(a) International human rights law and the right to education

In addition to the UDHR and ICESCR, as noted above, there are specific provisions in the International Convention on the Elimination of All Forms of Racial Discrimination,[132] the Convention on the Elimination of All forms of Discrimination Against Women,[133] the Convention Against Torture and Other Cruel, Inhuman or Degrading Treatment or Punishment,[134] the Convention on the Rights of the Child[135] and the International Convention on the Protection of the Rights of All Migrant Workers and Members of their Families.[136] In 1945, the United Nations Educational, Scientific and Cultural Organization (UNESCO), a specialised agency of the United Nations, was established with the purpose of contributing 'to peace and security by collaborating among the nations through education,

---

[131] Henrard, 'Education and Multiculturalism: The Contribution of Minority Rights?' 7 *IJMGR* (2000) 393 at p. 394.

[132] Article 5 of the Convention provides that 'States Parties undertake to prohibit and to eliminate racial discrimination . . . and to guarantee the right of everyone, without distinction as to race, colour, or national or ethnic origin, to equality before the law . . . in the enjoyment of . . . (e)(v) the right to education and training. . . .' Adopted 21 December 1965. Entered into force, 4 January 1969. 660 U.N.T.S. 195, 5 I.L.M. (1966) 352; see generally Okafor, and Agbakwa, 'Re-Imagining International Human Rights Education in Our Time: Beyond Three Constitutive Orthodoxies' 14 *Leiden Journal of International Law* (2001) 563.

[133] Articles 10 and 14 provide that 'States Parties shall . . . eliminate discrimination against women in order to ensure to them equal rights with men in the field of education . . . to ensure, on a basis of equality of men and women . . . the same conditions for career and vocational guidance, for access to studies . . . in educational establishments of all categories . . . ; this equality shall be ensured in pre-school, general, technical, professional and higher technical education, as well as in all types of vocational training; Access to the same curricula, . . . teaching staff . . . ; The elimination of any stereotyped concept of the roles of man and women at all levels and in all forms of education . . . , The same opportunities to benefit from scholarships . . . ; The same opportunities for access to programmes of continuing education, including adult and functional literacy programmes . . . ; Access to specific educational information to help to ensure the health and well-being of families, including information and advice on family planning'. 'States Parties shall . . . eliminate discrimination against women in rural areas . . . and . . . ensure to such women the right; . . . To obtain all types of training and education, formal and non-formal, including that relating to functional literacy.' New York, 18 December 1979 United Nations, *Treaty Series*, vol. 1249, p. 13.

[134] New York, 10 December 1984 United Nations, *Treaty Series*, vol. 1465, p. 85.

[135] Articles 28 and 29 of the Convention on the Rights of the Child (1989) provides that 'States Parties recognize the right of the child to education, and . . . shall . . . ; Make primary education compulsory and available free to all; . . . make [secondary education] available and accessible to every child . . . ; Make higher education accessible to all . . . ; Make educational and vocational information and guidance available and accessible to all children . . . ; Take measures to encourage regular attendance at schools and the reduction of drop-out rates . . . '. 'States Parties agree that the education of the child shall be directed to: . . . The development of the child's personality, talents and mental and physical abilities to their fullest potential; The development of respect for human rights . . . ; The development of respect for the child's parents, his or her own cultural identity, language and values. . . .'

[136] New York, 18 December 1990, UN Doc. A/RES/45/15. See Articles 30 and 43.

science and culture'.[137] The Convention against Discrimination in Education was adopted by the General Conference of UNESCO in December, 1960.[138] According to Article 1 of the UNESCO Convention, 'discrimination' in education includes 'any distinction, exclusion, limitation or preference which, being based on race, colour, sex, language, religion, political or other opinion, national or social origin, economic condition or birth, has the purpose or effect of nullifying or impairing equality of treatment in education'. However, exceptions to discriminatory practices include the establishment or maintenance of separate educational systems or institutions for pupils of the two sexes, provided there are no compromises on the quality and nature of education, and the establishment or maintenance of separate educational institutions for religious and linguistic reasons.[139]

The value of education in human development and the contribution which it makes in the advancement of human rights is a feature given credence by the Council of Europe,[140] the European Union,[141] the Organisation of American States[142] and the African Union.[143]

---

[137] See the Constitution of the United Nations Educational, Scientific and Cultural Organization, 16 November 1945, 4 U.N.T.S. 275. Article 1(1).

[138] Adopted 14 December 1960. Entered into force 22 May 1962. 429 U.N.T.S. 93.

[139] Ibid. Article 2(a)(b).

[140] See e.g. Resolution (78)41 on the Teaching of Human Rights (Adopted by the Committee of Ministers November 1978); The Declaration Regarding Intolerance – A Threat to Democracy (Adopted by the Committee of Ministers 29 April 1982); Declaration on the Freedom of Expression and Information, (Adopted by the Committee of Ministers, 29 April 1982); Recommendation R(81) 17 to Member States on Adult Education Policy (Adopted by the Committee of Ministers November 1981); Recommendation R(79)16 to Member States on the Promotion of Human Rights Research in the Member States of the Council of Europe (Adopted by the Committee of Ministers, September 1979); Recommendation R(83)13 to Member States on the Role of Secondary School in preparing Young People for Life (Adopted by the Committee of Ministers, September 1983). Also note, Council of Europe's European Convention on Human Rights (ECHR) Protocol (Protocol 1) to the Convention for the Protection of Human Rights and Fundamental Freedoms (Paris, 20.III.1952) Article 2 – Right to education: No person shall be denied the right to education. In the exercise of any functions which it assumes in relation to education and to teaching, the State shall respect the right of parents to ensure such education and teaching in conformity with their own religious and philosophical convictions. (Article 2, First Protocol to ECHR).

[141] See e.g. the Resolution of the European Parliament on Freedom of Education in the European Community (March 1984); Resolution of the Council and the Representatives of the Governments of the Member States meeting within the Council of 5 October 1995 on the fight against racism and xenophobia in the fields of employment and social affairs (November 1995); Decision of the European Parliament and of the Council adopting the third phase of the 'Youth for Europe' programme 818/95/EC, March 1995); Resolution of the Council and the Representatives of Member States' Governments meeting within the Council of 23 October 1995 on the response of educational systems to the problems of racism and xenophobia (November 1995). Also see Article 149, 150 EC; Community Charter of Fundamental Social Rights of Workers, adopted by the Heads of State or Government (11 Member States) on 9 December 1989, para 15.

[142] See the Charter of the Organization of American States, 119 U.N.T.S. 3, entered into force 13 December 1951 (Article 12); American Convention on Human Rights 'Pact of San Jose, Costa Rica' (B-32) O.A.S. Treaty Series No. 36, 1144 U.N.T.S. 123, entered into force 18 July 1978, reprinted in Basic Documents Pertaining to Human Rights in the Inter-American System, OEA/Ser.L.V/II.82 doc.6 rev.1 at 25 (1992) (Article 26); Additional Protocol to the American Convention on Human Rights in the Area of Economic, Social and Cultural Rights 'Protocol Of San Salvador' (A-52) OAS *Treaty Series* No. 69 (1988), signed November 17, 1988, reprinted in Basic Documents Pertaining to Human Rights in the Inter-American System, OEA/Ser.L.V/II.82 doc.6 rev.1 at 67 (1992) (Article 13) and Inter-American Convention on the Prevention, Punishment and Eradication of Violence Against Women, 33 I.L.M. 1534 (1994), entered into force 5 March 1995 (Article 8). For further consideration of these treaties see below chapter 9.

[143] See the African [Banjul] Charter on Human and Peoples' Rights, adopted 27 June 1981, OAU Doc. CAB/LEG/67/3 rev. 5, 21 I.L.M. 58 (1982), entered into force 21 October 1986 (Article 25); 7 HRLJ (1986) 403. African Charter on the Rights and Welfare of the Child, Addis Ababa, Ethiopia, July 1990 OAU Doc. CAB/LEG/24.9/49 (1990), entered into force 29 November 1999 (Article 11(2)) and the Resolution on Human and Peoples' Education (CM/Res. 1420 (LVI), adopted by the Council of Ministers of the Organisation of African Unity, 56th. Ordinary Session, Dakar, Senegal, 22–28 June 1992).

On 23 December 1994, the United Nations General Assembly adopted a resolution proclaiming 'the United Nations Decade for Human Rights Education (1 January–31 December 2004)'. In this resolution, the Assembly welcomed a plan of action for the decade with a request to the United Nations High Commission on Human Rights to ensure facilitation of the implementation of this plan.[144] On 19 December 2001, the General Assembly pronounced a 'United Nations Decade Literacy Decade (2003–2012)' in the form of a resolution which urged member States and related international agencies to 'promote the right for all and to create conditions for all for learning throughout life', whilst at the same time urging a stronger action at national and international levels to achieve educational goals.[145]

In 1998, the UN Human Rights Commission appointed Katarina Tomaševski as a Special Rapporteur on Education with an initial mandate up until 2001.[146] The mandate was extended for a further three years by the Commission in its Resolution of 16 April 2004 and in July 2004 Vernor Muñoz Villalobos (Costa Rica) was appointed as the Special Rapporteur on the Right to Education.[147] This mandate was endorsed and extended by the Human Rights Council in June 2008 for a further period of three years with Vernor Muñoz Villalobos continuing as Special Rapporteur on the Right to Education.[148] The work of the Special Rapporteur has involved three major functions. Firstly, an overview of the global developments in relation to the right to education is provided in an annual report. Secondly, country missions are carried out by the Special Rapporteurs to examine patterns of difficulties *in situ*. Finally, the Special Rapporteurs have engaged with concerned governments over complaints regarding the alleged violation of these rights. The Special Rapporteurs have consistently highlighted such factors as poverty, war and internal conflicts, child labour, prejudice and bias as impeding factors in the provision of education.[149] Furthermore, the Special Rapporteurs point to the absence of an enforceable claim upon governments to allocate specific budgets for educational purpose.[150] The Special Rapporteurs have also pointed to the discriminatory practices and gender bias in education and prompting the launch of the Ten Year United Nations Girl's Education Initiative at Dakar (April 2000). In an effort to eradicate gender bias and sexual discrimination in education, UNESCO drafted a working paper on Gender Equality in Basic Education – Strategic Framework, with special reference to non-formal education for girls and women.[151] The document pays specific attention to the issue of access and equity concerning girls' opportunities for primary schooling. Further closer collaboration has been devised between UNESCO and the ICESCR Committee on the Right to Education, particularly in relation to the eradication of sexual discrimination in education.

[144] See UN General Assembly Resolution 49/184, 'United Nations Decade for Human Rights' A/RES/49/184 (adopted 23 December 1994), para 7; for a detailed consideration see United Nations, *The Right to Human Rights Education: The United Nations Decade for Human Rights Education (1995–2004)* (United Nations, 1999).

[145] UN GA Res. 56/116 'United Nations Decade–Literacy Decade: Education for All' A/RES/56/116 (adopted 19 December 2001).

[146] Commission on Human Rights Resolution, Resolution 1998/33, (17 April 1998).

[147] Commission on Human Rights Resolution, Resolution 2004/25, 16 April 2004, E/CN.4/RES/2004/25.

[148] Human Rights Council, Resolution 8/4, A/HRC/8/L.5 (12 June 2008).

[149] Tomaševski, 'Removing Obstacles in the way of the right to education' 2001 www.right-to-education.org/ <last visited 20 May 2009>.

[150] Tomaševski 'Has the Right to Education a Future Within the United Nations? A Behind-the-Scenes Account by the Special Rapporteur on the Right to Education 1998–2004' 5 *HRLR* (2005) 205.

[151] Report of the Director-General on the implementation of and follow-up to the Framework for Action of the World Education Forum in Dakar, 162 EX/7, 2000 para 16.

Article 13 of the ICESCR – which, as noted above, builds upon Article 26 of the UDHR – provides for the right of everyone to education. Article 13 is, in the words of the Committee of ICESCR, 'the most wide-ranging and comprehensive article on the right to education in international human rights law'.[152] Whilst reinforcing the value of education to the advancement of human rights, Article 13 forms part of the substantial jurisprudence which international and regional organisations have accumulated on this subject.[153] As the most comprehensive statement on the subject, Article 13 represents a synthesis of the right to education. In accordance with the provisions for the thorough realisation of this right, States parties are committed to ensuring free, compulsory primary education in a range of forms including technical and vocational secondary education, making higher education accessible to everyone on the basis of capacity and merit, to making adequate provisions for adult education and for a system of schooling at all levels. Article 13(3) provides autonomy to parents (or the legal guardians) to select private schooling for their children. The provisions of Article 13 are further reinforced by Article 14. According to Article 14 all States parties undertake to adopt a detailed plan of action for the implementation of compulsory free education for everyone within two years (from the time of the ratification and acceptance of the treaty), if it does not already have such a system in place.

Both Articles 13 and 14 have been the subjects of General Comments.[154] In its General Comment No. 13 the Committee strongly emphasises the value of this right. It notes:

> Education is both a human right in itself and an indispensable means of realizing other human rights. As an empowerment right, education is the primary vehicle by which economically and socially marginalized adults and children can lift themselves out of poverty and obtain the means to participate fully in their communities. Education has a vital role in empowering women, safeguarding children from exploitative and hazardous labour and sexual exploitation, promoting human rights and democracy, protecting the environment, and controlling population growth. Increasingly, education is recognized as one of the best financial investments States can make. But the importance of education is not just practical: a well-educated, enlightened and active mind, able to wander freely and widely, is one of the joys and rewards of human existence.[155]

The Committee then goes on to expand on the various facets of this right. In relation to the provisions of this right, the Committee observes that, although variable, education should be made available to all without discrimination. Educational institutions should be physically and economically accessible to everyone. The remainder of General Comment No. 13 is dedicated to expanding further on various levels of education (e.g. secondary, technical, higher education, etc.). General Comment No. 11, on Plans of Action for Primary Education, represents a very useful guide to Article 14's provisions.[156] The

[152] CESCR General Comment No. 13, The Right to Education (Article 13) (8/12/99). (E/C.12/1999/10) (Twenty-first session), para 2.
[153] For useful information see www.pdhre.org/rights/education.html <last visited 28 June 2008>.
[154] CESCR General Comment No. 11, Plans of Action for Primary Education (Article 14) General Comment No. 11 (10/05/99). (E/C.12/1999/4) (Twentieth Session); CESCR General Comment No. 13, *The Right to Education* (Article 13) General Comment No. 13 (8/12/99). (E/C.12/1999/10) (Twenty-first session).
[155] CESCR General Comment 13, *The Right to Education* (Article 13) General Comment No. 13 (8/12/99). (E/C.12/1999/10) para 1.
[156] CESCR General Comment 11, *Plans of Action for Primary Education (Article 14)* General Comment No. 11 (10/05/99). (E/C.12/1999/4), (Twentieth Session).

Committee in this comment analyses the meaning of various terms and elaborates on the obligations undertaken by the States parties under this article. According to the Committee, 'compulsory' is meant

> to highlight the fact that neither parents, nor guardians, nor the State are entitled to treat as optional the decision as to whether the child should have access to primary education. Similarly, the prohibition of gender discrimination in access to education, required also by articles 2 and 3 of the Covenant, is further underlined by this requirement. It should be emphasized, however, that the education offered must be adequate in quality, relevant to the child and must promote the realization of the child's other rights.[157]

It also goes on to note that 'free of charge' is meant to ensure that education is free, without imposing any costs on the child, the parents or the guardians.[158] The Committee elaborates upon the State's obligations by noting that the States are required to formulate a plan of action covering all the requisite action necessary for the comprehensive realisation of this right within two years of their becoming parties to the treaty.[159] Furthermore, a State cannot avoid obligations on the grounds of lack of necessary resources. In situations where a State party lacks the necessary resources, there is also an obligation on the international community to provide support.[160] One controversial and debated question is as to whether the right to education is best realised where education is imparted in the indigenous language of the community in question. In multi-lingual States imposing such a requirement can be considerably onerous and yet at the same time this appears to be the natural culmination of recognising and realising fully the right to education as well as the right to culture and identity. As regards the right to education, minorities have raised other related issues such as the adequate and appropriate representation of their ethnic, cultural, religious or linguistic values.[161]

(v) Cultural rights

The rubric of the treaty accords great prominence to culture; the treaty is entitled the International Covenant on Social, Economic and Cultural Rights. However, in reality it is not until Article 15 that cultural life is addressed directly. Cultural rights within the Covenant are therefore the poor relation of social and economic rights. Steiner, Alston and Goodman make the pertinent point that cultural rights 'have attracted relatively little attention in this context. Rather, they have tended to be dealt within relation to the ICCPR, whether under its non-discrimination clause (Art. 2(1)), the minorities provision (Art. 27) or specific rights such as freedoms of expression, religion and association and the right to "take part in the conduct of public affairs". The consequence has been a clear neglect of the specifically economic and social rights dimensions of cultural rights.'[162]

---

[157] Ibid. para 6.
[158] Ibid. para 7. In its General Comment No. 17, HRC has emphasised that education is of fundamentally high significance for the proper development of a child's personality. See CCPR General Comment 17, General Comment No. 17: Rights of the Child (Article 24): 07/04/89 (Thirty-fifth session, 1989), para 3.
[159] Ibid. para 8.
[160] Ibid. para 9.
[161] Henrard, above n.131, at p. 399.
[162] Steiner, Alston and Goodman (eds), above n.1 at p. 276. Stavenhagen makes a similar observation by noting that the Covenant 'makes only modest proposals regarding cultural rights', Stavenhagen 'Cultural Rights: A Social Science Perspective' in Eide, Krause and Rosas (eds), above n.1, pp. 85–109, at p. 85.

The International Covenant on Economic, Social and Cultural Rights

6

According to Article 15, States parties recognise the right of everyone to take part in cultural life. There is also recognition on the part of States of the need to allow the individual the benefit of scientific progress and its applications[163] and to allow him '[t]o benefit from the protection of the moral and material interests from any scientific, literary or artistic production of which he is author'.[164] Steps undertaken by States to realise this right include 'those necessary for the conservation, the development and the diffusion of science and culture'.[165]

Culture represents a quintessential part of human existence; the absence of a cultural association makes it difficult to forge common identities and establish social values. 'Culture' or 'cultural life' remains an elusive concept. These terms are defined neither by the Covenant nor within general international law. There is also a failure to engage with situations where multifarious cultures exist alongside one another. It is often the tensions of competing or conflicting cultures within a State which has resulted in the dilemmas of multiculturalism.[166]

While a number of references could be found to cultural rights within human rights treaties, international law has remained deficient in according recognition to cultural rights as collective group rights; the comments made in relation to minority rights need to be recalled.[167] Cultural rights have to be viewed in the proper context of the existence of culture and collective existence, and therefore in essence representing collective rights. Cultural rights have a great affinity with people's rights to autonomy and self-determination. For many States the fear is that in the name of culture, minority groups would campaign for autonomy, leading to secession and the break up of existing State structures. In the context of individualistic human rights law, it is thus no surprise that cultural rights within the Covenant fail to receive pre-eminence.

6 IMPLEMENTATION MACHINERY[168]

Apart from the difficulties and controversies with the substantive nature of the rights contained in the International Covenant on Economic, Social and Cultural Rights (1966), the mechanisms to implement economic, social and cultural rights have not proved satisfactory. Under Articles 16 to 25 States parties are under an obligation to provide periodic reports. The Reporting Procedure is the only mechanism regarding the implementation of

---

163 Article 15(1)(b).
164 Article 15(1)(c).
165 Article 15(2).
166 Rehman, 'Islam, "War on Terror" and the Future of Muslim Minorities in the United Kingdom: Dilemmas of Multi-Culturalism in the aftermath of the London Bombings' 29 *HRQ* (2007) 831; Xanthaki, 'Multiculturalism and Extremism: International Law Perspectives' in Rehman and Breau (eds), *Religion, Human Rights Law and International Law: A Critical Examination of Islamic State Practices* (Martinus Nijhoff Publishers, 2007), pp. 443–464; Tierney (ed.), *Multiculturalism and the Canadian Constitution* (University of British Columbia Press, 2008).
167 See above chapter 5 and below chapter 12 and 13.
168 See *The Limburg Principles on the Implementation of the International Covenant on Economic, Social and Cultural Rights;* Alston, 'The Committee on Economic, Social and Cultural Rights' in Alston (ed.), *The United Nations and Human Rights: A Critical Appraisal* (Clarendon Press, 1992) pp. 473–507; O'Flaherty, *Human Rights and the UN: Practice before the Treaty Bodies* (Martinus Nijhoff Publishers, 2002) pp. 46–71; Leckie, 'The Committee on Economic, Social and Cultural Rights: Catalyst for Change in a System Needing Reform' in Alston and Crawford (eds), *The Future of UN Human Rights Treaty Monitoring* (Cambridge University Press, 2000) pp. 129–144.

the Covenant.[169] However, as discussed below, only recently has the United Nations been able to adopt an Optional Protocol to ICESCR (2008). In accordance with Article 16 of the ICESCR, State parties are under an obligation to submit reports to ECOSOC via the Secretary-General of the United Nations[170] on the measures they have adopted to give effect to the rights in the Covenant.[171] The reports need to inform of the progress made in achieving the observance of the rights within the treaty.[172] The United Nations Secretary-General is also required to transmit copies of these reports to the relevant specialised agencies.[173] According to Article 17, States may indicate factors and difficulties affecting the degree of fulfilment of the obligations. Initial reports must be submitted within two years of the Covenant coming into operation for the State, thereafter every five years.[174]

The Covenant as such does not provide for the creation of a treaty-body, and the responsibility for the implementation has been assigned to ECOSOC.[175] In order to perform its task of implementing the Covenant, ECOSOC set up a 15-member sessional working group, initially consisting of governmental representatives and subsequently of experts appointed by governments. The working group was not able to perform effectively, its track record being termed as 'disappointing'.[176] Amongst the many criticisms of the working group, the foremost ones were that its examination of reports was inadequate, superficial and politicised. It was claimed that the working group's conclusions lacked substance and failed to inform the States of the extent to which they were complying with their obligations within the Covenant. Furthermore, the attendance of members was irregular and members were not fully involved in the proceedings of the working group sessions.[177] Specialised agencies were also critical of the working group, claiming that they were not

---

[169] Proposal for having a complaints procedure are yet to become operation. See further Alston, *Establishing a right to petition under the Covenant on Economic, Social and Cultural Rights*, Collected Courses of the Academy of European Law: The Protection of Human Rights in Europe (European University Press, 1993) vol. IV, book 2 (1993) p. 115.

[170] Article 16(2)(a).

[171] Article 16(1).

[172] Ibid.

[173] Article 16(2)(b). The implementation mechanism instituted by ECOSOC and Article 18 of the ICESCR allow specialised agencies to arrange with the ECOSOC to submit reports which 'may include particulars of decisions and recommendations on such implementation adopted by [the specialised agencies] competent organs'. In pursuance of this mandate, the ILO has submitted a series of papers and reports see e.g. Twenty-sixth Report of the International Labour Organization under Article 18 of the International Covenant on Economic, Social and Cultural Rights, submitted in accordance with Economic and Social Council Resolution 1988 (LX) E/C.12/1999/SA/1 (11 November 1999); Report of the International Labour Organization:. 18/05/98 E/1998/17 (Report of the UN Agencies/Organs): Implementation of the International Covenant on Economic, Social and Cultural Rights–Day of General Discussion: Globalisation and Its Impact on the Economic and Social Rights, Monday 11 May 1998.

[174] ECOSOC Res. 1988/4, UN Doc. E/C/12/1989/4. See Steiner, Alston and Goodman (eds) above n.1, at p. 277. When the Covenant came into effect, States parties were required to present initial reports every three years dealing with only a third of the rights recognised in Part III of the Covenant (i.e. Articles 6–9, 10–12 and 13–15). A cycle of reporting for the States parties thus took nine years, denying any updated analysis of a States' obligation of all the rights contained in the Covenant. However, the change to submission of the complete initial State report after two years of the enforcement of the Covenant and thereafter every five years was brought into operation in order to enhance the effectiveness of the reporting procedures.

[175] See O'Flaherty, above n.160, at p. 57.

[176] Alston, 'Out of the Abyss: The Challenges Confronting the New UN Committee on Economic, Social and Cultural Rights' 9 *HRQ* (1987) 332 at p. 333.

[177] See the International Commission of Jurists, *Commentary: Implementation of the International Covenant on Economic, Social and Cultural Rights–ECOSOC Working Group*, ICJ Review No. 27, 28 December 1981; Westerveen, 'Towards a System for Supervising States' Compliance with the Right to Food' in Alston and Tomaševski (eds), above, n.24, pp. 119 –134.

6

The International Covenant on Economic, Social and Cultural Rights

adequately involved in the work of the group; the reports failed to provide a summary or to provide any recommendations on substantive issues.[178]

As a response to these criticisms, in 1985, ECOSOC changed the composition of the working group and established the Committee on Economic, Social and Cultural Rights.[179] The Committee held its first session in March 1987,[180] and by November 2008 it had held 41 sessions.[181] The Committee consists of 18 members elected by ECOSOC from a list submitted by State parties for a term of four years. Elections of half of the Committee take place every two years, with members being entitled to be re-elected. Only States parties are entitled to nominate persons for election to the Committee.[182] The members of the Committee serve in their personal capacity and (unlike the members of the sessional working group) not as State representatives.[183] The representation of the Committee is based on the criterion of equitable geographical distribution.

(i) Aims and objectives of State reporting system

In order to counter the deficiencies in the State reporting the Committee has elaborated on the aim of reporting, a task undertaken by the Committee in its first General Comment.[184] In its General Comment, the Committee considered

that it would be incorrect to assume that reporting is essentially only a procedural matter designed solely to satisfy each State party's formal obligation to report to the appropriate international monitoring body. On the contrary, in accordance with the letter and spirit of the Covenant, the processes of preparation and submission of reports by States can, and indeed should, serve to achieve a variety of objectives.[185]

The Committee articulated the following objectives:

■ (particularly in relation to the initial reports) to ensure that a comprehensive review is undertaken with respect to national legislation, administrative rules and procedures, and practices in an effort to ensure the fullest possible conformity with the Covenant.

■ to ensure that the State party monitors the actual situation with respect to each of the rights on a regular basis and is thus aware of the extent to which the various rights are, or are not, being enjoyed by all individuals within its territory or under its jurisdiction.

---

[178] See Alston, 'The Committee on Economic, Social and Cultural Rights' in Alston (ed.), above n.168, at pp. 480–481.

[179] Review of the Composition, Organization and Administrative Arrangements of the Sessional Working Group of Governmental Experts on the Implementation of the International Covenant on Economic, Social and Cultural Eights ECOSOC Resolution 1985/17 (1985), 28 May 1985. The Resolution decided to set up an expert body consisting of 18 expert members to examine State Reports, Tomuschat, above n.1, at p. 172.

[180] Alston and Simma, 'First Session of the UN Committee on Economic, Social and Cultural Rights' 81 *AJIL* (1987) 747, at p. 747.

[181] Forty-second session of the Committee was held during 4–22 May 2009. See www2.ohchr.org/english/bodies/cescr/cescrs42.htm <last visited 30 May 2009>.

[182] ESC Res. 1985/17, para c.

[183] ESC Res. 1985/17, para b.

[184] CESCR General Comment 1, *Reporting by States Parties* General Comment No. 1 (24/02/89), Third session, 1989, E/1989/22.

[185] Ibid. para 1.

- to enable the Government to demonstrate that such principled policy-making has in fact been undertaken.

- to facilitate public scrutiny of government policies with respect to economic, social and cultural rights and to encourage the involvement of the various economic, social and cultural sectors of society in the formulation, implementation and review of the relevant policies.

- to provide a basis on which the State party itself, as well as the Committee, can effectively evaluate the extent to which progress has been made towards the realization of the obligations contained in the Covenant. For this purpose, it may be useful for States to identify specific benchmarks or goals against which their performance in a given area can be assessed.

- to enable the State party itself to develop a better understanding of the problems and shortcomings encountered in efforts to realize progressively the full range of economic, social and cultural rights.

- to enable the Committee, and the States parties as a whole, to facilitate the exchange of information among States and to develop a better understanding of the common problems faced by States and a fuller appreciation of the type of measures which might be taken to promote effective realization of each of the rights contained in the Covenant.[186]

In March 2009, the Committee on Economic, Social and Cultural Rights adopted a new set of guidelines. The objective being 'to take into account the harmonized guidelines on reporting under the international human rights treaties (HRI/GEN/2/Rev.5), as well as the evolving practice of the Committee in relation to the application of the Covenant, as reflected in its concluding observations, general comments and statements'.[187] The revised guidelines provide as follows:

1. State reports submitted under the harmonized guidelines on reporting under the international human rights treaties consist of two parts: a common core document and treaty-specific documents. The common core document should contain general information about the reporting State, the general framework for the protection and promotion of human rights, as well as information on non-discrimination and equality, and effective remedies, in accordance with the harmonized guidelines.

2. The treaty-specific document submitted to the Committee on Economic, Social and Cultural Rights should not repeat information included in the common core document or merely list or describe the legislation adopted by the State party. Rather, it should contain specific information relating to the implementation, in law and in fact, of articles 1 to 15 of the Covenant, taking into account the general comments of the Committee, as well as information on recent developments in law and practice affecting the full realization of the rights recognized in the Covenant. It should also contain information on the

[186] Ibid. paras 2–9.
[187] Committee on Economic, Social and Cultural Rights, Guidelines on treaty-specific documents to be submitted by States parties under Articles 16 and 17 of the International Covenant on Economic, Social and Cultural Rights E/C.12/2008/2 (24 March 2009) para 3. For the Guidelines see www2.ohchr.org/english/bodies/cescr/docs/E.C.12.2008.2.doc <last visited 5 May 2009>.

6

The International Covenant on Economic, Social and Cultural Rights

concrete measures taken towards that goal, and the progress achieved, including – except for initial treaty-specific documents – information on the steps taken to address issues raised by the Committee in the concluding observations on the State party's previous report, or in its general comments.

3. In relation to the rights recognized in the Covenant, the treaty-specific document should indicate:

(a) Whether the State party has adopted a national framework law, policies and strategies for the implementation of each Covenant right, identifying the resources available for that purpose and the most cost-effective ways of using such resources;

(b) Any mechanisms in place to monitor progress towards the full realization of the Covenant rights, including identification of indicators and related national benchmarks in relation to each Covenant right, in addition to the information provided under appendix 3 of the harmonized guidelines and taking into account the framework and tables of illustrative indicators outlined by the Office of the United Nations High Commissioner for Human Rights (OHCHR) (HRI/MC/2008/3);

(c) Mechanisms in place to ensure that a State party's obligations under the Covenant are fully taken into account in its actions as a member of international organizations and international financial institutions, as well as when negotiating and ratifying international agreements, in order to ensure that economic, social and cultural rights, particularly of the most disadvantaged and marginalized groups, are not undermined;

(d) The incorporation and direct applicability of each Covenant right in the domestic legal order, with reference to specific examples of relevant case law;

(e) The judicial and other appropriate remedies in place enabling victims to obtain redress in case their Covenant rights have been violated;

(f) Structural or other significant obstacles arising from factors beyond the State party's control which impede the full realization of the Covenant rights;

(g) Statistical data on the enjoyment of each Covenant right, disaggregated by age, gender, ethnic origin, urban/rural population and other relevant status, on an annual comparative basis over the past five years.

6. Periodic reports should address directly the suggestions and recommendations of the previous concluding observations.[188]

(ii) Procedure

The Committee meets twice annually for three-week sessions, with its primary task being to examine State reports. The meetings are held in Geneva during April/May and November/December of each year. During 2000–01, the Committee was authorised to meet for one further extraordinary session of three weeks duration.[189] In one session the Committee normally considers up to five reports. Once a report is submitted, the Committee makes a decision about the session in which consideration would take place. After the submission of the report, it is likely to take 24 to 30 months for the report to be considered. The exact details of timetabling are available three months prior to consideration of the report. The reports which the Committee has agreed should be reviewed are passed on to a five-member working group of the Committee. The working group holds

---

[188] Ibid. paras 1–3, 6.
[189] The session took place in August/September 2000; O'Flaherty, above n.168, at p. 58.

closed meetings at the end of each session providing an initial consideration to the reports due for the next session. NGOs are allowed to submit written reports or to make oral presentations to the Committee at this stage.

In its consideration, the working group draws up a list of issues with the information before it, utilising information acquired from various inter-governmental and non-governmental sources. The idea behind this list is to

> identify in advance the questions which might most usefully be discussed with the representative of the reporting States. The aim is to improve the efficiency of the system and to facilitate the task of States' representatives by providing advance notice of many of the principal issues which will arise in the examination of the reports.[190]

In drafting the list, a serving member of the working group, the 'Country Rapporteur', plays an instrumental role. States parties are required to respond in writing to these questions prior to the consideration of the report. The reports are reviewed in a public session with the consideration of a single State report normally taking two days. Reports are normally introduced by the State representative. The discussion by the Committee is based around the list of questions previously prepared by its working group, issues arising therefrom, a country profile drawn by the Secretariat which incorporates information from a range of sources including international organisations such as the ILO and WHO, as well as information from NGOs.

During the session, the State representative is given the opportunity to respond to the questions on the list. After their consideration the Committee members summarise their views and make suggestions and recommendations. The consideration normally lasts for around three meetings, each consisting of three hours. Following the consideration of a State's report, the Committee produces its Concluding Observations, a practice followed since its second session.[191] Concluding Observations are issued as a public document in which various aspects of the report are analysed and usually consist of positive features in the report, the identification of difficulties and the concerns of the Committee. Suggestions and Recommendations are also made within the Concluding Observations. The Committee may include requests for the provision of additional information which had been made to the State representatives during the consideration of the report. Concluding Observations are issued at the end of each session and are included in the annual report of the Committee to ECOSOC. NGOs also have been allowed to make oral presentations at the start of each session (Rule 69(2)).[192] This provides the NGOs with an opportunity to comment on the reports which are due to be considered by the Committee. In accordance with Rule 69 of the ICESCR Committee's Rules of Procedure, NGOs are allowed to make submissions 'that might contribute to full and universal recognition and realization of the

---

[190] UN Doc. E/1995/22, Chap. III, para 23.

[191] Craven, above n.1, at p. 87.

[192] E/C.12/1990/4/Rev.1 (1 September 1993) Committee on Economic, Social and Cultural Rights Rules of Procedure of the Committee Provisional Rules of Procedure adopted by the Committee at its third session (1989) (embodying amendments adopted by the Committee at its fourth (1990) and eighth (1993) sessions). <http://daccessdds.un.org/doc/UNDOC/GEN/G93/183/98/PDF/G9318398.pdf?OpenElement> <last visited 29 May 2009>.

6

The International Covenant on Economic, Social and Cultural Rights

rights contained in the covenant'.[193] The NGOs have often produced alternative reports which represent a different and more accurate picture. It is not surprising that the Committee has benefited enormously from these alternative reports and other sources of information emanating from the NGOs. According to Leckie, the merits of alternative reports include:

> [drawing] attention to inaccuracies and distortions in a governmental report; they can provide new information and offer ideas for more appropriate policies and legislation. The preparation of alternative reports can also act as a catalyst in the emergence of new coalitions and movements between previously unconnected groups.[194]

In many respects the Committee's nature and role appears similar to that of the Human Rights Committee. However, unlike the Human Rights Committee, this Committee is not responsible to States parties but to ECOSOC, a main organ of the United Nations.[195] The primary difficulty in the implementation of the Covenant stems from the parties' reluctance to comply with their reporting obligations. Reports submitted by the States are often significantly overdue and have the characteristic of being excessively brief, incomplete or outdated. The other difficulties of implementation include the vast scope and, indeed, the vagueness of the nature of the rights themselves.[196] An associated issue is the ambivalence of many States towards economic, social and cultural rights of this nature. The relative lack of jurisprudence and case-law arising from international and domestic tribunals has not been helpful,[197] and there has been the added problem of attaining adequate and relevant information from States parties. There has been reluctance in developing the jurisprudence related to economic, social and cultural rights when compared to civil and political rights; the breadth of the Covenant's rights makes the Committee's analysis more difficult. Many of the economic, social and cultural rights concepts have not been considered in any depth at the international level or domestic level.[198] The development of such jurisprudence has

---

[193] Rule 69(1). This presentation of oral statements normally takes place in the first afternoon at the beginning of each of the committee's sessions.

[194] Leckie, 'The Committee on Economic, Social and Cultural Rights: Catalyst for Change in a System Needing Reform' in Alston and Crawford (eds), above n.168, at p. 134.

[195] For consideration of ECOSOC see chapter 3 above.

[196] Alston and Simma, 'Second Session of the UN Committee on Economic, Social and Cultural Rights' 82 *AJIL* (1988) 603 at p. 606.

[197] See Leckie, 'The Committee on Economic, Social and Cultural Rights: Catalyst for Change in a System Needing Reform' Alston and Crawford (eds), above n.168, at pp. 129–144.

[198] Note, however, the recent cases decided by South African Constitutional Court on economic, social and cultural rights, e.g. *Government of the Republic of South Africa and others* v. *Grootboom and others* 2000 (11) BCLR 1169. (CC) (Challenging failure of government to provide adequate housing under s.26 (right to adequate housing) and s.28 (Children's right to shelter) of the South African Constitution); *Bhe* v. *Magistrate Khayelitsha and others* 2005 (1) BCLR 1 (CC), 15 Oct. 2004 (Applicants and Public Interest Organisations challenged gender discriminatory inheritance laws); *Khosa and others* v. *Minister of Social Development and others* 2004 (6) BCLR 569 (CC) (allegations of exclusion of non-citizens from social grant entitlements being unconstitutional on grounds of Sections 27, 28, 9, 10 and 11 South African Constitution); *Minister of Health* v. *Treatment Action Campaign* (TAC) (2002) 5 SA 721 (CC) (Challenging restrictions on the provision of anti-retroviral drugs to HIV positive pregnant women, that led to huge numbers of infections and consequent deaths and there was an alleged violation of the right to health care services in s.27(1) and s.28(1)(c) of the South African Constitution); *Port Elizabeth Municipality* v. *Various Occupiers* 2004 (12) BCLR 1268 (CC) (Application made under *Prevention of Illegal Eviction from and Unlawful Occupation of Land Act 19 of 1998* (PIE) to challenge eviction as not being 'just and equitable'). The case also involved the question of negative as well as positive obligations on the State as to the right to housing. For further analysis see Chenwi, 'Putting

been one of the primary preoccupations of the Committee, a practice which, as we shall consider, is conducted in a variety of ways.

7 INNOVATIVE PROCEDURES

To make its work more effective the Committee has adopted a number of innovative procedures. The original provision in Article 17 required States parties to submit an initial report within one year of the Covenant's entering into force. However, the Committee, adopting a realist approach, devised rules to extend the date of submission to two years and thereafter every five years. During its twenty-fourth session in 2000, the Committee, in establishing a general rule, decided that a State party's next periodic report should be submitted five years after the Committee's consideration of the State's preceding report. However this period may be reduced on the basis of the following criteria and having regard to all the relevant circumstances: (i) the timeliness of the State party's submission of its periodic reports; (ii) the quality of all the information submitted by the State; (iii) the quality of dialogue between the Committee and the State; (iv) the adequacy of the State response to the Committee's Concluding Observations; and (v) the State's actual record as regards the implementation of the ICESCR.[199]

Furthermore, in order to deal with inordinate delays with the submission of reports, in its sixth session, the Committee appealed to the Council to allow it to list those States which have failed to submit their initial reports, notwithstanding the passage of 10 years. This in effect was aimed to embarrass or blacklist certain States. In addition, the Committee also adopted procedures of fast-tracking reports for consideration, notwithstanding their substantial delay or failure in submitting initial/periodic reports.[200]

Although it is anticipated that the State representative would be present at the time of consideration of the reports, the inability of States to send representatives has been established by the Committee as an invalid ground to delay the consideration of the State reports. The Committee has also adopted follow-up procedures as regards consideration of State reports. In accordance with these procedures the Committee requests the State party to inform the Committee in its next periodic report (or prior to such submission) of the steps that the State party has undertaken to comply with the recommendations issued in the Committee's Concluding Observations. In case of failure to provide the requisite information or failure to comply with the Committee's recommendations, the Committee may investigate the matter further including, *inter alia*, sending a investigating mission of one or two members of the Committee.

Flesh on the Skeleton: South African Judicial Enforcement of the Right to Adequate Housing of Those Subject to Evictions' 8 *Human Rights Law Review* (2008) 105; Despite the fact that economic, social and cultural rights have been adjudicated in some domestic courts establish justiciability under the ICESCR remains controversial. See the Report of the Open-ended working group to consider options regarding elaboration of an optional protocol to the International Covenant on Economic, Social and Cultural Rights on its first session (Geneva, 23 February–5 March 2004) UN Doc. E/CN.4/2004/44 (15 March 2004); also see Dennis and Stewart, 'Justiciability of Economic, Social and Cultural Rights: Should There be an International Complaints Mechanism to Adjudicate the Right to Food, Water, Housing and Health?' 98 *AJIL* (2004) 462.

[199] Committee on Economic, Social and Cultural Rights, Report on the Twenty-third and Twenty-fourth sessions (25 April 2000–12 May 2000, 14 August 2001–1 September 2001, 13 November 2000–1 December 2000) UN Doc. E/C.12/2000/21 para 637; O'Flaherty, above n.168, at p. 59.

[200] UN Doc. E/1992/23, 99 para 245.

The International Covenant on Economic, Social and Cultural Rights

6

NGOs play an important role in the promotion and protection of human rights. Considering their potential value in promoting economic, social and cultural rights, it is disappointing to note that no specific provisions had been made for NGOs to make a contribution to the Covenant's reporting and supervisory procedures.[201] The Committee, however, has made attempts to overcome this limitation. In recognition of the usefulness of their work and especially the production of alternative reports by the NGOs, the Committee has invited 'all concerned bodies and individuals to submit relevant and appropriate documentation to it'.[202] The Committee has also established procedures to invite the governments to provide additional information and to engage in dialogue on particular issues. 1994 saw the Committee seeking additional information from Panama, the Dominican Republic and the Philippines on the subject of forced eviction.[203] Similarly, additional information has been sought from a number of other States, including the United Kingdom.

From its third session, at the invitation of ECOSOC, the Committee has begun to prepare General Comments on various articles and provisions of the Covenant. We have already noted the reasoning and rationale behind formulating General Comments for ICCPR.[204] The Committee's decision to adopt General Comments has been based on the same rationale. The primary objective of the General Comments, according to the Committee, is to assist State parties to fulfil their obligations, and in particular

> to make the experience gained so far through the examination of these reports available for the benefit of all States parties in order to assist and promote their further implementation of the Covenant; to draw the attention of the States parties to insufficiencies disclosed by a large number of reports; to suggest improvements in the reporting procedures; and to stimulate the activities of the States parties, the international organizations and specialized agencies concerned in achieving progressively and effectively the full realization of the rights recognized in the Covenant.[205]

A number of significant Comments have been adopted by the Committee. These include, General Comment No. 1 (1989) on Reporting by States Parties,[206] General Comment No. 2 (1990) on International Technical Assistance Measures (Article 22),[207] General Comment No. 3 (1990) on the Nature of States Parties' Obligations (Article 2, para 1 of the Covenant),[208] General Comment No. 7 (1997) on the Right to Adequate Housing: Forced

---

[201] See Alston, above n.176, at p. 367.
[202] E/1992/23 at 100 para 386 (Report of the Committee, sixth session).
[203] See Human Rights Monitor, XXV/XXVI, 1994, p. 41 and XXVII, 1994, p. 17; Robertson and Merrills, above n.17, at p. 281.
[204] See above chapter 5.
[205] Office of the United Nations High Commissioner on Human Rights, *Committee on Economic, Social and Cultural Rights – Working Methods: Overview of the present working methods of the Committee* http://www2.ohchr.org/english/bodies/cescr/workingmethods.htm <last visited 1 May 2009>.
[206] CESCR General Comment No. 1. (General Comments) *Reporting by States Parties: 24/02/89* Third Session 1989, UN Doc. E/1989/22.
[207] CESCR General Comment No. 2. (General Comments) *International technical assistance measures (Art. 22): 02/02/90* Fourth Session, 1990, E/1990/23.
[208] CESCR General Comment No. 3. (General Comments) *The nature of States parties obligations (Art. 2, par.1): 14/12/90* Fifth Session, 1990, E/1991/23.

Evictions (Article 11, para 1 of the Covenant),[209] General Comment No. 8 on the Relationship between Economic Sanctions and the Respect for Economic, Social and Cultural Rights,[210] General Comment No. 5 (1994) on Persons with Disabilities,[211] General Comment No. 6 (1995) on the Economic, Social and Cultural Rights of Older Persons,[212] General Comment No. 14 (2002) on the Right to Highest Attainable Standard of Health (Article 12),[213] General Comment No. 16 (2005) on the Equal Right of Men and Women to the Enjoyment of All Economic, Social and Cultural Rights (Article 3 of the International Covenant on Economic, Social and Cultural Rights)[214] and General Comment No. 19 (2007) on the Right to Social Security (Article 9).[215] In the context of this Covenant, the General Comments produced by the Committee have been of particular value, as Tomuschat eloquently states 'the general comments particularizing the duties flowing from [ICESCR] are especially stimulating in that they make a tremendous effort to define the hard substance of economic and social rights'.[216]

In addition, the Committee has set aside one day in every session for a general discussion (DGD) on a specific issue or issues which allow specialised agencies and NGOs to contribute more effectively to the work of the Committee.[217] This reserved day is usually the Monday of the Committee's final week.[218] The DGD is a public event and allows governmental representatives, representatives from specialised agencies, national human rights institutions and non-governmental actors, including human rights activists, to take part in the general discussion.[219] According to the Committee the function of this day 'is twofold; the day assists the Committee in developing in greater depth its understanding of the relevant issues; and it enables the Committee to encourage inputs into its work from all interested parties'.[220] The agenda item for the proceedings of the day has been established as from the third session when the Committee considered the issue of the right to food. In the fourth session, the day of general discussion was devoted to the right of housing. In 1994 the Committee discussed the role of social security measures with particular reference to transition to a market economy and human rights education. In 1998 the one day of general discussion was dedicated to globalisation and its impact on the enjoyment of economic and social rights.[221] In 2003, the right to work formed the basis of the Committee's

---

[209] CESCR General Comment No. 7. (General Comments) *The right to adequate housing (Art. 11.1): forced evictions: 20/05/97* Sixteenth Session, 1997 E/1998/22, annex I.

[210] CESCR General Comment No. 8. (General Comments) *The relationship between economic sanctions and respect for economic, social and cultural rights: 12/12/97* E/1998/22 Seventeenth session, E/1990/22.

[211] CESCR General Comment No. 5. (General Comments): *Persons with Disabilities: 09/12/94*, Eleventh Session, 1994, E/1995/22.

[212] CESCR General Comment No. 6. (General Comments) *The economic, social and cultural rights of older persons:. 08/12/95* Thirteenth Session 1995, E/1996/22.

[213] CESCR General Comment No. 14, *The Right to Highest Attainable Standard of Health*, (Article 12) (11/08/00). (E/C.12/2000/4), (Twenty-Second Session) 25 April–12 May 2000.

[214] CESCR General Comment No. 16. (General Comments): *11/08/2005 The equal right of men and women to the enjoyment of all economic, social and cultural rights (art. 3 of the International Covenant on Economic, Social and Cultural Rights)*, Thirty-Fourth Session, E/C.12/2005/4.

[215] CESCR General Comment No. 19. (General Comments) *The right to social security (art. 9)* Thirty-Ninth Session, E/C.12/GC/19 (4 February 2008).

[216] Tomuschat, above n.1, at p. 190.

[217] Alston and Simma, above n.196 at p. 608.

[218] See O'Flaherty, above n.168, at p. 69.

[219] www2.ohchr.org/english/bodies/cescr/discussion090508.htm <last visited 30 May 2009>.

[220] UN Doc. E/C.12/2000/21, para 50.

[221] See Background paper submitted by ILO 21/04/98; E/C.12/1998/8.

day of general discussion. During its fortieth session, the Committee dedicated 9 May 2008 as the day for examining the 'Right to Take Part in Cultural Life'.[222] Furthermore, during its forty-first session (held 3–21 November 2008), the Committee dedicated half a day on 17 November 2008 for discussion on 'Discrimination and Economic, Social and Cultural Rights'.[223] This exercise of days for general discussion has been productive and has produced positive results. Commenting on some of these positive aspects, Alston notes:

> The discussions have provided an invaluable means by which the Committee has been able to open up its dialogue and has given it the opportunity to invite a much wider range of inputs from individuals or groups that feel they have something to offer to the Committee. The general discussions also enables the Committee to discuss broader, sometimes more theoretical issues which are directly relevant to its role of examining States reports and especially to the task of elaborating General Comments.[224]

The day of general discussion provides the opportunity for NGOs, Special Rapporteurs and UN specialised agencies to engage in the debates pertaining to the specific issue. One of the most positive achievements of the Committee's work has been its close association and co-ordination with UN agencies and the Special Rapporteurs. The Committee has drawn upon the expertise of relevant specialised agencies, the UN organs as well as experts working in related areas. It has therefore welcomed contributions and shared ideas with UN personnel including the UN Special Rapporteurs. The Committee was addressed in 1993 by the Special Rapporteur on the Issue of Impunity of the Sub-Commission on Prevention of Discrimination and Protection of Minorities and in 1994 by a delegate from the World Health Organization (WHO) in the context of human rights and HIV/AIDs. In 2001 the Committee was addressed by the Deputy High Commissioner, Dr. Bertrand Ramcharan. In order to assist States parties to ICESCR, the Committee has also adopted the practice of issuing statements. These statements are aimed at clarifying or confirming the Committee's stance on key international developments which are likely to impact on the implementation of the Covenant. Thus far the Committee has issued 16 such statements, the latest on 'The World Food Crisis' having been issued on 17 May 2008.[225]

The Committee has also initiated fact-finding missions for its members to visit States and assess for themselves situations involving violations of economic and social rights. The invitation and support of the relevant State, however, is necessary for a visit to take place. In further investigations of the issue of forced eviction in 1995, the Committee sent a fact-finding mission (which thus far remains the only mission) to Panama, which reported back to the Committee during the same year.[226]

---

[222] www2.ohchr.org/english/bodies/cescr/discussion090508.htm <last visited 30 May 2009>.

[223] Committee on Economic, Social and Cultural Rights, Half-day of General Discussion on 'Discrimination and Economic, Social and Cultural Rights' www2.ohchr.org/english/bodies/cescr/discussion17112008.htm <last visited 30 May 2009>.

[224] Alston, 'The Committee on Economic, Social and Cultural Rights' in Alston (ed.), above n.168, pp. 493–494.

[225] Committee on Economic, Social and Cultural Rights, Fortieth Session 28 April–16 May 2008 E/C.12/2008/1 (20 May 2008).

[226] See United Nations, *The Committee on Economic, Social and Cultural Rights*, Fact Sheet No. 16, Rev.1 (United Nations, 1991).

(i) Optional Protocol to the ICESCR[227]

Ever since the coming into operation of the Covenant, efforts have been made to draft an Optional Protocol similar in nature the Optional Protocol to the ICCPR. Considerable opposition, however, was engendered to any such attempts precisely due to the apparently weak and vague nature of the provisions contained within the ICESCR. Those in favour of introducing an Optional Protocol to the ICESCR pointed to the growing number of such instruments being appended to treaties with a high concentration of economic, social and cultural rights. These treaties have been adopted both at the global as well as at regional levels. In 1996, the ICESCR Committee adopted a draft Protocol providing for the consideration of communications for non-compliance with the treaty.[228] However the draft enthusiastically (and as it turned out rather naively) proposed to cover the scrutiny of all the substantive rights – from Article 1 to 15. Subsequently an independent expert was appointed, although his report did not prove particularly helpful. Further efforts were made by the now redundant Human Rights Commission to invigorate the debate through the renewal of the mandate of the independent expert, and by establishing an open-ended working group to consider the possibility of a communication mechanism. As the most significant milestone in the development of Economic, Social and Cultural Rights, on Wednesday 18 June, 2008, the United Nations Human Rights Council adopted the Optional Protocol to the International Covenant on Economic, Social and Cultural Rights. This Protocol allows persons to petition the Committee on ICESCR about the violation of their rights contained under the Covenant. The Council had recommended that at a signing ceremony to be held in Geneva in March 2009, the UN General Assembly adopts and opens for signature, ratification and accession the Optional Protocol to the International Covenant on Economic, Social and Cultural Rights. The Protocol is annexed to a Human Rights Council Resolution and was adopted by the Council in its eighth session.[229] The United Nations General Assembly unanimously adopted the Optional Protocol to the International Covenant on Economic, Social and Cultural Rights on 10 December 2008 with the recommendation that the Optional Protocol be opened for signature at a signing ceremony to be held in 2009.[230] This Protocol is due to be opened for signature in September 2009.

According to Article 1 of the Optional Protocol, States Parties to the Covenant joining the Protocol recognise the competence of the UN Committee on Economic, Social and Cultural Rights to receive and consider communications alleging violations of the economic, social and cultural rights set forth in the Covenant.[231] Article 2 provides that 'Communications may be submitted by or on behalf of individuals or groups of individuals, under the jurisdiction of a State Party, claiming to be victims of a violation of any of the economic, social and cultural rights set forth in the Covenant by that State Party.' Thus the text of the Protocol does not provide any *locus standi* to NGOs to submit any communications in their own right, although they may file communications on behalf of

---

[227] See Mahon 'Progress at the Front: The Draft Optional Protocol to the International Covenant on Economic, Social and Cultural Rights' 8 *Human Rights Law Review* (2008) 617.

[228] See *the Report of the Committee on the International Covenant on Economic, Social and Cultural Rights*, UN Doc. E/1997/22, 91, Annex IV; UN Doc. E/CN.4/1997/105, Annex.

[229] See A/HRC/8/L. 2/Rev. 1/Corr. 1. Human Rights Council Resolution 8/2.

[230] See FIDH, 'NGOs Celebrate Historic Adoption of Optional Protocol for Economic, Social and Cultural Rights at the United Nations' 11 December 2008 www.fidh.org/spip.php?article6113 <last visited 30 May 2009>.

[231] Optional Protocol to the International Covenant on Economic, Social and Cultural Rights, Article 1.

individuals or groups of individuals who are claiming to be victims.[232] Article 3 provides for admissibility criteria which are generally in line with the Optional Protocol of the ICCPR. Article 4 is an interesting provision through which '[T]he Committee may, if necessary, decline to consider a communication where it does not reveal that the author has suffered a clear disadvantage, unless the Committee considers that the communication raises a serious issue of general importance'. The obvious intention is to allow the Committee to concentrate on those communications which would lead to serious disadvantages and violations of rights contained in the Covenant. It would appear that the Committee would have discretion in making any such decisions; the Committee's future jurisprudence should hopefully provide certain guidelines on the operation of this provision.[233]

Within the Protocol, there are mechanisms for undertaking 'interim measures', through which 'the Committee may transmit to the State Party concerned for its urgent consideration a request that the State Party take such interim measures . . . to avoid possible irreparable damage to the victim or victims of the alleged violations'.[234] Article 8 of the Optional Protocol provides for a mechanism of the examination of the Communications, whereas Article 9 establishes a procedure for the follow-up to the views of the Committee. Article 10 caters for another implementation procedure – the inter-State complaints mechanism. In line with the ICCPR, States parties to the ICESCR must make an independent declaration if they are utilise this procedure; no communication shall be received by the Committee if it concerns a State party which has not made such a declaration.[235]

Furthermore, Article 11 of the Protocol also establishes an inquiry procedure, setting out that 'if the Committee receives reliable information indicating grave or systematic violations . . . the Committee shall invite that State Party to cooperate in the examination of the information and to this end to submit observations with regard to the information concerned'. However, as a prerequisite in order to trigger the inquiry procedure, the State party would need to make an independent declaration that it recognises the competence of the ICESCR Committee to operate under Article 11. The inquiry may include a visit to the territory of the State party concerned. According to the Optional Protocol, States are to take all appropriate measures to ensure that individuals under their jurisdiction are not subjected to any form of ill-treatment or intimidation as a consequence of communicating with the Committee pursuant to the Protocol.[236] The Optional Protocol will enter into force three months after the date of deposit with the UN Secretary-General of the 10th instrument of ratification or accession.

8 CONCLUSIONS

The analysis of the economic, social and cultural rights contained in ICESCR reveals many limitations and shortcomings. A particularly disturbing aspect has been the debate about the nature of many of the rights contained in the Covenant; whether they create immediately binding obligations or a mere programme of action. Through consideration of the provisions of ICESCR, the Committee's observations and General Comments, this chapter has established that economic, social and cultural rights retain the same legal value and

---

[232] See Mahon above n.227, at p. 634.
[233] Ibid. at p. 630.
[234] Optional Protocol to the International Covenant on Economic, Social and Cultural Rights Article 5.
[235] Ibid. Article 10(1).
[236] Ibid. Article 13.

binding effect as civil and political rights. Furthermore, international law and jurisprudence is increasingly approximating extra-territorial application to economic, social and cultural rights as has been the case with civil and political rights.[237] At the same time, on a realistic plane it has to be conceded that the implementation of economic, social and cultural rights has not been straightforward. The implementation mechanisms themselves have had to be revised and we are still awaiting the realisation of an individuals' complaints procedure.

The Committee, since its establishment in 1985, has done a commendable job in monitoring the Covenant. Of particular value have been its views, emergent from State reports and General Comments. In its consideration of State reports, the Committee has taken a broad approach, which encompasses human rights obligations incurred through the acceptance of ICESCR. Thus:

> in addition to asking questions on the status of ethnic minorities, natural children, women and men or discrimination on the basis of religion, alternative political philosophies and class bias [the Committee] has directed itself to the situation of those in particular regional areas, aliens (including the stateless, migrant workers and refugees) unmarried couples, and parents, people with AIDS, or physical and mental disabilities, homosexuals, the poor and the elderly.[238]

In particular the Committee has stressed the need for a comprehensive review of national legislation and administrative rules regarding the rights contained in the Covenant and of adequate scrutiny of governmental policies. The Committee has also highlighted the need for greater co-ordination in policy making, which would provide a basis for effective evaluation of the progress made in achieving the rights. Through its work the Committee has facilitated a better understanding of the problems and issues involved in the implementation of the Covenant as well as promoting exchange of information amongst States. Changes have also been introduced which have improved the work of the Committee. As noted earlier, the system of presenting initial reports at three-year intervals, each dealing with one-third of the rights, was changed by the Committee to a single comprehensive report to be submitted every five years. Further changes, as examined in our analysis, have been made to the State reporting mechanism with a view to making the system more effective. In addition, and in order to elaborate upon its jurisprudence and also to ensure greater

---

[237] ICESCR Committee criticised the Sri Lankan government for the housing and health and nutritional conditions for civilians displaced in the civil war. See *Concluding observation of the Committee on Economic, Social and Cultural Rights, Sri Lanka*, E/C.12/1/Add.24, 16 June 1998, para 7. The Committee has similarly been critical of economic suffering of the Palestinians by the State of Israel, and of Russia in conditions within Chechnya. See *Concluding Observations of the Committee on Economic, Social and Cultural Rights, Israel*, E/C.12/1/Add.90 26 June 2003, para 19 and *Concluding Observations of the Committee on Economic, Social and Cultural Rights: Russian Federation 12/12/2003*, E/C.12/1/Add.94, 12 December 2003 para 10. The UN Special Rapporteur on the Right to Food during 2002 reported that the use of food was a 'method of warfare against insurgents and civilian populations' by the Myanmar Government. The Special Rapporteur has similarly been critical of situations perpetuated in the Palestinian territory and in Afghanistan. E/CN.4/2002/58 Report by the Special Rapporteur on the right to food, Mr. Jean Ziegler, submitted in accordance with Commission on Human Rights resolution 2001/25, 10 January 2002. See also E/CN.4/2004/10/Add.2 31 October 2003 Report by the Special Rapporteur, Jean Ziegler Addendum Mission to the Occupied Palestinian Territories. The Special Rapportuer on the Right to Health has also expressed concern on the health of civilians in the city of Fallujah after the military operations by US military. E/CN.4/2005/51 2 February 2005, Report of the Special Rapporteur on the right of everyone to the enjoyment of the highest attainable standard of physical and mental health, Paul Hunt, Addendum, Summary of cases transmitted to Governments and replies receives, para 73. For the extra-territorial application of economic, social and cultural rights during times of armed conflict also see below chapter 21.

[238] Craven, above n.1, at pp. 169–170 (footnotes omitted).

appreciation of economic, social and cultural rights, the Committee has relied upon such useful strategies as issuing General Comments and Statements, and dedicating a day for a thematic discussion on key issues during the 'day for general discussion'. The adoption of the Optional Protocol to the International Covenant on Economic, Social and Cultural Rights on 10 December 2008 is a very welcome and positive development. The Protocol aims to set *at par* (at least in theoretical terms) the implementation mechanisms for civil and political rights and the economic, social and cultural rights. In reality it still remains highly speculative as to the extent to which States parties will share their enthusiasm in being subjected to the provisions of the Protocol.

A comment which relates to the role and position of NGOs in the present context appears necessary. NGOs have been the principal advocates of the vindication of individual human rights. Although over the years, their contribution (again largely through positive action undertaken by the Committee) has become more effective regarding the implementation of ICESCR, there continues to be some reluctance on the part of many NGOs to engage themselves in promoting economic, social and cultural rights. A predisposition in favour of civil and political rights is perhaps to be attributed to the origins and issues addressed by many of the NGOs. NGOs based in the developing world, in particular, have often treated violations of economic, social and cultural rights as ancillary to the breaches of civil and political rights.[239] Although some improvements have been made and some NGOs such as Amnesty International have taken a more active role in promoting economic, social and cultural rights in the overall framework there nevertheless remains a bias in the work of the NGO sector which needs to be removed.

The focus of the present chapter has been on ICESCR. Subsequent chapters of this book establish that economic, social and cultural rights have blended into civil and political rights, a feature particularly evident from a survey of the jurisprudence of the regional treaties of Europe, the Americas and Africa. The regional human rights systems have also accorded a degree of prominence to economic and social rights through the adoption of such treaties as the European Social Charter,[240] the revised European Social Charter (1996)[241] and the Additional Protocol to the American Convention on Human Rights in the Area of Economic, Social and Cultural Rights (1988).[242]

---

[239] According to Alston: 'for a variety of historical, ideological, pragmatic and other reasons, there remains a considerable reluctance on the part of many, if not most, human rights NGOs to become involved in this field. This is particularly the case with respect to those NGOs based in the West that do not have significant constituencies in the Third World. In the case of limited mandate organizations such as Amnesty International or Index on Censorship, the justification is the desire to maintain a narrow and precise focus. Other NGOs that purport to be concerned with either "the rights contained in the Universal Declaration" or "internationally recognized human rights" face a much more difficult task to justify their neglect of economic, social, and cultural rights. The situation in Central America today, for example, cannot be adequately or productively analyzed without taking full account of both sides of the human rights equation. In this sense, the much vaunted interdependence of the two sets of rights is not simply a hollow UN slogan designed to conceal an ideological split, but is an accurate reflection of the realities of the situation.' Alston, above n.176, at p. 372 (footnotes omitted).

[240] Adopted at Turin 18 October 1961. Entered into force, 26 February 1965. 529 U.N.T.S 89; ETS 35. See below chapter 9.

[241] Adopted 3 May 1996. Entered into force, 3 July 1999. ETS No. 163. See below chapter 9.

[242] Additional Protocol to the American Convention on Human Rights in the Area of Economic, Social and Cultural Rights, 'Protocol of San Salvador' OAS Treaty Series No. 69 (1988), entered into force 16 November 1999; 28 I.L.M. (1989) 156. See below chapter 10.

Part III

Regional protectionism of human rights

Europe and human rights (I)[1]

1 INTRODUCTION

European human rights law is not the product of a single monolithic mechanism. Instead there are several institutions which have established mechanisms for protecting human rights.[2] The role of at least three organisations is worthy of consideration: the Council of Europe, the European Union (EU) and the Organisation for Security and Co-operation in Europe (OCSE). The Council of Europe, the oldest of these institutions, has also had the most significant role in promoting human rights at the European level. The European Union, which remains politically the most viable and influential, has had only an indirect part to play in protecting human rights. However, increasingly human rights issues are being absorbed in the rapidly expanding EU, and there is now the future possibility of the accession of the EU to the European Convention on Human Rights.[3] Although having

---

[1] See Clayton and Tomlinson, *The Law of Human Rights* (Oxford University Press, 2009); Harris, O'Boyle, Bates and Buckley, *Harris, O'Boyle and Warbrick Law of the European Convention on Human Rights* (Oxford University Press, 2009); Mowbray and Harris, *Cases and Materials on the European Convention on Human Rights* (Butterworths, 2001); Janis, Kay and Bradley, *European Human Rights Law: Text and Materials* (Oxford University Press, 2000); Blackburn and Polakiewicz (eds), *Fundamental Rights in Europe: The European Convention on Human Rights and its Member States, 1950 2000* (Oxford University Press, 2001); Lester and Pannick, *Human Rights: Law and Practice* (Butterworths, 2004); Loux and McQueen, *Human Rights and Scots Law: Comparative Perspectives on the Incorporation of the ECHR* (Hart Publishing, 2002); Shelton, 'The Boundaries of Human Rights Jurisdiction in Europe' 13 *Duke J. Comp. & Int'l L.* (2003) 95; Clements, Mole and Simmons, *European Human Rights: Taking a Case Under the Convention* (Sweet & Maxwell, 1999); Barkhuysen, Van Emmerik and Van Kempen, *The Execution of Strasbourg and Geneva Human Rights Decisions in the National Legal Order* (Martinus Nijhoff Publishers, 1999); Van Dijk, Van Hoof, Van Rijn and Zwaak (eds), *Theory and Practice of the European Court of Human Rights* (Intersentia Publishing, 2006); Overy and White, *The European Convention on Human Rights* (Oxford University Press, 2006).

[2] These institutions sometimes act as parallels, while at other times they overlap with one another. See McCrudden and Chambers 'Introduction' in McCrudden and Chambers (eds), *Individual Rights and the Law in Britain* (Clarendon Press, 1994) pp. 1–38.

[3] Article 17 of Protocol 14 of the ECHR in revising Article 59(2) provides: 'The European Union may accede to this Convention'. Protocol No. 14 to the Convention for the Protection of Human Rights and Fundamental Freedoms, Amending the Control System of the Convention ETS No: 194 http://conventions.coe.int/treaty/en/treaties/html/194.htm <last visited 2 May 2009>. At the time of writing, Protocol 14 had yet to enter into force as *per* Article 19 of the Protocol which states: 'This Protocol shall enter into force on the first day of the month following the expiration of a period of three months after the date on which all Parties to the Convention have expressed their consent to be bound by the Protocol, in accordance with the provisions of Article 18.' Forty-six of the 47 States party to ECHR have ratified Protocol 14. Russia remains the only State not to have ratified Protocol 14, see New Europe, 'Merkel Calls on Russia to Adopt Protocol 14', 21 April 2008 (Issue: 778) www.neurope.eu/articles/85497.php <last visited 14 February 2009>; see further Caflisch, 'The Reform of the European Court of Human Rights: Protocol No. 14 and Beyond' 6 *HRLR* (2006) 403; Mowbary, *Cases and Materials on the European Convention on Human Rights* (Oxford University Press, 2007) at p. 48.

largely operated as an organisation aimed at promoting security and peace within Europe, the OSCE has taken a number of valuable human rights initiatives which are worthy of consideration.

Limitations of space make it impossible to study the work of each of the aforementioned organisations in great detail. Two chapters of this book are nevertheless dedicated to the study of European human rights law. The present chapter focuses on the position of the Council of Europe's European Convention on Human Rights (ECHR), an instrument which focuses largely on the provisions of civil and political rights. The next chapter, Chapter 8, considers the Council of Europe's European Social Charter (ESC). It then goes on to analyse the position and role of the EU and the OSCE in the protection of human rights.

2 THE COUNCIL OF EUROPE AND PROTECTION OF CIVIL AND POLITICAL RIGHTS

The Council of Europe is an inter-governmental organisation established in 1949 with the objective, *inter alia*, of strengthening democracy, human rights and the rule of law.[4] In its initial years, the membership of the Council of Europe was confined to the Western democratic European countries. It excluded Spain and Portugal until the mid-1970s. However, with the collapse of communism, several members of central and Eastern Europe have joined the Council. The current membership of the Council of Europe is 47 including all EU Member States. The Council of Europe has produced various important regional human rights treaties, the most prominent one being the ECHR.[5] The ECHR was adopted in 1950, came into operation in 1953 and currently provides protection to well over 800 million people.[6] The ECHR has the distinction of being the first and foremost of the human rights treaties with a procedurally developed judicial mechanism of accountability. Its extensive jurisprudence, as we shall examine in detail, has proved to be the inspirational force in the consolidation and practical realisation of international human rights norms. The institutions of the ECHR, the Court and the Committee of Ministers are based in Strasbourg, France.

During the Second World War (1939–45) Europe had been the scene of the most serious human rights violations. At the end of the war, it had become a major objective of the allied powers to punish those who had been involved in crimes against humanity during the war and to uphold human rights in the region. A regional human rights treaty protecting the fundamental civil and political rights was meant to act as a bulwark against the recurrence of the worst forms of human rights violations. The signing of the treaty was also aimed to encourage the extension of democracy in communist Europe and to suppress the spread of dictatorships and totalitarian ideologies in other parts of Europe.

As we have already noted, the UDHR was adopted in December 1948 by the United Nations General Assembly.[7] A natural progression from the Declaration on Human Rights

---

[4] According to Article 3 of the Statute each Member State 'must accept the principles of rule of law and the enjoyment by all persons within its jurisdiction of human rights and fundamental freedoms'. See Statute of the Council of Europe, adopted 5 May 1949. Entered into force August 1949. E.T.S. 1. For background reading see Robertson and Merrills, *Human Rights in Europe* (Manchester University Press, 1993) pp. 1–24.

[5] Signed at Rome, 4 November 1950. Entered into force 3 September 1953. 213 U.N.T.S. 221; E.T.S. 5. The Convention has over years been amended through 14 additional protocols.

[6] Feldman, *Civil Liberties and Human Rights in England and Wales* (Oxford University Press, 2002) at pp. 45–46.

[7] See above chapter 4.

was the formulation of a binding treaty with measures of implementation. Although it was not until 1966 that the International Covenants were adopted, consensus was easier to attain amongst the Western liberal States to draft a regional human rights treaty. The ECHR, despite being a regional convention, reflects the influence of and similarities with the principles contained in the Universal Declaration. The preamble of the ECHR, for example, refers to the Universal Declaration. Fundamental rights in the ECHR such as the prohibition of torture, the right to liberty and security and the right to a fair trial draw inspiration from similar provisions of the Declaration. However, there are also significant differences in the substantive provisions of the articles. Whereas the Universal Declaration considers civil, political, social, economic and cultural rights, the ECHR predominantly promotes and protects the civil and political rights.[8] This difference reflects the diversity of Constitutions adopted in Europe at the time – see e.g. the French Constitution of 1946, the Italian Constitution of 1948 and the German Basic Law of 1949.

The ECHR is divided into three sections. Section I provides a description and definition of the rights and fundamental freedoms provided in the treaty. Section II provides for the establishment of a court of human rights and explains the procedures, whereas Section III considers miscellaneous provisions such as reservations, denunciation, signature and ratification.[9] The substantive guarantees provided in the Convention are expanded by a number of additional Protocols.

The ECHR and its Protocols do not cover several important rights. The Convention, unlike the ICCPR, does not provide for the right to self-determination, which is recognised as one of the principal rights in international human rights instruments.[10] The vision of ECHR on minority or group rights is particularly thin.[11] There is also the failure to provide for economic, social and cultural rights.[12] Despite these omissions in the protection of rights, during the past six decades, the rights contained in the Convention have been utilised to protect individual rights. The Convention, as a living instrument, has been interpreted as in keeping with the changing values and traditions of European society.[13] It is described as a 'constitutional instrument of European Public Order'.[14] The ECHR, although

---

[8] The Counterpart of the ECHR is the European Social Charter which is considered in the next chapter.

[9] Starmer, *European Human Rights Law: The Human Rights Act 1998 and the European Convention on Human Rights* (Legal Action Group, 1999) pp. lxxi.

[10] See below chapter 14. ECHR is also limited in safeguarding many of the rights in the manner provided in ICCPR, e.g. Article 24 (family rights); Article 25 (rights of aliens); Article 26 (freestanding right to non-discrimination); see Higgins 'Foreword' in Harris and Joseph (eds), *ICCPR and UK Law* (Clarendon Press, 1995) pp. xi–xviii.

[11] The ECHR (and its Protocols) do not contain particular provisions protecting the rights of minorities. Some remedial action was taken by the Council of Europe to adopt a Framework Convention for the Protection of National Minorities; opened for signature 1 February 1995, entered into force 1 February 1998. E.T.S. 157; 34 I.L.M. (1995) 351. See Gilbert, 'The Council of Europe and Minority Rights' 18 *HRQ* (1996) 160. For consideration of regional treaties see below chapter 13.

[12] In emphasising upon the point that ECHR does not protect economic, social and cultural rights, it has been argued that its protection only extends to economic and social aspects of convention rights or collateral aspects of economic and social interests where these involve civil and political rights. See Warbrick 'Economic and Social Interests and the European Convention on Human Rights' in Baderin and McCorquodale (eds), *Economic, Social and Cultural Rights in Action* (Oxford University Press, 2007) pp. 241–256.

[13] See on issues of corporal punishment, *Tyrer* v. *UK* (1978) 2 E.H.R.R. 1; homosexuality, *Dudgeon* v. *United Kingdom* (1982) 4 E.H.R.R. 149.

[14] Meron, *The Implications of the European Convention on Human Rights for the Development of Public International Law* (Council of Europe, 2000) at p. 2.

7

Europe and human rights (I)

a regional instrument, has also had an enormous impact upon the development of norms in general international law.[15]

(i) Rights contained in the Convention

These are as follows:

Article 2   Right to life
Article 3   Prohibition of torture
Article 4   Prohibition of slavery and forced labour
Article 5   Right to liberty and security
Article 6   Right to a fair trial
Article 7   No punishment without law
Article 8   Right to respect for private and family life
Article 9   Freedom of thought, conscience and religion
Article 10   Freedom of expression
Article 11   Freedom of assembly and association
Article 12   Right to marry
Article 13   Right to an effective remedy
Article 14   Prohibition of discrimination
Article 15   Derogation in time of emergency
Article 16   Restrictions on political activities of aliens
Article 17   Prohibition of abuse of the rights
Article 18   Limitation on use of restrictions on rights

Protocol No. 1[16]
Article 1   Protection of property
Article 2   Right to education
Article 3   Right to free elections

Protocol No. 4[17]
Article 1   Prohibition of imprisonment for debt
Article 2   Freedom of movement
Article 3   Prohibition of expulsion of nationals
Article 4   Prohibition of collective expulsion of aliens

Article 1 of Protocol No. 6 Abolition of the death penalty[18]
Article 1 of Protocol No. 7 Procedural safeguards relating to expulsion of aliens[19]
Article 2 of Protocol No. 7 Right of appeal in criminal matters
Article 3 of Protocol No. 7 Compensation for wrongful conviction

[15] Meron identifies *inter alia* due process standards, environment, diplomatic protection, state responsibility and International Humanitarian Law as examples where ECHR has made substantial contributions to the development of the norms of International Law. See ibid. The Privy Council in *Pratt* v. *Attorney General of Jamaica* [1994] 2 AC 1 (Jamaica) approved the European Court of Human Rights' view expressed on the 'death-row' phenomenon.

[16] ETS No. 9, 213 U.N.T.S. 262. Entered into force 18 May 1954.

[17] ETS No. 46. Entered into force 2 May 1968.

[18] ETS No. 114. Entered into force 1 March 1985.

[19] ETS No. 117. Entered into force 1 November 1988.

Article 4 of Protocol No. 7 Right not to be tried or punished twice (*Ne bis in idem*)

Article 5 of Protocol No. 7 Equality between spouses

Protocol No. 12 General prohibition of discrimination[20]

Protocol No. 13 Abolition of the death penalty[21]

Institutional and Procedural Protocols

Protocol No. 11 Changes to the Convention machinery–Protocols 2, 3, 5, 8, 9, 10 were supplemented by Protocol 11[22]

Protocol No. 14 Amending the Control System of the Convention[23]

3 ANALYSIS OF SUBSTANTIVE RIGHTS

(i) The right to life and the prohibition of torture or inhuman or degrading treatment or punishment[24]

As we have already considered, the right to life is pre-emptory and the most fundamental of all human rights.[25] Within the Convention, the right to life is protected by Article 2, a right which is non-derogable even in times of war and public emergency.[26] The taking of life is prohibited save in the limited circumstances provided within the Article, a subject which we shall consider shortly. In relation to the substance of the right to life, the State is under two kinds of obligations. Firstly, there is a negative obligation not to take life and not to deprive an individual of his or her life save in limited circumstances which must be strictly in accordance with law. The second obligation is of a positive nature, which entails taking effective steps to protect the life of the individual concerned. Positive obligations include protecting individuals from agents of the State such as the police and security forces as well as non-State actors including terrorist organisations and other private individuals. The duty to take reasonable measures to protect life includes a duty to put in place 'effective criminal law provisions to deter the commission of offences against the person backed up by law-enforcement machinery for the prevention, suppression and sanctioning

---

[20] ETS No. 177. Adopted 26 June 2000. Opened for Signature 4 November 2000. Khaliq 'Protocol 12 to the European Convention on Human Rights: A Step Forward or a Step Too Far?' *Public Law* (2001) at 457. Protocol 12 entered into force 1 April 2005.

[21] ETS No. 187. Entered into force 1 July 2003.

[22] ETS No. 155. Entered into force 1 November 1998.

[23] ETS No. 194. http://conventions.coe.int/treaty/en/treaties/html/194.htm <last visited 15 May 2009>. See Council of Europe, *Reform of the European Human Rights System: Proceedings of the High Level Seminar Oslo, 18 October 2004* (2004). www.coe.int/t/e/human_rights/reformeurhrsystem_e.pdf <last visited 29 May 2007>; Mowbray, 'Faltering Steps on the Path to Reform of the Strasbourg Enforcement System' 7 *HRLR* (2007) 609.

[24] See Harris, 'The Right to Life Under the European Convention on Human Rights' 1 *Maastricht Journal of European Comparative Law* (1994) 122; Ni Aolain, 'The Evolving Jurisprudence of the European Convention Concerning the Right to Life' 19(1) *NQHR* (2001) 21; See also Rodley, *The Treatment of Prisoners Under International Law* (Clarendon Press, 1999).

[25] See above chapter 5.

[26] Harris, O'Boyle, Bates and Buckley, above n.1, at p. 37. Derogations are permissible in circumstances provided by Article 15(2). Article 15(2) provides that derogation from the Article is permissible 'in respect of deaths resulting from lawful acts of war'.

of breaches of such provisions'.[27] It also means requiring the proper investigation of all suspicious deaths, not merely those conducted by agents of the State.[28]

While these two components are firmly established, the remit of the obligation is not very clear. Thus, while the positive obligation includes taking reasonable steps to enforce the law to protect citizens, the State cannot be expected to prevent individuals from every attack.[29] Similarly, the breadth of obligations which might affect the right to life is uncertain. For instance, a question mark remains over the issue of State liability regarding poor housing, lack of food, medical attention, environmental pollution, road worthiness and workplace safety. This issue was considered but left unanswered in a case in which the parents of a seriously disabled child claimed that their daughter had not been allowed free medical treatment.[30]

In the context of the present Article, the meaning of the term 'life' has been the subject of considerable debate especially regarding the point at which life begins and ends. There is, for instance, substantial controversy regarding the rights of an unborn child.[31] In *Paton*

---

[27] *Osman* v. *UK* (2000) 29 E.H.R.R 245, para 115. On the facts of the case, the European Court did not find a violation of Article 2. The first and the second applicant, Mrs. Mulkiye Osman and her son Ahmet Osman were complaining of the failure of the UK authorities for their failure to act on warning signals that Paul Paget-Lewis posed to the physical safety of Mr. Osman and his family. After having formed an attachment with Mr. Ahmet Osman in 1986, Paget-Lewis had stalked and harassed Ahmet Osman and members of his family. On 7 March 1988, Paget-Lewis shot and killed Mr. Ali Osman and seriously wounded Mr. Ahmet Osman. The Court by a 17–3 majority held that there had been no violation of Articles 2 or 8. The Court however did find a violation of a violation of Article 6(1). The two applicants were awarded compensation of £10,000 each in accordance with Article 50. In relation to Article 2, the majority took the view that having regard to circumstances the police could not be criticised for attaching weight to the presumption of innocence or failing to use powers of arrest, search and seizure. The applicants had not been able to point to any decisive stage in the sequence of events when it could be said that the police knew or ought to have known that the lives of the Osman family were at real and immediate risk from Paget-Lewis.

[28] *Ergi* v. *Turkey* (2001) 32 E.H.R.R. 18; the applicant alleged the killing of the his sister by security services followed by ineffective investigation. It was held by the Court that while there were legitimate doubts as to the source of the bullet that killed the applicant's sister, there was insufficient evidence to prove that she was killed by security services. However the mere knowledge of the killing gave rise to a duty *ipso facto* on the part of the authorities under Article 2 to carry out an effective investigation into the circumstances which led to the death of the applicant's sister. The failure of the State to conduct an effective investigation resulted in a violation of Article 2. See also *McCann and others* v. *UK* (1996) 21 E.H.R.R. 97; *Kaya* v. *Turkey* (1999) 28 E.H.R.R. 1 – failure on the part of the Turkish authorities to carry out an effective investigation into the circumstances surrounding the death of the applicant's brother, Mr. Abdulmenaf Kaya, accordingly resulted in a violation of Article 2.

[29] *W* v. *UK*, Application No. 9348/81. In the case the applicant's brother was murdered by gunmen in Northern Ireland. It was held that while Article 2 places a positive obligation on States, '[t]hat, however, does not mean that a positive obligation to exclude any possible violence could be deduced from this article', para 12.

[30] On the facts of the case, the child had been provided adequate treatment; *X* v. *Ireland*, Application No. 6839/74. In another case which concerned the operation of a public vaccination scheme leading to the death of some young children, the Commission held that liability was possible when the State undertakes involvement in public vaccination scheme. On the facts of the case, it was held inadmissible as 'appropriate steps' had been taken for the safe administration of the scheme in the present instance; *X* v. *UK (Association of Parents* v. *UK)*, Application No. 7154/75 pp. 34–35.

[31] *Paton* v. *UK*, App. No. 8416/79 19 DR 244 (1980): in this case the European Commission appears to have taken the view that the context of Article 2 suggests that 'everyone' does not include those who are unborn: Farran, *The UK Before the European Court of Human Rights* (Blackstone Press, 1996) at p. 29. Also see *Open Door Counselling and Dublin Well Woman* v. *Ireland* (1993) 15 E.H.R.R. 244. The issue was primarily dealt under Article 10 Freedom of expression – the right to receive and impart information on obtaining abortion. The Court held that injunction in imparting information violated Article 10, but the decision is unconvincing as it was decided by a 15/8 majority. *Brüggemann and Scheuten* v. *Federal Republic of Germany*, (1981) 3 E.H.R.R. 244. Rehof, 'Article 3' in Alfredsson and Eide (eds), *The Universal Declaration of Human Rights: A Common*

v. *UK*,[32] the European Commission held that the abortion of a 10-week-old foetus under British law to protect the physical and mental health of the mother was not in breach of Article 2. In *H* v. *Norway*,[33] the Commission took the view that the abortion of a 14-week-old foetus was not contrary to Article 2 on the grounds that 'pregnancy, birth or care for the child may place the woman in a difficult situation of life'. The Commission considered the wide differences on the issue of abortion and allowed for a certain margin of appreciation. The decision is broader than *Paton* because the abortion was later in the pregnancy and the reasons given were social and did not relate to the health or medical condition of the mother. From the cases mentioned above, the Commission appears to have taken the view that Article 2 is applicable only to persons who are already born.[34] In *H* v. *Norway*, the Commission, however, did note that in certain circumstances Article 2 does offer protection to the unborn child without indicating what those circumstances were. As it is, currently the grounds for abortion are very wide, and in *Open Door Counselling* v. *Ireland*, the Human Rights Court itself left open the possibility of Article 2 placing restrictions on abortion.[35] In the case of *Boso* v. *Italy*, the European Court of Human Rights again found that an abortion conducted under Italian law did not violate Article 2 provisions – the Court taking the view that a fair balance had been struck between the interests of the woman and that of the foetus.[36] More recently, in *Vo* v. *France*, the European Court of Human Rights was asked to adjudicate as whether under Article 2 of the Convention foetuses enjoy the right to life.[37] The Court in reiterating its position noted that 'the unborn child is not regarded as a "person" directly protected by Article 2 of the Convention and that if the unborn do have a "right" to "life", it is implicitly limited by the mother's rights and interests'.[38] The Court therefore was able to avoid the problematic issue of whether Article 2 protection applied to foetuses by stating that 'there is no European consensus on the scientific and legal definition of the beginning of life'.[39] Confirming its earlier position in *Vo* v. *France*, the Court in its most recent pronouncement in *Evans* v. *United Kingdom* failed to extend Article 2 protection to embryos.[40]

Just as the rights of the unborn child have been controversial, problematic issues have arisen in relation to those who are approaching death. The exact point of death has generated legal challenges, as has the rights of those demanding a right to die. Article 2, an article on the right to life, has raised issues of euthanasia and death either through the

---

Standard of Achievement (Martinus Nijhoff Publishers, 1999), 89–101 at p. 97; for a consideration at the international level see Alston, 'The Unborn Child and Abortion under the Draft Convention on the Rights of the Child' 12 *HRQ* (1990) 156; Shelton, 'Abortion and the Right to Life in the Inter-American System: The Case of "Baby Boy"' 2 *HRLJ* (1981) 309; Hewson, 'Dancing on the Head of a Pin? Foetal Life and the European Convention' 13 *Feminist Legal Studies* (2005) 363. Also see below chapter 16.

[32] *Paton* v. *UK*, App. No. 8416/78 19 DR 244 (1980).

[33] *H* v. *Norway*, Application No. 17004/90 (1992) unreported, para 1. This case was held inadmissible as the State has not gone 'beyond its discretion which . . . it has in this sensitive area of abortion'.

[34] Fenwick, *Civil Liberties* (Routledge, 1998), p. 37.

[35] *Open Door Counselling and Dublin Well Woman* v. *Ireland* (1993) 15 E.H.R.R. 244, para 65 and 66.

[36] *Boso* v. *Italy* Application No. 50490/99.

[37] *Vo* v. *France* (2005) 40 EHRR 12. See Zampas and Gher 'Abortion as a Human Right – International and Regional Standards' 8 *HRLR* (2008) 249; Plomer, 'A Foetal Right to Life? The Case of *Vo* v. *France*' 5 *HRLR* (2005) 311.

[38] *Vo* v. *France* para 80.

[39] Ibid. para 82.

[40] *Evans* v. *UK* (2008) 46 E.H.R.R. 728.

assistance of family, a partner or in some cases medical staff.[41] In the Diane Pretty case, Mrs. Pretty claimed the right to death as a corollary to the right to life as contained in Article 2 of the ECHR. Diane Pretty, who was paralysed and terminally ill with motor neuron disease, had unsuccessfully appealed to the House of Lords claiming a reversal of the Director of Public Prosecution's decision for failing to provide surety to her husband that he would not be prosecuted for assisting her death. The House of Lords in a unanimous judgement dismissed her appeal. Mrs. Pretty's application to the European Court of Human Rights was also unsuccessful. The Court, whilst sympathetic to her position, was of the view that Article 2 did not contain a right to die, either through the assistance of an individual or with the support of public authorities. The Court was mindful of the 'margin of appreciation' to national authorities as well as the scope for abuse, were the existing ban on assisted suicides in the United Kingdom to be relaxed.[42] The debate on euthanasia has increasingly becoming more complex, as several countries have initiated legislation which may in restricted circumstances provide immunities to doctors from prosecution where they have assisted suicide.[43]

The general exceptions to the Article are provided in Article 2(2). These are exhaustive and must be narrowly construed. Article 2(2)(a) provides for death occurring as a result of self-defence. *McCann and Others* v. *UK*[44] was the first case dealt with by the Court concerning Article 2.[45] In this case three members of the provisional IRA were shot dead by British soldiers in Gibraltar. It was suspected that these IRA activists had remote control devices for a bomb to be detonated in a public place. The resulting damage, it was feared, would cause serious loss of life. The Commission by 11 to six votes held that shooting was justified under Article 2(2). The Court, however, disagreed. According to the Court the exception covers, but is not limited to, intentional taking of life. The question was the extent to which the State's response was proportionate to perceived threats posed by IRA members. Having considered all the circumstances of the case (including the planning and conduct of the operations by the British security forces and the decision to let the IRA members enter Gibraltar from Spain) it held that the United Kingdom had sanctioned killing by its agents in conditions giving rise to breach of Article 2. The Court noted:

> In sum, having regard to the decision not to prevent the suspects from travelling into Gibraltar, to the failure of the authorities to make sufficient allowances for the possibility that their intelligence assessments might, in some respects at least, be erroneous and to the automatic recourse to lethal force when the soldiers opened fire, the Court is not persuaded that the killing of the three terrorists constituted the use of force which was no more than absolutely necessary in defence of persons from unlawful violence within the meaning of Article 2 para (2)(a) (art. 2-2-a) of the Convention.[46]

---

[41] In *Widmer* v. *Switzerland*, the Commission held that the article does not require passive euthanasia (by which a person is allowed to die by not being given treatment) be a crime. Application No. 20527/92 (1993) unreported. A similar situation would appear to prevail in other human rights systems. On the position of euthanasia in the Inter-American Human Rights System see Davidson, 'The Civil and Political Rights Protected in the Inter-American Human Rights System' in Harris and Livingstone (eds), *The Inter-American System of Human Rights* (Clarendon Press, 1998) pp. 213–288 at p. 218.

[42] *Pretty* v. *UK* (2002) 35 E.H.R.R. 1, paras 39–42.

[43] See Hamilton, 'The Law on Dying' 95 *Journal of Royal Society of Medicine* (2002), 565.

[44] *McCann and others* v. *UK* (1996) 21 E.H.R.R. 97.

[45] Ni Aolain, above n.24, at pp. 28–31; see Joseph, 'Denouncement of the Death on the Rock: The Right to Life of Terrorists' 14 *NQHR* (1996) 5.

[46] *McCann and others* v. *UK* (1996) 21 E.H.R.R. 97, para 213.

The case emphasises a strict proportionality test under Article 2(2). Therefore, the use of deadly force to effect an arrest would never be justified, except in circumstances where there was certainty that the suspects would kill if allowed to escape. The other exceptions provided in Article 2(2) are quelling a riot[47] and to effect an arrest or prevent an escape.[48] It also needs to be emphasised that Article 2 does not prohibit capital punishment. In 1983, Protocol 6 was adopted, which prohibits the death penalty. The Protocol came into force in 1985 and is ratified by a majority of Member States; more recently this has been supplemented by Protocol 13.

(a) Prohibition of torture or inhuman or degrading treatment or punishment

According to Article 3 'No one shall be subjected to torture or to inhuman or degrading treatment or punishment'.[49] The rights contained in Article 3 are of a non-derogable nature even in times of war and public emergencies.[50] The prohibition of torture and inhuman or degrading treatment or punishment is expressed in absolute terms and no exceptions as such are attached to it.[51] In *Chahal* v. *UK*,[52] the European Court of Human Rights addressed this subject in clear and unambiguous language noting:

> [t]he Convention prohibits in absolute terms torture or inhuman or degrading treatment or punishment, irrespective of the victim's conduct . . . Article 3 . . . makes no provision for exceptions and no derogation from it is permissible under Article 15 . . . even in the event of a public emergency to the life of the nation.[53]

---

[47] *Stewart* v. *UK* (1985) 7 E.H.R.R. 453. The applicant, the mother of a child killed by a plastic bullet round in Northern Ireland, claimed a violation of Article 2. It was held by the European Commission that having regard to all the circumstances of the case, the deceased's death 'resulted from the use of force which was no more than "absolutely necessary" "in action lawfully taken for the purpose of quelling a riot . . ." within the meaning of Article 2 para 2 (c)', para 30. *Cf. Güleç* v. *Turkey* (1999) 28 E.H.R.R. 121. The applicant's 15-year-old son (Ahmet) was killed when security forces opened fire on demonstrators. The government claim was rejected by the Court that the force used to disperse demonstrators was proportionate and necessary within the exception of Article 2(2), paras 71–73.

[48] *Farrell* v. *UK* (1983) 5 E.H.R.R. CD466. *Kelly* v. *United Kingdom* (1993) 16 E.H.R.R. CD20. The applicant's 17-year-old son was shot dead by soldiers whilst driving a stolen car in the belief that occupants of the car were terrorists and had to be prevented from committing terrorist acts. The European Commission on Human Rights accepted the UK government's argument that the fatal shooting was for the purpose of apprehending the occupants of the stolen car, who were reasonably believed to be terrorists, in order to prevent their carrying out terrorist action. The Commission therefore rejected the application as being manifestly ill-founded.

[49] The Article draws its inspiration from Articles 5 of Universal Declaration on Human Rights (1948) and the American Declaration of Human Rights (1948). It also has close association with Article 7 of the ICCPR and Articles 5 of the ACHR (1969) and ACHPR (1981).

[50] Harris, O'Boyle, Bates and Buckley, above n.1, at p. 69.

[51] Article 3 also has the most developed and advanced jurisprudence of the non-refoulement principle in International Law. Examining the position adopted by the European Court of Human Rights in *Soering* and *Chahal* case (see below), Goodwin-Gill and McAdam conclude that Article 3 'has a broader application than Article 32 and 33 of the 1951 Convention and may provide protection from refoulement to people expressly excluded from refugee status'. Goodwin-Gill and McAdam, *The Refugee in International Law* (Oxford University Press, 2007) at p. 311. The broad non-refoulement principle has been challenged recently before the European Court of Human Rights in *Ramzy* v. *The Netherlands* Application No. 25424/05 (Decision of 27 May 2008).

[52] *Chahal* v. *UK* (1997) 23 E.H.R.R. 413.

[53] Ibid. para 79.

European societies have become increasingly intolerant towards accepting officially sanctioned brutality. In addition, the abolition of the death penalty in most countries within Europe has reduced the tolerance of State violence. The various categories of prohibition have different applications and the Article has been used in a variety of circumstances. In the case of *Ireland* v. *United Kingdom*,[54] the Court provided some useful guidelines regarding the provisions of Article 3. The Court in formulating a narrow approach took the view that 'torture' means deliberate, inhuman treatment causing very serious and cruel suffering, whereas 'inhuman treatment or punishment', means treatment or punishment that causes intense physical and mental suffering. In the Court's analysis, degrading treatment or punishment arouses in a victim a feeling of fear or anguish and inferiority capable of humiliating and debasing the victim, possibly breaking his or her physical or moral resistance. The meaning and scope of the Article can be illustrated through the facts of the *Ireland* v. *UK* case. The case is particularly useful in distinguishing torture from inhuman and degrading treatment or punishment.[55]

In this case the Irish government had brought proceedings against the United Kingdom alleging that persons taken into custody pursuant to the Civil Authorities (Special Powers) Act, Northern Ireland, 1922 were subjected to treatment which in convention terms amounted to torture, inhuman and degrading treatment contrary to Article 3. The Irish government also alleged that internment without trial amounted to a violation of the right to liberty and security of the person as provided in Article 5 and the right to fair trial accorded in Article 6 of the Convention. In addition, there was a claim of a violation of Article 14 (i.e. that the powers of detention and internment were exercised in a discriminatory manner). A particular source of concern was the methods of interrogation used by the British Security forces in Northern Ireland. They were engaged in the so-called 'interrogation in depth' or the five techniques, which were – (wall-standing) long periods of standing in a stressed position; (hooding) the placing of black hoods on heads; subjection to noise; deprivation of sleep pending interrogation; and deprivation of food and drink.

The European Commission in its report delivered to the Committee of Ministers in February 1976 took the view that measures of detention without trial were not in violation of Article 5 (the right to liberty and security). According to the Commission, the measures undertaken by the British government complied with the derogation entered under Article 15, which were not applied in a discriminatory manner. The Commission did not find violations of Article 14 (the prohibition of discrimination) but it did find that the use of the five techniques of interrogation constituted 'torture and inhuman treatment' contrary to Article 3.[56] The Commission's view, however, was not endorsed by the European Court of Human Rights. When the case, after being referred by the Irish Government, was considered by the Court, the Court drew a distinction between the various facets of Article 3, i.e. between torture on the one hand and 'inhuman' and 'degrading' treatment on the other. Torture as defined by the Court meant 'deliberate' inhuman treatment causing very serious and cruel suffering. Applying this test it held that the use of the 'five techniques' and

[54] *Ireland* v. *UK* (1978) 2 E.H.R.R. 25.
[55] See further Robertson and Merrills, *Human Rights in the World: An Introduction to the Study of the International Protection of Human Rights* (Manchester University Press, 1996) at pp. 139–140.
[56] According to the Commission 'the systematic application of techniques for the purpose of inducing a person to give information shows a clear resemblance to those methods of systematic torture which have been known over the ages . . . [T]he Commission sees in them a modern system of torture falling in the same category as those systems which have been applied in previous times as a means of obtaining information and confession'. *Ireland* v. *UK*, Series B, No. 23–I Com Rep (1971), para 794.

physical assaults did not amount to torture, although it constituted 'inhuman and degrading treatment'.[57] In concurrence with the Commission, the Court found that the measures of detention and internment without trial were covered by an Article 15 derogation made by the United Kingdom, and that their application was not in contravention of the non-discrimination provisions of Article 14. In the light of the serious consequence and the stigma attached to finding that a State conducted 'torture', a certain reluctance can be found in the Court's approach: the first finding of torture by the Court took place in 1996, with the Court finding Turkey as being involved in extreme interrogation techniques amounting to torture.[58] Acts of torture have subsequently been established in such actions as the rape of a detainee by a state official[59] and physical assaults including urination over the body as occurred in *Selmouni* v. *France*;[60] the latter judgment of the European Court of Human Rights resulting in the first finding of torture against a member of European Union.[61]

(b) Inhuman treatment, degrading treatment or punishment

While treatment needs to reach a minimum threshold before being designated as inhuman, the crucial factor which distinguishes it from torture is the absence of a deliberate intent to cause suffering. Inhuman treatment could be the result of conditions or treatment in a place of detention[62], withholding of food, water and medical treatment,[63] rapes and assault, ill treatment during preventative detention,[64] failure to provide medical treatment,[65] extradition or deportation,[66] mental torture, solitary confinement and severe mental

---

[57] The restrictive views adopted by the Court in relation to the meaning of torture have been criticised heavily. See Spjut, 'Torture under the European Convention on Human Rights' 73 *AJIL* (1979) 267; AI News Release (AI Index02/04/78) 19 January.

[58] *Aksoy* v. *Turkey* (1996) 23 E.H.R.R. 533 – Palestinian Hanging (suspension by the arms which are tied behind the back) amounted to torture, as it could only be inflicted deliberately; required preparation; was administered with the intention of gaining admissions; and caused serious pain and temporary paralysis of the arms. The other interrogation techniques used, which included blindfolding and electrocution were not considered in the light of the finding of torture.

[59] *Aydin* v. *Turkey* (1997) 25 E.H.R.R. 251, para 86.

[60] In this case, the Court established that 'the applicant was dragged along by his hair; that he was made to run along a corridor with police officers positioned on either side to trip him up; that he was made to kneel down in front of a young woman to whom someone said "Look, you're going to hear somebody sing"; that one police officer then showed him his penis, saying "Here, suck this", before urinating over him; and that he was threatened with a blowlamp and then a syringe . . . Besides the violent nature of the above acts, the Court is bound to observe that they would be heinous and humiliating for anyone, irrespective of their condition. The Court notes, lastly, that the above events were not confined to any one period of police custody during which – without this in any way justifying them – heightened tension and emotions might have led to such excesses. It has been clearly established that Mr. Selmouni endured repeated and sustained assaults over a number of days of questioning. Under these circumstances, the Court is satisfied that the physical and mental violence, considered as a whole, committed against the applicant's person caused "severe" pain and suffering and was particularly serious and cruel. Such conduct must be regarded as acts of torture for the purposes of Article 3 of the Convention.' *Selmouni* v. *France* (1999) 29 E.H.R.R. 403, paras 103–105.

[61] Mowbray and Harris, above n.1, at p. 95; Farer, *Confronting Global Terrorism and American Neo-Conservatism: the Framework of a Liberal Grand Strategy* (Oxford University Press, 2008) p. 107.

[62] *Denmark, Norway, Sweden* v. *Greece*, Applications No. 3321/67, No. 3322/67, No. 3323/67, No. 3344/67. The issues of overcrowding and inadequate heating, toilets, sleeping arrangements, food and recreation in Greek detention facilities led to a violation of Article 3.

[63] *Ireland* v. *UK* (1978) 2 E.H.R.R. 25. *Cyprus* v. *Turkey*, Application No. 8007/77, 13 DR 85 (1978); inhuman treatment has been established even where injuries might appear to be relatively slight, though constituting outward signs of physical force whilst under detention, *Tomasi* v. *France* (1993) 15 E.H.R.R. 1, para 113.

[64] *Tomasi* v. *France* (1993) 15 E.H.R.R. 1.

[65] *Hurtado* v. *Switzerland*, Application No. 17549/90, para 12.

[66] *Soering* v. *UK* (1989) 11 E.H.R.R. 439, para 88; *Chahal* v. *UK* (1997) 23 E.H.R.R. 413, para 107.

distress and anguish due to disappearance of a close relative.[67] In assessing whether punishment is inhuman, subjective consideration needs to be given to various factors including the physical and mental suffering, the applicant's sex, age, health and sensibilities, etc.[68] Degrading treatment arises from an ordinary everyday meaning: examples include refusal to allow the removal of soiled trousers and a change of clean clothing for over 24 hours during police detention and questioning before an investigating judge.[69] A further striking example was provided by racial discrimination as practised in British immigration restrictions. The 'Africanisation' policies operating during the 1960s meant that thousands of UK citizens of Asian origin based in East Africa were deprived of their livelihood and forced to emigrate. The efforts of these UK citizens to settle in the United Kingdom were frustrated by the passage of the Commonwealth Immigration Act 1968. The European Commission established a violation of Article 3.[70]

In order to constitute degrading punishment, the humiliation and debasement involved must attain a particular level, depending on, *inter alia*, the circumstances of the case, such as the nature and context of the punishment itself and the manner and methods of its execution.[71] Article 3 has been applied in a range of circumstances. Indeed, in many instances its provisions have been invoked to accord rights otherwise not contained in the Convention. The Convention does not provide for a right not to be deported or extradited. Similarly, the Convention does not cater for such rights as a right to a nationality, political asylum or a right of aboard (for a non-national). That said, the various facets of Article 3 have been used to assist applicants with some of the aforementioned claims. Instances of violation of Article 3 may include the deportation of a person who would be deprived of proper medical treatment,[72] or is likely to suffer from cruel or degrading punishment or be separated from his family as a result of extradition.[73] Indeed, Article 3 may also be deployed in circumstances where the source of risk to an individual emanates from the action of non-State agents such as terrorists or organised criminals.[74]

---

[67] *Kurt* v. *Turkey* (1999) 27 E.H.R.R. 373, paras 133–134. See also *Selçuk and Asker* v. *Turkey* (1998) 26 E.H.R.R. 477 paras 78–80 – the burning of people's homes by security forces.

[68] See *V* v. *UK* (1999) 30 E.H.R.R. 121, para 99.

[69] *Hurtado* v. *Switzerland*, Application No. 17549/90, para 12.

[70] *East African Asians* v. *UK* (1995) 19 E.H.R.R. CD1. 'The Commission was of the view that . . . the legislation applied in the present case discriminated against the applicants on the grounds of their colour or race. It has also confirmed the view, which it expressed at the admissibility stage, that discrimination based on race could, in certain circumstances, of itself amount to degrading treatment within the meaning of Article 3 of the Convention . . . The Commission recalls in this connection that, as generally recongised, a special importance should be attached to discrimination on the basis of race might, in certain circumstances, constitute a special form of affront to human dignity; and that differential treatment of a group of persons on the basis of race might therefore be capable of constituting degrading treatment when differential treatment on some other ground would raise no such question . . . The Commission considers that the racial discrimination, to which the applicants have been publicly subjected to the application of the above immigration legislation, constitutes an interference with their human dignity which, in the special circumstances described above, amounted to 'degrading treatment' in the sense of Article 3 of the Convention . . . It therefore *concludes*, by six votes against three votes, that Article 3 has been violated in the present cases, ibid. at p. 62; see Lester, 'Thirty Years on: The East African Case Revisited' [2002] *Public Law* 52.

[71] *Tyrer* v. *UK* (1978) 2 E.H.R.R. 1, paras 32–33; *cf. Campbell and Cosans* v. *UK* (1982) 4 E.H.R.R. 293, paras 28–31.

[72] *D* v. *UK* (1997) 24 E.H.R.R. 423, paras 50–53.

[73] See *Chahal* v. *UK* (1997) 23 E.H.R.R. 413, paras 106–107.

[74] *HLR* v. *France* (1998) 26 E.H.R.R. 29. On facts of the case it was held that there was no violation of Article 3 in the case of expulsion of a citizen of Columbia, since there was no 'relevant evidence' of risk of ill-treatment by non-state agents, whereby authorities 'are not able to obviate the risk by providing adequate protection', para 40.

An interesting example of the wide ambit of Article 3 to cover rights not expressly provided for in the Convention is illustrated through the *Soering* case. In *Soering* v. *UK*[75] the applicant, who was a West German national, in complicity with his girlfriend, murdered his girlfriend's parents. These offences were committed in the US state of Virginia, where he and his girlfriend were students. After having committed these offences they fled to the United Kingdom. The United States government, under the terms of the Extradition Treaty of 1972 between the United States and the United Kingdom, applied for the applicant and his girlfriend to be extradited to the United States. The girlfriend was extradited, and having pleaded guilty as an accessory to the murder was sentenced to 90 years' imprisonment. In the case of the applicant, the United Kingdom whilst agreeing to extradite him, had sought assurances that if convicted, he would not be awarded the death penalty. The applicant however appealed to the Strasbourg institutions. The death penalty, *per se*, is not prohibited by the Convention and the United Kingdom by extraditing Mr. Soering to the United States was not breaching any provisions of the Convention or general international law. The applicant's primary claim was based on the prospect of his suffering from inhuman or degrading treatment under Article 3 while waiting for his execution in the state of Virginia.

The European Court of Human Rights, in upholding Soering's claim, took the view that if he was extradited to Virginia there would be a real risk of his being placed on death row which would constitute a violation of Article 3. The Court acknowledged that the imposition of the death penalty, *per se*, is not in breach of Article 3. However, the Article 3 prohibition could be breached in conditions where the death penalty was imposed only after a six-to eight-year waiting period (the so called 'death-row' phenomenon). The fact that he was 18 when the offences were committed and psychiatric evidence of his mental instability were mitigating factors in favour of the applicant. Thus in the words of the Court:

> having regard to the very long period of time spent on death row in such extreme conditions, with ever present and mounting anguish of awaiting execution of the death penalty, and to the personal circumstance of the applicant, especially his age and mental state at the time of the offence, the applicant's extradition to the United States would expose him to a real risk of treatment going beyond the threshold set by Article 3.[76]

As in the case of *Soering*, there must exist a real risk, as opposed to a mere possibility, of facing inhuman or degrading treatment. The Court in *Soering* attempted to narrow down the ambit of its decision with the proviso that such a ruling would only be made in view of

---

[75] *Soering* v. *UK* (1989) 11 E.H.R.R. 439; *Case of Soering* v. *UK* http://cmiskp.echr.coe.int/tkp197/view.asp? item=1&portal=hbkm&action=html&highlight=Soering&sessionid=16663303&skin=hudoc-en <last visited 2 December 2008>. See Van Den Wyngaert, 'Applying the European Convention on Human Rights to Extradition: Opening Pandora's Box' 39 *ICLQ* (1990) 757; Lillich, 'The Soering Case' 85 *AJIL* (1991) 128.

[76] *Soering* v. *UK* (1989) 11 E.H.R.R. 439, para 111. Soering, as a remarkable decision was followed in *Pratt* v. *Attorney General of Jamaica* [1994] 2 AC 1 (Jamaica) where the Privy Council in approving the European Court's approach held 'in any case in which execution is to take place more than five years after sentence there will be strong grounds for believing that the delay is such as to constitute "inhuman or degrading punishment or treatment"'. As we have noted, the Human Rights Committee under the first Optional Protocol has held that death row, *per se* does not amount to cruel, inhuman or degrading treatment or punishment. See *Chitat Ng* v. *Canada*, Communication No. 469/1991 (7 January 1994), UN Doc. CCPR/C/49/D/469/1991 (1994) para 8.4; also see *Barrett and Sutcliffe* v. *Jamaica*, Communication No. 271/1988, UN Doc. CCPR/C/44/D/271/1988 at 71 (1992), p. 250.

Europe and human rights (I)

7

'the serious and irreparable nature of the alleged suffering risked'.[77] The narrow dicta has been followed in *Curz Varas* v. *Sweden*[78] and *Vilvarajah and four others* v. *UK*.[79]

Notwithstanding the stricter evidential requirements for substantiating Article 3 claims, European human rights jurisprudence also affirms that providing a real risk of torture is established, the conduct of the individual is not a relevant factor. In the *Chahal* case, the European Court of Human Rights re-affirmed and decided that since the right of individuals not to be tortured was absolute, it could not be trumped by considerations such as national security.[80] The *Chahal* judgment has posed particular problems for Council of Europe governments in that any attempts to remove foreign nationals to States where the concerned individuals are likely to be subjected to torture contravenes the prohibition contained in Article 3. Mr. Chahal, a Sikh from the Indian province of Punjab, had entered the United Kingdom illegally in 1971 though he was granted indefinite leave to remain in the country in 1974. Mr. Chahal subsequently married his wife who joined him from India. In the early part of the 1980s Mr. Chahal become actively engaged in the Sikh separatist movement. He visited Punjab in 1984 and claimed to have been detained and tortured by Indian police during his stay in India. In October 1985 Mr. Chahal was detained in the United Kingdom under the Prevention of Terrorism (Temporary Provisions) Act 1984 on suspicion of involvement of a conspiracy to assassinate the then Indian Prime Minister Mr. Rajiv Gandhi during his official visit to the United Kingdom.

In August 1990, the Home Secretary issued a deportation order for Mr. Chahal, since his presence in the United Kingdom was deemed not to be conducive to the public good for reasons of national security and to prevent international terrorism. On his part, after having exhausted all available domestic remedies in the United Kingdom, Mr. Chahal made an application to the European Commission on Human Rights alleging, *inter alia*, violations of Article 3 were he to be deported to India. The Commission unanimously decided that there would be a violation if Mr. Chahal was deported. The European Court of Human Rights upheld this position and in so doing made the following important observations:

> the national interests of the State could not be invoked to override the interests of the individual where substantial grounds had been shown for believing that he would be subjected to ill-treatment if expelled (79) Article 3 (art. 3) enshrines one of the most fundamental values of democratic society (see the above-mentioned *Soering* judgment, p. 34, para 88). The Court is well aware of the immense difficulties faced by States in modern times in protecting their communities from terrorist violence. However, even in these circumstances, the Convention prohibits in absolute terms torture or inhuman or degrading treatment or punishment, irrespective of the victim's conduct. Unlike most of the substantive clauses of the Convention and of Protocols Nos. 1 and 4 (P1, P4), Article 3 (art. 3) makes no provision for exceptions and no derogation from it is permissible under Article 15 (art. 15) even in the event of a public emergency threatening the life of the nation (see the *Ireland* v. *the United*

---

[77] *Soering* v. *UK* (1989) 11 E.H.R.R. 439, para 90.

[78] *Cruz Varas* v. *Sweden* (1992) 14 E.H.R.R. 1, paras 75, 76, 83. The claim for political asylum was, however, rejected due to a failure to substantiate that the first applicant Mr. Hector Cruz Varas would be exposed to real risk of being subjected to inhuman or degrading treatment upon his expulsion to Chile.

[79] *Vilvarajah and others* v. *UK* (1992) 14 E.H.R.R. 248, paras 102, 103, 109–112 (facts).

[80] *Chahal* v. *UK* (1997) 23 E.H.R.R. 413, paras 78–80; Bonner, 'Checking the Executive? detention without trial, Control Orders, Due Process and Human Rights' (2006) 12 *European Public Law* 45, at p. 53.

Kingdom judgment of 18 January 1978, Series A no. 25, p. 65, para 163, and also the *Tomasi* v. *France* judgment of 27 August 1992, Series A no. 241-A, p. 42, para 115). (80) The prohibition provided by Article 3 (art. 3) against ill-treatment is equally absolute in expulsion cases. Thus, whenever substantial grounds have been shown for believing that an individual would face a real risk of being subjected to treatment contrary to Article 3 (art. 3) if removed to another State, the responsibility of the Contracting State to safeguard him or her against such treatment is engaged in the event of expulsion (see the above-mentioned *Vilvarajah and Others judgment*, p. 34, para 103). In these circumstances, the activities of the individual in question, however undesirable or dangerous, cannot be a material consideration. The protection afforded by Article 3 (art. 3) is thus wider than that provided by Articles 32 and 33 of the United Nations 1951 Convention on the Status of Refugees.[81]

In the recent case of *Saadi* v. *Italy*, the European Court of Human Rights has reaffirmed the principles established in *Chahal*. In *Saadi*, the applicant Mr. Nassim Saadi was a Tunisian national, resident of Italy, who had entered Italy sometimes during 1996 and 1999. A residence permit had been issued to him for 'family reasons' by the Bologna police authority (*questura*) on 29 December 2000 which was due to expire on 11 October 2002. On 9 October 2002, Mr Saadi was arrested on suspicion of international terrorism and was placed in pre-trial detention. He along with five others was subsequently committed for trial in the Milan Assize Court. Prior to the decision made by the Milan Assize Court of Appeal, on 11 May 2005, a military court in Tunisia sentenced Mr. Saadi to 20 years' imprisonment for membership of a terrorist organisation operating abroad in time of peace and for incitement to terrorism. Mr. Saadi's trial and conviction had taken place *in absentia* in Tunisia.

Notwithstanding Mr. Saadi's trial and sentencing *in absentia*, a deportation order was issued on 8 August 2006 by the Italian Minister of the Interior. The Minister relied upon the provisions of Italian Legislative decree No. 144 of 27 July 2005 (entitled 'urgent measures to combat international terrorism' and later converted to statute law in the form of Law No. 155 of 31 July 2005). This deportation order to Tunisia was made on the basis that Mr. Saadi had taken an active part within an organisation that was responsible for providing logistical and financial support to persons belonging to fundamentalist Islamist cells in Italy and abroad. The Minister therefore had issued the deportation order because the applicant's conduct was contrary to public order and threatened Italian national security. On 11 August 2006, Mr. Saadi applied for political asylum, arguing that his trial *in absentia* in Tunisia had been motivated by political reasons. He claimed that if deported to Tunisia he would be subjected to torture and 'political and religious reprisals'. During the proceedings before the European Court of Human Rights evidence was submitted by the World Organisation against Torture, the Collective of the Tunisian Community in Europe, Amnesty International and Human Rights Watch that torture of alleged terrorists in Tunisia was routine and well documented, and that Mr Saadi faced the risk of being tortured if returned to Tunisia. The UK government acted as a third party intervener in the case and attempted to have the Court's previous ruling in *Chahal* v. *United Kingdom* overturned. The UK government argued that the right of a person to be protected from Article 3 treatment needs to be balanced with the risk that the person poses to the deporting State. The UK government argued that:

[81] *Chahal* v. *UK* (1997) 23 E.H.R.R. 413, paras 78–80.

Europe and human rights (I)

7

In the first place, the threat presented by the person to be deported must be a factor to be assessed in relation to the possibility and the nature of the potential ill-treatment. That would make it possible to take into consideration all the particular circumstances of each case and weigh the rights secured to the applicant by Article 3 of the Convention against those secured to all other members of the community by Article 2. Secondly, national-security considerations must influence the standard of proof required from the applicant. In other words, if the respondent State adduced evidence that there was a threat to national security, stronger evidence had to be adduced to prove that the applicant would be at risk of ill-treatment in the receiving country. In particular, the individual concerned must prove that it was 'more likely than not' that he would be subjected to treatment prohibited by Article 3. That interpretation was compatible with the wording of Article 3 of the United Nations Convention against Torture, which had been based on the case-law of the Court itself, and took account of the fact that in expulsion cases it was necessary to assess a possible future risk. . . . Lastly, the United Kingdom Government emphasised that Contracting States could obtain diplomatic assurances that an applicant would not be subjected to treatment contrary to the Convention. Although, in the above-mentioned *Chahal* case, the Court had considered it necessary to examine whether such assurances provided sufficient protection, it was probable, as had been shown by the opinions of the majority and the minority of the Court in that case, that identical assurances could be interpreted differently.[82]

In rejecting the arguments presented by the Italian government, as well as the intervener (the United Kingdom), and affirming the absolute nature of Article 3, the European Court of Human Rights made the following observations:

The Court notes first of all that States face immense difficulties in modern times in protecting their communities from terrorist violence . . . It cannot therefore underestimate the scale of the danger of terrorism today and the threat it presents to the community. That must not, however, call into question the absolute nature of Article 3. Accordingly, the Court cannot accept the argument of the United Kingdom Government, supported by the respondent Government, that a distinction must be drawn under Article 3 between treatment inflicted directly by a signatory State and treatment that might be inflicted by the authorities of another State, and that protection against this latter form of ill-treatment should be weighed against the interests of the community as a whole (see paragraphs 120 and 122 above). Since protection against the treatment prohibited by Article 3 is absolute, that provision imposes an obligation not to extradite or expel any person who, in the receiving country, would run the real risk of being subjected to such treatment. As the Court has repeatedly held, there can be no derogation from that rule. It must therefore reaffirm the principle stated in the *Chahal* judgment that it is not possible to weigh the risk of ill-treatment against the reasons put forward for the expulsion in order to determine whether the responsibility of a State is engaged under Article 3, even where such treatment is inflicted by another State. In that connection, the conduct of the person concerned, however undesirable or dangerous, cannot be taken into account, with the consequence that the protection afforded by Article 3 is broader than that provided for in Articles 32 and 33 of the 1951 United Nations Convention relating to

---

[82] *Saadi v. Italy*, Application No. 37201/06, paras 122, 123.

the Status of Refugees (see *Chahal*, cited above, § 80 and paragraph 63 above). Moreover, that conclusion is in line with points IV and XII of the guidelines of the Committee of Ministers of the Council of Europe on human rights and the fight against terrorism (see paragraph 64 above).[83]

The Court also refuted the argument presented by the UK government that in instances where the applicant presented a

threat to national security, stronger evidence must be adduced to prove that there is a risk of ill-treatment, the Court observes that such an approach is not compatible with the absolute nature of the protection afforded by Article 3 either. It amounts to asserting that, in the absence of evidence meeting a higher standard, protection of national security justifies accepting more readily a risk of ill-treatment for the individual. The Court therefore sees no reason to modify the relevant standard of proof, as suggested by the third-party intervener, by requiring in cases like the present that it be proved that subjection to ill-treatment is 'more likely than not'. On the contrary, it reaffirms that for a planned forcible expulsion to be in breach of the Convention it is necessary – and sufficient – for substantial grounds to have been shown for believing that there is a real risk that the person concerned will be subjected in the receiving country to treatment prohibited by Article 3.[84]

The Court also took the opportunity to pronounce on the validity of the so-called diplomatic assurances that the deported person would not be tortured or ill-treated by the receiving State. In its judgment, the Court noted that such diplomatic assurances do not *per se* offset an existing risk. It was of the view that:

the existence of domestic laws and accession to international treaties guaranteeing respect for fundamental rights in principle are not in themselves sufficient to ensure adequate protection against the risk of ill-treatment where, as in the present case, reliable sources have reported practices resorted to or tolerated by the authorities which are manifestly contrary to the principles of the Convention. Furthermore, it should be pointed out that even if, as they did not do in the present case, the Tunisian authorities had given the diplomatic assurances requested by Italy, that would not have absolved the Court from the obligation to examine whether such assurances provided, in their practical application, a sufficient guarantee that the applicant would be protected against the risk of treatment prohibited by the Convention. The weight to be given to assurances from the receiving State depends, in each case, on the circumstances obtaining at the material time. Consequently, the decision to deport the applicant to Tunisia would breach Article 3 of the Convention if it were enforced.[85]

Whilst both *Chahal* and *Saadi* were concerned with *ex ante* obligations of States to prevent torture occurring as a consequence of deportation or expulsion, Article 3 has also been relevant to *ex post facto* obligations of States (the obligation to prosecute or compensate the

---

[83] Paras 137, 138.
[84] Para 140.
[85] Paras 147–149. This intervention by the United Kingdom in the *Saadi* replicated the United Kingdom's efforts together with the governments of Lithuania, Portugal and Slovakia – in another pending case before the European court, *Ramzy* v. *The Netherlands* Application No. 25424/05 (Decision of 27 May 2008), involving deportation to Algeri.

7

Europe and human rights (I)

alleged victim). The case in question is *Al-Adsani* v. *UK*. In this case, Mr. Sulaiman Al-Adsani, a dual British–Kuwaiti national, alleged torture at the instruction of the Emir of Kuwait.[86] In 1992, Mr. Al-Adsani instituted legal proceedings in the United Kingdom against named individuals as well as against the government of Kuwait for physical and mental injuries caused to him through torture. In reliance upon the State Immunities Act 1978, the English High Court dismissed Mr. Al-Adsani's claim and a subsequent appeal to the House of Lords was denied in 1996. Mr. Al-Adsani brought proceedings before the European Court of Human Rights. In his claim Mr. Al-Adsani's did not suggest that acts of torture were committed by the United Kingdom nor was he arguing that UK authorities were to be held responsible for their failure to prevent torture. Rather, Mr. Al-Adsani's claim before the European Court of Human Rights was one of a procedural nature: he alleged *inter alia* that the United Kingdom had failed to allow him to pursue claims in national courts for acts of torture committed by foreign nationals in a foreign territory. The European Court of Human Rights dismissed the claim taking the position that the case did not concern the criminal liability of an individual for having conducted acts of torture. This case was, instead, about State immunity in a civil suit for damages in relation to alleged acts of torture committed outside the jurisdiction of the State. While recognising the special character of the prohibition of torture within international law, the Court was nevertheless 'unable to discern in the international instruments, judicial authorities or other materials before it any firm basis for concluding that, as a matter of international law, a State no longer enjoys immunity from civil suit in the courts of another State where acts of torture are alleged'.[87]

(ii) The right to liberty and security

Article 5 of the Convention deals with the right to liberty and security of the person. This provision is designed to control the exercise of powers of arrest and detention and is something which liberal constitutions have sought to achieve since the 17th century.[88] It protects liberty as well as security of the person. Articles 5(2)–(5) set out the procedures for such protection. According to Article 5(1) no deprivation of liberty is acceptable, save in accordance with a procedure prescribed by law.[89] In *Wintwerp* v. *Netherlands*,[90] the Court held that this meant that procedures must firstly be in accordance with national and conventional law including 'general principles contained in the Convention' and secondly they must not be 'arbitrary'. Article 5 applies even where the detention period is very short.

According to Article 5(1)(a) detention after conviction must be in accordance with applicable municipal law and with the Convention. This provision means that there must be a court judgment that justifies it and that the procedure that is followed to effect the

---

[86] *Al-Adsani* v. *Government of Kuwait and others* [1994] P.I.Q.R. P236; leave to appeal denied (1996) 107 ILR 536 (H.L. 1996); see Byres, 'Decisions of British Courts During 1996 Involving Questions of Public International Law' 67 *BYIL* (1996) 537.

[87] *Al-Adsani* v. *UK* (2002) 34 E.H.R.R. 11, http://cmiskp.echr.coe.int/tkp197/view.asp?item=1&portal=hbkm&action=html&highlight=al-adsani&sessionid=13711138&skin=hudoc-en <last visited 12 May 2009>. Judgment para 61; for commentaries on the case see 96 *AJIL* (2002) 677. This judgment of the Court has nevertheless come to be regarded as restrictive. Professor Shelton notes that 'the Court subordinated human rights jurisdiction to sovereign immunity . . .'. See Shelton above n.1 at p. 128; Voyiakis, '*Access to Court* v. *State Immunity*' 52 *ICLQ* (2003) 297.

[88] For a previous example see the Magna Carta 1215 c. 29.

[89] *Cf.* the *lettres de cachet* under the Ancien Regime in France.

[90] *Winterwerp* v. *The Netherlands* (1979–1980) 2 E.H.R.R. 387, para 39.

detention is lawful.[91] Article 5 does not require 'lawful conviction' but 'lawful detention'. The 'conviction' in para 5(1)(a) means, 'finding of guilt' and is taken to mean a conviction as a result of a trial by court.

Article 5(1)(b) means arrest or detention for non-compliance with lawful orders of a court or such arrest or detention in order to secure the fulfilment of any obligation prescribed by law.[92] According to Article 5(1)(c) lawful arrest or detention of a person is effected for the purpose of bringing him before the competent legal authority on reasonable suspicion of having committed an offence or where it is considered reasonably necessary to prevent him from committing an offence or fleeing after having done so. In cases of detention after arrest but before conviction it is imperative that the arrested person be brought promptly to trial and that the trial takes place in reasonable time. For an arrest to be lawful there must be reasonable suspicion of an honest belief (on the part of the person conducting the arrest) that the person being arrested has committed or is likely to commit an offence.[93] In *Fox, Campbell and Hartley* v. *United Kingdom*, the European Court declined to accept the UK authorities' position that the power of arrest was executed reasonably, in case of failure of the authorities to reveal the evidence upon which such an arrest was based, the only source of evidence that was being made available was the detained person's previous criminal record.[94]

Article 5(1)(d) deals with the detention of minors. The term 'minor' has an autonomous convention meaning, although it is generally taken to mean a person below the age of 18. Detention must also be for a lawful purpose. Article 5(1)(c) aims to protect society from vagrants, alcoholics, drug addicts and persons carrying infectious diseases. They may be restrained as a matter of social control (or even for their own protection), rather than because they have committed a criminal offence. Article 5(1)(f) allows for the arrest or detention of a person to prevent their unauthorised entry into a country or the arrest and detention of a person against whom action is being taken with a view to extradition and deportation. However, these individuals are given the right to have their detention or arrest reviewed in accordance with national laws.

The right to liberty and to security of the person has become a contentious right in the context of political events that reshaped the global picture in the aftermath of the terrorist offences in the United States on 11 September 2001. After the 9/11 attacks, the British government claimed that the United Kingdom faced a serious threat from terrorists within the country. It was, therefore, no longer possible for these individuals to remain at large, even in the absence of evidence substantial enough to bring charges against these suspected terrorists. The government felt it necessary to make derogations to Article 5(1) of the ECHR and Article 9 of the ICCPR[95] – provisions that accord individuals the right to liberty and prohibit detention without trial.[96] The government established a Human Rights Act (Designated Derogation Order 2001) in order to derogate from Article 5(1) of the ECHR.[97]

---

[91] Harris, O'Boyle, Bates and Buckley, above n.1, at p. 138.

[92] *Engel* v. *Netherlands*, (1976) 1 E.H.R.R. 647, para 69.

[93] *Fox, Campbell and Hartley* v. *UK* (1991) 13 E.H.R.R. 157, para 32.

[94] Ibid. paras 32–36. See Gearty, 'Political Violence and Civil Liberties' in McCrudden and Chambers (eds), above n.2, pp. 145–178, at 175.

[95] Dickson, 'Law Versus Terrorism: Can Law Win?' *EHRLR* [2005] 11; Justice, Response to the Joint Committee on Human Rights: Inquiry into UK Derogations from Convention Rights (May 2002), available at www.justice.org.uk/images/pdfs/derogations.pdf <last visited 1 May 2009>.

[96] See Michaelsen, 'Derogating from International Human Rights Obligations in the "War Against Terrorism"?: A British–Australian Perspective' 17 *Terrorism and Political Violence* (2005) 131.

[97] Human Rights Act 1998 (Designated Derogation) Order 2001 (Statutory Instrument 2001, No. 3644), (11 November 2001), available at www.opsi.gov.uk/si/si2001/20013644.htm <last visited 1 May 2009>.

7

During the adoption of Anti-Terrorism, Crime and Security Act 2001 (ATCSA), evidence had been presented to the Parliamentary Joint Committee on Human Rights (JCHR) with the proposition that such derogations would be unlawful.[98] It was also extraordinary that the UK was the only State member of the Council of Europe to have entered such a derogation provision as a consequence of the events of 11 September 2001.[99]

The ATCSA propelled into the consciousness of civil libertarians the saga of the Belmarsh detainees: held on mere suspicions under section 23 of the Act, and facing an environment almost as hostile and poisonous as their co-religionists in Guantánamo Bay. The Muslim men detained at Belmarsh high-security prison came to be referred to as the 'British Guantánamo Bay detainees'.[100] The suffering and humiliation of these men at the hands of the British executive resonated greatly with the minority communities of this country. The detention of these men continued to be a source of legal challenges raising profound questions about the limits of the executive power, discrimination on grounds of nationality and the role of the judiciary in pronouncing upon fundamental rights such as the right to liberty and freedom. In the first of the high-profile cases decided by the House of Lords on 16 December 2004, in an unprecedented sitting of nine judges, the Appellate Committee of the House of Lords, declared section 23 – the offending provision in Part IV of the 2001 Act – as incompatible to ECHR.[101] While a majority of their Lordships were inclined to favour the government's position, that there was a public emergency threatening the life of the nation, thereby validating the derogation under Article 15 of ECHR, they were not prepared (as a matter of judicial deference) to accept that detention provisions contained in the 2001 Act were necessary, proportionate and rational, or, as stated in the terms of Article 15, 'strictly required by the exigencies of the situation'.[102] The House of Lords resoundingly declared the detentions as disproportionate and unnecessary and, therefore, incompatible with the grounds as provided in Article 15 of ECHR.

The safeguards for the arrested person are contained in Article 5(2). Reasons for arrest (in a language the arrested person understands) need to be given promptly but not immediately.[103] Article 5(3) provides for the right to be brought promptly before judicial

---

[98] The Committee, in its report, had expressed substantial concerns both with the invocation of a public emergency threatening the life of the nations and the lack of adequate safeguards in relation to detention of powers. See Joint Committee on Human Rights Report on Anti-Terrorism, Crime and Security Bill, 2001–02 HL37, HC372, para 30 (16 November 2001).

[99] Thomas, 'September 11th and Good Governance' 53 *Northern Ireland Legal Q.* (2002) 366 at p. 381.

[100] Winterman, Press Release, BBC News, 'Belmarsh: Britain's Guantánamo Bay?', 6 October 2004. http://news.bbc.co.uk/1/hi/magazine/3714864.stm <last visited 15 May 2009>.

[101] *A and others* v. *Secretary of State for the Home Department* [2004] UKHL 56, paras 139, 155; for commentaries on the case see Dickson, above n.95, at 11; Walker, 'Prisoners of "War all the Time"' *EHRLR* [2005] 50; Shah, 'The UK's Anti-Terror Legislation and the House of Lords: The First Skirmish', 5 *HRLR* [2005] 403; Arden, 'Human Rights in the Age of Terrorism', 121 *LQR* (2005) 604; Elliott, 'United Kingdom: Detention without Trial and the "War on Terror"' 4 *IJCL* (2006) 553.

[102] European Convention for the Protection of Human Rights and Fundamental Freedoms, opened for signature 4 November 1950, 213 U.N.T.S. 221, E.T.S. No. 5 (entered into force 3 September 1953). Article 15(1) provides as follows: 'In time of war or other public emergency threatening the life of the nation any High Contracting Party may take measures derogating from its obligations under this Convention to the extent strictly required by the exigencies of the situation, provided that such measures are not inconsistent with its other obligations under international law.'

[103] *Fox, Campbell and Hartley* v. *UK* (1991) 13 E.H.R.R. 157, para 40; *Murray* v. *UK* (1995) 19 E.H.R.R. 193, para 68. The first applicant, Mrs. Murray, complained that her arrest – on suspicion of involvement in the collection of money for the purchase of arms for the IRA – and detention for two hours for questioning gave rise *inter alia* to violations of Article 5(1) and 5(2). It was held that there was no violation of Article 5(1) or (2) whilst the first applicant argued that Article 5(1)(c) had been breached since she was not arrested on 'reasonable suspicion' of having committed a criminal offence and that the purpose of her arrest and subsequent

authorities. An arrested person is entitled to a trial within a reasonable time or release pending trial.[104]

(iii) The right to fair trial

The right to a fair trial deals with the most significant right of any criminal justice system. In the light of the significance of Article 6, which provides the right to fair trial, it is not surprising that more applications have been received relating to Article 6 than any other provision of the Convention. The primary issue relates to the extent to which Strasbourg institutions should monitor national judicial systems to ensure the right to a fair trial. There is also the question of the margin of appreciation, in view of the substantial systems and standards of criminal justice proceedings. Significant differences exist between common law and civil law systems reflecting adversarial and inquisitorial systems of justice. Within common law systems (i.e. England and Ireland) criminal investigation is conducted entirely by the police.[105] In some civil law countries, the first investigation is conducted by the police, although after the identification of the suspect the case is handed over to an investigating judge who then decides whether a prosecution should be brought.[106] From an analysis of the jurisprudence of the Convention, a number of significant principles have emerged relating to the right to fair trial. Firstly, the scope of Article 6(1) extends not only to the guarantees of fair trial but also to access to the Courts themselves.[107] Secondly, this access to the Court must be 'effective'.[108] Thirdly, the right to a fair hearing, in criminal proceedings, includes a right to be present during hearings and that there is equality of opportunity to present one's case in accordance with established principles of natural justice. A significant feature of natural justice is that justice must not only be done, it must also be seen to be done. In *Piersack* v. *Belgium*[109] it

detention had not been to bring her before a 'competent legal authority'. According to the Court having regard to Article 5(1)(c) and its objective to further a criminal investigation mean thereby that the facts which raised a suspicion did not need to be of the same level as those necessary to justify a charge or conviction. Furthermore, there was no breach of Article 5(2) since it must have been apparent during the interview that she was being questioned on her involvement with collection of funds for purchase of arms and that the interview took place promptly after her arrest. Given social mobility, especially within Europe, this provision is of importance and requires the State to make available translators where possible.

[104] *Brogan and others* v. *UK* (1989) 11 E.H.R.R. 117. In Brogan, the Court by a margin of 12 to seven votes held that the seven-day detention period as permitted by under the United Kingdom's anti-terrorism legislation contravened the provisions of Article 5(3), paras 60–62. The United Kingdom's response to Brogan was to derogate *inter alia* from Article 5(3) under the derogation provisions of Article 15. In *Brannigan and McBride* v. *UK* (1994) 17 EHRR 539 93/19, para 54, the European Court of Human Rights held the derogation notice was valid therefore the applicants were unsuccessful in their complaint that detention violated Article 5(3) provisions.

[105] See Sprack, *Emmins on Criminal Procedure* (Oxford University Press, 2002).

[106] For the French Pre-trial system see Bell, 'The French Pre-trial System' in Walker and Starmer (eds), *Miscarriages of Justice: A Review of Justice in Error* (Blackstone Press, 1999), pp. 354–376. *Cf.* in Germany, there is no investigating Judge.

[107] *Golder* v. *UK* (1979–80) 1 E.H.R.R. 524, paras 35–36. In this case, a prisoner was accused of assaulting a prison officer during a disturbance in the prison. However, a different prison officer was able to vouch for his presence at the time in a different area of the prison. The refusal to allow the applicant the requested access to a solicitor, in order to pursue civil action for libel was held to be a violation of the right to access to the courts under Article 6(1).

[108] *Airey* v. *Ireland* (1979–80) 2 E.H.R.R. 305, paras 24–28. Mrs. Airey had attempted to gain a separation from her husband who was both physically and mentally abusive to herself and her children. However, he refused to sign the relevant deeds and the lack of legal aid and legal assistance in dealing with a complex procedure before the Irish High Court meant that the remedy of judicial separation was in reality ineffective. Therefore, the Court held a violation of Article 6(1); Thornberry, 'Poverty, Litigation and Fundamental Rights – A European Perspective' 29 *ICLQ* (1980) 250.

[109] *Piersack* v. *Belgium* (1985) 7 E.H.R.R. CD251, para 32.

was held that a breach of Article 6(1) had taken place with the appointment of a presiding trial judge who had earlier been the head of the section of public prosecutor's department and had investigated the applicant's case and instituted proceedings against him. Although there was no evidence that as a judge he had acted with bias, his position was still unacceptable and regarded as a violation of Article 6.

Fourthly, in accordance with Article 6(2) there is the right to be presumed innocent until proven guilty. This presumption was breached in *Allenet de Ribemont* v. *France*,[110] when a senior police officer made comments at a press conference that the applicant was one of the instigators of the murder. The Court held that Article 6(2) applied and the provisions of the Article had been breached. Although not yet charged, the applicant had been arrested and the statement was akin to a declaration of guilt which firstly encouraged the public to believe that the applicant was guilty and secondly prejudiced the assessment of facts by the court. The provisions here concern the actions of the State and do not, as such, affect the way in which allegations of criminal wrongdoing are reported in the media.

Fifthly, regard must be had to Article 6(3) which provides further guarantees of rights in criminal cases. Sixthly, the person charged with criminal offences must have 'adequate time and facilities for the preparation of his defence'. This provision pre-empts hasty trials. The term 'adequate facilities' means 'that the defendant had opportunity to organise his defence in an appropriate way and without restriction as to the possibility to put all relevant defence arguments before the trial court'. The provision also entails the right to be informed promptly in a language which he understands and in detail of the nature and cause of the action against him. He should also have adequate time and facilities to prepare his defence, to defend himself in person or through legal assistance of his own choosing, or if he has not sufficient means to pay for legal assistance to be given it for free when the interests of justice so require.

Seventhly, the right to a fair hearing needs to analysed as a whole. In *Barbera Messegue and Jabardo* v. *Spain*[111] a culmination of factors, such as the accused being driven over 300 miles the night before the trial and unexpected changes in the constitution and brevity of the trial, led the Court to find breach of Article 6(1).[112] Eighthly, the right to a fair trial also includes the right to trial within a reasonable time; an excessive delay in holding the trial or an excessive period of pre-trial detention would be a violation of that article. Hearings should be held in public and neither of the parties should be placed at a disadvantage.[113] There should also be fairness in the provision of evidence (e.g. the exclusion of illegally obtained evidence, the exclusion of hearsay evidence, the defence's access to evidence, the freedom from self-incrimination).[114] The Article also provides for a right to be able to cross-examine and to have a reasoned judgment, in criminal cases a right to be legally represented and to have access to legal aid.

(iv) Privacy, family life, home and correspondence

Article 8 protects an interesting set of rights. According to Article 8(1), everyone has the right to respect for his private and family life, his home and his correspondence. The

---

[110] *Allenet de Ribemont* v. *France* (1995) 20 E.H.R.R. 557, paras 36–37.

[111] *Barberà, Messegué and Jabardo* v. *Spain* (1989) 11 E.H.R.R. 360, para 89.

[112] *Cf.* in *Stanford* v. *UK*, Application No. 16757/90, paras 25–28, it was disputed that the accused was not able effectively to participate in the proceedings because he had not been able to hear some of the evidence in his trial. However when proceedings were looked at, in their entirety, including the fact that the accused had an experienced counsel and with whom he had been able to communicate and who had defended him well, it was held that the accused had a fair trial.

[113] *Borgers* v. *Belgium* (1993) 15 E.H.R.R. 92, paras 27–29.

[114] *Funke* v. *France* (1993) 16 E.H.R.R. 297, para 44; *Saunders* v. *UK* (1997) 23 E.H.R.R. 313, paras 72–76.

jurisprudence of the Convention confirms that 'private life', 'family life', 'home' and 'correspondence' are distinct although often overlapping interests. 'Private life' covers a wide range of issues, e.g. identity, moral and physical integrity, personal relationships and sexual relations.[115] In *X and Y* v. *Netherlands*, the Court unanimously took the view that ' "private life", [is] a concept which covers the physical and moral integrity of the person, including his or her sexual life'.[116] In *Dudgeon* v. *UK*, a homosexual relationship between adult men was regarded as a 'most intimate aspect of private life'.[117] In the category of personal and physical identity we can include cases concerning transsexuals, or those concerning changes of names, appearances and birth certificates.[118] 'Private life', however, has been accorded a wide meaning. The differing ages for homosexuals and heterosexuals, differing sexual orientation and discharge from armed forces, and *de facto* family relations based on

[115] See Karstan, 'Atypical Families and the Human Rights Act: The Rights of Unmarried Fathers, Same Sex Couples and Transsexuals' *EHRLR* [1999] 195.

[116] *X and Y* v. *The Netherlands*, Application No. 8975/80 (Judgment of 26 March 1985), para 22.

[117] *Dudgeon* v. *UK* (1982) 4 E.H.R.R. 149, para 52. A violation of the right to private life under Article 8 in conjunction with Article 14 was held to have taken place where the State had set differing ages of consent for heterosexual couples *vis-à-vis* homosexual couples. The Sexual (Offences) Amendment Act 2000 has now set the age of consent for gay men, lesbians and heterosexuals at 16 in England and at 17 in Northern Ireland. The Court found a similar violation of Article 8 for the criminalisation of homosexual activity in private between consenting adults: see *Norris* v. *Ireland*, (1991) 13 E.H.R.R. 186.

[118] See *Rees* v. *UK* (1987) 9 E.H.R.R. 56, paras 42–46. A female to male transsexual, R, had undergone gender reassignment surgery and had changed name, driving licence and had a passport issued. However, R was unable to change sex (on the birth certificate) and unable to marry (English Common Law marriage is only permitted between a 'man and a woman'). R argued that claiming to be a man when the birth certificate states otherwise is perjury under s.3(1) of the Perjury Act 191.1. The European Court found no violation of Article 8 and Article 12 – equating traditional marriage with persons of opposite biological sex. According to the Court, States are afforded a margin of appreciation in this area; *Cossey* v. *UK* (1991) 13 E.H.R.R. 622, paras 36, 42. Sex change male to female – the issues similar to *Rees*. The Court found again no violation of Article 8; *cf. B* v. *France* (1993) 16 E.H.R.R. 1, paras 49–62. Miss B was born and registered as a male. She undertook a surgical sex change operation in 1972. The French authorities refused to rectify her civil status certificate which included her sex on her birth certificate under French Law and her name on all identity documents including identity card, passport and voting card. The Court considered various factors – the purpose of French civil registers is to be 'updated throughout the life of the person concerned', in contrast to English birth certificates which simply 'record a historic fact', para 52. The case was therefore distinguishable from both *Rees* and *Cossey*. The Court held a violation of Article 8, as a fair balance had not been struck between the general public interest and the interest of the individual, para 63. In *Sheffield and Horsham* v. *UK* (1998) 27 E.H.R.R. 163, H had been born a man and went through a reassignment surgery in 1992. H was issued a new passport but was not allowed to change her name on the birth certificate. The Court, following *Rees* and *Cossey* decided that there had been no violation of Articles 8 or 12. In *X, Y and Z* v. *UK*, X a female to male transsexual had been in a long-term relationship (i.e. 13 years) with Y and the couple had a child Z through the procedure of artificial insemination. While Z was allowed to take X's name, X's application to be registered as Z's father was refused. The Court while recognising that family life was broader than marriage and marital relationships found no violations of Article 8, since according to the Court it could not be taken to mean placing an obligation on a State party to accord formal recognition as the father of a child who was in fact not the child's biological father. *X, Y and Z* v. *UK* (1997) 24 E.H.R.R. 143; however the Court has had a change of heart in more recent times. *Goodwin* v. *United Kingdom and I* v. *United Kingdom* concerned applicants who were both post-operative male to female transsexuals. G claimed that she had been the object of sexual harassment since her gender reassignment and had suffered from discrimination as regards the payment of her National Insurance contributions. G also complained that she was required to make payments until she was 65 and also alleged that her inability to change her National Insurance number allowed her employer to identify her previous gender identification details. I, the complainant alleged discrimination and inability to be admitted on a nursing course since she refused to present her birth certificate – the allegations of both applicants based on Article 8 and 12 were upheld by the Court. *Goodwin* v. *UK* (2002) 35 E.H.R.R. 18 and *I* v. *UK* (2003) 36 E.H.R.R. 53. Following this decision, the UK government brought in the Gender Recognition Act 2004, which *inter alia* accords the right of transsexuals to marry. It also provides them the right to be treated as having the sex they have adopted as their acquired gender.

relationships other than formal marriage have been treated as matters of private life.[119] In addition to sexual life, the collection and usage of information, census, photographs, medical data, fingerprinting and telephone tapping are all potential intrusions into private life.

According to the provisions of this article, 'home' has a broad meaning and has sometimes been taken to cover residence and business premises. Once the existence of a 'home' is established then the applicant is entitled to certain rights, e.g. the right to access and occupation, not to be expelled or evicted. Interests in the 'home' include the right to a peaceful enjoyment of residence, freedom or relief from noise, pollution, etc. In *Lopes Ostra v. Spain*[120] the applicant was successful in claiming that failure by the State to act to prevent or to protect her from serious pollution (fumes from a waste disposal plant dealing with waste from a tannery) constituted a failure to respect her home and private life. A failure to provide information about the risks inherent in residing at a hazardous and unsafe place would result in breaching the provisions of Article 8. In *Guerra v. Italy*,[121] a group of individuals from an Italian village successfully brought a claim for violation of Article 8. They complained of local government's maladministration in failing to provide essential information about the risks associated with a nearby chemical factory. The chemical factory was high risk and had a history of accidents. Although on previous occasions an explosion in the factory had led to the hospitalisation of 150 people with arsenic poisoning, none of the applicants in the present case had suffered a direct injury. The Court held that there was a violation of the Article, adjudicating that once the authorities became aware of the essential information and the risks and dangers involved in running the factory, they had delayed informing the applicants thereby depriving them from assessing the risks they and their families ran by continuing to live in the vicinity of the factory.[122]

'Correspondence' could be of a sensitive nature which needs to be protected (lawyer–client, lawyer–prisoner correspondence).[123] In *Malone v. UK*,[124] Mr. Malone, an antiques dealer had been tried and acquitted on charges of dishonesty. In 1978 he brought proceedings against the police alleging that since 1971 he had been under police surveillance, which included having his telephone tapped and his telephone calls 'metered' (a device that automatically records all numbers dialled). Mr. Malone also claimed that his correspondence had been intercepted and tampered with and sought a declaration from the English High

---

[119] See *Lustig-Prean and Beckett v. UK* (2000) 29 E.H.R.R. 548, para 104; *Smith and Grady v. UK* (2000) 29 E.H.R.R. 493, para 111; *Beck, Copp and Bazeley v. UK*, Application No. 48535/99, 48536/99 and 48537/99, paras 51–53. The Court held that the discharging of lesbians and gay men from the armed forces violated the right to private life as contained in Article 8.

[120] *López Ostra v. Spain* (1995) 20 E.H.R.R. 277, paras 51, 52 and 58. See Desgagné, 'Integrating Environmental Values into the European Convention on Human Rights' 89 *AJIL* (1995) 263.

[121] *Guerra and Others v. Italy*, (1998) 26 E.H.R.R. 357.

[122] Ibid. paras 59–60. See *McGinley and Egan v. UK* (1999) 27 E.H.R.R. 1, paras 101–103. This case related to nuclear tests carried out at Christmas Island, during which time servicemen were allegedly exposed deliberately to high levels of radiation and the health risks associated with this. The applicants claimed a violation of Article 8 in respect of lack of access to documents which would have enabled them to assess radiation levels. The Court held that while in such cases the State is under a positive obligation regarding the establishment of an 'effective and accessible procedure . . . which enables such persons to seek all relevant and appropriate information', in this case the State had fulfilled such obligations. *LCB v. UK* (1998) 27 E.H.R.R. 212; this case also related to the Christmas Island nuclear tests. However, the Court lacked jurisdiction regarding the complaints under Article 8. For a survey of literature see Hart, 'Environmental Rights' in English and Havers (eds), *An Introduction to Human Rights and the Common Law* (Hart Publishing, 2000) pp. 159–183; Churchill, 'Environmental Rights in Existing Human Rights Treaties' in Boyle and Anderson (eds), *Human Rights Approaches to Environmental Protection* (Clarendon Press, 1996) pp. 89–108.

[123] See *Silver v. UK* (1983) 5 E.H.R.R. 347, paras 91, 93–95, 105.

[124] *Malone v. UK* (1985) 7 E.H.R.R. 14.

Court. He argued, *inter alia*, that the interception, monitoring or recording of telephone conversations without his consent was unlawful, which violated Article 8 of the Convention. His claim in the English High Court was dismissed.[125] He then went to the European Court of Human Rights, which upheld his claim that there had been a violation of Article 8. According to the Court:

> [i]n view of the attendant obscurity and uncertainty as to the state of the law in this essential respect, the Court cannot but reach a similar conclusion to that of the Commission. In the opinion of the Court, the law of England and Wales does not indicate with reasonable clarity the scope and manner of exercise of the relevant discretion conferred on the public authorities. To that extent, the minimum degree of legal protection to which citizens are entitled under the rule of law in a democratic society is lacking.[126]

The Article places wide and far-reaching obligations on States parties in safeguarding respect for family life. The obligations are of a positive nature, an important illustration of which is provided by the case of *X and Y* v. *Netherlands*.[127] In this case, there had been a sexual assault on a 16-year-old mentally handicapped girl by an adult male of sound mind. It had not been possible to bring a criminal charge against the accused because the victim having attained the age of 16 and with a mental disorder was prevented under Dutch law to initiate a criminal 'complaint'. In the absence of criminal prosecution, the Dutch government had pointed to the possibility of civil remedies available to the girl. The European Court acknowledged the margin of appreciation which the State had and the difficulties which resulted as a consequence of action by a private individual as opposed to public bodies. However, according to the Court, civil remedies were inadequate and the absence of effective criminal remedy in these circumstances constituted a breach by the Dutch government to respect Y's right to a private life. Thus, according to the Court, positive obligations under Article 8 included ensuring the existence of civil as well as criminal remedies against sexual attacks. State responsibility and violation of Article 8 was thereby established because of the defectiveness in the Dutch law. The Court also confirmed the positive or horizontal nature of the obligations imposed by the Convention, in that the State responsibility was incurred for the failure on the part of the State to adopt measures 'designed to ensure respect for private life even in the sphere of individuals between themselves'.[128]

Family life has also been given an extensive meaning. In *Marckx* v. *Belgium*[129] it was held that Belgium had a positive obligation to make legislative provisions which safeguarded an illegitimate child's integration into the family, a failure of which had led to the violation of Articles 8 and 14. Violations under Article 14 took place because of discrimination between

---

[125] *Malone* v. *Metropolitan Police Commissioner* [1978 M. No. 3772]; [1979] 2 WLR 700.

[126] *Malone* v. *UK* (1985) 7 E.H.R.R. 14, para 79.

[127] *X and Y* v. *The Netherlands*, Application No. 8975/80, (Judgment of 26 March 1985, paras 27 and 30). See Van Bueren, 'Protecting Children's Rights in Europe – A Test Case Strategy' *EHRLR* [1996] 171.

[128] The Court noted 'that although the object of Article 8 (art. 8) is essentially that of protecting the individual against arbitrary interference by the public authorities, it does not merely compel the State to abstain from such interference: in addition to this primarily negative undertaking, there may be positive obligations inherent in an effective respect for private or family life (see *Airey* v. *Ireland* (1979–80) 2 E.H.R.R. 305, para 32). These obligations may involve the adoption of measures designed to secure respect for private life even in the sphere of the relations of individuals between themselves' *X and Y* v. *The Netherlands*, Application No. 8975/80, (Judgment of 26 March 1985), para 23.

[129] *Marckx* v. *Belgium*, (1979–80) 2 E.H.R.R. 330, paras 37 and 40–43.

Europe and human rights (I)

7

legitimate and illegitimate children. Violation of Article 8 occurred as discriminatory treatment was inconsistent with Belgium's duty to respect the mother's right to family life.

The Convention does not provide and protect the right to enter and stay in a member State. However, if the deportation of a family member makes it impossible to maintain the family, then the concerned State is under an obligation not to exclude that particular member. In *Berrehab* v. *Netherlands*,[130] the applicant was a Moroccan national whose right to stay in the Netherlands was dependent upon remaining married to a Dutch national. It was held that a violation of Article 8 had taken place when, after his divorce, his residence permit was not renewed. The violation had taken place because his removal from the Netherlands would make it impossible for him to maintain family ties with his daughter.[131] In *Moustaquim* v. *Belgium*,[132] a deportation order served on a young Moroccan national (second-generation immigrant in Belgium) violated Article 8(1). The applicant had been brought to Belgium as an infant and spent his childhood in his new country alongside seven of his brothers and sisters. He had strong family ties in Belgium and those ties could be enjoyed only whilst he remained in Belgium. This wide interpretation has led to changes in the immigration laws of several signatory States.

(a) Freedom of religion

Article 9 provides for freedom of thought, conscience and religion.[133] Modelled closely upon Article 18 of the Universal Declaration on Human Rights and subsequently developed by the ICCPR, freedom of thought, conscience and religion poses its own peculiarities. Article 9(1) provisions are best regarded as *freedoms* rather than rights *stricto sensu*.[134] As we shall be analysing in a subsequent chapter as a 'right' freedom of religion is difficult to both articulate and to implement within general international law.[135] Insofar as the Convention is concerned, the main focus of freedom of religion as exhibited in Article 9 established two principal features. Firstly, it accords protection to freedom of thought, conscience and religion. Secondly, it protects the manifestation of these freedoms. While restrictions can be placed on manifestation of this freedom, the literal reading of Article 9(1) provides for freedom of thought, conscience and religion as an unqualified right.

That said the phrases 'thought, conscience and religion' as used in the article have been difficult to define. In *X and Church of Scientology* v. *Sweden*,[136] the European Commission was faced with the question as to whether advertisement by the Church was to be attributed a commercial or religious purpose. After deciding that this advertisement was for commercial purposes and, therefore, not a manifestation of religion protected by the article, the Commission did not find it necessary to discuss whether Scientology is a religion. In *Arrowsmith* v. *UK*, the Commission accepted 'pacifism' as a philosophy which formed part of freedom of thought, conscience and religion. Although the ambit of defining

---

[130] *Berrehab* v. *The Netherlands* (1989) 11 E.H.R.R. 322.
[131] Ibid. para 29.
[132] *Moustaquim* v. *Belgium* (1991) 13 E.H.R.R. 802, paras 36, 46–47.
[133] See generally Taylor, *Freedom of Religion: UN and European Human Rights Law and Practice* (Cambridge University Press, 2005); Evans, *Religious Liberty and International Law in Europe* (Cambridge University Press, 1997); Evans, *Freedom of Religion under the European Convention on Human Rights* (Oxford University Press, 2001); Langlaude, 'Indoctrination, Secularism, Religious Liberty and the ECHR' 55 *ICLQ* (2006) 929.
[134] Harris, O'Boyle, Bates and Buckley, above n.1, at pp. 426–432.
[135] See below chapter 12.
[136] *X and Church of Scientology* v. *Sweden*. Application No. 7805/77, 16 DR 68 (1979), at 72, para 4.

'religion, thought or conscience' has been controversial, certain guidelines can nevertheless be derived from the European Human Rights case law: Article 9 protection has been extended to Druidism,[137] veganism,[138] Islam,[139] Krishna conscience movement,[140] Devine Light Zentrum[141] and Jehovah witnesses as determined in *Kokkinakis*.[142]

In terms of the substantive right, Article 9 provisions have resulted in a difficult balancing exercise, especially when freedom of religion has come into conflict with other human rights such as the right to freedom of expression or the right to private and family life.[143] A typical approach by the Commission and the Court has been to avoid the issues of freedom of religion. In *Hoffmann v. Austria*,[144] a custody dispute between the mother as a Jehovah's Witness, and the non-Jehovah's Witness father was treated as one of the rights to family life under Article 8. In *Khan v. UK*,[145] focus was placed upon the right to marry under Article 12. This meant that no violation was committed in the case of non-recognition of the marriage under national law in the instance of underage marriage, even though this was permissible in the applicant's religion.[146] Nevertheless, and ironically, the Commission and Court have often insisted that freedom of religion occupies the position of a fundamental right. In *Kokkinakis*, the Court took the view that the values contained in Article 9 were fundamental to the existence of a democratic society: 'It is, in its religious dimension, one of the most vital elements that go to make up the identity of believers and their conception of life, but it is also a precious asset for atheists, agnostics, sceptics and the unconcerned'.[147] While the State parties are accorded a 'margin of appreciation' as the case of *Kokkinakis*[148] establishes, any restrictions placed on freedom of religion or its manifestation by the State must be justifiable and proportionate. Mr. Kokkinakis had been arrested more

---

[137] *Chappell* v. *UK* (1988) 10 E.H.R.R. CD510, para 1. In this case the Commission held that the applicants assertion that the closing of Stonehenge during the midsummer solstice amounted to a violation of his rights under Article 9 to be manifestly ill-founded as the restriction was justified in order to protect Stonehenge and the surrounding area.

[138] *W* v. *UK*, Application No. 18187/91, para 1. This case concerned the refusal of a prison inmate to work in the prison print shop as his vegan beliefs prevented him from working with animal-tested products (dyes) according to his rights under Article 9. The claim was held to be inadmissible by the Commission as the interference with his rights was justified and proportionate to the aim of preserving good order in the prison.

[139] *Ahmad* v. *UK* (1982) 4 E.H.R.R. 126. The applicant, a teacher, was refused permission to attend a mosque during the hours of his employment. The Commission accepted that in this case, the education authority had to balance the applicant's religious position with the requirements of the education system as a whole. Therefore, it was held that there was no interference with the applicant's rights under Article 9(1)

[140] *ISKCON and 8 others* v. *UK* (1994) 18 E.H.R.R. CD133, para 2. This case relates to the use of a 19th century manor house by the International Society of Krishna Consciousness. It was held that the planning legislation and subsequent enforcement notice served were necessary in a democratic society and were, therefore, a justified interference with Article 9.

[141] *Omkarananda and the Divine Light Zentrum* v. *Switzerland*, Application No. 8118/77, pp. 112–113. The applicants complained that an expulsion order against an Indian national was aimed at the liquidation of the Devine Light Zentrum (DLZ). The Commission held the application to be manifestly ill-founded, as although the expulsion was 'likely to deeply shake the DLZ, cannot be considered as an interference with the second applicant's right under the same provision', para 6.

[142] *Kokkinakis* v. *Greece* (1994) 17 E.H.R.R. 397, paras 48–50.

[143] See Greer, ' "Balancing" and the European Court of Human Rights: A Contribution to the Habermas-Alexy Debate' 63 *Cambridge Law Journal* (2004) 412.

[144] *Hoffmann* v. *Austria* (1994) 17 E.H.R.R. 293.

[145] *Khan* v. *UK*, Application No. 11579/85.

[146] Ibid. pp. 253–255.

[147] Ibid. para 31.

[148] *Kokkinakis* v. *Greece* (1994) 17 E.H.R.R. 397.

than 60 times in addition to being interned and imprisoned on several occasions for proselytism, which was illegal in Greece, with criminal penalties attached. The Court held that in the absence of any pressing social need, the interference with the applicant's freedom of religion was not necessary in a democratic society.[149]

The European Court of Human Rights has been particularly keen to recognise the State's margin of appreciation, particularly in instances where the religious sensibilities of majority populations are brought into question: many of these cases relate to offending or outraging religious sentiments. However, it is also important to note that while freedom of religion is fundamental in many respects, views and practices based upon religions or religious interpretations, which violate or interfere with the enjoyment of the human rights of others, such as torture, female genital mutilation, underage marriages and forced marriages, cannot be permitted. In *Otto-Preminger-Institute* v. *Austria*,[150] the applicant institute attempted to show a film which was offensive to the religious sentiments of the Catholic people of Tyrol – a region with a largely Catholic population and where religion has a very influential role in people's lives. It was held that there was no violation of Article 10. In reaching this decision the Court was influenced by the religious views and beliefs of the majority Catholic population of Tyrol.[151] Similar approaches have emerged from case-law from the UK. In *X. Ltd. and Y* v. *UK* (the Gay News case),[152] the applicants were convicted in a private case of blasphemous libel due to a poem and illustration published in Gay News magazine detailing 'acts of sodomy and fellatio with the body of Christ immediately after His death and ascribed to him during His lifetime promiscuous homosexual practices with the Apostles and other men'.[153] The Commission held that the application of the blasphemy law was to be considered necessary in the circumstances of the case and there, therefore, followed no violation of convention rights.[154] In *Wingrove* v. *UK*,[155] the applicant's video, Visions of Ecstasy was refused a classification certificate on the basis of its infringement of the criminal law of blasphemy. This was again considered by the Court to be necessary in a democratic society and, thus, did not constitute a violation of convention rights.[156] On the other hand there is an apparent bias towards upholding values of the Christian religion *vis-à-vis* other religions, in particular Islam, and the religious sentiments of Muslims. Attempts to bring out a private prosecution were unsuccessful in the United Kingdom in *R* v. *Chief Metropolitan Stipendiary Magistrate, ex parte Choudhury*,[157] while the European Commission on Human Rights struck out an application as manifestly ill-founded since Article 9 of the European Convention on Human Rights did not provide absolute protection against religious sensitivities.[158] Such discrepancy in the application of laws (towards religions) has not only infuriated the Muslim community within the United Kingdom, but been the object of criticism by human rights scholars. Professors Bailey, Harris and Ormerod make the striking remark that:

---

[149] Ibid. paras 48–50; also see *Manoussakis and others* v. *Greece* (1997) 23 E.H.R.R. 387.
[150] *Otto-Preminger Institute* v. *Austria* (1995) 19 E.H.R.R. 34.
[151] *Otto-Preminger Institute* v. *Austria* (1995) 19 E.H.R.R. 34, para 56.
[152] *X. Ltd. and Y* v. *UK*, Application No. 8710/79.
[153] Ibid. p. 78.
[154] Ibid. p. 83.
[155] *Wingrove* v. *UK* (1997) 24 E.H.R.R. 1.
[156] Ibid. paras 64–65.
[157] *R* v. *Chief Metropolitan Stipendiary Magistrate, ex parte Choudhury*, [1990] 3 WLR 98, [1991] 1 QB 429.
[158] *Choudhury* v. *UK*, Application No. 17439/90, para 1.

Ex p Choudhury raises a question that has become increasingly relevant as the United Kingdom has become a more multi-religious society. Is it defensible that in *R v Lemon* the publisher of a poem that offended Christians could be guilty of blasphemy when in *Ex p Choudhury* the publishers of a novel that contained passages that were at least equally offensive to Muslims could not? The Law Commission addressed this question in their 1985 Report when recommending the abolition of the offences of blasphemy and blasphemous libel (the written form of blasphemy).[159]

After years of campaigning the blasphemy law in the United Kingdom has eventually been changed: the Criminal Justice and Immigration Act (2008) provides for the abolition of the common law offences of blasphemy and blasphemous libel.[160] According to section 79(1), 'The offences of blasphemy and blasphemous libel under the common law of England and Wales are abolished'.[161] The reform of the UK legislation is to be applauded since it removes the inherently discriminatory characteristic of the law towards faiths other than the Christian faith. That said, it is still a matter a conjecture as to whether the abolition of the common law offence of blasphemy, would in fact create an environment where genuine criticism, or satire and sarcasm of all religions and beliefs and followers of religions, could be conducted without fear of criminal prosecutions. Furthermore, while the belated revision of the UK domestic laws on blasphemy law undoubtedly represent a positive measure, disappointment has been expressed at the European human rights institutions for their apparent endorsement of a patently discriminatory law for such a sustained period of time.[162]

The Court has also been careful to ensure a wide margin of appreciation when faced with cases of the religious freedom of individuals, on the one hand, and the secularity of the State in question, on the other. In *Dahlab* v. *Switzerland*, it was held that prohibiting a primary school teacher from wearing a headscarf was permitted in the circumstances, despite the fact that she had taught in the same school for three years without action being taken and without complaints being made. The Court 'further noted that the impugned measure had left the applicant with a difficult choice, but considered that State school teachers had to tolerate proportionate restrictions on their freedom of religion'.[163] The neutrality of the State education system was held to be a legitimate aim when restricting freedom of religion. This sentiment was echoed in *Leyla Şahin* v. *Turkey*,[164] where the banning of headscarves by a university was declared justified and proportionate to the aim. In *Leyla Şahin*, the applicant Ms. Şahin complained that a rule established by Istanbul University prohibiting the wearing of the Islamic headscarf during classes and exams violated her Article 9 rights.[165] Ms. Şahin regarded wearing the headscarf as a religious

---

[159] Bailey, Harris and Ormerod, *Bailey, Harris and Jones: Civil Liberties: Cases and Materials* (Butterworths, 2001), at pp. 1050–1051.

[160] Criminal Justice and Immigration Act 2008 (2008 Chapter 4) www.opsi.gov.uk/acts/acts2008/ukpga_20080004_en_1 <last visited 30 May 2009>.

[161] Ibid. s.79(1).

[162] See Ghandhi and James, 'The English Law of Blasphemy and the European Convention on Human Rights' *EHRLR* [1998] 430.

[163] *Dahlab* v. *Switzerland*, Application No. 42393/98, p. 12.

[164] *Sahin* v. *Turkey* (2007) 44 E.H.R.R. 5. See also *Refah Partisi (the Welfare Party) and others* v. *Turkey* (2003) 37 E.H.R.R. 1.

[165] *Sahin* v. *Turkey* (2007) 44 E.H.R.R. 5, paras 85–101.

obligation. She insisted that the wearing of the headscarf was a matter of personal choice and that such a personal decision was not incompatible with the principles of secularism as guaranteed within the Turkish constitution.[166] The Turkish government contested the applicant's position and argued that the idea of secularism was vital to the Turkish State remaining a liberal democracy and that the headscarf represented an association with extreme 'religious fundamentalist movements' presenting a threat to Turkey's value of secularism.[167]

The Grand Chamber by a majority 16 votes to one decided that the ban on the headscarf was justified under Article 9(2). The Court noted that the restriction on the headscarf was 'necessary in a democratic society' and went on to make the following points of endorsement of the Turkish State's argument. The Court noted that:

> [a]s the Chamber rightly stated . . . the Court considers the notion of secularism to be consistent with the values underpinning the Convention. It finds that upholding that principle, which is undoubtedly one of the fundamental principles of the Turkish State which are in harmony with the rule of law and respect for human rights, may be considered necessary to protect the democratic system in Turkey.[168]

The Court's position is open to criticism, not only for endorsing an oppressive State restriction on Article 9, but also for its insensitivity towards women's rights and the personal autonomy of women in relation to manifestation and practice of religion.[169] Some critics may view the *Leyla Şahın v. Turkey* and *Dahlab v. Switzerland* cases as additional examples of an anti-Islamic bias on the part of the European human rights institutions. Notwithstanding these criticisms of bias on the part of European human rights institutions, the Commission and now the European Court of Human Rights has continued to insist on neutrality on the part of the State authorities in the exercise of their powers including registration of religious communities.[170]

(b) Freedom of expression, assembly and association

Article 10 contains the very important right to the freedom of expression. Article 10(1) provides that:

> [e]veryone has the right to freedom of expression. This right shall include freedom to hold opinions and to receive and impart information and ideas without interference by public authority and regardless of frontiers . . .

---

[166] Ibid. para 85.

[167] Ibid. paras 90–93.

[168] *Sahin v. Turkey* (2007) 44 E.H.R.R. 5, para 114.

[169] Ibid. Dissenting Opinion of Judge Tulkens, para 12; also see Evans 'The "Islamic Scarf" in the European Court of Human Rights' 7 *Melbourne Journal of International Law* (2006) 52; Vakulenko, ' "Islamic Headscarves" and the European Convention on Human Rights: An Intersectional Perspective' 16 *Social and Legal Studies* (2007) 190.

[170] See e.g. *Hasan and Chaush v. Bulgaria* (2002) 34 E.H.R.R. 55; also see *Holy Synod of the Bulgarian Orthodox Church (Metropolitan Inokentiy) and others v. Bulgaria*, Application Nos. 412/03 and 35677/04. See also Nathwani 'Religious cartoons and human rights – A critical legal analysis of the case law of the European Court of Human Rights on the protection of religious feelings and its implications in the Danish affair concerning cartoons of the Prophet Muhammad' *EHRLR* [2008] 488.

However, the right is not unlimited and the State has a wide margin of appreciation to restrict expression, as illustrated in *Handyside* v. *UK*.[171] In *Handyside*, the applicant had published a book called *The Little Red Schoolbook*, intended for school children age 12 and above. The book was meant to be for reference on issues such as education and learning, for both teachers and pupils, and contained a section on sex with sub-headings under pornography, contraceptives and other sexually intimate exercises. The applicant was convicted of having committed offences contrary to the Obscene Publications Acts 1959 and 1964. When the case came before the European Court of Human Rights, the Court took account of the variety of views that prevailed amongst the countries of the Council of Europe and, in particular, the importance of allowing domestic institutions the powers to decide in accordance with their moral and ethical values. Having regard to this margin of appreciation, the Court decided that there had been no violation of Article 10.[172]

More recently, there are signs that the Court is possibly shifting its position in accepting a narrower 'margin of appreciation' for States parties. This stance is reflected in the recent Chamber judgment of *Vereinigung Bildender Künstler* v. *Austria*.[173] In this case, the applicant association, Vereinigung Bildender Künstler Wiener Secession, was an organisation of artists established in the Secession building, Vienna, Austria. In an exhibition organised by the applicants, a painting entitled 'Apocalypse' was displayed. The painting which was a collage of 34 public figures – including Mother Teresa, the Austrian cardinal Hermann Groer and the former head of the Austrian Freedom Party (FPÖ) Jörg Haider – displayed these individuals as naked and depicting sexual activities taking place amongst them. Mr. Meischberger was shown as holding the ejaculating penis of Mr. Haider while at the same time being touched by two other FPÖ politicians and ejaculating on Mother Teresa. The domestic Austrian Court, the Vienna Court of Appeal, held that the painting in question represented a debasement of Mr. Meischberger's public standing and issued an injunction against the applicant association displaying the painting. The applicants claimed a right to be able to exhibit the painting as part of freedom of expression provided under Article 10.

The Chamber of the European Court refused to accept the Austrian State's position that the interference pursued the legitimate aim of protecting public morals. The Chamber was of the view that the painting, although outrageous in depicting Mr. Meischberger in such manner, was a caricature and the painting was satirical. Satire was a form of artistic expression which intentionally aimed to provoke its viewers. There was thus in the Court's judgment interference with an artist's right to such expression and the injunctions imposed by the domestic courts of Austria were therefore disproportionate to the aim pursued and therefore not necessary in a democratic society. A violation of Article 10 had taken place. Whilst acknowledging a possible shift in the Court's position, a cautionary approach needs to be taken. Although involving moral and religious sentiments, the case was brought as a violation of Article 10.[174]

Despite the existence of a 'margin of appreciation', it is not in every case that the Strasbourg institutions have allowed the domestic authorities to determine the rights and

---

[171] *Handyside* v. *UK* (1979–80) 1 E.H.R.R. 737.

[172] Ibid. paras 57 and 59. The same approach characterised the Court's position in *Müller and others* v. *Switzerland* (1991) 13 E.H.R.R. 212, paras 36 and 43 which concerned the confiscation of artistic works and the conviction of artists due to the works being deemed to be obscene publications. In *Otto-Preminger Institute* v. *Austria* (1995) 19 E.H.R.R. 34, which related to the display of a film, deemed to be offensive in a Catholic area, the Court ruled that the State was permitted a margin of appreciation.

[173] *Vereinigung Bildender Künstler* v. *Austria* (2008) 47 E.H.R.R. 5.

[174] For useful discussion on Freedom of Speech, see Barendt, *Freedom of Speech* (Oxford University Press, 2007).

7

freedoms of individuals. In the *Sunday Times* v. *UK* cases,[175] the applicants claimed that a court order prohibiting the publication of an article concerning 'thalidomide children' (i.e. children who were born deformed by reason of their mothers having taken thalidomide as a tranquilliser during pregnancy) constituted a violation of their rights as guaranteed by Article 10 of the Convention. The order had been made on the ground that the relevant Article might prejudice the proceedings which were pending before the English courts. The European Court of Human Rights held that the United Kingdom had violated the provisions of the Convention and ordered payment of a significant amount to the applicants for their costs.[176]

Article 11 provides for freedom of assembly and association as related freedoms. Peaceful assembly includes public meetings, demonstrations, marches, picketing and processions. Assembly needs to be peaceful, although any incidental breaches of peace would not render the assembly unlawful. The requirement of notification and permission is not normally regarded as interference, but bans because of the seriousness of interference require justification under Article 11(2). The interference under Article 11(2) must be 'in accordance with the law'. Freedom of association means that individuals are not to be compelled to become members of particular associations and there should be no discrimination against individuals who join specific organisations. Under the Convention, individuals have the freedom to form trade unions, and the State remains under an obligation to allow the establishment of trade unions. The State cannot make membership of a particular trade union compulsory. Breaches of the Convention law would be conducted through restrictive policies, or using public powers of interference.

(c) Non-discrimination issues under the Convention

Article 14 provides for the universally recognised norm of non-discrimination.[177] It is directly analogous to Article 2(1) of ICCPR. However, Article 14 has been restricted to protecting persons against discrimination only in respect of rights contained within the Convention, whereas Article 26 ICCPR extends the concept of non-discrimination in Article 2(1) to equality before the law. In the sense of not being an independent article, Article 14, is called a parasitic article. This limitation of Article 14 has now been redressed by the adoption of Protocol 12, which extends beyond the rights provided in the Convention to 'any right set forth by law'.[178] Protocol 12 removes the pre-condition that the rights affected must be contained within the Convention or one of the Protocols ratified by the State party. In other words, once a discriminatory practice is established, no corresponding violation of the substantive rights involved need to be found. Article 14 protects against discrimination, instead of promoting equality, although it would appear that different treatment of people in similar circumstances may be justified under

---

[175] *Sunday Times* v. *UK* (1979–80) 2 E.H.R.R. 245; *Sunday Times* v. *UK (No. 2)* (1992) 14 E.H.R.R. 229.

[176] *Sunday Times* v. *UK* (1979–80) 2 E.H.R.R. 245, paras 55–57 and 65–68; *Sunday Times* v. *UK (No. 2)* (1992) 14 E.H.R.R. 229, paras 52–56.

[177] See Harris, O'Boyle, Bates and Buckley, above n.1, at pp. 577–615; Goldston, 'Race Discrimination in Europe: Problems and Prospects' *EHRLR* [1999] 462.

[178] Article 1, Protocol 12 provides as follows: 'The enjoyment of any right set forth by law shall be secured without discrimination on any ground such as sex, race, colour, language, religion, political or other opinion, national or social origin, association with a national minority, property, birth or other status.'

Article 14.[179] On the whole, Protocol 12 has substantial advantages. It is comprehensive in nature and accords a broad application. Unlike the EU Race Directive or the UN Racial Discrimination Convention, Protocol 12 is applicable to racial and religious discrimination as well as discrimination on the grounds of national origin. The non-exhaustive nature of the Protocol gives it a potentially much broader scope to prevent discrimination: sexual minorities or other forms of minorities could seek solace in its provisions. That said, it needs to be noted that Protocol 12 does not provide any definition of discrimination and the elaboration of the provision will need to be tested in the light of the interpretation transmitted through the European Court's jurisprudence. The Protocol came into force 1 April 2005, although the United Kingdom has continued to refuse to sign or ratify it.

4 INSTITUTIONAL MECHANISMS AND IMPLEMENTATION MACHINERY

At the time of the enforcement of the ECHR, the institutional bodies comprised the European Commission on Human Rights, the European Court of Human Rights and the Committee of Ministers. Since 1 November 1998 when the 11th Protocol came into operation, the Commission was abolished and the functions of the Commission were merged into those of a permanent and full-time Court. The decision-making powers of the Committee of Ministers were also abolished by the 11th Protocol and the role of the Committee was limited to supervising the execution of judgments.[180] In addition, however, the Committee has since 1996 established a thematic monitoring procedure. Any member States may be requested to submit information, *inter alia*, on the role and application of democratic institutions, e.g. the police and judiciary, as well as reporting on such key areas as freedom of expression and information. A series of on-site visits have been conducted as part of the procedure.[181] Furthermore, the Committee also oversees the post-accession commitments made by new member States.[182]

Under the changes brought by Protocol 14, the Committee of Ministers may, by a vote of two-thirds of representatives, seek a ruling from the Court on the interpretation of a final judgement which is problematic.[183] This step is to be undertaken in case of disagreement regarding the meaning of the original judgment. A further change is brought about through the ability to bring infringement proceedings against a recalcitrant State. In situations where the Committee of Ministers considers that a High Contracting Party refuses to follow a final judgment, the Committee may, after serving formal notice on that Party and by a decision adopted by a majority vote of two-thirds of the representatives entitled to sit on the Committee, refer to the Court the question of whether that Party has failed to fulfil its obligations.[184] The Grand Chamber will then adjudicate as to whether the respondent

[179] *Rasmussen* v. *Denmark* (1985) 7 E.H.R.R. 37, paras 38–42; also note the extended scope of Article 14 as provided in more recent case-law, e.g. *Nachova and others* v. *Bulgaria* (2006) 42 E.H.R.R. 43; also see *DH* v. *Czech Republic* (2008) 47 E.H.R.R. 3.

[180] ECHR Article 46 (2). For a useful comparison with Inter-American human rights system see Harris, 'Regional Protection of Human Rights: The Inter-American Achievement' Harris and Livingstone (eds), above n.41, at pp. 1–29.

[181] Boyle 'Council of Europe, OSCE, and European Union' in Hannum (ed.), *Guide to International Human Rights Practice* (Transnational Publishers, 2004) pp. 143–170 at p. 144.

[182] Ibid. p. 144.

[183] Revised Article 46(3) ECHR, Article 16, Protocol 14.

[184] Ibid. Article 46(4) ECHR.

State has failed to follow the original judgment of the Court and inform the Committee of Ministers if there has been a breach of Article 46(1) ECHR by the State.[185] Whilst these infringement proceedings are likely to be rare, the extension in the powers of the Committee of Ministers is an added impetus to compliance and execution of the Court's judgments.

The Parliamentary Assembly is the democratic element of the Council of Europe. The 318 representatives and 318 substitutes are appointed from and by the national parliaments of member States and meet four times a year.[186] The Parliamentary Assembly adopts recommendations, resolutions and opinions which are used as guidelines for the Committee of Ministers and national governments and parliaments. It can also take action in the event that States do not meet their obligations. This includes refusing to ratify or withdrawing the credentials of a national delegation to the Assembly and as a last resort it may suspend a country's membership of the Council of Europe. The role that the Parliamentary Assembly has played in the Council of Europe's human rights regime cannot be overstated. In addition to being behind the inception of the European Convention on Human Rights, the Assembly also elects the judges to the European Court of Human Rights and the Commissioner for Human Rights.

The reformed Court of Human Rights performs the functions, both of the previously existent Commission and its own functions, thereby deciding upon both issues of admissibility and the merits of the cases. The Court sits in Committees of three judges, Chambers of seven judges and a Grand Chamber of 17 judges.[187] Protocol 14 of the ECHR extends the terms of the office of the Court judges to nine years, although they will not be re-elected thereafter.[188] In a particular case, the judge of the respondent State will sit *ex officio* as part of the chamber or the Grand Chamber. If the judge is unable to sit, the Court will choose someone from that State to sit in the capacity of a judge.[189] The ECHR also makes provisions for the possibilities of third-party intervention by a State or another interested party with the request, or with the leave, of the President of the Chamber.[190] The European Court of Human Rights is now accorded with a limited advisory jurisdiction.[191] This jurisdiction is, however, restricted to the Committee of Ministers.[192]

5 COMPLAINTS PROCEDURE UNDER PROTOCOL 11

(i) Preliminary procedures

The appropriate language for initiating proceedings is French or English as those are the official languages of the Court. The Rules of the Court however permit the usage of any

---

[185] Revised Article 31(b) ECHR, Article 10, Protocol 14.
[186] The representatives are organised into five different political groups within the Parliamentary Assembly, these are: Group of the European People's Party (EPP/CD); Socialist Group (SOC); European Democrat Group (EDG); Alliance of Liberals and Democrats for Europe (ALDE); Group of the European Unified Left (UEL).
[187] The judges who are elected by the Parliamentary Assembly sit in their individual capacity as either persons of judicial qualifications suited to the High Judicial office or are jurists of recognised competence. Their dismissal can only take place by vote of a two-thirds majority of judges.
[188] Revised Article 23 ECHR, Article 2, Protocol 14.
[189] Article 27(2).
[190] ECHR Article 36 and Rule 61. *Amicus curiae* had previously been submitted in a number of occasions e.g. *Chahal v. UK* (1997) 23 E.H.R.R. 413.
[191] See Article 47(1).
[192] Ibid.

language prior to admissibility and the President of the Court has the discretion to allow parties to continue use of the same language, as in the preliminary stages of the case.[193] Individual petitioners can lodge complaints of their own accord since lawyers are not required for proceedings before the Court. The Rules of the Court also make provision for legal aid for individual applicants. The funding is based on the financial assistance provided by the Council of Europe. Requests for legal aid should be made to the Court and decisions are based on the test of whether a particular individual would be eligible to obtain legal aid in his or her State. The financial assistance provided is not extensive but does allow for essential expenses including travel and living expenses in pursuit of a claim before the Court.[194]

(ii) Complaints procedure

The complaints procedure under the amended Convention is as follows.[195] The application should be addressed to the Registrar of the European Court of Human Rights, with whom all subsequent correspondence should be conducted.[196] Once an application is registered with the Secretariat a single judge is assigned. The judge makes a request for factual or other additional information and prepares a report on admissibility. Under Protocol 14,[197] a new entity, 'the single-judge formation', is devised under the revised Article 26 ECHR.[198] Under the provisions of Article 27 ECHR, the single judge may declare inadmissible an application or strike out of the Court's list applications brought under Article 34 ECHR, in instances where such decisions 'can be taken without further examination'.[199] According to the explanatory report, the single-judge formation is to reach such a decision 'in clear-cut cases, where the inadmissibility of the application is manifest from the outset'.[200] The judge's decision is final.[201] The single-judge formation is assisted by 'Rapporteurs' appointed by the Court's registry.[202] The single judge will be solely responsible for making a determination although the Rapporteurs provide assistance in filtering the cases (e.g. through assistance of the language and legal system of respondent States).[203] The single-judge format, working alongside Rapporteurs, is meant to provide a more effective filter for case-law.

In the case of inadmissibility, the applicant is sent a short note informing him or her of the decision of the committee – this is the stage where most applications are rejected. If the application is not declared inadmissible the case is forwarded to a committee or to a chamber for further examination.[204] However, if no such decision is taken then the

---

[193] Boyle 'Council of Europe, OSCE, and European Union' in Hannum (ed.), above n.181 at p. 152.
[194] Ibid. at p. 154.
[195] These changes were introduced through Protocol 11 (in effect 1 November 1998). Protocol 11 to the European Convention for the Protection of Human Rights and Fundamental Freedoms, adopted 11 May 1994. Entered into force 1 November 1998. E.T.S. 35; 33 I.L.M. (1994) 960; 15 *HRLJ* (1984) 86.
[196] The registry may point to the applicant any obvious grounds of inadmissibility such as non-exhaustion of domestic remedies. All applications will, however, be registered if the applicant insists. Boyle, above n.181, at p. 156.
[197] See above n.3; Protocol 14, at the time of writing, has yet to come into force.
[198] Article 6, Protocol 14.
[199] Ibid. Article 7.
[200] See Protocol 14 to the Convention for the Protection of Human Rights and Fundamental Freedoms, Amending the Control System of the Convention: Explanatory Report, ETS No. 194, para 67.
[201] Revised Article 27(2) ECHR, Article 7, Protocol 14.
[202] Revised Article 24, ECHR, Article 4, Protocol 14.
[203] Protocol 14 to the Convention for the Protection of Human Rights and Fundamental Freedoms, Amending the Control System of the Convention: Explanatory Report, ETS No. 194, para 58.
[204] Revised Article 27(3) ECHR, Article 7, Protocol 14.

application is to be referred to a chamber which has the task of deciding upon the admissibility as well as the merits of the case.[205]

The government is intimated and invited to present its observations on admissibility, which may lead to a friendly settlement. The government normally has six weeks to make comments or observations and to answer any pertinent questions. The latter may involve issues surrounding, for example, the exhaustion of domestic remedies, etc. The applicant is forwarded copies of the government's responses. A report is formulated which forms the basis of any subsequent action. The applicant and the government may also make oral submissions before the Chamber at the admissibility stage. In view of the heavy workload, oral hearings are becoming increasingly less likely, and if they do take place these provide a joint consideration to issues of admissibility and merit. The Chamber, whose deliberations are in private, then formulates (and communicates) its views on admissibility. It needs to be noted that all inter-State cases are to be decided by a chamber. According to the revised Article 28, under Protocol 14, the Committees (consisting of three judges) are in a position to unanimously declare it inadmissible or strike it out of its list of cases, where such a decision can be taken without further examination.[206] Alternatively, the Committee can declare the application admissible and simultaneously provide judgments on the merits of a case where the complaint 'is already the subject of well-established case-law of the Court'.[207] The objective of the amendment is to allow for an effective judicial processing in instances where similar issues have already been examined by the Court.[208]

The application must be submitted on the official form and should contain the following information:

- Name, DOB, nationality, sex, occupation and address of the applicant
- Name, occupation and address of the representative
- Name of the respondent State/States
- Statement of fact
- Statement of alleged violations of Convention rights
- Statement on applicant's compliance with admissibility requirements
- Observations on remedies.

(iii) Post-admissibility procedures

Once an application is declared admissible there are two possible courses of action which can be pursued simultaneously – attempts to reach a friendly settlement and a decision on the merits of the case. As under the previous procedure, once an application has been declared admissible, attempts are to be made to reach a friendly settlement.[209] On the instructions of the Chamber, the Registrar of the Court contacts the parties to see if there are possibilities for a friendly settlement. With this objective in mind, separate or joint

---

[205] Revised Article 29(1) ECHR, Article 9, Protocol 14.
[206] Revised Article 28(1)(a) ECHR, Article 8, Protocol 14.
[207] Revised Article 28(1)(b) ECHR, Article 8, Protocol 14. The Explanatory Report provides that an explanation as follows 'case-law which has been consistently applied by a Chamber. Exceptionally, however, it is conceivable that a single judgment on a question of principle may constitute "well-established case law", particularly when the Grand Chamber has rendered it'. Explanatory Report (CETS No. 194) para 68.
[208] Mowbray, 'Protocol 14 to the ECHR and Recent Strasbourg Cases', 4 *HRLR* (2004) 331, at p. 333.
[209] Revised Articles 38 and 39 ECHR, Articles 14 and 15 Protocol 14.

meetings could be organised. While the Court can offer its good offices and propose a settlement, the ultimate choice rests with the parties. There is however the obligation that any settlement reached must be approved by the Court as complying with the human rights set out in the Convention.[210] In the meantime, the Chamber continues to examine the merits of the case. It may invite the parties to furnish additional information and evidence. The Chamber may ask for additional evidence or written observations. It can also hold additional hearings of the case in order to decide upon its merits. Prior to giving a judgment, the Chamber may in certain circumstances relinquish its jurisdiction to the Grand Chamber. Such a relinquishment of jurisdiction takes place where a case raises serious questions regarding the interpretation of the Convention or where resolution of a question before the Chamber might have a result inconsistent with a previous judgment.[211] However, relinquishment is not possible if one party to the case objects.

The judgment by the Chamber becomes final in three circumstances: Firstly where the Parties declare non-intention in referring the case to the Grand Chamber,[212] secondly where three months have elapsed since Chamber has given its judgment[213] and finally where a referral request has been turned down by a panel of judges.[214] Within three months of the decision any party may in 'exceptional cases' request a referral to the Grand Chamber. The application is to be heard by a panel of five judges and accepted if 'the case raises a serious question affecting the interpretation or application of the Convention . . . or a serious issue of general importance'.[215] The judgments of the Grand Chamber are final, and binding upon the respondent State party.[216] The Committee of Ministers of the Council of Europe has the responsibility for supervising the execution of the judgment. The Council of Ministers also verifies as to whether adequate remedial action has been undertaken in response to the Court's judgment.

6   INTER-STATE APPLICATIONS

The ECHR does not have a State reporting procedure (similar in nature to international human rights treaty-based bodies)[217] but has both an inter-State and an individual

---

[210] Boyle, at p. 150. Once a settlement is agreed, it is binding on parties and brings the case to a close. In *Tahsin Acar v. Turkey* (2004) 38 E.H.R.R. 2, paras 83–86, rejected Turkey's request to strike out a case where a financial offer made by Turkey was rejected by the applicant. The Court's view appears to be that in instances of serious violation, there may well be an obligation on State parties to acknowledge a failure of domestic bodies and to undertake an investigation to that effect.

[211] ECHR Article 30.

[212] Ibid. Article 44(2)(a).

[213] Ibid. Article 44(2)(b).

[214] Ibid. Article 44(2)(c).

[215] Ibid. Article 43(2).

[216] Ibid. Article 44(1).

[217] See, however, ECHR Article 52 on reporting. According to Article 52, the Secretary General of the Council of Europe may request from States parties information to provide 'explanation of the manner in which its internal law ensures the effective implementation of any provisions of the Convention'. On the receipt of such a request, States parties are obliged to furnish such explanation. Tomuschat notes the absence of a 'well-organised' procedure to deal with information provided by States. There is a lack of regularity in seeking State reports. See Tomuschat, *Human Rights* (Oxford University Press, 2008) at p. 169. On 15 December 1999, a request was made by the Secretary-General of Council of Europe to Russia seeking 'explanations concerning the manner in which the convention is currently being implemented in Chechnya and the risk of violations which may result', ibid. at p. 169; Also see Trindade, 'Reporting in the Inter-American System of Human Rights Protection in Alston and Crawford (eds), *The Future of UN Human Rights Treaty Monitoring* (Cambridge University Press, 2000) pp. 333–346 at p. 334.

complaints procedure. The inter-State procedure allows a contracting State party to refer alleged breaches of the rights contained in the Convention (or the Protocols) to the Court by another State party.[218] In inter-State cases the only applicable admissibility requirements are *ratione materia, ratione persona, ratione loci, ratione temporis*, exhaustion of domestic remedies and the six months rule.[219] There is no limitation of the rule that 'substantially the same matter that has already been examined'[220] and 'contains no relevant new information'.[221] Nor is there the application of the rules of 'manifestly ill-founded'[222] or 'abusive' or 'politically motivated' or 'abuse of the right of petition'.[223]

There is no requirement of nationality or whether particular interests are at stake.[224] Unlike the ICCPR, there is no requirement to make an additional declaration for the system to be operative; the right to complain flows directly from ratification of the Convention.[225] A State may refer any alleged breach of the Convention. On the other hand, as we shall consider shortly, the individual can only claim breaches of the 'rights' contained in the Convention.[226] It also appears to be the case that in inter-State cases the principle of reciprocity does not apply. Therefore, a State would not be barred from complaining under an article because it has entered a reservation to the provision or has not ratified the (allegedly broken) provision of a protocol.[227]

It is equally irrelevant whether one State (or its government) has not been recognised by the other. Other differences from individual applications are that a State could challenge legislative measures *in abstracto*.[228] On the other hand, individuals must satisfy the victim requirement. In inter-State cases, applications are communicated automatically to the respondent government after the admissibility stage and there are separate proceedings on questions of admissibility and merits. Like other comparable treaty-based inter-State procedures, this procedure has not been used extensively, although there has been some jurisprudence.[229] A number of reasons can be advanced for the lack of popularity of the inter-State procedures. It is often seen as politically motivated and tends to strain relations (or is a product of strained relations) amongst States. Furthermore, it is not perceived as the most efficient method of resolving a dispute.[230] In inter-State cases both States parties must have ratified the Convention (Protocol).

---

[218] ECHR Article 33.

[219] Harris, O'Boyle, Bates and Buckley, above n.1, at p. 759.

[220] Article 35(2)(b).

[221] *Cyprus* v. *Turkey*, Application No. 8007/77, 13 DR 85 (1978), at 154–155 (1978) pp. 154–155, paras 47–50; *Ireland* v. *UK*, Series B, No. 23–I Com. Rep. (1971) p. 670.

[222] *France, Norway, Denmark, Sweden and The Netherlands* v. *Turkey* (1984) 6 E.H.R.R. 241.

[223] *Cyprus* v. *Turkey*, Application No. 8007/77, 13 DR 85 at 154–155 (1978) p. 156, paras 54–57.

[224] *Austria* v. *Italy*, Application No. 788/60, 4 YB 140 (1961).

[225] Ibid.

[226] Ghandhi, *The Human Rights Committee and the Right of Individual Communication: Law and Practice* (Ashgate, 1998) p. 27.

[227] *France, Norway, Denmark, Sweden and the Netherlands* v. *Turkey* (1984) 6 E.H.R.R. 241, where France was not barred from bringing a case against Turkey which concerned issues that were covered by the French reservation.

[228] Harris, O'Boyle, Bates and Buckley, above n.1, at p. 761.

[229] Since 1982, the procedure has only been used once. A total of 18 inter-State applications have been made. These relate to violations of rights in Northern Ireland, South Tyrol, Cyprus, Turkey and Greece.

[230] See e.g. *Ireland* v. *UK* (1978) 2 E.H.R.R. 25. Case discussed below.

7 INDIVIDUAL COMPLAINTS

In contrast to the inter-State procedure, the second procedure which has provided a significant amount of jurisprudence is the individual complaints procedure. As of 1 November 1998 when the 11th Protocol came into operation the individual complaints procedure has become automatic and a compulsory procedure for all States parties. According to Article 34:

> [t]he Court may also receive applications from any person, non-governmental organisation or group of individuals claiming to be the victim of a violation by one of the High Contracting Parties of the rights set forth in the Convention or the protocols thereto. The High Contracting Parties undertake not to hinder in any way the effective exercise of this right.

Complaints under Article 34 may be brought only by a person, a non-governmental organisation or group of individuals. This would include companies, minority shareholders, trusts, professional associations, trade unions, etc.[231] Non-governmental organisations or groups of individuals are broad categories but do not cover, for example, municipalities and local government organisations. In relation to individual complaints, over 90 per cent of the complaints are declared inadmissible and, thus, it is imperative to understand and comply with the admissibility requirements.

(i) *Ratione personae*

Complaints may only be brought by a person, non-governmental organisation or groups of individuals claiming to be victims of the violation of a convention right.

(ii) Complaints against whom?

Complaints may be brought only against a State or State bodies. This would cover the activities of such public bodies as the courts, the security forces or local or provincial governments.[232] A complaint could not be brought against the actions of private persons or private bodies (e.g. a newspaper). It is sometimes difficult to identify whether a particular body is a private organisation or a State body. Complex issues of State responsibility can arise in relation to the liability of such organisations as railway or broadcasting corporations. In these situations, factors such as the autonomy, financial independence and control over recruitment may determine the extent to which the organisation is acting as a non-State actor.

Actions by private individuals or private bodies may give rise to State responsibility in circumstances where the State is deemed to have secured particular rights, for example, the right to freedom of expression, to association, the right to form and join trade unions, the

[231] See *National Union of Belgian Police* v. *Belgium* (1979–80) 1 E.H.R.R. 578 and *Sunday Times* v. *UK* (1979–80) 2 E.H.R.R. 245.

[232] Harris, O'Boyle, Bates and Buckley, above n.1, at p. 787.

7

Europe and human rights (I)

right to education and the prohibition of inhuman or degrading treatment. In *Costello-Roberts* v. *UK*,[233] the issue before the European Court of Human Rights was whether the State was responsible for corporal punishment in private schools allegedly in breach of Article 3 and 8. In answering positively, the Court noted three points. Firstly, the State has an obligation to secure for children their right to education under Article 2 of the 1st Protocol and that a school's disciplinary system fell within the ambit of the right to education.[234] Secondly, in the United Kingdom, the right to education was ensured and guaranteed equally to pupils studying both at private and public schools, and thirdly the obligations imposed on the State cannot be absolved through delegating them to private organisations or individuals.[235]

An even more radical case of imposition of State liability for actions of private individuals is exemplified through *A* v. *UK*.[236] In this case a stepfather who had engaged in activities of beating his nine-year-old stepson was charged with occasioning actual bodily harm in the English courts. The stepfather had successfully relied on the defence of reasonable chastisement and was acquitted in the English courts. The European Court of Human Rights, however, rejected this defence and held that a breach of Article 3 had been committed. The Court held the United Kingdom government responsible because children and other vulnerable people were entitled to protection, even from private individuals, and the State was under an obligation to provide this protection.

It is also important to recognise that individuals cannot bring actions against those States that have not ratified the Convention or the relevant Protocol. Furthermore, the defendant must be a State party, and not an international agency or an international or regional organisation such as the United Nations or the European Union.[237]

(iii) Requirement of victim

The petitioner under Article 34 must claim to be directly affected or there must be a significant risk of being directly affected.[238] It is insufficient to establish a *mere* possibility, suspicion, conjuncture or future risk.[239] In *Open Door Counselling and Dublin Well Women* v. *Ireland*,[240] which concerned a Supreme Court injunction against the provision of information by applicant companies concerning abortion facilities outside Ireland, the Commission and the Court were of the view that women of child-bearing age could be regarded as victims as they belonged to a class of women which may be directly affected.

---

[233] *Costello-Roberts* v. *UK* (1995) 19 E.H.R.R. 112.

[234] Ibid. para 27.

[235] Ibid. para 27. Note, however, that on the facts of the case the Court did not find violations of Article 3 or Article 8.

[236] *A* v. *UK*, Application No. 25599/94 (Judgment of 23 September 1998). In the context of the Human Rights Act see Cooper, 'Horizonatility: The Application of Human Rights Standards in Private Disputes' in English and Havers (eds), above n.122, at pp. 53–69; Hunt, 'The "Horizontal Effect" of the Human Rights Act' *Public Law* (1998) 423.

[237] *CFDT* v. *European Communities/their Members* Application No. 8030/77, 13 D & R 231, para 3.

[238] See *Klass and others* v. *Federal Republic of Germany* (1979–80) 2 E.H.R.R. 214, where it was held by the Court that all users and potential users of telecommunication and postal services were 'directly affected' by legislation providing for secret surveillance, paras 33–34, 37. They thereby satisfied the victim requirement, despite the fact that they had not been subjected to such surveillance. Also consider *Norris* v. *Ireland* (1991) 13 E.H.R.R. 186, paras 32–34.

[239] *Tauira and 18 others* v. *France*, Application. No. 28204/95, 83-A DR 112 (1995), pp. 130–133, para 2.

[240] *Open Door Counselling and Dublin Well Woman* v. *Ireland* (1993) 15 E.H.R.R. 244, para 44.

In *Times Newspaper Ltd* v. *UK*,[241] the view was taken that a newspaper publisher could be regarded as a victim of an Article 10 violation (even without proceedings having been taken against him), where the law was not clear enough to be able to predict the risk of prosecution. In subsequent case-law the requirement of the victim has been more narrowly construed.

There also remains the possibility of being classed as an indirect victim, e.g. the widow of a person killed by terrorists and close family members or friends. This is applicable particularly in relation to serious violations of rights, e.g. those under Articles 2 or 3. The meaning of indirect victim has been taken to mean as those who are prejudiced by violations or have personal interests (e.g. parents, guardians, etc.).

(iv) Competence *ratione materiae*

These include the competence *ratione materiae*, which means that the individual cannot complain of breach of rights not contained in the Convention. Regardless of the extreme desirability in a particular instance or regardless of the serious nature of human rights violations, individuals cannot rely on those rights which are not contained in the Convention or the Protocols. Nor can the Court read into the provisions such rights as the right to die[242] or the right to asylum.[243] Thus, for example, individuals are not able to complain of the violation of such rights as pensions, social security, nationality or political asylum. However, recalling our earlier discussion, it needs to be noted that the Convention rights have sometimes been given a very broad meaning and applied in a range of circumstances. Thus, for example, while there is no right of political asylum, and freedom from expulsion or extradition, the applicants have been able to rely on Article 3. A distinction between individual and inter-State petitions also needs to be noted. In inter-State complaints a State can complain about any violation of the provisions of the Convention, whereas individuals can only complain about the rights contained within the Convention.

(v) Competence *ratione loci*

Competence *ratione loci* would limit the competence of the Court to analyse alleged breaches to taking place within the 'jurisdiction' of a particular State. Having said that 'jurisdiction' is not necessarily synonymous with territory, e.g. it would include State responsibility for acts conducted by agents outside its territory. This issue was considered in *Cyprus* v. *Turkey*.[244] In this case, the Turkish government argued for the application to be declared inadmissible *ratione loci*. The Turkish government's argument was that it could not be held responsible for acts outside its national territory. The European Commission, in rejecting the Turkish government's argument, took the view that the term 'jurisdiction' was not synonymous with territory. The real question related to authority and control of the State wherever exercised. Since the Turkish forces had landed in Cyprus and operated under the direction of the Turkish State, their actions extended the *de facto* jurisdiction of the Turkish State. The concept of jurisdiction was further highlighted in *Loizidou* v. *Turkey*, where the Court noted:

---

[241] *Times Newspapers Ltd* v. *UK*, Application No. 14631/89, para 2.
[242] See *Pretty* v. *the UK* (2002) 35 E.H.R.R. 1, paras 39–42.
[243] See e.g. *Chahal* v. *UK* (1997) 23 E.H.R.R. 413.
[244] *Cyprus* v. *Turkey*, Application No. 8007/77, 13 DR 85 (1978), paras 24–25.

[a]lthough Article 1 (art. 1) set limits on the reach of the Convention, the concept of 'jurisdiction' under this provision is not restricted to the national territory of the High Contracting Parties. According to its established case-law, for example, the Court has held that the extradition or expulsion of a person by a Contracting State may give rise to an issue under Article 3 (art. 3), and hence engage the responsibility of the State under the Convention (see the *Soering* v. *the United Kingdom* judgment of 7 July 1989, Series A no. 161, pp. 35–36, para 91; the *Cruz Varas and Others* v. *Sweden* judgment of 20 March 1991, Series A no. 201, p. 28, paras 69 and 70; and the *Vilvarajah and Others* v. *the United Kingdom* judgment of 30 1991, Series A no. 215, p. 34, para 103). In addition, the responsibility of Contracting Parties can be involved because of acts of their authorities, whether performed within or outside national boundaries, which produce effects outside their own territory (see the *Drozd and Janousek v. France and Spain* judgment of 26 June 1992, Series A no. 240, p. 29, para 91).[245]

However, a narrow and restrictive approach appears to have been adopted more recently. In *Bankovic and others* v. *Belgium and others*, the European Court of Human Rights restricted the ambit of jurisdiction, suggesting that extra-territorial jurisdiction can exist when as a result of military action, a State exercises effective control of an area outside of its national territorial jurisdiction.[246] Such recognition according to the Court was an exceptional measure and applicable where the State 'through the effective control of the relevant territory and its inhabitants abroad as a consequence of military occupation or through consent, invitation or acquiescence of the Government of that territory, exercises all or some of the public powers normally to be exercised by that Government'.[247] The *Bankovic* decision is disappointing and has been the subject of criticism[248] – the implications of a broader jurisdiction would be too sweeping in the prevailing circumstances. Even those commentators who advocate jurisdiction principles to be limited to 'effective control' regard *Bankovic* as a 'political' case.[249]

[245] *Loizidou* v. *Turkey* (Preliminary Objections) (1995) 20 E.H.R.R. 99, para 62.
[246] See *Banković and others* v. *Belgium and others*, Application No. 52207/99 (Decision of 12 December 2001), (2007) 44 E.H.R.R. 5.
[247] Ibid. para 71.
[248] Lawson, 'Life after Bankovic: On the Extraterritorial Application of the European Convention on Human Rights' in Coomans and Kamminga (eds), *The Extra-Territorial Application of Human Rights Treaties* (Intersentia, 2004), pp. 83–124; Oliver De Schutter, whilst citing the European Commission, makes the following useful observations 'whichever the firmness of its basis in the preparatory work of the Convention, it may nevertheless be asserted that the inadmissibility decision in the case of *Bankovic and others* constitutes a retreat from the previous case-law, both of the European Commission on Human Rights and Court itself. The European Commission of Human Rights has always stipulated that when agents of the States (not only diplomatic or consular agents but also armed forces) act outside the national territory "not only do they remain under its jurisdiction when abroad but [they also] bring any other person or property (within the jurisdiction) of that State, to the extent that they exercise over such persons or property. In so far as, by their acts or omissions, they affect such persons or property, the responsibility of the State is engaged"'. Schutter 'The Accountability of Multinationals for Human Rights Violations in European Law' in Alston (ed.) *Non-State Actors and Human Rights* (Oxford University Press, 2005) pp. 227–314, at p. 242; Byron, 'Blurring of the Boundaries: The Application of International Humanitarian Law by Human Rights Bodies,' 47 *VJIL* (2006–2007) 839 at p. 872.
[249] McGoldrick, 'The Interface Between Public Emergency Powers and International Law' 2 *IJCL*, (2004) 380 at p. 403. In *R. (Al Skeini and others) v. Secretary of State for Defence* [2007] UKHL 26, the House of Lords affirmed the *Bankovic* principle (ECHR applied to British military detention facilities but not to soldiers patrolling in Iraq); also see *R. (on the application of Al-Jedda) v. Secretary of State for Defence* [2007] UKHL 58 where the House of Lords held the binding United Nations Security Council Resolution which sanctioned the maintenance of public order took precedence over Article 5 of ECHR.

(vi) Exhaustion of domestic remedies

Once the initial requirements are satisfied the Court has to ascertain whether the particular application satisfies the criterion of admissibility in the light of Article 35 of the Convention. Article 35(1) provides as follows:

> The Court may only deal with the matter after all domestic remedies have been exhausted, according to the generally recognised rules of international law, and within a period of six months from the date on which the final decision was taken.

As we have already noted, the Article 35(1) rule on the exhaustion of domestic remedies is based on the rule of general international law that the State must have the opportunity to redress the alleged wrong. The task of ensuring that there are available 'adequate' and 'effective' remedies is an important requirement falling upon all contracting States parties. This requirement is intended to reduce the mass of complaints. It is more appropriate that in the first instance the domestic courts must be given the opportunity to provide remedies to the alleged wrongs.

Thus, the complainant is required to take action in order to redress their grievance at the national level. The applicant needs to pursue all possible and available remedies that are likely to be adequate and effective. The meaning of remedies 'likely to be adequate and effective' would depend upon the breach in question and upon the State jurisdiction. In principle the applicant must appeal to the highest court of appeal against an unfavourable decision. In States where there is a written constitution, applicants should take their cases through to the Constitutional Court, to the highest court of appeal. Mere doubt as to the prospect of failure is inadequate, although at the same time applicants need not go against settled and established legal opinion. Applicants need not pursue their case at the domestic forum if it is clear from established case-law that pursuing a particular remedy would be ineffective.[250]

(vii) Six months rule

The rule means that the application must be submitted to the Court within six months of the exhaustion of domestic remedies. Accordingly, the Court is restricted to dealing with cases only within a period of six months from the date from which the final decision was taken at the domestic level. The rule is intended to prevent a recurrence of old cases reappearing before the admissibility institutions. The six months will start running from the date of the final decision involving the exhaustion of all domestic remedies. The letter setting out the substance of the complaint (even in summary form and even where there has been no formal registration) triggers the process and must be conducted within six months of the final decision. The Court may refuse to accept the petition under this heading if, after the initial letter to pursue the action, there is a substantial period of inaction before the applicant submits further information. The principal exception to the six months rule

---

[250] *Johnston and others* v. *Ireland* (1987) 9 E.H.R.R. 203, paras 45–46 and *Open Door Counselling and Dublin Well Woman* v. *Ireland* (1993) 15 E.H.R.R. 244, paras 48–51.

relates to instances of continuing violations through the existence of offending legislation and administrative practices.[251]

(viii) Other restrictions

Article 35 further states that:

> (2) The Court shall not deal with any application submitted under Article 34 that
>
> (a) is anonymous; or
> (b) is substantially the same as a matter that has already been examined by the Court or has already been submitted to another procedure of international investigation or settlement and contains no relevant new information.

Article 35(3) as amended by Article 12 of Protocol 14 provides as follows:

> (3) The Court shall declare inadmissible any individual application submitted under Article 34 if it considers that:
>
> (a) the application is incompatible with the provisions of the Convention or the Protocols thereto, manifestly ill-founded, or an abuse of the right of individual application; or
> (b) the applicant has not suffered a significant disadvantage, unless respect for human rights as defined in the Convention and the Protocols thereto requires an examination of the application on the merits and provided that no case may be rejected on this ground which has not been duly considered by a domestic tribunal.[252]
>
> (4) The Court shall reject any application which it considers inadmissible under this Article. It may do so at any stage of the proceedings.

The applicant is required to disclose his or her identity but can request that his or her identity not be disclosed to the public.[253] Also, the application must not represent substantially the same matter in a different application; the Court will reject the application if the factual basis of the new application is the same as the previous one[254] or it is under consideration by another body. It does not matter if there are new legal arguments involved. The purpose of this rule is to prevent duplication of examination by international bodies. The term 'international investigation' has been taken to mean such bodies as the Human Rights Committee, other enforcement bodies (e.g. the ILO) and the European Court of Justice. It is equally irrelevant whether a particular body can render binding decisions. The application will be rejected if it is manifestly ill-founded or abuses the right of application.[255] The application will be held to be manifestly ill-founded if it discloses no breach of the rights

---

[251] Boyle above n.181 at p. 151.
[252] Revised Article 35 ECHR, Article 12, Protocol 14.
[253] Rule 47(3). Applicants (or their legal representatives) must also sign the application (Rule 45). European Court of Human Rights – Rules of Court – July 2007.
[254] See *X* v. *UK*, Application No. 8206/78, para 1 – unless there is 'relevant new information'.
[255] Article 35(3).

contained in the Convention or if the complainant fails to substantiate his or her application or has ceased to be the victim. The application would also be rejected if it is an abuse of the right of petition such as insulting, provocative or derogatory language, or merely political propaganda. However, provided there is substance in the complaint, the mere fact that it is initiated to gain political ground does not render it manifestly ill-founded. This provision is intended to prevent situations where attempts are being made to mislead the Court, or there is a deliberate refusal to co-operate with the Court. Protocol 14 has inducted a more controversial admissibility requirement, according to which:

> Paragraph 3 of Article 35 of the Convention shall be amended to read as follows:
>
> '(3) The Court shall declare inadmissible any individual application submitted under Article 34 if it considers that:
>
> (a) the application is incompatible with the provisions of the Convention or the Protocols thereto, manifestly ill-founded, or an abuse of the right of individual application; or
> (b) the applicant has not suffered a significant disadvantage, unless respect for human rights as defined in the Convention and the Protocols thereto requires an examination of the application on the merits and provided that no case may be rejected on this ground which has not been duly considered by a domestic tribunal.'

The new provisions amending Article 35(3) are enormously controversial in that the meaning of 'a significant disadvantage' remains yet to be established – these provisions would have to be clarified through the jurisprudence of the Chambers and Grand Chambers and will not become operational for a period of two years after Protocol 14 becomes effective, unless applied by the Chambers and Grand Chamber.[256]

8 REMEDIES BEFORE THE COURT

The European Court of Human Rights judgments are of a declaratory nature and cannot of themselves repeal inconsistent national law or judgments.[257] Equally, the State is not obliged to give direct effect to the decisions of the Court in national law. The defendant State, therefore, remains free to implement them in accordance with the rules of its national legal system.[258] One example where a State has refused to accept or comply with

---

[256] Article 20(2), Protocol 14 ECHR. See Mowbray, 'Protocol 14 to the European Convention on Human Rights and Recent Strasbourg Cases' 4 *HRLR* (2004), 331 at p. 334; also see Ruedin, 'De minimis non curat the European Court of Human Rights: the introduction of a new admissibility criterion (Article 12 of Protocol No. 14)' *EHRLR* [2008] 80.

[257] *Marckx* v. *Belgium*, (1979–80) 2 E.H.R.R. 330, para 58 cited in Harris, O'Boyle, Bates and Buckley, above n.1, at p. 25.

[258] Sometimes it is unclear whether steps undertaken (e.g. the legislation) have gone far enough. See Churchill and Young, 'Compliance with Judgments of the European Court of Human Rights and Decisions of the Committee of Ministers: The Experience of the UK' 62 *BYIL* (1991) 283.

the European Court's judgment is *Brogan* v. *UK*.[259] In this case the United Kingdom informed the Committee of Ministers that it could not repeal its legislation on the prevention of terrorism. The United Kingdom then made a derogation provision under Article 15, which was subsequently upheld by the Court.[260] In relation to the provision of remedies, Article 41 provides as follows:

> If the Court finds that has been a violation of the Convention or the protocols thereto, and if the internal law of the High Contracting Party concerned allows only partial reparation to be made, the Court shall, if necessary, afford just satisfaction to the injured party.

On the finding of a breach, the Court's powers are limited to the awarding of financial compensation and the granting of legal costs and expenses. As regards the award of compensation, the Court has made awards under two heads: pecuniary and non-pecuniary damage (e.g. loss of past and future earnings loss to property, loss of opportunity); and costs and expenses. In proceedings before the Court it is not possible to obtain specific relief. In *Selcuk and Asker* v. *Turkey*[261] applicants asked to be re-established in the village, a request that was turned down by the Court.[262] Furthermore, the Court also claims inherent powers to order provisional measures. In contrast to Article 41 of the Statute of ICJ and Article 63(2) ACHR there is an absence of authorising any provisional measures in the ECHR. Within the ECHR, the sole authority for adopting provisional measures derives from the European Court of Human Rights, Rules of Procedure.[263]

9 SIGNIFICANT PRINCIPLES EMERGENT FROM THE ECHR

(i) Reservations: Article 57

In accordance with general international law, ECHR allows States parties to make reservations to treaty previsions. Article 57 of ECHR provides:

> (1) Any State may, when signing this Convention or when depositing its instrument of ratification, make a reservation in respect of any particular provision of the Convention to the extent that any law then in force in its territory is not in conformity with the provision. Reservations of a general character shall not be permitted under this article.
>
> (2) Any reservation made under this article shall contain a brief statement of the law concerned.

---

[259] *Brogan and others* v. *UK* (1989) 11 E.H.R.R. 117.
[260] *Brannigan and McBride* v. *UK* (1994) 17 E.H.R.R. 539, paras 51 and 54. Harris, O'Boyle, Bates and Buckley, above n.1, at p. 27.
[261] *Selçuk and Asker* v. *Turkey* (1998) 26 E.H.R.R. 477.
[262] Ibid. paras 123–125. Shelton, *Remedies in International Human Rights Law* (Oxford University Press, 1999) p. 203.
[263] European Court of Human Rights, Rules of Court, Rule 39, July 2007.

The jurisprudence of the ECHR establishes 'a requirement of specificity . . . the exclusion of reservations which may render the convention ineffective and the severability of in-admissible reservations'.[264]

(ii) Derogation in time of emergency: Article 15

In exceptional circumstances States parties are permitted to take certain measures which interfere with or restrict the enjoyment of the rights provided in the Convention and the Protocols. In legal terms such restrictions and interference are termed as derogations. The permissibility of such restrictions is authorised by Article 15(1) of the Convention which provides that:

> [i]n time of war or other public emergency threatening the life of the nation any High Contracting Party may take measures derogating from its obligations under this Convention to the extent strictly required by the exigencies of the situation, provided that such measures are not inconsistent with its other obligations under international law.

However, these derogation provisions are subject to a number of conditions. These include, firstly, that these provisions have to be narrowly construed and are legitimate only to the extent that they are required by the exigencies of the situation. Secondly, that they are not inconsistent with other obligations of international law. Article 15(2) provides that it is not permissible to derogate from the provision relating to the right to life (except in respect of deaths resulting from lawful acts of war), from the right not to be tortured or subjected to inhuman or degrading treatment or punishment, the right not to be enslaved and the right not to be subjected to retrospective criminal penalties. Thirdly, the Secretary-General of the Council of Europe is to be informed of the measures which are taken with a detailed explanation of the reasons that led to such derogations.

Historically the European human rights institutions have accorded the so-called 'margin of appreciation' to States in their decision in the derogation of obligations. In criticising this approach, Provost makes the following observations:

> the commission and the court found that they could not ignore completely the state's appre-ciation of the situation. In the 'lawless' case, Waldock as president of the Commission noted that the rational for a 'margin of appreciation' was the nature of the task of characterisation in the context of an emergency threatening the life of the nation, being 'essentially a delicate problem of appreciating complex factors and of balancing conflicting considerations of public interests.' The Court in *Ireland* v. *United Kingdom* noted that the government concerned, being continuously and directly in contact with the situation in all its historical, economic, social, political and strategic dimensions, is in a better position than any other agent to assess whether the emergency has reached a level warranting the declaration of a State of emer-gency. The state's characterisation will therefore be left untouched if it is found to be reasonable within a margin of appreciation. The notion of a 'margin' of appreciation is eminently vague, and perhaps variable. The case-law of the European Commission and Court of Human Rights contains no indication of the breadth of this margin, apart from the

---

[264] Meron, above n.14, at 2.

statement in *Ireland* v. *United Kingdom* that it is 'wide' and the remark of Waldock on the part of the government, although not expressly presented as a relevant factor, seems to have the effect of narrowing the margin, as indicated by the stricter stand of the European Commission in the Greek case with respect to the declaration of a state of emergency by the Colonels' regime. Neither the Inter-American Court of Human Rights nor the Human Rights Committee has adopted ostensibly a margin of appreciation approach.[265]

(iii) Margin of appreciation

The Convention has been reliant on a concept which is termed as the 'margin of appreciation'. In essence it grants the domestic courts and institutions a measure of discretion to deal with a particular issue in accordance with their own moral, political, ideological and legal viewpoint. The notion of the margin of appreciation could best be illustrated by the *dicta* of the Court in *Handyside* v. *UK case*.[266] The Court noted:

the machinery of protection established by the Convention is subsidiary to the national systems safeguarding human rights . . . The Convention leaves to each Contracting State, in the first place, the task of securing the rights and liberties it enshrines. The institutions created by it make their own contribution to this task but they become involved only through contentious proceedings and once all domestic remedies have been exhausted . . . [I]t is not possible to find in the domestic law of the various Contracting States a uniform European conception of morals. The view taken by their respective laws of the requirements of morals varies from time to time and from place to place, especially in our era which is characterised by rapid and far-reaching evolution of opinions on the subject. By reason of their direct and continuous contact with the vital forces of their countries, State authorities are in principle in a better position than the international judge to give an opinion on the exact content of these requirements as well as on the 'necessity' of a 'restriction' or 'penalty' intended to meet them.[267]

10 CONCLUSIONS

The ECHR remains the most valuable treaty adopted by the Council of Europe. After nearly 60 years of existence the ECHR has firmly established itself as the leading human rights treaty. During the course of this chapter we have surveyed a range of rights that are protected by the ECHR. A number of modifications and advancements have been made by subsequent protocols to the substantive protection of rights. A significant addition to the protection of human rights has been through the application of Protocol 12. The case-law of the Convention is also impressive in the sense that the judgments of the European Court of Human Rights have influenced many States to change their laws or reformulate their administrative policies. Such a situation compares favourably with other systems of protecting human rights, where the system of implementation is hampered by the absence of

---

[265] Provost, *International Human Rights and Humanitarian Law* (Cambridge University Press, 2002) at pp. 287–288.
[266] *Handyside* v. *UK* (1979–80) 1 E.H.R.R. 737.
[267] Ibid. para 48.

bodies with the authority to deliver binding judgments. The success of the Convention and the expanding numbers of States parties to the treaty has exacerbated the difficulties in dealing effectively with the huge number of individual applications – currently around 40,000 every year.[268] The induction of Protocol 11 aimed to simplify the institutional mechanisms. It was also designed to allow individuals within member States access to the European Court of Human Rights, and to curtail the functions of the Committee of Ministers. However, the reformed system is still unable to produce all its intended results, particularly in relation to dealing with the enormous backlog of cases. While further reforms, primarily through Protocol 14, are anticipated, the Convention continues to suffer from the 'case overload crisis'.[269]

While the Convention has been hugely successfully, in the past 50 years a number of challenges have been presented. Firstly, there has been a significant change in the social, ideological and political values within Europe; the question arises as to the extent the text of the Convention could be used to interpret these rapidly changing values. The second and more significant issue relates to the position and nature of obligations that are undertaken by the States formerly part of the communist or socialist block. A number of these States have faced difficulties in complying with the standards of protecting civil and political rights within the Western States. In the light of their endemic political and economic problems there is almost an acceptance of the inability to match objective standards of protecting civil and political rights; such an approach however is a dangerous one, since it may lead to different standards even within the context of a regional treaty.

7

Europe and human rights (I)

---

[268] Greer, 'What's Wrong with the European Convention on Human Rights' 30 *HRQ* (2008) 680, at p. 682.
[269] Ibid. at p. 684.

8 Europe and human rights (II)[1]

1 INTRODUCTION

At the end of the Second World War, Europe needed an institutional framework to protect individual rights. At the same time the shattered infrastructure was in urgent need of re-development. Thus, in addition to the protection of civil and political rights there was also a desire for economic stability and prosperity.[2] Post-war Europe, however, was soon to be engulfed by an ideological and political conflict, and security considerations necessitated the establishment of a strong military alliance.[3] In the light of these security considerations, the Conference on Security and Co-operation in Europe (CSCE) was developed. The CSCE, as we shall consider in due course, has expanded into an active organisation, the Organisation for Security and Co-operation in Europe (OSCE).

   At the time of its inception in 1949, the Council of Europe's membership was largely drawn from Western liberal States. The aims of the organisation were directed towards acting as a bulwark against the spread of communism and totalitarianism and to protect largely well established civil and political rights. Hence, soon after the birth of the organisation, the European Convention on Human Rights was adopted.[4] It did not take long however to recognise that civil and political rights could not be protected without the promotion of economic and social rights. With the objective of promoting economic and social rights, the Council of Europe undertook to establish a regional treaty. The process of drafting took seven years and resulted in the adoption of the European Social Charter (ESC) (1961).[5] The Charter, as we shall consider in this chapter, has been criticised for its limited vision in granting adequate substantive rights. More significantly, there were substantial shortcomings in the implementation procedures which necessitated a thorough revision. The amended and revised Charter was adopted in 1996.[6]

---

[1] See Alston (ed.), *The EU and Human Rights* (Oxford University Press, 1999); Betten and Grief, *EU Law and Human Rights* (Longman, 1998); Betten and MacDevitt, *The Protection of Fundamental Social Rights in the European Union* (Kluwer Law International, 1996); Gomien, Harris and Zwaak, *Law and Practice of the European Convention on Human Rights and the European Social Charter* (Council of Europe Publishing, 1996); Robertson and Merrills, *Human Rights in the World: An Introduction to the Study of the International Protection of Human Rights* (Manchester University Press, 1996) pp. 160–196; Steiner, Alston and Goodman (eds), *International Human Rights in Context* (Oxford University Press, 2008) pp. 1014–1020.

[2] See Cassese, *International Law* (Oxford University Press, 2001) p. 398.

[3] Foster, *Foster on EU Law* (Oxford University Press, 2006) p. 8.

[4] See above chapter 7.

[5] Adopted at Turin 18 October 1961. Entered into force, 26 February 1965. ETS No. 035.

[6] Adopted 3 May 1996. Entered into force, 3 July 1999. ETS No. 163. See above chapter 7.

Parallel to these moves in the Council of Europe, the project of economic integration took shape with the signature of the ECSC Treaty of Paris and, more importantly, the 1957 Treaty of Rome which established the European Economic Community.[7] It must be emphasised that the Treaty of Rome envisaged an economic, rather than a political union and any rights conferred on individuals were incidental to that project. Over the years, however, the European Economic Community (or the European Union as it became known after the (1992) Treaty of Maastricht on European Union or TEU) has moved towards creating and protecting more explicit rights of citizenship and to a lesser extent what it terms as 'fundamental' rights. Since the TEU came into force in 1993, the criterion for membership of the EU contains the requirement that a European State must ensure the principles of liberty, democracy respect for human rights, fundamental freedoms and rule of law as pre-requisites.[8] It has a direct role to play in relation to discrimination on grounds of nationality and gender-based discrimination.

In the light of the broad nature of organisations such as the EU and OSCE, the present chapter will concentrate on elucidating their role in relation to the protection of human rights. Following our discussion on the ECHR in the previous chapter, this chapter has been divided into five sections. After these introductory comments, section 2 considers the Council of Europe's European Social Charter. Section 3 analyses the role and protection of human rights within the framework of the European Union. Section 4 provides consideration to the OSCE and its contribution to the promotion of human rights. The chapter ends with some concluding observations.

2 EUROPEAN SOCIAL CHARTER 1961 (REVISED 1996)[9]

A major criticism of the European Convention on Human Rights has been its almost exclusive focus on the protection of civil and political rights. As we noted, over time, this criticism, has been addressed, albeit to a limited extent, through two key processes. Firstly, a number of rights have been added through additional protocols to the ECHR which have a strong economic and social dimension.[10] Secondly, the broad interpretation accorded to many of the civil and political rights has highlighted the strong inter-linkage between these rights and economic, social and cultural rights.[11] Notwithstanding this indirect involvement, there has been a growing demand to have an effective regional treaty providing a more direct focus on social and economic rights.

The European Social Charter (ESC)[12] was adopted in Turin in 1961 by 11 Council of Europe Member States. The substantive rights and implementation mechanisms of the

---

[7] *European Union – Consolidated Versions of the Treaty on European Union and of the Treaty Establishing the European Community* (Consolidated Text) Official Journal C 321E of 29 December 2006.
[8] TEU Article 49; Article 6(1).
[9] Churchill and Khaliq 'Violations of Economic, Social and Cultural Rights: The Current Use and Future Potential of the Collective Complaints Mechanism of the European Social Charter' in Baderin and McCorquodale (eds), *Economic, Social and Cultural Rights in Action* (Oxford University Press, 2007) pp. 195–240; Harris, *The European Social Charter* (University Press of Virginia, 1984); Harris, 'A Fresh Impetus for the European Social Charter' 41 *ICLQ* (1992) 659; Harris, 'The System of Supervision of the European Social Charter – Problems and Options for the Future' in Betten (ed.), *The Future of European Social Policy* (Kluwer Law and Taxation Publishers, 1991) pp. 1–34.
[10] See e.g. the Right to Property and the Right to education (Protocol 1, Articles 1 and 2) Protocol 12, etc.
[11] See above chapter 7.
[12] European Social Charter of 1961, ETS No. 035.

Charter have been modified through a series of amendments. The ESC consists of a pre-amble, five parts and an appendix. The first additional Protocol, adopted in 1988, added several rights to the treaty.[13] Further additions and amendments have been made to the imple-mentation machinery through the Amending Protocols of 1991[14] and 1995.[15] In 1996, the revised European Social Charter[16] was opened for signature. The revised Charter updates and adds to the European Social Charter's substantive rights, incorporating in the document rights accorded in the 1961 European Social Charter and those provided in the additional Protocol of 1988.[17] Part I of the Charter establishes a number of principles, which con-tracting parties accept as policy aims. It does not establish specific legal obligations and includes such aims as the opportunity for everyone to earn a living in an occupation freely entered into, the right to just conditions of work, the right to safe and healthy working conditions, fair remuneration, children and young persons having the right to special pro-tection, and employed women, in cases of maternity, have the right to special protection.

Part II of the Charter lists a number of substantive rights. These substantive provisions are a consolidation and extension of the policy aim. The Charter is unique in the sense that it provides States with the discretion of not accepting all the provisions of the treaty. Accord-ing to Part III (Article A) of the revised Charter, each State party undertakes, *inter alia*:

(b) to consider itself bound by at least six of the following nine articles of Part II of this Charter: Articles 1, 5, 6, 7, 12, 13, 16, 19 and 20;

(c) to consider itself bound by an additional number of articles or numbered paragraphs of Part II of the Charter which it may select, provided that the total number of articles or numbered paragraphs by which it is bound is not less than sixteen articles or sixty-three numbered paragraphs.[18]

(i) Rights contained in the revised Charter

Article 1	The right to work
Article 2	The right to just conditions of work
Article 3	The right to safe and healthy working conditions
Article 4	The right to a fair remuneration
Article 5	The right to organise
Article 6	The right to bargain collectively
Article 7	The right of children and young persons to protection
Article 8	The right of employed women to protection of maternity
Article 9	The right to vocational guidance

---

[13] Additional Protocol to the European Social Charter, ETS No. 128 (1988) (opened for signature 5 May 1988; came into force 2 September 1992).

[14] Amending Protocol to the European Social Charter, ETS No. 142 (1991).

[15] Additional Protocol to the European Social Charter Providing for a System of Collective Complaints, ETS No. 158 (1995).

[16] European Social Charter (revised), ETS No. 163 At the time of writing the revised European Social Charter had received 25 ratifications. A total of 40 States had ratified either the revised Charter or the 1961 Charter.

[17] See Jaeger, 'The Additional Protocol to the European Social Charter providing for a System of Collective Complaints' 10 LJIL (1997) 69, at p. 71.

[18] The provisions in Part III Article A(b) are frequently referred to as 'hard core' articles.

Article 10 The right to vocational training

Article 11 The right to protection of health

Article 12 The right to social security

Article 13 The right to social and medical assistance

Article 14 The right to benefit from social welfare services

Article 15 The right persons with disabilities to independence, social integration and participation in the life of the community

Article 16 The right of the family to social, legal and economic protection

Article 17 The right of children and young persons to social, legal and economic protection

Article 18 The right to engage in a gainful occupation in the territory of other Parties

Article 19 The right of migrant workers and their families to protection and assistance

Article 20 The right to equal opportunities and equal treatment in matters of employment and occupation without discrimination on the grounds of sex

Article 21 The right to information and consultation

Article 22 The right to take part in the determination and improvement of the working conditions and working environment

Article 23 The right of elderly persons to social protection

Article 24 The right to protection in cases of termination of employment

Article 25 The right of workers to the protection of their claims in the event of the insolvency of their employer

Article 26 The right of all workers to dignity at work

Article 27 The right of all persons with family responsibilities to equal opportunities and equal treatment

Article 28 The right of workers' representatives to protection in the undertaking and facilities to be accorded to them

Article 29 The right to information and consultation in collective redundancy procedures

Article 30 The right to protection against poverty and social exclusion

Article 31 The right to housing

8

Europe and human rights (II)

The ESC contains a number of rights which are valuable to workers and employees. The right to just conditions of work,[19] for example, provides an undertaking from the States parties *inter alia* to allow individual employees reasonable daily and weekly working hours.[20] It also allows for public holidays with pay, and a minimum of four weeks' annual holiday with pay.[21] Through the right to safe and healthy working conditions States parties undertake to

formulate, implement and periodically review a coherent national policy on occupational safety, occupational health and the working environment. The primary aim of this policy shall be to improve occupational safety and health and to prevent accidents and injury to health arising out of, linked with or occurring in the course of work, particularly by minimising the causes of hazards inherent in the working environment.[22]

[19] Article 2.
[20] Article 2(1).
[21] Article 2(2).
[22] Article 3(1).

Comparable provisions can be found in a number of international instruments in relation to the rights of workers. Articles 6 and 7 of the ICESCR provide for the right to work and conditions of work. Similarly, the ILO Conventions – ILO Convention 132 on Holidays with Pay, C187 Promotional Framework for Occupational Safety and Health Convention and C183 Maternity Protection Convention – also establish standards for employees work conditions and provide for their rights including annual paid leave. In addition to this, the UN International Convention on the Protection of the Rights of All Migrant Workers and their Families guarantee rights for migrant workers and members of their families. However, none of the aforementioned instruments goes as far as the European Social Charter, particularly in respect of regulating the amount of holidays with pay that must be provided for workers.

An interesting and positive feature of the Charter is its protection of children and young persons at work.[23] In accordance with Article 7, States parties undertake to set a minimum age of 15 for allowing employment, subject to exceptions of light work, which does not affect their health, morals or education.[24] States also agree that persons in compulsory education are not to be employed in such a manner as would deprive them of the full benefit of their education.[25] In providing the right of employed women to maternity protection, States undertake to

provide either by paid leave, by adequate social security benefits or by benefits from public funds for employed women to take leave before and after childbirth up to a total of at least fourteen weeks.[26]

Other useful Articles secure the right to social security,[27] the right to social and medical assistance[28] and the right to social welfare services.[29] In the light of a substantial elderly population of Europe, it is important to have provisions protecting their rights.[30] While the Charter provides some protection to the migrant workers and their families,[31] one of its disappointing features is its approach, limiting the application of the majority of the rights to nationals of Contracting parties only.[32] It needs to be noted that the European

---

[23] Article 7.
[24] Article 7(1).
[25] Article 7(2).
[26] Article 8(1).
[27] Article 12.
[28] Article 13.
[29] Article 14.
[30] Article 23.
[31] Article 19.
[32] See Appendix to the Revised European Social Charter; Scope of the Revised European Social Charter in terms of persons protected, para 1. This states that '[w]ithout prejudice to Article 12, paragraph 4, and Article 13, paragraph 4, the persons covered by Articles 1 to 17 and 20 to 31 include foreigners only in so far as they are nationals of other Parties lawfully resident or working regularly . . . these articles are to be interpreted in the light of the provisions of Articles 18 and 19.' However, '[i]n 2004, the Committee recalled the possibility of extending Charter protection to foreign nationals of non-party states (Conclusions 2004, Statement of Interpretation, p. 10) . . . However, after stating the principle, the Committee added that these obligations did *"not in principle fall within the ambit of its supervisory functions"*. The Committee made it clear that it did not exclude *"that the implementation of certain provisions of the Charter could in certain specific situations require complete equality of treatment between nationals and foreigners, whether or not they are nationals of member States, Party to the Charter".*' Digest of the Case Law of the European Committee of Social Rights, 1 September 2008 www.coe.int/t/dghl/monitoring/socialcharter/Digest/DigestSept2008_en.pdf <last visited 28 May 2009>, pp. 182–183.

Committee on Social Rights has further developed the jurisprudence under the ESC. It found Italy as violating Article 31 (the right to housing) together with Article E (prohibition of discrimination) of the European Social Charter due to the policies and practices of racial segregation as applied to the Roma in the field of housing.[33] In a unanimous ruling, the Committee also held that the insufficiency of camping sites for nomadic Roma constitutes a violation of Article 31(1) of the Revised Charter, taken together with Article E; that forced eviction and other sanctions constitute a violation of Article 31(2) of the Revised Charter, taken together with Article E; and that the lack of permanent dwellings constitutes a violation of Articles 31(1) and 31(3) of the Revised Charter, taken together with Article E. In the significant case of *Autism-Europe* v. *France*, France was held to be in violations of the significant rights of Article 15(1) and Article 17(1) in their own right and also when read in conjunction with Article E of the Revised Charter.[34]

(ii) Implementation mechanism[35]

The ESC, as a regional treaty dealing with economic and social rights, parallels the ICE-SCR,[36] which, as we have considered, operates at the universal level.[37] The ESC mirrors similar weaknesses of implementation. The implementation mechanism of the ESC has been revised, which in addition to the reporting system, now provides for a collective complaints procedure. Primary monitoring of the treaty is conducted by a system of regular reports submitted by the State parties. Since the decision of the Committee of Ministers in 2006, the provisions of the Charter have been split up into four thematic groups and States now submit reports on one of these groups on an annual basis.[38] Therefore, States will, over the period of four years, cover all of the provisions of the Charter.

There also remains the possibility of occasional reports on unaccepted provisions.[39] These reports allow the European Committee of Social Rights (ECSR) (formerly the Committee

---

[33] See *European Roma Rights Centre (ERRC)* v. *Italy*, Complaint No. 27/2004, www.coe.int/t/e/human_rights/esc/4_collective_complaints/list_of_collective_complaints/RC27_on_merits.pdf <last visited 24 May 2009>. Roundtable Meeting on Housing Segregation in Italy 'Combating Housing Segregation and Social Exclusion of Roma and Sinti in Italy' 8 May 2006, www.errc.org/cikk.php?cikk=2594 <last visited 24 May 2009>. Also see *European Roma Rights Centre (ERRC)* v. *Bulgaria*, Complaint No. 31/2005, www.coe.int/t/e/human_rights/esc/4_collective_complaints/list_of_collective_complaints/MeritsRC31_en.pdf <last visited 24 May 2009>.

[34] See *Autism-Europe* v. *France*, Complaint No. 13/2002, www.autismeurope.org/portal/Portals/0/Decision%20November%202003.pdf <last visited 24 May 2009>.

[35] Harris, 'Lessons from the Reporting System of the European Social Charter' in Alston and Crawford (eds), *The Future of UN Human Rights Treaty Monitoring* (Cambridge University Press, 2000) pp. 347–360; Harris, 'The System of Supervision of the European Social Charter–Problems and Options for the Future' in Betten (ed.), above n.9, pp. 1–34.

[36] International Covenant on Economic, Social and Cultural Rights, New York, 16 December 1966, 993 U.N.T.S. 3; 6 I.L.M. (1967) 360.

[37] See above chapter 6.

[38] European Social Charter – Governmental Committee of the European Social Charter – New System for the presentation of reports on the application of the European Social charter – Proposal of the Governmental Committee (CM(2006)53). The four thematic groups are: Group 1, Employment, training and equal opportunities; Group 2, Health, social security and social protection; Group 3, Labour rights; Group 4, Children, families, migrants. https://wcd.coe.int/ViewDoc.jsp?id=996767&BackColorInternet=9999CC&BackColorIntranet <last visited 5 May 2009>.

[39] Article C of the revised European Social Charter and Article 22 of the 1961 European Social Charter. Article C states that '[t]he implementation of the legal obligations contained in this Charter shall be submitted to the same supervision as the European Social Charter'. See above for 'accepted' provisions and 'hard core' provisions, Part III Article A of the revised European Social Charter. See www.coe.int/t/dghl/monitoring/socialcharter/Presentation/Provisions_en.pdf <last visited 8 May 2009>.

of Independent Experts) to clarify the meaning of particular provisions and to comment on the problems that a State envisions that the acceptance of those provisions entail.[40] Requests for such reports have been rare, and there have thus far been only a few occasions when States have been called upon to submit these reports.

Two bodies are primarily involved in the monitoring of State reports: the ECSR and the Governmental Committee. The ECSR, a 15-member body of independent experts, is elected by the Committee of Ministers for a term of six years.[41] Members of the Committee sit in their individual capacity and are required not to perform any functions incompatible with the requirements of independence, impartiality and availability inherent in their office.[42] The other body, the Governmental Committee, consists of one representative of each of the Contracting parties.[43] Members of the Governmental Committee are usually civil servants, in charge of the national ministry responsible for implementing the ESC.[44] The Committee is authorised to allow no more than two international organisations of employers and no more than two international trade union organisations to send observers in a consultative capacity to its meetings.[45] It may also, at its discretion, consult representatives of non-governmental organisations with consultative status with the Council of Europe and having a particular competence in matters relating to the Charter.[46] The process is initiated through submission of the report to the Secretary General for its examination by ECSR. At the same time as sending the report to the Secretary General, the relevant State party is required to forward copies of this report to 'such of its national organisations as are members of the international organisations of employers and trade unions to be invited . . . to be represented at the meetings of the Sub-committee of the Governmental Social Committee'.[47] The reports received from these organisations and comments on these reports from the States Parties are sent to the Secretary General.[48] The ECSR may ask for additional information or clarification from the States parties.[49]

The ECSR provides a legal assessment of States' compliance with the provisions which it has accepted.[50] The conclusions made by the Committee are made available as a public document, and are communicated to the Parliamentary Assembly of the Council of Europe and to any other relevant organisations.[51] Once this stage is over, State reports, and the assessment made by the ECSR on these reports, are transmitted to the Governmental Committee.[52]

---

[40] Harris, 'Lessons from the Reporting System of the European Social Charter' in Alston and Crawford (eds), above n.35, at p. 350.

[41] The number of members was established by the Committee of Minister at 751st meeting of the Ministers' Deputies (2–7 May 2001). The 1961 ESC as amended by the 1991 Protocol Article 25(1) states that the Parliamentary Assembly elects members of the Committee: however, this has not yet been applied. www.coe.int/t/dghl/monitoring/socialcharter/ESCR/ESCRdefault_ en.asp <last visited 2 May 2009>. For the current list of members see www.coe.int/t/dghl/monitoring/socialcharter/ECSR/Members_en.asp <last visited 2 May 2009>.

[42] Article 25(1) and (4) 1961 ESC.

[43] Article 27(2) 1961 ESC.

[44] Harris, 'Lessons from the Reporting System of the European Social Charter' in Alston and Crawford (eds), above n.35, at p. 355.

[45] Article 27(2) 1961 ESC as amended by 1991 Protocol.

[46] Ibid.

[47] Ibid. Article 23(1).

[48] Ibid. Article 23(2).

[49] Ibid. Article 24(3).

[50] Ibid. Article 24(2).

[51] Ibid. Article 24(4).

[52] Ibid. Article 24(4).

The Governmental Committee examines those assessments where there are indications of non-compliance with the provisions of the Charter and, on the basis of social, economic and other policy considerations, prepares recommendations for the Committee of Ministers to adopt.[53] The recommendations prepared by the Governmental Committee are also passed on to the Parliamentary Assembly of the Council of Europe, which transmits its views to the Council of Ministers. In the light of comments made by the Governmental Committee and the Parliamentary Assembly, the Committee of Ministers issues recommendations to States which fail to comply with the Charter.

The Committee of Ministers adopts, 'by a majority of two-thirds of those voting with entitlement to voting limited to the Contracting Parties, on the basis of the report of the Governmental Committee, a resolution covering the entire supervision cycle and containing individual recommendations to the Contracting Parties concerned'.[54] The Secretary General of the Council of Europe transmits 'to the Parliamentary Assembly, with a view to the holding of periodical plenary debates, the reports of the Committee of Independent Experts and of the Governmental Committee, as well as the resolutions of the Committee of Ministers'.[55]

From the above description, the implementation mechanism might appear to be a straightforward one. However, in practice substantial difficulties arise because of a weak and cumbersome system of monitoring of the treaty. Many reasons can be advanced for the weaknesses in implementing the ESC. Giving the mandate to the Committee of Ministers was inappropriate because of the political nature of the body. Politicians have been reluctant to criticise States for fear of generating political tensions. Under the provisions of the original Charter, the Committee has to adopt recommendations by a two-thirds majority of its members. Given the limited membership of this Charter, for many years the Charter's Contracting Parties represented only about one-third of the Council of Europe's membership. This resulted in non-State parties criticising practices in a State, which had committed itself to fulfilling the Charter's obligations. There were other problems generated by the antagonism between the CIE (now ECSR) and the Governmental Experts. For example, a confrontation took place in the very first cycle of reporting, when the ECSR found 57 breaches from all seven States involved. As a reaction to this, the Governmental Committee produced its own less demanding interpretation of the Charter.[56]

National trade unions and employers' organisations are given the right to comment on national reports. However their role is limited in that they may only sit as observers at the meetings of the Committee of Governmental representatives. There are also no explicit provisions to the effect that their comments shall be taken into account by the supervisory bodies. This minor role for the employers and workers' representatives is another reason for the Charter's lack of popularity.

In the context of these issues the decision was taken in November 1990 to revise the Charter. A number of improvements were made in the supervisory system as well as an extension in the range and content of the rights. The 1991 Amending Protocol changed the voting requirements in the Committee of Ministers from a two-thirds majority of member states to a two-thirds majority of Contracting Parties, strengthening the role of the

---

[53] Ibid. Article 27(3).
[54] Ibid. Article 28(1).
[55] Ibid. Article 29.
[56] Harris, 'Lessons from the Reporting System of the European Social Charter' in Alston and Crawford (eds), above n.35, at p. 353.

Committee of Independent Experts and improving the consultation procedures with employers' and trade unions' representatives as well as with NGOs.[57] In addition, the 1991 Protocol enabled the ECSR to make direct contact with Contracting Parties in order to request clarification and additional information concerning their reports. Under the original provisions,[58] the CIE could only conclude that certain situations were unclear and, therefore, that they were not sure whether the Charter had been infringed.[59] They would have to wait two years to get the relevant information which might still be inconclusive.

The second major improvement has been the better definition of the Governmental Committee.[60] This is intended to avoid what had previously happened, namely that the governmental representatives more or less repeated the work of the experts and usually came to different conclusions. This offered the Committee of Ministers an opportunity to abstain from any further actions as there was no clear indication of a breach of the Charter. The amendment provides that in the light of the reports of the Committee of Independent Experts and of the Contracting Parties, the Governmental Committee shall select the situations which should, in its view, be the subject of recommendations by the Committee of Ministers.[61] In addition to a better description of the role of the Governmental Committee, there has also been a shift in the hitherto confrontational position adopted by the ECSR towards the Governmental Committee. The ECSR has also in the words of Professor Harris 'adopted a somewhat more measured approach. It is much slower to find a new party in breach of its obligations in its early reports. It has also moderated its approach to the application of some particularly delicate provisions or issues'.[62]

(a) Collective complaints procedure

In order to vitalise the ESC, a collective complaints procedure has been inducted into the protection accorded through the ESC. The process, which was initiated in 1990, culminated in the adoption of an additional Protocol of 1995, providing for a system of collective complaints.[63] The Protocol came into force on 1 July 1998, with the Complaints Mechanism being first initiated in October 1998. The Collective Complaints Procedure (CCP) as established through the Protocol does not allow individuals to make complaints: in other words there is no mechanism of individual petitioning. Nor are there any inter-State complaints procedures. Complaints can only be lodged by certain types of organisations against contracting States parties allegedly failing to comply with their obligations under the Charter. The four types of organisations eligible to launch complaints are detailed in the provisions of the Protocol.[64] Firstly, international organisations of employers and trade unions which act as observers during meetings of the Governmental Committee under the reporting system.[65] These organisations include the European Trade Union Confederation, the Union of Industrial Employers, the Confederation of Europe and the International Organisation of

---

[57] See Article 28(1) 1961 ESC (as amended by 1991 Protocol).
[58] Ibid. Article 24 1961 ESC.
[59] Ibid. Articles 24 and 27.
[60] Ibid. Article 27.
[61] Ibid. Article 27(3).
[62] Harris, 'The System of Supervision of the European Social Charter–Problems and Options for the Future' in Betten (ed.), above n.9, 1–34, at p. 10.
[63] Additional Protocol to the European Social Charter providing for a system of collective complaints, ETS No. 158 (adopted June 95, opened for signature 9 November 1995).
[64] Articles 1 and 2 1995 Protocol.
[65] Ibid. Article 1(a).

Employees. The second type of organisation includes Non-governmental Organisations with consultative standing with the Council of Europe and recognised in a list drawn by the Governmental Committee allowing them the right to make complaints under this system.[66] Thirdly, the procedure sanctions 'representative national organisations of employers and trade unions within the jurisdiction of the Contracting Party against which they have lodged a complaint'.[67] Fourthly, there is the final broad category of non-governmental organisations with 'particular competence' in the field to submit complaints.[68] A national NGO placed into this category can only make complaints if the State where the NGO is located has made a declaration allowing it to do so.[69] Furthermore, according to the procedure the NGOs of the second and fourth type are restricted to submitting complaints only in 'respect of those matters regarding which they have been recognised as having particular competence'.[70] The ECSR initially decides as to the admissibility of the complaint.[71] Once a complaint is held admissible it requires both the complainant as well as the defendant State party to present its views on the merits of the complaint.[72] On the basis of information that is available, ESCR draws up a report as to whether or not failure to ensure 'the satisfactory application' of one or more provisions of the Charter is found.[73] The findings of the report are forwarded to the Committee of Ministers, which makes the final decision. In articulating the nature of action required from the Committee of Ministers Article 9(1) of the 1995 Protocol provides:

> On the basis of the report of the Committee of Independent Experts, [now the ECSR] the Committee of Minsters shall adopt a resolution by a majority of those voting. If the [ECSR] finds that the Charter has not been applied in a satisfactory manner, the Committee of Ministers shall adopt, by a majority of two-thirds of those voting, a recommendation addressed to the Contracting Party concerned. In both cases, entitlement to voting shall be limited to the Contracting Parties to the Charter.

Despite the restrictions regarding the specificity of complainants, in contrast to other complaints mechanisms, the CCP does not set out a comprehensive or explicit list of admissibility requirements.[74] There is no time limit for bringing complaints, nor is there is a requirement to exhaust domestic remedies or (as in the case of ECHR) that a complaint is manifestly ill-founded.[75] The CCP, unlike the reporting system under the Charter, which is applicable to all States parties, applies to parties on an optional basis. Amongst the two possible ways in which CCP could be applicable to a State is: firstly through express ratification

---

[66] Ibid. Article 1(b).
[67] Ibid. Article 1(c).
[68] Ibid. Article 2(1).
[69] Ibid. Article 2(1).
[70] Ibid. Article 3.
[71] Ibid. Article 6. Unlike other human rights complaints mechanisms, the admissibility criterion also appear not to be rigorously applied; Churchill and Khaliq 'The Collective Complaints System of the European Social Charter: An Effective Mechanism for Ensuring Compliance with Economic and Social Rights?' 15 *EJIL* (2004) 417, at 432.
[72] Article 7(1) 1995 Protocol.
[73] Ibid. Article 8(1).
[74] Churchill and Khaliq, above n.71, at p. 213.
[75] See Chapter 7 above.

of 1995 Protocol; and secondly where a State party to the Revised Charter (but not a party to the Protocol) makes an express declaration under Article D2 of the Revised Charter expressing its agreement to be bound by the CCP. As noted above, complaints can be made regarding general situations and not about particular or individual cases.[76] The complaints procedure adds a new dimension and importance to the Social Charter; its impact is likely to be a beneficial one in generating greater interest in the Charter. That said, currently over half of State parties to the Charter have refused to accept the obligations under the CCP and this unfortunate trend appears likely to continue for the foreseeable future.

Many of the rights contained in the ESC have been addressed at various levels, and in some cases much more strongly at the European level through the European Union. This statement can be tested while contrasting Articles 2, 3, 7, 8, 20, 21, 25 and 29 of the ESC to comparable European Council Directives.[77] In a few instances, even the ECHR jurisprudence has been of greater assistance to disgruntled workers or employees.[78] Despite the shortcomings in the Charter, there are a number of positive features.[79] Although reports are usually delayed (not an unusual feature of international reporting procedures),

---

[76] *International Commission of Jurists* (ICJ) v. *Portugal* Complaint No. 1/1998 was the first complaint registered under CCP. The complaint made by the International Commission of Jurists against Portugal, Article 7 of ESC related to Children and Young People. The International Commission of Jurists alleged that notwithstanding an adequate legislative framework for the enforcement of minimum age for employment, illegal child labour persisted in Portugal and that the Portuguese Labour inspectorate was ineffective in enforcing labour laws related to child labour. ECSR was of the view that Portugal was not acting in conformity with its obligations under Article 7(1) ESC. The Committee of Ministers adopted a resolution taking note of the report and conclusion of CSR and Portugal to provide information on the steps towards compliance with requesting 1998 Resolution in the next reporting cycle for Charter. Resolution ChS(99)4 (adopted 15 December 1999: www/coe.fr/cm/ta/reschs/1999/99cx4.htm <last visited 11 May 2009> See Cullen, 'The Collective Complaints Mechanism of the European Social Charter' 25 *EL Rev* (Human Rights Survey HR) (2000) 18, at 26; also see Cullen, 'The Collective Complaints System of the European Social Charter: Interpretative Methods of the European Committee of Social Rights' 9 *HRLR* (2009) 61.

[77] Compare the following Article 2 ESC with Council Directive 93/104/EC of 23 November 1993 concerning certain aspects of the organisation of working time. Article 3 ESC with Article 137 TEC creates a legal basis for health and safety legislation, and there are too many subsequent Directives to number, all dealing with different dangers; Article 7 ESC with Council Directive 94/33/EC of 22 June 1994 on the protection of young people at work; Article 8 ESC with Council Directive 92/85/EEC of 19 October 1992 on the introduction of measures to encourage improvements in the safety and health at work of pregnant workers and workers who have recently given birth or are breastfeeding; Article 20 ESC with Article 141 TEC; Council Directive 75/117/EEC of 10 February 1975 on the approximation of the laws of the Member States relating to the application of the principle of equal pay for men and women; Council Directive 76/207/EEC of 9 February 1976 on the implementation of the principle of equal treatment for men and women as regards access to employment, vocational training and promotion, and working conditions; Council Directive 97/80/EC of 15 December 1997 on the burden of proof in cases of discrimination based on sex (also a couple of Directives on discrimination in social security); Article 21 ESC with Council Directive 91/533/EEC of 14 October 1991 on an employer's obligation to inform employees of the conditions applicable to the contract or employment relationship; Council Directive 94/45/EC of 22 September 1994 on the establishment of a European Works Council or a procedure in Community-scale undertakings and Community-scale groups of undertakings for the purposes of informing and consulting employees; Article 25 ESC with Council Directive 80/987/EEC of 20 October 1980 on the approximation of the laws of the Member States relating to the protection of employees in the event of the insolvency of their employer and Article 29 ESC with Council Directive 98/59/EC of 20 July 1998 on the approximation of the laws of the Member States relating to collective redundancies.

[78] See above chapter 7.

[79] It is also the case that some rights such as the right to strike is recognised as an important right under Article 6 of the ESC, with the ECSR interpreting this Article as requiring States to show the existence of strong objective justification for the imposition of restrictions on that right. By contrast within the EU context the right to strike in the light of the post *Viking* (*International Transport Workers' Federation* v. *Viking Line ABP* (C438/05) [2008] 1 C.M.L.R. 51) and post *Laval* (*Laval un Partneri Ltd* v. *Svenska Byggnadsarbetareförbundet and others* Case C-341/05 [2008] C.M.L.R. 9) environment appears to be less fundamental.

the States parties to ESC have made a point of making a definitive submission.[80] This action represents a major contrast with the situation at the international level, in particular in economic and social rights reporting. It is also to the credit of the ECSR that it reviews each of the State reports objectively and independently.

3 THE EUROPEAN UNION[81]

While the Council of Europe (COE) was focused on maintaining peace within Europe by means of co-operation in the field of human rights, the European Economic Community (which later became part of the EU) was founded in order to unite Europe both economically and politically.[82] The Treaty of Rome only indirectly concerned itself with human rights.[83] Amongst the few related provisions was Article 39 (previously Article 48) of the Treaty, which provided for the right of freedom of movement for community workers and Article 141 (previously Article 119) that established equal pay for equal work for men and women. The different approaches taken by the COE and the European Community (EC) meant that, historically, the protection afforded under Community law was different from the rights accorded under the ECHR. Within the Community sphere rights and protection were accorded to the individual not 'by virtue of his or her humanity, but [by reason of] one's status as a community national'.[84] Furthermore:

> the essentially economic character of the Communities . . . [made] the possibility of their encroaching upon fundamental human values, such as life, personal liberty, freedom of opinion, conscience etc very unlikely.[85]

---

[80] Harris, 'Lessons from the Reporting System of the European Social Charter' in Alston and Crawford (eds), above n.35, at p. 353.

[81] Alston (ed.), above n.1; Shaw, *Law of the European Union* (Palgrave, 2000); Betten and MacDevitt (eds), *The Protection of Fundamental Rights in the European Union* (Kluwer Law International, 2006); Hartley, 'The Constitutional Foundations of the European Union' 117 *LQR* (2001) 225; Jacobs, 'The Protection of Human Rights in the Members States of the EC: The Impact of Case-Law of the Court of Justice' in O'Reilly (ed.), *Human Rights and Constitutional Law: Essays in Honour of Brain Walsh* (Round Hall Press, 1992), pp. 243–250; Clapham, 'A Human Rights Policy for the European Community' 10 *YEL* (1990) 309; Mendelson, 'The European Court of Justice and Human Rights' 1 *YEL* (1981) 126; Mendelson, 'The Impact of European Community Law on the Implementation of European Convention on Human Rights' 3 *YEL* (1983) 99; McBride and Neville Brown, 'The United Kingdom, the European Community and the European Convention on Human Rights' 1 *YEL* (1981) 167; Meenan, *Equality Law in an Enlarged European Union: Understanding the Article 13 Directives* (Cambridge University Press, 2007).

[82] See McCrudden and Chambers 'Introduction' in McCrudden and Chambers (eds), *Individual Rights and the Law in Britain* (Clarendon Press, 1994) pp. 1–38, at 24.

[83] See Treaty Establishing the European Economic Community signed at Rome, 25 March 1957, as amended by subsequent treaties through the Treaty of Maastricht (1992), Treaty of Amsterdam (1997), the Treaty of Nice (2001) and Accession Treaty (2003) and Accession Treaty (2005); see *European Union – Consolidated Versions of the Treaty on European Union and of the Treaty Establishing the European Community* (Consolidated Text) Official Journal C 321E of 29 December 2006; see Douglas-Scott, 'Environmental Rights in the European Union – Participatory Democracy or Democratic Deficit?' in Boyle and Anderson (eds), *Human Rights Approaches to Environmental Protection* (Clarendon Press, 1996) pp. 109–128, at p. 109. Similarly, there was as such no recognition of complex 20th-century problems such as environment and pollution: see Sunkin, Ong and Wight, *Source Book on Environmental Law* (Routledge, 2002) at pp. 6–7.

[84] Twomey, 'The European Union: Three Pillars without a Human Rights Foundation' in O'Keeffe and Twomey (eds), *Legal Issues of the Maastricht Treaty* (Wiley, 1994) pp. 121–131 at p. 122.

[85] A.G. Toth, 'The Individual and European Law' 24 *ICLQ* (1975) 659 at p. 667.

However, the EC was concerned from the beginning with certain rights that affected its workers. Notably the guarantees of equality in respect of pay of men and women were established by the Treaty of Rome. Further inroads in respect of sex equality were hampered by the limitation of sex equality principles, and consequently prevented action being taken in respect of further marginalised groups such as black women or migrant women.[86] Another limitation on gender equality principles was its confinement to employment relationship.[87] However, these restrictions were removed by the Treaty of Amsterdam, by amending Article 3(2) of TEC, which states that:

> [i]n all the activities referred to in this Article, the Community shall aim to eliminate inequalities, and to promote equality, between men and women.

However, measures in respect of equality were clearly still limited to the realm of the competence of the European Community. Article 13, while making it possible to combat dual forms of discrimination as described above, was not limited in the same way as Article 3(2):

> [w]ithout prejudice to the other provisions of this Treaty and within the limits of the powers conferred by it upon the Community, the Council, acting unanimously on a proposal from the Commission and after consulting the European Parliament, may take appropriate action to combat discrimination based on sex, racial or ethnic origin, religion or belief, disability, age or sexual orientation.

That said, the interest of the European Community was limited; hence the EU's contemporary interest calls for an explanation. The accumulation of internal and external factors has elevated the subject of human rights as being a major issue. In the last quarter of the 20th century the Community perceptions have broadened and the protection of fundamental rights is now a significant concern. Since its establishment, the membership and influence of the European Community (now forming part of the European Union) has expanded and the EU is now actively engaged in taking initiatives for human rights protection. As an acknowledgement of their human rights commitments all EU Member States have become parties to the ECHR, ESC and the OSCE. The promotion and protection of human rights within the EU is now considered at all levels within this organisation.

The main reason why the EU is now concerned with human rights lies with the fact that it has expanded from a market-oriented institution to an organisation with a more inclusive agenda. In 1992, the Maastricht Treaty created the European Union and talked about a European citizenship. The Union was broader than a mere economic institution and this has been reflected in all subsequent treaties and developments. However, the growth of the influence of human rights in the European Community could even be seen prior to this; in 1986 the Single European Act established that European States were:

---

[86] Beveridge, 'Building against the Past: The Impact of Mainstreaming on EU Gender Law and Policy' 32 *EL Rev* (2007) 193–212, at p. 206.
[87] Ibid. p. 207.

> [d]etermined to work together to promote democracy on the basis of the fundamental rights recognized in the constitutions and laws of the Member States, in the Convention for the Protection of Human Rights and Fundamental Freedoms and the European Social Charter, notably freedom, equality and social justice.[88]

While the explicit recognition of human rights, particularly the ECHR, was a notable step forward, as will be discussed later, the ECJ put paid to idea of the EU acceding to the ECHR.

In 1993 the Copenhagen Criteria were established which stated that in order to accede to the European Union candidate countries must have achieved, 'stability of institutions guaranteeing democracy, the rule of law, human rights and respect for and protection of minorities',[89] thus affirming the EU's commitment to human rights. This was further echoed in the Treaty of Amsterdam, which amended Article 6 of the TEU to read:

> 1. The Union is founded on the principles of liberty, democracy, respect for human rights and fundamental freedoms, and the rule of law, principles which are common to the Member States.

Article 7 was amended so that sanctions could be brought against States which persistently breached Article 6(1). Additionally, the ECJ was given powers to ensure that the principles contained within Article 6(2) regarding the fundamental rights guaranteed by the ECHR were respected by the institutions of the EU.[90] Article 49 brought the TEU in line with the Copenhagen Criteria, demanding that applicant States respect the rights established in Article 6(1). In addition to sex equality, as discussed above, the Treaty of Amsterdam also made significant changes to the TEC in respect of combating 'discrimination based on sex, racial or ethnic origin, religion or belief, disability, age or sexual orientation'.[91]

The Treaty of Nice of 2001 led to a number of innovations in respect of human rights in the European Union. Article 7 of the TEU was altered from:

> 1 The Council, meeting in the composition of the Heads of State or Government and acting by unanimity on a proposal by one third of the Member States or by the Commission and after obtaining the assent of the European Parliament, may determine the existence of a serious and persistent breach by a Member State of principles mentioned in Article 6(1), after inviting the government of the Member State in question to submit its observations.[92]

---

[88] Preamble, Single European Act 1987 O.J. (L 169) 1.
[89] Ibid. p. 207. http://ec.europa.eu/enlargement/enlargement_process/accession_process/criteria/index_en.htm. http://ec.europa.eu/enlargement/enlargement_process/accession_process/criteria/index_en.htm <last visited 12 May 2009>.
[90] Article 46 TEU Article L of the Treaty of Amsterdam, para 13.
[91] Article 12 TEC Article 6.a.of the Treaty of Amsterdam para 7.
[92] Article 7 TEU Article F.1.1 of the Treaty of Amsterdam, para 9.

to:

> 1. On a reasoned proposal by one third of the Member States, by the European Parliament or by the Commission, the Council, acting by a majority of four-fifths of its members after obtaining the assent of the European Parliament, may determine that there is a clear risk of a serious breach by a Member State of principles mentioned in Article 6(1), and address appropriate recommendations to that State.[93]

This ensures that Article 7 of the EU Treaty can now be activated on the mere suspicion of a breach of fundamental rights. Article 7(2) and (3) provides that when a serious breach of fundamental rights is found, certain rights of the Member State can be suspended.

Over the past two decades, the perceptions over such matters as national security, terrorism and demands of human rights have weighed heavily on the policymaking of the Union members. In the immediate aftermath of the collapse of communism, Europe was confronted with concerns emanating from Eastern Europe and the Balkans. The conflicts and substantial acts of genocide, ethnic cleansing and violations of fundamental rights in Central and Eastern Europe, particularly in the former Yugoslavia, were particularly disturbing for the EU. Such distressing activities at the doorstep of the Union have raised substantial concerns regarding the effectiveness of the organisation to protect human rights. The escalation of the violence in the Balkans for a considerable period threatened to engulf Member States of the European Union.[94]

Since the terrorist events of 11 September 2001, EU Member States have also faced considerable disagreements both in foreign policy matters as well as individual domestic policies on sensitive issues such as national security, regulations regarding immigration and refugees. In 2003, the EU foreign policy agenda suffered a serious set-back when a number of States notably the United Kingdom, Spain, Italy and Denmark supported the United States' decision to invade Iraq, creating a rift between what was subsequently termed as the 'old' and 'new' Europe. One consequence of the engagement and involvement with the 'war on terror' were the reprisals instigated by terrorist groups led by Al-Qaeda in EU States: most prominently Spain and the United Kingdom.

Constitutional reform within Member States, particularly the United Kingdom, also provided an impetus to revisiting the subject at EU level.[95] The EU's expanding influence and interference with individual rights led to demands for greater accountability. The human rights debate has become entwined with the problems of the perceived democratic deficit within an increasingly powerful and bureaucratic Union.[96] The concerns of an ineffective apparatus to protect fundamental human rights have been addressed by Union institutions, albeit partially, through a variety of methods. Subsequent sections of this chapter analyse the issues of redress in greater detail.

---

[93] Article 7 TEU, Article 7 of the Treaty of Nice para 1.

[94] McGoldrick, 'The Tale of Yugoslavia: Lessons for Accommodating National Identity in National and International Law' in S. Tierney (ed.), *Accommodating National Identity: New Approaches in International and Domestic Law* (Kluwer Law International, 2000) pp. 13–64.

[95] See e.g. the position in the UK with the Human Rights Act (1998), and also in other States such as Spain, Belgium and the Netherlands.

[96] For useful discussion see Weiler and Wind (eds), *European Constitutionalism Beyond the State* (Cambridge University Press, 2003).

(i) Institutional structures and protection of human rights

The legal and institutional structure of the EU is relatively complex and beyond the scope of this book. However, a basic grasp of the relevant institutions and legal instruments is necessary in order to understand what follows, and this outline is intended for those who have never studied EU law. The need for a concise treatment means that this account is necessarily simplified and many subtleties are ignored.

EU law is based on a series of treaties, starting with the Treaty of Rome in 1957 and ending with the most recent effort to replace the 2004 Constitutional Treaty through the 2007 Reform Treaty (also known as the Treaty of Lisbon) whose future is at the moment uncertain.[97] These treaties provide the foundation for all EU law-making. The nature and composition of the institutions, the legislative procedures and, importantly, the substantive areas in which the EU is competent to act, are all laid down in the Treaties. This means that the EU can do nothing if not authorised to do so by the founding Treaties, or by secondary legislation which is ultimately derived from the founding Treaties.

In general terms, the Treaties have been consolidated into two Treaties, the Treaty establishing the European Community (abbreviated to TEC) and the Treaty establishing the European Union (abbreviated to TEU). The difference between the EC and the EU was laid down in the Treaty of European Union, signed at Maastricht in 1992.[98] This Treaty created the European Union, an entity much broader than the EC, made up of three pillars. The first, and most important, pillar is the European Community, the successor to the European Economic Community created at Rome in 1957 and focused around the creation of an internal market. The second pillar concerns co-operation in foreign and security policy, and the third concerns co-operation in police and criminal matters. The distinction between the first pillar and the other two pillars is important, because the law-making procedures and the way in which the law operates differs considerably. Human rights issues arise in the context of all three pillars.

While the EU may appear to be another branch of international law, in fact, the nature of the first pillar is supranational, rather than international. Two doctrines, developed by the Court of Justice, combine to give EC law its particular force within national legal systems. The doctrine of the supremacy of EC law, first declared in *Costa* v. *ENEL*[99] states that EC law should take priority over any domestic law, even domestic constitutional law. The doctrine of direct effect of EC law, first expressed in *Van Gend en Loos*[100] states that EC law, if it fulfils certain conditions relating to clarity and unconditionality, can take effect within domestic legal systems, even if national governments and legislatures have not properly transposed it into national legislation. Together, these doctrines give EC law a supreme role in national legal systems, even if national governments or legislatures oppose aspects of that law.

A number of institutions are involved in the EU legislative and policymaking procedures. The three main legislative institutions are the Commission, the Council of Ministers and the European Parliament. The Commission is made up of 27 independent

---

[97] See the Treaty of Lisbon amending the Treaty on European Union and the Treaty establishing the European Community, signed at Lisbon, 13 December 2007 Official Journal C 306, 17 December 2007.

[98] See *Treaty of Amsterdam Amending the Treaty on European Union, the Treaties Establishing the European Communities and Related Acts*, Official Journal C 340, 10 November 1997.

[99] *Costa* v. *Ente Nazionale per l'Energia Elettrica (ENEL)* Case 6/64 [1964] ECR 585.

[100] *Van Gend en Loos* v. *Nederlandse Belastingadministratie* Case C-26/62 [1963] ECR 1.

Commissioners, nominated by Member States and approved by the European Parliament, but who are supposed to act, independently of their State of origin, in the interests of the Union. The Commission has significant policymaking and law enforcement functions, and its role in the legislative process is that of making legislative proposals. The main legislative body is the Council (of Ministers) of the European Union.[101] It is made up of ministerial representatives from all Member State governments, and has the biggest role in legislating. It often has to do this in co-operation with the European Parliament, whose role in the legislative procedure has increased considerably in the past 10 years. Members of the European Parliament are directly elected by European citizens and represent their interests. At present the European Parliament is composed of 785 members (MEPs).

The most important non-legislative institution, whose role has been crucial in the development of human rights competence in the EU, is the Court of Justice. The Court is made up of judges drawn from the Member States. The Court has the final power of adjudication on matters pertaining to EU law, an ultimate power in respect of the interpretation of Treaties and legislation made by the Union institutions, and it may also pronounce as to whether Member States are implementing Union law properly. The jurisdiction and access of individuals to the Court is limited, in that individuals generally do not have the right to bring cases directly before the Court of Justice. The exception to this is staff cases, where the staff of the Community institutions can bring cases against their employers. Other than this, the Court hears cases in a number of different situations. It hears cases brought by the Commission against Member States, accusing them of failing to implement Community law.[102] National courts may refer questions of Community law to the Court in order to help them decide cases.[103] The Court also has the power, if asked to do so by one of the institutions or another interested party, to judicially review acts of the Community institutions.[104] Human rights issues are usually raised in the context of these last two types of action. As well as the Court of Justice, there exists a Court of First Instance. This Court hears staff cases and judicial review cases in the first instance. The parties can then appeal to the Court of Justice. The scope of the Court of First Instance's competence has been broadened by the Nice Treaty; the treaty provides for the creation of judicial panels.

(ii) European Court of Justice and human rights

The inadequate recognition given to fundamental rights in the founding treaty of the European Economic Community and a lack of interest in human rights was mirrored in the earlier jurisprudence of the European Court of Justice. During the early years of the Community, the Court was evasive and refused to rule on human rights issues on the grounds that human rights were not included in the Treaty of Rome.[105] In 1960, in a case concerning the German constitutional protection of the right to private property and the right to pursue a business activity, the Court took the view that Community law: 'does not contain any general principles, express or otherwise, guaranteeing the maintenance of vested rights.'[106] Over the years, however, the Court of Justice has gone through a significant

---

[101] Foster, above n.3, at p. 57.
[102] Article 226 TEC.
[103] Article 234 TEC.
[104] Article 230 TEC.
[105] Betten and Grief, above n.1, at p. 54.
[106] *Geitling and Nold* v. *High Authority of the European Coal and Steel Community* Joined Cases C-36–38/59 and 40/59 [1960] ECR 423 at p. 439.

change in its attitude towards human rights protection, largely prompted by its dialogues with national constitutional courts. This shift is evident in its case-law. In contrast to the position adopted in 1960, 15 years later, in the groundbreaking *Nold* judgment, the Court, dealing with a very similar situation involving one of the parties in the 1960 litigation, stated that 'fundamental rights form an integral part of the general principles of law, the observance of which it ensures'[107] and that 'it cannot therefore uphold measures which are incompatible with fundamental rights recognized and protected by the constitutions of those [Member] States'.[108] Such a shift in position has been ascribed to a range of factors, including the fact that the German and French constitutions were re-written with substantial commitments to basic rights and that with the ratification of all the original members of the EEC in 1974, both the Community and the Court were committed to protection of fundamental rights, in particular those contained within the constitutional frameworks of Member States.[109] In the *Nold* case the European Court of Justice took the position that:

> international treaties for the protection of human rights on which the Member States have collaborated or of which they are signatories, can supply guidelines which should be followed within the framework of community law.[110]

In another German case, *Haur* v. *Land Phalz*,[111] the applicant challenged a decision of German authorities refusing her permission to plant vines on her land. The question referred by German authorities to the ECJ led the Court to consider whether a council regulation which prohibited the new planting of vines for a period of three years infringed the right to property guaranteed by Article 1 of the First Protocol of the ECHR. The Court held that although the Protocol declares that every person is entitled to the peaceful enjoyment of their possession, it allows restrictions upon the use of property provided they are deemed necessary for the protection of general interests. After considering the constitutional rules of the Member States, the Court held the applicants' right to property had not been infringed since the planting restrictions in question were justified by objectives of general interest pursued by the Community – the immediate elimination of production surpluses and the long-term restructuring of the European wine industry.

The fact that these cases concerned the German Constitution should not be seen as coincidental. At the time of the *Nold* judgment, the Court of Justice and the German Constitutional Court were engaged in a debate (which continues to this day) concerning the reluctance of the German Constitutional Court to accept the supremacy of a body whose acts cannot be reviewed for violations of the wide-ranging fundamental rights contained within the German Basic Law. In the *Internationale Handelsgesellschaft* case, the Court of Justice accepted explicitly that it could review Community acts for violations of fundamental rights, but made it clear that it, rather than national constitutional courts, maintained that competence.[112]

---

[107] *Nold* v. *Commission of European Communities* Case C-4/73 [1974] ECR 491, para 13.
[108] Ibid.
[109] Foster, above n.3, at p. 98.
[110] *Nold* (C-4/73), see above n.107, para 13.
[111] *Hauer* v. *Land Pheinland-Pfalz* Case C-44/79 [1979] ECR 3727.
[112] *Internationale Handelsgesellschaft mbH* v. *Einfuhr- und Vorratsstelle fur Getreide und Futtermittel* Case C-11/70 [1970] ECR 1125. In this case the Court of Justice acknowledged (at p. 1134) that the 'protection of (human rights), whilst inspired by the constitutional traditions common to Member States, must be ensured within the framework of the structure and objectives of the Community.'

8

Europe and human rights (II)

A further step was taken in *Rutili* v. *Ministry for the Interior.*[113] In *Rutili,* French authorities prohibited an Italian national involved in political activities from residing in certain *départments* (regions). The ECJ held that limitations cannot be imposed on the right of a national of any Member State to enter the territory of another Member State, to stay there and to move freely within it unless his or her presence or conduct constitutes a genuine and sufficiently serious threat to public policy, concluding that:

> these limitations placed on the powers of Member States in respect of control of aliens are a specific manifestation of the more general principle, enshrined in Articles 8, 9, 10 and 11 of the Convention for the Protection of Human Rights and Fundamental Freedoms ... and in Article 2 of Protocol No 4 of the same Convention ... which provide, in identical terms, that no restrictions in the interests of national security or public safety shall be placed on the rights secured by the above-quoted articles other than such as are necessary for the protection of those interests 'in a democratic society'.[114]

The Court of Justice made it clear that provisions of Community law must be construed and applied by Member States with reference to principles of fundamental rights. Besides highlighting the Convention as a source of general principles to which it will have recourse, the ECJ's ruling suggested that provision of community law must be construed and applied by Member States with reference to those principles.

In a series of subsequent cases the ECJ went further in applying substantive principles of international human rights law. In *R* v. *Kirk (Kent)* the Court applied the principles of non-retroactivity of penal provisions (as in Article 7 ECHR) in the context of disputes concerning the validity of the British regulations prohibiting Danish vessels from fishing within the United Kingdom's 12-mile fishery zone.[115] In *Johnston* v. *CCRUC,* which concerned the legality of the policy of not issuing firearms to female members of the RUC, one question involved the applicants' right to effective judicial remedy. The ECJ ruled that Article 6 of the Equal Treatment Directive had to be interpreted in the light of the principle of judicial control, which reflects a general principle of law underlying the constitutional traditions common to Member States and is laid down in Articles 6 and 13 of the ECHR. The Court was of the view that:

> [b]y virtue of Article 6 the Directive No. 76/207, interpreted in the light of the general principle stated above, all persons have the right to obtain an effective remedy in a competent court against measures which they consider to be contrary to the principle of equal treatment for men and women.[116]

It followed that Article 53(2) of the Sex Discrimination (NI) Order 1976, according to which a certificate issued by the Secretary of State was conclusive evidence that derogation from the equality principle was justified, was contrary to the principle of effective judicial control. It has increasingly been acknowledged by the Court of Justice that, when acting

---

[113] *Rutili (Roland), Gennevilliers (France)* v. *Ministry of the Interior of the France* Case C-36/75 [1975] ECR 1219.
[114] *Rutili (Roland), Gennevilliers (France)* v. *Ministry of the Interior of the France* Case C-36/75 [1975] ECR 1219, para 32.
[115] *R.* v. *Kirk (Kent)* Case C-63/83 [1984] ECR 2689, para 22.
[116] *Johnston* v. *Chief Constable of the Royal Ulster Constabulary* Case C-222/84 [1986] ECR 1651, para 19.

within the framework of Community law, authorities within the domestic sphere are obliged to follow human rights principles. This view was taken a step further by Advocate General Jacobs in *Konstantinidis* v. *Stadt Altensteig-Standesamt*[117] when he noted that a person relying upon Articles 48, 52 or 59 TEC in relation to employment in another Member State is:

> entitled to assume that, where ever he goes to earn his living in the European Community, he will be treated in accordance with a common code of fundamental values, in particular those laid down in the European Convention on Human Rights.[118]

In addition to this, over the years the ECJ has recognised a number of rights, more frequently associated with international human rights law. These include: the right to human dignity;[119] the principle of equality;[120] non-discrimination;[121] freedom of association;[122] freedom of religion and belief;[123] right to a privacy;[124] respect for family life;[125] and freedom of opinion and publication.[126]

Despite this positive movement, significant gaps in human rights protection remain. The EU cannot be held accountable for human rights violations before the European Court of Human Rights, because the Union is not a party to the Convention.[127] It was hugely disappointing for human rights advocates when the Court of Justice ruled out the possibility of accession of the EU to the Convention, on the grounds that the treaties did not give the Union competence to do so.[128] However, if the Treaty of Lisbon is ratified by all EU Member States, under Article 6(2), the European Union will accede to the ECHR, with the proviso that 'such accession shall not affect the Union's competences as defined in the Treaties.'

(iii) Human rights and the EU treaties

The role of the Court of Justice in developing a human rights competence can be understood as a defensive tactic to bolster its argument that Community law is supreme throughout the Member States. However, it can also be viewed that increasing numbers of human

---

[117] *Konstantinidis* v. *Stadt Altensteig-Standesamt* Case C-168/91 [1993] ECR–I 1191.

[118] Ibid. p. 1211.

[119] *Casagrande* v. *Landeshauptstadt Munchen* Case C-9/74 [1974] ECR 773.

[120] *Klöckner-Werke AG and Hoesch AG* v. *High Authority of the European Coal and Steel Community* Joined Cases C-17/61 and C-20/61 [1962] ECR 653.

[121] *Defrenne* v. *SABENA* Case C-43/75 [1976] ECR 455.

[122] *Union Syndicale* v. *Council of the European Communities* Case C-175/73 [1974] ECR 917, 925.

[123] *Prais* v. *Council of Ministers of the European Communities* Case C-130/75 [1976] ECR 1589, 1599.

[124] *National Panasonic (UK) Ltd* v. *Commission of the European Communities* Case C-136/79 [1980] ECR 2033, 2056 *et seq.*

[125] *Commission of the European Communities* v. *Germany* Case C-249/86 [1989] ECR 1263.

[126] *VBVB and VBBB* v. *Commission of the European Communities* Cases C-43/82 and C-63/82 [1984] ECR 9, *et seq.*, 62.

[127] *CFDT* v. *European Communities/their Members* Application No. 8030/77, 13 D & R 231. See Harris, O'Boyle, Bates and Buckley, *Harris, O'Boyle and Warbrick Law of the European Convention on Human Rights* (Oxford University Press, 2009) at pp. 28–29.

[128] *Opinion 2/94*, [1996] ECR I-1759; CELS, Occasional Paper, *The Human Rights Opinion of the ECJ and its Constitutional Implications*, 1996; Economides and Weiler, 'Accession of the Communities to the European Convention on Human Rights: Commission Memorandum: Reports of Committees' 42 *MLR* (1979) 683; McGoldrick, *International Relations Law of the European Union* (Longman, 1997) pp. 174–180.

rights issues arise within the context of the European Union. Nevertheless, for many years it remained the only Community level forum in which human rights issues were discussed. It was not until the Maastricht Treaty of European Union (TEU) in 1992 that human rights were formally placed on the institutional agenda.[129] In many ways, Maastricht was to prove a significant watershed in the development of human rights protection within what was thenceforth to be known as the EU. Most symbolically, the obligation to protect human rights was inserted into the preamble of the founding treaty. This had no legal effect whatsoever, but it represented a first step towards the inclusion of some sort of human rights dimension into an apparently solely economic entity. This obligation was to be played out in two contexts: the EU's Foreign and Development Policy and the development of citizenship of the Union.

The TEU introduced, under what is known as the Second Pillar, a Common Foreign and Security Policy (CFSP). This policy allows for Member States, acting inter-governmentally, to take common action in the face of world events. One of the objectives of this policy is, under Article 11 TEU, stated to be the development and consolidation of democracy, the rule of law and respect for human rights and fundamental freedoms. Thus, the TEU gives Member States the power to act internationally in order to secure the respect of human rights.

This power, however, is limited by the weaknesses and difficulties which have plagued the CFSP itself. While the CFSP is perhaps more effective than is sometimes acknowledged, its human rights dimension has been accused of lacking consistency.[130] More hopeful was the inclusion within development co-operation policy of human rights conditionality, whereby Community aid or trade agreements are made conditional on the achievement of certain levels of human rights protection. This policy was institutionalised at Maastricht but had been incorporated into the Lomé Convention in 1990 and generalised by means of the Council Resolution of 28 November 1991 on human rights clauses in co-operation agreements. This resolution requires a carrot and stick approach to be taken. Financial resources are to be made available to beneficiary States to enable them to promote democracy and human rights. However, if human rights violations are identified, the EU has the power to withdraw aid until the problems are rectified.

One important criticism that has been made of the emphasis on human rights in external relations, is the fact that standards of protection are required of third countries which the EU itself does not grant to its own citizens. This potential hypocrisy is starkly illustrated within the Maastricht Treaty itself. In this treaty, the EU took an irreversible step towards the protection of individual rights by creating the concept of Citizenship of the Union. While this concept is an important symbol of the aspirations of the Union beyond the economic dimension, the citizenship provisions have been seen as somewhat hollow.[131] One important gap in the provisions is that no reference is made to the fundamental rights of those citizens, despite proposals from the European Parliament and the Spanish government that citizenship should incorporate a fundamental rights dimension. It would appear that giving EU citizens fundamental rights which could, potentially, be different from those granted by the Member States was a loss of sovereignty too far.

---

[129] For a general discussion see Twomey, 'The European Union: Three Pillars without a Human Rights Foundation' in O'Keefe and Twomey (eds), above n.84, pp. 121–131.

[130] Clapham, 'Human Rights in the Common Foreign Policy' in Alston (ed.), above n.1, pp. 627–683.

[131] d'Oliveira, 'Union Citizenship: Pie in the Sky?' in Rosas and Antola (eds), *A Citizens' Europe* (Sage Publications, 1995) pp. 58–84.

Furthermore, the development of the Third Pillar, known as Justice and Home Affairs, gave to the Union powers which, it can be argued, cried out for some sort of human rights dimension. These provisions related in the main to agreement surrounding issues of immigration, asylum and free movement within the territory of the Union, including police co-operation and the Schengen Information System (a data-sharing system operated by the police and immigration services of the various Member States). The Member States are not limited in these actions by human rights considerations. Under Article 35(5) TEU, the jurisdiction of the Court of Justice was excluded from all questions as to the validity of operations carried out by Member States with regard to the maintenance of law and order and the safeguarding of internal security, including all operations carried out by the police or other law enforcement services. This means that the review power developed by the Court of Justice and outlined in the previous section did not apply here.[132]

While the Maastricht Treaty was of fundamental importance, there were, nevertheless, significant problems with its provisions. The modifications made by the Amsterdam Treaty, signed in 1997, addressed mainly the more symbolic issues of protection.[133] As well as the mention of human rights within the preamble of the treaty, human rights and fundamental freedoms, as guaranteed by the ECHR and the constitutional traditions of the Member States, were recognised, under Article 6(2) TEU, as being one of the foundations of the Union. The Court of Justice, under Article 46(d) TEU, can, in the context of its existing powers of judicial review (which, in the main, are focused on First Pillar activity), review acts of the institutions against the principles contained in Article 6(2). Moreover, the obligation on Member States to comply with human rights standards gained very few teeth: Article 7 provided that a Member State who persistently violates human rights standards could have certain rights of membership suspended including voting rights. Further, Article 49 TEU made respect of human rights standards a condition of entry of new States to the EU.

Aside from the explicitly human rights-based dimension, other important steps were taken at Amsterdam. The Social Chapter of the Treaty, first inserted at Maastricht but weakened by the opt-out of the United Kingdom, was strengthened at Amsterdam. A new Article 13 TEC was added, giving the Community the power to legislate against discrimination on a wide range of grounds.[134] The burst of unprecedented racism and xenophobia prevalent in many EU States (through most noticeably the growth of the Far Right in Austria) and a need to balance the restrictive effects of EU immigration and asylum policies with steps to promoting integration of third country nationals, spurred swift action. Two Directives and an Action Plan were passed under Article 13, prohibiting racial discrimination in all circumstances, and discrimination in the workplace on the grounds of sex, race, age, disability, religion and, to a limited extent, sexual orientation.[135] The Racial Equality Directive – Directive 2000/43/EC – requires all EU States to forbid discrimination on the basis of

---

[132] Eicke, 'European Charter of Fundamental Rights – Unique Opportunity or Unwelcome Distraction' *EHRLR* [2000] 280.

[133] For a general discussion of the contribution of Amsterdam to human rights in the EU, see McGoldrick, 'The European Union after Amsterdam: An Organisation with General Human Rights Competence' in O'Keeffe and Twomey (ed.), *Legal Issues of the Amsterdam Treaty* (Hart Publishing, 1999) pp. 249–270.

[134] See Gearty, 'The Internal and External "Other" in the Union Legal Order: Racism, Religious Intolerance and Xenophobia in Europe' in Alston (ed.), above n.1 327–358 at p. 347.

[135] Council Directive 2000/43/EC of 29 June 2000 implementing the principle of equal treatment between persons irrespective of racial or ethnic origin (OJ L 180 19/7/2000, p. 22); Council Directive 2000/78/EC of 27 November 2000 establishing a general framework for equal treatment in employment and occupation (OJ L 303 2/12/2000, p. 16); Council Decision 2000/750/EC of 27 November 2000 establishing a Community action programme to combat discrimination (2001 to 2006) (OJ L 303 2/12/2000, p. 23).

ethnic or racial or racial origin in the areas of employment, education, healthcare, social protection, housing and access to goods and services.[136] The second Directive, which is only a Framework Directive, was adopted in November 2000. The Directive is limited to the field of employment though it is applicable on the basis of religion or belief, age, disability and sexual orientation.[137] Both Directives go further than current international law as they refer to both direct and indirect discrimination[138] as well as negative and positive protection.[139] Protection is also provided from religious discrimination. However, one of the most significant features of the two Directives is that they both provide for sanctions in the instances in which States fail to comply with them.[140] Increased compliance also has the bi-product of effecting discrimination against non-EU citizens, as State measures tend not to make a distinction between different categories of non-citizens.

Nevertheless, the limitations of EU human rights protection continue to be visible. Two major issues can be indicated. Firstly, Article 6(2) TEU states that the rights to be protected are those contained within the ECHR and the 'constitutional traditions common to the Member States'. This vague formula allows the Court of Justice to maintain a significant level of power as to the rights which it will protect. The fact that the rights protected extend beyond those contained within the ECHR is recognition of the limited nature of the Convention and the changing perceptions of fundamental rights. To that extent, the flexible approach which this represents is to be commended. However, the problem of distilling rights from constitutional traditions is significant. In some cases, the Court has adopted an almost mathematical approach. In others, however, clashes become apparent: what, for example, of the Irish constitutional protection of the right to life of the unborn child in conjunction with the, usually implicit and limited, freedom to choose to have an abortion which exists in many other Member States.[141]

In other cases the question is whether a fundamental right is in fact violated. Mention should be made here of the Banana Saga, where the German Constitutional Court required that the application of Regulation 404/93 on trade preferences should be modified in order to take account of the right of protection of private property, despite a finding by the Court of Justice that the Regulation did not violate fundamental rights.[142] This decision, taken in conjunction with the German Constitutional Court's earlier decision about the Maastricht Treaty,[143] demonstrates that the German court remains determined to have the last word on whether rights protected in the Basic Law are violated. Therefore, some sort of clarity is required as to the specific fundamental rights protected, as well as the jurisdiction of the various courts, in order that the power of the Court of Justice does not remain untrammelled.

---

[136] Bell, 'Combating Racism through European Laws: A Comparison of Racial Equality Directive and Protocol 12' in Chopin and Niessen (eds), *Combating Racial and Ethnic Discrimination: Taking the European Legislative Agenda Further* (Migration Policy Group and Commission on Racial Equality, 2002) pp. 7–34.

[137] See Skidmore, 'The EC Framework Directive on Equal Treatment in Employment: Towards a Comprehensive Community Anti-Discrimination Policy?' 30 *Industrial Law Journal* (2001) 126.

[138] Article 2 Racial Equality Directive, Article 2 Employment Framework Directive.

[139] The Employment Framework Directive also refers to reasonable accommodation in Article 5. Articles 5 and 6 Racial Equality Directive, Article 5, 7, 8 Employment Framework Directive.

[140] Article 15 Racial Equality Directive, Article 17 Employment Framework Directive.

[141] Difficulties have already been encountered on this issue – see *Society for the Protection of Unborn Children (Ireland) Ltd (SPUC)* v. *Grogan* Case C-159/90 [1991] ECR I-4685 and *Open Door Counselling and Dublin Well Woman* v. *Ireland* (1993) 15 E.H.R.R. 244.

[142] *Federal Republic of Germany* v. *Council of the European Union* Case C-280/93 [1994] ECR I-4973.

[143] *Brunner* v. *European Union Treaty* (2 Bv. R 2134/92 & 2159/92) [1994] 1 C.M.L.R. 57.

Secondly, the extent of the protection that can be provided is limited. The Court of Justice's power of review extends to Community acts and (under its own case law) to acts of the Member States when they are acting within an area of Community competence. The Court has no power to act against Member States violating the rights of Union citizens or residents in areas where the Community has no competence. Furthermore, the power is very limited when it comes to Second and Third Pillar issues. Under the Treaty of Amsterdam, immigration, asylum and free movement matters were moved to the First Pillar, under Title IV TEC. However, Article 68 TEC limits the scope of action of the Court of Justice, in that requests for preliminary rulings may be made only by the national court of last resort (rather than by any court) and the Court of Justice is given no jurisdiction in areas relating to the maintenance of law and order and the safeguarding of internal security.[144] The fundamental rights protected by the Court are, thus, perhaps better understood as obligations placed on the Community and on States in certain circumstances, rather than as clear rights possessed by individuals.

In other areas, while the rhetoric of human rights can be found in abundance, their positive inclusion within the full range of Community policy remains impossible. The acquisition of a full set of fundamental rights for Community citizens and residents, enforceable by the Court of Justice and national courts against both Community institutions and Member States, would appear to be the next obvious step. Indeed, if the Treaty of Lisbon comes into force, Article 6 of the TEU will establish that:

1. The Union recognises the rights, freedoms and principles set out in the Charter of Fundamental Rights of the European Union of 7 December 2000, as adapted at Strasbourg, on 12 December 2007, which shall have the same legal value as the Treaties. The provisions of the Charter shall not extend in any way the competences of the Union as defined in the Treaties. The rights, freedoms and principles in the Charter shall be interpreted in accordance with the general provisions in Title VII of the Charter governing its interpretation and application and with due regard to the explanations referred to in the Charter, that set out the sources of those provisions.

2. The Union shall accede to the European Convention for the Protection of Human Rights and Fundamental Freedoms. Such accession shall not affect the Union's competences as defined in the Treaties.

3. Fundamental rights, as guaranteed by the European Convention for the Protection of Human Rights and Fundamental Freedoms and as they result from the constitutional traditions common to the Member States, shall constitute general principles of the Union's law.[145]

Thus, ensuring that both the Charter of Fundamental Freedoms and the ECHR will be justiciable by the ECJ.[146]

---

[144] Ibid.

[145] Treaty of Lisbon amending the Treaty on European Union and the Treaty establishing the European Community, signed at Lisbon, 13 December 2007 Official Journal C 306 of 17 December 2007.

[146] The Charter will not be justiciable by the ECJ or any other court in the cases of the United Kingdom and Poland. See Protocol on the Application of the Charter of Fundamental Rights to Poland and to the United Kingdom, Official Journal C 306 of 17 December 2007.

(iv) The Charter of Fundamental Rights[147]

The acquisition of a comprehensive code of human rights, however, has been an issue fraught with complexity for the EU. The concern about State sovereignty which prevented the inclusion of a human rights dimension in the Maastricht citizenship provisions persists, and has in many ways intensified. A number of Member States, while prepared to countenance the preparation of a declaration of rights, would not accept a binding Charter. Further, the divergence between national constitutional traditions, which gave the Court so much discretion in turn made the task of agreeing on an acceptable text all the more difficult. However, in June 1999, at the European Council in Cologne, EU Heads of State committed themselves to the establishment of a Charter.[148] A body (confusingly known as the Convention) was set up, under the presidency of the former German President Roman Herzog, and included representatives from Member State governments, the Commission, the European Parliament and national parliaments; and that body produced a draft in October 2000. The ECJ, Council of Europe and European Court of Human Rights additionally had observer status. The draft was adopted by all 15 Member States at Nice in December 2000.

A striking aspect of the Charter is its scope. By focusing on fundamental rights rather than on the traditional, liberal democratic view of human rights, social and economic rights were included. The Convention had made it clear that they intended not to create new rights but to make explicit those rights which already exist, whether that be within the ECHR, other European or international agreements, or within the constitutions of Member States. Indeed, the Charter makes clear that the ECHR is to be used in order to interpret corresponding provisions.[149] However, the ECHR is seen as providing minimum standards and therefore this does not prevent the Charter from providing 'more extensive protection'. The rights contained in the Charter may be derogated from but under Article 52:

> 1. Any limitation on the exercise of the rights and freedoms recognised by this Charter must be provided for by law and respect the essence of those rights and freedoms. Subject to the principle of proportionality, limitations may be made only if they are necessary and genuinely meet objectives of general interest recognized by the Union or the need to protect the rights and freedoms of others.

The 54 Articles of the Charter are divided into six chapters: dignity, freedoms, equality, solidarity, citizens' rights and justice. Chapter One, on 'Dignity', covers the uncontroversial areas of the right to life, prohibition of torture and of slavery and forced labour. These rights are covered by the International Covenant on Civil and Political Rights and by all regional human rights treaties. Article 3, however, introduces a number of rights, hitherto not established within the traditional framework of human rights. Article 3(2) provides:

---

[147] Charter of Fundamental Rights of the European Union, Official Journal C 303 of 14 December 2007.
[148] Article 52(3) Charter of Fundamental Rights.
[149] Consolidated versions of the Treaty on European Union and the Treaty on the Functioning of the European Union, Official Journal C 115 of 9 May 2008.

In the fields of medicine and biology, the following must be respected in particular:

- the free and informed consent of the person concerned, according to the procedures laid down by law,

- the prohibition of eugenic practices, in particular those aiming at the selection of persons,

- the prohibition on making the human body and its parts as such a source of financial gain,

- the prohibition of the reproductive cloning of human beings.

While clearly influenced by the Council of Europe's Convention on Human Rights and Bio-Medicine,[150] the extent to which these provisions would influence developments in the European Union with regard to the field of medicine and biotechnology remains uncertain. The Charter prohibits only reproductive cloning. However, there is neither an authorisation nor prohibition of any other forms of cloning.

Chapter Two, on 'Freedoms', is generally unproblematic. The rights to liberty and security, to privacy, the right to marry and freedom of conscience, expression and assembly are familiar from international treaties including the ECHR. The social and economic rights included here involve the right to education, the right to work, the freedom to conduct a business and the right to property. Our earlier discussion has highlighted the distinctions which have traditionally been placed between civil and political rights and social and economic rights. Thus, for example, the right to education, often considered as an economic and social right, is provided in the UDHR (Article 26) and the International Covenant on Economic, Social and Cultural Rights Covenant (Article 13). It is not provided for in the International Covenant on Civil and Political Rights. Similarly, the right to education could not be established in the ECHR, although it was subsequently grafted on to it by the First Protocol to the treaty.[151] It is, therefore, positive to note the inclusion of civil, political, economic, social and cultural rights contained in the umbrella of one human rights document.

The idea of freedom also incorporates the right to asylum and protection against removal, expulsion and extradition under certain circumstances. The right to seek asylum has generated difficulties in international and domestic laws.[152] Although incorporated in Article 14 of the Universal Declaration of Human Rights, its subsequent affirmation within human rights treaties has been problematic. International law has similarly shown great weakness in forbidding expulsions and providing protection to individuals from extradition to States where they are likely to face serious risks. Although the ECHR (Protocol 4, Article 4) prohibits the collective expulsion of aliens, traditionally there has been a reluctance to condemn expulsions. Two recent and useful standard-setting norms aim to establish a more comprehensive regime protecting non-nationals against arbitrary expulsions. Firstly, the African Charter on Human and Peoples' Rights (AFCHPR)[153] provides, in Article 12(5), that:

---

[150] ETS No. 164 and Additional Protocol ETS No. 158; see Rehof, 'Article 3' in Alfredsson and Eide (eds), *The Universal Declaration of Human Rights: A Common Standard of Achievement* (Martinus Nijhoff Publishers, 1999) pp. 89–101 at p. 98.

[151] See Protocol 1 of ECHR, Article 2.

[152] For an analysis by the International Court of Justice see the *Asylum Case (Columbia v. Peru)*, Judgment 20 November 1950, (1950) ICJ Reports 266.

[153] African [Banjul] Charter on Human and Peoples' Rights, adopted 27 June 1981, OAU Doc. CAB/LEG/67/3 rev.5, 21 I.L.M. 58 (1982), entered into force 21 October 1986.

> The mass expulsion of non-nationals shall be prohibited. Mass expulsion shall be that which is aimed at national, racial, ethnic or religious groups.

The other provision, which has an application at the international level, is incorporated in the Statute of the International Criminal Court[154] which, in its definition of crimes against humanity, includes deportation or the forcible transfer of population.[155] The extradition and deportation of an individual has already raised complex issues of cultural relativism, and the European Court of Human Rights has had to deal with them in cases such as *Soering* v. *UK*[156] and *Chahal* v. *UK*.[157] Given that, under Title IV TEC, the Community is required to agree joint asylum and immigration policies, the inclusion of the right to asylum and protection against expulsion within the Charter could prove significant. It might equally dilute some of the insensitivity shown by the provisions of the European Union Directive on the mutual recognition of decisions on the expulsions of third country nationals; without substantial procedural human rights scrutiny, this Directive is likely to prejudice the position of third country nationals residing within the Union.[158] Finally, within the section on freedoms, the freedom of the arts and sciences,[159] including academic freedom, and the much-needed, but much-disputed, right to the protection of personal data[160] is incorporated under this heading.

Chapter Three is shorter and concerns 'Equality'. Article 21 prohibits discrimination on a wide range of grounds in an explicitly non-exclusive list. Further articles make more specific statements about cultural, religious and linguistic diversity,[161] and the cases of men and women,[162] children,[163] the elderly[164] and persons with disabilities.[165] These articles generally cover the ground of already existing binding legislation, particularly the new Framework Directive discussed earlier, although the extension of the rights beyond the workplace is significant. It is noticeable, however, that while discrimination on the grounds of sexual orientation is prohibited under the general Article 21, no more specific provisions on sexual orientation or transgendered people are included. Equally, no provisions making a direct reference to minorities or minority rights can be found. Given the recent upsurge in the issue of minority rights, it is disappointing not to have a detailed article on the rights of ethnic and religious minorities that are resident within the European Union.[166] Unfortunately, this can also be seen to lower current international standards, which is unacceptable.

---

[154] Rome Statute of the International Criminal Court, 2187 U.N.T.S. 90, *entered into force* 1 July 2002.

[155] See Article 7(2)(d) Statute of the International Criminal Court also see Henckaerts, *Mass Expulsion in Modern International Law and Practice* (Martinus Nijhoff Publishers, 1995).

[156] *Soering* v. *UK* (1989) 11 E.H.R.R. 439.

[157] *Chahal* v. *UK* (1997) 23 E.H.R.R. 413.

[158] See Council Directive 2001/40/EC of 28 May, 2001 on the Mutual Recognition of Decisions on the Expulsions of Third Country Nations (OJL149/34 28/05/2001).

[159] Article 13 EU Charter of Fundamental Rights.

[160] Article 8 EU Charter of Fundamental Rights See also Xanthaki, 'A European Criminal Record: Human Rights Considerations' in Xanthaki and Stefanou (eds), *Towards a European Criminal Record* (Cambridge University Press, 2008) pp. 79–103.

[161] Article 22 EU Charter of Fundamental Rights.

[162] Ibid. Article 23.

[163] Ibid. Article 24.

[164] Ibid. Article 25.

[165] Ibid. Article 26.

[166] See below chapter 13.

Chapter Four marks the point where more controversial material was included. Rights relating to 'Solidarity', which are in the main social rights, were not accepted as fundamental rights by all Member States. The ambitions that some parties had for this section have not been realised, and the rights contained within it are somewhat limited. Essentially, they cover workers' rights, such as collective bargaining,[167] health and safety[168] and the right not to be unfairly dismissed,[169] which are already contained within Community law. A number of the provisions contain references to the legal regimes of Member States, and the principle of subsidiarity appears to have been firmly at the forefront of the drafters' minds. The rights to social security,[170] healthcare[171] and consumer protection[172] are couched in particularly broad terms. The extent to which the jurisprudence of relevant provisions of the European Social Charter and the ECHR will influence the developments of the rights contained within this chapter remains uncertain.

Chapter Five, on 'Citizens' Rights', might again have been hoped to be significant, given the criticisms that have been made against the existing concept of Citizens of the Union. However, it remains limited. The majority of the rights in Chapter Five are already contained within binding Community law: the citizenship rights of Articles 17–22 TEC (which, it is made clear, apply only to citizens of the Union), and the provisions concerning the right of access to documents.

Finally, in Chapter VI, the rights to 'Justice' bring us back to familiar territory. Here we can find the right to a fair trial,[173] the right to a defence,[174] the right to a proportionate penalty[175] and the right not to be tried twice for the same offence.[176] The rights contained in this chapter are already a firmly established part of the International Criminal Justice System. The ECHR covers such rights as the right to fair trial in considerable detail and the European Commission and Court on Human Rights have built substantial jurisprudence on the subject over the past five decades.

Chapter VII represents a very important part of the Charter. It not only provides the level of protection but also explains the scope of the Charter rights. According to Article 51(1):

> The provisions of this Charter are addressed to the institutions and bodies of the Union with due regard for the principle of subsidiarity and to the Member States only when they are implementing Union law. They shall therefore respect the rights, observe the principles and promote the application thereof in accordance with their respective powers.

In relation to the level and sphere of protection, it is reassuring that the Charter adopts a wider and all-embracing approach. Thus, according to Article 53:

---

[167] Article 28 EU Charter of Fundamental Rights.
[168] Ibid. Article 31(1).
[169] Ibid. Article 30.
[170] Ibid. Article 34.
[171] Ibid. Article 35.
[172] Ibid. Article 38.
[173] Ibid. Article 47.
[174] Ibid. Article 48.
[175] Ibid. Article 49.
[176] Ibid. Article 50.

> Nothing in this Charter shall be interpreted as restricting or adversely affecting human rights and fundamental freedoms as recognised, in their respective fields of application, by Union law and international law and by international agreements to which the Union, the Community or all the Member States are party, including the European Convention for the Protection of Human Rights and Fundamental Freedoms, and by the Member States' constitutions.

The question of whether the Charter would be enforceable or not was a particular subject for discussion. Given the fact that the Court of Justice maintains a power to enforce human rights against Member States and institutions, it might be thought that a non-binding Charter would be impracticable.[177] However, a number of Member States (notably, but not exclusively, the United Kingdom) objected to the Charter having any binding status at all, despite the limited scope of Article 51. More fundamental, however, was probably the concern as to the symbolic power which a binding Charter would have as a part of a putative EU Constitution and as a claim to sovereignty. At the Nice Conference, where concerns of national interest and political horse-trading reigned supreme, anything with the potential of decreasing the power of Member States was not likely to meet with much success.

The Charter, therefore, remains purely declaratory and, at least in theory, of purely political importance. It was, however, drafted with the idea in mind that it could, at some point in the future, become binding.[178] A significant hope had been that the Charter would be incorporated in the (now defunct) Constitutional Treaty.[179] Furthermore, despite the intentions of the member States, the existing competence of the Union and of the Court of Justice raises the possibility that the provisions will have some legal impact. That possibility looked very real when, in his opinion in Case 173/99 *BECTU* v. *Secretary of State for Trade and Industry*,[180] Advocate-General Tizzano made explicit reference to Article 31(2) of the Charter, which states that workers have the right to paid annual leave. He further argued that, while the Charter is not itself binding, the statement of existing rights which it constitutes cannot be ignored in cases concerned with the nature and scope of a fundamental right elaborated in other, binding Community legislation. In cases such as the *BECTU* case, where the precise scope and application of the right is in dispute, the Charter is intended to serve as a substantive point of reference. This wide-ranging approach was, however, rejected by the Court of Justice. In its decision of 26 June 2001, the Court referred only to the 1989 Community Charter of the Fundamental Social Rights of Workers, and stated that the right to paid annual leave was 'a particularly important principle of Community social law' rather than, as Tizzano A-G had argued, a fundamental social right.[181] In a second case concerning the interpretation of the Working Time Directive, the same Advocate-General suggested that it was possible that that Directive itself could be challenged for infringing a

---

[177] Fredman, McCrudden and Freedland, 'An EU Charter of Fundamental Rights' *Public Law* (2000) 178 at p. 185.

[178] See, in particular, the speech of Roman Herzog, annexed to the report of the first meeting of the Convention held on 17/12/1999 (CHARTRE 4105/00), where he stated that 'we should constantly keep the objective in mind that the Charter which we are drafting must one day, in the not too distant future, become legally binding'.

[179] Arnull, 'From Charter to Constitution and Beyond: Fundamental Rights in the new EU' *Public Law* (2003) 774, at p. 777.

[180] *Broadcasting, Entertainment, Cinematographic and Theatre Union (BECTU)* v. *Secretary of State for Trade and Industry* Case 173/99, Preliminary Ruling, 8 February 2001.

[181] *R. (on the application of Broadcasting, Entertainment, Cinematographic and Theatre Union)* v. *Secretary of State for Trade and Industry*, (C-173/99) [2001] 3 C.M.L.R. 7.

fundamental social right.[182] It may, however, be significant that he argued that such a challenge would fail, and, in the light of the Court's decision in *BECTU*, it is unlikely that such an argument would succeed at present.

This role of the Charter is likely to be extended. In its human rights jurisdiction, while the Court of Justice may continue to claim the right to search national constitutional traditions for specific rights, the Charter may supersede the ECHR as the principal point of reference for deciding what rights are to be protected. In this context, the weakness of a non-binding Charter can be seen. The Court of Justice maintains its right to review on human rights grounds, and will make use of the Charter in doing that, but it also maintains the right to depart from the Charter if it so chooses. In a similar vein, while the Charter can be referred to in the context of the broader human rights dimension referred to above,[183] it does not bind the Union, which can either ignore rights contained within the Charter or enforce rights not contained therein.

(v) The Role of the Fundamental Rights Agency

In 2007 the Fundamental Rights Agency (FRA) replaced the European Monitoring Centre on Racism and Xenophobia (EUMC). Its role as established by Council Regulation (EC) 168/2007 is:

> to provide the relevant institutions, bodies, offices and agencies of the Community and its Member States when implementing Community law with assistance and expertise relating to fundamental rights in order to support them when they take measures or formulate courses of action within their respective spheres of competence to fully respect fundamental rights.[184]

The Regulation also provides for working methods and cooperation;[185] Organisation;[186] Operation;[187] and Financial Provisions.[188] The Agency splits its work into thematic areas, which are established by a five-year, multi-annual framework. In 2008 it was decided that the FRA will concentrate on the following thematic areas:

(a) racism, xenophobia and related intolerance;

(b) discrimination based on sex, race or ethnic origin, religion or belief, disability, age or sexual orientation and against persons belonging to minorities and any combination of these grounds (multiple discrimination);

(c) compensation of victims;

(d) the rights of the child, including the protection of children;

---

[182] *Bowden v. Tuffnells Parcels Express Ltd* (C-133/00) [2001] ECR I-7031.
[183] Indeed, even before the Charter was officially adopted by the Convention, its provisions were referred to in the report of the 'Three Wise Men' on the EU's sanctions against Austria (September 2001).
[184] Article 2.
[185] Chapter 2.
[186] Chapter 3.
[187] Chapter 4.
[188] Chapter 5.

(e) asylum, immigration and integration of migrants;

(f) visa and border control;

(g) participation of the EU citizens in the Union's democratic functioning;

(h) information society and, in particular, respect for private life and protection of personal data; and

(i) access to efficient and independent justice.[189]

Prior to the adoption of the Framework, the FRA had continued the work of the EUMC by concentrating on the area of racism and xenophobia. One of the most important elements of the FRA is to collect and analyse data on the protection of fundamental rights in Member States of the EU.[190] It also carries out comparative analysis of its findings. Examples of current projects include: EU-MIDIS (European Union Minorities and Discrimination Survey); a comparative report on the situation concerning homophobia and discrimination on grounds of sexual orientation in the EU; racism and social marginalisation: potential pathways to violent radicalisation; the situation regarding racism in sport in the European Union and positive initiatives to combat it; and the housing situation of Roma and travellers in the EU. It is clear from its current projects that the FRA is still very much focused on the areas of racism and xenophobia, which is positive as it was feared that the expansion of the mandate of the Agency would lead to the dilution of its work. Importantly, the FRA is independent and can, therefore, formulate opinions on the institutions of the EU as well as individual Member States. In order to prevent the duplication of work between the FRA and the Council of Europe a co-operation agreement has been established.[191]

Due to the fact that the FRA is in its infancy, it is unclear how successful it will be. However, it is primarily a monitoring agency, whose principal role is to collect and analyse data. It cannot receive individual complaints and neither can it take action in the event that fundamental rights are breached by member States. Even if the Charter of Fundamental Rights becomes binding, the ECJ will adjudicate in the instance of individual breaches and the EU will impose sanctions in the case of persistent and serious breaches.

(vi) Critical comments

The non-binding and unenforceable nature of the Charter is one of the aspects which has given rise to criticism. Weiler calls a non-binding Charter 'a symbol of European impotence and refusal to take rights seriously'.[192] The existence of a non-binding Charter does not add significantly to existing protection (apart, perhaps, from those substantive rights which are recognised within the Charter but not within the ECHR and which may be used by the Court of Justice in the exercise of its power of review). It may also be taken by critics as yet another vacuous declaration of enumerated rights. While the Convention claimed that the

---

[189] Regulation 4.1.a and b.

[190] Council Decision (2008/203/EC) implementing Regulation (EC) No. 168/2007 as regards the adoption of a Multi-annual Framework for the European Union Agency for Fundamental Rights for 2007–2012.

[191] Agreement between the European Community and the Council of Europe on the co-operation between the European Union Agency for Fundamental Rights and the Council of Europe. 2008 OJ (L 186) 7.

[192] Weiler, 'Editorial: Does the European Union Truly Need a Charter of Rights?' 6 *European Law Journal* (2000) 95.

Charter was drafted in the hope that it would become binding, much of it is drafted in grand, abstract and general terms (this is particularly noticeable in the solidarity provisions). Weiler argues that a commitment to human rights protection within the EU does not require yet another Declaration of Fundamental Rights, but rather the elaboration of a human rights policy, complete with a Commissioner, a staff and a budget, which is committed to searching out and facilitating the punishment of human rights violations.

These criticisms have to be taken on board. The non-binding nature of the Charter suggests that it is intended to be nothing more than a statement of principle, albeit the first statement of principle on human rights made by EU Member States in that capacity. Having said that, there are, nevertheless, positive features in the Charter. The breadth of the rights in the document and the inclusion of social and economic as well as civil and political rights are to be applauded. It is extremely encouraging to note the inclusion of a number of novel rights, which presumably have been incorporated as a response to new challenges from globalisation and more technology. The Charter also covers some of the more difficult areas. The inclusion of, for example, a right to asylum is also potentially helpful. However, a number of nettles have not been grasped, and some significant omissions have already been alluded to.

It is to be hoped that the Court of Justice will take the opportunity to make full use of the Charter within its existing jurisdiction. Nevertheless, the failure of the Member States to extend the scope of human rights protection within, and by, the EU is regrettable. Whether the hopes of the Convention that the Charter will, at some point in the not too distant future, become binding, remains to be seen. However, the steps taken by the Treaty of Lisbon certainly go a long way towards achieving this aim. All countries of the EU have ratified the Treaty of Lisbon, with the exception of the Czech Republic and Ireland. Ratification is still in progress in the Czech Republic after the Constitutional Court approved the compatibility of the Treaty with the Constitution in November 2008. Ireland on the other hand did not approve the Treaty at a referendum. It was anticipated that all States would ratify the Treaty of Lisbon by 1 January 2009.[193] This of course has not happened. As at 30 May 2009, 23 of the 27 Member States had ratified the treaty. The Charter may yet prove to be the first step along the long road towards really effective human rights protection within Europe, or it may remain an interesting, but ultimately toothless, document.

4 THE OSCE[194]

As shall be discussed in further detail, the Organization for Security and Co-operation in Europe (OSCE), as its name suggests, is an organisation primarily aimed at enhancing security and co-operation within Europe, with a focus on providing early warning, conflict prevention, crisis management and post-conflict rehabilitation.[195] The OSCE therefore is

---

[193] For recent developments see europa.eu/lisbon_treaty/index_en.htm <last visited 30 May 2009>.

[194] www.osce.org <last visited 12 May 2009> Brett, 'Human Rights and the OSCE' 18 *HRQ* (1996) 668; Robertson and Merrills, above n.1, at pp. 179–190; Sands and Klein, *Bowett's Law of International Institutions* (Sweet and Maxwell, 2001) pp. 199–201; Van Dijk, 'The Final Act of Helsinki–Basis for a Pan-European System' 11 *NYIL* (1980) 97; Bloed (ed.), *From Helsinki to Vienna: Basic Documents of the Helsinki Process* (Martinus Nijhoff Publishers, 1990); Sapiro, 'Changing the CSCE into the OSCE: Legal Aspects of a Political Transformation' 89 *AJIL* (1995) 631; Russell, 'The Helsinki Declaration: Brobdingnag or Lilliput?' 70 *AJIL* (1976) 244; Zellner, *On the Effectiveness of OSCE Minority Regime* (1999).

[195] See www.osce.org/publications/sg/2009/01/35857_1220_en.pdf <last visited 10 May 2009>.

not designed to concentrate, as such, on the promotion and protection of human rights. However, like the European Union, the OSCE over the years has had greater involvement with human rights issues. There are noticeable differences between the OSCE on the one hand and the EU and Council of Europe on the other. Unlike the EU and the Council of Europe which were premised on legally binding treaties, the OSCE is not founded as a legal body.[196] The principles emergent from the OSCE process are of the nature of political commitments rather than containing legal rights and obligations. This consequently means that unlike treaties, these commitments cannot be incorporated into domestic law, and national courts remain unable to rely upon these principles. Notwithstanding the absence of a legally binding regime, the OSCE has been highly successful. Ironically, it is the non-binding character of the regime which allowed and encouraged States such as the former Soviet Union to accept the fundamental principles of the organisation.[197] The OSCE comes within the framework of Chapter VIII of the UN Charter as a regional organisation.[198]

The OSCE also represents the single largest regional security organisation of the world. Prior to 1 January 1995, it was known as the Conference on the Security and Co-operation in Europe (CSCE). OSCE currently consists of 56 participating States from Europe, Central Asia and North America and is engaged, *inter alia*, in early-warnings, the prevention of conflicts and rehabilitation after a conflict has taken place. There are two broad phases in which the work of the organisation can be demarcated. The first phase 1973–90 reflected the Cold War dissensions followed by a brief spell of improved relations between the West and the Eastern Block. The second phase, as from 1990, has witnessed tumultuous changes in the political geography of Europe and the emergence of new global security concerns. The breakdown of the Soviet Union and the Warsaw Pact was followed by significant institutional developments within the organisation.

The initial developments of the organisation are rooted in the Conference on Security and Co-operation in Helsinki. The Conference, which began in 1973 with 33 participant States, including the United States and Canada, concluded in 1975 with the adoption of the Helsinki Final Act[199] and comprises of four parts, often being referred to as 'Baskets'. 'Basket I' relates to questions concerning the security in Europe and comprises of a Declaration on Principles Guiding Relations between Participating States; 'Basket II' is concerned with economic issues, science, technology and the environment; 'Basket III' addresses humanitarian and other issues; whereas 'Basket IV' deals with the follow-up process after the Conference. The Final Act is not a document dedicated to human rights, although 'Basket I' does contain important references to human rights. Principle VII 'Basket I' is

---

[196] Brett, above n.194, at p. 671.

[197] Brett correctly makes the point that '[I]t should not be forgotten that the Helsinki Final Act rather than the International Covenant on Civil and Political Rights (to which the Soviet Union was also a party and which came into force at about the same time) was the basis for the human rights groups that sprang up in the USSR itself as well as in Central Europe. Participating States were able to reach agreement on the Helsinki Final Act precisely because it would not be a legally binding document. The pursuit of legal rigor may sometimes be less useful to the cause of human rights in practice than political compromise'. Brett, above n.194, at pp. 676–677.

[198] See above chapter 3; Abass, *Regional Organisations and the Development of Collective Security: Beyond Chapter VIII of the UN Charter* (Hart Publishing, 2004) at p. 149.

[199] The Final Act of the Conference on Security and Cooperation in Europe, August 1. 1975, 14 I.L.M. (1975) 1292 (Helsinki Final Act). The agreement is often referred to as the Helsinki Accords. See Russell (1976) AJIL 242; Bloed and Van Dijk (eds), *Essays on Human Rights in the Helsinki Process* (Martinus Nijhoff Publishers, 1985); Buergenthal, 'The CSCE Rights System' 25 *George Washington Journal of International Law and Economics* (1991–1992) 333.

entitled 'Respect for human rights and fundamental freedoms, including freedom of thought, conscience and religion or belief'. This principle represents a commitment by the participating States to respect human rights, which include freedom of religion without distinctions as to race, sex, language, etc. Principle VII also contains an understanding that the participatory States:

> will promote and encourage the effective exercise of civil, political, economic, social, cultural and other rights and freedoms all of which derive from the inherent dignity of the human person and are essential for his free and full development.[200]

According to Principle VIII, participating States are committed to respecting the equal rights of peoples and their right to self-determination. 'Basket III', entitled 'Co-operation in humanitarian and other fields', is of considerable relevance.[201] It considers such issues as the reunification of families;[202] marriages between citizens of different States;[203] travel for personal and professional reasons;[204] trans-frontier information;[205] and flows and co-operation in culture and education.[206] The Helsinki Conference was followed by a number of follow-up intergovernmental conferences. These were held in Belgrade (1977–78),[207] Madrid (1980–83),[208] Vienna (1986–89)[209] and Helsinki (1992).[210]

The second, more vibrant phase began with the conclusion of the Vienna meeting of the CSCE conference. The Vienna Meeting, which had started in November 1986 concluded in January 1989. The Concluding Document of the Vienna Meeting represents a considerable advance in respect of human rights issues. Such developments can be seen in the light of easing tensions between the Western and Eastern European States and a willingness to address the subject of human rights within the Communist regimes.

The Concluding Document deals with a range of issues including security, culture, trade, education and the environment. In relation to human rights, the participating States agree to provide effective exercise of human rights guarantees and to establish provisions for effective remedies. The Concluding Document also aims to protect freedom of religion, freedom of movement and the rights of national minorities. The Vienna Meeting added a significant dimension to the human rights protection. It provided for a four-stage monitoring process for which it considers questions relating to the 'human dimension'. The four-stage monitoring procedure is initiated by an exchange of information on matters relating to human rights through diplomatic channels. The second stage is conducted by

---

[200] Principle VII.
[201] Basket III. For the text see Brownlie (ed.), *Basic Documents on Human Rights* (Clarendon Press, 1992) pp. 428–447.
[202] Para 1(b).
[203] Para 1(c).
[204] Para 1 (d).
[205] Para 2 (a)–(c).
[206] Paras 3 and 4.
[207] See Conference on Security and Co-operation in Europe: Concluding Document on the Belgrade Meeting in Follow-up to the Conference 8 March 1977. Reprinted 17 I.L.M (1978) 414.
[208] See Conference on Security and Co-operation in Europe: Concluding Document of the Madrid Session Meeting 9 September 1983. Reprinted 22 I.L.M. (1983) 1395.
[209] See Conference on Security and Co-operation in Europe: Concluding Document of the Vienna Meeting 15 January 1989. Reprinted 28 I.L.M. (1989) 531.
[210] See Conference on Security and Co-operation in Europe: Declaration and Decisions from Helsinki Summit, 10 July 1992. Reprinted 31 I.L.M. (1992) 1385.

holding bilateral meetings with other participating States and requesting them to exchange questions on human rights. In the third stage any State may bring relevant cases to the attention of other participating States, whereas in the final stage participating States may approach the relevant issues at the Conference of the Human Dimension as well as at the CSCE follow-up meetings.

Further improvements (both in the substantive recognition of rights and the procedures to implement these rights) were to take place in subsequent documents, in particular the Copenhagen Document.[211] Within the document, participating States show a range of commitments which include respect for the rule of law, justice and democracy.[212] There is an affirmation of fundamental rights and freedoms: freedom of expression;[213] the right to association;[214] the right of everyone to leave any country;[215] and the right to peacefully enjoy property.[216] A number of civil and political rights (e.g. the prohibition of torture and capital punishment) are also reaffirmed. The Copenhagen Document shows a particular interest in the position of national minorities.[217] Although the document is reluctant to define minorities it nevertheless emphasises linguistic, cultural and religious rights. In relation to implementation, the Copenhagen Document tightens up the mechanism by providing specific deadlines within which participating States are to act. In addition:

> [t]he participating States examined practical proposals for new measures aimed at improving the implementation of the commitments relating to the human dimension of the CSCE. In this regard, they considered proposals related to the sending of observers to examine situations and specific cases, the appointment of rapporteurs to investigate and suggest appropriate solutions . . .[218]

A number of these proposals (such as the provisions for on-site investigations by independent experts) have been given effect.[219] The usage of independent experts was the first step towards the involvement of what was previously a purely intergovernmental procedure. The procedure was invoked by the United Kingdom on behalf of the '"12" European Community States' and the United States in support of investigating attacks on unarmed civilians in Croatia and Bosnia and has also been used by several Eastern European States.[220] Other procedures have also been introduced such as the biennial review meeting, with the authority to draw attention to violations of human rights.

---

[211] See Document of the Copenhagen Meeting of the Conference on the Human Dimension of the Conference for Security and Co-operation in Europe. Adopted by the CSCE at Copenhagen 29 June, 1990. Reprinted 29 I.L.M. (1990) 1305.

[212] See I(1), (2), (3) and (5.1).

[213] See II(9.1).

[214] See II(9.3).

[215] See II(9.5).

[216] See II(9.6).

[217] See IV.

[218] Copenhagen Document, para 43.

[219] See Conference on Security and Co-operation in Europe: Document of the Moscow Meeting on the Human Dimension, Emphasizing Respect for Human Rights, Pluralistic Democracy, the Rule of Law, and Procedures for Fact-Finding, 3 October 1991. Reprinted 30 I.L.M. (1991)1670.

[220] See Brett, above n.194, at p. 682.

The Copenhagen Document was followed by the Paris Charter for a New Europe (the Paris Charter) in 1990.[221] The adoption of the Charter was also accompanied by a number of institutional and structural changes. The Paris Charter has led to the creation of the post of Secretary General and the High Commissioner on National Minorities. It also set up a schedule of meetings, which have led to further developments in the field of human rights. In subsequent years further institutional and procedural developments have taken place. The Office for Free Elections, established in 1990, evolved into the Office for Democratic Institutions of Human Rights (ODHIR), which was given the mandate to provide information on the implementation of human rights within the participating States. ODHIR also maintains a list of experts who can be used for mediation, fact-finding and conciliation purposes. Additionally, a handbook for field personnel is available in respect of how to deal with individual complaints.[222]

The fourth follow-up meeting was held in 1992 in Helsinki, in a politically transformed environment. The break-up of the Soviet Union and the Civil War in Yugoslavia had raised increasing concerns not only over security issues but also on the human rights front. These issues were addressed in the concluding document. In this document minority and group's rights are given distinct recognition and the scope of domestic jurisdiction is further curtailed in so far as the protection of human rights is concerned. The Helsinki Document also established the post of High Commissioner on National Minorities with the primary objective of bringing pressure on States to improve their individual and collective group rights record.[223] As we have already noted, at the beginning of 1995 the Conference, in the light of its achievement, reformed itself to be recognised as an Organisation. The Organisation thereafter formed a Secretariat, Senior Council, Parliamentary Assembly, Conflict Prevention Centre and as already noted, Office for Free Elections (later established as Democratic Institution for Human Rights). In December 1996 the Lisbon Declaration on a Common Comprehensive Security Model for Europe for the Twenty-First Century was adopted. The Declaration affirmed the security of Europe as indivisible as well as of universal concern. A subsequent Declaration was adopted in Istanbul in November 1999. In concluding a two-day seminar the OSCE called for a political settlement of the Chechnya dispute and adopted a Charter for European Security. In the new millennium, the transforming regional and global political geography re-invoked the need for all international organisations, including the OSCE, to revisit existing procedures and strategies. To meet these new challenges, on 7 December 2004, the OSCE Ministerial Council established a Panel of Experts to examine possible steps to strengthen the effectiveness of the OSCE.[224] The Chairman in Office of the OSCE was required to appoint a Panel of Experts which

---

[221] See Conference on Security and Co-operation in Europe adopted at Paris, 21 November. Reprinted 30 I.L.M. (1991)190.

[222] Individual Human Rights Complaints, A Handbook for OSCE Field Personnel, 1 October 2003, www.osce.org/odihr/item_11_13594.html <last visited 4 May 2009>.

[223] See CSCE Helsinki Decisions 31 I.L.M. (1992) 1385; A. de Zayas, 'The International Judicial Protection of Peoples and Minorities' in Brölmann, Lefeber and Zieck, (eds), *Peoples and Minorities in International Law* (Martinus Nijhoff Publishers, 1993) pp. 253–287 at p. 282; Bloed, 'The OSCE and the Issue of National Minorities' in Phillips and Rosas (eds), *Universal Minority Rights* (Åbo Akademi University Institute for Human Rights, Minority Rights Group (International), 1995) pp. 113–122. Post-Helsinki developments an increase in lower-level meetings and the post of Chairman-in-Office (C-i-O) was established. C-i-O position rotates amongst member States annually with the responsibility of coordinating fulfilment of the organisation's responsibility.

[224] OSCE, MC Decision No. 16/04, 7 December 2004.

would deliver a report with appropriate recommendations.[225] The appointed panel presented its report entitled 'Common purpose: Towards a more Effective OSCE' on 3 August 2005. The report was released to the public on 20 June 2005. The report highlights the current limitations of the OSCE with its largely political base. The report recommends structural changes leading to constitutional reforms based on a platform of an internationally binding instrument. Organisational reforms, according to the recommendations, included the setting up of committees – the Security Committee, a Human Dimension Committee and the Economic and Environmental Committee.

The political nature of the OSCE has often been seen as a weakness. However, this, as can be seen through the influence of the High Commissioner of National Minorities' work, in respect of the 'human dimension' has actually been positive. In some areas, the OSCE's work has been ground-breaking, for example the Hague, Oslo and Lund recommendations in respect of national minorities extend extensive rights. Additionally, while the decisions and recommendations of the OSCE are not legally binding, the influence of political pressure should not be underestimated.[226] The flexible nature of the obligations has in actual fact ensured that more States are likely to comply with them.[227]

(i) Human rights involvement through visits

As noted above, human rights protection was not envisaged as a primary function of the work of the CSCE. The past decade has seen a remarkable transformation in the role of the organisation. In this regard a number of procedures have already been referred to, although some mechanisms need a further brief survey. These include the short and long-term visits. In relation to the short-term visits, the OSCE sends a mission to a country to conduct a survey and to report back to the OSCE. Long-term visits are intended to monitor the human rights situation in a country over a period of time. These visits are conducted by around eight individuals nominated by the OSCE, and the visit lasts for up to six months. A number of missions have been conducted including those in Georgia, Estonia, Moldova, Latvia, Tajikistan, Ukraine and Chechnya.

(ii) High Commissioner for National Minorities

One of the most complex problems confronting the CSCE was the subject of minority rights, particularly within Central Europe. The difficulties in addressing the issue of group rights are dealt with in subsequent chapters. Suffice to note that within the United Nations and European human rights system collective group rights are accorded only very limited recognition. The disintegration of the Soviet Union and the escalation of civil wars in many parts of central and Eastern Europe reinvigorated the subject. In order to deal with the situation in 1992, the CSCE established the High Commissioner on National Minorities (HCNM). The primary responsibility of the HCNM is conflict prevention. HCNM is a person of 'eminent international personality . . . from whom an impartial performance of the function may be expected'.[228] HCNM is appointed for a three-year term which is renewable

---

[225] Ibid. para 3.
[226] Pentassuglia, *Minorities in International Law* (Council of Europe Publishing, 2002) p. 144.
[227] Ibid., at p. 144; Eide, 'The Oslo Recommendations regarding the Linguistic Rights of National Minorities: An Overview', 6 *IJMGR* (1999) 319, p. 324
[228] See Helsinki Summit, July 1992 above n.210 (Helsinki) Decision 8.

once.[229] Since his appointment, the HCNM has done a commendable task not only in attempt to resolve disputes but has also been instrumental in easing ethnic, racial and religious tensions in many parts of Central and Eastern Europe. With the involvement of American and United Kingdom forces in Afghanistan, and highly volatile situations developing in States bordering Afghanistan, it would appear that HCNM's role will remain critical in the near future.

On 1 July 2001 Swedish Ambassador Rolf Ekéus replaced the first High Commission Max Vander Stoel and was subsequently replaced by Knut Vollebaek from Norway in July 2007. One of the most significant contributions of the Office of the High Commissioner has been the conclusion of a set of recommendations to further the rights afforded to National Minorities. These are the Hague Recommendations regarding the Educational Rights of National Minorities; the Oslo Recommendations on the Linguistic Rights of National Minorities; and the Lund Recommendations on the Effective Participation of National Minorities in Public Life. While not being legally binding, these documents command a significant amount of political influence, as will be discussed later.[230]

(a) The Office for Democratic Institutions and Human Rights (ODIHR)

The Office for Democratic Institutions and Human Rights has a significant role to play in the establishment of democracy and monitoring of elections. As part of the Human dimension of the OSCE's objectives, the Office acts as the major point for observing and monitoring elections in emerging democracies of the world. Other focus areas include: democratisation; human rights; tolerance and non-discrimination; and Roma and Sinti issues. In addition to assisting participating States in respect of keeping their human dimension obligations, ODIHR also assists OSCE field missions by delivering training and regional coordination. ODIHR also contributes to the early warning and conflict prevention elements of OSCE's work. The Office significantly provides training programmes for developing States in developing election processes.

In respect of human rights ODIHR has two main functions. Firstly, it monitors and reports on States' compliance with their commitments, with emphasis on the areas of the death penalty, the right to liberty and a fair trial, and freedom of assembly and association. Secondly, the Office provides training and education and 'responds to specific concerns such as the protection of human rights in the global fight against terrorism'.[231] Significant work has also been completed in respect of the Roma and Sinti of Europe and tolerance and non-discrimination.

5 CONCLUSIONS

This chapter has analysed the position of three different institutions, all operating in the field of human rights. The comparisons between the work of the ESC and the EU produce interesting results. Since its establishment, the ESC has been operational with an insufficiently effective system of implementation. Two proposals have been put forward to make the system more effective. Firstly, to establish a European Court of Social Rights (similar in line with the European Court of Human Rights) and secondly, to add the rights

---

[229] Ibid. Decision 9.
[230] See below chapter 13.
[231] www.osce.org/odihr/13460.html <last visited 4 May 2009>.

of ESC in the form of an additional protocol to ECHR. Both these proposals have failed to be seriously considered by the Council of Europe. Over the years some positive developments have taken place to improve the implementation mechanism of the ESC through the introduction of a collective complaints procedure. However, judging from the record of the past 40 years, it remains clear that much needs to be done. A more serious threat to the ESC is that it remains undervalued and largely unknown even by European lawyers. By way of contrast to ESC, the EU represents a well established and effective organisation. The growth and expansion of the sphere of the EU in areas affecting economic, social and cultural rights is making it difficult to sustain a largely benign human rights treaty such as the ESC.

The development of OSCE from a purely security focused organisation to an entity which is actively engaged in the promotion and protection of human rights has to be welcomed. The OSCE has set up a number of institutions, which have in a short time proved their worth. A key institution is the HCNM that has raised major security concerns and has engaged in dispute resolution and highlighted major problems faced by the minority groups of the region. Given the recent political events the HCNM will continue to have an important role. The lawlessness in some of the territories of Eastern Europe provides a safe-haven for terrorist organisations to operate; in the 21st century the HCNM as well as the OSCE would have to directly confront the issue of terrorism.[232]

Notwithstanding the expansion and development of the OSCE, the lack of a constitutional founding treaty and a sound constitutional framework continues to undermine the Organisation. There are limitations placed because of a lack of legal rules and, therefore, the international legal personality of the organisation is a subject of contention.[233] This, in turn, leads to the inability to formulate legally binding decisions and instruments. Whilst a constitutional framework through treaty law appears to be a desirable course of action, there is, nevertheless, the risk that many Member States of the existing OSCE may not be willing to enter into such binding arrangements. In addition, and as has been pointed out, there is the risk of overlapping, multiplication of activities, both of the European and international organisations, with possible misuse of resources.[234] Despite the limitations of a political organisation operating in a legal domain, the OSCE carries weight and stature. The range of States including the United States, Canada and Russia and a membership covering the States of Central Asia makes it a vital tool for dealing with global and regional security matters.

---

[232] For further consideration of the subject of terrorism in international human rights law see below chapter 24.
[233] Odello, 'Thirty Years after Helsinki: Proposals for OSCE's Reform' 10 *Journal of Conflict and Security Law* (2005) 435 at 436.
[234] Ibid. at 449.

The inter-American system for the protection of human rights[1]

1 INTRODUCTION

The origins of American Unity and a movement towards humanitarian and libertarian notions date back to the nineteenth century.[2] One of the earliest attempts to forge inter-State co-operation was through the establishment of the International Union of American Republics in 1890. American unity had already been manifested by the proclamation of the so-called Monroe Doctrine, preventing any intervention from Europe in the affairs of the Americas.[3] These expressions of American unity were once more reflected through the establishment of the Pan-American Union at the end of the 19th century. However, it was at the end of the Second World War that real concrete steps were undertaken, insofar as the promotion and protection of human rights was concerned. At the ninth International Conference of American States in Bogotá, Colombia (1948) it was decided to replace the Pan-American Union with the Organisation of American States (OAS).[4] The OAS is a body comparable to the Council of Europe in terms of its institutional work for the promotion and protection of human rights in the Americas.[5]

The constitutional texts of the OAS are reflected through an array of documents. This includes the Charter itself as amended by its four protocols (Buenos Aires (1967),[6]

---

[1] See Harris and Livingstone (eds), *The Inter-American System of Human Rights* (Clarendon Press, 1998); Medina Quiroga, *The Battle of Human Rights: Gross, Systematic Violations and the Inter-American System* (Martinus Nijhoff Publishers, 1988); Buergenthal, 'The Inter-American System for the Protection of Human Rights' in Meron (ed.), *Human Rights in International Law: Legal and Policy Issues* (Clarendon Press, 1984) pp. 439–493; Robertson and Merrills, *Human Rights in the World: An Introduction to the Study of the International Protection of Human Rights* (Manchester University Press, 1996) pp. 197–237; Davidson, *Human Rights* (Open University Press, 1993) pp. 126–151; Buergenthal, 'The Advisory Practice of the Inter-American Human Rights Court' 79 *AJIL* (1985) 1; Buergenthal and Shelton, *Protecting Human Rights in the Americas* (N.P. Engel, 1995); Frost, 'The Evolution of the Inter-American Court of Human Rights: Reflections of Present and Former Judges' 14 *HRQ* (1992) 171; Shelton, 'The Jurisprudence of the Inter-American Court of Human Rights' 10 *AUJILP* (1994) 333; Pasqualucci, *The Practice and Procedure of the Inter-American Court of Human Rights* (Cambridge University Press, 2003).

[2] Robertson and Merrills, above n.1, at p. 197.

[3] Ibid. p. 197.

[4] Charter of the Organization of American States, 119 U.N.T.S. 3, entered into force 13 December 1951. Signed 1948.

[5] For the Council of Europe see chapters 7 and 8.

[6] 721 U.N.T.S. 324, O.A.S. T.S. 1–A (entered into force 27 February 1970). This Protocol incorporated the Inter-American Commission on Human Rights as an organ of the OAS (Article 51).

Cartagena de Indias (1985)[7] Washington (1992)[8] and Managua (1993)).[9] Further substantiation in the human rights field is provided by the American Declaration of the Rights and Duties of Man 1948,[10] the American Convention on Human Rights 1969,[11] the Inter-American Convention to Prevent and Punish Torture (1985),[12] the Additional Protocol to the American Convention on Human Rights in the Area of Economic, Social and Cultural Rights (Pact of San Salvador) (1988),[13] the Protocol to Abolish the Death Penalty (1990),[14] the Inter-American Convention on Forced Disappearance of Persons (1994),[15] the Inter-American Convention on the Prevention, Punishment and Eradication of Violence against Women (1994)[16] and the Inter-American Convention on the Elimination of All Forms of Discrimination Against Persons with Disabilities (1999).[17]

The Inter-American system is rather distinctive from other regional systems in that its origins lie in two distinct though inter-related instruments. Firstly, there is the OAS Charter system of human rights, which relies upon the OAS Charter and the American Declaration on the Rights and Duties of Man. Secondly, human rights protection is provided by the American Convention on Human Rights to those States members of the OAS which have voluntarily become parties to the Convention.[18] The two institutional systems operate through an inter-related organ, the Inter-American Commission on Human Rights. In both instances, the Inter-American Commission is vested with authority to receive communications from individuals and groups alleging violations of human rights contained within the American Declaration or the American Convention on Human Rights.

---

[7] O.A.S. Treaty Series, No. 66, 25 I.L.M. 527, entered into force 16 November 1988.

[8] 1–E Rev. OEA Documentos Oficiales OEA/Ser.A/2 Add. 3 (SEPF), 33 I.L.M. 1005, entered into force 25 September 1997.

[9] 1–F Rev. OEA Documentos Oficiales OEA/Ser.A/2 Add. 4 (SEPF), 33 I.L.M. 1009, entered into force 29 January 1996.

[10] O.A.S. Res. XXX, OAS Doc. OEA/Ser.L.V/II.82 doc.6 rev.1 at 17 (1992).

[11] 'Pact of San Jose, Costa Rica' (B-32) O.A.S. Treaty Series No. 36, 1144 U.N.T.S. 123, entered into force 18 July 1978, reprinted in Basic Documents Pertaining to Human Rights in the Inter-American System, OEA/Ser.L.V/II.82 doc.6 rev.1 at 25 (1992).

[12] (A-51) O.A.S. Treaty Series No. 67, entered into force 28 February 1987, reprinted in Basic Documents Pertaining to Human Rights in the Inter-American System, OEA/Ser.L.V/II.82 doc.6 rev.1 at 83, 25 I.L.M. 519 (1992). See Kaplan, 'Combating Inter-American Convention to Prevent and Punish Torture' 25 *Brooklyn Journal of International Law* (1989) 399; Davidson, 'No More Broken Bodies or Minds: The Definition and Control of Torture in the Late Twentieth Century' 6 *Canterbury Law Review* (1995) 25.

[13] (A-52) O.A.S. Treaty Series No. 69 (1988), signed 17 November 1988, reprinted in Basic Documents Pertaining to Human Rights in the Inter-American System, OEA/Ser.L.V/II.82 doc.6 rev.1 at 67 (1992).

[14] (A-53) Treaty Series No. 73 (1990), adopted June 8, 1990, reprinted in Basic Documents Pertaining to Human Rights in the Inter-American System, OEA/Ser.L.V/II.82 doc.6 rev.1 at 80 (1992).

[15] (A-60) 33 I.L.M.1429 (1994), entered into force 28 March 1996.

[16] 33 I.L.M. 1534 (1994), entered into force 5 March 1995. Note further the existence of a specialised organisation of the OAS – the Inter-American Commission of Women. The body dates back to the 1928 Sixth International Conference of American States (Havana). Each member of the OAS contributes one delegate to the organisation which meets once every two years. The objectives of the organisation include the promotion and protection of women's rights and the promotion of equality of participation in all aspects of life. On the subject of discrimination against women in Americans see Medina, 'Towards a More Effective Guarantee of the Enjoyment of Human Rights by Women in the Inter-American System' in Cook (ed.), *Human Rights of Women: National and International Perspectives* (University of Pennsylvania Press, 1994) pp. 257–284.

[17] AG/RES. 1608, 7 June 1999.

[18] It needs to be noted that there is no obligation on OAS Member States to becoming parties to ACHR. Out of the 35 OAS members, 10 have not become parties to the Convention.

2 THE OAS CHARTER SYSTEM AND THE AMERICAN DECLARATION OF THE RIGHTS AND DUTIES OF MAN

The OAS is a regional organisation and comes within the ambit of a regional organisation as provided in Article 52 of the United Nations Charter.[19] The OAS Charter system has similarities with that of the UN system.[20] Like the UN Charter, the OAS Charter contains a number of references to human or fundamental rights. According to Article 3(l) 'the American States proclaim the fundamental rights of the individual without distinction as to race, nationality, creed or sex'. Article 17 of the Charter goes on to provide that:

> [e]ach State has the right to develop its cultural, political, and economic life freely and naturally. In this free development, the State shall respect the rights of the individual and the principles of universal morality.

The Charter does not elaborate upon the meaning of the term 'rights of the individual' as used in Articles 3(1) and 17. The task of expanding on the meaning of human rights was undertaken by a declaration, the American Declaration of the Rights and Duties of Man, which was adopted at the same time as the adoption of the Charter.[21] This Declaration contains a variety of rights and also provides a set of duties of the individual towards the society. The following rights and duties are contained within the Declaration:

Article I	Right to life, liberty and personal security
Article II	Right to equality before law
Article III	Right to religious freedom and worship
Article IV	Right to freedom of investigation, opinion, expression and dissemination
Article V	Right to protection of honor, personal reputation, and private and family life
Article VI	Right to a family and to protection thereof
Article VII	Right to protection for mothers and children
Article VIII	Right to residence and movement
Article IX	Right to inviolability of the home
Article X	Right to the inviolability and transmission of correspondence
Article XI	Right to the preservation of health and to well-being
Article XII	Right to education
Article XIII	Right to the benefits of culture
Article XIV	Right to work and to fair remuneration
Article XV	Right to leisure time and to the use thereof
Article XVI	Right to social security
Article XVII	Right to recognition of juridical personality and civil rights

[19] As at 1 January 2009, the OAS consisted of 35 Member States. It is open to all American State, though Cuba is excluded from taking part in the system; see at Pasqualucci, above n.1, at p. 2.
[20] Davidson, above n.1, at p. 127; also see Gomez, 'The Interaction between the Political Actors of the OAS, the Commission and the Court' in Harris and Livingstone (eds), above n.1, pp. 173–211.
[21] American Declaration of the Rights and Duties of Man, O.A.S. Res. XXX, OAS Doc. OEA/Ser.L.V/II.82 doc.6 rev.1 at 17 (1992).

9

The inter-American system for the protection of human rights

Article XVIII	Right to a fair trial
Article XIX	Right to nationality
Article XX	Right to vote and to participate in government
Article XXI	Right of assembly
Article XXII	Right of association
Article XXIII	Right to property
Article XXIV	Right of petition
Article XXV	Right of protection from arbitrary arrest
Article XXVI	Right to due process of law
Article XXVII	Right of asylum
Article XXVIII	Scope of the rights of man
Article XXIX	Duties to society
Article XXX	Duties toward children and parents
Article XXXI	Duty to receive instruction
Article XXXII	Duty to vote
Article XXXIII	Duty to obey the law
Article XXXIV	Duty to serve the community and the nation
Article XXXV	Duties with respect to social security and welfare
Article XXXVI	Duty to pay taxes
Article XXXVII	Duty to work
Article XXXVIII	Duty to refrain from political activities in a foreign country

The role and position of the Declaration is comparable to UDHR.[22] Both the documents were drafted after the atrocities of the Second World War and attempt to uphold liberal democratic traditions of fundamental human rights. Amongst the significant differences is the list of duties for the individual contained in the American Declaration. The American Declaration (like the UDHR) was not intended to be legally binding. Like the UDHR, the legal status of the American Declaration has been a matter of some debate.

Both the Inter-American Commission on Human Rights and Inter-American Court of Human Rights have treated the Declaration as an authoritative interpretation of the Charter and thus having a binding effect. The Court in its Advisory Opinion No. 10[23] observed that:

> by means of an authoritative interpretation, the member states of the Organization have signaled their agreement that the Declaration contains and defines the fundamental rights referred to in the Charter. Thus the Charter of the Organization cannot be interpreted and applied as far as human rights are concerned without relating its norms, consistent with the practice of the organs of the OAS, to the corresponding provisions of the Declaration . . . [and that] for the member states of the Organization, the Declaration is the text that defines the human rights referred to in the Charter.[24]

[22] See above chapter 4. The American Declaration of Human Rights however was adopted seven months before the adoption of the UDHR.

[23] *Interpretation of the American Declaration of the Rights and Duties of Man Within the Framework of Article 64 of the American Convention on Human Rights*, Advisory Opinion OC-10/89, 14 July 1989, Inter-Am. Ct. H.R. (Ser. A) No. 10 (1989).

[24] Ibid. paras 43 and 45.

The Court in this opinion was inclined to take this view primarily because of the recognised position of the American Declaration in the revised Statute of the Inter-American Commission which places the Declaration *at par* with ACHR.[25] At the same time, such an elevated status for the Declaration has generated criticism from States which only accepted the Declaration considering it as a political statement rather than a legally binding instrument. The continuous objections from these States also make it difficult to establish the view that the Declaration represents regional customary law.[26]

3 THE INTER-AMERICAN COMMISSION ON HUMAN RIGHTS

(i) Background: one commission for the two systems

The jurisdiction of the Inter-American Commission on Human Rights extends to all OAS Member States. The Commission, which was established in 1959, is a product not of a binding treaty agreement but of a resolution of a consultation meeting between foreign affairs ministers.[27] The Commission started its work in May 1960 in pursuance of its Statute which was adopted the same year.[28] The Statute, as noted above, considered that the American Declaration provided a detailed expression of human rights. Although mandated since 1965 (with the addition of a new Article 9) to receive and deal with individual communications, the Commission concentrated on its advisory and recommendatory role. There remained reluctance towards the consideration of individual applications and the justification presented was that its sources and influence could be more effectively utilised in identifying human rights violations, holding meetings in any Member State of the OAS, and conducting on-site investigations leading to country studies.[29]

For several years after its creation, the status and position of the Inter-American Commission remained unclear. The Statute of the Commission defines it as an 'autonomous entity' of the OAS. It, therefore, meant that the Statute failed to provide the Commission with any exact legal status. This position was rectified by the Buenos Aires Protocol of 1967 which in amending the OAS Charter recognised the Commission as one of the 'principal organs'[30] of the organisation, through which it aimed to attain its purposes. The revised Charter came into operation in 1970.

With the Inter-American Commission becoming an institutional organ of the OAS Charter, the debate on the content of human rights and in particular the value of the

---

[25] Article (1)2 provided 'For the purposes of the present Statute, human rights are understood to be (a) The rights set forth in the American Convention on Human Rights, in relation to the States Parties thereto (b) The rights set forth in the American Declaration of the Rights and Duties of Man, in relation to the other member states'.

[26] For elaboration on customary law, see above chapter 2.

[27] See Resolution VIII of the Fifth Meeting of Consultation of Ministers of Foreign Affairs, Final Act, Santiago, Chile (12–18) August 1959. OAS. Off Rec. OEA/Ser F/II.5 (Doc. 89, English, Rev. 2) October, 1959 at 10–11. Available at www.oas.org/consejo/MEETINGS%20OF%20CONSULTATION/Actas/Acta%205.pdf <last visited 3 November 2007>; Tomuschat, *Human Rights: Between Idealism and Realism* (Oxford University Press, 2008) at p. 200; Robertson, 'Revision of the Charter of the Organisation of American States' 17 *ICLQ* (1968) 346.

[28] Statute of the Inter-American Commission on Human Rights, Basic Documents Pertaining to Human Rights in the Inter-American System, OEA/Ser.L/V/II.92, doc.31 rev.3, 3 May 1996.

[29] Cerna, 'The Inter-American Commission on Human Rights: Its Organisation and Examination of Petitions and Communications' in Harris and Livingstone (eds), above, n.1, 65–113 at p. 67.

[30] See Articles 53 and 106 OAS Charter.

ADHR was intensified.[31] It was also not clear whether there would be two Commissions in operation catering independently for the OAS Charter system and the American Convention respectively. The Inter-American Commission's new Statute (which came into force in 1979, following the coming into operation of the ACHR) confirmed the existence of a single Commission to serve both the OAS Charter and the American Convention.[32] Article 1(2) of the Commission's Statute provides:

> For the purposes of the present Statute, human rights are understood to be:
>
> (a) The rights set forth in the American Convention on Human Rights in relation to the States Parties thereto;
>
> (b) The rights set forth in the American Declaration of the Rights and Duties of Man, in relation to the other member states.

This meant firstly that all member States of OAS not party to ACHR continued to be bound by the standards of the Charter. Secondly, the mechanisms established by the Commission as a Charter institution were preserved. This also provided a treaty-like status to the American Declaration. The Commission also has a specific mandate to oversee all human rights obligations undertaken by OAS States.[33]

(ii) Structure and organisation of the Commission

According to Article 34 and 35 of the ACHR, the Commission comprises seven members who are nationals of the OAS. The members of the Commission must be people who have a 'high moral character with recognised competence in the field of human rights'.[34] They serve in their personal capacity for a period of four years and may be re-elected but only on one occasion. Members act in an independent capacity and not as State representatives.[35] Although not a requirement, most members have a legal background. The Commission represents all members of the OAS, and is not confined to the States parties of the ACHR.[36]

Members of the Commission are elected by the General Assembly of the OAS. The procedure for the election of members of the Commission requires that at least six months prior to the completion of the term of office of the member, the Secretary General is required to request that each member of the OAS, in writing, propose its list of candidates within 90 days.[37] Each government may propose up to three candidates who may be nationals of their own State or any other Member State. If three names are put forward then at least one is required to be a non-national.[38] Members are then elected by a secret ballot,

---

[31] Article 106 of the revised Charter provided that 'an inter-American convention on human rights shall determine the structure, competence and procedure of this [Inter-American] Commission, as well as those of other organs responsible for these matters'.

[32] *Statute of the Inter-American Commission on Human Rights, Basic Documents Pertaining to Human Rights in the Inter-American System*, OEA/Ser.L/V/II.92, doc.31 rev.3, 3 May 1996. See Norris, 'The New Statute of the Inter-American Commission on Human Rights' 1 *HRLJ* (1980) 379.

[33] Shelton, *Remedies in International Human Rights Law* (Oxford University Press, 1999) p. 122.

[34] Article 34 and 35 ACHR; Article 2(1) Statute of the Commission.

[35] Article 34 ACHR; Article 2(2) Statute of the Commission.

[36] Article 35 ACHR.

[37] Article 4(1) of Statute of the Commission.

[38] Ibid. Article 3(2).

with the candidates obtaining the highest number of votes being declared elected.[39] The Commission is supported by a secretariat, which carries out its day-to-day work. It prepares the working programme for each session and implements the Commission's decisions. It also prepares the draft reports and resolutions.

The Commission's sessions are held generally in Washington, but may also be held in any other member state of the OAS. The ordinary sessions are held twice every year, each session lasts for three weeks, during the course of which individual communications are given consideration.[40] In addition, there are also one or two extraordinary sessions each year. During the proceedings of the Commission oral hearings are conducted, during which representations can be made by individuals and NGOs.[41] The role and functions of the Commission are described in Articles 41 of ACHR which provides that:

[t]he main function of the Commission shall be to promote respect for and defense of human rights. In the exercise of its mandate, it shall have the following functions and powers:

(a) to develop an awareness of human rights among the peoples of America;

(b) to make recommendations to the governments of the member states, when it considers such action advisable, for the adoption of progressive measures in favor of human rights within the framework of their domestic law and constitutional provisions as well as appropriate measures to further the observance of those rights;

(c) to prepare such studies or reports as it considers advisable in the performance of its duties;

(d) to request the governments of the member states to supply it with information on the measures adopted by them in matters of human rights;

(e) to respond, through the General Secretariat of the Organization of American States, to inquiries made by the member states on matters related to human rights and, within the limits of its possibilities, to provide those states with the advisory services they request;

(f) to take action on petitions and other communications pursuant to its authority under the provisions of Articles 44 through 51 of this Convention; and

(g) to submit an annual report to the General Assembly of the Organization of American States.

These are the functions which the Commission used to perform prior to the ACHR becoming effective. As is evident, these are of a promotional character which includes making recommendations to member governments and requesting information on the human rights issues. The Commission also has the authority to prepare reports on human rights situation in any State of the OAS, and can use information from individuals and NGOs to prepare such reports. It submits annual reports to the OAS General Assembly, which includes resolutions on individual cases, reports on various States and recommendations for progress in human rights situations.[42] Articles 44–47 relate to those functions which

---

[39] Ibid. Article 5.

[40] Cerna, 'The Inter-American Commission on Human Rights: Its Organisation and Examination of Petitions and Communications' in Harris and Livingstone (eds), above n.1, 65–113 at p. 74.

[41] Shelton, above n.33, p. 122.

[42] Ibid. p. 122.

The inter-American system for the protection of human rights

apply specifically to the States parties to the ACHR. They focus on the individual and inter-State complaints procedures, specifically the competence of the Commission.

(iii) Complaints procedure

The procedure for acting upon individual complaints from the OAS Charter system and ACHR systems can be found in different sources. In the case of OAS Charter system the complaints procedure is provided by Articles 26–48 of the Commission's Rules of Procedure[43] whereas the complaint procedures under the ACHR is contained in Articles 44–55 of the Convention. Notwithstanding these sources, the actual practice of the Commission is similar although differences can be found in the post-admissibility stages. The differences result from the institutional structuring of the two institutions. While in the case of ACHR, the Commission has the option of transmitting cases to the Court, providing the relevant State has accepted the jurisdiction of the Court,[44] but no such possibilities exist in the case of the OAS Charter system. The absence of the Court also means that the final decisions in the OAS Charter systems are made by the Commission. The Commission (unlike the Court) cannot dispense legally binding judgments. Secondly, unlike the ACHR system, no obligations exist for the Commission to secure a friendly settlement.[45]

4 THE AMERICAN CONVENTION ON HUMAN RIGHTS (ACHR)

The ACHR (also known as the Pact of San José) alongside its protocols represents the second part of the inter-American Human Rights System. ACHR was adopted in 1969 and entered into force in 1978.[46] In 1988, an additional protocol was concluded extending its range of rights covered. In 1990, the death penalty was abolished through the addition of another protocol. There have been several sources of inspiration for the ACHR, including the ECHR and the ICCPR.[47] In terms of the implementation mechanisms, similarities could be traced between the European Convention and its American counterpart. At the time of its inception, the ACHR followed the pattern of the ECHR, being managed by a Commission and Court. Whereas, as noted earlier, the European Commission was abolished after the coming into operation of the 11th Protocol, the ACHR continues to rely upon its Commission and Court. The functions of the Inter-American Commission include admissibility and a possible friendly settlement. The recommendations of the Inter-American Commission are conducted on merit but are not legally binding. The functions of the Court are largely of a judicial decision-making nature. There are two processes of complaint allowed by the

---

[43] Rules of Procedure of the Inter-American Commission on Human Rights, reprinted in *Basic Documents Pertaining to Human Rights in the Inter-American System*, OAS/Ser.L/V/I.4 rev.12, 31 January 2007, Chapter II, Articles 26–48.

[44] Article 62 ACHR.

[45] Davidson, above n.1, at p. 135.

[46] As at 15 May 2009, 25 of the 35 members of the OAS have ratified the ACHR.

[47] It is, however, interesting to note a number of differences between ACHR and ICCPR. In the ACHR, there is no counterpart of Article 27 ICCPR; there are, however, no equivalent articles in ICCPR to right of reply (Article 14); right to property (Article 21); freedom from exile (Article 22(5)) and the right to asylum (Article 22(7)); and prohibition of the 'collective expulsion of aliens' (Article 21(9)).

Convention. Firstly, there is the contentious procedure which allows both individuals (and other non-State actors) to institute proceedings against a State party to the Convention and the inter-State complaints procedure. Secondly, there is the possibility of invoking the advisory jurisdiction of the Court.

In the light of the influence of the comparable international and regional human rights instruments, it is not surprising that many of the rights contained in the American Convention overlap or relate very closely to that of other regional and international human rights treaties. The ACHR contains traditional civil and political rights as well as economic, social and cultural rights. Many similarities can be found between the rights contained in the Convention, the International Covenants and the ECHR, although there are a number of significant differences. The ACHR contains a number of rights, not found in either the International Covenants or the ECHR. Having said that, the anticipation with which they will be implemented is more or less the same as with other international covenants.[48] The economic rights contained in the ACHR are supplemented by the Protocol. It is interesting to note that the differences in implementation follow the pattern of International Covenants and European Human Rights System. According to Article 1(1) of the ACHR States parties are to 'respect the rights and freedoms' and to 'ensure to all persons subject to their jurisdiction the free and full exercise of those rights and freedoms'. By contrast, Article 1 of the Additional Protocol to the American Convention on Human Rights in the area of Economic, Social and Cultural Rights (the Protocol of San Salvador) provides that the States parties take appropriate measure 'for the purpose of achieving progressively . . . the full observance of the rights recognized in the protocol'.

The following rights are contained in the Convention:

Article 3	Right to Juridical Personality
Article 4	Right to Life
Article 5	Right to Humane Treatment
Article 6	Freedom from Slavery
Article 7	Right to Personal Liberty
Article 8	Right to a Fair Trial
Article 9	Freedom from Ex post Facto Laws
Article 10	Right to Compensation
Article 11	Right to Privacy
Article 12	Freedom of Conscience and Religion
Article 13	Freedom of Thought and Expression
Article 14	Right of Reply
Article 15	Freedom of Assembly
Article 16	Freedom of Association
Article 17	Rights of the Family
Article 18	Right to a Name
Article 19	Rights of the Child
Article 20	Right to Nationality

[48] Davidson above n.1, at pp. 136–137.

5 ANALYSIS OF SUBSTANTIVE RIGHTS

(i) Right to life, liberty, the prohibition of enforced disappearances and torture

Article 4 protects the fundamental right to life. Article 4(1) provides that '[e]very person has the right to have his life respected'. The remainder of the Article however raises a number of issues without providing any definitive statement. It notes that the right to life 'shall be protected by law and, in general, from the moment of conception'. The question as to whether abortion is a violation of the Convention has been considered by the Inter-American Commission in a case arising from the United States, which is not a party to the Convention. After considering the *travaux préparatoires* of the American Declaration, the Commission concluded that the abortion of a foetus did not lead to a violation of the Declaration. The Commission also held *obiter* that the term 'in general' allowed discretion to States to determine the validity of their respective abortion laws.[49]

Article 4(1), like Article 6(1) of the ICCPR, goes on to prohibit the 'arbitrary' taking of life. The Inter-American Court has adopted a strict approach that 'arbitrary' means that any taking of life must not be the result of a disproportionate use of force by public authorities.[50] In line with the ECHR, the Inter-American Court has pronounced on the existence of both a positive and negative obligation on State parties.[51] Like the ICCPR, Article 4(2) represents what has been described as an 'abolitionist trend'.[52] It allows the death penalty only for the most serious offences, with a prohibition on the reintroduction of this penalty in States which have already abolished capital punishment and the prohibition of its extension to crimes which it currently does not apply. Article 4(4) provides that in 'no case shall capital punishment be inflicted for political offences or related common crimes'. This is an unusual provision and as Sapienza notes, its background can be traced to the spirit of co-operation in political matters existing in Latin America.[53] The move towards abolition of capital punishment was further reinforced through the adoption of the protocol to the American Convention on Human Rights to Abolish the Death Penalty (1990).

---

[49] See the *Baby Boy*, Case No. 2141 (United States), Res. 23/81, OEA/Ser. L/V/II.54, Doc. 9, rev. 1, 16 October 1981. For commentary on the case see Shelton, 'Abortion and the Right to Life in the Inter-American System: The Case of "Baby Boy"' 2 *HRLJ* (1981) 309; on the situation of States within the OAS see Schabas, 'Canadian Ratification of the American Convention on Human Rights' 16 *NQHR* (1998) 315.

[50] *Neira Alegria Case*, Judgment of 19 January 1995, Inter-Am.Ct.H.R. (Ser. C) No. 20 (1995), para 76.

[51] *Velásquez Rodríguez* Case, Judgment of 29 July 1988, Inter-Am.Ct.H.R. (Ser. C) No. 4 (1988), para 154.

[52] Davidson, 'The Civil and Political Rights Protected in the Inter-American Human Rights System' in Harris and Livingstone (eds), above n.1, 213–288 at p. 222.

[53] Sapienza, 'International Legal Standards on Capital Punishment' in Ramcharan (ed.), *The Right to Life in International Law* (Martinus Nijhoff Publishers, 1985) pp. 284–296, at p. 292.

In recognising the relevance of the right to life and restrictions on the application of the death penalty, in accordance with the provisions of Article 1 of the Protocol, States parties undertake not to apply 'the death penalty in their territory to any person subject to the jurisdiction'.[54] While no reservations to the Protocol are permissible, the instrument does allow State parties to reserve a right to apply the death penalty during war. However such an application needs to adhere strictly with the norms of international law and only for extremely serious crimes of a military nature.[55]

Enforced disappearances have been a recurrent theme in the unfortunate history of the States of Latin America and, in fact, led referrals by the Commission to the Inter-American Court in three contentious cases against Honduras. *Velásquez Rodríguez*, the first contentious case brought before the Inter-American Court of Human Rights, related to torture and enforced disappearance. As our discussion in a subsequent chapter confirms, the case and the judgment from this case has been of major significance in developing international standards on enforced disappearances.[56]

The Inter-American institutions have included the phenomenon of enforced disappearances as representing acts of torture or cruel, inhuman or degrading punishment or treatment.[57] Similarly prolonged periods of incommunicado detention,[58] rape,[59] the putting of hoods on the victims so as to suffocate them,[60] mock burials and mock executions,[61] and enforcement of malnutrition and starvation[62] have been categorised as torture. As already noted, the OAS system in recognising the significance of prohibiting, condemning and punishing all forms of torture adopted a regional convention in 1985.[63] Article 2 of the Convention defines torture as follows:

> For the purposes of this Convention, torture shall be understood to be any act intentionally performed whereby physical or mental pain or suffering is inflicted on a person for purposes of criminal investigation, as a means of intimidation, as personal punishment, as a preventive measure, as a penalty, or for any other purpose. Torture shall also be understood to be the use of methods upon a person intended to obliterate the personality of the victim or to diminish his physical or mental capacities, even if they do not cause physical pain or mental anguish.
>
> The concept of torture shall not include physical or mental pain or suffering that is inherent in or solely the consequence of lawful measures, provided that they do not include the performance of the acts or use of the methods referred to in this article.

---

[54] Article 1, Protocol to the American Convention on Human Rights to Abolish the Death Penalty (1990).

[55] Article 2(1), Protocol to the American Convention on Human Rights to Abolish the Death Penalty (1990).

[56] See below chapter 23.

[57] See *Lissardi and Rossi* v. *Guatemala*, Case 10.508, Report No. 25/94, Inter-Am.C.H.R., OEA/Ser.L/V/II.88 rev.1 Doc. 9 at 51 (1995).

[58] *Velásquez Rodríguez* Case, Judgment of 29 July 1988, Inter-Am.Ct.H.R. (Ser. C) No. 4 (1988).

[59] *Caracoles Community* v. *Bolivia*, Case 7481, Res. No. 30/82, March 8, 1982, OAS/Ser.L/V/II.57, Doc. 6 Rev. 1, at 20 September 1982, at 36 and *Raquel Martí de Mejía* v. *Perú*, Case 10.970, Report No. 5/96, Inter-Am.C.H.R., OEA/Ser.L/V/II.91 Doc. 7 at 157 (1996).

[60] *Lovato* v. *El Salvador*, Case 10.574, Report No. 5/94, Inter-Am.C.H.R., OEA/Ser.L/V/II.85 Doc. 9 rev. at 174 (1994).

[61] *Solano* v. *Bolivia*, Case No. 7823, Res. No. 32/82, Inter-Am.C.H.R., OEA/Ser.L/V/II.57, Doc. 6 Rev. 1.

[62] *Ruben Luis Romero Eguino* v. *Bolivia*, Case 2720, Inter-Am. C.H.R. 56, OEA/ser. L/V/II.47, doc.13 rev.1 (1979) (Annual Report 1978).

[63] See Kaplan, above n.12, at p. 399; Davidson, above n.12, at p. 25.

The Inter-American Commission (unlike the ECHR) has not distinguished between torture, inhuman and degrading treatment.[64] In a case relating to rape, in elaborating upon the meaning of torture, the Inter-American Commission has noted that there should be *mens rea* and *actus reas*, and that the act must be committed either by a public official or by an individual at the instigation of an officer.[65]

Enforced disappearances bear a strong relationship not only with torture, but an essential prerequisite to these disappearances are loss of personal liberty and inhumane treatment. The ACHR protects both the right to personal liberty and security[66] and provides for a right to humane treatment.[67] Article 7, while according the right to personal liberty, prohibits arbitrary arrests, imprisonment and loss of liberty, save for reasons established by law. Whereas the right to liberty is breached in the absence of lawful arrests[68] and for failure to comply with national laws,[69] the right to security is violated by threatening individuals with arbitrary arrest and detention.[70]

(ii) Equality and non-discrimination

Article 1(1), in placing obligations on States parties, provides for the State to respect the rights of all persons and to ensure to all persons

> subject to their jurisdiction the free and full exercise of those rights and freedoms, without any discrimination for reasons of race, color, sex, language, religion, political or other opinion, national or social origin, economic status, birth, or any other social condition.

The obligations in the Article are further reinforced through the provisions of Article 24, which affirms that 'all persons are equal before the law. Consequently, they are entitled, without discrimination, to equal protection of the law'. Equality, as is emphasised throughout this book, is the norm with the *jus cogens* character. This Article prohibits discriminatory practices in the provision of rights contained in the Convention and no derogations are permissible from the norm of non-discrimination. The value behind this principle of equality and non-discrimination was reiterated by the American Court in Advisory Opinion No. 4 Proposed Amendment to Naturalisation Provisions of the Political Constitution of Costa Rica[71] when it stated 'equality springs directly from the oneness of the human family and is linked to the essential dignity of the individual'.[72]

---

[64] Davidson, 'The Civil and Political Rights Protected in the Inter-American Human Rights System' in Harris and Livingstone (eds), above n.1, 213–288, at p. 230.
[65] *Raquel Martí de Mejía* v. *Perú*, Case 10.970, Report No. 5/96, Inter-Am. C.H.R., OEA/Ser.L/V/II.91 Doc. 7 at 157 (1996), at 182–188.
[66] Article 7.
[67] Article 5. According to Article 5(1) 'Every person has the right to have his physical, mental, and moral integrity respected'.
[68] Article 7(2).
[69] *Gangaram Panday Case*, Judgment of 21 January 1994, Inter-Am. Ct. H.R. (Ser. C) No. 16 (1994), para 47.
[70] *Garcia* v. *Peru*, Case 11.006, Report No. 1/95, Inter-Am. C.H.R., OEA/Ser.L/V/II.88 rev.1 Doc. 9 at 71 (1995).
[71] *Proposed Amendments to the Naturalization Provisions of the Constitution of Costa Rica*, Advisory Opinion OC-4/84, 19 January 1984, Inter-Am. Ct. H.R. (Ser. A) No. 4 (1984).
[72] Ibid. para 55.

The Court went on to approve the affirmative action policies in order to generate *de facto* equality and cited with approval the European Court of Human Rights in the *Belgian Linguistic Case*.[73]

Equality before the law has a substantial association with principles of natural justice, and most significantly to the right to fair trial, a right protected by Article 8 of the Convention. Article 8(1) in providing the right to fair trial states:

> Every person has the right to a hearing, with due guarantees and within a reasonable time, by a competent, independent, and impartial tribunal, previously established by law, in the substantiation of any accusation of a criminal nature made against him or for the determination of his rights and obligations of a civil, labor, fiscal, or any other nature.

The right to fair trial also includes in criminal cases a right to be presumed innocent until proven guilty.[74] It also incorporates the right of the accused to be assisted without charge for an interpreter,[75] prior notification of the charge,[76] adequate time and means for the preparation of defence,[77] right of assistance through counsel,[78] the right to examine witnesses and to obtain the appearance of witnesses of experts,[79] the right not to be compelled to be a witness against himself[80] (or not to make confession through coercion)[81] and a right to appeal.[82] The right to fair trial provides guarantees against the rule of double jeopardy,[83] and ensures that the trial should be held in public unless it is necessary to protect the interests of justice.[84] The right to fair trial is strengthened by Article 10 which provides that '[e]very person has the right to be compensated in accordance with the law in the event he has been sentenced by a final judgment through a miscarriage of justice'.

(iii) Privacy, religion, thought, expression, assembly and association

This section considers a number of rights which are distinct from one another though with overlapping features. Freedom of religion is inextricably related to freedom of thought and expression. A similar relationship could be found in cases of freedom of assembly and association. The right to privacy and honour is protected by Article 11 of the Convention.

---

[73] *Belgian Linguistic Case (No. 2)* (1979–1980) 1 E.H.R.R. 252. The European Court of Human Rights, 'following the principles which may be extracted from the legal practice of a large number of democratic States', has held that a difference in treatment is only discriminatory when it 'has no objective and reasonable justification', cited ibid. para 56. For further discussion on the European Convention jurisprudence see chapter 7 above.

[74] Article 8(2) ACHR.

[75] Ibid. Article 8(2)(a).

[76] Ibid. Article 8(2)(b).

[77] Ibid. Article 8(2)(c).

[78] Ibid. Article 8(2)(e).

[79] Ibid. Article 8(2)(f).

[80] Ibid. Article 8(2)(g).

[81] Ibid. Article 8(3).

[82] Ibid. Article 8(2)(h).

[83] Ibid. Article 8(4).

[84] Ibid. Article 8(5).

The violation of honour, according to the American Commission, represents not only moral and spiritual indignation, but could also include physical abuse.[85] Article 11 bears similarities to Article 8 of ECHR, and the Inter-American Commission has been influenced in its approach by the decision of the European Court of Human Rights. Although the ACHR, unlike the ECHR, does not provide an explicit clause justifying restrictions based on public interest, national security or public safety, such restrictions are implied in the provisions of the Article, and would be authorised by the Commission. Articles 12 and 13 in granting freedom of religion and thought are more explicit in recognising the authority of the State to place limitations. At the same time the Commission and Court have made it clear that any discretion given to the State has to be construed narrowly.[86] Pursing this line of narrowly construed discretion, the Court found that the practice of compulsory licensing of journalists in Costa Rica could not be justified on grounds of public order.[87]

(iv) Specialist rights

The ACHR contains a number of rights which have been of special concern for States from the Americas. Amongst these can be included the right to reply, and the right to name. Article 18 represents an interesting provision and in conferring the right to name, notes:

> Every person has the right to a given name and to the surnames of his parents or that of one of them. The law shall regulate the manner in which this right shall be ensured for all, by the use of assumed names if necessary.

Although the right to name is provided for in other international instruments, the inclusion of this right has been campaigned for particularly strongly by Latin American States. As we shall consider in due course, the incorporation of the Article relating to the right to identity, in the Convention on the Rights of the Child, was introduced by Argentina. Argentina campaigned for the incorporation of the right to identity as a reaction to its so-called 'dirty war'.[88] These exact sentiments were no doubt the driving force for the incorporation of this right in the ACHR. The American Commission has confirmed the relevance of this

---

[85] See *Rivas v. El Salvador*, Case 10.772, Report No. 6/94, Inter-Am. C.H.R., OEA/Ser.L/V/II.85 Doc. 9 rev. at 181 (1994). Discussed by S. Davidson, 'The Civil and Political Rights Protected in the Inter-American Human Rights System' in D.J. Harris and S. Livingstone (eds), above n.1, 213–288 at p. 256.

[86] See *Steve Clark v. Grenada*, Case 10.325, Report No. 2/96, Inter-Am. C.H.R., OEA/Ser.L/V/II.91 Doc. 7 at 113 (1996).

[87] *Compulsory Membership in an Association Prescribed by Law for the Practice of Journalism* (Arts. 13 and 29 of the American Convention on Human Rights), Advisory Opinion OC-5/85, 13 November 1985, Inter-Am. Ct. H.R. (Ser. A) No. 5 (1985), para 76. The Court also stated that the profession of journalism is in itself indistinguishable from the right to freedom of expression and, therefore, the profession itself is protected by the Convention, para 74. Also see *Nicolas Estiverne v. Haiti*, Case 9.855, Res. No. 20/88, Inter-Am. C.H.R., OEA/Ser.L/V/II.74, Doc. 10 rev.1, 24 March 1988, at 146; *Spadafora Franco v. Panama*, Case 9.726, Res. No. 25/87, Inter-Am. C.H.R., OEA/Ser.L/V/II.74, Doc. 10 rev.1, 23 September 1987 at 174.

[88] Fottrell, 'Children's Rights' in Hegarty and Leonard (eds), *Human Rights: An Agenda for the Twenty First Century* (Cavendish, 1999) pp. 167–179 at p. 172; Freestone, 'The United Nations Convention on the Rights of the Child' in Freestone (ed.), *Children and the Law: Essays in Honour of Professor H.K. Bevan* (Hull University Press, 1990) pp. 288–323 at p. 290. See chapter 16.

Article to Argentina by holding that the irregular adoption of the children of *desaparecidos*, disappearances and kidnapping violated Article 18.[89]

The right to property as an important right is contained in Article 21.[90] This right is contained in the UDHR,[91] the first Protocol of the ECHR[92] and the African Charter on Human and Peoples' Rights,[93] although due to a number of controversies could not be included in the international covenants. This provision is extremely useful for a region which has been vulnerable to denial of property rights, expropriation and nationalisation. The American Commission has accorded this right a special significance and has regarded it as being of great value for the enjoyment of other human rights.[94] As regards compensation ACHR Article 21(2) provides: 'No one shall be deprived of his property except upon payment of just compensation, for reasons of public utility or social interest, and in the cases and according to the forms established by law'. It is significant to note that the provisions call for 'just' compensation as opposed to 'full compensation' which points to less than full value of the property.[95]

While the overall rationale behind an Article dealing with the right to property appears acceptable, what is less certain is the inclusion of Article 21(3) which provides that '[u]sury and any other form of exploitation of man by man shall be prohibited by law'. This 'remarkable clause' was introduced by Honduras and accepted without any opposition. The reason for the inclusion of the provision appears to have been to prevent usury on tangible property and in the process to prevent exploitation by men against one another.[96] Nevertheless, the article perhaps appears more in tune with the values put forward by Islamic States on the prohibition of *riba*,[97] as opposed to the American States.[98]

The right to freedom of movement and residence also signifies a useful right, and is represented in other international human rights instruments. Of particular value in the context of the Americas, is the provision of the right to seek and gain asylum.[99] The *Asylum Case*

---

[89] See IACHR, 'A Study about the Situation of Minor Children who were Separated from their Parents and are claimed by Members of their Legitimate Families' [1988] *Inter-American Yearbook on Human Rights* 476 at 480.

[90] Article 21(1) provides as follows: 'Everyone has the right to the use and enjoyment of his property. The law may subordinate such use and enjoyment to the interest of society'. According to Article 21(2): 'No one shall be deprived of his property except upon payment of just compensation, for reasons of public utility or social interest, and in the cases and according to the forms established by law'.

[91] Article 17(1) provides that everyone has the right to own property alone as well as in association with others. Article 17(2) provides that no one shall be arbitrarily deprived of his property. On the UDHR see above chapter 4.

[92] According to Article 1 of Protocol 1 ECHR: 'Every natural or legal person is entitled to the peaceful enjoyment of his possessions. No one shall be deprived of his possessions except in the public interest and subject to the conditions provided for by law and by the general principles of international law'. See above chapter 7.

[93] Article 14 provides: 'The right to property shall be guaranteed. It may only be encroached upon in the interest of public need or in the general interest of the community and in accordance with the provisions of appropriate laws'. See below chapter 10.

[94] See *Marín et al.* v. *Nicaragua*, Case 10.770, Report No. 12/94, Inter-Am. C.H.R., OEA/Ser.L/V/II.85 Doc. 9 rev. at 293 (1994).

[95] Krause and Alfredsson make the point that such an interpretation in not necessarily out of line with that given under Protocol 1 of ECHR See Krause and Alfredsson 'Article 17' in Alfredsson and Eide (eds), *The Universal Declaration of Human Rights* (Martinus Nijhoff Publishers, 1999) pp. 359–378, at p. 371.

[96] Banning, *The Human Rights to Property* (Intersentia, 2002) at p. 62.

[97] *Riba* translates roughly as usury. The classical definition is 'surplus value without counterpart'.

[98] See Rehman, 'Islamic Perspectives on International Economic Law' in Qureshi (ed.), *Perspectives in International Economic Law* (Kluwer Law International, 2002) pp. 235–258.

[99] Article 22(7) provides 'Every person has the right to seek and be granted asylum in a foreign territory, in accordance with the legislation of the state and international conventions, in the event he is being pursued for political offenses or related common crimes'.

(*Columbia* v. *Peru*)[100] before the International Court of Justice confirms that the issues concerning asylum have formed a sensitive aspect in the complex political matrix of the region.[101]

(v) Economic, social and cultural rights

The ACHR is one of the first civil and political rights treaties to explicitly incorporate economic, social and cultural rights.[102] Article 26 provides that:

> [t]he States Parties undertake to adopt measures, both internally and through international cooperation, especially those of an economic and technical nature, with a view to achieving progressively, by legislation or other appropriate means, the full realization of the rights implicit in the economic, social, educational, scientific, and cultural standards set forth in the Charter of the Organization of American States as amended by the Protocol of Buenos Aires

The provisions in this Article have been supplemented by the Protocol on Economic, Social and Cultural Rights.[103] Although the overall picture in dealing with cultural rights has not been promising, particularly in relation to indigenous peoples, the Commission has taken the view that within international law there exists a prohibition on unrestricted assimilation of cultural and indigenous rights and that:

> special legal protection is recognized for the use of [the Nicaraguan population of Miskito origin's] language, the observance of their religion, and in general, all those aspects related to the preservation of their cultural identity. To this should be added the aspects linked to productive organization, which includes, among other things, the issue of the ancestral and communal lands.[104]

6 PROCEDURES UNDER THE AMERICAN CONVENTION ON HUMAN RIGHTS

(i) State reporting

There is no reporting procedure under ACHR similar to the ones conducted by the treaty-based bodies. There are, however, certain limited provisions in relation to reporting and are contained in Articles 42 and 43 of the treaty. These Articles provide as follows:

---

[100] *Asylum Case (Colombia* v. *Peru)*, Judgment 20 November 1950, (1950) ICJ Reports 266.
[101] See Shaw, *International Law* (Cambridge University Press, 2008) pp. 76–77.
[102] Additional Protocol to the American Convention on Human Rights in the Area of Economic, Social and Cultural Rights 'Protocol of San Salvador' (A-52) O.A.S. Treaty Series No. 69 (1988), signed 17 November 1988, *reprinted in* Basic Documents Pertaining to Human Rights in the Inter-American System, OEA/Ser.L.V/II.82 doc.6 rev.1 at 67 (1992). See Craven, 'The Protection of Economic, Social and Cultural Rights under the Inter-American System of Human Rights' in Harris and Livingstone (eds), above n.1, at pp. 289–321.
[103] Ibid.
[104] See Report on the Human Rights of a Segment of the Nicaraguan Population of Miskito Origin, O.A.S Docs. OEA/Ser. L/V/II.62, doc.10 rev.3 (1983), Part Two, B para 15, and OEA/Ser.LV/II.62, doc.26 (1984). Also see Macklem and Morgan, 'Indigenous Rights in the Inter-American System: The *Amicus Brief* of the Assembly of First Nations in *Awas Tingni* v. *Republic of Nicaragua*' 22 HRQ (2000) 569.

> **Article 42**
> The States Parties shall transmit to the Commission a copy of each of the reports and studies that they submit annually to the Executive Committees of the Inter-American Economic and Social Council and the Inter-American Council for Education, Science, and Culture, in their respective fields, so that the Commission may watch over the promotion of the rights implicit in the economic, social, educational, scientific, and cultural standards set forth in the Charter of the Organization of American States as amended by the Protocol of Buenos Aires.
>
> **Article 43**
> The States Parties undertake to provide the Commission with such information as it may request of them as to the manner in which their domestic law ensures the effective application of any provisions of this Convention.

(ii) Individual complaints procedure

Petitions are to be submitted in writing, stating the facts of the case, the details of the victim, the name of the State alleged to have violated the rights, and the alleged breaches. It is also important for the petition to confirm that domestic remedies have been exhausted and the communication satisfies other admissibility requirements. It is equally significant to assess the financial implications of the petitioning to the Commission. For invoking the Inter-American procedure legal aid is not generally available.[105]

Article 44 provides for the procedure for individual complaints. According to Article 44:

> [a]ny person or groups of persons, or any nongovernmental entity legally recognized in one or more member states of the Organization, may lodge petitions with the Commission containing denunciations or complaints of violation of this Convention by a State Party.

It needs to be noted that the States becoming parties to the ACHR automatically recognise the competence of the Commission to receive complaints from persons alleging violation of their rights. The petitioning system is also automatic for the States of the OAS Charter. The differences between the ACHR and the Optional Protocol of the ICCPR and the ECHR are worthy of consideration. While, according to Article 34 of the ECHR, only 'victims' may be authors of communications, Article 44 provides that 'any person or group of persons, or any nongovernmental entity legally recognized in one or more member states of the Organization, may lodge petitions with the Commission containing denunciations or complaints of violation of this Convention by a State Party'. Similarly, since any person, NGO or legally recognised entity may lodge a petition regardless of their being a victim of a violation, the ACHR is generous in that *actio popularis* applications are permissible.[106] 'Person' means a person who is alive and does not include entities such as banks and corporations.[107]

---

[105] See Cerna, 'The Inter-American Commission on Human Rights: Its Organisation and Examination of Petitions and Communications' in Harris and Livingstone (eds), above n.1, 65–113 at p. 79.

[106] Shelton, above n.1, at p. 342.

[107] See Cerna, 'The Inter-American Commission on Human Rights: Its Organisation and Examination of Petitions and Communications' in Harris and Livingstone (eds), above n.1, 65–113 at p. 78.

9

The inter-American system for the protection of human rights

(iii) Inter-State application

Like the ICCPR, ECHR and AFCHPR, the ACHR provides for an inter-State complaints mechanism. However, unlike ECHR (and in line with ICCPR) the State is required to make a declaration recognising the competence of the Commission to receive and examine communications from another State. Article 45(1) provides for this procedure, according to which:

> [a]ny State Party may, when it deposits its instrument of ratification of or adherence to this Convention, or at any later time, declare that it recognizes the competence of the Commission to receive and examine communications in which a State Party alleges that another State Party has committed a violation of a human right set forth in this Convention.

Communications under this procedure are only acceptable on the basis of reciprocity.[108] By way of contrast to the European Human Rights System, the inter-State application procedure has been used only once by a complaint brought by Nicaragua against Costa Rica.[109] In this complaint, Nicaragua alleged systematic discrimination against its nationals by Costa Rica. The Commission, however, decided that due to a failure to exhaust domestic remedies the complaint was inadmissible. The report of the Commission is, nevertheless, useful in providing further guidance on the inter-State procedure as well as taking the principled position of condemning 'all acts of discrimination or xenophobia against migrant persons of any origin' and re-asserting 'the obligation of states to protect individuals against discrimination, whether this occurs within the public sphere or among private parties'.[110]

(iv) Admissibility requirements

The procedure for admissibility of individual and inter-State complaints is provided for in Articles 46–47. Article 46 provides as follows:

> 1. Admission by the Commission of a petition or communication lodged in accordance with Articles 44 or 45 shall be subject to the following requirements:
>   (a) that the remedies under domestic law have been pursued and exhausted in accordance with generally recognized principles of international law;
>   (b) that the petition or communication is lodged within a period of six months from the date on which the party alleging violation of his rights was notified of the final judgment;
>   (c) that the subject of the petition or communication is not pending in another international proceeding for settlement; and
>   (d) that, in the case of Article 44, the petition contains the name, nationality, profession, domicile, and signature of the person or persons or of the legal representative of the entity lodging the petition.

---

[108] See Article 45.
[109] *Nicaragua v. Costa Rica*, Report No. 11/07, Inter-State Case 01/06, 8 March 2007; Alston, Steiner and Goodman (eds) *International Human Rights in Context* (Oxford University Press, 2008) p. 1038.
[110] *Nicaragua v. Costa Rica*, Report No. 11/07, Inter-State Case 01/06, 8 March 2007, para 310.

2. The provisions of paragraphs 1(a) and 1(b) of this article shall not be applicable when:

(a) the domestic legislation of the state concerned does not afford due process of law for the protection of the right or rights that have allegedly been violated;

(b) the party alleging violation of his rights has been denied access to the remedies under domestic law or has been prevented from exhausting them; or

(c) there has been unwarranted delay in rendering a final judgment under the afore-mentioned remedies.

The admissibility requirements of Article 46 are supplemented by the provisions of Article 47 which provides that:

The Commission shall consider inadmissible any petition or communication submitted under Articles 44 or 45 if:

(a) any of the requirements indicated in Article 46 has not been met;

(b) the petition or communication does not state facts that tend to establish a violation of the rights guaranteed by this Convention;

(c) the statements of the petitioner or of the state indicate that the petition or communication is manifestly groundless or obviously out of order; or

(d) the petition or communication is substantially the same as one previously studied by the Commission or by another international organization.

As we have analysed throughout this book, in order to invoke any international human rights procedure certain pre-requisites must be met. The ACHR, in common with other human rights systems, contains certain conditions.[111] According to the provisions of ACHR, the petitioner must have pursued and exhausted all domestic remedies, although as Shelton points out this requirement is 'less stringent than other human rights systems'.[112] In accordance with the general principles of international law, the petitioner is only required to pursue and exhaust those remedies which would adequately and effectively redress his grievances. He is not obliged to apply to domestic courts where there are no adequate remedies, or if there is an 'unwarranted delay'.[113] The Commission has developed in its jurisprudence, the meaning of the term 'unwarranted delay'.[114] The petitioner is also not obliged to follow his case in the domestic courts where he or she is being denied access to remedies[115] or is being prevented from exhausting domestic remedies,[116] or there has been a denial of justice because of lack of independent judicial determination of the case.[117]

---

[111] The executive secretariat of the Commission is given responsibility for enquires into admissibility requirements. A petition alleging violation of the Convention (or other treaty over which the Commission and the Court have jurisdiction) must be provided in writing with a statement of facts.

[112] Shelton, above n.1, at p. 344.

[113] Article 46(2)(c).

[114] See *Fabricio Proano* et al. v. *Ecuador*, Case 9.641, Res. No. 14/89, Inter-Am. C.H.R., OEA/Ser.L/V/II.76, Doc. 10, 12 April 1989; see *Rojas DeNegri and Quintana* v. *Chile*, Case 9.755, Res. No. 01a/88, Inter-Am. C.H.R., OEA/Ser.L/V/II.74, Doc. 10 rev.1, 12 September 1988, at 132; also see *Trujillo Oroza* v. *Bolivia* (Merits, 2000), Inter-Am. Ct. H.R. (Ser. C) No. 92, para 2(a).

[115] Article 46(2)(b).

[116] Ibid.

[117] Cerna, 'The Inter-American Commission on Human Rights: Its Organisation and Examination of Petitions and Communications' in Harris and Livingstone (eds), above n.1, 65–113 at p. 87.

As regards the burden of establishing whether adequate or effective domestic remedies exist and need to be pursued as a prerequisite, the Commission has tended to follow an approach favouring the petitioner.[118] This approach is closer in line to the one adopted by the Human Rights Committee, as opposed to the one adopted by the former European Commission on Human Rights. The probable reason for such a liberal approach is the difficulty an individual is likely to encounter in satisfying the principle, particularly through the provision of adequate evidence in his or her favour. The Inter-American Court has endorsed the Commission's approach. In the *Velásquez Rodríguez* Case,[119] the Court noted 'the state claiming non-exhaustion has an obligation to prove that domestic remedies remain to be exhausted and that they are effective'.[120]

The petitioner is also obliged to submit a claim to the Commission within a period of six months of the final decision of the domestic court.[121] The procedure has many similarities with those of the ECHR. Like the ECHR requirement, in the present instance the six months will start running from the date of the final decision involving the exhaustion of all domestic remedies. Final decision means a letter setting out the substance of the complaint. The Commission may refuse to accept the petition under this heading if, after the initial letter to pursue the action, there is a substantial period of inaction before the applicant submits further information. On the other hand, the Commission has shown flexibility in the application of the six months rule where the expiry of the time limit is attributable to the State[122] or in cases of continuing violations such as detention,[123] disappearances of the victims[124] or where the petitioner never receives a final judgment.[125]

Article 46(1)(c) requires that the 'subject of the petition or the communication is not pending in another international procedure'. This requirement is placed to avoid the petitioner instituting proceedings before another international procedure. However, this limitation does not apply where the general human rights situation concerning the case is being or has been considered by the United Nations Working Group on Enforced and Involuntary Disappearances,[126] or under the ILO Procedures.[127] The Inter-American Commission has also accepted petitions where simultaneous applications have been made

---

[118] The Commissions' Regulations provide 'When the petitioner contends that he is unable to prove exhaustion as indicated in this Article, it shall be up to the government against which this petition has been lodged to demonstrate to the Commission that the remedies under domestic law have not previously been exhausted, unless it is clearly evident from the background information contained in the petition'. Regulations of the Inter-American Commission on Human Rights, reprinted in Basic Documents Pertaining to Human Rights in the Inter-American System, OEA/Ser.L.V/II.82 doc.6 rev.1 at 103 (1992), Article 37(3).

[119] *Velásquez Rodríguez* Case, Judgment of 29 July 1988, Inter-Am. Ct. H.R. (Ser. C) No. 4 (1988).

[120] *Velásquez Rodríguez* Case, Judgment of 26 June 1987, Inter-Am. Ct. H.R. (Ser. C) No. 1 (1987) (Preliminary Objections), para 88.

[121] Article 46(1)(b).

[122] See Commission's Rules of Procedure 2001 Article 31(2).

[123] See *Paul Lallion* v. *Grenada*, Case 11.765 Report No. 124/99, Inter-Am. C.H.R., OEA/Ser.L/V/II.106 Doc. 3 rev. at 225 (1999), paras 22–23, where it was argued that the case was still admissible due to the continuing nature of the applicant' detention.

[124] See *Carlos A. Mojoli V.* v. *Paraguay*, Case 379/01, Report No. 84/03, Inter-Am. C.H.R., OEA/Ser.L/V/II.118 Doc. 70 rev. 2 at 412 (2003), paras 2526 and 33.

[125] See 2001 Rules of Procedure of the Inter-American Commission of Human Rights Article 32. See Article 32(2): in determining as to what constitutes a 'reasonable time', the Commission will consider 'circumstances of each case' independently.

[126] See *Munoz Yaranga* et al. v. *Peru*, Cases 9501–9512, Res. No. 1-19/88, Inter-Am. C.H.R., OEA/Ser.L/V/II.74, Doc. 10 rev.1, pp. 235–274.

[127] See the Commission's report, 54th Session 1981, Consideration of the ILO case 7579, *Jorge Salazar* v. *Nicaragua*.

by an unrelated third party.[128] This rule is adopted because of the view that the petitioner or his family members ought to be given precedence over NGOs.

(v) Procedure

If the communication is held admissible under Article 46 then the Commission goes on to consider whether it satisfies conditions under Article 47. The communication would fail if any of the requirements of Article 46 are not met. It would also fail if no violation of any of the rights in the Convention is found. The Commission refuses to accept jurisdiction *ratione personae* in cases filed in *abstracto*.[129] Similarly, there would be a failure if the petition is manifestly groundless or out of order. Finally, it would be inadmissible if the communication is substantially the same as one already studied by the Commission or studied by any other international organisation.

Once the communication is held to be *prima facie* admissible, there are two stages. In accordance with Article 48, the primary function of the Commission is to receive all necessary information and evidence up to and during the proceedings of the case.[130] On receipt of relevant information or after the passage of the established period, the Commission decides whether grounds exist for the consideration of the petition, and in cases where they do not, the Commission is authorised to close the case.[131] The second function for the Commission (which takes place if the case has not been closed[132] or if the petition has not been held admissible)[133] is to place itself at the disposal of parties with a view to reaching a friendly settlement.[134]

If a friendly settlement is reached, then, in accordance with Article 49, the Commission needs to draw up a report consisting of a brief statement of facts and the solution reached, which is transmitted to the Secretary General of the OAS. However, if it is not possible to reach a settlement, the Commission must draw up a report under Article 50 stating the

---

[128] *Lilian Celiberti de Casariego* v. *Uruguay*, Communication No. 56/1979 (29 July 1981), UN Doc. CCPR/C/OP/1 at 92 (1984).

[129] *González* v. *Costa Rica*, Case 11553, Res. No. 48/96, Inter-Am. C.H.R., OEA/Ser.L/VII.95, doc. 7 rev. (1996), paras 28–31. However, it has been held that a potential victim has the right to file petition. In *Hilaire, Constantine and Benjamin et al.*, although only one of the persons had in fact been executed it was held that all 32 persons who had been awarded death penalty were victims. *Hilaire, Constantine and Benjamin* v. *Trinidad and Tobago* (Merits) 21 June 2002, Inter-Am. Ct. H.R., (Ser. C) No. 94, paras 116–117. Similarly, according to the Court's dicta in *Suárez Rosero Case*, a right to petition arises when the law in itself is a violation of the Convention regardless of whether it was in fact imposed, *Suárez Rosero* v. *Ecuador (Merits)*, 12 November 1997, Inter-Am. Ct. H.R. (Ser. C) No. 35 para 98. The original jurisdiction under the Convention has been restricted to natural persons – Article 1(1). However, in *Cantos* v. *Argentina*, the Inter-American Court in adopting a broader interpretation accepted the petition of the owner of a business group consisting of various corporations. The Court aimed to adopt a pragmatic approach and held that business entities consist of voluntary associations of people and their claims should be treated in the same manner as persons bringing a claim. See *Cantos* v. *Argentina* (Preliminary Objections, 2001) Judgment of 7 September 2001, Inter-Am Ct H.R. (Ser. C) No. 85 (2001), paras 27–29.

[130] Article 48(1)(a) and Article 48(1)(e) (ACHR) (for the provision of information, time limits are prescribed. See Article 34 of the Commission's Regulations).

[131] Article 48(1)(b) (ACHR).

[132] Ibid. Article 48(1)(b).

[133] Ibid. Article 48(1)(c).

[134] Ibid. Article 48(1)(f). While the Court has recognised that the Commission has some discretion in reaching for a friendly settlement (see *Velásquez Rodríguez* Case, Preliminary Objections paras 42–46) it has been critical of the Commission for its reluctance in using the provision, since according to the provision, such action represents a mandatory requirement (see *Caballero Delgado and Santana* Case, Preliminary Objections, Judgment of 21 January 1994, Inter-Am.Ct.H.R. (Ser. C) No. 17 (1994), paras 25–30).

facts and its conclusions and transmit it to the relevant State party concerned within 180 days.[135]

Under Article 50(1) (and in cases where settlement is not reached) the Commission may make a recommendation or proposal which must not be published.[136] With the transmission of the report there commences a three-month period, during which the parties could settle the case, or the case could be referred to the Court either by the Commission or the State party itself.[137] If any of these actions do not take place, then the Commission has the option of presenting its opinion and recommendations as to the remedial course of action. In making such recommendation, the Commission is required to prescribe a timeframe within which these remedial actions need to be taken.[138] After the expiry of the three-month period, the Commission must decide whether the State has undertaken proper action and whether to publish its report.[139] There is no guidance from the Rules of Procedure. Nor is there any specification of the procedures which the Commission needs to follow when reaching decisions as to the submission of a case before the Court.[140] From the jurisprudence of the Court, it can be said that cases raising complex or controversial legal issues ought to be referred to the Court.[141]

7 THE INTER-AMERICAN COURT OF HUMAN RIGHTS[142]

The Inter-American Court of Human Rights was established in 1979 in pursuance of the ACHR. The Court has its permanent seat in San José, Costa Rica. The provisions relating to the Court are provided in Chapter VIII of the ACHR. According to Article 52, the Court is to consist of seven judges. Only States parties to the OAS Charter make the nominations, although the nominated person need not have the nationality of the State proposing such an appointment.[143]

Membership of the Court is limited to a maximum of one judge having the nationality of a State party to OAS.[144] The judges act in their individual capacity for a period of six years and are re-electable only once.[145] They are 'jurists of the highest moral authority and of

---

135 See Article 50 (ACHR).
136 See ibid. Article 50(2).
137 Ibid. Article 51(1).
138 Ibid. Article 51(1) and Article 51(2).
139 See Ibid. Article 51(3).
140 See *Baena Ricardo et al* v. *Panama* (Preliminary Objections) Judgment of 18 November 1999, Inter-Am. Ct. H.R. (Ser. C) No. 61 (1999), where the Court rejected Panama's objection that the Commission had used a telephone conference to make a formal decision to submit the case to the Court, see ibid. 32–40. Pasqualucci, above n.1, at p. 156.
141 *Compulsory Membership in an Association Prescribed by Law for the Practice of Journalism* (Arts. 13 and 29 of the American Convention on Human Rights), Advisory Opinion OC-5/85, 13 November 1985, Inter-Am. Ct. H.R. (Ser. A) No. 5 (1985).
142 Davidson, *The Inter-American Court of Human Rights* (Dartmouth, 1992); Dunshee de Abranches, 'La Corte Interamericana de Derechos Humanos' in *La Convencióan Americana sobre Derechos Humanos* (Organisation de los Estados Americanos, 1980), pp. 91–147; Cerna, 'The Structure and Functioning of the Inter-American Court of Human Rights (1979–1992)' 63 *BYIL* (1992) 135.
143 Article 53(2) ACHR; Article 4(1) Statute of the Inter-American Court on Human Rights, O.A.S. Res. 448 (IX-0/79), O.A.S. Off. Rec. OEA/Ser.P/IX.0.2/80, vol. 1 at 98, Annual Report of the Inter-American Court on Human Rights, OEA/Ser.L/V.III.3 doc.13 corr. 1 at 16 (1980), reprinted in Basic Documents Pertaining to Human Rights in the Inter-American System, OEA/Ser.L/V/II.82 doc.6 rev.1 at 133 (1992).
144 Article 52(2) ACHR; Article 4(2) of the Statute.
145 Article 54(1) ACHR; Article 5(1) of the Statute.

recognised competence in the field of human rights, who possess qualifications required for the exercise of the highest judicial functions'. The judges are nominated and elected for a term of six years by States parties to the American Convention with a staggered system of re-election every three years.[146] The term of office of an elected judge could be extended through re-election for a further one term.

There remains the possibility of appointing *ad hoc* judges. The circumstances of the *ad hoc* appointment of judges are provided for in Article 55. According to Article 55:

1. If a judge is a national of any of the States Parties to a case submitted to the Court, he shall retain his right to hear that case.

2. If one of the judges called upon to hear a case should be a national of one of the States Parties to the case, any other State Party in the case may appoint a person of its choice to serve on the Court as an *ad hoc* judge.

3. If among the judges called upon to hear a case none is a national of any of the States Parties to the case, each of the latter may appoint an *ad hoc* judge.

4. An *ad hoc* judge shall possess the qualifications indicated in Article 52.

5. If several States Parties to the Convention should have the same interest in a case, they shall be considered as a single party for purposes of the above provisions. In case of doubt, the Court shall decide.

The Court does not sit throughout the year but has two regular sessions.[147] However, there remains the possibility of asking for a special session and the Court has the power to order provisional measures and make interim judgments. The quorum of the Court is five members and, unlike the ECHR, the Court does not operate in Chambers.[148]

8 FORMS OF JURISDICTION

(i) Contentious jurisdiction

The Court has two forms of jurisdictions: a contentious and an advisory jurisdiction. Contentious jurisdiction itself is of two types: inter-State or individual complaints, although, as we have noted, the inter-State procedure has only recently been invoked. States may accept the contentious jurisdiction of the Court either unconditionally, conditionally or in specific cases.[149] In other words this jurisdiction is optional.[150] It also needs to be noted that only States and the Commission may submit a case to the Court.[151] The individual (unlike the new procedure under the ECHR) has no *locus standi* before the Court, although the

---

[146] Article 54 ACHR.
[147] Article 22(1) of the Statute; Article 11 Rules of Procedure of the Inter-American Court of Human Rights.
[148] Davidson, above n.142, at p. 46.
[149] Article 62(2).
[150] Not all parties to ACHR have accepted the jurisdiction of the Court.
[151] Article 61.

lawyers for petitioners have been listed at all stages.[152] For the Court to exercise its contentious jurisdiction, the proceedings before the Commission must have been completed and the case must be referred by the Commission or the State within three months after the initial report on the matter is transmitted to the parties. The Commission notifies the individuals if the case is submitted to the Court and the individual is accorded an opportunity to make observations. It needs to be noted that unlike the ECHR, the contentious jurisdiction of the Inter-American Court is very recent and the first case where breaches were found was decided in 1988 leading to the position that a number of Articles within the Convention have yet to be tested before the Court.[153]

According to Article 62, the contentious jurisdiction may only be initiated if the State party or States parties concerned have accepted the courts jurisdiction in such matters.[154] As noted above, the Court's jurisdiction cannot be invoked unless the procedures before the Commission have been fully completed.[155] Proceedings before the Court can be instituted through the filing of a petition to the Secretary General of the Court, stating *inter alia* the grounds and violations of human rights.[156] Once an application has been received, the Secretary of the Court notifies the Commission and all concerned State parties.[157] There is, at this point, a possibility of filing preliminary objections. On the receipt of these objections the Court may, at its discretion, deal with these preliminary objections in the following manner: it may admit all or some of the objections[158] or it may reject some or all the objections.[159] The Court can also join preliminary objections with the merits of the case.[160] After submission of written memorials, the Court allows the parties to make oral submission during the hearing of the case. Unless the Court determines otherwise, hearings before the Court are public and are held at the seat of the Court in San José, Costa Rica.[161]

---

[152] The 2001 Commission's Rules of Procedure provide for a broadening of rules – where the State concerned has accepted the Court's jurisdiction, the 2001 Rules provide for automatic referrals of a case 'unless there is a reasoned decision by an absolute majority of the members of the Commission to the contrary' – 2001 Rules of Procedure of Inter-American Commission on Human Rights, Article 44. A major factor in the Commission's decision making is the petitioner's position as to whether the case should be referred to the Court. The petitioner's desire to take the case to the Court increases the probability that the Commission will comply with the request; nevertheless the Commission still has the discretion as whether to take the case forward. Pasqualucci above n.1, at p. 19.

[153] Trindade, 'The Operation of the Inter-American Court of Human Rights' in Harris and Livingstone (eds), above n.1, 133–150 at p. 141.

[154] Article 62(3); any attempts to limit the jurisdiction of the Court through domestic law (e.g. mandating death penalty in convictions for murder) have been rendered unsuccessful. See *Benjamin* et al. v. *Trinidad and Tobago* (Preliminary Objections) 1 September 2001, Inter-Am. Ct. H.R. (Ser. C) No. 81, Operative Para 1; *Hilaire* v. *Trinidad and Tobago* (Preliminary Objections, 2001) 1 September 2001, Inter-Am. Ct. H.R. (Ser. C) No. 80 Operative para 1; *Constantine* et al. v. *Trinidad and Tobago* (Preliminary Objections), 1 September 2001, Inter-Am. Ct. H.R. (Ser. C) No. 82, Operative para 1.

[155] *The Matter of Viviana Gallardo* et al. Advisory Opinion No. G 101/81, Inter-Am. Ct. H.R. (Ser. A) (1984).

[156] Articles 26(1) and 26(2) Rules of Procedure of the Inter-American Court of Human Rights; Article 61 ACHR.

[157] Article 26 Rules of Procedure of the Inter-American Court of Human Rights.

[158] If the Court admits all the objections then the case is concluded without ever reaching the merits stage. See Pasqualucci, above n.1, at p. 172; The Court may, however, accept only one or few of all the preliminary objections raised – in this situation, the Court continues to hear other claims. In the *Las Palmeras Case*, the Court while accepting Columbia's objection that it did not have jurisdiction in determining on the violation by Columbia of Article 3 of the Geneva Convention 1949, nevertheless proceeded to hear the case on alleged violations under the American Convention on Human Rights; see *Las Palmeras* Case, Judgment on Preliminary Objections of 4 February 2000, Inter-Am. Ct. H.R. (Ser. C) No. 67 (2000), para 33 and operative para 2.

[159] In rejecting all or some of the preliminary objections, the Court proceeds to consider the merits of the case *vis-à-vis* the substantial (or outstanding) claims.

[160] Davidson, above n.142, at p. 52.

[161] See Article 58.

Once the case has been referred to the Court, it has the competence to review the Commission's findings regarding the factual issues as well as admissibility, *de novo*.[162] In relation to presumptions and circumstantial evidence, the Court has followed the jurisprudence of the Human Rights Committee and the European Court of Human Rights. Thus, ill-treatment of prisoners while in custody has been presumed to be the responsibility of the State unless proven otherwise;[163] or a presumption in favour of a victim's testimony regarding the conditions of detention, where the victim had been held incommunicado;[164] or in instances where the State is unwilling or unable to rebut the issues raised by the victim.[165] In discharging the burden on issues such as disappearances, the Court has accepted that the petitioner needs to establish that the State has either tolerated the practice of disappearances or has itself been engaged in such practices, whereupon the burden of proof shifts to the respondent State.[166]

Unlike the European Court of Human Rights, the Inter-American Court has addressed the issue of measuring damages for personal injury and wrongful deaths.[167] However, neither the European nor the Inter-American Court has awarded punitive damages yet. The *Velásquez Rodríguez*[168] and *Godinez Cruz* cases[169] were the first contentious cases before the Court, thereby allowing it the opportunity to expand on the Convention's provisions of reparations. Both the cases were brought against Honduras for the disappearances of the aforementioned individuals. In expanding on the meaning of reparations the Court observed:

> [r]eparation of harm brought about by the violation of an international obligation consists in full restitution (*restitutio in integrum*), which includes the restoration of the prior situation, the reparation of the consequences of the violation, and indemnification and patrimonial and non-patrimonial damages, including emotional harm.[170]

Having stated the general position, the Court articulated a number of important principles on reparations. It adopted the approach that international law (as opposed to national law) should provide the criterion for awarding reparations. It recognised the value in awarding damages for emotional harm in instances of human rights violations, which in its view should be based on the principles of equity, although it rejected the claim for punitive damages. The Court emphasised a duty upon the States to punish those responsible for disappearances and to prevent future reoccurrence of any such violations. In rejecting the contentions made by the Honduras government that damages should be paid out at a level equivalent to accidental death, the Court awarded damages including loss of earnings which the victim would have earned until the point of death. The salary was based upon

---

[162] 2001 Rules of Procedure, Inter-American Court of Human Rights, Article 14(1); these hearings are conducted before the plenary court.

[163] *Villagran Morales* et al. v. *Guatemala* (the *Street Children* Case) Merits, Judgment of 19 November 1999, Inter-Am. Ct. H.R. (Ser. C) No. 63 (1999), paras 128, 142 and 169.

[164] *Suarez Rosero* v. *Ecuador* (Merits, 1997) para 33.

[165] Ibid.

[166] See *Velásquez Rodríguez* Case, Judgment of 29 July 1988, paras 122–139.

[167] See *Velásquez Rodríguez* Case, Judgment of 29 July 1988, Inter-Am. Ct. H.R. (Ser. C) No. 4 (1988) paras 189–192; *El Amparo* Case, Judgment of 18 January 1995, Inter-Am. Ct. H.R. (Ser. C) No. 19 (1995).

[168] *Velásquez Rodríguez* Case, Judgment of 29 July 1988, Inter-Am. Ct. H.R. (Ser. C) No. 4 (1988).

[169] *Godínez Cruz* Case, Judgment of 21 January 1989, Inter-Am. Ct. H.R. (Ser. C) No. 5 (1989).

[170] *Velásquez Rodríguez* Case, Judgment of 21 July 1989, Inter-Am. Ct. H.R. (Ser. C) No. 7 (1989), para 26.

what the victim was earning at the time of his disappearance inclusive of the progressive increase of salary. In relation to the payment of damages, the Court ordered a payment within 90 days as a lump sum. Alternatively, the State could make the payment in six months although it would be subject to interest. In subsequent proceedings the Court ordered Honduras to compensate the victim for the loss in value of *lempira* (currency) from the point of judgment.[171]

In a later case the issue of awarding damages was further elaborated. In the *Aloeboetoe* case,[172] the State of Surinam accepted liability for the detention, abuse and murder of seven unarmed Bush men, suspected by the State police of subversive activities. The Court made an award of damages and in so doing took the innovative step of identifying the victim's successors through the application of the tribal customary laws of the Saramcas tribe. The Court also provided moral damages for psychological harm when the victims were taken illegally by the military and subsequently killed.[173] In the *Neira Alegria* case[174] the Court found a violation of Article 4 perpetrated by Peru. The case concerned the disappearance of three prisoners after a cell block in which they were detained was destroyed. The Court awarded compensation, to be fixed by agreement between the parties. The Court, however, reserved the right to review and approve the agreement, and to determine the amount in case of failure of any agreements. The Court has awarded damages to family members of the victim in instances where they have had to leave their jobs to search for missing relatives.[175] It has determined that material damages include financial expenses incurred whilst making such searches.[176]

Article 63 deals with the judgements of the Court. Article 63(1) provides:

> If the Court finds that there has been a violation of a right or freedom protected by this Convention, the Court shall rule that the injured party be ensured the enjoyment of his right or freedom that was violated. It shall also rule, if appropriate, that the consequences of the measure or situation that constituted the breach of such right or freedom be remedied and that fair compensation be paid to the injured party.

It needs to be noted that the Inter-American Court has a much broader jurisdiction under Article 63(1) in comparison to other regional human rights courts. Under the ECHR Article 41, the European Court of Human Rights is authorised to 'afford just satisfaction' to the injured party. The European Human Rights Court has restrictively applied these provisions for financial awards.[177] When awarding reparations or compensation the Inter-American Court of Human Rights has held that the concept of victim includes the next

---

[171] See Shelton, 'Reparations in the Inter-American System' in Harris and Livingstone (eds), above n.1, 151–172 at p. 156.

[172] *Aloeboetoe* et al. Case, Reparations (Art. 63(1) American Convention on Human Rights) Judgment of September 10, 1993, Inter-Am.Ct.H.R. (Ser. C) No. 15 (1994). Text in International Human Rights Reports, 1(2), 1994, 208. Also see Davidson, 'Remedies for violations of the American Convention on Human Rights' 44 *ICLQ* (1995) 405.

[173] See Shelton, above n.1, at pp. 364–370.

[174] *Neira Alegria* Case, Judgment of 19 January 1995, Inter-Am.Ct.H.R. (Ser. C) No. 20 (1995). American Society of International Law, *Human Rights Interest Group Newsletter*, 5(1), 1995, 29.

[175] *Bamaca Velásquez* v. *Guatamela* (Reparations) Inter-American Court of Human Rights 22 (February 2002) Ser. C., No. 91, para 54(a).

[176] *Trujillo Oroza* v. *Bolivia* (Reparations, 2002) paras 53(g) and 75.

[177] Mas makes the interesting observation that '[a] number of applicants have requested the Court to annul an internal decision or measure, to issue an injunction and to give some directions to the respondent State. The

of kin or dependants of the victim who have been affected through the violation of convention rights. The Inter-American Court has also emphasised the principle of *restituto interregnum* – namely full restitution to the previous situation. Unlike the ECHR, the American Court's judgments are not purely of a declaratory nature. These are specific enough to order measures which would provide an appropriate remedy including repealing, amending and adoption of national laws or judgments. In the *Paniagwa Morales* case,[178] people had been murdered after having been taken into custody. The Court ordered that the Guatemalan authorities establish a registry for all those who had been detained. As an example of amendment of laws, the Court has required Peru, in the *Loayza Tamaya*[179] and *Castillo Petruzzi*[180] cases, to reform various anti-terrorism and treason laws which would bring Peruvian laws into conformity with the American Convention on Human Rights. The Inter-American Court has also made certain specific orders, for example in *Mayanga (SUMO) Awas Tingri Community* v. *Nicaragua*, the Court required that the State demarcate and provide titles to the lands of the indigenous community. The Nicaraguan government, which had authorised forestry concessions on lands that were claimed by an indigenous community, was required by the Court to adopt 'legislative, administrative and any other measures required to create an effective mechanism for delimitation, demarcation, and titling of the property of indigenous communities, in accordance with their customary law, values, customs and mores'.[181] In the *Cantoral Benavides* case, the victim had been imprisoned by the State when he was 20 years of age. The Court ordered Peru to provide the victim with a scholarship for his studies and to provide his living expenses.[182]

The decisions of the Court are binding on States parties.[183] The contracting parties agree to abide by its judgment[184] and compensatory damages can be executed in the country concerned, in accordance with domestic procedures governing the execution of the judgments against the State.[185] The Court's judgment is final, and it is not possible to appeal against it.[186]

In the absence of a supervisory body similar to the Committee of Ministers to execute and supervise enforcement, there is no counterpart to the ECHR. If a State refuses to abide by the judgment of the Court, the Court is limited to documenting it in its annual report. The Court also has the power to award provisional measures.[187] It has the power to do so in emergency cases where there is a real threat of a violation taking place in the imminent

---

Court has answered that it had no jurisdiction to do so'. Mas, 'Right to Compensation under Article 50' in Macdonald, Matscher and Petzold (eds), *The European System for the Protection of Human Rights* (Martinus Nijhoff Publishers, 1993) pp. 775–790, at p. 778.

[178] *Paniagua Morales* et al. Case, Judgment of 8 March 1998, Inter-Am. Ct. H.R. (Ser. C) No. 37 (1998).
[179] *Loayza Tamayo* Case, Reparations (art. 63(1) American Convention on Human Rights), Judgment of 27 November 1998, Inter-Am. Ct. H.R. (Ser. C) No. 42 (1998), paras 159–164.
[180] *Castillo Petruzzi* et al. Case, Judgment of 30 May 1999, Inter-Am. Ct. H.R. (Ser. C) No. 52 (1999), para 222.
[181] *Mayagna (SUMO) Awas Tingni Community* v. *Nicaragua* (Merits), Inter-American Court of Human Rights 31 August 2001, Ser. C, No. 79, para 164 and operative para 3; see James, Anaya and Williams Jr, 'The Protection of Indigenous People's Rights Over Lands and Natural Resources Under the Inter-American Human Rights System' 14 *Harvard Human Rights Journal* (2001) 33.
[182] *Cantoral Benavides* Case, Judgment of 3 December 2001, Inter-Am Ct. H.R. (Ser. C) No. 88 (2001), paras 60 and 80.
[183] Article 63(1) (ACHR).
[184] Ibid. Article 68(1).
[185] Ibid. Article 68(2).
[186] Ibid. Article 66(1) and Article 67.
[187] Ibid. Article 63(2).

9

The inter-American system for the protection of human rights

future Article 63(2).[188] Although this power is at the discretion of the Court, the emphasis is upon cases of 'extreme gravity and urgency' with a real risk of irreparable damage.[189] According to the Court's jurisprudence there is an obligation to undertake measures to remedy the consequences of the violation, including a duty to investigate an offence and punish the perpetrators of the offences. These provisions were invoked in the *Velásquez Rodríguez*[190] and *Alemán Lacayo*[191] cases, and in the case of *Haitians and Dominicans of Haitian Origin in the Dominican Republic*.[192]

(ii) Advisory jurisdiction[193]

The second element of the Court's jurisdiction is it advisory jurisdiction. The rules regarding advisory jurisdiction are provided in Article 64 of the Convention. Article 64 provides:

1. The member states of the Organization may consult the Court regarding the interpretation of this Convention or of other treaties concerning the protection of human rights in the American states. Within their spheres of competence, the organs listed in Chapter X of the Charter of the Organization of American States, as amended by the Protocol of Buenos Aires, may in like manner consult the Court.

2. The Court, at the request of a member state of the Organization, may provide that state with opinions regarding the compatibility of any of its domestic laws with the aforesaid international instruments.

From the above provision, it is clear that the Court may provide an advisory opinion on the interpretation of ACHR and of other human rights treaties, concerning the protection of human rights in American states.[194] The intention has been to provide for the advisory jurisdiction 'in the broadest terms possible'.[195] Under the provisions of Article 64(2) the

---

[188] The Commission has also asserted this authority to award provisional measures based upon its Rules of Procedure. According to the 2001 Rules of Procedure, the Commission can request that 'the State party concerned adopt precautionary measures to prevent irreparable harm to persons'. See Rules of Procedure of the Inter-American Commission on Human Rights Article 25(1) www.oas.org/36ag/english/doc_referencia/Reglamento_CIDH.pdf <last visited 7 May 2009>; *Roach and Pinkerton* v. *United States*, Case 9.647, Res. No. 3/87, Inter-Am.C.H.R., OEA/Ser.L/V/II.71, Doc. 9 rev. 1, at 147.

[189] These provisional measures are, as the Court has emphasised mandatory and binding upon parties – *Constitutional Court Case (Peru) Provisional Measures*, Inter-American Court of Human Rights Order of 14 August 2000, Ser. E, para 14.

[190] *Velásquez Rodríguez* Case, Order of the Court of 15 January 1988, Inter-Am. Ct. H.R. (Ser. E) (1988). In these Provisional Measures, the Court ordered that the Government of Honduras adopt measures to prevent the infringement of the rights of those persons who had appeared or were to appear before the Court. Additionally the Court ordered that the Government investigate and bring to justice the perpetrators of these violations.

[191] *Alemán Lacayo* Case, Order of the Court of 2 February 1996, Inter-Am. Ct. H.R. (Ser. E) (1996). In this case the Court ordered that the Government of the Republic of Nicaragua take such measures necessary to protect the life and personal integrity of Dr. Alemán Lacayo as well as investigate the events and punish those responsible.

[192] *Case of Haitians and Haitian Origin in the Dominican Republican Republic*, Order of the Court of 18 August 2000, Inter-Am. Ct. H.R. (Ser. E) (2000). In this case the Court not only required that the Dominican Republic take measures to protect the lives and personal integrity of the concerned persons but also ordered that the State refrain from deporting, permit return and family reunification, provide information and investigate the situation.

[193] See Buergenthal, 'The Advisory Practice' above n.1, at p. 1.

[194] Article 64(1).

[195] *'Other Treaties' Subject to the Consultative Jurisdiction of the Court (Article 64 of ACHR)* Advisory Opinion OC-1/82, 24 September 1982, Inter-Am. Ct. H.R. (Ser. A) No. 1 (1982), para 17.

OAS Member States have the standing to invoke advisory jurisdiction as to whether their domestic laws are compatible with the ACHR or other treaties. Any Member State of the OAS may make a request for an advisory opinion; such requests not being restricted to States parties to the Convention.[196] While States not parties to ACHR may be less interested in this particular Convention, nevertheless, they would continue to have an interest in the interpretation of other human rights treaty obligations which they have incurred.[197] These opinion not only relate to the interpretation of instruments referred in Article 64, but any Member State could also seek an opinion as to whether its domestic legislation is compatible or not. The only main requirement is 'legitimate institutional interest', in the questions posed to the Court in the request.[198] The advisory opinions of the Court are not restricted to parties of OAS Member States but also authorise any organ of OAS listed in Chapter X of the Charter.[199] These organs are now listed in Chapter VIII of the Charter of the OAS as amended by the 1985 Protocol of Cartagena de Indias.

As regards *ratione materiae* (or subject matter) the court's jurisdiction consists of the following:

(a) Questions concerning the inter interpretation of the ACHR, Article 64(1) including the interpretation of its two protocols

(b) Questions related to the interpretation of 'Other treaties concerning protection of human rights in American States' under Article 64(1) and

(c) Requests pertaining to the whether a State's domestic laws are compatible with ACHR or 'Other treaties' under Article 64(2)

The Court, however, has emphasised that the organ petitioning for an advisory opinion must have the requisite *locus standi* to seek such a ruling.[200] The Inter-American Commission has been unequivocally recognised by the Court as having the competence to request advisory opinions,[201] and in practice has been the only organ to invoke the Court's advisory jurisdiction.[202] The procedure for invoking the advisory jurisdiction is initiated by making an application to the Court along with written observations. The Court then sets a date for a public hearing which is heard by the full Court. The ultimate decision to provide an advisory opinion is at the discretion of the Court. By virtue of the Courts' *amicus curiae* provisions, NGOs, academics and private individuals have been involved in the process of the Court's jurisdiction.[203]

---

[196] Article 64(1) (ACHR).

[197] Davidson, above n.142, at p. 101.

[198] *The Effect of Reservations on the Entry Into Force of the American Convention on Human Rights* (Arts. 74 and 75), Advisory Opinion OC-2/82, 24 September 1982, Inter-Am. Ct. H.R. (Ser. A) No. 2 (1982), para 14.

[199] Ibid.

[200] Ibid. The admissibility requirement is satisfied if submitted by an authorised entity (jurisdiction *ratione persona*), falls within the subject matter jurisdiction of the Court (jurisdiction *ratione materiae*) and contains any information that is required by ACHR. See Pasqualucci, above n.1, at p. 71.

[201] As the Court noted in *The Effect of Reservations on the Entry Into Force of the American Convention on Human Rights* Advisory opinion '[U]nlike some other OAS organs, the Commission enjoys, as a practical matter, an absolute right to request advisory opinions within the framework of Article 64(1) of the Convention' para 16.

[202] Trindade, 'The Operation of the Inter-American Court of Human Rights' in Harris and Livingstone (eds), above n.1, 133–150 at p. 142.

[203] See Shelton, above n.1, at p. 342; Shelton, 'The Participation of Non Governmental Organizations in International Judicial Proceedings' 88 *AJIL* (1994) 611, at 615.

Technically these opinions are advisory, however, through examination of the competence of the Court and its powers to interpret a particular provision, it can be said that it has considerable authority. For a State to disregard the advisory opinion of the Court is akin to breaching its obligations under the Convention. The Court's advisory jurisdiction has been used much more frequently than its contentious jurisdiction. A wide range of issues have been addressed by the Court in its advisory opinions. The Court has advised upon the relationship and inter-action of various systems of human rights protection with the opinion that the Convention creates immediate binding obligations for the ratifying State.[204] It has pronounced on the limitation of the use of the death penalty,[205] it has interpreted the provisions of the Convention[206] and has pronounced that the suspension of the remedies of *amparo* and *habeas corpus* (even in times of emergencies) as incompatible with the provisions of the Convention.[207]

In the first case considered by the Court, the *Other Treaties* advisory opinion,[208] the issue concerned the actual scope of the advisory jurisdiction of the Court, particularly the meaning of the reference in Article 64(1) to 'other treaties concerning the protection of human rights in the American System'. Peru had asked for an advisory opinion asking as to whether 'other treaties' meant treaties adopted within the framework of the Inter-American System, or was the term more general and included for example the UN Covenants and other non-American human rights treaties to which States outside the Americas may also be parties. The Court took the view that any human rights treaty may be the subject of an advisory opinion, although according to the Court there may be circumstances where it could refuse such a request if the case involved non-American States' obligations.[209] In the *Restrictions to the Death Penalty* advisory opinion[210] two primary issues were dealt with by the Court. Guatemala had made a reservation to Article 4(4) concerning the imposition of the death penalty, and the case emerged from a disagreement between the Commission and Guatemala. The first primary issue was, whether, in the absence of Guatemala having accepted the jurisdiction of the Court, it was still open to the Court to address the question. The Court took the view that since the case fell within the scope and competence of the Commission, the Court had jurisdiction to deal with the case.[211] Secondly, on the

---

[204] 'Other Treaties' Subject to the Consultative Jurisdiction of the Court (Art. 64 of the American Convention on Human Rights), Advisory Opinion OC-1/82, 24 September,1982, Inter-Am. Ct. H.R. (Ser. A) No. 1 (1982). and The Effect of Reservations on the Entry Into Force of the American Convention on Human Rights (Arts. 74 and 75), Advisory Opinion OC-2/82, 24 September 1982, Inter-Am. Ct. H.R. (Ser. A) No. 2 (1982), para 32.

[205] Restrictions to the Death Penalty (Arts. 4(2) and 4(4) of the American Convention on Human Rights), Advisory Opinion OC-3/83, 8 September 1983, Inter-Am. Ct. H.R. (Ser. A) No. 3 (1983).

[206] The Word 'Laws' in Article 30 of the American Convention on Human Rights, Advisory Opinion OC-6/86, 9 May 9, 1986, Inter-Am. Ct. H.R. (Ser. A) No. 6 (1986).

[207] Habeas Corpus in Emergency Situations (Arts. 27(2) and 7(6) of the American Convention on Human Rights), Advisory Opinion OC-8/87, 30 January 1987, Inter-Am. Ct. H.R. (Ser. A) No. 8 (1987) and Judicial Guarantees in States of Emergency (Arts. 27(2), 25 and 8 of the American Convention on Human Rights), Advisory Opinion OC-9/87, 6 October 1987, Inter-Am. Ct. H.R. (Ser. A) No. 9 (1987).

[208] 'Other Treaties' Subject to the Consultative Jurisdiction of the Court (Art. 64 of the American Convention on Human Rights), Advisory Opinion OC-1/82, 24 September 1982, Inter-Am. Ct. H.R. (Ser. A) No. 1 (1982).

[209] Ibid. para 21. Through the examples of the Castillo Petruzzi case (Preliminary Objections), paras 65–66 and 68–69 the Las Palmeras case (Preliminary Objections) para 34, it has been established that in contentious cases, the Inter-American Court does not have the jurisdiction to provide judgments on breaches of other treaties; see Pasqualucci, above n.1, at pp. 91–92.

[210] Restrictions to the Death Penalty (Arts. 4(2) and 4(4) of the American Convention on Human Rights), Advisory Opinion OC-3/83, 8 September 1983, Inter-Am. Ct. H.R. (Ser. A) No. 3 (1983).

[211] Ibid. paras 27–29.

substantive matter, the Court followed a much more traditional judicial approach. It held that Guatemala's reservations should be construed in a manner that was compatible to the objects and purposes of the Convention and at the same time leaving Guatemala's obligations under Article 2(4) intact. Although the Court did not find Guatemala's reservation as violating the objects and purposes of the Convention, the Court nevertheless made the following comment: 'a reservation which was designed to enable a State to suspend any of the non-derogable fundamental rights must be deemed to be incompatible with the object and purpose of the Convention and, consequently, not permitted by it'.[212]

In the *Interpretation of the American Declaration* case,[213] Columbia had asked for an advisory opinion of the Court regarding the status of the American Declaration on the Rights and Duties of Man, regarding the question whether under Article 64(1) of the ACHR it qualified as a treaty. The Court reversing the Commission's earlier approach took the view that it could not be regarded as a treaty. On the other hand, the Court did advance the position that the Declaration is an authoritative interpretation of the human rights provisions of the OAS Charter and in that sense is a source of international obligations. The importance given to the Declaration is valuable when the human rights record of the non-State parties of the ACHR are to be considered. In assessing the jurisprudence of the Court in its advisory jurisdiction, it has become evident that it has adopted a more robust approach than the ICJ. The Inter-American Court has stated that it should not refuse advisory jurisdiction because the subject-matter is based upon a dispute between States.[214]

9 FACT-FINDING MISSIONS OF THE INTER-AMERICAN COMMISSION

Article 18(g) of the Statute of the Inter-American Commission provides the Commission with a fact-finding investigative jurisdiction. It compares favourably to other fact-finding processes, in particular, the UN fact-finding missions.[215] Since its establishment, the Commission has conducted well over 60 *in loco* investigations of alleged violations of human rights in States belonging to OAS States. Commenting on the value of this investigation Trindade notes:

> . . . the IACHR has undertaken extensive fact-finding exercises, probably to a larger extent than any other international supervisory organ at least in so far as *in loco* observations are concerned. These are of particular significance as *in loco* investigations in Chile of 1974, the report on forced disappearances in Argentina of 1979, the report on the population of

---

[212] Ibid. para 61.
[213] *Interpretation of the American Declaration of the Rights and Duties of Man Within the Framework of Article 64 of the American Convention on Human Rights*, Advisory Opinion OC-10/89, 14 July 1989, Inter-Am. Ct. H.R. (Ser. A) No. 10 (1989).
[214] See *The Right to Information on Consular Assistance in the Framework of the Guarantees of the Due Process of Law*, Advisory Opinion OC-16/99, 1 October 1999, Inter-Am. Ct. H.R. (Ser. A) No. 16 (1999).
[215] See Bassiouni, 'Appraising UN Justice Related Fact-Finding Mission' 5 *Washington University Journal of Law and Policy* (2001) 37; Franck and Fairley, 'Procedural Due Process in Human Rights Fact-Finding by International Agencies' 74 *AJIL* (1980) 308; Weissbrodt and McCarthy, 'Fact-Finding by International Human Rights Organizations' 22 *Va.JIL* (1981) 1.

> Miskito origin in Nicaragua of 1984, and the reports on Haiti of 1993–1994, among others . . . The reports resulting from these mission have been instrumental in asserting the facts of a situation. Moreover, the publicity given to the reports has served to achieve certain of the objectives of a reporting system such as the monitoring of human rights, public scrutiny of legislative measures and administrative practices, exchange of information and the fostering of a better understanding of the problems encountered.[216]

These visits have, over time, reduced. Currently only a few visits take place with usually a single Commission member conducting a 'working visit' and issuing a press release at the end of the visit. Nevertheless during 2006, the Commission conducted on-site visits to Haiti, Columbia, the Dominican Republic, Argentina and Peru.[217] In conjunction with the fact-finding mission the Commission has included a chapter on 'Human Rights Development' in its annual reports. The objective of this information is to keep the OAS updated on human rights developments in the States of the region.

10 CONCLUSIONS

The promotion and protection of individual human rights within the Americas has been problematic. The region has witnessed substantial violations of human rights in the nature of torture, disappearances and mass killings. Repressive military regimes of the region violated human rights and victimised and persecuted unashamedly their political opponents. Confronted by hostile or unco-operative regimes it is to the credit of the inter-American system not only to have remained operational but also in a number of instances to have produced positive contributions to the protection of human rights and humanitarian law.[218]

This chapter has traced the developments through which the two largely incoherent inter-American systems are gradually progressing towards greater consistency and regularisation. Having said that, reliance upon the two distinct systems is unsatisfactory. The unsatisfactory nature of human rights protection is particularly evident in those States parties of the OAS which have not ratified the ACHR. The refusal to accept the obligations has a particularly strong impact regarding the obtaining of legally binding judgments as a result of the absence of recourse to the Inter-American Court. As Trindade correctly notes:

---

[216] Trindade, 'Reporting in the Inter-American System of Human Rights Protection' in Alston and Crawford (eds), *The Future of UN Human Rights Treaty Monitoring* (Cambridge University Press, 2000) pp. 333–346 at p. 342.

[217] See Annual Report 2006 (doc. OEEA/Ser L/V/II 127, Doc. 4 rev. 1, 3 March 2007) chapter II, section C. also noted by Tomuschat, above n.27, at p. 225.

[218] In *Salas* v. *United States*, the Inter-American Commission on Human Rights accorded a broad definition to provisions of the Inter-American Declaration to include the provisions of international humanitarian law. The Commission noted: '[w]here it is asserted that a use of military force has resulted in noncombatant deaths, personal injury, and property loss, the human rights of the noncombatants are implicated. In the context of the present case, the guarantees set forth in the American Declaration are implicated. The case sets forth allegations cognizable within the framework of the Declaration. Thus, the Commission is authorized to consider the subject matter of this case.' *Salas* v. *United States*, Case 10.573, Report No. 31/93, Inter-Am. C.H.R., OEA/Ser.L/V/II.85, doc.9 rev., Analysis, para 6 (1993).

> [t]he basis of the Court's compulsory jurisdiction provides yet another illustration of the unfortunate lack of automatic application of international jurisdiction. The Inter-American System of human rights protection will considerably advance the day that all OAS member States become parties to the American Convention (and its two Protocols) without reservations and all States Parties to the Convention accept unconditionally the Court's jurisdiction.[219]

Another important limitation is the lack of provisions in the Inter-American system to ensure compliance with the judgements of the Court. According to Article 65, the Court is required to submit to the General Assembly of the OAS, a report on its work during the previous year, in particular, the cases in which the Court's judgment has not been complied with.[220] Non-compliance or inadequate compliance continues to remain a substantial problem in human rights law. In this respect the largely political sanctions to ensure compliance represents an unsatisfactory feature of the Convention.[221]

There are significant limitations and weaknesses in the Inter-American human rights system. One of the primary difficulties is encountered with a system where a significant number of OAS States have failed to ratify or accede to the ACHR. This includes powerful and influential States such as the United States and Canada. In these instances the Inter-American Commission's mandate is limited to the application of the American Declaration of Human Rights and not the application of the ACHR. The second complexity is the lack of uniformity on the part of several members of the ACHR in failing to accept the compulsory jurisdiction of the Court. While a number of times, States have complied with the Court's judgments, there are, nevertheless, worrying instances of failure at a domestic level and failure to comply with recommendations of the Commission. Another considerable failing on the part of the OAS organs is in providing support for the Commission and the Court. The Inter-American system does not provide for a formal mechanism of the enforcement of the Court's judgments with the Court only required to present its annual report to the OAS General Assembly with the opportunity of referring the case when judgments have not been complied with. The General Assembly of the OAS may after discussing the issue of non-compliance adopt political steps against delinquent States. Unfortunately, political pressure has been ineffective – the Court's annual reports are not reviewed directly by the OAS General Assembly. Furthermore the General Assembly's responses have been attenuated towards non compliant States. 'No Comment' has been issued by the General Assembly for non compliance, nor has there been an appropriate response from the General Assembly. Thus, the denunciation of the Convention by Trinidad and Tobago was not commented upon by the OAS General Assembly nor did it react when Trinidad and Tobago rejected the provisional measures ordered by the Court in the death penalty case.[222]

Finally, like all international and regional human rights bodies, the OAS institutions suffer from a lack of adequate funding; sessions of the Court have been postponed.

[219] Trindade, 'The Operation of the Inter-American Court of Human Rights' in Harris and Livingstone (eds), above n.1, 133–150 at p. 136.
[220] Article 65 ACHR
[221] See Gomez, 'The Interaction between the Political Actors of the OAS, the Commission and the Court' in Harris and Livingstone (eds), above n.1, 173–211 at pp. 191–192.
[222] *James* et al. Case, Order of the Court of May 27, 1998, Inter-Am. Ct. H.R. (Ser. E) (1998). *James* et al. Case, Order of the Court of 2 December 2003, Inter-Am. Ct. H.R. (Ser. E) (2003).

9

The inter-American system for the protection of human rights

The growth in the caseload of the Court is partly a consequence of greater interest in the system and partly because of the Commission's Rules of Procedure 2001, whereby all cases against States which have accepted the Court's compulsory jurisdiction will be referred to the Court 'unless there is a reasoned decision by an absolute majority of the members of the Commission to the contrary'.[223] This has led to an increase in the workload of the Court and, therefore, demands additional court sessions.

Notwithstanding these limitations, the positive impact of the Inter-American Court can be gauged from the fact that in some instances a mere referral of the case has produced the desired results. Even with a blotted record of human rights violations, States have accepted responsibility for violations rather than face the prospect of an adverse judgment from the Inter-American Court of Human Rights. These States include Bolivia, Surinam, Peru and Ecuador. The Inter-American Court's advisory jurisdiction has also had a positive impact in bringing about changes in domestic laws and procedures.[224]

---

[223] Rules of Procedure of the Inter-American Commission on Human Rights 2001, entered into force 1 May 2001, approved by the Commission at its 109th special session held 4–8 December 2000, Article 44(1); Pasqualucci above n.1 at p. 347.

[224] Ibid. at p. 347.

10 The African system for the protection of human rights[1]

1 INTRODUCTION

Historically termed as the 'Black Continent', from pre-colonial to modern times Africa has witnessed substantial violations of human rights. In pre-colonial Africa, unfortunate practices such as human sacrifices, torture and infanticide were undertaken.[2] During the period of colonisation, Africa was economically and politically exploited and served as a ready producer for the slave trade and European expansionism.[3] For Africa, the transition from Colonialism to independent statehood has been a painful one. Post-Colonial Africa has witnessed substantial violations of individual and collective rights. The repressive one-party political systems and the dictatorial regimes under men like Idi Amin of Uganda (1971–79), Francisco Macías Nguema of Equatorial Guinea (1968–79), Jean-Bédel Bokassa of the former Central African Empire (1966–79), Omar Hasan Ahmad Al-Bashir of Sudan

---

[1] Flinterman and Ankumah, 'The African Charter on Human and Peoples' Rights' in Hannum (ed.), *Guide to International Human Rights Practice* (Transnational Publishers, 2004) pp. 171–188; Banda, *Women, Law and Human Rights: An African Perspective* (Hart Publishing, 2005); Starmer and Christou (eds), *Human Rights Manual and Sourcebook for Africa* (British Institute of International and Comparative Law, 2005); Davidson, *Human Rights* (Open University Press, 1993) pp. 152–162; Steiner, Alston and Goodman (eds), *International Human Rights in Context: Law, Politics, Morals* (Oxford University Press, 2008) pp. 1062–1083; Heyns, 'The African Regional Human Rights System: The African Charter' 108 *Penn. St. L. Rev.* (2004) 679; Quashigah and Okafor (eds), *Legitimate Governance in Africa: International and Domestic Legal Perspectives* (Kluwer Law International, 1999); Robertson and Merrills, *Human Rights in the World: An Introduction to the Study of the International Protection of Human Rights* (Manchester University Press, 1996) pp. 242–266; Murray, *Human Rights in Africa: From the OAU to African Union* (Cambridge University Press, 2004); Murray, 'International Human Rights: Neglect of Perspectives from African Institutions' 55 *ICLQ* (2006) 193; Murray, *The Role of National Human Rights Institutions at the International and Regional Levels: The Experience of Africa* (Hart Publishing, 2007); Evans and Murray, (eds) *The African Charter on Human and Peoples' Rights: The System in Practice, 1986–2006* (Cambridge University Press, 2008); Mutua, 'The African Human Rights Court: A Two Legged Stool?' 21 *HRQ* (1999) 342; Okafor, *The African Human Rights System, Activist Forces and International Institutions* (Cambridge University Press, 2007); Ouguergouz, *The African Charter of Human and People's Rights: A Comprehensive Agenda for Human Dignity and Sustainable Democracy in Africa* (Martinus Nijhoff Publishers, 2003); Umozurike, *The African Charter on Human and Peoples' Rights* (Martinus Nijhoff Publishers, 1997); Viljoen, *International Human Rights Law in Africa* (Oxford University Press, 2007); Viljoen, 'Africa's Contribution to the Development of International Human Rights and Humanitarian Law' 1 *African Human Rights Law Journal* (2001) 18; Wachira, *African Court on Human and Peoples' Rights: Ten Years on and Still no Justice* (Minority Rights Group, 2008).

[2] Umozurike, above n.1, at pp. 15–18.

[3] See Cassese, *International Law in a Divided World* (Clarendon Press, 1986) p. 52; Howard, 'Evaluating Human Rights in Africa: Some Problems of Implicit Comparisons' 6 *HRQ* (1984) 160 at p. 170; the claims for reparations for abuses conducted during the times of slavery and colonialism are hugely interconnected, see Plessis, 'Historical Injustices and International Law: An Exploratory Discussion of Reparations for Slavery' 25 *HRQ* (2003) 624.

(1989–) and Robert Mugabe of Zimbabwe (1980–) have been instrumental in the denial of all fundamental rights. Worst still, several African States notably Rwanda, Burundi and the Sudan have produced continuous waves of ethnic cleansing and genocide.

Amidst the gross violations of individual and collective rights, human rights have not been the strong point of African governments or African inter-governmental organisations.[4] Effective protection of human rights was rarely a factor influencing the policies of the Organization of African Unity (OAU), the principal regional African organisation between 1963 and 2002. The OAU was replaced by the African Union (AU) in 2002. This chapter deals with African Human Rights law, with its primary focus upon the African Charter on Human and Peoples' Rights (1986). In order to have an updated and complete understanding of the regional human rights machinery, it remains important to briefly examine the regional institutional framework of the African Union (AU).

(i) The African Union (AU)

The AU was established through the adoption of the Constitutive Act in the Lome Summit Togo on 11 July 2000.[5] The Durban Summit in 2002 launched the new organisation with the convening of the first Assembly of the Heads of States of the AU. The AU replaced the OAU and the references to OAU within existing treaties should now be read as the AU. The OAU Charter has been replaced and abrogated by the Constitutive Act of the AU. The primary and supreme organ of the Union is the Assembly of Heads of State and Government, which consists of Heads of States and Government or their duly accredited representatives.[6] It meets once every year with the possibility of having extraordinary sessions.[7] Amongst the functions of the Assembly are the determination of a common policy for the Union as well as devising and implementing the policies and decisions of the Union.[8] The Assembly makes its decisions by consensus or by a two-thirds majority of the Member States of the Union.[9] The Executive Council consists of the Executive Council of Ministers of the Union and is 'composed of the Ministers of Foreign Affairs or such other Ministers or Authorities as are designated by the Governments of Member States'.[10] It meets twice a year in ordinary session and can also convene in an extra-ordinary session at the request of any Member State and upon approval by two-thirds of all Member States. The Executive Council takes its decisions by consensus or by a two-thirds majority of the Member States. However, procedural matters, including the question of whether a matter is one of procedure or not, shall be decided by a simple majority.[11] In March 2004, the AU established the Pan-African

---

[4] For historical position see Umozurike, 'The African Charter on Human and Peoples' Rights' 77 *AJIL* (1983) 902; Umozurike, 'The Domestic Jurisdiction Clause in the O.A.U Charter' 311 *African Affairs* (1979) 197 at p. 199; D'Sa, 'Human and Peoples' Rights: Distinctive Features of the African Charter' 29 *JAL* (1985) 72 at p. 73.

[5] Lome, Togo, 11 July 2000 OAU Doc. CAB/LEG/23.15, entered into force 26 May 2001. On the African Union, see also Amnesty International, *African Union: A New Opportunity for the Promotion and Protection of Human Rights in Africa* (Amnesty International, 2002); Wing, Jackson and Levitt (eds), *The African Union and the New Pan-Africanism: Rushing to Reorganize or Timely Shift?* (American Society of International Law: University of Iowa, 2003).

[6] www.africa-union.org/root/au/organs/assembly_en.htm <last visited 20 May 2009>.

[7] Ibid.

[8] Ibid.

[9] Ibid.

[10] www.africa-union.org/root/au/organs/Executive_Council_en.htm <last visited 20 May 2009>.

[11] Ibid.

Parliament (PAP), which was aimed to be one of the foremost and effective organs of the Organisation.[12] For an initial period of five years, PAP is only assigned consultative and advisory duties though the ultimate aim after this time is to establish an institution with complete legislative powers.[13] Amongst the primary objectives of the Pan-African Parliament are the facilitation of effective implementation policies and objectives of the AU. The powers of the PAP include the examination and discussion of any matters including those of making recommendations related to matters concerning human rights, development of democracy and consolidation of the rule of law. The PAP comprises of 265 representatives. There are no direct elections to PAP, but representatives are elected by the legislatures of the 53 AU Member States. The initial seat of the PAP was in Addis Ababa, Ethiopia, but was later shifted to Midrand, South Africa. There are currently 10 Permanent Committees of the PAP aiming to deal with various sectors connected to the institution. The AU also consists of a Commission which operates as the Secretariat of the Union.[14] The Commission consists of the Chairman, and his or her deputy or deputies with the structure, functions and regulations of the Commission having been determined by the Assembly.[15] The AU also envisions a Court of Justice for the Organisation.[16] The Statute, composition as well as the functions of the Court are defined in a Protocol to the Court.[17] The AU also consists of a Permanent Representatives Committee, which is made up of Permanent Representatives to the Union and other Plenipotentiaries of Member States.[18] The work of the Executive Council is prepared by the Permanent Representatives Committee, which also acts upon the instructions of the Council. The Permanent Representatives Committee may also set up sub-committees and working groups in order to aid its work.[19] Furthermore, the Organisation establishes a number of specialised technical committees which are responsible to the Executive Council.[20] These are the Committee on Rural Economy and Agricultural Matters; the Committee on Monetary and Financial Affairs; the Committee on Trade, Customs and Immigration Matters; the Committee on Industry, Science and Technology, Energy, Natural Resources and Environment; the Committee on Transport, Communications and Tourism; the Committee on Health, Labour and Social Affairs; and the Committee on Education, Culture and Human Resources.[21]

After being ratified by a majority of Member States of the AU, the Protocol Relating to the Peace and Security Council (PSC) of the African Union came into force on 26 December 2003.[22] Following which the Fourth Ordinary Session of the Executive Council both elected the 15 members and adopted the Rules of the Procedure of the PSC. The PSC

---

[12] www.pan-african-parliament.org/default.aspx <last visited 20 May 2009>.
[13] www.pan-african-parliament.org/ABOUTPAP_GeneralOverview.aspx <last visited 20 May 2009>.
[14] www.africa-union.org/root/au/organs/The_Commission_en.htm <last visited 20 May 2009>.
[15] Ibid.
[16] www.africa-union.org/root/au/organs/Court_of_Justice_en.htm <last visited 12 May 2009>.
[17] www.africa-union.org/root/au/organs/Court_of_Justice_en.htm; www.africa-union.org/root/AU/Documents/ Treaties/Text/Protocol%20to%20the%20African%20Court%20of%20Justice%20-%20Maputo.pdf <last visited 12 May 2009>.
[18] www.africa-union.org/root/au/organs/Permanent_%20Representative_%20Committee_en.htm <last visited 12 May 2009>.
[19] Ibid.
[20] www.africa-union.org/root/au/organs/Specialized_Technical_Committee_en.htm <last visited 12 May 2009>.
[21] Ibid.
[22] www.africa-union.org/root/au/organs/The_Peace_%20and_Security_Council_en.htm <last visited 12 May 2009>.

has since then held a number of meetings that focus on conflict situations in Africa.[23] Furthermore, the PSC was aptly launched on Africa Day, 25 May 2004, at the level of Heads of State and Government of the Members of the PSC, in the presence of the representatives of the other AU Member States and AU Partners.[24] The AU also envisages a number of financial institutions whose rules and regulations are defined in protocols relating thereto – the African Central Bank, the African Monetary Fund, and the African Investment Bank.[25]

(ii) The African Union and human rights law

The OAU, from the point of its inception was consumed by the rhetoric of anti-colonialism, anti-racism and anti-apartheid movements. The preservation of State sovereignty, territorial integrity and non-interference in internal domestic affairs of States remained cardinal principles of the OAU.[26] The AU, which succeeded the OAU in 2002, has, in symbolic terms, accorded greater attention to the principle of human rights, democracy and rule of law.[27] The Constitutive Act of the AU, represents an improvement on the Charter of the OAU in its recognition of human rights values. In stating the objective of the AU, Article 3 provides the objectives of the AU as follows:

> (e) encourage international cooperation, taking due account of the Charter of the United Nations and the Universal Declaration of Human Rights;
>
> (f) promote peace, security, and stability on the continent;
>
> (g) promote democratic principles and institutions, popular participation and good governance;
>
> (h) promote and protect human and peoples' rights in accordance with the African Charter on Human and Peoples' Rights and other relevant human rights instruments.

The AU is to function in accordance with *inter alia* the following principles:

> Article 4 . . .
>
> (h) the right of the Union to intervene in a Member State pursuant to a decision of the Assembly in respect of grave circumstances, namely: war crimes, genocide and crimes against humanity;
>
> (i) peaceful co-existence of Member States and their right to live in peace and security;
>
> (j) the right of Member States to request intervention from the Union in order to restore peace and security;
>
> (k) promotion of self-reliance within the framework of the Union;

---

[23] Ibid.

[24] Ibid.

[25] www.africa-union.org/root/au/organs/Financial_Institutions_en.htm <last visited 12 May 2009>.

[26] Murray, *Human Rights in Africa* above n.1, pp. 11–15.

[27] See generally Magliveras and Naldi, 'The African Union – A New Dawn for Africa' 51 *ICLQ* (2002) 415; Maluwa, 'The Constitutive Act of the African Union and Institute Building in Post-Colonial Africa' 16 *Leiden JIL* (2003) 157; Packer and Rukare, 'The New African Union and its Constitutive Act' 96 *AJIL* (2002) 365.

(l) promotion of gender equality;

(m) respect for democratic principles, human rights, the rule of law and good governance;

(n) promotion of social justice to ensure balanced economic development;

(o) respect for the sanctity of human life, condemnation and rejection of impunity and political assassination, acts of terrorism and subversive activities;

(p) condemnation and rejection of unconstitutional changes of governments.

Notwithstanding virtuous expressions, the past decade has established the *de facto* continuation of disinterest in the projection of human rights law by the AU. The ineffectual policies of the OAU are reflected in the ideological and practical engagement of the AU within a number of key human rights bodies. The Constitutive Act of the AU failed to establish a specialist Commission relating to human rights and it, also, does not provide recognition to Africa's long-standing human rights institution, the African Commission on Human and Peoples' Rights.[28] The Constitutive Act similarly failed to make reference to potentially the most significant of regional human rights organs – the African Court of Human Rights, the Protocol to the Court having been adopted in 1998.[29] Similarly, it was not until July 2008, that a Protocol on the Statute of the African Court of Justice and Human Rights was adopted.[30]

2 THE AFRICAN CHARTER ON HUMAN AND PEOPLES' RIGHTS AND ITS DISTINCTIVE FEATURES[31]

A major exception to the otherwise genuine distaste for the promotion and implementation of human rights in Africa was the adoption of African Charter on Human and Peoples' Rights (AFCHPR).[32] The African Charter is also known as the Banjul Charter after Banjul, Gambia's Capital where the Charter was drafted. The Charter was adopted in June 1981 at the 18th Conference of Heads of State and Government of the OAU. It came into operation in October 1986. As shall be examined in due course, a Protocol to the Charter establishing an African Court on Human and Peoples' Rights was adopted in 1998. The Protocol came into force in 2004 with all States parties to the AU being eligible to become

---

[28] See Manby, 'The African Union, NEPAD, and Human Rights' 26 *HRQ* (2004) 983 at p. 987.

[29] The Protocol to the African Charter on Human and Peoples' Rights on the Establishment of an African Court on Human and Peoples' Rights; in highlighting some of shortcomings, Manby makes the observation that 'Despite its human rights language, the AU Constitutive Act does not refer to the continent's longest-standing human rights institution, the African Commission on Human and Peoples' Rights (ACHPR), responsible for monitoring compliance by states with the African Charter on Human and Peoples' Rights. Nor does it mention the protocol to establish an African Court on Human and Peoples' Rights (adopted in 1998, though it only came into force in January 2004); or the recently-created African Committee of Experts on the Rights and Welfare of the Child, monitoring the African Charter on the Rights and Welfare of the Child (adopted by the OAU in 1990 and entered into force in 1999). The authority of these institutions rests, independently, on individual states' ratification of their founding documents; but the explicit commitment of African states to the work of these human rights bodies was not secured at a crucial moment' Manby, above n.28, at p. 987.

[30] See Protocol on the Statute of the African Court of Justice and Human Rights (2008) Sharm El-Sheikh, Egypt, 1 July 2008. www.africa-union.org/root/au/Documents/Treaties/text/Protocol%20on%20the%20Merged%20 Court%20-%20EN.pdf <last visited 10 May 2009>.

[31] D'Sa, above n.4, at p. 73.

[32] African [Banjul] Charter on Human and Peoples' Rights, adopted June 27, 1981, OAU Doc. CAB/LEG/67/3 rev.5, 21 I.L.M. 58 (1982), entered into force 21 October 1986.

parties to the Charter (and the Protocol).[33] However in a further most significant development, the AU adopted the Protocol on the Statute of the African Court of Justice and Human Rights (2008). The 2008 Protocol replaces the Protocol to the African Charter on Human and Peoples' Rights on the Establishment of an African Court on Human and Peoples' Rights, (1998) and the Protocol of the Court of Justice of the African Union (2003).[34] This chapter deals with African human rights law, with its primary focus upon the protection accorded through the African Charter on Human and Peoples' Rights (the Charter).

(i) Incorporation of three generation of rights

Earlier chapters have considered the divisions and bifurcations between the three generations of rights. The Charter is the only human rights treaty to accord explicit protection to civil and political rights, economic, social, cultural as well as collective group rights. The Charter contains an elaborate list of traditional civil and political rights. These rights bear strong similarities to the ones contained in other international and regional treaties and include such fundamental rights as the right to equality before the law, the right to liberty, the right to a fair trial, freedom of conscience including religious freedom, freedom of association and freedom of assembly. In addition to the civil and political rights, there is a set of economic, social and cultural rights.[35] These include the right to education, the right to participate in the cultural life of one's community, and the right of the aged and disabled to special measures of protection.

Furthermore, and more exceptionally, the Charter also contains a number of collective rights, the so-called 'third-generation' rights. The idea of peoples' rights, in particular, the right to economic and political self-determination, forms a vital element within the constitutional workings of independent African States; it is also strongly represented within the African Charter, which as its title confirms is the only treaty upholding the rights of peoples alongside individual human rights. The Charter contains the important and well-established rights of peoples such as the right to existence and the right to self-determination. Associated with the right to self-determination is the condemnation of colonisation and domination of one people by another.[36] In addition, there are other innovate (though equally valuable) rights such as the 'right to a general satisfactory environment'. Environmental rights are increasingly being associated as part of the framework of international human rights law.[37] There is now substantial jurisprudence on the right to environment, although the contribution of the African Charter to the subject needs to be acknowledged.[38] As a pioneering treaty provision in international human rights law, Article 24 of

---

[33] Odinkalu and Christensen, 'The African Commission on Human and People's Rights: The Development of its Non-State Communication Procedures' 20 *HRQ* (1998) 235 at pp. 236–237.

[34] This replacement is subject to certain transitional arrangements (provided in Articles 5, 7 and 9 of the Protocol). See Article 1 of the Protocol on the Statute of the African Court of Justice and Human Rights (2008) www.africa-union.org/root/au/Documents/Treaties/text/Protocol%20on%20the%20Merged%20Court%20-%20EN.pdf <last visited 10 February 2009>.

[35] Odinkalu, 'Analysis of Paralysis or Paralysis by Analysis? Implementing Economic, Social, and Cultural Rights Under the African Charter on Human and Peoples' Rights' 23 *HRQ* (2001) 327.

[36] Article 19, Article 20(2).

[37] Boyle and Anderson (eds), *Human Rights Approaches to Environmental Protection* (Clarendon Press, 1996); Birnie and Boyle, *International Law and the Environment* (Clarendon Press, 1992) pp. 188–214; Rehman, 'The Role and Contribution of the World Court in the Progressive Development of International Environmental Law' 5 *APJEL* (2000) 387.

[38] See Tesi (ed.), *The Environment and Development in Sub-Saharan Africa* (Lexington Books, 2000).

the Charter has done much to highlight the existence of 'a general satisfactory environment' as a human right.[39]

(ii) Duties of the individual

The idea of duties, once again a distinctive feature of African societies is unprecedented in so far as human rights treaties are concerned.[40] However, the African Charter sets these out explicitly within Chapter II, Articles 27–29. It has been contended that the Charter includes a section on duties for the same reason as it includes a group of articles on economic and social rights. The primary reason had been that the States concerned wished to put forward a distinctive conception of human rights in which civil and political rights were seen to be counterbalanced by duties of social solidarity. Three general principles emerge from these provisions regarding the duties. Firstly, that every individual has duties towards his family and society, towards the State, 'other legally recognized communities, and the international community'.[41] Secondly, '[t]he rights and freedoms of each individual shall be exercised with due regard to the rights of others, collective security, morality and common interests'.[42] Thirdly, that everyone has the duty to respect and consider others without discrimination and to promote mutual respect and tolerance.[43] The individual also owes a duty to his family, national community, nation, and the African region as a whole.[44]

(iii) 'Claw-back' clauses

The Charter, unlike other international and regional human rights treaties, does not contain any derogation provisions – meaning thereby that States are not permitted to derogate from the provisions of Charter even in times of public emergency.[45] This laudable and distinctive feature of the Charter, nevertheless, has arguably allowed for other weaknesses in

---

[39] See Giorgetta, 'The Right to Healthy Environment' in Schrijver and Weiss (eds), *International Law and Sustainable Development: Principle and Practice* (Martinus Nijhoff Publishers, 2004) pp. 379–404, at p. 387. For regional environmental treaties within Africa see the African Convention on the Ban of the Importation of All forms of Hazardous Wastes in Africa and the Control of Transboundary movement of Such Wastes in Africa and the Control of Transboundary movement of Such Wastes generated in Africa 20 *Environmental Policy and Law* (1990) 173. See further the African Convention on the Conservation of Nature and Natural Resources, Algiers, Algeria, 15 September 1968, OAU Doc. CAB/LEG/24–I, entered into force 16 June 1969; Bamako Convention on the Ban of the Import into Africa and the Control of Transboundary Movement and Management of Hazardous Wastes within Africa, Bamako, Mali, 30 January 1991, 1 *African Year Book of International Law* (1993) 269–293, entered into force 22 April 1998.

[40] We have noted the existence of provisions on the duties of the individuals in the American Declaration of the Rights and Duties of Man (1948); see above chapter 9.

[41] Article 27(1) AFCHPR.

[42] Ibid. Article 27(2).

[43] Ibid. Article 28.

[44] Ibid. Article 29.

[45] The African Commission on Human and Peoples' Rights has held that States are not permitted to derogated from the provisions of the Charter, since no derogation clauses are contained within the Treaty *Article 19* v. *Eritrea*, Communication No. 275/2003 (2007). In *Media Rights Agenda* v. *Nigeria*, Communication No. 224/98 (2000) the African Commission affirmed that the lack of any derogation clause in the Africa Charter on Human and Peoples' Rights means that 'limitations on the rights and freedoms . . . cannot be justified by emergencies or special circumstances.' On the impressibility of derogating from the AFCHPR, see Manby 'Civil and Political Rights in the African Charter on Human and Peoples' Rights: Articles 1–7' in Evans and Murray (eds) above n.1, 171–212, at p. 176. Note however that Reservations that are compatible with the objects and purposes of the treaty are permissible and valid. See Viljoen, 'Communications under the African Charter: Procedure and Admissibility' Evans and Murray (eds), above n.1, 76–138, at p. 99.

the system. The Charter has been criticised for the vague nature of its provisions, and its so-called 'claw-back' clauses which authorise the State parties to deprive the individual, his or her rights.[46] The 'claw-back' clauses are used in relation to Articles 5–12 and have similarities to derogation clauses, save that in the case of the latter circumstances are explicitly stated in which rights may be limited. In so far as 'claw-back' clauses are concerned, a wide range of discretion is conferred upon the State to exclude the enjoyment of rights.[47] In each instance the State is permitted to justify limitations on the rights by reference to its own domestic laws. As we shall consider, these 'claw-back' clauses feature in many of the rights within the Charter. The impediment which exists due to the presence of 'claw-back' provisions has been challenged by the interpretative approach adopted by the African Commission on Human and Peoples' Rights. According to this approach, the usage of the phrase 'subject to law' is to be taken to mean as subject to international law as opposed to domestic law. As the Commission noted:

> [i]n regulating the use of this right . . . [freedom of association, under Article 10], the competent authorities should not enact provisions which would limit the exercise of this freedom. The competent authorities should not override constitutional provisions or undermine fundamental rights guaranteed by the constitution and international human rights standards.[48]

3 ANALYSING THE SUBSTANTIVE RIGHTS IN THE CHARTER

The Charter can be divided into three parts. Part one contains the rights and duties of the individual, part two considers the role and functions of the African Commission on Human and Peoples' Rights (the Commission), whereas part three provides for general procedural provisions. The principal executive organ for the implementation of the Charter has thus far been the Commission. However, it has established an African Court on Human and Peoples' Rights,[49] which as noted already merged with the African Court of

---

[46] Welch. Jr., 'The African Commission on Human and Peoples' Rights: A Five Year Report and Assessment' 14 *HRQ* (1992) 43 at p. 46. In an earlier edition of Murray and Evans (eds), *The African Charter on Human and Peoples' Rights: The System in Practice, 1986–2000* Christof Heyns regards this as 'perhaps the most serious flaw in the Charter if one interprets "law" as *domestic law*', Heyns, 'Civil and Political Rights in the African Charter' in Murray and Evans (eds), *The African Charter on Human and Peoples' Rights: The System in Practice, 1986–2000* (Cambridge University Press, 2002) pp. 137–177, at p. 142. (Italics provided).

[47] See Higgins, 'Derogations under Human Rights Treaties' 48 *BYIL* (1976–77) 281; Kiss, 'Permissible Limitations on Rights' in Henkin (ed.), *The International Bill of Rights: The Covenant on Civil and Political Rights* (Columbia University Press, 1981) pp. 290–310.

[48] *Civil Liberties Organisation in respect of the Nigerian Bar Association* v. *Nigeria*, Communication No. 101/93 (1995), para 16; in relation to the right to express and disseminate opinions, the Commission noted that '[a]ccording to Article 9(2) of the Charter, dissemination of opinions may be restricted by law. This does not however mean that national law can set aside the right to express and disseminate one's opinions guaranteed at the international level; this would make the protection of the right to express one's opinion ineffective. To permit national law to take precedence over international law would defeat the purpose of codifying certain rights in international law and indeed, the whole essence of treaty making' *Constitutional Rights Project, Civil Liberties Organisation and Media Rights Agenda* v. *Nigeria*, Communication Nos. 140/94, 141/94, 145/95 (1999) para 40.

[49] See Protocol to the African Charter on Human and Peoples' Rights on the Establishment of an African Court on Human and Peoples' Rights adopted 10 June 1998, OAU. Doc. CAB/LEG/66/5. The Protocol entered into force on 25 January 2004. Also see the Draft Protocol to the African Charter on Human and Peoples' Rights on the Establishment of an African Court on Human and Peoples Rights by the Assembly of Heads of State and Governments of the Organization of the African Unity, Conference of Ministers/Attorney-General on the

Justice to form a single Court and to establish the single Court known as 'The African Court of Justice and Human Rights'.[50] The Court will complement the work of the Commission. According to Article 1 of the African Charter, States parties recognise the rights, duties and freedoms in the Charter and undertake to adopt legislative or any other measures of compliance. The subsequent Articles provide a list of rights contained in the Charter. These are as follows:

Article 2	The right to non-discrimination
Article 3	The right to equality before the law
Article 4	The right to respect for life and the integrity of the person
Article 5	Freedom from exploitation and degradation, including slavery, torture and cruel, inhuman or degrading punishment
Article 6	The right to liberty and security of the person
Article 7(1)	The right to a fair trial
Article 7(2)	Freedom from retrospective punishment
Article 8	Freedom of conscience, the profession and free practice of religion
Article 9(1)	The right to receive information
Article 9(2)	The right to express and disseminate opinions
Article 10	Freedom of Association
Article 11	Freedom of Assembly
Article 12(1)	Freedom of movement
Article 12(2)	Right to leave any country and the right to return to his own country
Article 12(3)	Right to seek and obtain asylum
Article 12(5)	Prohibition of mass expulsion
Article 13(1)	The right to participate in government
Article 13(2)	The right to equal access to the public services
Article 13(3)	The right to of equal access to public property and to public services
Article 14	The right to property
Article 15	The right to work
Article 16	The right to health
Article 17(1)	The right to education
Article 17(2)	The right to participate in the cultural life of one's community
Article 17(3)	The duty of the State to promote and protect the moral and traditional values recognised by the community
Article 18(1)	Recognition of family as the natural unity and basis of society
Article 18(2)	Right of the family to be assisted as a custodian of morals and traditional values
Article 18(3)	Protection of the rights of women and children
Article 18(4)	Rights of the aged and disabled

Establishment of an African Court of Human and Peoples' Rights OAU/LEG/MIN/AFCHPR/PROT (1) Rev. 2 (1997). Also see Naldi and Magliveras, 'Reinforcing the African System of Human Rights: The Protocol on the Establishment of a Regional Court of Human and Peoples' Rights' 16 *NQHR* (1998) 431.

[50] See Protocol on the Statute of the African Court of Justice and Human Rights (2008), Sharm El-Sheikh, Egypt, 1 July 2008. www.africa-union.org/root/au/Documents/Treaties/text/Protocol%20on%20the%20Merged%20 Court%20-%20EN.pdf <last visited 10 February 2009>.

Article 19	Peoples' right to equality
Article 20(1)	Peoples' right to existence
Article 20(1)–(3)	Peoples' right to self-determination
Article 21(1)	Peoples' right to freely dispose of wealth and natural resources
Article 22	Peoples' right to economic, social and cultural development
Article 23	Peoples' right to national and international peace and security
Article 24	Peoples' right to a general satisfactory environment

(i) Non-discrimination and equality

Article 2 of the Charter reiterates the right to non-discrimination. This right, as we have noted throughout this study, represents the core of modern human rights law. It has been correctly established as the leading right within the context of a region, which has suffered from substantial acts of discrimination and inequalities. Article 2 provides:

> Every individual shall be entitled to the enjoyment of the rights and freedoms recognized and guaranteed in the present Charter without distinction of any kind such as race, ethnic group, color, sex, language, religion, political or any other opinion, national and social origin, fortune, birth or other status.

The terminology of the Article and the prohibited categories of discrimination are very similar to those employed in other human rights treaties. Like other human rights instruments distinctions based on race, ethnicity, colour, sex, language, political opinions and national and social origins, or birth are impermissible. The analysis of the provisions of this Article allows us to make a number of specific comments. Firstly, the terms used in the Article are not exhaustive; other possible grounds of discrimination, e.g. age, disability and sexual orientation,[51] are also covered by 'other status'. Secondly, the usage of the term 'fortune' represents an innovate basis of non-discrimination. From the *travaux préparatoires* the rationale for employing this term is not fully established. According to the *Oxford Advanced Learner's Dictionary*, 'fortune' means 'chance, especially regarded as a power affecting peoples' lives'.[52] It has been suggested by one commentator that its addition 'implied African recognition that enforcement of rights may depend upon a person's general circumstances or status in society'.[53] Thirdly, amongst this broad right to non-discrimination, certain sections of the community nevertheless deserve special attention. In the light of the frequent discrimination faced by women and children, protection of their rights on the basis of equality is an important concern.[54] The rights of women and children in the context of African regional human rights law have been further expanded by the Protocol to the African Charter on Human and Peoples' Rights on the Rights of Women

---

[51] See Murray and Viljoen 'Towards Non-Discrimination on the Basis of Sexual Orientation: The Normative Basis and Procedural Possibilities before the African Commission on Human and Peoples' Rights and the African Union' 29 *Human Rights Quarterly* (2007) 86.

[52] *Oxford Advanced Learner's Dictionary of Current English* (Oxford University Press, 1989) p. 486.

[53] Davidson, above n.1, at p. 154.

[54] See Van Bueren, *The International Law on the Rights of the Child* (Martinus Nijhoff Publishers, 1995) at p. 402.

in Africa[55] and the African Charter on the Rights and Welfare of the Child.[56] Furthermore, the AU has expressed its interest in promoting gender equality. The Constitutive Act of the AU provides that one of the principles of the Union is to be 'promotion of gender equality'.[57] According to the Protocol on Peace and Security members of the Council are to be 'elected on the basis of equal rights'.[58] Similarly, according to the Protocol of the African Court of Justice '[d]ue consideration shall be given to adequate gender representation in the nomination process'.[59] The Protocol to the Treaty Establishing African Economic Community to the Pan-African Parliament obliges States Parties to have at least one woman amongst their five member representatives in the Parliament.[60]

The right to non-discrimination is further reinforced by the provisions of Article 3 which emphasises the equality of all individuals before the law,[61] and equal protection of the law.[62] As already noted, equality and non-discrimination represent the fundamental principles of all international, regional and domestic frameworks. Equality includes *de jure* and *de facto* equality, confirming Umozurike's point that 'the Charter refers to substantive or relative and not material, formal or absolute equality'.[63] The notion of equality, therefore, allows for special measures and perhaps more radically reverse discrimination and affirmative action policies.

Non-discrimination and equality as broad overarching principles also encapsulate the concept of fairness in trial and freedom from retrospective punishment. The right to fair trial is covered by Article 7. Article 7(1) provides every individual with 'the right to have his cause heard'. This Article includes the right of appeal to competent national organs, and affirms a right to be presumed innocent until proved guilty by a competent court or tribunal. It also affirms the right to defence, including the right to be defended by counsel of his choice; and the right to be tried within a reasonable time by an impartial court or tribunal. Article 7(2) contains the cardinal principle of natural justice that no one may be condemned for an act or omission which did not constitute a legally punishable offence at the time it was committed. It provides that 'no penalty may be inflicted for an offence for which no provision was made at the time it was committed. Punishment is personal and can be imposed only on the offender'.

(ii) Right to life and prohibitions of torture and slavery

The right to life, as the supreme human right, has been protected by Article 4 of the Charter which provides as follows:

---

[55] Protocol to the African Charter on Human and Peoples Rights on the Rights of Women in Africa, Maputo, 13 September 2000 OAU Doc. CAB/LEG/66.6 (2000).

[56] African Charter on the Rights and Welfare of the Child, Addis Ababa, Ethiopa, July 1990 OAU Doc. CAB/LEG/24.9/49 (1990), entered into force 29 November 1999.

[57] Article 4(1)

[58] Protocol Relating to the Establishment of the Peace and Security Council of the African Union, Durban, South Africa, 10 July 2002, OAU Doc. CAB/LEG/23.22, entered into force, 26 December 2003. Article 5(1).

[59] Article 5(3).

[60] Protocol to the Treaty Establishing African Economic Community Relating to the Pan-African Parliament, CM/2198, (LXXIII), Annex I, Article 4(2).

[61] Article 3(1).

[62] Article 3(2).

[63] Umozurike, above n.1, at p. 30.

> Human beings are inviolable. Every human being shall be entitled to respect for his life and the integrity of his person. No one many be arbitrarily deprived of this right.

The Article in recognising the inviolability of human life confirms the entitlement of everyone to the right to life and integrity of person. At the same time, the Article is structured in an awkward manner, and does not address some fundamental issues. There is no explanation of the meaning of the term 'life' and it is not clear the extent to which the rights of the unborn child are protected. Furthermore, following the ICCPR, the Charter does not prohibit all forms of deprivation of life. Only 'arbitrary' deprivation of life is prohibited, although the meaning of arbitrariness is not defined. Some guidance may be obtained from the jurisprudence of the Human Rights Committee, which has spelled out the meaning in its consideration of individual cases and State reports.[64] Unlike, the ICCPR, no limitations are placed on the usage of capital punishment. The imposition of death penalty remains a controversial subject in international law, and a significant number of African States still retain this sentence.[65]

Article 5 provides for the right to the respect of the dignity in human beings. It also prohibits slavery, slave trade, torture, cruel, inhuman or degrading treatment or punishment and treatment. The prohibition of torture, inhuman degrading treatment or punishment as a norm of *jus cogens* and a principle of customary international law has been affirmed in all the international human rights instruments. The meaning of the term 'torture' and 'inhuman' or 'degrading treatment or punishment' has been expanded further by the Committee against Torture (CAT), and by regional human rights bodies (such as the European Commission and European Court of Human Rights).[66] Cruel, inhuman and degrading treatment and punishment has been addressed in considerable detail by the European Court of Human Rights in the context of corporal punishment. While the jurisprudence emergent from the African Commission on this subject is not substantial, domestic African courts have relied upon the ECHR's prohibition on corporal punishment. The Zimbabwean Supreme Court decision in *State* v. *Ncube and others*, represents the formulation of important principles. In this case, three persons had been found guilty of offences against children (the rape of an unspecified number over a period of two and a half years). All three men were sentenced to significant terms of imprisonment with labour and were also awarded sentences of whipping of six strokes. Their appeal to the Supreme Court concerning the sentence imposed was upheld. According to the Court, whipping as a punishment violated Section 15(1) of the Zimbabwean Constitution, a provision which prohibits torture and inhuman or degrading treatment or punishment.[67] In arriving at this

---

[64] See above chapter 5.

[65] See the recent decision of the Supreme Court of Uganda, in which the Court upheld death penalty. Uganda Government News: Supreme Court Upholds Death Penalty 'The Supreme Court has upheld the constitutional court decision emphasizing that the death penalty is constitutional and also directed for immediate measures to address the suffering of prisoners who have been sentenced to death' 21 January 2009 www.ugpulse.com/articles/daily/news.asp?about=Supreme%20Court%20upholds%20Death%20penalty%20 &ID=7697 <last visited 10 May 2009>.

[66] See chapters 5 and 7 above and below chapter 22.

[67] [1987] (2) ZLR 246 (SC) 267 B–C; 1988 (2) SA 702 (ZSC) 717 B–D; summaries of the case in International Commission of Jurists, *The Review*, No. 41 December 1988, 61; 14 *Commonwealth Law Bulletin* (1988) 593. Rodley, *The Treatment of Prisoners under International Law* (Clarendon Press, 1999) at p. 320.

decision the Court considered Article 3 of ECHR, comparative criminal and other case-law including *Tyrer v. UK*[68] and concluded that whipping was an affront to human dignity.[69]

It also needs to be appreciated that cruel, inhuman and degrading treatment is a subject impinging heavily upon cultural or religious relativism. In this context it is important to examine several different though nevertheless interconnected issues. Firstly, for some States arguably practising *Sharia*, the compatibility of punishments such as flogging, physical amputations and executions has raised problematic issues of compatibility with modern norms of human rights law. Secondly, some of the African States have been criticised for allowing such practices as female genital mutilation (FGM) or for criminalising adult homosexuality.[70] The practices of FGM and criminalisation of adult homosexuality have been based on cultures or traditions and are clearly not authorised within the *Sharia* or religious laws. Thirdly, there are the concern emerging from the practices of slavery and servitude. The African Charter clearly prohibits slavery and slave trade. However, various practices of servitude, in particular child labour, continue to take place. In addition to the prohibition of slavery and subjugation, the Charter provides for the right to liberty and security of person. Article 6 notes:

> Every individual shall have the right to liberty and to the security of his person. No one may be deprived of his freedom except for reasons and conditions previously laid down by law. In particular, no one may be arbitrarily arrested or detained.

The right to liberty and security of person is an important human right, and forms an essential ingredient of the human rights corpus. The Article while providing protection is unsatisfactory because of its vague and uncertain terminology. The usage of the term 'except for reasons and conditions laid down by law' as noted above, represents an example of the 'claw-back' clause as referred to earlier. The 'reasons and conditions' are not provided anywhere in the Charter, thus making it impossible to assess their conformity with other international human rights instruments. There is also the unhelpful use of the concept of 'arbitrary' in the arrest and detention of individuals.

---

[68] *Tyrer v. UK* (1978) 2 E.H.R.R. 1.

[69] *Ncube v. The State*, Supreme Court of Zimbabwe, 1988 LRC (Const) 442; Also see *State v. A Juvenile* (1989) (2) ZLR 61 where it was held that the corporal punishment of juveniles was unconstitutional. In *State v. Petrus and another* (1985) LRC (Const) 699 The Court of Appeal of Botswana held that while corporal punishment *per se* was not unconstitutional, the manner of punishment was. In exercising a 'value judgment', the Court held that repeated and delayed punishment resulted in the punishment being rendered degrading and unconstitutional. The Namibian Supreme Court held corporal punishment unconstitutional in respect of Article 8 of the Bill of Fundamental Rights enshrined in the Constitution in *Ex parte Attorney-General, In Re Corporal Punishment by Organs of State* (SA 14/90) [1991] NASC 2; 1991 (3) SA 76 (NmSc) (5 April 1991) (Namibia). A similar approach was adopted by the South African Constitutional Court in *State v. Williams* (1995) (3) SALR 632, where Justice Langa held that 'there is unmistakably a growing consensus in the international community that judicial whipping, involving as it does, the deliberate infliction of physical pain on the person of the accused, offends society's notions of decency and is a direct invasion of the right which every person has to human dignity' ibid. at p. 644. For analysis of the aforementioned case-law see Adjami, 'African Courts, International Law, and Comparative Case Law: Chimera or Emerging Human Rights' 24 *Mich. J. Int'l L.* (2002–2003) 103.

[70] See 21st Session Transcripts 75, in Murray, *The African Commission on Human and Peoples Rights and International Law* (Hart Publishing, 2000) p. 42 note 48; *Courson v. Zimbabwe*, Communication No. 136/94 (1995), paras 1–2 (complaint withdrawn and case not decided on merits) and ACHPR/Res.66(XXV)04: Resolution on the Situation of Women and Children in Africa.

(iii) Freedom of religion, expression, association and movement

Article 8 of the Charter provides for the right to freedom of conscience and religion. According to the Article:

> Freedom of conscience, the profession and free practice of religion shall be guaranteed. No one may, subject to law and order, be submitted to measures restricting the exercise of freedoms.

The right to freedom of religion constitutes an invaluable right in the context of a region which continues to suffer from serious persecutions based on religious differences.[71] Notwithstanding the value of this right, the provisions of the Article themselves have left a great deal to be desired. The meaning of 'free practice' is unclear, as it does not establish as to whether it incorporates the freedom to change religion or if it allows proselytism. Furthermore, the usage of the 'claw-back' clause of 'subject to law and order' can lead to unreasonable and unacceptable restrictions upon this freedom. Article 9 provides for an interesting right, the right to receive information. The Article also provides for a right of expression and the freedom to disseminate one's opinion. At the same time, the provisions of the Article can be highly restrictive as the ultimate discretion, to determine the boundaries of right to receive information and expression, is retained. Article 10 accords the right to association. Article 10(2) states that, subject to the obligation of solidarity provided for in Article 29, no one may be compelled to join an association. According to Article 11 all individuals have the right to assembly. This right again is subject to the 'claw-back' clause of being subject to 'necessary restrictions provided for by law in particular those enacted in the interest of national security, the safety, health, ethics and rights and freedoms of others'.

Article 12 provides for the freedom of movement and residence within the borders of a State. It also confirms that individuals have the right to leave any country including their own, and to return to their country.[72] Within this article there is also the right to seek and obtain asylum and for non-nationals not to be expelled save for a decision made in accordance with the law. Mass expulsion (aimed at expelling national, racial, ethnic or religious groups) is prohibited. This prohibition represents a highly valuable ordinance and is aimed to prevent recurrences similar to the expulsion of Asians from Uganda during Amin.[73] Mass expulsion as the most acute form of discrimination has been conducted against many ethnic, religious and racial groups in Africa. The induction of such a provision is a positive development of regional human rights law. That said, the issue of nationality has been a problematic area of international human rights law and the denial of citizenship as a tool for discrimination has been applied by a number of States, including those from Africa.

---

[71] Maxted and Zegeye, 'North, West and the Horn of Africa' in Minority Rights Group (eds), *World Directory of Minorities* (Minority Rights Group, 1997) pp. 388–463; Hodges, *Jehovah's Witnesses in Africa* (Minority Rights Group, 1985); Parfitt, *The Jews of Africa and Asia: Contemporary Anti-Semitism and Other Pressures* (Minority Rights Group, 1987); Verney *et al.*, *Sudan: Conflict and Minorities* (Minority Rights Group, 1995).

[72] Article 12(2).

[73] While traditional human rights instruments had not focused on expulsions it would now appear that mass expulsions on the basis of race, religion or ethnicity constituted a crime against humanity; see Article 7(2)(d) of the Statute of the International Criminal Court, http://untreaty.un.org/cod/icc/statute/romefra.htm <last visited 20 May 2009>.

International Conventions, including the International Convention on the Elimination of All Forms of Racial Discrimination and the African Charter do not specifically prohibit discrimination on the basis of nationality, so long as there is no discrimination against specific nationalities.[74]

(iv) Property rights in the Charter

Article 14 of the Charter states that the right to property shall be guaranteed and may only be restricted in the interest of public need or in the general interest of the community. In addition, expropriation of property would have to be in accordance with the provisions of the law. The grounds for expropriation are not elaborated upon nor are any examples provided. The right to property has been a controversial one.[75] The UDHR contains the right to property, as does Protocol 1 of the ECHR and the ACHR. The right to property, however, proved too divisive and it was not possible to incorporate it within the International Covenants. Socialist and developing countries argued against providing absolute guarantees for property rights. They campaigned for a right to be able to expropriate and nationalise foreign assets and to restrict the rights of foreign nationals more generally. A confirmation of this view is provided by Article 2(3) of the ICESCR which provides:

> Developing countries, with due regard to human rights and their national economy, may determine to what extent they would guarantee the economic rights recognized in the present Covenant to non-nationals

Issues regarding the disposal of property and natural wealth are further addressed in the context of peoples rights. Article 21 of the Charter provides all peoples with a right freely to dispose of their wealth and natural resources. At the same time, as we shall consider in the next section, the term 'peoples' is used almost synonymously with that of the 'State', thereby allowing the African governments an almost unquestionable discretion in relation to the usage, expropriation and exploitation of natural resources and property. Article 21 provides as follows:

> (1) All peoples shall freely dispose of their wealth and natural resources. This right shall be exercised in the exclusive interest of the people. In no case shall a people be deprived of it.
>
> (2) In case of spoliation the dispossessed people shall have the right to the lawful recovery of its property as well as to an adequate compensation.
>
> (3) The free disposal of wealth and natural resources shall be exercised without prejudice to the obligation of promoting international economic cooperation based on mutual respect, equitable exchange and the principles of international law.

---

[74] Article 1(3) of the International Convention on the Elimination of All Forms of Racial Discrimination (1965) provides 'Nothing in this Convention may be interpreted as affecting in any way the legal provisions of States Parties concerning nationality, citizenship or naturalization, provided that such provisions do not discriminate against any particular nationality'. For further discussion see below chapter 12.

[75] See Krause and Alfredsson, 'Article 17' in Alfredsson and Eide (eds), *The Universal Declaration of Human Rights: A Common Standard of Achievement* (Kluwer Law International, 1999) pp. 359–378.

10

The African system for the protection of human rights

(4) States parties to the present Charter shall individually and collectively exercise the right to free disposal of their wealth and natural resources with a view to strengthening African unity and solidarity.

(5) States parties to the present Charter shall undertake to eliminate all forms of foreign economic exploitation particularly that practiced by international monopolies so as to enable their peoples to fully benefit from the advantages derived from their national resources.

(v) Economic, social and cultural rights

In addition to civil and political rights, the African Charter also contains a number of economic, social and cultural rights. As we have already noted, the efforts to incorporate economic, social and cultural rights alongside civil and political rights within a single United Nations Covenant proved futile. It is, therefore, to the Charter's credit for having provided a combination of these rights, which also reconfirms the distinctive African concept of human rights.

Article 15 of the Charter provides for the right to work. This right is contained in the UDHR and the ICESCR. Amongst regional instruments it can be found in the ESC and Article 15 of the EU Charter of Fundamental Rights. Unlike any of the international and regional human rights instrument, Article 15 fails to deal with this right in any great detail. Furthermore, the right to work is not guaranteed *per se*, but guarantees that once employed a worker would have a right to work in equitable and satisfactory conditions and shall receive equal pay for equal work. Equal pay for equal work is also aimed at ensuring equality for women.

The Charter provides for the right to enjoy the best attainable state of physical and mental health. The provisions place States parties under an obligation to provide health and medical services for their populations. The right to health is an important right although its enforcement remains problematic. Article 16 in providing for this right, states:

(1) Every individual shall have the right to enjoy the best attainable state of physical and mental health.

(2) States parties to the present Charter shall take the necessary measures to protect the health of their people and to ensure that they receive medical attention when they are sick.

Article 17 covers a wide range of interrelated rights. According to the Article individuals are accorded the right to education, although there is no specification of the content of this right. The Article provides individuals the right to participate freely in the cultural life of the community and imposes an obligation on the State to promote and protect the morals and traditional values recognised by the community. The provision of the free exercise of the right to take part in community life is presumably intended for minority groups within States; although there is no reference to minorities in the entire Charter this provision is useful.[76]

---

[76] See Murray and Wheatley 'Groups and the African Charter on Human and Peoples' Rights' 25 *HRQ* (2003) 213.

(vi) The family as the natural unity and basis of society, rights of women and children

Article 18 is wide ranging, and covers at least four rights. It recognises family as the natural unit and basis of the society and establishes a duty upon the State to take care of the physical health and morals of the family. In its acknowledgement of the family as the natural and fundamental unit, the provisions draw upon Articles 23 ICCPR and Article 17 ACHR.[77] Article 18(2) reinforces these obligations with the duty on the State to assist the family unit in establishing it as the custodian of morals and traditional values. Article 18(3) is a comprehensive clause concerning prohibition of discrimination against women. According to this provision:

> The State shall ensure the elimination of every discrimination against women and also ensure the protection of the rights of the woman and the child as stipulated in international declarations and conventions.

These provisions appear to place substantial obligations in relation to protecting the rights of women and children. In the light of the construction of the article it has been contended that parties to the Charter are automatically bound by treaty law on women and children regardless of whether or not they have been ratified by the State.[78] Although an ambitious interpretation, this is a step in the right direction, and would also encourage the African Commission and the new African Court to draw inspiration from the jurisprudence of human rights bodies, in particular CEDAW and CRC. The African Commission has not yet dealt directly with case-law emerging from the right of women to non-discrimination.[79] Nevertheless, case-law on the subject has emerged from national courts. In the landmark decision of *Unity Dow* v. *Attorney-General of Botswana*[80] the Court of Appeal of Botswana held that a Statute which discriminated against women with respect to conferring citizenship and was therefore unconstitutional. Unity Dow, a Botswanese national complained of the operation of the Citizenship Act 1984. In 1979, a child had been born to Unity fathered by an American, Peter Dow. The law, then in force, established the child's nationality as Botswanese. In 1984, Unity and Peter were married and a further two children were born to the couple in 1985 and 1987 respectively. However, the effect of

---

[77] According to Article 17(1) of the ACHR 'The family is the natural and fundamental group unit of society and is entitled to protection by State and the Society'. For further consideration of ACHR see above chapter 9.

[78] Davidson, above n.1, at p. 154.

[79] Stefiszyw makes the point that 'out of over three hundred communications received by the African Commission, none have touched upon women's rights directly' Stefiszyw, 'The AU: Challenges and Opportunities for Women' 5 *African Human Rights Law Journal* (2005) 358 at p. 378; also see Murray, 'A Feminist Perspective on Reform of the African Human Rights System' 1 *African Human Rights Law Journal* (2001) 208.

[80] *Unity Dow* v. *Attorney General of Botswana*, CA. Civil Appeal No. 4/91 Appeal Court. For commentaries see Beyani, 'Towards a More Effective Guarantee of Women's Rights in the African Human Rights System' in Cook (ed.), *Human Rights of Women: National and International Perspectives* (Pennsylvania University Press, 1994) pp. 285–306, at p. 294; Goonesekere 'Law, Reform and Children in Plural Legal Systems: Some Experiences in Sub-Saharan Africa' in Ali, Goonesekere, Mendez, and Rios-Kohn, *Protecting the World's Children: Impact of the Convention on the Rights of the Child in Diverse Legal Systems* (Cambridge University Press, 2007) pp. 209–264, at p. 227.

the 1984 Citizenship Act was to deprive the two children of Botswanese nationality. Since the father was a foreign national, Unity Dow was successfully able to claim before the High Court that the Citizenship Act 1984 violated a number of her rights (including the right to equal protection of the law irrespective of sex (section 3), personal liberty (section 5), protection from being subjected to degrading treatment (section 7), freedom of movement (section 14) and protection from discrimination on the basis of sex (section 15) as guaranteed by the Constitution of Botswana. The Court of Appeal, in upholding the High Court's ruling held that the provisions of the Citizenship Act were discriminatory and, thus, contrary to the Constitution of Botswana.

In another highly significant decision *Uganda Association of Women Lawyers* v. *Attorney General*,[81] the Constitutional Court of Uganda affirmed that provisions within the Ugandan Divorce Act 1904 were contrary to the Constitution of Uganda. The Court held that sections 4(1) and (2), 5, 21, 22, 23 and 26 of the Divorce Act 1857 were discriminatory as well as inconsistent with, and in contravention of, the Constitution of Uganda. Section 4(1) of the Act had allowed the husband to petition for dissolution of marriage solely on the ground of adultery on the part of his wife. The wife, however, in order to petition had to establish a number of grounds. Section 5 of the Act required the husband to name an adulterer as a co-respondent in the petition: this was in effect to allow the husband to claim compensation in the form of damages but the provision was not applicable to the wife. Section 26 of the Act only allowed the successful husband as divorce petitioner to claim his wife's property. This provision denied the women any such rights. In this landmark judgment the Constitutional Court of Uganda unanimously held that the aforementioned provisions of the legislation contravened the equality provisions and the provisions of equality rights of men and women in marriage as contained in Article 21 and Article 31 of the Constitution of Uganda.[82]

The inequities faced by African women have been a major concern – a concern which led to the adoption of a specialised regional treaty on women's rights. In July 2003, the Assembly of the AU adopted the Protocol on the Rights of Women in Africa, which came into force in November 2005.[83] The Protocol has a range of rights and arguably goes much further than the United Nations Women's Convention (1979).[84] Amongst the far reaching rights are the right to dignity,[85] equal rights in marriage,[86] 'same rights' in separation, divorce and annulment of marriage,[87] right to participation in the political

---

[81] *Uganda Association of Women Lawyers* v. *The Attorney General*, Constitutional Petition No. 2 of 2003 [2004] UGCC 1 (10 March 2004).

[82] See the Constitution of Republic of Uganda 1995 www.trybunal.gov.pl/constit/constitu/constit/uganda/uganda-e.htm <last visited 15 May 2009>; for a useful commentary on the case see Ssenyonjo 'Towards Non-Discrimination against Women and De Jure Equality in Uganda: The Role of Uganda's Constitutional Court' 16 *African Journal of International and Comparative Law* (2008) 1.

[83] Protocol to the African Charter on Human and Peoples' Rights on the Rights of Women in Africa, adopted by the 2nd Ordinary Session of the Assembly of the Union, Maputo, CAB/LEG/66.6 (13 September 2000); reprinted in 1 *Afr. Hum. Rts. L.J.* 40, entered into force 25 November 2005; see Murray, 'Women's Rights and the Organization of African Unity and African Union: The Protocol on the Rights of Women in Africa', in Buss and Manji (eds), *International Law: Modern Feminist Approaches* (Hart Publishing, 2005) pp. 253–272; Wing and Smith, *The New African Union and Women's Rights*, 13 *Transnat'l L. & Contemp. Probs.* (2003) 33; Rebouché, 'Labor, Land, and Women's Rights in Africa: Challenges for the New Protocol on the Rights of Women' 19 *Harvard Human Rights Journal* (2006) 235.

[84] Murray, *Human Rights in Africa*, above n.1, at p. 151.

[85] Article 3.

[86] Article 6.

[87] Article 7.

and decision-making processes,[88] right to education and training,[89] economic and social welfare rights,[90] health and reproductive rights,[91] right to a positive cultural context,[92] right to a healthy and sustainable environment,[93] right to sustainable development,[94] widow's rights,[95] right to inheritance,[96] and special protection for elderly, disabled and distressed women.[97] One of the major concerns for women has been harmful practices such as female genital mutilation and scarification of women. In specifically prohibiting any such practices Article 5 provides as follows:

> States Parties shall prohibit and condemn all forms of harmful practices which negatively affect the human rights of women and which are contrary to recognised international standards. States Parties shall take all necessary legislative and other measures to eliminate such practices, including:
>
> (a) creation of public awareness in all sectors of society regarding harmful practices through information, formal and informal education and outreach programmes;
>
> (b) prohibition, through legislative measures backed by sanctions, of all forms of female genital mutilation, scarification, medicalisation and para-medicalisation of female genital mutilation and all other practices in order to eradicate them;
>
> (c) provision of necessary support to victims of harmful practices through basic services such as health services, legal and judicial support, emotional and psychological counselling as well as vocational training to make them self-supporting;
>
> (d) protection of women who are at risk of being subjected to harmful practices or all other forms of violence, abuse and intolerance.

The implementation of the Protocol is to be conducted through the national periodic reports under Article 62 of the AFCHPR, and through the African Commission and the African Court on Human and Peoples' Rights.[98]

Article 18(3) of the Banjul Charter also provides for the protection of the right of the child, and places an obligation to follow the principles enshrined in international treaty law. In order to further substantiate the legal regime in the rights of the child, African States themselves have entered into a specialised treaty concerning children, the African Charter

---

[88] Article 9.

[89] Article 12.

[90] Article 13.

[91] Article 14. The provisions contained in Article 14 represent the only 'the only legally binding human rights instrument that explicitly addresses abortion as a human right and affirms that women's reproductive rights are human rights'; Zampas and Gher, 'Abortion as a Human Right – International and Regional Standards' 8 *HRLR* (2008) 249 at p. 250.

[92] Article 17.

[93] Article 18.

[94] Article 19.

[95] Article 20.

[96] Articles 21.

[97] Articles 22–24.

[98] Articles 26 and 27; for a useful commentary on the Protocol see Musa, Mohammed and Manji (eds) *Breathing Life into the African Union Protocol on Women's Rights in Africa* (Fahamu & Solidarity for African Women's Rights, 2006).

on the Rights and Welfare of the Child (ACRWC) 1990.[99] In 1990, the OAU also adopted strategies for the African Decade for Child Survival, Protection and Development 1990–2000. Article 18(4) of the Banjul Charter provides that the aged and the disabled have the right to special measures of protection. Amongst the significant standard-setting development of children's rights, the most significant has no doubt been the adoption of ACRWC, although the impact of the Charter became less evident as a result of the long interval of nine years between its adoption in 1990 and its eventual enforcement in 1999. ACRWC aims to provide a distinctly African perspective on children's rights though the provisions within the Charter are inspired by those of the UN Convention on the Rights of the Child. ACRWC provides for wide ranging rights including a right to survival and development,[100] name and nationality,[101] freedom of expression,[102] thought, conscience and religion,[103] to education and to leisure,[104] recreation and cultural activities.[105] A number of useful safeguards for children are included in the Charter including the protection from abuse and torture,[106] from child labour[107] and from protection against harmful social and cultural practices.[108] The Charter aims to provide safeguards during armed conflict[109] and the rights of refugee children.[110] There are also safeguards for handicapped children.[111] An 11-member Committee – the African Committee of Experts on the Rights and Welfare of the Child – is appointed to oversee the enforcement of the Charter.[112] The members sit in an independent capacity and are appointed by the Assembly of Heads of State and Government on the nomination of States.[113] The functions of the Committee are, *inter alia*, to promote and protect the rights contained in the Charter, monitor the implementation of rights contained in the charter and interpretation of the provisions of the Charter.[114] The Charter provides for a reporting mechanism whereby States parties are required to submit to the Committee, within two years of entry into force of the Charter for the concerned State party and every three years thereafter reports on the implementation of the provisions of the Charter.[115] As a contrast to the UN Committee on the Rights of the Child, the African Charter on Child Rights and Welfare authorises its Committee to receive and consider communications from individuals and NGOs as regards matters contained in the Convention and is also mandated to investigate any issue falling within the ambit of the

---

[99] Adopted in July 1990, entered into force 29 October 1999, OAU Doc. CAB/LEG/TSG/Rev.1; see Lloyd, 'Evolution of the African Charter on the Rights and Welfare of the Child and the African Committee of Experts: Raising the Gauntlet' 10 *International Journal of Children's Rights* (2002) 179; Thompson, 'Africa's Charter on Children's Rights: A Normative Break with Cultural Traditionalism' 41 *ICLQ* (1992) 432.

[100] Article 5.

[101] Article 6.

[102] Article 7.

[103] Article 9.

[104] Articles 11 and 12.

[105] Article 12.

[106] Article 16.

[107] Article 15.

[108] Article 21 see further Van Bueren, 'Child Sexual Abuse and Exploitation: A Suggested Human Rights Approach' 2 *International Law Journal of Child Rights* (1994) 45.

[109] Article 22.

[110] Article 23.

[111] Article 13.

[112] Article 33.

[113] Articles 33 and 34.

[114] Article 42.

[115] Article 43.

Charter and report to the Assembly of Heads of State and Government on these matters.[116] In 2001, the Committee commenced its work, though there have been considerable delays in submission of State reports. By May 2008, when the Committee began its consideration of State reports, only a handful of reports had been submitted. The Committee has yet to implement the communications and the periodic reporting process fully and it is, therefore, necessary to clearly define the Committee's relationship with both the AFCHPR as well as the institutions of the AU.[117]

ACRWC contains a number of useful provisions which could articulate and expanded the principles within general international law. ACRWC defines a child as anyone below the age of 18:[118] this firm position advances the definition of a child stated in the UN Convention on the Rights of the Child and it is recommended that general international law confers the rights of child to all persons below 18. Notwithstanding these positives, ACRWC has been challenged for advancing irreconcilable principles of parental authority operational within the African Context *vis-à-vis* 'the best interests of the child'. Furthermore, as Rachel Murray points out 'the approach to the rights of the child has been, . . . set by the OAU/AU organs have not yet been linked with the Charter to develop a coherent whole.'[119]

4 THE MEANING OF PEOPLES' RIGHTS IN AFRICAN HUMAN RIGHTS LAW[120]

The impact of the concept of peoples' right to self-determination is nowhere more evident than in the African continent; Africa has emancipated itself from the shackles of colonialism, racial oppression and apartheid through reliance upon this concept. The term 'peoples' and 'the right to self-determination', therefore, forms a vital element within the constitutional working of independent African States as well as in the regional approach represented collectively. A number of State constitutions support the principle of peoples' rights, and the regional approach is reflected through a wide range of treaties including the Charter of the OAU, the Constitutive Act of the AU and the African Charter (AFCHPR).

---

[116] Article 44. It is possible for States to make reservations and hence opt-out of this procedure. Children are allowed to submit communication under universal human rights treaties if their own State is not a party to the African Charter. The complaints mechanism procedure has been described as follows 'a communication may be presented on behalf of a victim without his consent if the author is able to prove that the complaint has been brought in the supreme interest of the child. Communications are sent to all Committee members three months prior to each ordinary session. The Committee may set up a working group to meet before its sessions to consider whether a communication will be accepted. The working group then appoints a rapporteur. The Committee, working group or rapporteur brings the communication to the attention of the State concerned and requests an explanation or written statement within six months. The Committee may also request the presence of the person or group submitting the communication and the State party concerned for more information, clarification or observations'. See Child Rights Information Network: African Committee on the Rights of the Child www.crin.org/RM/acrwc.asp#ex <last visited 9 December 2008>.

[117] See Murray, *Human Rights in Africa*, above n.1 at pp. 171–172.

[118] Article 2.

[119] See Murray, *Human Rights in Africa*, above n.1, at pp. 171–172.

[120] See Murray and Wheatley, above n.76; Rehman, 'The Concept of "Peoples" in International Law with Special Reference to Africa' in Bakut and Dutt (eds), *Development in Africa for the 21st Century* (Palgrave, 2000) pp. 201–214; Kiwanuka, 'The Meaning of "People" in the African Charter on Human and Peoples' Rights' 82 *AJIL* (1988) 80.

The OAU, historically, played a huge role in the establishment of the rights of peoples. The preamble of the OAU Charter[121] reaffirmed the 'inalienable right of all people to control their own destiny'.[122] The purposes of the Charter included a commitment to intensify the collaboration of African States in order 'to achieve a better life for the peoples of Africa'.[123] Even though the OAU Charter supported the principles enshrined in the UN Charter and UDHR, the OAU did not have any particular vision on individual human rights or collective group rights.[124] The references to peoples were framed largely in the context of the right to sovereign State equality, and moves to eradicate colonialism.[125] There was no consideration of the right to self-determination apart from an emphasis on non-interference in the domestic affairs of States, and the guarantee for the '[r]espect for the sovereignty and territorial integrity and territorial integrity of each State and its inalienable right to independent existence'.[126]

The latter provision is the reconfirmation of the *uti possidetis juris* principle. The origins of the principle of *uti possidetis* can be traced back to the early 19th century, whereby the newly independent successor States of the former Spanish Empire in South and Central America were considered to have inherited the administrative divisions of the colonial empire as their new territorial boundaries.[127] The doctrine has come to be accepted as having universal significance and global application; in essence the application of the principle meant that the demarcations of boundaries under the colonial regimes corresponded to the boundaries of the new States that emerged.[128]

The *uti possidetis juris* principle received the complete support from the African heads of State at the time of adoption of the OAU Charter. Indeed, at the inaugural session of the Treaty, the Prime Minister of Ethiopia, echoing the sentiments of other heads of government, commented 'it is in the interest of all Africans now to respect the frontiers drawn on the maps, whether they are good or bad, by the former colonisers'.[129] Thus, while OAU Charter failed to elaborate on the subject of peoples' rights to self-determination, it,

---

[121] Now replaced and abrogated by the Constitutive Act of the AU.

[122] Preamble OAU Charter.

[123] Article 2(1)(b) OAU Charter.

[124] Ojo and Sesay, 'The OAU and Human Rights: Prospects for the 1980's and Beyond' 8 *HRQ* (1986) 89 at p. 96.

[125] Article 2(1)(c) and (d) OAU Charter.

[126] Article 3(3) OAU Charter.

[127] Shaw, *International Law* (Cambridge University Press, 2008) pp. 525–530; also see Shaw, *Title to Territory in Africa: International Legal Issues* (Oxford University Press, 1986).

[128] See Article 3(3) of the *OAU Charter*; Principle III of the *Helsinki Final Act* 1975, 1975 ILM 1292; Article 62 2(2)(a) VCLT 1969, 58 U.K.T.S, 1980, Cmnd 7964; Article 2 of the Vienna Convention on the Succession of States in Respect of Treaties (1978) 17 I.L.M 1488, 72 *AJIL* 971. For judicial acknowledgement of the principles see *Frontier Dispute Case (Burkina Faso v. Mali)* 1986 ICJ Reports 554; Naldi, 'The Case Concerning the Frontier Dispute (Burkina Faso/Republic of Mali): Uti Possidetis in an African Perspective' 36 *ICLQ* (1987) 893; *Temple of Peach Vihar Case (Merits) (Cambodia)*, 1962 ICJ Rep 6, 16, 29; *Rann of Kutch Arbitration* 1968, 50 ILR 2, 408; *Guinea-Guinea Bissau Maritime Delimitation Case* 77 ILR 1985, 635, 637; *Arbitration Tribunal in Guinea-Bissau v. Senegal*, 1990 83 ILR 1, 35; *Land, Islands and Maritime Frontier Case: El Salvador v. Honduras (Nicaragua Intervening)* 1992 ICJ Rep 351, 380; also see *Sovereignty over Certain Frontiers (Belgium v. the Netherlands)* ICJ Rep 1959, 209, in particular Judge Moeno Quitana's dissenting opinion, 252; *Avis Nos. 2 and 3 of the Arbitration Commission of the Yugoslavia Conference*, 31 I.L.M. 1497, 1499; *Taba Award (Egypt)* 80 ILR 1989, 224 in particular arbitrator Lapidoth's dissenting opinion; also see Klabbers and Lefeber, 'Africa: Lost between Self-Determination and *Uti-Possidetis*', in Brölmann, Lefeber and Zieck (eds), *Peoples and Minorities in International Law* (Martinus Nijhoff Publishers, 1993) pp. 33–76. See also Rehman, 'Re-Assessing the Right to Self-Determination: Lessons from the Indian Experience' 29 *AALR* (2000) 454.

[129] Cited in Klabbers and Lefeber, 'Africa: Lost between Self-Determination and *Uti-Possidetis*', in Brölmann, Lefeber and Zieck (eds), above n.128, at p. 57.

nevertheless, affirmed the African position on the inviolability and sanctity of boundaries inherited by the new States.

In contrast to the OAU Charter, the African Charter (AFCHPR) has a much stronger focus on the subject of peoples' rights. As the rubric of the treaty reflects, there is a special position accorded to peoples' rights. Indeed, the AFCHPR has the distinction of being the only international instrument to provide a detailed exposition of the rights of peoples. The peoples' rights, according to the Charter are spelt out in Articles 19–24 of the Treaty. These are the right of all peoples to equality,[130] to existence[131] and self-determination,[132] to dispose freely of wealth and natural resources,[133] to economic, social and cultural development,[134] to national and international peace and security,[135] and to a 'general satisfactory environment'.[136]

Notwithstanding a detailed exposition of the rights of peoples, the drafters of the AFCHPR deliberately avoided the complex issue of the definition of the term 'peoples'. The only affirmative view that emerges from a close scrutiny of the provisions of the Charter is that there is no single uniform meaning that could be attributed to the term 'peoples'. The Charter presents a variable approach, depending on the issues in question. Thus, as we have already noted, on the subject of the disposal of wealth and natural resources in Article 21, there is a large overlap between State and peoples and the terms could be used almost interchangeably. Similarly, according to Article 23(1), 'All peoples shall have the right to national and international peace and security'. The Article goes on to provide that 'the principles of solidarity and friendly relations implicitly affirmed by the Charter of the United Nations and reaffirmed by that of the Organization of African Unity shall govern relations between States'. Whilst it appears certain that peoples are the natural beneficiaries of the right to peace and security, the assumption appears to be that States themselves are to act as the representative of all the peoples within their respective jurisdictions in order to ensure the enjoyment of this right.[137]

On the other hand, the AFCHPR has provisions dealing with peoples' rights to equality and existence. As we have considered throughout this book, the right to equality and non-discrimination forms the basis of modern human rights law. The right to equality is an individual right, although it may also be applied to support particular group members *qua* individuals. In comparison to equality, the right to existence has a more direct application to groups within States. The right to existence is designed to protect, 'national, ethnical or religious groups' from genocide and physical extermination.[138] Therefore, in the context of the right to equality and existence, the only permissible view that could be formed is that 'peoples' represent collectivities such as ethnic, national or religious minorities within independent States.

---

[130] Article 19 AFCHPR.
[131] Article 20(1).
[132] Article 20(1)–(3).
[133] Article 21.
[134] Article 22.
[135] Article 23.
[136] Article 24.
[137] *Cf.* the provisions contained in the Universal Declaration of Human Rights (1948). Article 28 provides: 'Everyone is entitled to a social and international order in which the rights and freedoms set forth in this Declaration can be fully realized'. For discussion of the Universal Declaration of Human Rights see above chapter 4.
[138] See below chapters 13 and 14.

Article 20(1) of the AFCHPR, which provides for the right to existence, also accords peoples 'the unquestionable and inalienable right to self-determination'. The contrasting nature of the two rights and the manner of their proposed application, however, needs some analysis. The references to self-determination are closely associated with colonialism and oppression. It is only colonised and oppressed peoples who have the 'right to free themselves from the bonds of domination'.[139] Although the term 'oppression' is not defined, the limitation of being under colonial or minority racist regimes is firmly engrained. It is certainly not permissible for minorities or indigenous peoples to seek foreign assistance to further any claims towards self-determination. The reluctance to relate self-determination with minorities or indigenous peoples has been confirmed by the jurisprudence of the African Commission, which operates in pursuance of the Charter.

The African Commission, as we shall analyse in greater detail shortly, considers communications concerning group and peoples' rights. However, Article 56(2) of the Charter implies that in order for the communication to be admissible, allegations of violations of group rights must be compatible with the provisions of the Constitutive Act of the AU relating to respect of sovereignty and territorial integrity of the Members States of that organisation. In *Katangese Peoples' Congress* v. *Zaire*,[140] Mr. Gerard Moke, the author, was the President of the Katangese Peoples' Congress. He claimed that Zaire violated the Katangese peoples' right to self-determination. In its admissibility decision taken at its 16th Ordinary Session in October 1994, the Commission declared that the communication had 'no merit' under the AFCHPR because it was not compatible with Article 56(2) of the Charter. In its decision, the Commission firstly reasoned that the definition of 'peoples' and the content of the right are controversial, and then took the view that the issue in the present Communication was not self-determination for all Zaireoise as a people, but specifically for the Katangese. The Commission held that in these circumstances, it was obliged 'to uphold the sovereignty and territorial integrity of Zaire, a member of the OAU and a party to the African Charter on Human and Peoples' Rights.'[141] The other case related to the situation in Senegal, where rebels were trying to secede from the State.[142] In this case, the Commission refused to uphold this claim *inter alia* on the basis that such a claim by a Casamance group may prompt other groups in the region to take bring similar legal challenges. The Commission has made attempts to encourage the government to reach a settlement with the dissident group.

5 THE AFRICAN COMMISSION[143]

The African Commission is the main executive organ and is also in charge of implementing the provisions of the Charter.[144] The Commission consists 'of eleven members and are chosen from amongst African personalities of highest reputation, known for their high morality, integrity, impartiality and competence in matters of human and peoples' rights;

---

[139] Article 20(2).
[140] Communication 75/92 (1995).
[141] Communication 75/92 (1995), para 5.
[142] Tenth Annual Activity Report of the African Commission on Human and Peoples' Rights 1996–1997, ACHPR/ RPT/10th at 4. Annex VIII, *Rencontre Africaine Pour la Defense des droits de l'Homme (RADDHO)* v. *Senegal.*
[143] See Murray, above n.70; Odinkalu and Christensen, above n.33, at p. 235; Welch. Jr., above n.46, at p. 42; Ankumah, *The African Commission on Human and Peoples' Rights* (Martinus Nijhoff Publishers, 1996).
[144] Article 30 AFCHPR.

particular consideration being given to persons having legal experience'.[145] The Commission members are elected by Heads of States and Governments of the AU for a renewable term of six years from a list of persons nominated by State parties.[146] The Commission then appoints a Chairman and a Vice-Chairman for a two-year term. Since the demise of the OAU, its successor, the AU is the parent body and the Commission is required to report to it. The Commission holds session twice every year in spring and in fall and it alternates its meetings between Banjul and the Capitals of African States. The members of the Commission sit in their personal capacity. While each State party can nominate up to two individuals, no two members of the Commission may be nationals of the same State.[147] On 29 July 1987 an Assembly of Heads of State and Governments of OAU for the first time elected 11 members of the Commission, which was inaugurated in November of the same year.

While the AU is responsible for financing the Commission,[148] the Commission has been assigned a role establishing its independence from its parent body. The independence of the Commission's members is ensured in various ways. The members make a solemn declaration of impartiality and faithfulness,[149] with the headquarters of the Commission at a country other than the one home to the AU organs. Members of the Commission also enjoy diplomatic privileges and immunities.[150] A number of Rules of Procedure have been set up to deal with the organisation of the Commission's work, conduct of business, publication of documents and the participation in the Commission's sessions by state representatives. As a general rule, the Commission is to sit in private although final summary minutes of sessions, public or private, shall be 'intended for general distribution unless, under exceptional circumstances, the Commission decides otherwise'.[151] The Commission's reports to the AU Assembly are confidential unless the Assembly itself decides otherwise, while the annual report of the Commission is to be published following consideration by the Assembly.[152] The voting on draft resolutions, if a vote is requested, is by a simple majority. According to Article 41, the Secretary-General of AU is to appoint the Commission's Secretary.

It needs to be noted that the Commission's recommendations concerning protection activities require the endorsement of either the Assembly of Heads of State or AU. However, no such approval is required in relation to promotional activities.

The Commission is mandated to perform a number of functions. These are provided for in Article 45 and consist of:

(a) Promotional Role (Article 45(1)).

(b) Role of protecting human and peoples' rights (Article 45(2)).

(c) Interpreting the provisions of the Charter at the request of a State party, an institution of the OAU/AU or an African Organisation recognised by the OAU/AU (Article 45(3)).

(d) Performing 'any other tasks that may be entrusted to it by the Assembly of Heads of State and Government' (Article 45(4)).

---

[145] Ibid. Article 31.
[146] Ibid. Articles 33, 36.
[147] Ibid. Article 34.
[148] Ibid. Articles 41 and 42.
[149] Ibid. Article 38.
[150] Ibid. Article 43.
[151] Ibid. Article 51. Rule 39.
[152] Rules 77, 79.

According to Article 45(1) the promotional functions of the Commission consist of promoting Human and Peoples' Rights and in particular:

(a) To collect documents, undertake studies and researches on African problems in the field of human and peoples' rights, organize seminars, symposia and conferences, disseminate information, encourage national and local institutions concerned with human and peoples' rights, and should the case arise, give its views or make recommendations to Governments.

(b) To formulate and lay down, principles and rules aimed at solving legal problems relating to human and peoples' rights and fundamental freedoms upon which African Governments may base their legislations.

(c) Co-operate with other African and international institutions concerned with the promotion and protection of human and peoples' rights.

In the performance of its duties, the Commission 'may resort to any appropriate method of investigation' and may hear from the OAU Secretary-General 'or any other person capable of enlightening it'.[153] In its promotional programme the Commission has formulated a Programme of Action which consists of research and information for quasi-legislative co-operation.[154] As from 1990, the Commission has published its annual reports and distributed copies of the Charter. From 1991 to 2000, the Commission published a journal, the *Review of the African Commission on Human and Peoples' Rights*, with reviews and articles on the Charter and human rights issues.[155] A number of seminars have been organised involving such agencies and NGOs as UNESCO and the International Commission of Jurists.[156]

The constituting feature as well as the existing jurisprudence of the Commission reflects an emphasis on amicable resolution of disputes. While such emphasis is acceptable in the light of the provisions of the Charter, there have been occasions when such insistence and eagerness has led the Commission to overlook the admissibility and merit procedures altogether. The Commission has decided cases as being amicably resolved without consulting the author,[157] on the assumption that the matter would be satisfactorily resolved administratively,[158] and in the case of withdrawal of the case.[159] Another unsatisfactory aspect of the Commission's work is the reporting of its decisions. The approach taken by the Commission in a number of instances shows a considerable margin for improvement, particularly in relation to the substance and reasoning of the communication. A survey of the Commission's work tends to suggest that in recent years some improvement has been made. Nevertheless,

---

[153] AFCHPR, Article 46.
[154] See the Activity Report of the African Commission on Human and Peoples' Rights 9 *HRLJ* (1988) 326.
[155] Flinterman and Ankumah, above n.1, at p. 174. The Commission in the course of its promotional activities has also produced a Declaration of Principles on Freedom of Expression in Africa, Guidelines and Measures for the Prohibition and Prevention of Torture and a Resolution on the Rights of Indigenous Peoples Communities in Africa.
[156] Murray, above n.70, at p. 15.
[157] *Kalenga* v. *Zambia* (admissibility), Communication No. 11/88 (1990).
[158] *Comité Cultural pour la Democratie au Benin and Others* v. *Benin* (Merits), Communication Nos. 16/88, 17/88, 18/88 (1995), para 5.
[159] *Civil Liberties Organization* v. *Nigeria*, Communication No. 67/92 (1994).

they do not make reference to jurisprudence from national and international tribunals, nor do they fire the imagination. They are non-binding and attract little, if any, attention from governments and the human rights community'.[160]

Although the Commission has adopted a quasi-legal approach, as noted above, its decisions are non-binding.[161] Furthermore, the Charter decisions do not provide for any legally enforceable remedies nor have any procedures that have been established to obtain these remedies.

6   THE AFRICAN COURT OF JUSTICE AND HUMAN RIGHTS[162]

Lacunae and other additional limitations within the operation of the African Commission for Human and Peoples' Rights prompted calls for the establishment of the African Court of Human Rights.[163] The aforementioned weaknesses in the functions of the Commission and the desire to improve the system of protecting human rights led to a widespread calls for the establishment of the African Court.[164] The existence and successes of European and Inter-American Courts also provided strong precedents to establish a regional human rights court for Africa.

The African Court represented the fruition of a process consisting of various meetings and draft protocols. The Protocol to the African Charter on Human and People's Rights' on the Establishment of an African Court (also known as the Adis Protocol) was adopted in June 1998, and came into force on 25 January 2004.[165] During the January 2006 summit in Khartum, 11 judges of the Court were elected and the seat of the Court was determined to be in Tanzania. While appointed judges continued to meet, the Rules of Procedure of this Court have not yet been finalised.[166] The Court was provided with physical building, though – notwithstanding the passage of 10 years since the adoption of the Protocol setting up this Court – no cases were referred to it. However, events overtook the institutional developments within the AU system. As noted already, a further, substantially more

---

[160]   Mutua, above n.1, at p. 348.
[161]   Naldi and Magliveras, above n.49, at p. 432.
[162]   Protocol on the Statute of the African Court of Justice and Human Rights (2008) www.africa-union.org/root/au/Documents/Treaties/text/Protocol%20on%20the%20Merged%20Court%20-%20EN.pdf <last visited 10 May 2009>; for analysis see Kindiki, 'The Proposed Integration of the African Court of Justice and the African Court of Human and People's Rights: Legal Difficulties and Merits' 15 *RADIC* (2007) 138.
[163]   For useful background analysis see Viljoen, 'A Human Rights Court for Africa and African' 30 *Brook JInt Law* (2004–2005) 1; Van der Mei, 'The New African Court on Human and People's Rights: Towards an Effective Human Rights Protection Mechanism for Africa' 18 *Leiden Journal of International Law* (2005) 113; Hopkins, 'The Effect of the African Court on the Domestic Legal Orders of African States', (2002) 2 *African Human Rights Law Journal* 234; O'Shea, 'A Critical Reflection on the Proposed African Court on Human and Peoples' Rights', (2001) 1 *African Human Rights Law Journal* 285; Udombana, 'Toward the African Court on Human and Peoples' Rights: Better Late than Never', (2000) 3 *Yale Human Rights and Development Law Journal* 45; Mubangizi and O'Shea, 'An African Court on Human and Peoples' Rights', (1999) 24 *South African Yearbook of International Law* 256; Murray, 'A Comparison between the African and European Courts of Human Rights', (2002) 2 *African Human Rights Law Journal* 195.
[164]   Ojo and Sesay, above n.124, at p. 102.
[165]   See Protocol to the African Charter on Human and Peoples' Rights on the Establishment of an African Court on Human and Peoples' Rights adopted 10 June 1998, OAU Doc. CAB/LEG/66/5.
[166]   Ibid. Wachira, above n.1, at p. 20.

important development took place during 2008. The AU adopted the Protocol on the Statute of the African Court of Justice and Human Rights on 1 July 2008. The 2008 Protocol on the Statute of the African Court of Justice and Human Rights has replaced the Protocol to the African Charter on Human and Peoples' Rights on the Establishment of an African Court on Human and Peoples' Rights, (1998) and the Protocol of the Court of Justice of the African Union (2003).[167] The confirmation of a merger and the establishment of a single court is provided by Article 2 of the 2008 Protocol. It provides as follows:

> The African Court on Human and Peoples' Rights established by the Protocol to the African Charter on Human and Peoples' Rights on the Establishment of an African Court on Human and Peoples' Rights and the Court of Justice of the African Union established by the Constitutive Act of the African Union, are hereby merged into a single Court and established as 'The African Court of Justice and Human Rights'.[168]

The new Court once established shall have two sections – one General Affairs consisting of eight judges and a Human Rights section also consisting of eight judges.[169] The Court has been granted contentious, as well as advisory jurisdiction. In its capacity to deal with contentious cases, the Court is granted substantial and in some senses unusual jurisdiction. According to Article 28 of the Statute annexed to the Protocol, the Court has jurisdiction over all cases and legal disputes that are submitted to it which relate to:

(a) the interpretation and application of the Constitutive Act;

(b) the interpretation, application or validity of other Union Treaties and all subsidiary legal instruments adopted within the framework of the Union or the Organization of African Unity;

(c) the interpretation and the application of the African Charter, the Charter on the Rights and Welfare of the Child, the Protocol to the African Charter on Human and Peoples' Rights on the Rights of Women in Africa, or any other legal instrument relating to human rights, ratified by the States Parties concerned;

(d) any question of international law;

(e) all acts, decisions, regulations and directives of the organs of the Union;

(f) all matters specifically provided for in any other agreements that States Parties may conclude among themselves, or with the Union and which confer jurisdiction on the Court;

(g) the existence of any fact which, if established, would constitute a breach of an obligation owed to a State Party or to the Union;

(h) the nature or extent of the reparation to be made for the breach of an international obligation.[170]

---

[167] See Article 1 of the Protocol on the Statute of the African Court of Justice and Human Rights (2008) www.africa-union.org/root/au/Documents/Treaties/text/Protocol%20on%20the%20Merged% 20Court%20-%20EN.pdf <last visited 10 May 2009>.

[168] Ibid. Article 2.

[169] Article 16 of the Statute annexed to the Protocol.

[170] Ibid. Article 28.

As noted above, within Article 28, there is, a major innovative feature: in its adjudication, in addition to issues arising out of the application and interpretation of the African Charter, the Charter on the Rights and Welfare of the Child, the Protocol to the African Charter on Human and Peoples' Rights on the Rights of Women in Africa, the Court would have the power to consider 'any other legal instrument relating to human rights, ratified by the States parties concerned'.[171] The Statute annexed to the Protocol provides automatic access to submit cases to the Court to, *inter alia*, States parties to the Protocol, the African Commission on Human and People's Rights, the African Committee of Experts on the Rights and Welfare of the Child, the African intergovernmental organisations accredited to AU or its organs and African national human rights institutions.[172]

The Court however is not open to States not members of the AU nor does it provide jurisdiction to those AU member which have not ratified the Protocol.[173] Similarly the Statute in its Article 30, severely limits the possibility of individuals and NGOs to directly submit applications before the Court – their right of petitioning is made dependent on the relevant State party making a declaration allowing these entity a right to make such submissions.[174] In adopting this position, the Statute of the Court follows the course adopted by the Protocol establishing the African Court on Human and Peoples' Rights, Article 34(6) of which provides that 'At the time of the ratification of this Protocol or any time thereafter, the State shall make a declaration accepting the competence of the Court to receive cases under Article 5(3) of this Protocol. The Court shall not receive any petition under Article 5(3) involving a State Party which has not made such a declaration.'[175]

Article 34 of the Statute annexed to the 2008 Protocol establishes a procedure of submitting cases before the human rights section of the Court. According to Article 34(1):

> Cases brought before the Court relating to an alleged violation of a human or peoples' right shall be submitted by a written application to the Registrar. The application shall indicate the right (s) alleged to have been violated, and, insofar as it is possible, the provision or provisions of the African Charter on Human and Peoples' Rights, the Charter on the Rights and Welfare of the Child, Protocol to the African Charter on Human and Peoples' Rights on the Rights of Women in Africa or any other relevant human rights instrument, ratified by the State concerned, on which it is based.[176]

In its advisory capacity the Court may issue opinions *inter alia* on 'any legal question'.[177] This provision appears to be similar to Article 64(1) of ACHR. A range of bodies including AU Assembly, the Parliament, the Executive Council, the Peace and Security Council, Economic, Social and Cultural Council (ECOSOCC), the Financial Institutions as well as other organs of the AU authorised by the Assembly are eligible to request the Court for an

---

[171] Ibid. Article 28(c).
[172] Ibid. Article 30. Also included in the eligible entities are the Assembly, the Parliament and other Organs of the Union authorised by the Assembly. Ibid. Article 29(1)(b).
[173] Ibid. Article 29(2).
[174] Ibid. Article 30(f).
[175] See Amnesty International, *Document–African Union Summit in Addis Ababba: African Leaders Should Recommit to full Implementation of Human Rights* at p. 3 (AI Index: IOR63/001/2009, 31 January 2009).
[176] Article 34(1) of the Statute annexed to the Protocol.
[177] Ibid. Article 53(1).

advisory opinion.[178] The Courts' advisory opinions will not be of a binding nature, but like the ICJ, it is assumed that they will carry substantial persuasive authority. As indicated above, the single Court will consist of 16 judges, nationals of AU Member States who will be elected in their individual capacity by the Executive Council and appointed by the Assembly[179] from among 'among persons of high moral character, who possess the qualifications required in their respective countries for appointment to the highest judicial offices, or are juristconsults of recognized competence and experience in international law and/or, human rights law'.[180]

The judges would be elected through a secret ballot by a two-third majority of member State with voting rights, with those candidates eligible for appointment who obtain two-thirds majority and the highest number of votes.[181] In the election and appointment of Judges the Assembly is to ensure an equitable gender representation. The Judges are initially elected for a six-year term though they are eligible for re-election once.[182] The term of office of eight judges, four from each of the section elected during the first section would end after the first four years.[183] Article 9 of the Protocol to the Statute provides for the procedure of resignation as well as the suspension of a judge of the Court.

The Statute allows the Human Rights section to be competent to hear all cases relating to human and peoples' rights, while at the same time authorising the General Affairs section to all other cases.[184] There are provisions within one section of the Court to refer the matter to the Full Court if the section deems it necessary.[185] The quorum for the full Court is nine judges, whereas the quorum for each section is six.[186]

The Court will render its judgments stating reasons for the decision, within 90 days of having completed its deliberations.[187] The Executive Council would also be notified of the decision which shall then monitor the execution of the judgment on behalf of the Assembly.[188] Subject to provisions regarding an objection by one of the parties in relation to a judgment in default, the decisions of the Court shall be final,[189] and will be binding on States.[190] The parties are obliged to comply with the judgments of the Court within the timescale laid down by the Court. In case of failure to give effect to the judgment, the Assembly is authorised to impose sanctions by virtue of Article 23(2) of the Constitutive Act.[191] The extent to which the African Court has a role in awarding reparations remains unclear.[192] Article 45 however provides that '[W]ithout prejudice to its competence to rule on issues of compensation at the request of a party by virtue of paragraph 1(h), of Article 28 of the present Statute, the Court may, if it considers that there was a violation of a

---

[178] Ibid.
[179] Ibid. Article 7(1).
[180] Ibid. Article 4.
[181] Ibid. Article 7(2)(3).
[182] Ibid. Article 8(1).
[183] Ibid. Article 8(1).
[184] Ibid. Article 17.
[185] Ibid. Article 18.
[186] Ibid. Article 21.
[187] Ibid. Article 43(1)(2).
[188] Ibid. Article 43(6).
[189] Ibid. Article 46(2).
[190] Ibid. Article 46(1).
[191] Ibid. Article 46(5).
[192] See Pasqualucci, *The Practice and Procedure of the Inter-American Court of Human Rights* (Cambridge University Press, 2003) at p. 235.

human or peoples' right, order any appropriate measures in order to remedy the situation, including granting fair compensation'.

The practical ramifications of the 2008 Protocol and the Statute of the Court Annexed to the Protocol are yet to be determined, and it can not be said with any certainty that the new Court would fulfil the promise of an effective, organised and fully transparent judicial institution. The Statute of the Court shall come into force 30 days after the deposit of the instrument of ratification by 15 Member States.[193] It may be long time coming before the Statue comes into force and the single, Pan-African Court becomes operational. In the meanwhile, Article 7 of the Protocol provides for a provisional validity of the 1998 Protocol to the African Charter on Human and People's Rights to remain in force for period not exceeding one year or any other period determined by the Assembly after entry into force of the 2008 Protocol.[194]

7 PROTECTING HUMAN AND PEOPLES' RIGHTS

The African Charter (AFCHPR) provides for a State reporting procedure, an inter-State complaints procedure and what it terms as 'Other Communications' procedure. The State reporting procedure is contained in Article 62, the inter-State procedure is dealt with in Articles 47–54 whereas the 'Other Communications' procedure is provided for in Articles 55–59.

(i) State reporting procedure[195]

The Commission obtains reports from State parties with a view to ascertaining whether or not each State party has taken the necessary administrative, legislative or other measures to implement the Charter. According to Article 62, each State party is obliged to submit every two years from the date of the Charter's enforcement 'a report on the legislative or other measures taken, with a view to giving effect to the rights and freedoms recognized and guaranteed by the present Charter'. The reports are handled by the Assembly of Heads of State and Governments of [AU]. The reporting procedure has been treated as 'the backbone of the mission of the Commission'.[196]

The Charter does not specify any details as to the body to which the reports are to be submitted or provide guidelines on the structure of these reports and what subsequent action is required from these reports.[197] The established practice is that these reports are, with the approval of the Assembly, examined by the Commission. NGOs are allowed to submit alternative or shadow reports, but the efficiency and impact of these alternative reports is hindered due to the lack of access of NGOs to official State reports in which they are meant to highlight deficiencies. The Commission considers these reports in public

---

[193] Article 9 of the Protocol on the Statute of the African Court of Justice and Human Rights.
[194] Ibid. Article 7.
[195] See Evans and Murray, 'The State Reporting Mechanisms of the African Charter' in Evans and Murray (eds), above n.1, pp. 49–75.
[196] El-Sheikh, 'The African Commission on Human and Peoples Rights: Prospects and Problems' 7 *NQHR* (1989) 272 at p. 281.
[197] According to a number of commentators this silence was deliberate, not to threaten prospects of ratification. Heyns, *Human Rights Law in Africa, Vol. II* (Kluwer Law International, 1997) at p. 56.

sessions. The African Commission has provided certain guidelines on reporting procedures.[198] The reports need to provide detailed legislative measures and actual implementation for human rights protection.[199] After submission the reports are examined in public by the Commission. The Commission and the State representatives engage in a dialogue with the purpose of assisting and encouraging States to implement the Charter. After consultation regarding a report, the Commission communicates its observations and comments to the relevant State party. Despite these guidelines and efforts for improvements, States have been reluctant to produce reports. The Rules of Procedure in the African Commission do not attach sanctions for non-compliance with reporting procedures.[200] The few reports that have been produced are not satisfactory, with only 18 out of 53 States ever having submitted any report. Since 2001, the Commission has introduced the procedure of issuing Concluding Observations, although unfortunately neither State reports nor Concluding Observations are published.

(ii) Inter-State procedure

In addition to State reporting, the second principal function of the Commission is to ensure the protection of human rights through the complaints procedure. The Charter envisages two modes of inter-State complaints. Firstly, under Article 47 of the Charter if one State party has reason to believe that another State party has violated its obligations under the Charter, it may by written communication refer the matter to the State concerned. According to Article 47, this communication shall also be addressed to the Secretary-General of AU and Chairman of the Commission. Within three months of the receipt of the communication, the State to which the communication has been addressed shall give the enquiring State a written explanation or statement clarifying the issue. This should include all possible information and the action or redress available. 'If within three months from the date on which the original communication was received by the State', the issue is not settled satisfactorily through negotiations or other peaceful means then either State may bring the matter before the Commission.[201] The Commission then requests for further information from the State against whom complaint has been made. Parties can appear before the Commission and/or present written or oral statements. There also remains the possibility of an on-site investigation. The Charter makes clear that the primary objective is to secure friendly settlement. Not only is this the basic aim of the Commission but under Article 47 a complainant is encouraged to approach the other party directly with a view to settling the matter without involving the Commission. In advance

---

[198] See Guidelines for National Periodic Reports, Second Annual Activity Report of the African Commission on Human and Peoples' Rights 1988–1989, ACHPR/RPT/2nd Annex XII (Documents of the African Commission) at p. 49. According to this, 'the aim of the exercise is to show the degree of actual satisfaction of the rights, duties and freedoms of the Charter; the reporting obligations extend to the practice of the Courts and administrative organ of the State Party and other relevant facts'. Ibid. para 9. These guidelines were amended (by a rather simplistic set of guidelines) in 1998. See Amendment of the General Guidelines for the preparation of Periodic Report by States parties, Doc/03/27 (XXIII). These latter guidelines have been the subject of criticism for their inadequacy.

[199] See Gaer, 'First Fruits: Reporting By States under the African Charter on Human and Peoples Rights' 10 NQHR (1992) 29.

[200] Umozurike, above n.1, at pp. 71–72. See Rule 84 of the Rules of Procedure of the African Commission on Human and Peoples' Rights, adopted on 6 October 1995.

[201] Article 48.

of the European and American Conventions, Article 47 reflects the African States preference for informed methods of dispute settlement. However, such an approach is prone to criticism as 'too State-centric'[202] with the Commission appearing to settle 'inter-State disputes rather than serving as a watchdog of human rights transgressions'.[203]

The alternative mechanism of inter-State complaints is contained in Article 49. According to this procedure, a State party may refer the matter directly to the Commission if it considers that another State party has violated any of the provisions of the Charter. The reference to the Commission would be by a communication to the Chairman, Secretary-General of the AU and the relevant State party. In line with other international procedures the Commission can only deal with the matter if all local remedies have been exhausted.[204] However, there remains the usual exemption to those cases where remedies are 'unduly prolonged'.[205] Furthermore, the matter in question must not have already been settled through an international procedure or settlement.[206]

The Commission has wide powers. It can ask States to provide information and they are entitled to appear before it and submit oral and written representations. Article 52 provides that when the Commission has obtained from the States concerned 'and from other sources' all the information it deems necessary, its task is to make attempts to reach 'an amicable solution based on the respect of Human and Peoples' Rights'.[207] Failing this, the Commission is required to prepare a report (containing facts and its findings) and send it to the States concerned and to Heads of State and Government. According to Article 53, while transmitting its report, the Commission may make appropriate recommendations to the Assembly of Heads of State and Government. The Commission is also required to submit a general report on its activities to each Ordinary Session of Assembly of Heads of States and Government.[208] Although a number of attempts were made in the past,[209] in actual effect, inter-State procedure has thus far only been used once with a complaint being brought forward by the Democratic Republic of Congo against Burundi, Rwanda and Uganda.[210] It was, as Chaloka Beyani elaborates, the first instance where the Commission dealt with a case involving sexual offences and violations of international humanitarian law.[211] In dealing with the procedural matters, the Commission noted that while the procedure of notifying a respondent State is permissive it is not mandatory.[212] On the merits of the case, the Commission found that the respondent States had violated the provisions of the AFCHPR and international human rights law and international

---

[202] Ojo and Sesay, above n.124, at p. 89.

[203] Ibid. p. 96.

[204] Article 50.

[205] Ibid.

[206] See Rules of Procedure, Rule 93(2)(c).

[207] Article 52.

[208] Article 54.

[209] A complaint was received from Sudan complaining of violations by Ethiopian troops in Sudanese territory in 1997. Since Ethiopia was at the time not a party to the Charter, the Commission advised Sudan that subject-matter was beyond the jurisdiction of the Commission. A previous attempt had been made by Libya against the United States in 1987 concerning the removal of Libyan soldiers from Chad. The communication was held inadmissible as US is not a party to the treaty. See Nmehielle, *The African Human Rights System: Its Laws, Practice and Institutions* (Brill, 2001) at p. 202.

[210] *Democratic Republic of the Congo v. Burundi, Rwanda and Uganda*, Communication No. 227/99 (2006). Beyani, 'Recent Developments in the African Human Rights System 2004–2006' 7 *HRLR* (2007) 582.

[211] Beyani, 'Recent Developments in the African Human Rights System 2004–2006' 7 *HRLR* (2007) 582 at p. 598.

[212] *Democratic Republic of the Congo v. Burundi, Rwanda and Uganda*, Communication No. 227/99 (2006) para 57.

humanitarian law.[213] A contemporaneous complaint was filed by Congo before the International Court of Justice.[214] In the case against Rwanda, the World Court decided that it lacked jurisdiction. However the International Court of Justice did find that Uganda had violated its obligations under international law and international humanitarian law.[215]

(iii) Other communications

In addition to the inter-State mechanisms for protecting human rights, the African Charter also has another complaints procedure which is entitled 'Other Communications'. Much like its European Counterpart, this procedure has been more readily used. To date the Commission had received well over 300 communications. Article 55 of the Charter provides that the Commission's Secretary is to prepare a list of non-State communications and to pass them to members of the Commission.[216] The decision whether to consider the communication is conducted by the Commission members by a simple majority.[217] The Secretary to the Commission prepares a list of all communications received and dealt by the Secretariat. Each communication is designated to a Commissioner who acts as the Rapporteur. According to the Rules of Procedure, the Commission may through the Secretary seek further clarifications regarding the Communication.[218] Long delays have characterised the admissibility procedure regarding Communications.[219] A Communication should provide all possible details regarding the violation of rights. Although a communication could be presented in any of the working languages of the AU, in the light of the limited resources, it is desirable to submit communications in either French or English, or as Professor Viljoen suggests both in English and French.[220]

The powers of the Commission under Article 55 are mandatory, i.e. the African Commission's competence to deal with individual or other non-State Communications is accepted automatically, as soon as a State ratifies the Charter. The following are the conditions of Admissibility:

> The Communication must indicate the author(s) even if they request anonymity.[221]

The Commission requires the authors to provide their names and addresses even if they desire to remain anonymous in respect of the State party concerned.[222] It must be noted in the present context that there are no limitations as to who may file petition. Unlike the position in ECHR, there is no 'victim' requirement. There is no requirement that the

---

[213] Ibid. paras 68 and 77.

[214] See *Case Concerning Armed Activities in the Territory of Congo (Democratic Republic of Congo v. Rwanda)* [2006] ICJ Reports 1.

[215] Ibid. para 219. Also see Higgins, 'Human Rights in the International Court of Justice' 20 *LJIL* (2007) 745.

[216] Article 55(1).

[217] Article 55(2).

[218] Rules of Procedure, Rule 104.

[219] Communication No. 44/90, *Peoples' Democratic Organisation for Independence and Socialism v. The Gambia* was received in 1990 and finding on admissibility was conducted in 1995.

[220] Viljoen, 'Communications under the African Charter: Procedure and Admissibility' in Evans and Murray, (eds), above n.1, pp. 76–138, at p. 91.

[221] Article 56(1).

[222] The full details of address are required so that the author can be contacted promptly; see *Dioumessi and others v. Guinea*, Communication No. 70/92 (1994) (1995).

authors are the victims of a violation of the rights contained in the Charter or family members of the victim.[223] The author does not need to be a national of the State party to the Charter[224] nor needs to be based within the State against whom the complaint is made.[225] Indeed, one advantage for not having the 'victim' requirement is that the authors do not have to establish that they have been directly affected by particular laws or practices.[226] Several communications have unsurprisingly been put forward by NGOs – a concession which carries the risk of opening flood-gates. The communication must, nevertheless, be against a State party to the Charter. A number of communications have been held inadmissible as they were either instituted against non-African States, non-States parties or against non-State entities.[227]

> **The Communications must be compatible with the Charter of AU 'or' the African Charter.[228]**

The difficulties in providing a literal reading to the term 'or' have been pointed out.[229] It would appear that a sensible construction of the provisions requires the communication to be compatible with both the Constitutive Act of the AU (previously the Charter of the OAU) and the African Charter, and thus the substitution of 'or' in Article 56(2) with 'and'.[230] It also means that attempts on the part of minority groups or indigenous peoples to claim a right to self-determination would not be admissible since these arguably conflict with AU provisions on the territorial integrity and sovereignty of the State.[231] In this context our discussion earlier in the chapter needs to be recalled. The Commission has used these provisions to hold communications inadmissible if they fail to show a *prima facie* violation

---

[223] *Free Legal Assistance Group, Lawyers Committee for Human Rights, Union InterAfricaine des Droits de l'Homme, Les Témoins de Jehovah v. Zaire*, Communication Nos. 25/89, 47/90, 56/91, 100/93 (1995).

[224] *Lawyers Committee for Human Rights v. Tanzania*, Communication No. 66/92.

[225] *Baes v. Zaïre* (admissibility) Communication No. 31/89 (1995), Maria Baes – a Danish national – submitted a communication on behalf of a Zairian colleague at the University of Zaire, Dr. Kondola. Although the Communication was inadmissible, the author's nationality was not a factor material to the decision.

[226] Viljoen, 'Communications under the African Charter: Procedure and Admissibility' in Evans and Murray, (eds), above n.1, pp 76–138, at p. 103.

[227] See e.g. *El-Nekheily v. OAU*, Communication No. 12/88 (1988).

[228] Article 56(2).

[229] Odinkalu and Christensen, above n.33, at p. 252.

[230] Relying upon the Commission's decision in *Katangese Peoples' Congress v. Zaire*, Communication No. 75/92 (1995), Viljoen takes the view that communications have to be compatible with the African Charter as well as the OAU Charter. See Viljoen, 'Communications under the African Charter: Procedure and Admissibility' in Evans and Murray (eds), above n.1, pp. 76–138, at p. 95.

[231] In *Katangese Peoples' Congress v. Zaire*, Communication No. 75/92 (1995), the Kantangese Peoples' Congress, claiming to be the national liberation movement for the people of Kantaga in Zaire, petitioned the Commission claiming the right to independence and secession under Article 20(1) of the Charter. According to the Commission territorial integrity of all Member States of the OAU must be preserved. The Commission's approach reflects the AU position that secession in the name of self-determination is impossible although the Commission hinted at two exceptions from this general principle. Firstly, independence based arguments are sustainable where there is substantial evidence of violations of human rights and these violations lead to a questionable territorial unity of the State, and secondly where there is evidence of a group being deprived of participation in government as provided for in the African Charter. On the facts of the case, neither of these conditions were satisfied; hence the communication was held inadmissible.

of any of the Articles[232] or provide a general allegation[233] or have failed to be specific,[234] are not directed against a State,[235] against a State which is not a party to the Charter,[236] has been submitted by an incompetent person, was not based upon event that took place within the period of the Charter's application,[237] or related to events that took place outside the territory of the State party.[238]

> The Communications must not be insulting, and not written in a disparaging manner which is directed against the State, its institutions or against the AU.[239]

The Commission has used this requirement to hold communications inadmissible where the allegation has been that, for example, 'Paul Biya [the President of Cameroon] must respond to crimes against humanity' or 'regime of torturers', and 'government barbarisms'.[240] While the requirement of a communication to be non-insulting is not uncommon, the Commission has, nevertheless, been criticised for showing a bias and approaching the issues very subjectively.[241]

> Communications are not based exclusively on news disseminated through the mass media.

This is a rather unusual requirement that the complaint must not be based exclusively on news disseminated through mass media. This requirement while aimed at preventing spurious petitions, possibly represents a distinctly African approach. At the same time it also potentially counteracts to a small extent the lack of a 'victim' requirement.

---

[232] *Korvah* v. *Liberia* (admissibility), Communication No. 1/88 (1988). The communication was based on the lack of discipline in Liberian Security Police and the immorality of the Liberian people and the national security risk caused by American financial experts. The Commission held that it was not able to ascertain that the communication contained allegations amounting to any violations of the provisions within the Charter.

[233] *Hadjali Mohamad* v. *Algeria* (admissibility), Communication No. 13/88 (1994).

[234] *Centre for the Independence of Judges and Lawyers* v. *Algeria*. Communication Nos. 104/94, 109/94, 126/94 (1994), para 6. The communication was held inadmissible due to the lack of any specific places, dates and times for the violations of the provisions of the Charter. *Congress for the Second Republic of Malawi* v. *Malawi* (admissibility), Communication 63/93 (1992).

[235] See Communication 12/88, *Mohamed El-Nekheily* v. *OAU*, Seventh Activity Report 1993–1994, Annex (Documents of the African Commission, p. 339).

[236] Two Communications were submitted against Morocco, which at the relevant periods was not a party to the OAU (*Austrian Committee Against Torture* v. *Morocco*, Communication No. 20/88 (1989). A further communication was submitted claiming violations by four States, none of these States being a party to the Charter at the relevant time (*International PEN* v. *Malawi, Ethiopia, Cameroon, Kenya*, Communication No. 19/88 (1989)).

[237] *Njoka* v. *Kenya*, Communication 142/94 (1995). The Commission held the Communication inadmissible as it related to event that took place before Kenya becomes a party to the Charter. In line with other, human rights bodies, the Commission has, however, indicated the possibility of the 'continuous violation' exception – circumstances where the violation is continuous and persists to the time of the State becoming party to the Convention.

[238] For a considerable controversy over 'effective' control outside the territory of the State see above chapter 7.

[239] Article 56(3).

[240] *Ligue Camerounaise des Droits de l'Homme* v. *Cameroon*, Communication No. 65/92 (1997) para 13. Tenth Activity Report 1996–1997, Annex X (Documents of the African Commission, p. 562). This decision has been criticised as 'unfortunate and regrettable' by Viljoen in Viljoen, 'Communications under the African Charter: Procedure and Admissibility' in Evans and Murray (eds), above n.1, pp. 76–138, at p. 108.

[241] Odinkalu and Christensen, above n.33, at p. 255. On several occasions cases have been referred by the Commission to the Assembly, which unfortunately has not taken any action – see *Constitutional Rights Project and Civil Liberties Organisation* v. *Nigeria*, Communication 102/93 (1998); *Achuthan and Amnesty International* v. *Malawi*, Communication Nos. 64/92, 68/92 and 78/92 (1995).

Communications are sent after exhausting all local remedies, unless the remedies are unduly prolonged.

We have already noted exhaustion of all available remedies as an admissibility requirement is part and parcel of all international procedures. Pending complaints are not admissible.[242] Local remedies mean the provision of any form of domestic legal action which could lead to the resolution of the dispute. This includes remedies of a judicial nature including review or appeals.[243] A number of exceptions apply to this general rule. There would be no requirement of exhausting local remedies where all opportunities of redress have been closed[244] or where the procedures are excessively prolonged or cumbersome.[245] In a number of instances, however, the approach adopted by the African Commission has been much narrower. This position is reflected by the case of the *Kenya Human Rights Commission* v. *Kenya*.[246] In this case university staff in Kenya decided to form an umbrella trade union named the Universities Academic Staff Union (UASU) and submitted the application for registration in May 1992. Not having heard from the university authorities for six months they decided to go on strike. Their application for registration was rejected by the university registrar in 1993. The university staff instituted legal proceedings in December 1993 to challenge the decision made by the registrar. Although, the proceedings were still before the Kenyan courts on 27 December 1993, President Moi alleged that the Kenyan government would never allow the registration of UASU, a statement that was repeated a number of times. Despite this almost confirmed position of the government, in October 1995, the Commission decided that although 'the President gave indication that any challenge would not be effective' the complainant had to await the outcome of national procedures and thus declared the Communication inadmissible.[247] Such an attitude is unfortunate and fails to comply with the recognised exceptions whereby the authors of the communication are exempted from utilising those remedies which would prove to be 'inadequate' or 'ineffective'.

The Commission's more recent jurisprudence tends to be more in line with other international bodies. The Commission has pronounced on occasions the meaning of 'effective' remedies and 'unduly prolonged procedure'.[248] Thus, in one case where an appeal against the death sentence lay before the Governor it was held that such an appeal created 'a discretionary, extraordinary remedy which was of a non-judicial nature'. The Commission,

---

[242] *Civil Liberties Organisation* v. *Nigeria*, Communication No. 45/90 (1994).

[243] *Ngozi Njoku* v. *Egypt*, Communication No. 40/90 (1997).

[244] *Civil Liberties Organisation* v. *Nigeria*, Communication No. 67/91 (1993). Section 4 of the State Security (Detention of Persons) Decree barring any legal challenge.

[245] *Mekongo Louis* v. *Cameroon*, Communication No. 59/91 (1994). Where the case was pending for 12 years. *Lawyers' Committee for Human Rights* v. *Tanzania*, Communication No. 66/92 (1994) (rejection of bail applications and delay in appeal procedures). However the Commission has insisted on the initiation of legal proceedings *International PEN (in respect of Kamal al-Jazouli)* v. *Sudan*, Communication No. 92/93 (1995) – where the Commission was of the view that '[t]he fact that the Government has in general terms denied the existence of incommunicado detentions in Sudan does not amount to saying that the case has been tried in Sudanese Courts'. Ibid.; *Peoples' Democratic Organisation for Independence and Socialism* v. *The Gambia*, Communication No. 44/90 (1996) where the Commission held that the technical possibility of taking the appeal to the Privy Council would result in rendering the 'local remedies' requirement as unduly prolonged.

[246] *Kenya Human Rights Commission* v. *Kenya* (admissibility), Communication 135/94 (1995).

[247] Ibid. para 17.

[248] *Lawyers Committee for Human Rights* v. *Tanzania*, Communication 66/92, a two-year delay in bringing the applicant to trial since ostensibily no judge was available to hear the case.

therefore, held that it was not necessary to exhaust such a remedy.[249] The Commission has in line with other international procedures required the author of the communication to adduce *prima facie* evidence that he or she has either exhausted all domestic remedies, or that the existing remedies are inadequate and ineffective. Once the author can establish the *prima facie* evidence, then the burden of proof shifts upon the defendant State.

> Communications are submitted within a reasonable period from the time local remedies are exhausted or from the date the Commission is seized of the matter.[250]

Contrary to the rigid admissibility requirements of the ECHR, of petitioning within six months from the 'date on which the final decision was taken' (Article 35) the African Charter does not provide for any time limitation for the submission of communications. The Commission has not directly provided the details of the timeframe in which communications are to be submitted after the exhaustion of domestic remedies requirement is fulfilled, although some guidelines are available in the light of decisions. Thus, in one case a communication was held admissible despite the author having spent more than 12 years pursuing a discretionary remedy.[251] Similarly in another case a communication was held admissible even though after 16 years the final appeal was still pending.[252] This approach although apparently hugely favourable to the author in the context of African judicial and political mechanisms is a realistic one and must be commended.

> Communications do not deal with cases which have been settled by the States involved in accordance with the principles of the United Nations Charter, or the AU Constitutive Act (previously the Charter of the OAU) or the African Charter.[253]

Insofar as restrictions relate to international procedure these limitations apply only to those communications which have actually been *settled* by use of another procedure. Therefore, presumably concurrent communications are not barred from consideration by the Commission.[254] Cases, therefore, have been held inadmissible when a decision has been made by such international bodies as the Human Rights Committee.[255] The Commission has decided to hold a communication as inadmissible which received attention under UN ECOSOC Resolution 1503 procedure.[256] However, a change brought about in the Rules of

---

[249] *Constitutional Rights Project* v. *Nigeria (in respect of Wahab Akamu, G. Adega and Others)*, Communication No. 60/91 (1995); in an environment of massive violations of human rights including arrests, torture and extra-judical killings the Commission has acknowledged local remedies are *prima facie* not available or effective, Communication 25/89, 47/90, 56/91 and 100/93; Communication 275/2003, *Article 19* v. *Eritrea*, Communication No. 275/2003 (2007).

[250] Article 56(6).

[251] *Mekongo Louis* v. *Cameroon*, Communication No. 59/91 (1994).

[252] *Modise* v. *Botswana*, Communication No. 97/93 (1997), paras 19–22.

[253] Article 56(7).

[254] *Ngozi Njoku* v. *Egypt*, Communication No. 40/90 (1997), para 58. Simultaneous communications had been made before the Commission and the Human Rights Committee. The UN Working Group of the Sub-Commission on the Prevention and Protection of Minorities did not entertain the communication, which led to the African Commission to take the view that the matter had not been 'settled' under Article 56(7), therefore, the communication was held admissible, paras 55–56.

[255] *Mpaka-Nsusu* v. *Zaire*, Communication No. 15/88 (1994).

[256] See *Amnesty International* v. *Tunisia*, Communication No. 69/92 (1994).

Procedure, allowing the Commission only to preclude consideration to '[t]he extent to which the same issue has been settled by another international investigation or settlement body'[257] would arguably allow it to be more flexible in its approach.[258]

(iv) Article 58 communications[259]

The Charter makes reference and elaborates upon the procedure regarding cases that are 'special'. According to Article 58(1) when it appears after deliberations of the Commission that one or more communications apparently relate to special cases which reveal the existence of a series of serious or massive violations of human and peoples' rights, the Commission shall draw the attention of the Assembly of the Heads of State and Governments of the AU to these special cases. The Assembly of Heads of State and Government may then request the Commission to undertake a detailed study. This would result in making a report on the facts of the case, the findings of the Commission and its recommendations on the particular situation.[260]

According to Article 58(3) the Chairman of Assembly is authorised to request an in-depth study in all the cases of emergency. However, there is no discussion of the position relating to those cases that are 'not special'.[261] Two views can be put forward here. Firstly, that the Commission has no role to play in these instances, thereby confirming the situation that the role of the Commission is to identify special cases and refer them to the Assembly in the hope that they will be passed back for further investigation. Hence any other case which does not fall within this category would be inadmissible. The second, more positive and forthright view is that in 'non-special' cases, the Commission has the same functions as under the inter-State procedure, i.e. conduct investigation, attempt reconciliation and report conclusions to the Assembly.[262]

Article 59(1) establishes the requirement of confidentiality. It notes that all the measures undertaken in accordance with the provisions of Chapter III shall remain confidential until a time when the Assembly of Heads of State and Government decides to disclose the measures. A report shall nevertheless be published by the Chairman of the Commission upon the decision of Heads of State and Government.[263] The report on the activities of the Commission is also published by its Chairman after it has been considered by the Assembly of Heads of States and Governments.[264] There are no explicit provisions relating to interim or provisional measures which the Commission could authorise the use of in order to prevent irreparable harm. The Rules of Procedure of the Commission, however, provides the Commission with such powers and the Commission has deployed these powers in a number of cases.[265]

[257] Rules of Procedure, Rule 104(1)(g).
[258] See Odinkalu and Christensen, above n.33, at p. 268.
[259] Ibid. at p. 239; see generally Viljoen, 'Communications under the African Charter: Procedure and Admissibility' in Evans and Murray (eds), above n.1, pp. 76–138.
[260] Article 58(2).
[261] See Murray, 'Decisions by the African Commission on Individual Communications under the African Charter on Human and Peoples' Rights' 46 *ICLQ* (1997) 412 at p. 413; Bendek, 'The African Charter and Commission on Human and Peoples Rights: How to make it more Effective' 11 *NQHR* (1993) 25 at p. 31.
[262] See Odinkalu and Christensen, above n.33, at p. 244.
[263] Article 59(2).
[264] Article 58(3).
[265] Rules of Procedure, Rule 111; See *Interights (on behalf of Safia Yakubu Husaini* et al.*) v. Nigeria*, Communication No. 269/2003 (2005); Communications 137/94; 139/94; 154/96 and 161/97; *International PEN and others v. Nigeria*, Communication Nos. 137/94, 139/94, 154/96 and 161/97 (1998).

(v) Procedure

The procedure adopted by the Commission is that it brings any communication received to the attention of the State party concerned. Communications are registered by the Secretariat, who also assigns it a number. On receipt of a communication, the Commission informs the concerned State party that a complaint has been lodged against it and requests the submission of the State party's comments as regards admissibility.[266] A Commissioner is thereafter appointed as Rapporteur for the case. The Rules of Procedure allow the State party three months from the date of notification to respond.[267] Communications are considered in closed or private meetings.[268] Failing any response from the State concerned, at the end of three months, the Commission has the authority to hold the communication admissible. In practice, however, the Commission has not been particularly efficient, with the issue of admissibility being decided upon a matter of years rather than months after the submission of the communication. The Commission has also shown a willingness to review the decision on admissibility if the State subsequently does decide to provide relevant evidence or information.

The Rules of Procedure require the Commission to notify both the author and the State party concerned if a decision has been made to hold a communication admissible.[269] The Rules also allow for seeking additional supplementary information.[270]

If a communication is held as being inadmissible, the case is closed with the parties being informed of such a decision.[271] However, upon being admissible, there is a time limit of three months provided to the State party to submit its views.[272] All submissions made by States are to be disclosed to the author.[273] The Assembly of Heads of State and Government is also entitled to have information regarding the communications that have been declared admissible.[274] More recently the Commission has decided to invite State representatives as well as the author for oral hearings.[275] It is also encouraging to note that States are attending the sessions of the Commission as a matter of routine and participating in the proceedings. After the presentation of all the available evidence and any oral hearings, the Commission deliberates in private in accordance with the provisions of Article 59 of the Charter.[276] Thus, after the consideration of a communication, the Commission submits its report to the Assembly of the Heads of State and Government. This report can, however, only be published after the formal decision of the Assembly. In its initial phases the reporting of case-law was unsystematic. However since 1994, the Commission in its Annual Activity

---

[266] Rules 112 and 117(1).
[267] Rule 117(4).
[268] Rule 106.
[269] Rule 119(1).
[270] Rules 117(1) and 119(2) and (3).
[271] Rule 118(1).
[272] Rule 119(2).
[273] Rule 119(3).
[274] See Rules 113, 117.
[275] Communication 83/92, 88/93 and 91/93, *Degli (on behalf of N Bikagni) Union Interafricaine des Droits de l'Homme, Commission International des Juristes* v. *Togo*, Communication Nos. 83/92, 88/93 and 91/93 (1994). The Botswana Centre for Human Rights which has an observer status with the Commission was referred the case. The lack of financial resources have a part to play in often restricting the authors of the communications from attending and participating in oral hearings. NGOs have on occasion represented authors, or organisations other than their own which submits the communication. The Commission has some times referred cases to NGOs for representation.
[276] Odinkalu and Christensen, above n.33, at p. 274.

Report has produced its views in their entirety concerning all cases that have been submitted during the session. To its credit, the Assembly has authorised the Commission to publish some highly embarrassing reports, insofar as the State parties are concerned. These include a 2000 opinion on the treatment of black people in Mauritania, and the 2002 decision of the Commission on the treatment of Ogani people by the Nigerian government.

(a) Human rights initiatives focusing on peace-building and security

The AU (and during its currency, the OAU) focused on a number of initiatives related to Peace-building and Security within Africa. Africa has faced a historic problem of refugeeism and the problems of mass displacement of people has increased in recent decades. According to the UN High Commissioner for Refugees (UNHCR) African States were home to 2.8 million refugees during 2004, a figure which amounts to 30 per cent of the total number of refugees in the world. These figures were maintained by the end of 2008 and beginning of 2009. A 2002 study commissioned by the UN found that 13.5 million or more than half of the world's 25 million internally displaced persons were in Africa (concentrated in Angola, the DRC and Sudan). Tentative figures during 2008–09 suggest around 13 million internally displaced persons in Africa. About one in 50 African people have, therefore, been displaced from their home, or sought protection across borders.[277] Aware of the increase in political turmoil and consequent influx of refugees and displacement of peoples, the OAU adopted the Convention Governing the Specific Aspects of Refugee Problems in Africa in 1969. The treaty emulates the UN Convention Relating to the Status of Refugees 1951, though not without substantial differences. Thus, according to Article 1 of the OAU Convention, a refugee:

1. ... [s]hall mean every person who, owing to well-founded fear of being persecuted for reasons of race, religion, nationality, membership of a particular social group or political opinion, is outside the country of his nationality and is unable or, owing to such fear, is unwilling to avail himself of the protection of that country, or who, not having a nationality and being outside the country of his former habitual residence as a result of such events is unable or, owing to such fear, is unwilling to return to it.

2. The term 'refugee' shall also apply to every person who, owing to external aggression, occupation, foreign domination or events seriously disturbing public order in either part or the whole of his country of origin or nationality, is compelled to leave his place of habitual residence in order to seek refuge in another place outside his country of origin or nationality.

3. In the case of a person who has several nationalities, the term 'a country of which he is a national' shall mean each of the countries of which he is a national, and a person shall not be deemed to be lacking the protection of the country of which he is a national if, without any valid reason based on well-founded fear, he has not availed himself of the protection of one of the countries of which he is a national.

The Convention, whilst representing the reality of the African situation, broadens the UN definition in allowing victims of external aggression or calamities disturbing public order

---

[277] See Norwegian Refugee Council Global IDP Project, *Internally Displaced People: A Global Survey* (2002) www.reliefweb.int/rw/rwb.nsf/AllDocsByUNID/73cbe6109243c30285256c400067aa32 <last visited 21 November 2007>.

The African system for the protection of human rights

10

to claim a refugee status. It also arguably extends the principle of *non-refoulement* as presented in Article 2(3) as being an absolute one by making it impossible to be rejected at a State border.[278] Despite this broader perspective, the OAU Convention does not engage with the issues of mass influx of people with the processes and procedures of determining refugees being left generally at the discretion of individual States. Furthermore, the rights of refugees are not appropriately articulated nor is any specific body assigned the task of monitoring the Convention.[279] In order to deal with the growing number of refugees and displaced populations, the OAU established various procedures and committees including the so-called 'Commission of Ten' in 1964 and the Bureau for the Placement and Education of African Refugees in 1968.[280] The growth of political turmoil necessitates a more co-ordinated approach on the part of the AU. Thus far, the African Commission on Human and Peoples' Rights has mandated a Special Rapporteur on Refugees, Asylum-Seekers, Migrants and Internally Displaced Persons in Africa.[281]

Since the adoption of the AFCHPR, the African Commission has appointed Special Rapporteurs, with a range of mandates. Although there is no legal basis under the AFCHPR, the Commission established Special Rapporteurs in order to deal more effectively with gross violations of human rights. A Special Rapporteur on Summary, Arbitrary and Extra-Judicial Execution was put in place. A Special Rapporteur on the Conditions of Women in Africa has been established. Further Special Rapporteurs are the Special Rapporteur on Prisons and Conditions of Detention in Africa and the Special Rapporteur on Freedom of Expression, Refugees and Internally Displaced Persons and human rights defenders. The AU has also appointed the Special Rapporteur on Summary, Arbitrary and Extra-Judicial Executions, Prisons and other Conditions composed of NGOs and Commissioners for the examination of such areas as indigenous populations and fair trials.[282] The African Commission has also instituted on-site visits. These visits which commenced in 1995 include activities in the nature of fact-finding, promotional visits and usage of good office by the Commission.

The Conference on Security, Stability, Development and Co-operation was adopted at the 36th Ordinary Session of the Assembly. This is a standing conference, designed to be a process as opposed to a one-off event. The Conference was established in recognition of the fact that:

> problems of security in many African countries had impaired their capacity to achieve the necessary level of infra and inter-African cooperation that is required to attain the integration of the continent and critical to the continent's socio-economic development and transformation.[283]

The CSSDCA is organised into separated calabashes, however, the Memorandum of Understanding on the Security, Development and Cooperation Calabashes has enabled an all-inclusive approach to the work of the Conference.[284] This includes a common set of benchmarks for monitoring compliance, as well as core values and goals and the

---

[278] Murray, *Human Rights in Africa*, above n.1, at pp. 220–221.
[279] Ibid. p. 189.
[280] Ibid. pp. 195–201.
[281] Resolution from the 36th Ordinary Session, Dakar, Senegal 7 December 2004, renewed November 2007.
[282] In the Context of Africa see Murray, *Human Rights in Africa*, above n.1, at p. 51.
[283] AHG/Decl.4 (XXXVI), CSSDCA Solemn Declaration, para 6.
[284] Decision of 75th Ordinary Session of the Council of Ministers, Addis Ababa, March 2002.

commitments, obligations and actions necessary for realising these. Despite being an African document, the Conference is inspired by the OSCE and as a consequence the two organisations have worked closely together.[285]

Furthermore, the Commission has also adopted resolutions on a number of human rights issues on Africa. With the growth of African human rights law, a number of additional regional human rights treaties have been adopted. As we have already examined, the OAU, in 1990, adopted the Charter on the Rights and Welfare of the Child. The Charter which is the primary regional instrument dealing with children's rights came into force in 1999. Similarly in 2003, the Protocol to the African Charter on Human and People's Rights on the Rights of Women in Africa was adopted, which came into force in November 2005. The OAU also established the Women's Committee on Peace and Development with a view to further enhancing the role of women in decision-making processes relating to peace and development.[286] Amongst the 16 members of the Committee, six women come from senior government positions, five represent NGOs whereas five are elected in a personal capacity. Amongst the wide ranging role of the Committee the central theme is that of 'bringing women and a gender perspective into the mainstream of decision-making in preventing, managing and resolving conflicts'.[287] While the Committee has not been able to play a prominent role in the prevention and resolution of conflicts, the Committee will arguably be provided with greater prominence under the auspices of the AU. The AU has also promoted the cause of human rights through an active participation in peacekeeping forces. In 2004, the African Union Mission in Sudan was established which has over time consisted of over 7000 peacekeepers. In 2007, the AU Mission in Somalia (AMISOM) had been established with several thousand peacekeepers.

(b) Darfur, Sudan (AMIS)

Since an uprising against the government of Sudan in February 2003 by rebel movements in Darfur, the people, at the hands of both the government and the Janjaweed, have been subjected to 'serious violation of international human rights and humanitarian law. These included indiscriminate attacks, killing of civilians, torture, enforced disappearances, destruction of villages, rape and other forms of sexual violence, pillaging and forced displacement'.[288] In response to this, the Addis Ababa Agreement of 28 May 2004 enabled the African Union to become involved in the crisis. Initially AMIS (African Union Mission to Sudan) consisted of only a 300-strong protection force and 60 military observers.[289] It quickly 'became clear that the size and mandate of AMIS were insufficient to make a significant impact on the situation in Darfur',[290] and later on the same year this was

---

[285] Council of Ministers (Seventy-sixth Ordinary Session/Eleventh Ordinary Session of the AEC), 28 June–6 July 2002, Durban, South African. Report of the Secretary-General on the Implementation of the CSDCA.

[286] Report of the Secretary-General on the Implementation of the African Platform of Action: Women, Peace and Development (announced at the fortieth anniversary celebrations of the Economic Commission for Africa, April 1998).

[287] See Rule 3(2)(a), Terms of Reference and Rules of Procedure, OAU/ECA/AF/WM/PD6(1).

[288] Zwanenburg, 'Regional Organisation and the Maintenance of International Peace and Security: Three Recent Regional African Peace Operations' 11 JCSL (2006) 483, at p. 494, Report of the International Commission of Inquiry on Darfur to the United Nations Secretary-General, 25 January 2005.

[289] African Union Assembly of Heads of State and Government, 3rd Ordinary Session, Decision on Darfur, 8 July 2004 AU/Dec.54(III).

[290] Zwanenburg, above n.288, at p. 495.

increased to 3320 personnel by the African Union Peace and Security Council, which included a Civilian Police Component of 815.[291] The Mission, which then became known as AMIS II, was notably expanded with the blessing of the Sudanese government and Parliament.[292] The size of the Mission was again increased in April 2005 to 6171 personnel including 1560 Civilian Police, in recognition of the continuing violence and the inadequacy of the resources.[293] The AU mission continually faced issues regarding lack of funds, personnel and expertise. The size of Darfur also made monitoring the area particularly difficult.

On 31 July 2007 the UN Security Council approved the merger of AMIS II and the UN Mission to Sudan.[294] The merger had initially been planned for September 2006, however, it was delayed due to opposition from the Sudanese government. UNAMID had an initial mandate of one year and became operative on 31 December 2007. The merger has had a significant impact on the capabilities of the Missions and has led to a significant increase in personnel, with the mandate authorising up to 19,555 military personnel, 6432 police and 5105 civilians.[295] However, as of January 2009 the actual strength of the force was only 9995 uniformed personnel. In addition to the mandate of the Mission being extended for another year in July 2008,[296] the budget of the Mission for the coming year was also decided as being $1,569,255,200.[297]

(c) Somalia

Somalia has been consistently described as a failed State. Made up of a former British protectorate and an Italian colony, since it was created in 1960, Somalian history has been particularly turbulant.[298] More recently, after President Siad Barre was overthrown by opposing clans in 1991, after 21 years of power, Somalia plunged into civil war. In 2004, after years of peace talks, warlords and politicans finally signed a deal to establish a Parliament, which went on to appoint a President.[299] However, the stability of this interim arrangement have been called into question frequently, most significiantly when Islamists seized control of Southern Somalia including Mogadishu in 2006. Although, by the end of 2006 the administration had managed to regain control, this sparked off a resurgence in violence.[300] In response to this, the African Union Mission to Somalia (AMISOM) was established by the African Union Peace and Security Council on 19 January 2007,[301] with the approval of the United Nations.[302]

---

[291] www.amis-sudan.org/index.html <last visited 11 May 2009>; also see www.crisisgroup.org/home/index.cfm?id=3060 <last visited 10 May 2009>.

[292] Zwanenburg, above n.288, at p. 495.

[293] Ibid. Communique PSC/PR/Comm. (XXVIII), AUPSC 28th Meeting 28 April 2005.

[294] UN Security Council Resolution 1769, 31 July 2007.

[295] www.un.org/Depts/dpko/missions/unamid/facts.html <last visited on 11 September 2008>.

[296] UN Security Council Resolution 1828, 31 July 2008.

[297] UN Doc. A/C.5/62/30.

[298] http://news.bbc.co.uk/1/hi/world/Africa/country_profiles/1072592.stm <last visited 11 May 2009>. www.crisisgroup.org/home/index.cfm?id=1232&l=1 <last visited 10 May 2009>.

[299] http://news.bbc.co.uk/1/hi/world/Africa/country_profiles/1072592.stm <last visited 11 May 2009>.

[300] http://news.bbc.co.uk/1/hi/world/Africa/country_profiles/1072592.stm <last visited 11 May 2008>.

[301] African Union Peace and Security Council, 69th Meeting, 19 January 2007, Addis Ababa, Ethiopia. PSC/PR/Comm(LXIX).

[302] UN Security Council Resolution 1744 (2007), 20 February 2007.

The initial mandate of AMISOM was just six months, but this has been extended every six months by the UN Security Council.[303] There are currently around 1600 troops from Uganda and Burundi taking part in the Mission, despite the fact that it was initially anticipated that the Mission would have 8000 troops.[304] Nigeria, Ghana and Malawi have as of yet failed to supply troops for the Mission. On 20 August 2008 the Somalian Transitional Federal Government and a faction of an Eritea-based opposition alliance signed the 'Djibouti Peace Deal'.[305] However, AMISOM will remain in place in order to police the peace. This mission, as with AMIS, suffers significantly due to a lack of funding and personnel. In June 2008, the African Union Peace and Security Council called for a UN Peacekeeping team to re-enforce the African Union Mission and to 'support the long-term stabilization and post-conflict restoration in the country'.[306] The United Nations Security Council 1831 extended the existing mandate of AMISOM in August 2008 for a further six months. In its Resolution 1863, adopted on 16 January 2009, the Security Council expressed an intention to have in place a peacekeeping force in Somalia. Although extending AMISOM's mandate for a further six months, Resolution 1863 called upon the United Nations Secretary-General to develop a mandate for the proposed peacekeeping force by 15 April 2009 with a view to replacing AMISOM.

(d) Elsewhere

There have been a significant number of conflicts in recent years in Africa, which threaten peace and security in large areas of the continent. Current conflicts include the Ivorian Civil War, the Casamance Conflict in Senegal, the Niger Delta Conflict in Southern Nigeria, the Ituri Conflict (a sub-conflict of the Second Congo War) and the War in Chad (which is also linked to the conflict in Darfur and the Central African Republic Bush War). In a number of these, the AU has been involved in trying to broker peace. There is still political fall-out from the Second Congo War, the North-South Conflict in Sudan, the Ugandan conflict with the Lord's Resistance Army and the Central African Republic Bush War. The AU was also successfully involved in the Anjouan conflict in Comoros, when the Government of Comoros backed by AU troops, regained control of the island after fraudulent local elections.

8   CONCLUSIONS

The continent of Africa represents a serious test for those wanting to ensure an effective system of protecting individual and collective group rights.[307] The modern history of Africa has been an unfortunate one, and the transition from repressive colonial regimes to independent statehood has not been satisfactory. In many instances, soon after independence, dictatorial and authoritarian regimes took charge of the newly independent States and

---

[303] The mandate of ANISOM was extended on 17th July 2008 for a further six months. UN Security Council Resolution 1831 (2008).

[304] www.irinnews.org/report.aspz?ReportId=79903 <last visited 11 May 2009>, 'Somalia: Peacekeeping mission extends as parties sign Djibouti Peace Accord'.

[305] Ibid.

[306] Ibid.

[307] See generally Murray, 'The African Charter on Human and Peoples' Rights 1987–2000' 1 *African Human Rights Law Journal* (2001) 1.

The African system for the protection of human rights

10

showed little regard for human dignity and human rights. At the beginning of the new millennium, Africa continues to witness substantial violations of human rights; the recurrent genocidal campaigns in Burundi, Rwanda and Sudan confirm the existence of a major human tragedy. This chapter has presented an overview of the African human rights law, which has been aptly described as:

> the newest, the least developed or effective . . . the most distinctive and most controversial of the three [i.e. the European, the Inter-American and the African] established human rights regimes.[308]

The African human rights system is primarily based around the AFCHPR, which as our discussion has revealed contains a number of weaknesses. These weaknesses and limitations are derived not only from the substantive provisions of the Charter but also from the mechanisms of implementation. The African Commission, the principal executive organ, has performed a commendable task, although its work remains limited in many respects. The work of the Commission needs to be recognised and placed centrally with an established role in the AU's human rights policies and practices.[309] Although it was expected that the African Commission would 'enhance interaction and coordination with the different organs of the African Union in order to strengthen the African Mechanism for the Promotion and Protection of Human and Peoples Rights' such an expectation is still to be realised.[310]

The need for having a body to deliver authoritative and binding judgments led to demands for the establishment of a Court of Human Rights. The establishment of the Court was a very positive feature, although there continue to be many concerns. Firstly there is a major question-mark over the relationship between the African Commission and the new African Court. The (Addis) Protocol does not elaborate or clarify the situation and limits itself to noting that the Court will complement the protective role of the Commission.[311]

However, notwithstanding the passage of a considerable period, members of the African Commission and Judges of the Court 'have shied away from jointly discussing [the issues of complimentarity]'.[312] It probably would be the case that the Commission would have the initial more conciliatory jurisdiction with the Court deciding the actual disputes. Following the precedent of the ECHR, the merger of Commission and Court may be a long-term possibility. At the same time, a careful approach needs to be taken so as not to provoke conflicts similar to those generated between the Inter-American Commission on Human Rights and the Inter-American Court of Human Rights.[313] Secondly, as noted already, one of the serious difficulties has been the preparation of the single instrument leading to the merger of the African Court of Human Rights with that of the African Court of Justice. Despite being on the agenda since 2005, it took until the 13th Ordinary Session of the Executive

---

[308] Steiner, Alston and Goodman, above n.1, at p. 504.

[309] In the Context of Africa see Murray, *Human Rights in Africa*, above n.1, at p. 71.

[310] Assembly/AU/Dec.6 (II), Draft Decision on Sixteenth Annual Activity Report of the African Commission on Human and People's Rights – Doc.Assembly/AU/7(II).

[311] Van der Mei, 'The New African Court on Human and People's Rights: Towards an Effective Human Rights Protection Mechanism for Africa' 18 *Leiden Journal of International Law* (2005) 113 at p. 123.

[312] Wachira, above n.1, at p. 15.

[313] Harris, 'Regional Protection of Human Rights: The Inter-American Achievement' in Harris and Livingstone (eds), *The Inter-American System of Human Rights* (Clarendon Press, 1998) pp. 1–29 at p. 3.

Council in June 2008 for it finally to recommend that the Assembly adopt the Draft Single Instrument on the Merger of the African Court of Human and Peoples' Rights and the Court of Justice of the African Union.[314] As discussed above the Protocol on the Statute of the African Court of Justice and Human Rights went on to be adopted by the AU Assembly during its 11th Ordinary Session in Sharm El Sheikh, Egypt in July 2008.[315] In its decision the Assembly called

> on Member States to sign and ratify the Protocol on the Statute of the African Court of Justice and Human Rights as expeditiously as possible so as to enable the Protocol enter into force and ensure the speedy operationalization of the merged Court.

The African Court of Justice has not become operational, despite the fact that the requisite number of ratifications to the Protocol have been made.[316] However, there are significantly more parties to the Protocol on the African Court of Human and Peoples' Rights.[317] This could indicate a lack of political will in respect of the African Court of Justice and, therefore, also for the merged African Court. The protocol to the African Court of Justice and Human Rights provides:

> [t]he Protocol to the African Charter on Human and Peoples' Rights on the Establishment of an African Court on Human and Peoples' Rights shall remain in force for a transitional period not exceeding one (1) year or any other period determined by the Assembly, after entry into force of the present Protocol, to enable the African Court on Human and Peoples' Rights to take the necessary measures for the transfer of its prerogatives, assets, rights and obligations to the African Court of Justice and Human Rights.[318]

There is, however, no provision that deals with the situation that a party to the Protocol establishing the African Court on Human and Peoples' Rights does not ratify the new Protocol: thus indicating that States parties to the former Protocol will be left without a regional court to refer to on human rights issues and limiting the jurisdiction of the Court. Notwithstanding the adoption of the 2008 Protocol confirming the merger of the African Court of Human Rights and the African Court of Justice (ACJ), the viability, practicability as well as the effectiveness of this experiment still needs to be tested.[319]

---

[314] Decision on the Single Legal Instrument on the merger of the African Court on Human and Peoples' Rights and the Court of Justice of the African Union DOC.EX.CL/431(XIII). Decision on the Merger of the African Court on Human and Peoples' Rights and the Court of Justice of the African Union – (Doc. Assembly/AU/6 (V)), Assembly/AU/Dec.83 (V) For further discussion see Murray, *Human Rights in Africa*, above n.1, at pp. 68–69.

[315] Assembly/AU/Dec.196 (XI), Decision on the Single Legal Instrument on the Merger of the African Court on Human and Peoples' Rights and the African Court of Justice Doc.Assembly/AU/13 (XI).

[316] www.africa-union.org/root/au/Documents/Treaties/List/Protocol%20on%20the%20Court%20of%20Justice.pdf <last visited on 12 September 2008>.

[317] The Protocol to the African Charter on Human and Peoples' Rights on the Establishment of an African Court on Human and Peoples' Rights has at the times of writing 24 ratifications as opposed to 15 for the Protocol to the Court of Justice of the African Union. www.africa-union.org/root/au/Documents/Treaties/List/Protocol%20on%20the%20African%20Court%20on%20Human%20and%20Peoples%20Rights.pdf <last visited 12 May 2009>.

[318] Article 7 Protocol on the Statute of the African Court of Justice and Human Rights.

[319] Viljoen and Baimu, 'Courts for Africa: Considering the Coexistence of the African Court on Human and Peoples' Rights and the African Court of Justice' 22 *NQHR* (2004) 241.

10

The African system for the protection of human rights

11 Additional human rights mechanisms[1]

1 INTRODUCTION

In the earlier chapters of this study we examined the European, American and African mechanisms for the protection of human rights at a regional level. In addition to Europe, the Americas and Africa, additional regional human rights schemes do operate, although as we shall examine, considerable question marks remain regarding their effectiveness. This chapter investigates four additional regimes of human rights protection. Firstly, an examination is conducted of the Islamic schemes of human rights protection. As is common knowledge, Islam and Muslims are the subjects of considerable international attention.[2] Within the Islamic jurisprudence there is considerable debate over the position of human rights. Moreover, the position of religious minorities, women and children form a highly contentious part of this debate. Our study will present an overview of the position and arguments regarding the *Sharia vis-à-vis* human rights. The study considers the approaches adopted by the Organisation of Islamic Conference (OIC). Secondly, the human rights regime under the Arab League will be considered. While the Arab Charter does make references to Islam and *Sharia*, the system cannot be regarded primarily as religious and, therefore, this requires a separate consideration from the Islamic scheme of human rights protection. Thirdly, no study on regional human rights would be complete without some reference to the position adopted by the most populous of the regional organisations – the South Asian Association for Regional Cooperation (SAARC). The chapter briefly considers the human rights initiatives undertaken by SAARC. Fourthly, the chapter considers the position and engagement of human rights issues by the Association of South-East Asian Nations (ASEAN).

---

[1] See generally Ali, 'The Conceptual Foundations of Human Rights: A Comparative Perspective' 3 *European Public Law* (1997) 261; Ali, *Gender and Human Rights in Islam and international law: Equal before Allah, Unequal before Man* (Kluwer Law International, 2000); Ali and Rehman 'Freedom of Religion versus equality in International Human Rights Law: Conflicting Norms or Hierarchical Human Rights (A case study of Pakistan)' 21 *Nordic Journal of Human Rights* (2003) 404; Baderin (ed.), *Islam and International Law* (Ashgate, 2007); Rehman, *Islamic State Practices, International Law and the Threat from Terrorism: A Critique of the 'Clash of Civilizations' in the New World Order* (Hart Publishing, 2005); Rehman and Breau (eds), *Religion, Human Rights and International Law: A Critical Examination of Islamic State Practices* (Martinus Nijhoff Publishers, 2007); Karns and Mingst, *International Organizations: The Politics and Processes of Global Governance* (Lynne Reinner Publishers Inc, 2005); Sands and Klein, *Bowett's Law of International Institutions* (Sweet & Maxwell, 2001); Shaw, *International Law* (Cambridge: University Press, 2008) pp. 1204–1331.

[2] See Rehman, 'Islamophobia after 9/11: International Terrorism, *Sharia* and Muslim Minorities in Europe – The Case of the United Kingdom' 3 *European Yearbook of Minority Issues* (2003/4) 217; Rehman, 'Accommodating Religious Identities in an Islamic State: International Law, Freedom of Religion and the Rights of Religious Minorities' 7 *IJMGR* (2000) 139.

2 ISLAM AND HUMAN RIGHTS LAW

Amidst the wider debate about the 'war-on-terror', and the 'clash of civilisations', *Sharia's*[3] compatibility with modern norms of human rights law forms a critical and charged debate.[4] Muslims constitute approximately 25 per cent of the total world population.[5] Projected estimates are that by the first quarter of the 21st century, Muslims are likely to reach 30 per cent of the global population.[6] The continued relevance of Islam and Islamic law is highlighted by the consistent invocation of the *Sharia* principles within international, regional and domestic courts.[7] *Sharia* is not only relevant for those States which actively promote and claim to implement Islamic law within their domestic legal system, but Islamic legal principles have become increasingly of great relevance in States such as the United Kingdom, France and the United States which have significant Muslim minorities.[8] Requirements of the *Sharia* have been invoked in such contentious matters as the veil, headscarves and the wearing of *jilbab* at work and in educational institutions,[9] the formalities and capacity to enter a marriage,[10] the validity of arranged or forced marriages,[11] the recognition of polygamous marriages,[12] the consequence of the *talaq* (unilateral divorce by the husband)[13] and Muslim religious obligations during employment.[14] These sections

[3] Meaning Islamic law.

[4] See generally Rehman, '*Islamic State Practices*' above n.1.

[5] www.islamicweb.com/begin/results.htm <last visited 12 May 2009>.

[6] Huntington, *The Clash of Civilizations and the Remaking of World Order* (Simon & Schuster, 1996) at p. 117; McGoldrick, Multiculturalism and Its Discontents' in Ghanea and Xanthaki (eds), *Minorities, Peoples and Self-Determination* (Martinus Nijhoff Publishers, 2005) pp. 211–235, at p. 228.

[7] LIAMCO award 20 ILM (1981) 37 at 201; *Sahin* v. *Turkey* (2007) 44 E.H.R.R. 5. See also *Refah Partisi (the Welfare Party) and others* v. *Turkey* (2003) 37 E.H.R.R. 1; *R. (on the application of Begum)* v. *Denbigh High School Governors* [2006] H.R.L.R. 21.

[8] Poulter, *English Law and Ethnic Minority Customs* (Butterworths, 1986); Poulter, *Ethnicity, Law and Human Rights: The English Experience* (Clarendon Press, 1998).

[9] See *R. (on the application of Begum)* v. *Denbigh High School Governors* [2006] H.R.L.R. 21 (wearing of *jilbal*, a covering more extensive than *hijab*). On veil, see *Azmi* v. *Kirklees Metropolitan Borough Council* [2007] E.L.R 125, [2007] I.C.R. 1154. See *Bradford Corporation* v. *Patel* (1974) unreported (Conviction of a Muslim father under the provisions of the 1944 Education Act for failing to send his daughter to co-educational school on religious grounds).

[10] On under-age marriages see *Alhaji Mohamed* v. *Knott* [1969] 1 QB 1, [1968] 2 WLR 1446, [1968] 2 All ER 563. See the Immigration Rules, para 277 (Home Office, UK Border Agency www.ukba.homeoffice.gov.uk/policyandlaw/immigrationlaw/immigrationrules/part8/spouses_civil_partners/ <last visited 1 May 2009>. Poulter, 'The Claim to a Separate Islamic System of Personal Law for British Muslims' in Mallat and Connors (eds), *Islamic Family Law* (Graham & Trotman, 1990) pp. 147–166.

[11] See *Hirani* v. *Hirani* (1983) 4 FLR 232 (although the particular case concerned a Hindu girl). Also note the 'primary purpose' rule, *Halsbury's Law of England* (Butterworths, 1992) paras 95–97. Are arranged marriages *per se* indicative that the primary purpose of marriage is immigration to the UK? *R.* v. *Immigration Appeal Tribunal, ex p. Iqbal (Iram)* [1993] Imm. A.R. 270.

[12] See *Quorasishi* v. *Quorasishi* [1983] FLR 706; See the Immigration Rules, paras 278–280 (Home Office, UK Border Agency www.ukba.homeoffice.gov.uk/policyandlaw/immigrationlaw/immigrationrules/part8/spouses_civil_partners/ <last visited 1 May 2009>. *Bibi* v. *Chief Adjudication Officer* [1998] 1 FLR 375; [1998] 1 FCR 301; [1997] Fam. Law 793 (case concerning entitlement to widow's pension in polygamous marriages).

[13] *Quazi* v. *Quazi* [1980] AC 744; *Chaudhary* v. *Chaudhary* [1985] 2 WLR 350; Family Law Act 1986 (Part II); on Immigration see *R.* v. *Secretary of State for Home Department, ex p. Fatima (Ghulam)* [1986] 2 WLR 693 (refusal of entry into UK for fiancé for non-recognition of first divorce through transnational Talaq). See UK Visas Enquires www.ukvisas.gov.uk/servlet/Front?pagename=OpenMarket/Xcelerate/ShowPage&c=Page&cid=1038489156801 <last visited 23 November 2006>.

[14] See *Ahmad* v. *Inner London Education Authority* [1978] QB 36, [1977] 3 WLR 396, [1978] 1 All ER 574, CA, [1976] I.C.R. 461, EAT (Court of Appeal); *Ahmad* v. *UK* (1982) 4 E.H.R.R. 126.

assess the question of compatibility of the *Sharia* with modern international human rights law, which is followed by an examination of relevant Islamic organisations.

(i) The sources and content of the *Sharia*[15]

Islamic law is often referred to as the *Sharia*. The concept of *Sharia*, however, is not confined to legal norms, but conveys a more holistic picture; the Arabic translation of *Sharia* is 'the road to the watering place'.[16] The *Sharia*, therefore, does not simply represent religious laws, but covers a wide range of secular laws and ordinances.[17] These include areas as diverse as commercial law, criminal law, constitutional and administrative law, and provide a substantial code of humanitarian and human rights laws.[18] A variety of primary and secondary sources constitute the *Sharia*.[19] At the apex, is the primary source of the *Qur'an*,[20] which is accompanied and interpreted by the *Sunna*[21] of Prophet Muhammad.[22] In addition to the primary sources, *Ijma*,[23] *Qiyas*[24] and *Ijtihad*[25] represent the secondary sources. Amongst these secondary sources, jurists have also added the practices of Islamic rulers and caliphs, their official instruction to commanders and statesmen; constitutional laws and internal legislation of Islamic States both historic as well as modern.[26] The *Qur'an*,

---

[15] See Denny, *An Introduction to Islam* (Macmillan Pub Co, 1993) at p. 67; Mulla, *Principles of Mahamedan Law* (P.L.D. Publishers, 1990) p. xiv; Gibb, *Mohammedanism: An Historical Survey* (Oxford University Press, 1949) p. 1; Bassiouni, 'Sources of Islamic Law and the Protection of Human Rights in the Islamic Criminal Justice System' in Bassiouni (ed), *The Islamic Criminal Justice System* (Oceana Publications, 1982) pp. 3–54.

[16] Landau, *Islam and the Arabs* (George Allen and Unwin Ltd, 1958) at p. 141; Oba, 'Islamic Law as Customary Law: The Changing Perspective in Nigeria' 51 *ICLQ* (2002) 817 at p. 819; Doi, *Shariah: The Islamic Law* (Taha Publishers, 1998) at p. 2; Adamec, *Historical Dictionary of Islam* (The Scarecrow Press, 2001) at p. 241.

[17] Moinuddin, *The Charter of the Islamic Conference and Legal Framework of Economic Cooperation Among its Member States: A Study of the Charter, the General Agreement for Economic, Technical and Commercial Co-operation and the Agreement for Promotion, Protection and Guarantee of Investments Among Member States of the OIC* (Clarendon Press, 1987) at p. 6; Rehman, 'Islamic Perspectives on International Economic Law' in Qureshi (ed.), *Perspectives in International Economic Law* (Kluwer Law International, 2002) pp. 235–258, at p. 236.

[18] Mahmassani, 'The Principles of International Law in the Light of Islamic Doctrine' (1966) 117(I) *Recueil des Cours de l'Académie de Droit International* 205 at p. 229; Rahim, *The Principles of Muhammadan Jurisprudence According to the Hanafi, Maliki, Shafi'i and Hanbali Schools* (Luzac, 1911); Badr, 'Islamic Law: Its Relations to Other Legal Systems' 26 *American Journal of Comparative Law* (1978) 188.

[19] Coulson, *A History of Islamic Law* (Edinburgh University Press, 1964) pp. 9–20.

[20] Muslim Holy Book.

[21] For the elaboration and meaning of *Sunna*, see below.

[22] With all references to Prophet Muhammad the terminology (Peace be Upon Him) shall be assumed.

[23] Meaning consensus of the *Ummah* (the community of Believers). Ijma provided essential tools for the muslim community to reach agreements over contentious issues. According to an established *Sunna* the Prophet is reported to have said 'My People will never agree together on an error' cited in Weeramantry, *Islamic Jurisprudence: An International Perspective* (Palgrave MacMillan, 1988) at p. 39.

[24] Broadly meaning 'analogy' or 'deduction'. In the absence of concrete answers from the primary sources of the *Sharia*, Muslim jurists look for an analogous situation in which to make a decision. According to a well-recited *Hadith*, the role *Qiyas* was confirmed at the time when Prophet Muhammad (whiling sending Mu 'adh b. Jalal to Yemen to take the position of a *qadi*) asked him the following question: 'How will you decide when a question arises?' He replied, 'According to the Book of Allah' – 'And if you do not find the answer in the Book of Allah?' – 'Then according to the *Sunna* of the Messenger of Allah' – 'And if you do not find the answer either in the *Sunna* or in the Book?' – 'Then I shall come to a decision according to my own opinion without hesitation' Then the Messenger of *Allah* slapped Mu 'adh on the chest with his hand saying: 'Praise be to *Allah* who has led the Messenger of Allah to an answer that pleases him'. 'Kiyas' in Gibb and Kramers (eds), *Shorter Encyclopaedia of Islam* (Cornell University Press, 1953) at p. 267.

[25] Ijtihad is term that refers to the use of independent legal reasoning in search of an opinion. Ijtihad conveys a sense of exertion, a sense of struggle and has the same meaning as *Jihad*. For further elaboration see Rehman, *Islamic State Practices*, above n.1, at p. 14.

[26] Bassiouni regards the consistent practice of Muslim Heads of State (the *Khalifas*) as secondary sources of Islam. See Bassiouni, 'Protection of Diplomats under Islamic Law' (1980) 74 *AJIL* 609 at 609. Hamidullah, *Muslim*

according to the Muslim belief, represents the accumulation of the verses revealed by God to the Prophet Muhammad.[27] According to the Muslim faith, every word of the *Qur'an* is divine and cannot be challenged. Neither the Prophet Muhammad nor any other human being had any influence over the contents of the divine book.[28] The compilation of the Holy Book in a single volume was conducted in the years which followed the Prophet's death.[29] The *Qur'an* is aimed at establishing basic standards for the Muslim societies and guiding these communities in terms of their rights and obligations. At the time of its revelation, it provided a set of progressive principles. It advances such values as compassion, good faith, justice and religious ethics. The *Qur'an*, however, is a religious text and *per se* is not a legal document.

The *Sunna*, the second principal source of Islam, represents model behaviour and is referred to as the tradition and practices of Muhammad, the Prophet of Islam. The *Sunna* of the Prophet has been expanded through the practices of Prophet Muhammad's followers and other Islamic leaders. While the *Qur'an* was recorded within a relatively short time, the recording of the *Sunna* took a much longer period.[30] There is a significant debate over the authenticity and accuracy of some of the *Sunna* and there have been comments as to the possibility of fabrication in the recording of the *Sunna*. Commenting on this subject, Coulson makes the point that 'the extent of [Muhammad's] extra Qur'ānic law-making is the subject of the greatest single controversy in early Islamic legal theory'.[31]

(ii) Understanding the scope of the *Sharia*

For an appropriate understanding of the scope and application of the *Sharia* the following factors need to be highlighted. Firstly, it has to be emphasised that the totality of the *Sharia* and Islamic human rights law, its interpretation and application do not represent the ultimate expression of the will of the Almighty.[32] Islamic scholars have often found themselves restricted in the debate surrounding the *Sharia* because of existing perceptions that the totality of the Islamic legal system is the word of God: any analysis or attempts to review the *Sharia* would be tantamount to heresy. Such assertions are, however, misleading since there exists a clear distinction between the varied Islamic legal systems (which represent evolutionary processes and in common with other legal system need constant review and change) and the fundamental principles of Islam which remain unalterable. Thus, notwithstanding the fact that the *Sharia* regards the *Qur'an* and *Sunna* as its principal sources, distinctions and varying interpretations are inevitable features between divine ordinances

---

Conduct of State: Being a Treaties on Siyar, that is Islamic Notion of Public International Law, Consisting of the Laws of Peace, War and Neutrality, Together with precedents from Orthodox Practices and Precedent by a Historical and General Introduction (Sh Muhammad Ashraf, 1977) at p. 28; Khadduri, *War and Peace in the Law of Islam* (The John Hopkin Press, 1955) at p. 44; Hussain, *Issues in Pakistan's Foreign Policy* (Progressive Publishers, 1988) at p. 100.

[27] Weeramantry, above n.23, at p. 26; Denny, above n.15, at 63; Landau, above n.16, at p. 25; Lombardi, 'Islamic Law as a Source of Constitutional Law in Egypt: The Constitutionalization of the *Sharia* in a Modern Arab State' (1998) 37 *Col.J.T.L.* 81 at p. 92.

[28] Denny, above n.15, at p. 63.

[29] Ibid.

[30] Mahmassani, above n.18, at p. 229.

[31] Coulson, n.19 above, at p. 22.

[32] An-Na'im, *Toward an Islamic Reformation: Civil Liberties, Human Rights and International Law* (Syracuse University Press, 1990); Baderin, *International Human Rights and Islamic Law* (Oxford University Press, 2003) at p. 33.

vis-à-vis manmade principles that regulate societies. *Sharia*, in this sense, is in fact no more than the understanding of early Muslims of the sources of Islam.[33] The Muslim jurists who developed the *Sharia* during the second and third centuries did so in accordance with their personal understanding and comprehension of the word of God. It is arguable that *Sharia* represents the human endeavour to understand and implement the core values and principles specifically referred to in the principal sources of Islam.[34]

Secondly, (contrary to common assumptions) *Sharia* principles are neither rigid nor stagnant and can in fact be applied in evolving situations.[35] There is a substantial possibility of evolution in order to accommodate modern human rights law. It is, therefore, as one scholar has argued, 'no slight irony and tragedy that the *Sharia*, which has the idea of mobility built into its very meaning, should have become a symbol of rigidity for so many in the Muslim world'.[36]

Thirdly, in formulating principles of the *Sharia*, there have been substantial complexities faced by Islamic jurists. A particularly complex issue arose in attempts to find compatibility between the legally authoritative through competing injunctions of the *Qur'anic* verses and the *Sunna*.[37] The *Qur'an* (although the primary source of the *Sharia*) is not a legal text and in fact there is little in the *Qur'an* with a strictly legal content. From over 6000 verses of the *Qur'an*, strict legal content is arguably attached to only around 120 verses.[38] Save for a few specific offences there is no indication of criminal sanctions.[39] Some legal rules can be identified regarding the rights of individuals (e.g. women and religious minorities), even though they have been the subject of debate and argumentation. Particular complications have arisen in articulating legal principles from the above mentioned Islamic legal sources, some of these overlap or are in competition with each other. A useful mechanism for dealing with competing norms and values has been through the adoption of *Naskh*.[40] The principle of *Naskh* allows for a process of abrogation or repeal of laws with respect to the legal efficacy of the primary sources of the *Sharia*. The revelation of the *Qur'an* coincides with the metamorphosis undergone by the Arab community over a period of 23 years. During this phase, two broad processes are of particular significance

---

[33] An-Na'im, above n.32.

[34] Weiss, *The Spirit of Islamic Law* (University of Georgia Press Athens, 1998) at p. 116.

[35] The issue of human involvement and interpretation of the divine line has been a subject of debate amongst both oriental and Western scholars. Two leading scholars of comparative law make the point that '[o]ne of the consequences is that Islamic law is in principle immutable, for it is the law revealed by God. Western legal systems generally recognize that the content of law alters as it is adapted to changing needs by the legislator, the judges, and all other social forces which have a part in the creation of law, but Islam starts from the proposition that all existing law comes from ALLAH who at a certain moment in history revealed it to man through his prophet MUHAMMAD. Thus Islamic legal theory cannot accept the historical approach of studying law as a function of the changing conditions of life in a particular society. On the contrary, the law of ALLAH was given to man once and for all: society must adopt itself to the law rather than generate laws of its own as a response to the constantly changing stimulus of the problems of life', Zweigert and Kötz, *Introduction to Comparative Law* (Clarendon Press, 1998) at p. 304.

[36] Hassan, 'The Role and Responsibilities of Women in the Legal and Ritual Tradition of Islam', paper presented at a biannual meeting of a Trialogue of Jewish-Christian-Muslim scholars on 14 October 1980 at the Joseph and Rose Kennedy Institute of Ethics, Washington, DC, USA at p. 4.

[37] See An-Na'im, above n.32, at p. 16.

[38] See Badr, 'Islamic Law: Its Relations to Other Legal Systems' 26 *American Journal of Comparative Law* (1978) 188, at p. 188. Ali, 'The Conceptual Foundations of Human Rights' above n.1, p. 266. Glenn, *Legal Traditions of the World* (Oxford University Press, 2000) at p. 159.

[39] An-Na'im, above n.32, at p. 20.

[40] *Naskh* is a concept derived from the Arabic language usually referred to as 'abrogation'; it shares the same roots with as the term that appear in the phrase *al-nāsikh wal-mansūkh* 'the abrogating and abrogated [verses]'.

in terms of the substance of the message contained in the *Qur'an*: the Meccan stage and the Medina stage.[41] The Meccan *Surras* are more charitable while the verses revealed in Medina show strains of actual governance, and are reflective of concrete legal and administrative problems that were confronted during that phase. Due to the changes in the context of Islam through the violent disruption to the otherwise peaceful message of Islam, there are noticeable differences of approaches in the Mecca and Medina stages. While the validity of the verses of the *Qur'an* remains intact and not in doubt, the concept of *Naskh* has been deployed to challenge the legal efficacy of those verses which are deemed as being out of context, and not suited to the contemporary requirements.

The aforementioned consideration establishes that without challenging the authenticity of the *Qur'an* and *Sunna*, considerable jurisprudential disagreements have arisen as to the legal content within a number of their provisions.[42] The process of distinguishing a body of positive rules proved a taxing exercise which led to an emphasis upon *ijtihad*.[43] To formulate a cohesive set of Islamic laws differing weight was afforded to the competing ordinances from the *Qur'an* and the *Sunna*, and jurists extensively relied on the techniques of analogy and deduction. Arguments about the application and the interpretation of the *Sharia* and *Siyar*,[44] nevertheless, materialised, and over a period of time led to the creation of various schools of thought.[45]

(iii) Islamic international human rights law

Three inter-governmental organisations have been at the forefront of advancing Islamic Human Rights Law. These are the Islamic Council, the League of Arab States and the OIC. However, as previously stated, the League of Arab States is primarily a non-religious organisation and therefore will be considered separately. These organisations have been active in promoting human rights values and have in fact advanced alternative models of human rights protection. These organisations were particularly active during the last quarter of the 20th century and attempted to respond to the entry into force of the International Covenants and drafting of other international human rights instruments. In 1981, the Islamic Council adopted the Universal Islamic Declaration of Human Rights in Paris. In 1990, the OIC adopted the Cairo Declaration on Human Rights in Islam. These instruments are no doubt influenced by international human rights instruments and by and large share common values of equality, non-discrimination. That said, there are noticeable differences over key controversial areas such as the rights of women and the rights of religious minorities. There is equivocacy and ambivalence on sensitive issues of gender and the norm of religious equality within an Islamic State. Such ambivalence is also reflected in contemporary State practices within the Islamic world.

---

[41] For further information on the content of the *Qur'an* and attempts at ascertainment of dates of the revelation of the various *surras* see Denny, above n.15, at 138–143.

[42] An-Na'im, 'Religious Minorities under Islamic Law and the Limits of Cultural Relativism' 9 *HRQ* (1987) 1 at p. 15.

[43] Weiss, 'Interpretation in Islamic Law: The Theory of Ijtihad' 26 *American Journal of Comparative Law* (1978) 199, at p. 200.

[44] Broadly defined as 'Islamic International Law'.

[45] Weiss elaborates upon the crucial distinctions in the interpretation of the *Sharia* between *Sunni* and *Shia* Schools of thought; see Weiss above n.43, at pp. 210–212. For a consideration of the *Shia* School of thought see Ramzani, 'The Shi'i System: Its Conflict and Inter-action with Other Systems' (1959) *Proceedings of the American Society of International Law* 53; Qureshi, 'The Politics of Shia Minority in Pakistan: Context and Development' in Vajpeyi and Malik (eds), *Religious and Ethnic Minority Politics in South Asia* (Riverdale Company Publishers, 1989) pp. 109–138.

(iv) Controversy over women's rights and rights of religious minorities

Sharia's compatibility with women's rights in modern international law is a contentious subject and is frequently debated. According to one interpretation of the *Sharia* men and women have been designated different roles within the society, with women having a more subservient position. The concept of *Quwama*[46] is frequently deployed to legitimise the subservience of women. Proponents of such an interpretation rely on the *Quranic* verse 4:34 according to which 'Men have *qawama* [guardianship and authority] over women because of the advantage they [men] have over them [women] and because they [men] spend their property in supporting them [women].' Historical interpretation of the afore-mentioned verse has allowed men to claim guardianship and superiority over women. For example, such an interpretation has led to women being excluded from holding public office, or exercising authority over men. The superiority of men over women is deployed to a point of physically disciplining women in case of serious misconduct on the part of the latter. It has, however, been convincingly argued that the *Quranic* verse, viewed in a holistic manner, in fact cannot be interpreted as sanctifying discrimination. *qawama* could only be utilised in social environments where men provided financial and material support to women. However, in contemporary modern societies, since men are not expected to spend their property on women, and that since men and women are equal in all respects, the concept of *qawama* has also become inapplicable.

There are additional general principles commonly derived from the *Sharia*. A number of primary sources of the *Sharia* are deployed to enforce the argument of *hijab*[47] for women or to prevent women from interaction with men. The subjection of women to discrimination in criminal justice processes is also justified on the basis of the *Sharia*. Women in this interpretation of the law are incompetent witnesses in serious criminal cases regardless of their knowledge of the facts or their competence as individuals. In civil law, two women's testimony equates to that of an adult Muslim man.

Furthermore, according to classical interpretations of the *Sharia*, while a male Muslim is allowed to marry 'woman (women) of the book' which includes Christians, Jews and Zoroastrians, a Muslim female is restricted to entering into marriage only with Muslims. A valid marriage can be contracted from the age of puberty, classical *Sharia* equating puberty with the age of majority. Under *Hanafi* Islamic legal tradition, a lawful marriage could only take place with the complete and absolute consent of both the spouses. In practice, however, there continue to be cases, where consent is vitiated (generally from the female) through indirect or direct pressures.[48] Complications have also arisen in modern Islamic State practices whereby classical *Sharia* arguments have been advanced in relation to the role and consent of the *wali* (guardian), e.g. in the marriage of adult women.[49]

Certain Islamic schools also granted authority to the parent or the guardian (*wali*) to enforce child marriages, with the so-called 'option of puberty' whereby marriage is

---

[46] Broadly defined as 'guardianship and authority'.

[47] Meaning 'curtain or covering'. The Arabic terminology connotes 'to cover, to veil, or to shelter'. Within Islamic parlance the concept of *hijab* is taken to be mean as modest dress for Muslim women, which within most legal system refers to as covering for women in public of all the body save for face, feet and hands.

[48] For a useful analysis see Mullally, 'As Nearly as May Be: Debating Women's Human Rights in Pakistan' 14 *Social and Legal Studies* (2005) 341.

[49] According to classical and rigid interpretations of the *Shafi* and *Malaki* Schools (in contrast to the *Hanafi* School) an adult virgin needs the consent of the *wali*; for an recent analysis and juridical interpretation see *Hafiz Abdul Wahid* v. *Asma Jahangir* KLR (1997) (Shariat Cases) 121.

rescindable upon attaining puberty or majority. Islamic jurists however point to the fact that many of these practises including the 'option of puberty' is based on juristic interpretations of Islamic family laws and is stated neither in the *Quran* nor is it derived from the *Sunna*.

A fundamental subject of controversy is the institution of polygamy.[50] While there are some differences in the approach within Islamic legal schools, polygamy is legitimised both by the *Quran* and the *Sunna*. This continuing legitimacy of polygamy is reflected in modern Islamic States practices, whereby an overwhelming majority of States authorise polygamous marriages, albeit with a variety of restrictions and sanctions. The rules relating to Islamic family laws, including polygamy, have led to numerous reservations by Islamic States to the Convention on the Elimination of All Forms of Discrimination against Women 1979.[51] Within its historical context there were possible rational arguments for retaining polygamy. Besides, it is also the case that the primary source of the *Sharia*, the *Qur'an*, has laid down substantial onerous pre-conditions before rendering polygamous unions acceptable. Islam, therefore, it has been contended, essentially requires monogamous unions.[52]

Furthermore, all Islamic schools permit *Talaq*,[53] with the right to divorce being regarded as 'unencumbered' within the Sunni School of *Hanafi* tradition.[54] In this interpretation, a Muslim man who has attained the age of puberty has the absolute right to divorce his wife without having to cite any reasons for such an action. The *Talaq* can be pronounced even in the absence of and without the involvement of the wife in the process.[55] Within general interpretations of *Sharia*, women are granted a right to divorce, although they have a significantly inferior and (depending on the school of thought) onerous task in respect of obtaining divorce, invariably reliant upon a judicial decree. A *khul* (also known as *khula*) divorce can be obtained by the wife although it requires the consent of the husband and the wife is required to forgo part of (or the entirety of) the dowry.[56] In practice, the limited possibilities of obtaining divorce, (e.g. *Talaqi Tafwiz*) which is a delegated right of *Talaq* and is provided by Islamic law, is frequently denied to them through various procedural formalities.[57] These historical interpretations unfortunately continue to be reflected in modern times. A majority of Islamic States continue to retain polygamy and the Convention on the Elimination of All Forms of Discrimination against Women (1979) and this attracts considerable reservations from Islamic States.

The position and role of religious minorities within the *Sharia* are matters of intense controversy. According to classical *Sharia*, there are crucial distinctions between the Muslims (believers of Allah and his Prophet Mohammad, as the final Prophet); *ahal al-kitab* (the Peoples of the Book) and the pagans (the non-believers, infidels).[58] In their modern incarnation, Muslim States have not been able to establish a consensual view on the

---

[50] Rehman, 'The *Sharia*, Islamic Family Laws and International Human Rights Law: Examining the Theory and Practice of Polygamy and *Talaq*' 21 *International Journal of Law, Family and Policy* (2007) 108 at p. 114.

[51] Rehman, 'Women's Rights: An International Law Perspective' in Mehdi and Shaheed (eds) *Women's Law in Legal Education and Practice: North-South Co-operation* (New Social Science Monograph, 1997) at pp. 106–128; see further below chapter 15.

[52] Rehman, above n.50, pp. 114–117.

[53] Meaning divorce.

[54] Esposito, *Women in Muslim Family Law* (Syracuse University Press, 1982) at p. 31.

[55] Ibid.

[56] *Cf.* in the exceptional Pakistani case of *Khurshid Bibi* v. *Mohd Amin* PLD 1967 SC 97, the Supreme Court held that as a matter of principle a husband's consent is not required in *Khul* cases.

[57] In the *Nikah Nama* (marriage certificate) this possibility for the woman retaining the option of divorce is frequently struck out.

[58] Mayer, *Islam and Human Rights: Tradition and Politics* (Westview Press Ltd, 1995) at p. 127.

meaning and content of freedom of religion within the Islamic jurisprudence. The substantial disparities and ambivalence in approach becomes evident through a survey of the practices and instruments adopted by Islamic States. Reservations (and declarations) are frequently put in place that make specific human rights norms subject to their compatibility with the *Sharia*. These reservations (and declarations) are not followed by an elaboration as to the exact position of the *Sharia* on that particular subject. Human rights obligations are also frequently drafted in an imprecise manner, which allows for a variety of interpretations.

In the English version of the Universal Islamic Declaration of Human Rights (1981) Article X on Rights of Minorities provides that:

(a) The Qur'anic principle 'There is no compulsion in Religion' shall govern the religious rights of non-Muslim minorities.

(b) In a Muslim country religious minorities shall have the choice to be governed in respect of their civil and personal matters by Islamic law or by their own laws.[59]

The aforementioned provisions are not explicit as to whether these principles are to be applied to all non-Muslims or are limited to the *ahalal-kitab*.[60] Neither do they articulate the substantive rights which non-Muslim minorities have within an Islamic State. There are also significant differences between the English and the Arabic versions, suggesting the possibility of the divergent views of the drafters of the Declaration. Modern juristic opinion that finds international human rights provisions such as Article 18 of the Universal Declaration on Human Rights[61] and Article 18[62] and 27[63] of the International Covenant on Civil and Political Rights compatible with the *Sharia* emphasises an egalitarian and broad interpretation of Islamic values.[64] The contemporary differences of interpretations of the *Sharia*, and its compatibility with contemporary norms of international human rights, can be established through a survey of the practices of Islamic States.

An interesting example is provided by the contrasting positions adopted at the time of the drafting of the Universal Declaration of Human Rights. A number of Islamic States were actively involved in the preparation and drafting of the Declaration. Muslim representatives, such as Fereydoun Hoveida of Iran, served on the drafting committee of the Declaration, alongside the French Professor Rene Cassin.[65] Similarly, Pakistan, a State carved-out of Colonial India specifically for protecting the identity and interests of Muslims, actively took part in the preparation of the Declaration with the view that '[i]t was imperative that the peoples of the World should recognise the existence of a code of civilised behaviour which would apply not only in international relations but also in domestic affairs'.[66] On the other hand, the *travaux préparatoires* of the Declaration reveals

---

[59] Article X (Rights of Minorities) Universal Islamic Declaration of Human Rights.
[60] Mayer, above n.58 above, pp. 131–133.
[61] For discussion on Article 18 see above chapter 4.
[62] For discussion on ICCPR see above chapter 5.
[63] See above chapter 5 and below chapter 13.
[64] See Mahmassani, *Arkan Huquq-al-Insan* (*Arkan Huquq-al-Insan* (Beirut: Dar-'ilmli'-Malayin) 1979, pp. 260–264; Haider (ed.), *Islamic Concept of Human Rights* (Book House, 1978).
[65] Mayer, above n.58, at p. 11.
[66] Pakistan's Representative Begum Ikram-ullah, GAOR 3rd Session, Part I, third Committee, 90th meeting, 1 October 1948, 37.

that Article 18 provisions, particularly the clause relating to the 'freedom to change religion or belief', generated considerable debate and disagreement amongst the Islamic States. The provision allowing the freedom to change religion or belief had been initiated by Lebanon, a State which during the '1940s and 1950s was an oasis of toleration, where large Christian, Muslim and Druze communities coexisted in a pluralistic society'.[67] There was, however, an interesting confrontation between two States – Saudi Arabia and Pakistan – both attempting to justify their position on the basis of Islamic Law.[68]

The Saudi Arabian representative Mr. Al-Barudy objected to the terminology as proposed in Article 18 of the Declaration on the basis *inter alia* of its incompatibility with the ordinances of Islam. In opposition to the Saudi Arabian position, the Pakistani representative Muhammad Zafar-ullah Khan relied upon the *Qur'anic* verse which notes 'let he who chooses to believe, believe and he who chooses to disbelieve, disbelieve' and went on to argue that:

[t]he Moslem religion was a missionary religion: it strove to persuade men to change their faith and alter their ways of living, so as to follow the faith and way of living it preached, but it recognised the same right of conversion for other religions as for itself.[69]

Pakistan found no discord between the provisions of the Declaration and of the ordinances of Islam.[70] The Declaration was subsequently adopted with the consent of all Islamic States, except for Saudi Arabia.[71]

---

[67] Mayer, above n.58, at p. 142.

[68] See Kelsay, 'Saudi-Arabia, Pakistan and the Universal Declaration on Human Rights' in Little *et al.* (eds), *Human Rights and Conflict of Cultures: Western and Islamic Perspectives on Religious Liberty* (University of South Carolina Press, 1988) at pp. 33–52; Tahzib, *Freedom of Religion or Belief: Ensuring Effective International Legal Protection* (Martinus Nijhoff Publishers, 1996) at pp. 72–74. On the sensitive question of apostasy in Islamic law and its compatibility with modern human rights law see AA An-Nai'm, 'The Islamic Law of Apostasy and its Modern Applicability: A Case from the Sudan' (1986) 16 *Religion*, 197.

[69] UN Doc. A/PV. 182, 890.

[70] During the preparation of the Convention on the Prevention and Punishment of the Crime of Genocide (1948) Pakistan had paid a particular emphasis on the cultural contributions of religious groups and communities within the states and had also proposed an article according to which 'genocide also [meant] . . . acts committed with the intent to destroy the religion or culture of a religious, racial or national group: (i) Systematic conversions from one religion to another by means of or by threats of violence (ii) Systematic destruction or desecration of places and objects of religious worship and desecration and destruction of objects of cultural value'. The failure of having such a provision included in the text of the Convention proved a major disappointment to the Pakistani delegation. In the plenary session Pakistan's representative Begum Ikram-ullah said 'it must be realised that very often a people did not differ from its neighbours by its racial characteristics but by its spiritual heritage. To deprive a human group of its separate culture could thus destroy its individuality as completely as physical inhalation. Moreover, those guilty of the crime of mass extermination committed that crime because the existence of a community endowed with a separate cultural life was intolerable to them. In other words physical genocide was only the means, the end was the destruction of a peoples spiritual individuality'. GAOR 3rd Session, Part I, 178th meeting, 9 December 1948, 817. This commitment was made evident in Pakistan's bilateral treaty with India in 1950 whereby both the States undertook to 'ensure the Minorities. . . . complete equality of citizenship, irrespective of religion . . . freedom of occupation, speech and worship . . .' Agreement between India and Pakistan Concerning Minorities (1950) 131 UNTS (1950) para (a). Freedom of religion and support for the religious minorities was strongly advocated by Pakistan during the drafting stages of ICCPR. Article 27 of the ICCPR was treated as 'the most important in the entire Covenant' A/C3/SR1104, 14 November 1961, para 15.

[71] The Declaration was adopted on 10 December 1948 with 48 votes in favour none against and eight abstentions. In addition to Saudi Arabia, South Africa and the Soviet Block States abstained from voting. See Robertson and Merrills, *Human Rights in the World: An Introduction to the Study of the International Protection of Human Rights* (Manchester University Press, 1996) at p. 28.

Notwithstanding the explicit provisions of Article 18 within the Universal Declaration, allowing for the right to change religion or belief, the existence of any such freedom or right in general international law has been cast into doubt by the opposition of a number of Islamic States. Many of these States while purporting to follow the *Sharia*, differ in their position. Some challenge the legitimacy of the freedom to change religion and base their arguments upon its incompatibility with apostasy rules within Islam, while others acknowledge the existence of such a freedom but are reluctant to forcefully assert their position. As a consequence of opposition from certain Islamic States it proved impossible to incorporate the express provision to authorise the freedom to change religion or belief in all of the subsequent international instruments.

(v) Islamic institutions and approaches towards human rights law

Many of the historic controversies are reflected in modern human rights schemes adopted by Islamic institutions and Islamic States. A case in point is the Universal Islamic Declaration of Human Rights (1981),[72] which is a document prepared by a number of Islamic States including Egypt, Pakistan and Saudi Arabia under the auspices of the Islamic Council (a private London based organisation, working in conjunction with the Muslim World League, an international non-governmental organisation). The Universal Islamic Declaration does not contain any specific provision sanctifying polygamy. Article XIX (a), however, notes that '[e]very person is entitled to marry, to found a family and to bring up children in conformity with his religion, traditions and culture. Every spouse is entitled to such rights and privileges and carries such obligations as are stipulated by the Law'.

Upon divorce, Article XX (c) of the Universal Islamic Declaration stipulates that '[e]very married woman is entitled to: . . . seek and obtain dissolution of marriage (*Khul'a*) in accordance with the terms of the Law'. While this provision appears to consecrate gender equality with regard to divorce, the reference made to 'the Law' requires closer examination. According to explanatory note 1(b) of the Declaration, 'the term "Law" denotes the *Shari'a*, i.e. the totality of ordinances derived from the *Qur'an* and the *Sunnah* and any other laws that are deduced from these two sources by methods considered valid in Islamic jurisprudence'. As a consequence, Article XX of the Universal Islamic Declaration does not provide an inalienable equal right of divorce to women and men, the exercise of the right is conditioned by the terms of the *Sharia*. The words of the *Sharia* will ultimately be the only provisions relevant to determining whether the regime of divorce differs according to gender. On post-divorce maintenance, Article XX (b) provides that every woman is entitled:

> in the event of divorce, [to] receive during the statutory period of waiting *(iddah)* means of maintenance commensurate with her husband's resources, for herself as well as for the children she nurses or keeps, irrespective of her own financial status, earnings, or property that she may hold in her own rights.

---

[72] For an analysis of the Declaration see Mayer, above n.58, at p. 22.

The limitation imposed up to a period of *iddah*,[73] constitutes a restriction to divorced women's entitlement to post-divorce maintenance.

On the subject of succession, Article XX (d) of the Universal Islamic Declaration states that '[e]very married women is entitled to: . . . inherit from her husband, her parents, her children and other relatives according to the Law'. This article also arguably encompasses two kinds of discrimination. Firstly, here also, equality is conditioned by the terms of the *Sharia*. Secondly, there is no reference to any possibility for the woman to be responsible for her financial means and being able to transmit it in case of her death.

(vi) The Organisation of the Islamic Conference (OIC)

The OIC was established in Rabat, Kingdom of Morocco, on 12 Rajab 1389H (25 September 1969). Its establishment was a reaction against a Zionist arson attack upon *Al-Aqsa* in occupied Jerusalem on 21 August 1969. Motivated to defend the faith and integrity of the Muslim people, a large group of States united by this common cause covenanted in their first meeting held in Rabat to liberate Jerusalem and Al-Aqsa from Zionist occupation.[74] Now existing as an inter-governmental organisation with 56 Members States, the OIC continues to pool its resources and efforts in its endeavour to present a unified voice and protect the interests of Muslim people and the Muslim world community. The Organisation now has 57 Member States, over four continents.[75]

A permanent General Secretariat was created and a Secretary General was appointed at the First Islamic Conference of Ministers of Foreign Affairs. After the first epochal meeting in Rabat, the Islamic Conference of Foreign Ministers approved the Charter of the Organisation.[76] This was replaced by a new version of the Charter in March 2008. Pursuant to Article 1 of the Charter, the Organisation's objectives are:

1. To enhance and consolidate the bonds of fraternity and solidarity among the Member States;

2. To safeguard and protect the common interests and support the legitimate causes of the Member States and coordinate and unify the efforts of the Member States in view of the challenges faced by the Islamic world in particular and the international community in general;

---

[73] *Iddat* is a period of waiting imposed upon a woman who has been divorced or whose husband has died, after which a new marriage is permissible. The divorced woman is bound to observe *iddat* for three menstrual cycles i.e. the period of three complete courses of menstruation. If the marriage is terminated by the death of a husband then the widow, if not pregnant, is under obligation to observe the *iddat* for a period of four months and ten days. If the wife is pregnant at the time of termination of her marriage (whatever the cause of termination may be) then her *iddat* will expire with the delivery of a child.

[74] Huntington, above n.6, at p. 176.

[75] www.oic-oci.org/page_detail.asp?p_id=52 <last visited 10 May 2009>.

[76] The OIC Charter was approved and adopted in the third Islamic Conference of Foreign Ministers held in Jeddah in March 1972. The initial Charter was registered in conformity with Article 102 of the United Nations Charter on 1 February, 1974. An Amended Charter was adopted at the 11th Islamic Summit on 14 March 2008 in Dakar, the Republic of Senegal. For the text of the amended Charter see www.oic-oci.org/oicnews/is11/english/Charter-en.pdf <last visited 10 May 2009>; For the initial Charter of 1972 see http://Arabian-union.org/reference/oic_charter_text.htm <last visited 10 May 2009>; also see Sands and Klein, above n.1, at p. 148.

3. To respect the right of self-determination and non-interference in the domestic affairs and to respect sovereignty, independence and territorial integrity of each Member State;

4. To support the restoration of complete sovereignty and territorial integrity of any Member State under occupation, as a result of aggression, on the basis of international law and cooperation with the relevant international and regional organisations;

5. To ensure active participation of the Member States in the global political, economic and social decision-making processes to secure their common interests;

6. To promote inter-state relations based on justice, mutual respect and good neighbourliness to ensure global peace, security and harmony;

7. To reaffirm its support for the rights of peoples as stipulated in the UN Charter and international law;

8. To support and empower the Palestinian people to exercise their right to selfdetermination and establish their sovereign State with Al-Quds Al-Sharif as its capital, while safeguarding its historic and Islamic character as well as the Holy places therein;

9. To strengthen intra-Islamic economic and trade cooperation; in order to achieve economic integration leading to the establishment of an Islamic Common Market;

10. To exert efforts to achieve sustainable and comprehensive human development and economic well-being in Member States;

11. To disseminate, promote and preserve the Islamic teachings and values based on moderation and tolerance, promote Islamic culture and safeguard Islamic heritage;

12. To protect and defend the true image of Islam, to combat defamation of Islam and encourage dialogue among civilisations and religions;

13. To enhance and develop science and technology and encourage research and cooperation among Member States in these fields;

14. To promote and to protect human rights and fundamental freedoms including the rights of women, children, youth, elderly and people with special needs as well as the preservation of Islamic family values;

15. To emphasize, protect and promote the role of the family as the natural and fundamental unit of society;

16. To safeguard the rights, dignity and religious and cultural identity of Muslim communities and minorities in non-Member States;

17. To promote and defend unified position on issues of common interest in the international fora;

18. To cooperate in combating terrorism in all its forms and manifestations, organised crime, illicit drug trafficking, corruption, money laundering and human trafficking;

19. To cooperate and coordinate in humanitarian emergencies such as natural disasters;

20. To promote cooperation in social, cultural and information fields among the Member States.

The Organisation is further inspired by the following principles enshrined in Article 2 of the Charter:

1. All Member States commit themselves to the purposes and principles of the United Nations Charter;

2. Member States are sovereign, independent and equal in rights and obligations;

3. All Member States shall settle their disputes through peaceful means and refrain from use or threat of use of force in their relations;

4. All Member States undertake to respect national sovereignty, independence and territorial integrity of other Member States and shall refrain from interfering in the internal affairs of others;

5. All Member States undertake to contribute to the maintenance of international peace and security and to refrain from interfering in each other's internal affairs as enshrined in the present Charter, the Charter of the United Nations, international law and international humanitarian law;

6. As mentioned in the UN Charter, nothing contained in the present Charter shall authorize the Organisation and its Organs to intervene in matters which are essentially within the domestic jurisdiction of any State or related to it;

7. Member States shall uphold and promote, at the national and international levels, good governance, democracy, human rights and fundamental freedoms, and the rule of law;

8. Member States shall endeavour to protect and preserve the environment.

Article 2(7) is of particular significance as it recognises that Member States will undertake to promote the values of human rights, democracy and rule of law. The practical implementation of democracy, human rights and the *modus operands* of good governance schemes remain to be seen.

(a) Institutions of the OIC

The Conference is composed of main bodies, secondary organs, specialised institutions and standing committees. Pursuant to Article 5 of the OIC Charter, the Organisation establishes 11 organs, these are:

1. Islamic Summit

2. Council of Foreign Ministers

3. Standing Committees

4. Executive Committee

5. International Islamic Court of Justice

6. Independent Permanent Commission of Human Rights

7. Committee of Permanent Representatives

8. General Secretariat

9. Subsidiary Organs

10. Specialised Institutions

11. Affiliated Institutions

This marks a substantial increase from the three main bodies established under the 1972 Charter: (i) the Conference of Kings and Heads of State and Government, (ii) the Conference of Foreign Ministers, and (iii) the General Secretariat and Subsidiary Organs. The Islamic Summit has the same composition as, and therefore takes the place of, the Conference of Kings and Heads of States and Government and is the supreme authority of the Organisation.[77] It compulsorily meets once every three years, and additionally when the interests of Muslim nations warrant it, to lay down and coordinate the Organisation's policy.[78] The Council of Foreign Ministers meets once a year and whenever the need arises, to consider means of implementing its general policy and resolutions, to adopt new resolutions, and to examine the financial and administrative reports and approve the budget.[79] Under Article 11, the OIC established four Standing Committees these are:

1. Al Quds Committee
2. Standing Committee for Information and Cultural Affairs (COMIAC)
3. Standing Committee for Economic and Commercial Cooperation (COMCEC)
4. Standing Committee for Scientific and Technological Cooperation (COMSTECH).

Notably the new Charter establishes an Independent Permanent Commission on Human Rights, with the mandate to 'promote the civil, political, social and economic rights enshrined in the organisation's covenants and declarations and in universally agreed human rights instruments, in conformity with Islamic values'.[80] The General Secretariat, in accordance with Chapter XI of the 2008 Charter, is the executive organ of the Organisation. The Secretariat is headed by a Secretary-General, who is elected by the Council of Foreign Ministers.[81] The Secretariat is entrusted with the 'implementation of the decisions, resolutions and recommendations of the Islamic Summits, and Councils of Foreign Ministers and other Ministerial meetings'.[82] Additionally, the General Secretariat prepares meetings of the Islamic Summits and the Councils of Foreign Ministers.[83] Currently the headquarters of the Secretariat are in Jeddah, with the aim of moving them to Al-Quds (Jerusalem) upon 'the liberation of the city'.[84]

The Charter also establishes that the International Islamic Court of Justice will be the principal judicial organ of the OIC, when its Statute enters into force.[85] The International Islamic Court of Justice (IICJ) will be located in Kuwait and will be the principal judicial organ of the OIC. Its composition will constitute seven members elected by the Islamic Council of Foreign Ministers (CFM). The remit of the Court will be disputes between Member States, the issuing of opinions as requested by the Islamic Summit, the CFM or by any organ of the OIC with the prior approval of the CFM, and the interpretation of the Charter of the Organisation.[86]

---

[77] Article 6, OIC Charter.
[78] Ibid. Articles 7, 8 and 9 OIC Charter.
[79] Ibid. Article 10.
[80] Ibid. Article 15.
[81] Ibid. Article 16.
[82] Ibid. Article 17(b).
[83] Ibid. Article 20.
[84] Ibid. Article 21.
[85] Ibid. Article 14.
[86] For a critical examination see Hussain, above n.26, at pp. 90–117. See also OIC Resolutions on Legal Affairs, Adopted by the 35th Session of the Council of Foreign Ministers (Session of Prosperity and Development),

There are a number of secondary organs and institutions that collaboratively work towards the attainment of the Organisation's objectives – subsidiary organs, specialised institutions, affiliated institutions and standing committees (categorised by the degree of autonomy they each enjoy *vis-à-vis* the Organisation) – and these have been steadily proliferating in both numbers and in terms of areas covered. Notably, by the third year of the World Decade for Cultural Development, an initiative inaugurated by the United Nations in 1988 under the auspices of UNESCO, the Organisation of the Islamic Conference had already built Islamic colleges and cultural institutes and centres for the purpose of disseminating Islamic culture and proliferating the teaching of Arabic, the language of the Holy *Qur'an*, and other languages.

Several additional institutions have been established within the framework of the OIC and in accordance with the resolutions adopted by the Islamic Conference of Foreign Ministers. Member States automatically become members of these organs and their budgets are approved by the Council of Foreign Ministers. These additional institutions include the Statistical, Economic, Social Research and Training Centre for Islamic Countries (SESRIC) (located in Turkey), the Islamic University of Technology (IUT) (Bangladesh), the Islamic Centre for the Development of Trade (ICDT) (Morocco), the Research Center for Islamic History, Art and Culture (IRCICA) (Turkey) and the International Islamic Fiqh Academy (IIFA) (Saudi Arabia).

The remit of the subsidiary organs is both research and operational. Several of the organs are creating and publishing databases of information collected through surveys and research. In their operational capacity, the organs set up programmes for the dissemination of expertise, training, and resources for the benefit of all Member States.[87] At present there are seven subsidiary organs. In establishing these agencies, the OIC commented that:

> The undermentioned Centres are established within the framework of the Organization of the Islamic Conference in accordance with a resolution adopted by the Islamic Conference of Kings and Heads of State and Government or the Islamic Conference of Foreign Ministers. Member States shall automatically become members of these organs and their budgets shall be approved by the Islamic Conference of Foreign Ministers.[88]

The OIC has been actively engaged in drafting and adopting numerous resolutions and instruments which engage with human rights issues. The present analysis is limited to three initiatives which are directly relevant to the subjects examined in this study: these are the Cairo Declaration on Human Rights in Islam (1990), the OIC Covenant on the Rights of the Child in Islam and the OIC Convention on Terrorism (1999).

(b) The Cairo Declaration on Human Rights in Islam[89]

The Cairo Declaration on Human Rights in Islam (CDHRI) was adopted and issued at the 19th Islamic Conference of Foreign Ministers in Cairo on 5 August 1990. CDHRI was

---

OIC/CFM-35/2008/LEG/RES/FINAL, Resolution No. 1/35-LEG on the International Islamic Court of Justice and cooperation among Islamic States in the judicial field.

[87] See Subsidiary Organs, www.oic-oci.org/oicnew/page_detail.asp?p_id=64#FIQH <last visited 3 May 2009>.

[88] www.oic-oci.org/english/main/subsidiary%20organs.htm <last visited 9 May 2009>.

[89] *Cairo Declaration on Human Rights in Islam*, 5 August 1990, UN GAOR, World Conf. on Hum. Rts., 4th Sess., Agenda Item 5, UN Doc. A/CONF.157/PC/62/Add.18 (1993).

adopted by the 45 Foreign Ministers of the OIC with the aim that the Declaration should serve as guiding principles in issues of human rights. As its title indicates, the Declaration represents non-binding guiding principles for members of the OIC. CDHRI has a preamble and consists of 25 Articles in total. As a document inspired and influenced heavily by the Islamic faith and the Islamic *Sharia*, the Declaration makes consistent references to Islam and *Sharia*. The preamble affirms the:

> civilizing and historical role of the Islamic Ummah which God made the best nation that has given mankind a universal and well-balanced civilization in which harmony is established between this life and the hereafter and knowledge is combined with faith.

The preamble also affirms the view that fundamental rights and universal freedoms within Islam form an integral part of the Islamic faith which cannot be suspended or violated.

According to Article 1 of the Declaration all human beings are part of one family and are united by submission to God and are descendants of Adam. All men are equal in terms of dignity, obligations and rights. The Article appears to recognise the principle of non-discrimination on the basis of *inter alia*, religion even though the references to God and Adam begs the question as to the extent which non-believers or atheists could be accommodated within the provisions of non-discrimination. Article 2 protects the right to life 'and it is prohibited to take away life except for a *Shari'ah*-prescribed reason'. This, however, opens up the possibility of sanctioning the death penalty for offences within *Shariah*. Similarly, the Declaration entitles all individuals 'to inviolability and the protection of his good name and honour during his lifetime and after his death'.[90]

Article 3 deals with provisions of humanitarian law and appears to be consonant with the customary norms established by Geneva Conventions.[91] The Declaration accords protection to all individuals from arbitrary arrest, torture, maltreatment or indignity.[92] It also guarantees the presumption of innocence, with the guilt of an individual to be proven through a trial in 'which he [the defendant] shall be given all the guarantees of defence'.[93] No one, according to the Declaration, is to be used for medical or scientific experiments.[94] There is also a prohibition on the taking of hostages, regardless of the purpose, a feature which confirms customary humanitarian and treaty law.[95]

The most controversial aspect of the Declaration, however, relates to the rights of women, children and the position of *Sharia* within the State. Article 5 of the Declaration provides as follows: 'The family is the foundation of society, and marriage is the basis of its formation. Men and women have the right to marriage, and no restrictions stemming from race, colour or nationality shall prevent them from enjoying this right.' While common grounds of discrimination like race, colour and nationality are duly included in this provision, no mention is made to religious-based discrimination in marriage. The provision does not appear to include any reference to the situation of non-Muslims who could be governed by this instrument. In practice, the situation is even less equal as *Sharia* law often

---

[90] Article 4 Cairo Declaration.
[91] See below chapter 21.
[92] Article 20 Cairo Declaration.
[93] Ibid. Article 19(e).
[94] Ibid. Article 20.
[95] Ibid. Article 21.

commands that women cannot marry non-Muslim men but that Muslim men can marry non-Muslim women. The religious logic behind this is that in Islam the child endorses the religion of his or her father in order to ensure the continuance of the Islamic faith.

More generally, the Declaration is hesitant in according complete gender equality to woman: women thus are accorded 'equal human dignity', 'own rights to enjoy', 'duties to perform', 'own civil entity', 'financial independence', and the 'right to retain her name and lineage'. Notwithstanding these references, the Declaration fails to provide equal rights to women in all spheres of public and private life with the subservience of women being reinforced with the husband having been granted responsibility for the support and welfare of the family. Article 6 provides as follows:

(a) Woman is equal to man in human dignity, and has rights to enjoy as well as duties to perform; she has her own civil entity and financial independence, and the right to retain her name and lineage.

(b) The husband is responsible for the support and welfare of the family.

Article 7 of the Declaration deals with the rights of children. It provides that:

(a) As of the moment of birth, every child has rights due from the parents, society and the state to be accorded proper nursing, education and material, hygienic and moral care. Both the fetus and the mother must be protected and accorded special care.

(b) Parents and those in such like capacity have the right to choose the type of education they desire for their children, provided they take into consideration the interest and future of the children in accordance with ethical values and the principles of the Shari'ah.

(c) Both parents are entitled to certain rights from their children, and relatives are entitled to rights from their kin, in accordance with the tenets of the Shari'ah.

Critics of the Article point to equivocal approach on the subject of abortion. The right of the parents to choose the type of education for their children is limited to the ethical values and principles of the *Sharia*. Parents and others in similar situations are also entitled to certain rights from their children although they are again circumscribed to act within the *Sharia*.

The position of other faiths and religions *vis-à-vis* Islam also raises particular issues within the Declaration. The right to hold public office can only be exercised in accordance within the *Sharia*.[96] Enforcement of the criminal justice system of the *Sharia* implies the application of corporal punishments to both Muslims and non-Muslims.[97] The Declaration appears rather vague in its position in respect of an absolute freedom of religion. Article 10 provides that:

---

[96] Ibid. Article 23(b) Cairo Declaration.

[97] Ibid. Article 19(d) provides: 'There shall be no crime or punishment except as provided for in the *Shari'ah*.' The Declaration preserves capital punishment: Article 2(a) notes: 'Life is a God-given gift and the right to life is guaranteed to every human being. It is the duty of individuals, societies and states to protect this right from any violation, and it is prohibited to take away life except for a *Shari'ah*-prescribed reason.'

Islam is the religion of unspoiled nature. It is prohibited to exercise any form of compulsion on man or to exploit his poverty or ignorance in order to convert him to another religion or to atheism.

It is, nevertheless, unclear as to whether it is permissible for individuals to convert to another religion or belief in instances where there is no exploitation or ignorance involved. In other words, the explicit provisions of the Universal Declaration on Human Rights as regards absolute freedom of religion and including the freedom of the individual to change his or her religion or belief are absent from the Islamic Declaration.

The Declaration positively asserts a right to free expression, although this right is tied to the prerequisite that those views 'would not be contrary to the principles of *Shari'ah*'[98] – presumably the Islamic State being the adjudicator of the quality and appropriateness of these views. Furthermore, this right is accompanied by a right to 'advocate what is right, and propagate what is good'[99] and a prohibition against violating the 'sanctities and the dignity of Prophets'.[100] As well as this, it is not permitted to 'undermine moral and ethical values or disintegrate, corrupt or harm society or weaken its faith',[101] 'arouse nationalistic or doctrinal hatred'[102] or commit 'incitement to any form of racial discrimination'.[103] The penultimate Article of the Declaration, Article 24, further restricts the ambit of the rights through subjecting all rights and freedoms to the Islamic *Sharia*. The concluding Article, Article 25 declares Islamic *Sharia* as the only 'source of reference for the explanation and clarification to any of the articles of this Declaration'.

The current Secretary-General of the OIC, in December 2007, expressed the wish to establish an 'independent permanent body to promote Human Rights in the Member States in accordance with the provisions of the OIC Cairo Declaration on Human Rights in Islam and to elaborate an OIC Charter on Human Rights'.[104] The Independent Permanent Commission on Human Rights was established under Article 15 of the 2008 Charter: however, this has yet to become operational.

(c) OIC Covenant on the Rights of the Child in Islam (2004)

In 2004, the OIC adopted the Covenant on the Rights of the Child in Islam. Much like the Cairo Declaration, this Covenant is influenced by the Muslim ideals and targets the position of children within Muslim societies, although there is recognition of international instruments such as the Convention on the Rights of the Child.[105] The Covenant considers children:

---

[98] Ibid. Article 22(a).
[99] Ibid. Article 22(b).
[100] Ibid. Article 22(c).
[101] Ibid.
[102] Ibid. Article 22(d).
[103] Ibid.
[104] www.oic-oci.org/oicnew/topic_detail.asp?t_id=708 <last visited 3 May 2009>.
[105] *OIC Covenant on the Rights of the Child in* Islam (2004), OIC Doc. OIC/0-IGGE/HRI/2004/Rep.Final. On Children's rights within Muslim Jurisdictions see Ali 'A Comparative Perspective of the United Nations Convention on the Rights of the Child and the Principles of Islamic Law: Law Reform and Children's Rights in Muslim Jurisdictions' in Ali, Goonesekere, Mendez and Rios-Kohn, *Protecting the World's Children: Impact of the Convention on the Rights of the Child in Diverse Legal Systems* (Cambridge University Press, 2007) at pp. 142–208.

as part of the vulnerable sector of society, bear the burden of the greater suffering as a result of natural and man-made disasters leading to tragic consequences, such as orphanage, homelessness, and exploitation of children in military, harsh, hazardous or illegitimate labor and [considers] the suffering of refugee children and those living under the yoke of occupation or languishing or displaced as a result of armed conflicts and famines thus fostering the spread of violence among children and increasing the number of physically, mentally, and socially disabled children.[106]

According to the definition provided by Article 1, a child means 'every human being who, according to the law applicable to him/her, has not attained maturity'. The term 'maturity' is not demarcated by any age and, therefore, remains a vacuous description for legal application. With this induction of an ambiguous concept such as 'maturity' the definition can be criticised as unhelpful. The Covenant is based on highly ambitious objectives, as provided in Article 2. The Article provides:

Article Two – Objectives
This Covenant seeks to realize the following objectives:

1. To care for the family, strengthen its capabilities, and extend to it the necessary support to prevent the deterioration of its economic, social, or health conditions, and to habilitate the husband and wife to ensure fulfillment of their role of raising children physically, psychologically, and behaviourally.

2. To ensure a balanced and safe childhood and ensure the raising of generations of Muslim children who believe in their creator, adhere to their faith, are loyal to their country, committed to the principles of truth and goodness in thoughts and in deeds, and to the sense of belonging to the Islamic civilization.

3. To generalize and deepen interest in the phases of childhood and adolescence and to provide full care for them so as to raise worthy generations for society.

4. To provide free, compulsory primary and secondary education for all children irrespective of gender, color, nationality, religion, birth, or any other consideration, to develop education through enhancement of school curricula, the training of teachers, and the provision of opportunities for vocational training.

5. To provide opportunities for the child to discover his/her talents and to recognize his/her importance and place in the society through the family and relevant institutions, and to encourage children to participate in the cultural life of society.

6. To provide the necessary care for children with special needs and for those who live in difficult conditions as well as address the causes that lead to such conditions.

7. To provide all possible assistance and support for Muslim children in all parts of the world in coordination with governments or through international mechanisms.

These objectives are to be attained through a number of principles. These include the respect of the Islamic *Sharia*, as well as the objectives and principles of the OIC. Article 5 of the Covenant provides for the equality of children before the law 'regardless of sex, birth, race, religion and language, political affiliation, or any other consideration affecting the

---

[106] Preamble OIC Covenant on the Rights of the Child.

right of the child, the family, or his/her representative under the law or Shari'a'. The right to life is guaranteed to all children under Article 6. While the fetus is protected, unlike the American Convention on Human Rights such protection is not stated as extending from the moment of conception.[107] The child is accorded a right to a 'good' name and to be registered with the relevant authorities.[108] The child also has the right to a nationality and has the right to know his or her parents and relatives.[109] The Covenant places an obligation on States to protect the family from disintegration and provide all available resources.[110] The Covenant recognises that every child has the ability to formulate his or her own views and has the right to express these freely although these must not be contrary to the *Sharia*.[111] While the child is entitled to respect of personal life, parents have the entitlement 'to exercise Islamic and humane supervision'.[112] A child has both freedom of expression and freedom of assembly.[113]

The noble ideas of upbringing of children as established in Article 11 are to be reinforced through education and the development of culture. In consonance with the provisions of ICESCR, the Covenant enjoins States to provide '[c]ompulsory, free primary education for all children on an equal footing'.[114] Furthermore, States are obliged to provide free compulsory secondary education.[115] The emphasis of education, however, should be based upon fundamental *Sharia* principles,[116] with Muslim children being able to join private institutions so long as these private institutions respect the doctrines of the *Sharia* and observe State regulations.[117]

According to Article 13, the child is entitled to rest and to have times of 'legitimate' activities. The Covenant also contains provisions on appropriate social and living standards.[118] The Covenant places emphasis upon the physical and psychological health of the child including the provision of preventative medical care, disease and malnutrition.[119] The protection of the child's health necessitates '[n]on-interference . . . in medically altering the colour, shape, features or sex of the fetus except for medical necessities'.[120] The Covenant, however, includes the right of a male child to circumcision, a feature unique to this particular instrument.[121] As part of the scheme of protecting children, the Covenant places obligations on States parties to take all necessary measures to protect children from *inter alia* the illegal use of drugs, intoxication and harmful substances and all forms of torture, inhumane treatment including smuggling, kidnapping or trafficking.[122] The Covenant prohibits all forms of sexual abuse, and extends protection to engagement in hazardous work.[123]

---

[107] See Article 4, American Convention on Human Rights (1969). See also above chapter 9.
[108] See Article 7(1) OIC Covenant on the Rights of the Child.
[109] Ibid.
[110] Ibid. Article 8(1).
[111] Ibid. Article 9(1).
[112] Ibid. Article 9(2).
[113] Ibid. Articles 9 and 10.
[114] Ibid. Article 12(2)(i).
[115] Ibid. Article 12(2)(ii).
[116] Ibid. Article 12(1).
[117] Ibid. Article 12(4).
[118] Ibid. Article 14.
[119] Ibid. Article 15.
[120] Ibid. Article 15(6).
[121] Ibid. Article 15(5).
[122] Ibid. Article 17.
[123] Ibid. Articles 17(3) and 18(1).

There is also an obligation to protect children from armed conflicts and wars.[124] Article 21 of the Covenant accords protection to refugee children and requires States parties to allow the enjoyment of rights contained in this Covenant to refugee children. Articles 22 to 26 deal with procedural matters including an undertaking on the part of the States parties to establish an Islamic Committee on the Rights of the Child.[125] The Committee is to be composed of representatives of all States parties and aims to meet every two years from the date of entry into force of the Covenant. The meetings of the Committee are to take place at the headquarters of the OIC with the underlying objective of examining the progress of the implementation of the Covenant. Two-thirds of the States parties constitute a quorum and the workings of the Committee are to be governed by the rules of procedure for the meeting of the conferences of the OIC.[126] The Covenant allows ratifying States to enter into reservations (and their subsequent withdrawal) although in each case such action has to be notified to the Secretary General of the OIC.[127] The Covenant is due to come into force on the 30th day following the date of deposit with the Secretary General of the OIC of the 20th instrument of ratification.[128]

(d) Convention of the OIC on Combating International Terrorism (1999)

The OIC has repeatedly taken the position that the subject of international and regional terrorism needs to be reviewed comprehensively. Such a comprehensive review would include the examination of substantive issues. Conceptual and definitional problems would also need to be revisited. In its Ninth Summit, in Doha, the State of Qatar, during 12–13 November 2000, the final communiqué dealt with the issue of definition of terrorism in the following terms:

> The Conference expressed again its support for the convening of a conference under the aegis of the United Nations to define the concept of terrorism and make a distinction between terrorism and people's struggle for national liberation.[129]

This position had been repeated in the Declaration that emerged from the Ninth Summit, where the OIC took the view that:

> We again condemn all forms and manifestations of terrorism whatever its source as reflected in the unanimous adoption of the Agreement of the Organization of the Islamic Conference on Combating Terrorism, and in the repeated promises for the convening of a World Conference under the auspices of the United Nations to address this phenomenon in an effective manner away from racism and bias and to consider effective ways and means to eradicate it. We reaffirm here that a clear separation must be made between terrorism, on the one hand, and people's struggle for national liberation including the struggle of the Palestinian people and the elimination of foreign occupation and colonial hegemony as well as for regaining the right to self-determination, on the other hand.[130]

[124] Ibid. Article 17(5).
[125] Ibid. Article 24(1).
[126] Ibid. Article 24(2).
[127] Ibid. Article 25(1).
[128] Ibid. Article 23(1).
[129] Ninth OIC Summit, Doha, State of Qatar, 16–17 Sha'ban 1421 H, 13 November 2002 (Final Communiqué).
[130] Ibid.

The OIC has been at the forefront in its efforts to deal with international, regional and domestic terrorism. The primary instrument in this regard is the Convention of the OIC on Combating International Terrorism. The Convention was adopted at Ouagadougou on 1 July 1999. The preamble of the Treaty is of particular significance since it not only condemns terrorism as a violation of the *Sharia* principles but also establishes the essential relationship between terrorist acts and breach of fundamental human rights. The preamble of the Convention provides *inter alia*:

> [p]ursuant to the tenets of the tolerant Islamic Sharia which reject all forms of violence and terrorism, and in particular specially those based on extremism and call for protection of human rights, which provisions are paralleled by the principles and rules of international law founded on cooperation between peoples for the establishment of peace;
>
> Abiding by the lofty, moral and religious principles particularly the provisions of the Islamic Sharia as well as the human heritage of the Islamic Ummah.

The preamble goes on to affirm principles of general international law *inter alia* sovereignty, territorial integrity, political independence and non-intervention in domestic affairs. There is also an important acknowledgement of the right to self-determination and a firm belief that 'terrorism constitutes a gross violation of human rights, in particular the right to freedom and security, as well as an obstacle to the free functioning of institutions and socio-economic development, as it aims at destabilizing States'. With such strong preambular condemnation of international terrorism, the text of the treaty provides a detailed definition of terrorism. However, as terrorism is considered in the context of human rights in a later chapter, the discussion here will be limited.[131]

The Convention, presents a strong affirmation of the right of self-determination.[132] Accordingly, peoples' struggle against foreign aggression and colonial or racist regimes is not to be considered a terrorist crime.[133] Self-determination is a well-established right in international law, and as we have noted already, one with a *jus cogens* character. The international community remains under an obligation to support peoples struggling for their right to self-determination. There is, thus, a substantial risk of conflict between a people's struggle for self-determination, which involves an armed uprising and resistance on the one hand and the complete prohibition of terrorist activities and all forms of violence on the other. This apparently conflicting approach has been regarded as generating 'a great amount of confusion'[134] and has been criticised in various quarters.[135] There is substance in such criticism. For members of the OIC the availability of the struggle of liberation and self-determination is only legitimate when conducted 'in accordance with the principles of international law'.[136] When applied within the domestic context of Member States such provisions bring out disconcerting features. Many of the States have inherently

---

[131] See below chapter 24.
[132] See Article 2(a) OIC Convention of the Organisation of the Islamic Conference on Combating International Terrorism.
[133] Article 2(a) OIC Convention on Terrorism.
[134] Report by the International Bar Association's Task Force on International Terrorism, *International Terrorism: Legal Challenges and Responses* (Ardsley NY: Transnational Publishers) 2003 at p. 2.
[135] Ibid.
[136] Article 2(a) OIC Convention on Terrorism.

undemocratic systems of governance; denials of the 'internal' right to self-determination and the negation of rule of law is widespread.[137]

(e) The Role of the OIC and its Member States in the Aftermath of 11 September 2001

In the aftermath of attacks in the United States on 11 September 2001 there was condemnation of terrorist acts by individual members of Al-Qaeda as well as by the organisation itself. All Member States expressed their deepest regrets and passed condolences to the families of individuals who died on 11 September. This expression of tragedy was without any exceptions or reservations. There was also the urgency to distance Islam and *Sharia* from the motives of the terrorist hijackers. The same sentiments were advanced by the OIC in its final communiqué of the ninth extra-ordinary session of the Islamic Conference of Foreign Minster (ICFM), in Doha, Qatar. The Conference stressed that:

> such shameful terrorist acts [of 11 September, 2001] are opposed to the tolerant message of Islam which spurns aggression, calls for peace, co-existence, tolerance and respect among people, highly prizes the dignity of human life and prohibits killing of the innocent. It further rejected any attempts alleging the existence of any connection or relation between the Islamic faith and the terrorist acts as such are not in the interest of the multilateral efforts to combat terrorism and further damage relations among peoples of the world. It stressed the need to undertake a joint effort to promote dialogue and create links or contacts between the Islamic world and the west in order to reach mutual understanding and building brides of confidence between the two civilizations.[138]

The resolve to condemn terrorism in all its forms was apparent in the Kuala Lumpur Declaration on International Terrorism adopted at the extraordinary session of the Islamic Conference of the Foreign Ministers on Terrorism.[139] In this Declaration the Ministers present their response to the 11 September attacks.[140] Invoking Islamic solidarity, they recall the earlier measures that had been adopted by the OIC for combating international terrorism, in particular the OIC Convention on Terrorism, the Code of Conduct for Combating International Terrorism, the Declaration of the Ninth extraordinary Session of ICFM and other relevant Resolutions passed by the Conference.[141] In two important provisions the Declaration firstly reaffirms the commitment to 'the principles and true teachings of Islam which abhor aggression, value peace, tolerance and respect as well as prohibiting the killing of innocent people'[142] and rejects 'any attempt to link Islam and Muslims to terrorism as terrorism has no association with any religion, civilization or nationality'.[143] There is an absolute and unequivocal condemnation of terrorism in all its manifestations and forms; the Declaration regarding terrorism as a serious threat to

---

[137] See Rehman, *The Weaknesses in the International Protection of Minority Rights* (Kluwer Law International, 2000).

[138] Final Communiqué of the Ninth Extraordinary Session of the Islamic Conference of Foreign Ministers, Doha, Qatar, 10 October 2001.

[139] Declaration on International Terrorism adopted at the extraordinary session of the Islamic Conference of the Foreign Ministers on Terrorism, Kuala Lumpur, adopted 3 April 2002, text available at www.oic-oci.org/english/conf/fm/11_extraordinary/declaration.htm <last visited 12 May 2009>.

[140] Ibid. Article 1.

[141] Ibid. Article 2.

[142] Ibid. Article 4.

[143] Ibid. Article 5.

international peace and security and a grave violation of human rights.[144] There is also a reiteration of the norms of international law, in particular, the support of peoples under colonial, alien and foreign occupation. The Declaration acknowledges the strength and binding nature of all relevant United Nations Security Council Resolutions, in particularly Security Council Resolution 1373.[145] There is also an interest in expediting the accession or ratification of relevant international Conventions and Protocols relating to terrorism. The struggle of the Palestinian peoples for self-determination is commended and members advocate the necessity for an independent Palestinian State to be established. By the same token there is the condemnation of Israel for the:

> escalating military campaign against the Palestinian people, including the daily brutalization and humiliation of its civilians, resulting in mounting casualties, strangulation of the Palestinian economy, systematic and indiscriminate destruction of houses and residential facilities as well as infrastructure, institutions and structures of the Palestinian National Authority.[146]

There is urgency on the part of the Foreign Ministers to address the main causes of terrorism. The Declaration pleads against unilateral action against any Islamic country, on the ostensible basis of combating international terrorism. While such a unilateralist approach is seen as contrary to international law, this has precisely been the course adopted by the United States against several States members of the Organisation. The most recent example has been the use of military force against Iraq. The Kuala Lumpur Declaration presents a Plan of Action, whereby a 13-member open-ended Ministerial Level OIC Committee on International Terrorism is established.[147] The Committee is required to present its recommendations to Member States and to the ICFM for consideration and action. The mandate of the Committee is to undertake:

1. Measures to strengthen OIC cooperation and coordination in combating international terrorism;

2. Ways of expediting the implementation of the OIC Code of Conduct and the Convention on Combating International Terrorism;

3. Measures in projecting the true image of Islam. These include holding seminars and workshops to promote a better understanding of Islam and its principles;

4. Measures in strengthening dialogue and understanding among different civilizations, cultures and faiths, for instance, by building on initiatives such as the United Nations Dialogue Among Civilizations and the OIC-EU Joint Forum on Harmony and Civilization;

5. Other measures, as appropriate and in accordance with the Charter of the OIC as well as Summit and ICFM resolutions, in response to developments affecting Muslims and Islam arising from action to combat terrorism.

---

[144] Ibid. Article 7 notes: 'We unequivocally condemn acts of international terrorism in all its forms and manifestations, including state terrorism, irrespective of motives, perpetrators and victims as terrorism poses a serious threat to international peace and security and is a grave violation of human rights'.
[145] Ibid. Plan of Action, Articles 6 and 7.
[146] Ibid. Article 12.
[147] Ibid. Plan of Action.

A number of sessions have been held since the Kuala Lumpur Declaration, the most recent being that of the 35th session of International Conference of Foreign Ministers in Kampala, Republic of Uganda during 18–20 June 2008.[148] However, only very limited steps have, thus far, been undertaken to effectively implement the provisions of the Kuala Lumpur Declaration.

3 LEAGUE OF ARAB STATES

The League of Arab States was established in March 1945 by Syria, Lebanon, Jordan, Iraq, Egypt and Yemen. The rationale for the creation League, as evidenced by the Alexandria Protocol, was to show Arab unity, at a time when Arab Nation States were eager to exert influence in the region. There are now 22 Member States of the League,[149] which has its headquarters in Cairo. The Arab League operates within a Council, that consists of the Foreign Minister of each Member State.[150] The Council meets two times every year.[151] There is also the possibility of calling a special session at the behest of any two Member States.[152] The League has also had periodic summits of the Heads of States, in these instances these replace the normal council sessions. The League has a Secretary-General[153] and operates through 17 specialised agencies dealing with such issues as economic and social development, educational, cultural and scientific affairs and broadcasting.[154] Furthermore, the 15 permanent committees deal with issues such as women and human rights.[155] The resolutions of the League can be adopted by a simple majority. While the resolutions of the League are binding, these resolutions only bind those members which vote in favour of them.[156] The membership of the League is limited to Arab States, and therefore excludes such non-Arab States as Turkey and Iran, which reduces the effectiveness of the organisation.

The region as well as the League has been plagued by conflict including substantial territorial disputes. One of the primary preoccupations of the League has been its continuing support of the Palestinians in their conflict with Israel. In other disputes involving Arab States themselves, the League has turned out to be a rather ineffective medium for conflict resolution. The League was unable to deal appropriately with Yemen's civil war or with the protracted Iran–Iraq War. The League condemned the military invasion of Kuwait by Iraq

---

[148] See final report of the 35th session of the Council of Foreign Ministers, Kampala, Republic of Uganda 10–20 June 2008 OIC/35-CFM/2008/FINAL REPORT www.oic-oci.org/35cfm/english/res/35CFM-FINAL%20 REPORT.pdf <last visited 15 May 2009>.

[149] In addition to the seven founding States, these include Algeria, Bahrain, Comoros, Djibouti, Kuwait, Mauritania, Morocco, Oman, Palestine, Qatar, Saudi Arabia, Somalia, Sudan, Tunisia and the United Arab Emirates. In addition to this both Venezuela (2006) and India (2007) have Observer Status with the League.

[150] Article III *Charter of the League of Arab States*, 22 March 1945. Text available at www.mfa.gov.eg/ MFA_Portal/en-GB/Foreign_Policy/Treaties/Charter+of+the+League+of+Arab+States.htm <last visited 15 May 2009>.

[151] Ibid. Article XI.

[152] Ibid.

[153] Ibid. Article XII.

[154] History of Establishment, www.diplomacy.edu/arabcharter/league_hist.asp <last visited 10 May 2009>.

[155] The Arab Commission of Human Rights was created in 1968, the purpose of which is the promotion of human rights and the dissemination of information. See M. Amin Al-Midani, 'The League of Arab States and the Arab Charter on Human Rights', www.acihl.org/articles.htm&article_id=6 <last visited 10 May 2009>.

[156] Article VII Charter of the League of Arab States.

377

in 1990. Over the issue of Iraq, post-1990, the League has remained divided. Some members of the League actively opposed Saddam Hussein's regime. Prior to the invasion of Iraq in March 2003, a number of the League members attempted to avert the conflict through negotiations and pressuring Saddam Hussein to disarm. At the same time there were some members of the League who expressed support over the United States's decision to invade Iraq and remove the regime via military means.[157]

The Arab League is institutionalised with a Council, Committees and a Secretariat. There is also a Joint Defense Council, Permanent Military Committee, and Economic Council. The League has been involved in initiatives relating to economic social and cultural co-operation. In terms of economic developmental steps, initiatives have included efforts to create a common market (Arab Economic Union) and the Arab Development Bank. Its noticeable failures have been in the area of political cohesion and co-operation. The League, as we shall discuss shortly, has made efforts to develop a human rights mechanism – the success of which has been only partial.

(i) Arab Charter of Human Rights

On 22 May 2004, the League of Arab States adopted a revised version of the Arab Charter on Human Rights (Charter 2004), which entered into force on 15 March 2008.[158] It was the second attempt by the League to adopt such a document since 1994 when the League of Arab States attempted to adopt the first Arab Charter of Human Rights. There are significant differences between these two versions, reflected in differences in provisions and the expanded nature of the revised Charter (with its 53 Articles as opposed to the previous 43 Articles). The revised Charter does not make any references to the previous version, even in the preamble, thereby confirming an ambition to establish a new beginning in respect of Arab Human Rights protection.[159] To its credit, the Arab League, in drafting the Charter, adopted an inclusive process actively engaging in consultative process both with NGOs as well as inter-governmental organisations. The revised Charter was a product of efforts on the part of the League of Arab States to 'modernize' existing institutions.[160] Additional institutions envisaged to form part of the package include an Arab Parliament, a regional Security Council and an Arab Court of Justice. While the ideal of establishing additional institutions and revamping the human rights systems appears attractive, in reality many of these proposals have not been welcomed by members of the League. Hence, it is not surprising to note that, thus far, the only concrete achievement is the production and the enforcement (since March 2008) of the revised Arab Charter. Even this has not been entirely successful, with the Charter attracting criticism from such influential quarters as the former UN High Commissioner for Human Rights, Louise Arbour, who stated, 'concerns included the approach to death penalty for children and the rights of women and non-citizens'.[161]

The preamble of the Charter makes specific reference to 'eternal principles of fraternity, equality and tolerance among human beings consecrated by the noble Islamic religion and

---

[157] Note e.g. the position of neighbours of Iraq.
[158] 12 *International Human Rights Reports* (2005) 893.
[159] Rishmawi, 'The Revised Arab Charter on Human Rights: A Step Forward?' 5 *HRLR* (2005) 361, at p. 363.
[160] See the Statement by Amr Mousa, the then Secretary-General of the Arab League in Resolution of the Council of Ministers of the Arab League 6184, March 2002 and 6243, September 2002 (available in Arabic).
[161] 'UN News Centre, Arab rights charter deviates from international standards,' says UN official www.un.org/apps/news/story.asp?NewsID=25447&Cr=human&Cr=rights <last visited 10 May 2009>.

the other divinely-revealed religions'.[162] Thus, while the influence of Islam and other divine faiths are inescapable, the bias against other ideologies, for example, secularism, could also be easily inferred. The preamble of the Charter also identifies Zionism as a form of racism and condemns it as a violation of human rights and a threat to peace and security. In this sense, the Charter seems to be biased particularly against Zionism and the relationship of Arab States with the State of Israel being a matter of concern. This has been another point of criticism from the United Nations, the former High Commissioner emphasising:

> to the extent that it equates Zionism with racism, we reiterated that the Arab Charter is not in conformity with General Assembly Resolution 46/86, which rejects that Zionism is a form of racism and racial discrimination.[163]

The Charter, in Article 1, places emphasis on the national identity of Arab States and the peoples occupying these States and in this way puts the notion of human rights as of paramount value to these people. Although, the Charter echoes the Vienna Declaration (1993) in declaring all human rights as 'universal, indivisible, interdependent and indissoluble' there is much reluctance in the articulation of this relationship. Article 1 of the Charter provides:

> The present Charter seeks, within the context of the national identity of the Arab States and their sense of belonging to a common civilization, to achieve the following aims:
> 1. To place human rights at the centre of the key national concerns of Arab States, making them lofty and fundamental ideals that shape the will of the individual in Arab States and enable him to improve his life in accordance with noble human values.
> 2. To teach the human person in the Arab States pride in his identity, loyalty to his country, attachment to his land, history and common interests and to instill in him a culture of human brotherhood, tolerance and openness towards others, in accordance with universal principles and values and with those proclaimed in international human rights instruments.
> 3. To prepare the new generations in Arab States for a free and responsible life in a civil society that is characterized by solidarity, founded on a balance between awareness of rights and respect for obligations, and governed by the values of equality, tolerance and moderation.
> 4. To entrench the principle that all human rights are universal, indivisible, interdependent and interrelated.

In common with the International Covenants and the African Charter, Article 2 focuses on the right of self-determination. The positive assertion of economic and political self-determination are countered by references to the principles of territorial integrity and national sovereignty, confirming the *uti possidetis* principle.[164] The categorisation of racism and foreign occupation alongside Zionism presumably established exceptions to the

---

[162] Preamble of the Revised Arab Charter on Human Rights, 22 May 2004, *reprinted in* 12 *Int'l Hum. Rts. Rep.* 893 (2005), entered into force 15 March 2008.
[163] 'UN News Centre, Arab rights charter deviates from international standards,' says UN official, www.un.org/apps/news/story.asp?NewsID=25447&Cr=human&Cr=rights <last visited 10 May 2008>.
[164] The Arab Charter, Article 2.

prohibition on the armed struggle by peoples claiming the right to self-determination. Article 2 provides that:

1. All peoples have the right of self-determination and to control over their natural wealth and resources, and the right to freely choose their political system and to freely pursue their economic, social and cultural development.
2. All peoples have the right to national sovereignty and territorial integrity.
3. All forms of racism, Zionism and foreign occupation and domination constitute an impediment to human dignity and a major barrier to the exercise of the fundamental rights of peoples; all such practices must be condemned and efforts must be deployed for their elimination.
4. All peoples have the right to resist foreign occupation.

On the whole, the Charter appears to devote a considerable space for rights that are widely associated with universal human rights such as equality and non-discrimination. Article 3 establishes that:

1. Each State party to the present Charter undertakes to ensure to all individuals subject to its jurisdiction the right to enjoy the rights and freedoms set forth herein, without distinction on grounds of race, colour, sex, language, religious belief, opinion, thought, national or social origin, wealth, birth or physical or mental disability.
2. The States parties to the present Charter shall take the requisite measures to guarantee effective equality in the enjoyment of all the rights and freedoms enshrined in the present Charter in order to ensure protection against all forms of discrimination based on any of the grounds mentioned in the preceding paragraph.
3. Men and women are equal in respect of human dignity, rights and obligations within the framework of the positive discrimination established in favour of women by the Islamic Shariah, other divine laws and by applicable laws and legal instruments. Accordingly, each State party pledges to take all the requisite measures to guarantee equal opportunities and effective equality between men and women in the enjoyment of all the rights set out in this Charter.

Reference to non-discrimination on the basis of religious belief is worthy of appreciation in this regional context, where religious affiliations continue to carry great weight. Similarly, and perhaps more significantly, reference to non-discrimination on the basis of physical and mental disability must be acknowledged as a highly positive step given the considerable disadvantages faced by the individuals suffering from disabilities.

The provisions of Article 3(3) contain seeds of ambiguity. While affirming its commitment towards universal human rights, this Charter provision argues for gender equality within the 'framework of the positive discrimination established in favour of women by Islamic Shariah, other divine laws and by applicable laws and legal instruments'. As noted earlier, considerable debate surrounds the issue of women's rights in *Sharia*, and the ambiguity generated by such provisions render a legally binding document subject to substantial criticism.

Article 4 provides for derogations to a number of rights in times of public emergency that threaten the life of the nation. These derogations are, however, restricted firstly by limitations placed on the non-derogable nature of certain rights. Secondly, in the case of those rights which may be derogated from during times of public emergencies, States are required to make official pronouncements of such derogations. Thirdly, such measures must strictly be required by the exigencies of the situation; and fourthly, must never be inconsistent with other obligations undertaken by States parties including the obligation of non-discrimination on the grounds of race, colour, sex, language, religion or social origin. Finally, a State party making such a derogation must notify other States parties through the offices of the Secretary General the provisions which are being derogated from and subsequently the date on which that State shall terminate the derogation.

The Charter follows the pattern of other international instruments in providing and safeguarding key individual rights such as the right to life;[165] the right not to be subjected to torture, inhuman or degrading treatment;[166] the right to be free from slavery;[167] and the right to liberty and security of the person.[168] At the same time, the Charter's provisions contain ambiguities and uncertainty. These include difficulties in articulating the meaning of 'inherent' right of life or arbitrary deprivation of life. The ambiguous nature of Article 7(1) which states that, '[s]entence of death shall not be imposed on persons under 18 years of age, unless otherwise stipulated in the laws in force at the time of the commission of the crime', means a person at any age under 18 might be sentenced to death if so stipulated by law. It implies that even a child might be sentenced to death which clearly contradicts universal principles of human rights and grants States a right to sentence anyone to death at any age if he or she meets the above mentioned criteria. Torture, cruel, inhuman or degrading treatment or punishment remains impermissible and yet as we shall analyse, many States in the region retain punishments which would, according to the Committee against Torture, violate the provisions of the Convention against Torture.[169]

Another set of rights cover the rules of justice including equality before the law, due process and the right to a fair trial. Article 12 affirms the principle of equality for all before the law.[170] It places obligations on States parties to ensure an independent and impartial judicial system with a right of a legal remedy for all. The right of equality before courts of law and the corresponding right of fair trial and innocence until proven guilty are articulated by Article 13 and 16 respectively.[171] A further group of rights include such rights as the right to freedom of movement;[172] right of respect for private and family life;[173] rights of minorities;[174] the right of political asylum;[175] liberty of thought, belief and religion;[176] the right to private property;[177] the right of information and liberty of opinion, expression and

---

[165] Ibid. Articles 5, 6 and 7.
[166] Ibid. Article 8.
[167] Ibid. Article 10.
[168] Ibid. Article 14.
[169] See below chapter 22.
[170] The Arab Charter, Article 12.
[171] Ibid. Article 13 and 16.
[172] Ibid. Article 26.
[173] Ibid. Article 33.
[174] Ibid. Article 25.
[175] Ibid. Article 28.
[176] Ibid. Article 30.
[177] Ibid. Article 31.

research;[178] and the right to full consent to marriage.[179] The Article on the rights of minorities, Article 25, appears to be in consonance with general international law provisions in that individuals belonging to minorities are accorded rights including the right to profess and practice their own religion. The apparently broad nature of the right is certainly an improvement on a historically narrow interpretation of the rights of religious minorities under classical Islamic doctrine.[180]

Article 26 which relates to the right of freedom of movement, however, has been the subject of criticism in its restriction on 'the right to freedom of movement and to freely choose his residence' as such actions must be 'in conformity with the laws in force'. The criticism has focused around the sanctification of national regulations – Saudi Arabia – a case in point, where freedom of movement for women is restricted on the basis of a certain interpretation of the *Sharia*.[181] The Charter, therefore, unfortunately does not rectify many of the contradictions which were generated by Arab States in placing reservations on Article 15(4) of the Convention on the Elimination of All Forms of Discrimination Against Women (1979) that requires States to 'accord to men and women the same rights with regard to the law relating to the movement of persons and the freedom to choose their residence and domicile'.

In addition to the established civil and political rights, the Charter also contains a number of economic, social and cultural rights. These include the right to work;[182] the right to form trade unions;[183] the right to social security;[184] and the right to an adequate standard of living.[185] Finally, there are the so-called third generation rights. The right to development, an otherwise controversial right in the context of general international law, is accorded the elevated status of 'a fundamental human right'.[186]

A positive initiative is the recognition of the rights of persons with mental and physical disability within the Charter.[187] As shall be considered in a subsequent chapter, it is only recently that the international community has begun to appreciate the concerns emerging from the violations of the rights of peoples with disabilities and, therefore, the incorporation of Article 40 is to be welcomed. Article 40 provides:

1. The States parties undertake to ensure to persons with mental or physical disabilities a decent life that guarantees their dignity, and to enhance their self-reliance and facilitate their active participation in society.

2. The States parties shall provide social services free of charge for all persons with disabilities, shall provide the material support needed by those persons, their families or the families caring for them, and shall also do whatever is needed to avoid placing those persons in institutions. They shall in all cases take account of the best interests of the disabled person.

---

[178] Ibid. Article 32.
[179] Ibid. Article 33(1).
[180] See earlier discussion in relation to Universal Islamic Declaration of Human Rights.
[181] Rishmawi, above n.159, at p. 367.
[182] The Arab Charter, Article 34.
[183] Ibid. Article 35.
[184] Ibid. Article 36.
[185] Ibid. Article 38.
[186] Ibid. Article 37.
[187] Ibid. Article 40.

3. The States parties shall take all necessary measures to curtail the incidence of disabilities by all possible means, including preventive health programmes, awareness raising and education.

4. The States parties shall provide full educational services suited to persons with disabilities, taking into account the importance of integrating these persons in the educational system and the importance of vocational training and apprenticeship and the creation of suitable job opportunities in the public or private sectors.

5. The States parties shall provide all health services appropriate for persons with disabilities, including the rehabilitation of these persons with a view to integrating them into society.

6. The States parties shall enable persons with disabilities to make use of all public and private services.

The Charter represents a step forward in comparison with a previous version, yet there are certain gaps that need to be filled. These gaps are caused by the fragmented nature of legislation where democracy and the rule of law are yet to flourish adequately. Furthermore, the Arab States still have not clarified the position of Islam in their legislation, even though the majority of their constitutions declare Islam as a source of legislation. They have not identified the areas where Islam plays a primary role; whether it is public or private law. Only after these gaps are filled will Arab States be able to enforce the present Charter correctly. One major point of criticism which is carried over from the previous version of the Charter is the lack of an effective enforcement mechanism. The Charter provides for the establishment of an Expert Committee consisting of seven members.[188] The Committee receives periodic reports from States parties,[189] although there are no mechanisms for individual complaints similar in nature to the European, American and African regional human rights systems. This has been recognised as:

a major constraint on guaranteeing effective access to justice for victims, especially as most Arab countries have yet to sign up to the UN complaints systems, although a number of them are subject to the complaints mechanism of the African Charter on Human and Peoples' Rights 1982.[190]

The prospects of establishing an Arab Court of Human Rights are simply too remote at this stage. Despite being a non-religious document the Charter also has a distinct Islamic flavour, reflecting the State religion of all of the League's Member States. While not as clearly grounded in Islam as the Cairo Declaration, '[r]egrettably, this conservatism of the Cairo Declaration is actually reflected in some of the substantive provisions of the revised Charter'.[191] This conservatism is reflected in provisions effecting women such as Article 3(3) and Article 26. However, this is not necessarily reflective of the approach of the majority of Arab States, with one commentator expressing the view that

---

[188] Ibid. Article 45(1).
[189] Ibid. Article 48.
[190] Rishmawi, above n.159, at p. 365.
[191] Ibid. at p. 367.

> [i]t is disappointing that the Charter adopted the lowest common denominator rather than the most progressive interpretation.[192]

Notwithstanding the various substantive and procedural limitations, the Arab Charter is a significant step in the right direction – having established an acceptable framework it should be possible to consolidate substantive and procedural matters through additional and subsequent protocols.

4 SOUTH-ASIA AND HUMAN RIGHTS LAW[193]

> Like embroidery, regional co-operation will have to be fashioned patiently, stitch by stitch. The strength of the fabric will be determined by the weakest of the threads.[194]

South Asia is beset with ethnic, religious, and domestic political conflicts persistently leading to substantial violations of human rights.[195] There is an economic and political imbalance, resulting in the abuse of individual and collective rights, poverty, hunger, malnutrition, illiteracy, and environmental degradation. There are considerable violations of the rights contained in the Universal Declaration of Human Rights and the International Covenants.[196] Against the backdrop of the enormous complications faced by South Asia, this discussion considers the issues pertaining to the protection and promotion of human rights. A particular focus is upon the South Asian Association for Regional Cooperation (SAARC) which, it is contended, is an organisation capable of providing a suitable platform for peaceful dialogue within South-Asia.[197]

(i) The South-Asian mosaic and the enormity of problems

Aspirations of peace, security and respect for human rights within South Asia are confounded by the enormity of the region's historical and political problems. The political geography of the region reflects the mosaic and heterogeneous character of the nations from which it is formed.[198] South Asia stretches from the Durrand line (which separated British India from Afghanistan) in the north-west to the Burmese border in the east, from the Himalayas in the north to Dondra Head in Southern Sri Lanka. This densely inhabited

---

[192] Ibid. at p. 368.

[193] Yamazaki, 'Human Rights Conditions and Human Rights Movement in the Asian Region' 10 *Kagawa Law Review* (1990) 211.

[194] The late Rajiv Gandhi, Prime Minister of India, Bangalore (Public Statement), 18 November 1986.

[195] See Rehman and Roy 'South-Asia' in World Directory of Minorities (eds), *World Directory of Minorities* (Minority Rights Group, 1997) at pp. 535–587.

[196] The International Bill of Rights consists of the *Universal Declaration of Human Rights*, GA Res. 217A (III), UN Doc. A/810 at 71 (1948), the International Covenant on Civil and Political Rights, New York, 16 December 1966 United Nations, 999 U.N.T.S. 171; 6 I.L.M. (1967) 368 and the International Covenant on Economic, Social and Cultural Rights, New York, 16 December 1966, 993 U.N.T.S. 3; 6 I.L.M. (1967) 360.

[197] See Ahson, *SAARC: A Perspective* (Bangladesh, 1992); Bokhari, 'South Asian Regional Cooperation: Progress, Problems, Potential and Prospects' 35 *Asian Survey* (1985) 371; Muni, 'SARC: Building Regionalism From Below' 35 *Asian Survey* (1985) 391.

[198] Rehman and Roy, 'South–Asia', above n.195, at p. 534; Rehman, 'Re-Assessing the Right to Self-Determination: Lessons from the Indian Experience' 29 *Anglo-American Law Review* (2000) 454–475.

region has a population of approximately one fifth of the World's total population, and is concentrated in about 3 per cent of the total land mass.[199] A distinctive history is attached to South Asia. The region has the most ancient of the World's civilisations and is the birth-place of two of the most widely practised world religions.[200] South Asia has braced waves of invaders, refugees and immigrants and has a greater number of followers of Islam than in any other country of the Middle East or North Africa. With more languages spoken than the entire continent of Europe and having a population larger than Africa and Latin America combined, South Asia resembles a continent rather than a set of countries.[201] The picture is extremely complex and bewildering: peoples are segregated on the basis of their castes and creeds, their social order and rank in life determined at the time of birth. There exist extremes of poverty, deprivation and hopelessness and yet South Asia, in many ways, discloses an aesthetically rich and peaceful social order. Religions splinter into denomina-tions of sects and factions, languages branch out into dialects and the ethnic equation is imbalanced, with peoples of different colours and shades living next to each other.

The South Asian mosaic has also been a source of some of the gravest tragedies of human history, with a legacy of terrorism, violation of human rights and continuing threats to regional and international peace and security. The partition of British India and the emergence of Pakistan and India in 1947 were accompanied by the largest inter-country transfer of population of the 20th century.[202] Almost a million people were killed during this period. Approximately eight million people migrated from India to Pakistan, while there was a similar exodus of Hindus and Sikhs from Pakistan to India.[203] What happened in India and Pakistan led to further decolonisation. Ceylon (which adopted the name Sri Lanka in 1972) and Burma gained independence in 1948 and the Maldives in 1965.[204] The new States that emerged, in common with those that had not been directly colonised, such as Afghanistan and Nepal, have had to face serious issues affecting peace, security and human rights. The existence of arbitrary boundaries; the absence of sound political cul-tures; the suppression of values including democracy and human rights; and the repression of ethnic, religious and linguistic communities have all contributed to threats to peace; extremism in Afghanistan and in Kashmir; the repression of Bengalis of East Pakistan; the scarcity of rule of law in Pakistan, Bhutan, Nepal and India; and the discriminatory practices against the Tamils of Sri Lanka present some of the unfortunate examples.[205]

11

Additional human rights mechanisms

---

[199] Ali, *A New History of India and Pakistan* (Pakistan Book Centre, 1992); 'South Asia Poorer Than Black Africa' *Times* 2 May 1997.

[200] Hinduism and Buddhism.

[201] Rehman and Roy, 'South–Asia', above n.195, at pp. 534–537.

[202] For historical surveys in English see Collins and Lapierre, *Freedom at Midnight* (Collins, 1975); Kuper, *Genocide: Its Political Use in the Twentieth Century* (Yale University Press, 1981); Moon, *Divide and Quit* (Chatto & Windus, 1962); Khosla, *Stern Reckoning: A Survey of the Events Leading up to and Following the Partition of India* (Oxford University Press, 1989); Ghai, *The Partition of the Punjab 1849–1947* (Munshiram Manoharlal Publishers, 1986).

[203] Souza and Crisp, *The Refugee Dilemma* (Minority Rights Group, 1985) at p. 6; Rehman, 'Self-Determination, State-Building and the Muhajirs: An International Legal Perspective of the Role of the Indian Muslim Refugees in the Constitutional Developments of Pakistan' 3 *Contemporary South Asia* (1994) at p. 111; Whitaker *et al.*, *The Biharis in Bangladesh* (Minority Rights Group, 1977) at p. 7.

[204] See Rehman and Roy 'South-Asia', above n.195, at p. 534.

[205] On Tamils see Schwarz, *The Tamils of Sri Lanka* (Minority Rights Group, 1988); on minority rights in Pakistan see Rehman, above n.137; on indigenous peoples rights within South Asia see Rehman, 'Indigenous Peoples at Risk: A Survey of Indigenous Peoples of South Asia' in Burman and Verghese (eds), *Aspiring To Be: The Tribal, Indigenous Condition* (Konark Publishers, 1998) pp. 72–121; Ali and Rehman, *Indigenous Peoples and Ethnic Minorities of Pakistan: Constitutional and Legal Perspectives* (Routledge, 2001).

Several factors have led to the non-fulfilment of basic guarantees provided by several of the constitutions of the South Asian region. These include the suspension of fundamental rights as a result of military and civilian dictatorships (e.g. the Indian Emergency 1975–77) and also a lack of political will to substantially implement the progressive legislation contained within the constitutional frameworks. A cursory survey of the States in the region reveals a range of assimilative strategies such as the treatment of Bengalis in Pakistan that amounted to a complete annihilation of a civilisation, culture and language.[206] In Nepal and Bhutan there is considerable evidence of the forced assimilation of minorities.[207] Attempts to subjugate the Nepali-speaking Southern Bhutanese and to eradicate their culture, along with other repressive measures, have resulted in the creation of more than 100,000 refugees. Pakistan and Bangladesh have had long periods of military dictatorships, which prevented any autonomous development on the part of ethnic minorities and indigenous peoples. Additionally, the emphasis on an Islamic system of government, and its associated rhetoric, continues to be used to repress the rights of religious minorities.[208]

(ii) International and regional institutions and difficulties in protecting and promoting human rights: case studies of East Pakistan and Kashmir

(a) East Pakistan

The nine-month civil war in Pakistan (March–December 1971) resulted not only in grave violations of human rights, but also conceived the first (and until recently the only) successful secessionist movement of the post-colonial era.[209] It is alleged that the conflict resulted in one to three million civilian deaths, with the civil war creating 10 million refugees.[210] Throughout the conflict, while the United Nations Security Council remained bitterly divided, unwilling and unable to take any form of action, the deliberations of the General Assembly and other United Nations organs reflected a concern more for State sovereignty than regional peace and security or the protection of human rights. The government of Pakistan remained adamant that the situation in East Pakistan was confined to Article 2(7) of the United Nations Charter; essentially a matter for the domestic jurisdiction for Pakistan. The majority of the States within the United Nations Security Council and the General Assembly agreed with the argument advanced by Pakistan.[211]

---

[206] See Nanda, 'Self-Determination in International Law: The Tragic Tale of Two Cities – Islamabad (West Pakistan) and Dacca (East Pakistan)' 66 *AJIL* (1972) 321; Nanda, 'A Critique of the United Nations inaction in Bangladesh Crisis' 49 *Denver Law Journal* (1972) 53.

[207] Stokke, 'Nepal' in *Human Rights in Developing Countries Yearbook, 1993* (Nordic Human Rights Publications, 1993); Skar, 'Nepal, Indigenous Issues and Civil Rights: the Plight of Rana Tharu' in Barnes, Gray and Kingsbury (eds), *Indigenous Peoples of Asia* (Association of Asian Studies, 1995) pp. 173–194; Dhakal and Strawn, *Bhutan: A Movement in Exile* (Nerala Publications, 1994); US Department of State, *Bhutan: Released by the Bureau of Democracy, Human Rights, and Labor* (US Department of State, 2004).

[208] See Rehman and Roy 'South-Asia', above n.195, at pp. 534–537.

[209] Jahan, *Pakistan: Failure in National Integration* (Columbia University Press, 1972); Choudhury, 'Bangladesh: Why it Happened' (1972) 48 *International Affairs*, 242; Noman, *Pakistan: A Political and Economic History Since 1947* (Kegan Paul International, 1990).

[210] Mascarenhas, *The Rape of Bangladesh* (Vikas Publications, 1971); Macdermot, 'Crimes Against Humanity in Bangladesh' 7 *International Lawyer* (1973) 476.

[211] International Commission of Jurists, *The Events of East Pakistan: A Legal Study* (Geneva) 1972, at 85. Salzberg, 'UN Prevention of Human Rights Violations: The Bangladesh Case' 27 *International Organization* (1973) at 115; According to the then United States Ambassador to the UN, George Bush, the Pakistani military action in March 'does not justify the actions of India in intervening militarily and places in jeopardy the territorial integrity and political independence of its neighbour Pakistan'. S/VP. 1611 (12 December 1971) at 11.

There were serious political differences on the issue of East Pakistan in the Security Council and it was 'seized' of the matter only after active hostilities broke out between India and Pakistan in December 1971 – nine months after the civil war had started. Ultimately, when it did begin its deliberations on 4 December 1971, the political and ideological differences immediately came to surface. The issue became a pawn in the hands of the major powers, with the United States and China supporting Pakistan and asking for an immediate cease-fire and Indian military withdrawal, and the Soviets siding with India and insisting on immediate political settlement in East Pakistan. Ultimately, these political and ideological differences prevented any form of action with a Resolution drafted by the Soviet Union failing to be adopted.[212]

Given this *impasse* in the Security Council, the matter was then referred to by the General Assembly, which could take action under the Uniting for Peace Resolution.[213] There was a sense of urgency in the General Assembly and a strong consensus on the ways things should operate. It must, however, be noted that this consensus suggests that the prime concern of the members was upon the insistence of the territorial integrity, and the retention of the status quo at the expense of democracy, human rights and regional peace and security.[214] A similarly disappointing approach was adopted by the UN Commission on Human Rights and the Sub-Commission on the Prevention of Minorities and Protection of Human Rights (now replaced by the Human Rights Council and the Human Rights Council's Advisory Committee respectively).[215] The East Pakistan saga also led to the eventual involvement of the International Court of Justice. Prior to the independence of India, British India was a member of the Permanent Court of International Justice, predecessor to the present day International Court of Justice. By virtue of their membership of the United Nations, both India and Pakistan are *ipso facto* members of the Court. On 9 July 1949, Pakistan made the declaration under Article 36(2) of the Statute of Court accepting the compulsory jurisdiction of the Court.[216]

India has continued with the Declaration made by British India, whose obligations it inherited after independence in 1947.[217] Proceedings before the International Court were instituted by the Pakistani government against India as a tactical move to obtain the release of its prisoners of war and to prevent any trials for genocide. Pakistan relied upon Article 41 and Article 66 of the Statute and the Rules of the Court, and pending the decision on the merits of the case, the Pakistani government sought the following interim measures:[218]

----

[212] United Nations (Draft) Security Council Resolution S/10428 (6 December 1971).

[213] Uniting for Peace Resolution (adopted 3 November 1950) UN GA Res. 377(V), GAOR, 5th Sess. Supp. 20, at 10. For a consideration of the value of the Resolution in International Law see above chapter 3.

[214] Kuper, *The Prevention of Genocide* (Yale University Press, 1985) at p. 58.

[215] On Human Rights Council and its Advisory Committee, see above chapter 3.

[216] Article 36(2) of the Statute of the International Court of Justice, 26 June 1945, 59 Stat. 1055, 3 Bevans 1179 provides as follows: 'The states parties to the present Statute may at any time declare that they recognize as compulsory ipso facto and without special agreement, in relation to any other state accepting the same obligation, the jurisdiction of the Court in all legal disputes concerning: a. the interpretation of a treaty; b. any question of international law; c. the existence of any fact which, if established, would constitute a breach of an international obligation; d. the nature or extent of the reparation to be made for the breach of an international obligation.'

[217] Hussain, above n.26 at p. 202.

[218] See *The Trial of Pakistani Prisoners of War (Pakistan v. India)* [1973] ICJ Pleadings pp. 3–7.

Additional human rights mechanisms

11

(a) That the process of repatriation of prisoners of war and civilian internees in accordance with international law, which has already begun, should not be interrupted by virtue of charges of genocide against a certain number of individuals detained by India.

(b) That such individuals, who are in the custody of India and are charged with alleged acts of genocide, should not be transferred to 'Bangladesh' for trial till such time as Pakistan's claim to exclusive jurisdiction and the lack of any other Government or authority in this respect has been adjudged by the Court.

The case before the International Court of Justice proved short-lived. The case did not proceed to a discussion of the merits.[219] It was settled by an agreement between India and Pakistan in August 1973, leading Pakistan to drop the case against India.[220] Through a subsequent agreement involving India, Pakistan and Bangladesh (signed in Delhi on 7 April 1974) it was agreed that no trials for crimes against humanity or genocide were to be conducted; all outstanding issues were to be resolved through diplomatic channels instead of having recourse to courts including the International Court of Justice.[221]

(b) The Kashmir conflict

Kashmir has a bitter and painful political history, the roots of the conflict going back to the partition of India in 1947.[222] The main constitutional instruments for determining the future position of the princely states such as Kashmir was the Indian Independence Act of 1947, section 7(1)(b) of which provided that:

The suzerainty of His Majesty over the Indian States lapses, and with it, all treaties and agreements in force at the date of the passing of this Act between His Majesty and the rulers of the Indian states, all functions exercisable by His Majesty at the date with respect to Indian states or the rulers thereof and all powers, rights, authority or jurisdiction exercisable by His Majesty at that date in or in relation to Indian states, by treaty, grant usage, sufferance or otherwise.[223]

Notwithstanding the presence of a number of complexities surrounding the issue of succession, the strict legal position appears to be that with the lapse of the treaties and agreements with the British government, sovereignty reverted to the princely States which then had the options of accession, merger and integration with the Dominions of India or Pakistan.[224] In practice, however, the vast majority of States decided to accede to India or Pakistan before the Indian Independence Act came into force on 15 August 1947.[225] In the

[219] Ibid. at p. 1; for commentary see Levie, 'Legal Aspects of the Continued Detention of Pakistani Prisoners of War by India' 67 *AJIL* (1973) 512.

[220] Paust and Blaustein, 'War Crimes Jurisdiction and Due Process: The Bangladesh Experience' 11 *Vanderbilt Journal of Transnational Law* (1978), 1; Press Release, 17 April 1973 reprinted in Paust and Blaustein, *War Crimes Jurisdiction and Due Process: A Case Study of Bangladesh* (Unpublished Documents, 1974) at p. 54; India–Pakistan Agreement on Repatriation of Prisoners of War (1973) 12 ILM at (1973) 1080–1084.

[221] Paust and Blaustein, 'War Crimes Jurisdiction and Due Process: The Bangladesh Experience', above n.220, at p. 1.

[222] Lamb, *Kashmir: A Disputed Legacy, 1846–1990* (Roxford Books, 1991); Azmi, *Kashmir: An Unparalleled Curfew* (Panfwain Printing Press, 1990); Ataov, *Kashmir and Neighbours: Tale, Terror, Truce* (Ashgate, 2002).

[223] For the text of the Act see Mahmood, *Constitutional Foundations of Pakistan* (Jang Publishers, 1989) at p. 31.

[224] Ibid. pp. 31–33.

[225] See Poulose, *Succession in International Law A Study of India, Pakistan, Ceylon and Burma* (Orient Longman, 1974) at pp. 30–56.

case of the State of Jammu and Kashmir, the Hindu ruler of a Muslim majority state vacillated in making a decision as to whether to accede to India or Pakistan. His hesitation and indecisiveness provided the opportunity for an 'invasion' of the territory by the so-called 'Azad Kashmir Army' made up of some of the tribal peoples of Pakistan. Under the pressure of this invasion, in October 1947, the ruler of Jammu and Kashmir decided to appeal to India for help and acceded to India. The accession to India took place on the condition that, on the restoration of order, a referendum would be held in order for the people to determine their political destiny.[226] Indian troops were rushed into the territory and stopped the advance of the tribal army from Pakistan. The Line of Control established as a result of this action became the border between India and Pakistan, and also the line dividing the territory of Jammu and Kashmir between the Indian and Pakistani jurisdictions.

Jammu and Kashmir was subsequently to become a victim of the proxy war between India and Pakistan with the Kashmiri people becoming the main victims of this conflict. If there is to be criticism of Pakistan's insistence upon Article 2(7) provisions of the United Nations Charter in East Pakistan, India has adopted a not too dissimilar approach to accusations of its violations of fundamental human rights in Kashmir.[227] Despite the protracted nature of the conflict, the role of the United Nations was ineffective. On 1 January 1948 India took the question of Kashmir before the United Nations Security Council with a formal complaint against Pakistan. India's complaint was lodged under Article 35 of Chapter VI, a Chapter (as noted in our earlier discussion) dealing with 'Pacific Settlement of Disputes'.[228] The subject of the complaint soon got entangled by claims of aggression and counter-claims of genocide. The Security Council, in its response adopted two resolutions. In its first Resolution of 17 January 1948 the Security Council asked both the governments to refrain from aggravating the situation and to appraise the Security Council of any material changes to the situation.[229] By its second Resolution of 20 January 1948, the Council established a Commission (the United Nations Commission for India and Pakistan – UNCIP). The UNCIP consisted of three members, one nominated by India, another by Pakistan and the third by the two States. The number was increased to five, two nominated by each State. The UNCIP, based on its views and detailed negotiations with the two protagonists, adopted two resolutions.[230] The essence of these resolutions adopted on 13 August 1948 and 5 January 1949, was the withdrawal of troops, demilitarisation of

---

[226] On 27 October, 1947, Lord Mountbatten, the then Governor-General of India, in accepting the Kashmir Maharaja's offer of accession of the state with India noted as follows: 'In the special circumstances mentioned by your Highness, my Government has decided to accept the accession of Kashmir State to the Dominion of India. In consistence with their policy that, in the case of any State where the issue of accession has been the subject of dispute, the question of accession should be decided in accordance with the wishes of the peoples of the State, it is my Government's wish that, as soon as law and order have been restored in Kashmir and her soil cleared of the invader, the question of the State's accession should be settled by a reference to the people.' Letter of His Highness the Governor-General of India addressed to His Highness the Maharaja of Jammu and Kashmir, 27 October 1947 cited in Hasan (ed.), *Documents on the Foreign Relations of Pakistan: The Kashmir Question* (Pakistan Institute of International Affairs, 1966) at pp. 57–58.

[227] Article 2(7) of the Charter provides: 'Nothing contained in the present Charter shall authorize the United Nations to intervene in matters which are essentially within the domestic jurisdiction of any state or shall require the Members to submit such matters to settlement under the present Charter; but this principle shall not prejudice the application of enforcement measures under Chapter VII.'

[228] For legal analysis of validity of Security Council's Resolution's under Chapter VI see above chapter 3.

[229] Resolution adopted at the Two Hundred and Twenty-Ninth meeting of the Security Council 17 January 1948 (S/651).

[230] For the text of these Resolutions see Sharma and Bakshi (eds), *Kashmir and the United Nations* (Anmol Publications, 1995) at pp. 44–48.

the region, and the future of the territory to be decided through a free and impartial plebiscite.[231] None of the objectives laid down by the UNCIP could, however, be achieved. India, in the meanwhile, has progressed towards a complete accession of Kashmir, through the use of the Kashmir Constituent Assembly. Despite the conflict being the source of two wars (1947–49 and 1965), a threat to peace and security (most recently in 1999), and encouraging terrorism and fundamentalism, the Security Council has never undertaken binding action under Chapter VII of the UN Charter. On its part, India claims to have satisfied the right to self-determination, through local elections and using the Kashmir Constituent Assembly as the ultimate constitutional mouthpiece. India continues to accuse Pakistan of continued military support of the 'Azad Kashmir Army' and of encouraging militancy and terrorism in the region.[232] Pakistan in turn, lays the blame upon India for the denial of the right of self-determination to the people of Kashmir.[233]

The lack of enthusiasm of both India and Pakistan to resolve the dispute through peaceful means is also evident in their reluctance to approach the International Court of Justice. Both India and Pakistan have accepted the compulsory jurisdiction of the Court, although their accompanying declarations are very restrictive in scope. Pakistan's declaration pursuant to Article 36(2) excludes from the jurisdiction of the Court all disputes relating to questions which fall exclusively within the domestic jurisdiction of Pakistan.[234] A similar restrictive approach is adopted by India. In its most recent declaration entered upon on 15 September 1974, India excludes from the jurisdiction of the International Court of Justice, *inter alia*, those matters which are essentially within its domestic jurisdiction. In order to ensure that no challenges regarding international frontiers with Pakistan and Bangladesh are raised before the World Court, India's declaration excludes the Court's jurisdiction in respect of all disputes with present or previous Commonwealth Member States. Furthermore, the Court is denied jurisdiction in disputes 'relating to or connected with facts or situations of hostilities, armed conflicts, individual or collective actions taken in self-defence, resistance to aggression'[235] and disputes with India concerning or relating *inter alia* to its frontiers or any other matter concerning boundaries.[236] The intention of such a narrow and limited declaration is clearly to forestall efforts to have the Kashmir issue adjudicated by the World Court.

(iii) Regional mechanisms for the protection of human rights within South Asia: South Asian Association for Regional Co-operation (SAARC)

There is a great measure of accuracy in the observation made by Sands and Klein that 'Asia is characterised by a singular lack of regional organisations as compared with Europe, the Americas and Africa. The reasons for this are not entirely clear, although it may not be

---

[231] Resolution adopted at the meeting of the United Nations Commission for India and Pakistan on 5 January 1949 (Doc No. 5/1196, para 15, dated the 10 January 1949).

[232] Rehman 'South-Asia' in Green (ed.), *State of the World's Minorities* (Minority Rights Group, 2006) at p. 116.

[233] See Hussain, *Kashmir Dispute: An International Law Perspective* (National Institute of Pakistan Studies, 1998); Wirsing, 'Kashmir Conflict: The New Phase' in Kennedy (ed.), *Pakistan: 1992* (Westview Press Ltd, 1993) at pp. 133–165.

[234] See www.icj-cij.org/icjwww/ibasicdocuments/ibasictext/ibasicdeclarations.htm <last visited 20 May 2009> for the text of the Declaration.

[235] Ibid.

[236] Ibid.

unrelated to the broad range of geopolitical interests and cultural groupings within the region'.[237] The foremost regional organisation insofar as South Asia is concerned is the South Asian Association for Regional Co-operation (SAARC). SAARC, which consists of eight States of South Asia, and was formally established in December 1985.[238] While the idea of regional co-operation had been mooted for a considerable time, the foremost proponent of establishing such a South Asian organisation was the late President of Bangladesh, President Zia-ur-Rahman. President Zia-ur-Rahman was also responsible for producing a draft document, the blueprint for the new organisation. This document was analysed by the Foreign Ministers of seven States. Further deliberations over a document proposing the establishment of South-Asia regional organisation took place in New York during a summit in August–September 1980. Following further meetings in Kathmandu (November 1981), Islamabad (August 1982) and Dhaka (March 1983), a Foreign Ministerial meeting was organised in New Delhi in August 1983.[239] During the meeting held in New Delhi, the Foreign Ministers adopted a Declaration on South Asian Regional Cooperation with the induction of an Integrated Programme of Action, promising co-operation in Agriculture, Rural Development, Telecommunications, Meteorology and Health and Population Activities. The organisation itself was formally launched in Dhaka on 7–8 December 1985.[240] The Charter of SAARC has been formulated with the objective *inter alia* of promoting the welfare of the peoples of South-Asia through an improvement in the quality of their lives, to advance economic growth, progress at the social and cultural level, and to provide all individuals with the opportunity to live in dignity and to realise their full potential; to encourage trust, mutual understanding, collective self-reliance and appreciation of each other's existence. With a firm agenda based on regional cooperation, SAARC as an organisation is committed to sovereign equality and the resolution of disputes through peaceful means.[241]

(iv) Institutions of SAARC

The institutions of SAARC are multi-layered with the highest authority conferred to the Summit consisting of Heads of State or Governments. The Summit, designed to meet annually has thus far had 15 meetings, the latest being held in Colombo from 2–3 August 2008.[242] The Council of Ministers, which consists of Foreign Ministers of Member States, has the principal responsibility for reviewing existing policies and devising new strategies for further cooperation.[243] The Council is mandated to meet twice each year, with the possibility of extraordinary sessions.[244] The Standing Committee, which consists of Foreign

---

[237] Sands and Klein, above n.1, at p. 227.

[238] The current membership of SAARC comprises of Bangladesh, Bhutan, India, Maldives, Nepal, Pakistan and Sri Lanka. On 3 April 2007, Afghanistan became the eighth SAARC member.

[239] See Information and Publications Division, *From SARC to SAARC: Milestones in the Evolution of Regional Cooperation in South-Asia* (vol. 1 and vol. 2) (1990). *From SARC to SAARC: Milestones of Regional Cooperation in South-Asia* (vol. 1 and vol. 2) (Nepal, 1990).

[240] www.saarc-sec.org/ <last visited 13 May 2009>; Kashyap, (ed.) *SAARC* (Lok Sabha Secretariat, 1988) at pp. 7–11; Bhargara, Nongartz and Sobhan (eds), *Shaping South Asia's Future: Role of Regional Co-operation* (Vikas Publishing House, 1995).

[241] The full text of the SAARC Charter can be found at: www.saarc-sec.org/data/docs/charter.pdf <last visited 30 April 2009>.

[242] www.saarc-sec.org/?t=1 <last visited 13 May 2009>.

[243] Article IV(1) Saarc Charter.

[244] Ibid. Article IV(2).

Additional human rights mechanisms

Secretaries, has the overall responsibility for monitoring and co-ordination of projects and programmes.[245] The Committee is also in charge of financing these projects, and initiating further measures for co-operation.[246] There have, thus far, been 35 sessions of the Committee, the most recent one being held in Colombo in July 2008.[247] A programme Committee consisting of senior civil servants has been established to assist the Standing Committee for scrutinising the budget and for finalising its activities. In order to achieve the objectives, as outlined in the Charter, a range of so-called Technical Committees were set up.[248] The Technical Committees plan specialised projects and programmes and have responsibility for monitoring implementation. The seven Technical Committees currently cover Agriculture and Rural Development; Health and Population Activities; Women, Youth and Children; Environment and Forestry; Science and Technology and Meteorology; Human Resources Development; and Energy.[249] In order to facilitate the implementation of the Technical Committees, a number of Regional Centres were set up. These include the SAARC Agricultural Information Centre (SAIC), SAARC Tuberculosis Centre (STC), SAARC Documentation Centre (SDC), SAARC Meteorological Research Centre (SMRC), and SAARC Human Resources Development Centre (SHRDC).

In order to achieve its objectives relating to economic growth, SAARC has established a number of institutions and agreements, which include the Committee on Economic Cooperation, SAARC Preferential Trading Arrangement (SAPTA) and South Asian Free Trade Area (SAFTA). Many of the institutions, under the auspices of SAARC, may at first appear not directly relevant to the promotion and protection of human rights. On the other hand, several instruments adopted by SAARC deal with collective group rights or engage with subjects of human security and terrorism. Thus, SAARC has also provided the platform for a number of regional treaties, notably the Regional Convention on Suppression of Terrorism (1987),[250] SAARC Regional Convention on Narcotic Drugs and Psychotropic Substances (1990),[251] and the SAARC Convention on Prevention of Trafficking of Women and Children for Prostitution (2002).[252]

Notwithstanding existing differences, SAARC States have in principle come around to agreeing on some of the fundamental principles of human rights and group rights and in this regard the SAARC Regional Convention on the Suppression of Terrorism, deserves a particular mention.[253] This Convention also reaffirms the fundamental international law principles of *aut dedere aut judicare* for example Member States undertake to extradite or submit the alleged offender for the purpose of prosecution.[254] The city of Colombo is established as the base for STOMD (SAARC Terrorist Offences Monitoring Desk),

---

[245] Ibid. Article V(1)(a).

[246] Ibid. Article V(1)(b) and (e).

[247] See www.lankamussuib.org/content/view/597/9/ <last visited 30 January 2009>.

[248] Article VI Saarc Charter.

[249] See www.saarc-sec.org/t=2 <last visited 13 May 2009>. For a detailed consideration see Khan (ed.), *SAARC and the Superpowers* (University Press Ltd, 1991).

[250] 4 November 1987. Text available http://untreaty.un.org/English/Terrorism.asp <last visited 31 January 2009>.

[251] For text of the Convention see www.saarc-sec.org/publication/conv-narcotic.pdf <last visited 13 May 2009>.

[252] For text of the Convention see www.saarc-sec.org/publication/conv-traffiking.pdf <last visited 13 May 2009>.

[253] For the text of the Convention see Bassiouni, *International Terrorism* (Transnational Publishers, 2001) at p. 385.

[254] For an analysis of this principle and of terrorism in general international law see below chapter 24.

which collates, analyses and disseminates information about terrorist incidents, tactics and strategies. It is also to the credit of the Organisation that in its 12th summit (at Islamabad, 4–6 January 2004) the Council of Ministers signed the Additional Protocol to SAARC Regional Convention on the Suppression of Terrorism.[255] The primary objective of the Protocol is not only to prevent terrorist actions (such as those witnessed on 26–29 November 2008)[256] but also to eradicate all forms of the financing of terrorism.[257]

A further, possibly more tangible contribution of SAARC, is what has been termed as the 'Promotion of People-to-People Linkage'.[258] Despite their close regional proximity, many States of the region have traditionally shown an inbuilt distrust of each other. Communication has been difficult. Hurdles and artificial barriers exist in commerce, trade, and travel amongst citizens of these countries. In order to facilitate growth of trade and commerce, SAARC has established a Chamber of Commerce and Industry (SCCI). A scheme providing for visa-free travel for certain categories of individuals has been put in place, and a sub-group of SAARC lawyers and legal professionals called 'SAARCLAW' has been established with the view to bringing together the legal community for legal harmonisation. From this brief overview, it can be stated with confidence that in its limited lifespan SAARC has shown positive and constructive results. The achievements are particularly significant given the violent and turbulent geo-political history of the region. Having said that, in practice SAARC continues to be a minor player in so far as the resolution of regional disputes are concerned. The intransigence of the two larger States, Pakistan and India, over a number of issues including Kashmir has been a major disappointment. Similarly, SAARC has had an unimpressive record in dealing with notable conflicts such as those involving the Tamils in Sri Lanka, the Addivasis of the Chittagong Hill Tracts (in Bangladesh), Nepali-speaking Bhutanese (residing in Nepal) and the Maoist Rebels (in Nepal).[259]

5 ASSOCIATION OF SOUTH-EAST ASIAN NATIONS (ASEAN)

In contrast to Europe and Latin American, the East Asian regional movement has been described as 'both belated and limited'.[260] The reasons for this belated movement are varied and include 'persistence of Cold War divisions on the Korean peninsula and communist states in the region (China, Vietnam and North Korea); the diversity of cultures and levels of development, an absence of experience with cooperation; low levels of interdependence; and the absence of the idea that Asia-Pacific (or East Asia or the Pacific) might constitute a region'.[261]

In 1967 ASEAN was established by Indonesia, Singapore, Malaysia, the Philippines and Thailand. It was subsequently joined by Brunei Darussalam in 1984, and at the end of the

---

[255] www.saarc-sec.org/main.php?t=2.4 <last visited 13 May 2009>.

[256] BBC 'As it happened: Mumbai attacks 29 Nov' http://news.bbc.co.uk/1/hi/world/south_asia/7756073.stm <last visited 30 May 2009>.

[257] www.saarc-sec.org/main.php?t=2.4 <last visited 30 May 2009>.

[258] www.saarc-sec.org/ <last visited 30 May 2009>. Chapter 11 Promotion of People-to-People Linkage and SAARC Professional Associations.

[259] For a consideration of these conflicts see Rehman and Roy, 'South Asia', above n.195 at pp. 571–572.

[260] Karns and Mingst, n.1 above, p. 189.

[261] Ibid.

Additional human rights mechanisms

Cold War, Vietnam in 1995, Laos and Myanmar (Burma) in 1997 and Cambodia in 1999. The primary reasons behind the formation of the organisation were the promotion of regional security and economic development. ASEAN is based on the principle of non-intervention in the internal affairs of other Member States. Non-intervention does not necessarily mean non-involvement in others affairs: however, it does mean that States must refrain from criticing each other and providing no support to opposition movements. An important ASEAN working method is the process of informal consultation and consensus building as opposed to legal procedures. Importantly, if there is no consensus, the Members agree to disagree and continue by focusing upon cooperation in other areas. This serves the purpose of conflict avoidance as opposed to conflict resolution.

For the first two decades, the focus of the organisation was upon regional security and stability. The 1989 Manila Declaration marked a significant change in the focus of the Organisation through the setting up the ASEAN Plan of Action for Economic Cooperation. In 1992 Member States agreed to establish the ASEAN Free Trade Area (AFTA) within 15 years. This was subsequently shortened in 1994 to 11 years. In 1994, the ASEAN Regional Forum (ARF) was created in order to promote a multilateral security dialogue. The 1995 Bangkok Treaty created the South East Asian Nuclear Weapons Free Zone. In addition, following the setting up of Asian-Pacific Economic Cooperation, ASEAN initiated a series of dialogue programmes with outside powers, including the EU Member States, South Korea, China, India and Japan.

The Treaty of Amity and Cooperation provided for a High Council of Ministers to deal with disputes, however, this mechanism has never been used. The core structures provided for are the various ministerial level meetings that now extend well beyond the foreign and trade ministries. From the beginning of the millennium, ASEAN has expanded considerably its agenda including such spheres as human rights, social and public policies and the environment. How effective this, remains to be seen. Historically, ASEAN has never been a regional integration project, but in 2003, Singapore and Thailand, two of the economically strongest members proposed creating a common market. ASEAN has been involved in conflict management by avoiding dealing with regional protracted issues. Asian-Pacific Economic Cooperation was established in 1989 to facilitate intergovernmental dialogue on economic policy issues with the goal of sustaining growth and development. An important unstated purpose, especially for the Asian members, is to support a process of confidence-building amongst countries of the region that had no tradition of multilateral co-operation and were reluctant to create a regional organisation that might compete with ASEAN or lead to domination by the US or Japan. The annual summits have raised APEC's profile and reformed the idea of Asia-Pacific as a region.

Recently the Organisation has moved towards establishing a human rights mechanism to monitor human rights protection in the region. This was instigated by the 1993 UN Vienna Declaration and Program of Action, which raised the need 'to consider the possibility of establishing regional and sub-regional arrangements for the promotion and protection of human rights where they do not already exist'.[262] Both the ASEAN Inter-Parliamentary Organization and the Ministerial Meeting, in 1993, agreed that ASEAN should consider establishing such a regional human rights mechanism.[263] The Working Group for an

---

[262] See www.aseanhrmech.org/aboutus.html <last visited 20 May 2009>.
[263] Ibid.

ASEAN Human Rights Mechanism was subsequently established in Manila in 1995.[264] The culmination of the work of the Working Group has been the inclusion in the newly adopted ASEAN Charter of an article establishing such a human rights body. Article 14 of the Charter states:

1. In conformity with the purposes and principles of the ASEAN Charter relating to the promotion and protection of human rights and fundamental freedoms, ASEAN shall establish an ASEAN human rights body.
2. This ASEAN human rights body shall operate in accordance with the terms of reference to be determined by the ASEAN Foreign Ministers Meeting.[265]

The ASEAN Charter has now been ratified by all Member States of the Organisation, after Indonesia, Thailand and the Philippines deposited their instruments of ratification in November 2008. The Charter came into force in December 2008, and consequently, at the time of writing, it remains to be seen the effect that the Charter will have on the human rights protection in the region. 'The most controversial part of the charter is a proposed human rights body, details of which will be hammered out for approval at an ASEAN summit in Thailand, now scheduled to taken place in February [2008].'[266] While the details of the Human Rights Body are yet to be established as Phan correctly points out 'the ASEAN Charter is a treaty and Article 14 is a legal obligation, ASEAN states are bound to follow it. It is, however, too early for any sense of accomplishment'.[267] The draft Agreement on the Establishment of the ASEAN Human Rights Commission, from the Working Group in 2000 perhaps gives some indication of the format that the body will take.[268] The numerous suggestions include:

- A declaration of principles.
- A commission with monitoring, promotional, and recommendatory functions. It may also receive complaints from states and/or individuals. It may cover all rights, or initially, be issue-specific where it focused only on the rights of migrants or other vulnerable groups. Another option is having human rights commissions in all ASEAN countries. A mechanism can be born when they begin coordinating efforts.
- A court which could render binding decisions.[269]

The ASEAN vision 2020 reiterates further the commitment of the Organisation to human rights, placing emphasis on 'A Community of Caring Societies', particularly non-discrimination and social and economic rights.[270] Additionally, the vision states that:

---

[264] Ibid.
[265] ASEAN Charter www.aseansec.org/ASEAN-Charter.pdf <last visited 13 May 2009>.
[266] *International Herald Tribune*, 'Asean charter comes into force', www.iht.com/articles/ap/2008/12/15/asia/AS-ASEAN-Charter.php <last visited 13 May 2009>.
[267] Phan, 'The Evolution Towards an ASEAN Human Rights Body' 9 *Asia-Pacific Journal on Human Rights and the Law* (2008) 1, p. 11.
[268] Draft Agreement on the Establishment of the ASEAN Human Rights Commission www.aseanhrmech.org/downloads/draft-agreement.pdf <last visited 13 May 2009>.
[269] See www.aseanhrmech.org/aboutus.html <last visited 13 May 2009>.
[270] ASEAN Vision 2020 www.aseanhrmech.org/downloads/Asean-Vision-2020.pdf <last visited 13 May 2009>, pp. 3–4.

Additional human rights mechanisms

11

> We envision our nations being governed with the consent and greater participation of the people with its focus on the welfare and dignity of the human person and the good of the community.[271]

The Hanoi Plan of Action elaborated that in order to achieve ASEAN's goals it would be necessary to exchange information amongst the Member States in respect of human rights as well as to work towards the full implementation of international human rights standards in respect of women and children.[272]

In 2007 ASEAN established the Committee on the Implementation of the ASEAN Declaration on the Protection and Promotion of the Rights of Migrant Workers, reaffirming its commitment to human rights.[273] The Declaration on the Protection and Promotion of the Rights of Migrant Workers will be discussed in more depth in a later chapter.[274] The Declaration provides for both documented and undocumented migrant workers, and places obligations on receiving States, sending States and on ASEAN itself.[275] Paragraph 5 of the Declaration places receiving States under the obligation to '[i]ntensify efforts to protect the fundamental human rights, promote the welfare and uphold human dignity of migrant workers'.

As is evidenced by the above discussion, ASEAN has become increasingly involved and committed to human rights. The eventual establishment of a human rights body, with the competence to deal on a regional level with human rights violations will be a huge step forward for the Organisation. However, while ASEAN's commitment to human rights on paper has grown, it remains to be seen how effective its mechanisms will be, particularly in the light of some of its more repressive member States, such as Myanmar.

6 CONCLUSIONS

This chapter has considered a range of mechanisms and schemes involved with the promotion and protection of human rights. A survey was conducted of the Islamic scheme of human rights protection. While the egalitarian and humanitarian spirit of the *Sharia* becomes evident, a critical investigation into many of the issues also raises dissensions and inconsistencies amongst modern Islamic States, applications of the *Sharia*. As has been explored the position of women, religious minorities, and children generates considerable controversy in the context of the instruments adopted by Organisation of Islamic Conference as well as the League of Arab States. Within this context attempts to devise and apply human rights standards and the debate of universalism *vis-à-vis* cultural and religious relativism attains considerable significance.[276] In common with ASEAN and the EU, the

---

[271] Ibid. p. 4.
[272] ASEAN Hanoi Plan of Action. www.aseanhrmech.org/downloads/Hanoi-Plan-of-Action.pdf <last visited 13 May 2009>, paras 4.8–4.9.
[273] Selected Human Rights Documents, Statement of the Establishment of the ASEAN Committee on the Implementation of the ASEAN Declaration on the Protection and Promotion of the Rights of Migrant Workers, 8 *Asia-Pacific Journal on Human Rights and the Law* (2007) p. 112.
[274] See below chapter 19.
[275] Declaration on the Protection and Promotion of the Rights of Migrant Workers www.aseansec.org/19264.htm <last visited 13 May 2009>.
[276] For a consideration of these issues see above chapter 1.

objectives of SAARC are not only to promote political and economic collaboration but also include the promotion of regional and political stability. In this endeavour, and in contrast to both ASEAN and the EU, SAARC continues to remain less effective. One reason is the relative delay in the establishment of the organisation itself, though as Bhargara *et al.* elaborate there is an overarching psychological and cultural impediment. They note:

> ASEAN in 1967 and SAARC in 1985 adopted declarations at the political level which led to the founding of the two associations. Long before ASEAN was born, the people of South-East Asia had been conditioned to the culture of consensus. On the other hand, such a consensus was missing in South Asia, and SAARC started as an exercise in economic, social and cultural cooperation and excluded from its purview, bilateral and contentious issues.[277]

SAARC Member States continue to have significantly divergent perspectives on issues ranging from the role of religion and the armed forces in the governance of the State, constitutionalism, democracy and human rights. This form of diversity is not unique when compared to other regional organisations although possibly the greatest stumbling block in the development of SAARC is the protracted conflict and lack of trust between two of the most powerful member States – India and Pakistan. Amidst the organisational problems facing SAARC is the plethora of summits and meetings, which 'appear to be more of a fan fare than substantial, result oriented work'.[278] In common with financial difficulties being faced by the EU, ASEAN and other international and regional organisations, SAARC is confronted by substantial monetary shortages. However, in the case of SAARC, the situation is more acute since this organisation is almost entirely dependent on the financial support of India and Pakistan. A significant weakness in the work of SAARC is the absence of legislative powers, similar in nature to the European Parliament. An inability to challenge administrative, political and legal decisions made by South Asian States remains a fundamental defect in the system: there is no European style Court of Justice or Court of Human Rights; there are no effective enforcement procedures for the legal issues addressed by SAARC; and enforcement is largely dependent on the goodwill of Member States. While ASEAN is to establish a human rights body in the near future it remains to be seen what powers this body will have and how effective it will be.

The League of Arab States has recently made significant headway through the adoption of the Arab Charter on Human Rights. Despite the controversy surrounding elements of the Charter, particularly the references to Zionism, large parts of it compare favourably to international instruments such as the Universal Human Rights Declaration and the ICCPR. As with SAARC, the lack of an effective enforcement mechanism is of concern. The OIC Cairo Declaration has been described as 'a major compromise on human rights',[279] and due to its non-binding nature, is not a particularly effective method of protecting human rights. However, the 2004 OIC Covenant on the Rights of the Child and the move to establish an independent and permanent human rights commission on human rights in the 2008 Charter, marks a recent shift towards providing more comprehensive human rights protection.

---

[277] Bhargava, Bongartz and Sobhan, above n.240, p. 52.
[278] Muni, 'South-Asian Association for Regional Cooperation' in Khan (eds), *SAARC and the Superpowers* (Bangladesh University Press, 1991) pp. 55–73, at 64.
[279] See Rishmawi, above n.159, at p. 367.

Part IV

Group rights

12 Equality and non-discrimination[1]

1 INTRODUCTION

> Respect for human rights and fundamental freedoms without distinction of any kind is a fundamental rule of international human rights law. The speedy and comprehensive elimination of all forms of racism and racial discrimination, xenophobia and related intolerance is a priority task for the international community.[2]

The principles of equality and non-discrimination represent the twin pillars upon which the whole edifice of the modern international law of human rights is established. The claim to equality 'is in a substantial sense the most fundamental of the rights of man. It occupies the first place in most written constitutions. It is the starting point of all liberties'.[3] This chapter considers the various mechanisms adopted by the international community to develop equality and non-discrimination as an established principle of international and constitutional law. Notwithstanding the enormous significance of the norm of equality and non-discrimination within general international law, this chapter recommends a cautious and critical approach for a variety of reasons. Firstly, 'equality' and 'non-discrimination' are in themselves controversial terms with immense uncertainty as to their precise scope and content. Thus, according to one authority 'equality is a notion exposed to different philosophical interpretations; its meaning in the various legal systems is not always the same'.[4] Secondly, there is a substantial debate as to the means of creating real and meaningful equality. Should affirmative action policies be approved or even enforced as a means of

---

[1] See Banton, *International Action against Racial Discrimination* (Clarendon Press, 1996); Fredman, *Discrimination and Human Rights: The Case of Racism* (Oxford University Press, 2001); Gearty, 'The Internal and External "Other" in the Union Legal Order: Racism, Religious Intolerance and Xenophobia in Europe' in Alston (ed.), *The EU and Human Rights* (Oxford University Press, 1999) pp. 327–358; Keane, *Caste-based Discrimination in International Human Rights Law* (Ashgate, 2007); Lerner, *The UN Convention on the Elimination of All Forms of Racial Discrimination* (Sijthof & Noordhoff, 1980); Lerner, *Group Rights and Discrimination in International Law* (Martinus Nijhoff, 2003); McKean, *Equality and Discrimination under International Law* (Clarendon Press, 1983); Skogly, 'Article 2' in Alfredsson and Eide (eds), *The Universal Declaration of Human Rights: A Common Standard of Achievement* (Kluwer Law International, 1998) pp. 75–87; Van Dyke, *Human Rights, Ethnicity and Discrimination* (Greenwood Press, 1985); and Vierdag, *The Concept of Discrimination in International Law – With Special Reference to Human Rights* (Martinus Nijhoff, 1973).

[2] *Vienna Declaration and Programme of Action* (1993) UN Doc. A/49/668 (adopted 25 June, 1993), para 15.

[3] Lauterpacht, *An International Bill of the Rights of Man* (Columbia University Press, 1945) at p. 115.

[4] Lerner, *Group Rights and Discrimination*, above n.1, at p. 30. Craven, *The International Covenant on Economic, Social and Cultural Rights: A Perspective on its Development* (Clarendon Press, 1995) p. 154. Also see Judge Tanaka's dissenting opinion in *South West Africa* (Second Phase) 1966 ICJ Report 6.

overcoming past inequality? Thirdly, it is important to realise that international law has not progressed dramatically enough to eradicate all forms of discriminations. Various facets of discrimination, in particular discrimination on the basis of religion or belief and gender, remain neglected. The position in relation to gender-based discrimination is considered in Chapter 16. As regards the situation concerning discrimination on grounds of religion or belief, the picture is most depressing. Although there are references to religious non-discrimination in the United Nations Charter and the international bill of rights[5] (unlike racial or gender discrimination) it has not been possible to draft a specific treaty condemning discrimination based on religion or belief.

2 EQUALITY AND NON-DISCRIMINATION WITHIN INTERNATIONAL LAW

Since the adoption of the United Nations Charter, the principles of equality and non-discrimination have proved to be the linchpins of the human rights regime. As noted earlier, the references contained within the Charter concentrate on equality and non-discrimination – references which have been provided meaning through the Universal Declaration of Human Rights.[6] Equality and non-discrimination are prominent features of both the ICCPR (1966) and the ICESCR (1966).[7] In addition to the general pronouncement condemning discrimination and upholding the norm of equality, the United Nations has also dealt with specific forms of discrimination through various treaties and instruments. The norms of racial equality and non-discrimination have been further strengthened by the International Convention on the Elimination of All Forms of Racial Discrimination (1966).[8] As we shall see in due course, discrimination against women and against children has been condemned and outlawed by the Convention on Elimination of All Forms of Discrimination against Women[9] and the Convention on the Rights of the Child (1989)[10] respectively. Inequality and Discrimination in Education has been addressed by the UNESCO Convention against Discrimination in Education.[11] Similarly discrimination against disabled people has been addressed by the Convention on the Rights of Persons with Disabilities.[12]

The theme of equality and non-discrimination has been most forcefully asserted by the United Nations in its more comprehensive 1992 Declaration on the Rights of Persons Belonging to National or Ethnic, Religious and Linguistic Minorities[13] and the United Nations World Conference on Human Rights, Vienna Declaration and Programme of

[5] See above chapters, Part I and II.
[6] See above chapters, Part II.
[7] Ibid.
[8] New York, 7 March 1966 United Nations, *Treaty Series*, vol. 660, p. 195.
[9] New York, 18 December 1979 United Nations, *Treaty Series*, vol. 1249, p. 13. See below chapter 15.
[10] New York, 20 November 1989 United Nations, *Treaty Series*, vol. 1577, p. 3. See below chapter 16.
[11] 14 December 1960, 429 U.N.T.S. 93, *entered into force* 22 May 1962.
[12] *Convention on the Rights of Persons with Disabilities*, New York, 13 December 2006 UN Doc. A/61/611. See below chapter 17.
[13] UN Doc. A/Res/47/135 Adopted by the General Assembly, 18 December 1992. See the Preamble, Articles 1, 2, 3(1), 4(1) of the Declaration. See below chapter 13.

Action of the World Conference.[14] Again, as we have analysed already, equality and non-discrimination also form the critical mass of the regional instruments. These include the ECHR,[15] the EU treaties[16] the Charter of the OAS,[17] the ADHR,[18] the AFCHPR,[19] the Arab Charter on Human Rights,[20] the OIC[21] and South-Asian regional human rights instruments. Non-discrimination and equality has also been the main concern in the instruments adopted by International Labour Organization.[22]

3 RELIGIOUS DISCRIMINATION AND INTERNATIONAL LAW[23]

Freedom of religion is a subject which throughout human history has been the source of profound disagreements and conflict.[24] The chronicles of humanity have seen the growth and extinction of many religions and beliefs. A promise of eternity, of absolute truth and providence, a hallmark of many of the world religions, has acted as the great determinant of human existence. The overpowering nature of religion, however, has also been used as a weapon for generating intolerance, and as an instrument for the persecution and ultimate destruction of religious minorities. Religious intolerance and repression were the great predisposing factors of history.[25] Within the texts of religious scriptures, forms of genocide of religious minorities were sanctioned. The tragic wars of the medieval and Middle Ages,

---

[14] Vienna Declaration and Programme of Action, adopted by the World Conference on Human Rights, UN Doc. A/CONF.157/23 12, July 1993 para 5 (pt 1).

[15] Convention for the Protection of Human Rights and Fundamental Freedoms ETS No. 005 213 U.N.T.S. 222, entered into force Sept. 3, 1953. See above chapter 7.

[16] See above chapter 8. Treaty Establishing the European Coal and Steel Community, April 18, 1951, 261 UNTS 140; Cmnd 7461.

[17] 119 U.N.T.S. 3, entered into force December 13, 1951. See above chapter 9.

[18] American Declaration on the Rights and Duties of Man, OAS Res. XXX, OAS Doc. OEA/Ser.L.V/II.82 doc.6 rev.1 at 17 (1992). See above chapter 9.

[19] adopted June 27, 1981, OAU Doc. CAB/LEG/67/3 rev. 5, 21 I.L.M. 58 (1982), *entered into force* Oct. 21, 1986. See above chapter 10.

[20] League of Arab States, Revised Arab Charter on Human Rights, May 22, 2004, reprinted in 12 Int'l Hum. Rts. Rep. 893 (2005), entered into force March 15, 2008. See above chapter 11.

[21] See above chapter 11.

[22] Equal Remuneration Convention (ILO No. 100), 165 U.N.T.S. 303, *entered into force* 23 May 1953, Discrimination (Employment and Occupation) Convention (ILO No. 111), 362 U.N.T.S. 31, *entered into force* 15 June 1960. For discussion of the ILO Conventions and indigenous rights see chapter 14 below.

[23] See Benito, *Elimination of All Forms of Intolerance and Discrimination Based on Religion or Belief* (United Nations, 1989); Clark, 'The United Nations and Religious Freedom' 11 *NYUJILP* (1978) 197; Dickson, 'The United Nations and Freedom of Religion' 44 *ICLQ* (1995) 327; Evans, *Religious Liberty and International Law in Europe* (Cambridge University Press, 1997); Evans, 'Time for a treaty? The legal sufficiency of the declaration on the elimination of all forms of intolerance and discrimination' (2007) *Brigham Young University Law Review*, 617; Evans, *Freedom of Religion under the European Convention on Human Rights* (Oxford University Press, 2001); Ghanea (ed.), *The Challenge of Religious Discrimination at the Dawn of the New Millennium* (Martinus Nijhoff, 2004); Rehman, 'Accommodating Religious Identities in an Islamic State: International Law, Freedom of Religion and the Rights of Religious Minorities' 7 *IJMGR* (2000) 139; Sullivan, 'Advancing the Freedom of Religion or Belief through the UN Declaration on the Elimination of Religious Intolerance and Discrimination' 82 *AJIL* (1988) 487; Tahzib, *Freedom of Religion or Belief: Ensuring Effective International Legal Protection* (Martinus Nijhoff, 1995); and Taylor, *Freedom of Religion: UN and European Human Rights Law and Practice* (Cambridge University Press, 2005).

[24] See Krishnaswami, *Study of Discrimination in the Matter of Religious Rights and Practices*, UN Publication Sales E. 60.X.IV.2 1960; Benito, above n.23; Neff, 'An Evolving International Legal Norm of Religious Freedom: Problems and Prospects' 7 *CalWILJ* (1973) 543.

[25] See Whitaker, *Report on the Question of the Prevention and Punishment of the Crime of Genocide*, UN Doc. E/CN.4/Sub.2/1985/6, pp. 6–7.

Equality and non-discrimination

the Crusades and the *Jihads* translated these religious ordinances to complete and thorough effect.[26]

Religious intolerance is unfortunately not simply a matter of historical disposition. Intolerance based on religious beliefs continues to provide lacerative and tormenting concerns to the possibility of congenial human relationships.[27] During the modern era of the United Nations, the international community of States has made tremendous strides in formulating standards regarding the promotion of individual human rights. It is recognised that freedom of religion represents an essential concern for modern human rights law. Discrimination on the grounds of religion or belief is condemned and forms a necessary feature of the United Nations human rights regime.[28] The UDHR and the ICCPR contain specific provisions relating to freedom of religion. The United Nations Declaration on the Elimination of All Forms of Intolerance and of Discrimination based on Religion or Belief (1981) is dedicated entirely to the issue of religious freedom.[29] Freedom of Religion is also recognised by regional human rights instruments such as Article 9 of the ECHR[30] Article III of the ADHR, Article 12 of ACHR[31]; Article 8 of the AFCHPR,[32] Article 30 of the Arab Charter on Human Rights and South-Asian Regional human rights instruments.[33]

4 INCONSISTENCIES WITHIN INTERNATIONAL STANDARDS AND DIFFICULTIES IN IMPLEMENTATION

The aforementioned provisions from the international bill of rights represent strong commitments undertaken by the international community, and alongside the provisions of the Declaration on the Elimination of All Forms of Intolerance and of Discrimination Based on Religion or Belief (1981) and the United Nations Declaration on the Rights of Persons Belonging to National or Ethnic, Religious and Linguistic Minorities (1992) give an appearance of a strong consensus on issues regarding freedom of religion and protecting the rights of religious minorities. However, in reality, much of this consensus is superficial, as there are serious inconsistencies and disagreements both in the meaning and in the substance of the right to freedom of religion.

Notwithstanding persistent references to the term 'religion' or 'belief' within international and national instruments, it has not been possible to explain the terms in a definitive manner. Attempts to incorporate a definition in the United Nations Declaration on the

---

[26] Kuper, *International Action Against Genocide* (Minority Rights Group, 1984) p. 1; Kuper, *Genocide: Its Political Use in the Twentieth Century* (Yale University Press, 1981) pp. 12–14; Kelsay and Johnson (eds), *Just War and Jihad: Historical and Theoretical Perspectives on War and Peace in Western and Islamic Traditions* (Greenwood Press, 1991).

[27] For examples of religious intolerance and repression of religious minorities see Boyle and Sheen (eds), *Freedom of Religion and Belief: A World Report* (Routledge, 1997); Minority Rights Group International (ed.), *World Directory of Minorities* (Minority Rights Group, 1997).

[28] See Articles 1(3) and 13 of the United Nations Charter; Articles 1, 2, 18, Universal Declaration on Human Rights (1948); Article 2, Convention on the Prevention and Punishment of the Crime of Genocide (1948), Articles 2, 18, 26 and 27 of the International Covenant on Civil and Political Rights (1966) Article 2 International Covenant on Economic, Social and Cultural Rights (1966) UN Declaration on the Rights of Persons Belonging to National or Ethnic, Religious and Linguistic Minorities (1992). HRC General Comment No. 22 on The right to Freedom of Thought, Conscience and Religion, *CCPR/C/21/Rev.1/Add.4.*

[29] UN Doc. A/36/55 25 November 1981.

[30] See above chapter 8.

[31] See above chapter 10.

[32] See above chapter 11.

[33] See above chapter 12.

Elimination of All Forms of Intolerance and of Discrimination Based on Religion or Belief (1981) could not succeed.[34] The text of the Declaration represents a fragile compromise between States pursuing widely different ideological bases. Thus, at the insistence of the Eastern European States, the term 'whatever' was inserted between the words 'religion' and 'belief' in the third pre-ambular paragraph as well as in Article 1. This insertion was aimed at extending the scope of the protection to theistic and non-theistic and atheistic beliefs and values.[35] The lack of consensus on the definition of 'religion' or 'religious minorities' has produced unfortunate consequences. In some instances, States have denied the existence of religions and persecuted religious minorities as heretics and political enemies of the State. In other cases, certain groups have been forcibly excluded from the mainstream religious faith and declared a religious minority. Thus, for example, the constitution of the Islamic Republic of Iran affords recognition to Jews, Christians and Zoroastrians as minorities. However, there is a complete refusal to accord any official and constitutional recognition to more than 300,000 Bahais.[36] Conversely, notwithstanding a firm belief on the part of the Ahmaddiyyas of Pakistan to be followers of Islam, they have been denounced as non-Muslims and forcibly relegated to the status of a religious minority.[37]

The next area of substantial controversy where international law has faltered is the issue of 'freedom to change one's religion or belief'. As noted earlier, the UDHR (1948) expressly authorises the right to change religion or belief.[38] The International Covenant on Civil and Political Rights, while not in a position to make as explicit a statement as the Universal Declaration, nevertheless grants the 'freedom to have or to adopt' a religion or belief.[39] The text of the 1981 Declaration, the most recent of the international instruments on religion fails however to make any reference to the 'right' to change religion or belief.[40] The omission of such a provision is unfortunate, and represents what one commentator has termed as 'a downward thrust in the drafting process'.[41] The fact of the matter, however,

---

[34] The European Commission on Human Rights has treated pacifism as a philosophy coming within the ambit of the right to freedom of thought, conscience and belief *Arrowsmith v. UK* App. No. 7050/75, 19 DR 5 (1980). Also see the United States Supreme Courts in *Davies v. Beason* 1889, 133 USS.Ct Report 333, at p. 342 and *The Commissioner, Hindu Religious Endowments Madras v. Sri Lakshmindra Thiratha Swamiar of Sri Shirur Mutt* AIR 1954 SC 282. For scholarly views see Dinstein, 'Freedom of Religion and the Protection of Religious Minorities' in Dinstein and Tabory (eds), *The Protection of Minorities and Human Rights* (Martinus Nijhoff, 1992) pp. 145–169 at p. 146.

[35] See UN Doc. A/C.3/3R. 43 (1981).

[36] According to Article 13 of the Iranian Constitution 'Zoroastrian, Jewish and Christian Iranians are the only recognized religious minorities, who, within the limits of law, are free to perform their religious rites and ceremonies, and to act according to their own canon in matters of personal affairs and religious education'. Constitution of the Islamic Republic of Iran of 24 October 1979, as amended to 28 July 1989. See Blaustein and Flanz, *Constitutions of the Countries of the World* (Oceana Publications, 1973) Vol. viii; See further Ghanea, *Human Rights, the UN and the Bahá'ís in Iran* (Brill, 2003) at p. 102.

[37] See Kennedy, 'Towards the Definition of a Muslim in an Islamic State: The Case of the Ahmadiyya in Pakistan' in Vajpeyi and Malik (eds), *Religious and Ethnic Minority Politics in South Asia* (Riverdale Company Publishers, 1989) pp. 71–108; Ayaz, *Submission Made before the Working Group on Minorities* (Geneva) May, 1998.

[38] Article 18 of the Universal Declaration of Human Rights. See above chapter 4. It is important to note that tensions arose during the drafting of UDHR.

[39] Article 18 ICCPR.

[40] Article 8 of the 1981 Declaration, however, states that 'Nothing in the present Declaration shall be construed as restricting or derogating from any right defined in the Universal Declaration of Human Rights and the International Covenants on Human Rights'.

[41] Ramcharan, *Towards a Universal Standard of Religious Liberty in Commission of the Churches on International Affairs* (Unpublished, 1987) at p. 9.

is that during the drafting stages of the 1981 Declaration there had arisen major disagreements between various blocs; in order for this Declaration and subsequent treaties such as the Convention on the Rights of the Child to be adopted, it became necessary to omit all references to freedom to change religion or belief. The *travaux préparatoires* of the Convention on the Right of the Child and the reservations drawn in relation to Article 14 of the Convention dealing with the issue of freedom of religion confirm this point.[42]

In terms of substance, a religion or belief often tends to be a conglomeration of various values, claims and rights. Religious freedom has several dimensions. A religion is not simply a personal belief, but invokes teachings, practices, worship, observance and public as well as private manifestations of these beliefs and values.[43] There is a strong tendency amongst religions to invoke complete and absolute submission, and in the process they are likely to affect many aspects of human life including matrimonial and family affairs, family planning, care of children, inheritance, public order, food and diet, freedom of expression and association.[44] The collective dimension of religious freedom raises complex issues within the individualistic framework of human rights in domestic and international law.[45]

A particularly serious difficulty arises from the claims made by religions or beliefs to have a complete and absolute 'monopoly of truth'.[46] It is this claim to a monopoly of the truth which has served 'as a basis of countless holy, divine or just wars' and 'crusades' waged against so-called 'heretics' or 'infidels'.[47] Religions and beliefs also have the tendency to become rigid, and their followers intolerant towards other competing religious values and philosophies. This intolerance, as Macaulay puts it, can lead a follower to view that:

> [I] am in the right and you are wrong. When you are stronger, you ought to tolerate me; for it is your duty to tolerate truth. But when I am stronger, I shall persecute you; for it is my duty to persecute you.[48]

International law, like national laws, is confronted with the problem of religious extremism and rigidity. In view of the variance in State practices, international law has faced substantial difficulties in formulating established principles governing freedom of religion and non-discrimination for all religions. As one commentator has remarked:

---

[42] See Johnson, 'Cultural and Regional Pluralism in the Drafting of the UN Convention on the Rights of the Child' in Freeman and Veerman (eds), *Ideologies of Children's Rights* (Martinus Nijhoff, 1992) pp. 95–114 at p. 98.

[43] See the General Comment by the Human Rights Committee, General Comment 22 on Article 18 of the ICCPR (48th Session) 20th July, 1993.

[44] *Kokkinakis* v. *Greece*, (1994) 17 E.H.R.R. 397: European Commission on Human Rights in *Ahmad* v. *UK* (1982) 4 E.H.R.R. 126 (Time off work for Friday prayers); European Commission on Human Rights *Choudhury* v. *United Kingdom*, Application No. 17439/90, 12 HRLJ (1991) 172 (Blasphemy). See also *Testigos de Jehová* v. *Argentina*, Case 2137, Inter-Am. C.H.R., Annual Report 1978 (prosecution of Jehovah's witnesses for unwillingness to swear oath to military service, to recognise the State and symbols of the State). Also see the US Supreme Court in *Church of Lukimi Babalu Aye, Inc. & Ernesto Pichardo* v. *City of Hialeah*, 508 U.S. 520 (1993) (rituals) and the Indian Supreme Court in *Mohammed Ahmed Khan* v. *Shah Bano* 1985 AIR SC 945 (Muslim personal laws).

[45] See Gilbert, 'Religious Minorities and their Rights: A Problem of Approach' 5 *IJMGR* (1997) 97.

[46] Tahzib, above n.23, at p. 30.

[47] Ibid. p. 31.

[48] Macaulay, *Critical and Historical Essays* (Longman, Roberts & Green, 1870) at p. 336.

> [t]he question of religion takes international law to the limits of human rights, at least in so far as the law functions in a community of states. It is quite meaningless, for example, to the adherents of a religion to have their beliefs or practices declared to be contrary to 'public morality'. To the believer, religion is morality itself and its transcendental foundation grounds it more firmly in terms of obligations than any secular rival, or the tenets of other religions. All religions are to a greater or lesser extent 'fundamentalist' in character in they recognize that theirs is the just rule, the correct avenue to truth.[49]

The difficulties inherent in the issue of freedom of religion become prominent when contrasted with the international developments in relation to the prohibition of racial discrimination and apartheid. While in its early years the United Nations approached the issue of racial and religious discrimination with equal vigour, with the emergence of new States, it was the issue of racial (not religious) discrimination which attracted international concern.[50] The abolition of racial discrimination and the demolition of colonialism, apartheid and racial oppression were less controversial subjects and suited the interests of the majority of the Member States of United Nations. On the other hand, the issue of freedom of religion and religious non-discrimination was extremely sensitive, and even an inquiry into the treatment of religious practice within the General Assembly provoked angry responses. In its Resolution 1510 (XV) of 12 December 1960, the General Assembly condemned 'all manifestations and practices of racial, religious and national hatred in the political, economic, social, education and cultural spheres of the life of society as violations of the Charter of the United Nations and the Universal Declaration of Human Rights'.[51] However, serious differences emerged in relation to possible action to combat racial and religious discrimination. In the end as a compromise it was decided to create separate instruments dealing with race and religion. According to Tahzib:

> [t]he decision to separate the instruments on religious intolerance from those on racial discrimination constituted a compromise solution designed to satisfy a number of conflicting viewpoints. Western states insisted on addressing both matters in a joint instrument. Communist states were not anxious to deal with religious matters. Arab states were eager to displace the question of anti-Semitism. African and Asian states considered the question of religious intolerance a minor matter as compared with racial discrimination. By separating the issues, the Communist, Arab, African and Asian states could delay, if not prevent, the adoption of special instruments or religious intolerance.[52]

In 1962, the General Assembly requested the Economic and Social Council to prepare a draft declaration and Convention on the Elimination of All Forms of Racial Discrimination. The General Assembly in its Resolution 1904 (XVIII) adopted on 20 November 1963, proclaimed the Declaration on the Elimination of All Forms of Racial Discrimination. Two years later, the United Nations General Assembly adopted with overwhelming support the Convention on the Elimination of All Forms of Racial Discrimination. No such fortunes have accompanied efforts to draft an international treaty on the elimination of

---

[49] Thornberry, *International Law and the Rights of Minorities* (Clarendon Press, 1991) at p. 324.
[50] Lerner, *Group Rights and Discrimination*, above n.1, at p. 84.
[51] GA Resolution 1510 (XV) Manifestations of racial and national hatred, para 1.
[52] Tahzib, above n.23, at p. 142.

discrimination based on religion or belief.[53] The farthest the United Nations has gone in terms of drafting a specific instrument on religious freedom is a General Assembly Declaration adopted in 1981. Despite the passage of nearly 30 years since the Declaration was adopted, efforts to devise a binding instrument on Freedom of Religion or Belief have proved a failure. Furthermore, there is considerable scepticism over the possibility of concluding such a treaty in the near future.[54]

In its capacity as a General Assembly Resolution, the Declaration is not a binding document *per se*. Even as a political and moral expression the image of the Declaration has been tarnished through many deviations and disagreements amongst States. It is probably the case that the constitutional provisions and legislation overwhelmingly satisfy the broad and generalised requirements of a non-discriminatory stance on the basis of religion, though even here a number of cases point in the opposite direction.[55] Freedom of religion or belief itself is a conglomeration of various rights and values and is capable of manifestation in innumerable ways.[56] 'Religion' or 'Belief' is in many instances regarded as providing a complete code of life, determining every pattern of social behaviour. Its pronouncements affect every aspect of life, including matrimonial and family affairs, public order, freedom of expression and association, freedom to preach and freedom to manifest one's religion as matter of conscience and faith.[57] Domestic and international tribunals have often been confronted with the faithfuls belonging to different religions and sects and raising questions of a serious nature.[58] Therefore, although the plethora of international treaties since 1945 clearly reflect the view that the fundamental principle of the international law of human rights is that all individuals are to be treated equally and ought not to be discriminated against merely on the basis of their belonging to a certain ethnic, religious or linguistic group, it is argued that the strength of the prohibition in each case differs. Hence, while the legal norms in relation to the prohibition of racial discrimination are regarded as a fairly uncontroversial example of *jus cogens*,[59] the same cannot be said with certainty in relation to the prohibition of discrimination based on religion.

[53] Alston, 'The Commission on Human Rights' in Alston (ed.), *The United Nations and Human Rights: A Critical Appraisal* (Clarendon Press, 1992) p. 134.

[54] See the proceedings of Conference, Freedom of Religion (Unpublished, Geneva, June 2008).

[55] Article 19 of the Iranian Constitution provides as follows: 'All People of Iran, whatever the ethnic group or tribe to which they belong, enjoy equal rights: color, race, language, and the like do not bestow any privilege.' Thus, the Constitution excludes religion as a criterion for non-discrimination, an action which cannot be treated as non-deliberate. See Blaustein and Flanz, above n.36.

[56] See the Human Rights Committee, *General Comment 22, Article 18*, 48th. Session, 1993.

[57] See the cases before the Human Rights Committee e.g. *Singh Bhinder* v. *Canada*, Communication Nos. 208/1986, UN Doc. CCPR/C/37/D/208/1986 (1989); *Coeriel* et al. v. *Netherlands*, Communication No. 453/1991 (9 December 1994), UN Doc. CCPR/C/52/D/453/1991 (1994).

[58] See UK cases: *R. (on the application of Begum)* v. *Denbigh High School Governors*, [2006] H.R.L.R. 21; *Ahmad* v. *Inner London Education Authority* [1978] QB 36, [1977] 3 WLR 396, [1978] 1 All ER 574, CA, [1976] I.C.R. 461, EAT; ECHR cases *Sahin* v. *Turkey* (2007) 44 E.H.R.R. 5; the US Supreme Court in *Church of Lukimi Babalu Aye, Inc. & Ernesto Pichardo* v. *City of Hialeah*, 508 U.S. 520 (1993); also see the jurisprudence under the European Convention on Human Rights (1950) e.g. *Kokkinakis* v. *Greece* (1994) 17 E.H.R.R. 397; *Otto-Preminger Institute* v. *Austria* (1995) 19 E.H.R.R. 34. Note also Pakistani and Indian case-law, see e.g. *Navendra* v. *State of Gujarat* AIR 1974 SC 2098; *Jagdishwar Anand* v. *P.C.*, Calcutta (1984) SC 51; *Ratilal Panchad Ghandhi and others* v. *State of Bombay and others AIR* (SC) *(1954)*, 388; *Rev. Stainsislans* AIR 1975 MP 163; *Saifuddin Saheb* AIR 1962 SC 853; *Commissioner of Hindu Religious Endowments Madras* v. *Sri Lakshmandra* AIR (1954) SC 388; *Sarwar Hussain* AIR (1983) All 252; *State of Bombay* v. *Narasu Appa Mali* AIR 1952 Bombay 1984; *Mohammed Ahmed Khan* v. *Shah Bano Begum* 1985 AIR SC 945. For the position in the UK see Employment Equality (Religion or Belief) Regulation 2003, SI 2003/1660 (in force since 2 December 2003) and adopted in pursuance of the EU's Framework Directive 2000/78/EC (2000).

[59] Brownlie, *Principles of Public International Law* (Oxford University Press, 2008) pp. 510–511.

In view of the existing dissensions it is difficult to expect the emergence of a greater measure of consensus. As noted earlier, there are no immediate prospects for the adoption of a specific treaty focusing on the Elimination of Religious Discrimination. Having said that, while a radical shift in the existing position seems impossible to attain, the ingenuity of a number of human rights processes has led to positive developments towards reducing discrimination and intolerance on grounds of religion. These processes include a more constructive usage of existing procedures, as well as a greater consciousness of the issues of religious discrimination in group rights discourses and standard-setting mechanisms. Using Article 18 of the ICCPR as its base, the Human Rights Committee has invoked the reporting, individual communication and General Comment procedures within the Covenant to elaborate upon the meaning and scope of the right to religious non-discrimination.[60] Religious communities are the beneficiaries of the emerging jurisprudence on group rights. The United Nations General Assembly Declaration on the Rights of Persons Belonging to National or Ethnic, Religious and Linguistic Minorities 1992, places a special emphasis on non-discrimination and equality for members of religious minorities. The ILO Convention No. 169 on Indigenous and Tribal Peoples 1989 presents undertakings from States to protect and preserve the beliefs and spiritual well-being of the indigenous peoples.[61] The States parties to the Convention on the Rights of the Child 1989 commit themselves not to discriminate against the child, irrespective of religious beliefs and his or her minority or indigenous background.[62]

A significant element in furthering the human rights norms has been the usage of the institution of Rapporteurs, focusing on a thematic, geographical or territorial basis.[63] The institution of Rapporteurs and their role has been particularly valuable not only in publicising instances of violations based on religious intolerance but also in persuading governments to follow the guidelines provided by the Declaration on the Elimination of All Forms of Intolerance and of Discrimination Based on Religion or Belief (1981) and the Declaration on the Rights of Persons Belonging to National or Ethnic, Religious and Linguistic Minorities (1992). In this regard the contributions made by the Special Rapporteurs on Religious Intolerance (formerly of the United Nations Commission on Human Rights and now of the United Nations Human Rights Council) are of enormous significance and deserve a fuller analysis.[64] The initial appointment of the Rapporteur had been authorised by the Commission on Human Rights in its Resolution 1986/20.[65] This appointment was to last for a period of one year, during which period the Rapporteur was mandated *inter alia* to examine incidents and governmental actions in all parts of the world inconsistent with the provisions of the Declaration on the Elimination of All Forms of Intolerance and Religious Discrimination, and to recommend measures in order to

12

Equality and non-discrimination

---

[60] It has recently been recommended that the Human Rights Committee and its jurisprudence on Article 18 should be followed closely to develop the subject of Freedom of Religion or Belief (Geneva, June 2008).

[61] See Articles 5(a), 7(a) and 13.

[62] See Articles 2 and 30.

[63] See above chapter 3; Van Boven, 'The United Nations Commission on Human Rights and Freedom of Religion or Belief' in Lindholm *et al.* (eds), *Facilitating Freedom of Religion or Belief: A Deskbook* (Martinus Nijhoff, 2004) pp. 173–188.

[64] See Evans, *Religious Liberty and International Law in Europe* (Cambridge University Press, 1997) pp. 245–250; Evans, 'Strengthening the Role of the Special Rapporteur on Freedom of Religion or Belief' 1 *Religion and Human Rights* (2006) 75; Wiener, 'The Mandate of the Special Rapporteur on Freedom of Religion or Belief – Institutional, Procedural and Substantive Legal Issues' 2 *Religion and Human Rights* (2007) 3.

[65] 10 March 1986 (42nd Session).

remedy such violations. Mr. d'Almeida was appointed the first Special Rapporteur and he produced his initial report in 1987. Resolution 1987/15 extended the mandate of the Rapporteur for a further year. This mandate has since been extended by subsequent Resolutions of the Commission,[66] and the Human Rights Council.[67] Mr. d'Almeida's mandate was continually extended by the Human Rights Commission until 1993 at which point he was succeeded by Mr. Abdelfattah Amor. Mr. Amor was succeeded by Ms. Asma Jahangir in July 2004 and she continues to be the Special Rapporteur on Freedom of Religion or Belief. In the meanwhile, and at the request of the Rapporteur the title of mandate holder was changed from Special Rapporteur on Religious Intolerance to the Special Rapporteur on Freedom of Religion or Belief in 2001,[68] with the Commission on Human Rights requesting the mandate holder to continue his examination of 'incidents and governmental actions in all parts of the world that were incompatible with the provisions of the Declaration'.[69]

From 1988, the Special Rapporteurs have submitted annual reports, which are extremely instructive not only in highlighting incidents of religious intolerance but also in providing constructive solutions and making valuable recommendations.[70] The work of the Special Rapporteur is characterised by a number of activities, and as Carolyn Evans elaborates, has shifted considerably over the past 20 years.[71] The initial reports submitted by Mr. d'Almeida Ribeiro presented a broad framework with the generalised examination of human rights violations, religious intolerance and religious-based discrimination in specific States. This trend of examining more specifically the violations of religious communities continued under Rapporteur Amor. Asma Jahangir in her current mandate has made greater efforts to focus on highlighting violations of rights of individuals and communities by States and taking steps to prevent such violations and abuse.

A central and emergent role of the Special Rapporteur on Freedom of Religion or Belief therefore, is to outline allegations of violations of rights, to record the responses (if any) from the State concerned and in turn to transmit their concerns regarding violations of freedom of Religion taking place in specific States. The Special Rapporteurs have also deployed the system of 'urgent appeals' where a particular individual or a group is under imminent threat. Individual Rapporteurs have varyingly relied on such techniques as developing dialogue amongst communities when attempting to introduce greater tolerance and understanding.[72] Another significant feature of Special Rapporteur work is *in situ* visits and their follow-ups, which are valuable

---

[66] See the Commission's Resolutions 1988/55; 1990/27; 1995/23.

[67] See the Council's Resolution 6/37, 34th Meeting, 14 December 2007, which extended the mandate of the Special Rapporteur for a further three years. For further analysis of the roles and positions of the Special Rapporteurs see chapter 3 above.

[68] See Evans, 'Strengthening the Role of the Special Rapporteur' above n.64, at p. 77.

[69] Commission on Human Rights, UN Doc. E/CN.4/RES/2001/42, para 9. ECOSOC Decision 2000/261 and GA Res. 55/97.

[70] See E.CN.4/1988/45 and Add.1; E.CN.4/1989/44; E.CN.4/1990/46; E.CN.4/1991/56; E.CN.4/1992/52; E.CN.4/1993/62 and Corr and Add.1; E.CN.4/1994/79; E.CN.4/1995/91 and Add.1; E.CN.4/1996/95 and Add.1 and 2; E.CN.4/1997/91 and Add.1 and also the General Assembly at the 50th., 51st. and 52nd. and 53rd. Sessions (A/50/440; A/51/54/542 and Add.1 and 2; A/52/477 And Add.1) E.CN.4/1998/6, E/CN.4/2004/64, E/CN.4/2005/61, E/CN.4/2006/5, A/HRC/4/21, A/HRC/6/5.

[71] See Evans, 'Strengthening the Role of the Special Rapporteur', above n.64, at pp. 78–79.

[72] Both of these very characteristics during Professor Amor's period – discussed by Evans, 'Strengthening the Role of the Special Rapporteur', above n.64, at pp. 86–88.

both for gathering opinions and comments on all alleged incidents and government action incompatible with the Declaration, and for analysing and passing on the experience and positive initiatives of States pursuant to General Assembly Resolution 50/183 and Commission on Human Rights Resolution 1996/23.[73]

A highly significant advantage of these visits is the first-hand information and experience of individuals and communities most directly affected by violations of freedom of religion. The previous Special Rapporteur, Professor Abdelfattah Amor, during his tenure, made important visits to countries including China,[74] Pakistan,[75] Greece[76] and India.[77] The present Rapporteur Asma Jahangir has also placed a high degree of value on *in situ* visits and has visited Nigeria, Sri Lanka and France amongst many others. Several meaningful objectives have been attained through these visits. Not only have they allowed the Special Rapporteur to form a firmer view on the nature and extent of violations of the rights of religious communities, but in some instances the Rapporteur has been able to extract valuable concessions from the governments concerned.[78] In recent years, the United Nations mandate holders, in particular the Special Rapporteurs have increasingly adopted a practice of issuing joint initiatives including visits and joint communications. In the light of the fact, that freedom of religion issues often involve other violations of fundamental rights such as arbitrary detentions, torture and denials of freedom of expression, such an approach appears highly sensible. During 2005, 25 of the 75 communications sent by Asma Jahangir were sent jointly with another Rapporteur. In describing the advantages of such joint communications, Jahangir notes that:

(a) They give a greater strength, legitimacy and credibility to the action undertaken because they express the common voice of several mandate holders;

(b) They increase the efficiency of the research process owing to the joint effort of several mandates and, thus, different expertise;

(c) They generally improve the format and content of communications sent to Governments thanks to a sustained coordination among the mandates, especially at the level of the office of the High Commissioner for Human Rights.[79]

One strong example of a joint communication was the communiqué forwarded by United Nations Special Rapporteur on Torture,[80] along with the UN Special Rapporteurs on the

---

[73] *Report submitted by Mr Abdelfattah Amor, Special Rapporteur in accordance with the Commission on Human Rights Resolution* 1996/23, E/CN.4/1997/91, para 44.

[74] See E/CN.4/1995/91; November 1994.

[75] See E/CN.4/1996/95.Add.2. June 1995.

[76] See A/51/542/Add.1. June 1996.

[77] See E/CN.4/1997/91/Add.1. December 1996.

[78] On the role of Rapporteurs see above chapter 2.

[79] See *Report of the Special Rapporteur of the Commission on Human Rights on Freedom of Religion or Belief*, Asma Jahangir www2.ohchr.org/english/issues/religion/docs/A_60_399.pdf A/60/399 (30 September 2005) <last visited 29 November 2008>.

[80] See Economic and Social Council, *Situation of detainees at Guantánamo Bay*, Report of the Chairperson of the Working Group on Arbitrary Detention, Ms. Leila Zerrougui; the Special Rapporteur on the independence of judges and lawyers, Mr. Leandro Despouy; the Special Rapporteur on torture and other cruel, inhuman or degrading treatment or punishment, Mr. Manfred Nowak; the Special Rapporteur on freedom of religion or belief, Ms. Asma Jahangir and the Special Rapporteur on the right of everyone to the enjoyment of the highest attainable standard of physical and mental health, Mr. Paul Hunt. E/CN.4/2006/120 (15 February 2006) http://news.bbc.co.uk/1/shared/bsp/hi/pdfs/16_02_06_un_guantanamo.pdf <last visited 11 April 2009>.

right of everyone to the highest attainable standard of physical and mental health, the independence of judges and lawyers, and freedom of religion or belief, and the Chairperson of the Working Group on Arbitrary Detention calling for the immediate closure of Guantánamo Bay.[81] Although a planned joint visit by the United Nations Special Rapporteurs to the detention centre did not materialise due to the lack of co-operation by the United State authorities, the joint communiqué, nevertheless, had a strong psychological impact at the global level.[82] A lack of co-operation by a State is one, albeit significant, impediment in the operation of the Special Rapporteur. There are several others: the rise in religious extremism post 11 September 2001, the absence of a treaty focusing exclusively on freedom of religion or belief, the lack of human and financial resources and perhaps significantly the inherent tensions and aggravation within domestic legal systems on issues surrounding freedom of religion or belief and the rights of religious minorities.

While acting in her capacity as the Special Rapporteur on Freedom of Religion or Belief, the current Rapporteur, Asma Jahangir, has also been at the forefront of acting as a vanguard of human rights which relate directly to freedom of religion such as the freedom of expression and the freedom of speech. This feature came to light very strongly during the debates within the United Nations on attempts at establishing the offence of 'Defamation of Religions'. The subject of 'Defamation of Religions' had been raised by the Organisation of Islamic Conference (OIC) during the time of the UN Human Rights Commission, but has been engineered with intensity since the first session of the UN Human Rights Council. Ever since 1999, Pakistan on behalf of the OIC has proposed resolutions before the now defunct Human Rights Commission on 'Defamation of Religions' with an obvious focus on defamation against Islam. The issue has of course acquired considerable and added significance in the light of the Danish Cartoon saga caricaturing cartoons of Prophet Mohammad, the Prophet of Islam. The Special Rapporteur on racism and xenophobia was requested to prepare a report on defamation of Religion. Similarly, the High Commissioner was asked to present a report on defamation of Religion. Both reports were considered in September 2007.

In March 2008, the OIC member States aided by a group of African States was able to have a resolution adopted on the Defamation of Religion. According to Human Rights Council Resolution 7/19 adopted on 27 March 2008, the Council:

> . . . *expressed deep concern* at attempts to identify Islam with terrorism, violence and human rights violations and emphasizes that equating any religion with terrorism should be rejected and combated by all at all levels;

> 3. *Further expresses deep concern* at the intensification of the campaign of defamation of religions and the ethnic and religious profiling of Muslim minorities in the aftermath of the tragic events of 11 September 2001;

> 4. *Expresses its grave concern* at the recent serious instances of deliberate stereotyping of religions, their adherents and sacred persons in the media and by political parties and groups in some societies, and at the associated provocation and political exploitation;

[81] Ibid. para 96.
[82] Ibid.

5. *Recognizes that*, in the context of the fight against terrorism, defamation of religions becomes an aggravating factor that contributes to the denial of fundamental rights and freedoms of target groups and their economic and social exclusion;

6. *Expresses concern* at laws or administrative measures that have been specifically designated to control and monitor Muslim minorities, thereby stigmatizing them and legitimizing the discrimination that they experience;

The idea of preventing defamation of religions appears to be a noble one. However, there are substantial difficulties with having wholesale acceptance of the offence of defamations of religion, since essentially this would prevent dissemination of ideas and beliefs rather than protecting individuals or communities. Freedom of expression of course has limits and this freedom has to be restricted in cases where it constitutes 'incitement to discrimination, hostility or violence' (Article 20 ICCPR). Furthermore, freedom of expression cannot be allowed to intimidate, humiliate and insult an individual or community of believers. That said, the test for assessing as to whether such incitement, discrimination, hostility, humiliation or insult has taken place is through its impact on the relevant individual or upon the community and cannot be attached in abstract to a religion or belief. The UN Special Rapporteur on Freedom of Religion or Belief has rightly noted that 'the right to freedom of religion or belief protects primarily the individual and to some extent the collective rights of the community concerned but it does not protect religions or beliefs per se'. She goes on to make the point that defamation of religion 'may offend people and hurt their religious feeling but it does not necessarily or at least directly result in a violation of their rights, including their right to freedom of religion'. An offence of defamation of religion runs the risk of jeopardising any form of criticism of religion or faith – and indeed as we have noted during the course of this study, it is important to have a critical approach to those aspects of religions, beliefs or ideologies, which do not accord with the consistently changing notions of human rights law. It also remains the case that the legislation in a number of countries based on the concept of defamation of religion can lead to serious violations of rights of the individuals. The case of Pakistan has been noted already. Pakistan retains blasphemy laws with stringent criminal penalties; blasphemy laws unfortunately have been used as a weapon of political exploitation and undermining the rights of religious minorities.

5 RIGHT TO RACIAL EQUALITY AND NON-DISCRIMINATION IN INTERNATIONAL LAW

(i) The International Covenants

As noted above the underlying theme of the international bill of rights are the concepts of equality and non-discrimination. The comment is particularly apt in its application to ICCPR. As one commentator has rightly stated 'equality and non-discrimination constitute the most dominant single theme of the [Civil and Political Rights] Covenant'.[83] According to Article 2(1) of ICCPR, each State party undertakes to:

[83] Ramcharan, 'Equality and Non-Discrimination', in Henkin (ed.), *The International Bill of Rights: The Covenant on Civil and Political Rights* (Columbia University Press, 1981) pp. 246–269 at p. 246.

12

Equality and non-discrimination

> respect and to ensure to all individuals within its territory and subject to its jurisdiction the rights recognized in the present Covenant, without distinction of any kind, such as race, colour, sex, language, religion, political or other opinion, national or social origin, property, birth or other status.[84]

Article 3, while providing for equality for men and women, states:

> The States Parties to the present Covenant undertake to ensure the equal rights of men and women to the enjoyment of all civil and political rights set forth in the present Covenant.

Article 3 has been elaborated upon in the Human Rights Committee's General Comments No. 4 and 28.[85] The recognition of the need for affirmative action is particularly pertinent.[86] General Comment No. 28, also discusses practices of concern including 'prenatal sex selection and abortion of female foetuses. States parties should ensure that traditional, historical, religious or cultural attitudes are not used to justify violations of women's right to equality before the law and to equal enjoyment of all Covenant rights'.[87]

---

[84] See above chapter 4.

[85] General Comment No. 4: Equality between the sexes (Art. 3). (Thirteenth session, 1981) updated and replaced by General Comment No. 28 General Comment No. 28: Equality of rights between men and women (article 3), CCPR/C/21/Rev.1/Add.10.

[86] General Comment No. 4, paras 2 and 3 had provided as follows: 'Firstly, article 3, as articles 2 (1) and 26 in so far as those articles primarily deal with the prevention of discrimination on a number of grounds, among which sex is one, requires not only measures of protection but also affirmative action designed to ensure the positive enjoyment of rights. This cannot be done simply by enacting laws. Hence, more information has generally been required regarding the role of women in practice with a view to ascertaining what measures, in addition to purely legislative measures of protection, have been or are being taken to give effect to the precise and positive obligations under article 3 and to ascertain what progress is being made or what factors or difficulties are being met in this regard . . . Secondly, the positive obligation undertaken by States parties under that article may itself have an inevitable impact on legislation or administrative measures specifically designed to regulate matters other than those dealt with in the Covenant but which may adversely affect rights recognized in the Covenant. One example, among others, is the degree to which immigration laws which distinguish between a male and a female citizen may or may not adversely affect the scope of the right of the woman to marriage to non-citizens or to hold public office.' General Comment No. 28, para 3 provides that 'the obligation to ensure to all individuals the rights recognized in the Covenant, established in articles 2 and 3 of the Covenant, requires that States parties take all necessary steps to enable every person to enjoy those rights. These steps include the removal of obstacles to the equal enjoyment of such rights, the education of the population and of State officials in human rights, and the adjustment of domestic legislation so as to give effect to the undertakings set forth in the Covenant. The State party must not only adopt measures of protection, but also positive measures in all areas so as to achieve the effective and equal empowerment of women. States parties must provide information regarding the actual role of women in society so that the Committee may ascertain what measures, in addition to legislative provisions, have been or should be taken to give effect to these obligations, what progress has been made, what difficulties are encountered and what steps are being taken to overcome them.' Note, General Comment No. 28 has updated and replaced General Comment No. 4.

[87] General Comment No. 28, para 5.

Article 25 provides that:

> Every citizen shall have the right and the opportunity, without any of the distinctions mentioned in article 2 and without unreasonable restrictions:
>
> (a) To take part in the conduct of public affairs, directly or through freely chosen representatives;
>
> (b) To vote and to be elected at genuine periodic elections which shall be by universal and equal suffrage and shall be held by secret ballot, guaranteeing the free expression of the will of the electors;
>
> (c) To have access, on general terms of equality, to public service in his country.

One of the primary articles on equality and non-discrimination is Article 26 according to which:

> All persons are equal before the law and are entitled without any discrimination to the equal protection of the law. In this respect, the law shall prohibit any discrimination and guarantee to all persons equal and effective protection against discrimination on any ground such as race, colour, sex, language, religion, political or other opinion, national or social origin, property, birth or other status.

Article 2(2) of the ICESCR provides that:

> The States Parties to the present Covenant undertake to guarantee that the rights enunciated in the present Covenant will be exercised without discrimination of any kind as to race, colour, sex, language, religion, political or other opinion national or social origin, property, birth or other status.[88]

Article 2(1) and 26 of ICCPR vary in their terminology. Article 2(1) uses the term 'distinction' while Article 26 invokes the phrase 'discrimination'. It also needs to be noted that Article 2(2) of the ICESCR relies upon the term 'discrimination'. The ambiguity generated by the differential use of the terms 'distinction' and 'discrimination' is exacerbated by the fact that there is no definite attempt to define either of these terms,[89] although it is probably the case that the terms have been used interchangeably. While analysing the *travaux préparatoires*, Craven takes the view that the usage of the term 'discrimination' in ICESCR (as opposed to 'distinction') was a term more suitably applied for setting in to operation affirmative action policies.[90] Within the Covenants there is also the absence of any explicit provisions relating to policies of affirmative action which tends to reinforce the anti-collective stance. As noted above, the Human Rights Committee has, however, taken the view that affirmative action policies are provided for by the provisions of the Covenant.[91]

---

[88] GA Res. 2200 A, 21 UN GAOR, (Supp. No. 16) 49–50.

[89] McKean, above n.1, at pp. 148–152.

[90] Craven, above n.4, at p. 161.

[91] See McGoldrick, *The Human Rights Committee: Its Role in the Development of the International Covenant on Civil and Political Rights* (Clarendon Press, 1991) pp. 275–276.

(ii) International Convention on the Elimination of All Forms of Racial Discrimination (The Race Convention)

The adoption and entry into force of the Race Convention provided a significant step towards the attempt to combat racial discrimination at the global level.[92] The Race Convention was adopted on 21 December 1965[93] and entered into force on 4 January 1969. The Convention was adopted by 106 votes to none. Although Mexico abstained initially, it later declared an affirmative vote in support of the provisions of the Convention.[94] The speed and number of State ratifications represent the general consensus on the issues relating to prohibition of racial discrimination. It currently stands as one of the most widely ratified treaties in the international arena.[95]

While the Declaration on the Elimination of Racial Discrimination provided the driving force for the incorporation of both substantive and normative articles of the Convention, it would be fair to suggest that the adoption of the Convention within two years of the Declaration has its roots in the political support of the newly emerging States of Africa and Asia, who have been particularly strong in condemning racial discrimination and apartheid.[96] The provisions of the Convention, although undeniably a major advance in the cause of eliminating racial discrimination, nonetheless raise a number of complex questions reflecting the existent weaknesses in international law relating to the prohibition of discrimination.

(a) Complications in the definition of 'discrimination' and the scope of the Convention

The preamble to the Convention while introducing the matters under consideration, places emphasis on equality and upon the importance of removing racial barriers. Unlike the Declaration, the Convention does contain a definition of 'racial discrimination' which means:

> any distinction, exclusion, restriction or preference based on race, colour, descent, or national or ethnic origin which has the purpose or effect of nullifying or impairing the recognition, enjoyment or exercise, on an equal footing, of human rights and fundamental freedoms in the political, economic, social, cultural or any other field of public life.[97]

The importance of the contents of the definition need to be noted. 'Racial discrimination' is given a broad meaning which according to the terms of the Convention may be based on a variety of factors like race, colour, descent, national or ethnic origin. According to the definition, four kinds of acts could be regarded as discriminatory: any distinction, exclusion, restriction or preference. For any of these acts to constitute discrimination they must be based on (a) race, (b) colour, (c) descent, (d) national origin or (e) ethnic origin,

---

[92] See Meron, 'The Meaning and Reach of the International Convention on the Elimination of all Forms of Racial Discrimination' 79 *AJIL* (1985) 283 at p. 283.

[93] New York, 7 March 1966 United Nations, *Treaty Series*, vol. 660, p. 195.

[94] Thornberry, above n.49, at p. 259.

[95] As at 30 July 2009, there were 173 States parties to the Race Convention.

[96] See Humphrey, 'The UN Charter and the Universal Declaration of Human Rights' in Luard (ed.), *The International Protection of Human Rights* (Thames & Hudson, 1967) pp. 39–56 at p. 56.

[97] Article 1(1).

and should have the purpose or effect of impairing or nullifying the recognition, enjoyment or exercise on an equal footing of human rights and fundamental freedoms in the political, economic, social, cultural or any other field of public life.[98] The definition has been used as the basis of other human rights treaties.[99] Identification of group as pertaining to 'race' remains a highly controversial subject. Professor Cassese makes the valid point that 'race is a notion whose scientific validity has been debunked by anthropologists; it must nevertheless be perforce interpreted and applied when used in a legal provision'.[100] Notwithstanding the difficulties faced in identification of an entity as a race or as a group, the Committee on the Elimination of All Forms of Racial Discrimination – CERD – has in its 'General Recommendation' noted that membership of a group, 'shall, if no justification exists to the contrary, be based upon self-identification by the individual concerned'.[101]

In comparison to the ICCPR, it appears that the Race Convention has a broader perspective for, unlike the ICCPR, which is limited to rights addressed in that particular instrument, Article 1(1) applies to racial discrimination 'which has the purpose or effect of nullifying or impairing the recognition, enjoyment or exercise of human rights and fundamental freedoms'.[102] However, in another respect the scope of the Race Convention is far more limited as it only deals with racial discrimination and any discrimination based on grounds of religion, sex or political opinion are *prima facie* outside its scope. The definition of racial discrimination raises a number of intriguing though controversial issues.[103] There is a constant debate over the nature of equality that is aspired to: how far is the separation of different groups on the basis of ensuring equality compatible with the provisions of the Covenant? How far does the Convention impose obligations or extend itself in prohibiting discrimination in private life as opposed to public life – with the meaning as to what constitutes 'public life' itself being the subject of controversy.[104]

It is equally important to note the situations where the Convention (as provided in other paragraphs of Article 1) is not applicable. The Convention is not applicable in cases of 'distinctions, exclusions, restrictions or preferences' made by a State party between citizens and non-citizens and cannot be interpreted as affecting the laws regulating nationality, citizenship[105] or naturalisation, 'provided that such provisions do not discriminate against any particular nationality'.[106] Hence, while distinctions made solely on the basis of race, colour, descent, national or ethnic origin are impermissible,[107] the provisions of Article 1(2) appear

---

[98] Ibid.
[99] See the Convention on Elimination All forms of Discrimination against Women (1979) below chapter 15.
[100] Cassese, *International Criminal Law* (Oxford University Press, 2008) p. 138.
[101] General Recommendation No. 8: Identification with a Particular Racial or Ethnic Group (Art 1, para 1 and 4):. 22/08/90, General Recommendation No. 8 (General Comments).
[102] See Article 1; Meron, above n.92, at p. 286.
[103] See Vierdag, above n.1.
[104] At first sight the usage of the terminology may restrict the activities contained therein to public life (see Article 1(1)). However, a number of other provisions indicate a broader approach, e.g. see Article 2(1)(d). Similarly, Article 5 provides for a number of rights not necessarily coming within the ambit of public life. To reconcile these apparently conflicting approaches it has been suggested that the term public life is used in the wider sense encompassing all sectors of organised life of community, an interpretation presented in support of the rejection of draft proposal of the limiting of the scope of Article 1(1) of the Convention. See McDougal, Lasswell and Chen, *Human Rights and World Public Order: The Basic Policies of an International Law of Human Dignity* (Yale University Press, 1980) p. 593.
[105] Article 1(2).
[106] Ibid. Article 1(3).
[107] Ibid. Article 1(3).

objectionable as permitting *de facto* discrimination on the basis of nationality. The provisions of the Article represent the unfortunate reality that non-nationals can be denied equal treatment under international law.[108] The denial of citizenship as a tool for discrimination has been applied in several States.[109] The Committee on the Elimination of All Forms of Racial Discrimination has made concerted efforts to interpret the provisions of Article 1(2) so as to emphasise that discrimination based solely on fundamental human rights, such as the right to equality, nevertheless remains impermissible. According to the Committee:

> [a]lthough some of these rights, such as the right to participate in elections, to vote and to stand for election, may be confined to citizens, human rights are, in principle, to be enjoyed by all persons. States parties are under an obligation to guarantee equality between citizens and non-citizens in the enjoyment of these rights to the extent recognized under international law.[110]

Article 2 of the Race Convention sets out State obligations in detail with the aim of pursuing 'by all appropriate means and without delay a policy of eliminating racial discrimination in all its forms and promoting understanding among all races'. The parties not only undertake to refrain from permitting discriminatory acts, but promise to take positive steps through legislative and administrative policies to prohibit and condemn racial discrimination. Article 2(1) reads as follows:

> States parties condemn racial discrimination and undertake to pursue by all appropriate means and without delay a policy of eliminating racial discrimination in all its forms and promoting understanding among all races, and, to this end:
>
> (a) Each State Party undertakes to engage in no act or practice of racial discrimination against persons, groups of persons or institutions and to ensure that all public authorities and public institutions, national and local, shall act in conformity with this obligation;
>
> (b) Each State Party undertakes not to sponsor, defend or support racial discrimination by any person or organizations;
>
> (c) Each State Party shall take effective measures to review governmental, national and local policies, and to amend, rescind or nullify any laws and regulations which have the effect of creating or perpetuating racial discrimination wherever it exists;

---

[108] In further highlighting this unfortunate reality Provost makes the following observations '[t]he *travaux preparatoires* of the Universal Declaration and the Political Covenant reveal unambiguously that the reference to 'national origins' in those instruments was meant to proscribe distinctions between citizens born in the country and citizens who had been naturalised, and not between nationals and aliens' Provost, *International Human Rights and Humanitarian Law* (Cambridge University Press, 2002) at pp. 215–216.

[109] In illustration the discriminatory position in Bahrain, Bahrain Women's Association submitted to the Human Rights Council that 'Bahraini women who marry non-Bahraini citizen are denied the right to extend their citizenship to their children, who therefore have limited access to high education, health care, land ownership, political participation and employment. This inequality not only denies women their basic rights as citizens, it also denies children their right as human beings. It stated that although Bahrain mentioned in its report that "a draft law on citizenship is being debated", this draft remains the same since it does not permit Bahraini mothers to transmit their nationality to their children. Lately, even this draft was withdrawn from the parliament. The numbers of children from Bahraini mothers who do not have a nationality are increasing'. Human Rights Council, June 2008 A/HRC/8/L. 2/Rev. 1/Corr. 1, para 13.

[110] General Recommendation No. 30. Discrimination Against Non Citizens: 01/10/2004, para 3.

(d) Each State Party shall prohibit and bring to an end, by all appropriate means, including legislation as required by circumstances, racial discrimination by any persons, group or organization;

(e) Each State Party undertakes to encourage, where appropriate, integrationist multiracial organizations and movements and other means of eliminating barriers between races, and to discourage anything which tends to strengthen racial division.

Article 2(1), imposes a twofold obligation on parties: one positive and the other negative. The negative obligation prevents parties or their agents from undertaking acts or practices of racial discrimination against persons or institutions. The second, positive, obligation is conducted through effective, concrete measures to bring to an end any form of racial discrimination. Hence, while Article 2(1)(a) prevents a State party from sponsoring, defending or supporting racial discrimination by any persons or organisations, Article 2(1)(c) and (d) impose on States parties positive obligations to take effective measures to eradicate the possibility of racial discrimination by any person, group of persons or organisation. Article 2(1)(e) perhaps reveals the essence of the whole section, stating that the aim of each State party is to encourage integration of racial groups in the nation-State.

One of the most significant features of the Convention is the exception to the general rule of equality for all individuals. The provisions relating to affirmative action find expression in Articles 1(4) and 2(2).[111] According to Article 1(4):

Special measures taken for the sole purpose of securing adequate advancement of certain racial or ethnic groups or individuals requiring such protection as may be necessary in order to ensure such groups or individuals equal enjoyment or exercise of human rights and fundamental freedoms shall not be deemed racial discrimination, provided, however, that such measures do not, as a consequence, lead to the maintenance of separate rights for different racial groups and that they shall not be continued after the objectives for which they were taken have been achieved.

This is complemented by Article 2(2), which represents details of the obligations undertaken by the States parties, who:

[S]hall, when the circumstances so warrant, take, in the social, economic, cultural and other fields, special and concrete measures to ensure the adequate development and protection of certain racial groups or individuals belonging to them, for the purpose of guaranteeing them the full and equal enjoyment of human rights and fundamental freedoms. These measures shall in no case entail as a consequence the maintenance of unequal or separate rights for different racial groups after the objectives for which they were taken have been achieved.

---

[111] For similar provisions see Article 2(3) of the Declaration, Article 5 of the Indigenous and Tribal Populations Convention (ILO No. 107), 328 U.N.T.S 247; Cmnd. 328, entered into force 2 July 1959. According to UNESCO Convention provision of separate schools by States parties will not be deemed discriminatory. Also see the UNESCO Declaration on Race and Racial Prejudice 1978 UN Doc. E/CN.4/Sub.2/1982/2/Add.1, annex V Article 9(2).

The two provisions are of potentially considerable significance for attempts to establish regimes of genuine equality for individuals. The insertion of these provisions are necessary as the Convention [aims] 'not only to achieve *de jure* equality, but also *de facto* equality, allowing the various ethnic, racial and national groups to enjoy the same social development. The goal of *de facto* equality is considered to be central to the Convention'.[112] The essence of both these articles of the Race Convention is that, although permitting for special measures, they are designed to be of a temporary nature. Their essential purpose is to generate equality in real terms. McKean's view is that Article 1(4) and 2(2) provide a synthesis

> which incorporates the notion of special temporary measures, not as an exception to the principle but as a necessary corollary to it, demonstrates the fruition of the work of the Sub-Commission and the method by which the twin concepts of discrimination and minority protection can be fused into the principle of equality.[113]

A number of provisions of the Convention have a very broad scope and in practice may seem rather over-ambitious. Article 4, for instance, and primarily for this reason, has been regarded as one of the most controversial of articles within the Convention.[114] According to it:

> State Parties condemn all propaganda and all organizations which are based on ideas or theories of superiority of one race or group of persons of one colour or ethnic origin, or which attempt to justify or promote racial hatred and discrimination in any form, and undertake to adopt immediate and positive measures designed to eradicate all incitement to, or acts of, such discrimination and, to this end, with due regard to the principles embodied in the Universal Declaration of Human Rights and the rights expressly set forth in article 5 of this Convention, inter alia:
>
> (a) Shall declare an offence punishable by law all dissemination of ideas based on racial superiority or hatred, incitement or racial discrimination, as well as all acts of violence or incitement to such acts against any race or group of persons of another colour or ethnic origin, and also the provision of any assistance to racist activities, including the financing thereof;
>
> (b) Shall declare illegal and prohibit organizations, and also organized and all other propaganda activities, which promote and incite racial discrimination, and shall recognize participation in such organizations or activities as an offence punishable by law;
>
> (c) Shall not permit public authorities or public institutions, national or local, to promote or incite racial discrimination.

---

[112] Eide, *Possible Ways and Means of facilitating the Peaceful and Constructive Solution of Problems Involving Minorities* E/CN.4/Sub.2/1993/34, para 95.

[113] McKean, above n.1, p. 159.

[114] Korengold, 'Lessons in Confronting Racist Speech: Good Intentions, Bad Results and Article 4(a) of the Convention on the Elimination of All Forms of Racial Discrimination' 77 *Minnesota Law Review* (1993) 719.

The provisions of Article 4 carry far-reaching implications. States parties not only take upon themselves the prohibition of discriminatory acts, but also undertake to declare illegal and prohibit organisations and activities which attempt to disseminate opinions of racial superiority inciting racial discrimination. The scope of the obligations imposed are also far wider than those of other international provisions such as Article 20(2) of ICCPR. Article 4 uses a very wide and strong terminology and the question arises as to the resolution of any conflict of rights which is inherent in the provisions of the article.[115]

According to Article 5, States undertake to prohibit and to eliminate racial discrimination in all its forms and to guarantee the right of everyone without distinction as to race, colour or national or ethnic origin to equality before the law. The article then goes on to enumerate a number of rights, including both civil and political rights as well as economic, social and cultural rights. Article 6 provides remedies for those who have been involved in racial discrimination, be it in their official or unofficial capacity. It provides:

> State Parties shall assure to everyone within their jurisdiction effective protection and remedies, through the competent national tribunals and other States institutions, against any acts of racial discrimination which violate his human rights and fundamental freedoms contrary to this Convention, as well as the right to seek from such tribunals just and adequate reparation or satisfaction for any damage suffered as a result of such discrimination.

It has been suggested that a liberal interpretation of the provisions of the article, particularly bearing in mind the phrase 'just and adequate reparation or satisfaction' for any damage suffered as a consequence of racial discrimination, would be a considerable advance over previous instruments such as Article 8 of the UDHR, Article 2 of ICCPR, and Article 7(2) of the Declaration on the Elimination of All forms of Racial Discrimination which have dealt with the subject previously.[116] In accordance with Article 7, States parties undertake to adopt immediate and effective measures, particularly in the field of teaching, education, culture and information, with a view to combating prejudices which lead to racial discrimination and to promote understanding, tolerance and friendship among nations and racial or ethnic groups.

(b) Issues of implementation

We have already noted that there exists a broad consensus on the issue of the prohibition of racial discrimination. This consensus is evidenced through an analysis of international treaty law as well as customary law. As far as the Race Convention is concerned, its unique position is reflected through the degree of its ratifications and by the readiness of States to endorse its provisions by the necessary amendments to their domestic legislation. A closer analysis, even that of the issue of racial equality, however, discloses a number of weaknesses in implementation. Discrimination based on race, colour, ethnicity, language, religion and culture is a historical as well as a contemporary phenomenon. The consequences of traditional practices of discrimination have produced complex problems in contemporary

---

[115] Which right is to be given priority (freedom of expression as against non-discrimination) UN Docs E/CN.4/837, paras 73–83; E/3873, paras 144–188; A/6181, paras 60–74.
[116] Lerner, *Group Rights and Discrimination*, above n.1, at pp. 60–61.

terms; it is largely recognised that legal prohibitions *per se* would not be completely effective in societies with an ancient history of rivalries between communities or where there are vast economic, educational and cultural differences amongst various groups.

The differences are generally a result of prejudice and past acts of discrimination. As Meron rightly points out:

> Past acts of discrimination have created systematic patterns of discrimination in many societies. The present effects of past discrimination may be continued or even exacerbated by facially neutral policies or practices that, though not purposely discriminatory, perpetuate the consequences of prior, often intentional discrimination. For example, when unnecessarily rigorous educational qualifications are prescribed for jobs, members of racial groups who were denied access to education in the past may be denied employment.[117]

In providing an example of language-based discrimination, Henrard alludes to the situation when only one language is used as a medium of instruction in a multilingual state and a seemingly equal baseline proves to entail serious substantive inequalities for those who are not taught in their mother tongue.[118] Craven, in supporting the concept of *de facto* equality makes a similarly valid point that 'the concept of discrimination in international law, while requiring strict scrutiny of any differential treatment based on a suspect classification, does not automatically prohibit differential treatment if justified by some socially relevant objective'.[119] CERD, itself has also commented and as we shall be elaborating in more detail, not all forms of discrimination are automatically invidious, and, therefore, have to be viewed from the perspective of actual impact or effect.[120] In order to overcome past disabilities, a strong case can be made for affirmative action. However, if there is logic in the argument for overcoming past acts of discriminatory behaviour, there is also a strong lobby which would not be in favour of a *prima facie* discriminatory treatment in order to compensate for previous acts. In order to overcome past acts of discrimination going back to earlier generations, would it be fair and just to give priority to the contemporary less meritorious claims?

The Race Convention, as has been seen, provides for affirmative action policies. On the other hand, a closer analysis of the *travaux préparatoires* and the reservations entered against the articles relating to the provisions of affirmative action provides complexity to the issues. It, hence, remains unclear whether the broad consensus which is represented in the general principles of the Convention is also reflected in the provisions related to affirmative action. It may well be that at present, in view of the lack of clarity regarding State practice, it is difficult to unequivocally accept the view that the principles relating to affirmative action exist in customary international law. Another recurrent problem, which deserves attention, is the nature of the political and administrative structures in various States. There are a number of patently undemocratic regimes which perpetuate on the basis of the exploitation of conflicts within the society. One has only to consider the problems

---

[117] Meron, above n.92, p. 289 (footnotes omitted). The language in which education is imparted can discriminate minority linguistic groups. See Henrard, 'Education and Multiculturalism: the contribution of Minority Rights?' 7 *IJMGR* (2000) 393, at p. 395.

[118] Ibid. p. 393.

[119] Craven, above n.4, at p. 184.

[120] General Recommendation No. 14: Definition of Discrimination (Art. 1. para 1) (Forty-Second Session 1993) para 2.

confronted by such States as Nigeria, Rwanda, Burundi and a number of other African, Latin American and Asian States to appreciate the problems confronted.[121]

The problems of racial, ethnic and religious tensions are confronted by most States, regardless of their official admission. Whereas these tensions are evident in the advanced industrialised States of North America and Western Europe,[122] extreme forms of racial and ethnic divisions have taken place in States which have gained their independence in the latter half of the twentieth century. Tribal, ethnic and racial antagonism has been witnessed in many of the States of Africa. Similarly, acute divisions have been evident in Asia, with the prime examples of Sri Lanka, and India. In Malaysia, for instance, as Van Dyke explains in some detail, the issues of religion, race and linguistic identities are intertwined and discrimination by the Malays, 'the Bumiputras', persists against the Chinese, Indians and others.[123] In Sri Lanka through a culmination of discriminatory legislation and governmental policies, there has been a sustained effort to discriminate against the Tamils. The early restrictive and discriminatory laws relating to citizenship, and the linguistic and religious policies while working against the Tamils, represent an unfortunate picture.[124] In view of the socio-economic, political and historical difficulties it is not surprising to see that a complete end to all forms of racial discrimination is an enduring and painstaking task. The implementation mechanisms which exist in pursuance of States' conventional obligations certainly provide a reflection of the difficulties inherent in combating racial discrimination.

(iii) The Committee on the Elimination of Racial Discrimination (CERD)[125]

The key international implementation mechanism which has been devised as far as the elimination of racial discrimination is concerned is the procedure adopted under the Race Convention. The main vehicle for the performance of the Convention and for measures of implementation is CERD. The rules providing for the constitution and the functions of the CERD are stated in Article 8 and supplemented by the Committee's Rules of Procedure. CERD consists of 18 individuals serving for a period of fours years. They are elected from a list of persons nominated by the State parties from among their own nationals, each State party, however, may only nominate one person from its nationals. The experts are of high moral standing, and although elected by State parties, act in their personal capacity.[126] CERD, presently convenes twice every year, for a three to four week session; each session being held in February/March and August respectively. CERD is involved in all the procedures concerned with the implementation of the Convention. These systems consist of (a)

---

[121] For coverage of the pertinent issues see Minority Rights Group International (ed.), above n.27.

[122] Consider e.g. the ethnic tensions and riots in Bradford, UK.

[123] Van Dyke, above n.1, at p. 111.

[124] Nissan, *Sri Lanka: A Bitter Harvest* (Minority Rights Group, 1996); Hyndman, 'The 1951 Convention Definition of Refugee: An Appraisal with Particular Reference to the Case of Sri Lankan Tamil Applicants' 9 *HRQ* (1987) 49. Note the violation of Tamils and their rights during the Sri Lankan Army campaign of 2009.

[125] See Partsch, 'The Committee on the Elimination of Racial Discrimination' in Alston (ed.), above n.53, at pp. 339–368; Bernard-Maugiron, '20 Years After: 38th. Session of the Committee on the Elimination of Racial Discrimination' 8 *NQHR* (1990) 395; Lerner, 'Curbing Racial Discrimination – Fifteen Years CERD' 13 *IYHR* (1983) 170; Bayefsky, 'Making the Human Rights Treaties Work' in Henkin and Hargrove (ed.), *Human Rights: An Agenda for the Next Century* (American Society for International Law, 1994) pp. 229–296; Buergenthal, 'Implementing the UN Racial Convention' 12 *Texas International Law Journal* (1977) 187.

[126] Article 8(1).

a reporting procedure,[127] (b) an inter-State complaints procedure,[128] (c) an *ad hoc* conciliation commission to deal with inter-State complaints,[129] (d) petitions by individuals or groups on an optional basis,[130] and (e) petitions by inhabitants of colonial territories.[131] The key mechanism to date remains that of State reporting upon which we shall focus our attention. Article 9(1) provides that:

> State Parties undertake to submit to the Secretary-General of the United Nations, for consideration by the Committee, a report on the legislative, judicial, administrative or other measures which they have adopted and which give effect to the provisions of this Convention:
>
> (a) within one year after the entry into force of the Convention for the State concerned; and
>
> (b) thereafter every two years and whenever the Committee so requests. The Committee may request further information from the State Parties.

According to Article 9(2):

> The Committee shall report annually, through the Secretary-General, to the General Assembly of the United Nations on its activities and may make suggestions and general recommendations based on the examination of the reports and information received from State Parties. Such suggestions and general recommendations shall be reported to the General Assembly together with comments, if any, from State Parties.

States who are overdue in their submission of reports can produce consolidated reports. CERD has insisted that the reporting obligation is a substantial one and imposes an obligation on State parties to provide detailed information on a range of governmental activities and should be sufficiently exhaustive so as to inform of the situations or circumstances outside of the ambit of the governmental activities.[132] However, CERD has adopted a flexible approach in terms of the submission of periodic reports. In its revised procedure, it has decided that '[i]n a case where the period between the date of the examination of the last periodic report and the scheduled date for the submission of the next periodic report is less than two years, the Committee may suggest in its concluding observations that the State party concerned, if it so wishes, submit the latter report jointly with the periodic report to be submitted at the following date fixed in accordance with Article 9 of the Convention'.[133]

(a) Procedure

The reporting procedure is designed to obtain information regarding legislative and administrative practices of the States parties. They also help in the identification of the

---

[127] Article 9.
[128] Article 11.
[129] Rules 72–79 Rules of Procedure of CERD; HRI/GEN/3/Rev.3, pp. 81–84.
[130] Article 14.
[131] UN Fact Sheet No. 12 on the Committee of the Elimination of Racial Discrimination, www.unhchr.ch/html/menu6/2/fs12.htm <last visited 2 April 2009>.
[132] General Guidelines for the preparation of State Reports; see O'Flaherty, *Human Rights and the UN: Practice before the Treaty Bodies* (Brill, 2002) p. 80. Compilation of Guidelines on the Form and Content of the Reports to be Submitted by States Parties to the International Human Rights Treaties, HRI/GEN/2/Rev.4, pp. 53–61.
[133] UN Docs. CERD/C/SR.1446 and CERD/C/SR.1454, para 46; see O'Flaherty, above n.132, at p. 80.

overall policies which affect the position of racial or other less advantaged groups. Once a report is submitted it may take up to 12 months before consideration of the report. A confirmed list of reports due for consideration can be provided three months before the session. The Committee meets for two sessions a year, each of three weeks.[134] These sessions take place in February/March and August respectively and are held in Geneva. There are two three hours meetings each day. Once in receipt, each of the reports is assigned to a Country Rapporteur. The Country Rapporteur may have specialist knowledge about the state of affairs of the particular country and undertakes a detailed study of the report and identifies key issues arising from it. He also prepares a list of questions to be put to the State representative, although there is no standard practice in relation to the nature and content of these questions.[135]

State reports are considered in public sessions. Reports are normally introduced by the representative of the State. After the report has been introduced by the State representative, the Country Rapporteur addresses the Committee and presents his or her views of the report. Then it is up to the discretion of the members of CERD to make comments on the report. Once comments have been made by members of CERD, it is conventional for the State representative to provide answers or brief explanations of the issues raised. Alternatively he may offer to provide answers to outstanding issues either in the form of additional information or in the next report.[136]

After having considered the report from the State, CERD adopts its 'Concluding Observations'. The initial draft of the 'Concluding Observations' is prepared by the Country Rapporteur through the assistance of the Secretariat. The 'Concluding Observations' comprise a critique of the State report and of the response of the State representative to the scrutiny of the Committee, noting positive and negative feature and presenting suggestions and recommendations. The Committee has since 1995 adopted 'Concluding Observations' in meetings which are open to the public. 'Concluding Observations' are issued after 24 hours of their having been adopted by CERD, and are included in the annual report of the General Assembly of the United Nations. These observations can be accessed from the OHCHR website. Despite the often considerable delay in receiving State reports, with frequent and significant omissions or lack of information, the flexibility and ingenuity with which the Committee has performed its task has made the reporting procedure a success. Its flexibility in receiving delayed reports, the usage of a variety of sources of information alongside the content of the report, guidance as to the content of the State reports, and accommodating a system of examination of reports have all contributed towards a positive element.

The experience of CERD has revealed that a number of States regularly misconceive their obligations under the Convention. While some States have perceived no reporting obligations if they claim that racial discrimination does not exist within their States,[137] many others have felt under no obligation to report periodically if they have not instituted

---

[134] See Banton, 'Decision-Taking in the Committee on the Elimination of Racial Discrimination' in Alston and Crawford (eds), *The Future of UN Human Rights Treaty Monitoring* (Cambridge University Press, 2000) pp. 55–78.
[135] O'Flaherty, above n.132, at p. 83.
[136] See O'Flaherty, above n.132, at p. 82.
[137] Note e.g. the position adopted by Yemen and the comments given to its reports by CERD A/47/18 para 178. Banton, above n.1, at p. 300.

any further measures to combat discrimination.[138] Confusion has also been reported where a State declares that the ratification of treaty provisions is self-executory and the State party itself does not have to take any action to make changes in the constitutional or legal framework.[139] A frequent occurrence noted by CERD has been the delay in the preparation and submission of these reports. Thus, for example, Bangladesh's Seventh through Ninth periodic reports were due from July 1992–July 1996. Nepal submitted its consolidated ninth through to 13th reports after a delay of nine years. In order to deal with these inordinate delays, CERD has devised a procedure whereby compliance with the terms of Convention is considered in the light of the last report submitted. In instances where the relevant State party has failed to submit an initial report, CERD takes into consideration all information that has been submitted to it by the State party as well as any other information that is available to the Committee. Such a procedure can prove significant in forcing an otherwise recalcitrant State to submit reports – since State reports generally tend to present a more positive picture, the absence of submission is likely to result in adverse comments from CERD. A so-called 'second-round review' of State parties is also conducted by CERD in instances of failure of submission of a report within five year after the initial consideration of the above mentioned procedure.[140] Concerns of incomplete and unsatisfactory information of legislative, judicial and administrative mechanisms regarding implementation have regularly been put forward by CERD.

(b) Inter-State complaints procedure

The inter-State procedure under Articles 11–13 is supervised by CERD, with provisions for subordinate *ad hoc* conciliation commissions in the case of more serious disputes.[141] The provisions of the aforementioned articles are similar in nature to that of the ICCPR,[142] and other regional human rights instruments. In the case of the ICCPR however, the inter-State procedure applies only to States which have specifically recognised the competence of the Committee to receive reports.[143] In contrast to ICCPR, the inter-State complaints procedure contained in the Race Convention is obligatory and does not require a specific declaration.[144] This procedure has not been used frequently, although some States have made allegations against other States (non-parties) of having generated difficulties in their implementation obligations.[145]

---

[138] See generally Lerner, *The UN Convention*, above n.1.
[139] Ibid. p. 116.
[140] O'Flaherty, above n. 132, at p. 84.
[141] Articles 12 and 13.
[142] See Articles 41 and 42 of ICCPR.
[143] Article 41.
[144] See Rodley, 'United Nations Human Rights Treaty Bodies and Special Procedures of the Commission on Human Rights – Complementarity or Competition' 25 *HRQ* (2003) 882 at p. 888.
[145] Although not relevant to the inter-State procedure established in the Race Convention, the International Court of Justice examined Article 22 provisions of the Race Convention in a recent inter-State dispute between Georgia and Russia. The ICJ confirmed it had jurisdiction under Article 22 ICERD to conclude on the Convention's interpretation (although it didn't find specific violations against Russia, calling on both parties to refrain from racial discrimination See *Application of the International Convention on the Elimination of All Forms of Racial Discrimination (Georgia v. Russian Federation) Request for the indication of provisional measures Summary of the Order* (15 October 2008) www.icj-cij.org/docket/files/140/14809.pdf <last visited 2 April 2009>.

(c) Individual or group communications

Individual or group communications under the Convention operate on the basis of an optional system, with States parties being required to make a Declaration accepting the procedure.[146] In contrast to the Human Rights Committee, CERD has thus far considered very few communications. Since 1984, the Article 14 mechanism has been in operation although its significance has not matched that of the first Optional Protocol under ICCPR. Article 14(1) provides for a provision whereby a State Party:

> may at any time declare that it recognizes the competence of the Committee to receive and consider communications from individuals or groups of individuals within its jurisdiction claiming to be victims of a violation by that State Party of any of the rights set forth in this Convention. No communication shall be received by the Committee if it concerns a State Party which has not made such a declaration.[147]

According to Article 14(1), individuals or groups of individuals may submit communications. 'Groups of individuals', however, does not mean organisations.[148] According to Article 14(2), a State party agreeing to this procedure 'may establish or indicate a body within its national legal order which shall be competent to receive and consider petitions from individuals and groups of individuals within its jurisdiction who claim to be victims'. Hence, there exists the probability 'of a double safeguard against the embarrassment which may be caused to a State party by individual or group petitions'.[149] The attenuated nature of the provisions of the article are reflected through a careful reading, and the usage of the term 'petition' rather than 'communication' has led cynics to point out that the provisions are meant only 'to deliver the message'.[150] The Committee obtains all relevant information largely through written communications. CERD, after having considered this information then decides firstly whether the complaint is admissible and if so it provides an 'opinion' on the merits of the case. CERD is not a court and does not provide binding judgments. All steps under Article 14 are confidential until the Committee adopts its opinion. Opinions are reported in CERD's annual report together with a summary of information made available to the Committee. Firstly, the applicant has to communicate the case through the Secretariat. Once the communication has been submitted, the case is appointed a Working Group, the object of this exercise being the preparation of the case for the admissibility process. The designated Working Group may seek further information and clarifications.[151]

As noted above, after the submission of a communication the Working Group undertakes a preliminary enquiry into the admissibility of the communication. Admissibility

---

decisions are made in plenary hearings of the Committee, and can be reviewed subsequently in the light of change in circumstances. It is also possible for CERD to make a decision both on the admissibility as well as the merit of the case at the same time.[152] The admissibility requirements have strong similarities with other international procedures. The applicant must have exhausted all domestic remedies, and the communication must not be an abuse of the right of petition.[153] Anonymous applications are not acceptable, although the name of the complainant could be withheld at the individual's request. The communication must pertain to the violation of a Convention right conduct by a State party to the Convention.[154] However, unlike the First Optional Protocol of ICCPR, there is no requirement of the 'same matter' rule which in theory could also lead to simultaneous communications. In order to prevent such an occurrence, a number of States have entered reservations that they will only recognise the Committee's competence if the subject matter is not being or has not been considered under another international procedure.[155]

At the time of considering admissibility, the government concerned is invited to comment on any relevant issues. Final decisions on admissibility are made in the plenary session of the Committee. An admissibility decision is sent to both the State and the individual. In so far as the submission of the communication is concerned, a duly appointed representative can bring an application on behalf of an alleged victim or victims, though the representative making such a submission needs to establish the consent or authority of the victim. All (reasonable) domestic remedies must have been exhausted before a communication could be declared admissible. Article 14 provides a unique provision of having established national bodies to consider the petitions. It would appear that this provision is not obligatory. Thus, an application would still be successful in the absence of having followed such a procedure. There is no time limitation provided by the provisions of the Article itself although, according to the Rule of Procedure, the communication must be submitted within six months after all domestic remedies have been exhausted. This provision can be waived in exceptional circumstances.[156]

Once admissible, the State concerned is requested to offer its views within three months.[157] CERD is required to examine the merits of communication based upon all the evidence and information available from the parties. It may also rely upon documentation obtained from the United Nations bodies or specialised agencies that 'may assist in the disposal of the case'.[158] There is also the possibility of interim measures to safeguard the individual concerned and to avoid irreparable damage.[159] CERD has adopted the practice of making suggestions and recommendations even in instances where no violations have been found.[160] Once CERD establishes a view that there is sufficient evidence to proceed on the merits of the case, it formulates its opinion and makes any recommendations.

---

[152] Rule 94(7) of the Rules of Procedure of CERD; HRI/GEN/3/Rev.3. For an example of its operation, see *Kamal Quereshi* v. *Denmark* in the 2005 report of the Committee to the General Assembly, A/60/18, pp. 142–53.

[153] Rule 91(d) and (e) of the Rules of Procedure of CERD.

[154] UN Doc. HRI/GEN/3 pp. 89–96.

[155] See Lewis-Anthony and Scheinin, in Hannum (ed.), above n.148, at p. 48.

[156] Rules of Procedure of the Committee on the Elimination of Racial Discrimination, Rule 91(f) HRI/GEN/3/Rev.3.

[157] Ibid. Rule 94, para 2, UN Doc. CERD/C/35/Rev.3.

[158] Ibid. Rule 95, para 2.

[159] Ibid. Rule 94, para 3.

[160] Lewis-Anthony and Scheinin in, Hannum (ed.), above n.148, at p. 55.

The decisions made by CERD require the presence of two-thirds of its members, with a majority vote in favour of the decision.[161] However, the general practice of CERD has been to adopt opinions through consensus. Members are entitled to append individual opinions if they wish to do so. CERD has no power to make pecuniary or non-pecuniary awards. However, it is entitled and does make recommendations to the relevant State party. The State party is asked to inform CERD of the measures it has taken to comply with its opinions. Like the HRC, CERD, has adopted follow up procedures to deal with cases subsequent to their adoption.[162] A Special Rapporteur may be appointed in order to establish the measures which have been taken in response to the Committee's suggestions and recommendations.[163] In order to fulfil this role '[t]he Special Rapporteur(s) may establish such contacts and take such action as is appropriate for the proper discharge of the follow-up mandate'.[164]

While the wording of the article indicates the limitations in the powers of CERD, with the Committee dealing with the obvious hurdle of State sovereignty, the provisions relating to petitioning provide a considerable advance since the procedure allows racial or ethnic groups the right to petition before an international tribunal. Although, unlike the Optional Protocol, group petitions are acceptable, the scope is narrow in comparison both to Article 34 of ECHR and Article 44 of ACHR, which allow any person, non-governmental organisation or group of individuals to address petitions.

Jurisprudence

At the time of writing the Committee had dealt with 40 communications, with an additional three living cases waiting to be considered.[165] Of these, 17 had been found to be inadmissible by the Committee and no violation had been found in the case of a further 12 communications.[166] The Committee has, however, taken the perhaps unusual step of making recommendations to the State party, even when no violation has been found.[167] Although 53 States accept the jurisdiction of the Committee, communications have only been received in respect of nine States.[168] The most common complaint referred to the Committee relates to employment, either the subjection of the author to racist abuse in the work environment or difficulties in gaining employment as a result of racism. In *A. Yilmaz-Dogan* v. *The Netherlands*, the termination of the author's employment during her pregnancy due to the belief that foreign workers take advantage of sick leave after they have had children,[169] was held to be a violation of the author's right to work.[170] The failure of the

---

[161] UN Doc. HRI/GEN/3 pp. 89–96; Lewis-Anthony and Scheinin in, Hannum (ed.), above n.148, at p. 55.

[162] See the amended Rule 95 (as of 15th August 2005) of the Rules of Procedure of CERD. E/CN.4/2006/86 (27 February 2006).

[163] Ibid. Rule 95(6)

[164] Ibid. Rule 95(7).

[165] www2.ohchr.org/english/bodies/cerd/stat4.htm <last visited 2 April 2009>.

[166] www2.ohchr.org/english/bodies/cerd/stat4.htm <last visited 2 April 2009>.

[167] See *Michel L.N. Narrainen* v. *Norway*, Communication No. 3/1991 where the Committee recommended that 'to the State party that every effort should be made to prevent any form of racial bias from entering into judicial proceedings which might result in adversely affecting the administration of justice on the basis of equality and non-discrimination. Consequently, the Committee recommends that in criminal cases like the one it has examined, due attention be given to the impartiality of juries, in line with the principles underlying article 5(a) of the Convention', despite finding that it was not in a position to interpret Norwegian rules on Criminal Procedure. Paras 9.5–10. See also *B.M.S.* v. *Australia*, Communication No. 8/1996.

[168] www2.ohchr.org/english/bodies/cerd/stat4.htm <last visited 2 April 2009>.

[169] *A. Yilmaz-Dogan* v. *The Netherlands*, Communication No. 1/1984, para 2.2.

[170] Ibid. para 10.

police or other authorities to properly investigate instances of racist abuse and discrimination has been held to be a violation of Article 6 of the Convention, as has been the lack of an effective legal remedy.[171] The naming of a sports stand with a racially offensive name, despite the lack of intent was held to be unacceptable. However, in this case, as the State party had already taken steps to rectify the situation, the Committee simply recommended that the sign be taken down.[172] Offensive comments made by a politician against the Somali ethnic group, which were not sufficiently investigated by the authorities were held to have violated Articles 2(1)(d), 4 and 6 of the Convention.[173]

6 THEMATIC DISCUSSIONS

CERD has exhibited considerable ingenuity in developing innovative procedures and practice for an effective implementation of the Convention as well as raising awareness on matters pertaining to Racial Discrimination. One of these mechanisms is 'thematic discussions', a practice which has been instituted since 2000. In reliance upon its mandate under Article 9, CERD has deployed the practice of convening thematic discussions on matters of racial discrimination, though commonly affecting a number of States. In its first such exercise, CERD conducted a discussion of 'Discrimination against Roma'.[174] This discussion which took place over two meetings, each of three hours duration was preceded by consultative meeting of CERD with intergovernmental and non-governmental organisations.[175] Topics of discussion included the ability of Roma to maintain their identity, problems with the lack of statistical data, issues surrounding the police, employment, media stereotyping and the lack of political sensitivity.[176] Relying upon the information from various agencies, CERD was able to produce its General Comment on Discrimination against Roma. The next Thematic discussion was on the topic of Discrimination based on Descent. While it was felt at the event that defining this concept would be unwise, issues such as caste based discrimination, discrimination faced by Asians as a result of 11 September 2001, issues surrounding indigenous and minority groups and inheritance-based discrimination, were all discussed.[177] The discussion on non-citizens and racial discrimination was based mainly on the plight of refugees and asylum seekers. Stateless persons living in Arab countries, particularly Palestinians were of particular concern as were Haitians in the Dominican Republic.[178] The Declaration on the Prevention of Genocide was the product of thematic discussions.[179] In August 2008 the latest discussion took place on Special Measures and Affirmative Action. Thematic discussions are of great value not only in raising pertinent issues connected with racial discrimination but are also useful for State parties in developing their legislative and administrative policies. The discussion is open to all

---

[171] See *Kashif Ahmad* v. *Denmark*, Communication No. 16/1999, *L. R.* et al. v. *Slovak Republic*, Communication No. 31/2003, *The Jewish community of Oslo; the Jewish community of Trondheim; Rolf Kirchner; Julius Paltiel; the Norwegian Antiracist Centre; and Nadeem Butt* v. *Norway*, Communication No. 30/2003.
[172] *Stephen Hagan* v. *Australia*, Communication No. 26/2002.
[173] *Mohammed Hassan Gelle* v. *Denmark*, Communication No. 34/2004.
[174] Report in UN Doc. A/55/18 paras 442–453.
[175] O'Flaherty, above n.132, at p. 94.
[176] CERD/C/SR.1423.
[177] CERD/C/SR.1531 Thematic Discussion on Discrimination Based on Descent, Summary Record.
[178] CERD/C/SR.1624.
[179] CERD/C/66/1.

States parties, as well as the intergovernmental and non-governmental organisations involved with the subject.

7 CONCLUSIONS

Discrimination exists in various forms and its potentially evil manifestations are capable of affecting every member of society. As far as racial discrimination is concerned, it is highly persuasive to argue that there is now an absolute prohibition of it in international law. Discrimination based on race or ethnic origin is, however, only one facet of a wider phenomenon. Religious or linguistic discrimination, although associated with discrimination in general and categorised in the same bracket, alongside racial discrimination represent evil in their own right with far-reaching implications.

It may well be possible to argue that the general prohibition existing in international law against discrimination on grounds of *inter alia* sex, race, ethnicity, religion and language belongs to the category of peremptory norms of *jus cogens*. However, in reality the consensus formed on the issue of the prohibition of discrimination based on the grounds of race and ethnicity cannot be said to match the relative lack of concern shown on grounds of religion or sex. The issue of religion as we have seen in this chapter remains a difficult one in international law.

Even in the case of racial discrimination, the apparent international consensus may have many elements of superficiality. We have already noted that, while unanimity lies in the ideal of equality and a non-discriminatory society, considerable differences exist in achieving genuine equality and overcoming previous discrimination. Despite the large number of ratifications to the Race Convention, the issue of affirmative action has remained divisive. It is submitted that State practice is equivocal without giving any firm guidelines on the position as regards customary law. The Race Convention makes explicit provisions as to affirmative action and the issue is highly significant if progress is to be made in the direction of attaining genuine equality.

A number of tensions precipitate when the matter of taking measures to prohibit racial discrimination is considered, more particularly that of obligations on the part of States to outlaw organisations which incite racial hatred. Article 4 of the Race Convention has already generated debate, controversies and reservations. There can often be a fine dividing line between racist expressions as opposed to rightful expressions based on Freedom of Speech. Such delicate balance is also evident, as we have considered, in the contestations of the right to freedom of expression and speech *vis-à-vis* freedom of religion or belief. The United Nations' Special Rapporteur on Freedom of Religion or Belief has presented a defence for freedom of expression in the context of establishing an offence of defamation of religion. Yet at the same time it also remains the case that liberties which a tolerant society bestows would surely include as much a right to free expression of views and values as it would to prevent racial and religious-based abuse and violence. Within its own procedures, CERD also devised an early warning and urgent action procedure. According to this system, the Committee examines a case whereby there is a serious cause of concern. The procedure is not dependent on the State party having submitted a report. It has been invoked in a number of cases and allows the CERD to name the relevant party in public session and then or later in the session the situation is considered in public. Thus, in 1993 the Committee obtained information on the events taking place in the former Yugoslavia as a matter of urgency. Requests for further information can also be made. After its review of the situation CERD expresses its opinion and usually asks the relevant State to submit a report. It also may bring events to the attention of the High Commissioner for Human Rights, the Secretary-General of the United Nations or to the General Assembly or the Security Council, etc. Once a State is placed under this procedure it continues to remain under the scrutiny for an apparently indefinite period.[180] CERD, however, has the discretion to remove a particular State from its list, which it has previously considered under this procedure.[181]

The role of CERD is in some ways analogous to that of the Human Rights Committee working under the auspices of the ICCPR, and the responses which the States make to these two committees are also similar.[182] However, in contrast to the individual petitions before the Human Rights Committee, the individual and group petitions before CERD have so far not been rigorously invoked. CERD only became competent to receive Communications in 1982. Hence, it still remains speculative as to what role these petitions might play in the enforcement procedures.

---

[180] O'Flaherty, above n.132, at p. 90.
[181] Ibid.
[182] See above chapter 4.

13 The rights of minorities[1]

> Each nation has a unique tone to sound in the symphony of human culture; each nation is an indispensable and irreplaceable player in the orchestra of humanity.[2]

1 INTRODUCTION

Minorities, as groups, exist everywhere in various forms and sizes. There are ethnic, linguistic, cultural, racial, religious, linguistic, sociological and political minorities in practically every State of the world. State practice has been inconsistent and incoherent in so far as the protection of minority rights is concerned. Some States have adopted generous policies in not only recognising the existence of minorities but also in protecting their cultural and linguistic identity. However, there have been other States where genocide and physical extermination of minority groups has taken place. In their practices, many States continue to refuse to recognise that minorities are present within their territorial jurisdiction or have used forcible mechanisms of assimilation.[3] In view of the ambiguities emergent from State practices, international law has historically found it difficult to provide firm guidelines in defining 'minorities', and in articulating a detailed set of rights. An underlying theme in relation to the subject is that by way of contrast to individual human rights, minority rights – as collective rights – may pose more substantial threats to the territorial integrity of States or to those who form the government of those States.

At the time of the establishment of the League of Nations, an elaborate regime of minority rights treaties was established. The mechanisms that were adopted by the League of Nations to protect minorities were limited in nature and the minority protection regime collapsed well before the start of the Second World War. With the establishment of the United Nations, emphasis shifted to the position of individual human rights. The United

---

[1] See Alfredsson and Zayas, 'Minority Rights: Protection by the United Nations' 14 *HRLJ* (1993); Brölmann, Lefeber and Zieck (eds), *Peoples and Minorities in International Law* (Martinus Nijhoff Publishers, 1993); Rehman, *The Weaknesses in the International Protection of Minority Rights* (Kluwer Law International, 2000); Ali and Rehman, *Indigenous Peoples and Ethnic Minorities of Pakistan* (Curzon Press, 2001); Thornberry, *International Law and the Rights of Minorities* (Clarendon Press, 1991); Thornberry, *Minorities and Human Rights Law* (Minority Rights Group, 1991); Fottrell and Bowring (eds), *Minority and Group Rights in the New Millennium* (Brill, 1999); Weller, *Universal Minority Rights: A Commentary on the Jurisprudence of International Courts and Treaty Bodies* (Oxford University Press, 2007); Rehman, 'Minorities' in Cane and Conaghan (eds), *The New Oxford Companion to Law* (Oxford University Press, 2008) pp. 791–793.
[2] Claude Jr., *National Minorities: An International Problem* (Harvard University Press, 1995) p. 85.
[3] See Wirsing (ed.), *Protection of Minorities. Comparative Perspectives* (Pergamon Press, 1981).

Nations Charter contains several references to human rights. The Universal Declaration of Human Rights (UDHR) is committed to promoting individual rights and non-discrimination. There is no reference to minorities in either the United Nations Charter or the UDHR.[4] The Human Rights Commission, one of the principal functional commissions of the ECOSOC, nevertheless, established a Sub-Commission whose specific mandate included the prevention of discrimination and protection of minority rights. After the establishment of the Sub-Commission, efforts were made to project the subject of minority rights in the international arena. However, such efforts were stalled far too frequently, not only because of divisions over substantive claims put forward by minorities, but the subject of definition and identification has proved an intractable one.

2 DEFINITION OF MINORITIES[5]

The issue of defining minorities in independent States has been problematic. In 1966 Special Rapporteur Francesco Capotorti was assigned to the task of preparing a study pursuant to Article 27 of the ICCPR. In producing a detailed examination of the Rights of the Persons Belonging to Ethnic, Religious and Linguistic Minorities, Capotorti also formulated a definition, which is generally regarded as authoritative. According to his definition a 'minority' is a:

> group numerically inferior to the rest of the population of a State, in a non-dominant position, whose members–being nationals of the State–possess ethnic, religious or linguistic characteristics differing from those of the rest of the population and show, if only implicitly, a sense of solidarity, directed towards preserving their culture, traditions, religion or language.[6]

This definition proposed by Capotorti has been challenged and criticised on a number of grounds. The primary feature of the definition seems to be a combination of both objective and subjective elements in ascertaining a minority group.[7] Objective criteria would involve a factual analysis of a group as a distinct entity within the State '[P]ossessing stable ethnic, religious or linguistic characteristics that differ sharply from those of the rest of the population'.[8] The subjective criteria would be found on the basis that there exists 'a common will in the group, a sense of solidarity, directed towards preserving the

---

[4] See Eide, 'The Non-inclusion of Minority Rights: Resolution 217C (III)' in Alfredsson and Eide (eds), *The Universal Declaration of Human Rights: A Common Standard of Achievement* (Martinus Nijhoff Publishers, 1999) pp. 701–723 at p. 723.

[5] Rehman, 'Raising the Conceptual Issues: Minority Rights in International Law' 72 *Australian Law Journal* (1998) 615; Andrýsek, *Report on the Definition of Minorities* (Netherlands Institute of Human Rights, 1989); Rodley, 'Conceptual Problems in the Protection of Minorities: International Legal Developments' 17 *HRQ* (1995) 48.

[6] Capotorti, Special Rapporteur, *Study on the Rights of Persons Belonging to Ethnic, Religious and Linguistic Minorities UN Sales No E. 78.XIV.2, 1991*, 96, para 568.

[7] 'The prevailing approach to the definition of minorities [is one] which intermingles objective and subjective criteria'. Shaw, *International Law* (Cambridge University Press, 2008) p. 298.

[8] Sohn, 'The Rights of Minorities' in Henkin (ed.), *The International Bill of Rights: The Covenant on Civil and Political Rights* (Columbia University Press, 1981) pp. 270–289 at p. 278.

distinctive characteristics of the group'.[9] However, it could be argued that in view of the rather onerous considerations of evaluating both the objective and the subjective criterion, identification of a minority group might prove to be a difficult task.

The second proposition which needs to be addressed is that of the numerical strength of the group in question. It seems acceptable that the numerical strength must at least account for 'a sufficient number of persons to preserve their traditional characteristics',[10] hence a single individual could not form a minority group. On the other hand, it is contended that to put in place an absolute principle that in order to be recognised as a minority, an entity must necessarily be 'numerically inferior' places an unnecessarily heavy burden on the group and may well be factually incorrect. The minority concept, controversial as it is, cannot be treated in such a restrictive manner. A consideration of the case of the Bengalis of East Pakistan clearly reinforces this point. At the time of its emergence as an independent State, Pakistan was divided into two 'wings' of unequal sizes: East Bengal (subsequently renamed East Pakistan) and Western Pakistan. East Bengalis constituted nearly 54 per cent of the total population and in this sense the provincial population formed a numerical majority. On the other hand, the Bengalis had very little share in the political and constitutional affairs of the State. They were heavily discriminated against and suffered from the characteristic minority syndromes.[11] This minority syndrome was also evident in cases of the Black African majorities of South Africa and Rhodesia under the apartheid regimes.

Amongst the contemporary situations, the tragedies of 'ethnic cleansing' in the two Central African States of Rwanda and Burundi also defy this conception of a minority being necessarily 'numerically inferior'. As a fact of *realpolitik*, minorities are possibly undermined not so much by their weaknesses in numbers, but by their exclusion from power. As one commentator has aptly pointed out, 'the distinction . . . between nations and minorities is one of power. The element of power or powerlessness is the distinguishing characteristic of national and minority discourses'.[12] It may well be that a definition similar in nature to that of the one provided by Professor Palley, with its focus on the power-politics of a group may be more appropriate in these circumstances. According to her, a minority is 'any racial, tribal, linguistic, religious, caste or nationality group within a nation state and which is not in control of the political machinery of the state'.[13] Capotorti's insistence on numerical inferiority to the rest of the population would also generate difficulties in multi-minority situations where no single group forms an ascertainable majority. The *World Directory of Minorities* lists a number of States where it is difficult to isolate this straight forward majority–minority numerical relationship.[14]

The third issue to arise out of the Capotorti definition is that of the position of non-nationals within the State.[15] Non-nationals could form a significant proportion of a State's

---

[9] Ibid. at p. 279.

[10] UN Doc. E/CN.4/703 (1953), para 200.

[11] See Dinstein, 'Collective Human Rights of Peoples and Minorities' (1976) 25 *ICLQ* 102 at p. 112.

[12] Cullen, 'Nations and Its Shadow: Quebec's Non-French Speakers and the Courts' 3 *Law and Critique* (1992) 219 at p. 219.

[13] Palley, *Constitutional Law and Minorities* (Minority Rights Group, 1978) p. 3; also see Fawcett, *The International Protection of Minorities* (Minority Rights Group, 1979), p. 4; Laponce, *The Protection of Minorities* (University of California Press, 1960) pp. 8–9.

[14] See Minority Rights Group (ed.), *World Directory of Minorities* and Indigenous Peoples www.minorityrights.org/directory <last visited 6 October 2008>, see, for example, Uganda, Nigeria and Zambia.

[15] See Weis, *Nationality and Statelessness in International Law* (Sijthoff and Noordhoff, 1979).

13

The rights of minorities

population, and although the main thrust of the development of international law of human rights has devoted itself to a consideration of the plight of nationals within the State, the rights of the non-nationals, as individuals, are also increasingly becoming a concern of human rights law. Indeed, as Lillich correctly points out:

> the question of rights of aliens is inextricably linked to the contemporary international human rights law movement because it poses a clear test of relevance and enforceability of international human rights norms which have developed since World War II.[16]

Non-nationals include migrant workers, refugees and Stateless persons and the phenomenal increase in their numbers in recent years has brought considerable attention to their position in international human rights law.[17] Subsequent chapters in this book examine the vulnerabilities of migrant workers,[18] refugees and stateless persons,[19] both from a human rights perspective as well as imperilled minority groups. The *travaux préparatoires* of the ICCPR are not extremely helpful on the matter, though whatever guidance that can be obtained points more in the direction of the exclusion of non-nationals from the category of minorities as envisaged in Article 27.[20] The Special Rapporteur Capotorti has also taken the position that since foreigners are able to take advantage of protection bestowed upon them within customary international law and other international agreements, this provision should exclude non-nationals.[21] On the other hand, it needs to be noted that Article 27 of the International Covenant on Civil and Political Rights, unlike Article 25, refers to persons, as opposed to citizens.[22] It is also significant to note the views put forward by the Human Rights Committee in its general comment on Article 27. According to the Committee:

---

[16] Lillich, *The Human Rights of Aliens in Contemporary International Law* (University Press, 1984) p. 2; 'the whole human rights movement may be seen as an attempt to extend the minimum international standards from aliens to nationals', Akehurst, *A Modern Introduction to International Law* (Harper Collins, 1987) p. 91.

[17] See Weis, above n.15; Goodwin-Gill and McAdam, *The Refugee in International Law* (Oxford University Press, 2007) pp. 285–354; D'Souza and Crisp, *The Refugee Dilemma* (Minority Rights Group, 1985); Hathaway, *The Law of Refugee Status* (Butterworths, 1991); Weissbrodt, *The Human Rights of Non-Citizens* (Oxford University Press, 2008).

[18] See below chapter 20.

[19] See below chapter 19.

[20] See the additional draft clause to [Article 27] that was proposed by Yugoslavia limiting the Article to 'citizens', UN Doc. A/C.3/SR.1103 para 54; the Indian delegate Mr. Kaslival 'wondered whether the committee would not prefer to replace the word "persons" by "citizens"'. According to Mrs. Afnan, the Iraqi delegation understood 'the obligation of a state within its own territory could only be towards its own citizens. It was in that sense that she understood the word "person" used in the Article', UN Doc. A/C.3/SR.1104, para 7; also note the Pakistani position UN Doc. A/C.3/SR. 1104, para 17; *cf.* the position of the representative from Equador Ibid. para 45.

[21] Capotorti, above n.6 at p. 12, para 57. for a challenge to these assertions see Cholewinski, *Migrant Workers in International Human Rights Law: Their Protection in Countries of Employment* (Clarendon Press, 1997) at pp. 54–55.

[22] Attempts to replace in Article 2(1) the term individuals with 'nationals' or 'citizens' could not succeed. UN Doc. A.C.3/SR. 1103, para 38; The exclusive focus of Capotorti has come under considerable academic criticism. According to Tomuschat 'One can not fail to observe that the word employed [in Article 27] is "persons", not "nationals"'. C. Tomuschat, 'Protection of Minorities under Article 27 of the International Covenant on Civil and Political Rights' (1983) *Völkerrecht als Rechtsordnung, Internationale Gerichtsbarkeit, Menschenrechte, Festschrift für Herman Mosler*, 945, at p. 960; similarly Dinstein is critical of this view of the special Rapporteur 'this interpretation cannot be endorsed'. Dinstein, 'Freedom of Religion and the Protection of Religious Minorities' in Dinstein and Tabory (eds), *The Protection of Minorities and Human Rights* (Martinus Nijhoff Publishers, 1992) pp. 145–169 at p. 157.

[t]he terms used in article 27 indicate that the persons designed to be protected are those who belong to a group and who share in a common culture, a religion and/or a language. Those terms also indicate that the individuals designed to be protected need not be citizens of the State party. In this regard, the obligations deriving from article 2.1 are also relevant, since a State party is required under that article to ensure that the rights protected under the Covenant are available to all individuals within its territory and subject to its jurisdiction, except rights which are expressly made to apply to citizens, for example, political rights under article 25. *A State party may not, therefore, restrict the rights under article 27 to its citizens alone.*[23]

13

The Committee's views on the position of those groups whose degree of permanence could be questioned are also interesting. The Committee spells out its views in para 5.2 of the Comment:

[a]rticle 27 confers rights on persons belonging to minorities which 'exist' in a State party. Given the nature and scope of the rights envisaged under that article, it is not relevant to determine the degree of permanence that the term 'exist' connotes. Those rights simply are that individuals belonging to those minorities should not be denied the right, in community with other members of their group, to enjoy their own culture, to practise their religion and speak their language. Just as they need not be nationals or citizens, they need not be permanent residents. *Thus, migrant workers or even visitors in a State party constituting such minorities are entitled not to be denied the exercise of those rights.*[24]

Notwithstanding these views put forward by the Human Rights Committee, there remains a prevalent confusion as to the national status of claimant groups. Several of the recent minority rights instruments make reference to the term 'National'. This includes the United Nations Declaration on the Rights of Persons Belonging to National or Ethnic, Religious and Linguistic Minorities (1992)[25] and Council of Europe's Framework Convention for the Protection of National Minorities (1994).[26] This has provided some States with the opportunity to claim a limitation on the scope of minority status – a criticism reiterated in the fifth session of the Working Group on Minorities.[27] In the view of these States, nationality is the essential pre requisite for making any claims to the status of a minority. South Asia provides a number of examples, including those of the Biharis of Bangladesh, the Tamils of Sri Lanka and the Nepali-speaking Bhutanese, where the relevant State has exploited the nationality issue in order to discriminate against and persecute a minority group.

Another area on which Capotorti's definition could be challenged is its narrowness by concentrating almost exclusively upon what has been termed as 'minorities by will' and overlooking the position of 'minorities by force'. 'Minorities by will' and 'minorities by force' are terms engineered by Laponce.[28] Explaining the distinctions between the two

[23] Para 5.1. Italics added. Human Rights Committee, General Comment No. 23 (Fiftieth Session 1994) Report of the Human Rights Committee 1 GAOR 49th Session, Supp. No. (A/49/40) pp. 107–110.
[24] Ibid. para 5.2; italics added.
[25] Adopted by the General Assembly 18 December 1992, GA Res. 135, UN GAOR 47 Sess. 49 at 210, UN Doc. A/Res/47/135. 32 I.L.M. (1993) 911.
[26] Opened for signature 1 February 1995, entered into force 1 February 1998. E.T.S. 157; 34 I.L.M. (1995) 351.
[27] See *Report of the Working Group on Minorities on its Fifth Session* E/CN.4/Sub.2/1999/21 paras 19–20.
[28] Laponce, above n.13, pp. 12–13.

kinds of minorities, he comments: 'two fundamentally different attitudes are possible for a minority in its relationship with the majority: it may wish to be assimilated or it may refuse to be assimilated. The minority that desires assimilation but is barred is a minority by force. The minority that refuses assimilation is a minority by will.'[29]

3 ANALYSING THE SUBSTANTIVE RIGHTS OF MINORITIES

It is well established that the rights of minorities are inter-related and are dependant upon the rights of the individual. Minority rights are built upon the existing framework of rights of the individual human being. The right to existence, the right to equality, non-discrimination, freedom of religion or belief, expression and culture, therefore, are integral parts of individual and minority rights. The rights of minorities, however, have a collective dimension.[30] As we shall see in greater detail, the minority right to existence is not exclusive to the physical existence of members of a particular minority but would also include, *inter alia*, a cultural, religious, linguistic existence, without which the group in question would lose its distinctiveness.[31] In the context of group rights the right to equality and non-discrimination often raises issues of affirmative active and positive discrimination for the groups that have historically been deprived of equal opportunities.[32] Freedom of religion and of cultural, linguistic and political autonomy for minorities is often related to notions of self-determination and possibly independent statehood.[33] This latter claim of political self-determination leading to secession and independence poses a major threat to the existing world order – States and the governments in charge are very sceptical of encouraging any such claims.

(i) The right to life and physical existence

The right to life and physical existence represents the most fundamental rights of all individuals. The right is protected in all human rights instruments.[34] It is an unfortunate historical and contemporary feature of human existence, that individuals have in many cases been deprived of their right to life because of their religion, culture, race or colour. The activity of physical destruction of minority groups is a long and painful one. In more modern times it has been labelled as genocide.[35] Raphael Lemkin, a Polish jurist of Jewish origin, is accredited with developing the modern principles relating to the crime of genocide and for coining the term itself.[36]

---

[29] Ibid.

[30] Thornberry, *International Law and the Law of Minorities,* above n.1, at p. 57.

[31] Ibid.

[32] See McKean, *Equality and Discrimination under International Law* (Clarendon Press, 1983); Lerner, *Group Rights and Discrimination in International Law* (Martinus Nijhoff Publishers, 1991); Banton, *International Action against Racial Discrimination* (Clarendon Press, 1996).

[33] See Rehman, 'Autonomy and the Rights of Minorities in Europe' in Wheatley and Cumper (eds), *Minority Rights in the New Europe* (Kluwer Law International, 1999) pp. 217–231.

[34] See the UDHR Article 3; ECHR Article 2, and the Sixth Protocol (1983), ICCPR Article 6, ACHR Protocol to American Convention on Human Rights to Abolish the Death Penalty; AFCHPR, Article 4.

[35] Whitaker aptly describes this activity as 'the ultimate crime and gravest violation of human rights it is possible to commit'. Special Rapporteur B. Whitaker, *Revised and Updated Report on the Question of the Prevention and Punishment of the Crime of Genocide* UN Doc. E/CN.4/Sub.2/1985/6, 5.

[36] Lemkin, *Axis Rule in Occupied Europe* (Carnegie Endowment for International Peaces, 1944) p. 79; Porter, 'What is Genocide? Notes towards a Definition' in Porter (ed.), *Genocide and Human Rights: A Global Anthology* (University Press of America, 1982) p. 5.

In international legal discourse the usage of the term 'genocide' is a relatively new one, and appeared for the first time during the Nuremberg trials in a separate category. Its recognition as a crime in international law was a direct consequence of the atrocities committed during the Second World War. After the establishment of the United Nations, international law confirmed genocide as a crime through the Convention on the Prevention and Punishment of the Crime of Genocide[37] (hereafter the Convention). According to Article I of the Convention:

> The Contracting Parties confirm that genocide, whether committed in time of peace or in time of war, is a crime under international law which they undertake to prevent and to punish.

According to Article II, genocide consists of:

> any of the following acts committed with intent to destroy, in whole or in part, a national, ethnical, racial or religious group, as such:
>
> (a) Killing members of the group;
>
> (b) Causing serious bodily or mental harm to members of the group;
>
> (c) Deliberately inflicting on the group conditions of life calculated to bring about its physical destruction in whole or in part;
>
> (d) Imposing measures intended to prevent births within the group;
>
> (e) Forcibly transferring children of the group to another group.

Despite the coming into operation of the Genocide Convention, there have been several instances where minority groups have faced death and destruction.[38] A number of cases have highlighted weaknesses both in the substance as well as implementation in the Convention. The protected groups in the Convention are 'national, ethnical, racial or religious . . .'.[39] The Convention makes no reference to political and 'other' groups. Several cases reveal that political opponents have been a primary target of destruction and this omission is particularly unfortunate. The Convention does not criminalise the destruction of a culture, language or a religion.[40] Thus, individuals may be deprived of their cultural upbringing, their language or their faith and yet those responsible cannot be held accountable under this Convention. There is no explanation in relation to the meaning of 'national' or 'ethnical' 'racial' or 'religious' group as used in Article II. There has also been a lack of clarity as to what amounts to genocide. Whilst it is established that killing members of the group and causing serious bodily or mental harm amounts to genocide, the nature of such harm has been a matter of contention. Serious bodily or mental harm presumably has to

[37] Convention on the Prevention and Punishment of the Crime of Genocide, adopted 9 December 1948. Entered into force 12 January 1951. 78 U.N.T.S 277.
[38] Rehman, above n.1, p. 58.
[39] Article II.
[40] Rehman, above n.1, p. 58.

be given its natural and generally understood meaning. It is only in more recent times that rape and sexual violence has been categorised as amounting to genocide, a position that was confirmed by the Trial Chamber in the case of *Prosecutor* v. *Jean-Paul Akayesu*.[41] It noted that:

> rape and sexual violence, the Chamber wishes to underscore the fact that in its opinion, they constitute genocide in the same way as any other act as long as they were committed with the specific intent to destroy, in whole or in part, a particular group, targeted as such. Indeed, rape and sexual violence certainly constitute infliction of serious bodily and mental harm on the victims and are even, according to the Chamber, one of the worst ways of inflict harm on the victim as he or she suffers both bodily and mental harm.[42]

The trial chamber also took the view that forms of sexual violence and mutilation, including sterilisation and forced birth control, separation of sexes and prohibitions of marriages constituted genocide if all the aforementioned activities are intended to impose measures to prevent births within the group. The definition, however, retains elements of causational uncertainty when examining the meaning of 'deliberately inflicting on the group conditions of life calculated to bring about its physical destruction'.[43] In order to trigger genocide, it would presumably be deliberate actions as opposed to omission which are required.[44] The provision related to forcible transfer of children has also been questioned in that such a transfer may only be temporary, but not have a permanent effect in removing children from the community.[45]

A further gap in the Convention is the absence of a prohibition on demographic changes which could transform the proportion of a population.[46] Forced expulsions are not within the ambit of the Genocide convention, a point re-emphasised by Professor Cassese when he notes: '[i]t would seem that Article IV does not cover the conduct currently termed in non-technical language "ethnic cleansing", that is the forcible expulsion of civilians belonging to a particular group from an area, a village, or a town. In the course of drafting of the Genocide Convention, Syria proposed an amendment designed to add a sixth class of acts of genocide: "Imposing measures intended to oblige members of a group to abandon their home in order to escape the threat of subsequent ill-treatment". However, the draftsmen rejected this proposal.'[47] Recent International instruments have covered some ground to condemn forced or mass expulsions, and the jurisprudence emerging from international criminal tribunals have, at least in some cases, regarded the forcible expulsion of ethnic, racial or religious groups as constituting genocide.[48] It is positive to note that the Statute of the International Criminal Court regards mass expulsions as a crime against humanity.

---

[41] See *Prosecutor* v. *Jean-Paul Akayesu* Trial Chamber, Case No. (ICTR-96-4-T) para 7.8.1.

[42] Ibid.

[43] Article II (c).

[44] De Than and Shorts, *International Criminal Law and Human Rights* (Sweet & Maxwell, 2003) at p. 78.

[45] Ibid.

[46] Ermacora, 'The Protection of Minorities before the United Nations' 182 *Rec. des cours* (1983) 251–366 at p. 314.

[47] Cassese, *International Criminal Law* (Oxford University Press, 2003) at pp. 98–99.

[48] See Judge Riad express affirmation and recognition of 'ethnic cleansing' as a form of 'genocide' *The Prosecutor* v. *Kradžić and Mladić*, confirmation of indictment (IT-95-18-I) of 16 November 1995.

Similarly forced expulsions are likely to breach the provision of ICESCR on the right to housing.[49]

Modern day developments have created new threats to the survival of certain groups which were not covered by the provisions of the Convention. Activities such as the use of nuclear and chemical explosions, toxic environmental pollution, acid rain or the destruction of rain forests threaten the existence of peoples in several parts of the world.[50] The commission of the crime of genocide requires two necessary ingredients: *actus reus*, which is the physical action of destruction, in whole or in part, of a national, ethnical, racial or religious group, and *mens rea*, which is the mental element or the intent to commit such a crime. The crime of genocide requires a specific intent. Thus, no offence would be committed, regardless of the ruthlessness of the act and the barbarity of its consequences, without a specific intent of committing genocide.[51] In reiterating this point, the ICTY Trail chamber in the Akayesu case noted that:

> Genocide is distinct from other crimes inasmuch as it embodies a special intent or *dolus specialis*. Special intent of a crime is the specific intention, required as a constitutive element of the crime, which demands that the perpetrator clearly seeks to produce the act charged. Thus, the special intent in the crime of genocide lies in 'the intent to destroy, in whole or in part, a national, ethnical, racial or religious group, as such'.[52]

At the level of implementation several situations have confirmed the ineffectiveness of the Convention in the actual prevention and punishment of the crime of genocide. Genocide of minorities has taken place in a number of States. These States include both those which are parties to the Convention and those which have not ratified the Convention. A number of genocidal conflicts have taken place in the newly independent States of Asia and Africa. It would perhaps not be inaccurate to suggest that the minorities in the post-colonial States of Africa have suffered the most adverse consequences. The historical and contemporary position of many groups, including the Tutsis and Hutus in Rwanda and Burundi, the Ibos in Nigeria and the indigenous Africans of Southern Sudan provide an unfortunate commentary. On 1 July 1962, Rwanda declared its independence with Grégoire Kayibanda as President of the First Republic. However, independence triggered a large-scale genocide of the Tutsi minority, resulting in the massacre of approximately 20,000 Tutsi men, women and children.[53] In neighbouring Burundi, the genocidal conflict between Tutsis and Hutus went on for several years, resulting in the massacre of hundreds of thousands. Immediately after 1962, when Burundi gained her political independence, relations began to turn sour between the minority Tutsis and majority Hutus. In 1965, with the failure of a Hutu-backed coup attempt, several thousand Hutus were massacred. This triggered a bloody genocidal conflict resulting in the massacre of thousands of Tutsis, but more significantly of at least

---

[49] See Article 11 Right to Adequate Housing. Discussion by Craven, *The International Covenant on Economic, Social and Cultural Rights: A Perspective on its Development* (Clarendon Press, 1995) pp. 340–344.

[50] Whitaker, above n.35, p. 17.

[51] Robinson, *The Genocide Convention: A Commentary* (Institute of Jewish Affairs, 1960) pp. 58–59; Cassese, *International Criminal Law*, above n.47, pp. 141–144.

[52] See *Prosecutor* v. *Jean-Paul Akayesu* Trial Chamber, Case No. (ICTR-96-4-T) para 6.3.1; also see the ICTR in Kayishema and Ruzindan (paras 87–118) and Rutaganda (paras 44–63).

[53] Minority Rights Group (ed.), *World Directory of Minorities* (Minority Rights Group, 1997) pp. 505–509; Kuper, *Genocide: Its Political Use in the Twentieth Century* (Yale University Press, 1983) p. 62.

100,000 Hutus.[54] This conflict between the Hutus and Tutsis in both Rwanda and Burundi has continued unabated, leading in part to considerable accusations of negligence, indifference and complicity on the part of the international community in this genocidal conflict.[55]

On 23 October 1993, the Hutu President of Burundi, Melchior Ndadaye, was assassinated during an attempted coup by Burundi Tutsi soldiers. Hutu extremists used this assassination for a claim to Hutu-power not only in Burundi but also in Rwanda. In Rwanda, during 1994 the orgy of 'ethnic cleansing' resurfaced with unprecedented vigour. Thus '[i]n the weeks following the assassination of the Rwandan President Juvénal Habyarimana, somewhere between 500,000 and one million people were massacred in a genocide directed against the country's Tutsi ethnic minority as well as moderate Hutus'.[56] The atrocities committed during this time are graphically presented in the testimony that has emerged in the Criminal Trials conducted by the ICTR.[57] During the Trial of Jean-Paul Akayesu, one expert witness provided the testimony that:

> the Achilles' tendons of many wounded persons were cut to prevent them from fleeing. In the opinion of the Chamber, this demonstrates the resolve of the perpetrators of these massacres not to spare any Tutsi. Their plan called for doing whatever was possible to prevent any Tutsi from escaping and, thus, to destroy the whole group. Witness OO further told the Chamber that during the same meeting, a certain Ruvugama, who was then a Member of Parliament, had stated that he would rest only when no single Tutsi is left in Rwanda . . . many Tutsi bodies were often systematically thrown into the Nyabarongo river, a tributary of the Nile. Indeed, this has been corroborated by several images shown to the Chamber throughout the trial. She explained that the underlying intention of this act was to send the 'Tutsi back to their place of origin', to 'make them return to Abyssinia', in keeping with the allegation that the Tutsi are foreigners in Rwanda, where they are supposed to have settled following their arrival from the Nilotic regions.[58]

The 1994 wave of genocide and ethnic cleansing has been the most tragic in the history of the region. Notwithstanding a few successful trials of those involved in genocide and other crimes against humanity by the ICTR, many perpetrators remain at large and it seems unlikely that retribution and punishment could be dispensed to any more than a small proportion of individuals involved.[59] Ever since the creation of independent Sudan in 1956, the peoples of the southern regions have suffered from a form of 'colonial or alien domination' and the resulting conflict between the relatively prosperous and dominant north and the poor and underdeveloped south has caused the virtual extermination and liquidation of

---

[54] Ibid., p. 63.

[55] Alvarez, 'Crimes of States/Crimes of Hate: Lessons from Rawanda' 24 *Yale Journal of International Law* (1999) 365.

[56] Schabas, 'Justice, Democracy and Impunity in Post-Genocide Rwanda: Searching for Solutions to Impossible Problems' 7 *Criminal Law Forum* (1996) 523, at p. 523.

[57] See *Prosecutor* v. *Jean-Paul Akayesu* Trial Chamber, Case No. (ICTR-96-4-T).

[58] Ibid. paras 119 and 120.

[59] See the Judgment of 2 September 1998 *Prosecutor* v. *Jean-Paul Akayesu* Case No. (ICTR-96-4-T) convicting Jean-Paul Akayesu for crimes of genocide; also note the guilty plea by Jean Kambanda for acts of genocide by Rwanda's former Prime Minister–Sentence delivered on 4 September, 1998. www.un.org/ictr 1 March 1999.

thousands of southerners.[60] The rigour and upsurge of religious fundamentalism[61] which has been characterised in many parts of the world is typically reflected in the mood of the Khartoum government; religious, racial minorities and political opponents becoming unfortunate victims of a policy of discrimination, persecution, physical extermination and genocide. The case of southern Sudan epitomises a tragic tale of attempts at forced cultural, linguistic and religious assimilation, of Arabisation and of 'starvation deployed as a weapon against civilians'.[62] The agreements which have been made – most notably, the Southern Provinces Self-Government Act 1972, and the Koka Dam Agreement 1986 – unfortunately became a casualty of intolerance on the part of successive Khartoum governments and the political immaturity of rebel factions of the south.[63] The consequences, however, have been highly tragic for the minority groups of southern Sudan. According to recent reports, as a result of the persistent repression nearly 80 per cent of the entire population of southern Sudan has been displaced with about two million people having perished since 1983. The representatives from southern Sudan have attempted to raise this matter in the international forums, including the sessions of Working Group of Indigenous Populations; the practical international response however appears less than encouraging. An offshoot of the wider Sudanese conflict is reflected in the civil war in Darfur region of the country. Sudan's western region of Darfur has been plagued by conflict since the early 1970s. The people of Darfur region accuse the central government of neglect, economic exploitation and cultural and tribal imperialism. From the United Nations investigations it is now well-established that the government of Sudan in conjunction with Janjweed have been responsible for substantial violations of international humanitarian law as well as international human rights law.[64]

Large-scale genocide of minority groups has taken place in the Middle East and Asia.[65] It is not possible to provide a detailed analysis of the position in every State, although a reference to prime instances of genocide seems necessary. The Kurds, as a Minority Rights Group report comments, 'are the fourth most numerous people in the Middle East. They

---

[60] Hannum, *Autonomy, Sovereignty and Self-Determination: The Accommodation of Conflicting Rights* (University of Pennsylvania Press, 1990) pp. 308–327. Kuper says that during 1955–1972 nearly 500,000 southern Sudanese were killed, were victims of civil war, famine or disease. Nearly one million became refugees: Kuper, *Genocide*, above n.53, at p. 69.

[61] See the study produced by M.P. Moya, Special Rapporteur, *The Rise of Islamic Radicalism and the Future of Democracy in North Africa, Sub Committee on the Mediterranean Basin, Draft Interim Report*, May 1994.

[62] Kuper, 'Theoretical Issues Relating to Genocide' in Andreopoulos (ed.), *Genocide: Conceptual and Historical Dimensions* (University of Pennsylvania Press, 1994) pp. 31–46, at p. 42.

[63] See generally Eprile, *Sudan: The Long War* (1972); Morrison, *The Southern Sudan and Eritrea: Aspects of Wider African Problems* (1973); for extracts of the 1972 and 1986 agreements see Hannum, *Documents on Autonomy and Minority Rights* (Martinus Nijhoff, 1993) pp. 688–701.

[64] For details see Report of the International Commission of Inquiry on Darfur to the United Nations Secretary-General. The conflict has led to the displacement of over 2.5 million people and 500,00 deaths. On 14 July 2008, 10 charges of war crimes, genocide and crimes against humanity were filed against Sudan's President Omar al-Bashir. Sudan is not a party to the International Criminal Court and has in the past failed to cooperate with the Court by refusing to hand over two nationals previously indicated for war crimes and crimes against humanity. See Walker and Strucke, 'Darfur genocide charges for Sudanese President Omar al-Bashir' 14 July 2008 *Guardian*. As evident through the recent responses of the African Union as well as the International Criminal Court (October 2008, BBC website) the prospect of accountability for serious crimes including genocide in Darfur, appear remote.

[65] There are many painful instances, which though grave in magnitude would require volumes – for the case of Cambodia see Hannum, 'International Law and the Cambodian Genocide: The Sounds of Silence' (1989) 11 *HRQ*, 82; Hawk and Coomaraswamy, *Minorities in Cambodia* (Minority Rights Group, 1995).

constitute one of the largest races, indeed nations, in the world today to have been denied an independent State. Whatever the yardstick for national identity, the Kurds measure up to it'.[66] However, the atrocities which have been committed against the now fragmented Kurdish people, and the inadequate international response towards the plight of the Kurds in Iran, Iraq, Turkey and Syria remains one of the most unfortunate stories of human history. There is evidence to suggest that the Kurds have been made victims of genocide and that they have been and continue to be persecuted and discriminated against within the entire region.[67]

In the case of Iraq, memories of recent repression, persecution and genocide have attracted more international attention. These atrocities have resulted in the extermination and displacement of hundreds of thousands of innocent men, women and children. During the 'reign of terror' perpetuated by the former President Saddam Hussain, the Kurds, alongside other minorities such as the Shi'ites and the Marsh Arabs became victims of a genocidal campaign. During the presidency of Saddam Hussain, there were constant attacks made on Kurdish villages. The Kurds received the treatment of belonging to the fifth column during the Iran–Iraq war. In 1987, the Kurds became the victims of chemical attacks by the Iraqi forces.[68] During the month of April, a number of villages in the Sulaymaniya province and in the Balisan valley were attacked by mustard gas, leaving hundreds of innocent people dead or permanently disabled.[69] Unfortunately, as the Minority Rights Group report goes on to state, '[a]lthough news of these chemical attacks was disseminated internationally, no steps were taken to restrain Iraq. Furthermore, although a United Nations Commission investigated and confirmed the alleged use of chemical weapons by Iraq against Iran, it did not investigate allegations of their use against Iraqi Kurds, since it was not authorized to do so'.[70]

On 17 March 1988, the Iraqis used poisonous gas in Halabja, killing at least 5000 people, with several thousand blinded, wounded and injured[71] and there are reports that similar attacks continued thereafter, particularly in the immediate aftermath of the cease-fire with Iran. Some international attention in recent years has been focused on the position of the Kurds in Iraq, which may in itself be due to political reasons. The limited protection which had been provided to the Kurds in the immediate aftermath of the Gulf crisis, through the creation of 'safe havens', fell far short of adequate and permanent protection for the Kurdish people. The legal basis under which the limited enforcement action was undertaken is open to question; certainly it was difficult to accept the view that the Security

---

[66] McDowall, *The Kurds* (Minority Rights Group, 1991) p. 5. See also Minority Rights Group and Diyarbakir Bar Association, *A Quest for Equality: Minorities in Turkey* (Minority Rights Group, 2007) also available at www.minorityrights.org/4572/reports/a-quest-for-equality-minorities-in-turkey.html <last visited 21 May 2009>.

[67] For the discriminatory position of Kurds in Turkey see Articles 3 and 42 of the Constitution of Turkish Republic reprinted in Blaustein, Flanz, *Constitutions of the Countries of the World* (Oceana Publications, 1973–1984) vol. xxi; AI, *Escalation in Human Rights Abuses against Kurdish Villages*, July 1993 AI Index EUR 44/64/93; AI, *A Time for Action*, AI Index EUR 44/13/94 February 1994; AI, *Turkey, More People 'Disappear' Following Detention*, AI Index: EUR 44/15/94; AI *Turkey, Selahattin Sinsek: 12 Years in Prison After Unfair Trial* AI Index: EUR 44/EUR 44/09/93; AI *Turkey, Student Soner Onder Still Held*, July 1993 AI Index EUR 44/66/93.

[68] The use of chemical and biological weapons had been a longstanding and worrying feature of the First Gulf war between Iraq and Iran. See Roberts, 'The Laws of War: Problems of Implementation in Contemporary Conflicts' 6 *Duke Journal of Comparative and International Law* (1995–1996) 11 at p. 46.

[69] McDowall, above n.65, p. 38.

[70] Ibid.

[71] Ibid. p. 38.

Council Resolution 688, as such, was sufficient to provide such a firm legal basis.[72] The attempts by the United States and the United Kingdom (the bombing campaigns in December–January 1998/1999) to destroy the military arsenal of Iraq and to protect the no-fly zone did not result in major successes. The build up to the invasion by the United States and its Allies in 2003, saw a human rights argument advanced by the United States and the United Kingdom. Saddam Hussein's dictatorial regime and Iraq's repression of its ethnic communities – in particular the genocidal activity against the Kurds – were put forward as grounds for justifying invasion and removal of the regime.[73] After the invasion of Iraq by the United States and allied forces and the capture of the former dictator, the new Iraqi regime established an Iraqi High Tribunal. Saddam Hussian was charged with crimes against humanity and genocide. In November 2006, the Tribunal handed down death sentence to Saddam Hussein and two other men for the killing of 148 men and boys from the town of Dujail in 1982.[74] The allied invasion has been heavily criticised as an illegal act in international law, and the trial of Saddam Hussein as breaching international human rights standards of fair trial.[75] That said, the fact, nevertheless remains that such rare actions of accountability have been possible only through military invasion and the actual defeat of the regime (and not through consensus as was envisaged in the Genocide Convention). Notwithstanding the removal of the regime of Saddam Hussein and the apparent induction of Kurdish autonomy, the future of Iraqi Kurds remains a matter of contention.[76]

In so far as persecution of Kurds is concerned, such action has been continuing in the entire region including Iraq's neighbours Turkey and Iran. The recent initiative on the part of the Turkish government to wipe out the PKK rebels and the allegations of brutality and violations of the human rights of the Kurdish population endorse this point.[77] There is also substantial evidence to support the view that the genocide of religious groups (regardless of whether their minority status is recognised or not) in several countries – primarily those of the Middle East and Asia – has taken place. The plight of the Bahá'ís in Iran is a chilling reminder of what fundamentalist States can do to dissident religious and ideological groups. Politicians and statesmen are generally extremely careful not to accept responsibility for genocide, though the example of Iran has shown that when fundamentalism takes over other faculties, this may not necessarily be the case. In this context the statement of Hujjab'l-Islam Qazi, President of the Revolutionary Court in Shiraz is revealing. He notes:

---

[72] See Alston, 'The Security Council and Human Rights; Lessons to be Learned From the Iraq Kuwait Crisis and its Aftermath' (1990–91) 13 *AYBIL*, 107; Hampson, 'Liability for War Crimes' in Rowe (ed.), *The Gulf War 1990–91 in International and English Law* (1993) pp. 241–260; Farer, 'Human Rights and Foreign Policy: What the Kurds Learned (A Drama in One Act)' (1992) 14 *HRQ*, 62; Freedman and Karsh, *The Gulf Conflict 1990–91: Diplomacy and War in the New World Order* (Routledge, 1993). Iraq has consistently denied any violations of the rights of the Kurds; see *Report of the Working Group on Minorities on its Fifth Session* E/CN.4/Sub.2/1999/21, para 26.

[73] See the Authorization of Military Force Against Iraq Resolution of 2002–U.S. Public Law No. 107–243. 16 October 2002. 116 STAT. 1498–9.

[74] Human Rights Watch, 'Iraq: Saddam Husain Put to Death' 30 December 2006 hrw.org/english/docs/2006/12/30/iraq14950.htm <last visited 4 August 2008>.

[75] Peterson, 'Unpacking Show Trials: Situating the Trial of Saddam Hussein' 48 *Harv. Int. L.J.* (2007) 257.

[76] For further analysis see Minority Rights Group, *Kurds* www.minorityrights.org/?lid=5748&tmpl=printpage <last visited 15 February 2009>.

[77] See US Cautions Turkey on Iraq Incursion. Rebels Urge Urban Violence www.iraqupdates.com/p_articles.php/article/27821 <last visited 16 February 2009>; Turkish army kills 79 PKK rebels in Iraq as offensive widens www.haaretz.com/hasen/spages/957135.html <last visited 16 February 2009>.

13

The rights of minorities

The Iranian nation has determined to establish the government of God on earth. Therefore it cannot tolerate the perverted Bahá'ís who were instruments of Satan and the followers of devil and of the super powers and their agents . . . It is absolutely certain that in the Islamic Republic of Iran there is no place for the Bahá'ís and Bahá'ísm . . . Before it is too late the Bahá'ís should recant Bahá'ísm, which is condemned by reason and logic. Otherwise the day will soon come when the Islamic nation will deal with them in accordance with its religious obligations, as it has dealt with other hypocrites . . . The Muslim nation will, God willing, fulfil the prayer of Noah [from the Koran]: 'And Noah said, Lord, leave not a single family of Infidels on the Earth: For if thou leave them, they will beguile thy servants and will beget only sinners, infidels'[78]

Genocidal conflicts have also arisen in most other parts of the world. Although religious cleavages, as in the case of India, Lebanon, Northern Ireland, Cyprus and the former Yugoslavia have sometimes been the key element in starting such conflict, as the situation in Pakistan illustrates, ethnic and linguistic dissonance can be equally destructive.[79] Indeed, as the cases of Tibet, Sri Lanka and more recently those of the former Yugoslavia and the former USSR illustrate it is quite possible that a combination of several factors can lead to such genocidal conflicts.[80]

Although atrocities have occurred in virtually every republic of the former Yugoslavia, it would appear that the Muslims in Bosnia-Herzegovina have been the prime targets of genocide, victims of Serbian aggression. Exact figures are difficult to obtain and probably are not of extreme significance; the fact of the matter is that, while several millions have become displaced or have become refugees, uncountable numbers have perished, have been tortured or gang raped or become victims of the 'systematic policies of ethnic cleansing'.[81] The rather insignificant role which the United Nations has played in the actual physical protection of the minorities of the former Yugoslavia creates disillusionment of any hope that a 'New World Order' has emerged.[82]

In the case of States who are parties to the Genocide Convention, the binding legal obligations of the treaty have not proved sufficient to prevent genocide.[83] The Convention has not been able to overcome the hurdle of State sovereignty and provide a satisfactory mechanism for the trial and punishment of those involved in committing genocide. The real test of the efficacy of any human rights instrument is its effective implementation.

---

[78] Cited in Frelick, 'Refugees: Contemporary Witnesses to Genocide' in Fein (ed.), *Genocide Watch* (Yale University Press, 1992) pp. 45–58 at p. 47; also see various newsletters produced by Bahá'í International Community; see Ghanea, *Human Rights, the UN and the Bahá'ís in Iran* (Brill, 2003); *The Report submitted by Special Rapporteur, Angelo Vidal d'Almeida Ribeiro complied in accordance with Resolution 1986/20 of the Commission on Human Rights* E/CN.4/1988/45, p. 5. An-Na'im's paper also contains a catalogue of measures taken against the Bahá'ís in Iran, see An-Na'im, 'Religious Minorities under Islamic Law and the Limits of Cultural Relativism' (1987) 9 *HRQ*, 1, at p. 1, p. 13; Cooper, *The Bahá'ís of Iran* (Minoritiy Rights Group, 1991) pp. 7–8.

[79] See *World Directory of Minorities*, above n.14.

[80] Rehman, 'Accomplices or Globo-Cop? Genocide Alive in Bosnia' paper presented at the Conference on *The Law and Politics of Yugoslavia* (1993).

[81] The Guardian Education, 'Nation States: Recipe for International Disasters' *Guardian*, 23 February, 1993. See symposium, 'The Yugoslav Crisis: New International Law Issues'; Chinkin, 'Rape and Sexual Abuse of Women in International Law' 5 *EJIL* (1994) 326; Petrovic, 'Ethnic Cleansing: An Attempt at Methodology', ibid. 342.

[82] Ignatieff, 'Ugly Face of a New World Order' *Sunday Times*, 7 November 1993; Pajic, *Violation of Fundamental Rights in the Former Yugoslavia: The Conflict of Bosnia-Herzegovina* (Occasional Paper No. 2, David Davies Memorial Institute of International Studies, 1993).

[83] The Former Yugoslavia provides a prime example of this situation.

Human rights instruments generally suffer from the absence of adequate implementation machinery which in the face of principles of State sovereignty remains seriously ineffective. At the same time, the implementation mechanisms within the Genocide Convention have not come into operation or have proved fundamentally flawed.[84] According to Article V of the Convention:

> The Contracting Parties undertake to enact, in accordance with their respective Constitutions, the necessary legislation to give effect to the provisions of the present Convention, and, in particular, to provide effective penalties for persons guilty of genocide or any of the other acts enumerated in article III.

The provision implies that each State party would introduce legislation which would meet the requirements of Article V. States are given considerable latitude as to the application of this provision within their constitutional framework. This has also meant a difference in interpretation of the various provisions nationally, both by legislatures and judiciary. A number of States have not adopted any specific measures implying that they regarded the treaty as self-executing. Finland and Poland are two key examples of States which have treated the Convention as directly applicable in their domestic laws.[85] Most States have claimed that their existing legislation satisfies the requirements of the Convention. The Special Rapporteur M. Ruhashyankiko in his report provides a number of examples where States have responded in this manner.[86] Egypt, for instance, stated:

> In application of these constitutional principles, Egyptian penal law contains provisions guaranteeing the individual's right to the physical and psychological safety of his person and the protection of his freedom. The penal code devotes a special chapter to the crimes of homicide and assault (Articles 230–251) and prescribes the death penalty for any person who leads such a band or holds a position of command therein. Any person who has joined such a band without taking part in its organisation or with holding a position of command therein is liable to a penalty of a term of hard labour or hard labour for life (Article 89).[87]

Ruhashyankiko's report similarly reveals that the domestic legislation introduced by a number of States is based on the provisions of the Convention. Indeed, in some cases the legislation uses terminology of Article II verbatim.[88] However, the legislation, though incorporated by a few States, raises questions as to whether it complies with the provisions of Article II of the Convention. The case of Israel is the classic example as its legislation,

---

[84] See Hannum, *Guide to International Human Rights Practice* (Transnational Publishers, 2004); Sohn, 'Human Rights: Their Implementation and Supervision by the United Nations' in Meron (ed.), *Human Rights in International Law: Legal and Policy Issues* (Clarendon Press, 1984) pp. 369–401.

[85] Ruhashyankiko, *The Study of the Question of the Prevention and Punishment of the Crime of Genocide*, UN Doc. CN.4/Sub.2/416, 141. On Finland, see Törnudd, *Finland and International Norms of Human Rights* (Brill, 1986); LeBlanc, *The United States and the Genocide Convention* (Duke University Press, 1991) p. 126.

[86] See Ruhashyankiko, above n.85, at p. 142.

[87] Ibid. p. 142.

[88] See the legislation introduced by UK (*Genocide Act 1969*), Ch 12, 40 *Halsbury's Statutes of England* 387–90, 3rd edn.; also see the *War Crimes Act 1991*; Richardson, 'War Crimes Act 1991' 55 *MLR* (1992) 73–87; Ganz, 'The War Crimes Act 1991: Why No Constitutional Crisis', ibid. pp. 87–95; for Canada see *Can.Rev. STAT. Supp* 1, 171–181, 1970.

although similar to the Convention, is deemed only to apply to crimes committed 'against the Jewish people' with the implication that other groups are not covered by the law.[89]

In his report, the Special Rapporteur provides a detailed analysis of efforts made by a number of States to incorporate legislative measures to adopt the Convention in their domestic laws; this includes those States who have had a satisfactory record of protection of minority rights. Some States, albeit, a handful (e.g. Ethiopia, Peru and Paraguay) have also incorporated a broader category so as to accord protection to political or social groups. Ethiopia's Penal Code of 1957 (Article 281) deploys genocide to include *political groups*.[90] Peru's Criminal Code (Article 129), Paraguay's Criminal Code (Article 308) and Lithuania's Criminal Code (Article 71) includes genocide as 'social group'.[91] In another study, Marschik surveys the penal codes of a number of European States to confirm that these States have legislated in accordance with the provisions of the Genocide Convention to prohibit and punish the crime of genocide.[92]

There are a number of States which, although claiming to have incorporated the Genocide Convention, have failed to respect its provisions. Although a number of East European States could be mentioned in this respect, the main focus lies on the States of Latin America, Africa and Asia. One prime example in the context of Africa is that of Rwanda. Despite its unfortunate record on physical protection of minorities, Rwanda has maintained that its domestic legislation contains adequate protection against acts of genocide.[93]

As far as the implementation of the Convention is concerned, according to Article VI of the Convention 'Persons Charged with genocide . . . shall be tried by a competent tribunal of the State in the territory of which the act was committed, or by such international penal tribunal as may have jurisdiction with respect to those Contracting Parties which shall have accepted its jurisdiction'. The Convention in its final draft presents two alternatives; that of a trial in the territory where the offence took place or trial by an international penal tribunal.

In relation to trial in the territory of the offence, the primary problem is that genocide in most instances is committed by the governments in power, and as long as those governments remain in power, it is almost impossible to rely on this territorial principle. The cases of Germany and Japan after the Second World War, as the defeated powers, were exceptional in providing the allied powers a forum – probably a manifestation of a prerogative of the victors against the losers. However, in most cases of genocide, it is the governments within the States that are involved, and unless and until they are removed, the difficulty remains of trying those who have been involved in committing genocide. It is quite possible for a genocidal regime to stay in power for a long time and defy international law and municipal laws.[94] It is equally possible that the stance of successive governments might be

---

[89] See the Nazi and Nazi Collaborators (Punishment) Law 1950.

[90] Kissi, 'Genocide in Cambodia and Ethopia' in Gellately and Kiernan (eds), *The Spectre of Genocide: Mass Murder in Historical Perspective* (Cambridge University Press, 2003) pp. 307–324 at p. 308.

[91] See Ferdinandusse, *Direct Application of International Criminal Law in National Courts* (Asser Press, 2006) at p. 241.

[92] See Marschik, 'The Politics of Prosecution: European National Approaches to War Crime' in McCormack and Simpson (eds), *The Law of War Crimes: National and International Approaches* (Kluwer Law International, 1997) pp. 65–101.

[93] Ruhashyankiko, above n.85, pp. 150–151.

[94] The example of the arrest and extradition of the former President of Yugoslavia, President Milošević also confirms the position. It was only possible to extradite the former President after the overthrow of his government. Milošević's trial before ICTY began in 2002, but he died in March 2006 before the ICTY reached a verdict.

based on the policy of genocide and forced assimilation of certain minority groups. Professor James Crawford reconfirmed this view by noting that '[t]he national jurisdiction envisaged by Article VI does not seem to work'.[95] Professor Antonio Cassese regards these the provisions of Article VI as 'odd or rather ingenuous' in stipulating that 'persons accused of genocide must be prosecuted and tried by the judicial authorities of the territory in which "the act was committed" (plus a future international criminal court that in 1948 looked like a radiant daydream)'.[96]

The one rare instance where the national jurisdiction (as envisaged by the Convention) was invoked was in Rwanda in 1994, where the domestic courts were allowed to prosecute alleged authors of genocidal acts committed against the Tutsi minority. However, even on this occasion, *real politic* was evident. Professor Cassese makes the point that 'this was only possible due to the rare circumstance that the victims of the genocide, the Tutsi, had seized power in Rwanda (the Tutsi-led party having in 1994 deposed the Hutu-led government that planned and waged the genocide), and were, therefore, strongly intent on bringing prosecutions for genocide, not least since the fact of the genocide legitimized the minority Tutsi's hold on power'.[97]

There also persists a strong view that the difficulties in the operation of the Convention are exacerbated by the apprehension of the accused: the point has recently been reiterated through the difficulties in arresting and trying Radovan Karadzic and Ratko Mladic, two of the people indicted by the Yugoslav tribunal.[98] Karadzic was spectacularly arrested on 21 July 2008 in Serbia after 12 years on the run from charges of war crimes and genocide.[99] Karadzic's capture, transfer to the Yugoslav tribunal for trail and the outcome of this trail remains the subject of much speculation.[100] The other fugitive Ratko Mladic is yet to be captured.

Although, by Article VII, States parties to the Convention pledge to grant extradition wherever appropriate, political interests and subjective opinion seriously hamper a smooth operation of the provision. It is quite possible for the accused to flee a State which is not a contracting party to the Convention. Since international law does not impose any specific obligations on States to comply with each other to extradite individuals, the last and perhaps the only course of action would be to resort to illegality to assume jurisdiction.[101] Professor Roberts makes the valid point that 'war criminals [and those involved in crimes against humanity and genocide] can avoid prosecution by going to a country which does

---

[95] Crawford, 'Prospects of an International Criminal Court' *CLP* (1995) 303 at p. 319.

[96] Cassese, *International Criminal Law* (Oxford University Press, 2008) at p. 128.

[97] Ibid. at p. 280.

[98] See *Prosecutor* v. *Karadzic*, Case IT-95-5-R61; *Prosecutor* v. *Mladic*, *Case* IT-95-18-R61.

[99] Borger, 'Radovan Karadzic, Europe's Most wanted Man, Arrested for War Crimes' *Guardian* 22 July 2008 www.guardian.co.uk/world/2008/jul/22/warcrimes.internationalcrime <last visited 15 November 2008>.

[100] Gordy, 'Radovan Karadzic: The Politics of An Arrest' www.opendemocracy.net/article/radovan-karadzic-the-politics-of-an-arrest <last visited 15 November 2008>.

[101] Harris and Kushen, 'Surrender of fugitives to the War Crimes Tribunals for Yugoslavia and Rwanda: Squaring International Legal Obligations with the US Constitution' 7 *CLF* (1996) 561 at p. 587; Bridge, 'The Case of an International Court of Criminal Justice and the formulation of International Criminal Law' 13 *ICLQ* (1964) 1255 at p. 1258. On Rwanda, Cissé, 'The End of a Culture of Impunity in Rwanda? Prosecution of Genocide and War Crimes before Rwandan Courts and the International Criminal Tribunal for Rwanda' 1 *Yearbook of International Humanitarian Law* (1998) pp. 161–188. Note, however, the views of Professor Meron, where he advances the view that increasingly genocide is being recognised a crime for which universal jurisdiction exists, see Meron, 'International Criminalization of Internal Atrocities' 89 *AJIL* (1995) 554 at p. 569.

not have the political desire to punish him or her and does not have the extradition agreements with those who do'.[102] Even if the accused is captured and tried in the State in which the offences were committed, the sensitivity of the issue of genocide might make the possibility of fair trial very remote.

If the option of conducting trials on territorial basis seems impractical, the second alternative to have an international criminal court has proved even more illusive. The large scale violations of human rights in the former Yugoslavia, Rwanda and elsewhere highlighted the need for a permanent international criminal court. In the absence of a permanent court, the United Nations Security Council acting under Chapter VII of the United Nations Charter, in its Resolution 827 (1993)[103] and Resolution 955 (1994)[104] established the *ad hoc* tribunals for former Yugoslavia and Rwanda.

The jurisdictional and territorial limitations of the *ad hoc* tribunals of the aforementioned tribunals were obvious, generating an unprecedented momentum towards the creation of a court with a universal jurisdiction. The General Assembly, which had requested the ILC in 1990[105] to draft a statute for an international criminal court, reiterated its request underlying the significance and urgency of the matter.[106] A draft produced by a working group of the ILC was discussed in 1993 by the General Assembly.[107] The revised draft was discussed again in 1994 by the Sixth Committee, by an Ad Hoc Committee on the Establishment of an International Criminal Court and by a Special Preparatory Committee on the Establishment of an International Criminal Court. The Special Preparatory Committee during its three sessions in 1996, 1997 and 1998 focused on preparing the text of the draft Statute.

The text submitted by the Preparatory Committee to the Rome Conference in June 1998 consisted of 116 Articles. A number of these Articles were essentially in draft format, with crucial details yet to be finalised.[108] It is, thus, to the credit of the participants of the Rome Conference that within the space of six weeks a Statute was adopted. Having said that, the Statute contains many weaknesses, there are a number of serious inconsistencies and agreement could not be reached on several key issues. It is also significant to note that many of the provisions within the Statute were heavily criticised by the United States, which also decided publicly to indicate that it had to vote against the Statute.[109]

As regards the substantive issues, various criticisms could be made. The principle of complementarity which grants priority to national jurisdictions *vis-à-vis* the Court could seriously undermine the system of accountability. The priority accorded to national courts is also in stark contrast to the position adopted by the Yugoslavia and Rwanda Tribunals.[110]

---

[102] Roberts, 'The Laws of War: Problems of Implementation in Contemporary Conflicts' 6 *Duke Journal of Comparative and International Law* (1995–1996) 11 at p. 37.

[103] See S.C Res. 827, 48 UN SCOR (3217th mtg.) UN Doc S/RES/827 (1993) reprinted 32 ILM 1203.

[104] See S.C Roes 955, UN SCOR (3453rd mtg.) UN Doc S/RES/955 (1994) reprinted 33 ILM 1600.

[105] GA Res. 45/41 UN GAOR, 45th. Sess. Supp. No. 49, p. 363, UN Doc. A/RES/45/41 (1990).

[106] GA Res. 47/33 UN GAOR, 47th. Sess. 73rd mtg., at 3, UN Doc. A/RES/47/33 (1992).

[107] Crawford, 'The ILC's Draft Statute for an International Criminal Tribunal' 88 *AJIL* (1994) 140 at p. 140; Crawford, 'The ILC Adopts a Statute for an International Criminal Court' 89 *AJIL* (1995) 404.

[108] Kirsch and Holmes, 'The Rome Conference on an International Criminal Court: The Negotiating Process' 93 *AJIL* (1999) 2 at p. 3.

[109] Scheffer, 'The United States and the International Criminal Court' 93 *AJIL* (1999) 12.

[110] GA Res. 47/33 UN GAOR, 47th. Sess. 73rd. mtg., at 3, UN Doc. A/RES/47/33 (1992). Sarooshi, 'The Statute of the International Criminal Court' 48 *ICLQ* (1999) 387 at p. 395. Sarooshi also highlights the position that 'decisions of the Court will not, in general terms, prevail over a State's other treaty obligations' at p. 390 and that 'there is no obligation under the Statute to waive [State or diplomatic] immunity' at p. 392 (footnotes omitted).

These jurisdictional requirements highlight the limitations under which the Court would have to operate. The Statute authorises the Court to exercise jurisdiction for crimes as stated therein if consent has been provided by the State of the territory of the crime or the consent of the State of the nationality of the accused.[111] The ICC would also have jurisdiction if a referral is made by the Security Council acting under Chapter VII powers of the UN Charter. The jurisdictional point had strongly been resisted by the United States as it would establish an arrangement whereby '[United States] armed forces operating overseas could conceivably be prosecuted by the ICC even if the United States had not agreed to be bound by the treaty. The United States took the position that such an overreaching by the ICC could inhibit its use of the military to meet alliance obligations and to participate in multinational operations, including humanitarian intervention to save civilian lives'.[112] Furthermore, in the view of David Scheffer, the United States Ambassador at the Rome Conference, the position of non-parties was jeopardised through the amendment provisions as provided in Article 121(5). These provisions allow 'for the addition of new crimes to the jurisdiction of the Court or revisions of existing crimes in the treaty [entailing] an extraordinary and unacceptable consequence. After the States parties decide to add a new crime or change the definition of an existing crime, any state that is a party can decide to immunise its nationals from prosecution for the new or amended crime. Nationals of non-parties, however, are subject to potential prosecution'.[113]

The political dimension and role of the Security Council is underlined by the provision which authorises the Council to refer the matter to the Court even if crimes are committed in non-State parties, by the nationals of States not parties to the Statute and in the absence of any consent by the State of the nationality of the accused or by the territorial State.[114] In so far as the crimes over which the Court would have jurisdiction are concerned, these include genocide, crimes against humanity, war crimes and crimes of aggression.[115] While the list is limited to the 'most serious crimes', the emergent consensus is more apparent than real. The crime of genocide encapsulating the definition accorded by the Genocide Convention proved to be the least controversial. The Genocide Convention, however, as we have been analysing, presents serious limitations and weaknesses. Furthermore, notwithstanding the apparent inherent jurisdiction which is granted to the Court in the case of genocide it would form an uneasy relationship with the jurisdictional basis of the Genocide Convention. The position taken by the Statute is objectionable on three grounds. Firstly, it tends to overlook the 'territorial jurisdictional' aspect in the Genocide Convention which, as we have noted has hitherto remained the predominant one. Secondly, it brings into issue the position of States which are not parties to the Genocide Convention. Are they to be bound even by those treaty provisions from the Genocide Convention which are not settled and possibly do not form part of customary law? Thirdly, if the inherent jurisdiction of the International Criminal Court in matters of genocide could be sustained on the ground that Article 6 provisions had customary value, further explanation would need to be given for the position of States who decline to become parties to the Statute of the International Criminal Court.

---

[111] See Article 12 of the Statute.

[112] Arsanjani, 'The Rome Statute of the International Criminal Court' 93 *AJIL* (1999) 22 at p. 26.

[113] Scheffer, above n.60, at p. 20; also see Wedgwood, 'The International Criminal Court: An American View' 10 *EJIL* (1993) 93.

[114] Arsanjani, above n.112, at p. 26.

[115] Article 5 of the Rome Statute.

In relation to other crimes, the expanded nature of crimes against humanity and war crimes raised considerable debate and disagreement. While the wider inclusive view is welcoming, the operations and actual reliance upon these aspects by the Court remains speculative. Finally, there is the crime of aggression which, although incorporated, nevertheless generated unacceptable levels of controversy over its definition. As a compromise it was decided that notwithstanding incorporation, the Court would only be able to exercise jurisdiction in relation to crimes of aggression once a definition had been agreed upon. Judging by the protracted and controversial history of the definitional issues, a consensus definition of aggression may be a long way away. The aforementioned jurisdictional and substantive limitations constitute a considerable hurdle to attaining the ultimate objectives of the Statute – the accountability and punishment of individuals involved in serious crimes against international law. The final hurdle, which is the most critical one as well, concerns the lack of strength in the existing International Criminal Court. Three of the Five Permanent members of the Security Council – the United States, Russian Federation and China – have refused to become parties to Rome Statute.[116] Although, as at the beginning of 2009, there are over 100 State parties, the rather mediocre position which the Court retains is already becoming evident through its limited business thus far. In the meantime, and in so far as the punishment of those involved in breaching the right to physical existence is concerned, the global situation cannot be taken to represent a serious note of optimism. Many minority groups continue to suffer as the provisions of international criminal law (and more specifically those of the Genocide Convention) remain insufficient to punish the perpetrators of these crimes.

(ii) The right to religious, cultural and linguistic autonomy[117]

Religious, linguistic and cultural autonomy is not a novel concept for minorities. Its history stretches to the time when minorities as distinct groups came to be recognised. Medieval and modern history presents many revealing instances of the granting of autonomy to religious minorities. A clear example of autonomy was presented by the League of Nations through its system of minority treaties at the end of World War One. The intervening years between the two world wars saw a number of imaginative attempts to realise meaningful autonomy such as the Aaland Islands, the Free City of Danzig and the Memel territory. The mechanisms installed to protect minorities proved defective and alongside the minority treaties themselves collapsed well before the Second World War.[118]

The legal and political developments that took place after the Second World War more or less resulted in the erosion of any independent concern that previously existed for ethnic, linguistic and religious minorities and for their aspirations of autonomy and existence

---

[116] For Commentaries see Jia, 'China and the International Criminal Court: Current Situation' 10 *Singapore Year Book of International Law* (2006) 1; Tuzmukhamedov, 'The ICC and Russian Constitutional Problems' 3 *Journal of International Criminal Justice* (2006) 621.

[117] For useful commentaries on the subject see Hannum, *Autonomy, Sovereignty and Self-Determination: The Accommodation of Conflicting Rights* (University of Pennsylvania Press, 1990); Lapidoth, 'Some Reflections on Autonomy', *Mélanges Offerts à Paul Reuter* (1981) 379; Lapidoth, *Autonomy-Flexible Solutions to Ethnic Conflicts* (United States Institute of Peace Press, 1997); Kardos, 'Human Rights: A Matter of Individual or Collective Concern?' in Pogany (ed.), *Human Rights in Eastern Europe* (Edward Elgar, 1995) pp. 169–183; see also the proceedings of the colloquium, *Autonomy and Self-Determination: Theories and Application*, at the Institute of International and European Law, University of Liverpool, England, (27 May 1997).

[118] See Claude Jr., above n.2; Kelly, 'National Minorities in International Law' 3 *JILP* (1973) 253–273 at p. 258.

as distinct entities. The interest in the position of minorities that could be ascertained was largely of an indirect nature, namely the United Nations preoccupation with upholding individual human rights and concern with non-self-governing territories. In the present context the provisions of Chapter XI of the Charter need to be noted. Chapter XI concerns non-self-governing territories and Article 73 applies to territories 'whose peoples have not yet attained a measure of self-government'. A focus of this nature upon territorial elements meant a lack of consideration for ethnic, linguistic and religious groups who were without a territorial base.

The issue of self-government became almost synonymous with independence from former colonies. At the same time United Nations bodies started relying heavily on the concept of individual human rights and non-discrimination neglecting the subject and concerns of minorities.[119] The United Nations Charter in solely confining itself to references on human rights and non-discrimination appears to have taken the view that minority rights could be adequately protected in a regime of non-discrimination.[120] Despite the absence of any specific mention of minorities or their rights within the UN Charter or UDHR, minorities have been able to benefit from a number of concepts enshrined in these instruments.

Within the UDHR, there is mention of a number of rights, which can be treated as forming the basis of minority protection. The Declaration specifically provides in Articles 1 and 2, the right of equality and non-discrimination.[121] The right to freedom of thought, conscience and religion is stated in Article 18, the right to freedom of opinion and expression is provided in Article 19, the right to peaceful assembly and association in Article 20, the right to education in Article 26 and the right to freely participate in the cultural life of the community in Article 27.[122] All these rights provide the necessary foundation for providing individual members a claim for autonomy. Although the Universal Declaration has no explicit references to minorities, subsequent international instruments have provided greater attention to minority or group rights. The International Convention on the Elimination of All Forms of Racial Discrimination,[123] while placing emphasis on the elimination of racial discrimination, also aims to protect racial minority groups. Article 1 of the Convention defines racial discrimination as 'any distinction, exclusion, restriction or preference based on race, colour, descent, or national or ethnic origin'. The inclusion of 'national or ethnic groups' adds to the protection afforded by CERD to minority groups. It provides an explicit recognition to affirmative action policies[124] and allows minority groups to institute a complaints procedure.[125] The ICESCR[126] represents a strong recognition of the

---

[119] 'From the very beginning of the United Nations, emphasis has been put on the development of non-self-governing territories towards independence' Sohn, 'Models of Autonomy within the United Nations Framework' in Dinstein (ed.), *Models of Autonomy* (Transaction Books, 1981) pp. 5–22 at p. 9.

[120] Claude Jr., above n.2, at p. 211.

[121] See above chapter 4.

[122] Ibid.; see Henrard, 'Education and Multiculturalism: the contribution of Minority Rights?' 7 *IJMGR* (2000) 393.

[123] Adopted 21 December, 1965. Entered into force, 4 January 1969. 660 U.N.T.S. 195, 5 I.L.M (1966) 352; see above chapter 12.

[124] See Articles 1(4) and 2(2).

[125] See Article 14(1).

[126] Adopted at New York, 16 December, 1966. Entered into force 3 January, 1976. GA Res. 2200A (XXI) UN Doc. A/6316 (1966) 993 U.N.T.S. 3, 6 I.L.M. (1967) 360. Craven notes that the Covenant 'arguably recognises the different needs of ethnic minorities particularly as regards their cultural identity'. Craven, above n.49, at p. 188; see above chapter 7.

value of cultural rights in the human rights context.[127] According to Article 15 of ICESCR, States undertake to recognise that everyone has the right to 'take part in cultural life'.[128] There is also recognition of legitimate differences in beliefs and traditions in Articles 13(3) and 13(4). Under Article 13, parents are given the right to establish and choose schools other than those established by public authorities. The most significant of international treaties in respect to protecting minority rights has been the ICCPR.[129] Article 27 of the ICCPR is of special importance for minorities as it is the main provision in current international law which attempts to provide direct protection to ethnic, linguistic and religious minorities. Article 27 provides as follows:

> In those States in which ethnic, religious or linguistic minorities exist, persons belonging to such minorities shall not be denied the right, in community with other members of their group, to enjoy their own culture, to profess and practice their own religion, or to use their own language.

The article, however, does not take a straightforward approach in extending protection to minorities. It is drafted in an awkward manner and appears to suggest that while the majority of States comprise of homogenous groups, the issue of minorities is confined to only a few. The aim behind such wording appears to be to provide protection only to the long established minorities and to prevent or discourage the formation of new minority groups. This phraseology invites States to deny the existence of minorities within their boundaries. Many States have indeed not hesitated to do so.[130]

The obligations in the article require States 'not to deny the right [to persons belonging to minorities] to enjoy their own culture, to profess and practice their own religion, or to use their own language'. The wording of the provision, contrary to other articles, is negative in tone.[131]

The obligations that are to be imposed upon State parties have also been a matter of considerable debate. The text is not strong enough to place States and governments under the obligation of providing special facilities to members of minorities. The sole obligation that was placed on the States was not to deprive or deny members of the minority groups

---

[127] See above chapter 5.

[128] Ibid.

[129] Adopted at New York, 16 December, 1966. Entered into force 23 March 1976. GA Res. 2200A (XXI) UN Doc. A/6316 (1966) 999 U.N.T.S. 171; 6 I.L.M. (1967) 368. There is no reference in the Covenant to according positive group rights or requirements that States should promote minority Rights, Craven, *above* n.49, at p. 158. Craven however argues that the Covenant 'arguably recognised the different needs of ethnic minorities particularly as regards their cultural identity'. Although Article 15 merely states that everyone has the right to 'take part in cultural life' a recognition of legitimate differences in belief and traditions is to be found in Article 13(3) and (4). Under that Article, parents have the right to establish and choose schools other than those established by the public authorities. Similarly the reference to self-determination in Article 1 of the Covenant may be interpreted as implying that minorities have a right to pursue their own economic, social and cultural development 'without excessive interference from the authorities'. Craven, above n.49, at pp. 188–189.

[130] Mr. Kaliswali of India had warned that such phraseology 'might encourage dictatorial States to refuse to recognise the rights of minorities living in their territory, simply by denying their existence' 9 UN ESCOR, Commission on Human Rights, UN Doc. E/CN.4/SR. 368–71 (1951) para 37.

[131] In contrast see e.g. Article 18(1): Every one shall have the right to freedom of thought, conscience and religion. Article 24(3) Every child has the right to require a nationality.

the status they were already enjoying.[132] Article 27 is not only weak due to not placing positive obligations on State parties, but it is also limited in scope as far as the issue of *locus standi* is concerned. The jurisprudence emanating from the operation of the First Optional Protocol confirms that the provisions of the article are limited to persons. Cases such as *Sandra Lovelace* v. *Canada*[133] establish the possibility of vindication of minority rights using Article 27. At the same time, the article has proved inadequate in satisfying many of the claims put forward by minority groups in particular when they straddle along the claims of self-determination.[134] Minorities as groups are not entitled to bring actions before the Committee; however, minorities as a group of individuals who allege a violation of their rights are permitted to bring an action before the Committee.[135] Nor has it been possible to claim violations of Article 1 under the Optional Protocol to the ICCPR.[136]

The Human Rights Committee has dealt with minority rights in the context of Article 27 in a significant number of cases. The vast majority of these relate to ethnic minorities with very little jurisprudence relating to linguistic and religious minority groups. In *Lovelace* v. *Canada*,[137] a Maliseet Indian lost the rights and status associated with the minority after she married a non-Maliseet Indian man. The Human Rights Committee decided that as she was ethnically a Maliseet Indian and was brought up on a reserve and maintained ties to the reserve during her marriage, she must still belong to the minority. While there is no right to live on a reserve under Article 27, *per se*, her access to culture and to language was interfered with, as there was no place outside the reserve where such a possibility existed. Therefore, the loss of rights amounted to a violation of Article 27. In *Länsman* v. *Finland*,[138] it was held that the quarrying of land traditionally used for reindeer breeding, that was also a sacred place in the Old Sami religion, did not constitute a violation of Article 27, as the quarrying was of a limited nature and the reindeer herding had not been adversely affected. It is, however, important to note that in this judgment it was emphasised that ethnic communities have the right to use modern methods when carrying out traditional trades. In contrast in *Lubicon Lake Band* v. *Canada*[139] it was held that the expropriation of land by the Provincial government in order to lease it to private enterprise constituted a violation of Article 27. Economic and social activities, which are part of the culture of the community,

---

[132] According to Capotorti during the discussions at the Commission: 'It was generally agreed that the text submitted by the Sub-Commission would not, for example, place States and governments under obligation of providing special schools for persons belonging to ethnic, religious and linguistic minorities. Persons who comprised of ethnic, religious or linguistic minorities could as such request that they should not be deprived of the rights recognised in the draft article. The sole obligation imposed upon them was not to deny that right.' Capotorti above n 6, at p. 36.

[133] *Sandra Lovelace* v. *Canada*, Communication No. 24/1977 (30 July 1981), UN Doc. CCPR/C/OP/1 at 83 (1984).

[134] See *Lubicon Lake Band* v. *Canada*, Communication No. 167/1984 (26 March 1990), UN Doc. Supp. No. 40 (A/45/40) at 1 (1990). Also see General Comment 23(50) Article 27, UN Doc. CCPR/C/21/Rev. 1/Add.5 (1994) at para 3.1.

[135] See e.g. *Lubicon Lake Band* v. *Canada*, Communication No. 167/1984 (26 March 1990), UN Doc. Supp. No. 40 (A/45/40) at 1 (1990) and *Diergaardt* v. *Namibia*, Communication No. 760/1997, UN Doc. CCPR/C/69/D/760/1997 (2000).

[136] CCPR/C/33D/197/1985, 10 August 1988; Human Rights Committee, 33rd. session; Prior decisions CCPR/C/WG/27/D/197 1985; CCPR/C/29D/197 1985 (admissibility 25 March 1987).

[137] *Sandra Lovelace* v. *Canada*, Communication No. 24/1977 (30 July 1981), UN Doc. CCPR/C/OP/1 at 83 (1984).

[138] Communication No. 511/1992, views adopted on 26 October 1994, CCPR/C/52/D/511/1992.

[139] Communication No. 167/1984 (26 March 1990), UN Doc. Supp. No. 40 (A/45/40) at 1 (1990).

are protected by Article 27. In *Kitok* v. *Sweden*[140] it was held that legislation with the reasonable and objective aim of the continued viability and welfare of the minority as a whole was not a violation of Article 27.[141] The requirement of obtaining a fishing licence for fishing out of season on land not part of the reserve, especially when the reserve in question was abundant with fish, was not considered a violation of Article 27 in *Howard* v. *Canada*.[142]

In respect of religious minorities, the HRC has yet to hear any cases in respect of Article 27. However, a number of cases have been brought in respect of Article 18[143] and Article 26.[144] The rights of linguistic minorities have been dealt with in *Ballantyne* et al. v. *Canada*,[145] *Guesdon* v. *France*[146] and *Cadoret and Bihan* v. *France*.[147] In *Ballantyne* it was held that rules preventing the use of the English language in advertising in Quebec did not violate the rights of the English Linguistic minority, as they constituted the majority in Canada and, therefore, did not fall within the ambit of Article 27. However, a violation of Article 19, freedom of expression was found. *Guesdon* v. *France* and *Cadoret and Bihan* v. *France*, concerned the rights of the Breton minority in France to use the Breton language in court proceedings. The authors were all charged with defacing road signs in the French language, in order to protest at the lack of Breton road signs. The HRC, however, avoided the issues of considering the legality of the French declaration[148] regarding Article 27 by holding that there were no issues raised relevant to the article. Instead the Court considered the merits of the case under Article 14, the right to a fair trial, and found no violation as the authors were perfectly capable of expressing themselves in French. The HRC, however, was not able to avoid considering the legality of the French declaration, and in *Hopu and Bessert* v. *France*[149] held that it was unable to consider the claims under Article 27, as the French declaration operates as a reservation. This decision is somewhat disappointing. The Human Rights Committee neglected to consider the compatibility of the French declaration with the objectives and purposes of the ICCPR and simply accepted that it did not have the competence to consider the claim.[150]

---

[140] Communication No. 197/1985 UN Doc. CCPR/C/33/D/197/1985.

[141] See also *Apirana Mahuika* et al. v. *New Zealand*, Communication No. 547/1993, UN Doc. CCPR/C/70/D/547/1993 (2000), where fishing quotas were held to be reasonable as the Maori had been consulted regarding the regulation of fishing activities and the overriding purposes of such provisions was the sustainability of Maori fishing activities.

[142] Communication No. 879/1999, UN Doc. CCPR/C/84/D/879/1999 (2005).

[143] *Karnel Singh Bhinder* v. *Canada*, Communication Nos. 208/1986, UN Doc. CCPR/C/37/D/208/1986 (1989).

[144] *Waldman* v. *Canada*, Communication No. 694/1996, UN Doc. CCPR/C/67/D/694/1996 (1999).

[145] Communications Nos. 359/1989 and 385/1989, UN Doc. CCPR/C/47/D/359/1989 and 385/1989/Rev.1 (1993).

[146] Communication No. 219/1986, UN Doc. CCPR/C/39/D/219/1986 (1990).

[147] Communication No. 323/1988, UN Doc. CCPR/C/41/D/323/1988 (1991).

[148] 'In the light of article 2 of the Constitution of the French Republic, the French Government declares that article 27 is not applicable so far as the Republic is concerned.' www2.ohchr.org/english/bodies/ratification/docs/DeclarationsReservationsICCPR.pdf <last visited 12 October 2008>.

[149] Communication No. 549/1993, UN Doc. CCPR/C/60/D/549/1993/Rev.1 (1997).

[150] Note, however, that in its recent Concluding Observations of the Report Submitted by France, HRC has made the following observations: 'the Committee . . . remains unable to share the view of the State Party that the abstract principle of equality before the law and the prohibition of discrimination represents sufficient guranatees for the equal and effective enjoyment by persons belonging to ethnic, religious or linguistic minorities of the rights set out in the Covenant. (article 26 and article 27) . . . The State Party should review its position concerning formal recognition of ethnic, religious or linguistic minorities in accordance with the provisions of Article 27 of the Covenant', Concluding Observations of the Human Rights Committee: France CCPR/C/FRA/CO/4 (31 July 2008) para 11.

4 MODERN INITIATIVES IN INTERNATIONAL LAW

Since the adoption of the ICCPR a number of recent initiatives have reinforced the international provisions relating to minority protection. The primary instrument at the global level is the United Nations General Assembly's Resolution 47/135 of 18 December 1992.[151] The Declaration represents a concerted effort on the part of the international community to overcome some of the limitations in Article 27 of the ICCPR.[152] According to Article 1(1), States:

> shall protect the existence and the national or ethnic, cultural, religious or linguistic identity of minorities within their respective territories and shall encourage conditions for the promotion of that identity.

Article 2(1) confirms and elaborates upon the position of Article 27 of ICCPR. The provisions of this article present a more positive attitude compared with the tentative position adopted by Article 27. It provides:

> Persons belonging to national or ethnic, religious and linguistic minorities (hereinafter referred to as persons belonging to minorities) have the right to enjoy their own culture, to profess and practice their own religion, and to use their own language, in private and in public, freely and without interference or any form of discrimination.

Article 2(2) provides for wide-ranging participatory rights to persons belonging to minorities in 'cultural, religious, social, economic and public life'. The provision is significant as the recognition and authorisation of such rights form an essential element of the concept of autonomy. Similarly, Article 2(3) provides for effective participation at national and regional levels and on matters which necessarily affect the position of minorities. Article 2(4) authorises persons belonging to minorities to establish and maintain their own institutions, a matter indispensable to the autonomous existence of minorities. Hence, Article 2 as a whole, could be taken to bear significant value in recognising autonomy for minorities, even though the right to autonomy itself failed to be incorporated in the Declaration. Article 3 of the Declaration also carries a similar message. It reinforces the collective dimension with encouragement of the communal enjoyment of rights without discrimination of any sort. Article 4 provides that:

> (1) States shall take measure to ensure that persons belonging to minorities may exercise fully and effectively all their human rights and fundamental freedom without any discrimination and in full equality before the law.
>
> (2) States shall take measures to create favourable conditions to enable persons belonging to minorities to express their characteristics and to develop their culture, language, religion, traditions and customs except where specific practices are in violation of national law and contrary to international standards.

---

[151] UN Doc. A/Res/47/135.
[152] Dickson, 'The United Nations and Freedom of Religion' 44 *ICLQ* (1995) at p. 354.

(3) States should take appropriate measures so that, wherever possible persons belonging to minorities have adequate opportunities to learn their mother tongue

(4) States should, where appropriate, take measures in the field of education, in order to encourage the knowledge of the history, traditions, language and culture of the minorities existing with in their territory. Persons belonging to minorities should have adequate opportunities to gain knowledge of the society as a whole

(5) States should consider appropriate measures so that persons belonging to minorities may participate fully in the economic progress and development in their country.

Articles 5, 6, and 7 also carry considerable value. According to Article 5, 'legitimate interests' of the persons belonging to minorities would be taken in account when formulating national policies or programmes of co-operation and assistance among States. The emphasis of Articles 6 and 7 is upon international co-operation in understanding the minority question in a more tolerant and rational manner. The Declaration has many positive elements. Aspects of ethnic, cultural and linguistic autonomy appear within the text of the Declaration and represent a considerable advance. The communal aspects of existence of minorities is more pronounced, the references relating to State sovereignty and territorial integrity although integral to the Declaration are framed in a more accommodating manner. They are less confrontational to aspirations of autonomy and distinct identity.

The Declaration, however, is a General Assembly Resolution and its impact on the development of international law is not clear. Many of the substantive provisions of the Declaration are themselves framed in a rather general manner providing a number of States to claim that they already respect minority rights.[153] States may also prevent legitimate expression of minorities in the pretext of being 'incompatible with national legislation'.[154] Even as a political and moral expression there have been controversies as to the rights of minorities and concern for State sovereignty and territorial integrity resurfaced frequently. The right to autonomy was not acceptable and even the 'lower level' right to 'self-management' failed to be incorporated.[155] The manner and circumstances of the adoption of the Declaration, as its critics would argue, was probably more in response to the inability of the United Nations to take appropriate action to protect the rights of minorities, even after the East–West détente and the ending of the Cold War.

One ingenious method of overcoming historical weaknesses in the implementation of minority rights mechanisms was through the setting up of a Working Group on Minorities. The Working Group, which was established in 1995, helped to eradicate some of the criticisms regarding the weaknesses existent in the practical realisation and implementation of the Declaration, before its winding down in 2006. The Working Group on Minorities

---

[153] Hence the position adopted by Poland in the Human Rights Commission may be unduly optimistic according to which: 'Even though the text, was not perfect, it did appear to fulfil two essential requirements: firstly, it constituted a comprehensive international instrument in the field of protection of minorities, all of whose rights were clearly specified, and secondly, it clearly set out the commitments by which States could universally agree to be bound in so sensitive a sphere. It was thus a sound document, in line with the general approach to the question of international standards for the protection of the rights of minorities, and which, while ensuring a satisfactory balance between the rights of the nation as a whole.' UN Doc. E/CN.4/1992/SR.18, para 20.

[154] See Articles 2(3) and 4(2) of the Declaration.

[155] Thornberry, 'International and European Standards on Minority Rights' in Miall (ed.), *Minority Rights in Europe: The Scope for a Transnational Regime* (Pinter Publishers, 1994) pp. 14–21 at p. 20.

was also influential in promoting the issue of minority rights at the global level, and notwithstanding its brief history created a lasting impression within the United Nations as an effective forum for deliberation and producing mutual understanding between minorities and their governments.

The origins of the Working Group can be traced through the recommendations of Professor Asbjørn Eide. These recommendations, initially presented in his report entitled *Possible Ways and Means of Facilitating the Peaceful and Constructive Solutions of Problems Involving Minorities*, were endorsed by the Human Rights Sub-Commission, which made a further recommendation to the Commission on Human Rights in its Resolution 1994/4 of August 1994.[156] The establishment of the Working Group was authorised by the Human Rights Commission[157] and subsequently endorsed by the Economic and Social Council in July 1995.[158] On 3 March 1995, the Human Rights Commission in its Resolution 1995/24 authorised the setting-up of the Working Group initially for a period of three years. The Working Group was to consist of five members of the Sub-Commission on Human Rights and to meet for five working days every year. The mandate of the Working Group was constituted as follows:

(a) Review the promotion and practical realisation of the Declaration.

(b) Examine possible solutions to problems involving minorities, including the promotion of mutual understanding between and among minorities and governments.

(c) Recommend further measures, as appropriate, for the promotion and protection of the rights of persons belonging to national or ethnic, religious and linguistic minorities.

In accordance with the mandate of the Working Group its sessions consisted of public meetings as well as private (closed) sessions. For the most part the sessions were open to individuals belonging to minority groups, representatives from inter-governmental organisations, non-governmental organisations, State representatives and scholars interested in the subject. The sessions of the Working Group not only succeeded in promoting the practical realisation of the United Nations Declaration but also acted as an excellent forum for debate, deliberation and constructive dialogue. Delegates representing various non-governmental organisations and other bodies were able to highlight their concerns, and where appropriate make recommendations for necessary action. Issues of autonomy were at the forefront of a number of debates, both minority groups as well as the State observers being participants in these debates.

The Working Group was able to enhance the overall jurisprudence of minority rights through a number of initiatives. Members of the Working Group produced commentaries on the Declaration, as well as on the various rights contained therein. Professor Asbjørn Eide, the chairman of the Working Group, made a substantial impression on the proceedings and continuing success of the Working Group.[159] Other members of the Working

---

[156] See Sub-Commission on the Prevention of Discrimination and Protection of Minorities Res. 1994/4 (19 August 1994).

[157] See Commission on Human Rights Res. 1995/24 (3 March 1995).

[158] See ECOSOC Res. 1995/31 (25 July 1995).

[159] E/CN.4/Sub.2/AC.5/1998 WP.1 and observations thereon from governments, specialised agencies, non-governmental organisations and experts E/CN.4/Sub.2/AC.5/1999 WP.1.

Group similarly provided valuable input. In March 1999, Mustafa Mehdi presented a working paper on Multicultural and Intercultural Education on the Protection of Minorities[160] as did another member of the Working Group on Universal and Regional Mechanisms for Minority Protection.[161]

In the Working Group's session of May 1999 numerous significant proposals were put forward, including the establishment of a database on minorities and enhanced strategies for further involvement of regional and sub-regional agencies.[162] The Working Group on Minorities held its 12th and final session in August 2006. However, it was not apparent at the time that this was to be the last session and consequently cooperation between the Working Group and the Independent Expert on Minority Issues was established.[163] In 2007, it was decided that the Sub-Commission on the Promotion and Protection of Human Rights was to be abolished, which led to the winding down of the Working Group. This development was of great concern to those involved in minority rights issues, who feared a weakening of the UN human rights framework and stressed the need for a similar mechanism in order to prevent conflict in addition to promoting and protecting minority rights.[164]

In its final session the Working Group in its recommendations proposed:

> 2. ... that the sessions of the Working Group on Minorities or a similar future mechanism, if the Human Rights Council decides to establish one, should be intersessional and have a duration of five working days, and recommends that such a mechanism should ensure access to and participation by minority representatives from all regions of the world and serve as a forum for dialogue and mutual understanding on minority rights issues.[165]

The Working Group on Minorities during its time made a significant impact through its interpretation of the UN Declaration on Minorities. However, the mechanism itself was significantly weaker than other UN special mandate holders and it was not until the introduction of the concept of the Independent Expert on Minority Issues that there was a Minority Rights mandate on a par with the other Special Rapporteurs.[166] The Working Group made a positive contribution to Minority Rights in so far as it allowed minorities that would usually be excluded from national and local decision-making to raise their concerns at an international level, it enabled minorities to learn about international standards and in some cases allowed minority groups to engage in dialogue with governments.[167] However, commentators have also criticised the Working Group for its lack of sustained discussion and government response, the *ad hoc* nature of the proceedings were a weakness

---

[160] E/CN.4.4/AC.5/1999 WP.5.
[161] E/CN.4/Sub.2/AC.5/1999 WP. 6 May 1999.
[162] E/CN.4/Sub.2/AC.5/1999 WP.9.
[163] Report on the Working Group on Minorities on its Twelfth Session, UN Doc. A/HRC/Sub.1/58/19 24 August 2006.
[164] Letter for the High Commission on National Minorities of the Organization of Security and Cooperation in Europe addressed to the President of the Human Rights Council, UN Doc. A/HRC/6/9 7 September 2007.
[165] Report on the Working Group on Minorities on its Twelfth Session, UN Doc. A/HRC/Sub.1/58/19 24 August 2006, para 2.
[166] Hadden, 'The United Nations Working Group on Minorities', 14 *IJMGR* (2007) p. 285.
[167] Ibid. pp. 289–290.

as was the fact there was no consistency regarding the attending minorities. 'In more general terms, there has been an absence of any sustained agenda or programme and no clear objective in respect of the adoption or publication of agreed conclusions or recommendations by the Working Group.'[168] It is likely that the issues of the Working Group were in part symptomatic of its weak mandate.

In 2005 Ms. Gay McDougall was appointed as the first Independent Expert on Minority Issues in accordance with the Commission on Human Rights Resolution 2005/79. In accordance with para 6 of the resolution, the Independent's expert's role includes:

(a) To promote the implementation of the Declaration on the Rights of Persons Belonging to National or Ethnic, Religious and Linguistic Minorities, including through consultations with Governments, taking into account existing international standards and national legislation concerning minorities;

(b) To identify best practices and possibilities for technical cooperation by the Office of the United Nations High Commissioner for Human Rights at the request of Governments;

(c) To apply a gender perspective in his or her work;

(d) To cooperate closely, while avoiding duplication, with existing relevant United Nations bodies, mandates, mechanisms as well as regional organizations;

(e) To take into account the views of non-governmental organizations on matters pertaining to his or her mandate.[169]

This mandate was extended by the Human Rights Council in resolution 7/6 of 27 March 2008 for a further three years and the role of the Independent Expert was extended to include:

(f) To guide the work of the Forum on Minority Issues, as decided by the Council in its resolution 6/15;

(g) To submit annual reports on his/her activities to the Council, including recommendations for effective strategies for the better implementation of the rights of persons belonging to minorities.[170]

The Independent Expert on Minorities in her role carried out a number of duties including receiving information from a variety of agencies, submitting annual reports and undertaking country visits at the invitation of the respective government.[171] Thus far, she has carried out missions to Hungary, Ethiopia, France, and the Dominican Republic. In her reports she has focused on the rights of the Roma, immigrant communities, linguistic minorities and the multiple forms of discrimination faced by minority women.[172]

13

The rights of minorities

---

[168] Ibid. p. 291.
[169] Human Rights Commission Resolution 2005/79, para 6.
[170] Human Rights Council Resolution 7/6 on the Mandate of the Independent Expert on Minority Issues, para 3.
[171] www2.ohchr.org/english/issues/minorities/expert/index.htm <last visited 8 October 2008>.
[172] See Report of the Independent Expert on Minority Issues, Addendum, Mission to Hungary, UN Doc. A/HRC/4/9/Add.2, Addendum, Mission to France, UN Doc. A/HRC/7/23/.Add.2.

The thematic priorities of the Independent Expert are also to:

1. Increase the focus on minority communities in the context of poverty alleviation, development and the Millennium Development Goals (MDGs) . . .

2. Increase the understanding of minority issues in the context of promoting social inclusion and ensuring stable societies . . .

3. Mainstream the consideration of minority issues within the work of the United Nations and other important multilateral forums.[173]

The Forum on Minority Issues was established by Human Rights Council Resolution 6/15 of 28 September 2007, in order to replace the Working Group on Minorities. The work of the Forum is to be guided by the Independent Expert in accordance with Resolution 7/6. However, the Forum will also provide support for the Independent Expert including thematic contributions and expertise.[174] The Chairperson of the Forum appointed in May 2008 was Ms. Viktória Mahácsi.[175] The Forum will meet annually for just two working days.[176] The first session of the Forum on Minority Issues took place on 15 and 16 December 2008 in Geneva, the thematic focus of which was 'Minorities and the right to education'.[177] It remains to be seen whether the Forum on Minority Issues manages to have as much of an impact as the Working Group, but it is disappointing that the Human Rights Council did not heed the recommendation of the Working Group in its final session that the mechanism 'be intersessional and have a duration of five working days'.[178] The limited timeframe, within which the Forum is required to work, will no doubt have an effect on its impact.

5 REGIONAL PROTECTION OF MINORITY RIGHTS: AN OVERVIEW

Many of the difficulties which have characterised the United Nations approach towards minorities have been reflected at the regional level. The continents of Europe, America and Africa have established regional institutions for the protection of human rights, although concern for minority rights has not been a strength of any of these systems. The provisions of the European Convention on Human Rights as well as the jurisprudence arising from the Strasbourg institutions has reflected difficulties in advancing the cause of minorities as distinct entities; it is the absence of the focus on group rights that is problematic.[179] The ECHR contains a number of provisions relevant to protecting the interests of minorities.

---

[173] www2.ohchr.org/english/issues/minorities/expert/objectives.htm <last visited 8 March 2009>.

[174] www2.ohchr.org/english/bodies/hrcouncil/minority/forum.htm <last visited 8 March 2009>.

[175] www2.ohchr.org/english/bodies/hrcouncil/minority/forum.htm <last visited 8 March 2009>.

[176] Human Rights Council Resolution 6/15 Forum on Minority Issues, para 3.

[177] www2.ohchr.org/english/bodies/hrcouncil/minority/forum.htm <last visited 8 October 2008>.

[178] Report on the Working Group on Minorities on its Twelfth Session, UN Doc. A/HRC/Sub.1/58/19 24 August 2006, para 2.

[179] See Harris, O'Boyle, Bates and Buckley, *Law of the European Convention on Human Rights* (Oxford University Press, 2009) at p. 602; Poulter, 'The Rights of Ethnic, Religious and Linguistic Minorities' 2 *EHRLR* (1997) 254; Weller (ed.) *The Rights of Minorities in Europe: A Commentary on the Framework Convention for the Protection of National Minorities* (Oxford University Press, 2006); Malloy, *National Minority Rights in Europe* (Oxford University Press, 2005).

However, it is only Article 14 (an article providing for a regime of non-discrimination) and Protocol 12, providing for a general prohibition of discrimination, that direct references to minorities are made.

The European Court and Commission have not been forthcoming in advancing the cause of minorities. Efforts to adopt a minority rights protocol have thus not borne fruition. The Council of Europe has however been successful in adopting two treaties which are directly relevant to minorities in Europe. The European Framework Convention for the Protection of National Minorities (FCNM) 1994[180] is the first binding instrument which has an exclusive focus on minorities. The treaty came into operation in 1998. The Convention emphasises on the usual non-discriminatory norms. It provides for equality, prohibiting discrimination on grounds 'belonging to a national minority'.[181] The States parties also undertake to adopt 'measures in the fields of education and research to foster knowledge of the culture, history, language and religion of their national minorities and of the majority'.[182] There is an undertaking to promote minority languages[183] and educational rights.[184] In accordance with Article 17, parties are also under obligation 'not to interfere with the right of persons belonging to national minorities to establish and maintain free and peaceful contacts across frontiers with persons lawfully staying in other States, in particular those with whom they share an ethnic, cultural, linguistic or religious identity, or a common cultural heritage'.[185]

In spite of these positive features, the Convention has many weaknesses. The Framework Convention, like other minority rights instruments fails to define the term 'national minority'. This has been further exacerbated by the 'margin of appreciation' employed, which allows States parties to decide upon the minority group they deem to qualify for protection under the FCNM. This has led to the exclusion of so-called 'new minorities' by a large number of States and in some cases the additional limitation of an exhaustive list of minorities to which the FCNM is to be applied.[186] However, the Advisory Committee, while adopting such a flexible approach, has emphasised that any reservation or declaration must be in accordance with the principles of international law and the fundamental principles contained in Article 3 FCNM. As in the *Greco-Bulgarian Communities* case, the PCIJ held that 'the existence of communities is a question of fact; it is not a question of law',[187] it is unlikely that exhaustive lists of applicable minorities are in accordance with the principles of international law. It has further emphasised that the definition of a minority employed by a State must 'not be a source of arbitrary or unjustified distinctions'.[188] The Advisory Committee has been extremely critical of States which it deems to have unreasonably restricted the definition of 'national minority'.[189] Article 6(1) states:

---

[180] For the text of the Convention see 16 *HRLJ* (1995) 98.
[181] Article 4(1).
[182] Article 12(1).
[183] Articles 10–11.
[184] Articles 12–14.
[185] Article 17(1).
[186] See reservations by Denmark on 22 September 1997, Germany 11 May 1995 and Poland 20 December 2000.
[187] *Greco-Bulgarian Communities* Case (PCIJ, 1930, Ser. B, No.17, p. 22).
[188] Advisory Committee on the Framework Convention for the Protection of National Minorities, Opinion on Denmark Adopted on 22 September 2000, ACFC/INF/OP/I(2001)005, para 14. Advisory Committee on the Framework Convention for the Protection of National Minorities, Opinion on Germany Adopted on 1 March 2002, ACFC/INF/OP/I(2002)008, para 14.
[189] Advisory Committee on the Framework Convention for the Protection of National Minorities, Opinion on Germany Adopted on 1 March 2002, ACFC/INF/OP/I(2002)008, para 17.

> The Parties shall encourage a spirit of tolerance and intercultural dialogue and take effective measures to promote mutual respect and understanding and co-operation among all persons living on their territory, irrespective of those persons' ethnic, cultural, linguistic or religious identity, in particular in the fields of education, culture and the media.

The use of 'all persons living on their territory' indicates that States may not limit the scope of this provision at all and, therefore, it must all extend to include 'new minorities'.[190] In its consideration of the State Report of Germany, the Advisory Committee suggested that the articles are applied to minorities on an article-by-article basis.[191] While this will certainly increase the rights afforded to 'new minorities', and can thus be seen as a positive move, there is still the danger that doing so will create a hierarchy of both minorities and minority rights.[192]

The Convention also does not detract from the path of according individual rights as opposed to the collective group rights.[193] The authors of the text of the Framework Convention reiterate this point in an explanatory note, commenting that the application of the provisions of the Convention 'does not imply the recognition of collective rights'.[194] They also point out that the notion of collective rights is separate and distinct from the issue of enjoyment of rights by individuals who belong to minority groups.[195]

In addition, a number of provisions of the Framework Convention are structured in such a manner that there is an apparent distinction in the nature of obligations undertaken by States parties. For example, under Article 7, States parties undertake to ensure respect for the rights of persons belonging to a minority to enjoy freedom of peaceful assembly, association, expression, thought, conscience and religion. On the other hand, in a number of instances where positive action is required to promote the collective group rights dimension the articles are framed in a manner which suggests an orientation towards 'progressive realisation' rather than an existence of immediate binding obligations, reminiscent of the principles enshrined in ICESCR. Examples of the latter construction are apparent from the usage of the term 'undertake to recognise' or 'not to interfere with'.

There is little in the Convention for minorities from the standpoint of autonomy. The closest the Convention comes to the subject of autonomy is in the article which provides that '[t]he Parties shall create the conditions necessary for the effective participation of persons belonging to national minorities in cultural, social and economic life and in public

---

[190] Hoffman, 'The Framework Convention for the Protection of National Minorities: An Introduction', in Weller (ed.) *A Commentary on the European Framework Convention for the Protection of National Minorities* (Oxford University Press, 2006) p. 17.

[191] Advisory Committee on the Framework Convention for the Protection of National Minorities, Opinion on Germany Adopted on 1 March 2002, ACFC/INF/OP/I(2002)008, para 18, Second Opinion on Germany Adopted on 1 March 2006, ACFC/OP/II(2006)001, para 10.

[192] See the discussion by the German Government: Comments of the Federal Government of Germany on the Opinion of the Advisory Committee, GVT/COM/INF/OP/I(2002)008, p. 6, Second Report Submitted by Germany Pursuant to Article 25, Paragraph 1 of the Framework Convention on the Protection of National Minorities, ACFC/SR/II(2005)002 paras 5–8.

[193] See Wheatley, 'The Framework Convention for the Protection of National Minorities' 1 *EHRLR* (1996) 583; 'The Framework Convention is predicated upon the rights of individuals and not collective rights of the minority group' Ibid. p. 584.

[194] See the Framework Convention for the Protection of National Minorities and Explanatory Report (1995) para 13, 22.

[195] See Aarnia, 'Minority Rights in the Council of Europe: Current Developments' in Phillips and Rosas (eds), *Universal Minority Rights* (Minority Rights Group International, 1995) pp. 123–133 at p. 131.

affairs, in particular those affecting them.'[196] The weak nature of obligations contained in the article have been a subject of criticism.[197] Furthermore, this article represents a retreat from the statements already advanced through Recommendation 1201 (1993) of the Parliamentary Assembly of the Council of Europe.[198] However, considering the already restrictive approach taken by States parties to the FCNM, it is likely that including a provision on autonomy may have considerably limited the number of States willing to ratify the Convention, particularly as a binding right to autonomy can be considered as seriously infringing on State sovereignty. The final and most significant of weaknesses in the Convention is that it does not have a complaints procedure. The Convention establishes general principles which are not directly applicable at national level, with implementation being the 'prerogative of the States'.[199] States parties are required to submit reports to an advisory committee of the Committee of Ministers on the measures – legislative and administrative – in order to ensure compliance with the treaty. The Advisory Committee also undertakes on-site visits as part of its investigations which allows the committee members to meet the officials from governments and others in non-governmental sectors. The reports submitted by the Advisory Committee is reviewed by the Committee of Ministers, which then adopts its conclusions with appropriate recommendations. It would be useful to further advance the possibility of NGOs and minority groups to comment or State reports to make suggestions when State practices are being considered by the Advisory Committee.[200] The flexible nature of the rights contained within FCNM and the margin of appreciation employed regarding the definition of a minority, means that the Convention itself does not lend itself to judicial interpretation or application.[201]

The Council of Europe has also adopted the European Charter for Regional or Minority Languages (1992). The Charter, a binding treaty, as its title suggests aims to protect the regional and minority languages spoken within Europe. States parties to the Charter undertake to encourage and facilitate the regional and minority languages, *inter alia*, 'in speech and writing, in public and private life'. There is also an undertaking to encourage the usage of these languages in studies, in education,[202] in administration of justice,[203] public services,[204] in media,[205] in social and economic life,[206] and to establish institutions in order to advise 'authorities on all matters pertaining to regional or minority languages'.[207] Implementation of the treaty is to be conducted through periodic reports to the Secretary-General

---

[196] Article 15.
[197] Gilbert treats the provisions of Article 15 as 'some what timid' Gilbert, 'The Council of Europe and Minority Rights' 18 *HRQ* (1996) 160 at p. 196.
[198] Article 11 of the Recommendation provided as follows: 'In the regions where they are in a majority the persons belonging to a national minority shall have the right to have at their disposal appropriate local or autonomous authorities or to have a special status, matching the specific historical and territorial situation and in accordance with the domestic legislation.'
[199] Wheatley, above n.193, at p. 585.
[200] Boyle, 'Europe: The Council of Europe, the OSCE, and the European Union' in Hannum (ed.), *Guide to International Human Rights Practice* (Transnational Publishers, 2004) pp. 143–170.
[201] Hoffman, 'The Framework Convention for the Protection of National Minorities: An Introduction', in Weller (ed.), *A Commentary on the European Framework Convention for the Protection of National Minorities*, above n.187, at p. 6.
[202] Article 8.
[203] Article 9.
[204] Article 10.
[205] Article 11.
[206] Article 13.
[207] Article 7(4).

of the Council of Europe in a manner prescribed by the Committee of Ministers.[208] The first report is to be presented within a year following entry into force of the Charter with respect to the State concerned and thereafter at three-year intervals.[209] These reports are to be examined by a Committee of Experts, consisting of one member from each State party,[210] nominated by the relevant State, appointed for a six-year term and eligible for reappointment.[211] Issues relevant to the undertakings of the State concerned may be brought to the attention of the Committee of Experts. France[212] and Turkey, major States members of the Council of Europe, have as yet not signed the FCNM whereas Belgium, Iceland, Greece and Luxembourg have not ratified the FCNM.

In the light of other information (including State reports) the Committee of Experts prepares a report for the Committee of Ministers. This report is accompanied with the comments which the Parties have been requested to make and may be made public by the Committee of Ministers. These report are required to contain, in particular, the proposals of the Committee of Experts to the Committee of Ministers for the preparation of such recommendations of the latter body to one or more of the Parties as may be required. The Secretary-General of the Council of Europe is required to make a bi-annual detailed report to the Parliamentary Assembly on the application of the Charter. The Committee of Ministers may, after the entry into force of the Charter, invite non-member States of the COE to accede to the Charter.[213]

In addition to work done by the Council of Europe, significant contributions in the field of minority rights are made by another inter-governmental organisation, the Organization of Security and Co-operation in Europe (OSCE).[214] The concern shown for the subject of minority rights within the OSCE stretches back to the Helsinki Final Act. As we noted in an earlier chapter, significant progress was made in this direction during the course of the 'Follow-up meetings' leading up to and beyond the Copenhagen Document.[215] The Copenhagen Document is valuable for the propagation of minority rights. There are important provisions relating to autonomy. Article 35 provides:

> The participating States note the efforts undertaken to protect and create conditions for the promotion of the ethnic, cultural, linguistic and religious identity of certain minorities by establishing, as one of the possible means to achieve these aims, appropriate local and autonomous administrations corresponding to the specific historical and territorial circumstances of such minorities and in accordance with the policies of the State concerned.

The Organization for Security and Co-operation in Europe is similar in nature to the European Union: both are inter-governmental organisations. Whilst the OSCE and the EU were not designed initially for promoting human rights *per se*, both the organisations became involved with this subject. There are, however, significant differences between the OSCE and both the EU and the Council of Europe. The OSCE is not a legal body, and unlike

---

[208] Article 15(1).
[209] Article 15(2).
[210] Article 16.
[211] Article 17.
[212] In the light of France's Declaration regarding Article 27 ICCPR, this is hardly surprising.
[213] Shaw, above n.7, at p. 278.
[214] Wright 'The OSCE and the Protection of Minority Rights' 18 *HRQ* (1996) 190.
[215] See above chapter 8.

the EU and the Council of Europe its foundations have not been laid on legally binding treaties. The principles that emerge from the OSCE process are necessarily political commitments as opposed to legal rights and obligations. As noted earlier, this means that unlike treaties, these commitments cannot as such be incorporated into domestic law, and national courts are unable to rely upon these principles. Despite the absence of legally binding regime, the OSCE has proved to be a success; it is possibly the non-binding character of the regime which encouraged States such the former Soviet Union to accept the fundamental principles of the organisation. The OSCE also has the distinction of being the only security organisation in Europe considered as a regional organisation within the framework of Chapter VIII of the UN Charter.

The OSCE, which prior to 1 January 1995 was known as the Conference on the Security and Co-operation in Europe (CSCE), represents the largest regional security organisation in the world. It has 56 participating States from Europe, Central Asia and North America and is engaged, *inter alia*, in early-warnings, the prevention of conflicts and rehabilitation after a conflict has taken place. The development of the organisation can be broken down into two phases. The first period corresponds roughly to 1973–1990 which reflected tensions through increasing détente between the West and Eastern Europe. The second phase, since 1990, has witnessed the breakdown of the Soviet Union and the Warsaw pact and considerable institutional development of the organisation.[216]

In order to deal with the situation in 1992, the CSCE crested the post of the High Commissioner on National Minorities (HCNM), at the Helsinki meeting of the OSCE.[217] The primary responsibility of the HCNM is in conflict prevention. In order to conduct his responsibilities the HCNM adopts a strategy of 'early warning' and 'early action' as regards 'tensions involving national minority issues which have not yet developed beyond an early warning stage, but, in the judgment of the High Commissioner, have the potential to develop into a conflict within the OSCE area'.[218] A long-term perspective allows for a consistent dialogue, exchange of ideas and cooperation between the parties, leading to de-escalation of tensions and the ultimate resolution of disputes. The High Commissioner has performed a number of services for minority groups. His interventions to diffuse potentially volatile situations and his role as a mediator remain the most important ones.

HCNM is a person of 'eminent international personality . . . from whom an impartial performance of the function may be expected'.[219] HCNM is appointed for a three-year term which is renewable once.[220] Since his appointment, the HCNM has been impressive not only in attempt to resolve disputes but has also been instrumental in easing ethnic, racial and religious tensions in many parts of the European continent. Since the involvement of American and United Kingdom forces in the Middle East, and highly volatile situation developing in States of Central Asia and Eastern Europe, the role of HCNM's role has acquired even greater significance. On 1 July 2001 the Swedish Ambassador Rolf Ekéus replaced the first High Commission Max Vander Stoel. Ambassador Rolf Ekéus's term of office was extended for another three years on 1 July 2004. On 7 July 2007, a former Norwegian foreign minister Ambassador Knut Vollebaek

---

[216] For further institutional human rights developments of the organisation see chapter 8 above.
[217] See Helsinki Document 1992, Reprinted 13 *HRLJ* (1992) 284.
[218] See www.osce.org/hcnm/13022.html 'OSCE: High Commissioner on National Minorities' <last visited 1 March 2008>.
[219] See Helsinki Summit, July 1992 *above* n.127 (Helsinki) Decision 8.
[220] Ibid. Decision 9.

The rights of minorities

13

was appointed OSCE HCNM for a period of three years. In addition to dealing with specific situations in the various Member States of OSCE, the High Commissioners have also made recommendations on subjects that affect a number of States such as education, use of language and participation in public affairs, the use of minority languages in the broadcast media and policing in multi-ethnic societies. The need to integrate diversity has also been stressed as a crucial element in preventing conflict by the various High Commissioners.[221] While the overriding purpose of the Office of the High Commissioner is conflict prevention this has not prevented a focus on Roma and Sinti issues.[222]

As a natural consequence of the work of HCNM, the OSCE has developed several sets of recommendations which deal with the rights of minorities with the ultimate goal of conflict prevention. These recommendations have been developed with the Copenhagen Document of the Conference on the Human Dimension (CSCE) 1991 in mind. This is still the most far-reaching document dealing with the rights of national minorities, covering such issues as education, language, cross-border contacts, political representation and participation in public affairs, in its detailed clauses.[223] It is important to note, however, that an acceptable definition of a 'national minority' has yet to be found.[224] The Hague Recommendations regarding the Educational Rights of National Minorities, in common with the other Recommendations, are derived from pre-existing legally binding international instruments. In the respect of the Hague Recommendations, the right to education in ICESCR and the Convention on the Rights of the Child, Article 27 ICCPR and the UNESCO Convention on the Prevention of Discrimination in Education have been cited as sources of international law.[225] The purpose of such a political document is essentially to add meat to the bones of the pre-existing minority rights framework. Eide, has pointed out that '[s]ince they are more precise, they will also reduce the likelihood of disputes and agreements'.[226] However, this also has the more negative side of reducing the flexibility of the system, which has been seen by many as one of its strong points.[227] The flexible nature of OSCE standards reflects the varying situation of different national minorities, and States are more likely to accept flexible standards as opposed to strict ones. The Hague Recommendations while providing for education in minority languages and a compulsory curriculum regarding the histories, traditions and cultures of national minorities, also places obligations on the minority groups in question:

> Paragraph 1, in particular, highlights the spirit of these *Recommendations* the right of persons belonging to national minorities to maintain their identity can only be fully realized if they acquire a proper knowledge of their mother tongue during the educational process. At the same time, persons belonging to national minorities have a responsibility to integrate into the wide national society through the acquisition of a proper knowledge of the State language.[228]

---

[221] www.osce.org/hcnm/item_2_129.html <last visited on 11 March 2009>.

[222] See e.g. Seminar on the Roma in the OSCE Region, 14–15 June 2000, Bratislava.

[223] Bloed, 'The OSCE and the Issue of National Minorities', in Philips and Rosas (eds), *Universal Minority Rights* (Minority Rights Group International, 1995) p. 114.

[224] Ibid. p. 115.

[225] Eide, 'The Hague Recommendations regarding the Educational Rights of National Minorities: Their Objective' 4 *IJMGR* (1996) 163, p. 164.

[226] Ibid. p. 164.

[227] Pentassuglia, *Minorities in International* Law (Council of Europe Publishing, 2002) p. 144. Eide, 'The Oslo Recommendations regarding the Linguistic Rights of National Minorities: An Overview', 6 *IJMGR* (1999) 319, p. 324.

[228] Eide, 'The Hague Recommendations regarding the Educational Rights of National Minorities: Their Objective' 4 *IJMGR* (1996) 163 p. 167.

Similarly, the Oslo Recommendations regarding the Linguistic Rights of National Minorities and the Lund Recommendations on the Effective Participation of National Minorities in Public Life are also based around pre-existing legal standards. The Oslo Recommendations deal with subjects as far reaching as 'names', 'religion' and 'the media'. The Lund Recommendations deal with two main topics, the participation of the national minority in the 'governance of the State as a whole, and self-governance over certain local or internal affairs'.[229] It is important to bear in mind when considering the Recommendations that their primary purpose is conflict prevention and as such:

> [t]he Recommendations do not propose an isolationist approach, but rather one which encourages a balance between the right of persons belonging to national minorities to maintain and develop their own identity, culture and language and the necessity of ensuring that they are able to integrate into the wide society as full and equal members.[230]

As the Recommendations are simply political documents, they do not contain any legal weight. That said, '[a]lthough non-compliance with a non-legally binding commitment may not *per se* generate international legal responsibility, a violation of "politically" binding agreements is thus as unacceptable as a violation of norms of international law'.[231] Despite their non-binding character, the Recommendations have frequently been used by policy and law-makers as a point of reference.[232] 'OSCE agreements not only often constitute "progressive development" of existing legal norms, but also lead to the creation of law.'[233] The Recommendations have even been used as if they were binding legal instruments by the High Commissioner on National Minorities, Max van der Stohl, when dealing with governments.[234]

The Office for Democratic Institutions and Human Rights (ODHIR) has a considerable role in establishing democratic governance and monitoring of elections. As part of the human dimension of the OSCE's objectives, the Office is of great importance in observing and monitoring elections in emerging democracies of the world. The Office also provides training programmes for developing States in developing election processes. ODIHR plays an important role regarding the rights of non-'national' minority groups, with a specific focus on Roma and Sinti issues and tolerance and non-discrimination. There is an obvious overlap between the work of the High Commissioner on National Minorities and the Office for Democratic Institutions and Human Rights.[235]

---

[229] 'The Lund Recommendations on the Effective Participation of National Minorities in Public Life and Explanatory Note' 12 *IJMGR* (2005) 297, p. 300.

[230] 'The Oslo Recommendations regarding the Linguistic Rights of National Minorities and Explanatory Note', February 1998, 6(3) *IJMGR* (1999) 359, p. 370.

[231] Pentassuglia, *Minorities in International Law* (2002) p. 144.

[232] 'The Lund Recommendations on the Effective Participation of National Minorities in Public Life and Explanatory Note' 12 *IJMGR* (2005) 297, p. 299.

[233] Bloed, 'The OSCE and the Issue of National Minorities', in Philips and Rosas (eds), *Universal Minority Rights* (Minority Rights Group International, 1995) p. 116.

[234] Bowring, 'European Minority Protection The Past and Future of a "Major Historical Achievement" ' 15 *IJMGR* (2008) 413, p. 424 (see particularly footnote 59).

[235] See e.g. OSCE Supplementary Human Dimension Meeting, The Role of National Institutions against Discrimination in Combating Racism and Xenophobia, with a Special Focus on Persons Belonging to National Minorities and Migrants. www.osce.org/documents/odihr/2008/10/33849_en.pdf <last visited 11 October 2008>.

When addressing Roma and Sinti issues the ODIHR has recognised that there are several areas which require action, including racist violence, unemployment, poverty, illiteracy and high infant mortality. The Office's work with Roma and Sinti culminated in 2003 with its 'Action Plan on Improving the Situation of Roma and Sinti within the OSCE Area'.[236] This plan outlined the importance of combating racism and discrimination through legislation and law enforcement, the police and the mass media. In addition to this, the improvement of socio-economic factors such as housing and living conditions, unemployment and healthcare were addressed along with the importance of improving access to education and enhancing participation in public and political life.

Within the ambit of tolerance and non-discrimination falls Islamophobia, anti-Semitism, racism and xenophobia, and freedom of religion and belief. In order to achieve its objectives the ODIHR carries out a number of activities including, inter-cultural dialogue, education, engaging with civil society and law enforcement training. The Office specifically aims to reduce hate crime. The main activities of the Office in this respect include collecting data and information regarding hate crime, collecting and disseminating information on best practices, monitoring incidents of intolerance and discrimination and, finally, giving support to States when dealing with instances of intolerance.

The African Charter on Human and Peoples Rights, as we have seen, contains a number of rights designated as people's rights.[237] These rights as group rights have the potential of being of great significance to minorities. On the other hand, it is equally true that individual State practice, the AU as an organisation and the African Commission as the principal organ of the Charter have shown great reluctance in equating minorities as peoples. The fear largely is that such an equation would lead minorities to claim a right of self-determination resulting in the break up of existing States. The use of peoples' rights in the OAU Charter refers primarily to the eradication of oppressive and colonial rule. It is feared now that the large amount of minorities that exist in African States, if granted minority rights, could lead to the further destabilisation of the region. However, cultural rights are not considered such a threat, such as those provided by Article 17 of the Protocol to the African Charter on Human and Peoples' Rights on the Rights of Women, which states that:

1. Women shall have the right to live in a positive cultural context and to participate at all levels in the determination of cultural policies.
2. States Parties shall take all appropriate measures to enhance the participation of women in the formulation of cultural policies at all levels.

Latin America has seen problems arising out of minority rights, though a serious debate has arisen in relation to the rights of indigenous peoples. This is a subject to which we shall direct our attention to in the next chapter.

6 CONCLUSIONS

Minority Rights has been a problematic issue for international law to handle. Although international law primarily deals through the medium of States, and minorities generally

---

[236] PC.Dec/566 of 27 November 2003, Decision No. 55. Action Plan on Improving the Situation of Roma and Sinti within the OSCE Area.
[237] See above chapter 10.

have no *locus standi*, the treatment which minorities receive from their States has increasingly become a matter of international concern. International law, however, has historically found it difficult to deal with the problems around minorities. Like the poor, the weak and the inarticulate, they have since time immemorial proven as natural victims of persecution and genocide. Even in the contemporary period of relative tolerance and rationality, minorities are often subjected to persecution, discrimination and genocide. The stance of international law remains tentative and extremely cautious, for minorities pose questions of a serious nature; they exist in myriad forms, with their own social, political, cultural and religious particularities. Often transcending national frontiers, minorities are extremely capable of appealing to the sensitivities of their international sympathisers. Most national boundaries are arbitrarily drawn and a number of States contain turbulent factions artificially placed within their borders, often cutting across frontiers.

After considerable hesitation, there are now a number of notable initiatives. At the United Nations level, Article 27 of the ICCPR continues to represent the leading provision dealing with minority rights. It is however inadequate and there is need for reform – on a practical level, the Human Rights Committee has not been able to adequately support cases emerging from disgruntled minorities. The UN Declaration on Minorities has been a positive step though much remains to be done. The Declaration needs to be converted in a binding treaty, and States must acknowledge more firmly their commitment to protecting minority rights. The appointment of the Independent Expert on Minority Issues (2005) with an extended mandate in 2008 is a positive step, as is the establishment of the Forum on Minority Issues by the Human Rights Council in September 2007. However, it is only with the passage of time that a fuller impact of these latter initiatives would become evident.

At the regional level, the Council of Europe's adoption of the Framework Convention for the Protection National Minorities and the European Charter for Regional or Minority Languages represents important developments. The OSCE has also brought the subject of minority rights to the forefront of its agenda, recognising the importance of such rights in order to ensure peace and prevent future conflict. It is, however, an unfortunate reality that the regions where some of the worst minority rights violations take place, for example, South Asia, the Middle East and Africa remain devoid of initiatives to protect minorities.

13

The rights of minorities

14 The rights of 'peoples' and 'indigenous peoples'[1]

> [n]early forty years ago a Professor of Political Science who was also the President of the United States, President Wilson, enunciated a doctrine which was ridiculous, but which was widely accepted as a sensible proposition, the doctrine of Self-determination. On the surface it seemed reasonable: Let the people decide. It was in fact ridiculous because the people cannot decide until somebody decides who are the people.[2]

1 INTRODUCTION

The identification of an entity as 'peoples' in international law, particularly in the post-colonial period, has proved to be controversial. The primary reason for this controversy is that if an entity is recognised as a 'people', it becomes a lawful claimant to the right of self-determination, a right which also includes independent statehood.[3] The definitional debate as to the precise meaning of 'peoples' has taken place ever since the term was used in the United Nations Charter. The Charter attaches the 'Right of Self-Determination' to 'Peoples'.[4] The United Nations Secretariat commenting upon the term 'peoples' in the Charter stated that '[p]eoples refers to a group of human beings, who may or may not comprise States or

---

[1] See Anaya, *Indigenous Peoples in International Law* (Oxford University Press, 1996); Barnes, Gray and Kingsbury (eds), *Indigenous Peoples of Asia* (Association for Asian Studies/University of Michigan, 1993); Brownlie, *Treaties and Indigenous Peoples: The Robb Lectures* (Clarendon Press, 1992); Castellino, *International Law and Self Determination: The Interplay of the Politics of Territorial Possession with Formulations of Post Colonial National Identity* (Martinus Nijhoff Publishers, 2000); Castellino and Dominguez Redondo, *Minority Rights in Asia* (Oxford University Press, 2006); Heinz, *Indigenous Populations, Ethnic Minorities and Human Rights* (Quorum Verlag, 1988); Gilbert, *Indigenous Peoples Land Rights under International Law: From Victims to Actors* (Transnational Publishers Inc, 2006); Gilbert, 'Historical Indigenous Peoples' Land Claims: A Comparative and International Approach to the Common Law Doctrine on Indigenous Title' 56 *ICLQ* (2007) 583; Kingsbury, ' "Indigenous Peoples" in International Law: A Constructivist Approach to the Asian Controversy' 92 *AJIL* (1998) 414; Thornberry, *Indigenous Peoples and Human Rights* (Manchester University Press, 2002); and Xanthaki, *Indigenous Rights and United Nations Standards: Self-Determination, Culture and Land* (Cambridge University Press, 2007).
[2] Jennings, *The Approach to Self-Government* (Cambridge University Press, 1956) pp. 55–56.
[3] Professor Malcolm Shaw appropriately points out '[t]he issue of what in law constitutes a "People" has proved to be one of the great controversies of the Post-World War II era. The reason for this has been the development of the concept of self-determination'. Shaw, 'The Definition of Minorities in international law' in Dinstein and Tabory (eds), *The Protection of Minorities and Human Rights* (Martinus Nijhoff Publishers, 1992), 1–31 at p. 2.
[4] See below.

472

Nations',[5] leading to the view, although a minority one, that the provisions of the Charter allowed secession for minorities.[6] International law is similarly moving towards allowing indigenous peoples a right to self-determination, and hence similar difficulties arise in identifying and defining 'indigenous peoples'.

Since the Charter became operational, the term 'peoples' has become a significant feature of many international and national instruments although there has often been an inconclusive debate as to its meaning and scope. Notwithstanding the difficulties in identifying the term 'peoples', it is important to acknowledge and explore the meaning and content of the term 'Peoples' Right to Self-Determination'. It is equally important to understand the relevance of considering the position of indigenous peoples in debates on self-determination. Indigenous peoples' claim to be recognised as 'peoples' and their demand to self-determination includes a right to independent statehood.

2 PEOPLES' RIGHT TO SELF-DETERMINATION

Self-determination in its modern form can be related to the experiences of the American, French and Bolshevik Revolutions with their emphasis on popular sovereignty.[7] Although it is used widely by politicians and nationalists, in international law the concept remained in an embryonic form until the events of the First World War when US President Wilson, the leading exponent of this ideal, attempted to assert his wishes in various forms.[8] However, President Wilson was soon to discover, presenting utopian ideals was one thing, yet putting them into practice quite another. The fundamental difficulty with the otherwise attractive, and even sensible proposition, was the identification of its potential beneficiaries. Beset by the inherent contradictions of different, though competing and equally worthy 'selves', the uncertainty in ascertaining the proper mode of 'determination' and its content and the conflict of self-determination with the cardinal principles of sovereign equality, duty of non-intervention, the maintenance of the *status quo*, preservation of peace and security and the sanctity of international treaties, the Wilsonian ideal failed to flourish.[9] On a universal level, its application could not be taken seriously; it was generally ignored at the Paris Peace Conference 1919, and was not even mentioned in the final draft of the Covenant of the League of Nations. Despite the fact that the final territorial settlements proved disappointing, self-determination left some of its mark in the form of the mandate system,[10] minority rights treaties[11] and was sometimes reflected in the judgments of the Permanent Court of International Justice.[12]

---

[5] UNCIO Docs. XVIII, 657–658.

[6] UNCIO Docs. XVII, 142.

[7] Franck, 'Post-Modern Tribalism and the Right to Secession' in Brölmann, Lefeber and Zieck (eds), *Peoples and Minorities in International Law* (Martinus Nijhoff Publishers, 1993) pp. 3–27 at p. 6; Pomerance, *Self-determination in Law and Practice: The New Doctrine in the United Nations* (Martinus Nijhoff Publishers, 1982); Rigo Sureda, *The Evolution of the Right of Self-Determination: A Study of United Nations Practice* (Sijthoff, 1973) p. 17.

[8] Shaw, *Title to Territory in Africa: International Legal Issues* (Oxford University Press, 1986) pp. 60–61; Nawaz, 'The Meaning and Range of the Principle of Self-Determination' 82 *Duke LJ* (1965) 82 at p. 82.

[9] Pomerance, above n.7, at pp. 1–9.

[10] See Article 22 of the Covenant of League of Nations, 28 June 1919, 112 B.F.S.P 1.

[11] Thornberry, 'Is there a Phoenix in the Ashes? – International Law and Minority Rights' 15 *Tex.ILJ* (1980) 421 at p. 453.

[12] See e.g. *Minority Schools in Albania* [1935] PCIJ Ser A/B Nos. 64, 17.

Despite repeated references to it by both politicians and lawyers, during the inter-war years self-determination failed to be recognised as part of general international law;[13] this position being confirmed by the Council of the League of Nations in the *Aaland Island* case.[14] Although the events in Europe in the 1930s and during the course of the Second World War forced the allied powers to focus on the issue of human rights, references to self-determination remained ambivalent, only rarely making its appearance. The Atlantic Charter of August 1941 makes reference to it, but the Dumbarton Oaks proposals do not.

The United Nations Charter makes express reference to self-determination on two occasions. According to Article 1, one of the purposes of the UN is to 'develop friendly relations among nations based on respect for equal rights and self-determination of all peoples and to take other appropriate measures to strengthen universal peace'.[15] The other reference is made in Article 55, according to which '[w]ith a view to the creation of conditions of stability and well-being which are necessary for peaceful and friendly relations among nations based on respect for the principle of equal rights and self-determination of peoples, the United Nations shall promote' followed by a number of objectives. Chapter XI, which was subsequently to form the basis of decolonisation, also implicitly recognises the principle of self-determination, although the term itself is not used.

There seems to be some debate as to whether it was, in fact, the intention of the drafters of the UN Charter to provide for a legally binding right of self-determination,[16] although the view may seem persuasive that Charter provisions in relation to self-determination did create binding legal obligations, albeit in a rather vague and imprecise manner. In any event, as Professor Higgins points out, the self-determination principle – as enunciated in the Charter – was inherently conservative and radically different from how it came to be understood subsequently.[17] Whatever the legal position regarding self-determination may have been at the time the Charter came into operation, the rapid changes in the UN have ensured its conspicuous existence as a legal right, although its primary focus has been directed towards decolonisation. Notwithstanding the fact that a number of States have adopted a negative stance on the issue,[18] it seems certain that the right to self-determination is applicable even in the post-colonial world.

---

[13] Kirgis Jr., 'The Degrees of Self-Determination in the United Nations Era' 88 *AJIL* (1994) 304 at p. 304; Thornberry, 'Self-Determination, Minorities and Human Rights: A Review of International Instruments' 38 *ICLQ* (1989) 867 at p. 871.

[14] *The Aaland Island Case*, LON Official J Special Supp No. 1. Aug. 1920 3, 5; Hannikainen and Horn (eds), *Autonomy and Demilitarisation in International Law: The Aland Islands in a Changing Europe* (Kluwer Law International, 1997).

[15] Article 1(2) of the United Nations Charter (1945). 26 June 1945, 59 Stat. 1031, T.S. 993, 3 Bevans 1153.

[16] Hannum, *Autonomy, Sovereignty and Self-Determination: The Accommodation of Conflicting Rights* (University of Pennsylvania Press, 1990) p. 33; Blum, 'Reflections on the Changing Concept of Self-Determination' 10 *Israel L.R.* (1975) 509 at p. 511; see also the views of Gross as discussed by Emerson, in Emerson, 'Self-Determination' 65 *AJIL* (1971) 459 at p. 461; Brownlie, *Principles of Public International Law* (Oxford University Press, 2008) pp. 580–581.

[17] 'The concept of self-determination did not then, originally, seem to refer to a right of dependant peoples to be independent, or indeed, even to vote'. After a discussion of Chapter XI and XII she concludes 'It can now be seen that self-determination is not provided for the text of the United Nations Charter – at least in the sense that it is generally used'. Higgins, *Problems and Process: International Law and How We Use It* (Oxford University Press, 1995) at p. 112; also see Emerson, 'Colonialism, Political Development and the United Nations' in *International Organization* (1965) pp. 484–503.

[18] See e.g. the Indian reservation to Article 1 of the ICCPR. According to this reservation, entered at the time of the ratification of the Covenant 'With reference to article 1 . . . the Government of the Republic of India declares that the words "the right of self-determination" appearing in this article apply only to the peoples under the foreign domination and that these words do not apply to sovereign independent States or to a

As we have already noted, this view is forcefully asserted in the common article of the ICCPR and ICESCR.[19] Article 1 has been referred to not as a 'human right[s]' article but as one providing for 'collective right of peoples'.[20] The right to self-determination has also been the subject of a General Comment by the Human Rights Committee. In its General Comment, emphasising upon the significance of this right, the Committee notes that:

> [i]n accordance with the purposes and principles of the Charter of the United Nations, article 1 of the International Covenant on Civil and Political Rights recognizes that all peoples have the right of self-determination. The right of self-determination is of particular importance because its realization is an essential condition for the effective guarantee and observance of individual human rights and for the promotion and strengthening of those rights. It is for that reason that States set forth the right of self-determination in a provision of positive law in both Covenants and placed this provision as article 1 apart from and before all of the other rights in the two Covenants.[21]

Claims to self-determination have also been invoked in a number of cases before the Committee. However, as Article 1 refers to the rights of peoples and the communications procedure concerns individuals, all claims under Article 1 have been held inadmissible.[22] The difference between the rights is evidenced not only by the wording of the provision; Article 1 refers to the rights of '[a]ll peoples', it is also evidenced by the separation of the rights within the Covenant itself. Article 1 is in Part I of the ICCPR, whereas the substantive rights which claims can be brought under are in Part III. In the *Lubicon Lake Band* case it was held that the First Optional Protocol only provides remedies for the rights set out in Part III of the Covenant.[23] It has, on the other hand, been possible for indigenous groups to invoke their rights as individuals or as groups of individuals under Article 27 of the ICCPR.[24] While it is not possible for individuals to submit communications under Article 1, it is nevertheless important to bear in mind that the Committee has held 'the provisions

section of a people or nation – which is the essence of national integrity' UN Centre for Human Rights, *Human Rights: Status of International Instruments* (1987) 9 UN Sales No. E.87.XIV.2; Although there are inconsistencies in India's position, the views expressed in the reservation were reaffirmed by her representative to the Human Rights Committee stating that 'the right to self-determination in international context [applies] only to dependent territories and people' UN Doc. CCPR/C/SR. 498 (1984) 5; HRC has urged India to review its reservations, 'with a view to withdrawing them': *Concluding observations of the Human Rights Committee India. 04/08/97 (CCPR/C/79/Add.81)* CCPR/C/79/Add.81; 4 August 1997. For further discussion on the right to self-determination see above chapter 5.

19 See above chapters 5 and 6.
20 Nowak, *UN Covenant on Civil and Political Rights: CCPR Commentary* (N.P. Engel, 2005) p. 14.
21 Human Rights Committee, *The Right to Self-determination of Peoples (Art. 1). 13/04/84*. CCPR General Comment 12. (General Comments) para 1.
22 *Sandra Lovelace* v. *Canada*, Communication No. 24/1977 (30 July 1981), UN Doc. CCPR/C/OP/1 at 83 (1984); *Lubicon Lake Band* v. *Canada*, Communication No. 167/1984 (26 March 1990), UN Doc. Supp. No. 40 (A/45/40) at 1 (1990).
23 *Lubicon Lake Band* v. *Canada*, Communication No. 167/1984 (26 March 1990), UN Doc. Supp. No. 40 (A/45/40) at 1 (1990). 'The Optional Protocol provides a procedure under which individuals can claim that their individual rights have been violated. These rights are set out in part III of the Covenant, articles 6 to 27, inclusive'. Ibid. (para 32.1).
24 *Sandra Lovelace* v. *Canada*, Communication No. 24/1977 (30 July 1981), UN Doc. CCPR/C/OP/1 at 83 (1984); *Lubicon Lake Band* v. *Canada*, Communication No. 167/1984 (26 March 1990), UN Doc. Supp. No. 40 (A/45/40) at 1 (1990).

of Article 1 may be relevant in the interpretation of other rights protected by the Covenant, in particular Articles 25, 26 and 27'.[25]

In our survey of instruments, we have analysed the role and position of the right to self-determination as enshrined in the AFCHPR.[26] The Convention Concerning Indigenous and Tribal Peoples in Independent Countries (ILO) No. 169[27] also implies the right to self-determination, but without defining the concept.[28] The Organization for the Security and Co-operation in Europe (OSCE) has laid down a certain emphasis on the continuing role of self-determination.[29] The Helsinki Final Act, although a political commitment, has carried substantial influence in affirming the right to self-determination. Article VIII of the Act provides as follows:

> The participating States will respect the equal rights of peoples and their right to self-determination . . . By virtue of the principle of equal rights and self-determination of peoples, all peoples always have the right, in full freedom, to determine, when and as they wish, their internal and external political status, without external political interference, and to pursue as they wish their political, economic, social and cultural development.

Customary international law affirms the view that self-determination is a binding legal right. We have already noted that the General Assembly Resolutions are not *per se* binding, though they can be instrumental in providing evidence of State practice, and can in certain circumstances be regarded as interpreting the provisions of the Charter.[30] In this context it is important to note the highly authoritative UN General Assembly Resolutions which have been treated as authoritative interpretations of the Charter, and generally regarded as reflective of customary law, for example Declaration on the Granting of Independence to Colonial Territories and Peoples GA Res. 1514 (XV) (1960) and the Declaration of the Principles of International law Concerning Friendly Relations and Co-operation Amongst States in Accordance with the Charter of the United Nations GAR 2625 (XXV), 1970. There are many other General Assembly Resolutions which reaffirm this normative value.

Judicial discussion is heavily in support of this assertion. *Dicta* from the Advisory Opinion of the World Court in the *Namibia*[31] and the *Western Sahara* cases[32] are strong arguments to substantiate the point.[33] A further reconfirmation of this view came through

---

[25] *Diergaardt (late Captain of the Rehoboth Baster Community)* et al. v. *Namibia*, Communication No. 760/1997, UN Doc. CCPR/C/69/D/760/1997 (2000), para 10.3.

[26] Article 20(1). See above chapter 10.

[27] 72 ILO Official Bull. 59, 28 I.L.M. (1989) 1382, entered into force 5 September 1991.

[28] See Lerner, *Group Rights and Discrimination in International Law* (Martinus Nijhoff Publishers, 1991) p. 29.

[29] See above chapter 8; Wright, 'The OSCE and the Protection of Minority Rights' 18 *HRQ* (1996) 190; Koskenniemi, 'National Self-Determination Today: Problems of Legal Theory and Practice' 43 *ICLQ* (1994) 241 at p. 242.

[30] See above chapter 3.

[31] *Legal Consequences for States of the Continued Presence of South Africa in Namibia (South West Africa) notwithstanding Security Council Resolution 276 (1970)*, Advisory Opinion 21 June 1971, (1971) ICJ Reports 16.

[32] *Western Sahara*, Advisory Opinion 16 October 1975, (1975) ICJ Reports 12.

[33] See the *Namibia* case 'the subsequent developments of international law in regard to non-self governing, as enunciated in the Charter of the United Nations, made the principle of self-determination applicable to all of them . . .' (1971) ICJ Reports, 6, 31; *Western Sahara*, Advisory Opinion 16 October 1975, (1975) ICJ Reports 12, pp. 31–33 and Judge Dillard's celebrated opinion especially at 122. For a succinct discussion see Cassese, 'The International Court of Justice and the Right of Peoples to Self-Determination' in Lowe and Fitzmaurice (eds), *Fifty Years of the International Court of Justice: Essays in Honour of Sir Robert Jennings* (Cambridge University Press, 1996) pp. 351–363.

the World Court's judgment in the *East Timor Case (Portugal v. Australia)*.[34] In this case the Court found itself unable to look into the possible substantive breach of self-determination. According to the Court such a course would:

> necessarily [involve ruling] . . . upon the lawfulness of Indonesia's conduct as a prerequisite for deciding on Portugal's contention that Australia violated its obligation to respect Portugal's status as administering Power, East Timor's status as a non-self governing territory and the right of the people of the Territory to self-determination and to permanent sovereignty over its wealth and natural resources.[35]

The Court, however, reconfirmed the value inherent in the right to self-determination. Thus according to the Court, 'Portugal's assertion that the right of peoples to self-determination, as it evolved from the Charter and from United Nations practice has *erga omnes* character, is irreproachable . . . it is one of the essential principles of contemporary international law'.[36] It could be convincingly argued that the inherent principles enshrined in the right to self-determination form part of the norms of *jus cogens*;[37] and their character of rights *erga omnes*[38] have been firmly engrained in the substance of international law. A recent practical manifestation of the right could be found in the reunification of Germany, the break-up of the former Soviet Union and Yugoslavia, and the emergence of East Timor as an independent State. In February 2008, Kosovo issued a declaration of independence from Serbia and was subsequently recognised as an independent State by 50 other States, including the United States and member States of the European Union. However, Serbia has always opposed such a move and at the time of writing the International Court of Justice had begun to consider the legality of Kosovo's declaration.[39]

The right to self-determination, as shall be considered in a subsequent chapter, has also reshaped the laws relating to armed conflict. Protocol I, additional to the Geneva Conventions (1949), transfers the status of conflicts involving peoples fighting against colonial domination and alien occupation and against racist regimes while exercising a right to self-determination. By virtue of Protocol I these conflicts are regarded as international armed conflicts as opposed to internal conflicts. Article 1(4) of Protocol I provides that:

> The situations referred to in the preceding paragraph include armed conflicts in which peoples are fighting against colonial domination and alien occupation and against racist regimes in the exercise of their right of self-determination, as enshrined in the Charter of the United Nations and the Declaration on Principles of International Law concerning Friendly Relations and Co-operation among States in accordance with the Charter of the United Nations.

---

[34] *East Timor Case (Portugal v. Australia)*, Judgment 30 June 1995, (1995) ICJ Reports 90.

[35] Ibid. para 33.

[36] Ibid. para 29.

[37] See Gros Espiell, Special Rapporteur, *Implementation of United Nations Resolutions Relating to the Right of Peoples under Colonial and Alien Domination to Self-Determination*, Study for the Sub-Commission on Prevention of Discrimination and Protection of Minorities, UN Doc. E/CN.4/Sub.2/390, 1977, 17–19, paras 61–71; Gros Espiell, 'Self-Determination and *Jus Cogens*' in Cassese (ed.) *UN Law/Fundamental Rights: Two Topics in International Law* (Sijthoff & Noordhoff, 1979) pp. 119–135; ILC, *Draft Articles on State Responsibility*, Part I, Article 19 3(b).

[38] See *Barcelona Traction, Light and Power Company, Limited Case (Belgium v. Spain)*, Judgment 5 February 1970, (1970) ICJ Reports 3.

[39] UN News Centre, 'UN World Court to Give Opinion on Legality of Kosovo Independence' www.un.org/apps/news/story.asp?NewsID=28492&Cr=Kosovo&Cr1 8 October 2008 <last visited on 16 May 2009>.

However, unfortunately, neither Protocol I nor the Declaration on Friendly Relations to which Article 1(4) alludes provides a definition of 'peoples' or 'the right to self-determination'. Even if it is possible to locate a 'people', as discussed in a subsequent chapter, it is certain that not all peoples fighting for their right to self-determination are entitled to claim the protection from the regime of IHL.[40] As established by Protocol I, Article 96(3), in order for the regime of international armed conflict to apply, the authority representing the people in their struggle of the right to self-determination must make a declaration.[41] Confusion ensues in situations where is there is no recognised or established authority representing the people or where several factions have emerged each claiming to be the representing authority of the people. The authority making the declaration under Article 96(3) must have the characteristics of armed forces as established in Article 43 of the Protocol: it must be an organised force under responsible command, equipped with an internal disciplinary system charged with *inter alia* enforcing compliance with humanitarian law.[42] Notwithstanding these conditions, and as shall be examined in due course, there is an element of subjective judgement regarding the recognition of the fulfilment of the requirements contained in Article 1(4). There are likely to be further complications in many new conflicts that have arisen recently – Iraq and Afghanistan as well as the on-going fallout from the US-led 'war on terror'.

(i) Form and content of the right to self-determination

The substance and meaning of the right to self-determination needs to be reconsidered. Under the banner of the right to self-determination the emergent State practice has focused almost exclusively on casting off colonial rule and attaining independent statehood.[43] This focus, however, represents only one aspect of the right to self-determination: the 'external' aspect. The right to self-determination also has an 'internal' aspect, the essence of which is participatory democracy for all individuals and autonomy for minority groups. The applicable standards of democracy are to be acquired from the existing body of human rights, standards which are enshrined and adequately elaborated in the International Bill of Human Rights.[44] The principle of autonomy is associated with, and reliant upon, the effective application of democracy and the respect for individual human rights. At the same time, the principle of autonomy carries a special significance for minorities and indigenous

---

[40] See above chapter 21.
[41] Article 96(3), Protocol I. Also see below chapter 21.
[42] Article 43 provides as follows: 'Article 43(1) The armed forces of a Party to a conflict consist of all organized armed forces, groups and units which are under a command responsible to that Party for the conduct or its subordinates, even if that Party is represented by a government or an authority not recognized by an adverse Party. Such armed forces shall be subject to an internal disciplinary system which, inter alia, shall enforce compliance with the rules of international law applicable in armed conflict. 43(2): Members of the armed forces of a Party to a conflict (other than medical personnel and chaplains covered by Article 33 of the Third Convention) are combatants, that is to say, they have the right to participate directly in hostilities. 43(3): Whenever a Party to a conflict incorporates a paramilitary or armed law enforcement agency into its armed forces it shall so notify the other Parties to the conflict.'
[43] In the Context of Africa see Murray, *Human Rights in Africa: From the OAU to African Union* (Cambridge University Press, 2004) at pp. 11–13.
[44] See Article 21 of the Universal Declaration on Human Rights, GA Res. 217A (III), UN Doc. A/810 at 71 (1948); and Article 25 of the New York, 16 December 1966 United Nations, 999 U.N.T.S. 171; 6. I.L.M. (1967) 368. *ICCPR.*

peoples. Successful regimes of autonomy ensure that minority groups are able to preserve their existence and identity and also have control over their own affairs.[45] An excellent example of this are the Sami Parliaments in Finland,[46] Norway[47] and Sweden,[48] which grant the Sami control over their own affairs. While these Parliaments are not unified, they frequently come together to deal with cross-border issues. This interpretation reflects self-determination as a continuum of rights; forming a natural lineage between meaningful expressions of autonomy and democracy at one end of the spectrum and respect for individual human rights on the other. Self-determination as a legal right has clearly stood the test of time. However, times have changed and so must the psychology of international law. If it is not to exhaust itself or be degenerated into perpetual anarchy, the rigid and unaccommodating vision of the right to self-determination must take on board a more humane and conciliatory dimension.[49] Indeed, it is contended that what the 'external' version of self-determination has failed to achieve – a more participatory role for majorities as well as minorities – could be achieved through democratic 'internal' self-determination which would also incorporate the principle of autonomous development. This interpretation of self-determination advocated is neither radical nor novel. In actual fact it closely matches the views of self-determination's modern architect, US President Woodrow Wilson. According to one leading source:

> 'Self-determination' as conceived by Wilson, was an imprecise amalgam of several strands of thought, some being associated in his mind with the notion of 'self-government', others newly hatched as a result war-time developments, but all imbued with a general spirit of democracy ('Consent of the governed'). Thus, Wilson had long held the idea that every people had the right to select its own form of government – an idea that might be termed 'internal' self-determination.[50]

It is therefore argued that at the present time the most positive direction that the right of self-determination could take is through an emphasis on its 'internal' or democratic aspect. While there is no guarantee that a democratic regime would be the ultimate panacea for the protection of individual or collective rights, one is reminded of Sieghart's comment that '[o]n the whole . . . democracy tends to march with respect of human rights and respect for human rights tends to march with freedom under the law'.[51] The principle of democracy is a valuable one and needs to be firmly established within the existing political

---

[45] Hannum, *Autonomy, Sovereignty and Self-Determination: The Accommodation of Conflicting Rights* (University of Pennsylvania Press, 1990) at p. 473; Rehman, 'The Concept of Autonomy and Minority Rights in Europe' in Cumper and Wheatley (eds), *Minority Rights in the 'New' Europe* (Kluwer Law International, 1999) pp. 217–231.

[46] www.samediggi.fi/index.php?lang=fi <last visited 22 May 2009>.

[47] www.samediggi.no/artikkel.aspx?AId=1&MId1=1&back=1 <last visited 22 May 2008>.

[48] www.sametinget.se/ <last visited 22 May 2009>.

[49] Thornberry, 'The Democratic and Internal Aspect of Self-Determination' in Tomuschat (ed.), *Modern Law of Self-Determination* (Martinus Nijhoff Publishers, 1993) pp. 100–138.

[50] Promerance, above n.7, at p. 1.

[51] Sieghart, *The Lawful Rights of Mankind: An Introduction to the International Legal Code of Human Rights* (Oxford University Press, 1986) p. 156.

framework of modern States.[52] As we shall shortly examine, insofar as the application of democracy is relevant to indigenous peoples, it would emphasise heavily on economic, social and cultural aspects of self-determination.[53] This includes, but is not limited to, 'the right to free disposition of natural resources' and 'permanent sovereignty over natural wealth and resources'.[54]

3 INDIGENOUS PEOPLES IN INTERNATIONAL LAW: THE ISSUE OF DEFINITION

In many States, the indigenous populations constitute numerical minorities whose weak political organisation prevents them from expressing their unique needs. Consequently, many of their demands are absorbed by those of other minority groups.[55] However, these populations are unique. Being indigenous, their heritage is connected to the land, land that was usually conquered by the present-day majority in a manner that severely reduced their original numbers and left the survivors subjugated to a foreign majority.[56] Genocide, persecution and discrimination, subjugation and mistreatment of indigenous persons was a historically acceptable practice which continues to persist in various forms. Such abuse and maltreatment of indigenous populations has the added element of having been practised as a global – rather than regional or short-lived – phenomenon.

Having been relentlessly victimised in the contemporary age, many indigenous peoples remain in conditions which governments of modern States regard as less developed. Efforts to retain their aboriginal and autonomous way of life have met with repressive measures, stretching from forced assimilation to genocide. As noted earlier, unfortunately, persecution and discrimination against indigenous peoples still exists in many societies, and the continuing use of a number of discriminatory laws provides a sad commentary on their state of affairs.[57] Having had an artificial life pattern imposed upon them, many indigenous

---

[52] On the concept and application of democracy, see Crawford, 'Democracy in International Law' 64 *BYIL* (1993) 116, Stein, 'International Integration and Democracy: No Love at First Sight' 95 *AJIL* (2001) 489; Burchill, *Democracy and International Law* (Ashgate Publishing Ltd, 2006); Marks, *The Riddle of all Constitutions: International Law, Democracy, and the Critique of Ideology* (Oxford University Press, 2000); Wheatley, *Democracy, Minorities, and International Law* (Cambridge University Press, 2005); Frank 'The Emerging Right to Democratic Governance' 86 *AJIL* (1992) 46; Von Prondzynski, *Law, Sovereignty and Democracy* (Inaugural lecture, 1992); Jonge, 'Democracy and Economic Development in the Asia-Pacific Region: The Role of Parliamentary Institutions' 14 *HRLJ* (1993) 301; Axworthy, 'Democracy and Development: Luxury or Necessity' in Mahoney and Mahoney (eds), *Human Rights in the Twenty First Century: A Global Challenge* (Martinus Nijhoff Publishers, 1993) pp. 721–727; Rizvi, *South Asia in a Changing International Order* (Sage, 1993) pp. 122–146; Jalal, *Democracy and Authoritarianism in South Asia* (Cambridge University Press, 1995).

[53] Nowak, above n.20, pp. 24–26.

[54] Ibid. pp. 24–25.

[55] See e.g. O'Shaugnnessy, *What future for the Amerindians of South America* (Minority Rights Group, 1987); Wilson, *Canada's Indians* (Minority Rights Group, 1982); Creery, *The Inuit (Eskimo) of Canada* (Minority Rights Group, 1983); Vakhtin, *Native Peoples of the Russians Far North* (Minority Rights Group, 1992); Jones, *The Sami of Lapland* (Minority Rights Group, 1982); Stephen and Wearne, *Central America's Indians* (Minority Rights Group, 1984).

[56] Clinebell and Thomson, 'Sovereignty and Self-Determination: The Rights of Native Americans under International Law' 27 *Buff LR* (1978) 669; Kuper, *International Action against Genocide* (Minority Rights Group, 1984) p. 5; Davidson, 'The Rights of Indigenous Peoples in Early International Law' 5 *Canterbury Law Review* (1994) 391.

[57] See International Labour Conference, *Report of the Committee of Experts on the Application of Conventions and Recommendations*, 64th session, 1978.

communities suffer from disease, ill-health and disabilities.[58] A United Nations document eloquently summarises their contemporary position:

> Often uprooted from their traditional lands and way of life and forced into prevailing national societies, indigenous peoples face discrimination, marginalisation and alienation. Despite growing political mobilization in pursuit of their rights, they continue to lose their cultural identity along with their natural resources. Some are in imminent danger of extinction.[59]

While similar concerns are shared as regards both indigenous peoples and minorities, there remains a pronounced view that the indigenous peoples belong to a distinct category.[60] This, in fact, is the established view of the indigenous peoples themselves mainly grounded on the argument that indigenous claims are far more substantial than minorities in general – ranging from collective rights to self-determination (including a possible right to secession). Unfortunately, in some cases, there is also a reaction to State practice which refuses to accord any distinct and separate recognition to indigenous peoples; accordingly, such State practices tend to regard indigenous peoples as minorities. Bangladesh's approach towards the *Adivasis* of the Chittagong Hill Tracts provides one clear example: the conventional stance put forward by successive governments is that all Bengalis are indigenous. Although there are ethnic and religious differences, Bangladesh refuses to accept that distinctions based on indigenousness could be applied to its peoples.[61] Other States follow a similar line.[62]

While several States have proved extremely sensitive in respect of the definitional issue, many of the indigenous groups themselves have asserted a prerogative to define their 'nations'.[63] In the midst of these conflicts, it is not surprising that tensions are perceived

---

[58] According to the UN Special Rapporteur on Human Rights and Disability: 'At various sessions of the Sub-Commission, non-governmental organizations concerned with protection of the human rights of indigenous populations have reported that the risk of disability among those populations is extremely high because their working conditions are often exhausting and highly dangerous, their level of living is usually lower than that of the rest of the population and the preventive-medical services available to them are often of very poor quality. Furthermore, disabled persons belonging to such groups do not usually have access to suitable rehabilitation services or adequate government help. In short, the characteristics making up a vulnerable group, which in the case of disabled persons is subject to twofold discrimination were highlighted by almost everyone who spoke on this topic.' Despouy, *Human Rights and Disabled Persons*, Human Rights Studies Series No. 6, UN Sales No. E.92XIV.4 (1992), available at www.un.org/esa/socdev/enable/dispaperdes0.htm <last visited 30 May 2009>, para 153.

[59] United Nations, *Indigenous People: International Year 1993: Promoting the Rights of Indigenous People* (UN Department of Public Information, 1992) at p. 1.

[60] See the proceedings of the 11th meeting of the United Nations working group on indigenous rights 18 UN Doc. E/CN.4/Sub.2/1992/33, 1992, 19; Shaw, 'The Definition of Minorities in international law' in Dinstein and Tabory (eds), above n.3, pp. 13–16; Lerner, 'The Evolution of Minority Rights in International Law' in Brölmann, Lefeber and Zieck (eds), above n.6, 77–101 at p. 81.

[61] For a confirmation of this view see *Report of the Working Group on Indigenous Populations on its Fourteenth Session* E/CN.4/Sub.2/1996/21, 14 para 34.

[62] Barsh mentions that in addition to Bangladesh, 'the [former] USSR, India and China have also maintained that there are no "indigenous" peoples in Asia, only minorities, and that as Soviet Ambassador V. Sofinsky told the Sub-Commission in 1985 "indigenous" situations only arise in the Americas and Australasia where there are "imported" populations of Europeans'. Barsh, 'Indigenous People: An Emerging Object of International Law' 80 *AJIL* (1986) 369 at p. 375.

[63] Ibid. p. 376.

no matter what definition is accorded to the term 'indigenous peoples' or 'indigenous communities'. Thus, neither general international law nor regional custom provides a recognised and fully accepted definition of 'indigenous peoples'.[64] The most widely publicised definition of indigenous peoples and communities is the one put forward by the United Nations Special Rapporteur José R Martínez Cobo. According to him:

Indigenous communities, peoples and nations are those which, having continuity with pre-invasion and pre-colonial societies that developed on their territories, consider themselves distinct from other sectors of the societies now prevailing in those territories, or parts of them. They form at present non-dominant sectors of society and are determined to preserve, develop and transmit to future generations their ancestral territories and their ethnic identity, as the basis of their continued existence as peoples, in accordance with their own cultural patterns, social institutions and legal systems.

The historical continuity may consist of the continuation, for an external period reaching into present, of one or more of the following factors:

(a) Occupation of ancestral lands, or at least of part of them;

(b) Common ancestry with the original occupants of the lands;

(c) Culture in general, or in specific manifestation (such as religion, living under a tribal system, membership of international community, dress, means of livelihood, life-style etc.);

(d) Language (whether used as the only language, as mother-tongue, as the habitual means of communication at home or in the family, or as the main preferred, habitual general or normal language);

(e) Residence in certain parts of the country, or in certain regions of the World;

(f) Other relevant factors.[65]

According to Article 1(1) of the ILO Convention 169, adopted in 1989, the Convention applies to:

(a) Tribal peoples in independent countries whose social, cultural and economic conditions distinguish them from other sections of the national community, and whose status is regulated wholly or partially by their own customs or traditions or by special laws or regulations;

(b) Peoples in independent countries who are regarded as indigenous on account of their descent from the populations which inhabited the country, or a geographical region to which the country belongs, at the time of conquest or colonisation or the establishment of present State boundaries and who, irrespective of their legal status, retain some or all of their own social, economic, cultural and political institutions.

[64] Anaya, above n.1, pp. 3–5; McCandles, 'Indigenous Peoples: The Definitional Debate in Minority Rights Group' in *Outsider* (Minority Rights Group, 1996) p. 1.
[65] Special Rapporteur, José R Martínez-Cobo, *Study of the Problem of Discrimination Against Indigenous Populations*, UN Doc. E/CN.4/Sub.2/1986/7/Add.4, 1986, 29, paras 378–380.

Article 1(2) goes on to provide:

> Self-identification as indigenous or tribal shall be regarded as a fundamental criterion for determining the groups to which the provisions of this Convention apply.

A number of distinct features are evident in the definitions provided by Martínez Cobo as well as by the 1989 Convention. These include self-identification, non-dominance, historical continuity with pre-colonial societies, ancestral territories and ethnic identity.[66] Other attempts that have been made to elaborate the concept of 'indigenous' also rely to an extent on these criteria. Thus, according to Professor Anaya:

> [t]oday the *indigenous* refers broadly to the living descendants of preinvasion inhabitants of land dominated by others. Indigenous peoples, nations or communities are culturally distinctive groups that find themselves engulfed by settler societies born of the forces of empire and conquest.[67]

Similarly, the World Council of Indigenous Peoples defines 'indigenous peoples' as 'natives usually descendants of earlier population of a particular country composed of different ethnic or racial groups, but who have no control over the government'.[68] This discussion reveals the tensions and divisive nature of the probable definition of 'indigenous' peoples in international law. It is also the case that indigenous peoples, themselves, like other groups or communities, are capable of differing radically from each other. Hence, a safer form of identification for the purposes of international law may be on the basis of the above-mentioned criteria, rather than rigid definitions.

4 RIGHTS OF INDIGENOUS PEOPLES

Many of the claims made by indigenous peoples coincide with those of other minorities. The desire for autonomy and recognition as collective entities forms part of the vocabulary of the indigenous peoples as well as some minority groups, although the thrust and vibrancy of these may differ significantly. Historical association with land and environment dispenses a distinct flavour to the demands made by the indigenous peoples. Their claims include, *inter alia*, that of collective property rights to land and natural resources, the recognition of the special nature and form of the relationship between individual members and tribes, and the right to impose obligations on individual members which may not necessarily be aspired to by other minorities.[69]

International instruments have in recent years attempted to consider the position of indigenous people and a number of specialist instruments have been adopted which aim

---

[66] Kingsbury, ' "Indigenous Peoples" as an International Legal Concept' in Barnes, Gray and Kingsbury (eds), above n.1, 13–34 at p. 26.

[67] Anaya, above n.1, at p. 3.

[68] Cited in Roxanne, *What to Celebrate in the United Nations Year of Indigenous Peoples?* (National University of Singapore, 1993) p. 5.

[69] Neithem, ' "Peoples" and "Populations" Indigenous Peoples and the Rights of Peoples' in Crawford (ed.), *The Rights of Peoples* (Clarendon Press, 1988) pp. 107–126; Rehman, 'International Law and Indigenous Peoples: Definitional and Practical Problems' 3 *Journal of Civil Liberties* (1998) 224.

to concentrate solely on indigenous populations.[70] This rather sudden resurgence of interest may be taken as an acknowledgement, at least in part, that the cause of indigenous peoples raises specific issues of concern which ought to be focused upon. The organisation, which has shown a significant interest in the plight of indigenous peoples and more generally in its efforts to 'establish universal and lasting peace' through means of social justice, is the International Labour Organization (ILO).[71] The ILO, ever since its inception in 1919, made evident its interest by establishing a Committee of Experts on Native Labour, finally adopted in 1926.[72] A natural projection of this agenda was reflected in the adoption of various conventions and recommendations including the Forced Labour Convention 1930 (ILO Convention 29),[73] the Recruiting of Indigenous Workers Convention 1936 (ILO Convention 50),[74] the Contracts of Employment (Indigenous Workers) Convention 1939 (ILO Convention 64),[75] the Penal Sanctions (Indigenous Workers) Convention 1940 (ILO Convention 65)[76] and the Contracts of Employment (Indigenous Workers) Convention 1947 (ILO Convention 86).[77]

Significant work towards the cause of protecting indigenous peoples was conducted under the auspices of the ILO in the form of the study on 'Indigenous Peoples Living and Working Conditions of Aboriginal Population in Independent Countries'.[78] The study published in 1953, bears its mark in the two texts adopted at the 40th session of the organisation, Recommendations No. 104 and the ILO Convention 107 Concerning the Protection and Integration of Indigenous and other Tribal and Semi-tribal Populations in Independent Countries (1957).[79] The adoption of the 1957 Convention was a significant step forward in projecting the views and aspirations of the indigenous peoples.[80] The Convention, however, was a product of its time with a considerable imprint of an assimilationist ideology. According to its definition, indigenous peoples are populations, 'whose social and economic conditions are at a less advanced stage than the stage reached by the other sections of the national community'.[81] In 1986, the ILO organised the meetings of representatives of indigenous peoples under the emblem of 'Meeting of experts'. The meeting forcefully advocated the case for the revision of the Convention, noting that 'the integrationist language of Convention No 107 is outdated, and that the application of this principle is destructive in the modern world'.[82]

---

[70] See e.g. Barsh, above n.62; Barsh, 'Revision of the ILO Convention No. 107' 81 *AJIL* (1987) 756; Barsh, 'United Nations Seminar on Indigenous Peoples and States' 83 *AJIL* (1989) 599 at p. 762.

[71] Preamble to the *Constitution of the ILO*, 62 Stat. 3485; 15 U.N.T.S. 35, entered into force 9 October 1946; Brownlie (ed.), *Basic Documents in International Law* (Clarendon Press, 1981) p. 45; Wolf, 'Human Rights and the International Labour Organization' in Meron (ed.), *Human Rights in International Law: Legal and Policy Issues* (Clarendon Press, 1984) pp. 273–305.

[72] See Hannum (ed.), *Documents on Autonomy and Minority Rights* (Martinus Nijhoff Publishers, 1993) p. 8.

[73] 39 U.N.T.S. 55, entered into force 1 May 1932.

[74] 40 U.N.T.S. 109, entered into force 8 September 1939.

[75] 40 U.N.T.S. 281, entered into force 8 July 1948.

[76] 40 U.N.T.S. 311, entered into force 8 July 1948.

[77] 161 U.N.T.S. 113, entered into force 13 February 1953.

[78] ILO, *Studies and Reports, New Series No, 35* (1953).

[79] *Indigenous and Tribal Populations Convention* (ILO No. 107), 328 U.N.T.S 247; Cmnd. 328, entered into force July 2 1959. *Indigenous and Tribal Populations Recommendation* (ILO No. 104) adopted on 26 June 1957.

[80] For a critical examination see Xanthaki, above n.1, at pp. 49–70.

[81] *ILO Indigenous and Tribal Populations Convention* 107 Article 1(1)(a).

[82] *Report of the Meeting of Experts*, para 46; See *Partial Revision of the Indigenous and Tribal Populations Convention, 1957* (No. 107) Report 6(1), International Labour Conference, 75th Sess. (1988), 100.

Indeed, a prominent theme of the Convention is the emphasis on assimilation of indigenous peoples with other sections of the community, even at the cost of abandoning their heritage. This overwhelming feeling of discontent provided the impetus to the adoption of a revised Convention Concerning Indigenous and Tribal Peoples in Independent Countries (ILO) No. 169.[83] The 1989 Convention is a reflection of a more liberal attitude and biased against hitherto prevalent integrationist and assimilation orientations; its moderating effect on what according to its preamble were 'the assimilationist orientation of the earlier standards' is worthy of appreciation. In the words of a commentator the 1989 Convention is 'international law's most concrete manifestation of the growing responsiveness to indigenous peoples' demands. Convention 169 is a revision of the ILO's earlier Convention 107 of 1957, and it represents a marked departure in world community policy from the philosophy of integration or assimilation underlying the earlier Convention'.[84]

On the substantive front, a number of features of the 1989 Convention reflect a degree of promise. Article 2, for instance, while improving upon the 1957 Convention, reinforces the idea that governments have the responsibility to protect the rights of peoples through their participation. It stresses the importance of the participation of the peoples concerned, actions to protect their rights with emphasis upon the need to respect social and cultural identity, their customs and traditions and their institutions. These acts shall ensure equality of rights and opportunities, full realisation of the social, economic and cultural rights of the indigenous peoples, and would eliminate the socio-economic gaps.

While Article 3, in line with the norm of non-discrimination in international treaties, prohibits discrimination in the enjoyment of human rights and fundamental freedoms, Article 4 enjoins special measures for safeguarding the institutions, property, labour, culture and environment of indigenous peoples in a manner which is not inconsistent with their freely expressed wishes. Article 5 reaffirms the fundamental principle of recognising, respecting and promoting the social, cultural and religious values. The significance of Article 6 lies primarily in the fact that it requires governments to consult indigenous peoples in matters affecting them, allowing and establishing means for free participation and establishing means for development of their institutions. Article 7 reflects the cherished ideals of autonomy by stating that:

> [t]he peoples concerned shall have the right to decide their own priorities for the process of development as it affects their lives, beliefs, institutions and spiritual well-being and the lands they occupy or otherwise use, and to exercise control, to the extent possible, over their own economic, social and cultural development.

In addition, they shall participate in the formulation, implementation and evaluation of plans and programmes for national and regional development which may affect them directly. Amongst the Convention's other positive features is a contribution made in cultural provisions. Xanthaki points to Article 32 which obliges States parties to 'facilitate contact and cooperation between indigenous and tribal peoples across borders, including activities in the economic, social, cultural, spiritual and environmental fields'.[85] The contrast that she highlights between this binding treaty and the non-binding provisions of the

---

[83] (ILO No. 169) 72 ILO Official Bull. 59, 28 I.L.M. (1989) 1382, entered into force 5 September 1991.
[84] Anaya, above n.1, p. 47.
[85] Article 32. Xanthaki above n.1 at p. 75.

UN Declaration on the Rights of Persons belonging to Ethnic, National, Religious and Linguistic Minorities (1992) reflect the advances of Convention 169 over other related instruments.[86]

The advance of the 1989 Convention is considerable over its predecessor, and deserves our attention insofar as it relates specifically to the position of indigenous peoples and their rights. Xanthaki in presenting a matured reflection of the Convention notes:

> Convention No. 169 makes a substantial advance on Convention No. 107 in several areas. Its most important contribution to indigenous rights, but also to human rights, is arguably its multicultural outlook and its insistence on perceiving indigenous peoples as equal partners in the development and evolution of the national society. This is evident in the emphasis on collective rights that recognise indigenous identities but also in the principles of participation and cooperation with indigenous peoples applied in all areas of indigenous activities and the emphasis on effective implementation of these principles. More specific successes of the text include the strengthening of land rights; the introduction of the issue of natural resources; the principle of self-identification; and the many references to collective rights. Also important are the repeated references in the Convention to special measures, especially in view of the general cautiousness of other minority and human rights instruments. The Convention represents a minimum for the satisfactions of indigenous claims. Ten years since its adoption and while other international bodies discuss indigenous issues in the United Nations and elsewhere, standards are constantly evolving. The work of the Committee of Experts has surprisingly not been given attention. Yet, the Committee has applied the Convention in a constructive manner and has ensured that the interpretation of the text is in accordance with the evolving standards of international law.[87]

Having said this, the 1989 Convention, in many ways, falls short of providing an adequate expression to the claims of indigenous peoples. There are a number of issues in the Convention where there is very little international consensus including land rights, the right to autonomy, self-determination and international personality. For example, although Part II of the Convention deals in considerable detail with the subject of land, in its drafting stages considerable disagreements emerged evidenced by more than 100 amendments and a final version that reflects a compromise amongst divergent interests.[88]

The right to self-determination has also proved to be particularly contentious and it needs to be borne in mind that while the Convention does apply to 'peoples' a number of State representatives were unhappy with the usage of the term 'peoples' and wanted it replaced with 'populations'.[89] The Convention itself has grudgingly granted indigenous peoples a limited recognition to this right, although the adoption of this text was only possible through the addition of an extra paragraph curtailing the effect of whatever the right has to offer. This occurs in the form of Article 1(3) which provides:

---

[86] Ibid. pp. 75–76.
[87] Ibid. pp. 90–91.
[88] See Lerner, above n.28 at p. 109; Swepston, 'Economic, Social and Cultural Rights under the 1989 ILO Convention' in Horn (ed.), *Economic, Social and Cultural Rights of the Sami, International and National Aspects* (Northern Institute for Environmental and Minority Law, 1988) pp. 38–46, at p. 43.
[89] Lerner, above n.28.

486

[t]he use of the term *peoples* in this Convention shall not be construed as having any implications as regards the rights which may attach to the term under international law.

5 INDIGENOUS PEOPLES AND THE UN SYSTEM

Efforts on the part of other international organisations have recently begun to match those of the ILO. The rights of the indigenous peoples were canvassed strongly by the United Nations Working Group on Indigenous Populations. The creation of the Working Group on Indigenous Populations was proposed by the United Nations Sub-Commission on Prevention of Discrimination and Protection of Minorities in September 1981,[90] and endorsed and approved by the Commission on Human Rights in its Resolution of March 1982.[91] The ultimate authorisation was provided by the Economic and Social Council in 1982,[92] with the first annual meeting of the Working Group taking place in August of the same year.[93] The Working Group was a subsidiary organ of the Sub-Commission on the Prevention of Discrimination and Protection of Minorities and was comprised of five individuals who were members of the Sub-Commission (drawn from different regions) who acted in their capacity as independent experts, rather than as representatives of their governments.

The Working Group derived inspiration from Rapporteur José R. Martínez-Cobo's study, with many of the themes being used as a basis for developing international standard-setting on indigenous rights. The original mandate of the Working Group comprised of the following two parts:

(a) to review developments pertaining to the promotion and protection of the human rights and fundamental freedoms of indigenous populations

(b) give special attention to the evolution of standards concerning the rights of indigenous populations through out the world.[94]

For its first few sessions the Working Group concentrated on collecting useful data on cases and information as regards different forms of violations that take place against indigenous peoples. The information revealed killings, torture, inhuman and degrading treatment amounting to genocide and ethnocide. Serious violations of land rights of indigenous peoples all over the world through forcible occupation or destruction came to light. Indigenous peoples also used the forum of the Working Group sessions to publicise their experiences of forcible assimilation and erosion of their cultural and spiritual existence. The early successes were the result of an enthusiastic and ingenious approach that was adopted by the Working Group. Indeed, at

---

[90] See Sub-Commission Res. 2 (XXXIV) 8 September 1981.
[91] Commission on Human Rights Res. 1982/19, 10 March.
[92] See ECOSOC Res. 1982/34, 7 May.
[93] Hannum, above n.16, p. 84.
[94] ECS/Res. 1982/34, UN ESCOR, Supp. No. 1, UN Doc. E/1982/82 (1982) pp. 26–27.

its first session, the Working Group took the almost unprecedented step of allowing oral (and written) interventions from all indigenous organizations which wished to participate in its work, not limiting such participation to those with formal consultative status. Approximately 380 persons took part in its sixth session in 1988, including representatives from over 70 indigenous organizations and observers from 33 Countries. As a result of this wide participation, the Working Group [has] provided meaningful forum for exchange of proposals regarding indigenous rights and for the exposition of indigenous reality throughout the world. While the Working Group reiterate[ed] at each session that it is not a 'chamber of complaints' and has no authority to hear allegations of human rights violations, it [has] nevertheless permitted very direct criticism of government practices by NGOs, as a means of gathering data upon which standards will eventually be based.[95]

Although review of the developments pertaining to indigenous peoples remained a significant feature of the sessions, from 1985 until its dissolution in 2007, the Working Group paid particular attention to universal standard-setting for indigenous peoples. In this regard a valuable contribution of the Working Group was its determined effort to draw up a Declaration on the Rights of the Indigenous Peoples. In 1985 approval was given by the Sub-Commission supporting the Working Group in its decision to prepare a draft Declaration on the Rights of the Indigenous Peoples for adoption by the General Assembly of the United Nations.[96] Three years later, a first complete draft Declaration was produced, a document largely representing the views of the indigenous peoples.[97] Further refinements and the views of governments were incorporated into the 1989 draft of the Declaration.[98] There then followed a period of deliberations and discussion within the Working Group involving all the concerned parties – representatives from the indigenous groups as well as the concerned States. With the progressive development of the draft Declaration:

more and more governments responded with their respective pronouncements on the content of indigenous peoples' rights. Virtually every state of the Western Hemisphere came to participate in the Working Group discussion on the declaration. Canada, with its large indigenous population took a leading role. States of other regions with significant indigenous populations also became active participants, especially Australia and New Zealand. The Philippines, Bangladesh and India are just three of the other numerous states that at one time or another made oral or written submission to the Working Group in connection with the drafting of the declaration.[99]

(i) The United Nations Declaration on the Rights of Indigenous Peoples

The process leading to the adoption of the United Nations Declaration on the Rights of Indigenous Peoples spanned over almost a quarter of a century, corresponding to the

---

[95] Hannum, above n.16, p. 84.
[96] Sub-Commission Res. 1985/22 (29 August 1985).
[97] Universal Declaration on Indigenous Rights: A Set of Preambular Paragraphs and Principles UN Doc. E/CN.4/Sub.2/1988/25 at p. 2 (1988).
[98] See the first Revised Text of the Draft Universal Declaration on the Rights of Indigenous Peoples UN Doc. E/CN.4/Sub.2/1989/33 (1989).
[99] See Anaya, above n.1, at p. 52.

emergence of the international indigenous peoples' movement as a global development.[100] This movement began in the 1970s and accelerated during the 1980s. As noted already, as a result of the continuing investigations into the wide-spread discrimination of indigenous peoples, the UN established a Working Group on Indigenous Populations in 1982. In 1993, the Working Group produced its final version of the draft Declaration.[101] A year later in 1994, the Sub-Commission approved and adopted without any changes the Working Group's draft, which was then submitted for the consideration of the Human Rights Commission.[102] However, in March 1995, the Commission decided to establish yet another working group, an open-ended inter-sessional working group with a view to elaborating the draft Declaration.[103] The procedure for participation in the inter-sessional working group was generous and allowed virtually everyone interested to deliberate and contribute to its work without prior accreditation. The final progression of the Declaration, however, proved to be a time consuming and onerous task; by its third session, the inter-sessional working group had adopted at first reading only two articles of the draft Declaration without any changes.[104] After a considerable period of gestation, political maneuvering and intense lobbying, the Declaration was finally adopted on 13 September 2007.[105] The adoption of the Declaration on the Rights of Indigenous Peoples is seen by many as a triumph for indigenous peoples' rights worldwide. However, the adoption of the Declaration also signified the end of the Working Group on Indigenous Populations, which, following the Human Rights Council's Resolution 6/36 was replaced by the Expert Mechanism on the Rights of Indigenous Peoples.

The Declaration is crucial in enabling a coherent approach to indigenous rights, shifting the body of indigenous rights into the legal and normative international order. The Declaration is constructed from a number of different sources including the Universal Declaration of Human Rights, the Convention on the Rights of the Child, Convention on the Elimination of Discrimination against Women, Convention on the Elimination of Racial Discrimination, the Genocide Convention, the ILO Convention 169 and other human rights conventions.[106] A significant difference between the Declaration, and the other aforementioned sources, is that the collective rights enshrined in the Declaration apply to indigenous peoples as peoples under international law, rather than as mere 'populations'.[107] The question of whether a specific arrangement for indigenous peoples is necessary has been central to the debate about the Declaration on the Rights of Indigenous Peoples – on one hand it can be argued that a specific regime is not necessary due to the rights enshrined within general human rights law, while on the other hand, it can be argued that due to the unique collective rights that indigenous peoples have, a precise blueprint is absolutely necessary to

---

[100] Oldham and Frank, ' "We the peoples . . .": The United Nations Declaration on the Rights of Indigenous Peoples' 24 *Anthropology Today* (2008) 4 at p. 5.
[101] See Annex to the Report of the Working Group on Indigenous Populations on its 11th Session. UN Doc. E/CN.4/Sub.2/1993/29 Annex 1 (1993).
[102] See UN Doc. E/CN.4/1995/2, E/CN.4/Sub.2/1994/56, p. 105.
[103] See Commission on Human Rights Res. 1995/32 (3 March 1995).
[104] See Ms. Erica-Irene A. Daes, E/CN.4/Sub.2/1998/16, para 19.
[105] Declaration on the Rights of Indigenous Peoples UN Doc. A/RES/61/295.
[106] Commission on Human Rights, Discrimination against Indigenous Peoples, *Technical review of the United Nations draft declaration on the rights of indigenous peoples*, UN Doc. E/CN.4/Sub.2/1994/2.
[107] Ibid. Also see Beteille, 'The Indian heritage – A Sociological Perspective' in Balasubramaniam and Appaji Rao (eds), *The Indian Human Heritage* (Sangam Books Ltd, 1998) pp. 87–94. This is an important differentiation when closely examining the right to self-determination under international law.

allow for the full realisation of the rights subsumed in international human rights law.[108] Synthesising these individual and collective rights between the State *vis-à-vis* the indigenous peoples is the primary aim of the Declaration, and, indeed, of indigenous peoples worldwide.[109]

The Declaration is intended to serve 'as a standard of achievement to be pursued in a spirit of partnership and mutual respect'[110] between States and indigenous peoples, providing 'the minimum standards for the survival, dignity and well-being of the indigenous peoples of the world'.[111] The Preamble, like the ICESCR Article 10, refers to moral responsibility, and homogenising the universal reach and the scope of the Declaration as an international tool for the promotion of indigenous peoples' rights. In highlighting the significance of the Declaration, the Committee on the Elimination of All Forms of Racial Discrimination – a treaty body in charge of implementation of the Convention on the Elimination of All Forms of Racial Discrimination (1965) has reiterated that States should use the Declaration 'as a guide to interpret [their] obligations under the Convention relating to indigenous peoples'.[112] Although the Declaration is not a legally binding instrument but is, according to Oldham and Franck, 'in some respects declaratory of customary international law'.[113] The Declaration is already (at least in certain quarters) being invoked as reflecting international customary law and binding upon domestic courts. For example, in the recent landmark decision in the Belize Supreme Court, the Court concluded that 'this Declaration, embodying as it does, general principles of international law relating to indigenous peoples and their lands and resources, is of such force that the defendants, representing the government of Belize, will not disregard it[114].'

Indigenous peoples' rights can constitute a *sui generis* category of rights, according to Berman, 'aris[ing] *sui generis* from the historical condition of indigenous peoples as distinctive societies with the aspiration to survive as such'.[115] The final text of the Declaration points towards this as it links the rights with the historical injustices indigenous peoples have suffered. Authoritative working definitions provide a basis upon which to identify the *sui generis* nature of indigenous peoples within the international order.[116] Recent case law,

---

[108] Gilbert, 'Indigenous Rights in the Making: The United Nations Declaration on the Rights of Indigenous Peoples', 14 *IJMGR* (2007) 210–212

[109] See Declaration on the Rights of Indigenous Peoples UN Doc. A/RES/61/295. Preamble: 'indigenous individuals are entitled without discrimination to all human rights recognised in international law, and that indigenous peoples possess collective rights which are indispensable for their existence, well-being and integral development as peoples.'

[110] Ibid. Preamble.

[111] Ibid. Article 43.

[112] Concluding Observations of the Committee on the Elimination of Racial Discrimination CERD/C/USA/CO/6, at para 29 (8 May 2008). http://daccessdds.un.org/doc/UNDOC/GEN/G08/419/82/PDF/G0841982.pdf?OpenElement <last visited 17 May 2009>. For further analysis of the Committee see above chapter 12.

[113] Oldham and Franck, above n.100, pp. 5–6.

[114] *Cal (on behalf of the Maya Village of Santa Cruz) and others & Coy (on behalf of the Maya Village of Conejo) and others v. Attorney-General of Belize and Minister of Natural Resources and Environment Claims Nos. 171 and 172 of 2007*, Supreme Court of Belize, Judgment of 18 October 2007, unreported.

[115] Berman, 'Are Indigenous Populations Entitled to Internal Juridical Personality?' 79 *ASIL Proc.* (1989) 189 at p. 190.

[116] Kirby's definition which was used by the UNESCO International Meeting of Experts on Further Study of the Concept of the Rights of Peoples, UNESCO HQ, Paris, 27–30 November 1989. According to the Kirby definition, a people is: '1. a group of individual human beings who enjoy some or all of the following common features: a. a common historical tradition; b. racial or ethnic identity; c. cultural homogeneity; linguistic unity; e. religious or ideological affinity; f. territorial connection; g. common economic life. 2. the group must be of a certain number which need not be large but which must be more that a mere association of individuals

including the *Awas Tingni* case,[117] the *Saramaka People* case[118] and the *Maya Village* case[119] significantly support the development and the implementation of a specific legal approach to indigenous peoples' rights. In the *Maya Village* case, the Court noted that Belize was party to such treaties which have consistently upheld the rights of indigenous peoples over their lands and resources, including the ICCPR, Race Convention and the OAS Charter. This case on behalf of the Maya Village of Santa Cruz in Belize represented a resounding success for the Declaration on the Rights of Indigenous Peoples. The Supreme Court noted throughout that Belize is obliged not only by the Belize Constitution but also by international treaty and customary international law to recognise, respect and protect Maya customary land rights. The presiding Judge, Chief Justice Conteh set it out thus:

> I am therefore, of the view that this Declaration, embodying as it does, general principles of international law relating to indigenous peoples and their lands and resources, is of such force that the defendants, representing the Government of Belize, will not disregard it.[120]

In their judgment, para 120, the Supreme Court noted that Belize was party to such treaties which have consistently upheld the rights of indigenous peoples over their lands and resources. Accordingly, the Court concluded that Belize is:

> bound, in both domestic law in virtue of the Constitutional provisions that have been canvassed in this case, and international law, arising from Belize's obligation there under, to respect the rights to and interests of the claimants as members of the indigenous Maya community, to their lands and resources which are the subject of this case.[121]

Moreover, the judgment interpreted the Declaration on the Rights of Indigenous Peoples as containing principles of general international law, despite General Assembly Resolutions not ordinarily binding Member States,[122] while concluding that Article 46 of the Declaration 'requires that its provisions shall be interpreted in accordance with the principles of justice, democracy, respect for human rights, equality, non-discrimination, good

---

within a State; 3. the group as a whole must have the will to be identified as a people or the consciousness of being a people–allowing that group or some members of such groups, through sharing the foregoing characteristics, may not have that will or consciousness; and possibly; 4. the group must have institutions or other means of expressing its common characteristics and will for identity', at p. 279 available at www.unesdoc.unesco.org/images/0008/000851/085152fo.pdf <last visited 18 May 2009>.

[117] *The Mayagna (Sumo) Awas Tingni Community* v. *Nicaragua*, Judgment of 31 August 2001, Inter-Am. Ct. H.R., (Ser. C) No. 79 (2001), para 148.

[118] *Saramaka People* v. *Suriname*, Judgment 28 November 2007, Inter-Am. Ct. H.R. (Ser. C) No. 172 (2007).

[119] *Cal (on behalf of the Maya Village of Santa Cruz) and others & Coy (on behalf of the Maya Village of Conejo) and others v Attorney-General of Belize and Minister of Natural Resources and Environment Claims Nos. 171 and 172 of 2007*, Supreme Court of Belize, Judgment of 18 October 2007, unreported. Available at http://209.85.229.132/search?q=cache:AIcMFoix4bMJ:www.law.arizona.edu/Depts/iplp/advocacy/maya_belize/documents/ClaimsNos171and172of2007.pdf+peoples+and+their+lands+and+resources,+is+of+such+force+that+the+defendants,+representing+the+Government+of+Belize,&cd=2&hl=en&ct=clnk&gl=uk <last visited 15 May 2009>. Also see Campbell and Anaya 'The Case of the Maya Villages of Belize: Reversing the Trend of Government Neglect to Secure Indigenous Land Rights' 8 *HRLR* (2008) 377.

[120] Ibid. para 132.

[121] Ibid. para 134.

[122] Article 132 – 'But where these resolutions or Declarations contain principles of general international law, states are not expected to disregard them'. On the potential binding nature of the General Assembly Resolutions see above chapter 2.

governance and good faith'. Emerging national developments are important for the 'weight' the Declaration will acquire as part of international law.

The United Nations has recently placed particular emphasis on the rights of indigenous peoples. In addition to the establishment of the Expert Mechanism on the Rights of Indigenous Peoples, the Special Rapporteur on the situation of human rights and fundamental freedoms of indigenous peoples, the Permanent Forum on Indigenous Issues and the UN Voluntary Fund for Indigenous Peoples all ensure that indigenous issues and rights remain on the UN agenda.

In 2008 Professor S. James Anaya replaced Professor Roldolfo Stavenhagen as the Special Rapporteur on the situation of human rights and fundamental freedoms of indigenous peoples. The mandate of the Special Rapporteur dates back to 2001.[123] In this role the Special Rapporteur can receive information and communications from a number of different sources, including governments, indigenous people or their communities and organisations.[124] Additionally, the role includes formulating recommendations and proposals and examining ways of overcoming existing obstacles to the enjoyment of human rights by indigenous peoples.[125] The Rapporteur is expected to work in conjunction with the Permanent Forum as well as attend the Expert Mechanism meetings.[126]

Since 2001, the Rapporteur has carried out a number of country visits at the invitation of receiving States. These have included visits to Guatemala, Canada, New Zealand, Kenya and recently Bolivia.[127] The reports on these visits – which are often challenging – are published alongside the Annual Report to the Human Rights Council and include conclusions and recommendations in respect of the situation of indigenous peoples in the country in question.[128] One of the most important roles that the Rapporteur fulfils is receiving communications regarding alleged violations of indigenous peoples' human rights. These take two forms – urgent appeals or allegation letters – and are published on the Rapporteur's webpage.[129] Unlike other human rights communication procedures at the UN, there are no formal requirements that need to be fulfilled in order for the Communication to be admissible.[130] Consequently, Communications have been submitted by States wishing to elaborate upon the situation of indigenous peoples' in their territory,[131] peoples trying to protect their land,[132] victims of civil war[133] and the African Commission.[134]

The Expert Mechanism on the Rights of Indigenous Peoples replaced the Working Group on 14 December 2007 in accordance with resolution 6/36 of the Human Rights Council. It is unclear at the time of writing how effective this mechanism will be, as it only held its first session from 1–3 October 2008.[135] Initially, the Mechanism met for a period of

---

[123] Commission on Human Rights Resolution 2001/57, 24 April 2001 see also Human Rights Council Resolution 6/12, 28 September 2007.

[124] www2.ohchr.org/english/issues/indigenous/rapporteur/mandate.htm <last visited 22 May 2009>.

[125] Ibid.

[126] Ibid.

[127] www2.ohchr.org/english/issues/indigenous/rapporteur/visits.htm <last visited 22 May 2009>.

[128] www2.ohchr.org/english/issues/indigenous/rapporteur/visits.htm <last visited 22 May 2009>.

[129] www2.ohchr.org/english/issues/indigenous/rapporteur/communications.htm <last visited 22 May 2009>.

[130] Ibid. See also www2.ohchr.org/english/issues/indigenous/rapporteur/submit.htm <last visited 22 May 2009>.

[131] UN Doc. E/CN.4/2002/97/Add.1, Commission resolution 2001/57, Addendum, Selected summaries of communications examined by the Special Rapporteur in 2001/2002, para 3.

[132] Ibid. para 7.

[133] Ibid. para 8.

[134] Ibid. para 17.

[135] www2.ohchr.org/english/issues/indigenous/ExpertMechanism/index.htm <last visited 22 May 2009>.

three days in Geneva but this can now be extended to up to five days.[136] The Expert Mechanism is made up of five experts and is intended to serve as a body that will provide thematic assistance on the subject of indigenous issues to the Human Rights Council.[137] The five experts who are appointed by the President of the Human Rights Council for a period during 2008–10 are: Ms. Catherine Odimba Kombe (Congo), Ms. Jannie Lasimbang (Malaysia), Mr. John Bernhard Henriksen (Norway), Mr. José Carlos Morales Morales (Costa Rica) and Mr. José Mencio Molintas (Philippines). The main body of work will comprise research and studies, however the Mechanism may also submit proposals to the Human Rights Council for its consideration. It is supported by the Office of the UN High Commission for Human Rights.[138]

The UN Permanent Forum on Indigenous Issues (UNPFII) is an advisory body to the Economic and Social Council of the UN, established by Resolution 2000/22 on 28 July 2000.[139] Its first session was held in May 2002, and thereafter it has held annual two-week sessions in New York, although they may also take place in Geneva.[140] The eighth session of the UNPFII was conducted during 18–29 May 2009 in New York. There are 16 independent experts in the Forum – eight are elected by governments and eight directly by indigenous organisations.[141] The mandate of the Forum is three-fold:

- to provide expert advice and recommendations on indigenous issues to the Council, as well as to programmes, funds and agencies of the United Nations, through the Council

- to raise awareness and promote the integration and coordination of activities related to indigenous issues within the UN system

- to prepare and disseminate information on indigenous issues.[142]

In addition, workshops are held in order to complement the Forum's recommendations.[143] Recent topics of meetings and workshops have included climate change,[144] indigenous languages,[145] protection of the environment[146] and the relationship between indigenous peoples and industrial companies.[147] At its Fifth Session the Forum also appointed a number of its members as Special Rapporteurs who represented the results of this research at the Sixth Session of the Forum in May 2007. Consequently, further research is being carried out on two of the areas of research: firstly, on the 'Oil Palm and Other Commercial Tree Plantations, Monocropping: Impacts on Indigenous Peoples; Land Tenure and Resource

---

[136] Human Rights Council Resolution 6/36 – Expert Mechanism on Indigenous Issues, of 14 December 2007 para 8.
[137] Ibid. paras 1 and 3.
[138] Ibid. paras 1(a) and (b).
[139] UN ECOSOC Resolution 2000/22 of 28 July 2000.
[140] www.un.org/esa/socdev/unpfii/en/about_us.html <last visited 21 May 2009>.
[141] www.un.org/esa/socdev/unpfii/en/members.html <last visited 21 May 2009>.
[142] www.un.org/esa/socdev/unpfii/en/about_us.html <last visited 21 May 2009>.
[143] www.un.org/esa/socdev/unpfii/en/ourwork.html <last visited 21 May 2009>.
[144] International Expert Group Meeting, on Indigenous Peoples and Climate Changes, Darwin, Australia 2–4 April 2008.
[145] UNPFII Expert Group Meeting on Indigenous Languages, New York, 8–10 January 2008.
[146] International Expert Group Meeting on Indigenous Peoples and Protection of the Environment, Khabarovsk, Russian Federation, 27–29 August 2007.
[147] International Workshop on Perspectives of Relationships between Indigenous Peoples and Industrial Companies, Salekhard, Russian Federation, 1–4 July 2007.

Management Systems and Livelihoods'; and secondly on the 'Indigenous Traditional Knowledge'.[148] The Seventh Session of the Forum was held in New York between 21 April–2 May 2008 and analysed the Special theme of 'Climate change, Bio-Cultural Diversity and Livelihoods: the Stewardship Role of Indigenous Peoples and New Challenges'.[149]

The Forum is further supported by the Inter-agency Support Group (IASG), the purpose of which is to allow 'the UN system and other intergovernmental organizations to analyze recommendations made by the Forum with a view to facilitating comprehensive and coordinated responses to the UNPFII'.[150] IASG has some 31 members, including the Office of the High Commissioner for Human Rights, the Secretariat for the Convention on Biological Diversity, the World Health Organization and the European Union.[151] The work of this agency is invaluable, as the issues facing indigenous peoples often go beyond pure human rights violations, into the arena of the economic, social and cultural continuation and development of the group. It is impressive that such widely varying organisations see fit to work towards the same goals in respect of indigenous peoples, again highlighting the importance now placed upon 'indigenous' by the international community.

The UN Voluntary Fund for Indigenous Peoples was established by General Assembly Resolution 40/131 in 1985, in order to enable indigenous peoples to take part in the work of the UN Working Group on Indigenous Populations, and this has been continued through to the Expert Mechanism.[152] Initially, it was intended that indigenous representatives should take part in the deliberations of the Working Groups but this was quickly broadened in order to enable indigenous representatives to attend the working group as observers.[153] Financial support is provided for the indigenous representatives through voluntary contributions, from governments, non-governmental organisations and private and public entities.[154]

Other UN activities relevant to indigenous peoples include the adoption of Guidelines on Indigenous Peoples' Issues in February 2008. These guidelines are intended to assist UN Country teams in integrating indigenous issues into other areas of their work.[155] The International Decade of the World's Indigenous People ran from 1995 to 2004 and has been followed by a Second International Decade from 2005 to 2014. In addition to this, an Indigenous Children's Discussion Day has been establish under the Convention on the Rights of Children.

The numerous activities and mechanisms being held under the auspices of the United Nations, in a number of bodies, has aided the promotion of indigenous rights greatly. Although the Working Group was wound down following the adoption of the Declaration on Indigenous Issues, it has been replaced by a new mechanism. Indeed, indigenous rights are now the concern of several mechanisms, including the Permanent Forum and the Committee of Experts and, as discussed earlier, the Human Rights Committee (HRC) and the Committee on the Elimination of Racial Discrimination (CERD). Indigenous rights cover a number of areas, not just traditional human rights law and, therefore, there is a great need for other UN bodies to become involved, which has been achieved through the IASG. There is little doubt that of late indigenous rights are enjoying an increased profile at an international level. If the varying bodies and mechanisms can work cohesively

---

[148] www.un.org/esa/socdev/unpfii/en/special_rapporteurs.html <last visited 21 May 2009>.
[149] UNPFII, www.un.org/esa/socdev/unpfii/en/session_seventh.html <last visited 17 May 2009>.
[150] www.un.org/esa/socdev/unpfii/en/iasg.html <last visited 21 May 2009>.
[151] www.un.org/esa/socdev/unpfii/en/iasg.html <last visited 21 May 2009>.
[152] www2.ohchr.org/english/about/funds/indigenous/ <last visited 21 May 2009>.
[153] Ibid. See also, General Assembly Resolution 56/140.
[154] www2.ohchr.org/english/about/funds/indigenous/ <last visited 21 May 2009>.
[155] www2.ohchr.org/english/issues/indigenous/docs/guidelines.pdf <last visited 21 May 2009>.

and not duplicate the efforts of other bodies, indigenous rights could finally be awarded the priority they deserve.

(ii) Issues arising from the UN Declaration on the Rights of Indigenous Peoples (2007)

(a) Continuing the definitional debate

As examined earlier, 'indigenous' is a relative concept that relates *inter alia* strongly to the land. Colonisation from both Western imperialists and non-Western colonisers has played a huge part in determining the destiny as well as the claims presented by indigenous peoples. Adding to the difficulty, and as already discussed, in identifying a holistic definition of indigenous peoples is the need to identify and treat indigenous people as distinct from minorities. There remains a pronounced view, codified in the UN Declaration on the Rights of Indigenous Peoples that indigenous peoples belong to a distinct category whereby distinct rights are conferred upon them collectively.[156] The emphasis within the Declaration on the Rights of Persons Belonging to National or Ethnic, Religious and Linguistic Minorities is upon effective participation in the society of which the minority is a part; indigenous rights seek autonomous decision-making. Indigenous peoples' participation in wider society is secondary to the primary right to determine the ways and means in which the groups participate, including legislative and administrative procedures.[157] Indigenous rights, to a large extent, aim at consolidating and strengthening the distinctiveness of these peoples from other groups in society and allow them to establish and maintain separate institutions. Minority rights, on the other hand, are formulated as the rights of individuals to preserve and develop their separate group identity within the process of integration.[158] International instruments relating to minorities rule out the entitlement of self-determination to minorities differentiating them in a very fundamental respect from the rights of peoples.[159] As already noted, what further separates minority rights from indigenous rights is that the instruments concerning indigenous peoples are intended to allow for a high degree of autonomous development.

The United Nations in its 2008 Development Group Guidelines on Indigenous Peoples' Issues makes the point that 'the prevailing view today is that no formal definition [of indigenous peoples] is necessary for the recognition and protection of their rights'.[160] It goes on to say that 'this [lack of definition] should in no way constitute an obstacle . . . in addressing the substantial issues affecting Indigenous Peoples'. The text of the UN Declaration on the Rights of Indigenous Peoples does not contain a definition of 'indigenous'. The definitional question led to substantial disagreements during the drafting stages. Whilst several States took the view that the incorporation of a definition represented an essential

---

[156] See Declaration on the Rights of Indigenous Peoples, the Permanent Forum on Indigenous Issues etc.

[157] See Article 4 'Indigenous peoples, in exercising their right to self-determination, have the right to autonomy or self-government in matters relating to their internal and local affairs, as well as ways and means for financing their autonomous functions' and Article 18 'Indigenous peoples have the right to participate in decision-making in matters which would affect their rights, through representatives chosen by themselves in accordance with their own procedures, as well as to maintain and develop their own indigenous decision-making institutions'.

[158] Sami letter to the Council of Europe 2002, www.austlii.edu.au/au/journals/AILR/2002/1.html <last visited 17 October 2008>.

[159] Alfredsson, 'Minority Rights: Protection by the United Nations' 14 *Human Rights Law Journal* (1993) at 1.

[160] United Nations Development Group Guidelines on Indigenous Peoples Rights February 2008 www2.ohchr.org/english/issues/indigenous/docs/guidelines.pdf <last visited 15 May 2009>.

The rights of 'peoples' and 'indigenous peoples'

14

feature of the Declaration, others were of the view that 'applying the concept universally would lead to dilution of the issue, thus harming the true beneficiaries of the rights enshrined in the declaration'.[161] Thus, while the text of the Declaration does not contain any specific definition of 'indigenous peoples', the theme of self-identification nevertheless was highlighted. According to the Article 9 of the Declaration: 'Indigenous peoples and individuals have the right to belong to an indigenous community or nation, in accordance with the traditions and customs of the community or nation concerned.' Similarly Article 33(1) establishes that: 'Indigenous peoples have the right to determine their own identity or membership in accordance with their customs and traditions. This does not impair the right of indigenous individuals to obtain citizenship of the States in which they live.' The approach enshrined within the Declaration therefore bears considerable resonance with the self-identification themes of the ILO Convention 169.

As one of the four Member States voting against the Declaration on the Rights of Indigenous Peoples, the United States of America stated that the failure of the Declaration on the Rights of Indigenous Peoples to define 'indigenous peoples' is 'debilitating to the effective application and implementation of the Declaration' and will 'subject [the declaration] to endless debate especially if entities not properly entitled to such status seek to enjoy the special benefits and rights contained in the declaration'.[162] Bangladesh abstained from voting, citing the lack of an explicit definition of indigenous peoples. Others favoured the flexibility that a non-codified definition retained according to the facts, law and history of each case.[163] Despite the lack of a formal definition, indigenous peoples nevertheless have established rights recognised by international law. The protection accorded to indigenous peoples cannot be diminished by citing a lack of a formal definition.

The Working Group on Indigenous Populations' working paper on the concept of 'indigenous people' listed the following factors that have been considered relevant to the understanding of the concept of 'indigenous' by international organisations and legal experts:

- Priority in time, with respect to the occupation and use of a specific territory;
- The voluntary perpetuation of cultural distinctiveness, which may include the aspects of language, social organization, religion and spiritual values, modes of production, laws and institutions;
- Self-identification, as well as recognition by other groups, or by State authorities, as a distinct collectively; and
- An experience of subjugation, marginalization, dispossession, exclusion or discrimination, whether or not these conditions persist.[164]

---

[161] Report on the 1st Session of the WGDD, UN Doc. E/CN.4/1996/84, p. 7 cited in Gilbert, 'The United Nations Declaration on the Rights of Indigenous Peoples: Towards Partnership and Mutual Respect' www.liv.ac.uk/law/ielu/docs/UN_Declaration_on_the_Rights_of_Indigenous_Peoples-JG.pdf <last visited 17 November 2008>.

[162] Explanation of the vote by Robert Hagan, US Advisor, on the Declaration on the Rights of Indigenous Peoples to the UN General Assembly, with Annex: Observations of the US with respect to the Declaration on the Rights of Indigenous Peoples, USUN Press Release # 204 (07) www.twnside.org.sg/title2/resurgence/206/cover3.doc <last visited 18 May 2009>.

[163] As concluded in the *Report of the African Commission's Working Group of Experts on Indigenous Populations/Communities*, 'there is no global consensus about a single final definition . . . A strict definition of *indigenous peoples* is neither necessary nor desirable'.

[164] Working paper on the concept of 'indigenous people' of the Working Group on Indigenous Populations (E/CN.4/Sub.2/AC.4/1996/2).

As noted above, the crucial feature emergent both from the ILO Convention No. 169 and the UN Declaration is the determination that the status of indigenous peoples applies through 'self-identification'. Article 33 of the United Nations Declaration on the Rights of Indigenous Peoples refers to the rights of indigenous peoples to decide their own identities and procedures of belonging.[165] There has been an ongoing debate in many regions of the world, in particular South Asia, as to whether the term 'indigenous' can be used to describe tribal populations, and consequently what reach the Declaration has in this region. India has consistently favoured the use of the word 'tribal' to describe its indigenous peoples; nowhere within the Constitution is the term 'indigenous' used. India has been anxious to gain support for its position that it has no 'indigenous' people; rather the government argues, the entire population of India is considered to be indigenous. This same position was adopted by India throughout the drafting process of the UN Declaration on the Rights of the Indigenous Peoples. Thus, Mr. Ajai Malhotra from India noted 'in an explanation of the vote before the vote [in the Human Rights Council] said India had consistently favoured the rights of indigenous peoples, and had worked for the Declaration on the Rights of Indigenous Peoples. The text before the Council was the result of 11 years of hard work. The text did not contain a definition of "indigenous". The entire population of India was considered to be indigenous. With regards to the right to self-determination, this was understood to apply only to peoples under foreign domination, and not to a nation of indigenous persons. With this understanding, India was ready to support the proposal for the adoption of the draft Declaration, and would vote in its favour'.[166] Scepticism, however, was evident amongst a number of States of South Asia. At the adoption of the draft Declaration by the Human Rights Council on 29 June 2006 Pakistan, a member of the Council, voted in favour of the declaration. All States of South Asia, save for Bangladesh, voted in the United General Assembly for the adoption of the Declaration on 13 September 2007. Bangladesh was most fervent and also perturbed at the absence of a definition within the Declaration and hence abstained from voting in the Human Rights Council and the United Nations General Assembly.

A specific preambular paragraph has been added to the Declaration, acknowledging that 'the situation of indigenous peoples varies from region to region and from country to country and that the significance of national and regional particularities and various historical and cultural backgrounds should be taken into consideration'. A broad interpretation of this paragraph allows Scheduled Tribes and *Adivasis* in India, Bangladesh and

14

The rights of 'peoples' and 'indigenous peoples'

---

[165] Declaration on the Rights of Indigenous Peoples UN Doc. A/RES/61/295.

[166] See www.unog.ch/80256EDD006B9C2E/(httpNewsByYear_en)/BE82C77003776B9EC125719C005D5994? OpenDocument <last visited 25 February 2009>. This mentality was confirmed at the time of the vote on the UN Declaration. For Mr. Ajai Malhotra from India: 'While the Declaration did not define what constituted indigenous peoples, the issue of indigenous rights pertained to peoples in independent countries who were regarded as indigenous on account of their descent from the populations which inhabited the country, or a geographical region which the country belonged, at the time of conquest or colonization or the establishment of present State boundaries and who, irrespective of their legal status, retained some or all of their socio-economic, cultural and political institutions.' India's neighbour Pakistan, through its representation, expressed similar views. According to Mr. Bilal Hayee, the representative from Pakistan 'his country had voted said his country had voted in favour of the Declaration both in the Human Rights Council and in the Assembly. Although the Declaration did not define indigenous peoples, he hoped that its adoption would fulfil the aims of the International Decade for the rights of indigenous peoples and enable them to maintain their cultural identity, with full respect for their values and traditions'. See www.un.org/News/Press/docs/2007/ga10612.doc.htm General Assembly Sixty-First Plenary Session 13 September 2007 <last visited 23 February 2009>.

Pakistan to qualify as indigenous peoples because they are culturally different from mainstream Indian society despite being internally colonised and dominated.

Indeed, as Alpa Shah argues, the term 'indigenous peoples' has become an important tool for empowerment for tribal and *Adivasi* peoples[167] as according to research carried out by Ghosh, India has the second largest indigenous population in the world.[168] Crispin Bates, on the other hand, proposes that the term *Adivasi* is a colonial invention and that we need to admit in one sense that all Indians are *Adivasis*.[169] He argues that complex migration patterns in India mean that it is impossible to establish who the original settlers in a particular region are, unlike for example, within the United States or Canada. In order to address this anomaly in the application of indigenous within India, Bangladesh and Pakistan, the Indigenous Rights in the Commonwealth project, initiated by the Commonwealth Policy Studies Unit, has used the following criteria to differentiate between indigenous and non-indigenous in South Asia:

(1) Prior origin in a territory

(2) Subjugation by external political structures such as the nation states

(3) Cultural distinctiveness from majority population, including a special relationship based on cultural mores, with their lands,

(4) Self definition as indigenous or 'first peoples'.[170]

This definition has allowed for the identification of over 100 million members of the *Adivasi* population in South Asia, subsequently making it the largest component of indigenous peoples in the Commonwealth project. Sanders believes that the term 'indigenous peoples' has come to absorb elucidations such as 'tribal' and 'hill-people', and that its use is consistent with current United Nations and academic discussions regarding indigenous peoples. The Declaration allows for a homogenisation of the way that rights concerning indigenous peoples are applied by States and standardises the application under international standard setting. The Declaration applies to South Asia and, therefore, as it allows for the flexible interpretation of the term 'indigenous peoples' not only can this lead to the development of customary international law, the text also requires States and the international community to respect the 'spirit of the declaration'.

(b) Land rights

Throughout the Declaration, the special relationship between indigenous peoples and their land has been emphasised[171] while the emerging jurisprudence of HRC and CERD also

---

[167] Shah, 'The Dark Side of Indigenity', 5/6 *History Compass* (2007) 1806–1832 See also Xaxa, 'Tribes as Indigenous Peoples of India', 34 *Economic and Political Weekly* (1999) 3589–3596.

[168] Ghosh, 'Between Global Flos and Local Dams: Indigenousness, Locality and the Transanational Sphere in Jharkhand, India' 21 *Cultural Anthropology* (2006) 402.

[169] Bates, 'Lost Innocence and the loss of innocence: Interpreting Adivasi movements in South Asia' in Barnes, Gray and Kingsbury (eds), above n.1, pp. 103–194.

[170] Kapur, 'Indigenous Rights in India–Outlook and Challenges in the First Decade of the Twenty-First Century' (Commonwealth Policy Studies Unit, 2003) www.cpsu.org.uk/downloads/Indigenous_Rights_in_India.pdf <last visited 21 May 2009>.

[171] Indeed, the entire Declaration could be interpreted as an implicit reiteration of land rights; without their land, many indigenous peoples would not be able to enjoy any of the rights mentioned in the Declaration while other instruments that can be invoked for protection rely strongly on the promotion of land rights to recognise indigenous collective rights.

emphasise the collective nature of this relationship.[172] Although the Declaration does not go so far as the ILO Convention No. 169 Article 14(2), it does, in Article 26(3) state that 'States shall give legal recognition and protection to these lands, territories and resources' in order to provide an effective demarcation of indigenous lands. Gilbert argues that this demarcation is further achieved as a result of the Declaration 'indigenising' the general right to property.[173] Defining what these land rights refer to, however, is another widely debated topic, with the Declaration referring to, in Article 26(1), 'traditionally owned or otherwise occupied, used or acquired'.[174] Some clarification for this is provided in Article 26(2) whereby indigenous peoples must 'possess' the land. Articles 25–30 of the Declaration are dedicated to the protection of the rights of indigenous peoples over their traditional lands and resources. Conversely, States are required to give legal recognition to these lands, territories and resources and this legal recognition shall be conducted with due respect to the 'customs, traditions and land tenure systems of the indigenous peoples concerned'.[175] However, the Declaration does not specify what exactly the resources, which indigenous peoples have the right 'to own, use, develop and control',[176] are. The Supreme Court of the Philippines has decided that indigenous peoples are entitled only to surface resources, leading to a fairly narrow interpretation of Article 26, restricting its meaning exclusively to surface resources. For those who historically have been forcibly evicted, for private enterprise or other reasons,[177] Article 8 of the Declaration provides that States shall provide effective mechanisms for the prevention of, and redress for: '[a]ny action that has the *aim or effect* of depriving them of their integrity as distinct peoples, or of their cultural values or ethnic identities' and '[a]ny action which has the aim or effect of dispossessing them of their lands, territories or resources',[178] while Article 28 provides for the right to redress. However, the right to redress does not automatically encompass the return of lands; it can include monetary compensation which fails to recognise that land is the essence of many indigenous peoples' culture and heritage.

In the *Yakye Axa* case, the Inter-American Court of Human Rights explained that compensation granted to indigenous peoples 'must be guided by the meaning of the land for them'.[179] Additionally, in this case, the Court also awarded damages for harm, 'not just as it pertains to its subsistence resources, but also with regards to the spiritual connection the

---

[172] CERD, Convention on the Elimination of Racial Discrimination General Recommendation XXIII, 18 August 1997, HRI/GEN/1/Rev.7 at 215, para 5. For a discussion on collective land rights, see Gilbert, *Indigenous Peoples' Land Rights Under International Law*, above n.1, pp. 05–115.

[173] See Gilbert, 'Indigenous Rights in the Making: The United Nations Declaration on the Rights of Indigenous Peoples', 14 *IJMGR* (2007) 210–212.

[174] Article 26, Declaration on the Rights of Indigenous Peoples.

[175] Ibid. Article 26(3).

[176] Ibid. Article 26(2).

[177] *Saramaka People* v. *Suriname*, Judgment 28 November 2007, Inter-Am. Ct. H.R. (Ser. C) No. 172 (2007) and see the 5th and 6th Amendments to the Constitution of India whereby the state has an addendum where by it can retake lands if for State use. However, this applies usually to private companies/mega projects and or National Parks.

[178] Article 8 (2a and 2b) Declaration on the Rights of Indigenous Peoples. In the draft Declaration, the terms 'cultural genocide' and 'ethnocide' were included, which would have allowed indigenous peoples recourse to international criminal prosecution.

[179] *Indigenous Community Yakye Axa* v. *Paraguay*. Judgment of 17 June 2005 Inter-Am. Ct. H.R. (Ser. C) No. 125 (2005), at para 149 (referring to, *inter alia*, para 131, which states that 'this Court has underlined that the close relationship of indigenous peoples with the land must be acknowledged and understood as the fundamental basis for their culture, spiritual life, wholeness, economic survival, and preservation and transmission to future generations').

Saramaka people have with their territory'.[180] In a wider context, the United Nations Intergovernmental Forum on Forests recommended that the valuation of forests should 'reflect the social, cultural, economic and ecological context and consider values that are important to local and/or indigenous communities'.[181] To further re-emphasise the importance of land rights for indigenous peoples, Article 32 of the Declaration places the emphasis on free and informed consent concerning matters relating to indigenous land,[182] a matter that has been the focus of considerable discussion in the UN Permanent Forum; CERD has also stressed the rights of indigenous peoples, in its recommendations, to give their informed consent through self-chosen representatives relating to development activities, including: mining, oil and gas operations[183]; logging[184]; the establishment of protected areas[185]; dams; resettlement;[186] and other decisions affecting the status of territorial rights.[187] The Concluding Observations from the CERD 70th Session noted as a concern the reports of adverse effects of economic activities, concluding that the State should explore ways to hold transnational corporations registered in Canada accountable.[188] These concluding observations highlight the responsibilities that the State has toward indigenous peoples; namely, to monitor the actions of corporations involved in development on indigenous peoples' lands. Moreover, in its concluding observations on the United States under Article 9 of the Convention, CERD emphasised that the State must allow indigenous peoples free participation in decisions affecting them. It further reiterated that the

---

[180] *Saramaka People* v. *Suriname*, Judgment 28 November 2007, Inter-Am. Ct. H.R. (Ser. C) No. 172 (2007).

[181] *Report of the Intergovernmental Forum on Forests on its Third Session*, UN Doc. E/CN.17/IFF/1999/25, at p. 20, para 1. Available at: www.daccessdds.un.org/doc/UNDOC/GEN/N00/228/81/PDF/N0022881.pdf?OpenElement <last visited 21 May 2009>.

[182] *Cf.* CERD and ILO C169.

[183] See e.g. Guyana, 04/04/2006, CERD/C/GUY/CO/14, at para 19, where the Committee recommended that Guyana seek the informed consent of concerned indigenous communities prior to 'authorizing any mining or similar operations which may threaten the environment in areas inhabited by these communities'. Guatemala, 15/05/2006, CERD/C/GTM/CO/11, para 19; and Suriname, 18/08/2005, Decision 1(67), CERD/C/DEC/SUR/4, para 3.

[184] See e.g. Cambodia, 31/03/98, CERD/C/304/Add.54, at paras 13 and 19. Where the Committee noted that 'rights of indigenous peoples have been disregarded in many government decisions, in particular those relating to citizenship, logging concessions and concessions for industrial plantations"' and recommended that Cambodia 'ensure that no decisions directly relating to the rights and interests of indigenous peoples are taken without their informed consent'.

[185] See e.g. Botswana. 23/08/2002, UN Doc. A/57/18, paras 292–314, at para 304 (concerning the Central Kalahri Game Reserve); and Botswana, 04/04/2006, CERD/C/BWA/CO/16, at para 12. India, 05/05/2007, CERD/C/IND/CO/19, at para 19 where the Committee held that India 'should seek the prior informed consent of communities affected by the construction of dams in the Northeast or similar projects on their traditional lands in any decision-making processes related to such projects and provide adequate compensation and alternative land and housing to those communities'.

[186] India, 05/05/2007, CERD/C/IND/CO/19, at para 20, where it was noted that the 'State party should also ensure that tribal communities are not evicted from their lands without seeking their prior informed consent and provision of adequate alternative land and compensation'; and Botswana, 04/04/2006, CERD/C/BWA/CO/16, at para 12, where the Committee recommended that the State 'study all possible alternatives to relocation; and (d) seek the prior free and informed consent of the persons and groups concerned'. See also Laos, 18/04/2005, CERD/C/LAO/CO/15, para 18.

[187] Australia. CERD/C/AUS/CO/14, 14 April 2005, at para 11, 'the State party [should] refrain from adopting measures that withdraw existing guarantees of indigenous rights and that it make every effort to seek the informed consent of indigenous peoples before adopting decisions relating to their rights to land'; and United States of America, 14/08/2001, A/56/18, para 380–407, at para 400 which concerned 'plans for expanding mining and nuclear waste storage on Western Shoshone ancestral land, placing their land up for auction for private sale, and other actions affecting the rights of indigenous peoples'.

[188] CERD/C/CAN/CO/18 para 17.

Declaration on the Rights of Indigenous Peoples is applicable to all United Nations Member States, regardless of whether they voted in the affirmative.[189]

(c) Right of self-determination

The Declaration on the Rights of Indigenous Peoples limits the right to external self-determination through Article 46(1) which reads: '[n]othing in this Declaration may be interpreted as . . . encouraging any action that would dismember or impair, totally or in part, the territorial integrity or political unity of sovereign and independent States'. Against this background stands Article 3 which reaffirms that indigenous peoples have the right to self-determination, taken together with Article 4 which provides that '[i]ndigenous peoples, in exercising their right to self-determination, have the *right to autonomy or self-government in matters relating to their internal and local affairs*'. Aspects of self-determination (apart from 'external' self-determination in the form of secession) are not excluded and autonomy is provided for in the Declaration as a right. As already analysed, a recognised right to autonomy and self-governance would be a precious item in the armoury of indigenous peoples.[190]

This *prima facie* right to autonomy in matters relating to internal affairs suggests that within the Declaration the right as provided in Article 3 can only be realised through internal, as opposed to external self-determination. Article 3 states '[b]y virtue of that right [to self-determination] they freely determine their political status and freely pursue their economic, social and cultural development'. Indigenous peoples are, by virtue of the Declaration, therefore, constrained to the recognition of self-determination within existing national boundaries. The ability of indigenous peoples to construct and maintain their autonomy is provided in Article 5 which confirms that '[i]ndigenous peoples have the right to maintain and strengthen their distinct political, legal, economic, social and cultural institutions'. Indigenous peoples are not, as Article 3 suggests, able to 'freely determine' their political development to the extent of secession or political independence; rather, they have the right, to determine their autonomous development within established international boundaries. The Declaration accords indigenous peoples the freedom to identify and choose in which way they exist according to tradition and heritage. This principle of self-identification can be seen as 'part of the evolution of a right to self-determination for indigenous peoples'[191] citing their ability to self determine their identity in line with the Declaration. Moreover, Articles 33 and 34 provide not only for self-identification, but additionally allow indigenous peoples structures and membership in accordance with their with own procedures and international human rights standards, this includes 'juridical systems or customs'; Article 14 affords indigenous peoples the right to 'establish and control' educational systems and institutions providing education in indigenous languages; Article 35 determines the responsibility of individuals to their communities; Article 16 provides rights in respect of the media; and Article 24 in respect of traditional medicines and the right to the 'highest attainable standard of health'. Whereas, Article 20(1) provides that

---

[189] Observations Considering Reports Submitted by State Parties Under Article 9 of the Convention, Addressing the United States of America on 7 March 2008.

[190] See Pentassuglia, 'State Sovereignty, Minorities and Self-Determination: A Comprehensive Legal View', 9 *IJMGR* (2002) 303 at p. 320. Similarly, see Heintze, 'Implementation of Minority Rights through the Devolution of Powers – The Concept of Autonomy Reconsidered' 9 *IJMGR* (2002) 325 at p. 329. This distinction has been pointed out by the Chairperson-Rapporteur of the UN Working Group on Minorities, Asbjørn Eide, in 'Working Paper on the relationship and distinction between the rights of persons belonging to minorities and those of indigenous peoples', 10 July 2000, E/CN.4/Sub.2/2000/10 at paras 10 and 15.

[191] Ibid. pp. 216–218.

'[i]ndigenous peoples have the right to maintain and develop *their* political, economic and social systems or institutions'; and Article 18 refers to the right to maintain indigenous decision-making institutions. As noted above, the wide-ranging principle of self-determination, insofar as it authorises 'peoples' to secession is inapplicable to indigenous peoples. The Declaration, however, authorises other forms of self-determination including indigenous representation in international fora. To assert, as the United States, Canada, Australia and New Zealand did, that the principle of self-determination is inapplicable to indigenous peoples is contrary to international legal standards[192] and in effect contravenes their own domestic policies.[193] The interpretation of self-determination for the purposes of this Declaration should be: 'the freedom for indigenous peoples to live well, to live according to their own values and beliefs, and to be respected by their non-indigenous neighbours.'[194]

(d) Cultural rights

By analysing the language of articles on cultural rights included in the Declaration, the strengths and weaknesses of the language can be identified. The standards set in the Declaration will be compared with those in the general human rights instruments as well ILO Convention No. 169. The Declaration establishes rights in respect of:

- Cultural, spiritual and linguistic identity (Articles 11–13): Rights to practice and revitalize culture and the transmission of histories, languages etc; and the protection of traditions, sites, ceremonial objects and repatriation of remains.

- Education, information and labour rights (Articles 14–17): Right to education, including the right to run their own educational institutions and teach in their own language; cultures to be reflected in education and public information; access to media (both mainstream and indigenous specific); and rights to protection of labour law and freedom from economic exploitation.

- Participatory, development and other economic and social rights (Articles 18–24): Rights to participation in decision-making, through representative bodies; rights to their own institutions to secure subsistence and development; special measures to be adopted to address indigenous disadvantage and ensure non-discriminatory enjoyment of rights; guarantees against violence and discrimination for women and children; right to development; and access to traditional health practices and medicines

The approach advocated in the Declaration may require the revision of traditional ideas held by majority or dominant cultural groups about national culture and identity. The rights of indigenous peoples to culture includes the right to the enjoyment and protection

---

[192] 'Canada Condemns UN Declaration on Rights of Indigenous Peoples' http://www.shunpiking.com/ol0406/0406-index.htm 19 October 2007. It is worth noting here that all four of these countries have domestic laws relating to the ownership and management of indigenous lands by indigenous peoples. See section 35 of Canada's constitution, Treaty of Waitangi Act 1975 of New Zealand. *Mabo (No. 2)*, the High Court of Australia rejected the principle of *terra nullius* and recognised the rights of Indigenous peoples to native title in land where there had been a continuing connection with the land and in the absence of a supervening act of sovereignty on the part of governments or parliaments. Under United States domestic law, the United States government recognises Indian tribes as political entities with inherent powers of self-government as first peoples.

[193] Ibid., USA approach, but it is interesting to compare that to the remarks made at the US National Security Council on 18 January 2001, where criteria to determine who was indigenous included the following: *self-determination*, aboriginal status, and distinct culture and customs.

[194] Daes, 'Striving for self-determination for Indigenous Peoples' Professor Erica-Irene Daes, Former Chair – United Nations Working Group on Indigenous Populations, Kly and Kly (eds), *In Pursuit of the Right to Self-Determination* (Clarity Press Inc., 2001) pp. 50–62, at p. 58.

of their own cultures in a wider, multicultural world.[195] In order to fully recognise these rights, however, there must be effective participation, with the free, prior and informed consent of indigenous peoples within the State. In the Convention on the Elimination of All Forms of Racial Discrimination general recommendations, States have been called upon to ensure that 'members of Indigenous Peoples have equal rights in respect of effective participation' and that 'no decisions are taken without their informed consent'.[196] The Declaration, as noted already, uses this idea of free, prior and informed consent, superseding the free and informed consent (Article 19) of the ILO 169. Free, prior and informed consent will underpin effective participation culturally, socially and economically. UN Treaty Monitoring bodies have also made various references to the principle of 'free, prior and informed Consent' in their decision-making.[197] In the report of its 27th session (2001) the UN Committee on Economic, Social and Cultural Rights also highlighted the need to obtain indigenous peoples' consent in relation to resource exploitation affecting the indigenous peoples of Columbia. The Committee observed 'with regret that the traditional lands of indigenous peoples have been reduced or occupied, without their consent, by timber, mining and oil companies, at the expense of the exercise of their culture and the equilibrium of the ecosystem'.[198]

The emphasis within the Declaration on participation is key to reconciling the interests of the State and indigenous peoples, especially in the light of international developments. Much development occurs within tribal lands and the Declaration serves to mitigate the effects of this by ensuring that if such development takes place, benefits can flow to the indigenous peoples. It should be highlighted that the provisions of the Declaration will not be satisfied through mere consultation with indigenous peoples; rather there is an emphasis throughout the Declaration on the need for informed consent on the part of the indigenous communities involved and an emphasis on the importance of cultural autonomy. Article 25 expressly affirms the rights of indigenous peoples to maintain and strengthen their distinctive spiritual relationship with their lands and, thus, the provisions in the Declaration are implicitly related to cultural autonomy. This is particular to legal regimes regarding indigenous peoples; the maintenance of a culture closely linked to particular use of land and natural resources is a main element distinguishing minorities from indigenous peoples.[199] As José Martínez Cobo has stated: it is 'basic to [indigenous peoples] existence as such and to all their beliefs, customs, traditions and culture'.[200] Thus, those provisions of the Declaration that envisage the right of indigenous peoples to free, prior and informed consent, in relation to the approval of any project affecting them, are of vital importance.[201]

[195] A/59/150. Fifty-ninth session, Programme of activities of the International Decade of the World's Indigenous People (1995–2004) report of Rodolfo Stavenhagen, Special Rapporteur on the situation of human rights and fundamental freedoms of indigenous people, 12 August 2004.

[196] Para 4(d) Convention on the Elimination of Racial Discrimination General Recommendation XXIII, 18 August 1997, HRI/GEN/1/Rev.7 at 215 para 2.

[197] See Part II above.

[198] E/C.12/1/Add.74, para 12.

[199] Nuuk Conclusions and Recommendations on Indigenous Autonomy and Self-Government, Report of the Meeting of Experts to review the experience of countries in the operation of schemes of internal self-government for Indigenous Peoples, 24–28 September 1991, E/CN.4/1992/42/Add.1.

[200] Cobo, *Study of the Problem of Discrimination Against Indigenous Populations*, United Nations Special Rapporteur (1987). E/CN,4/Sub.2/1986/7/Add.4, p. 16.

[201] Article 32(2), Declaration. Article 15(2), ILO Convention No. 169 contemplates such a hypothesis where States retain the ownership of sub-soil resources, providing that in such cases procedures aimed at the consultation of indigenous groups shall be established. See also Article XVIII(5), Proposed American Declaration on the Rights of Indigenous Peoples.

Many of the relevant provisions of the Declaration directly refer to, imply or underscore the right of free, prior and informed consent in relation to rights affirmed in Treaties, Agreements and other Constructive Arrangements between States and indigenous peoples as well as other rights. Articles 19, addressing the adoption of legislative and administrative measures, and Article 32, which addresses development activities affecting indigenous peoples' lands and natural resources, do contain some of the broadest affirmations in the Declaration of the right to free, prior and informed consent for indigenous peoples. The provisions spelling out the terms and criteria for restitution, redress and compensation in cases of land and resource rights violations are equally relevant. Article 10, which affirms that indigenous peoples shall not be forcibly removed or relocated from their lands or territories without their free, prior and informed consent, is also of direct relevance to the issue of land, as the central issue in most Treaty rights violations being carried out around the world.[202] Article 12 of the ILO Convention No. 169 allows for indigenous and tribal peoples 'to take legal proceedings either individually, or through their representative bodies'. In order for this article to be effective, synthesis of provisions in the Declaration and in the ILO Conventions are necessary.

(e) The right to health

The right to health is, as has been noted throughout this study, a fundamental part of human rights law and of our understanding of a life in dignity. As this study has examined, the right to the enjoyment of the highest attainable standard of physical and mental health (to give it its full name) has been a long-standing concern of international human rights law. Internationally, it was first articulated in the 1946 Constitution of the World Health Organization (WHO): the preamble defines health as 'a state of complete physical, mental and social well-being and not merely the absence of disease or infirmity'.[203] The emphasis to achieve 'the highest attainable standard to physical and mental health' has been referenced within the constitutions of various States, other Declarations and Conventions, and in case-law. For example, the Constitution of India (1950) in Part IV, Article 47 articulates the duty of the State to raise the level of nutrition and the standard of living and to improve public health.[204] Provisions of the ILO Convention No. 169, for example in Article 20 (2)(c), provides that the State should provide medical and social assistance while in Article 25(1–3), although it states that traditional practices should be considered, the overall emphasis is upon the government providing services in co-ordination with other 'cultural, social and economic measures in the country'.[205] Article 24 of the UN Declaration provides as follows:

---

[202] 'The UN Declaration on the Rights of Indigenous Peoples, Treaties and the Right to Free, Prior and Informed Consent: The Framework For a New Mechanism for Reparations, Restitution and Redress', submitted by the International Indian Treaty Council as a Conference Room Paper for the United Nations Permanent Forum on Indigenous Issues Seventh Session (UNPFII7) 9 March 2008.

[203] The Constitution was adopted by the International Health Conference held in New York from19 June to 22 July 1946, signed on 22 July 1946 by the representatives of 61 States (*Off. Rec. Wld. Hlth Org.*, 2, 100), and entered into force on 7 April 1948. Amendments adopted by the Twenty-sixth, Twenty-ninth, Thirty-ninth and Fifty-first World Health Assemblies (resolutions WHA26.37, WHA29.38, WHA39.6 and WHA51.23) came into force on 3 February 1977, 20 January 1984, 11 July 1994 and 15 September 2005 respectively.

[204] See the Constitution of India, http://indiacode.nic.in/coiweb/welcome.html <last visited 18 May 2009>.

[205] Article 25(4) UN Declaration on the Rights of Indigenous Peoples.

1. Indigenous peoples have the right to their traditional medicines and to maintain their health practices, including the conservation of their vital medicinal plants, animals and minerals. Indigenous individuals also have the right to access, without any discrimination, to all social and health services.

2. Indigenous individuals have an equal right to the enjoyment of the highest attainable standard of physical and mental health. States shall take the necessary steps with a view to achieving progressively the full realization of this right.

Furthermore, within the Declaration, emphasis is placed upon utilising traditional medical care, Article 29(3) provides that States are to 'take effective measures to ensure, as needed, that programmes for monitoring, maintaining and restoring the health of indigenous peoples, as developed and implemented by the peoples affected by such materials, are duly implemented'. The International Covenant on Economic, Social and Cultural Rights (Article 2(2)) and the Convention on the Rights of the Child (Article 2(1)) identify the following non-exhaustive grounds of discrimination: race, colour, sex, language, religion, political or other opinion, national or social origin, property, disability, birth or other status. According to the Committee on Economic, Social and Cultural Rights, 'other status' may include health status (e.g., HIV/AIDS) or sexual orientation. States have an obligation to prohibit and eliminate discrimination on all grounds and ensure equality to all in relation to access to healthcare and the underlying determinants of health. In its General Comment No. 14 on the right to health, the Committee on Economic, Social and Cultural Rights noted:

In the light of emerging international law and practice and the recent measures taken by States in relation to indigenous peoples, the Committee deems it useful to identify elements that would help to define indigenous peoples' right to health in order better to enable States with indigenous peoples to implement the provisions contained in article 12 of the Covenant. The Committee considers that indigenous peoples have the right to specific measures to improve their access to health services and care. These health services should be culturally appropriate, taking into account traditional preventive care, healing practices and medicines. States should provide resources for indigenous peoples to design, deliver and control such services so that they may enjoy the highest attainable standard of physical and mental health. The vital medicinal plants, animals and minerals necessary to the full enjoyment of health of indigenous peoples should also be protected. The Committee notes that, in indigenous communities, the health of the individual is often linked to the health of the society as a whole and has a collective dimension. In this respect, the Committee considers that development-related activities that lead to the displacement of indigenous peoples against their will from their traditional territories and environment, denying them their sources of nutrition and breaking their symbiotic relationship with their lands, has a deleterious effect on their health.[206]

---

[206] CESCR General Comment 14, *The Right to Highest Attainable Standard of Health*, (Article 12) General Comment No. 14 (11/08/00). (E/C.12/200/4). para 27.

The rights of 'peoples' and 'indigenous peoples'

14

The International Convention on the Elimination of All Forms of Racial Discrimination (Article 5) also stresses that States must prohibit and eliminate racial discrimination and guarantee the right of everyone to public health and medical care, as does CEDAW (Articles 11(1), 12 and 14), and CRC (Article 24). Many States with large indigenous populations have ratified the CRC and CEDAW. The latter conventions, as shall be discussed in due course, apply with equal vigour to all persons with disabilities including indigenous persons.[207]

As shall be examined, the newly adopted Convention on the Rights of Persons with Disabilities requires States to promote, protect and ensure the full and equal enjoyment of all human rights and fundamental freedoms by persons with disabilities, including their right to health, and to promote respect for their inherent dignity (Article 1). Article 25 of the UN Convention further recognises the 'right to the enjoyment of the highest attainable standard of health without discrimination on the basis of disability' and elaborates upon measures States should take to ensure this right.[208] These measures include ensuring that persons with disabilities have access to and benefit from those medical and social services needed specifically because of their disabilities, including early identification and intervention, services designed to minimise and prevent further disabilities as well as orthopaedic and rehabilitation services, which enable them to become independent, prevent further disabilities and support their social integration. Similarly, States must provide health services and centres as close as possible to people's own communities, including in rural areas. Furthermore, the non-discrimination principle requires that persons with disabilities should be provided with 'the same range, quality and standard of free or affordable health care and programmes as provided to other persons', and States should 'prevent discriminatory denial of health care or health services or food or fluids on the basis of disability' (see generally Articles 25 and 26 of the Convention). Importantly, States must require health professionals to provide care of the same quality to persons with disabilities as to others, including on the basis of free and informed consent. To this end, States are required to train health professionals and to set ethical standards for public and private healthcare. The Convention on the Rights of the Child (Article 23) recognises the right of children with disabilities to special care and to effective access to healthcare and rehabilitation services. Disabled children from indigenous communities are also to be provided the same level of special care and effective access to healthcare and rehabilitation services. There are marked disparities in how States treat indigenous persons with disabilities. For example, in his concluding recommendations, the Special Rapporteur for the ICESCR found that Australia had significant resources for the improvement of the treatment of indigenous peoples with disabilities,[209] while in Bolivia the exploitation of indigenous children with disabilities was tied into trafficking, exploitation and child labour.[210]

It remains to be seen as to the extent to which a holistic interpretation of the entire Declaration would be incorporated within State practices. The Declaration is no doubt a positive step in recognising the rights of indigenous peoples. Nevertheless, this is only a first step – the status of the Declaration as a customary principle of international law is yet to be established. A binding UN Convention appears to be only a distant possibility.

---

[207] See below chapters 15 and 16.
[208] World Health Organization, Mental Health Atlas: 2005 (Geneva, 2005).
[209] ICESCR Concluding Recommendation, E/2001/22 (2000) 66, para 375.
[210] CRC Concluding Remarks, CRC/C/16 (1993), 13, at para 36.

6 OTHER INITIATIVES

At the global and regional levels indigenous peoples continue to receive attention. A number of modern instruments contain article references to indigenous peoples. Rights of the indigenous children are the subject of attention in the Convention on the Rights of the Child. According to Article 30 of the Convention:

> In those States in which ethnic, religious or linguistic minorities or persons of indigenous origin exist, a child belonging to such a minority or who is indigenous shall not be denied the right, in community with other members of his or her group, to enjoy his or her own culture, to profess and practise his or her own religion, or to use his or her own language.

Legal literature as well as international instruments are increasingly acknowledging the strength of the bond between indigenous peoples and the environment. Although environmental agendas are not always in agreement with indigenous agendas, the ILO Convention No. 169 Concerning Indigenous and Tribal Peoples in Independent Countries,[211] the Rio Declaration on Environment and Development[212] and the Convention on Biological Diversity[213] make specific reference to this relationship.[214] In many other instruments, while direct references are missing, the jurisprudence emanating from their implementation organs is concerned with indigenous issues. The Human Rights Committee has dealt with indigenous claims pertaining to non-discrimination, minority rights and the right to self-determination. Concern is also evident in United Nations treaties which do not deal directly with indigenous peoples.

We have already noted that the AFCHPR makes substantial references to peoples' rights; indigenous peoples may be able to claim many of these rights. Indigenous issues are also on the agenda of the African Commission on Human and Peoples' Rights. In its Resolution on the Rights of Indigenous Peoples/Communities, the Commission reiterated and confirmed the decision to establish a working group to consider the concept of indigenous peoples and to devise mechanisms for their protection. The sub-commission established under the African Commission on Human and Peoples' Rights adopted the Report of the African Commission's Working Group on Indigenous Populations/Communities which confirms that indigenous groups are 'discriminated in particular ways because of their particular culture, mode of production and marginalized position within the state'.[215] Despite this consciousness the notion of the rights of indigenous peoples is an on-going issue in Africa. The European and American human rights systems have also developed jurisprudence on indigenous rights. Within Europe although the problem of indigenous rights

---

[211] (ILO No. 169) 72 ILO Official Bull. 59, 28 I.L.M. (1989) 1382, entered into force 5 September 1991.

[212] UN Doc. A/CONF.151/26 (vol. I); 31 ILM 874 (1992); see in particular Principle 22.

[213] Signed June 5 1992; 818 ILM 1992; see in particular the preamble and Article 10 of the Convention.

[214] Fabra, 'Indigenous Peoples, Environmental degradation and Human Rights: a Case Study' in Boyle and Anderson (eds), *Human Rights Approaches to Environmental Protection* (Clarendon Press, 1996) pp. 244–263; Bilderbeek (ed.), *Bio-Diversity in International Law* (IOS Press, 1992) pp. 36–41.

[215] The African Commission's Work on Indigenous Peoples in Africa, Indigenous Peoples in Africa: The Forgotten Peoples? (2006) at p. 12, www.achpr.org/english/Special%20Mechanisms/Indegenous/ACHPR%20WGIP%20Report%20Summary%20version%20ENG.pdf <last visited 10 May 2009>.

14

The rights of 'peoples' and 'indigenous peoples'

exists, it is less visible when compared with the situations in Australia and the Americas.[216] The European Convention on Human Rights does not contain any explicit provisions on minority rights or the right of self-determination. Members of the minorities have nevertheless used the Convention rights to claim violation of their group rights. In *G and E* v. *Norway*, two members of the Lapp minority complained that the proposed hydroelectric project would flood traditional reindeer grazing grounds.[217] The Commission acknowledged that the construction of the dam amounted to an interference with the Article 8 right to private and family life of members of the Lapp minority that breeds its reindeers in the valley, which would be inundated as a consequence of the construction of the dam. However, the Commission held that land to be flooded constituted too small an interference and even if it did this would be justifiable under Article 8(2). The minimalisation of the interests of the Lapp minority *vis-à-vis* the credit towards the authorities' attitude and the State's economic interests have been subjected to criticism.[218] In *Buckley* v. *UK*, an enforcement notice against a Gypsy family was held not to constitute a violation of Article 8(1) of the ECHR.[219] By contrast in the *Chapman, Beard, Jane Smith, Lee* and *Coster* cases against the United Kingdom,[220] the European Court of Human Rights acknowledged that the traditional indigenous living of the Roma need to be supported within the context of Article 8. In the *Chapman* case, the Court made the following useful observations:

> Nonetheless, although the fact of being a member of a minority with a traditional lifestyle different from that of the majority of a society does not confer an immunity from general laws intended to safeguard assets common to the whole society such as the environment, it may have an incidence on the manner in which such laws are to be implemented. As intimated in the *Buckley* judgment, the vulnerable position of gypsies as a minority means that some special consideration should be given to their needs and their different lifestyle both in the relevant regulatory planning framework and in arriving at the decisions in particular cases. To this extent there is thus a positive obligation imposed on the Contracting States by virtue of Article 8 to facilitate the gypsy way of life.[221]

The issue of indigenous peoples has been elevated in the Inter-American Institute, a specialised agency of OAS.[222] The Institute organises congresses and conferences on indigenous issues and has also provided technical and advisory services to members of OAS and to indigenous peoples.[223] The Inter-American Commission of Human Rights has

---

[216] Hannum, 'The Protection of Indigenous Rights in the Inter-American System' in Harris and Livingstone (eds), *The Inter-American System of Human Rights* (Clarendon Press, 1998) pp. 323–343, at p. 325.

[217] *G. and E.* v. *Norway* (1983) Application No. 9278/81 (Eur. Comm. H. R).

[218] See Henrard, *Devising an Adequate System of Minority Protection* (Kluwer, 2000) at p. 102.

[219] (1996) 23 E.H.R.R. 101.

[220] *Chapman* v. *UK* (2001) 33 E.H.R.R. 18, para 129; *Smith* v. *UK* (2001) 33 E.H.R.R. 30; *Lee* v. *UK* (2001) 33 E.H.R.R. 29; *Beard* v. *UK* (2001) 33 E.H.R.R. 19; *Coster* v. *UK* (2001) 33 E.H.R.R. 20.

[221] *Chapman* v. *UK*, para 96.

[222] See the Inter-American Commission on Human Rights, *Inter-American Year Book on Human Rights 1969–70* (1976) pp. 73–83; also see Inter-American Commission on Human Rights, *Report on the work accomplished by the Inter-American Commission on Human Rights during its 29th session* (October 16–27), 1972 OAS Doc. OAS/Ser L/V/II.29 Doc. 40 rev.1 1973, 63–65.

[223] Hannum, 'The Protection of Indigenous Rights in the Inter-American System' in Harris and Livingstone (eds), above n.216, at p. 325.

also addressed a number of cases from indigenous peoples[224] and has also engaged in country reports focusing on indigenous rights.[225] Since 1992, the Commission has also been engaged in the drafting of the American Declaration on the Rights of Indigenous Peoples.

7 CONCLUSIONS

The right to self-determination forms a critical though controversial aspect of modern human rights law and has been incorporated in the International Covenants and other modern human rights documents.[226] While during the decolonisation phase the right to self-determination was deployed to claim an independent State, its meaning, purposes and objectives have been questioned by many States in the post-colonial era. The right to self-determination continues to be invoked by many dissatisfied minority groups, who often equate self-determination as secession or independent statehood. Modern States, on the other hand, are extremely reluctant to grant an explicit right of self-determination to minority groups, fearing rebellion and secession. This conflict arising out of the right to self-determination has been painful. It has led to destruction and more recently resulted in violations of human rights through terrorist activities.[227]

Indigenous peoples have a special claim to the right to self-determination. Being indigenous to the lands, their rights were violated by more powerful foreign forces. As this chapter has analysed, there is a growing recognition of the injustices that have been faced by indigenous peoples. International law has taken some steps, albeit limited, to grant a measure of autonomy and land rights to indigenous peoples. A very significant step was undertaken through the adoption of ILO Convention No. 169. Some of the modern international law instruments have also shown sensitivity towards issues which concern indigenous peoples. There is, however, a lot that needs to be done. Despite the numerous mechanisms adopted within the framework of the Commission on Human Rights, and more recently the Human Rights Council, as well as under ECOSOC, the United Nations struggled for decades to adopt the Declaration on the Rights of Indigenous Peoples.

The adoption of the United Nations Declaration on the Rights of the Indigenous Peoples (2007) is a significant step in standard-setting and ultimate realisation of the rights of indigenous peoples. The Declaration, in its capacity of a United Nations General Assembly Resolution, is not *per se* a binding document. Nevertheless, a number of its provisions are of such fundamental character, that they represent customary international laws and therefore bind all States. Despite the normative values of these provisions contained in the Declaration, their implementation represents a real challenge to the international community.

---

[224] Case No. 1690, (Colombia), OEA/Ser.L/V/II.29, doc. 41, rev. 2, 14 March 1973 at 63; Case No. 1802, (Paraguay), OEA/Ser.L/V/II.43, doc. 21, 20 April 1978, at 36. Also see Report on the Situation of Human Rights of a Segment of the Nicaraguan Population of Miskito Origin OAS OEA/Ser.L/V/II.62. doc 10 rev. 3 (1983) and OEA/Ser.L/V/II.62 doc 26 (1984), discussed by Hannum, 'The Protection of Indigenous Rights in the Inter-American System' in Harris and Livingstone (eds), above n.216, at pp. 326–331.

[225] See IACHR Report on H. 332 fn. 48–52.

[226] See above chapters 5 and 6.

[227] See below chapters 20 and 24.

It is recommended that although an apparently ambitious project at the moment, the Human Rights Council must continue its work on the drafting and ultimately adoption of a binding treaty which would protect the rights of the indigenous peoples, along with the establishing of a corresponding treaty body. It would also be highly beneficial, if the various mechanisms established under the UN system were able to co-ordinate their work effectively to prevent repetition and overlap in order to maximise the use of resources and emphasise particularly important issues concerning indigenous peoples.

15 The rights of women[1]

1 INTRODUCTION

From the very moment of her birth, the girl child confronts a world which values her existence less than that of boys. Girls face obstacles in education, nutrition, health and other areas solely because of their sex. They are viewed as having a 'transient presence' to be married young and then judged by their ability to procreate. As they mature into women, they are thrust into a cycle of disempowerment that is very likely to be their daughter's destiny as well.[2]

The issue of the rights of women remains highly divisive in most societies and regions of the world. These divisions are reflected in the developing norms of the international law of human rights. Discriminatory practices and violations of the rights of women are a historical as well as a contemporary phenomenon.[3] Gender equality was neither promoted

---

[1] See Ali, *Gender and Human Rights in Islam and International Law: Equal Before Allah, Unequal Before Man?* (Kluwer, 2000); Bayefsky, 'The Principle of Equality or Non-Discrimination in International Law' 11 *HRLJ* (1990) 1; Buss and Manji, *International Law: Modern Feminist Approaches* (Hart, 2005); Banda, *Women, Law and Human Rights: An African Perspective* (Hart, 2005); Charlesworth and Chinkin, *The Boundaries of International Law: a Feminist Analysis* (Manchester University Press, 2000); Charlesworth, Chinkin and Wright 'Feminist Approaches to International Law' 85 *AJIL* (1991) 613; Chinkin, 'Women's Human Rights and Religion: How do they Co-Exist?' in Rehman and Breau, *Religion, Human Rights and International Law: A Critical Examination of Islamic State Practices* (Martinus Nijhoff, 2007) pp. 53–80; Cook, 'Women's International Human Rights Law: The Way Forward' 15 *HRQ* (1993) 230; Eisler, 'Human Rights: Toward an Integrated Theory for Action' 9 *HRQ* (1987) 287; Galey, 'International Enforcement of Women's Rights' 6 *HRQ* (1984) 463; Hevener, 'An Analysis of Gender Based Treaty Law: Contemporary Developments in Historical Perspective' 8 *HRQ* (1986) 70; Knop (ed.), *Gender and Human Rights* (Oxford University Press, 2004); Meron, 'Enhancing the Effectiveness of the Prohibition of Discrimination Against Women' 84 *AJIL* (1990) 213; Morsink, 'Women's Rights in the Universal Declaration' 13 *HRQ* (1991) 229; Mullally, *Gender, Culture and Human Rights: Reclaiming Universalism* (Hart, 2006); Reanda, 'Human Rights and Women's Rights: The UN Approach' 3(2) *HRQ* (1981) 11; Rehman, 'The *Sharia*, Islamic Family Laws and International Human Rights Law: Examining the Theory and Practice of Polygamy and *Talaq*' 21 *International Journal of Law, Policy and the Family* (2007) 108; Tinker, 'Human Rights for Women' 3(2) *HRQ* (1981) 32; Wright, 'Economic Rights and Social Justice: A Feminist Analysis of Some International Human Rights Conventions' 12 *AYIL* (1992) 241.

[2] United Nations, *Human Rights and the Girl Child* (1993).

[3] Schuler (ed.), *Freedom from violence Women's strategies from Around the World* (Pact, 1992); 'significant numbers of the world's population are routinely subjected to torture, starvation, terrorism, humiliation, mutilation and even murder simply because they are female'; Bunch, 'Women's Rights as Human Rights: Toward a Re-Vision of Human Rights' 12 *HRQ* (1990) 486 at p. 486; McDougal, Lasswell and Chen, *Human Rights and World Public Order: The Basic Policies of an International Law of Human Dignity* (Yale University Press, 1980) at p. 612.

by religious ideologies, nor was it advocated by philosophers of the Enlightenment. It is ironic that in the great revolutions in France, the United States and Russia, champions of equality had a limited vision on matters of women's rights and gender-based equality.[4]

In contemporary terms the discriminatory nature of the treatment which women receive transcends national frontiers and can be visualised as a global issue rather than a regional or national concern. Even amongst social and cultural entities proud and confident of their human rights standards, women are more frequent victims of violence, abuse, poverty and discrimination.[5] In many societies women are perceived as inherently inferior, intellectually deficient and physically and emotionally subservient to men.[6] In these traditions, women continue to be subjected to such abhorrent practices as genital mutilation, sales, forced marriages, pressure to bear male off-spring, marital rape and honour killings.[7] While in the event of scarcity of resources men's demands are given priority, women are often denied educational, professional and economic opportunities. There are also denials of inheritance and property rights, and discouragement or refusal of women to take part in public and social life, at national as well as international level.[8]

If the civic order breaks down leading to anarchy and civil war women are most vulnerable to torture, physical abuse and rape. The treatment accorded to women in domestic and international conflicts suggests that amongst the civilian population, it is women who are most vulnerable to abuse; targets of torture, slavery, mass rape and other crimes against humanity. As Chapter 21 analyses, it is only recently that modern international humanitarian laws began to address the violence conducted against women during armed conflicts.[9] Women constitute the greatest proportion of world refugees and as refugees are often subjected to abuse and victimisation.[10]

---

[4] Olympe de Gouge, 'The Rights of Woman' (Pythia, 1989); Robinson (ed.), *Mary Shelley: Collected Tales and Stories* (John Hopkins University Press, 1976).

[5] Knop (ed.), above n.1; Buss and Manji, above n.1; Charlesworth, Chinkin and Wright, above n.1, at p. 639; McDougal, Lasswell and Chen, above n.3, at p. 618; Marshall, 'Violence Against Women in Canada by Non-State Actors: The State and Women's Human Rights' in Mahoney and Mahoney (eds), *Human Rights in the Twenty-First Century: A Global Challenge* (Martinus Nijhoff, 1993) pp. 319–333; MacKinnon, 'On Torture: A Feminist Perspective on Human Rights' in Mahoney and Mahoney (eds), ibid. at 21–31.

[6] Dearden., *Arab Women* (Minority Rights Group, 1983); Rounaq, *Women in Asia* (Minority Rights Group, 1982); Harris, *American Women Writers to 1800* (Oxford University Press, 1983); Ivan-Smith, Tandon and Connors, *Women in Sub-Saharan Africa* (Minority Rights Group, 1988).

[7] Raday, 'Culture, Religion and Gender' 1 *IJCL* (2003) 663.

[8] Makram-Ebeid, 'Exclusion of Women from Politics' in Mahoney and Mahoney (eds), above n.5, 89–94; Wikler, 'Exclusion of Women from Justice: Emergency Strategies for Reform' in Mahoney and Mahoney (eds), above n.5, 950–108; Waring, 'The Exclusion of Women from "Work" and Opportunity' in Mahoney and Mahoney (eds), above n.5, 109–117; McDougal, Lasswell and Chen, above n.3, at p. 616.

[9] See below chapter 21. Charlesworth and Chinkin, above n.1, at ch.10; Human Rights Watch, *Struggling To Survive: Barriers to Justice for Rape Victims in Rwanda* (Parts III and IV) (2004) http://hrw.org/reports/2004/rwanda0904/ <last visited 30 January 2009>; Sellars 'Individual('s) Liability for Collective Sexual Violence' in Knop (ed.), above n.1; Women's Initiatives for Gender Justice, www.iccwomen.org/ <last visited 30 January 2009>; Tabory, 'The Status of Women in Humanitarian Law' in Dinstein and Tabory (eds), *International Law at a Time of Perplexity* (Brill, 1989) pp. 941–951; Chinkin, 'Rape and Sexual Abuse of Women in International law' 5 *EJIL* (1994) 326; Petrovic, 'Ethnic Cleansing – An Attempt at Methodology' 5 *EJIL* (1994) 342. On the violation of rights of women during the Gulf War (1990–91) see Hampson, 'Liability for War Crimes' in Rowe (ed.), *The Gulf War 1990–1991 in International and English Law* (Routledge, 1993) p. 241 at p. 248. On former Yugoslavia see Salzman, 'Rape Camps as a Means of Ethnic Cleansing: Religious, Cultural and Ethical Responses to Rape Victims in the Former Yugoslavia' 20 *HRQ* (1998) 348; Pajic, *Violation of Fundamental Rights in the Former Yugoslavia: The Conflict of Bosnia-Herzegovina* (Occasional paper No. 2, David Davies Memorial Institute of International Studies, 1993) at p. 7. Ni Aolain, 'Radical Rules: The Effects of Evidential and Procedural Rules on the Regulation of Sexual Violence in War' 60 *Albany Law Review* (1997) 883.

[10] See below chapter 18; '[During] refugee movements, women and girls risk further violations of their human rights, and have repeatedly been targeted as victims of rape and abduction. Their passage to safety may have to

2 RIGHTS OF WOMEN AND THE HUMAN RIGHTS REGIME

Women face discrimination, intimidation, harassment, torture and physical abuse not simply by State organs but also by their own family and other non-State organs. A major problem which has led to a negative impact on the position of women is the reluctance of international human rights law to intervene in what is perceived as private (as opposed to the public) matters.[11] Attempts to combat discrimination and violence against women in the private domain have raised substantial opposition. Intrusion into private and family life is not viewed as desirable for law enforcement bodies. Such an intrusion is seen as contrary to the social, cultural and religious values prevalent in many societies.[12] Within the sanctity of the home, women, in many parts of the world, are regularly subjected to mental and physical violence or sexual abuse of the nature of incest, rape, 'dowry deaths', wife battering, genital mutilation, prostitution and forced sterilisation.[13] In these social structures women have to undergo a persistent cycle of rejection, subordination and shame. Women face multiple disadvantages based on grounds such as race, religion, national and social origin.[14] Old age and disability have a substantially negative impact on the lives of women.

be bought at the price of sexual favours, and even within the relative security of a refugee camp or settlement and bearing additional responsibilities as heads of household, they face discrimination in food distribution, access to health, welfare and education services – doubly disadvantaged as refugees and as women'. Goodwin-Gill and McAdam, *The Refugee in International Law* (Oxford University Press, 2007) at p. 473; Byrnes, 'The "Other" Human Rights Treaty Body: The Work on the Committee on the Elimination of Discrimination Against Women' 14 *YJIL* (1989) 1–67 at p. 64; Wallace, 'Making the Refugee Convention Gender Sensitive: The Canadian Guidelines' 45 *ICLQ* (1996) 702.

[11] Engle, 'After the Collapse of the Public/Private Distinction: Strategizing Women's Rights' in Dallmeyer (ed.), *Reconceiving Reality: Women and International Law* (American Society of International Law, 1993) at p. 143; 'International Human Rights and Feminisms: When Discourses Keep Meeting' in Buss and Manji (eds), above n.1, at p. 47; Subedi, 'Protection of Women Against Domestic Violence: The Response of International Law' 2 *EHRLR* (1997) 587; McGillivray, 'Reconstructing Child Abuse: Western Definition and Non-Western Experience' in Freeman and Veerman (eds), *Ideologies of Children's Rights* (Martinus Nijhoff, 1992) pp. 213–236 at p. 213.

[12] Byrnes, 'Women, Feminism and International Human Rights Law: Methodological Myopia, Fundamental Flaws or Meaningful Marginalisation?' 12 *AYIL* (1988–89) 205 at 215.

[13] See CEDAW, General Recommendation No. 14, Female Circumcision, (ninth session, 1990) UN Doc. A/45/38/ (where the Committee expresses its concern at 'the continuation of the practice of female circumcision and other traditional practices harmful to the health of women') www.un.org/womenwatch/daw/cedaw/recommendations/recomm.htm#recom14 <last visited 17 February 2009>. According to one study, an estimated 130 million women and girls have been forced into FGM, and around two million girls face the danger of some form of mutilation on a yearly basis, Rahman and Toubia, *Female Genital Mutilation* (Zed Books Ltd, 2000) at p. 6; Dorkenoo and Elworthy, *Female Genital Mutilation: Proposals for Change* (Minority Rights Group, 1992); Dorkenoo, *Cutting the Rose: Female Genital Mutilation-the Practice and its Prevention* (Minority Rights Group, 1995); Slack, 'Female Circumcision: A Critical Appraisal' 10 *HRQ* (1987–1988) 437; Gunning, 'Arrogant Perceptions, World Travelling and Multicultural Feminism: The Case of Female Genital Surgeries' 23 *CHRLR* (1991–1992) 189 at p. 238; Skrobanek, 'Exotic, Subservient and Trapped: Confronting Prostitution and Traffic in Women in Southeast Asia' in Schuler (ed.), above n.3, at pp. 121–137; Seager and Olson (eds), *Women in the World: An International Atlas* (Pluto Press, 1986); Van Bueren, *The International Law on the Rights of the Child* (Brill, 1995) at pp. 262–292; Boulware-Miller, 'Female Circumsion Challenges to the Practice as a Human Rights Violation' 8 *Harvard Women's Law Journal* (1985) 155.

[14] See Human Rights Committee General Comment No. 28, para 30 www.unhchr.ch/tbs/doc.nsf/0/13b02776122d4838802568b900360e80 Equality of Rights between Men and Women (Article 3) 29 March 2000 *CCPR/C/21/Rev.1/Add.10, General Comment No. 28* <last visited 9 November 2008>; Committee on the Elimination of Racial Discrimination, its General Recommendation XXV Concerning Gender-Related Dimensions of Racial Discrimination 20 March 2000 (56th session) www.unhchr.ch/tbs/doc.nsf/(Symbol)/76a293e49a88bd23802568bd00538d83?Opendocument <last visited 19 November 2008>.

Disabled women, as the Committee on Economic, Social and Cultural Rights has noted, suffer from 'double discrimination'.[15]

It is encouraging to note that the United Nations has undertaken positive steps to combat discrimination and violence against women in both the public and private domain. The United Nations Convention on the Elimination of All Forms of Discrimination against Women,[16] the primary focus of this chapter, prohibits discrimination in 'any other field'.[17] At the same time it is important to note that difficulties have arisen in enforcing the norm of non-discrimination in the domestic or private sphere. Such difficulties are apparent through a large number of reservations to significant provisions contained in the Convention, e.g. Article 16.

Violence against women – an activity frequently conducted within the confines of family and home – has been dealt with specifically by the United Nations. In December 1993, the United Nations General Assembly adopted a Declaration on the Elimination of Violence against Women.[18] The United Nations has also appointed a Special Rapporteur on violence against women. An optional protocol to the Convention was adopted by the United Nations General Assembly in 1999.[19] The protocol allows individuals and groups to complain to the Committee on the Elimination of Discrimination Against Women (CEDAW) for violations of the rights contained in the Convention.

(i) Women and violence during armed conflict

Women and girls are the frequent targets of violence and sexual humiliation in times of distress, civil war or internal and international armed conflicts.[20] The rape of women during armed conflict is an unfortunate though regular occurrence; recent conflicts such as those in the former Yugoslavia and Rwanda graphically reflect the targeted rape of women from the opposing religious or ethnic grouping as a war tactic. As the Trial Chamber of the ICTR in the Trial of Jean-Paul Akayesu found, there was

> sufficient credible evidence to establish beyond a reasonable doubt that during the events of 1994, Tutsi girls and women were subjected to sexual violence, beaten and killed on or near the bureau communal premises, as well as elsewhere in the commune of Taba. Witness H, Witness JJ, Witness OO, and Witness NN all testified that they themselves were raped, and all, with the exception of Witness OO, testified that they witnessed other girls and women being raped. Witness J, Witness KK and Witness PP also testified that they witnessed other

[15] Committee on Economic, Social and Cultural Rights, General Comment No. 5, *Persons with Disabilities* (Eleventh Session, 1994) UN Doc. E/C.12/1994/13 (adopted) 25 November, 1994, para 19.

[16] International Convention on the Elimination of All Forms of Discrimination against Women, New York, 18 December 1979 United Nations, *Treaty Series*, vol. 1249, p. 13.

[17] Article 1, Convention on the Elimination of All forms of Discrimination against Women (1979). As has been discussed in earlier chapters, the scope of international human rights law has expanded to include violations of rights conducted by individuals in the private 'realm'. See discussion in chapter 1 above and the cases discussed in chapter 1.

[18] General Assembly Resolution 48/104 of 20 December 1993.

[19] Optional Protocol to the Convention on the Elimination of All Forms of Discrimination against Women, New York, 6 October 1999 UN Doc. A/RES/54/4.

[20] Human Rights Watch, 'Seeking Justice, The Prosecution of Sexual Violence in the Congo War' www.hrw.org/en/reports/2005/03/06/seeking-justice-0 <last visited 15 March 2009>.

girls and women being raped in the commune of Taba. Hundreds of Tutsi, mostly women and children, sought refuge at the bureau communal during this period and many rapes took place on or near the premises of the bureau communal – Witness JJ was taken by Interahamwe from the refuge site near the bureau communal to a nearby forest area and raped there. She testified that this happened often to other young girls and women at the refuge site. Witness JJ was also raped repeatedly on two separate occasions in the cultural center on the premises of the bureau communal, once in a group of fifteen girls and women and once in a group of ten girls and women. Witness KK saw women and girls being selected and taken by the Interahamwe to the cultural center to be raped. Witness H saw women being raped outside the compound of the bureau communal, and Witness NN saw two Interahamwes take a woman and rape her between the bureau communal and the cultural center. Witness OO was taken from the bureau communal and raped in a nearby field. Witness PP saw three women being raped at Kinihira, the killing site near the bureau communal, and Witness NN found her younger sister, dying, after she had been raped at the bureau communal. Many other instances of rape in Taba outside the bureau communal – in fields, on the road, and in or just outside houses – were described by Witness J, Witness H, Witness OO, Witness KK, Witness NN and Witness PP. Witness KK and Witness PP also described other acts of sexual violence which took place on or near the premises of the bureau communal – the forced undressing and public humiliation of girls and women. The Chamber notes that much of the sexual violence took place in front of large numbers of people, and that all of it was directed against Tutsi women.[21]

Furthermore, the Human Rights Committee in its General Comment No. 28 stated that '[w]omen are particularly vulnerable in times of internal or international armed conflicts. States parties should inform the Committee of all measures taken during these situations to protect women from rape, abduction and other forms of gender-based violence'.[22] This has been echoed in the Committee on the Elimination of Discrimination Against Women's General Recommendation on violence against women, which states that, '[w]ars, armed conflicts and the occupation of territories often lead to increased prostitution, trafficking in women and sexual assault of women, which require specific protective and punitive measures'.[23] Article 8(2)(b)(xxii) of the Rome Statute further highlights the specific impact of armed conflict on women, establishing that '[c]ommitting rape, sexual slavery, enforced prostitution, forced pregnancy, as defined in article 7, paragraph 2 (f), enforced sterilization, or any other form of sexual violence also constituting a grave breach of the Geneva Conventions' amount to war crimes.[24] The ICRC has also commissioned a number of reports into the impact of armed conflict on women.[25]

[21] See *Prosecutor* v. *Jean-Paul Akayesu*, Judgment Decision of 2 September 1998, Trial Chamber, Case No. (ICTR-96-4-T), para 449. http://69.94.11.53/default.htm <last visited 7 February 2009>.
[22] General Comment No. 28: *Equality of rights between men and women (article 3): 29/03/2000.* CCPR/C/21/Rev.1/Add.10, General Comment No. 28, para 8.
[23] CEDAW General Recommendation 19 on Violence against women, www.un.org/womenwatch/daw/cedaw/recommendations/recomm.htm#recom19 <last visited 17 February 2009>, para 16.
[24] Rome Statute of the International Criminal Court, UN Doc. A/CONF.183/9.
[25] Women Facing War, ICRC Study on the Impact of Armed Conflict on Women, www.icrc.org/Web/eng/siteeng0.nsf/htmlall/p0798 <last visited 16 February 2009>.

3 COMBATING DISCRIMINATION AGAINST WOMEN AND THE INTERNATIONAL HUMAN RIGHTS MOVEMENT

Attempts to combat discrimination against women and to establish *de jure* and *de facto* equality have a substantial history. As we have noted in this book, the norm of equality and non-discrimination, especially gender-based equality and non-discrimination represents the core of the modern human rights regime.[26] The international bill of rights is established on the principle of non-discrimination between men and women. The UDHR and the International Covenants contain various provision confirming gender equality and non-discrimination.[27] As we considered in earlier chapters, gender equality as a commitment is evident in the provisions of all regional human rights treaties.[28] By virtue of Article 1 of the ECHR, States parties undertake to 'secure to everyone' the rights contained in the Convention. According to Article 14:

> The enjoyment of the rights and freedoms set forth in this Convention shall be secured without discrimination on any ground such as sex . . .

The guarantees on non-discrimination in ECHR are further strengthened by Protocol 12.[29] Protocol 12 extends beyond the rights provided in the Convention to 'any right set forth by law'.[30] Such an extension is clearly to the benefit of disadvantaged groups, such as women, who have suffered from various discriminatory norms, and practices which are not necessarily covered by the rights set forth in ECHR itself.

The African and American regional human rights systems also prohibit discrimination *inter alia* on grounds of sex. In 1994, the General Assembly of the OAS adopted the Inter-American Convention on the Prevention, Punishment and Eradication of Violence Against Women at Belém do Pará.[31] According to the Preamble of the Convention, 'violence against women pervades every sector of society regardless of class, race or ethnic group, income, culture, level of education, age or religion and strikes at its very foundations'. The Convention prohibits physical, sexual and psychological violence against women, which explicitly includes violence in the home (Article 2). The Convention provides a number of rights including the right to life, liberty, integrity, fair trial, association, religion, legal protection and freedom from torture (Article 4). The Convention contains an undertaking on the part of States which includes to do more than merely investigating, prosecuting and punishing violence against women. In line with the Women's Convention, there is an undertaking to modify social and cultural patterns of conduct of men and women to counteract prejudices and customs based on the inferiority of women and stereotyping of roles (Article 8). The illegality and unacceptability of discrimination on the basis of sex is now regarded a firmly accepted principle of general international law, and applies to all States as well as to

---

[26] See above Part II.

[27] See above Part II and III.

[28] See above chapters 7–11.

[29] Protocol No. 12 to the Convention for the Protection of Human Rights and Fundamental Freedoms ETS No. 177; (Opened for Signature, Rome Date: 04/11/00). See above chapter 7.

[30] Article 1, Protocol 12 provides as follows: 'The enjoyment of any right set forth by law shall be secured without discrimination on any ground such as sex, race, colour, language, religion, political or other opinion, national or social origin, association with a national minority, property, birth or other status.'

[31] Signed 9 June 1994. Entered into force 3 March 1995. 33 I.L.M. (1994) 1534. See above chapter 9.

international organisations. The AU Protocol to the African Charter on Human and Peoples' Rights on the Rights of Women in Africa,[32] came into force on 26 November 2005 after Togo became the 15th State to ratify the Protocol. Importantly, Article 2(2) of the Protocol states that:

> States Parties shall commit themselves to modify the social and cultural patterns of conduct of women and men through public education, information, education and communication strategies, with a view to achieving the elimination of harmful cultural and traditional practices and all other practices which are based on the idea of the inferiority or the superiority of either of the sexes, or on stereotyped roles for women and men.

This provision echoes Article 5(a) of Women's Convention. However, unlike the Women's Convention, the African Protocol contains a provision dealing specifically with 'the rights to life, integrity and security of the person'.[33] This provision provides that:

> Article 4.
> 2. States Parties shall take appropriate and effective measures to:
> (a) enact and enforce laws to prohibit all forms of violence against women including unwanted or forced sex whether the violence takes place in private or public;
> (b) adopt such other legislative, administrative, social and economic measures as may be necessary to ensure the prevention, punishment and eradication of all forms of violence against women;
> (c) identify the causes and consequences of violence against women and take appropriate measures to prevent and eliminate such violence;
> (d) actively promote peace education through curricula and social communication in order to eradicate elements in traditional and cultural beliefs, practices and stereotypes which legitimise and exacerbate the persistence and tolerance of violence against women;
> (e) punish the perpetrators of violence against women and implement programmes for the rehabilitation of women victims;
> (f) establish mechanisms and accessible services for effective information, rehabilitation and reparation for victims of violence against women;
> (g) prevent and condemn trafficking in women, prosecute the perpetrators of such trafficking and protect those women most at risk;
> (h) prohibit all medical or scientific experiments on women without their informed consent;
> (i) provide adequate budgetary and other resources for the implementation and monitoring of actions aimed at preventing and eradicating violence against women;
> (j) ensure that, in those countries where the death penalty still exists, not to carry out death sentences on pregnant or nursing women;
> (k) ensure that women and men enjoy equal rights in terms of access to refugee status determination procedures and that women refugees are accorded the full protection and benefits guaranteed under international refugee law, including their own identity and other documents.

---

[32] Adopted on the 11 July 2003. *Protocol to the African Charter on Human and Peoples Rights on the Rights of Women in Africa*, Maputo, 13 September 2000 OAU Doc. CAB/LEG/66.6 (2000), Banda, above n.1.
[33] Article 4 of the Protocol on the Rights of Women in Africa.

The European Union, although per se not a human rights institution, has taken the unequivocal stance on non-discrimination of women and gender equality.[34] There is a growing concern on matters of sexual discrimination and violation of women's rights amongst member States of the Arab league. The South-Asian Association for Regional Co-operation (SAARC) has frequently raised the issue of violations of the rights of the children and women. The years 1991–2000 were designated as the 'SAARC Decade of Girl Child'.[35] In the light of the evidence presented some jurists have adopted the view that discrimination on the basis of gender forms part of customary international law, some even attaching a stature of a norm *jus cogens* to the prohibition of gender based discrimination.[36] In our study, we shall discover that while there is an overall consensus in prohibiting gender discrimination, there are also substantial disagreements on the various aspects of women's positions in particular societies and States. Hence, a more cautious and realistic approach is recommended.

4 THE ROLE OF THE UNITED NATIONS

The United Nations Charter contains a number of references providing for gender equality and non-discrimination. According to Article 1(3) of the Charter one of the purposes of the United Nations is:

> [T]o achieve international co-operation in solving international problems of an economic, social, cultural, or humanitarian character, and in promoting and encouraging respect for human rights and for fundamental freedoms for all without distinction as to . . . sex.

Soon after the establishment of the United Nations, the United Nations' Economic and Social Council, in accordance with Article 68 of the Charter, set up a Commission on the Status of Women (CSW). As we have noted, CSW is one of the nine ECOSOC Functional Commissions.[37] The CSW was established as a functional commission of the ECOSOC to

---

[34] See e.g. Articles 2, 3, 13, 137 and 141 Treaty establishing the European Community as well as the draft EU Constitution; Council Directive 75/117/EEC of 10 February 1975 on the approximation of the laws of the Member States relating to the application of the principle of equal pay for men and women; Council Directive 76/207/EEC of 9 February 1976 on the implementation of the principle of equal treatment for men and women as regards access to employment, vocational training and promotion, and working conditions; Council Directive 97/80/EC of 15 December 1997 on the burden of proof in cases of discrimination based on sex. See also the Community Framework Strategy on Gender Equality (2001–2005) COM(2000)335 Final Council Regulation 2836/98/EC on *Integrating of Gender Issues in Development Co-Operation*. Also see the proposed new Directive amending Equal Treatment Directive 1976.

[35] See Rehman, 'Women's Rights: An International Law Perspective' in Mehdi and Shaheed (eds), *Women's Law in Legal Education and Practice: North-South Co-operation* (New Social Science Monograph, 1997) pp. 106–128 at p. 117; Ahsan, *SAARC: A Perspective* (University of California Press, 1992).

[36] Ali and Rehman, 'Freedom of Religion versus Equality in International Human Rights Law: Conflicting Norms or Hierarchical Human Rights? (A Case Study of Pakistan)' 21 *Nordic Journal of Human Rights* (2003) 404; also see note Brownlie's omission of gender-based discrimination in his analysis of *jus cogens*, Brownlie, *Principles of Public International Law* (Oxford University Press, 2008) at p. 511; For elaboration of the concept see above chapter 2.

[37] www.un.org/womenwatch/daw/csw/index.html <last visited 23 January 2009>.

prepare recommendations and reports for the Council on promoting women's rights in political, economic, civil, social and educational fields.[38] The Commission also makes recommendations to the Council on urgent problems requiring immediate attention in the field of women's rights. The object of the Commission is to promote the implementation of the principle that men and women shall have equal rights. Its mandate was expanded in 1987 by the Council in its resolution 1987/22. Following the 1995 Fourth World Conference on Women, the General Assembly mandated the Commission to integrate into its work programme a follow-up process to the Conference, in which the Commission should play a significant role, regularly reviewing the critical areas of concern in the Platform for Action. ECOSOC Resolution 1996/6 additionally altered the terms of reference of CSW by broadening its mandate to include 'emerging issues, trends and new approaches to issues affecting equality between women and men'.

The Commission, which initially began with 15 members, now consists of 45 members elected by the Economic and Social Council for a period of four years. Members, who are appointed by governments, are elected on the following basis: 13 from African States; 11 from Asian States; four from Eastern European States; nine from Latin American and Caribbean States; and eight from Western European and other States. The Commission meets normally on an annual basis for a period of eight working days.

The status of the members of the CSW resembled that of the former Commission on Human Rights (in the sense that members act as representatives of States rather than in their personal capacity) and as in the case of the Human Rights Commission the course of the proceedings and their outcome reflected the governmental stance on human rights issues.[39] Unlike the former Human Rights Commission, the CSW has not been able to develop its role much further than promotional, educational and standard-setting activities. Indeed, for sometime the future of the CSW remained under threat and there has been a pronounced resistance to the idea of expanding the scope and authority of CSW to receive and consider petitions similar in nature to those received under ECOSOC 1503 procedure. The specificity of the work of CSW, with an exclusive focus of women's human rights also generated some concern, and as we shall notice in due course there have been attempts to mainstream gender equality.

Notwithstanding its limitations the CSW should be accredited and commended for its contribution to establishing new standard-setting mechanisms. A number of international conventions were formulated under the sponsorship of CSW including the 1952 Convention on the Political Rights of Women,[40] the 1957 Convention on the Nationality of Married Women[41] and the 1962 Convention on Consent to Marriage, Minimum Age for Marriage and Registration of Marriages.[42] The most significant achievement of the Commission remains its role in the drafting of the Convention on the Elimination of All Forms of Discrimination Against Women (1979).[43]

---

[38] By its Resolution 11(II) of 21 June 1946.
[39] See ECOSOC Res. E/1979/36; Davidson, *Human Rights* (Open University Press, 1993).
[40] 193 U.N.T.S. 135, entered into force 7 July 1954.
[41] 309 U.N.T.S. 65, entered into force 11 August 1958.
[42] 521 U.N.T.S. 231, entered into force 9 December 1964. For a consideration of these instruments see Galey, 'Promoting Non-Discrimination against Women: The United Nations Commission on the Status of Women' 23 *International Studies Quarterly* (1979) 273.
[43] New York, 18 December 1979 United Nations, *Treaty Series*, vol. 1249, p. 13.

5 THE CONVENTION ON THE ELIMINATION OF ALL FORMS OF DISCRIMINATION AGAINST WOMEN

The Convention on the Elimination of All Forms of Discrimination Against Women (hereafter the Women's Convention) was adopted by the General Assembly of the United Nations on 18 December 1979 and came into force on 3 September 1981. Like the Race Convention and the Convention against Torture, the Women's Convention was also preceded by a United Nations General Assembly Declaration.[44] The Declaration on the Elimination of All Forms of Discrimination against Women was adopted in 1967.[45] The outcome of years of discussion, debates and ultimate compromises, the Convention asserts many of the fundamental rights of women. It constitutes a comprehensive attempt at establishing universal standards on the rights of women. The Convention is one of the widely ratified human rights treaties, and can be regarded as a milestone towards reaching the goal of standard-setting for gender-based equality.

In the preamble to the Convention, the State parties acknowledge the fact that 'extensive discrimination against women continues to exist'.[46] The preamble also acknowledges the detrimental effect that discrimination has on the development of nations, thereby linking gender equality with development. The family, as well as the society, is hampered by the denial of women's full and adequate participation in the political, economic, social, legal and cultural activities. Significantly, within the preamble there is the recognition of a link between gender-based discrimination and exploitation for political and economic goals. Article 1, following the definition as provided in the Convention on Elimination of All Forms of Racial Discrimination,[47] defines discrimination as:

> any distinction, exclusion or restriction made on the basis of sex which has the effect or purpose of impairing or nullifying the recognition, enjoyment or exercise by women, irrespective of their marital status, on a basis of equality of men and women, of human rights and fundamental freedoms in the political, economic, social, cultural, civil or any other field.

The definition in the Convention differs from the Race Convention in that firstly, it omits any reference to the term 'preference'. Secondly, the Women's Convention appears to have a wider sphere of influence, applying in the 'political, economic, social, cultural, civil or any other field' in comparison to the 'political, economic, social, cultural or any other field of public life' as stated in Article 1 of the Race Convention. This wider sphere includes the eradication of distinctions and discrimination in private life. CEDAW (Committee on the Elimination of Discrimination Against Women) has in its General Recommendation 19 reminded States parties to include information on steps taken to eliminate gender-based violence in their reports, violence against women coming within the Convention's definition of discrimination, since such violence is directed at women and affects women disproportionately.[48]

---

[44] Declaration on the Elimination of All Forms of Racial Discrimination – GA Res. 1904(XVIII) 20 November 1963, Declaration Against Torture – GA Res. 3452(XXX) 9 December 1975.

[45] General Assembly Resolution 2263(XXII) of 7 November 1967. However, in the case of the Race Convention the time-span between the adoption of GA Resolution and a binding treaty was shorter as compared to the Women's convention.

[46] See Preamble to the Convention.

[47] See Article 1 of the Convention on the Elimination of All Forms of Racial Discrimination (1965); see above chapter 12.

[48] CEDAW General Recommendation No. 19 www.un.org/womenwatch/daw/cedaw/recommendations/recomm.htm#recom19 <last visited 17 February 2009>, para 6. UN Doc. HRI/GEN/I/Rev.5, at p. 216.

(i) Issues of discrimination and of *de facto* equality

Article 2 of the Women's Convention represents what has been aptly described as the 'core of the Convention'.[49] According to this article, States parties condemn discrimination against women in all its forms and agree to eliminate discrimination. The agreement is to eliminate discrimination 'by all appropriate means and without delay'. The sub-sections of Article 2 spell out details of this undertaking. According to Article 2(a), States parties undertake to:

> embody the principle of the equality of men and women in their national constitutions or other appropriate legislation if not yet incorporated therein and to ensure, through law and other appropriate means, the practical realization of this principle.

In accordance with Article 2(b), States parties are under an obligation to 'adopt appropriate legislative and other measures, including sanctions where appropriate, prohibiting all discrimination against women' and Article 2(c) obliges States to 'establish legal protection of the rights of women on an equal basis with men and to ensure through competent national tribunals and other public institutions the effective protection of women against any act of discrimination'. The underlying commitment of Article 2(d)–(g) is to prevent discrimination against women, to ensure the abolition of all discriminatory law, regulations, customs and practices.[50] Amongst the various subsections of the Article, Article 2(e) is worth a specific mention. The Article represents an undertaking on the part of the parties to take 'all appropriate measures to eliminate discrimination against women by any person, organization or enterprise'. In adopting a holistic approach and condemning discrimination by any person or organisation, this provision further reinforces the reach of the Convention beyond the public sphere.

The provisions of Article 2 are particularly valuable in identifying and establishing a regime of non-discrimination and gender equality. As we shall see in due course, CEDAW has started dealing with individual communications under the Optional Protocol to the Convention. In its future analysis and application of Article 2, the Committee can usefully benefit from related jurisprudence of the ICCPR and ECHR. The discussion that follows therefore considers case-law emerging from other human rights treaty provisions.

In *Shirin Aumeeruddy-Cziffra and 19 other Mauritian women* v. *Mauritius*,[51] Aumeerddy-Cziffra and 19 women brought forward a claim against Mauritius under the first optional protocol to ICCPR. These women complained that two pieces of legislation on immigration and deportation resulted in gender discrimination which violated the right to found a family and home and removed protection of courts of law breaching Article 2(1), 3, 17, 23, 25 and 26 of ICCPR. To further their complaints as violating norms of gender equality on non-discrimination, the authors argued that, under the new laws:

---

[49] Nordenfield UN Doc. CEDAW/C/SR.35; UN Doc. A/39/45 Sec. 190.
[50] See Article 2(f).
[51] *Shirin Aumeeruddy-Cziffra and 19 other Mauritian women* v. *Mauritius*, Communication No. 35/1978 (9 April 1981), UN Doc. CCPR/C/OP/1 at 67 (1984).

> alien husbands of Mauritian women lost their residence status in Mauritius and must now apply for a 'resident permit' which may be refused or removed at any time by the Minister of Interior. These new laws, however, do not affect the status of alien women married to Mauritian husbands who retain their legal right to residence in the country. The authors further contend that under the new laws alien husband of Mauritian woman may be deported under a ministerial order which is not subject to Judicial Review.[52]

The Committee while accepting that Mauritius could justifiably place restrictions on entry and expulsion of aliens, nevertheless, found the pieces of legislation as discriminatory since they subjected foreign spouses of Mauritian women to the restriction, but not foreign spouses of Mauritian men.[53] The issue of gender discrimination was similarly raised in *Lovelace* v. *Canada*.[54] After finding violations of Article 27, the Committee did not feel the need to examine the subject of sex discrimination,[55] although in his individual opinion Mr. Bouziri took the view that Canadian legislation discriminated against Indian women.[56]

Article 3 represents a substantial obligation on the State parties to undertake all appropriate measures to 'ensure the full development and advancement of women'. As an important provision, Article 3 has frequently been the subject of analysis of CEDAW in State reports. CEDAW in its review of reports has been critical of many States for failing to ensure compliance with this Article. In its Concluding Observations on the Report submitted by Cameroon, the Committee notes with concern that:

> inadequate allocation of resources for the advancement of women, with the resultant incomplete execution of programmes and projects, seriously jeopardizes the improvement of women's living conditions.[57]

Article 4 of the Convention sanctions policies of affirmative action or reverse discrimination. According to this article, temporary measures aimed at accelerating *de facto* equality are not to be regarded as discriminatory. In its General Recommendation No. 5, the Committee notes that:

---

[52] Ibid. para 1.2.

[53] Ibid. para 9.2(b)2(ii)3.

[54] *Sandra Lovelace* v. *Canada*, Communication No. 24/1977 (30 July 1981), UN Doc. CCPR/C/OP/1 at 83 (1984). For commentaries see Bayefsky, 'The Human Rights Committee and the Case of Sandra Lovelace' 20 *CYBIL* (1982) 244; McGoldrick, 'Canadian Indians, Cultural Rights and the Human Rights Committee' 40 *ICLQ* (1991) 658; also see *Jeanette Lavell* case (Canada), *A-G of Canada* v. *Jeanette Lavelle, Richard Isaac* et al. v. *Yvonne Bedard (1974), SCR 1349*; and *Martinez* case (United States), *Santa Clara Pueblo* v. *Martinez* 436 US 49 (1978) raising similar issues.

[55] Paras 13.2–19.

[56] Ibid. p. 175. See also Mullally, 'The UN, Minority Rights and Gender Equality: Setting Limits to Collective Claims' 14 *International Journal on Minority and Group Rights* (2007) 263.

[57] Concluding Observations (Comments) of the Committee on the Elimination of All Forms of Discrimination Against Women: Cameroon 26/06/2000; A/55/38; para 47; Concluding Observations (Comments) of the Committee on the Elimination of All Forms of Discrimination Against Women: India 01/02/2000; A/55/38 para 56.

the reports, the introductory remarks and the replies by States parties reveal that while significant progress has been achieved in regard to repealing or modifying discriminatory laws, there is still a need for action to be taken to implement fully the Convention by introducing measures to promote *de facto* equality between men and women.... [The Committee] Recommends that States Parties make more use of temporary special measures such as positive action, preferential treatment or quota systems to advance women's integration into education, the economy, politics and employment.[58]

This was again reiterated in a further General Recommendation on Temporary Special Measures.[59] However, these extraordinary steps to remedy past discrimination must not result in establishing separate standards and must be discontinued 'when the objectives of equality of opportunity and treatment have been achieved'. A number of States have adopted specific positions on Article 4(1). Several developing States, including Bangladesh, India and Pakistan, have a quota system for women in the fields, *inter alia*, of employment and higher education. Such initiatives representing affirmative action have been applauded by CEDAW in its consideration of State reports.[60] At the same time, the subject of affirmative action is a controversial one. Article 4 is similar in nature and scope to Article 1(4) and 2(2) of the Convention on the Elimination of Racial Discrimination (save that it applies to women) and the debates arising out of its provisions have been similarly divisive.[61]

(ii) Modifying social and cultural patterns to eliminate practices based on ideas of inferiority

Societal patterns have frequently led to ideas of inferiority of women – many of the practices noted in the introductory section of this chapter represent stereotypical attitudes established in male-dominated patriarchal societies. One of the principal objectives of the Women's Convention is to change perceptions and traditional (usually negative) image of women in many cultures and tradition, and in this regard Article 5(a) represents a significant commitment. According to the provisions of Article 5(a) States parties have to undertake 'all appropriate measures':

[To] modify the social and cultural patterns of conduct of men and women, with a view to achieving the elimination of prejudices and other customary and all other practices which are based on the idea of inferiority or the superiority of either of the sexes or on stereotyped roles for men and women.

---

[58] CEDAW General Recommendation No. 5 (seventh session, 1988), Temporary Special Measures www.un.org/womenwatch/daw/cedaw/recommendations/recomm.htm#recom5 <last visited 17 February 2009>.

[59] CEDAW General Recommendation No. 25 (13th session, 2004), Article 4(1) Temporary Special Measures www2.ohchr.org/english/bodies/cedaw/comments.htm <last visited 17 February 2009>.

[60] Concluding Observations (Comments) of the Committee on the Elimination of All Forms of Discrimination Against Women: Bangladesh 24/07/1997; A/52/38/Rev.1 para 416; Concluding Observations (Comments) of the Committee on the Elimination of All Forms of Discrimination Against Women: India 01/02/2000; A/55/38 para 32.

[61] See above chapter 12.

However, there is no specification as to what those 'appropriate measures' could amount to. Some elaboration has been provided by CEDAW in its General Recommendation No. 19 whereby the Committee observes that traditional attitudes representing stereotyped roles for men and women perpetuate practices of violence or coercion, forced marriages, dowry deaths and female circumcision.[62] The Committee goes on to observe that:

> Such prejudices and practices may justify gender-based violence as a form of protection or control of women. The effect of such violence on the physical and mental integrity of women is to deprive them the equal enjoyment, exercise and knowledge of human rights and fundamental freedoms. While this comment addresses mainly actual or threatened violence the underlying consequences of these forms of gender-based violence help to maintain women in subordinate roles and contribute to the low level of political participation and to their lower level of education, skills and work opportunities ... These attitudes also contribute to propagation of pornography and the depiction and other commercial exploitation of women as sexual objects, rather than as individuals.[63]

A number of States have been the object of criticism by CEDAW for their failure to comply with Article 5 or entering reservations to the Article. Thus, for instance, the Republic of Ireland has been criticised for the provisions of Article 41.2 of the Irish Constitution, which according to the Committee 'reflect a stereotypical view of the role of women in the home and as mothers'.[64] India, is one of the States which has made a declaration in relation to Article 5(a), representing tensions, and male hegemony within the society.[65] Other States entering reservations to Article 5(a) are Niger,[66] Malaysia[67] and New Zealand–Cook Islands.[68] In addition to the practices of female genital mutilation and polygamous marriages, the Committee has expressed its concern over a range of approaches. There are, however, practices over which it has not been possible to formulate any firms views. It is debatable, for example, whether such practices as wearing of headscarves as compulsory dress code to ensure women's modesty contravenes the provisions of this Article. Conversely, it remains highly problematic, the approach adopted in several States whereby there is a banning of headscarves for women or other religious symbolism in educational institutions or other public institutions.[69] In the *Leyla Sahin* case, the European Court of Human Rights did not

---

[62] UN Doc. HRI/Gen 1/Rev. 1, para 11.

[63] Ibid. paras 11 and 12.

[64] Concluding Observations of the Committee on the Elimination of Discrimination Against Women: Ireland. CEDAW/C/IRL/CO/4-5 (Concluding Observations/Comments) (22 July 2005), para 24.

[65] The Indian declaration notes: 'With regard to articles 5(a) ... of the Convention on the Elimination of All Forms of Discrimination Against Women, the Government of the Republic of India declares that it shall abide by and ensure these provisions in conformity with its policy of non-interference in the personal affairs of any Community without its initiative and consent.'

[66] Niger's reservation states that 'the Government of the Republic of Niger expresses reservations with regard to the modification of social and cultural pattern of conduct of men and women'.

[67] Malaysia's reservation is based upon and subject to the *Shariah* principles on division of inherited property.

[68] The Cook Island reserve the right not to apply Article 2(f) and Article 5(a) to the extent that customs governing the inheritance of certain Cook Islands chief titles may be inconsistent with those provisions.

[69] See the Turkish Constitutional Court's decision invalidating a bylaw of the Institution of Higher education which had permitted exception of 'modern clothing' in the form of wearing of headscarves. See Constitutional Court of Turkey Decision 1989/652. This was reaffirmed by the Turkish Constitutional Court on 5 June 2008, in its decision vetoing legislation permitting female university students to wear the headscarf. In June 2008, Moroccan woman married to a French national and residing in Paris was refused French nationality on the basis of her 'insufficient assimilation' into France. See 'France rejects Muslim woman over radical practice of Islam' 12 July 2008, www.guardian.co.uk/world/2008/jul/12/france.islam <last visited 3 February 2009>.

find a violation of Article 9 of the European Convention of Human Rights, when the Turkish State had denied access to university facilities to a female medical student while wearing the *hijab* (the headscarf) in accordance with her religious convictions.[70] In a further disappointing stance, the United Kingdom's House of Lords held that insistence on wearing a *jilbab* (use of enhanced covering for women) was neither a right recognised under Article 9 of the ECHR, nor was this a pre-requisite for establishing an Islamic right to identity.[71] The role and stance which is increasingly being adopted by overzealous courts raise tensions; the potential for conflict remains over the right to manifest one's religious beliefs *vis-à-vis* Article 5 of the Woman's Convention.

Article 6 considers the important issue of female sexual slavery and the suppression of trafficking in women. In condemning such activities it requires States parties to take all appropriate steps to end trafficking in women and exploitation and prostitution of women. In its General Recommendation 19, CEDAW has noted that poverty and unemployment, as well as armed conflicts, encourage such activities as trafficking in women, and prostitution. The Committee has also expressed concern at the newer forms of exploitation: sex tourism, exploitation of migrant women workers and marriages of women from poorer

---

[70] The case of *Leyla Şahin* v. *Turkey* (2007) 44 E.H.R.R. 5. The European Court of Human Rights noted: 'In democratic societies, in which several religions coexist within one and the same population, it may be necessary to place restrictions on freedom to manifest one's religion or belief in order to reconcile the interests of the various groups and ensure that everyone's beliefs are respected' (see *Kokkinakis*, cited above, p. 18, para 33). This follows both from paragraph 2 of Article 9 and the State's positive obligation under Article 1 of the Convention to secure to everyone within its jurisdiction the rights and freedoms defined therein. The Court has frequently emphasised the State's role as the neutral and impartial organiser of the exercise of various religions, faiths and beliefs, and stated that this role is conducive to public order, religious harmony and tolerance in a democratic society. It also considers that the State's duty of neutrality and impartiality is incompatible with any power on the State's part to assess the legitimacy of religious beliefs or the ways in which those beliefs are expressed (see *Manoussakis and others* v. *Greece* (1997) 23 E.H.R.R. 387 para 47; *Hasan and Chaush* v. *Bulgaria* (2002) 34 E.H.R.R. 55 para 78; *Refah Partisi (the Welfare Party) and others* v. *Turkey* (2002) 35 E.H.R.R. 3 para 81 and that it requires the State to ensure mutual tolerance between opposing groups (see *United Communist Party of Turkey and others* v. *Turkey* (1998) 26 E.H.R.R. 121 para 57). Accordingly, the role of the authorities in such circumstances is not to remove the cause of tension by eliminating pluralism, but to ensure that the competing groups tolerate each other (see *Serif* v. *Greece* (2001) 31 E.H.R.R. 20, para 53). Pluralism, tolerance and broadmindedness are hallmarks of a 'democratic society'. Although individual interests must on occasion be subordinated to those of a group, democracy does not simply mean that the views of a majority must always prevail: a balance must be achieved which ensures the fair and proper treatment of people from minorities and avoids any abuse of a dominant position (see, *mutatis mutandis*, *Young, James and Webster* v. *UK* (1982) 4 E.H.R.R. 38 para 63, and *Chassagnou and others* v. *France* (2000) 29 E.H.R.R. 615 para 112). Pluralism and democracy must also be based on dialogue and a spirit of compromise necessarily entailing various concessions on the part of individuals or groups of individuals which are justified in order to maintain and promote the ideals and values of a democratic society (see, *mutatis mutandis*, *the United Communist Party of Turkey and others*, cited above, pp. 21–22, para 45, and *Refah Partisi (the Welfare Party) and others*, cited above para 99). Where these 'rights and freedoms' are themselves among those guaranteed by the Convention or its Protocols, it must be accepted that the need to protect them may lead States to restrict other rights or freedoms likewise set forth in the Convention. It is precisely this constant search for a balance between the fundamental rights of each individual which constitutes the foundation of a 'democratic society' (see *Chassagnou and Others*, cited above, para 113. Ibid. paras 106–108. For a fuller discussion of these issues see McGoldrick, *Human Rights and Religion: The Islamic Headscarf Debate in Europe* (Hart, 2006); Marshall, 'Conditions for Freedom?: European Human Rights Law and the Islamic Headscarf Debate' 30 *HRQ* (2008) 631.

[71] *R. (on the application of Begum)* v. *Denbigh High School Governors*, [2006] H.R.L.R. 21; *R. (on the application of S.B)* v. *Headteacher and Governors of Denbigh High School*, [2005] H.R.L.R. 16; Clare Dyer, *Muslim Girl Loses fight over Jilbab*, 23 March 2006, available at http://education.guardian.co.uk/schools/story/0,,1737482,00.html <last visited 3 February 2009>; see also Blair, 'R (SB) v. Headteacher and Governors of Denbigh High School: Human Rights and Religious Dress in Schools', 17 *Child & Family L.Q.* (2005) 399; Rehman, 'Islam, "War on Terror" and the Future of Muslim Minorities in the United Kingdom: Dilemmas of Multi-Culturalism in the Aftermath of the London Bombings' 29 *HRQ* (2007) 831.

15

The rights of women

countries with foreign and wealthier men from developed States. In order to combat the evil of trafficking of women, the international community has adopted a number of specific international instruments. These include the Convention for the Suppression of the Traffic in Persons and of the Exploitation of the Prostitution of Others 1949,[72] the Protocol to Prevent, Suppress and Punish Trafficking in Persons, Especially Women and Children (supplementing the 2000 UN Convention Against Transnational Organized Crime),[73] the Council of Europe Convention on Action against Trafficking in Human Beings[74] and the Optional Protocol to the United Nations Convention on the Rights of the Child on the sale of children, child prostitution and child pornography.[75] Although frequently associated with and indeed resulting in prostitution, as the International Law Association (ILA) study establishes, trafficking in not confined to prostitution or to the sex industry.[76] In fact the practice is much wider covering such forms of exploitation as slavery, servitude and forced labour. The ILA study presents the worrying figures of hundreds of thousands of women and young children been trafficked all over the world – these practices are not confined to any one region or only to the developing world.[77]

(iii) Representation in public life and the issue of nationality

Article 7 of the Convention deals with the elimination of discrimination against women in the political and public life of the country. It attempts to ensure that women have a right to vote, and have a right to be elected to office with participatory rights in policy formulation, at all the governmental levels. It also attempts to ensure that women are able to participate in the activities of non-governmental organisations. Whilst a majority of States accord equality to women in public life, there remain unfortunate remnants of legislative enactments and administrative policies barring women from political participation at the governmental level. Examples of such discriminatory practices could be found in State laws excluding women from public offices,[78] exclusion from voting rights[79] and exclusion from

---

[72] Convention for the Suppression of the Traffic in Persons and of the Exploitation of the Prostitution of Others 96 U.N.T.S. 271, entered into force 25 July 1951.

[73] Protocol to Prevent, Suppress and Punish Trafficking in Persons, Especially Women and Children Adopted by Resolution A/RES/55/25 of 15 November 2000 at the 55th session of the General Assembly of the United Nations.

[74] Council of Europe Convention on Action against Trafficking in Human Beings CETS No. 197.

[75] Adopted by the General Assembly May 25 2000. GA. Res. 263, UN GAOR, 54 Sess., Supp. 49; UN Doc. A/Res/54/263.

[76] See the International Law Association, Committee on Feminism and International Law 'Women and Migration: Interim Report on Trafficking in Women' Rapporteur Annette Lansink, Berlin Conference 2004, pp. 242– 279.

[77] Ibid. at p. 248.

[78] Note the position of Kuwait. See also Kuwait's reservation to Article 25(b) of the ICCPR, which seeks to restrict the Covenant's right of citizens to vote and to be elected, making it subject to provisions in Kuwaiti law that bar women from voting and standing for office and severely limit the rights of naturalised citizens. The reservation asserts: 'the Government of Kuwait wishes to formulate a reservation with regard to article 25(b). The provisions of this paragraph conflict with the Kuwaiti electoral law, which restricts the right to stand and vote in elections to males. It further declares that the provisions of the article shall not apply to members of the armed forces or the police'. The text of Article 25(b) explicitly prohibits restriction of the right to vote and to be elected on the basis of discrimination prohibited in article 2 of the Covenant: every citizen shall have the right and the opportunity, without any of the distinctions mentioned in article 2 and without unreasonable restrictions: [. . .] b) To vote and to be elected at genuine periodic elections which shall be by universal and equal suffrage and shall be held by secret ballot, guaranteeing the free expression of the will of the electors [. . .].

[79] Note the position of Saudi Arabia.

religious courts.[80] This subject was recently raised by the Human Rights Committee in its analysis of the State Report from Kuwait. The Committee in its concluding comments expresses its concern that:

> in spite of constitutional provisions on equality, Kuwait's electoral laws continue to exclude entirely women from voting and being elected to public office. It notes with regret that the Amir's initiatives to remedy this situation were defeated in Parliament.[81]

CEDAW has shown concern on many occasions at the low levels of women in public offices and women in ministerial posts.[82] It has elaborated on the provisions of the Convention through its General Recommendation No. 23 (1997) on women in political and public life.[83] In this Recommendation, the Committee took the view that the obligations contained in Article 7 are not specific to those contained expressly in subparagraphs a, b and c, and extend to all aspects of public and political life. Therefore, according to the Committee a broad construction needs to be given to the meaning of 'public and private life'. The Committee also endorsed special provisions as contained in Article 4 of the Convention.[84]

In its consideration of Kazakhstan's initial report, the Committee expressed its concern at the very low representation of women in decision-making bodies including an 11 per cent representation in the National Parliament.[85] Such views on gender equality unfortunately continue to invoke the displeasure of States, leading some of them to place reservations to the Article, particularly in relation to the representation of women in armed forces and national security systems.[86]

According to Article 8, State parties are under an obligation to take all appropriate measures to ensure that women have the opportunity to represent their government at all international levels. In its General Recommendation on the Implementation of Article 8, the Committee notes that:

> States parties take further direct measures in accordance with article 4 of the Convention to ensure the full implementation of article 8 of the Convention and to ensure to women on equal terms with men and without any discrimination the opportunities to represent their Government at the international level and to participate in the work of international organizations.[87]

---

[80] Note the position of Israel.
[81] Concluding Observations (Comments) of the Human Rights Committee Kuwait. 19/07/2000 A/55/40, paras 452 407, at para 461.
[82] Concluding Observations (Comments) of the Committee on the Elimination of All Forms of Discrimination Against Women: Cameroon 26/06/2000; A/55/38; paras 56–57.
[83] CEDAW General Recommendation No. 23 Women in Public and Political Life (16th session, 1997) www.un.org/womenwatch/daw/cedaw/recommendations/recomm.htm#recom23 <last visited 17 February 2009>.
[84] Ibid. para 5.
[85] See the Initial Report of Kazakhstan CEDAW/C/KAZ/I, 490th, 491st and 497th meetings (18 and 23 January 2001), para 54. Such concern has been reiterated in the recent observations of the Committee, where the Committee states that 'while noting the proposal for quotas aimed at having no less than 30 percent of women in political institutions, which the delegation states was included in the draft law on equal rights and equal opportunities, the Committee is concerned about the continuing underrepresentation of women in public and political life and in decision-making positions, including in Parliament, local representative bodies, the executive bodies of the Government and local government, as well as in diplomacy' CEDAW/C/KAZ/CO/2 (2 February 2007), para 21.
[86] See UN website (appendix on further information on Reservations).
[87] CEDAW General Recommendation, No. 8 Implementation of Article 8. UN. Doc. A/43/38. www.un.org/womenwatch/daw/cedaw/recommendations/recomm.htm#recom8 <last visited 17 February 2009>.

15

The rights of women

Article 9 deals with the complex though highly important issue of nationality rights. The Article emphasises equal rights for women in acquiring, changing and retaining nationality. States parties are required to ensure that:

> neither marriage to an alien nor change of nationality by the husband during marriage shall automatically change the nationality of the wife, render her stateless or force upon her the nationality of the husband.[88]

Issues relating to nationality are vexed and controversial ones in general international law. Matters concerning nationality and citizenship have traditionally been seen as falling within the jurisdictional domain of sovereign States. International consensus is particularly thin when it comes to the capacity of women to change or retain their nationality and to pass it on to their children. It has, hence, not been surprising that the article has attracted reservations from a number of States. Several States continue to insist on granting the child the nationality of the father.[89] Iraq has placed reservations on Article 9(1) and (2) while Jordan, Morocco and Tunisia have reserved this position as regards Article 9(2).[90] On 4 January 2004, Egypt withdrew is long-standing reservation to Article 9(2).[91]

An analysis of the available State reports reveals a divergence of rationale behind the imposition of reservations, although the possible unifying thread amongst these reservations would appear to be the argument of preservation of family solidarity and cultural integrity. In relation to the inheritance of nationality, the arguments have little weight and indeed on occasions reflect a misconstruction of the principles of gender equality.[92] In its General Recommendation 21, CEDAW has pointed out that adult women – in equality with men – should be able to change their nationalities and 'nationality should not be arbitrarily removed because of marriage or dissolution of marriage or because her husband or father changes his nationality'.[93]

(iv) Educational, employment and health rights

Women frequently suffer from inequality of opportunities in education and vocational and professional training. Article 10 of the Convention attempts to eradicate such discrimination and inequality. Article 11 deals with elimination of discrimination at the workplace

---

[88] Article 9(1).

[89] See *Unity Dow* v. *The Attorney General of Botswana*, CA. Civil Appeal No. 4/91 Appeal Court. Case also considered in chapter 10 above.

[90] See further www.law.emory.edu/ifl/legal/iraq.htm <last visited 20 November 2008>; see the UNDP, *Arab Human Development Report* (2005) p. 181; http://wrn.crtda.org.lb/en/Country+Analysis:+Morocco <last visited 3 February 2009>.

[91] See www2.ohchr.org/english/bodies/ratification/docs/EgyptArt9(2)CEDAW.pdf; http://66.102.9.104/search?q=cache:2gD26SztpOkJ:www2.ohchr.org/english/bodies/cedaw/docs/co/TunisiaCO27.pdf+tunisia+Article+9+reservations&hl=en&ct=clnk&cd=13&gl=uk <last visited 3 February 2009>.

[92] Egypt, for instance, had justified inheritance to father's nationality alone 'to prevent a child's acquisition of two nationalities, since this may be prejudicial to his future' but went on to plead that 'It is clear that the Child's acquisition of his father's nationality is the procedure most suitable for the child and that this does not infringe upon the principles of equality between men and women, since it is the custom for a woman to agree, on marrying an alien, that her children shall be of the father's nationality'. See UN Doc. CEDAW/SP/13Rev.Add 1, 18. See Arzt, 'The Application of International Human Rights Law in Islamic States' 12 *HRQ* (1990) 202 at p. 219.

[93] CEDAW General Recommendation No. 21 Equality in Marriage and Family Relations (13th session 1994), www.un.org/womenwatch/daw/cedaw/recommendations/recomm.htm#recom21 <last visited 17 February 2009> para 6.

and in the field of employment. The Article recognises the right to work as an inalienable right of all human beings.[94] States parties undertake to adopt all appropriate measures to ensure equal opportunities in employment and to provide a free choice of profession and employment. There is also an undertaking to provide equal remuneration, right to social security and a right to protection of health and to safety in working conditions. Right to employment also needs to take account of the factors which concern women; in this context Article 11(2) is of enormous value. The provisions of Article 11(2) are also noteworthy since they move away from the sameness/equal treatment approach and recognise the biological uniqueness of pregnancy.

According to Article 11(2), States undertake to prohibit dismissals on grounds *inter alia* of pregnancy.[95] Instead, the commitment is to introduce maternity leave with pay or comparable social benefits without loss of former employment, seniority or social allowances. There is also an undertaking to provide special protection to women during their pregnancies, and to encourage the provision of necessary supporting social services to enable family obligations to operate in conjunction with obligations of employment. The provisions of this Article are enormously beneficial to women the world over. In many regions, women are deprived of equal opportunities of employment. Women of child bearing ages are particularly at a disadvantage as employers are reluctant to offer employment opportunities or have been known to terminate employment when these women become pregnant. Discriminatory actions are witnessed in the developing, as well as the developed, world. It is equally unfortunate to note that financially stable States such as Singapore and notably, Australia, have maintained reservations to Article 11.[96] CEDAW, in its General Recommendation 19 has pointed to the fact that gender-specific violence, including sexual harassment at the workplace can have a substantial impairing effect on equality in employment.[97] In its General Recommendations 5 and 25, CEDAW recommends the usage of temporary mechanisms, *inter alia*, preferential treatment or quota system to enhance women's integration into such fields as employment.[98]

Article 12 of the Convention deals with the important subject of equality in healthcare, including family planning assistance. CEDAW has made a General Recommendation in pursuance of Article 12.[99] The right to health has also been a subject of a General Comment

---

[94] Article 11(1)(a).

[95] In this context it is important to note that in establishing a normative content of the right to work for women, the ICESCR Committee in its General Comment has noted 'Article 3 of the Covenant prescribes that States parties undertake to "ensure the equal right of men and women to the enjoyment of all economic, social and cultural rights". The Committee underlines the need for a comprehensive system of protection to combat gender discrimination and to ensure equal opportunities and treatment between men and women in relation to their right to work by ensuring equal pay for work of equal value. In particular, pregnancies must not constitute an obstacle to employment and should not constitute justification for loss of employment. Lastly, emphasis should be placed on the link between the fact that women often have less access to education than men and certain traditional cultures which compromise the opportunities for the employment and advancement of women'. The General Comment, the Committee on the Economic, Social and Cultural Rights, The Right to Work, General Comment No. 18 Adopted on 24 November 2005 E/C.12/GC/18 6 (6 February 2006), paras 6 and 7.

[96] This reservation was raised as a subject of concern. See CEDAW, 522nd meeting, 13 July 2001.

[97] CEDAW General Recommendation No. 19 Violence against Women (11th Session) 1992, www.un.org/womenwatch/daw/cedaw/recommendations/recomm.htm#recom19 <last visited 17 February 2009>, para 17.

[98] CEDAW General Recommendation No. 5 Temporary Special Measures (Seventh Session) 1988 www.un.org/womenwatch/daw/cedaw/recommendations/recomm.htm#recom5 <last visited 17 February 2009>; General Recommendation No. 25, Temporary Special Measures (13th Session) 2004, Article 4(1) www2.ohchr.org/english/bodies/cedaw/comments.htm <last visited 17 February 2009>, para 22.

[99] CEDAW, General Recommendation 24, Women and Health (Article 12) Doc A/54/38/Rev. 1, chapter 1 www.un.org/womenwatch/daw/cedaw/recommendations/recomm.htm#recom24 <last visited 17 February 2009>.

15

The rights of women

by the Committee on the ICESCR.[100] In its General Recommendation 24, CEDAW has urged States parties to report on their health legislation and policies for women.[101] They are also required to provide information on health conditions, conditions hazardous to the health of women and on related diseases.[102] The Committee has recommended that States should base healthcare policies affecting women with particular regard, *inter alia*, to biological, socio-economic and psychological factors.[103] In addition, in General Recommendations 14 and 15, CEDAW has invited States parties to include information relating to healthcare issues that specifically affect women in their individual State reports. This includes the measures taken in order to eliminate female genital mutilation and about the effects of HIV/AIDs on the situation of women.

The General Comment, made by the Committee on ICESCR, is a useful elaboration on women's health rights jurisprudence. The Committee notes:

> To eliminate discrimination against women, there is a need to develop and implement a comprehensive national strategy for promoting women's right to health throughout their life span. Such a strategy should include interventions aimed at the prevention and treatment of diseases affecting women, as well as policies to provide access to a full range of high quality and affordable health care, including sexual and reproductive services. A major goal should be reducing women's health risks, particularly lowering rates of maternal mortality and protecting women from domestic violence. The realization of women's right to health requires the removal of all barriers interfering with access to health services, education and information, including in the area of sexual and reproductive health. It is also important to undertake preventive, promotive and remedial action to shield women from the impact of harmful traditional cultural practices and norms that deny them their full reproductive rights.[104]

The ICESCR Committee's reference to reproductive services as well as equality in reproductive rights is a critical one, with the subject eventually gaining the recognition it deserves. Women, in many societies continue to be denied the right to make decisions as regards their reproductive activity. In many traditions, abortion is socially and morally unacceptable, even in instances where continued pregnancy poses serious threat to the life of the mother. In highlighting and exemplifying this problem, Christina Zampas and Jaime Gher make the point that '[a]t present, Chile, El Salvador and Nicaragua have legislation eliminating all exceptions to the countries' abortion prohibitions, even when a woman's life is at risk, thus giving women no recourse when their lives are imperilled during pregnancy'.[105] The International Conference on Population and Development held in Cairo (1994), as well as the Beijing, Fourth World UN Conference on Population and Development (1995) emphasised this right. The Human Rights Committee has called for repeal of harsh and restrictive abortion laws to prevent unwanted pregnancies and unsafe

---

[100] ICESCR General Comment 14, *The Right to Highest Attainable Standard of Health* (Article 12) General Comment No. 14 (11/08/00). (E/C.12/2000/4).
[101] See above n.99, para 9.
[102] Ibid. para 10.
[103] Para 12(a)–(c).
[104] See above n.100, para 21.
[105] Zampas and Gher, 'Abortion as a Human Right – International and Regional Standards' 8 *HRLR* (2008) 249 at p. 256.

abortions.[106] Furthermore, CEDAW has expressed its concern over restrictions in accessing contraceptive methods and a lack of family planning services. Amongst recommendations advanced by the Committee are an enhancement of family planning clinics and services in order to reduce unsafe abortions and maternal mortality.[107]

(v) Social and economic rights

Article 13 represents important provisions related to economic and social rights. It emphasises equality of rights, particularly the right to family benefits, the right to bank loans, mortgages, other forms of financial credit and the right to participation in recreational activities. Women often suffer from inequalities in obtaining benefits, loans and credit from governmental agencies, banks and building societies. The provisions of the Article aim, *inter alia*, to prevent sex discrimination in the payment of social securities and similar benefits. In *Broeks* v. *Netherlands*, Ms. Broeks appealed to the Human Rights Committee under the First Optional Protocol claiming violations of Article 26 of ICCPR and Article 9 in conjunction with Articles 2 and 3 of ICESCR.[108] Ms. Broeks had been dismissed by her employer because of illness. At first she received payments as unemployment benefits, but the Dutch government discontinued these since she was not the 'breadwinner' in her household as was required by the Netherlands Unemployment Benefits Act. The Human Rights Committee found violations of Article 26 of ICCPR, because the Statute was discriminatory in its treatment of women *vis-à-vis* men, and no grounds could be ascertained to justify such a distinction between men and women.[109] Similarly, gender discrimination has been found by the Human Rights Committee where a woman was not allowed to claim before domestic courts in relation to matters arising from matrimonial property.[110] The offending legislation in Peru had provided that when a woman is married only the husband is entitled to represent matrimonial property before the Courts, a provision which violated the terms of Article 26.[111]

---

[106] See Concluding Observations of the Human Rights Committee concerning: Chile, 18 May 2007, CCPR/C/CHL/CO/5 at para 8; El Salvador, 22 August 2003, CCPR/CO/78/SLV at para 14; Madagascar, 11 May 2007, CCPR/C/MDG/CO/3 at para 14; and Poland, 2 December 2004, CCPR/CO/82/POL at para 8.

[107] See Concluding Observations of CEDAW on: Chile, 9 July 1999, A/54/38 at paras 209 and 228; Greece, 1 February 1999, A/54/38 at para 207; Hungary, 9 May 1996, A/51/38 at para 254; Lithuania, 16 June 2000, A/55/38 at para 158; Ukraine, 9 May 1996, A/51/38 at para 287; Concluding Observations: Burundi, 2 February 2001, A/56/30 at para 62, Chile, 9 July 1999, A/54/38 at para 229; Chile, 25 August 2006, CEDAW/C/CHI/CO/ at para 20; Georgia, 1 July 1999, A/54/38 at para 112; Greece, 1 February 1999, A/54/38 at para 208; Ireland, 1 July 1999, A/54/38 at para 186; Kazakhstan, 2 February 2001, A/56/38 at paras 76 and 106; Lithuania, 16 June 2000, A/55/38 at para 159; Mongolia, 2 February 2001, A/56/38 at para 274; Nicaragua, 31 July 2001, A/56/38 at para 301; and Slovenia, 12 August 1997, A/52/38/Rev.1 at para 119.

[108] *S. W. M. Broeks* v. *The Netherlands*, Communication No. 172/1984 (9 April 1987), UN Doc. Supp. No. 40 (A/42/40) at 139 (1987); see also Cook, 'Women' in Joyner (ed.), *United Nations and International Law* (Cambridge University Press, 1997) pp. 181–207 at p. 199.

[109] *Broeks* v. *Netherlands* above n.108, para 14.

[110] See *Graciela Ato del Avellanal* v. *Peru*, Communication No. 202/1986 (28 October 1988), UN Doc. Supp. No. 40 (A/44/40) at 196 (1988).

[111] Ibid. para 10.2. Article 16 claim was also 'on the right to recognition' held admissible although the HRC did not provide a separate finding on Article 16. See Frostell and Scheinin 'Women' in Eide, Krause and Rosas *Economic, Social and Cultural Rights* (Brill, 2001) pp. 331–352 at p. 339. Restriction on property rights for women was also adjudicated by the European Court of Human Rights in the *Marckx* case (App. No. 6833/74) (acting for herself and on behalf of her daughter) alleged *inter alia* that discrimination based on Belgian law whereby unmarried mothers were required to adopt their own children in order to establish inheritance rights, constituted a violation of Article 14 ECHR in conjunction with Article 8 and Article 1, Protocol 1.

Article 14 deals with the specific position of rural women whose work is often not acknowledged. The Article is a detailed expression of the rights belonging to women in rural areas and provides as follows:

1. States Parties shall take into account the particular problems faced by rural women and the significant roles which rural women play in the economic survival of their families, including their work in the non-monetized sectors of the economy, and shall take all appropriate measures to ensure the application of the provisions of the present Convention to women in rural areas.

2. States Parties shall take all appropriate measures to eliminate discrimination against women in rural areas in order to ensure, on a basis of equality of men and women, that they participate in and benefit from rural development and, in particular, shall ensure to such women the right:

   (a) To participate in the elaboration and implementation of development planning at all levels;
   (b) To have access to adequate health care facilities, including information, counselling and services in family planning;
   (c) To benefit directly from social security programmes
   (d) To obtain all types of training and education, formal and non-formal, including that relating to functional literacy, as well as, inter alia, the benefit of all community and extension services, in order to increase their technical proficiency;
   (e) To organize self-help groups and co-operatives in order to obtain equal access to economic opportunities through employment or self employment;
   (f) To participate in all community activities;
   (g) To have access to agricultural credit and loans, marketing facilities, appropriate technology and equal treatment in land and agrarian reform as well as in land resettlement schemes;
   (h) To enjoy adequate living conditions, particularly in relation to housing, sanitation, electricity and water supply, transport and communications.

According to Article 15, equality before the law in matters of civil law must be accorded to women, including the legal capacity to contract, to own and to administer property, to move and to choose a residence and domicile. Under this Article, States parties are obliged to ensure the conformity of their national legislation with this rule. In addition, any contract or legal document whose effect 'is directed at restricting the legal capacity of women shall be deemed null and void'.[112] The granting of equality before law has proved controversial. There have been complex issues emerging, particularly from property and land rights, and inheritance, with reliance being placed on customary laws or religious values to justify the refusal to bring about equality of treatment.[113]

Women are in many traditions and cultures excluded or denied equal distribution of property or land upon divorce or death of a partner. Such practices have been the object of

---

[112] Article 15(3).

[113] See the *Pastory* case (*Bernado Ephrahim v. Holaria Pastory and Gervazi Kaizilege*, Civil Appeal No. 70 of 1989, High Court at Mwanza). The Tanzanian High Court held that customary law barring women from selling clan land, represented unconstitutional discrimination. *Cf. Veneria Magaya* case (*Veneria Magaya v. Nakyi Shonhiwa Magaya*) (SC 210/98). The Zimbabwean Supreme Court refused to invalidate customary law according preference to male inheritance.

criticism by CEDAW. In its General Recommendation No. 21 on Equality in Marriage and Family Relations, CEDAW notes that laws which grant men a larger share upon divorce are discriminatory.[114] These practices, according to the Committee, seriously affect a woman's ability to divorce her husband, support her family and live as a dignified human being.[115] In its General Recommendation No. 21, the Committee urges that account be taken of the non-financial contribution made by women.[116]

CEDAW has highlighted several particularly pertinent obligations in General Recommendation No. 19. Regarding Article 15 the Committee noted that a woman is denied legal autonomy if she is unable to enter into a contract, access financial credit or needs a male relative's permission to do so. Secondly, if a woman's legal capacity is diminished either by the State, or when individuals or institutions can do so lawfully, this amounts to a denial of equality and constitutes a restriction on the ability of women to provide for themselves and their families or dependants. Thirdly, the Committee noted, from State reports, that women can not always change their nationality if they so wish, which again constitutes a violation of Convention rights. Finally, migrant workers who are female should be allowed the same rights as men regarding the right to be joined by their spouses, partners and children as well as family re-unification during their period of work in another State.[117]

It is also important to note that such a significant article has attracted reservations from many States. These reserving States continue to feel reluctant to allow women the legal and contractual capacity equal to men. Women have often been excluded from inheritance and property ownership through legal disabilities. Women are, thus, in some parts of world legally dependent on matters of contract and litigation. Amongst States entering reservations are Thailand and Brazil. The primary objection that has emanated from Islamic States, such as Morocco, Jordan and Oman, and relates to the application of Article 15(4). The apparent reasoning behind the reservations to Article 15(4) is the conflict with their personal laws.

In its observation, the Human Rights Committee has expressed its concern not only at the continued existence of the institution of polygamy but also at the deprivation of women from their due share in inheritance. In presenting its concluding comments to the report by Gabon, the Human Rights Committee expresses the view that:

> The Committee notes that there are customs and traditions in the State party, having a bearing on, among other things, equality between men and women, that may hamper the full implementation of some provisions of the Covenant. In particular, the Committee deplores the fact that polygamy is still practiced in Gabon and refers to its general comment No. 28, which states that polygamy is incompatible with equality of treatment with regard to the right to marry. 'Polygamy violates the dignity of women. It is an inadmissible discrimination against women' (CCPR/C/21/Rev.1/Add.10, para. 24). The Committee also observes that a number of legislative provisions in Gabon are not compatible with the Covenant, including article 252 of the Civil Code requiring a woman to be obedient to her husband. Lastly, the

---

[114] CEDAW General Recommendation No. 21. Equality in Marriage and Family Relations, www.un.org/womenwatch/daw/cedaw/recommendations/recomm.htm#recom21 <last visited 17 February 2009>, para 28.
[115] Ibid.
[116] For exclusion of women from membership of indigenous communities see *Lovelace* v. *Canada* Communication No. R.6/24, UN Doc. Supp. No. 40 (A/36/40) at 166 (1981).
[117] On the position of Migrant workers see below chapter 20.

Committee notes that, in the event of her husband's death, a woman inherits only the usufruct of a quarter of the property left by her husband, and only after her children.

The State party must review its legislation and practice in order to ensure that women have the same rights as men, including rights of ownership and inheritance. It must take specific action to increase the involvement of women in political, economic and social life and ensure that there is no discrimination based on customary law in matters such as marriage, divorce and inheritance. Polygamy must be abolished and article 252 of the Civil Code repealed. It is the duty of the State party to do everything necessary to ensure that the Covenant is respected.[118]

(vi) Marriage and family relations

In accordance with Article 16, States parties agree to undertake all appropriate measures to eliminate discrimination against women in all matters relating to marriage and family relations. Assurances are provided by States that men and women shall have the same right to enter into marriage, the same right freely to choose a spouse and to enter into marriage only with their free and full consent. States also agree that both parties to marriage would have the same rights and responsibilities during its existence and at the time of its dissolution. By virtue of this Article, States undertake to adopt measures to allow women, on the basis of equality, to plan a family, or the parenting of children and all other relevant issues such as guardianship, wardship, trusteeship and adoption of children, or similar institutions where these concepts exist in national legislation. According to Article 16(2) '[t]he betrothal and the marriage of a child shall have no legal effect, and all necessary actions, including legislation, shall be taken to specify a minimum age for marriage and to make the registration of marriages in an official registry compulsory'.

Through the provisions of Article 16, States parties undertake to eliminate discrimination in matters relating to marriage and family relations. The Article emphasises upon equal rights in choosing a spouse and in the entering and the dissolution of marriage.

The Committee took the view in General Recommendation No. 19 that family violence, such as forced marriage, dowry deaths, acid attacks and female circumcision, remains on of the most insidious forms of violence against women and that it is prevalent in all societies.[119] Therefore, the Committee stated that:

States parties should ensure that laws against family violence and abuse, rape, sexual assault and other gender-based violence give adequate protection to all women, and respect their integrity and dignity. Appropriate protective and support services should be provided for victims.[120]

---

[118] Concluding Observations of the Human Rights Committee: Gabon. 10/11/2000. CCPR/CO/70/GAB. (Concluding Observations/Comments) Seventieth session, para 9; for a similar observation that States parties have to abolish polygamy as it constitute sex discrimination see Concluding Comments on Mali (2003) UN Doc. CCPR/CO/77/MLI.

[119] CEDAW General Recommendation No. 19 Violence against Women, www.un.org/womenwatch/daw/cedaw/recommendations/recomm.htm#recom19 <last visited 17 February 2009> para 11.

[120] CEDAW General Recommendation No. 19, Violence against Women www.un.org/womenwatch/daw/cedaw/recommendations/recomm.htm#recom19 <last visited 17 February 2009> para 24(b).

In its General Recommendation 21, CEDAW notes that '[a]n examination of State parties' Reports discloses that there are countries which, on the basis of custom, religious beliefs or the ethnic origins of particular groups of people permit forced marriages or remarriages'.[121] In addition, CEDAW has noted that a *de facto* union is frequently not given adequate legal protection and that children of such unions do not always enjoy the same status as those born in wedlock.[122] Finally, the Committee has also noted with alarm the number of States parties which have entered reservations to Article 16, particularly when a reservation has also been entered regarding Article 2. These reservation often state 'that compliance with the provisions may conflict with a commonly held vision of the family based, *inter alia*, on cultural or religious beliefs or on the country's economic or political status.[123]

The Convention establishes equality of rights of men and women in the raising of the family and in the ownership of family property. The rights granted to women in Article 16 raised opposition in many quarters, particularly from several Islamic States. A number of the Islamic States have registered their reservations to this Article. These include Algeria, Egypt, Iraq, Jordan, Kuwait, Lebanon, Libya, Maldives, Morocco, Tunisia and Oman (grounds and specific provisions). Bangladesh and Mauritius initially made reservations to Article 16(1)(c) and (f) and Article 16(1)(g) respectively, which they have subsequently removed. Malaysia also has withdrawn its initial reservations as regards Article 16(b), 16(d), 16(e) and 16(h). Furthermore there are other States which have entered reservations on *inter alia* religious grounds – these are Israel, India and Singapore.

The viewpoints of the State representatives and the State reports reveal that the rights contained in this Article conflict directly with existing cultural and religious norms. While many Islamic States question the compatibility of the *Sharia, vis-à-vis* the provisions of Article 16, Islamic States are by no means the only ones to have entered reservations.

6 RESERVATIONS AND THE ATTEMPTS TO FIND CONSENSUS ON THE PROVISIONS OF THE CONVENTION

During the course of this chapter we have come across a number of reservations that have been made by State parties to the various provisions. While international law does permit reservations and derogations to be made in certain circumstances, the question arises as to the extent States can make such reservations without compromising their commitments to the Convention. The existing disagreement over women rights are reflected vividly through the significant number of reservations. A complex although significant element in the entire debate surrounding this subject is the influence of socio-cultural and religious perspectives. While the impact of human rights law has been significant, many societies hold their distinct religious, cultural and societal ordinance in the highest esteem.

The prioritisation of international human rights norms risks being labelled as an attempt at imposing Western cultural imperialism. This imposition of cultural imperialism is evident from the State responses, and while such reaction can be discerned from many non-Western States, the Islamic States have very strongly asserted the superiority of their

121 CEDAW General Recommendation No. 21, Equality in Marriage and Family Relations www.un.org/womenwatch/daw/cedaw/recommendations/recomm.htm#recom21 <last visited 17 February 2009>, para 16.
122 CEDAW General Recommendation No. 21, para 18.
123 CEDAW General Recommendation No. 21, para 41.

religious and moral values. According to these States, Islam is not merely a religion, it is a complete code of life, a complete recipe for social and moral behaviour. Such an attitude initially prompted Bangladesh to enter a reservation to noting that 'The Government of the People's Republic of Bangladesh does not consider as binding upon itself the provisions of articles 2, 13(a) and 16(1)(c) and (f) as they conflict with *Sharia* law based on *Holy Quran* and *Sunna*'. The reservation to Articles 13 and 16(1)(f) was withdrawn in 1997, although the continuing reservation to Article 2 means that both the letter and spirit of the laws in Bangladesh very much represents the superiority of *Sharia* over any other law. The issue of compatibility becomes more complex, since there is neither a single unified view of the *Sharia*, nor is there any detailed official view on women's rights in Islam. Islamic States vary radically in their approaches towards the position of women in Muslim States. Thus the vision of the Talaban in Afghanistan or the views of the Saudi Arabian regime on the *Sharia* and women's rights is very different from the position adopted by the Libyan, Maldives, Malaysian or Pakistan governments. Considering the position of women in a number of Islamic States, sceptics argue that religion has very often been used as an instrument of domination and exploitation. This view appears to be substantiated when the breadth, plurality and accommodating nature of the *Sharia* is analysed.[124] Religion has not only been a factor influencing women's rights in theocracies, but State's propounding secular traditions have also been confronted by the sensitivities of religious communities.[125]

As discussed earlier, the significant number of reservations do pose a serious challenge though it is not just the issue of numbers. More worrying, as Dr. Siobhan Mullally eloquently notes, is the reason presented for such 'opting out' by States: these include not just religious grounds, but also as in the case of the United States, constitutional practices protecting private sphere.[126] In highlight the serious dangers of reservations to the Woman's Convention as well as the burgeoning jurisprudence on women's rights, Dr. Mullally makes the following pertinent points:

> Taken together, the text of the Convention and the 'jurisprudence' of the Committee, give us an international instrument that is potentially very far-reaching indeed. As gender equality is increasingly mainstreamed into the work of other human rights treaty bodies, notably the Human Rights Committee, the scope of international human rights law has greatly expanded, holding out greater possibility for the transformation of domestic laws.

---

[124] See the consideration on Universalism and Regionalism in the introductory chapter. See also Rehman, 'Accommodating Religious Identities in an Islamic State: International Law, Freedom of Religion and the Rights of Religious Minorities' 7 *IJMGR* (2000) 139; also see Rehman, above n.1; Abiad, *Sharia, Muslim States and International Human Rights Treaty Obligations: A Comparative Study* (British Institute of Comparative and International Law, 2008).

[125] *Mohammed Ahmed Khan* v. *Shah Bano Begum Supreme Court of India* (1985), 2 Sup. Ct Cases 556 *Shah Bano* case is a striking illustration of judicial activism where the Supreme Court intervened to protect the rights of Muslim women from the antiquated and unjust application of Muslim personal laws *cf. Ahmedabad Women Action Group and others* v. *Union of India* (1997) Sup. Ct Cases 573 (Indian Supreme Court dismissed challenges to Muslim practices of polygamy and triple Talaq); *Open Door Dublin Well Woman* v. *Ireland* (193) 15 E.H.R.R. 224 92/67; *Abdul Waheed* v. *Asma Jehangir (Saima Waheed case)* PLD 1997 Lah. 301, where the Court held that Saima Waheed was permitted to marry the man of her choice. In the *Mary Roy* case, the Indian Supreme Court avoided the discriminatory provisions of the Christian succession Act 1916 to avoid discriminatory inheritance law against a Christian women based in Kerala. *Mary Roy* v. *State of Kerala* AIR (1986) SC 1011.

[126] Mullally, above n.1, chapter 6.

536

Reservations, however, seek to limit this transformative potential and the scope of international human rights standards. This transformative potential is limited, in particular, by general reservations that seek to make a treaty obligation subject to conformity with something outside of the treaty, such as religious doctrine or domestic laws and customs. In such cases, States parties and the monitoring bodies are essentially being asked 'to sign a blank cheque'. There is likely to be ongoing disagreement as to the content of the proposed alternative canon of interpretation, as where different adherents of the same religious group disagree on the meaning or scope of a particular doctrine. Where a general reservation appeals to domestic laws and customs, further uncertainties are created as such laws and customs may vary over time. Reservations to article 2 of [the Women's Convention] – the core norm of obligation – pose a particularly 'acute problem' for [the Women's Convention]. A number of States have specifically 'reserved' on article 2. Others states have entered reservations that do not invoke any specific provision of [the Women's Convention] but are broad enough to encompass article 2. Saudi Arabia states that in case of contradiction between any term of the Convention and the norms of Islamic law, 'the Kingdom is not under an obligation to observe the contradictory terms of the Convention.' Pakistan's ratification of the Convention was accompanied by a declaration stating that accession was subject to the provisions of its Constitution. General reservations such as these envisage an enduring inconsistency between state law and practice and the requirements of the Convention. State sovereignty and the defence of domestic jurisdiction reappears, this time in the guise of an unyielding assertion of difference. The divisions between the public and the private that the Convention seeks to overcome are re-asserted.[127]

7 THE COMMITTEE ON THE ELIMINATION OF DISCRIMINATION AGAINST WOMEN (CEDAW)[128]

Part V of the Convention establishes the Committee on the Elimination of Discrimination against Women (CEDAW), a body of 23 experts. CEDAW is elected by States parties with individual members to serve in their personal capacity.[129] The Committee is elected by States Parties for four year terms. CEDAW members are required to be 'of high moral standing and competence in the field covered by the Convention'.[130] Historically CEDAW Committee Secretariat, unlike other treaty-based Committees, was not provided by the office of the High Commissioner of Human Rights. However, as of 1 January 2009 all responsibility for servicing CEDAW has been shifted to the Office of the High Commissioner for Human Rights.[131] Like the Human Rights Committee and the Economic, Social and Cultural Rights Committee, expenses of CEDAW are borne from the UN budget. Prior to 1994 CEDAW used to meet in New York and Vienna although the

---

[127] Ibid. chapter 6. pp. 100–102 (footnotes omitted).
[128] See Byrnes, above n.10; Jackson, 'The Committee on the Elimination of Discrimination against Women' in Alston (ed.), *The United Nations and Human Rights: A Critical Appraisal* (1992) pp. 444–472; Bustelo, 'The Committee on the Elimination of Discrimination against Women at the Crossroads' in Alston and Crawford (eds), *The Future of UN Human Rights Treaty Monitoring* (Cambridge University Press, 2000) at pp. 79–111; Martínez, 'Human Rights of Women' 5 *Washington University Journal of Law and Policy* (2001) 157; Wadstein, 'Implementation of the UN Convention on the Elimination of All Forms of Discrimination against Women' 6 *NQHR* (1988) 5.
[129] Article 17.
[130] Article 17(1).
[131] See Release of Information by the Division for the Advancement of Women (May 2009).

New York sessions were much more publicised. Since its 13th session in 1994, the Committee's sessions have mostly been held in New York. However, as noted above, in January 2008 the Secretariat of CEDAW moved to Geneva, which has allowed a greater number of sessions to be held in Geneva.

According to Article 20, CEDAW is required to meet for a period of not more than two weeks, every year. However, the rapid expansion of the State membership meant that more time was needed to consider State reports. As of 1990, a pre-sessional working group has been used to review reports and to prepare questions for state representatives. In addition to the pre-sessional working-group the CEDAW has also set up additional working groups: one aims to suggest ways to expedite the Committee's task, with others being instrumental in producing General Comments. In the light of unexpected workload, the General Assembly since 1990 has also allowed the Committee to meet on an exceptional basis for an extra one week per year. An amendment to Article 20 to enhance the meeting period was introduced in 1995. However, the operation of such an amendment is dependent upon a two-thirds majority of the States accepting this and it has not yet come into force.[132] In the meantime, the General Assembly has approved the holding of three, three-week sessions every year (pending the entry into force of the amendment), each preceded by a one-week pre-sessional working group session, pending the entry into force of the amendment, from 2010 onwards.[133] The sessional meetings of the Committee have been held in January and June of each year. However, in 2008 the Committee held three sessions due to the General Assembly in Resolution 62/218 having extended the meeting time and chambers for 2008/09. This included allowing the Committee to meet five times over the period and three of these in Parallel Chambers on an exceptional and temporary basis. Two of these five sessions were permitted to be held in New York.[134]

CEDAW's overall structure and composition resembles the Human Rights Committee, although the membership of the Committee is predominantly female. The Committee also has the largest membership of any of the United Nations Treaties. The members of CEDAW come from a range of professions. Members are nominated by States but serve in their personal capacity and not as government representatives. Until recently CEDAW has not had a judicial or quasi-judicial function. Its sole task, previously, was reviewing the State reports but this has changed significantly since the Optional Protocol came into operation. The Committee's main task was one of implementing the Convention, an exercise, thus far, conducted within the framework of reporting procedures.[135] The Optional Protocol to the Convention authorising communications from individuals or groups of individuals, as well as an enquiry procedure, was adopted by the General Assembly on 6 October 1999 and came into force on 22 December 2000.[136]

The present reporting procedure as provided in the Convention, in common with other reporting procedures, has proved less than satisfactory. Reports are often delayed, out-dated and inadequate, with most State parties placing emphasis upon the legislative

---

[132] *Amendment to article 20, paragraph 1 of the Convention on the Elimination of All Forms of Discrimination against Women*, New York, 22 November 1995 UN Doc. CEDAW/SP/1995/2.

[133] General Assembly Resolution 62/218 *cf.* GA Res. 51/68.

[134] Statement by Ms. Dubravka Simonovic, chairperson on the Elimination of Discrimination against Women, 52nd session (25 February–7 March 2008).

[135] Article 29 provides that two or more States parties can refer a dispute arising from the interpretation and implementation of the Convention to arbitration and, if the dispute is not settled, it can be referred to the ICJ. This procedure has thus far not been used.

[136] GA Res. 54/4. See below.

mechanisms relating to gender equality. We have already noted CEDAW's concern at the lack of information or data on issues related to women's rights. There is also a complaint about reports being ineffective in their exposition of steps undertaken to eliminate *de facto* discrimination against women. To deal with the subject of outdated reports, in its sixteenth session in 1997, the Committee took a formal decision to encourage the submission of up to two consolidated reports.[137] In order to assist State Parties in reporting, CEDAW has adopted guidelines for their preparation of initial and subsequent reports.[138] These were subsequently replaced by the Reporting Guidelines of CEDAW in conjunction with the Harmonized Guidelines on the Reporting under the international human rights treaties in 2007.[139] In the initial reports States need to pay particular regard to the criterion set out in Section D of the Harmonized Guidelines and Section C.5. of the Reporting Guidelines of CEDAW, which are as follows:

D.1. General

D.1.1. This report is the State party's first opportunity to present to the Committee the extent to which its laws and practices comply with the Convention which it has ratified. The report should:

(a) Establish the constitutional, legal and administrative framework for the implementation of the Convention;

(b) Explain the legal and practical measures adopted to give effect to the provisions if the Convention;

(c) Demonstrate the progress made in ensuring enjoyment of the provisions of the Convention by the people within the State party and subject to its jurisdiction.

D.2. Contents of the reports

D.2.1. A State party should deal specifically with every article in Parts I, II, III and IV of the Convention; legal norms should be described, but that is not sufficient: the factual situation and the practical availability, effect and implementation of remedies for violation of provisions of the Convention should be explained and exemplified.

D.2.2. The report should explain:

(1) Whether the Convention is directly applicable in domestic law on ratification, or has been incorporated into the national Constitution or domestic law so as to be directly applicable;

(2) Whether the provisions of the Convention are guaranteed in a Constitution or other laws and to what extent; or if not, whether its provisions can be invoked before and given effect to by courts, tribunals and administrative authorities;

(3) How article 2 of the Convention is applied, setting out the principal legal measures which the State party has taken to give effect to Convention rights; and the range of remedies available to persons whose rights may have been violated.

---

[137] Report of CEDAW, GAOR 52nd Session, Supp. No. 38 (A/52/38/Rev.1), Part 1, Decision 16 (III).

[138] UN Doc CEDAW/2/7/Rev 3 (26 July 1996).

[139] www2.ohchr.org/English/bodies/cedaw/docs/AnnexI.pdf <last visited on 5 February 2009> and HRI/GEN/2/Rev.4 (21 May 2007).

D.2.3. Information should be given about the judicial, administrative and other competent authorities having jurisdiction with respect to the implementation of the provisions of the Convention.

D.2.4. The report should include information about any national or official institution or machinery which exercises responsibility in implementing the provisions of the Convention or in responding to complaints of violations of those provisions, and give examples of their activities in this respect.

D.2.5. The report should outline any restrictions or limitations, even of a temporary nature, imposed by law, practice or tradition, or in any other manner on the enjoyment of each provision of the Convention.

D.2.6. The report should describe the situation of non-governmental organizations and women's associations and their participation in the implementation of the Convention and the preparation of the report.

C.5. Data and Statistics

C.5. While general factual and statistical information should be included in the common core document, the Convention-specific document should include specific data and statistics disaggregated by sex which are relevant to the implementation of each article of the Convention and the general recommendations of the Committee in order to enable the Committee to assess progress in the implementation of the Convention.

For the preparation of second and subsequent reports, the States need particularly to consider the following:

E. Subsequent periodic reports

E.1. In general, the subsequent periodic reports of States parties should focus on the period between the consideration of their previous report and the presentation of the current reports. There should be two starting points for such reports:

(a) The concluding comments (particularly 'Concerns' and 'Recommendations') on the previous report;
(b) An examination by the State party of the progress made toward and the current implementation of the Convention within its territory or jurisdiction and the enjoyment of its provisions by those within its territory or jurisdiction.

E.2. Periodic reports should be structures so as to follow the articles of the Convention. If there is nothing new to report under any article, it should be so stated. Periodic reports should also highlight any remaining obstacle to the participation of women on an equal basis with men in the political, social, economic and cultural life of the State party.

E.3. The State party should refer again to the guidance on initial reports and on annexes, insofar as these may also apply to periodic reports.

E.4. There may be circumstance where the following matters should be addressed:

(a) A fundamental change may have occurred in the State party's political and legal approach affecting Convention implementation: in such a case a funll article-by-article report may be required;

(b) New legal and administrative measures may have been introduced which require the annexure of texts, and judicial or other decisions.[140]

Furthermore, the Reporting Guidelines of CEDAW add:

E.3. There should be at least three starting points for such subsequent Convention-specific documents:

(a) Information on the implementation of concluding observations (particularly 'Concerns' and 'Recommendations') to the previous report and explanations for the non-implementation or difficulties encountered;

(b) An analytical and result-oriented examination by the State party of additional legal and other appropriate steps and measures undertaken towards the implementation of the Convention;

(c) Information on any remaining or emerging obstacles to the exercise and enjoyment by women of their human rights and fundamental freedoms in the civil, political, economic, social, cultural or any other field on the basis of equality with men, as well as information on measures envisages to overcome these obstacles.

E.4. Periodic Convention-specific documents should in particular address the impact of measures taken, and should analyse trends over time in eliminating discrimination against women and ensuring women's full enjoyment of their human rights.

E.5. Periodic Convention-specific documents should also address the implementation of the Convention with respect to different groups of women, in particular those subject to multiple forms of discrimination.

E.6. Where a fundamental changes has occurred in the State party's political and legal approach affecting the implementation of the Convention or new legal or administrative measures have been introduced by the State party which require the annexure of texts, and judicial or other decisions, such information should be provided in the Convention-specific document.

(i) The Optional Protocol[141]

The Optional Protocol to CEDAW was opened for signature on 10 December 1999 and required 10 ratifications to come into operation. It came into force on 22 December 2000. As at 17 July 2009, there are 97 parties to the Protocol. In its 24th session (January–February 2001), the Committee adopted the Rules of Procedure for the Optional Protocol. The Protocol provides for an individual complaints procedure and also provides for

[140] HRI/GEN/2/Rev.4 (21 May 2007) p. 64.

[141] See Sokhi-Bulley, 'The Optional Protocol to CEDAW: First Steps' 6 *HRLR* (2006) 143; Byrnes, 'Using International Human Rights Law and Procedures to Advance Women's Human Rights' in Askin and Koenig (eds), *Women and International Human Rights Law* (Transnational Pubishers, 2000) pp. 79–118.

a procedure under which the Committee can inquire into serious and systematic violations of the Convention. The overall pattern and the admissibility procedure are based on the First Optional Protocol of ICCPR. A number of interesting distinctions exist and need to be mentioned. Firstly, the Optional Protocol to the Women's Convention allows 'individuals or groups of individuals' to submit complaints to CEDAW. This represents a more generous rule when compared to the First Optional Protocol to ICCPR which only allows 'individuals' to submit communications.[142] In practice, however, as we have already considered, the Human Rights Committee and the existing rules of procedure have adopted a more flexible and realistic approach in relation to the submission of communications.[143] Secondly, Article 8 establishes that:

1. [i]f the Committee receives reliable information indicating grave or systematic violations by a State Party of rights set forth in the Convention, the Committee shall invite that State Party to cooperate in the examination of the information and to this end to submit observations with regard to the information concerned.

2. . . . Where warranted and with the consent of the State Party, the inquiry may include a visit to its territory . . .

3. After examining the findings of such an inquiry, the Committee shall transmit these findings to the State Party concerned together with any comments and recommendations.

4. The State Party concerned shall, within six months of receiving the findings, comments and recommendations transmitted by the committee, submit its observations to the committee.

There are no parallel provisions in the First Optional Protocol to ICCPR. This procedure draws upon a similar procedure in the Convention against Torture.[144] Thirdly, no allowance is made within the Optional Protocol to the Women's Convention for reservations; a reaction to the difficulties that have arisen under the ICCPR, with Trinidad and Tobago attempting to withdraw from their obligations.[145] Fourthly, in common with the ICCPR and Convention against Torture, the OP-Women's Convention makes provision for 'interim measures . . . to avoid possible irreparable damage'.[146] Finally, there remains the overarching problem of dealing with the rights as provided in Women's Convention itself. Tomuschat makes the point that CEDAW 'will have to face up to considerable difficulties when beginning its work under the OP-CEDAW'.[147] This prediction was first of all due to the fact that the CEDAW was not framed as a text which enunciates rights of women, but has been formulated according to the 'duties model'.[148]

A State party is under an obligation to disseminate information about the Communications Procedure on its own territory under the Protocol.[149] Additionally, States must take all appropriate steps to ensure that individuals under their jurisdiction are not subjected to ill-treatment as a consequence of communicating with the Committee. The functions of the Committee include the gathering of information, by means of written

---

[142] This formula is similar in nature to that of the Race Convention Article 14(1). See above chapter 12.
[143] See above chapter 5.
[144] See below chapter 22.
[145] See above chapter 5.
[146] Article 5(1) OP-CEDAW.
[147] Tomuschat, *Human Rights: Between Idealism and Realism* (Oxford University Press, 2008) at p. 173.
[148] Ibid. at p. 173.
[149] HRI/GEN/2/Rev.4 (21 May 2007) p. 64.

exchanges with the parties (the State and the complainant) to consider the admissibility and merits of the complaint in question and to issue its 'views' accordingly. It is important to note that CEDAW is not a court and does not, therefore, issue binding judgments and has no enforcement mechanisms regarding its 'views'. All exchanges with the Committee are in written format and there is no allocation of financial assistance in order to enable authors to take a case to the Committee. The procedure is confidential until the adoption of 'views' by CEDAW. However, an author or the State may make information public unless the Committee has explicitly requested otherwise.

As with the Human Rights Committee Individual Complaints Procedure, a communication must overcome two stages. Firstly, the consideration of the admissibility of the Communication and secondly, of the merits. However, the Committee may decide on the admissibility and merits of a communication together. The Committee may also request interim measures to prevent irreparable harm to the author of the Communication.[150] In order to file a Communication, the applicant initially needs to contact the Secretariat. The Secretariat may then request that the author(s) complete a questionnaire concerning the case. It is important to note that the Complaints Form under CEDAW's Optional Protocol is not the same as the Complaints Form used by the other treaty bodies. At this or any other stage, authors are free to maintain contact with members of the Secretariat to obtain advice and guidance. The Committee may also issue a questionnaire in order to obtain more information from the author of the complaint.[151]

Communications are brought to the attention of the Committee at its next regular session.[152] The Committee may establish a Working Group or designate a Rapporteur to assist it in its consideration of communications at any stage of the proceedings.[153] After having been received by the Committee the communications are brought to the attention of the State party with a request for a response within six months regarding a complaint's admissibility and merits.[154] If the State wishes the Communication to be rejected as inadmissible, any arguments should be submitted within two months.[155] The Committee may also request further information from both the State party or the author, subject to fixed limits.[156]

A Communication is held inadmissible where:

(a) The same matter has already been examined by the Committee or has been or is being examined under another procedure of international investigation or settlement;

(b) It is incompatible with the provisions of the Convention;

(c) It is manifestly ill-founded or not sufficiently substantiated;

(d) It is an abuse of the right to submit a communication;

(e) The facts that are the subject of the communication occurred prior to the entry into force of the present Protocol for the State Party concerned unless those facts continued after that date.[157]

---

[150] Article 5 Optional Protocol, Rule 63 of the Rules of Procedure of CEDAW. See also *A.T. v. Hungary*, CEDAW Communication No. 2/2003, UN Doc. CEDAW/C/32/D/2/2003 (2005).

[151] Rule 58(3) of the Rules of Procedure of CEDAW.

[152] Rule 59(1) of the Rules of Procedure of CEDAW.

[153] Rule 62(1) of the Rules of Procedure of CEDAW.

[154] Rule 69(3) of the Rules of Procedure of CEDAW.

[155] Rule 69(5) of the Rules of Procedure of CEDAW.

[156] Rule 69(8) of the Rules of Procedure of CEDAW.

[157] Article 4(2) of the Optional Protocol.

15

The rights of women

In addition to this, domestic remedies must be exhausted[158] and the Communication cannot be anonymous.[159] The case may be reopened in the case of an inadmissibility decision if further information is provided indicating reasons for the review of the decision.[160]

When formulating its views the Committee makes use of all information available to it, including information from individuals and the State party, as well as organisations such as the UN and related treaty bodies.[161] Views are determined by a simple majority and may include recommendations.[162] Individual opinions may also be appended to the view formed on a specific communication.[163]

States are required to provide a written response to the views of the Committee within six months of their issuance. This should include information regarding the action taken in respect of the views and recommendations of the Committee.[164] The Committee may then request further information, including a request to incorporate such information in its reports pursuant to Article 18.[165] The issues arising from the views of the Committee are monitored either by a Special Rapporteur or by a Working Group.[166] The Rapporteur or Working Group should maintain contact and take appropriate action and recommend further action to be undertaken by the Committee.[167] The Committee includes information on any follow-up activities in its annual report.[168] In addition to this, at its 24th session the Committee decided to set up a working group to monitor the progress of the Protocol.

Since it came into force on 22 December 2000 the Committee has only published its findings regarding 10 different Communications. Of these, five have been held inadmissible for either failure to exhaust domestic remedies or *ratione temporis*.[169] Of the remaining five Communications, violations have been found in four of the Communications. In *Dung Thi Thuy Nguyen* v. *The Netherlands*,[170] it was held that there was no violation of

---

[158] Article 4(1) of the Optional Protocol.
[159] Article 3 of the Optional Protocol.
[160] Rule 70(2) of the Rules of Procedure of CEDAW.
[161] Ibid. Rule 72(1) and (2).
[162] Ibid. Rule 72(5).
[163] Ibid. Rule 72(6).
[164] Ibid. Rule 73(1).
[165] Ibid. Rule 73(2) and (3).
[166] Ibid. Rule 73(4).
[167] Ibid. Rule 73(5).
[168] Ibid. Rule 73(7).
[169] See *B.-J.* v. *Germany*, Communication No. 1/2003, UN Doc. CEDAW/C/36/D/1/2003 (2004), the Communication which alleged gender-based discrimination under the statutory regulations on the legal consequences of divorce was held inadmissible both *ratione temporis* and for failure to exhaust domestic remedies. *Cristina Muñoz-Vargas y Sainz de Vicuña* v. *Spain*, Communication No. 7/2005, UN Doc. CEDAW/C/39/D/7/2005 (2007), regarding the succession to titles of nobility and the preference given to male heirs, was held inadmissible *ratione temporis*. *Rahime Kayham* v. *Turkey*, Communication No. 8/2005, UN Doc. CEDAW/C/34/D/8/2005 (2006), the Communication regarding legislation banning the headscarf in Universities as gender-discrimination as the provision only adversely affected the rights of women was held inadmissible for failure to exhaust domestic remedies. *N.S.F.* v. *UK*, Communication No. 10/2005, UN Doc. CEDAW/C/38/D/10/2005 (2007), regarding the right to claim asylum when facing gender-based persecution in county of origin was held inadmissible due to a failure to exhaust domestic remedies and a failure to allege the gender-aspect of the claim before the British courts. *Constance Ragan Salgado* v. *UK*, Communication No. 111/2006, UN Doc. CEDAW/C/37/D/11/2006 (2007), regarding the inability of a woman to register her child as a British citizen as at the time of birth citizenship was only derived from the father's descent was held inadmissible both *ratione temporis* and for the failure to exhaust domestic remedies.
[170] Communication No. 3/2004.

544

the Convention when States had separate rules for self-employed women and salaried women when providing maternity cover. More specifically:

> [t]he Committee notes that article 11, paragraph 2 (b), does not use the term 'full' pay, nor does it use 'full compensation for loss of income' resulting from pregnancy and childbirth. In other words, the Convention leaves to States parties a certain margin of discretion to devise a system of maternity leave benefits to fulfil Convention requirements. The Committee notes that the State party's legislation provides that selfemployed women and co-working spouses as well as salaried women are entitled to paid maternity leave – albeit under different insurance schemes.[171]

In *A.T. v. Hungary*,[172] *Şahide Goekce (deceased) v. Austria*[173] and *Fatma Yildrim (deceased) v. Austria*,[174] the Committee dealt with cases of domestic violence, which in two of the cases had resulted in death. The Committee held on all three occasions that the State party had a duty to protect the women from domestic violence and although provisions to do this were in place they were not effective.[175] Violations were found, in the latter two cases, regarding Articles 2(a) and (c) through (f), Article 3 in conjunction with Article 1 and, also, Recommendation No. 19. In the first case, violations were found of Articles 2(a), (b) and (e) as well as Article 16. In *A.S. v. Hungary*,[176] the Committee considered the case of a Roma woman coerced into being sterilised. Although she had signed a consent form, she was not informed of the consequences of the sterilisation and was not in a fit state to make an informed decision.[177] The Committee found violations of Articles 10(h), 12 and 16(1)(e).[178] In all four cases where the Committee has found violations of the provisions of the Convention, it has also provided lengthy recommendations for the violating State in its judgments.[179]

Inquiry Procedure under the Optional Protocol

The Inquiry Procedure provides for the investigation of reliable indications of grave or systematic violations by a State party to the Optional Protocol of the rights set forth in the Convention. The procedure is not applicable if the State in question at the time of ratification or accession to the Optional Protocol declared that it does not recognise the competence of the Committee, in this respect.[180] This is a confidential procedure but requires summaries to

---

[171] Ibid. para 10.2.
[172] Communication No. 2/2003.
[173] Communication No. 5/2005.
[174] Communication No. 6/2005.
[175] *A.T. v. Hungary*, CEDAW Communication No. 2/2003, UN Doc. CEDAW/C/32/D/2/2003 (2005), paras 9.2–9.3, *Şahide Goekce (deceased) v. Austria*, Communication No. 5/2005, UN Doc. CEDAW/C/39/D/5/2005 (2007), paras 12.1.1–12.1.2, *Fatma Yildrim (deceased) v. Austria*, Communication No. 6/2005, UN Doc. CEDAW/C/39/D/6/2005 (2007), paras 12.1.1–12.1.2.
[176] Communication No. 4/2004.
[177] Ibid. paras 11.2–11.3.
[178] Ibid. para 11.5.
[179] *A.T. v. Hungary*, CEDAW Communication No. 2/2003, UN Doc. CEDAW/C/32/D/2/2003 (2005), para 9.6, *A.S. v. Hungary*, Communication No. 4/2004, UN Doc. CEDAW/C/36/D/4/2004 (2006), para 11.5, *Şahide Goekce (deceased) v. Austria*, Communication No. 5/2005, UN Doc. CEDAW/C/39/D/5/2005 (2007), para 12.3, *Fatma Yildrim (deceased) v. Austria*, Communication No. 6/2005, UN Doc. CEDAW/C/39/D/6/2005 (2007), para 12.3.
[180] Rule 76 of the Rules of Procedure of CEDAW.

be adopted in CEDAW's annual report to the General Assembly. States Parties are also under an obligation to 'ensure that individuals under its jurisdiction are not subjected to ill-treatment as a consequence of communicating with the Committee pursuant to the present Protocol'.[181]

> **Article 9**
>
> 1. The Committee may invite the State Party concerned to include in its report under article 18 of the Convention details of any measures taken in response to an inquiry conducted under article 8 of the present Protocol.
> 2. The Committee may, if necessary, after the end of the period of six months referred to in article 8.4, invite the State Party concerned to inform it of the measures taken in response to such an inquiry.

The Committee's Rules of Procedure explain the manner in which the Protocol is to be implemented. It appears that an inquiry can be initiated on the basis of information received from any source.[182] All such information which appears to be submitted under the inquiry procedure must be registered and made available to the Committee by the Secretary-General.[183] The Committee may instruct the Secretary-General to investigate the reliability of the information and to seek further or corroborating information.[184]

Once information is considered to be reliable and indicative of grave or systematic violations of rights set forth in the Convention, the State party concerned is invited to comment within a stated time limit.[185] Other possible sources of information, e.g. NGOs and individuals, may also be invited to submit further information and the Committee shall decide the form and the manner in which such additional information may be obtained.[186] The Committee may then decide to conduct an inquiry to be conducted by one or more of its members, assisted by relevant experts regarding the Convention, in accordance with any modalities determined by the Committee, and invite the government to afford its co-operation including, if appropriate, the provision of facilities for the conducting of one or more visiting missions.[187] The visits may involve conducting of sworn hearings and the State party may be informed by the Committee that it shall take all appropriate steps to ensure that those heard are not intimidated or subjected to ill-treatment. During the period of an inquiry, the Committee may defer consideration of any report of a State party submitted under Article 18 of the Convention. After examining the findings of the inquiry, the Committee transmits the findings together with its comments and recommendations to the State party and may invite it to indicate, within six months, measures taken in response thereto.[188] The Committee may also request that a State party include details of such measures in its reports under Article 18 of the Convention.[189]

---

[181] Article 11 Optional Protocol to CEDAW.
[182] Rule 77 of the Rules of Procedure.
[183] Rule 78 of the Rules of Procedure.
[184] Rule 82 of the Rules of Procedure.
[185] Rule 83(1) of the Rules of Procedure.
[186] Rule 83(3) of the Rules of Procedure.
[187] Rules 84 and 86 of the Rules of Procedure.
[188] Rules 89 and 90(1) of the Rules of Procedure.
[189] CEDAW has conducted an inquiry into Mexico, as regards 'allegations of the abduction, rape and murder of women in the Ciudad Juárez area of Chihuahua, Mexico, in particular that, since 1993, more than 230 young women and girls, most of them maquiladora workers, had been killed in or near Ciudad Juárez'. In finding

In pursuance of Article 18 of the Convention, States parties undertake to submit reports of legislative, judicial, administrative and other measures adopted to give effect to the provisions of the Convention within one year as an initial report, and every four years thereafter. Article 21, provides for the reporting procedures. CEDAW reports annually to the General Assembly through ECOSOC. Its reports may be transmitted by the Secretary-General to the Commission on the Status of Women for its information. Individuals and NGOs are not authorised to address the Committee directly. On the other hand, specialised agencies can be present at the time when reports are being submitted and considered by the Committee.[190]

(ii) General recommendations

In addition to considering State reports, CEDAW may also make General Recommendations and suggestions which are included in the report. CEDAW has made a number of General Recommendations on various significant though controversial issues. General Recommendations are similar to the General Comments issued by the Human Rights Committee or those provided by the Committee on ICESCR. They are aimed at States parties and usually consist of the Committee's view of the obligations assumed under the Convention. General Recommendations have been issued by CEDAW to expand into areas not covered by the Convention, e.g. violence against women and female circumcision. CEDAW has, thus far, adopted 25 General Recommendations. Those General Recommendations adopted during the Committee's first decade of existence were short and of a limited nature in dealing with issues such as the content of reports and reservations to the Convention and resources. Thus, for example, the brevity of General Recommendation No. 5 (1988) where the Committee called upon States parties to make greater use of 'temporary special measures such as positive action, preferential treatment or quota system to advance women's integration into education, the economy, politics and employment'[191] needs to be noted.

Since its 10th session the Committee has decided to adopt the practice of issuing General Recommendations on specific provisions of the Convention and on the relationship between the Convention Articles. This is what has been described by CEDAW as 'crosscutting' themes. CEDAW has issued a number of comprehensive and detailed General Recommendations offering States Parties guidance on the application of the Convention in specific situations. Thus, for example, its General Recommendation No. 19 (1992) considered the issue of violence against women.[192] General Recommendation No. 23 (1997) related to women in political and public life[193] and General Recommendation No. 21 (1999) was

---

allegations of these violations CEDAW recommended *inter alia*, 'Incorporate a gender perspective into all investigations, polices to prevent and combat violence, and programmes to restore the social fabric, bearing in mind the specific characteristics of gender-based violence against women, its causes and consequences, and the specific social responses that the situation requires, with a view to eliminating discrimination and establishing gender equality', CEDAW Optional Protocol Article 8 Examinations Concerning Gender Discrimination CEDAW A/59/38 part II (2004) para 268.

[190] Article 22 CEDAW.

[191] CEDAW General Recommendation No. 5 Temporary Special Measures (Seventh Session, 1988) www.un.org/womenwatch/daw/cedaw/recommendations/recomm.htm#recom5 <last visited 17 February 2009>.

[192] CEDAW General Recommendation No. 19 Violence against women (11th Session, 1992) www.un.org/womenwatch/daw/cedaw/recommendations/recomm.htm#recom19 recom5 <last visited 17 February 2009>.

[193] CEDAW General Recommendation No. 23 Women in Political and Public Life (16th Session, 1997) www.un.org/womenwatch/daw/cedaw/recommendations/recomm.htm#recom23 <last visited 17 February 2009>.

concerned with women and health.[194] General Recommendation No. 25 on Article 4 para 1 – Temporary Special Measures,[195] expanded upon General Recommendation No. 5, and thus aims to further accelerate *de facto* equality between men and women. In addition to General Recommendations, the Committee has also adopted a number of suggestions. Suggestions, as opposed to General Recommendation are usually aimed at United Nations entities.

(iii) Procedure

At the end of each session, a decision is made on the States whose reports will be considered at the next session. The listing is published in the Committee report and available from the UN Secretariat. States are made aware of this listing and have until 1 September to withdraw from being considered, should they wish to do so. Each report is designated a Country Rapporteur upon receipt. The work of the Rapporteur is split into three phases. The initial phase is based around preparing a draft list of issues and questions for the Pre-Session Working Group that is to consider the report. This is then followed by the consideration of the report and, finally, the preparation of draft Concluding Comments.[196] Reports are considered by a Pre-Session Working Group, five days in advance of the normal session in order to give States parties time to respond.[197] The Working Group draws up a list of issues and questions to be addressed by the State party with particular attention being paid to the Concluding Comments of previous State Reports.[198]

The purpose of the Pre-Session Working Group is to prepare a list of questions to be put before the State representative during the consideration of the report by CEDAW. In its scrutiny, CEDAW is assisted by information from the Secretariat and non-governmental organisations. NGO documentation is made available to members of the working group.[199] Initial reports are considered by up to three meetings. In comparison, periodic reports are reviewed by pre-sessional group and questions already posed, therefore the consideration is for a shorter period of up to one and a half meetings.

In common with other procedures, the Committee invites a representative from the State Party to introduce the report prior to its consideration. After the presentation of reports, CEDAW members may ask additional questions, seek additional information or clarify certain points.[200] Following the consideration of the report by CEDAW, it then proceeds to its 'Concluding Comments'. These typically include CEDAW's view on the report, an introduction to the comments, positive aspects in the report, factors and difficulties in the implementation of the Convention, and principal areas of concern and recommendations.[201] The Concluding Comments are included in the annual report to the General Assembly and the Commission on the Status of Women as well as being distributed

---

[194] CEDAW General Recommendation No. 24 Women and Health (20th Session, 1999) www.un.org/ womenwatch/daw/cedaw/recommendations/recomm.htm#recom24 <last visited 17 February 2009>.

[195] CEDAW General Recommendation No. 25 Temporary Special Measures (30th Session, 2004) www2.ohchr.org/ english/bodies/cedaw/comments.htm <last visited 17 February 2009>.

[196] UN. Doc. CEDAW/C/2007/I/4/Add.1 Ways and Means of Expediting the Work of the Committee on the Elimination of Discrimination against Women, Overview of the Working Methods of the Committee on the Elimination of Discrimination against Women, para 8.

[197] Ibid. para 10.

[198] Ibid. para 9.

[199] Ibid. para 34.

[200] Ibid. paras 14 and 15.

[201] Ibid. para 23.

through the Office of the UN High Commissioner for Human Rights.[202] Since 1990, the Committee has decided that it would review up to eight initial reports.

Similar to other reporting procedures, State reports are often characterised by unsatisfactory coverage of issues. In many cases the reports are prepared by governmental officials who do not fully comprehend the provisions of the Convention. In these circumstances credit needs to be given to CEDAW for going beyond the strict parameters of its mandate. It has on a number of instances raised issues and concerns (e.g. in relation to abortion on the reports from the Republic of Ireland)[203] regarding matters not strictly covered by the Convention.

It is also the case that State reports often vary in quality, volume and substance. Often there is little information on the implementation of the Convention with reports being excessively self-congratulatory and avoiding controversial areas. An uncompromising and unsympathetic attitude by governmental officials towards NGOs often results in little NGO involvement in crucial stages in compiling the report. To an extent, CEDAW can itself be criticised for having made insufficient use of information from other bodies. Within the Convention, there are no explicit provisions relating to the participation of NGOs. Article 22 of the Convention has, thus far, invoked limited interest from specialised agencies.

The Exceptional Report Procedure

In 1993 CEDAW, whilst making use of Article 18 of the Convention, requested reports on an exceptional basis from certain States of the former Yugoslavia.[204] It subsequently took the position that it would adopt such a procedure in order to 'look into similar grave violations of human rights being experienced by women in any part of the world'.[205] In relation to reports that have been submitted by States of the former Yugoslavia, CEDAW has adopted the following procedure:[206]

1. Tabling of reports at the upcoming session without sending them for attention of the Working Group;
2. Permitting the state representative to orally introduce the report at the session;
3. Inviting questions by members;
4. Permitting responses by the State representatives;
5. Adopting and publishing brief comments for inclusion in the annual report.

In 1999, CEDAW provided further clarification of the purpose of this procedure as being, 'to obtain and examine the information on an actual or potential violation of women's rights, where there is special cause for concern about such violation'.[207] The criterion for requesting an exceptional report are: (a) the existence of 'reliable and adequate information indicating grave or systematic violations of women's human rights'; and (b) the violations should be 'gender-based or directed at women because of their sex'. The exceptional reports should

---

[202] Ibid. para 26.
[203] UN Doc. A/60/38(SUPP) para 397.
[204] See O' Flaherty, 'Treaty Bodies Responding to States of Emergency: The Case of Bosnia and Herzegovina' in Alston and Crawford, above n.128, pp. 439–460.
[205] UN Doc. A/48/38; Chap 1. sect. B. Reports have since been requested from Democratic Republic of Congo (Zaire) and Rwanda. Rule 48(5) Rules of Procedure of the Committee on the Elimination of Discrimination against Women, UN Doc. A/56/38 (Annex. I).
[206] UN Doc. A/48/38, paras 729–776 and A/50/38, paras 553–591.
[207] Decision 21/1 in UN Doc. A/54/38/Rev.1 (SUPP), Chapter I, p. 47.

focus on whatever particular issues have been identified by the Committee.[208] NGOs may direct the attention of members of the Committee to situations that call for requesting of exceptional reports. Furthermore, NGOs may submit reports once the reports have been submitted.

(iv) Recent initiatives

In light of the significant violations of women's rights, the international community has undertaken a number of initiatives. Women's rights, as a subject, have been considered in various contexts and by a number of recent international instruments. We have already considered the adoption of the Optional Protocol to the Convention on the Elimination of All Forms of Discrimination against Women. The Optional Protocol forms part of a sustained campaign to ensure equality of treatment for women in all spheres of life, and also to provide an impetus in addressing their needs. These campaigns also include the Nairobi Forward-looking Strategies for the Advancement of Women (1985)[209] the Vienna Declaration and Programme of Action adopted by the World Conference on Human Rights (1993)[210] and the Fourth World Conference on Women held in Beijing in September 1995.[211] The objective of the Beijing Conference included, *inter alia*, reviewing the progress made since the Nairobi Conference and to adopt a 'Platform for Action'. This 'Platform for Action' was intended to concentrate on key obstacles which are preventing the advancement of women. The document suggested and proposed to various agencies, including the governments, NGOs, the private sector and individuals, strategies for the removal of barriers in the path of equality and further progression of women's rights. Further developments have taken place after the Beijing Conference.

During its 55th session, the General Assembly adopted a resolution which is a follow-up to the Beijing Conference and was intended to review the progress made in the five years proceding the Conference.[212] The General Assembly also invited ECOSOC to continue to promote a co-ordinated follow-up programme for the implementation of the outcomes of the major UN Conferences and to ensure gender mainstreaming as an integral part of the activities of its mandate. At the same time there was a reaffirmation of the need to mobilise resources at all levels for the promotion of an active policy of adopting a gender perspective by the United Nations. In 2005, a review and appraisal of the Beijing Platform for Action was held at the Commission on the Status of Women in New York. In addition to reviewing the implementation of the Beijing Platform for Action the Commission also considered 'current challenges and forward-looking strategies for the advancement and empowerment of women and girls'.[213] The Declaration adopted at the review welcomed the progress made towards achieving gender equality but also recognised the need for further action to be taken in order to implement the Beijing Platform for Action.[214]

---

[208] Ibid.
[209] See Report of the World Conference to Review and Appraise the Achievements of the United Nations Decade for Women: Equality, Development and Peace, Nairobi, 15–26 July 1985 (United Nations publication, Sales No. E.85.IV.10), chap. I, sect. A.
[210] World Conference on Human Rights: *The Vienna Declaration and Programme of Action*, June (1993), UN Doc. A/CONF.157/23 12 July 1993.
[211] A/CONF.177/20, 1995; 35 I.L.M. (1996) 401. The Beijing Conference as noted above was the fourth world conference on women. Earlier conferences had been held in Mexico City (1975), Copenhagen (1980) and Nairobi (1985) which adopted the Forward-looking Strategies for the Advancement of Women.
[212] Bejing +5 (2000) GA/Res/55/71.
[213] www.un.org/womenwatch/daw/Review/English/49sess.htm <last visited 22 September 2008>.
[214] E/CN.6/2005/L.1 paras 2 and 3.

8 VIOLENCE AGAINST WOMEN

The Vienna Declaration and Programme of Action places emphasis upon the rights of women as human rights. The Declaration notes:

> The human rights of women and of the girl-child are an inalienable, integral and indivisible part of universal human rights. The full and equal participation of women in political, civil, economic, social and cultural life, at the national, regional and international levels, and the eradication of all forms of discrimination on grounds of sex are priority objectives of the international community.[215]

One of the recommendations that were made by the Vienna Declaration was to call 'upon the General Assembly to adopt the draft declaration on violence against women and [to urge] States to combat violence against women in accordance with its provisions'.[216] The majority of domestic violence goes on behind closed doors, the information that is leaked out to international monitoring bodies presents a horrific and unfortunate picture. Reports of forms of domestic violence represent a source of serious concern. A serious criticism of the Women's Convention has been the absence of specific provisions condemning violence against women, an omission which is unacceptable in the light of everyday instances of violence against women in every region of the world.[217] This criticism is visible through the analysis of such treaty-based bodies as the Human Rights Committee and the Committee against Torture.[218]

In order to overcome this lacuna, the United Nations General Assembly adopted a Declaration on the Elimination of Violence against Women.[219] The Declaration provides an expansive definition to the term 'violence against women' in Article 1, taking it to mean:

> any act of gender-based violence that results in, or is likely to result in, physical, sexual or psychological harm or suffering to women, including threats of such acts, coercion or arbitrary deprivation of liberty, whether occurring in public or in private life.

Article 2, in elaborating upon the meaning of violence, provides examples such as:

> (a) Physical, sexual and psychological violence occurring in the family, including battering, sexual abuse of female children in the household, dowry-related violence, marital rape, female genital mutilation and other traditional practices harmful to women, non-spousal violence and violence related to exploitation;

---

[215] Ibid. Section I, para 18, p. 34.
[216] Ibid. Section II.38, p. 54.
[217] Subedi, above n.11, at p. 595; this point has been established by CEDAW in its consideration of State reports.
[218] See Human Rights Committee, Sixty fourth session, *Concluding observations of the Human Rights Committee: Libyan Arab Jamahiriya*. 06/11/98. CCPR/C/79/Add.101. (Concluding Observations/Comments), para 17. On the Committee against Torture See Byrnes, 'The Committee against Torture' in Alston (ed.), above n.128, 509–546 at p. 519; see below chapter 22.
[219] GA Res. 48/104 of 20 December 1993.

(b) Physical, sexual and psychological violence occurring within the general community, including rape, sexual abuse, sexual harassment and intimidation at work, in educational institutions and elsewhere, trafficking in women and forced prostitution;

(c) Physical, sexual and psychological violence perpetrated or condoned by the State, wherever it occurs.

The Declaration calls upon all States to condemn violence against women and not to invoke any custom, tradition or religious consideration to justify the continuation of any such violence.[220] This provision is particularly aimed at those societies which continue to vindicate such policies as female circumcision, *sati*[221] or dowry as part of divine ordinance or an integral part of their culture and traditions. In addition, the Declaration adopts a much wider approach in condemning psychological violence and marital rape. Marital rape remains a problematic family law issue in many States, including the United Kingdom.[222]

The UN Declaration is a General Assembly Resolution and is not *per se* a legally binding instrument.[223] However, as we have noted in an earlier chapter, General Assembly Resolutions present evidence of State practice which alongside the requisite *opinio juris* can lead to the establishment of customary international law. The fact that the Resolution was adopted without a vote, but by consensus amongst States, has added to its weight and authority. Subsequent developments, particularly since the Beijing Conference may lead the provisions in the Declaration to represent customary law.

Whatever may be the precise legal position of the provisions contained in the Declaration, it is already obvious that the Resolution has had a considerable impact in developing the law relating to women's rights and has provided substantial ammunition to CEDAW to scrutinise practices which contravene the provisions of the Declaration. CEDAW in its recent survey of reports has shown concern at the lack of available information on the incidence and types of violence against women, particularly at home.[224] It has expressed grave concern at the incidents of so-called 'honour killings',[225] acid throwing, stoning and dowry death,[226] dowry, *sati* and the *devadasi* system.[227] In a number of instances, it has lamented the inability of government to take effective action to enforce laws, or to provide immediate relief to women who are victims of such violence. The unfortunate position of women suffering from violence and the threat of violence has led to other courts and tribunals extending human rights protection. There is, therefore, an increased willingness to recognise gender-based persecution as a ground for granting asylum. In a case decided by the Judicial Committee of the House of Lords, their Lordships

---

[220] Ibid. Article 4.
[221] The self-immolation of a widow on her husband's funeral pyre.
[222] See *R. v. R. (Rape: Marital Exemption)* [1992] 1 AC 599; *S.W. v. UK*, Ser. A 335-B, 1995 and *C.R. v. UK*, Ser. A 335-C, 1995. Sexual Offences Act 2003; for commentaries on the revisions in law, see Ashworth, *Principles of Criminal Law* (Oxford University Press, 2006) pp. 337–351; concern has been expressed at the continuation of instances of martial rape. See e.g. Concluding Observations/Comments by the Human Rights Committee for Uzbekistan, 26/04/2001 CCPR/CO/71/UZB, para 19; see also Concluding Comments by CEDAW on the report by Egypt para 344, see Egypt's 3rd and Combined 4th and 5th Periodic Reports, CEDAW/CIEGY/3 and CEDAW/C/EGY at its 492nd and 493rd meetings (4–19 January 2001). A/56/38 p. 36, para 344.
[223] On the value of General Assembly Resolutions see above chapter 3.
[224] Iraq A/55/38 (SUPP), p. 66, para 189.
[225] Ibid. para 193.
[226] See Bangladesh, above n.60, para 436.
[227] See India, above n.60, para 68.

held that women suffering from domestic violence could be recognised as a 'particular social group' and thereby are able to rely upon the protection afforded under the Geneva Convention Relating to the Status of Refugees 1951 and therefore allowed their appeal.[228]

Given the widespread nature and growing concern over violence against women, the United Nations Human Rights Commission, in 1994, appointed a Special Rapporteur on Violence against Women, for a period of three years, which has subsequently been extended every three years for a further period.[229] The Special Rapporteurs, during their terms in office, have made a number of visits to countries and produced several valuable reports. Violence against women was a subject that highlighted a particular source of concern in the Beijing Conference[230] and the follow-up to the Conference.[231]

9 CONCLUSIONS

The Convention on the Elimination of All Forms of Discrimination against Women has been described as the international bill of rights for women. Its many positive aspects include coverage of a fairly comprehensive range of rights and a useful State reporting mechanism, which has more recently been supplemented by an individual complaints procedure. Despite these positive features, the Convention, nevertheless, suffers from significant substantive and procedural weaknesses. The language of the Convention 'is considerably closer to that of a political declaration than that of an international treaty'.[232] The Convention fails to address some of the more fundamental issues such as violence against women; it does not makes any references to sexual orientation or lesbian women, and apart from the reference in Article 12 to health, no particular recognition of reproductive rights. While some remedial attempts have been made by the United Nations in the absence of

[228] See Article 1A(2) Geneva Convention Relating to the Status of Refugees 1951. *Islam (A.P.) v. Secretary of State for the Home Department; R. v. Immigration Appeal Tribunal and another ex parte Shah (A.P.) (Conjoined Appeals)* www.parliament.the-stationery-office.co.uk/pa/ld199899/ldjudgmt/jd990325/islam, 25 March 1999, (Internet edition: 27 October, 2001). See also Wallace, above n.10, at p. 702; see however, the following: Sinha, 'Domestic Violence and U.S. Asylum Law: Eliminating the "Cultural Hook" for Claims Involving Gender-Related Persecution' 76 *New York University Law Review* (2001) 1562; Anker, 'Refugee Status and Violence Against Women in the "Domestic" Sphere: The Non-State Actor Question' 15 *Georgetown Immigration Law Journal* (2001) 391.

[229] See the most recent report by the Special Rapporteur on Violence against Women Promotion and Protection of All Human Rights, Civil, Political, Economic, Social and Cultural Including the Right to Development, Report of the Special Rapporteur on violence against women, its causes and consequences, Yakin Ertürk: Indicators on violence against women and State response 29 January 2008 www2.ohchr.org/english/bodies/hrcouncil/docs/7session/A-HRC-7-6.doc <last visited 7 February 2009>.

[230] 'Violence against women both violates and impairs or nullifies the enjoyment by women of human rights and fundamental freedoms. Taking into account the Declaration on the Elimination of Violence against Women and the work of Special Rapporteurs, gender-based violence, such as battering and other domestic violence, sexual abuse, sexual slavery and exploitation, and international trafficking in women and children, forced prostitution and sexual harassment, as well as violence against women, resulting from cultural prejudice, racism and racial discrimination, xenophobia, pornography, ethnic cleansing, armed conflict, foreign occupation, religious and anti-religious extremism and terrorism are incompatible with the dignity and the worth of the human person and must be combated and eliminated. Any harmful aspect of certain traditional, customary or modern practices that violates the rights of women should be prohibited and eliminated. Governments should take urgent action to combat and eliminate all forms of violence against women in private and public life, whether perpetrated or tolerated by the State or private persons', see above n.211, para 224.

[231] See FWCW 'Platform for Action Violence against Women' Strategic objective D.1–D.3.

[232] Reanda, 'The Commission on the Status of Women' in Alston (ed.), above n.128, pp. 265–303 at p. 287.

15

The rights of women

specific provisions, e.g. prohibiting violence, recognising sexual orientation and reproductive rights through the jurisprudence of CEDAW, within the treaty this still represents a significant omission.

It is also the case that the Convention was a product of years of debate and argument. Needless to say, the instrument that finally emerged was a product of political compromises, many of them fundamental to the entire debate relating to women's human rights.[233] A majority of the States would have been unwilling to proceed towards completion of the instruments if this contravened their fundamental precepts. One lingering reminiscent of this conciliatory stance is the reservations clause as provided in the Convention.[234]

Out of all the human rights treaties, the Women's Convention has attracted the highest number of reservations, some of them so sweeping and overriding in nature that the issue of good faith and principle of integrity of the instrument inevitably comes into question. The factors that have led States to place reservations include cultural relativism and religious intolerance.[235] CEDAW has consistently encouraged States to review and withdraw their reservations. A number of Islamic States have disputed the compatibility of provisions. Unlike the Race Convention, which provides that reservations are to be considered incompatible if at least two-thirds of the State parties object to it, the Women's Convention provides no similar provisions as to whether reservation is valid, except the possibility of reference to the International Court of Justice under Article 29. States which are unhappy with a reservation can enter an objection to the reservation and then raise the matter at meetings of State parties or other bodies such as ECOSOC or the General Assembly. The realisation of the purposes and principles set forth in the Convention through a system of periodic reporting has not been satisfactory. While the adoption of the Optional Protocol to the Convention (which allows individuals to bring a complaint before CEDAW) is a very commendable undertaking, it is probably too early to predict the extent to which this procedure will be relied upon or the extent to which the Protocol will prove to be a vehicle for positive change for women's rights. Judging from the current state of affairs, it might be overly optimistic to assume that the Protocol would have an impact anywhere near to that of the first Optional Protocol to the ICCPR.

There are other defects and weaknesses as well. In comparison to other treaty-based bodies, CEDAW has remained at a disadvantage when acquiring adequate information on violations of the rights set forth in the Convention. There is a need for a greater formal and informal participation of NGOs and specialised agencies such as the International Labour Organisation.[236] The overall position of CEDAW (again when compared with other treaty-based bodies) represents a relatively weak position. The Committee has had to adopt a more mundane and conciliatory stance, reasons for which include a weaker threshold of implementing authority, limited resources in terms of time and finances, and often evident divisions within CEDAW members themselves.

---

[233] On definitional aspects see UN Doc. E/CN.6/589–591 (1974); UN Doc. E/CN.6/AC.1/L.4. On Reservations see 54 UNESCOR Supp. (No. 5).

[234] Clark, 'The Vienna Convention Reservations Regime and the Convention on Discrimination against Women' 85 *AJIL* (1991) 281. Also see Cook, 'Reservations to the Convention on the Elimination of All Forms of Discrimination against Women' 30 *VJIL* (1990) 643.

[235] Steiner, Alston and Goodman (eds), *International Human Rights in Context: Law, Politics, Morals* (Oxford University Press, 2008) at pp. 1124–1130.

[236] See O'Flaherty, *Human Rights and the UN: Practice before the Treaty Bodies* (Brill, 2002) at pp. 111–112.

16 | The rights of the child[1]

1 INTRODUCTION

Violations of the rights of children represent a common occurrence in many parts of the world.[2] These violations take the form of torture, cruel, inhuman or degrading treatment, disappearances, excessive work and labour, prostitution, sexual abuse and slavery. Children also represent a significant proportion of the global refugee or stateless population. Millions of children around the world are at a serious risk of starvation and malnutrition; according to one estimate malnutrition, starvation and disease leads to the death of 40,000 children every day.[3]

As a response to these violations efforts have been made to establish a regime of international protection of the rights of children. During the 20th century the movement to protect children was given impetus by Save the Children International Union, an international NGO established shortly after the First World War.[4] In 1924, Save the Children International Union drafted a Declaration, which is more commonly known as the Declaration of Geneva or the Declaration of the Rights of the Child.[5] This Declaration was

---

[1] Fortin, *Children's Rights and the Developing Law* (Butterworths, 2003); Freestone (ed.), *Children and the Law: Essays in Honour of Professor H.K. Bevan* (Hull University Press, 1990); Fotrell (ed.), *Revisiting Children's Rights: 10 Years of the UN Convention on the Rights of the Child* (Kluwer Law International, 2000); Ali, Goonesekere, Mendez, and Rios-Kohn, *Protecting the World's Children: Impact of the Convention on the Rights of the Child in Diverse Legal Systems* (Cambridge University Press, 2007); Archard and Macleod (eds), *The Moral and Political Status of Children* (Oxford University Press, 2002); Ensalaco and Majka (eds), *Childrens' Human Rights: Progress and Challenges for Children Worldwide* (Rowman and Littlefield Publishers, 2005); Detrick, Doek, Cantwell and Martenson, *The United Nations Convention on the Rights of the Child: A Guide to the 'Travaux préparatoires'* (Martinus Nijhoff Publishers, 1992); McGoldrick, 'The United Nations Convention on the Rights of the Child' 5 *IJLF* (1991) 132; Arts and Popovski (eds), *International Criminal Accountability and the Rights of Children* (Hague Academic Press, 2006); Hallet and Prout (eds), *Hearing the Voices of Children: Social Policy for a New Century* (Routledge, 2003); See Alston, Parker and Seymour (eds), *Children, Rights and the Law* (Clarendon Press, 1992); Van Bueren, *The International Law on the Rights of the Child* (Martinus Nijhoff Publishers, 1995); and Freeman and Veerman (eds), *Ideologies of Children's Rights* (Martinus Nijhoff Publishers, 1992).

[2] The Convention on the Rights of the Child confirming this point notes in its preamble that 'in all countries in the world, there are children living in exceptionally difficult conditions': Preamble to the Convention on the Rights of the Child (1989). According to Freeman 'there are countries which today are systematically exterminating children as if they were vermin. Poverty, disease, exploitation are strife in every part of the globe', Freeman, 'The Limits of Children's Rights' in Freeman and Veerman (eds), above n.1, 29–46 at p. 31; Rogers and Roche, *Children's Welfare & Children's Rights: A Practical Guide to the Law* (Hodder and Stoughton, 1994).

[3] Van Bueren, above n.1, at p. 293. Van Bueren, 'Combating Child Poverty – Human Rights Approaches' 21 *HRQ* (1999) 680.

[4] See Cohen, 'The Role of Non-Governmental Organizations in the Drafting of the Convention on the Rights of the Child' 12 *HRQ* (1990) 137. See Save the Children website: www.savethechildren.org <last visited 1 March 2009>.

[5] See Cohen, 'Natural Law and Legal Positivism' in Freeman and Veerman (eds), above n.1, 53–70 at p. 60.

adopted by the Fifth Assembly of the League of Nations.[6] The Declaration provides for the fundamental rights of children such as the right to normal development, the right to be fed, relief from distress and protection from exploitation, and subsequently has proven to be the inspiration behind subsequent international child rights instruments.

Efforts to promote the rights of children continued after the Second World War. The United Nations Charter (1945)[7] while containing references to human rights does not refer to children's rights. The UDHR (1948) contains important provisions for children, although the emphasis is upon protection and non-discrimination, rather than granting specific, independent rights to a child as a person.[8] Article 25(2) of the Declaration provides that '[m]otherhood and childhood are entitled to special care and assistance. All children, whether born in or out of wedlock, shall enjoy the same social protection.' Article 26 instructs compulsory and free education at elementary level. It also provides for parents to 'have a prior right to choose the kind of education that shall be given to their children.'[9] The ICESCR (1966)[10] contains Articles regarding education[11] and health,[12] issues particularly connected to children. The ICCPR has several Articles which protect such valuable rights as the right to life, liberty and security of persons; rights that are applicable to individuals including children.[13] The Covenant also addresses children's rights in Article 24, which provides that:

1. Every child shall have, without any discrimination as to race, colour, sex, language, religion, national or social origin, property or birth, the right to such measures of protection as are required by his status as a minor, on the part of his family, society and the State.

2. Every child shall be registered immediately after birth and shall have a name.

3. Every child has the right to acquire a nationality.

The Human Rights Committee, which implements the ICCPR has also elaborated on the provisions of Article 24 through its consideration of State reports and its General Comment on the Article.[14]

2 INTERNATIONAL INSTRUMENTS ON THE RIGHTS OF THE CHILD

As far as children's rights as a distinct category of human rights law is concerned, the real impetus was provided with the adoption of the United Nations General Assembly Declaration on the Rights of the Child in 1959.[15] The Declaration, which consists of 10 substantive principles and a preamble, enumerates the most fundamental rights of the child in

---

[6] Record of the Fifth Assembly, Supplement No. 23 LONOJ, 1924.
[7] 26 June 1945, 59 Stat. 1031, T.S. 993, 3 Bevans 1153; see above chapter 2.
[8] GA Res. 217A (III), UN Doc A/810 at 71 (1948); see above chapter 4.
[9] Article 26(3) UDHR.
[10] New York, 16 December 1966, 993 U.N.T.S. 3; 6 I.L.M. (1967) 360.
[11] Article 13 ICESCR.
[12] Article 12 ICESCR.
[13] New York, 16 December 1966 United Nations, 999 U.N.T.S. 171; 6 I.L.M. (1967) 368.
[14] Human Rights Committee, General Comment 17: Rights of the Child (Article 24): 07/04/89 (Thirty fifth Session, 1989).
[15] Unlike the UDHR, this General Assembly Resolution was adopted without any abstentions GA Res. 1386(XIV), 20 November 1959.

international law. The principal aim is to provide for a range of rights including the right to a name and nationality, housing, recreation and medical services. The Declaration considers the position of physically, mentally and socially handicapped children and children without a family. It proved instrumental in developing concrete international standards and in particular the drafting of the Convention on the Rights of the Child. The year 1979 was designated by the United Nations General Assembly as the Year of the Child.[16] During 1979, the UN General Assembly authorised the Commission on Human Rights to draft a Convention focusing on the Rights of the Child. A Working Group established by the Commission started work on drafting of the Convention, a task that was completed with the adoption of the Convention on the Rights of the Child in 1989.[17]

The Convention came into force in September 1990. It is the most valuable treaty in the armoury of human rights law which protects and defends the rights of children the world over. Notwithstanding the fact that the Convention is more comprehensive than any other human rights treaties it has attracted the greatest number of ratifications.[18] The rights provided in the Convention have been supplemented by the Optional Protocol to the Convention on the Rights of the Child on the Involvement of Children in Armed Conflict[19] and the Optional Protocol to the Convention on the Rights of the Child on the Sale of Children, Child Prostitution and Child Pornography.[20] Other important international developments have included the International Labour Organization Convention 182 concerning the Prohibition and Immediate Action for the Elimination of the Worst Forms of Child Labour,[21] the UN Declaration on Social and Legal Principles relating to the Protection and Welfare of Children, with special reference to Foster Placement and Adoption Nationally and Internationally[22] and the United Nations Standard Minimum Rules for the Administration of Juvenile Justice ('The Beijing Rules').[23]

Children's rights have also been integrated into the wider human rights debate. We have already noted a developing human rights jurisprudence emergent from international bodies such as the European Court of Human Rights, and the Human Rights Committee.[24] The subject is increasingly being addressed by various international and regional bodies.[25] The International Criminal Court is authorised to consider specific aspects of children's rights as it qualifies the conscription of children under 15 years of age as a crime.[26] International

---

[16] GA Res. 31/169.

[17] New York, 20 November 1989 United Nations, *Treaty Series*, vol. 1577, p. 3.

[18] There are currently 193 States party to the Convention. All States apart from the United States and Somalia have ratified the convention. The ratifications of Convention have 'regrettably' been accompanied by a high pro portion of reservations and interpretative declaration. See Schabas, 'Reservations to the Convention on the Rights of the Child' 18 *HRQ* (1996) 4/2, at p. 472.

[19] New York, 25 May 2000 UN Doc. A/RES/54/263.

[20] Ibid.

[21] Convention Concerning the Prohibition and Immediate Action for the Elimination of the Worst Forms of Child Labour (ILO No. 182), 2133 U.N.T.S.161, entered into force, 9 November 2000.

[22] UN Declaration on Social and Legal Principles relating to the Protection and Welfare of Children, with special reference to Foster Placement and Adoption Nationally and Internationally, GA Res. 41/85, 3 December 1986.

[23] Standard Minimum Rules for the Administration of Juvenile Justice, GA Res. 40/33, 29 November 1985.

[24] See above chapters 5 and 7; Kilkelly, 'The Best of Both Worlds for Children's Rights? Interpreting the European Convention on Human Rights in the Light of the UN Convention on the Rights of the Child' 23 *HRQ* (2001) 308.

[25] Kilkelly, 'Strengthening the Framework for Enforcing Children's Rights: An Integrated Approach' in Ensalaco and Majka (eds), above n.1, pp. 53–79.

[26] In its definition of 'war crimes' the Statute of the Court includes the offence of 'Conscripting or enlisting children under the age of fifteen years into armed forces or groups or using them to participate actively in hostilities', Statute of the International Criminal Court (1998) Article 8 (e)(vii).

16

The rights of the child

economic agencies and intergovernmental bodies such as GATT/WTO have been reacting to sensitive issues of child exploitation and child labour.[27] The focus of this chapter is upon the Convention on the Rights of the Child, although brief consideration is provided to the jurisprudence emerging from regional or national instruments.

3 THE CONVENTION ON THE RIGHTS OF THE CHILD[28]

The basic thrust of the Convention is that the child has independent rights and the primary focus of the Convention is to operate in 'the best interests of the Child'.[29] According to Professor Van Bueren, the Convention is essentially about what she terms as the 'four Ps'. These are:

> the participation of children in decisions affecting their own destiny; the protection of the children against discrimination and all forms of neglect and exploitation; the prevention of harm to children; and the provisions of assistance for basic needs.[30]

There are many positive features of the Convention. The substantive Articles (Articles 1–41) are meant to cover all kinds of civil, political, economic, social and cultural rights. This is a detailed and comprehensive set of rights. The Convention confirms the fundamental rights, which are applicable to everyone. There is coverage of laws and regulations that affect children during armed conflicts. Rights, which are of a general character and have been applied in other human rights treaties, include the right to life, freedom of expression, freedom of religion, respect for privacy and the right to education. In addition to reiterating fundamental human rights, the Convention also establishes a regime of innovative rights. According to Cohen 'of the thirty-eight Articles . . . which are devoted to substantive rights, at least ten of these have never been recognised for children in any other international instrument'.[31] The innovative rights, which shall be considered in due course, include those contained in Articles 8, 10, 12–16, 25, 37 and 40.

The Convention also provides children with fundamental protection such as the right to be shielded from harmful acts or practices, to be protected from commercial or sexual exploitation, physical or mental abuse, or engagement in warfare. The Convention allows for the participation of the child in various matters concerning his or her welfare, e.g. the right to be heard on decisions affecting one's own life. It is fairly strong as regards provisional as well as protectional aspects. Within the Convention, the wishes of children are given much more prominence. Notwithstanding the many positive aspects in the Convention, there are also difficulties and tensions inherent in the text. The Convention

---

[27] See Ehrenberg, 'The Labor Link: Applying the International Trading System to Enforce Violations of Forced and Child Labour' 20 *YJIL* (1995) 361.

[28] New York, 20 November 1989 United Nations, *Treaty Series*, vol. 1577, p. 3 (entry into force 2 September 1990, in accordance with Article 49).

[29] See Article 3(1).

[30] Van Bueren, above n.1, at p. 15.

[31] See Cohen, 'Natural Law and Legal Positivism' in Freeman and Veerman (eds), above n.1, 53–70 at p. 61.

represents tensions between the rights of the parents, guardians and even the State *vis-à-vis* those of the child. The Convention has also proved disappointing in terms of elucidating rules regarding children in armed conflicts, e.g. protection of children. Furthermore, the language of several articles is weak and vague.

4 ANALYSING THE SUBSTANTIVE PROVISIONS

The Convention can be broken down into three parts: a Preamble, the Substantive articles (Article 1–41), and measures of implementation (Article 42–45). A Committee known as the Committee on the Rights of the Child is established by the Convention – the Committee is in charge of supervising the implementation of the Convention. The Convention is based upon four 'general principles' which are as follows:

- non-discrimination (Article 2),
- best interests of the child (Article 3),
- survival and development (Article 6),
- participation (Article 12).

These general principles represent essential underlying values and provide guidance in that each right is fulfilled and respected. They thereby act as a constant referencing point for the implementation and monitoring of children's rights. In its various General Comments as well as observations on States' reports, the Committee on the Rights of the Child has insisted that compliance with the aforementioned general principles form an essential basis for respecting all other provisions of the Convention. The value of these guiding principles can be ascertained through a perusal of the text as well as the Preamble to the Convention; the latter spelling out the principles and their inter-relationship with other international human rights provisions. The Preamble makes reference to the human rights provisions of the United Nations Charter, to the UDHR and the International Covenants on Human Rights. There are also references to the principles derived from the Declaration of the Rights of the Child of 1924 and to the Declaration of the Rights of the Child (1959).[32]

(i) Definitional issues and the obligations of States parties to non-discrimination

The Convention accords the child with a definition. According to Article 1, for the purposes of the Convention a child is 'every human being below the age of eighteen unless, under the law applicable to the child, majority is attained earlier'. The provision represents a compromise since States parties differ in their views on the age of majority. At the same time the phrase 'unless, under the law applicable to the child, majority is attained earlier' puts the helpfulness of the article in doubt. According to McGoldrick:

---

[32] See the Preamble to the Convention on the Rights of the Child (CRC).

Article 1 clearly permits the national law of a State to provide that majority is attained at an age earlier than eighteen. Although that individual is then entitled to all the human rights of an adult, the special protection applicable to children no longer covers them. A minimum age limit for the declaration of majority by national laws should have been included.[33]

Article 1 uses the term 'human being' and the most common deduction appears to be that it is applicable to a child who is born; a foetus, thus, cannot claim to have rights under the Convention. At the same time, the Convention specifically incorporates in its preamble, the terminology from United Nations Declaration (1959) which applies 'special safeguards and care, including appropriate legal protection, before as well as after birth'.[34] The position, as we have noted already, continues to remain ambiguous, and uncertainty exists in other regional and international human rights instruments.[35]

As noted already, Article 2 alongside Articles 3, 6 and 12 represent the four main general principles of the Convention and therefore deserve a focused analysis. Article 2 sets out the obligation, according to which:

---

[33] McGoldrick, above n.1, at p. 133. Also see Human Rights Committee General Comment 17: Rights of the Child (Article 24) (35th Session) adopted 5 April 1989, para 4. Concern has been expressed by HRC in instances where children under the age of 10 are held in detention on remand (Concluding Observations on Guyana, 2000 UN Doc. CCPR/C/79/Add.121, para 16); similar concern has been expressed in the case of Sri Lanka with a low age of criminal responsibility and the stipulation within the Penal Code by which a child above 8 years of age and under 12 years of age can be held to be criminally responsible. See 1995 UN Doc. CCPR/C/79/Add 56. The Committee on the Rights of the Child has expressed its concern where judicial officers are granted a discretion to decide that a person under the age of 18 has reached majority at an earlier age. See the Committee on the Rights of the Child, Forty-First Session, Consideration of Reports Submitted by States Parties under Article 44 of the Convention, Concluding Observations: Saudi Arabia CRC/C/SAU/CO/2 (17 March 2006) para 25. As considered below, in may States, capital punishment continues to be applied to persons below the age 18.

[34] The strength of the preambular paragraph is however watered down by a statement in the *travaux préparatoires* which notes 'in adopting this preambular paragraph, the working-group does not intend to prejudice the interpretation of Article 1 or any other provisions of the Convention by the States parties', UN Doc. E/CN.4/1989/48, para 43. See Alston, 'The Unborn Child and Abortion under the Draft Convention on the Rights of the Child' 12 *HRQ* (1990) 156.

[35] Attempts to incorporate an article in UDHR prohibiting abortion proved unsuccessful. See Samnøy, 'The Origins of the Universal Declaration of Human Rights' in Alfredsson and Eide (eds), *The Universal Declaration of Human Rights* (Kluwer Law International, 1998) pp. 3–22 at p. 14; According to Sarah Joseph, Jenny Schultz and Melissa Castan, 'neither the CRC nor the ICCPR makes any significant express attempt to elicit rights for unborn children . . . The CRC Preamble does refer to the need for appropriate legal protection applicable "before as well as after birth". However, this Preamble essentially represents a compromise between the irreconcilable views of two groups of countries concerning the moment when childhood begins; it is unlikely to be interpreted as a prohibition on abortion. Certainly, HRC comments have indicated that *prohibition* of abortion is more likely to breach the ICCPR than the *permissibility* of abortion', Joseph, Schultz and Castan *The International Covenant on Civil and Political Rights: Cases, Materials, and Commentary* (Oxford University Press, 2005) at p. 630 (italics provided). Also see Article 2 ECHR, Article 4(1) ACHR. In the context of inter-American human rights law see the *'Baby Boy'* case (United States), Case No. 2141, Res. 23/81, Inter-Am. C.H.R., OEA/Ser. L/V/II.54, Doc. 9, rev. 1, 16 October 1981; for commentary on the case see Shelton, 'Abortion and the Right to Life in the Inter-American System: The Case of 'Baby Boy' 2 *HRLJ* (1981) *HRLJ* 309. The issue of the rights of the unborn child and the right to seek abortions of unborn children remains contentious and is coloured heavily with religious, political and social perspective. In many traditions which are influenced by Christian (in particular Catholic) Islamic or Hindu faith, States continue to retain rigorous laws in restricting abortions. As noted in an earlier chapter, Chile, El Salvador and Nicaragua are three countries in the Americas eliminating all exception to abortion. Similarly, within the Islamic world serious restrictions exist over abortion. In the European Human Rights context the European Court of Human Rights, however, has determined that 'the unborn child is not regarded as a "person" directly protected by Article 2 of the Convention and that if the unborn do have a "right" to "life", it is implicitly limited by the mother's rights and interests' *Vo v. France*, (2005) 40 E.H.R.R. 12, para 80. Discussed above in chapter 8. See further Zampas and Gher 'Abortion as a Human Right – International and Regional Standards' 8 *HRLR* (2008) 249; Plomer, 'A Foetal Right to Life? The Case of *Vo v. France*' 5 *HRLR* (2005) 311.

1. States Parties shall respect and ensure the rights set forth in the present Convention to each child within their jurisdiction without discrimination of any kind, irrespective of the child's or his or her parent's or legal guardian's race, colour, sex, language, religion, political or other opinion, national, ethnic or social origin, property, disability, birth or other status.

2. States Parties shall take all appropriate measures to ensure that the child is protected against all forms of discrimination or punishment on the basis of the status, activities, expressed opinions, or beliefs of the child's parents, legal guardians, or family members.

This Article is aimed at ensuring the applicability of the international norm of non-discrimination insofar as children are concerned. The terminology employed here is similar to the non-discriminatory provisions in other human rights treaties, in particular the ICCPR and ICESCR. In common with the two international covenants, the term 'discrimination' is not defined in the Convention. As we have been considering throughout this study, the concept of 'respect' and 'ensure' impose positive as well as horizontal obligations on the State. In the context of children's rights, the horizontal application of rights places obligations on States parties to render unlawful breaches of the convention by non-State actors and private individuals.[36] The deployment of the terminology of 'jurisdiction' as opposed to 'territory' is also meaningful and, in the light of our analysis, in particular that of the Human Rights Committee and the European Court of Human Rights arguably covers a wide range of activities, which are not necessarily confined to the territorial boundaries of a State.[37] The Convention borrows the terms race, colour, sex, language, religion, political or other opinion, national, ethnic or social origin, and property from related human rights instruments and the Committee on the Rights of the Child has relied upon existing human rights jurisprudence in its analysis. The usage of the phrase 'birth' in Article 2(1) is arguably meant to ensure that children born out of wedlock or those through the process of artificial insemination receive non-discriminatory treatment.[38] The Convention, in line with other human rights instruments[39] and case-law emergent from treaties,[40] aims to eradicate all forms of discrimination against children born out of wedlock. Discriminatory regulations and practices for illegitimacy are applied routinely

---

[36] See Harris, O'Boyle, Bates and Buckley, *Harris, O'Boyle and Warbrick Law of the European Convention on Human Rights* (Oxford University Press, 2009) at pp. 21–22.

[37] See in particular, above, chapters 5 and 7.

[38] Lopatka, 'The Rights of the Child are Universal: The Perspective of the UN Convention on the Rights of the Child' in Freeman and Veerman (eds), above n.1, 47–52 at p. 49.

[39] See e.g. Article 25(2) Universal Declaration of Human Rights which requires treatment of all children 'whether born in or out of wedlock'; the ACHR also notes that the States 'shall recognise equal rights for children born out of wedlock and those born in wedlock'. For consideration of this Article see Davidson, 'The Civil and Political Rights Protected in the Inter-American Human Rights System' in Harris and Livingstone (eds), *The Inter-American System of Human Rights* (Clarendon Press, 1998) pp. 213–288 at p. 270. The ICCPR requires children not to be discriminated on grounds of birth and the ICESCR prohibits 'for reasons of parentage'. HRC has expressed concern over State legislation and practices where discrimination persists against children born out of wedlock. (See Concluding Observations on the Libyan Arab Jamahirya 1998 UN Doc. CCPR/C/79/Add.80.) The European Social Charter (1961) accords rights 'irrespective of marital status and family relations'.

[40] See *Marckx* v. *Belgium* (1979–80) 2 E.H.R.R. 330 (inferior legal status of unmarried mother and her child constituted a violation of Articles 8 and 14); *Johnston and others* v. *Ireland* (1987) 9 E.H.R.R. 203 (where child is born out of wedlock and this state of affairs results in a failure of respect for child's family life, a violation of Article 8 takes place); for discussion see Davidson, 'The European Convention on Human Rights and the "Illegitimate" Child' in Freestone (ed.), above n.1, at pp. 75–106; Kilkelly, *The Child and the European Convention on Human Rights* (Dartmouth Publishing Co., 1999).

across many cultures and traditions and have been the object of concern for the Committee on the Rights of the Child. In its concluding observations on Saudi Arabia, the Committee makes the following observations:

> The Committee recommends that the State party review relevant domestic laws and administrative regulations in order to ensure full respect for the equality between girls and boys in the enjoyment of all rights in the Convention, and in order to ensure that children born out of wedlock, children of non-Saudi nationals (migrants) and children begging on the streets are not discriminated against. The Committee encourages the State party to further strengthen its proactive and comprehensive efforts to eliminate de facto discrimination on any grounds and against all vulnerable groups of children, including through public education campaigns to prevent discrimination and combat negative attitudes in society. The State party should pursue such efforts in close cooperation with community and religious leaders with a view to promoting change in persisting patriarchal socio-cultural traditions and attitudes, especially towards girls in particular.[41]

Discrimination on the basis of gender, including against girl-children, is impermissible, both in international human rights treaty law and under customary international law.[42] That said, gender-based discrimination and that against the girl-child, unfortunately, is continually practiced and in some cases officially sanctioned. There are tragic reports of abortions of the female foetus, and stereotypical images continue to provide preferential treatment for boys. There are also instances where forms of gender-based discrimination are written into existing legislation: one regular example being that of laws defining different minimum ages of marriages prescribed for boys and girls.[43]

The features listed within Article 2(1) are not exhaustive; instead the terminology 'other status' takes account of various other bases for discrimination. Thus the Committee has legitimately expressed concern at the treatment faced by children belonging to ethnic or indigenous communities,[44] refugee or asylum-seeking children;[45] discrimination against children living in institutions, discrimination against children with various forms of disabilities[46] and children affected by infectious diseases.[47] Discrimination against children

---

[41] Consideration of Reports Submitted by State Parties under Article 44 of the Convention, Concluding Observations: Saudi-Arabia, Forty-First Session, CRC/C/SAU/CO/2 17 March 2006, para 28.

[42] In its General Comment No. 28, HRC makes the following observation: '[t]he obligation of states to protect children (article 24) should be carried out equally for boys and girls. States should report on measures taken to ensure that girls are treated equally to boys in education, in feeding and in health care, and provide the Committee with disaggregated data in this respect. States should eradicate, both through legislation and any other appropriate measures, all cultural or religious practices which jeopardize the freedom and well-being of female children' (para 28). See Human Rights Committee, *General Comment No. 28: Equality of rights between men and women (article 3): 29/03/2000* CCPR/C/21/Rev.1/Add.10.

[43] UNICEF, *Implementation Handbook for the Convention on the Rights of the Child* (UNICEF, 2002) p. 23.

[44] Consideration of Reports Submitted by State Parties under Article 44 of the Convention, Concluding Observations: Bulgaria Forty-Eight Session, CRC/C/BGR/CO/2 23 June 2008, para 24; Consideration of Reports Submitted by State Parties under Article 44 of the Convention, Concluding Observations: Hungary Forty-first Session, CRC/C/HUN/CO/2 17 March 2006, para 19.

[45] Consideration of Reports Submitted by State Parties under Article 44 of the Convention, Concluding Observations: Georgia Forty-Eight Session, CRC/C/GEO/CO/2 23 June 2008, para 21.

[46] Consideration of Reports Submitted by State Parties under Article 44 of the Convention, Concluding Observations: Azerbaijan, Forty-First Session, CRC/C/AZE/CO/2 17 March 2006, para 24.

[47] Consideration of Reports Submitted by State Parties under Article 44 of the Convention, Concluding Observations: Eriteria Forty-Eight Session, CRC/C/ERI/CO/3 23 June 2008, para 25.

with HIV/AIDS has manifested particularly strongly in limitations placed *inter alia* on their access to health, education, care and housing. In its concluding observations on Eritrea, the Committee expressed concern at the discrimination not only against girl-children and nomadic and pastoralist minorities, but also children living in poverty and children affected by and/or infected with HIV/AIDS.[48]

In order to comply with the provisions fully, States parties are required to undertake an active approach. The Committee on the Rights of the Child has emphasised adopting this approach on several occasions. In its concluding observations to Egypt, the Committee noted that: 'the principle of non-discrimination, as provided for under article 2 of the Convention, must be vigorously applied. A more active approach should be taken to eliminating discrimination against certain groups of children, in particular girl children and children in rural areas. With regard to the gap in literacy and school enrolment mentioned in the report, obstacles facing girls should be adequately addressed so that they can enjoy their right to go to school; further measures might be taken to increase the awareness of parents in this regard.'[49] The States parties need to confirm as to whether the principle of discrimination related to children has been incorporated in the State constitutions or within domestic legislation and also to confirm that the grounds provided in Article 2 are reflected in established legal provisions. The Committee has urged States parties to consistently review their legislation and administrative practice to eradicate discrimination against children. Furthermore, States parties need to provide information within their reports on the steps that are taken to prevent and combat discrimination in law as well as in practice.

An active approach is required within the provisions of Article 2 also include positive action, including in particular cases, having resort to affirmative action policies or special measures. Thus the Committee notes:

> This non-discrimination obligation requires States actively to identify individual children and groups of children the recognition and realization of whose rights may demand special measures. For example, the Committee highlights, in particular, the need for data collection to be disaggregated to enable discrimination or potential discrimination to be identified. Addressing discrimination may require changes in legislation, administration and resource allocation, as well as educational measures to change attitudes. It should be emphasized that the application of the non-discrimination principle of equal access to rights does not mean identical treatment.[50]

Article 2(1) not only prohibits discrimination against the child, but also against 'his or her parent's or legal guardian's race, colour, sex etc'. Children, obviously suffer from various forms of discrimination because of the many attributes they inherit from the parents. Article 2(2) represents an undertaking on the part of States parties to protect the child from being discriminated as a consequence of status, activities or beliefs of the child's parents,

---

[48] Ibid. para 25.
[49] Consideration of Reports Submitted by State Parties under Article 44 of the Convention, Concluding Observations: Egypt Third Session CRC/C/15/Add.5. Concluding Observations/Comments, 18/02/93 para 12.
[50] Committee on the Rights of the Child, General measures of implementation of the Convention on the Rights of the Child (Articles 4, 42 and 44, para 6) General Comment No. 5. CRC/GC/2003/5 27 November 2003 at p. 4.

legal guardians or family members. One clear example of parental action affecting discrimination faced by children is the failure of the parents to enter a valid marriage agreement. The religion, language or political or other opinions of the parents, legal guardian or family members are factors which frequently attract discrimination – as this study examines both within this chapter and in others, children are targets of genocide as well as persecution based on religion, ethnicity and language inherited. In their reports, State parties are required to provide information on measures undertaken to ensure the protection of children against discrimination as a consequence of the status, activities, belief or opinions of the child's parents or legal guardian or family members.

(ii) Best interest of the child

Article 3, as noted earlier, represents a guiding principle of the Convention; the Convention having built around the principle that all measures undertaken must take into account the best interests of the child.[51] Best interest of the child principle is clearly established by Article 3, which provides that:

1. In all actions concerning children, whether undertaken by public or private social welfare institutions, courts of law, administrative authorities or legislative bodies, the best interests of the child shall be a primary consideration.

2. States Parties undertake to ensure the child such protection and care as is necessary for his or her well-being, taking into account the rights and duties of his or her parents, legal guardians, or other individuals legally responsible for him or her, and, to this end, shall take all appropriate legislative and administrative measures.

3. States Parties shall ensure that the institutions, services and facilities responsible for the care or protection of children shall conform with the standards established by competent authorities, particularly in the areas of safety, health, in the number and suitability of their staff, as well as competent supervision.

In light of its significance, States parties are required to recognise that this principle is a primary consideration in all its activities concerning children and that it is established within the constitutional framework or within relevant national legislation. States parties are required to provide further particulars and details of the manner in which this principle is applied by public as well as private bodies. The principle requires active measures within government as well as legislative and judicial bodies. 'Every legislative, administrative and judicial body or institution is required to apply the best interests principle by systematically considering how children's rights and interests are or will be affected by their decisions and actions – by, for example, a proposed or existing law or policy, or administrative action or court decision, including those which are not directly concerned with children, but indirectly affect children'.[52] The Committee on the Right of the Child has elaborated on the provision and it notes that the 'article refers to actions undertaken by "public or private

---

[51] See generally Alston and Gilmour-Walsh, *The Best Interests of the Child: Towards a Synthesis of Children's Rights and Cultural Values* (International Child Development Centre, UNICEF, 1996).

[52] General measures of implementation of the Convention on the Rights of the Child (Articles 4, 42 and 44, para 6) Thirty-fourth session 19 September–3 October 2003 CRC/GC/2003/5 27 November 2003 at p. 4.

social welfare institutions, courts of law, administrative authorities or legislative bodies" '.[53] The Committee on the Rights of the Child has emphasised on the critical importance of best interests throughout its consideration of State reports.[54] It has recently, in the case of Kazakhstan, expressed concern that 'this principle is not adequately respected and imple mented in all regulations as well as in practice in all domains and for all children'.[55] In its interaction with the United Kingdom, the Committee noted that '[Article 3 provisions] relating to the best interest of the child, should guide the determination of policy-making at both the central and local levels of government'.[56]

The significance of the provisions of Article 3 is underlined by the fact that these provisions cannot be the subject of any reservation.[57] This significance is further highlighted in the jurisprudence of domestic courts where, for example, in the United States, a US district court recognised the conventional 'best interest' principle as a principle of customary international law.[58] The usage of the word 'a primary' instead of 'the primary' consideration however allows for other factors to be taken into account.[59] In deciding what is in the best interest of the child, the wishes of the child are to be considered. Issues of cultural relativism do, nevertheless, enter the debate making it difficult for international tribunals to formulate definitive judgments.[60] As regards the application of the rights, the Convention – in line with the division produced by the International Covenants – distinguishes between civil and political rights of the child *vis-à-vis* economic, social and cultural rights. There is, thus, a difference between the civil and political rights of the child as opposed to economic, social and cultural rights of the child.[61] The civil and political rights obligations are of immediate application, whereas in the case of economic, social and cultural rights, the States parties are to 'undertake such measures to the maximum extent of their available

16

---

[53] Committee on the Rights of the Child, General measures of implementation of the Convention on the Rights of the Child (Articles 4, 42 and 44, para 6) General Comment No. 5. CRC/GC/2003/5 27 November 2003 at p. 4.

[54] Thus, for example, in its concluding observations to the report from Maldives, the Committee 'recommends that the State party fully incorporate article 3 of the Convention into all legislation and practices concerning children and raise awareness of the meaning and practical application of the principle of the best interests of the child. The Committee recommends that the State party review its legislation critically to ensure that the main thrust of the Convention, namely that children are subjects of their own rights, is adequately reflected in domestic legislation and that the best interests of the child be a primary consideration in all decision-making regarding children, including custody decisions'. Forty-fifth session Concluding Observations: Maladives CRC/C/MDV/CO/3 (13 July 2007) para 41, Consideration of Reports Submitted by States Parties under Article 44 of the Convention.

[55] Forty-fifth session Concluding Observations: Kazakhstan CRC/C/KAZ/CO/3 (19 June 2007) Consideration of Reports Submitted by States Parties under Article 44 of the Convention para 28.

[56] Eighth session Concluding Observations: *Concluding observations of the Committee on the Rights of the Child: United Kingdom of Great Britain and Northern Ireland. 15/02/95 CRC/C/15/Add.34. (Concluding Observations/ Comments)* Consideration of Reports Submitted by States Parties under Article 44 of the Convention para 24.

[57] Goodwin-Gill and McAdam, *The Refugee in International Law* (Oxford University Press, 2007) at p. 323.

[58] See *Beharry v. Reno*, 181 F. Supp. 2d 584, 603–605 (E.D.N.Y. 2002) discussed in Aleinikoff and Chetail, *Migration and International Legal Norms* (Asser Press, 2003) at p. 101.

[59] *Cf.* the English Children's Act 1989, which makes the Child's interests the paramount factor. In this comparison we see that the Child's interests are not given as much weight in the Convention as under national law. This represents one significant criticism of the Convention.

[60] Above chapter 1.

[61] *Cf.* Van Bueren, above n.1, at p. 692 where emphasising upon the interaction between civil and political rights she goes as far as to suggest that 'it is even arguable that the economic and social rights of children have become part of international customary law'. Also see Nolan, 'A Role for the Courts in Ensuring the Enforcement of the Socio-Economic Rights of the Child: Overcoming the "Counter-majoritarian Objection"' in Alen *et al.* (eds), *The UN Children's Rights Convention: Theory Meets Practice* (Intersentia, 2007) at pp. 333–357.

resources and, where needed, within the framework of international co-operation'.[62] States, in their reports under Article 44 of the Convention, have often relied on the lack of resources to justify their failure to meet the requirements of the Convention. This argument has, however, been criticised by the Committee on the Rights of the Child on numerous occasions.[63]

(iii) Developmental rights of the child

The right to life (as noted throughout this book) is the most fundamental of human rights.[64] This significance of this right is underlined through its recognition as providing the guiding principles for the convention. In the case of children, the relevance of the right could not be overstated. Article 6 provides as follows:

1. States Parties recognize that every child has the inherent right to life.
2. States Parties shall ensure to the maximum extent possible the survival and development of the child.

The ambit of this right is very wide as it includes pre-natal and post-natal care, nourishment and proper development.[65] As established by Article 6(2) the right to life is interlinked with the child's right to development. The Committee has further emphasised that it 'expects States to interpret "development" in its broadest sense as a holistic concept, embracing the child's physical, mental, spiritual, moral, psychological and social development. Implementation measures should be aimed at achieving the optimal development for all children'.[66] In accordance with this Article, States parties are required to specify steps undertaken to ensure the child's right to life and to effort taken to create an environment conducive to allowing maximum possible development and survival of the child including his or her mental, physical, moral, social and psychological development sufficient to reaffirm their inherent human dignity and also to prepare them as full members of the society. This right therefore means not only the adequate and inherent right to life but also the child'ń emotional, psychological, social, cognitive and cultural development. The developmental entitlement also incorporates certain programmes and opportunities that impact upon the qualitative aspect of survival. In this regard and intimately connected to this aspect of the right are the provisions contained in Article 31 which recognises the right of the child to rest, leisure, play, and participation in cultural life.[67] The right to life also

---

[62] Article 4 of the Convention on the Rights of the Child (CRC).
[63] See e.g. Consideration of Reports submitted by States Parties Under Article 44 of the Convention: Concluding Observations of the Committee on the Rights of the Child: Egypt, UN GAOR, Committee on the Rights of the Child 3rd. Session UN Doc. CRC/C/15/Add.5 (1993); Jordan, UN GAOR, Committee on the Rights of the Child 6th. Session UN Doc. CRC/C/15/Add.21 (1994).
[64] See Article 2 ECHR, Article 4 ACHPR, Article I ADHR and Article 4 AFCHPR. Article 19 ACHR provides that 'Every minor child has the right to measures of protection required by his condition as a minor on the part of his family, society and the State'.
[65] See Article 24.
[66] Committee on the Rights of the Child, General measures of implementation of the Convention on the Rights of the Child (Articles 4, 42 and 44, para 6) General Comment No. 5. CRC/GC/2003/5 27 November 2003 at p. 4.
[67] Concepcion, The Convention on the Rights of the Child After Ten Years: Success or Failure' www.wcl.american.edu/hrbrief/v7i2/child10years.htm <last visited 13 May 2009>.

includes freedom from malnutrition, starvation and disease. It is unfortunate that poverty continues to undermine the existence of millions of children not only within the developing world, but also within the developed industrialised States.[68] According to available statistics, child poverty has risen in 17 of the 24 most industrialised States over the past 12 years. Within the developing world 40 per cent of all children (over half a billion in total) struggle to survive on less than US$ 1 per day.[69] In elaborating upon the evils of child poverty, a UNICEF report makes the appropriate comment that '[M]illions of children around the world miss out on their childhood as a result of poverty – it threatens each and every right. Poverty deprives children of the capacities they need to survive, develop and thrive. It prevents them from enjoying equal opportunities. It makes children more vulnerable to exploitation, abuse, violence, discrimination and stigmatisation'.[70] Child poverty and starvation impacts upon all the rights accorded to children within the Convention.

In addition to existing child poverty, it remains a fact that in some regions of the world, starvation has been adopted as a deliberate policy of extermination of certain individuals or groups.[71] In such situations children are the primary casualties. Article 7 of the Convention confers upon children the important right to registration after birth, a right to name and to nationality, and the right to have knowledge of his parents. A 'right to identity', which can be considered an unusual right, is accorded to the child by virtue of Article 8. This Article was sponsored by Argentina with its tragic experiences of the so-called 'Dirty war' and child disappearances.[72] It was prompted by the same feelings as those which led to the incorporation of Article 18 of the ACHR.[73] Article 8 (in combination with Article 30) would also be valuable to children belonging to minority or indigenous groups in preserving their family traditions as well their linguistic, cultural and religious identity.[74]

Article 9 reinforces a significant factor concerning the development of the child. It imposes an obligation on States to make sure that children are never separated from their parents against their will, unless after due judicial determination such action is considered necessary to be in the best interest of the child. Examples provided in the Article include situations where abuse or neglect had been conducted by the parents or where the parents are living separately and the child's place of abode needs to be decided.[75] The Article also confers on the child the right to maintain personal contact with both of the separated parents.[76] The aims of Article 9 are further strengthened by Article 10, through encouraging States Parties to allow entrance and departure of parents by States, in order to facilitate union or contact with their children. The rights of children and parents to leave any country and to enter their own country is only subject to such restrictions as are prescribed by

[68] See UNICEF, *Child Poverty* (2006) www.unicef.org.uk/campaigns/publications/pdf/child_poverty06.pdf <last visited 11 May 2009>.
[69] Ibid. at p. 1.
[70] Ibid. at p. 1.
[71] Leo Kuper points to Sudan where 'starvation [has been] deployed as a weapon against civilians'. See Kuper, 'Theoretical Issues Relating to Genocide' in Andreopoulos (ed.), *Genocide: Conceptual and Historical Dimensions* (University of Pennsylvania Press, 1994) pp. 31–46 at p. 42.
[72] Fottrell, 'Children's Rights' in Hegarty and Leonard (eds), *Human Rights: An Agenda for the Twenty First Century* (Cavendish, 1999) pp. 167–179 at p. 172; Freestone, 'The United Nations Convention on the Rights of the Child' in Freestone (ed.), above n.1, 288–323 at p. 290.
[73] See above chapter 9.
[74] See Rehman, *The Weaknesses in the International Protection of Minority Rights* (Kluwer Law International, 2000) at p. 173.
[75] Article 9(1) CRC.
[76] Article 9(3) CRC.

law, which are necessary to protect the national security, public order (*ordre public*), public health or morals, or the rights and freedoms of others and are consistent with the other rights that are recognised in the Convention.[77] The applicability of this provision has been a problematic one, especially in respect of the immigration laws of many States including the United Kingdom.[78] Domestic legislation and administrative practices purporting to separate children from parents have received the attention of human rights tribunals. The ECHR does not include any articles establishing identical rights, but it has, nevertheless, been relied upon by individuals claiming that deportation or refusal to enter the State would mean separation from their children.[79]

Article 11 ordains that States take appropriate measures to prevent the illicit trafficking of children, their abduction and non-return from abroad. Several important regional and international conventions to prevent child abduction have come into operation to reinforce international law concerning child abduction and child custody. These include the Hague Convention on the Civil Aspects of International Child Abduction (1980)[80] and the European Convention on Recognition and Enforcement of Decisions Concerning Custody of Children and Restoration of Custody of Children (1980).[81]

Another subject, crucial to the development of children, is one of adoption. Article 20 attempts to cater for the adoption of the child, although as the provisions confirm there are widespread religious and cultural differences on this subject. Within the *Sharia* (the Islamic legal system), adoption *per se* is not permissible, although the concept of *Kafalah* exists whereby the child can be taken care of, in situations where the biological parents cannot do so. However *Kafalah* arguably is a weaker concept as it does not permit the child to adopt the family's name or confer property or other rights.[82] The *travaux préparatoires* of the Convention reflect substantial disagreements between the Islamic block on the one hand and Western States on the other.[83] As a consequence the original text, which was drafted in 1982, had to be altered.[84] The final text of the treaty represents a compromise, applying only to those States which recognise the institution of adoption.[85] Article 21, while sanctioning inter-country adoption, attempts to ensure that the interests of the child are

---

[77] Article 10(2) CRC.

[78] Freeman, 'The Limits of Children's Rights' in Freeman and Veerman (eds), above n.1, 29–46 at p. 40.

[79] See Article 8 ECHR. *Berrehab* v. *Netherlands*, (1989) 11 E.H.R.R. 322 (violation of Article 8 where a Moroccan national after divorce from a Dutch National was refused renewal of residence permit which made it impossible for him to maintain family ties with his daughter); *Moustaquim* v. *Belgium*, (1991) 13 E.H.R.R. 802 (a deportation order served on a young Moroccan national violated Article 8(1). The applicant had been brought to Belgium as an infant and spent his childhood in his new country alongside seven of his brothers and sisters.) See discussion above chapter 7.

[80] Cmnd 8281 (1980).

[81] ETS No. 105, Cmnd 8155 (1980).

[82] Van Bueren, above n.1, at p. 95; for an elaboration of *Kafalah* see Ali, 'A Comparative Perspective of the United Nations Convention on the Rights of the Child and the Principles of Islamic Law: Law Reform and Children's Rights in Muslim Jurisdictions' in Ali, Goonesekere, Mendez and Rios-Kohn, *Protecting the World's Children: Impact of the Convention on the Rights of the Child in Diverse Legal Systems* (Cambridge University Press, 2007) pp. 142–208; Ali, 'Rights of the Child Under Islamic Law and Laws of Pakistan: A Thematic Overview', 2 *Journal of Islamic State Practices in International Law* (2006) 1; Ishaque, 'Islamic Principles on Adoption: Examining the Impact of Illegitimacy and Inheritance Related Concerns in Context of a Child's Right to an Identity' 22 *International Journal of Law, Policy and the Family* (2008) 393.

[83] The issue of adoption has contributed to reservations from several Islamic States. See Schabas, 'Reservations to the Convention on the Rights of the Child' 18 *HRQ* (1996) 472.

[84] UN Doc. E/1982/12/Add.1, C, para 76.

[85] Johnson, 'Cultural and Regional Pluralism in the Drafting of the UN Convention on the Rights of the Child' in Freeman and Veerman (eds), above n.1, 95–114 at p. 105.

upheld. States parties undertake to ensure the rights of the child in inter-country adoptions. They also guarantee that such adoptions will be undertaken by competent authorities who will safeguard the interests of everyone involved and that such placements are not going to result in 'improper financial gain' for any party.[86]

(iv) Respect for the views of the child

Articles 12 of the Convention deals with the vital right of being heard, particularly in relation to the matters which affect the person and interests of the child. By virtue of Article 12(1), States undertake to 'assure to the child who is capable of forming his or her own views the right to express those views freely in all matters' which affect the child. As a key provision, establishing general guiding principles for the convention, Article 12(1) establishes an undertaking for States parties to assure that any child capable of forming a view has the right to express freely views in all matters affecting him or her. Furthermore there is an obligation to give due weight to the child's views having regard to the child's age and maturity. Article 12(2) lays particular emphasis on the

> opportunity to be heard in any judicial and administrative proceedings affecting the child, either directly, or through a representative or an appropriate body, in a manner consistent with the procedural rules of national law.

Article 12 articulates a number of values. Firstly, it confirms an undertaking that children are active subjects of rights and that their involvement and views are to be given due weight and recognition. Article 12, as we shall examine, forms the basis of various other rights of the child, such as the right to freedom of expression (Article 13) and freedom of thought, conscience and religion (Article 14). Secondly, the provisions within Article 12 recognise the child's right of *involvement in* and *participation in* decision-making as opposed to having a completely autonomous power of independent decision-making. The references to 'due weight' in Article 12(1) and 'evolving capacity' in Article 5 and Article 14 reconfirm this principle of *involvement in* decision-making. Thirdly, since the Convention does not establish any lower age limit on the child's right to express views freely, it would be contrary to the spirit of the Convention to have any artificial age limits in taking account of the child's views. The Committee has expressed disappointment in instances where States have set minimum age on the right of the child to be heard, as in custody proceedings following a divorce between parents.[87] Fourthly, the right to express views is not undermined where the child is not fully matured or has not yet attained a certain level of understanding: the obligation remains to take into consideration the views of the child giving 'due weight in accordance with the age and maturity of the child'. Fifthly, the child's right to express his or her views is also not undermined in cases of inability of the child to communicate his or her views – such limitations could be placed upon children with disabilities. Sixthly, the right to express views must be exercised 'freely' and without any coercion or pressure on the child. Seventhly, the child has the right to express in 'all matters' that affect him or her.

---

[86] Article 21(d) CRC.
[87] Twenty Fifth Session Finland: Concluding Observations: Consideration of Reports Submitted by States Parties under Article 44 of the Convention 16/10/2000 CRC/C/15/Add.132. (Concluding Observations/Comments) paras 29 and 30.

'All matters' is a term with a wide meaning and by definition applies to all matters that affect the relationships, interests and concerns of the child. Article 12(2) in establishing a link with Article 12(1) also provides a certain amount of specification. The child's views are particularly important and the child must be provided with an opportunity to be heard in 'judicial and administrative proceedings affecting [him or her]'. Judicial proceedings include civil proceedings including divorce, custody, judicial application of residence, immigration and asylum matters, etc. Administrative proceedings would incorporate a vast body of processes including formal decision-making regarding education, health, planning, child protection and administration of juvenile justice.[88]

The failings on the part of the States not to involve children in decision-making or allowing their expression of views has been criticised by the Committee on the Rights of the Child. In its concluding observations to the report submitted by India, the Committee expressed concern that 'that traditional attitudes towards children in society, especially girls, still limit the respect for their views within the family, at school, in institutions and at the community government level. [It further noted] with regret that there are virtually no legal provisions guaranteeing children's participation in civil proceedings affecting their rights and well-being'.[89] The Committee went on to make the following recommendation that the State party:

(a) Promote, within the family, the schools, institutions, as well as in judicial and administrative proceedings, respect for the views of children, especially girls, and facilitate their participation in all matters affecting them, in accordance with article 12 of the Convention;

(b) Provide educational information to parents, teachers, government administrative officials, the judiciary, children themselves and society at large on the right of children to have their views taken into account and to participate in all matters affecting them; and

(c) Regularly review the extent to which children's views are taken into consideration, including their impact on relevant policies and programmes.[90]

Similarly, in its recent review of the State Report from the United Kingdom, the Committee on the Rights of the Child expressed concern that 'there has been little progress in enshrining article 12 in education law and policy. Furthermore, the Committee is concerned that insufficient action has been taken to ensure that the rights enshrined in article 12 are applied to children with disabilities'.[91]

---

[88] UNICEF, *Implementation Handbook for the Convention on the Rights of the Child* (2002) p. 166.

[89] Thirty-fifth Session Concluding Observations: *Concluding observations of the Committee on the Rights of the Child: India* CRC/C/15/Add.228 26 February 2004. *(Concluding Observations/Comments)* Consideration of Reports Submitted by States Parties under Article 44 of the Convention para 36.

[90] Ibid. para 37.

[91] Forty Ninth Session United Kingdom of Great Britain and Northern Ireland Concluding Observations: Consideration of Reports Submitted by States Parties under Article 44 of the Convention CRC/C/GBR/CO/4 20 October 2008 para 32.

(v) Freedom of expression, thought, conscience and religion and association and assembly

Article 13 provides the child with the right to freedom of expression which includes:

> freedom to seek, receive and impart information and ideas of all kinds, regardless of frontiers, either orally, in writing or in print, in the form of art, or through any other media of the child's choice.[92]

The exercise of the right is, however, subject to restrictions. These restrictions are to be established by law and are to be laid down to ensure 'respect of the rights or reputations of others'[93] or 'for the protection of national security or of public order (*ordre public*), or of public health or morals'.[94] The provisions of Article 13 can be criticised for the vague terminology, which allows States parties to apply their own standards to justify the exclusion of children from effective enjoyment of their rights.

Article 14, which deals with the right of the child to freedom of thought, conscience and religion, is a problematic one.[95] The Article has attracted widespread reservations from contracting States parties.[96] As already noted, it is difficult to state if the right to freedom of religion or belief is fully established in international law – certainly in the light of divisions amongst States the parameters of any such right are not clearly drawn.[97] Article 14(1) notes that 'States Parties shall respect the right of the child to freedom of thought, conscience and religion'. However, attempts to incorporate a right for the child to changes his or her religion proved abortive.[98] Article 14(2) places an obligation on States to allow parents to direct their children to exercising this right and Article 14(3) notes that freedom to manifest one's religion or beliefs can be subjected only to minimalist limitations that are established by law and are necessary for public safety, public order, health or morals, or for the protection of fundamental rights and freedoms of others. There are significant tensions inherent in the provisions of this article. The Convention is reluctant to allow substantial rights to the child *vis-à-vis* the family, parents and the State. In real life, children live with their parents and in societies with strongly assertive religious or cultural values, which may conflict with the child's interests, needs and wishes.

Article 15 provides for the recognition of the right to freedom of association and to freedom of peaceful assembly.[99] The limitation clause associated to Article 15 is taken from

---

[92] Article 13(1) CRC

[93] Ibid. Article 13(2)(a).

[94] Ibid. Article 13(2)(b).

[95] See generally Langlaude, *The Right of the Child to Religious Freedom in International Law* (Martinus Nijhoff Publishers, 2007).

[96] One significant area of disagreement and consequent reservations has been the issue of child rights to 'have' or 'to adopt' a religion. The final text of Article 14 does not make any references to the right of the child to 'have' or 'to adopt' a religion, a result principally from the divided views of the Muslim majority *vis-à-vis* other States. See Langlaude, 'Children and Religion under Article 14 UNCRC: A Critical Analysis' 16 *International Journal of Children's Rights* (2008) 475 at p. 484; Brems, 'Article 14: The Right to Freedom of Thought, Conscience and Religion' Alen, Vande Lanotte, Verhellen, Ang, Berghmans and Verheyde (eds), *A Commentary on the United Nations Convention on the Rights of the Child* (Martinus Nijhoff Publishers, 2006) pp. 1–39.

[97] See above chapter 12.

[98] UN Doc. E/CN.4/1984/71 (1984) paras 13–33. See Van Bueren, above n.1, at pp. 157–58; Johnson, 'Cultural and Regional Pluralism in the Drafting of the UN Convention on the Rights of the Child' in Freeman and Veerman (eds), above n.1, pp. 95–114.

[99] In its original format the article included the right to privacy. However, due to significant differences, two instead of one article was drafted See UN Doc. E/CN.4/1987/25 (1987) paras 111–118.

Article 22 of ICCPR, the right to peaceful assembly.[100] Article 16 prohibits arbitrary or unlawful interference with privacy, family, home or correspondence. The article also makes it unlawful to attack the honour and reputation of the child. Article 17 ensures that the child has access to information and materials from a diverse range of national and international sources. This is an innovative right and usefully highlights the significance of mass media in the development of the rights of the child. Article 18 obliges States parties to ensure recognition of the principle that both parents have common responsibilities for the upbringing and development of the child.[101] Article 18 is intrinsically connected to an earlier article, Article 5, according to which:

> States Parties shall respect the responsibilities, rights and duties of parents or, where applicable, the members of the extended family or community as provided for by local custom, legal guardians or other persons legally responsible for the child, to provide, in a manner consistent with the evolving capacities of the child, appropriate direction and guidance in the exercise by the child of the rights recognized in the present Convention.

Both Article 18 and Article 5 represent important provisions of the Convention. While accepting the realities of parental influences and the rights and duties of the wider family, the article is, nevertheless, reticent in dealing with situations where the interests of child are not 'consistent with the evolving capabilities of the child'. Reference to the notion of 'evolving capabilities' has already been made although it needs to be noted that 'evolving capabilities' are neither defined nor exemplified in the text of the Convention.

(vi) Measures to combat violence, abuse, exploitation and maltreatment of children

Article 19 obliges States parties to take the necessary appropriate action 'to protect the child from all forms of physical or mental violence, injury or abuse, neglect or negligent treatment, maltreatment or exploitation, including sexual abuse, while in the care of parent, parents or legal guardian'.[102] These appropriate actions include 'legislative, administrative, social and educational measures'.[103] Article 19(2) goes on to provide that:

> [s]uch protective measures should, as appropriate, include effective procedures for the establishment of social programmes to provide necessary support for the child and for those who have the care of the child, as well as for other forms of prevention and for identification, reporting, referral, investigation, treatment and follow-up of instances of child maltreatment described heretofore, and, as appropriate, for judicial involvement.

Article 19 is a very broad article as no definition is provided of 'physical or mental violence, injury or abuse, neglect or negligent treatment, maltreatment or exploitation, including sexual abuse'. According to Professor Van Bueren:

---

[100] McGoldrick, above n.1, at p. 142.
[101] Article 18(1) CRC.
[102] Ibid. Article 19(1).
[103] Ibid. Article 19(1).

the terms neglect and abuse are intentionally undefined in order to avoid the danger that a definition of child abuse and neglect could unwittingly be based upon either arbitrary or ethnocentric assumptions. In general terms child neglect involves either the inability or the deliberate refusal to care for a child with the result that a child's development is impaired. It is also clear that abuse and neglect includes all acts or omissions where the sole motivation is the desire to harm the child.[104]

Following the jurisprudence of the European Convention on Human Rights, the States have a positive obligation to ensure the provision of civil and criminal proceedings against those involved in sexual offences against children.[105] Subsequent articles of the Convention also deal with child abuse through such unfortunate practices such as economic exploitation, illicit usage of drugs, sexual abuse and trafficking of children. Article 32 deals with some of most critical issues relating to the rights of the child. It provides as follows:

1. States Parties recognize the right of the child to be protected from economic exploitation and from performing any work that is likely to be hazardous or to interfere with the child's education, or to be harmful to the child's health or physical, mental, spiritual, moral or social development.

2. States Parties shall take legislative, administrative, social and educational measures to ensure the implementation of the present article. To this end, and having regard to the relevant provisions of other international instruments, States Parties shall in particular:

   (a) Provide for a minimum age or minimum ages for admission to employment;
   (b) Provide for appropriate regulation of the hours and conditions of employment;
   (c) Provide for appropriate penalties or other sanctions to ensure the effective enforcement of the present article.

Notwithstanding the abolition of slavery and the slave trade, child slavery and servitude is still being practised in many regions of the world. In addition, there are millions of children employed in rigorous labour in many parts of the world.[106] Children provide employers with a stable source of cheap labour. They are capable of putting in long hours and are unlikely to question their employers over working conditions and wages. It is estimated that around 165 million 5–14-year-old-children are inducted into child labour, with over 100 million employed in rigourous full-time labour.[107] Child labour is institutionalised in many regions of the world (e.g. Pakistan, Bangladesh and India). As the Committee on the Rights of the Child noted in its Concluding Observations on the State report submitted by

---

[104] Van Bueren, above n.1 at p. 88; *Costello Costello-Roberts* v. *UK* (1995) 19 E.H.R.R. 112; *A* v. *UK*, Application No. 25599/94 (Judgment of 23 September 1998).

[105] See *X and Y* v. *The Netherlands*, Application No. 8975/80 (Judgment of 26 March 1985). (Victim having attained the age of 16 and with a mental disorder was prevented under Dutch law to initiate a criminal 'complaint'. The European Court of Human Rights held unanimously that civil remedies were inadequate and the absence of effective criminal remedy in these circumstances constituted a breach by the Dutch government to respect Y's right to private life.) For further discussion, see above chapter 7.

[106] Samet, 'Child Labor and the New Millennium' 21 *Whittier L. Rev.* (1999–2000) 69; Cullen, *The Role of International Law in the Elimination of Child Labor* (Martinus Nijhoff Publishers, 2007).

[107] Scouts, 'World Day Against Child Labour–12 June: Creating a Better World' (2008) www.scout.org/en/information_events/news/2008/world_day_against_child_labour_12_june <last visited 12 May 2009>.

India, the institutionalisation of labour is reinforced through official complacency or connivance in the lack of enforcement of minimum age standards for employment and a reluctance to deploy appropriate penalties for those engaged in child labour.[108] In its Concluding Observation on the Report submitted by Bangladesh, the Committee expressed concern at the continued widespread acceptance of the phenomenon of child labour within Bangladeshi society and the vulnerability of child workers within the domestic sphere and their physical and sexual abuse.[109] Article 32 not only complements existing human rights provisions, but extends them to a significant extent. The UDHR and the ICCPR prohibit slavery, servitude and forced labour for everyone, including children. Article 10(3) ICESCR imposes a duty on States parties to protect children and young persons from economic and social exploitation. Article 32 requires States to set age limits below which it would be punishable to employ a child for labour. The article also makes it punishable by law to employ children in work harmful to their morals or health. Child labour and exploitation for commercial and economic purposes has been an issue raised in a number of quarters. A useful study was prepared by Mr. A. Bouhdiba in 1981, which prompted the UN Sub-Commission's Working Group on Contemporary Forms of Slavery to propose a '35–point Programme of Action for the Elimination of Exploitation of Child Labour'.[110] This proposal was adopted by UN Commission on Human Rights in 1991.[111]

The ILO Convention No. 138 places an obligation on States to ensure effective protection of children from labour.[112] There is also increasing pressure on international trading organisations to impose sanctions on States which allow the practice of child labour.[113] Article 33 ordains that States take all necessary measures to protect children from the illicit use of narcotic drugs and psychotropic substances. Article 34 is also a very significant article of the Convention. Children suffer from all forms of sexual exploitation and abuse which the article is designed to criminalise. According to this article, States are under an obligation to prevent inducement or coercion in any unlawful sexual activity.[114] Child pornography, prostitution, sale as servants and bonded labour and ritual and satanic abuse are also widespread phenomenon. Article 34(a) aims to protect the child from inducement or coercion to engage in any unlawful sexual activity. This includes sexual exploitation or abuse. Exploitation of children in activities such as prostitution, unlawful sexual practices

---

[108] See Committee on the Rights of the Child, Concluding Observations: India Thirty-Fifth Session, CRC/C/15/Add.228 (26 February 2004) para 72.

[109] See Committee on the Rights of the Child, Concluding Observations: Bangladesh Thirty-Fourth Session, CRC/C/15/Add.221 (27 October 2003) para 69.

[110] Bouhdiba, *Exploitation of Child Labour* (United Nations publication, Sales No. E. 82.XIV.2) see also Sub-Commission Res. 1990/31 and Commission's Res. 1991/54, Pt II, para 10.

[111] See Eide, 'The Sub-Commission on Prevention of Discrimination and Protection of Minorities' in Alston (ed.), *The United Nations and Human Rights: A Critical Appraisal* (Clarendon Press, 1992), pp. 211–264 at p. 234.

[112] Article 1. Convention concerning Minimum Age for Admission to Employment (ILO No. 138), 1015 U.N.T.S 297, entered into force, 19 June 1976.

[113] See Ehrenberg, above n.27, at p. 361; Cullen, 'The Limits of International Trade Mechanisms in Enforcing Human Rights: The Case of Child Labour' 7 *International Journal of Children's Rights* (1999) 1.

[114] International treaty bodies have also expressed concerned at the sexual abuse of children. HRC has expressed such concern in its response to the report from Sri Lanka. The Committee notes: 'while the committee welcomes the proposed changes to legislation for offences committed against children, such as incest and the sexual exploitation of children, it is concerned about the situation of economic and sexual exploitation both with respect to the use of children in domestic service and the prostitution of boys' (1995) UN Doc. CCPR/C/79Add.56; also see Levesque 'Sexual Use, Abuse and Exploitation of Children' (1994) 60 *Brooklyn Law Review* 959.

and exploitation through pornography are also prohibited.[115] The international community has advanced further on attempting to prevent abuse through the adoption of the Optional Protocol on the Sale of Children, Child Prostitution and Child Pornography.[116] As we shall be examining shortly, the Protocol came into force on 18 January 2002, and is intended to be a major step forward in the international campaign to prevent and criminalise the sale of children for prostitution and child pornography.

One of the more problematic areas within international and national family law relates to sexual abuse that takes place within the confines of the home and family. As with many other Articles in the Convention, international human rights law provides protection to the child from sexual abuse conducted by non-State personnel. However, in practice often protection from sexual and physical abuse remains ineffective, largely due to lack of disclosure and detection. Sexual, physical and emotional exploitation is conducted in many societies under the garb of religious, cultural or personal family practices.[117] According to McGillivray:

[i]n a dysfunctional relationship [the] interpretive power displaces the child's view, making disclosure unlikely and detection difficult. The value given to the archetype of the family as a private cohesive unit joined by ties of blood, affection and economic interdependence contributes to the ideology of family loyalty. Children fear breaching the family compact by disclosing problems to outsiders and recant where family cohesiveness is threatened.[118]

---

[115] The United Nations Human Rights Committee has expressed concern over the practices being conducted in several States e.g. in its response to Mexico, HRC notes 'the committee also deplores the situation of street children, which is constantly worsening. These are the children who are at greatest risk of sexual violence and who are exposed to the practices of sexual trafficking. The State should take effective measures for the protection and rehabilitation of these children in accordance with article 24 of the covenant, including measures to end prostitution, child pornography and the sale of children'. Concluding Observations of the Human Rights Committee Mexico 27/07/99 CCPR/C/79/Add.109 (27 July 1999) para 15. In relation to Costa Rica, the Human Rights Committee notes 'the committee is deeply concerned at the high incidence of commercial sexual exploitation of children, apparently often related to tourism . . . The Committee urges the State party to take further measures to eradicate this phenomenon, in cooperation as appropriate with other States, through the investigation and prosecution of the crimes in question'. Concluding Observations of the Human Rights Committee Costa Rica 08/04/99 CCPR/C/79/Add.107 (8 April 1999), para 18; Kent, 'Little Foreign Bodies: International Dimension of Child Prostitution' in Freeman and Veerman (eds), above n.1, pp. 323–346; Ennew, The Sexual Exploitation of Children (Polity Press, 1986).

[116] Optional Protocol to the Convention on the Rights of the Child on the sale of children, child prostitution and child pornography, New York, 25 May 2000 UN Doc. A/RES/54/263; see Dennis, 'Newly Adopted Protocols to the Convention on the Rights of the Child' 94 AJIL (2000) 789.

[117] Note the concluding comments of the Committee on the Elimination of All Forms of Discrimination Against Women on India, where the Committee expresses its concerns over the narrow definition of rape within the Indian Penal Code, failure to take effective action to prevent child marriages and the continuing sexual exploitation of children. CEDAW/C/IND/CO3 (2 February 2007) para 22. Levesque, Sexual Abuse of Children: A Human Rights Perspective (Indiana University Press, 1999). On child forced marriages see Clark and Richards, 'The prevention and prohibition of forced marriages: a comparative approach' 57 ICLQ (2008) 501. Commenting in the context of the Pakistani society, Hussain makes the valid point that 'child sexual abuse does not occur in isolation. Like most other forms of violence it is perpetuated by popular culture, myths surrounding sexuality, flawed and outdated methods of teaching and parenting children and irresponsible families who prefer silence above the safety of their children, so that they can protect their "honour". Indifferent and outdated teaching methods and irresponsible parenting are central to appropriating children's physical and emotional security and boundaries which in turn made them vulnerable to rampant sexual molestation', Hussain 'The Sexual Exploitation and Sexual Abuse of Children in Pakistan' in Mehdi and Shaheed (eds), Women's Law in Legal Education and Practice: North-South Co-operation (New Social Science Monograph, 1997) 233–244 at p. 234.

[118] McGillivray, 'Re-Construction Child Abuse: Western Definition and Non-Western Experience' in Freeman and Veerman (eds), above n.1, 213–236 at p. 216.

16

The rights of the child

The Committee on the Rights of the Child has on several occasions expressed concern not only at the continuing sexual abuse of children within the confines of family but also at the absence of penal legislation to sanction such behaviour.[119] Whilst international human rights law remains limited in adopting an interventionist approach in the context of family laws and cultural practices, harrowing and tragic cases of sexual abuse and incest continue to emerge from all parts of the world.[120] By virtue of Article 35, States endeavour to take all appropriate and necessary action to prevent child abduction and the sale and trafficking of children. According to Article 36, 'States Parties shall protect the child against all other forms of exploitation prejudicial to any aspects of the child's welfare'. Article 37 echoes the traditional human rights approach. It provides for the prohibition of 'torture or other cruel, inhuman or degrading treatment or punishment' of the child. Widespread divergences exist on the subject of corporal punishment of children.[121] However, the Committee on the Rights of the Child, has taken the position that corporal punishment is inconsistent with the provisions of the Convention on the Rights of the Child.[122] In its General Comment No. 8, which elaborates on the Rights of Children to Protection from Corporal Punishment and Other Cruel or Degrading Forms of Punishment, the Committee reiterated its firm position that eliminating violent and humiliating punishments for children needs to be an unqualified and immediate obligation of all States parties.[123]

The Committee has consistently expressed concern at the legislative provisions providing exceptions to the practice of corporal punishment from various countries, including during its consideration of the reports from the United Kingdom. The concern according to the Committee was that this so-called 'reasonable chastisement', may 'pave the way for subjective and arbitrary interpretation'.[124] In its consideration of the fifth and sixth periodic reports from the United Kingdom, the Committee on the Elimination of Discrimination against Women, also 'note[d] with concern that corporal punishment is lawful in the home and constitutes a form of violence against children' and advanced recommendations for legislative prohibition.[125]

It can be argued that following the jurisprudence of regional and domestic courts, a general norm is emerging in international law, which regards all forms of corporal punishment of children as violating the provisions of Article 37.[126] Nevertheless, a lacunae exists within

---

[119] See Committee on the Rights of the Child, Forty-First Session, Consideration of Reports Submitted by States Parties under Article 44 of the Convention Concluding observations: Saudi Arabia CRC/C/SAU/CO/2 (17 March 2006), para 51(b). See Committee on the Rights of the Child, Forty-Fourth Session, Consideration of Reports Submitted by States Parties under Article 44 of the Convention Concluding observations: Mali CRC/C/MLI/CO/2 (3 May 2007) para 46(a)–(e).

[120] See Brown and Wellman, 'How two girls were trapped by shame, fear and the love of their own children' Times Online (26 November, 2008); Weaver and Connelly, 'Austrian Cellar Case Man Admits Abduction and Incest' *Guardian* newspaper 28 April 2008; for commentaries see Evans, 'Falling Angels? The Material Construction of Children as Sexual Citizens' 2 *International Law Journal of Child Rights* (1994) 1; Van Bueren, 'Child Sexual Abuse and Exploitation: A Suggested Human Rights Approach' 2 *International Law Journal of Child Rights* (1994) 45; Cordeiro 'Sexual Abuse in Children and Teenagers – A Perspective from Portugal' 2, *International Law Journal of Child Rights* (1994) 105.

[121] For further consideration see above chapter 5.

[122] See Report on the Seventh Session, UN Commission on the Rights of the Child, Annex 4, at 63, UN Doc. CRC/C/34 (November 1994).

[123] See the right of the child to protection from corporal punishment and other cruel or degrading forms of punishment (Articles 19, 28, para 2 and 37, *inter alia*). General Comment No. 8 (2006) 02/03/2007, para 22.

[124] See UN Doc. CRC/C/15 Add. 34 para 16.

[125] CEDAW/C/GBR/CO/6, 18 July 2008.

[126] See the Zimbabwean Supreme Court decision in *Ncube* v. *The State*, *Supreme Court of Zimbabwe*, 1988 LRC (Const) 442. Also see *State* v. *A Juvenile* (1989), (2) ZLR 61 (Zimbabwe), where it was held that the corporal

the domestic UK framework, through which physical punishment of children has continued to be delivered. The United Kingdom was recently criticised by the Council of Europe's Commissioner for Human Rights, Thomas Hammarberg, in his memorandum on corporal punishment, where by pointing to the gaps in existing legislation, he expressed substantial concerns over the numbers of children suffering from chastisement. He noted:

> The UK is one of the few European countries which have neither achieved full prohibition of corporal punishment nor committed themselves publicly to it. Worse, it is in a small minority whose laws actually persist in allowing parents and some other carers to justify some level of violence as 'reasonable' when it is regarded as discipline. This situation is unacceptable and must be changed.[127]

Article 37 also provides for a ban on capital punishment and life imprisonment (without the possibility of release) to be imposed for offences committed by persons below 18 years of age.[128] It provides for prohibiting unlawful or arbitrary deprivation of liberty, and provides for the requisite safeguards.[129] The prohibition of capital punishment for those under 18 is a particularly valuable provision with implications on the issue of the definition of childhood and the overall campaign for the abolition of the death penalty in international law. Notwithstanding the provisions of Article 37(a) and Article 6(5) ICCPR, capital punishment has been awarded to 17-year-olds.[130]

A number of such situations have arisen in the United States. In several cases filed in the United States and brought before the Inter-American Commission on Human Rights, the petitioners had argued that a norm of customary international law existed prohibiting the application of the death penalty to individuals below the age of 18.[131] In *Roach and Pinkerton* the Inter-American Commission accepted the view that 'in the OAS member

punishment of juveniles was unconstitutional. In *State* v. *Petrus and another* [1985] LRC (Const) 699 (CA) (Botswana). The Court of Appeal of Botswana held that while corporal punishment *per se* was not unconstitutional, the manner of punishment was. In exercising a 'value judgment', the Court held that repeated and delayed punishment resulted in the punishment being rendered degrading and unconstitutional. The Namibian Supreme Court held corporal punishment unconstitutional in respect of Article 8 of the Bill of Fundamental Rights enshrined in the Constitution in *Ex parte Attorney-General, In Re: Corporal Punishment by Organs of State* (SA 14/90) [1991] NASC 2; 1991 (3) SA 76 (NmSc) (5 April 1991). *Tyrer* v. *UK* (1978) 2 E.H.R.R. 1 (judicial corporal punishment of 15-year-old boy violating article 3); *A* v. *UK*, Application No. 25599/94 (judgment of 23 September 1998) (caning of a 9-year-old boy by step-father violation of Article 3). See also the Human Rights Committee's General Comments (forty-fourth session 1992). In the Committee's view 'the prohibition in article 7 (on torture, cruel, inhuman or degrading treatment or punishment) relates not only to acts that cause physical pain but also to acts that cause mental suffering to the victim. In the Committee's view, moreover, the prohibition must extend to corporal punishment, including excessive chastisement ordered as punishment for a crime or as an educative or disciplinary measure. It is appropriate to emphasize in this regard that Article 7 protects, in particular, children, pupils and patients in teaching and medical institutions' para 5.

[127] Council of Europe, '"UK must improve children's protection and ban corporal punishment" Reports Commissioner Hammarberg'. Press release – 710(2008 Strasbourg, 09.10.2008 https://wcd.coe.int/ViewDoc.jsp?id=1351691&Site=DC <last visited 12 May 2008>.

[128] Article 37(a) CRC.

[129] Ibid. Article 37(b).

[130] In many States, capital punishment continues to be applied to persons below the age of 18. These States include China, Democratic Republic of Congo (DRC), Iran, Pakistan and the United States. www.amnestyusa.org/abolish/juveniles.html <last visited 9 May 2009>.

[131] Note Article 6(5) ICCPR which provides that 'Sentence of death shall not be imposed for crimes committed by persons below eighteen years of age'.

States there is a recognised norm of *ius cogens* which prohibits the State execution of children'[132] but it could not refute the United States' contention on the absence of any customary rules for the determination of the age of majority.[133] However, more recently in *Michael Domingues*,[134] *Napoleon Beazley*[135] and *Douglas Christopher Thomas*,[136] the Inter-American Commission has held that:

> 84. In the Commission's view, the evidence canvassed above clearly illustrates that by persisting in the practice of executing offenders under age 18, the U.S. stands alone amongst the traditional developed world nations and those of the inter-American system, and has also become increasingly isolated within the entire global community. The overwhelming evidence of global state practice as set out above displays a consistency and generality amongst world states indicating that the world community considers the execution of offenders aged below 18 years at the time of their offence to be inconsistent with prevailing standards of decency. The Commission is therefore of the view that a norm of international customary law has emerged prohibiting the execution of offenders under the age of 18 years at the time of their crime.
>
> 85. Moreover, the Commission is satisfied, based upon the information before it, that this rule has been recognized as being of a sufficiently indelible nature to now constitute a norm of *jus cogens*, a development anticipated by the Commission in its Roach and Pinkerton decision.[137]

Nevertheless, as the Inter-American Commission does not have binding jurisdiction, the United States initially completely disregarded its decisions. The execution of Napoleon, Beazley and Douglas Christopher Thomas went ahead while the case was still pending before the Commission as the United States chose to disregard the Commission's request for a stay of execution. However, in *Roper* v. *Simmons*,[138] the Supreme Court held by a 5–4 majority that the execution of juvenile offenders violated the Eighth and Fourteenth Amendments of the American Constitution. It was also held that the execution of offenders who were under the age of 18 when their crimes were committed violates, 'evolving standards of decency'.[139] Perhaps more significantly, in this case the American Supreme Court also recognised the importance of international law, when noting that:

---

[132] *Roach and Pinkerton* v. *United States*, Case 9.647, Res. No. 3/87, Inter-Am.C.H.R., OEA/Ser.L/V/II.71, Doc. 9 rev.1.

[133] The Inter-American Commission found the US in violation for its pattern of 'legislative arbitrariness through out the United States which results in the arbitrary deprivation of life and inequality before the law' (para 173). For commentaries see Fox, 'Inter-American Commission on Human Rights finds the United States in Violation' 82 *AJIL* (1988) 601; Shelton, 'The Decision of IACHR of 27 March 1987 in the Case of Roach and Pinkerton: A Note' 8 *HRLJ* (1987) 355; Weissbrodt, 'Execution of Juvenile Offenders by the United States Violates International Human Rights Law' 3 *AUJILP* (1988) 339.

[134] *Michael Domingues* v. *US (Merits)*, Case 12.285, Report No. 62/02, Inter-Am. C.H.R., OEA/Ser.L/V/II.116, Doc. 33, 22 October 2002.

[135] *Napoleon Beazley* v. *United States*, Case 12.412, Report No. 101/03, Inter-Am. C.H.R., OEA/Ser./L/V/II.114 Doc. 70 rev. 1 at 804 (2003).

[136] *Douglas Christopher Thomas* v. *United States*, Case 12.240, Report No. 100/03, Inter-Am. C.H.R., OEA/Ser./L/V/II.114 Doc. 70 rev. 1 at 790 (2003).

[137] *Michael Domingues* v. *US (Merits)*, Case 12.285, Report No. 62/02, Inter-Am. C.H.R., OEA/Ser.L/V/II.116, Doc. 33, Oct. 22, 2002, paras 84–85.

[138] *Roper* v. *Simmons*, Opinion of the Court Supreme Court Case No. 03-633, Argued 13 October 2004, 543 US (2005).

[139] *Roper* v. *Simmons*, Stevens, J. concurring, Supreme Court Case No. 03-633, Argued 13 October 2004, 543 US (2005), p. 1.

[i]t is proper that we acknowledge the overwhelming weight of international opinion against the juvenile death penalty, resting in large part on the understanding that the instability and emotional imbalance of young people may often be a factor in the crime.[140]

It is also interesting to note that the United States, upon its ratification of the ICCPR, entered a reservation to Article 6(5) of the Covenant.[141] This reservation has been considered as 'incompatible with the objects and purposes of the Covenant' by the Human Rights Committee and has called for its withdrawal.[142] While the situation regarding the execution of juvenile offenders in the United States has been brought in line with international standards, the punishment of life without parole for juvenile offenders remains an issue. A recent Human Rights Watch Report estimates that there are currently 2380 people serving sentences of life without parole in the United States for crimes that they committed when under the age of 18.[143] In comparison, there are a total of seven people serving such terms throughout the whole of the rest of the world and only 10 countries have retained the sentence of life without parole in their domestic legal systems for under 18s.[144] It is also estimated that of those currently serving life sentences without parole in California, 45 per cent of them did not actually commit the murder in question, rather they were convicted of aiding and abetting.[145]

(vii) Children in wars and conflicts

Article 22 aims to ensure that the child receives the protection of international refugee and humanitarian law. Article 22(1) provides that:

States parties shall take appropriate measures to ensure that a child who is seeking refugee status or who is considered a refugee ... shall ... receive appropriate protection and humanitarian assistance in the enjoyment of applicable rights set forth in the present Convention and in other international human rights or humanitarian instruments ...

The protection applies regardless of whether the child is unaccompanied by his or her parents.[146] According to Article 22(2), States are to provide co-operation with the UN and other intergovernmental agencies to trace the parents or other members of the family of any refugee child or to obtain information with a view to reunification with their family.

---

[140] *Roper* v. *Simmons*, Opinion of the Court, Supreme Court Case No. 03-633, Argued 13 October 2004, 543 U.S (2005) p. 24. For a commentary on the case see Van Zyl Smit, 'The Abolition of Capital Punishment for Persons Under the Age of Eighteen Years in the United States of America. What Next?' 5 *Human Rights Law Review* (2005) 393.

[141] The US reservations provides as follows: '(2) That the United States reserves the right, subject to its Constitutional constraints, to impose capital punishment on any person (other than a pregnant woman) duly convicted under existing or future laws permitting the imposition of capital punishment, including such punishment for crimes committed by persons below eighteen years of age' See International Covenant on Civil and Political Rights New York, 16 December 1966, Reservations and Declarations www2.ohchr.org/english/bodies/ratification/4_1.htm <last visited 15 February 2009>.

[142] See Report of the Human Rights Committee UN Doc. A/50/40 (1995) para 279.

[143] Human Rights Watch Report, 'When I Die, They'll Send Me Home, Youth Sentenced to Life Without Parole in California', 29(1) January 2008 (G).

[144] Ibid.

[145] Ibid.

[146] Article 22(1) CRC.

Whilst the provisions of Article 22 are to be welcomed, the overall regime catering for refugee children is inadequate and has been criticised. In advancing their criticism, Goodwin-Gill and McAdam make the point that:

> neither the 1951 Convention [on the status of refugees] nor the Convention on the Rights of the Child, so far as they address the situation of children as refugees, provide an entirely satisfactory legal basis. The 1951 Convention does little more than recommend measures to ensure family unity and protection, and provide for access at least to primary education. Article 22 of the Convention on the Rights of the Child (CRC89) endorses the entitlement of refugee children to 'appropriate protection and humanitarian assistance', but essentially by cross-referencing the body of the Convention and other international instruments, while emphasizing cooperation in tracing and family reunion.[147]

Additional safeguards are provided by Article 38, which aims to ensure the compliance and respect for the rules of international humanitarian law applicable to children in armed conflicts. The obligations of the article are to prohibit the creation of child soldiers. Article 38(2) and Article 38(3) ordains States Parties to undertake all feasible steps to ensure that those below the age of 15 years do not take a direct part in hostilities, and not to recruit under fifteens into their armed forces.[148] Even when recruiting those who have attained the age of 15 (but have not yet reached 18) States parties undertake to give priority to those who are the oldest.[149]

It is of importance to appreciate that during times of unrest and war children need greater protection than during peacetime. At the same time, it is unfortunately the case that in times of war children are abused and are prone to be coerced into becoming combatants.[150] A vast majority of contemporary armed conflicts are of a localised nature and examples of such internal conflicts can be found in many regions of the world. In these armed conflicts children are frequently used as combatants. Children also represent the highest number of casualties and suffering. Until recently the Geneva Convention Relative to the Protection of Civilian Persons in Times of War (1949),[151] supplemented by the Protocols Additional to the Geneva Conventions of 1949 Relating to the Protection of Victims of International Armed Conflict (1977)[152] and the Protection of Victims of Non-International Armed Conflicts[153] have remained the most pertinent treaties protecting the rights of the child in international humanitarian law. The Fourth Geneva Convention on the Protection of Civilians (1949) contains a number of provisions aimed at protecting

---

[147] Goodwin-Gill and McAdam, *The Refugee in International Law* (Oxford University Press, 2007) at p. 475. See also UNHCR, *Family Protection Issues*, UN Doc. EC/49/SC/CRP.14, 4 June 1999, in 11 IJRL 583 (1999).

[148] Article 38(2) and Article 38(3). Van Bueren, above n.1, at p. 275; for an interesting and thought-provoking analysis of the opposition of the United States and United Kingdom in relation to raising the minimum age of recruitment to 18, see Van Bueren, 'The International Legal Protection of Children in Armed Conflict' 43 *ICLQ* (1994) 809 at p. 814.

[149] Article 38(3) CRC.

[150] Gardam, 'The Law of Armed Conflict: A Feminist Perspective' in Mahoney and Mahoney (eds), *Human Rights in the Twenty-First Century: A Global Challenge* (Martinus Nijhoff, 1993) pp. 419–436; Elahi, 'The Rights of the Child Under Islamic Law: Prohibition of the Child Soldier' 19 *Columbia Human Rights Law Review* (1988) 259.

[151] Geneva 12 August 1949, 75 U.N.T.S. 287, entered into force 21 October 1950.

[152] 1125 U.N.T.S. 3, entered into force 7 December 1978.

[153] 1125 U.N.T.S. 609, entered into force 7 December 1978.

children and also provides general protection to those children living in occupied or un-occupied territories.[154] Article 77(2) of Additional Protocol I of the Geneva Conventions bans the recruitment of soldiers under the age of 15. Article 8(2)(b) the Rome Statute of the International Criminal Court 1998, regards the recruitment or 'use' of soldiers under the age of 15 as a 'war crime'.[155] Article 77 of Additional Protocol I of the Geneva Conventions also provides that, '[c]hildren shall be the object of special respect and shall be protected against any form of indecent assault. The Parties to the conflict shall provide them with the care and aid they require, whether because of their age or for any other reason'.[156] The combined effect of the Geneva Conventions is to accord protection to children living in occupied or unoccupied territory and also regulates child participation in hostilities.

The HRC, in pursuance of its mandate to provide General Comments, has also commented on the prohibition of child recruitment in armed conflicts. In its General Comment, HRC notes, 'the Committee wishes to draw the attention of States parties to the need to include in their reports information on measures adopted to ensure that children do not take a direct part in armed conflict'.[157]

A further advancement towards according protection to children has been conducted through the adoption of the Optional Protocol on the Involvement of Children in Armed Conflict – which as noted above is one of two Optional Protocols to the Convention on the Rights of the Child.[158] Whilst a detailed analysis of the Protocol shall be conducted in due course, it is pertinent to note Article 3(1) of the Protocol which provides:

> States Parties shall raise in years the minimum age for the voluntary recruitment of persons into their national armed forces from that set out in article 38, paragraph 3, of the Convention on the Rights of the Child, taking account of the principles contained in that article and recognizing that under the Convention persons under the age of 18 years are entitled to special protection.[159]

Amongst regional instruments there is the African Charter on the Rights and Welfare of the Child (ACRWC) which takes a specific interest and in protecting children in times of civil unrest and internal conflict. Article 22(3) deals with children caught up in international and internal armed conflicts. In accordance with the provisions of Article 22(3) States are required to 'take all necessary measures to ensure that no child shall take a direct part in hostilities and refrain in particular, from recruiting any child.' Under Article 2 of this Charter, the child is defined as 'every human being below the age of 18 years'. Possibly the most significant development has been the adoption and coming into force of the Rome Statute of International Criminal Court which denounces the conscription of children as a

---

[154] See Articles 14, 17, 23–27, 40, 50, 51, 68, 76, 81, 82, 89, 94 and 132 of the Fourth Geneva Convention.

[155] ICC Statute, Article 8(2)(b)(xxvi) – (e)(vii); Statute of the Special Court for Sierra Leone, Article 4(c).

[156] 1125 U.N.T.S. 3, entered into force 7 December 1978; see also UNHCR, Refugee Children: Guidelines on Protection and Care (1994), 19; also see 'UNHCR Policy on Refugee Children' UN Doc. EC/SCP/82 (6 August 1993); 'Report of the Working Group on Refugee Women and Refugee Children' UN Doc. EC/SCP/85 (5 July 1994).

[157] General Comment 17, para 3; also see Maslen, 'The Use of Children as Soldiers: the Right to Kill and be Killed' 4 International Journal of Children's Rights (1998) 455.

[158] New York, 25 May 2000 UN Doc. A/RES/54/263.

[159] See Article 3(1).

war crime[160] – indeed the first trial being conducted by the Court relates to charges of enlisting chlidern under the age of 15 and using them in active hostility in from September 2002 to August 2003 by the defendant Thomas Lubanga Dyilo, the founder and leader of the Union des Patriotes Congolais (UPC).[161]

(viii) Concerns of disability and health

The Convention also accords rights to mentally and physically disabled children. In its Article 23, States parties recognise the rights of mentally and physically disabled children to have a decent life and to ensure that they live a life of dignity, self-reliance and can participate in the life of the community. This is an extremely important provision, as disabled children are prone to abuse, violence and suffering. Inherent in the article is the provision of non-discrimination, as provided in Article 2. The article provides for special care and encourages the State to extend available resources.[162]

The provision of the rights enumerated in Article 24 are interrelated to those in Article 6, the right to life for the child. Article 24 expands on this right, noting that the States parties recognise the right of 'the child to the enjoyment of the highest attainable standard of health and to facilities for the treatment of illness and rehabilitation of health'[163] and that they 'shall strive to ensure that no child is deprived of his or her right of access to such health care services'.[164] Particular emphasis needs to be placed on: reducing the mortality rate of children;[165] the provision of medical and healthcare;[166] combating malnutrition and disease;[167] providing maternal pre-natal and post-natal healthcare;[168] and ensuring that parents, children and others involved in the upbringing of the child have the adequate knowledge and education that is essential, *inter alia*, for child health and hygiene.[169] These provisions are much more specific than other human rights provisions including the right to health recognised by Article 12 of ICESCR.[170] While, unlike Article 11 of the ICESCR, there is no specific reference to the right to food, there is recognition of the need to combat malnutrition.[171] Making reference to the Convention on the rights of the child, in its General Comment on the Right to Health the Committee on the International Covenant on Economic, Social and Cultural Rights has noted:

---

[160] Article 7(2)(b)(xvi) includes as 'war crimes': conscripting or enlisting children under the age of 15 years into the national armed forces or using them to participate actively in hostilities. For the text of the Statute see http://untreaty.un.org/cod/icc/statute/romefra.htm <last visited 18 May 2009>. See further chapter 20 below.

[161] The trial commenced on 26 January 2009 See www.icc-cpi.int/menus/icc/situations%20and%20cases/situations/situation%20icc%200104/related%20cases/icc%200104%200106/democratic%20republic%20of%20the%20congo?lan=en-GB <last visited 15 May 2009>.

[162] Article 23(2) CRC.

[163] Ibid. Article 24(1).

[164] Ibid.

[165] Ibid. Article 24(2)(a).

[166] Ibid. Article 24(2)(b).

[167] Ibid. Article 24(2)(c).

[168] Ibid. Article 24(2)(d).

[169] Ibid. Article 24(2)(e).

[170] According to Article 12 of ICESCR, States Parties 'recognize the right of everyone to the enjoyment of the highest attainable standard of physical and mental health' and that steps are to be taken by States 'to the present Covenant to achieve the full realization of this right shall include those necessary for: (a) The provision for the reduction of the stillbirth-rate and of infant mortality and for the healthy development of the child; (b) The improvement of all aspects of environmental and industrial hygiene; (c) The prevention, treatment and control of epidemic, endemic, occupational and other diseases (d) The creation of conditions which would assure to all medical service and medical attention in the event of sickness'.

[171] McGoldrick, above n.1, at p. 146.

[t]he Convention on the Rights of the Child directs States to ensure access to essential health services for the child and his or her family, including pre- and post-natal care for mothers. The Convention links these goals with ensuring access to child-friendly information about preventive and health-promoting behaviour and support to families and communities in implementing these practices. Implementation of the principle of non-discrimination requires that girls, as well as boys, have equal access to adequate nutrition, safe environments, and physical as well as mental health services. There is a need to adopt effective and appropriate measures to abolish harmful traditional practices affecting the health of children, particularly girls, including early marriage, female genital mutilation, preferential feeding and care of male children. Children with disabilities should be given the opportunity to enjoy a fulfilling and decent life and to participate within their community.[172]

According to Article 24(3), States parties shall take all effective and appropriate measures with a view to abolishing traditional practices prejudicial to the health of children. As an important improvisation, the intention had been to target such practices as female infanticide, male preference, neglect and abuse of children and female circumcision. During the drafting of the Convention, the issue of female circumcision aroused significant tensions and disagreements.[173] In order to prevent stalling the work on this particular Article, it was decided that no examples (including that of female circumcision) could be referenced in the text of the Article itself.[174] As noted earlier, the practice of female circumcision continues to take place in many parts of the world, although there is equally a strong condemnation of this activity in many quarters. Indeed the abhorrence and condemnation of female circumcision has been so strong that it has now been established that in circumstances where protection is not afforded to women or girls at risk of this practice it may constitute a grounds for a claim of refugee status, under 'particular social group'.[175]

Article 25 of the Convention provides that:

> States Parties recognize the right of a child who has been placed by the competent authorities for the purposes of care, protection or treatment of his or her physical or mental health, to a periodic review of the treatment provided to the child and all other circumstances relevant to his or her placement.

There is, however, no elaboration of 'competent authorities' or 'periodic review'. Article 26 recognises the right of children to State benefits such as social security and social insurance. The right to social security as an important right has been recognised by Article 9 ICESCR and Article 12 of the European Social Charter. Article 27 of the CRC provides that States

---

[172] ICESCR General Comment 14, *The Right to Highest Attainable Standard of Health* (Article 12) General Comment No. 14 (11/08/00). (E/C.12/200/4), para 22.

[173] For a multitude of literature see chapter 15.

[174] UN Doc. E/CN.4/1986/42.

[175] See the Cases of *Fornah and K* v. *Secretary of State for the Home Department* [2006] UKHL 46 [2007] 1 AC 412 in 19(1) I.J.R.L. (2007) pp. 96–144, paras 11–16 and 32, see also *Mademoiselle X* (19 September, 1991). Case is considered in (1992) *Public Law* 196, England and Wales (*Yake* v. *Secretary of State for the Home Department*, 19 January 2000, unreported; *P and M* v. *Secretary of State for the Home Department* [2004] EWCA Civ 1640, [2005] Imm AR 84), the United States (*In re Kasinga* 21 I & N Dec. 357 (BIA 1996), *Abankwah* v. *Immigration and Naturalization Service* 185 F 3d 18 (2d Cir 1999), *Mohammed* v. *Gonzales* 400 F 3d 785 (9th Cir 2005), Australia (*RRT N97/19046*, unreported, 16 October 1997), Austria (GZ 220.268/0-XI/33/00, unreported, 21 March 2002), and Canada (*Re B(PV)* [1994] CRDD No. 12, 10 May 1994; and *Compendium of Decisions, Immigration and Refugee Board*, February 2003, pp. 31–35).

'recognize the right of every child to a standard of living adequate for the child's physical, mental, spiritual, moral and social development'.

(ix) Educational rights

According to Article 28(1) States parties recognise the right of the child to education, and with a view to achieving this right progressively and on the basis of equal opportunity, they shall, in particular:

(a) Make primary education compulsory and available and free to all;

(b) Encourage the development of different forms of secondary education, including general and vocational education, make them available and accessible to every child, and take appropriate measures such as the introduction of free education and offering financial assistance in case of need;

(c) Make higher education accessible to all on the basis of capacity by every appropriate means;

(d) Make educational and vocational information and guidance available and accessible to all children;

(e) Take measures to encourage regular attendance at schools and the reduction of drop-out rates.

The provisions develop the obligations inherited from Article 26(1) of the UDHR and Articles 13 and 14 of the ICESCR. As already mentioned, Articles 13 and 14 of the ICESCR have been the focus of substantial attention from the Committee on the International Covenant on Economic, Social and Cultural Rights, with the right to education being the subject of two General Comments by the Committee.[176] While commenting on the right to primary education the Committee noted that:

[i]n line with its clear and unequivocal obligations under article 14, [relating to primary education] every State party is under a duty to present to the Committee a plan of action[177] . . . This obligation needs to be scrupulously observed in view of the fact that in developing countries, 130 million children of school age are currently estimated to be without access to primary education, of whom about two thirds are girls.[178]

---

[176] ICESCR General Comment 11, *Plans of action for Primary Education (Article 14)* General Comment No. 11 (10/05/99). (E/C.12/1999/4); CESCR General Comment 13, *The Right to Education* (Article 13) General Comment No. 13 (8/12/99). (E/C.12/1999/10).

[177] According to ICESCR General Comment No. 11, para 8: '[t]he plan must cover all of the actions which are necessary in order to secure each of the requisite component parts of the right and must be sufficiently detailed so as to ensure the comprehensive realization of the right. Participation of all sections of civil society in the drawing up of the plan is vital and some means of periodically reviewing progress and ensuring accountability are essential.'

[178] ICESCR General Comment No. 11, para 3.

The article is important as many States, particularly those from Asia and Africa, continue to invest poorly in education.[179] Although there is increasing emphasis on primary education for children being compulsory, many children for economic or social reasons are forced to remain illiterate. The provisions of Article 28 are complemented by Article 29, which the Committee has treated as one of 'far-reaching importance'.[180] The Committee on the Rights of the Child noted in its first General Comment that:

> Article 29(1) not only adds to the right to education recognized in article 28 a qualitative dimension which reflects the rights and inherent dignity of the child; it also insists upon the need for education to be child-centred, child-friendly and empowering; and it highlights the need for educational processes to be based upon the very principles it enunciates. The education to which every child has a right is one designed to provide the child with life skills, to strengthen the child's capacity to enjoy the full range of human rights and to promote a culture which is infused by appropriate human rights values. The goal is to empower the child by developing his or her skills, learning and other capacities, human dignity, self-esteem and self-confidence. 'Education' in this context goes far beyond formal schooling to embrace the broad range of life experiences and learning processes which enable children, individually and collectively, to develop their personalities, talents and abilities and to live a full and satisfying life within society.[181]

Article 30 is based on Article 27 of ICCPR. It deals with the rights of minority children. Criticisms are shared with those of Article 27, there is no definition of 'minorities' or persons of indigenous origins; the article itself is drafted in a negative manner and is party to the same shortcomings that are attached to Article 27.[182] The Committee on the Rights of the Child has more recently through its jurisprudence, however, attempted to establish concrete principles as well as scope of the protection available to children belonging to minorities and indigenous communities. In establishing a nexus between Article 27 of the ICCPR and Article 30 of the Convention, the Committee in its General Comment No. 11 (January 2009), focused on indigenous children and makes the observation that:

> Both articles specifically provide for the right, in community with other members of his or her group, to enjoy his or her own culture, to profess and practice his or her own religion or to use his or her own language. The right established is conceived as being both individual and collective and is an important recognition of the collective traditions and values in indigenous cultures. The Committee notes that the right to exercise cultural rights among indigenous peoples may be closely associated with the use of traditional territory and the use of its resources.[183]

16

The rights of the child

---

[179] See e.g. HRCP, *State of Human Rights in Pakistan in 1998* (1999) pp. 6–15.
[180] Article 29(1): The Aims of Education 08/02/2001. CRC General Comment 1, CRC/GC/2001/1, para 1.
[181] Ibid. para 2.
[182] See Xanthaki, *Indigenous Rights and United Nations Standards: Self-Determination, Culture and Land* (Cambridge University Press, 2007) at pp. 198–199.
[183] Committee on the Rights of the Child, General Comment No. 11 (2009) Indigenous children and their rights under the Convention (Fiftieth Session) CRC/C/GC/11, para 16.

It has, as we shall examine shortly, also held a discussion day on the indigenous child, whereby it emphasised to States the significance of taking all necessary measures for the protection of the identity of indigenous children.[184]

(x) Criminal justice rights

A number of the provisions within Article 40 draw inspiration from the Beijing Rules. Aspects of the Beijing Rules have developed into recognised rules of criminal law within the domestic jurisdictions of States, although there are many others which do not, as such, have a binding effect and belong to the regime of 'soft law'.[185] These 'soft laws', however, can prove significant in the development of norms of customary international law or binding treaty law. Article 40 caters for wide diversity in the penal systems. Some States have juvenile courts, separate regimes of administering offences conducted by children, whereas others treat children in more or less the same manner as adults.[186] The article confirms many principles including the principle of non-retroactivity of penal law,[187] presumption of innocence,[188] being informed promptly of charges,[189] the matter being decided promptly by a competent, independent and impartial authority[190] and non-compulsion of confession.[191] As a response arising out of the concerns related to the treatment of children within criminal justice systems, the Committee has provided detailed guidelines through its General Comment. In this comment, the Committee reminds States of the essential requirements of a satisfactory juvenile justice system. It notes:

> A comprehensive policy for juvenile justice must deal with the following core elements: the prevention of juvenile delinquency; interventions without resorting to judicial proceedings and interventions in the context of judicial proceedings; the minimum age of criminal responsibility and the upper age limits for juvenile justice; the guarantees for a fair trial; and deprivation of liberty including pre-trial detention and post-trial incarceration.[192]

Within the general comment, the Committee goes on to elaborate the various facets of this comprehensive system of the juvenile justice system.[193]

5 IMPLEMENTATION OF THE CONVENTION[194]

The second part of the Convention, dealing with its implementation, is provided for in Articles 42–45. Supervision of the Convention is conducted by a 18-member Committee

---

[184] Recommendations, Day of General Discussion on the Rights of Indigenous Children, 3 October 2003.
[185] See above chapter 2.
[186] Van Bueren, above n.1, at pp. 179–180.
[187] Article 40(2)(a) CRC.
[188] Ibid. Article 40(2)(b)(i).
[189] Ibid. Article 40(2)(ii).
[190] Ibid. Article 40(2)(iii).
[191] Ibid. Article 40(2)(iv).
[192] Committee on the Rights of the Child, General Comment No. 10 (2007) Children's Rights in Juvenile Justice CRC/C/GC/10 Forty-Fourth Session (9 February 2007) 4.
[193] Ibid.
[194] O'Flaherty, *Human Rights and the UN: Practice before the Treaty Bodies* (Martinus Nijhoff Publishers, 2002) pp. 147–175; Cohen, Hart and Kosloske, 'Monitoring the United Nations Convention on the Right of the Child: The Challenge of Information Management' 18 *HRQ* (1996) 439.

called the Committee on the Rights of the Child.[195] The members of the Committee are drawn from States which are party to the treaty. Members serve in their individual capacity.[196] They are to be 'of high moral standing and of recognized competence in the field'.[197] Each member's term of office is for four years, with the possibility of re-election.[198] The only mechanism for the implementation of the Convention is through a system of periodic reports submitted by States parties.

Under Article 44, the Committee is obliged to forward a biannual report of its activities to the General Assembly via ECOSOC.[199] The Committee initially started with one session per year. However, with the growing number of States, it soon became evident that this time would be insufficient. Since 1994 three sessions per year have been the standard practice. These sessions are normally held in January, May and September in Geneva. Each of the sessions lasts for three working weeks and is followed by a meeting of one week's duration of a Working Group to prepare for the next session.

The Convention requires a State report to be submitted within two years of its entry into force and, thereafter, every five years.[200] According to Article 44(2), reports submitted by the States 'shall indicate factors and difficulties, if any, affecting the degree of fulfilment of the obligations' of the provisions within the Convention. Reports are also aimed at providing adequate information of an analysis of the Convention's implementation. The first meeting of the Committee was held in 1991, and the scrutiny of reports started in 1993. In its sessions during 1991–92, the Committee concerned itself with practical issues such as drafting provisional rules of procedure and reporting guidelines. In order to improve guidance on initial reports by State parties, the Committee has issued guidelines regarding the form and content of these reports.[201] These guidelines aim at providing a clear indication of the nature and depth of information required, and also to impose some degree of uniformity on the production of reports.[202] The Committee has also produced guidelines on periodic reports.[203] In accordance with the provisions of the Convention, the Committee has asked the governments to publish their reports within their countries.[204] It has also been suggested by the guidelines that summary records of States parties' dialogue with the Committee, alongside the Concluding Observations, be published. The guidelines recommend a thematic approach for the reports adopting the following structure. Information should be provided as regards the implementation of the following:

---

[195] Article 43. An Amendment to increase the number of members of the Committee from 10 to 18 was adopted by the General Assembly–GA Res. 50/155 21 December 1995. The amendment entered into force on 18 November 2002 upon being approved by two-thirds of States parties.

[196] Article 43(2) CRC.

[197] Ibid. Article 43(2).

[198] Ibid. Article 43(6).

[199] Ibid. Article 44(5).

[200] Ibid. Article 44(1).

[201] General Guidelines Regarding the Form and Content of Initial Reports to be Submitted by States Parties under Article 44, para 1(a) of the CRC, UN Doc. CRC/C/5.

[202] Lansdown, 'The Reporting Procedure under the Convention on the Rights of the Child' in Alston and Crawford (eds), *The Future of UN Human Rights Treaty Monitoring* (Cambridge University Press, 2000) 113–128 at p. 114.

[203] General Guidelines Regarding the Form and Content of Periodic Reports to be Submitted by States Parties under Article 44, para 1(b) of the CRC, UN Doc. CRC/C/58/Rev.1, 29 November 2005.

[204] Article 44(6) CRC.

- General Measures of Implementation (Articles 4, 42, and 44(6)).
- Definition of the Child (Article 1).
- General Principles (Articles 2, 3, 6 and 12).
- Civil rights and freedoms (Articles 7, 8, 13–17, and 37(a)).
- Family environment and alternative care (Articles 5, 9–11, 18(1–2), 19–21, 25, 27(4), 39).
- Basic health and welfare (Articles 6, 18(3), 23, 24, 26, 27(1–3)).
- Education, leisure and cultural activities (Articles 28, 29, 31).
- Special measures of protection (Articles 22, 30, 32–36, 37(b)–(d), 38, 39, 40).

The guidelines direct our attention to four underlying principles in relation to compliance with and scrutiny of the Convention rights. These concern non-discrimination (Article 2), the best interest of the child (Article 3), the right to life, survival and development (Article 6), and the right of children to participate in decisions affecting them (Article 12).[205] In providing consideration to any issue, these underlying factors need to be relied upon. An article placed within one band will not fall neatly into a single aspect of the rights of the child. Such a categorisation, however, places emphasis upon the integration of civil and political rights with those of social, economical and cultural rights and the re-affirmation of the view of the indivisibility of these sets of rights.

At the end of each session of the Committee, one week is allocated to the consideration of the questions to be addressed to the States parties due to appear in the next session.[206] A working group from amongst the Committee members is established for the purpose of identifying key areas within the report which raise concern or need further clarification. This pre-sessional Working Group meets in private, no government representatives are allowed to attend and no public record of the discussion is produced. NGOs are, however, invited to attend the pre-sessional Working Group.[207] With the input of NGOs and other UN agencies, the Committee writes its list of issues to be presented to the government.[208] A list of issues for transmission to the States parties is compiled with a request for written replies to be considered together with the issues drawn up by members serving as 'country rapporteurs'.[209] In addition, other sources of information derived from NGOs and agencies such as the ILO, UNICEF and UNHCR are collated.[210]

A State report, once submitted, is likely to be considered by the Committee within 18 months of submission, although it is difficult to predict at which session the report will be

---

[205] General Guidelines Regarding the Form and Content of Periodic Reports to be Submitted by States Parties under Article 44, para 1(b) of the CRC, UN Doc. CRC/C/58/Rev.1, 29 November 2005, para 21.

[206] Overview of the Reporting Procedures, UN Doc. CRC/C/33 24 October 1994, para 7.

[207] Committee of the Rights of the Child – Working Methods, www2.ohchr.org/english/bodies/crc/workingmethods. htm#a2a <last visited 30 October 2008>.

[208] See Cullen and Morrow, 'International Civil Society in International Law: The Growth of NGO Participation' 1 *Non-State Actors and International Law* (2001) 7 at p. 18.

[209] There are significant benefits derived from through this procedure. With the NGO input the committee members become much more aware of the actual situation. The committee members can also raise concrete issues and criticises the misinformation within State reports. Government reports are often weak in terms of measures of implementing the Convention rights and the Committee is better placed to show its concerns in its concluding observations. The NGO produced alternative reports underlines the weakness in the official position. The encouragement to NGOs is to submit this alternative report on behalf of the National NGO body as whole. The consolidated report is likely to be more authoritative and comprehensive and avoids duplication.

[210] Overview of the Reporting Procedures, para 10. www2.ohchr.org/english/bodies/crc/workingmethods.htm#a2a <last visited 30 October 2008>.

receiving consideration. Two, three-hour plenary sessions are allocated to each country report. At the plenary sessions the governmental representative appears before the Committee. At these sessions NGO representatives are invited to present their comments on the country reports and to identify major areas of concern. Those NGO representatives who wish to make submissions to the Working Group should inform it in advance and must provide evidence of the relevance of their intervention and interest.

Reports are considered in public sessions. They are introduced by the State Representative. The relevant United Nations agencies are also invited to attend. The proceedings of the Committee are based on the categorisation as provided within the Convention guidelines. The discussion on each of the categories is introduced by comments of the State representative, followed by questions and comments of members of the Working Group and concluded by responses of the State representative. At the end of the consideration, the Committee members summarise their observations and make suggestions and recommendations. The State representative may make a final statement and provide a response to the Committee's observations.

After the completion of its review of the report, the Committee in a closed meeting produces Concluding Observations in which the Committee presents it opinion on the adequacy or inadequacy of the report, positive as well as negative features of the report, and considers any possible difficulties of implementation. The Committee also puts forward the issues which it perceives to be a matter of concern and ends with suggestions and recommendations. The Concluding Observations are issued at the end of each session in the form of public documents and are included in the biannual report to the United Nations General Assembly. These Concluding Observations are also transmitted to UN specialised agencies such as the UNICEF. If the Committee takes the views that the report or the information submitted by the State is of insufficient merit, it may decide only to provide preliminary Concluding Observations and request further information to be submitted for consideration at a future session where a conclusive form of Concluding Observations may be issued. Alternatively, the Committee may decide upon providing definitive Concluding Observations, at the same time requesting further supplementary information.

(i) Protocols to the Convention on the Rights of the Child

In an analysis of the expanding rights, as well as the monitoring of these rights, it would be most pertinent to examine, allbeit briefly, the two Optional Protocols to the Convention to the Rights of the Child: the Optional Protocol to the Convention on the Rights of the Child on the Sale of Children, Child Prostitution and Child Pornography (OP–CRC–SC) and the Optional Protocol to the Convention on the Rights of the Child on the Involvement of Children in Armed Conflict (OP–CRC–AC).

OP–CRC–SC Protocol was opened for signature, ratification and accession by the United Nations General Assembly Resolution on 25 May 2000.[211] The Optional Protocol has been ratified by 132 States and entered into force in January 2002. The Protocol, in its preamble, takes notes of the concerns emerging from the increased trafficking in children for purposes of sale, prostitution and pornography.[212] There is also concern at the growth in such practices as sex tourism and sexual exploitation of children.[213] In accordance with

[211] New York, 25 May 2000 UN Doc. A/RES/54/263.
[212] Preamble.
[213] Ibid.

the provisions of Article 1, States parties categorically and unequivocally agree to prohibit the sale of children, child prostitution and child pornography.[214] Article 2 provides a definition of the meaning of the terms 'Sale of Children', 'Child Prostitution' and 'Child Pornography'.

Article 2 establishes the following definition for the purposes of the Protocol:

(a) Sale of children means any act or transaction whereby a child is transferred by any person or group of persons to another for remuneration or any other consideration;

(b) Child prostitution means the use of a child in sexual activities for remuneration or any other form of consideration;

(c) Child pornography means any representation, by whatever means, of a child engaged in real or simulated explicit sexual activities or any representation of the sexual parts of a child for primarily sexual purposes.

In accordance with Article 3, each State party is required as a minimum to prohibit and attach criminal sanctions for anyone 'Offering, delivering or accepting' a child for the purposes of sexual exploitation,[215] transfer of organs for profit,[216] or engagement into forced labour.[217] Furthermore, it is also prohibited and criminalised to induce consent improperly, as an intermediary, for the purposes of child adoption.[218] Article 3 also criminalises any attempts to offer or to procure a child for the purposes of prostitution,[219] as well as producing, distributing, disseminating or otherwise publishing pornographic images of children.[220] Attempts to procure sexual exploitation of children through prostitution or through child pornography are also to be sanctioned by the criminal law of States parties.[221] According to Article 4 of the Protocol, a State party is required to establish jurisdiction when the aforementioned offences referred in Article 3 are committed either in its territory or on board a ship or aircraft registered in that State.[222] Additional grounds for jurisdiction include instances where either the victim is a national of the State party, or habitually resident therein,[223] or in circumstances where the alleged offender is present in the State party's jurisdiction and it fails to refuse to extradite the individual to another State on the basis of his or her nationality.[224] The Convention affirms that Article 3 offences are extraditable with the States undertaking to provide each other with all possible assistance in

---

[214] Ibid.
[215] Article 3(1)(a)(i)(a).
[216] Article 3(1)(a)(i)(b).
[217] Article 3(1)(a)(i)(c).
[218] Article 3(1)(ii). As Dennis makes the point, intercountry adoptions was a matter of concern for the United States since 'many U.S. jurisdictions prospective adopting parents to reimburse birth parents reasonable expenses, such as medical and legal fees, counselling services, and living expenses, while waiting for the adoption to be completed . . . During the final negotiating session both Japan and the United States stated their understanding that "applicable international legal instruments on adoption" meant the Hague Convention, and that since they were not parties to that instrument, they would not be bound to penalize the conduct barred by it', Dennis, 'Newly Adopted Protocols to the Convention on the Rights of the Child', 94 *AJIL* (2000) 789 at pp. 793–794.
[219] Article 3(1)(ii)(b).
[220] Article 3(1)(ii)(c).
[221] Article 3(2).
[222] Article 4(1).
[223] Article 4(2)(a)(b).
[224] Article 4(3).

relation to investitagations, provision of evidence, etc.[225] There is also an undertaking to take steps to seize or confiscate materials, goods and proceeds emanating from the criminalised activities as well as to ensure closure of premises used for committing any actions criminalised under the Protocol.[226] In accordance with provisions of Article 8, States parties undertake to adopt measures to protect the rights of child victims, particularly through the legal processes and ensuring their rights in accordance with the principle of the best interests of the child. According to Article 9, States parties also undertake to adopt measures including legislative and administrative measure to prevent offences against children as contained in the Protocol. There is also an undertaking to promote awareness through information as regards the offences, and to ensure that all possible measures are undertaken to ensure full integration of child victims within society.[227] The reporting procedure to the Protocol is contained in Article 12. Within two years of the Protocol coming into force for the State party, the relevant party undertakes to submit a report to the Committee on the Rights of the Child as regards the measures it has undertaken to implement the provisions of the Protocol.[228] Following the submission of the Report, each State party is required to submit to the Committee on the Rights of the Child in accordance with Article 44, any further information as regards the implementation of the Protocol.[229] Other States that are parties to the Protocol are required to submit a report every five years.[230] Furthermore, the Committee on the Rights of the Child may request from States parties additional relevant information relevant to the implementation of the Protocol.[231] The Protocol is open to any State that is a party to the Convention on the Rights of the Child or has signed the parent convention.[232] It came into force three months after the deposit of the 10th ratification or accession.[233]

OP–CRC–AC, was also opened for signature, ratification and accession by the United Nations General Assembly Resolution on 25 May 2000.[234] The Optional Protocol entered into force in January 2002 and has been ratified by 128 parties. The preamble to the Protocol highlights the global concern at the increasing involvement and targeting of children in armed conflict and consequently a highly adverse impact upon their lives. The preamble makes reference to positive developments in international humanitarian and criminal law for the protection of children in armed conflict and for the prohibition of their conscription in armed conflicts. In this regards the Rome Statute (particularly the inclusion therein as a 'war crime' of conscripting or enlisting children below the age of 15 years in international or non-international armed conflicts) and the ILO Convention No. 182 are specifically mentioned.[235] According to Article 1 of the Protocol, States Parties are committed to take all 'feasible measures' to ensure that those members of their armed forces that have not attained the age of 18, do not take a direct part in hostilities.[236] The

---

[225] Articles 5 and 6.
[226] Article 7.
[227] Article 9(2).
[228] Article 12(1).
[229] Article 12(2).
[230] Article 12(2).
[231] Article 14.
[232] Article 13.
[233] Ibid.
[234] New York, 25 May 2000 UN Doc. A/RES/54/263.
[235] Preamble.
[236] Article 1.

term 'feasible measures' represent a compromise to accommodate those States (e.g. the United States and United Kingdom) who retain a policy of recruiting 17-year-olds and therefore, in strict military terms, could not guarantee that these person would in all circumstances be prevented from taking a direct part in armed conflict or hostilities.[237]

The language in relation to conscription of children is particularly stern: Article 2 prohibits the compulsory recruitment of persons below the age of 18 years into armed forces.[238] A similar prohibition lies on use or recruitment of persons below 18 on armed groups unconnected with the State. As is tragically happening in various internal or international armed conflicts, insurgents or armed groups regularly make use of children as part of their forces and military arsenal, and the Protocol makes an attempt to prevent such abominable practices. While such an undertaking is not always in the control of the States, ratifying States are nevertheless under an obligation to take all 'feasible measures' to prevent recruitment of under-18s by non-State actors.[239]

Although it is almost universally agreed that the minimum age for conscription into armed forces would not be below 18, State practice varies significantly on the subject of voluntary recruitment and participation in hostilities. Almost half of the States, including the United States, the United Kingdom and Australia allow for voluntary recruitment of persons below 18.[240] An ultimate comprise, incorporated at the behest of the United States, is that States parties undertake to raise the minimum age for voluntary recruitment into national armed forces (from the previously established 15 years by Article 38(3) of the Convention on the Rights of the Child) having regard to the fact that those below 18 are entitled to special protection.[241] In accordance with the provisions of this Protocol, States parties undertake to make binding declarations establishing a minimum age at which they will permit voluntary recruitment into national armed forces.[242] Those States continuing to permit voluntary recruitment into their armed forces of individuals below 18 are required to ensure that such recruitment is genuinely voluntary;[243] that it is carried out with the informed consent of the individual's parent or legal guardian,[244] is agreed upon with full proof of the age,[245] and the individual is provided with complete information of the duties involved in the military service.[246] Since the United States retains annually over 50,000 17-year-olds on active-duty, albeit with full proof of age and full parental consent, the United States was insistent on these aforementioned provisions.[247]

States parties commit themselves to take steps to ensure implementation with the provisions of the Protocol within their jurisdiction and to provide all possible assistance to other States and relevant international agencies.[248] The implementation mechanisms of OP–CRC–AC are the same as that of OP–CRC–SC, as are the procedural rules on entry into force.

In order to provide assistance and collaborative support towards adequate implementation of the Convention on the Rights of the Child and OP–CRC–AC, the UN has appointed

---

[237] Dennis, above n.218, at p. 791.
[238] Article 2.
[239] Article 4.
[240] Dennis, above n.218, at p. 790.
[241] Article 3(1).
[242] Article 3(2).
[243] Article 3(3)(a).
[244] Article 3(3)(b).
[245] Article 3(3)(d).
[246] Article 3(3)(c).
[247] Dennis, above n.218, at p. 791.
[248] Articles 6 and 7.

a Special Representative of the Secretary-General for Children and Armed Conflict, as well a Special Rapporteur on the Sale of Children, Child Prostitution and Child Prongraphy. Radhika Coomaraswamy (the former Special Rapporteur on Violence against Women 1994–2003) was appointed by the Secretary-General as the Special Representative for Children and Armed Conflict in April 2006. Her appointment was reconfirmed by the current Secretary-General Ban Ki-moon in February 2007. Ms. Coomaraswamy, since her appointment, has outlined a number of key objectives which include: (i) supporting global initiatives to end grave violations; (ii) promoting rights-based protection for children affected by armed conflict; (iii) making children and armed conflict concerns an integral aspect of peacekeeping and peacebuilding; and (iv) raising awareness with regard to all issues relating to children and armed conflict.[249] Reports have been compiled on Iraq, Chad, Myanmar and Somalia.[250] Currently the focus is on Afghanistan, which was visited by the Special Representative in June/July 2008.[251] The officeholder looks at a wide range of issues varying from child soldiers to sexual violence and from refugee and internally displaced children to HIV/AIDs.[252]

The UN Special Rapporteur on the sale of Children, Child Prostitution and Child Pornography also plays an invaluable role in enforcing the OP–CRC–SC. This mandate was established by the Human Rights Commission Resolution 1990/68 in 1990. The duration of the mandate has been extended since that time, most recently by the Human Rights Council in its Resolution 7/13 in 2008, for a period of three years. The current mandate holder is Ms. Najat M'jid Maala from Morocco. The Optional Protocol has been ratified by 132 States and entered into force in January 2002. The position of the Special Rapporteur predates the adoption of OP–CRC–SC and has been operational from 1991. In light of the significance of the work of the Special Rapporteur, the mandate was extended in March 2008 for a further three years. The Special Rapporteur performs a number of functions including visits and exchanges with governments, promoting strategies and measures and making recommendations. Country Missions take place annually; recently this has included Mexico in 2007, Ukraine in 2006 and Greece in 2005. The Annual Report of the Special Rapporteur includes a study into a substantive area, in 2008 this was a 'assistance and rehabilitation programmes for child victims of trafficking and sexual commercial exploitation' and in 2007, the 'sale of children's organs and rapid-response programs for abducted or disappeared children'.

6 INNOVATIVE FEATURES AND OTHER INITIATIVES

In comparison with other reporting treaty-based procedures, NGOs have a more prominent and formally acknowledged role to play within the Convention on the Rights of the Child. According to Article 45 of the Convention, the specialised agencies, the United Nations Children's Fund and other United Nations organs are entitled to be represented at the consideration of the State reports. Thus, for example, when consideration is given to

---

[249] Special Representative of the Secretary General for Children and Armed Conflict www.un.org/children/conflict/english/radhika-coomaraswamy.html <last visited 22 May 2009>.
[250] Office of the Special Representative of the Secretary-General for Children and Armed Conflict www.un.org/children/conflict/english/index.html <last visited 30 May 2009>.
[251] Office of the Special Representative of the Secretary-General for Children and Armed Conflict – Visit to Afghanistan www.un.org/children/conflict/english/afghanistan-june-2008.html <last visited 30 May 2009>.
[252] Office of the Special Representative of the Secretary-General for Children and Armed Conflict – Issues www.un.org/children/conflict/english/issues.html <last visited 30 May 2009>.

provisions related to employment or labour, the ILO representatives can attend the proceedings of the Committee as of right. The article also authorises the Committee to request submission of reports from the UN Children's Fund (UNICEF) and other UN bodies on areas falling within the scope of their activities. It can also invite these and other expert bodies (which implicitly includes the NGOs) to provide expert advice on areas falling within their respective mandates.[253] The Committee can, therefore, consult the ILO, as well as other relevant UN bodies, on issues arising out of child labour in a particular State. This is a unique provision amongst human rights instruments and the Committee has responded by inviting NGOs to submit alternative reports, which provide the Committee with a fuller and more critical analysis of the state of children's rights in a country.

The Convention also provides for NGOs to have a recognised and formalised function and this is also reflected in the Rules of the Procedure. The Committee has made use of this formal position of NGOs as important providers of information. NGOs have also established a Group for the Convention on the Rights of the Child, with a full-time Geneva based co-ordinator, facilitating the flow of information to the Committee and encouraging NGO contributions at the international and national level. This allows for a more effective contribution to the work of the Convention. NGOs provide support to the Committee in a number of ways. This includes providing information to the Country Rapporteurs during the initial consideration of the State Report, in order to help develop a list of issues for the Working Group's consideration. During the Working Group's deliberations, NGOs are generally invited for only a three-hour session during which time the relevant State report is being considered. After the Working Group has considered the report, it is possible for NGOs to obtain the list of issues and the replies of the relevant government. This then aids the NGOs when compiling final submissions which are submitted to the Committee prior to its final consideration of the State Report in question.

Article 45(b) authorises the Committee to transmit, at a State's request, 'technical advice or assistance' to 'the specialized agencies, the United Nations Children's Fund, and other competent bodies'. The object is to enable those States which are experiencing difficulties in implementing the Convention to have access to and support from all the relevant competent bodies. In accordance with Article 45(c) the Committee may recommend that the General Assembly request the Secretary-General to undertake on its behalf studies relevant to issues concerning child rights. Article 45(d) allows the Committee to make suggestions and general recommendations based on information received through Articles 44 and 45. These suggestions and general recommendations are transmitted to the concerned State party and to the General Assembly.

The Committee has also adopted a number of initiatives. The Committee has for some years now devoted one day every year to a general discussion of a specific issue. Rule 75 of the Rules of Procedure sanctions such an activity. It provides:

[i]n order to enhance a deeper understanding of the content and implications of the Convention, the Committee may devote one or more meetings of its regular sessions to a general discussion on one specific article of the Convention or related subject.[254]

---

[253] Article 45(a)(b); Cohen, above n.4, at p. 146.
[254] Rules of Procedure of the Committee on the Rights of the Child, Rule 75, UN Doc. CRC/C/4/Rev.1, 25 April 2005.

This provision has been used to set aside a series of 'Days of General Discussion' on a range of topics.[255] The first such discussion took place in 1992 on the subject of children in armed conflict; the second in 1993 related to the economic exploitation of Children; and the third in 1994 on the role of the family. In 1998, the Committee devoted a day to discuss 'Children living in a world with HIV/AIDS'. Other topics covered have included, and as noted earlier, the rights of indigenous children (2003), State violence against children (2000) and children without parental care (2005). In September 2008, the Day of Discussion was held on the theme of 'The Rights of the Child to Education in Emergency Situations'.[256] These discussions are attended by members of the Committee, NGOs and international organisations. They have been very useful in developing greater appreciation of the role of the Committee and providing a forum of consideration and debate. Such a debate may also influence international State practice and lead to the formulation of new Standards regarding the rights of the Child. Days of general discussion are normally announced in the report of the session immediately preceding that in which it is proposed they occur. The announcement may be accompanied by a paper by the Committee on the topic.[257] All those who are interested and concerned are invited to make written representations to the Committee.

Members of the Committee have also undertaken missions to various countries. These missions allow members of the Committee to consider and discuss issues arising out of the implementation of the Convention with the representative of the State, relevant organisations and NGOs. The practice was discontinued in 1997 but was re-established again in 2003.[258] Traditionally, all the Committee members have been able to participate in these missions. However, for the future it is more likely that a selected group of Committee members will be on each of these trips.[259]

A number of significant UN bodies have been established in order to protect the rights of the child. As noted in our earlier consideration, these include the Office of the Special Representative of the Secretary-General for Children and Armed Conflict. The Office of the Special Representative works in conjunction with UNICEF and other key UN entities. One of the most noteworthy aims of the Office is to place children in conflict situations on the UN Security Council Agenda.[260] The United Nations Study on Violence Against Children was completed in October 2006 by the Independent Expert for the Secretary-General Study on Violence against Children. The study looked at violence in five different settings, including: the home and family; schools and educational settings; care and justice institutions; the work-places; and the community.[261] The report made 12 recommendations which included the prohibition of violence against children, the prioritsation of prevention, ensuring accountability and ending impunity and strengthening international commitment.[262] In October 2007, the Independent Expert presented his progress report on the implementation of the study to the General Assembly of the UN.[263] It is apparent from the

---

[255] O'Flaherty, above n.194, at p. 174.
[256] See Committee on the Rights of the Child, Day of General Discussion www2.ohchr.org/english/bodies/crc/discussion2008.htm <last visited 30 October 2008>.
[257] O'Flaherty, above n.194, at p. 174.
[258] Committee of the Rights of the Child – Working Methods www2.ohchr.org/english/bodies/crc/workingmethods.htm <last visited 30 May 2009>.
[259] On Mission see O'Flaherty, above n.194, at pp. 174–175.
[260] Office of the Special Representative of the Secretary-General for Children and Armed Conflict – Actions www.un.org/children/conflict/english/actions.html <last visited 30 May 2009>.
[261] UN Doc. A/61/299, 29 August 2006.
[262] UN Doc. A/61/299, 29 August 2006.
[263] UN Doc. A/62/209, 7 August 2007.

progress report that while the study has had an international effect and led to action being taken all over the world, it is also far too soon to evaluate the overall success of the report.[264] The study requires time in order for the recommendations to be implemented properly.

(i) Regional initiatives to protect the rights of children

In common with the global initiatives, efforts have been made at the regional level to protect the rights of children. Brief consideration has already been provided to the European, African and inter-American systems and other systems in relation to children's rights, although it is pertinent to make reference to the certain specific regional instruments focusing on children's rights.[265] The Council of Europe's Convention on the Exercise of Children's Rights emulates the Convention on the Rights of the Child.[266] However, the provisions within this Convention largely establish or strengthen procedural rights which can be exercised by children themselves or are exercisable through other bodies.[267] The Convention provides the child *inter alia* of rights to be informed[268] and to express his or her views in judicial proceedings,[269] and a right to apply for the appointment of a special representative in such proceedings.[270] The Convention places obligations on judicial authorities which include involving the child in the decision-making process,[271] keeping the child informed of relevant judicial proceedings,[272] acting speedily and in relevant cases appointing a representative.[273] A Standing Committee has been established to review the implementation of the Convention and to provide advice and assistance.[274]

Within the African Union, the African Charter on the Rights and Welfare of the Child (ACRWC)[275] has been established. This is monitored by the African Committee of Experts on the Rights and Welfare of the Child.[276] Provisions within the ACRWC are modelled closely on the Convention on the Rights of the Child, though in consonance with the African values a number of responsibilities are also placed on children. As noted in an earlier chapter, ACRWC provides for a wide set of rights for the children including a right to survival and development,[277] name and nationality,[278] freedom of expression,[279] thought, conscience and religion,[280] to education and to leisure,[281] and recreation and cultural activities.[282] The

---

[264] UN Doc. A/62/209, 7 August 2007 pp. 20–21.

[265] See Part III above.

[266] Council of Europe, European Convention on the Exercise of Children's Rights, ETS No. 160, Strasbourg, 25.I.1996 http://conventions.coe.int/Treaty/en/Treaties/Html/160.htm <last visited 18 May 2009>.

[267] See Council of Europe, European Convention on the Exercise of Children's Rights, ETS No. 160 (Explanatory Note) http://conventions.coe.int/Treaty/EN/Reports/HTML/160.htm <last visited 18 May 2009>.

[268] Article 3 (a).

[269] Article 3 (b).

[270] Article 4.

[271] Article 6.

[272] Article 6(b).

[273] Article 7.

[274] Chapter III.

[275] Addis Ababa, Ethiopa, July 1990 OAU Doc. CAB/LEG/24.9/49 (1990), entered into force 29 November 1999.

[276] For more information see www.africa-union.org/child/home.htm <last visited 30 May 2009>.

[277] Article 5.

[278] Article 6.

[279] Article 7.

[280] Article 9.

[281] Articles 11 and 12.

[282] Article 12.

useful safeguards for children built within the Charter include the protection from abuse and torture,[283] from child labour[284] and from protection against harmful social and cultural practices.[285] The Charter aims to provide safeguards during armed conflict[286] and the rights of refugee children.[287] There are also safeguards for handicapped children.[288] The African Committee of Experts on the Rights and Welfare of the Child, which was established in 2001, has a variety of functions, which include promoting and protecting the rights enshrined in the Charter and to monitor this, it interprets the provisions of the Charter and performs such tasks that may be entrusted to it by the Assembly of the Head of States.[289] Despite being a relatively young mechanism the Committee has managed to hold thematic discussions on a number of important and topical subject areas, including children and armed conflict, and the impact of HIV/AIDs, poliomyelitis and malaria on children.[290]

Although lacking a binding document, the inter-American system has adopted a series of Resolutions and has also established a number of mechanisms. Amongst the major instruments are the OAS General Assembly Resolution on Children and Armed Conflict[291] and the inter-American Year of the Child and the Adolescent.[292] The prominent mechanisms and initiatives include the Inter-American Children's Institute[293] and Rapporteur-ships on the Rights of Children.[294] Within its jurisprudence the inter-American Court of Human Rights has also pronounced on cases involving children including the landmark case of *Villagran–Morales* v. *Guatemala*.[295] This case concerned the unfortunate beatings, torture and deaths of five street children. In recognising a positive duty to protect children who did not have the protection of their families, the court also regarded the Convention on the Rights of the Child as having the status of *corpus juris* for protecting children in Guatemala.[296]

Amongst the Islamic world, the issue of children's rights has also received attention. The Organisation of Islamic Conference (OIC), as noted already, adopted a Covenant on the Rights of the Child in Islam.[297] The Covenant is heavily influenced by the Islamic ideals and targets the position of children within Muslim societies. At the same time the recognition of international instruments such as the Convention on the Rights of the Child within the

---

[283] Article 16.
[284] Article 15.
[285] Article 21 see further Van Bueren, 'Child Sexual Abuse and Exploitation: A Suggested Human Rights Approach' 2 *International Law Journal of Child Rights* (1994) 45.
[286] Article 22.
[287] Article 23.
[288] Article 13.
[289] For more information see www.africa-union.org/child/home.htm# <last visited 30 May 2009>.
[290] For more information see www.africa-union.org/child/home.htm# <last visited 30 May 2008>.
[291] AG/RES. 1709 (XXX-O/00) Resolution adopted at the first plenary session 5 June 2000.
[292] AG/RES. 1733 (XXX-O/00) Resolution adopted at the first plenary session 5 June 2000.
[293] For more information see www.iin.oea.org/iin/English/index.shtml <last visited 30 October 2008>.
[294] For more information see www.cidh.org/relatorias.eng.htm <last visited 30 May 2009>.
[295] (The *Street Children* case) Merits, Judgment of November 19, 1999, Inter-Am. Ct. H.R. (Ser. C) No. 63 (1999).
[296] See Van Bueren and Wanduragala, 'Annual Review of International Family Law' in *The International Survey of Family Law* (2001) 1 at p. 4. The Court ordered reparations for the deaths of the children and also ordered Guatemala to name an educational centre after the name of the children and to place a plaque in the Centre with the names of children inscribed in their memory. *Villagran Morales* et al. v. *Guatemala* (the *Street Children* case) Reparations, Judgment of May 26, 2001, Inter-Am Ct. H.R. (Ser. C) No. 77 (2001), paras 103 and 115. See Pasqualucci, *The Practice and Procedure of the Inter-American Court of Human Rights* (Cambridge University Press, 2003) at p. 252.
[297] (2004), OIC Doc. OIC/0-IGGE/HRI/2004/Rep.Final.

Covenant reinforces the point that children's rights within the Islamic ethos are not incompatible with international standards.[298] Many of the rights contained in the Convention on the Rights of the Child are also represented in the OIC Covenant. The Covenant contains such key rights as the right to life, equality, nationality, education, and physical and psychological health.[299] The South Asian Association for Regional Cooperation (SAARC) has also undertaken a number of initiatives to raise awareness and to improve the condition of children a regional level. SAARC has also provided the platform for a number of regional treaties including the SAARC Convention on Regional Arrangements for the Promotion of Child Welfare in South Asia (2002) and the SAARC Convention on Prevention of Trafficking of Women and Children for Prostitution (2002). Furthermore, SAARC recognised 1990 as the SAARC Year of Girl Child and the decade 2001–10 has been observed as the SAARC Decade of the Rights of the Child. Although, in real concrete terms, much needs to be done to improve the plight of the children of South Asia, SAARC has at the very least proved instrumental in raising awareness as regards the rights of children.[300]

7 CONCLUSIONS

The value and significance of the Convention on the Rights of Child was confirmed through its unanimous approval by the United Nations General Assembly in 1989 and its having attracted the highest number of ratifications amongst international treaties. As noted eloquently by one commentator 'it is clear that in addition to its legally binding nature, the CRC also enjoys a certain moral force'.[301] The details and breadth of the rights contained in the Convention have been analysed in this chapter. Our discussion has also presented an overview of the operations of the Committee on the Rights of the Child. Despite the many positives emerging from the work of the Committee on the Rights of the Child there are concerns and there remains significant room for improvement. One of the outstanding concerns is the volume of work which the Committee has to deal with. The United Nations has agreed to provide further resources to the Committee. In terms of the substance of the State reports, many of the apprehensions are reflected in the work of other treaty-bodies, for example, the inadequacy and insufficiency of the information provided. The Committee on the Rights of the Child frequently comments upon this in its Concluding Observations. With the enormous workload in the past two decades the Committee is increasingly under pressure. There is currently a backlog of reports. However, if the reports are being produced on time, it is inevitable that a delay in their consideration will take place. This will in turn lead to a situation where their consideration would be conducted at a point in time when the reports themselves would be outdated.

Another concern which the Committee has drawn attention to in its consideration of the reports has been the inadequate attention to some sets of rights from States. These

---

[298] On Children's rights within Muslim Jurisdictions see Ali 'A Comparative Perspective of the United Nations Convention on the Rights of the Child and the Principles of Islamic Law: Law Reform and Children's Rights in Muslim Jurisdictions' in Ali, Goonesekere, Mendez and Rios-Kohn, *Protecting the World's Children: Impact of the Convention on the Rights of the Child in Diverse Legal Systems* (Cambridge University Press, 2007) pp. 142–208.

[299] For further details see above chapter 11.

[300] For further details on SAARC see above chapter 11; also see www.saarc-sec.org/?t=2.8.2 'Children and Youth' <last visited 23 May 2009>.

[301] Kilkelly, 'Strengthening the Framework for Enforcing Children's Rights: An Integrated Approach' in Ensalaco and Majka (eds), above n.1, 53–79 at p. 54.

include firstly the four guiding principles (Articles 2, 3, 6 and 12) and also Articles 13–16 (freedom of expression, religion, conscience and thought, privacy) and Article 23 (disability), etc. It is important that the Committee is able to assess the implementation of all the rights contained in the Convention. On a procedural matter, the pre-sessional Working Groups have proved very useful. They allow for NGO input and for effective scrutiny. Even in this regard, there are some negative points. After a lengthy session of the Committee, members are often exhausted and frequently too few are present. The Committee members tend to show a relative lack of interest which is disappointing for the NGOs.

Having considered some of the weaknesses and limitations in the work of the Committee, the overall contribution of the Committee and the Convention must not be overlooked. The Convention has motivated almost every State in the world to improve the position of children within its jurisdiction. As we have noted, serious disagreements remain on the scope and nature of many of the rights contained in the Convention. At the same time, there is a fundamental recognition that the international community must act in the best interest of the child and must ensure his or her welfare and respect his or her innocence and integrity. The two additional Protocols to the Convention on the Rights of the Child deal with sensitive yet highly critical areas of child protection. Their adoption is a welcome addition and has been rightly described as 'represent[ing] major advances in international efforts to strengthen and enforce norms for the protection of the most vulnerable children, who desperately need the world's attention'.[302]

16

The rights of the child

---

[302] Dennis, above n.218, at p. 789.

17 Rights of the persons with disabilities[1]

1 INTRODUCTION

[A]pproximately 10 per cent of the world's total population – have a disability of one form or another. Over two thirds of them live in developing countries. While their living conditions vary, they are united in one common experience: being exposed to various forms of discrimination and social exclusion. This negative attitude, which is rooted in ignorance, low expectations and prejudice, leads to exclusion and marginalisation of persons with disabilities. This phenomenon also deprives societies of active participation and contribution by a significant societal group.[2]

A natural consequence of the enormous diversity in the human species is the presence of people with varying abilities, some with lesser abilities than others. People with lesser abilities and impairments – often classified as physical and mental disabilities – inevitably form part of all States and societies, and yet discrimination, exclusion and neglect of disabled persons is visible in every society. Historically, people with disabilities have suffered from the 'invisibility' syndrome: since disabled people were viewed with disgrace and shame, they were frequently forced to remain within the confines of the home. They have been systematically discriminated against and excluded from human activity and human rights (e.g. education, employment, sport, cultural activities) to the extent that within many societies, persons with disabilities were regarded as sub-humans; shameful and disgraceful creatures not worthy of recognition as humans. Some societies identified persons with disabilities as 'diseased' for whom a cure or 'medical' solution was required.[3] The Standard Rules on Equalization of Opportunities for People with Disabilities, adopted by the UN General

---

[1] Degener and Quinn, *Human Rights and Disability: The Current Use and Future Potential of United Nations Human Rights Instruments in the Context of Disability* (2002) HR/PUB/02 at p. 1; Despouy, *Human Rights and Disabled Persons*, Human Rights Studies Series No. 6, UN Sales No. E.92XIV.4 (1992), available at www.un.org/esa/socdev/enable/dispaperdes0.htm <last visited 3 June 2008>; Kayess and French, 'Out of Darkness into Light? Introducing the Convention on the Rights of Persons with Disabilities' 8 *HRLR* (2008) 1; Lawson, 'The United Nations Convention on the Rights of Persons with Disabilities: New Era or False Dawn' 34 *Syracuse Journal of International Law and Commerce* (2007) 563; and Stein, 'Disability Human Rights' 95 *California Law Review* (2007) 75.

[2] Office of the United Nations High Commission for Human Rights www.unhchr.ch/disability/intro.htm <last visited 8 April 2009>.

[3] Melish, 'The UN Disability Convention: Historic Process, Strong Prospects and Why the U.S. Should Ratify' 14 Human Rights Brief (2007) 37, at p. 44. www.wcl.american.edu/hrbrief/14/2melish.pdf?rd=1 <last visited 8 April 2009>.

Assembly identify 'ignorance, neglect, superstition and fear' as significant social factors which have resulted in the isolation of disabled persons and which has impeded their development.[4] Persons with disabilities have frequently been victimised, targeted and harassed. During natural catastrophes, humanitarian crises or armed conflicts persons with disabilities have been abused and targeted.[5] While injuries caused during conflicts, wars and internal disturbances render millions of peoples disabled, those already having disabilities become the primary targets of abuse during these conflicts. Disabled persons became a major target of the Nazi Holocaust during the Second World War. It was, therefore, unfortunate as well as disappointing to note that the newly formed United Nations failed to condemn the Nazi atrocities against disabled persons with the same vigour with which it condemned atrocities against other minorities and vulnerable communities.[6]

In contemporary societies – in which much of the historic discrimination and ostracism persists – human rights law continues to express reluctance to engage fully with disability and provide full and proper recognition to the rights of disabled persons as human rights. As in the past within many existing societies, persons with disabilities are viewed as those not in need of fundamental human rights but are all too frequently bracketed as being physically or mentally retarded and needing medical attention or medical solutions.[7] Those with disabilities have been seen as the objects of treatment or charity rather than the holders of rights. The oppression of disabled persons has denied or diminished personhood, thereby reducing citizenship and civil participation.[8] The medical model of disability has powerfully influenced how disability has been understood throughout all strata of society, especially within the field of mental health/disability. Many people have historically been – and still are today – institutionalised on the basis of their disability.[9] The World Health Organization states that 'there is increasing worldwide concern about people with mental health disorders being incarcerated in prisons rather than being cared for in mental health facilities. Unfortunately, prisons have become *de facto* mental hospitals (without treatment) in a number of countries'.[10] According to the Treatment Advocacy Centre, on any given day, there are four times the number of people suffering from schizophrenia, bipolar disorder and serious depression in the nation's jails and prisons as there are in hospitals.[11] The Human Rights Committee in its concluding observations on Krgystan in 2000 expressed serious concerns on 'the detention of persons on mental health grounds and the apparent lack of possibility of challenging such detention is of concern'.[12] This situation is indicative of the global picture of those who are mentally ill: the lack of facilities available to them means that they are likely to face the criminal justice system.[13] Thus for example, those who are mentally disabled suffer grave threats to their substantive right to life as part of the punitive features of criminal justice systems such as the United States which approved the execution of death row prisoners with an IQ of less than 70 until 2002,[14] and continues to executes those with mental illnesses. In many other countries (developed as well as developing), the rights of the disabled person remain under threat due to a punitive and highly insensitive criminal justice system.

There has been a distinct lack of adequate policies, programmes, laws and resources to address the issue of mental disability. For example, in 2001, most middle- and low-income countries devoted less than 1 per cent of their health expenditure to mental health.[15] As a result, mental health care, including essential medication, such as psychotropic drugs, is inaccessible or unaffordable to many. Access to all types of health care for persons with psychosocial or intellectual disabilities is complicated due to the stigma and discrimination to the sufferers, contrary to the obligation on States to provide access to health care on an equal footing. The Special Rapporteur on the Right of Everyone to the Enjoyment of the Highest Attainable Standard of Physical and Mental Health, Paul Hunt raised concerns about treatment of those with mental disability in Peru where:

> there is an almost universal lack of rehabilitation services and community-based mental health and support services. The centralized and institutionalized model of care denies those with mental disabilities the rights to be treated and cared for in the community in which they live, and to live and work in the community, as far as possible.[16]

Persons with mental disabilities frequently suffer from denials of fundamental rights, including the right to adequate and appropriate action, as well as the right to a dignified life. A clear connection has been established between poverty and disability with a fifth of the world's poorest people also suffering from various forms of disability. Elwan makes the point that 'the links between poverty and disability go two ways – not only does disability add to the risk of poverty, but conditions of poverty add to the risk of disability'.[17] Moreover, what counts as a disability in a given place, to begin with, is uniquely dependent on economic factors, so that what may not be much of a disability in some corners of the world will be a considerable one in others. Megret gives a simple example; 'a mild vision impairment will not be a disability in a country where glasses are widely available, nor is there any risk of the short-sighted, for example, being the object of stigma. In a country where glasses are not available, conversely, even a mild, easily corrected impairment may constitute a disability for many jobs and lead to exclusion and marginalization'.[18]

---

[13] www.amnesty.org/library/index/ENGAMR510032006 <last visited 8 April 2009>.

[14] See e.g. *Atkins* v. *Virginia* 536 U.S. 304 (2002).

[15] Saxena, Sharan and Saraceno, 'Budget and financing of mental health services: baseline information on 89 countries from WHO's Project Atlas' 6 *Journal of Mental Health Policy and Economics* (2003) 135–143.

[16] Right of Everyone to the Enjoyment of the Highest Attainable Standard of Mental and Physical Health: Report: Assenmum/Submitted by the Special Rapoorteur on the Right of Everyone to the Enjoyment of the Highest Attainable Standard of Physical and Mental Health, Paul Hunt. E/CN.4/2005/51/Add.3, para 64.

[17] Elwan, 'Poverty and Disability: A Survey of the Literature' (Social Protection Discussion Paper Series Paper No. 9932, 1999) http://siteresources.worldbank.org/DISABILITY/Resources/280658-1172608138489/PovertyDisabElwan.pdf <last visited 1 November 2008>, p. 34.

[18] Megret, 'The Disabilities Convention: Towards a Holistic Concept of Rights', 12 *International Journal of Human Rights* (2008) 261 at p. 269.

As this chapter explores, although human rights developments regarding disability since the formation of the United Nations have seen some improvement, the overall picture continues to remain dismal. More than 650 million people, 10 per cent of the total global population, suffer from various forms of mental, sensory or physical disabilities, constituting the 'world's largest minority'.[19] Persons with disability have not traditionally been considered a minority, [20] although Kayess and French argue that the Convention on the Rights of Persons with Disabilities has 'finally empowered the world's largest minority to claim their rights and to participate in international and national affairs on an equal basis with others who have achieved specific treaty recognition and protection'.[21] They believe that the current approach to achieving substantive equality, as reflected in disability non-discrimination laws, can be classed as a minority rights approach.[22] The problem with this approach is that it assumes that the identification of the beneficiaries as a group is possible, while creating a hierarchy for social resources, which may be few and far between. More importantly, this approach emphasises difference and deviation from the norm, rather than social diversity and the holistic membership of a community, further discriminating and ostracising those with disabilities to such an extent they are forced into refugeeism or relocation.[23] However, minority rights have traditionally been applied to groups that identify along ethnic, racial, cultural, national, religious or linguistic lines. Additionally, it is vital that the individual members of the group in question not only choose to belong to such a group but also that they have the will to maintain the distinct characteristics of the group as a whole.[24] The rights required for disabled persons to enjoy human rights do not require the maintenance of group identity within the meaning of minority rights. Rather they require provisions prescribing non-discrimination (particularly affirmative action) and equality before the law to be enacted both *de jure* and *de facto*, as is the case regarding other marginalised groups, which are not necessarily minorities, such as women. There is also, as will be discussed later, an element of 'reasonable accommodation'. While there is little doubt that disabled persons are a 'minority' within the normal meaning of the term and require extra protection as a result, it is unlikely that they can be beneficiaries of the regime of 'minority rights' within the meaning of the term under international law.

---

[19] Kayess and French, above n.1, at p. 4.

[20] Degener, 'Disabled Persons and Human Rights: The Legal Framework', in Degener and Koster-Dreese (eds), *Human Rights and Disabled persons: Essays and Relevant Human Rights Instruments* (Martinus Nijhoff, 1995) pp. 20–33.

[21] Kayess, and French, above n.1, at p. 1.

[22] See Fredman, 'Providing Equality. Substantive Equality and the Positive Duty to Provide' 21 *South African Journal of Human Rights* (2005) 163.

[23] Disabled persons have also been categorised as 'social group' within the definition of a refugee. Disability through HIV has featured before refugee tribunal. The courts have recognised that in instances such as the HIV which leads an individual to 'social stigma and ostracism' from family and friends and having been forced to live in street does amount to persecution with in the categorisation of the 1951 Convention. Reference V95/02084, RRT, 23 February 1996 at 7; discussed by Foster, *International Refugee Law and Socio-Economic Rights* (Cambridge University Press, 2007) pp. 228–229. Furthermore the discrimination faced by disabled persons has also been recognised as amounting to persecution. In allowing the application of a disabled person, a Canadian Tribunal made the following observation: 'The repeated and persistent injury and annoyance suffered by the disabled persons of Burkina Faso . . . greatly undermine the fundamental rights of disabled persons, in particular their right to work to support themselves, thus potentially jeopardizing their survival in a country where medical care is not free of charge and where there is no system of state protection for those persons and they rely solely on the aid of their family or charities to survive.' See OGW (Re) No. MA1-08719 [2002] CRDD No. 53, 16 April 2002 at para 16; also see IPJ (Re) No. A99-01121 [2000] CRDD No. 141.

[24] See chapter 13 above for the definition of a minority in international law.

Disabled people are routinely subjected to victimisation and violence while being specifically targeted in times of war or armed conflict. Even within human rights circles – both academic and non-governmental – disabled people fail to get their due share of attention. References to disability and disabled peoples within most human rights textbooks are only incidental. Indeed, some commentators regard disability as the 'invisible element of international human rights law'.[25] As our discussion explores, such ignorance follows the unfortunate trend which until recently was adopted by the international regime of human rights law. The present chapter analyses the rights of the disabled under international law. It examines the civil, political, economic and social rights that are accorded in international law to disabled peoples and also assesses the difficulties in the implementation of these rights. The efforts within the UN have resulted in the adoption of the International Convention on the Rights of Persons with Disabilities (CRDP) and the Optional Protocol to the Convention.[26] On 3 May 2008, the Convention on the Rights of Persons with Disabilities and its Optional Protocol entered into force. In order to mark such a momentous occasion a special ceremony took place in the General Assembly Hall in New York on 12 May 2008. This chapter examines the provisions and prospects of the instrument.

2 THE UNITED NATIONS AND THE RIGHTS OF THE DISABLED PEOPLES

The universality and indivisibility of human rights means that all human rights are applicable to all persons, regardless of any disability or characteristic. In its preamble, the UDHR calls for equality before the law for everyone.[27] In advocating non-discriminatory practices, the Declaration emphasises in Article 1 that '[a]ll human beings are born free and equal in dignity and rights'. Furthermore, the Declaration itself is built on a number of fundamental principles including respect for inherent dignity.[28] Kittay maintains that equal dignity is due to all human beings by virtue of their capacity to create themselves,[29] or by virtue of their ability to behave as moral autonomous agents or as self-respecting members of a society characterised by just principles of fair social co-operation.

This sense of 'equal dignity' is generally aligned with an understanding of dignity as 'empowerment' as Beyleveld and Brownsword believe.[30] As dignity is based on a certain capacity or capability, to treat someone with dignity is not merely to refrain from doing certain things to them, but involves allowing them to exercise that capacity or capability, which is how the Convention can be seen to interpret the concept of 'human dignity'.[31]

Megret refers to the 'pluralization' of human rights, whereby human rights as law and ideology has recognised the needs of specific groups or categories as worthy of specific

---

[25] Kayess and French, above n.1, at p. 12.

[26] The CRPD and the Optional Protocol were adopted by the General Assembly during its 61st Session: See GA Res. 61/611 (13 December 2006) A/61/611; 15 IHRR 255.

[27] UN General Assembly resolution 217 A(III) of 10 December 1948, Universal Declaration of Human Rights, 10 December 1948.

[28] Article 3(a) UDHR; see chapter 5 above.

[29] Mirandola, *Oration on the Dignity of Man* (Gateway, 1956).

[30] See Beyleveld and Brownsword (eds), *Human Dignity in Bio-Ethics and Bio-Law* (Oxford University Press, 2001).

[31] Kittay, 'Equality, Dignity and Disability' in Lyons and Waldron (eds), *Perspectives on Equality: The Second Seamus Heaney Lectures* (Liffey Press, 2005) pp. 95–122.

human rights protection.[32] He believes that group specific rights, such as those provided by the Convention on the Rights of Persons with Disabilities propose a much more holistic concept of what rights entail for certain persons, in the same mould as the Convention on the Elimination of Racial Discrimination despite not being specifically described as an anti-discrimination convention.[33] However, the Convention goes further than the Race Convention or the Womens' Convention, specifically spelling out in substantial detail how States should go about ensuring the rights of persons with disabilities. Furthermore, the General Assembly mandate, under which the Convention was developed, uses the word 'integral' which signifies a shift in the rights of the disabled to being a core constituent of international human rights law, rather than existing as complementary to other core instruments.[34]

Both the International Covenant on Economic, Social and Cultural Rights (ICESCR) and the International Covenant on Civil and Political Rights (ICCPR) contain rights which can be directed towards supporting the rights of disabled persons. The jurisprudence of the Covenants has acknowledged the applicability of rights to disabled persons.[35] The right of everyone to just and favourable conditions of work, including adequate remuneration, extends to disabled persons,[36] as does the recognition that one has an adequate standard of living for himself and his family, including adequate housing and clothing.[37] The right to the highest attainable standard of physical and mental health and education are rights most needed by persons with disabilities. Article 10(2) of the ICESCR provides that special protection is to be accorded to mothers for a reasonable period before and after childbirth. These provisions carry direct relevance for women and children whose disabilities occur during the process of childbirth. Article 10(2) of the ICESCR provides: 'Special protection should be accorded to mothers during a reasonable period before and after childbirth.

---

[32] Megret, 'The Disabilities Convention: Human Rights of Persons with Disabilities or Disability Rights?' 30 *Human Rights Quarterly* (2008) 494 at p. 495.

[33] Megret, above n.18 at p. 269.

[34] GA Res. 56/168, 19 December 2001, A/56/583/Add.2.

[35] The Committee on ICESCR has noted that although the treaty does not explicitly refer to persons with disability, Article 2(2) has broader perspective and the terminology of 'or other status' incorporates persons with disabilities (HRI/GEN/1/Rev 8, Add.1). The Committee goes on to note in this comment, both 'de jure and de facto discrimination against persons with disability have a long history and take various forms'. They range from invidious discrimination, such as the denial of access to educational opportunities, to more 'subtle' forms of discrimination such as segregation and isolation achieved through the imposition of physical and social barriers' *Persons with disabilities:* 09/12/94. CESCR General Comment 5 (General Comments) Eleventh Session 1994 E/1995/22, para 15. In this General Comment, the Committee on ICESCR makes the following highly pertinent observations: 'The central importance of the International Covenant on Economic, Social and Cultural Rights in relation to the human rights of persons with disabilities has frequently been underlined by the international community. Thus a 1992 review by the Secretary-General of the implementation of the World Programme of Action concerning Disabled Persons and the United Nations Decade of Disabled Persons concluded that "disability is closely linked to economic and social factors" and that "conditions of living in large parts of the world are so desperate that the provision of basic needs for all – food, water, shelter, health protection and education – must form the cornerstone of national programmes". Even in countries which have a relatively high standard of living, persons with disabilities are very often denied the opportunity to enjoy the full range of economic, social and cultural rights recognized in the Covenant.' Ibid. para 1.

[36] Article 7 ICESCR. In its General Comment No. 5, the Committee has also emphasised the integration of persons with disabilities into the workforce. According to the Committee, States parties need to support any physical barriers from within the workplace which place restrictions upon persons with disabilities. Furthermore, the Committee emphasises the transportation which 'is crucial to the realization by persons with disabilities of virtually all rights recognised in the Convention'. Ibid. para 23. The ICESCR Committee also notes that 'the double discrimination suffered by women with disabilities is often neglected'. The Committee, in the comment urges States parties to the Covenant to address and priorities the position of women with disabilities, with a focus on the implementation of their rights under the Covenant.

[37] Article 11 ICESCR.

During such period working mothers should be accorded paid leave or leave with adequate social security benefits.'

Disabled persons are particularly vulnerable to violations of political rights and civil liberties and, therefore, all of the rights contained in the ICCPR apply with full force to disabled persons. That said, a number of references are made to equality of rights for all, though persons with disabilities can rely upon these only by implication. Similarly, persons with disability and disability *per se* do not specifically feature in the two International Covenants.[38] It could be argued that all the rights contained in the ICCPR apply with full force to the persons with disability, although again the absence of references directly dealing with disability remains an unfortunate omission.[39] This shortcoming within the international covenants raises several pertinent issues. Firstly, and as noted consistently in this study, the rights contained within the international bill of rights are applicable to everyone and are therefore also conferred on disabled persons. Secondly, and more importantly, notwithstanding their universal applicability, disabled persons are often denied their rights. Reasons for breaches include the inability or unwillingness on the part of the State to undertake action to prevent violation of rights of disabled persons including violations conducted by non-State actors and private individuals. A further reason for violation of rights of disabled persons is the failure to provide any positive action to ensure provisions of the rights of the disabled persons. Thirdly, there also remains a debate as to the most effective means of ensuring the rights of disabled persons – as we shall examine in due course, there is now an increasingly popular view which perceives positive action beyond policies of positive discrimination or affirmative action to ensure elimination of discrimination against disabled persons.

Other human rights treaties, i.e. the Convention on the Elimination of Racial Discrimination, the Convention on the Elimination of All Forms of Discrimination against Women, the Convention Against Torture and the International Convention on the Protection of the Rights of All Migrant Workers and Members of their Families, whilst being group-focused, nevertheless do not directly engage with the subject of disability. Amongst international human rights treaties, the Convention on the Rights of the Child (CRC) provides an exception. Article 23 of the CRC places an obligation on States parties to allow for the full and decent life of disabled children in conditions which guarantee their dignity and promote self-reliance.[40] Positive obligations on the States parties include measures to provide for disabled children's active participation in the community and recognition of their right

---

[38] Kayess and French, above n.1, at p. 12.

[39] The jurisprudence of the Human Rights Committee on disability is also limited.

[40] Article 23(1) CRC provides that: 'States Parties recognize that a mentally or physically disabled child should enjoy a full and decent life, in conditions which ensure dignity, promote self-reliance and facilitate the child's active participation in the community.' The Committee on the Rights of the Child has also provided a General Comment on the Rights of Children with Disabilities, where the Committee makes the following observations: 'It is estimated that there are 500–650 million persons with disabilities in the world, approximately 10% of the world population, 150 million of whom are children. More than 80% live in developing countries with little or no access to services. The majority of children with disabilities in developing countries remain out of school and are completely illiterate. It is recognized that most of the causes of disabilities, such as war, illness and poverty, are preventable which also prevent and/or reduce the secondary impacts of disabilities, often caused by the lack of early/timely intervention. Therefore, more should be done to create the necessary political will and real commitment to investigate and put into practice the most effective actions to prevent disabilities with the participation of all levels of society.' The Rights of Children with Disabilities CRC/C/GC/9 27 February 2007 (Forty-third session) General Comment No. 9 (2006), para 1.

to special care.[41] Such special care is to be provided to the child through assistance accorded to the parent of the child and others in charge of such care. Assistance provided to children with disabilities is to be free of charge, wherever possible, having regard to the financial circumstances of the children and those in charge of their care. These children are to have access to education, training, healthcare services and recreational activities in such manner as is conducive for the complete social, cultural and educational development of children including their fullest societal integration.[42] States parties also undertake to promote information in the fields of preventative healthcare and medical care, as well as psychological and functional treatment of children with disabilities, including the dissemination of information regarding methods for their rehabilitation, vocational services and their education.[43] The aim of such exchange of information is to enhance State capabilities and skills in order to widen their experience in the area.[44] Particular account is to be taken of the needs of the position of disabled children within the developing countries.[45]

A number of other United Nations instruments have been useful in developing the armoury of international laws on disability. Article 1 of the UNESCO Convention against Discrimination in Education, for example, guarantees equal access to education of all types and levels and prohibits the limitation of any person or group of persons to education of an inferior standard.[46] Persons with disabilities must, therefore, be provided with equal access to education, which is of a comparable standard to that available to non-disabled persons and, therefore, there is a requirement of 'reasonable accommodation'. This includes access to the school and classrooms and the availability of learning aides such as Braille books. The ILO Convention concerning Vocational Rehabilitation and Employment (Disabled Persons) recognises the rights of disabled persons to appropriate training and employment, not only in specialised institutions and sheltered workshops, but also in open labour markets, and stipulates that employers' and workers' organisations – together with governments and organisations of disabled persons – share the responsibility for helping disabled persons to realise their rights.[47] The definition of discrimination in Article 1 of the ILO Convention concerning Discrimination in Respect of Employment and Occupation (1958) does not specifically include a distinction based on the disability of a person; however, as under Article 1(2), the term discrimination includes 'such other distinction, exclusion or preference which has the effect of nullifying or impairing equality of opportunity or treatment in employment or occupation as may be determined by the Member concerned after consultation with representative employers' and workers' organisations', discrimination on the ground of disability may come within the provisions of the Convention, if so determined by the Member State.[48]

---

[41] Article 23(1)(2) CRC.
[42] Article 23(2) CRC.
[43] Article 23(4) CRC.
[44] Article 23(4) CRC.
[45] Article 23(4) CRC.
[46] UNESCO Convention against Discrimination in Education, 14 December 1960, 429 U.N.T.S. 93, entered into force 22 May 1962.
[47] Article 23(4). Vocational Rehabilitation and Employment (Disabled Persons) Convention (ILO No. 159), 1401 UNTS 235, entered into force 20 June 1935.
[48] Discrimination (Employment and Occupation) Convention (ILO No. 111), 362 U.N.T.S. 31, entered into force 15 June 1960.

(i) The UN effort towards a focused approach to disability

Until the adoption of the Convention on the Rights of Persons with Disabilities in December 2006, disability presented a major lacuna in the United Nations consideration of the human rights of vulnerable, victimised and disadvantaged groups. Attempts during 1987–88 to formulate a treaty concerning the rights of those with disabilities were thwarted within the General Assembly.[49] Nascent efforts to devise a binding instrument can be discerned from the range of 'soft law' documents, including the Declaration on the Rights of Disabled Persons[50] and the General Assembly's Declaration on the Rights of Mentally Retarded Persons.[51] The first significant development in the acknowledgement of the rights of the disabled was conducted through the proclamation of the 'International Year of the Disabled' in 1981 by the United Nations General Assembly.[52] This International Year was celebrated under the slogan 'Full Participation and Equality'. In its 1981 General Assembly Declaration, whilst recognising the contributions made by disabled persons, nonetheless, the Assembly lamented the large-scale discrimination conducted against them. The Assembly urged member States to make all possible efforts to consolidate and build upon the progress made as a result of the International Year of the Disabled with a view to full integration of the disabled people within their societies.[53] The Assembly invited member States to submit national reports to the UN Secretary General on the implementation of the Plan of Action for the International Year of Disabled Persons.[54] The Assembly requested the Secretary-General to convene in 1982 a meeting of the Advisory Committee of the International Year of Disabled Persons in order to finalise the World Programme of Action Concerning Disabled Persons.[55] The Assembly requested each Regional Commissions to provide high priority to formulate and implement regional programmes for the equalisation of opportunities for disabled persons and welcomed governmental contributions and donations from the private sector toward the UN Trust Fund for the International Year of the Disabled Persons.[56] In addition, it urged closer co-operation between the developed and developing world to support the rights of the disabled peoples through the transfer of technology and the exchange of information.[57]

In order to implement the provisions of the 1981 Declaration, the General Assembly adopted the World Programme of Action Concerning Disabled Persons (WPA) in 1982, which established essential guidelines for a global strategy to promote 'equality' and 'full participation' for people with disabilities.[58] The WPA was premised on the platform of prevention, rehabilitation and the equalisation of opportunities. In its Resolution 1984/31 the former Commission on Human Rights and its Sub-Commission in its Resolution 1984/20 called for a thorough study to be conducted in order to establish a connection between

---

[49] See Dhir, 'Human Rights Treaty Drafting through the Lens of Mental Disability: The Proposed International Convention on Protection and Promotion of the Rights and Dignity of Persons with Disabilities' 41 *Stan. J.Int. Law* (2005) 181.

[50] Declaration on the Rights of Disabled Persons, GA Res. 3447 (XXX) (9 December 1975).

[51] Declaration on the Rights of Mentally Retarded Persons, GA Res. 2856, UN GAOR 26th Session, Supp No. 9 (UN Doc A/8429, 20 December 1971).

[52] GA Res. A/RES/36/77 (8 December 1981) (International Year of Disabled Persons).

[53] Ibid. para 3.

[54] Ibid. para 4.

[55] Ibid. para 5.

[56] Ibid. paras 10 and 12.

[57] Ibid. para 15.

[58] GA Res. 37/52, UN GAOR, 37th Sess. (Supp No. 51) at 185, UN Doc. A/37/52 (3 December 1982).

disability on the one hand and serious violations of human rights on the other. These resolutions also called for concrete suggestions and recommendations in providing remedies for these situations.[59] During 1984, the UN produced a study detailing the relationship between disability and human rights. The UN Sub-Commission on the Prevention of Discrimination and the Protection of Minorities appointed a Special Rapporteur who produced his report in 1993 on the subject of disability and human rights.[60] In 1993, the UN General Assembly undertook a significant step in advancing the case of people with disabilities through the adoption of a Resolution entitled the Equalization of Opportunities for People with Disabilities (Standard Rules).[61] The Rules, which are extensive and comprehensive in nature, can be categorised as a universal approach to the Rights of the People with Disabilities.[62] These Rules *inter alia* stress pre-conditions of equality, opportunities for access to services and facilities, and the involvement and participation of disabled persons within the mainstream. The same period witnessed considerable efforts to heighten awareness of problems facing persons with disabilities in a variety of international fronts including references within the Vienna Declaration and Programme of Action, which reaffirmed the fundamental rights of all persons including disabled persons (1993),[63] the Cairo Programme of Action (1994),[64] the Report of the World Summit for Social Development (Copenhagen Declaration, 1995)[65] and the Beijing Declaration and Platform for Action, Fourth World Conference on Women (1995).[66]

In April 2000, the former UN Human Rights Commission adopted a resolution in which the Commission recognised that violations of the principles of equality and non-discrimination constituted breaches of the UN human rights instruments as well as United Nations Standard Rules on Equalization of Opportunities for Persons with Disabilities.[67] The Commission also encouraged non-governmental organisations active in the protection of the rights of the disabled persons to cooperate with each other and to provide

---

[59] See Despouy, above n.1, para 15.

[60] Ibid.

[61] GA Res. 48/96, 20 December 1993, A/RES/48/96, Supp No. 49, Annex at 202–11, available at www.un.org/documents/ga/res/48/a48r096.htm <last visited 31 March 2009>.

[62] GA Res. 48/96, Annex, UN GAOR, 48th Sess. (Supp No. 49) UN Doc. A/Res/48/96/Annex (20 December 1993).

[63] Vienna Declaration and Programme of Action adopted by the World Conference on Human Rights, UN Doc. A/CONF.157/23 12, July 1993, B. Equality, Dignity and Tolerance: 6(63) 'The World Conference on Human Rights reaffirms that all human rights and fundamental freedoms are universal and thus unreservedly include persons with disabilities. Every person is born equal and has the same rights to life and welfare, education and work, living independently and active participation in all aspects of society. Any direct discrimination or other negative discriminatory treatment of a disabled person is therefore a violation of his or her rights. The World Conference on Human Rights calls on Governments, where necessary, to adopt or adjust legislation to assure access to these and other rights for disabled persons' para 63. The Conference called upon the General Assembly and the Economic and Social Council to adopt the draft standard rules on the equalization of opportunities for persons with disabilities, during their meetings in 1993. Ibid. para 6(65). www.unhchr.ch/huridocda/huridoca.nsf/(Symbol)/A.CONF.157.23.En <last visited 7 April 2009>.

[64] See Cairo Programme of Action, Chapter VI (E) www.iisd.ca/Cairo/program/p00000.html <last visited 8 April 2009>.

[65] Report of the World Summit for Social Development. UN.doc. A/CONF.166/9 (19 April 1995) www.un.org/documents/ga/conf166/aconf166-9.htm <last visited 1 November 2008>. See C. Equality and Social Justice, para 74 (h) F. Violence, Crime and Problem of Illicit Drugs and substance abuse, para 79(h).

[66] Beijing Declaration and Platform for Action, Fourth World Conference on Women, 15 September 1995, A/CONF.177/20 (1995) and A/CONF.177/20/Add.1 (1995), para 132. www1.umn.edu/humanrts/instree/e5dplw.htm <last visited 8 April 2009>.

[67] Commission on Human Rights, 'Human Rights of Persons with Disabilities' www.unhchr.ch/huridocda/huridoca.nsf/(Symbol)/E.CN.4.RES.2000.51.En?Opendocument <last visited 7 April 2009> (25 April 2000) Resolution 2000/51.

17

Rights of the persons with disabilities

information and assistance to such agencies as the office of the High Commissioner for Human Rights. The Commission invited the UN High Commissioner for Human Rights, in co-operation with the UN Special Rapporteur on Disability, to investigate mechanisms for strengthening the protection and monitoring of human rights of persons with disabilities to solicit suggestions and proposals from the relevant parties and particularly panels of experts.[68] Subsequently, various efforts were made *inter alia* highlighting various dimensions of disability and integrating the debate on disability in the activities of treaty-based bodies as well as non-treaty-based mechanisms. In its response to this request, the High Commissioner commenced a study, examining the treatment of the rights of the disabled persons within the existing treaty-based human rights system.[69] Prior to the publication of the study in 2002, the United Nations established an Ad Hoc Committee to consider proposals for a Comprehensive and Integral Convention on the Protection and Promotion of the Rights and Dignity of Persons with Disabilities.[70] The Ad Hoc Committee held its first and second sessions, during 2002–03, alongside delegates from States, intergovernmental and non-governmental agencies and disabled persons organisation.[71] The Ad Hoc Committee established a working group to devise an initial first draft of the Convention. After having met in January 2004, the Working Group produced a draft text known as the 'working group draft text'.[72] After considerable revisions and negotiations the Ad Hoc Committee was able to formulate a draft text of the Convention and an Optional Protocol in December 2006. The texts were then referred to the General Assembly, where the text was adopted on 13 December 2006. Notwithstanding the substantial disagreements and controversies during the drafting stages, the emergent Convention has nevertheless been recognised as the 'most rapidly negotiated [Convention] ever'.[73] The Convention is the outcome of an engaging process involving State representatives and non-governmental organisations with consultative as well as non-consultative standing before the United Nations.[74] As noted in the introductory chapter of this book, the Convention highlights a new trend in international human rights treaty law.[75] The Convention is a product of an unprecedented degree of involvement of NGOs and civil society actors. These non-governmental organisations and civil society actors were adamant and in the end were successful in having a document produced which guaranteed right to persons with disabilities on an equal footing with those of all other persons in the State.[76]

---

[68] Ibid.
[69] See Report of the United Nations High Commissioner for Human Rights and Follow-Up to the World Conference E/CN.4/2002/18/Add.1 (12 February 2002).
[70] GA Res. 58/168 UN Doc. A/RES/56/168 (19 December, 2001) The Resolution established an Ad Hoc Committee 'to consider proposals for a comprehensive and integral international convention 'to promote and protect the rights and dignity of persons with disabilities, based on the holistic approach in the work done in the fields of social development, human rights and non-discrimination and taking into account the recommendations of the Commission on Human Rights and the Commission for Social Development'.
[71] Report of the Ad Hoc Committee on a Comprehensive and Integral International Convention on Protection and Promotion of the Rights and Dignity of Persons with Disabilities (2nd Session), 3 July 2003, A/58/118 and Corr. 1, Part IV (15) 1, available at www.un.org/esa/socdev/enable/rights/a_58_118_e.htm <last visited 8 April 2009>.
[72] Report of the Working Group to the Ad Hoc Committee, Draft Articles for a comprehensive and integral international Convention on the Protection and Promotion of the Rights and Dignity of Persons with disabilities, Annex I, A/AC.265/2004/WG/1, available at www.un.org/esa/socdev/enable/rights/ahcwgreport.htm <last visited 8 April 2009>.
[73] Kayess and French, above n.1, at p. 2.
[74] Lawson, above n.1 at p. 588.
[75] See chapter 1 above.
[76] Lawson, above n.1 at pp. 588–590.

(ii) The UN Convention on the Rights of Persons with Disabilities (CRPD): fundamental principles

The unusually detailed preamble to the Convention explicitly refers to the human rights, equality and non-discriminatory provisions in the UN Charter, as well as the International Bill of Rights. The preamble also highlights the principle of equality enshrined in other human rights treaties, notably the International Convention on the Elimination of All Forms of Racial Discrimination, the Convention on the Elimination of All Forms of Discrimination against Women, the Convention against Torture and Other Cruel, Inhuman or Degrading Treatment or Punishment, the Convention on the Rights of the Child, and the International Convention on the Protection of the Rights of All Migrant Workers and Members of Their Families. The preamble, whilst recognising the significance of international cooperation for the improvement of the living conditions of persons with disabilities, underlines the necessity of promoting and protecting the human rights of individuals with disabilities. It emphasises the gender, age civil, political, economic, social and cultural perspectives related to disability. The fundamental objectives of the Convention are provided in Article 1, which aims 'to promote, protect and ensure the full and equal enjoyment of all human rights and fundamental freedoms by all persons with disabilities, and to promote respect for their inherent dignity'.[77] Furthermore, the Convention is built upon a number of fundamental principles including:

(a) Respect for inherent dignity, individual autonomy including the freedom to make one's own choices, and independence of persons;

(b) Non-discrimination;

(c) Full and effective participation and inclusion in society;

(d) Respect for difference and acceptance of persons with disabilities as part of human diversity and humanity;

(e) Equality of opportunity;

(f) Accessibility;

(g) Equality between men and women;

(h) Respect for the evolving capacities of children with disabilities and respect for the right of children with disabilities to preserve their identities.[78]

Source: The United Nations is the author of the original material.

The CRPD does not provide any definition of 'disability' or 'persons with disabilities'. Attempts at finding a definition within the United Nations circles, as we have examined in other contexts, have proved hopelessly futile and it was feared that efforts at a definition would prove counter-productive.[79] Instead of formulating a definition, Article 1 of the

---

[77] Article 1 International Convention of the Rights of Persons with Disabilities and its Optional Protocol, UN GAOR, 61st Sess., Item 67(b), UN Doc. A/61/611 (6 December 2006) (CPRD).

[78] Article 3 CRPD.

[79] Again as in other instances (e.g. in minorities/indigenous peoples) there were disagreements and diversions on the part of both the representatives from disability organisations and States. The International Disability Caucuses (IDC) argued that a definition would unduly narrow and disempower many in the category of disability. IDC also emphasised on disability as an evolving concept. The participating States were (from their perspective) concerned that an excessively broad definition would lead to the inclusion of even those persons not generally recognised as facing disability within the domestic context.

CRPD notes that '[p]ersons with disabilities include those who have long-term physical, mental, intellectual or sensory impairments which in interaction with various barriers may hinder their full and effective participation in society on an equal basis with others'.

As part of their general obligations, States parties undertake to ensure the full realisation of all human rights and fundamental freedoms for persons with disabilities without any discrimination, undertaking to adopt all appropriate measures including incorporating legislative, administrative or other measures as provided in the Convention and to take account of the promotion and protection of disabled persons in governmental policies and programmes. States parties are to ensure equality for persons with disabilities and also to modify or abolish prevailing laws or discriminatory practices,[80] to refrain from activities contrary to the provisions of the Convention[81] and to undertake all appropriate steps to ensure that neither the public authorities, any persons, organisation nor private enterprise breach these provisions.[82] Articles 4(1)(d) and 4(1)(e) confirm that the provisions of the Convention are fully applicable, for public authorities and governmental bodies. States parties also commit to undertake all appropriate measures to eliminate discrimination by private agencies, organisations and individuals. Furthermore, States parties are required to conduct and promote research and development of most appropriate goods, services and facilities aiding and benefiting disabled persons.[83] This undertaking incorporates the promotion of research and development, and the availability of new technologies (which includes information, communications technology, mobility aids, etc.) as well as the prioritisation of their availability at affordable cost.[84] States parties also agree to provide information and other forms of assistance in relation to these new assistive technologies and undertake to promote training of professional workers in the field for better provisions of assistance and services.[85] As regards the provision of economic, social and cultural rights, States parties undertake to achieve progressively the full realisation of these rights.[86] In developing laws and implementation strategies, States parties are required actively and closely to consult persons with disabilities, including children, through their representative organisations.[87] Article 4(4) confirms that the CRPD should not in any sense be regarded as a reason for derogation from other, stronger, obligations imposed either by national or international law.[88] States parties, therefore, cannot argue that the CRPD sets a lower threshold than other human rights treaties and thereby provides justification from not applying a higher standard.[89]

The Convention makes a significant effort to transcend the domestic/international divide. Domestic law, as Goldsmith and Posner argue, 'is not a pure reflection of moral principles, but instead limits them as necessary to accommodate the need for clear guidelines, the time and expense of judges, the distribution of political power and other constraints'.[90] The provisions of the Convention present a balanced approach in developing a relationship between international law and its domestic application. The Convention

---

[80] Article 4(1)(b) CRPD.
[81] Article 4(1)(d) CRPD.
[82] Article 4 (1)(d)(e) CRPD.
[83] Article 4(1)(f) CRPD.
[84] Article 4(1)(g) CRPD.
[85] Article 4(1)(h) CRPD.
[86] Article 4(2) CRPD.
[87] Article 4(3) CRPD.
[88] Article 4(4) CRPD.
[89] Lawson, above n.1, at p. 592.
[90] Goldsmith and Posner, *The Limits of International Law* (Oxford University Press, 2005) at p. 201.

recognises 'the importance of international cooperation for improving the living conditions of persons with disabilities in every country'.[91] States parties to the Convention, in accordance with Article 32, 'will undertake appropriate and effective measures in this regard, between and among States and, as appropriate, in partnership with relevant international and regional organizations'. Controversy raged over this Article throughout negotiations, as developed countries elucidated the concern that there would be an expectation from developing countries for increased aid in order for them to fully implement the Convention. Moreover, the danger that developing countries would refuse to implement the Convention, citing lack of resources and aid, was mooted. The resulting Article 32 strongly emphasises the importance of national responsibility, yet reiterates the importance of international cooperation in supporting domestic initiatives.

Many civil and political rights contained in the Convention, for example, are matched with corresponding economic and social ones, and vice versa. For instance, the Convention requires States to guarantee such a classic civil and political right as 'freedom of expression and opinion'.[92] However, in order to secure these rights, it is imperative that the State party secures – or at least engages with – economic and social efforts. The Convention reiterates that States parties must take 'all appropriate measures to ensure that persons with disabilities can exercise their right to freedom of expression and opinion'. In some cases, it is the domestic law itself which stipulates that disabled children must attend special schools, which is tantamount to official segregation, while the Convention further establishes that States parties are to provide an inclusive form of education. Article 24 of the Convention provides that:

1. States Parties recognize the right of persons with disabilities to education. With a view to realizing this right without discrimination and on the basis of equal opportunity, States Parties shall ensure an inclusive education system at all levels and life long learning directed to:

   (a) The full development of human potential and sense of dignity and self-worth, and the strengthening of respect for human rights, fundamental freedoms and human diversity;

   (b) The development by persons with disabilities of their personality, talents and creativity, as well as their mental and physical abilities, to their fullest potential;

   (c) Enabling persons with disabilities to participate effectively in a free society.

2. In realizing this right, States Parties shall ensure that:

   (a) Persons with disabilities are not excluded from the general education system on the basis of disability, and that children with disabilities are not excluded from free and compulsory primary education, or from secondary education, on the basis of disability;

   (b) Persons with disabilities can access an inclusive, quality and free primary education and secondary education on an equal basis with others in the communities in which they live;

   (c) Reasonable accommodation of the individual's requirements is provided;

   (d) Persons with disabilities receive the support required, within the general education system, to facilitate their effective education;

---

[91] Preamble, CRDP.
[92] Article 21 CPRD.

> (e) Effective individualized support measures are provided in environments that maximize academic and social development, consistent with the goal of full inclusion.
>
> 3. States Parties shall enable persons with disabilities to learn life and social development skills to facilitate their full and equal participation in education and as members of the community. To this end, States Parties shall take appropriate measures, including:
>
> (a) Facilitating the learning of Braille, alternative script, augmentative and alternative modes, means and formats of communication and orientation and mobility skills, and facilitating peer support and mentoring;
>
> (b) Facilitating the learning of sign language and the promotion of the linguistic identity of the deaf community;
>
> (c) Ensuring that the education of persons, and in particular children, who are blind, deaf or deafblind, is delivered in the most appropriate languages and modes and means of communication for the individual, and in environments which maximize academic and social development.
>
> 4. In order to help ensure the realization of this right, States Parties shall take appropriate measures to employ teachers, including teachers with disabilities, who are qualified in sign language and/or Braille, and to train professionals and staff who work at all levels of education. Such training shall incorporate disability awareness and the use of appropriate augmentative and alternative modes, means and formats of communication, educational techniques and materials to support persons with disabilities.
>
> 5. States Parties shall ensure that persons with disabilities are able to access general tertiary education, vocational training, adult education and lifelong learning without discrimination and on an equal basis with others. To this end, States Parties shall ensure that reasonable accommodation is provided to persons with disabilities.

Source: The United Nations is the author of the original material.

A holistic reading of the Convention ensures that civil rights, moreover, are presented as ways of protecting economic or social rights. For example, the repetition of the prohibition of discrimination is further qualified in the context of economic and social rights. Accordingly, as Megret says, the Convention is noteworthy for integrating into it both negative and positive rights. Articles 18 (liberty of movement and nationality) and 22 (respect for privacy) are a case in point whereby both negative and positive rights relate to the right. On the one hand, persons with a disability should 'not be deprived . . . of their ability to obtain, possess, and utilize documentation of their nationality' (a negative right), but at the same time they should 'have the right to acquire and change a nationality' (a positive right). Furthermore, individuals both have the right to 'not be subjected to arbitrary or unlawful interference' with their privacy (negative), and to 'the protection of the law against such interference' (positive). There is, throughout the Convention, a tendency to systematically highlight both the negative and positive dimensions of all relevant rights. That said, the provision of positive rights is likely to entail expenses on the part of the State. Article 20 provides an example containing the right to personal mobility and the right to freedom of expression entailing sign language, Braille, etc.

(iii) Equality and non-discrimination

Equality and non-discrimination for persons with disabilities are themes which are underlined throughout the CRPD. Article 5 of the Convention emphasises the principle of equality and non-discrimination. As our previous discussion has established, notions of equality and non-discrimination are themselves highly controversial with significant outstanding debate as to the nature and content of their meaning.[93] State parties undertake to prohibiting all forms of discrimination on the basis of disability through *de facto* equal and effective legislative protection against discrimination on all grounds. Article 5(3) states that '[i]n order to promote equality and eliminate discrimination, States Parties shall take all appropriate steps to ensure that reasonable accommodation is provided'. Article 2 defines 'reasonable accommodation' as being:

> necessary and appropriate modification and adjustments not imposing a disproportionate or undue burden, where needed in a particular case, to ensure to persons with disabilities the enjoyment or exercise on an equal basis with others of all human rights and fundamental freedoms.

Source: The United Nations is the author of the original material.

The 'reasonable accommodation' of disabled persons guarantees formal equality although the concept goes much further than this. It prohibits both 'direct' and 'indirect' discrimination. More importantly, it also takes into account the needs and requirements of each individual as the case may be. In the context of employment for a person with disability, 'reasonable accommodation' would ensure that the employer makes all reasonable efforts to provide a working environment where the disabled person is not placed at a disadvantage or discriminated against *vis-à-vis* those who are not disabled. It is this 'more individualistic and contextual approach' which is a key distinctive feature of the 'reasonable accommodation' concept.[94] Thus, reasonable accommodation prescribes that there should not only be equality but also that measures are taken in order to create a so-called 'level playing field', so far as it is 'reasonable' and possible to do so. This could be achieved, for example, through the removal or alteration of physical features, policies, practices, etc. which would otherwise place disabled people at a disadvantage when compared to non disabled people. While equality *de jure* and *de facto* is always desirable,

> [o]n the other hand, to insist on strict equality between persons with disabilities and other persons would be to ignore real differences. A formal anti-discrimination law, for instance, may proscribe disability discrimination but fail to move beyond the 'equality as neutrality' philosophy and take the further vital step of requiring 'reasonable accommodation' of the difference of disability. This kind of 'equality' is plainly hollow. It confers illusory benefits and invites cynicism vis-à-vis the law. Although the endeavour to accommodate real differences within a theory of equality may result in paradox and pose its own set of problems, it seems necessary to make equality meaningful and to produce real change.[95]

---

[93] See above chapter 12.

[94] See Waddington and Hendriks, 'The Expanding Concept of Employment Discrimination in Europe: From Direct and Indirect Discrimination to Reasonable Accommodation' 18 *The International Journal of Comparative Labour Law and Industrial Relations* (2002) 403 at p. 425. For an excellent analysis see Lawson, *Disability and Equality Law in Britain: The Role of Reasonable Adjustment* (Hart, 2008).

[95] Quinn and Degener, above n.1, at p. 16.

In *Hamilton* v. *Jamaica*,[96] the author, an inmate on death row who was also paralysed in both legs, claimed that the prison authorities had failed to make proper provision for his condition, particularly in respect of slopping out and climbing onto his bed. In essence his claim was based on an absence of the 'reasonable accommodation' of his needs.[97] The Human Rights Committee held that the above conditions were a violation of Article 10 of the ICCPR, the right to be treated with humanity and dignity. This confirms 'an awareness on the part of the Committee that it is not enough to treat all persons the same, but that added allowance (or "reasonable accommodation") may be necessary to make rights "real" for people with disabilities'.[98] This approach has been transferred to the Convention on the Rights of Persons with Disabilities, and reasonable accommodation has become a necessary aspect of the rights of disabled people.

Article 5(4) notes that '[s]pecific measures which are necessary to accelerate or achieve *de facto* equality of persons with disabilities shall not be considered discrimination under the terms of the present Convention'. No elaboration is provided as to the content of 'specific measures'. However, key strategies would include affirmative actions policies, quota system, imposition of mechanisms ensuring accommodation of personal needs (e.g. flexible working conditions, legislating for sign languages and Braille, screen-reading software in computers, telephone-typewriters, etc.). While using a terminology very similar to that of Convention the Elimination of All Forms of Discrimination against Women, these provisions are broader in the sense that they are not restricted to any limitation or restrictions.[99] The concept of discrimination is elucidated within the Convention itself. According to Article 2, discrimination is defined as meaning:

> any distinction, exclusion or restriction on the basis of disability which has the purpose or effect of impairing or nullifying the recognition, enjoyment or exercise, on an equal basis with others, of all human rights and fundamental freedoms in the political, economic, social, cultural, civil or any other field. It includes all forms of discrimination, including denial of reasonable accommodation.

For the most part, this definition follows other definitions provided in human rights instruments, most notably the Race Convention. There is however one significant addition – CRDP incorporates the 'denial of reasonable accommodation' as constituting discrimination. Article 12 of the Convention affirms the right of persons with disabilities to have equal recognition as persons before the law and to guarantee that they will enjoy legal capacity in all aspects of life on the basis of complete equality with others. This is a highly significant provision in that it would prevent States from declaring individuals legally incapable and hence devoid of any authority to make legally effective decisions.[100] States parties agree to undertake appropriate measures to ensure that persons with disabilities are legally entitled to own or inherit property, have equality in access to banking facilities including loans, mortgages or other forms of credit and are not arbitrarily deprived of their property rights. It is in the light of this Article, Kittay's assertion that the Convention attempts to

[96] *Hamilton* v. *Jamaica*, Communication No. 616/1995, UN Doc. CCPR/C/66/D/616/1995 (1999).
[97] Quinn and Degener, above n.1 at p. 73.
[98] Ibid. p. 4.
[99] Lawson, above n.1 at p. 599.
[100] Ibid. p. 596.

ensure respect for dignity by allowing people to use their own capacities appears to be valid.[101] Article 12, more than any other Article in the Convention, reflects this interpretation of dignity – it requires States to move away from systems of total or plenary guardianship towards mechanisms of supported decision-making (where a person who needs assistance in making some decisions is given appropriate support to make such decisions but is nevertheless allowed to make such decisions by him or herself).

Equal access to justice for persons with disabilities is guaranteed through the provisions of Article 13. States parties are required to ensure that disabled persons have access to justice on the basis of equality including provisions for procedural and age-appropriate accommodation. States parties are to facilitate the effective role of disabled persons as direct or indirect participants allowing them to be witnesses as well as being involved in all legal proceedings. According to the provisions of Article 14, persons with disabilities are ensured liberty and security of person on an equal basis. They are not to be deprived arbitrarily or unlawfully of their liberty, and existence of any disability could never be a pretext for such a justification for deprivation of liberty. If disabled persons are deprived of their liberty, the Convention provides assurances that such deprivation would be based on equality with others and that persons with disabilities would be entitled to guarantees as provided in international human rights law.[102]

Article 17 aims to ensure the physical and mental integrity of all persons who have disability on the basis of equality with others. The article aims to ensure non-interference with both the physical bodies and minds of persons with disabilities. The primary reason for incorporation of this provision was to prevent compulsory testing of persons with psychological or social impairments.[103] As noted earlier, Article 18 provides for liberty of movement and nationality, with States parties recognising that persons with disabilities are to be ensured freedom of movement, right to choose their residence and a right to nationality on an equal footing with other nationals. Furthermore, States parties agree that the disabled persons, in equality with others, have the right to acquire and change nationality and will not be deprived of their nationality arbitrarily on the basis of their disability. Persons with disabilities have the right to utilise the documents of their nationality or make use of relevant processes for immigration that are necessary for the right to liberty of movement. In common with other citizens of the State, persons with disabilities have the right to leave any country including their own. Persons with disabilities are not to be deprived of the right to return to their own country arbitrarily or on the basis of their disability. Article 18(2) provides that children with disabilities are to be registered after birth and have the right to a name, the right to acquire a nationality, the right to know their parentage and the right to be cared for by their parents. Article 19 is a highly significant article in that it allows disabled persons the choice of living independently as well as in their community and the right to participate fully in the life of their community. Article 19 provides:

> States Parties to the present Convention recognize the equal right of all persons with disabilities to live in the community, with choices equal to others, and shall take effective and appropriate measures to facilitate full enjoyment by persons with disabilities of this right and their full inclusion and participation in the community, including by ensuring that:

---

[101] Kittay, above n.31, at p. 95.
[102] Article 14(2) CRDP.
[103] Kayess and French, above n.1 at p. 29.

(a) Persons with disabilities have the opportunity to choose their place of residence and where and with whom they live on an equal basis with others and are not obliged to live in a particular living arrangement;

(b) Persons with disabilities have access to a range of in-home, residential and other community support services, including personal assistance necessary to support living and inclusion in the community, and to prevent isolation or segregation from the community;

(c) Community services and facilities for the general population are available on an equal basis to persons with disabilities and are responsive to their needs.[104]

(iv) Vulnerable communities within disabled persons

Article 6 and Article 7 focus on the position of vulnerable communities within and amongst disabled persons exist. Disabled women and girls represent a particularly vulnerable group. Elwan, while summarising established research, notes that:

the difficulties faced by disabled girls can start at birth, and that if disabled girls are allowed to survive, they can face discrimination within the family, receive less care and food, and be left out of family interactions and activities. They also have less access to health care and rehabilitation services, and fewer education and employment opportunities. Disabled girls and women are at high risk of being abused physically and mentally, sometimes by those within the household. Abuse from outside the family is often unreported because of the additional shame to the family which is already stigmatized for having a disabled daughter.[105]

In protecting the rights of women and girls with disabilities, Article 6 provides recognition that such women and girls 'are subject to multiple discrimination'[106] and that States are required to ensure full and equal enjoyment of their fundamental human rights. States parties are required to take all appropriate measures to ensure the full development and empowerment of women and girls with disabilities. According to Article 7 of the Convention, States parties are required to take all necessary measures to ensure the full enjoyment of the rights of children with disabilities. Article 7, whilst upholding the fundamental principle of the best interest of the child, notes that States parties are to ensure that children with disabilities have the rights to express views freely on issues that affect them with due weight being accorded to those views depending on their age and maturity. Concluding observations from the Committee on the Rights of the Child raise concerns about the absence of programmes addressing children with mental disability in various countries including Bangladesh[107] and Ireland.[108] Article 7 recommends that awareness raising initiatives be put in place with appropriate support and resources in order to facilitate the active participation in the community of children with mental disabilities. One of

---

[104] For a very useful articulation of the issues involved see Parker and Clements, 'The UN Convention on the Rights of Persons with Disabilities: a new right to independent living?' 4 *EHRLR* (2008) 508.

[105] Elwan, 'Poverty and Disability: A Survey of the Literature' http://siteresources.worldbank.org/DISABILITY/Resources/280658-1172608138489/PovertyDisabElwan.pdf p. 29 <last visited 8 April 2009>.

[106] Article 6(1) CRPD.

[107] Bangladesh, CRC, CRC/C/66 (1997) 22 at paras 143 and 165.

[108] Ireland, CRC, CRC/C/73 (1998) 14 at para 100.

the fundamental objectives of the Convention is to raise awareness in the society about persons with disabilities and to fundamentally change societal attitudes towards such persons. According to the provisions of Article 8, States parties undertake to adopt effective, immediate and appropriate steps to raise awareness at all levels of society regarding persons with disability and to foster respect for the rights and dignity of disabled persons. States agree to combat stereotypes, prejudices and harmful practices that are related to disabled persons and to raise awareness about the capabilities and contributions of persons with disabilities.[109]

In order to inject such awareness Article 8(2) advances a number of strategies, which include effective public awareness campaigns, nurturing receptiveness towards the rights of disabled persons, promoting positive perceptions and greater social awareness towards persons with disabilities, greater recognition of the skills, abilities and merits of persons with disabilities, promoting awareness training programmes amongst the general public and encouraging positive media portrayal of persons with disabilities.

(v) Independence, accessibility and participation in all aspects of life

Independence, self-reliance and participation in all aspects of life for persons with disabilities represent primary themes emerging from the Convention. In accordance with Article 9, States parties undertake to enable persons with disabilities full participation in every aspect of life and to live an independent life. This situation is premised on the basis that States parties would undertake all appropriate measures to ensure persons with disabilities access to the physical environment, to transportation, communication and all forms of information in complete equality with others.[110] According to Article 9, such measures include the identification, as well as elimination, of obstacles in the accessibility to buildings, transportation and all forms of facilities. States parties also agree to develop, monitor and implement minimum standards and guidelines to accessibility of facilities, to ensure that private facilities which are open to the public are also accessible to persons with disabilities, to provide training for all those involved with disabled persons and to provide in all public facilities signage in Braille and other sources of assistance to facilitate accessibility to buildings.[111] Notwithstanding the detailed nature of Article 9, the provisions have been criticised for their failure to specify which buildings are to be accessible and also for the failure of Article 9 to establish any target dates to meet these standards.[112]

Personal mobility within the Convention is ensured through the provisions of Article 20, according to which States parties are required to undertake effective measures to ensure the maximising of personal mobility for persons with disability at affordable costs.[113] However, it is unclear what constitutes an affordable cost. States parties are to facilitate

---

[109] CRDP Article 8(1)(b)(c).
[110] See Article 9(1) CRDP.
[111] See Article 9(2) CRPD.
[112] Justesen and Justesen, 'An Analysis of the Development and Adoption of the United Nations Convention Recognizing the Rights of Individuals with Disabilities: Why the United States Refuses to Sign this UN Convention' 14 *Human Rights Brief* (2007) 36, at p. 39. www.wcl.american.edu/hrbrief/14/2melish.pdf?rd=1 <last visited 8 April 2009>.
[113] See Article 20(a) CRPD.

access to mobility aids, devices, providing training in mobility skills for persons with disabilities and to specialist staff dealing with disabled persons and encouraging further technological advances for the assistance of disabled persons. Since the obligations are immediately binding upon States parties, these provisions appear to blur the line between traditionally recognised civil and political rights *vis-à-vis* economic, social and cultural rights.[114]

Freedom of expression and opinion for disabled persons is guaranteed by Article 21, which also provides that States parties must ensure the provision of information in accessible formats, without additional cost for disabled persons, accepting and facilitating the usage of such communicative mechanisms as sign language, Braille, augmentative or alternative communication, and encouraging both mass media as well as private bodies to provide information accessible to persons with disabilities.

(vi) Right to life, security and the prohibition from inhuman and degrading treatment

The Convention, whilst having a specific focus on disabled persons, affirms and guarantees many of the fundamental human rights including the inherent right to life, and effective enjoyment of rights on the basis of equality, to ensure safety and the protection of disabled persons during situations of armed conflict, man-made or humanitarian disasters. The right to life, despite being a fundamental right and recognised within all constitutions and international instruments, is nevertheless of critical importance in the context of the catalogue of rights designed for persons with disabilities. The need for an emphasis on the significance of this right is made evident since in many societies, persons with disabilities are particularly prone to losing their right to life through persistent denials of fundamental necessities such as food, water and housing. The right to life also incorporates a positive obligation on the State – this is to ensure that disabled persons are not deprived of essentials which sustain life, with an obligation to provide all such essentials which result in a healthy and positive life. Article 10 of the Convention provides for the Right to Life with States parties affirming 'that every human being has the inherent right to life and shall take all necessary measures to ensure its effective enjoyment by persons with disabilities on an equal basis with others'.

The provisions of Article 10 are, however, incomplete in a number of respects.[115] There is no explicit prohibition of pre-birth negative selection of foetuses with impairments nor does the article have a view on genetic science targeting the elimination of impairment-related human diversity, through, for example, the negative selection of embryos based on genetic imperfections.[116] Such silence has been predicted as the CRDP's 'greatest failing'.[117] The use of abortion in the situation where a genetic imperfection has been detected pre-birth has become a well-established practice. In a number of countries where abortion is either prohibited or only permitted in order to preserve the physical health of the mother, an exception is made in the case of foetal impairment, e.g. Mexico, Panama, Burkina-Faso,

---

[114] Kayess and French, above n.1, at p. 29.
[115] See chapter 5 for an analysis of the right to life in the context of ICCPR.
[116] Kayess and French, above n.1 at p. 29. *Cf.* recent discussion in the UK relating to the selection of embryos with a disability: http://news.bbc.co.uk/1/hi/health/7287508.stm <last visited 8 April 2009>.
[117] Kayess and French, above n.1, at p. 29.

Kuwait, Poland, Qatar and the Republic of Korea.[118] This is, however, not a consistent practice and the ethical implications remain similar to those associated with pre-fertilisation negative selection of embryos. We have already noted the prohibition from torture, cruel, inhuman or degrading treatment or punishment within international and regional instruments.[119] Article 15 emphasises this prohibition with specific reference to persons with disabilities and disallows the subjection of any person without his or her free consent to scientific or medical experimentation. Disabled persons are frequently made the victims of exploitation, physical or mental abuse as well as violence. In prohibiting such exploitation or violence, States parties undertake to provide appropriate legislative, administrative, social and education measures to protect persons with disabilities within the home as well as from society in general. In prohibiting such violence and abuse, a gender-based perspective is of vital importance as is highlighted by Article 16. All programmes and facilities designed to serve persons with disabilities are to be adequately monitored by independent authorities.[120] Article 16 also places an obligation on States parties to promote the physical, cognitive and psychological rehabilitation and social integration of disabled persons who are victims of forms of exploitation and abuse, including the provision of protection services in an environment of welfare, self-respect and dignity of the person.[121] States parties undertake to put in place laws and policies to ensure that instances of abuse and exploitation are identified and persons involved in such activities are prosecuted and apprehended.[122]

The right to respect for personal and private life has been affirmed by all international human rights instruments. The Convention, with its focus on disabled persons, affirms this right. Article 22 ensures that persons with disabilities are not subject to any unlawful interference in their privacy, family, home and correspondence. They are not to be subjected to invasion of their privacy in respect of other forms of communication nor is it permitted to attack their reputation and honour.[123] All information regarding the person, health and rehabilitation will be protected by the State.[124] A continuum of the right to privacy is the respect for home and family life, which is guaranteed by Article 23. According to the provisions of Article 23, States parties are required to undertake effective and adequate measures to eliminate all forms of discrimination against disabled persons as regards issues of marriage, family, parenthood and relationships. Disabled persons of marriageable age have the right to marry and found a family on the basis of free and full consent in the selection of their spouses; disabled persons have the right to decide upon the number of children and spacing of children and have appropriate access to family planning education and the means to conduct family planning.[125] Furthermore, disabled persons have the right to retain their fertility on an equal basis with other persons in any community.[126] Article 23(2) places an obligation on States parties to ensure that disabled persons have equal rights and responsibilities in relation to guardianship, wardship, trusteeship, adoption of children or

---

[118] The World's Abortion Laws, May 2007. www.reproductiverights.org/pdf/pub_fac_abortionlaws.pdf <last visited 2 April 2009>.
[119] See part II and III; for an analysis of the Convention against Torture see below chapter 23.
[120] Article 16(3) CRPD.
[121] Article 16(4) CRPD.
[122] Article 16(5) CPRD.
[123] Article 22(1) CPRD.
[124] Article 22(2) CPRD.
[125] Article 23(1)(b) CPRD.
[126] Article 23(1)(c) CPRD.

similar institutions, where these concepts exist in national legislation. Article 23(3) reiterates that children with disabilities have equal rights in respect of family life. No concealment or segregation of children with disabilities is permitted, nor should disabled children be separated from their parents, save for an order from a competent judicial authority which determines that such an action is necessary in the best interest of the child.

(vii) The right to education, health and employment

The right to education, although recognised as a fundamental human right, is frequently denied to the poor, needy and disabled. While emphasising the right to education for children with disabilities, the Special Rapporteur on Human Rights and Disability makes the point that:

education should, as far as possible, be provided within the ordinary school system, without any discrimination against handicapped children or adults. However, this condition is not always met, because of the prejudices of the authorities and teachers, of the parents of other children, or even of the parents of disabled children. Consequently, in many instances where the child's disability does not constitute an obstacle in itself, discrimination prevents him from entering the ordinary school system. In some cases, it is the law itself which stipulates that disabled children must attend special schools, which is tantamount to official segregation. In other cases, the obstacle to school attendance is the lack of means of transport, both in cities and in rural areas, although the phenomenon is much more common in the latter. Shortcomings in building design have a similar effect, making access to school buildings and movement inside them difficult, and also barring access to toilets etc., a very common phenomenon.[127]

The Convention recognises this right and makes it applicable for persons with disabilities. According to Article 24, States parties recognise the right to education for disabled persons and should ensure its application without discrimination. States parties are to apply the right to education at all educational levels and enable life-long learning directed towards the full development of the potential of disabled persons as well as enabling persons with disabilities to participate effectively in a free society. In order to achieve this end, States parties are to ensure that disabled persons are not excluded from the general system of education at any level of education and that disabled persons are able to access education at primary and secondary levels, which should be free.[128] States parties are to ensure the reasonable accommodation of disabled persons, and ensure that all possible provisions are made to maximise the academic and social development of the disabled person.[129] In addition, States parties are required to facilitate 'the learning of Braille, alternative script, augmentative and alternative modes, means and formats of communication . . . facilitating peer support and mentoring'.[130] States parties are also to facilitate 'the learning of sign language and the promotion of linguistic identity of the deaf community' and to ensure the education of blind persons is undertaken in the most appropriate language and mode.[131]

---

[127] Despouy, above n.1 at para 186; see also Bell, 'Disabled rules: how will the new UN Convention on the Rights of Persons with Disabilities Impact on Children' 248 *Childright* (2008) 24.

[128] Article 24(2)(a)(b) CRPD.

[129] Article 24(2)(c)(e) CRPD.

[130] Article 24(3)(a) CRPD.

[131] Article 24(3)(b)(c) CRPD.

To ensure the realisation of the right to education, States parties undertake to adopt all provisions for the employment and training of those teaching persons with disabilities, with qualifications such as sign language, Braille, and to train professionals and staff who work at all levels of education.[132]

An important and developing human right is the right to health. Persons with disabilities can have special needs and are particularly vulnerable towards the denial of this right. Under the provisions of Article 25, States parties undertake to take all appropriate measures to ensure access to health services on a gender-sensitive basis. Furthermore, the obligations include the dispensation of healthcare on a non-discriminatory basis, the provision of health services required specifically on the basis of their disabilities including early identification and intervention to minimise or prevent future disabilities.[133] There must not be any discrimination in the provision of health insurance and insurance for life where such insurance is permitted under the provisions of domestic law.[134] States parties are to take all effective steps to ensure that disabled persons are as able to attain and maximise their independence as non-disabled persons and are able participate fully in all aspects of life.[135] With this view, comprehensive facilitation and rehabilitation plans are to be introduced especially in areas of health, employment, education and social services.[136]

The right to work and employment constitutes a highly significant right and carries an added value in the context of disabled persons. Unfortunately, evidence suggests that persons with disabilities often face discrimination and exclusion when obtaining employment. Whilst in the developed world, unemployment figures for persons with disabilities are disproportionately high, in most developing States, the 'employment prospects of disabled persons are minimal or nonexistent'.[137] In recognising the right to employment, States parties to the Convention undertake to incorporate within this right the opportunity to gain a living through freely selected work.[138] States parties agree to take legislative measures to prohibit all forms of discrimination on the basis of disability in employment including conditions of recruitment, hiring, working conditions, etc.[139] States are to protect the rights of persons with disabilities alongside other employees to ensure just and favourable conditions of work, including equal opportunities and equal remuneration for work.[140] Equality in working conditions incorporates health and safety conditions, ensuring persons with disabilities are able to exercise their labour and trade union rights on an equal basis and enabling person with disabilities effective and appropriate access to vocational and placement programmes and training initiatives.[141] States parties are to promote employment opportunities for disabled persons in the labour market and the opportunities of career advancement, promotion, self-employment and to encourage entrepreneurship.[142] States parties undertake to employ disabled persons in the public sector and to promote the

---

[132] Article 24(4) CRPD.
[133] Article 25(a)(b) CRPD.
[134] Article 25(e) CRPD.
[135] Article 26(1) CRPD.
[136] Article 26(1) CRPD.
[137] Despouy, above n.1, at para 187.
[138] Article 27(1) CRPD.
[139] Article 27(1)(a) CRPD.
[140] Article 27(1)(b) CRPD.
[141] Article 27(1)(c)(d) CRPD.
[142] Article 27(1)(e)(f) CRPD.

employment of disabled persons in the private sector through such policies as quota systems, affirmative action or other incentives.[143] States parties are obliged to ensure that disabled persons are not held in servitude or slavery or slave-like practices or other forms of forced labour.[144]

States parties recognise, under Article 28, the right of disabled persons to an adequate standard of living for themselves and for members of their families. Such a right includes having adequate food, clothing and housing, and the continuous improvement of their living conditions. The following measures are included:

(a) To ensure equal access by persons with disabilities to clean water services, and to ensure access to appropriate and affordable services, devices and other assistance for disability-related needs;

(b) To ensure access by persons with disabilities, in particular women and girls with disabilities and older persons with disabilities, to social protection programmes and poverty reduction programmes;

(c) To ensure access by persons with disabilities and their families living in situations of poverty to assistance from the State with disability-related expenses, including adequate training, counselling, financial assistance and respite care;

(d) To ensure access by persons with disabilities to public housing programmes;

(e) To ensure equal access by persons with disabilities to retirement benefits and programmes.[145]

(viii) Right to participation in political, public and cultural life, recreation and sport

According to the provisions of Article 29, States parties undertake to allow disabled persons to partake, on an equal basis, in political rights 'and fully participate in political and public life on an equal basis with others, directly or through freely chosen representatives, including the right and opportunity for persons with disabilities to vote and be elected'.[146] States parties are required to ensure that all voting procedures and related facilities are accessible to and comprehensible by disabled persons.[147] States parties are also obliged to protect the rights of persons with disabilities to vote by secret ballot in public elections and to stand for elections, to hold public offices and to facilitate the use of new technologies wherever required.[148] States parties must also ensure the participation of disabled persons in non-governmental organisations and associations related to the public and political life of the State and allow the formation of organisations of persons with disabilities to represent themselves at all levels.[149]

Disabled persons are frequently deprived of cultural and recreational facilities in many societies, due, in part, to the prohibitive cost of such facilities for individuals. In accordance with Article 30, States parties recognise the right of disabled persons to involve themselves

[143] Article 27(1)(g)(h) CRPD.
[144] Article 27(2) CRPD.
[145] Article 28(2) CRPD.
[146] Article 29(a) CRPD.
[147] Article 29(a)(i) CRPD.
[148] Article 29(a)(ii) CRPD.
[149] Article 29(b) CRPD.

on an equal basis with others in cultural life and to ensure that such persons enjoy access to cultural materials in formats that are suitable to their own needs.[150] States parties also recognise the need of persons with disabilities to have access to films, the theatre and television, and in modes that are comprehensible and accessible to them and that they can enjoy access to cultural performances, libraries and tourism services, etc.[151] According to Article 35(2), States agree to take appropriate measures to enable disabled persons opportunities to develop their creative potential to the fullest possible extent for their own selves as well as for the enhancement and enrichment of the entire society. Intellectual property rights should not constitute a barrier for disabled person in accessing cultural materials.[152] The article also establishes that disabled persons are entitled to a specific linguistic and cultural identity, including sign language.[153] All appropriate and adequate measures are to be taken for the encouragement and participation of disabled person in the field of sports and other recreational activities.[154] States parties must ensure that disabled persons have the opportunity to organise and develop disability-specific sporting and recreational activities and to encourage the provision of adequate and appropriate instruction, training and resources, to ensure the availability of appropriate venues, to ensure that children with disabilities have equal access to participation in sporting activities and to ensure that disabled persons have access to services from those involved in the organisation of recreational, tourism, leisure and sporting activities.[155]

(ix) Implementation of the Convention

Article 31, provides for the collection of statistical and data-related information on the part of States parties. Article 32 obliges States parties to 'recognize the importance of international cooperation and its promotion, in support of national efforts for the realization of the purpose and objectives of the present Convention'.[156] States parties:

will undertake appropriate and effective measures in this regard, between and among States and, as appropriate, in partnership with relevant international and regional organizations and civil society, in particular organizations of persons with disabilities. Such measures could include, *inter alia*:

(a) Ensuring that international cooperation, including international development programmes, is inclusive of and accessible to persons with disabilities;

(b) Facilitating and supporting capacity-building, including through the exchange and sharing of information, experiences, training programmes and best practices;

(c) Facilitating cooperation in research and access to scientific and technical knowledge;

(d) Providing, as appropriate, technical and economic assistance, including by facilitating access to and sharing of accessible and assistive technologies, and through the transfer of technologies.[157]

---

[150] Article 30(1)(a) CRPD.
[151] Article 30(1)(b)(c) CRPD.
[152] Article 30(3) CRPD.
[153] Article 30(4) CRPD.
[154] Article 30(5) CRPD.
[155] Article 30(5)(a)–(e) CRPD.
[156] Article 32(1) CRPD.
[157] Article 32(1) CRPD.

Article 33 represents a highly significant provision according to which States parties undertake to designate focal points for the appropriate implementation of this Convention. States parties are to provide due attention to the establishment or designation of a co-ordination mechanism within government to facilitate related action in different sectors and at different levels. States parties are required to maintain and strengthen a framework of effective implementation of the Convention.[158] When devising such a mechanism, States parties are required to take the principles relating to the status and function of national institutions for the protection and promotion of human rights into account.[159] Civil society is also to be involved, participating in the monitoring process.[160]

In common with other treaty-based bodies, the Convention is also to be implemented through the assistance of a Committee.[161] This Committee is known as the Committee on the Rights of Persons with Disabilities.[162] In accordance with Article 34(2), after the entry into force of the Convention, the Committee was formed which consisted initially of 12 experts.[163] Since the ratification or accession of 60 States, the membership has been increased to 18 members.[164] Similar to other Committees formed from human rights treaties, members of this Committee act in their personal capacity and are of high moral standing and possess recognised competence in the field of expertise covered by the present convention.[165] In presenting nominations, States parties are to actively consider the involvement and participation of persons with disabilities.[166] However, no specific provisions have been made for the inclusion of persons with disabilities. Such absence has been the source of criticism in that:

> this lack of recognition of the expertise that individuals with disabilities can bring to the Convention not only as a result of life experience, but as professionals who happen to also have disabilities reinforces the stereotypical and discriminatory perceptions that the majority of experts likely cannot be individuals with disabilities.[167]

The Committee members are elected by States parties, with due consideration being given to a number of factors, including geographical distribution, representation of different forms of civilisation and principal legal systems and participation of experts with disabilities.[168] Committee members are elected through a secret ballot from those individuals who are nominated by States parties from amongst their own nationals.[169] An absolute majority would determine the election of the Committee members, with the presence of two-thirds of States constituting a quorum.[170] The initial elections were held within six months of the Convention coming into force.[171] The Committee members serve for a four-year term and

---

[158] Article 33(2) CRPD.
[159] Article 33(2) CRPD.
[160] Article 33(3) CRPD.
[161] Article 34(1) CRPD.
[162] Article 34(1) CRPD.
[163] Article 34(2) CRPD.
[164] Article 34(2) CRPD.
[165] Article 34(3) CRPD.
[166] Article 34(3) CRPD.
[167] Justesen and Justesen, above n.112, at p. 39.
[168] Article 34(4) CRPD.
[169] Article 34(5) CRPD.
[170] Article 34(5) CRPD.
[171] Article 34(6) CRPD.

are eligible for re-elections only once.[172] The term of six of the members elected at the first election is due to expire at the end of two years.[173] After the first election, the names of these six members are to be chosen by lot by the chairperson of the meeting.[174] The Convention also contains provisions regarding the eventuality of the death or resignation of any Committee member.[175] The Committee will devise its own rules of procedure.[176] The Secretary-General provides for staff and facilities for the effective performance of the Committee.[177] Committee members receive their emoluments from United Nations resources on such terms and conditions as decided by the General Assembly, with the Committee members being entitled to those facilities, privileges and immunities available to experts on mission for the United Nations.[178]

Article 35 details the implementation mechanism of this Convention which is principally conducted through State reporting. States parties are required to submit to the Committee, through the offices of the Secretary-General, comprehensive reports on measures which have been taken by each State party in order to give effect to the provisions of the Convention and the progress that has been made.[179] The initial report is due within two years after the entry into force of the Convention for the State party concerned, whereas subsequent reports are due every four years and whenever the Committee so requests.[180] Information already provided in the initial report need not be repeated in subsequent reports.[181] State reports are to point to the factors which affect compliance with the provisions and objectives of the Convention.[182] The Committee will decide on its guidelines that are applicable to the contents of the reports.[183] The Committee examines each report that is submitted to it and makes comments, suggestions and general recommendations, forwarding these to the relevant State party.[184] The State party may respond to any of the issues highlighted by the Committee, with the Committee having the option to request any further related information or clarification.[185] In instances where a State party is significantly overdue with its reports, the Committee may, at its own discretion, notify the State party of the need to examine the implementation of the report on the basis of any reliable information that is otherwise made available to the Committee.[186] If the State party does not provide a report within three month of notification, the Committee will invite the representative of the State party to consider convention obligations during the examination.[187] If the State party does submit the report prior to the deliberation of the Committee, then the Committee will consider the contents of the report.[188] The UN Secretary-General

---

[172] Article 34(7) CRPD.
[173] Article 34(7) CRPD
[174] Article 34(7) CRPD.
[175] Article 34(9) CRPD.
[176] Article 34(10) CRPD see the Provisional Rules of Procedure for the Conferences of States Parties to the Convention on the Rights of Persons with Disabilities UN Doc. CRPD/CSP/2008/3 14 October 2008.
[177] Article 34(11) CRPD.
[178] Article 34(12)(13) CRPD.
[179] Article 35(1) CRPD.
[180] Article 35(1)(2) CRPD.
[181] Article 35(4) CRPD.
[182] Article 35(5) CRPD.
[183] Article 35(3) CRPD.
[184] Article 36(1) CRPD.
[185] Article 36(1) CRPD.
[186] Article 36(2) CRPD.
[187] Article 36(2) CRPD.
[188] Article 36(2) CRPD.

makes reports available to all States parties.[189] States parties are required to make these reports widely available for public information and facilitate the access of these reports.[190] The States that are party to the Convention are also obliged to transmit these reports to specialised agencies and other competent bodies.[191] Co-operation is intended and anticipated between States parties and members of the Committee.[192] The specialised agencies and other United Nations organs are authorised to be present at the consideration of State reports by the Committee.[193] The Committee can, therefore, invite relevant specialised agencies, intergovernmental as well as non-governmental bodies, to provide expert opinion on the implementation of the Convention in areas falling within the scope of their respective mandates.[194] The Committee is required to report to the General Assembly and to the Economic and Social Council every two years and can make suggestions and general recommendations based on its examination of State reports and information.[195] The States parties undertake to meet on a regular basis in the form of a Conference of States parties for consideration of any matters relevant to the implementation of the Convention.[196] A Conference was convened within six months of the Convention coming into force, and subsequent meetings are to be called by UN Secretary-General biennially or as decided by the Conference of States Parties.[197]

(x) The Optional Protocol to CRDP

At the time of adopting the Convention, an Optional Protocol to the Convention was also adopted. The Convention in essence follows the path of the ICCPR's First Optional Protocol. According to the provisions of the Protocol, a State party agrees to recognise the competence of the Committee 'to receive and consider communications from or on behalf of individuals or groups of individuals subject to its jurisdiction who claim to be victims of a violation by that State Party of the provisions of the Convention'.[198] However, no communication is to be received or given any consideration by the Committee if it concerns any State which has not become a party to the Protocol.[199] The Committee considers a communication inadmissible in circumstances where the communication is anonymous,[200] or it constitutes an abuse of the right of submission or is incompatible with the provisions of the Convention,[201] or the same matter has already been examined by the Committee or it has been or is being examined under another procedure of international investigation or settlement.[202] In line with all other international procedures, any consideration by the

---

[189] Article 36(3) CRPD.
[190] Article 36(4) CRPD.
[191] Article 36(5) CRPD.
[192] Article 37(1) CRPD.
[193] Article 38(a) CRPD.
[194] Article 38(a) CRPD.
[195] Article 39 CRPD.
[196] Article 40(1) CRPD.
[197] Article 40(2) CRPD. The first session of the Conference of the States Parties to the Convention took place on 31 October and 3 November 2008 in New York.
[198] Article 1(1) Optional Protocol to the Convention on the Rights of Persons with Disabilities (OP-CRPD).
[199] Article 1(2) OP-CRPD.
[200] Article 2(a) OP-CRPD.
[201] Article 2(b) OP-CRPD.
[202] Article 2(c) OP-CRPD.

Committee can only take place where all reasonably available domestic remedies have been exhausted.[203] Furthermore, the communication must not be manifestly ill-founded or not sufficiently substantiated,[204] and the facts of the communication must have taken place after the communication has come into force for the State party concerned, unless those facts were of a continuing nature and took place both prior and post entry into force of the Convention for the particular State party.[205] According to Article 3 of the Protocol, the Committee brings communications submitted to it confidentially to the attention of the relevant State party.[206] The concerned State party must respond to the issues raised within a period of six months, through written explanations or statements providing clarification of the issue or any remedial action undertaken by the State.[207] After the receipt of the communication, the Committee may transmit to the State party concerned for urgent considerations that interim measures be undertaken so as to avoid possible irreparable damage to the victim or victims of the alleged violation.[208] This does not, however, affect the substance of the Convention nor does this imply a determination on admissibility or on the merits of the communication in question.[209] The Committee holds closed meetings while examining communications and after its examination of a communication, the Committee forwards its suggestions and recommendations, both to the petitioner and the relevant State party.[210]

Article 6 provides that:

(1) If the Committee receives reliable information indicating grave or systematic violations by a State Party of rights set forth in the Convention, the Committee shall invite that State Party to cooperate in the examination of the information and to this end submit observations with regard to the information concerned.

(2) Taking into account any observations that may have been submitted by the State Party concerned as well as any other reliable information available to it, the Committee may designate one or more of its members to conduct an inquiry and to report urgently to the Committee. Where warranted and with the consent of the State Party, the inquiry may include a visit to its territory.

(3) After examining the findings of such an inquiry, the Committee shall transmit these findings to the State Party concerned together with any comments and recommendations.

(4) The State Party concerned shall, within six months of receiving the findings, comments and recommendations transmitted by the Committee, submit its observations to the Committee.

(5) Such an inquiry shall be conducted confidentially and the cooperation of the State Party shall be sought at all stages of the proceedings.

[203] Article 2(d) OP-CRPD.
[204] Article 2(e) OP-CRPD.
[205] Article 2(f) OP-CRPD.
[206] Article 3 OP-CRPD.
[207] Article 3 OP-CRPD.
[208] Article 4(1) OP-CRPD.
[209] Article 4(2) OP-CRPD.
[210] Article 5 OP-CRPD.

17

Rights of the persons with disabilities

According to Article 7 of the Optional Protocol 'the Committee may invite the State Party concerned to include in its report under article 35 of the Convention details of any measures taken in response to an inquiry conducted under Article 6 of the Protocol'.[211] The Committee may ask the State Party to inform it of any of the measures taken in respect of the inquiry, after the end of a period of six months.[212] Article 8 provides States parties can declare that they do not recognise the competence of the Committee in respect of Articles 6 and 7 at the time of signature or ratification of the Protocol.[213]

(xi) Developments

There are 63 States parties to the Convention as of 30 July 2009. To become binding the Convention needed to have obtained at least 20 ratifications. The Optional Protocol has 40 ratifications; in order to become binding it required 10 ratifications. The Convention and the Protocol are, therefore, in full force. Countries which have signed, but not yet ratified the Convention, agree to uphold the spirit of the Convention, and not to pass any legislation in contravention of the provisions contained within the Convention.

The Convention however has attracted a varied set of reservations and declarations. Both Malta and Poland have entered reservations regarding Article 25(a). Malta's national legislation considers the termination of pregnancy through induced abortion as illegal and subsequently observed that the Convention does not create any abortion rights and, therefore, it cannot be interpreted to constitute support, endorsement or promotion of abortion. Poland entered a reservation stating that 'The Republic of Poland understands that Articles 23(1)(b) and 25(a) shall not be interpreted in a way conferring an individual right to abortion or mandating State party to provide access thereto'.[214] Further reservations were made regarding Article 11,[215] Article 12[216] and Article 29(a)(i).[217] The government of the Republic of El Salvador ratified the text of the Convention and its Optional Protocol to the extent that its provisions do not 'prejudice or violate the provisions of any of the precepts, principles and norms enshrined in the Constitution of the Republic of El Salvador, particularly in its enumeration of principles'.[218]

---

[211] Article 7(1) OP-CRPD.

[212] Article 7(2) OP-CRPD.

[213] Article 8 OP-CRPD.

[214] See www.un.org/disabilities/default.asp?id=475 <last visited 8 April 2009> for the reservations concerning the Convention.

[215] 'The Government of Mauritius signs the present Convention subject to the reservation that it does not consider itself bound to take measures specified in article 11 unless permitted by domestic legislation expressly providing for the taking of such measures.' Ibid.

[216] 'The Arab Republic of Egypt declares that its interpretation of article 12 of the International Convention on the Protection and Promotion of the Rights of Persons with Disabilities, which deals with the recognition of persons with disabilities on an equal basis with others before the law, with regard to the concept of legal capacity dealt with in paragraph 2 of the said article, is that persons with disabilities enjoy the capacity to acquire rights and assume legal responsibility ('ahliyyat al-wujub) but not the capacity to perform ('ahliyyat al-'ada'), under Egyptian law.' Ibid.

[217] 'Pursuant to Article 29 (a)(i) and (iii) of the Convention, while the Government of Malta is fully committed to ensure the effective and full participation of persons with disabilities in political and public life, including the exercise of their right to vote by secret ballot in elections and referenda, and to stand for elections, Malta makes the following reservations: With regard to (a)(i) At this stage, Malta reserves the right to continue to apply its current electoral legislation in so far as voting procedures, facilities and materials are concerned. With regard to (a)(iii) Malta reserves the right to continue to apply its current electoral legislation in so far as assistance in voting procedures is concerned.' Ibid.

[218] Ibid. www.un.org/disabilities/default.asp?id=475 <last visited 8 April 2009>.

(xii) National policies in respect of the Convention

As a signatory to the Convention, all States parties' existing and future legislation and programmes will need to be in line with all the rights and responsibilities set down in the Convention. Article 33 of the Convention requires States parties to establish specific mechanisms to strengthen the implementation and monitoring of the rights of women, men and children with disabilities at the national level. Provisions include: designating a focal point or focal points within government for implementation; establishing or designating a co-ordination mechanism within government to facilitate related action in different sectors and at different levels; and establishing an independent framework, such as a national human rights institution, to promote and monitor implementation of the Convention.[219] This aims to go some way towards eradicating the marked disparities in how States treat those with disabilities. According to Quinn and Degener, there are some 40 States that have systemic disability rights laws, many of which are 'outdated or of questionable utility.'[220] For example, in his concluding recommendations, the Special Rappoteur for the ICESCR found that Australia had significant resources for improvement in the treatment of indigenous peoples with disabilities,[221] while in Bolivia, the exploitation of indigenous children with disabilities was tied into trafficking, exploitation and child labour.[222] This is despite Australia and Bolivia both having their own domestic disability legislation guaranteeing the full participation in society of disabled persons. As noted by the President of the General Assembly on the day that the Convention was adopted, the treaty's consensus acceptance 'is a great opportunity to celebrate the emergence of comprehensive guidelines the world so urgently needs'.[223]

In Australia, the Disability Discrimination Act was passed in 1992. The objectives of the Act are:

> to eliminate, as far as possible, discrimination against persons on the ground of disability in the areas of: work, accommodation, education, access to premises, clubs and sport; and the provision of goods, facilities, services and land; and existing laws; and the administration of Commonwealth laws and programs; and to ensure, as far as practicable, that persons with disabilities have the same rights to equality before the law as the rest of the community; and to promote recognition and acceptance within the community of the principle that persons with disabilities have the same fundamental rights as the rest of the community.[224]

In India, two national instruments were passed: the Rehabilitation Council of India Bill and the Persons with Disabilities (Equal Opportunities, Protection of Rights and Full

---

[219] Article 33 CRPD.
[220] Degener and Quinn, 'A Survey of International, Comparative and Regional Disability Law' in Breslin and Yee (eds), *Disability Rights Law And Policy: International And National Perspectives* (Transnational Publishers, 2002) pp. 3–129, at p. 120.
[221] ICESCR Concluding Recommendation, E/2001/22 (2000) 66, para 375.
[222] CRC Concluding Remarks, CRC/C/16 (1993) 13 at para 36.
[223] Statement by H.E. Sheikha Haya Rashed Al Khalifa, President of the United Nations General Assembly, at the Adoption of the Convention on the Rights of Persons with Disabilities (13 December 2006), available at www.un.org/ga/president/61/statements/statement20061213.shtml <last visited 8 April 2009>.
[224] Section 3. Preamble, Disability Discrimination Act Australia, 1992 http://unpan1.un.org/intradoc/groups/public/documents/apcity/unpan004021.pdf <last visited 8 April 2009>.

Participation) Act.[225] Disability India states that these Acts are 'guided by the philosophy of empowering persons with disabilities and their associates. The endeavor of the Act has been to introduce an instrument for promoting equality and participation of persons with disability on the one hand, and eliminating discriminations of all kinds, on the other'.[226]

In the United Kingdom, the Amended Disability Discrimination Act aims to end the discrimination which many persons with disabilities face. The Act, in its preamble, makes it unlawful to discriminate against disabled persons in connection with employment, the provision of goods, facilities and services or the disposal or management of premises; to make provision for the employment of disabled persons; and to establish a National Disability Council.[227]

In the United States, civil rights law regarding persons with disabilities is based on a number of laws among which the Americans with Disabilities Act (ADA) is the most fundamental and comprehensive law protecting those with disabilities. The ADA prohibits discrimination on the basis of disability in employment, state and local government, public accommodations, commercial facilities, transportation and telecommunications.[228] Examples of further national legislation are the Civil Rights of Institutionalized Persons Act,[229] the Individuals with Disabilities Education Act[230] and the Rehabilitation Act.

Stein and Lord believe that the Convention will:

> [engage] domestic-level disability laws on three interrelated levels . . . [1] each State must decide whether it will ratify the CPRD, and then adjust its own national level schemes . . . accordingly . . . [2] each State must assess its individual socio-legal circumstances and determine how to most expediently to balance antidiscrimination prohibitions with equality measures . . . [3] each State must resolve unsettled interpretations of existing disability-related principles.[231]

Consequently, they argue that the Convention will be able 'to prompt unprecedented national-level action in the form of law and policy transformation on disability rights'.[232]

3 REGIONAL HUMAN RIGHTS LAW AND DISABILITY

(i) The European system

At the regional European level, the role of both the Council of Europe and the European Union remains of great relevance in the promotion of the rights of persons with disabilities.

[225] See the Persons with Disabilities (Equal Opportunities, Protection Of Rights And Full Participation) Act 1995 www.disabilityindia.org/pwdacts.cfm <last visited 8 April 2009>.
[226] See Acts in Disability www.disabilityindia.org/mod1.cfm <last visited 8 April 2009>.
[227] See Disability Discrimination Act 1995 (c. 50) 1995 Chapter 50 www.opsi.gov.uk/acts/acts1995/ukpga_19950050_en_1#Legislation-Preamble <last visited 8 April 2009>.
[228] The Americans with Disabilities Act 1990, www.ada.gov/pubs/ada.htm <last visited 1 November 2008>.
[229] Civil Rights of Institutionalized Persons Act, Public Law 96–247, 42 U.S.C. 1997.
[230] Individuals with Disabilities Education Act of 1990, 20 U.S.C. para 1400 et seq. and Individuals with Disabilities Education Act Amendments of 1997, 20 U.S.C. para 1400 et seq.
[231] Stein and Lord, 'The United Nations Convention on the Rights of Persons With Disabilities as a Vehicle for Social Transformation', in National Monitoring Mechanisms on the Rights of Persons with Disabilities, Comisión Nacional de los Derechos Humanos, Mexico, May 2008, www.rindhca.org/nuevo/mecanismosNls.pdf at p. 114 <last visited 8 April 2009>.
[232] Ibid.

The leading regional human rights treaty produced by the Council of Europe, the European Convention on Human Rights, has had considerable influence in developing the legal regime concerning the rights of persons with disabilities. The European Convention for the Protection of Human Rights and Fundamental Freedoms is designed to protect individuals' fundamental rights and freedoms. This Convention contains the classical human rights guarantees, including the right to life (Article 2), the right not to be subject to torture or to inhuman or degrading treatment or punishment (Article 3), the right to liberty and security of person (Article 5), and the right to respect for private and family life, home and correspondence (Article 8).[233] These rights apply to all persons, regardless of their characteristics. Two articles that are particularly interesting in regard to disability are Article 14, the anti-discrimination clause, which refers to sexual, racial, linguistic, religious and political discrimination, but does not explicitly mention disabled persons and Article 5 which states that '[e]veryone has the right to liberty and security of person. No one shall be deprived of his liberty save the following cases and in accordance with a procedure prescribed by law'. This has the qualification of 'prescribed by law' which has the potential to create restrictions on liberty for those with mental disabilities, although this has been specifically addressed in domestic legislation.[234]

The European Court of Human Rights has provided ancillary recognition to disability rights in various substantive rights, thereby producing substantial jurisprudence as regards the rights of persons with disabilities. The European Court has made use of a number of articles within the Convention, in particular Articles 3,[235] 5,[236] 6 and 8,[237] to substantiate the rights of disabled persons.

The European Social Charter which works as the counterpart to the ECHR, addresses rights such as the right to employment, or the right to social security, and was the first human rights treaty to explicitly mention disability. The new Article 15 of the Revised European Social Charter recognises the right of persons with disabilities 'to independence, social integration and participation in the life of the community', and commits Contracting Parties:

---

[233] Convention for the Protection of Human Rights and Fundamental Freedoms, ETS 5, www.echr.coe.int/NR/rdonlyres/D5CC24A7-DC13-4318-B457-5C9014916D7A/0/EnglishAnglais.pdf <last visited 8 April 2009>. See Articles 2, 3, 5 and 8.

[234] See the Disability Alliance discussion on the UK's Mental Capacity Act 2005 www.disabilityalliance.org/mencapact.htm <last visited 8 April 2009>.

[235] The withdrawal of medical treatment could amount to inhuman treatment (Article 3, D v. UK (1997) 24 E.H.R.R. 423); B.B. v. France, Application No. 30930/96. (finding Article 3 violation whereby a citizen of Congo suffering from AIDS would be deported to the country of origin without access to adequate medical care); disabled individuals who are detained or otherwise imprisoned must not be allowed to undergo degrading treatment (Price v. UK (2002) 34 E.H.R.R. 53) where the applicant was inter alia refused to take battery charger for her wheelchair to prison and required the assistance of male staff in order to use the toilet.

[236] In Winterwerp v. The Netherlands (1979–1980) 2 EHRR 387, the Court established three preconditions for detention under Article 5(1)(e) thereby constituting an exception to the right of liberty and security of persons – these preconditions are firstly that the medical disorder relied upon to justify detention must be established objectively by medical experts, secondly the nature or degree of the disorder must be serious enough so as to justify detention and thirdly dentition should only be as long as the condition persists. See Winterwerp v. The Netherlands (1979–1980) 2 E.H.R.R. 387 para 37.

[237] Nasri v. France (1996) 21 E.H.R.R. 458 it was held that the deportation of a man who was unable to speak or hear would result in violation of Article 8. The State is also held liable where it is unable to protect a mentally handicapped girl from abuse and rape, see X and Y v. The Netherlands, Application No. 8975/80 (Judgment of 26 March 1985).

> (1) to take the necessary measures to provide persons with disabilities with guidance, education and vocational training . . .
>
> (2) to promote their access to employment through all measures tending to encourage employers to hire and keep in employment persons with disabilities in the ordinary working environment and to adjust the working conditions to the needs of the disabled . . .
>
> (3) to promote their full social integration and participation in the life of the community in particular through measures, including technical aids, aiming to overcome barriers to communication and mobility and enabling access to transport, housing, cultural activities and leisure.[238]

Other articles, such as Article 11 oblige States to 'remove as far as possible the causes of ill-health' and 'to provide advisory and educational facilities for the promotion of health' and are implicitly related to disabled persons.[239]

The European Union has undertaken considerable work in the area of non-discrimination and human rights for persons with disabilities. On 24 July 1986, a Recommendation on the Employment of Disabled People within the European Community was adopted.[240] This Recommendation established the principle of equal opportunities for disabled persons in training and employment. In subsequent resolutions and decisions, the organs of the Union have reiterated the policy for the rehabilitation of disabled persons, whereby member States are called on to strengthen preventive measures to overcome impairments, and handicaps facing those with disabilities, and implement a comprehensive and co-ordinated policy of rehabilitation. These include the Resolution on the Human Rights of Disabled People (1996),[241] the Resolution on Threats to the Right to Life of Disabled Persons (1996)[242] and, finally, the Resolution on the Commission's Communication on Equality of Opportunity for People with Disabilities (1997).[243] In December 2000, the Council of Ministers of the European Union adopted a (binding) general Framework Directive on equal treatment in employment prohibiting direct and indirect discrimination on the grounds of religion or belief, age, disability or sexual orientation.[244] Further resolutions have included Equal Opportunities for Pupils and Students with Disabilities in Education and Training, and 'eAccessibility' which set out to improve the access of people with disabilities to the knowledge based society.[245] The objectives of the recommendations

---

[238] Council of Europe, European Social Charter (Revised), 3 May 1996. ETS 163. See above chapter 9.

[239] Article 11 Council of Europe, European Social Charter (Revised).

[240] See Official Journal No. L225/443 of 12 August 1986.

[241] A4-0391/96 of 12 December 1996.

[242] B4-0650/96 of 23 May 1996.

[243] European Commission's Communiqué of August 10, 1996 on equal opportunities for people with disabilities – New strategy of European Community with regard to people with disabilities. The December 20, 1996 Resolution of the Council of Europe on equal opportunities for people with disabilities.

[244] European Parliament's Resolution on the Communication from the Commission to the Council, the European Parliament, the Economic and Social Committee and the Committee of the Regions – Towards a barrier-free Europe for people with disabilities: COM(2000) 284–C5-0632/2000 – 2000/2296(COS) See www.mhe-sme.org/en/our-work/disability-and-mental-health/EU-developments.html <last visited 8 April 2009>.

[245] See e.g. Council Resolution of 5 May 2003 (on equal opportunities for pupils and students with disabilities in education and training) 2003/C 134/04: Official Journal No. C 134 of 07/06/2003, Council Resolution of 15 July 2003 on promoting the employment and social integration of people with disabilities (2003/C 175/01), The Communication to the Council, the European Parliament, the Economic and Social Committee, and the Committee of Regions, regarding eAccessibility, COM (2005) 425. See http://ec.europa.eu/information_society/policy/accessibility/eincl/policy/index_en.htm <last visited 8 April 2009>.

are to encourage and promote the full participation of disabled persons within their chosen society.

In July 2007, the first provisions of the EU regulation on the Rights of Disabled Air-passengers entered into force. The overall aim of the regulation is to guarantee equal treatment for all passengers, including 'any person with reduced mobility or sensory impairment, intellectual disability or any other cause of disability, age, and whose situation needs appropriate attention and the adaptation to his or her particular needs of the service made available to all passengers'.[246] In addition, the European Commission published a Communication on the Analysis of the Situation of People with Disabilities in the European Union and proposed new objectives for the Disability Action Plan 2008–09.[247] By 2010, the European Commission has stated that it wants to see improvements in the employment prospects, accessibility and independent living of disabled people. Disabled people are involved in the process on the basis of the European principle: '[n]othing about disabled people without disabled people'.[248] The CRDP will be the first UN human rights treaty that the EU has signed and has pledged to accede to.[249]

(ii) Organization of American States

The Organization of American States (OAS) has declared 2006–16, the 'Decade of the Americas for the Rights and Dignity of Persons with Disabilities'. The OAS has also prepared a Programme of Action which establishes objectives as well as specific measures to be taken in such areas as education, employment, accessibility and political participation.[250] There is no reference regarding disability in the Charter of the Organization of American States, although Article 34 states that in order to accelerate their economic and social development the Member States agree to dedicate every effort to achieve the following basic goals:

> (g) Fair wages, employment opportunities and acceptable working conditions for all;
>
> (h) Rapid eradication of illiteracy and expansion of educational opportunities for all;
>
> (i) Protection of man's potential through the extension and application of modern medical science; . . .
>
> (k) Adequate housing for all sectors of the population;
>
> (l) Urban conditions that offer the opportunity for a healthful, productive, and full life.[251]

---

[246] Regulation (EC) No. 1107/2006 of the European Parliament and of the Council of 5 July 2006.

[247] Communication from the Commission to the Council, The European Parliament, The European Economic and Social Committee and the Committee of the Regions, Situation of Disabled People in the European Union: the European Action Plan 2008–2009 (SEC(2007)1548).

[248] Proclamation of the, the UN General Assembly decided on the World Programme of Action for Disabled People, 3 December 1982.

[249] www.myhandicap.com/com-handicap-un-conference.html <last visited 4 April 2009>.

[250] OAS Permanent Council, Committee on Juridical and Political Affairs, Program of Action, Decade of the Americas for Persons with Disabilities (2006–2016), OEA/Ser.G, CP/CAJP-2362/06 corr.1 (2006).

[251] Charter of the Organization of American States, 119 U.N.T.S. 3, entered into force 13 December 1951. Inter-American Democratic Charter. Lima, 2001, AG/RES. 1 (XXVIII-E/01).

Explicit and implicit rights are visible in the American Declaration on the Rights and Duties of Man which are binding through the OAS Charter. Article I states, '[e]very human being has the right to life, liberty and the security of his person'. Furthermore, Article II provides that '[a]ll persons are equal before the law and have the rights and duties established in this Declaration, without distinction as to race, sex, language, creed or any other factor'.[252]

Two other articles of the American Declaration of the Rights and Duties of Man are clearly relevant. Article XI states that '[e]very person has the right to the preservation of his health through sanitary and social measures relating to food, clothing, housing and medical care, to the extent permitted by public and community resources'.[253] In addition, Article XVI proclaims the right of every person to enjoy the protection of the State 'from the consequences of unemployment, old age and any disabilities arising from causes beyond his control that makes it physically or mentally impossible for him to earn a living'.[254] The American Convention on Human Rights, likewise, does not explicitly mention the rights of disabled persons, however, under Article 1(1):

> [t]he States Parties to this Convention undertake to respect the rights and freedoms recognized herein and to ensure to all persons subject to their jurisdiction the free and full exercise of those rights and freedoms, without any discrimination for reasons of race, color, sex, language, religion, political or other opinion, national or social origin, economic status, birth, or any other social condition.

It would not be a departure from the intention of the drafters to include disability within the concept of 'any other social condition'.

The Additional Protocol to the American Convention on Human Rights in the Area of Economic, Social, and Cultural Rights,[255] specifically refers to the rights of persons with disabilities. According to Article 18, '[e]veryone affected by a diminution of his physical or mental capacities is entitled to receive *special attention* to help him achieve the greatest possible development of his personality'.[256] States parties agree to undertake programs aimed at providing persons with disabilities with the resources and environment needed for attaining this goal and to provide special training to the families of the handicapped. The Inter-American Convention on the Elimination of all Forms of Discrimination against People with Disabilities[257] is aimed at the prevention and elimination of all forms of discrimination against persons with disabilities and the promotion of their full integration into society. The Convention entered into force in 2001 and is in four parts:

---

[252] American Declaration on the Rights and Duties of Man, OAS Res. XXX, OAS Doc. OEA/Ser.L.V/II.82 doc.6 rev.1 at 17 (1992). For a detailed consideration of the Inter-American human rights system see above chapter 9.

[253] Article XI ADRDM.

[254] Article XVI ADRDM.

[255] Additional Protocol to the American Convention on Human Rights in the Area of Economic, Social and Cultural Rights 'Protocol of San Salvador' (A-52) OAS *Treaty Series* No. 69 (1988), signed 17 November 1988, *reprinted in* Basic Documents Pertaining to Human Rights in the Inter-American System, OEA/Ser.L.V/II.82 doc.6 rev.1 at 67 (1992).

[256] See UN Official Journal No. L225/443 of 12 August 1986.

[257] Inter-American Convention on the Elimination of All Forms of Discrimination Against Persons With Disabilities, AG/RES. 1608, 7 June 1999.

(1) the objectives concerning the prevention and elimination of discrimination and the integration of persons with disabilities into society;

(2) the obligations of States parties;

(3) definitions of discrimination and disability; and

(4) implementation mechanisms. States parties undertake to adopt the legislative, social, educational, labour-related, or any other measures needed to achieve the goals of the Convention, and to co-operate with one another in helping to prevent and eliminate discrimination against persons with disabilities.

Article V states that:

[t]o the extent that it is consistent with their respective internal laws, the states parties shall promote participation by representatives of organizations of persons with disabilities, nongovernmental organizations working in this area, or, if such organizations do not exist, persons with disabilities, in the development, execution, and evaluation of measures and policies to implement this Convention.

The Convention also establishes a Committee for the Elimination of All Forms of Discrimination against Persons with Disabilities.[258]

(iii) The African Union

The African human rights system is the 'youngest' regional system. As noted earlier, one of the most distinctive features of the African Charter on Human and Peoples' Rights is its recognition of collective rights. It views individual and peoples' rights as being linked. The other distinctive features have been discussed in Chapter 10. More specifically as regards disability. Article 18(4) of the Charter provides that the disabled have the right to special measures of protection in keeping with their physical or moral needs, although what constitutes a moral need has yet to be qualified by relevant jurisprudence. Article 16(1) provides that '[e]very individual shall have the right to enjoy the best attainable state of physical and mental health'.[259]

The Protocol to the African Charter on Human and Peoples' Rights on the Rights of Women in Africa contains a number of relevant provisions, which deserve a specific mention.[260] Article 23, in according special protection to women with disabilities, establishes that States parties are to ensure such protection and take specific measures 'commensurate with the [disabled women's] physical, economic and social needs to facilitate their access to employment, professional and vocational training as well as their participation in decision-making'.[261] There is a further undertaking to ensure that women are protected from discrimination and violence, including sexual abuse.[262] The African Charter on the Rights and

---

[258] Article VI Inter-American Convention on the Elimination of All Forms of Discrimination Against Persons With Disabilities.

[259] African [Banjul] Charter on Human and Peoples' Rights, adopted 27 June 1981, OAU Doc. CAB/LEG/67/3 rev. 5, 21 I.L.M. 58 (1982), entered into force 21 October 1986.

[260] Protocol to the African Charter on Human and Peoples Rights on the Rights of Women in Africa, Maputo, 13 September 2000 OAU Doc. CAB/LEG/66.6 (2000).

[261] Article 23(a) Protocol to the African Charter on Human and Peoples' Rights on the Rights of Women in Africa.

[262] Article 23(b) Protocol to the African Charter on Human and Peoples' Rights on the Rights of Women in Africa.

Welfare of the Child (1990) contains specific provisions for handicapped children, noting that all mental or physically disabled children have the right to dignity, promotion of self-reliance and satisfaction of physical and moral needs.[263] Article 13, furthermore, places an obligation on States parties to ensure that disabled children have 'effective access to training, preparation for employment and recreation opportunities in a manner conducive to the child achieving the fullest possible social integration, individual development and his cultural and moral development'.[264] Most of the provisions of the African Children's Charter are modelled on the articles of the CRC. The main difference lies in the existence of provisions concerning children's duties, in line with the African Human Rights Charter.

The decade 2000–09 has been proclaimed the Africa Decade of Disabled People. It is an initiative of the non-governmental community in Africa. The goals of the Decade are to promote awareness and commitment to full participation, equality and empowerment of persons with disabilities in Africa. In February 2002, the AU organised in Addis Ababa, in collaboration with regional organisations of persons with disabilities, the Pan-African Conference on the Africa Decade of Disabled Persons to consider a 'Plan of Action for the Decade'. The Action Plan calls upon OAU Member States and governments to study the situation of persons with disabilities with a view to formulating measures favouring the equalisation of opportunities, full participation and their independence in society. In 2003 the Secretariat for the Decade of Persons with Disabilities was established by the South African Government, the African Rehabilitation Institute (ARI) and a number of continental disability organisations. The Secretariat believes that 'the new institutional framework should include an inclusive civil society representation that ensures that the groups of society most affected by poverty are represented/included in all the processes undertaken.'[265]

As a result of the African Union Regional Conference, held in September 2008, a statement on the Millennium Development Goals was released. The aims were to establish a Specialist Agency on Disability in the league of UNICEF and UNIFEM in order to provide leadership and global accountability on matters related to disabled people. They also called on governments to move and support a motion during the UN General Assembly, calling for the establishment of a new UN Special Agency on Disability; to provide leadership, co-ordination, harmonisation and enhanced monitoring and reporting.[266] The Disability Movement has indicated that it now bases its strategy on the new UN Convention on the Rights of Persons with Disabilities.[267]

(iv) Other systems of regional protection

No particular instruments on disability have been adopted in Asia, but workshops spanning all of Asia and regional meetings were held to discuss the Convention on the Rights of Persons with Disabilities in preparation for the second session of the Ad Hoc Committee on a Comprehensive and Integral International Convention on Protection and Promotion

---

[263] Article 13(1) African Charter on the Rights and Welfare of the Child, Addis Ababa, Ethiopia, July 1990 OAU Doc. CAB/LEG/24.9/49 (1990), entered into force 29 November 1999.

[264] Article 13(2) ACHPR.

[265] Letter from A.K. Dube, to the President of the African Union in response to the Regional Conference regarding Disability in Nairobi, Kenya 15–17 September 2008. See www.africandecade.org/document-repository/Letterto%20AU%20chair.pdf <last visited 8 April 2009>.

[266] Ibid.

[267] Update, September 2008, www.africandecade.org/reads/monthly-updates/update-september-2008 <last visited 8 April 2009>.

of the Rights and Dignity of Persons with Disabilities in New York.[268] The UN ESCAP (Economic and Social Commission for Asia and the Pacific) proclaimed the Asian and Pacific Decade of Disabled Persons (1993–2002) and the Agenda for Action for the decade at the 48th Commission Session in 1992. In the Agenda for Action, 'Regional Cooperation' was considered essential to provide disabled persons with 'full-participation and equality' within their chosen State.[269] In May 2002, the last year of the UN ESCAP Asian and Pacific Decade of Disabled Persons, a resolution on '[p]romoting an inclusive, barrier-free and rights-based society for people with disabilities in the Asian and Pacific region in the twenty-first century' was adopted with full support from 29 countries at the ESCAP 58th Commission Session.[270]

4 CONCLUSIONS

Persons with disabilities have for far too long been part of the single largest 'silent minority' of the world. Historically persons with disabilities have been excluded from an appropriate social interaction; they have either been symbols of disgrace and shame or were treated as 'diseased' persons needing cure and a medical solution.[271] International human rights, since its development post-1945, remained reluctant to engage with and consider the situation of persons with disabilities. Despite initial opposition to the adoption and controversies in the formulation of the text of the CRPD, the treaty was one of the most rapidly negotiated internationally binding instruments. The concluded treaty has also been welcomed with unusual enthusiasm. As this chapter has highlighted, there are numerous positive features contained within CRPD. The CRDP brings to an end the stereotypical views about persons with disability in that the Convention aims:

> to transition disability policy away from a 'medical' or 'social welfare' model based on sorting and separating persons with disabilities onto 'parallel tracks' or exclusive living spaces, toward a 'social' or 'human rights' model that focuses on *capability* and takes *inclusion, individual dignity, personal autonomy and social solidarity* as the principle points of departure. Under this approach, the disability problematic is no longer how to provide for those deemed 'unable' to integrate into mainstream society, but rather how to make society accessible to all persons, on an equal, non-separate basis.[272]

Disability, as an issue facing all societies and States requires a fundamental change in human psychology and societal perceptions. Furthermore, as the CRPD has underlined, in order to adequately cater for the rights of the disabled an expanded body of rights must be incorporated in the existing human rights paradigm. A scheme of this sort includes additional 'second generation' rights such as the social protection and poverty reduction,[273] awareness raising,[274] 'third generation' rights such as international co-operation which

---

[268] A/58/118 & Corr.1 Second Session, New York, 16–27 June 2003.
[269] Economic and Social Commission for Asia and the Pacific, Asia and Pacific Decade of Disabled Persons – Country Perspectives (United Nations, New York, 1999) UN Doc. ST/ESCAP/2014 See www.unescap.org/esid/psis/disability/decade/publications/apdcp.pdf <last visited 8 April 2009>.
[270] UN Doc. A/58/61–E/2003/5 Annex – part 2.
[271] See Melish, above n.3, at p. 37.
[272] Ibid. at p. 44.
[273] Article 28(2)(b) CRPD.
[274] Article 8 CRPD.

includes co-operation in international developmental programmes[275] as well as the so-called 'fourth generation' rights (e.g. accessible environment)[276] and 'fifth-generation' rights (e.g. the right to leisure, recreation and tourism).[277]

Notwithstanding the unusual enthusiasm and rapid ratification of the CRPD, the greatest challenge lies (as with all human rights treaties) with the implementation of the treaty. The obligations contained within CRPD require a disciplined and focused approach towards the enforcement of traditionally categorised human rights through a disability-specific focus. Furthermore, the provisions of the Convention invoke systematic policies for ensuring genuine equality and non-discrimination for persons with disabilities; this requires a long-term human, societal, economic and emotional commitment.

The Committee on Economic, Social and Cultural Rights recalls the principle of non-discrimination in access to employment by persons with disabilities in its General Comment No. 5 (1994) on persons with disabilities. 'The "right of everyone to the opportunity to gain his living by work which he freely chooses or accepts" (art.6(1)) is not realized where the only real opportunity open to disabled workers is to work in so-called "sheltered" facilities under substandard conditions.'[278] States parties must take measures enabling persons with disabilities to secure and retain appropriate employment and to progress in their occupational field, thus facilitating their integration or reintegration into society.[279]

---

[275] Article 32 CRPD.
[276] See Article 3 and 9 CRPD.
[277] See Article 30 CRPD.
[278] See the General Comment No. 5 (1994), *09/12/94 CESCR General Comment 5. (General Comments)* para 21.
[279] Ibid.

18 Rights of refugees and internally displaced persons[1]

1 INTRODUCTION

Since time immemorial, torture, inhuman and degrading treatment, religious and political persecution and other violations of human rights have forced people to flee. Political, racial, religious, economic and environmental upheavals during the 20th century and at the beginning of the new millennium highlight the relevance of refugee law for human rights law. The gross violation of the rights of refugees and displaced persons is a growing concern for international human rights and humanitarian law. Today's contemporary world faces mass crises of refugees and internally displaced persons (IDPs). There are currently 16 million refugees worldwide and more than 51 million internally displaced persons.[2] Most of the refugees and displaced persons originate from the developing States of Africa, Asia and Latin America. Approximately 50 per cent of these refugees are women and girls, while around 44 per cent are children.[3] Poverty, undernourishment and underdevelopment are a significant cause of exodus and yet international refugee law continues to take a restrictive approach towards violations of social and economic rights.[4] Refugees often face substantial difficulties in seeking asylum; receiving States are wary of the burdens which are placed through an influx of refugees. Restrictions and limitations are placed by many States to discourage movement and travel to their territorial jurisdiction through such strategies as strict visa control and carrier sanctions. Since the events of 11 September 2001 the heightened threat of terrorism has resulted in further exclusionary policies towards asylum-seekers.[5] Regarded as a burden and frequently associated with filth and crime, refugees and asylum-seekers are stigmatised.

Upon arrival at the border, asylum-seekers are often denied proper procedures to submit claims for refugee status. Asylum-seekers are detained and in some instances forcibly repatriated. Even on recognition of a refugee status, these individuals may be denied access

---

[1] Chimni (ed.), *International Refugee Law: A Reader* (Sage, 2000); Feller, Turk and Nicholson, *Refugee Protection in International Law* (Cambridge University Press, 2003); Goodwin-Gill and McAdam, *The Refugee in International Law* (Oxford University Press, 2007); Goodwin-Gill, 'Refugees and Responsibility in the Twenty-First Century: More Lessons Learned from the South Pacific' 12 *Pacific Rim Law and Policy Journal* (2003) 23; Hathaway (ed.), *Reconceiving International Refugee Law* (Martinus Nijhoff, 1997); Nicholson and Twomey (eds), *Refugee: Rights & Realities* (Cambridge University Press, 1999).

[2] UNHCR: 2007 Global Trends: Refugees, Asylum-seekers, Returnees, Internally Displaced and Stateless persons, June 2008 www.unhcr.org/statistics/STATISTICS/4852366f2.pdf <last visited 15 March 2009> at p. 1.

[3] Ibid. p. 12.

[4] See Foster, *International Refugee Law and Socio-Economic Rights* (Cambridge University Press, 2007).

[5] See below chapter 24.

to basic services, such as adequate healthcare, education and housing. In the context of IDPs, individual humanitarian assistance could be restricted or linked to military or other political advantages that are sought between the warring factions in the conflict. With its human rights perspective, this chapter aims to provide an overview of the key international initiatives dealing with refugees and displaced persons. It examines the difficulties inherent in these initiatives – both international and regional – and underlines the limitations of existing State practice. It finally concludes with a number of observations on improving the situation.

2 ESTABLISHING A NEXUS BETWEEN REFUGEEISM AND MASS DISPLACEMENT WITHIN HUMAN RIGHTS LAW

The nexus between international human rights law and refugeeism and mass internal displacement has been described as 'multidimensional and global'.[6] Refugees and IDPs are the victims of gross violations of human rights such as genocide, war crimes, crimes against humanity and torture – much of the existing human rights jurisprudence has been built around the unfortunate stories of refugees and IDPs. The rights of refugees imbibe fundamental human rights, civil and political, as well as economic, social and cultural rights. Many universally recognised human rights are directly applicable to refugees. These include the right to life, protection from torture and ill-treatment, the right to a nationality, the right to freedom of movement, the right to leave any country, including one's own, and to return to one's country, and the right not to be forcibly returned. These rights are affirmed, among other civil, political, economic, social and cultural rights, for all persons, citizens and non-citizens alike, in the Universal Declaration of Human Rights (UDHR), the International Covenant on Civil and Political Rights (ICCPR), and the International Covenant on Economic, Social and Cultural Rights (ICESCR), which together make up the International Bill of Human Rights. By the same account, modern human rights treaties encounter and deal with core concepts derived from laws relating to refugees. Clark and Crépeau make the point that:

> [i]t is no longer possible to interpret or apply the Refugee Convention without drawing on the text and jurisprudence of other human rights treaties. Conversely it is not possible to monitor the implementation of other human rights treaties, where refugees are concerned, without drawing on the text of the Refugee Convention and related interpretive conclusions of the UNHCR Executive Committee.[7]

The relationship between human rights law and refugee law can be established from the text of all modern human rights instruments as well as from the provisions of the 1951 Refugee Convention. The rights contained within the UDHR are applicable to all individuals, which includes refugees and IDPs. In addition, specific provisions of the Declaration are particularly valuable in order to reinforce the human rights of asylum seeker and IDPs.

---

[6] Office of the High Commissioner for Human Rights, 'Fact Sheet No. 20, Human Rights and Refugees' www.ohchr.org/EN/PublicationsResources/Pages/FactSheets.aspx <last visited 15 March 2009>, p. 1.

[7] Clark and Crépeau, 'Mainstreaming Refugee Rights: The 1951 Refugee Convention and International Human Rights Law' 17 *NQHR* (1999) 389 at p. 389.

Article 14 of UDHR has a particular relevance to refugees and provides that '[e]veryone has the right to seek and to enjoy in other countries asylum from persecution'. The initial provisions were broader but were subsequently tightened to refuse asylum-seekers the ability to gain asylum as a right.[8] Article 15 provides for a right of everyone to acquire a nationality. Article 13 provides for everyone the 'right to freedom of movement and residence within the borders of each State'.

One fundamental principle – which now informs the entirety of the human rights regime – is that of *non-refoulement*. Initially contained within the 1951 Refugee Convention, the principle of *non-refoulement* has been incorporated and inducted within the jurisprudence of ECHR, ICCPR and the Torture Convention. *Non-refoulement* is a principle of customary international law,[9] and also arguably that of *jus cogens* character.[10]

3 INTERNATIONAL LAW AND THE PROTECTION OF REFUGEES[11]

One of the characteristics of the earlier attempts at dealing with refugees was to adopt a group or category approach, and it was deemed sufficient that a person (within that category) was outside his or her country of origin and was without the protection of his or her government.[12] The first real attempt at an international level to provide legal protection was conducted under the auspices of the League of Nations.[13] The League defined refugees as categories, in relation to the States of origin. In accordance with such a concept of 'refugees', the Convention Relating to the International Status of Refugees was adopted in 1933 and entered into force in 1935.[14] During and after the Second World War millions were displaced or became refugees. In 1946 the International Refugee Organization (IRO) was formed.[15] This was a non-permanent body aiding in large-scale resettlement helping specified categories, e.g. victims of Nazi and Fascist persecution. The persecution of minorities and mass displacement forced at least the European States (which at that point consisted of a majority within the UN) to consider the issue seriously. Replacing the IRO, the United Nations General Assembly in its Resolution 319(IV)A of 3 December 1949 established the Office of the United Nations High Commissioner for Refugees for a period of three years. Its mandate has since that time been renewed. On 14 December 1950, the General Assembly adopted the Statute of the UNHCR.[16] In 1951 the UN Convention Relating to the Status of Refugees was adopted and entered into force in April 1954, which was further supplemented by the 1967 Protocol.[17]

---

[8] Goodwin-Gill and McAdam, above n.1, at pp. 359–360. See also above chapter 4.

[9] Goodwin-Gill and McAdam, above n.1, at p. 211.

[10] Goodwin-Gill and McAdam, above n.1, at p. 218, Allain, 'The Jus Cogens Nature of Non-Refoulement' 13 *IJRL* (2001) 533.

[11] Feller, 'The Evolution of International Refugee Protection Regime' 5 *Washington University Journal of Law and Policy* (2001a) 129.

[12] Goodwin-Gill and McAdam, above n.1, at p. 16.

[13] Ibid. pp. 16–20.

[14] 159 *LNTS* No. 3663.

[15] 1946 Constitution of the International Refugee Organization, entered into force 20 August 1948, 18 *UNTS* 3 – reprinted in Goodwin-Gill and McAdam, above n.1 Annexe 1.1.

[16] UN Doc. A/RES/428 (V) 14th December 1950.

[17] 1951 Convention relating to the Status of Refugees 189 *UNTS* 150, 1967 Protocol relating to the Status of Refugees 606 *UNTS* 267.

(i) The Refugee Convention 1951

The 1951 Convention together with its Protocol represent the primary instruments dealing with refugee law. The Convention, was adopted on 28 July 1951 and is currently ratified or acceded to by 144 States.[18] It is often referred to as the 'Magna Carta of international refugee law'[19] since it provides the fundamental charter of rights afforded to the refugee and also provides for measures of implementation. Notwithstanding the considerable criticism of the Convention, it is the only binding international instrument dealing with refugees. It is a limited instrument and while attempting to deal with the question of the status of refugees, does not provide any solution against remedying the causes. The Convention is also more about State responsibilities rather than individual rights. The Convention provides a definition of 'refugee', a definition which, as we shall consider, despite modification has remained inadequate and controversial. The 1967 instrument, although a separate instrument, removed the time-limitation which had been adopted by the 1951 Convention and provided the option of expanding the scope of applicability of the Convention to beyond the frontiers of Europe. Both the 1951 Convention and the 1967 Protocol permit reservations. However, the sanctity of certain provisions is absolute and cannot be undermined. These provisions relate to Article 1 (definition), Article 33 (*non-refoulement*), Article 3 (non-discrimination), Article 4 (religion) and Article 16(1) (access to courts).[20] States that presented reservations to any one of the above, or limit the application of these provisions breach general international law. In addition to the *refoulement* principle, the Convention also established other principles, which included the fundamental principle of non-discrimination (Article 3).

Broadly speaking, the 1951 Refugee Convention contains three elements: the definition of a refugee in Article 1, which shall be analysed shortly, the principle of *non-refoulement* in Article 33 and the rights and obligations of refugees and the obligations placed upon States.

(ii) The principle of non-refoulement under the 1951 Convention

Article 33(1) of the Convention establishes that:

> No Contracting State shall expel or return ('refouler') a refugee in any manner whatsoever to the frontiers of territories where his life or freedom would be threatened on account of his race, religion, nationality, membership of a particular social group or political opinion.

The method of entry into a country, legal or otherwise does not affect the right of refugees to *non-refoulement* under Article 31 of the Convention. It is, however, important to note that the principle of *non-refoulement* and, indeed, the Refugee Convention, do not contain a right to asylum in itself and, therefore, there is no right of entry. *Non-refoulement* is

---

[18] As of 1 October 2008, 144 States were party to the Convention and 144 were party to the Protocol. However, only 141 States were party to both documents, with Monaco, Madagascar and St. Kitts and Nevis having only ratified the Convention and Cape Verde, the United States and Venezuela having only ratified the protocol. www.unhcr.org/protect/PROTECTION/3b73b0d63.pdf <last visited 13 October 2008>.

[19] See *Refugee* Vol. 2, No. 123 (2001) www.unhcr.org/home/PUBL/3b5e90ea0.pdf <last visted 22 February 2009> at p. 2.

[20] Goodwin-Gill and McAdam, above n.1, at p. 508.

simply the right of refugees not to be returned to a country where they are likely to fear for their life or freedom. Goodwin-Gill and McAdam, however, add that as a result of States' practice, since the conception of the Convention, it is also reasonable to infer that 'the concept now encompasses both non-return and non-rejection'.[21] This means that temporary admission to a State is permitted until the individual's refugee claim for asylum has been processed. Both direct return to a country of persecution and 'chain-*refoulement*' constitute a violation of Article 33.[22] The concept of *non-refoulement* has additionally been added to by international human rights treaties, most notably Article 3 of the Convention against Torture, as well as the newly evolving concept of complementary or subsidiary protection. Despite the fact that the principle is constantly evolving and is 'massively affirmed',[23] States have increasingly attempted to avoid application by ensuring that refugees are not legally admitted on to State territory despite their factual presence. One of the most worrying trends regarding *non-refoulement*, is States attempting to avoid their obligations through the creation of legal loopholes. These evasive measures take varying forms. Safe Third Country arrangements and Safe Country of Origin presumptions are most notable within the EU. However, these arrangements are particularly worrying as they do not take account of the fact that countries can become rapidly unstable, or of the situations of unrepresented minority groups within all of these countries. The situation of the Roma within several Central European States is of particular concern here. Deterrent measures such as visa requirements and sanctions being placed on unwitting carriers of potential refugees and asylum-seekers are also becoming increasingly prevalent.

An increasingly used avoidance technique is that of the establishment of 'international areas or zones' within ports of entry into States. The purpose of this is to retain the right to turn back asylum-seekers or refugees that have arrived through more traditional methods, before they are actually deemed to be on State territory. Noll has gone so far as to claim that the right to *non-refoulement* is in fact the 'right to transgress an administrative border'.[24] However, as Goodwin-Gill and McAdam have correctly asserted, '[n]o State, by treaty or practice, appears to have abandoned the territory comprised by its ports of entry; the extent of national control exercised therein sufficiently contradicts any assertion of their purely international character'.[25] As long as a State maintains control over its territory, its international obligations remain applicable and to claim otherwise can be deemed to be a breach of good faith and even Convention obligations if this were to negatively affect the access of refugees and asylum-seekers to protection and *non-refoulement*.

The need to establish what is acceptable within the boundaries of *non-refoulement*, through an authoritative interpretation of the Convention, is becoming increasingly important, as States more and more frequently attempt to limit the scope of its application and essentially undermine the spirit of both the Convention and the provision. While States continue to avoid their obligations under Article 33 of the Refugee Convention through a refusal to accept that its provisions apply extra-territorially, there is, without doubt, a need for an authoritative interpretation of treaty obligations.

---

[21] Goodwin-Gill and McAdam, above n.1, at p. 208.
[22] 'Chain-*refoulement*' is where a State deports to a third State which is likely to return the refugee to the State of origin where they are likely to face persecution. See *T.I* v. *UK* ECtHR 2000.
[23] Clark, 'Rights Based Refuge, the Potential of the 1951 Convention and the Need for Authoritative Interpretation' 16 *IJRL* 4 (2004) 584, p. 589.
[24] Noll, 'Seeking Asylum at Embassies: A Right to Entry under International Law' 17 *IJRL* (2005) 542 at p. 548.
[25] Goodwin-Gill and McAdam, above n.1, at p. 255.

(iii) Obligations upon States parties under the Refugee Convention

The 1951 Refugee Convention has been appropriately termed as 'a human rights document'.[26] Yet, at the same time, as noted above, the only major human rights treaty that lacks a clearly defined reporting procedure is the Convention relating to the Status of Refugees. In accordance with Article 35(2) of the Refugee Convention, the State parties to the Convention undertake to provide the Office of the High Commissioner for Refugees with information and statistical data concerning the condition of refugees and the implementation of the Convention.[27] While the UNHCR is able to advise and comment upon the application of the Convention, its precarious situation regarding funding may inhibit this.[28] The UNHCR is directly dependent upon State contributions, unlike other treaty bodies that are funded through the UN system. It is clear that this situation may impact on UNHCR's ability to criticise the actions of donor States. Countries from the European Union as well as Australia and the United States, that are known to creatively interpret provisions of the Convention including the definition of the refugee and the principle of *non-refoulement*, are also the donors that UNHCR is most dependent upon. This system can only be seen to significantly weaken UNHCR and must impact on its ability to carry out its work.

It has also been purported that the Refugee Convention lacks an authoritative interpretation and the diplomatic nature of the UNHCR has not lent itself to resolving this issue.[29] While other binding human rights instruments have treaty bodies, enabled to authoritatively interpret the provisions and in some cases hear complaints, the UNHCR is very much limited in its work. In many ways the Refugee Convention is very much dependent upon the good faith of the States that apply it. As has been discussed above, this is not always the case, especially regarding *non-refoulement*. The deliberate use of 'narrow and ungenerous definitions of those entitled to protection',[30] highlights the urgent need for a treaty body with wider powers to work alongside UNHCR. However, the current climate surrounding both refugees and migrants, does not lend itself to such a change. Fitzpatrick continues that '[t]he Convention's reliance on good faith determination of refugee status by States parties contributes to its potential marginalization in an era of retrenchment'.[31]

The use of human rights law to further substantiate asylum claims, together with the advent of complementary protection, has placed an additional burden on UNHCR. Unlike other treaty bodies, the UNHCR lacks the ability directly to criticise other States, never mind interpret the Convention. In fact, the only body with the competency to authoritatively rule or indeed advise on the Refugee Convention in conjunction with other UN Human Rights treaties is the ICJ.[32] However, with the constant evolution of asylum-based human rights, it is unlikely that the ICJ will ever be asked to rule or advise upon an unreasonable amount of cases. Therefore, it has been suggested that the only way forward is through the Refugee Convention being given a treaty committee with the ability to

---

[26] See Aleinikoff, 'The Refugee Convention at Forty: Reflections on the International Journal of Refugee Law Colloquim' 3 *IJRL* (1991) 617 at p. 625.

[27] Article 35(2).

[28] Statute of the Office of the United Nations High Commissioner for Refugees, UN Doc. A/RES/428 paras 8(a) and (b).

[29] Clark, above n.23, at p. 606.

[30] Fitzpatrick, 'Revitalizing the 1951 Convention' 9 *Harvard Human Rights Journal* (1996) 229 at p. 237.

[31] Ibid. at p. 252.

[32] On the role of the ICJ within international law, see above chapter 4.

interpret refugee law, in conjunction with other human rights treaty committees and produce advisory comments.[33]

As previously stated, the 1951 Convention establishes a number of non-derogable rights for refugees. In addition to this, it places a number of obligations on receiving States and as such constitutes a 'statement of the minimum rights of refugees'.[34] These rights and obligations fall within the categories of Welfare, Gainful Employment, Juridical Status and Administrative Measures. Essentially, their purpose is to provide refugees with a minimum standard of living and provide for their immediate needs. However, due to the ambiguity of the terminology used, the content of the rights in practice varies considerably from State to State. Regarding the right of association, Article 15 and the right to engage in wage earning employment,[35] refugees ought to receive the same treatment as aliens from most favoured nations. At the same time other rights demand that refugees should receive the same treatment as is generally afforded to aliens.[36] This has led to huge disparities between the rights afforded to refugees and the extent to which governments fulfil their obligations, based purely on the way they treat other aliens on their territory.[37]

While the Refugee Convention has its issues, it remains the only universal binding treaty regarding refugee law. Although its ambiguities have been the cause of significant criticism, it is still followed by the States that are party to it, with the majority of States that have tried to limit the rights contained therein through evasive tactics such as through interpretation as opposed to direct breach. The major stumbling block has been the inability of UNHCR to prevent States from avoiding the application of *non-refoulement* through 'devised fictions'.[38]

(iv) Defining 'refugees' in international law

Article 1 A(2) of the 1951 Refugee Convention provides the following definition of a 'refugee':

> As a result of events occurring before 1 January 1951 and owing to well-founded fear of being persecuted for reasons of race, religion, nationality, membership of a particular social group or political opinion, is outside the country of his nationality and is unable or, owing to such fear, is unwilling to avail himself of the protection of that country; or who, not having a nationality and being outside the country of his former habitual residence as a result of such events, is unable or, owing to such fear, is unwilling to return to it.

A number of characteristics emerge from the definition of refugees. Firstly, Article 1B(1)(a) provides that 'events occurring before 1 January 1951' must be understood to mean 'events occurring in Europe before 1 January 1951'. The limitation of time and geography was however subsequently removed by the 1967 Protocol. Secondly, that they are outside their country of origin. Thirdly, they are unable, or owing to fear, unwilling to seek or take advantage of the protection of that country. Fourthly, such inability or unwillingness arises

---

[33] Clark, above n.23, at p. 607.
[34] Goodwin-Gill and McAdam, above n.1, at p. 506.
[35] Article 17.
[36] See e.g. Article 21 (Housing).
[37] Hathaway, *The Rights of Refugees under International Law* (Cambridge University Press, 2005) pp. 192–193.
[38] Goodwin-Gill and McAdam, above n.1, at p. 206.

as a consequence of a well-founded fear of being persecuted. Fifthly, the individual concerned fears persecution which is based on reasons of race, religion, nationality, membership of a particular social group or political opinion: thus a nexus has to be established between fear of persecution and one of the reasons provided in the Convention. Each of these characteristics is of great importance and the following discussion aims to elaborate upon them. However, it is important to note that the definition of a refugee has been the subject of much criticism. Fitzpatrick asserts that '[t]he vagueness of the refugee definition is unsatisfactory because it permits a kind of local option for asylum adjudicators either to permit adaptation to new realities or to deny claims that fail to follow the archaic scenario'.[39]

(a) Outside the country of origin

In order to be recognised as a refugee, it is of critical importance that the person in question is outside his or her country of origin. He or she must have crossed the international State boundary. This, of course, excludes internally displaced persons (IDPs) as will be discussed later on in this chapter. While the Refugee Convention ensures that refugees are entitled to a significant number of rights and safeguards from the receiving State, persons belonging to that State are not entitled to the same rights. Whereas, the presumption is, no doubt, that the State in question already provides its citizens with rights, it can also be said that this group of people as internally displaced persons can be extremely vulnerable.

(b) Inability or unwillingness to seek or to take advantage of the protection of country of origin

There are numerous reasons why a person may be unable to seek or take advantage of the protection of their country of origin. The most common and established ground is that the State itself is responsible for the persecution. However, increasingly, it is not the State that is committing the persecution but private individuals or non-State entities. There has been considerable disagreement over whether private individuals can be responsible for persecution, as the presumption has been that this is a matter for national criminal law and the State provides protection from this. However, if non-State entities or private individual are able to act with impunity either due to the inaction, tolerance, approval of the government, or indeed the inability of the government, then it would seem that the victim is indeed subject to persecution.[40] While the definition of a refugee has nothing within it that indicates that the persecution must be committed by State authorities, receiving States have in the past been unwilling or reluctant to accept that in such cases there is no other recourse for the victim than claiming refugee status. Fitzpatrick has asserted that '[t]he dangers posed by this vagueness are apparent in the tendency of asylum adjudicator to respond unevenly to innovative claims from protection . . . to insist that non-state actors are incapable of inflicting persecution'.[41] The UNHCR Handbook, does state, however, that non-State agents, and as such private individuals, can be responsible for persecutory acts, if they 'are

---

[39] Fitzpatrick, above n.30, at p. 239.
[40] See jurisprudence of the Committee against Torture, e.g. *Elmi* v. *Australia* CAT 120/98; *cf. H.M.H.I* v. *Australia* CAT 177/01.
[41] Fitzpatrick, above n.30, at p. 239.

knowingly tolerated by the authorities, or if the authorities refuse, or prove unable to offer effective protection'.[42] Despite State reluctance, most notably in cases of domestic violence and other gender-related claims, the situation has started to change. The UNHCR Guidelines relating to Gender Persecution clearly state that '[e]ven though a particular state may have prohibited a persecutory practice . . . the State may nevertheless continue to condone or tolerate the practice, or may not be able to stop the practice effectively. In such cases, the practice would still amount to persecution'.[43]

State-like entities such as *de facto* authorities and insurgents, where the State does not exert control over areas of its territory, as well as failed States, are also likely to generate claims of persecution where the victim is unable or unwilling to seek the protection of the country of origin. While the persecution itself does not have to be committed by the State, there is still without doubt a link between protection and fear of persecution. In the event that persecution is committed by a private individual, only if the State in question fails to provide adequate protection for its citizens will this give rise to a claim for refugee status. As such, the lack of action on behalf of the authorities must be part of an overall problem or situation; the incompetence of an individual police officer or public official is not sufficient.

(c) Reasons for persecution

The Convention provides for five grounds upon which a person can seek refugee status. These are race, religion, nationality, membership of a particular social group or political opinion. It is not necessary that the claimant actually has the characteristics or beliefs that led to persecution, rather that the persecutor believes them to have such a characteristics or beliefs. As such, imputed characteristics are sufficient to establish a link between the claimant and one of the Convention grounds for claiming refugee status. An understanding of the aforementioned characteristics or grounds necessitates an exploration of international human rights law. Thus, as regards 'race' the International Convention on the Elimination of All Forms of Racial Discrimination and the jurisprudence of CERD retain the primary position.[44] Race and racial discrimination, as has been examined, provides multifarious examples leading to persecution and displacement of individuals and communities.[45] Religion, perhaps more than other characteristics continues to be the cause of conflict and persecution. Our earlier examination has already explored many of the tensions which are precipitated through religious differences.[46] Religious minorities have historically been targeted and victimised: specific examples in the context of the refugee law are the persecution of French Huguenots which forced thousands to flee in 1685 and take refuge in England and Prussia,[47] and the exodus of Jews under the Nazi regime.[48]

---

[42] *UNHCR Handbook on Procedures and Criteria for Determining Refugee Status under the 1951 Convention and the 1967 Protocol relating to the Status of Refugees*, HCR/IP/4/Eng/REV.1, para 65.

[43] *UNHCR Guidelines on International Protection: Gender-Related Persecution within the context of Article 1A(2) of the 1951 Convention and/or its 1967 Protocol relating to the Status of Refugees*, HCR/GIP/02/01, para 11.

[44] See above chapter 12.

[45] Ibid.

[46] Ibid.; also see above chapter 2.

[47] See above chapter 12.

[48] See below chapter 13.

Recent times have also witnessed the mass refugee movements of Baha'is of Iran[49] and Ahmadiyyas of Pakistan to various parts of the world, to name only a few instances.[50]

The 1951 Convention provides for the ground of persecution on the basis of 'nationality'. However, the scope of nationality is never fully established. It has been described as 'somewhat odd' since the concept of being recognised as a refugee is premised on the fact that the State or the State agents are engaged in the persecution of its own nationals. In the political reorganisation that emerged since the Second World War citizens of one State would frequently find themselves on the wrong side of the border. Controversies with the meaning of 'nationality' have already been explored and it would appear that the 1951 Convention definition takes on the broader interpretation of 'nationality' including within its ambit members of ethnic, religious, cultural minorities or communities. More obvious examples of 'nationality' are groups of people that deem themselves as belonging to a particular nationality that is not connected to a recognised State. This could include groups such as Kurds, Baluchis and Kosovars. Minority groups that are traditionally resident in one country but also maintain links with their 'home' country are also possible recipients of protection under the term 'nationality'. Russian minorities in Baltic States are an example of this.

A further ground of persecution, under the Convention definition of a refugee, is based on membership of a particular 'social group'. 'Social group' is a broad category and can accommodate a range of entities. Gender, was not included as a possible basis for having a well-founded persecution for the purpose of claiming refugee status. The lacuna in the Convention definition has been recognised and claims have been established by women on the basis of violence by society or domestic violence. It is, however, important to note that gender denotes the way in which society expects males and females to behave and the roles it has created for them, in contrast to sex which is a purely biological construct. As a result, as gender is not static but is relevant to the particular society and time in which it is discussed, the roles assigned are likely to change over time. UNHCR has stressed that 'it should be noted that harmful practices in breach of international human rights law and standards cannot be justified on the basis of historical, traditional, religious or cultural grounds'.[51] However, it is also vital to note that while discrimination and persecution on the basis of gender usually affects women, this is not always the case. Other groups which, by their mere existence, challenge the values and roles established by patriarchal societies also frequently encounter persecution on the basis of gender, this includes homosexuals, transsexuals and transgendered people. While, without doubt, discrimination occurs frequently on the basis of gender, the absence of gender as a Convention ground for claiming refugee status leads to the issue as to whether the treatment encountered must be linked to a Convention ground (e.g. social group, political opinion and religion). In other words can gender *per se* constitute a distinct ground for claiming a refugee status? A response to these issues could be provided in the following manner. While gender has been established as a factor behind many occurrences of persecution, this in itself is not enough to claim refugee status. Persecution due to gender must also be linked with a Convention ground, whether 'religion', 'political opinion' or 'social group'. Periodic attempts to include gender within the

---

[49] See Ghanea, *Human Rights, the UN and the Bahá'ís in Iran* (Brill, 2003).
[50] See Rehman, *The Weaknesses in the International Protection of Minority Rights* (Kluwer Law International, 2000) pp. 142–153; Rehman, 'Minority rights and the constitutional dilemmas of Pakistan' 19 *NQHR* (2001) 417.
[51] *UNHCR Guidelines on International Protection: Gender-Related Persecution*, above n.43 at para 5.

refugee definition have failed,[52] indicating that many States are uneasy with this concept. However, the 'proposition that all violence against women is political, or in its slightly less radical variant, that all violence against women should be presumed to be political unless and until the State is shown to provide effective protection',[53] perhaps indicates where this uneasiness stems from. It is unlikely that States that do not protect women or other groups persecuted on the grounds of gender sufficiently or, indeed, partake in persecution them-selves, will ever accept 'gender' as a Convention ground. So, while 'gender' may be included within 'social group', as highlighted by *Islam and Shah*,[54] gender does not of itself constitute a ground for persecution that could give rise to a claim for refugee status. Instead, as with sexual minorities, claims based on 'gender' must establish that they belong to a social group, which is discriminated against and persecuted as a group. Alternatively, and as often is the case, women have to claim refugee status on political or religious grounds.[55]

Additionally, it must also be established that the treatment encountered is sufficiently severe to qualify as persecution and does not fall short of the mark as discrimination. In addition to fitting within one of the Convention grounds, 'the persecution must be causally linked to that membership'.[56] This can be whether the claimant was initially persecuted for Convention reasons or, more importantly, regarding gender, if the State's inaction was for Convention reasons. As has been examined already, the subject of violence against women is extremely controversial – many societies are particularly sensitive when it comes to women's rights and violence against women or domestic violence is perceived a matter in which the State or the international community has no role to play.[57] However, as previ-ously discussed, private individuals can indeed be the perpetrators of persecution, pro-vided that the State does not or is unable to provide sufficient protection for the victim.[58] Additionally, 'refusal to conform to the gender-specific roles of a given society can lead to abuse . . . in such cases; women are persecuted because they transgress the roles that are imposed upon them'.[59] Forms of persecution that are inflicted upon women, simply as a result of gender, are innumerable. 'Genital mutilation, infanticide, forced marriage, spousal abuse, involuntary abortion, mandatory sterilisation, sexual assault, dowry-related murders, honour crimes, widow burning, mandatory dress codes, and trafficking in women' are all mentioned by Laviolette.[60] UNHCR added in its guidelines, 'punishment for the transgression of social mores'.[61] Additionally, '[w]here the penalty or punishment for non-compliance with, or breach of, a policy or law is disproportionately severe and has a gender dimension, it would amount to persecution'.[62]

---

[52] Goodwin-Gill and McAdam, above n.1 at p. 82.

[53] Ibid. at p. 81.

[54] See below for further discussion of *Islam and Shah*.

[55] See Sinha, 'Domestic Violence and U.S. Asylum Law: Eliminating the "Cultural Hook" for Claims Involving Gender-Related Persecution' 76 *New York University Law Review* (2001) 1562; Anker, 'Refugee Status and Violence Against Women in the "Domestic" Sphere: The Non-State Actor Question' 15 *Georgetown Immigration Law Journal* (2000/2001) 391.

[56] Heyman, 'Domestic Violence and Asylum: Toward a Working Model of Affirmative State Obligations', 17 *IJRL* (2005) 729 at p. 730.

[57] See above chapter 16.

[58] Ibid.

[59] Laviolette, 'Gender-Related Refugee Claims: Expanding the Scope of the Canadian Guidelines' 19 *IJRL* (2007) 169 at p. 173.

[60] Ibid. p. 173.

[61] UNHCR Guidelines on International Protection: Gender-Related Persecution, above n.43, para 3.

[62] Ibid. para 12.

As mentioned above, in respect of persecution on the grounds of gender, refugee status is occasionally claimed in respect of 'religion', in so far as religious custom may assign women certain roles, which in turn leads to their persecution in the event that they try to break away from this custom. Regarding 'political opinion', this is to be interpreted broadly, as 'to incorporate any opinion on any matter in which the machinery of State, government, society, or policy may be engaged'.[63] This includes, if women have or are believed to have expressed opposition to male cultural dominance or the roles imposed upon women by society. An imputed opinion is also sufficient to qualify as Convention grounds: for example, in many patriarchal societies it is believed that women hold the same political opinions as their male relatives.

In respect of women as a 'social group', within the meaning of the definition of a refugee, the group should 'share a common characteristic, other than their risk of being persecuted' or who are otherwise perceived by society to constitute a group, these characteristics are 'often innate, unchangeable or otherwise fundamental to identity, conscience or the exercise of one's human rights'.[64] Taking into account the widespread violence and abuse that takes place in many societies, a further sub-categorisation was developed in the UK case of *Islam and Shah*. In *Islam and Shah* the House of Lords recognised that women in particular societies were recognised as a 'social' group.[65] The applicants were successful since they were able to establish that they suffered violence in their country of origin and they had been abandoned by their husbands, who falsely accused them of adultery. Both women were forced to flee and sought refugee status in the United Kingdom. They lacked any male protection and feared persecution by the local community for sexual misconduct if returned to Pakistan.[66] The State sanctioned or at least tolerated the persecution that the women were likely to suffer.

Children – perhaps more than women – occupy a vulnerable position.[67] In many societies, children are subjected to violence, and refugee claims have been recognised in a number of States in instances where children face the risk of being force to live on the streets in order to escape violence at home,[68] or are otherwise abandoned because of death or absence of family.[69] Commenting on the position of refugee or displaced children, the Special Rapporteur on Human Rights and Disability makes the following sobering observations. He notes that:

> it would not be right to ignore the tragic situation of displaced or refugee children, of whom there are approximately 15 million today and who, in addition to the risks from the conflicts themselves, must suffer the heart-rending trauma of being uprooted. In many cases they are also forced to change residence frequently. The displaced are frequently subjected to military controls when travelling from one temporary camp to another, and they are not allowed to

---

[63] Ibid. para 32.
[64] Ibid. para 29.
[65] *Islam v. Secretary of State for the Home Department, R v. Immigration Appeal Tribunal and Secretary of State for Home Department ex parte Shah* [1999] 2 WLR 1015.
[66] See Goodwin-Gill, 'Judicial Reasoning and "Social Group" after Islam and Shah' 11 *IJRL* (1999) 537; Vidal, '"Membership of a Particular Social Group" and the Effect of Islam and Shah' 11 *IJRL* (1999) 528.
[67] See Russell, 'Unaccompanied Refugee Children in the United Kingdom' 11 *IJRL* (1999) 126. See above chapter 17.
[68] See MZR(Re). Nov97-03500 [1999] CRDD No. 118, 31 May 1999.
[69] See QDS (Re), Nos. A99-00215, A99-00256, A99-00258 [1999] CRDD No. 235, 30 September 1999.

resume their normal lives. Unlike refugees, who because they have crossed frontiers can have the immediate support and protection of the United Nations High Commissioner for Refugees, displaced persons usually have greater difficulty in obtaining international protection since they remain in their own countries. This raises a series of problems when one or both parties to the conflict limit or prevent access to aid and rehabilitation.[70]

Additional factors come into play when assessing the right of a child to claim asylum. Whether the child in question is accompanied by an adult and who will act in the child's best interests, are of particular importance. The particularly vulnerable nature of children, as established above, is also of relevance. When it comes to assessing the claims and needs of the child the following instruments provide useful guidance: the UN Convention on the Rights of the Child, relevant regional and national laws, the provisions of the Refugee Convention and other relevant regional and national laws.[71] The UNHCR Guidelines on Determining the Best Interests of the Child also attempts to address the unique situation of child refugees.

Children may be unaccompanied as a result of a variety of factors. Goodwin-Gill and McAdam mention, 'abduction, when they are sent out of the country of origin by parents who remain behind, or when parents return home. Military recruitment of minors, detention or internment of parents, and the actions of aid workers have also led to children being separated from their families'.[72] Regardless of the reason for their being unaccompanied, unaccompanied children are in a particularly vulnerable situation. While accompanied children have an adult to act in their best interests, unaccompanied children are left to face the asylum system alone. Generally speaking, accompanied children will be awarded or not awarded status 'in the context of family unity'.[73]

The Convention on the Rights of the Child, establishes that 'the best interests of the child shall be a primary consideration in all actions affecting children'.[74] The special protection required by children who are seeking refugee status is also highlighted in Article 22 of the Convention on the Rights of the Child. It provides as follows:

1. States Parties shall take appropriate measures to ensure that a child who is seeking refugee status or who is considered a refugee in accordance with applicable international or domestic law and procedures shall, whether unaccompanied or accompanied by his or her parents or by any other person, receive appropriate protection and humanitarian assistance in the enjoyment of applicable rights set forth in the present Convention and in other international human rights or humanitarian instruments to which the said States are Parties.

2. For this purpose, States Parties shall provide, as they consider appropriate, co-operation in any efforts by the United Nations and other competent intergovernmental organizations or non-governmental organizations co-operating with the United Nations to protect and assist such a child and to trace the parents or other members of the family of any refugee

---

[70] Despouy, *Human Rights and Disabled Persons*, Human Rights Studies Series No. 6, UN Sales No. E.92XIV.4 (1992), available at www.un.org/esa/socdev/enable/dispaperdes0.htm <last visited 15 March 2009> para 132.

[71] See above chapter 17. See also McAdam, 'Seeking Asylum under the Convention on the Rights of the Child: A Case for Complementary Protection' 14 *International Journal of Children's Rights* (2006) 251.

[72] Goodwin-Gill and McAdam, above n.1, at p. 477.

[73] Ibid. p. 130.

[74] Article 3 UN Convention on the Rights of the Child. For analysis see above chapter 18.

> child in order to obtain information necessary for reunification with his or her family. In cases where no parents or other members of the family can be found, the child shall be accorded the same protection as any other child permanently or temporarily deprived of his or her family environment for any reason, as set forth in the present Convention.[75]

Goodwin-Gill and McAdam suggest that taking Article 1A(2) of the Refugee Convention along with Article 3 of the CRC and acting in the best interests of the child 'may also constitute a complementary ground of protection in its own right'.[76] This may be particularly relevant in cases of generalised violence against the children.

The UNHCR Guidelines of May 2008 emphasise the importance of family reunification in cases of unaccompanied minors, unless this is likely to result in abuse or neglect.[77] However, adoption in cases of prolonged separation may be considered to be in the best interests of the child. The Guidelines also establish procedure in the case that the parents of the child in question have been returned to their country of origin,[78] and in cases of severe harm by the parents.[79]

The Refugee Convention of 1951, despite providing for basic rights including protection and primary education, has not proven to be satisfactory when dealing with the situation of refugee children, particularly unaccompanied minors. The UN through the Convention on the Rights of the Child and the UNHCR's Guidelines, have attempted to establish a framework, in order to deal with the unique situation of child refugees.

The issue of sexual minorities is also one that easily falls within the concept of 'social group' and gender. Patriarchal societies often discriminate and persecute sexual minorities as a result of their breaking away from societal norms and the roles assigned to them. While '[s]ocial, political, and legal disapproval of homosexuality is often a reaction to the non-compliance to gender and social roles that a simple expression of contempt for the sexual practices of homosexuals',[80] punishment for 'homosexual conduct' is usually tantamount to persecution. This includes in many cases corporal punishment, and in countries such as Iran, the death penalty.

(d) Well-founded fear of persecution

A claim for refugee status must be based upon the claimant's 'well-founded fear of persecution' on the basis of one of the grounds enumerated within Article 1A. However, the highly subjective concept of 'well-founded fear' requires that decision-makers address whether the claimant's beliefs are reasonable and justified. Thus, this ensures the inconsistent application of the definition from State to State and, indeed, by different adjudicators within the same State. The UNHCR Handbook attempts to clarify what is meant by 'well-founded fear'. However, the suggestion that attention should be paid not only to the objective situation in the country but also to look at the credibility of the claimant's fear and his or her ability to cope with the persecution suffered, does not seem to clarify the matter. 'An

---

[75] *UNHCR Guidelines on Determining the Best Interests of the Child*, May 2008 p. 14.
[76] Goodwin-Gill and McAdam, above n.1, at p. 324. See also McAdam, above n.71.
[77] *UNHCR Guidelines on Determining the Best Interests of the Child*, above n.62, at p. 31.
[78] Ibid. p. 33.
[79] Ibid. p. 38.
[80] Laviolette, above n.59, at p. 185.

evaluation of the subjective element is inseparable from the assessment of the personality of the applicant, since psychological reactions of different individuals may not be the same in identical conditions.[81] Such an approach is necessary when dealing with such a subjective element of a right. The UNHCR suggests evaluating whether the fear of suffering persecution is reasonable, '[e]xaggerated fear, however, may be well-founded if, in all the circumstances of the case, such a state of mind can be regarded as justified'.[82] Whether, the claimant has already been the victim of persecution may also aid him or her in proving that his or her fear of persecution is 'well-founded', but this is not a requirement.[83] Therefore, evaluating whether a claimant's fear of persecution is justified is subject to a number of conditions, ranging from the psychological health of the claimant to the situation in the country of origin. The 1951 Convention does not define 'persecution', thus ensuring that, 'the elasticity of the definition of persecution depends upon the political will of Member States implementing the Convention'.[84] Persecution is associated with torture and in this context our examination and understanding of the constituent elements of 'torture' as well as jurisprudence on 'torture' remains highly relevant.[85] The broader definition of persecution may also incorporate 'cruel, inhuman or degrading treatment or punishment'.[86] The counters of cruel, inhuman and degrading treatment or punishment are malleable and yet to be firmly established. Again, the UNHCR suggests that 'due to variations in the psychological make-up of individuals and in the circumstance of each case, interpretations of what amounts to persecution are bound to vary'.[87] Particularly where discrimination is involved the UNHCR has suggested that persecution can be claimed on 'cumulative grounds'. Whereas an act of discrimination in itself may not be sufficient to claim refugee status, where this is combined with 'other adverse factors (e.g. a general atmosphere of insecurity in the country of origin)'[88] or 'where a person has been the victim of a number of discriminatory measures',[89] this may be enough to establish persecution.

Refugee status cannot be used as a means of avoiding punishment for a criminal law offence in the country of origin. That said, there are certain circumstances where the prosecution or punishment can amount to persecution. Thus, where the crime committed, discriminates against a certain sector of society, linked to Convention ground for claiming refugee status, for example the practice of Pentecostalism within Eritrea (religion) or taking part in homosexual acts in Iran (social group). Furthermore, the Refugee status is established if the punishment to be received is excessive, as long as this is linked to an enumerated ground, such as punishment in Saudi Arabia or Iran for not wearing a veil (social group, political opinion or religion).

A further question relates to persecution based on economic discrimination. State practice generally tends to bifurcate between 'economic migrants' and refugees. On the other hand, the line between economic discrimination and denial of fundamental rights is frequently blurred. Discrimination such as instances of deliberate denials of employment or deprivation of opportunities to earn a living ought to be considered as sufficiently

---

[81] *UNHCR Handbook*, above n.42, at para 40.
[82] Ibid. para 41.
[83] Ibid. para 45.
[84] Fitzpatrick, above n.30, at p. 240.
[85] See below chapter 22 and the case-law of the Committee against Torture.
[86] Goodwin-Gill and McAdam, above n.1, at pp. 90–91.
[87] *UNHCR Handbook*, above n.42, at para 52.
[88] Ibid. para 53.
[89] Ibid. para 55.

serious to be categorised as persecution.[90] Other instances of socio-economic rights could be categorised as 'persecution'. Denial of the right to receive education has been recognised as a form of persecution for the purposes of the Convention.[91] Similarly, deliberate and systematic denial of healthcare could also form the basis of a successful refugee claims. A common thread in the successful reliance on the violations of socio-economic rights is that denials of rights have been deliberate and discriminatory and have been based on one or more grounds as laid out in the 1951 Convention. The notion of persecution is specifically incorporated in the Statute of the International Criminal Court, when describing crimes against humanity.[92]

(v) Loss of refugee status

There are four sets of circumstances where a refugee may lose his status. This is, firstly, by reason of a voluntary action, such as for example, when the individual concerned him or herself suggests that the well-founded fear of persecution no longer exists. Evidence of such voluntary action would be the re-availment of the protection of the individual's country of origin or return to the country. Secondly, by reason of change of circumstances, which include political or other circumstances which remove the grounds of the previously held well-founded fear of persecution. A change from dictatorial to democratic regime would be a sound basis or improvement of human rights in the country. Thirdly, by reason of protection accorded by other States or international agencies; and finally in the case of serious criminal or such related activities. The latest provisions regarding the loss of refugee status is provided in Article 1F, which states:

F. The provisions of this Convention shall not apply to any person with respect to whom there are serious reasons for considering that:

(a) he has committed a crime against peace, a war crime, or a crime against humanity, as defined in the international instruments drawn up to make provision in respect of such crimes;

(b) he has committed a serious non-political crime outside the country of refuge prior to his admission to that country as a refugee;

(c) he has been guilty of acts contrary to the purposes and principles of the United Nations.

---

[90] The UK courts have recognised that a person's inability to secure employment for a convention reason, presents a 'serious issue' of an examination as to whether this amounts to persecution. *He* v. *Secretary of State for the Home Department* [2002] EWCA 1150, [2002] Imm AR 590 at paras 26, 38. Similar position has been advanced by Australian Courts see *Prahastono* v. *Minister for Immigration and Multicultural Affairs* (1997) 7 FCR 260 at 267.

[91] See *Ali* v. *Canada (Minister of Citizenship and Immigration)* [1997] 1 FCD 26.

[92] ICC Statute, Article 7: 'For the purpose of this Statute, "crime against humanity" means any of the following acts when committed as part of a widespread or systematic attack directed against any civilian population, with knowledge of the attack. . . . (h) Persecution against any identifiable group or collectivity on political, racial, national, ethnic, cultural, religious, gender as defined in paragraph 3, or other grounds that are universally recognized as impermissible under international law, in connection with any act referred to in this paragraph or any crime within the jurisdiction of the Court'. Article 7(2)(g) defines 'persecution' as meaning 'the intentional and severe deprivation of fundamental rights contrary to international law by reason of the identity of the group or collectivity'.

The offences mentioned and assumed in Article 1(F) are of a very serious nature. Exclusion clauses in human rights documents, by their very nature, have an exceptional nature. Article 1(F) should only be utilised when the crimes committed are so grave that the perpetrators are undeserving of protection.[93] Due to the grave consequences that exclusion could have on the claimant, it has also been urged that States apply this clause with extreme caution.[94] The aim of the exclusion clause is not to protect a country from potential criminals, this is provided by Articles 32 and 33(2), but rather not to offer protection to those who may have themselves committed acts amounting to persecution.[95] It is perhaps useful here to highlight the difference between the exclusion clause contained within Article 1(F) and Articles 32 and 33(2). Whereas Article 1(F) is concerned with refusal of refugee status to those who have committed certain acts, primarily prior to claiming refugee status, Articles 32 and 33(2) deal with future risk, that is they are concerned with the behaviour of a refugee after status has been granted.[96] As such, they do not remove status (unlike a violation of Article 1(F)), from a person who already has been granted status but rather repeal the right to *non-refoulement*. It has been suggested that a decision regarding Articles 32 and 33(2) be best made at asylum review hearings.[97] It should also be noted, that while status can be withdrawn or denied due to one of the reasons enumerated in Article 1(F), this does not mean that States are obliged to take any further action. In fact, as a result of human rights obligations, it is prohibited for States to return individuals, if they are to face torture, under Article 3 ECHR and Article 3 of the Convention against Torture, regardless of the fact as to whether or not they are excluded from refugee status.[98] Therefore, it has been correctly argued that Article 3 of the Convention against Torture provision provides a stronger guarantee in that unlike Article 33 of the Convention on the Status of the Refugees, Article 3 permits no exceptions to the principle of *non-refoulement*.[99] As we shall be examining in due course, Article 3 of the Convention against Torture is non-derogable in nature, emphasises the fundamental right of *non-refoulement* and is now considered part of customary international law.[100]

Article 1(F)(a) addresses the most serious international crimes that an individual can commit. 'Crimes against peace', 'war crimes' and 'crimes against humanity' are terms derived from Article VI of the International Military Tribunal (IMT) Charter and have

---

[93] *UNHCR Guidelines on International Protection*: Application of the Exclusion Clauses: Article 1(F) of the 1951 Convention relating to the Status of Refugees, HCR/GIP/03/05, para 2.

[94] Ibid. para 2.

[95] The European Council on Refugees and Exiles, Position on Exclusion from Refugee Status PP1/03/2004/Ext/CA 16 *IJRL* (2004) 257, p. 258

[96] *UNHCR Guidelines on International Protection*: Application of the Exclusion Clauses above n.93, at para 4.

[97] Blake, 'Exclusion from Refugee Protection: Serious Non Political Crimes after 9/11' 4 *Eur. J. Migrat. Law* (2002) 425, p. 431.

[98] *Chahal* v. *UK* (1996) 23 E.H.R.R. 413, See also, Lambert, 'Protection Against *Refoulement* from Europe: Human Rights Law Comes to the Rescue' 48 *ICLQ* (1999) 515.

[99] Goodwin-Gill and McAdam, above n.1, at p. 301. The view taken by the Canadian Supreme Court in *Suresh* v. *Canada* [2002] 1 SCR 3, which attempted to balance individuals interests with those of the State's national security has been criticised by the Human Rights Committee 'Consideration of Reports: Concluding Observations on Canada'. UN doc. CCPR/C/79/Add.105 (7 April 1999), para 13. Also note the position of the European Court of Human Rights in *Selmouni* v. *France* (1999) 29 E.H.R.R. 403, para 95.

[100] Kjærum, 'Article 14' in Alfredsson and Eide (eds), *The Universal Declaration of Human Rights: A Common Standard of Achievement* (Kluwer Law International, 1999) pp. 279–295 at p. 285. However, note that by its nature Article 3 *non-refoulement* provisions are restricted to acts of torture – this is in contrast to Article 7 ICCPR, Article 3 ECHR and Article 5 ACHR which are not restricted to torture. See Goodwin-Gill and McAdam, above n.1, at p. 302.

been used subsequently by major instruments of international criminal law.[101] The IMT Charter principles influenced the 1949 Geneva Conventions and the 1977 Protocols. These principles were subsequently deployed by the Statutes of international tribunals for the former Yugoslavia and Rwanda and the Statute of the International Criminal Court.[102] It is for the prosecution to establish that the individual concerned has committed the crimes and acts in question.[103] This provision applies regardless of when the crimes were committed. Therefore, refugee status can be removed for crimes committed after it has being granted. 'Crimes against peace', were defined in the London Charter as being the 'planning, preparation, initiation or waging of a war of aggression, or a war in violation of international treaties, agreements, or assurances, or participation in a common plan or conspiracy for the accomplishment of any of the foregoing'. 'War crimes', have been established as, 'wilful killing and torture of civilians, launching indiscriminate attacks on civilians, and wilfully depriving a civilian or a prisoner of war of the rights of fair and regular trial', amongst other things.[104] Whereas 'crimes against humanity' have been characterised by their nature as a widespread or systematic attack on the civilian population by way of genocide, murder, rape and torture.[105] As Article 1(F)(a) addresses the most heinous of crimes, that are widely documented in international law, there is little confusion as to what falls within this provision. The seriousness of the crimes is of particular relevance when considering that:

[s]ince the commission of such crimes may themselves amount to persecution, the perpetrators should not benefit from refugee protection. By excluding them from refugee status, the integrity of the international system of refugee protection shall be preserved. Thus, the exclusion clause must be understood as a reinforcement of the central purpose of international refugee law, namely the protection of those fleeing persecution.[106]

Article 1(F)(b) deals with 'serious non-political crime', this provision, however, only deals with crimes committed outside the State of refuge and prior admission as a refugee. The provisions of Article 1(F)(b) are meant to avoid a situation where a criminal is provided sanctuary as a refugee. The provision excludes 'serious non-political' crimes. These undoubtedly include crimes against physical integrity, life and liberty.[107] Thus, in cases of fugitives escaping from crimes such as murder, manslaughter, rape, serious and aggravated assaults, robbery and drug-offences, they would be excluded from the ambit of the Refugee Convention. UNHCR expressly exclude 'minor crimes' and 'prohibitions on the legitimate exercise of human rights' from the definition of 'serious non-political crimes'.[108]

---

[101] International Military Tribunal Charter, also known as the London Charter and the Nuremburg Charter, in Agreement for the Prosecution and Punishment of the Major War Criminals of the European Axis (London Agreement), 8 August 1945, 58 Stat. 1544, E.A.S. No. 472, 82 U.N.T.S. 280. See below chapter 20.

[102] See below chapters 20 and 21.

[103] See the Canadian cases of *Ramirez* v. *Minister of Employment and Immigration* [1992] 2 FC 306, (FCA), para 5; *Xie* v. *Minister of Citizenship and Immigration* [2004] FCA 250, (2004) 243 DLR (4th) 395.

[104] UNHCR Guidelines on International Protection: Application of the Exclusion Clauses, above n.93, at para 12.

[105] Ibid. para 13.

[106] The European Council on Refugees and Exiles above n.95, at p. 258.

[107] Goodwin-Gill and McAdam, above n.1, at p. 177.

[108] UNHCR Guidelines on International Protection: Application of the Exclusion Clauses above n.93, at para 14.

Historically, States have given asylum or at least some measure of protection to the perpetrators of political crimes in other States, as is evidenced by extradition treaties.[109] However, the concept of political crime is particularly difficult to define. Blake suggests that:

> [s]ome offences are inherently political: treason, sedition, the adherence to a particular religious or political group held in disfavour, the propagation of ideas the state opposes and the like; some are political in context such as offences of violence and disorder committed in the course of political action to change a regime or its policies; some are made political in the hands of the prosecutor selectively targeting for prosecution and excessive punishment of political or ethnic opponents for apparently neutral offences.[110]

While some crimes are inherently political, it is often necessary to examine the motive of the perpetrator in order to establish the nature of the act. Additionally, the concept of 'political' varies considerably from State to State, further confusing the situation. It is often necessary to consider the nature of the State in which the crime was committed. In the event that there is no recourse to democratic means, it is more justifiable to resort to violent means than in democratic States where more peaceful alternatives are available.[111] As shall be considered in due course, denial of the right to self-determination as well as the refusal to authorise legitimate political dissent led many organisations to be labelled as 'terrorist' by repressive and undemocratic States.[112] Therefore, a more elaborate set of criteria is necessary in order to decide what is meant by a 'non-political crime'. In *T* v. *Secretary of State for the Home Department*, Lord Lloyd attempted a description of the required characteristics of a political crime, stating:

> only if (1) it is committed for a political purpose, that is to say, with the object of overthrowing or subverting or changing the government of a State or inducing it to change its policy; and (2) there is a sufficiently close and direct link between the crime and the alleged political purpose. In determining whether such a link exists, the court will bear in mind the means used to achieve the political end, and will have particular regard to whether the crime was aimed at a military or governmental target, on the one hand, or a civilian target on the other, and in either event whether it was likely to involve the indiscriminate killing or injuring of members of the public.[113]

The UNHCR in its Guidelines on the Exclusion Clauses further elaborates:

> A serious crime should be considered non-political when other motives (such as personal reasons or gain) are the predominant feature of the specific crime committed. Where no clear link exists between the crime and its alleged political objective or when the act in question is disproportionate to the alleged political objective, non-political motives are predominant. The motivation, context, methods and proportionality of a crime to its objectives are important factors in evaluating its political nature. The fact that a particular crime is designated as non-political in an extradition treaty is of significance, but not conclusive in itself.[114]

---

[109] Blake, above n.97, at p. 429.
[110] Ibid. p. 430.
[111] Ibid. p. 433.
[112] See below chapter 24; also above chapter 14.
[113] *T* v. *Secretary of State for the Home Department* [1996] AC 742 at p. 788.
[114] *UNHCR Guidelines on International Protection*: Application of the Exclusion Clauses, above n.93 at para 14.

18

Rights of refugees and internally displaced persons

However, as shall be examined in relation to terrorism, it is often a problematic subject to decide whether a particular offence has been committed due to personal reasons or gain, or the action in question was a consequence of genuine political motives. The serious nature of the offence, in particular if it has been disproportionate, should in principle outweigh the political nature of the offence. That said, controversy surrounds the entire debate on 'terrorism', 'terrorist offences' and 'offences of a political nature'.[115] It has not been possible to agree on a definition of 'terrorism' nor has it been possible to draft a global treaty dealing with acts of terrorism.[116]

Terrorism poses a substantial danger to international law and humanitarian values and has been roundly condemned by all international human rights instruments. The UDHR, in its final article states that nothing in the Declaration 'may be interpreted as implying for any State, group or person any right to engage in any activity or to perform any act aimed at the destruction of any of the rights contained in the Declaration'. Similar warnings are pronounced by Article 17 ECHR and Article 5 of ICCPR. As shall be noted shortly, a range of international and national instruments engage, condemn and criminalise various forms of terrorist activities.[117] A consequence of the failure to formulate agreed principles on terrorism has had an impact on refugee law; States may exclude individuals based on their alleged terrorist activities and thereby deny them both a refugee status and deprive them of the protection under the *non-refoulment* principle. Using the definitions of 'political' crimes above, it would be difficult to justify many terrorist acts on the grounds of proportionality, especially as they are primarily not aimed at the political figures that the individual terrorist or organisation may have a grievance against and are generally of a indiscriminate nature. Indeed, UNHCR in its guidelines established that '[e]gregious acts of violence, such as acts those commonly considered to be of a "terrorist" nature, will almost certainly fail the predominance test, being wholly disproportionate to any political objective'.[118] At the same time it is important to note that Article 1(F)(b) does not exclude all political violence against regimes.[119] Nevertheless, Blake notes that activity conducted abroad against a foreign regime of dubious democratic credentials is now seen to impact on the security of the host state'.[120] Thus leading to the suggestion, that whether violent political crime can be deemed as proportionate or not, may not be considered when excluding potential refugees from the ambit of the Convention.

In the United Kingdom, Article 55 of the Immigration, Asylum and Nationality Act 2006 authorises the Secretary of State to certify that the removal of the appellant would be conducive to the public good. Section 34 requires that in any appeal, no account is to be taken of the seriousness of the events or fear which may be relevant to an individual's claim to refugee status, or of any threat to his or her life or freedom; rights of appeal and review are restricted.[121] A thorny question which gained prominence in the aftermath of 11 September relates to the status of refugees whom the State authorities seek to expel on the basis of Article 1F(b) and Article 33(2) but face the risk of torture or ill-treatment if deported or expelled to their country of origin. As considered earlier, the jurisprudence as established

---

[115] See below chapter 24.
[116] Ibid.
[117] Ibid.
[118] *UNHCR Guidelines on International Protection*, above n.93, para 15.
[119] Blake, above n.97, at p. 438.
[120] Ibid. p. 431.
[121] Bruin and Wouters, 'Terrorism and the Non-Derogability of *Non-refoulement*' 15 *IJRL* (2003) 5.

by Article 3 ECHR and Article 3 of the Convention Against Torture appears to affirm that the prohibition of torture is absolute and cannot be subject to national security considerations.[122] However, it also needs to be noted that the prohibition from expulsion under the Convention Against Torture only applies in cases of the likely threat of torture and does not extend to cruel, inhuman and degrading treatment or punishment.[123]

Article 1(F)(c) is a broad provision which excludes a person from claiming refugee status if he or she has been guilty of acts which are contrary to the purposes and principle of the United Nations – these would include violations of human rights, terrorist activities or serious obstruction in the course of justice. The UNHCR has urged States to interpret this provision narrowly. However, it should also be noted that if a crime falls within Article 1(F)(c), there is a high chance that it also falls within one of the previous two exclusion clauses as well. The guidance given by UNHCR indicates that to fall within the ambit of this provision, the crime in question must be of an international nature and be a threat to peace.[124] In all likelihood, this is likely to be committed by someone in a position of power either in a State or a State-like entity. However, as noted above, terrorist activity can fall within this category but 'involves an assessment as to the extent to which the act impinges on the international plane – in terms of its gravity, international impact, and implications for international peace and security'.[125]

There is a need for caution when approaching exclusion clauses due to the potential devastating consequences for those individuals to whom they are to be applied. There is, additionally, a need to balance the threat posed by the individual with the severity of harm they are likely to suffer if returned to their country of origin.[126] However, although international human rights law has at least prevented those likely to be subjected to torture from being returned, the likelihood of indefinite internment without trial (against international human rights standards) is high. In the event that there is enough evidence to suggest that someone is involved in terrorist acts or serious crimes, and yet cannot be returned to their country of origin, surely a fair trial would be a far more legitimate way of dealing with the issue.[127]

4 REGIONAL APPROACHES TO REFUGEES

(i) Europe

The Treaty of Amsterdam (1997)[128] shifted asylum and immigration out of the intergovernmental decision-making process and into the area where legally binding instruments

---

[122] In *Chahal* v. *UK*, the European Court of Human Rights made the following, now celebrated remarks, 'Article 3 enshrines one of the most fundamental values of democratic society . . . The Court is well aware of the immense difficulties faced by States in modern times in protecting their communities from terrorist violence. However, even in these circumstances, the Convention prohibits in absolute terms torture or inhuman or degrading treatment or punishment, irrespective of the victim's conduct . . . Article 3 makes no provision for exceptions and no derogation from it is permissible under Article 15 even in the event of a public emergency threatening the life of the nation'. *Chahal* v. *UK* (1996), para 79; see also Andrysek, 'Gaps in International Protection and the Potential for Redress through Individual Complaints Procedure' 9 *IJRL* (1997) 392; and Lambert, above n.98.

[123] See discussion below in chapter 22.

[124] UNHCR Guidelines on International Protection: Application of the Exclusion Clauses, above n.93, para 17.

[125] Ibid.

[126] Blake, above n.97, at p. 427.

[127] Note the interesting position adopted by the United Kingdom through e.g. 'control orders'.

[128] Treaty of Amsterdam Amending the Treaty on European Union, the Treaties Establishing the European Communities and Related Acts, Official Journal C 340, 10 November 1997.

of harmonisation can be legislated by the Council of Ministers and a measure of judicial control exercise by the European Court of Justice. A new Treaty title 'Visas, asylum, immigration and other policies related to freedom of movement of persons' established a number of objectives: in particular within five years of the Treaty's entry into force, the European Council was required to 'adopt measures on asylum in accordance with the Geneva Convention of 28 July 1951 and the Protocol of 1967 relating to the status of refugees and other relevant treaties'.[129] Article 63 of the Treaty Establishing the European Community (TEC) also set out the framework for the development of EU minimum standards in regards to the temporary protection of displaced persons. Within the EU the relevant initiatives are the 2004 EU 'Qualification Directive'[130] for third country nationals or stateless persons (incorporating the 1951 Convention and 1967 Protocol as well as subsidiary protection under the 1950 European Convention on Human Rights and Fundamental Freedoms and State Practice) and the 2001 'Temporary Protection Directive'.[131]

The 2004 EU Qualification Directive, provides 'subsidiary protection',[132] that is an additional layer of protection provided by States on top of their 1951 Convention obligations based on the principle of *non-refoulement* and international human rights law. Under Article 2(e) of the Directive:

> 'person eligible for subsidiary protection' means a third country national or a stateless person who does not qualify as a refugee but in respect of whom substantial grounds have been shown for believing that the person concerned, if returned to his or her country of origin, or in the case of a stateless person, to his or her country of former habitual residence, would face a real risk of suffering serious harm as defined in Article 15, and to whom Article 17(1) and (2) do not apply, and is unable, or, owing to such risk, unwilling to avail himself or herself of the protection of that country.

Under Article 15, serious harm, as mentioned in Article 2(e) is defined as:

> (a) death penalty or execution; or
>
> (b) torture or inhuman or degrading treatment or punishment of an applicant in the country of origin; or
>
> (c) serious and individual threat to a civilian's life or person by reason of indiscriminate violence in situations of international or internal armed conflict.

---

[129] Article 63 TEC; G at p. 39.

[130] Council Directive 2004/83/EC of 29 April 2004 on minimum standards for the qualification and status of third country nationals or stateless persons as refugees or as persons who otherwise need international protection and the content of the protection granted.

[131] Council Directive 2001/55/EC of 20 July 2001 on minimum standards for giving temporary protection in the event of a mass influx of displaced persons and on measures promoting a balance of efforts between Member States in receiving such persons and bearing the consequences thereof.

[132] Outside the EU system this is known as 'complementary protection'.

Article 15(c) has been of particular concern for jurists, with Goodwin-Gill and McAdam pointing out:

> [w]hether or not the provision requires individuals actually to be singled out is unclear. To demand this would establish a higher threshold than is required for either Convention-based protection or under the EU Temporary Protection Directive. For article 15(c) to provide meaningful protection, it would seem that States will have to be relatively generous in determining the 'individual' aspect of the risk.[133]

Furthermore, exclusions do apply and are provided under Article 17(1) and (2). These provisions echo Article 1(F) and 33(2) of the 1951 Convention, however, some important differences should be noted. Article 17 of the Qualification Directive excludes those who have committed crimes against peace, war crimes or crimes against humanity,[134] along with those who have committed serious crimes,[135] those who have 'been guilty of acts contary to the purposes and principles of the United Nations'[136] and those considered a 'danger to the community or to the security of the Member State'.[137] Additionally, Article 17(2) extends these crimes 'to persons who instigate or otherwise participate in the commission of the crimes or acts mentioned therein'. Notably Article 17(1)(b) of the Directive includes all serious crime, while the 1951 Convention was careful only to exclude 'serious non-political crime'. The failure to exempt political crime from the scope of the exclusion clause could be used to exclude those who have taken part in opposition political movements in their State of origin, that would be deemed legitimate within a democratic State. While it can be assumed that those who find themselves in such a situation would be able to avail themselves of the protection afforded by the 1951 Convention, this limitation on the scope of applicability of the Qualification Directive is of concern. Additionally, the exclusion of those considered to be a danger to the security of the State goes further than the 1951 Convention. The Refugee Convention does not exclude such a person from qualifying as a refugee, it excludes them from benefiting from the principle of *non-refoulement* under Article 33, and thereby excludes them from the other provisions contained in the Convention.

The Qualification Directive has been praised for being 'the first supranational instrument to seek to harmonize domestic complementary protection', and has codified what were previously *ad hoc* arrangements.[138] However, there are a number of issues that have been raised with the protection extended. In addition to the ambiguity surrounding the protection offered by Article 15(c), the Directive has been criticised for codifying the minimum standard of protection offered by States and therefore, creating a hierarchy within those to which protection is extended.[139] The Directive also omits certain catgories of people needing protection.[140] Furthermore:

---

[133] Goodwin-Gill and McAdam, above n.1, at p. 328.
[134] Article 17(1)(a). *Cf.* Article 1.F(a) 1951 Convention.
[135] Article 17(1)(b). *Cf.* Article 1.F(b) 1951 Convention.
[136] Article 17(1)(c). *Cf.* Article 1.F(c) 1951 Convention.
[137] Article 17(1)(d). *Cf.* Article 33(2) 1951 Convention.
[138] McAdam, 'The European Union Qualification Directive: The Creation of a Subsidiary Protection Scheme' 17 *IJRL* (2005) 461 at pp. 461–462.
[139] Ibid. p. 462. Goodwin-Gill and McAdam, above n.1, p. 329.
[140] Ibid. p. 462. Goodwin-Gill and McAdam, above n.1, p. 329.

> [i]t is well documented that some States interpret the Convention definition extremely narrowly, in order to provide subsidiary protection to the majority of applicants for international law protection, since it is regulated outside the international law regime, subject to greater domestic discretion and frequently provides a lower level of protection.[141]

(ii) Africa

The OAU/AU Convention Governing the Specific Aspects of Refugee Problems in Africa 1969, is a binding regional treaty which has extended refugee protection past that granted by the 1951 Convention and the 1967 Protocol. There are several particularly innovative concepts contained within the OAU/AU Refugee Convention. These are contained within Article 1, on the definition of a refugee; Article 2, which includes *non-refoulement*, temporary refuge and burden sharing; and Article 5 on voluntary repatriation.

Despite Article 1(1) of the 1969 Convention being consistent with the definition of a refugee contained within the 1951 Refugee Convention and 1967 Protocol, Article 1(2) significantly extended the scope of the 1951 Convention. This states that:

> The term 'refugee' shall also apply to every person who, owing to external aggression, occupation, foreign domination or events seriously disturbing public order in either part or the whole of his country of origin or nationality, is compelled to leave his place of habitual residence in order to seek refuge in another place outside his country of origin or nationality.

Thus, it introduced the 'group-based conception' into international refugee law.[142] Article 1(2) removed the condition of an individualised threat to the life of the claimant as well as the conditions of deliberateness and discrimination.[143] 'They allowed the grant of refugee status to asylum seekers whose fears were grounded in the accidental but nonetheless dangerous consequences of intensive fighting and associated random lawlessness in their countries of origin.'[144] Within this extended definition of a refugee, it is also important to note that there is no reason for the asylum-seeker in question to establish a 'well-founded fear', in the same way as with Article 1(1) and the Refugee Convention 1951. Instead the general situation in the country is to be taken into account. However, the terminology used within Article 1(2) has been criticised for the lack of a firm definition, this particularly applies to 'external aggression'.[145]

As noted earlier, within the OAU/AU convention the principle of *non-refoulement* is declared without any exceptions. Meaning that the right to *non-refoulement* in the OAU/AU Convention has been also extended, in comparison with Article 33 of the 1951 Convention.

---

[141] Ibid. p. 464.

[142] Fitzpatrick, above n.30, at p. 234.

[143] Turner, 'Liberian Refugees: A Test of the 1969 OAU Convention Governing the Specific Aspects of the Refugee Problem in Africa' 8 *Geo. Imm. L. J.* (1994) 281 at p. 298; Arboleda, 'Refugee Definition in Africa and Latin America: The Lessons of Pragmatism' 3 *IJRL* (1991) 185 at p. 195. See also Okoth-Obbo, 'Thirty Years On: A Legal Review of the 1969 OAU Refugee Convention Governing the Specific Aspects of Refugee Problems in Africa' 20 *Refugee Survey Quarterly* (2001) 79.

[144] Arboleda, ibid. p. 195.

[145] Ibid. p. 195.

This ensures that while it is not mandatory to grant refugee status to anyone considered a threat to national security, he may not be returned to 'a territory where his life, physical integrity or liberty would be threatened'.[146] The concept of temporary residence is also contained within Article 2:

> Where a refugee has not received the right to reside in any country of asylum, he may be granted temporary residence in any country of asylum in which he first presented himself as a refugee pending arrangement for his resettlement in accordance with the preceding paragraph.[147]

This is not mandatory, as indicated by the language 'may be granted temporary residence', however, in the event that an asylum-seeker does not qualify as a refugee within the terms of the Convention it is still possible for them to be awarded temporary residence. This, however, is at the discretion of the State and is without the safeguards that a refugee would be granted. This concept is basically codifying what was previously considered to be a customary norm.[148] Also contained within Article 2 is the concept of burden sharing, attempting to lighten the burden of countries of first refuge by appealing to 'the spirit of African solidarity'.[149]

The inclusion of voluntary repatriation within the OAU/AU Convention highlights the economic and social difficulties of the region. While the emphasis in this clause must be placed upon 'voluntary', in order not to breach the principle of *non-refoulement*, this clause is aimed, again, at relieving the burden on receiving States and communities. As has been highlighted by Turner, '[v]oluntary repatriation is the most viable and durable solution for Africa because of the poverty of many African nations, which makes them incapable of integrating large numbers of refugees'.[150] The large numbers of refugees that cross borders in order to avoid internal aggression makes this clause all the more vital: the vast majority of refugees also intend to return to their country of origin once the threat to their life has dissipated. The awareness of the difficulties that States may face in honouring their obligations under the OAU/AU Convention is highlighted by Article 2(1) which proclaims that member States 'shall use their best endeavours . . . to receive refugees and to secure the settlement'.[151]

The reasons for extending the Refugee Convention of 1951 are numerous. However, it can be said that this was a response to the situation in the region at the time of the negotiation and adoption of the Convention. This reflected 'the realities of Africa during a period of violent struggle for self-determination and national development'.[152] The reasons for flight became less clear cut than in the immediate aftermath of World War Two in Europe, and the OAU Convention merely intended to reflect this fact. However, it can also be said that the OAU Convention highlights the inadequacies of the 1967 Protocol. The Protocol fails to ensure the applicability and appropriateness of international refugee law to the situation in Africa. Fitzpatrick asserts that:

[146] Article 2(3) OAU Convention.
[147] Article 2(5) OAU Convention.
[148] Turner, above n.143, at p. 299.
[149] Article 2(4) OAU Convention.
[150] Turner, above n.143, at p. 298.
[151] Article II.
[152] Arboleda, above n.143, at p. 186.

Rights of refugees and internally displaced persons

18

the roughly contemporaneous drafting of the 1969 Organization of African Unity (OAU) Convention Governing the Specific Aspects of Refugee Problems in Africa indicated that policy-makers, including the UNCHR, were well aware of the new dimensions of the refugee challenge by the time the Protocol was drafted.[153]

(iii) The Americas

Latin America has been historically known for its generous asylum regime concerning political refugees. However, it is only recently and with the conception of the Cartagena Declaration of 1984 that this has been formally extended to include other groups. The Cartagena Declaration is a non-binding document and notably is not connected to a regional organisation in the same way as the OAU/AU Convention. Instead it came from a colloquium of *ad hoc* specialists in addition to government representatives.[154] While there was not a political will for a binding document relating to refugee issues, this Declaration, partly due to its flexible and practical nature, has been widely used and is thought to have 'concretized regional, customary international law principles with respect to the protection and assistance of refugees'.[155] It should also be noted that the Declaration was introduced at a time when many Latin American countries were not party to the Refugee Convention and Protocol or had only recently ratified them.[156] Nevertheless, the Cartagena Declaration has been described as 'an innovative and creative regional approach for guaranteeing protection to those who require it that goes well beyond in its proposal of a broad definition of refugee'.[157]

While being described as analogous to the OAU/AU Convention and taking the lead from the OAU/AU regarding the extension of the refugee definition,[158] the definition of a refugee contained within the Cartagena Declaration extends the concept even further to include:

refugees persons who have fled their country because their lives, safety or freedom have been threatened by generalized violence, foreign aggression, internal conflicts, massive violation of human rights or other circumstances which have seriously disturbed public order.

The inclusion of 'massive violation of human rights' is of particular note. This broader definition, similarly to the OAU/AU Convention, has enabled group determinations of status when States are faced with large-scale influxes of asylum seekers.[159] Another point of expansion has been that '[t]he Declaration includes the protection and treatment that should be offered to refugees during the entire cycle of forced displacement'.[160] Article 11 of the Cartagena Declaration has been considered pioneering due to the suggestion that a study be made:

---

[153] Fitzpatrick, above n.30, at pp. 233–234.
[154] Goodwin-Gill and McAdam, above n.1, at p. 38.
[155] Arboleda, above n.143, at p. 205.
[156] Discussion Document UNHCR, 'The Refugee Situation in Latin America: Protection and Solutions Based on the Pragmatic Approach of the Cartagena, Declaration on Refugees of 1984' 18 *IJRL* (2006) 252, p. 262.
[157] Ibid.
[158] Cartagena Decl. III 3.
[159] Discussion Document UNHCR, above n.156, at p. 268.
[160] Ibid. p. 262.

in countries in the area which have a large number of refugees, of the possibilities of integrating them into the productive life of the country by allocating to the creation or generation of employment the resources made available by the international community through UNHCR, thus making it possible for refugees to enjoy their economic, social and cultural rights.[161]

Additionally, '[i]n certain matters the Cartagena Declaration on Refugees of 1984 has undoubtedly been a pioneer. We refer specifically to the problem of internally displaced persons'.[162]

Despite the non-binding nature of the Cartagena Declaration, the Inter-American Commission has attempted to use it, along with the 1951 Convention, in the interpretation of Article 22(7) of the American Convention on Human Rights (1969) which states that: 'every person has the right to seek and be granted asylum in a foreign territory', as well as Article XXVII of the American Declaration of the Rights and Duties of Man (1948). This is part of the 'clear strategy of harmonization and standardisation of international law' exercised by the Court and Commission.[163] However, it is also important to note that the three largest refugee-receiving States within the Inter-American system, the United States, Canada and the Bahamas, are neither party to the Convention nor accept the jurisdiction of the Court.[164] This clearly limits the use of international refugee law and the Cartagena Declaration at a regional level. However, the Commission is still able to consider refugee issues in these three States in light of the Inter-American Declaration. There is, however, a focus on the civil and political rights of refugees and asylum seekers in comparison with the Cartagena Declaration which also considers economic, social and cultural rights.[165]

Despite the pioneering nature of the Cartagena Declaration and its use by the Inter-American Commission, it has been criticised for its wide reach and difficulty in interpreting its previously unused terminology.[166] However, the UNHCR in its discussion of the Declaration stated that:

[t]he Cartagena Declaration on Refugees of 1984 is one of the principal contributions of our region to the progressive development of International Refugee Law, and, as outlined in this document, many of the advances in the matter of the protection of refugees in Latin America are inspired and founded on the principles established in said regional instrument of non-binding character.[167]

The Mexico Declaration of 2004,[168] has been the latest step in the Latin American system of refugee protection. While not adding substantially to the Cartagena Declaration, the Mexico Declaration highlights some outstanding issues that have yet to be adequately addressed in reality. The Declaration made a point of '[r]eaffirming the principles of the

---

[161] Cartagena Decl. III 11.
[162] Discussion Document UNHCR, above n.156, at p. 266.
[163] Sandoval, 'A Critical View of the Protection of Refugees and IDPs by the Inter-American System of Human Rights: Re-assessing its Powers and Examining the Challenges for the Future' 17 *IJRL* (2005) 43 at p. 64.
[164] Ibid. p. 54.
[165] Ibid. pp. 64–65.
[166] Discussion Document UNHCR, above n.156, at p. 261.
[167] Discussion Document UNHCR, above n.156, at p. 269.
[168] Declaration of Mexico, OAS Doc. OEA/Ser.K/XXVII.2 REMIC-II/DEC. 1/04 cor. 1.

Rights of refugees and internally displaced persons

18

indivisibility and interdependence of all human rights and the need to provide comprehensive protection to refugees that guarantees the full enjoyment of their rights, in particular, civil, economic, social and cultural rights'.[169] Additionally, the need for finding a balance between fighting terrorism and the protection of refugee and human rights was highlighted.[170] The Plan of Action additionally stressed the importance of strengthening 'humanitarian and social programmes in border areas, emphasizing a geographic approach instead of a population approach, so that receiving communities benefit on equal footing with refugees and other persons in need of protection'.[171]

The fact that Latin American countries and the OAU/AU were willing to broaden the definition of refugee and extend protection to groups of people that would not be granted status under the 1951 Convention and 1967 Protocol reflects badly on countries in the West. While African and Latin American countries have been both economically and politically unstable, they have been willing to extend this definition on humanitarian grounds, in order to reflect the situation in their respective regions. The West, in contrast, has maintained a restrictive approach, even trying to limit the definition in some situations, despite being in a much better position both economically and politically to deal with large-scale influxes.

(iv) Non-refoulement

The principle of *non-refoulement* forms the core of the rights of the refugees. A central element of international protection for the refugee is the right not to be forcibly returned or expelled to a situation which would threaten one's life or freedom. This principle, known as the *non-refoulement* principle, as previously mentioned, is embodied in Article 33 of the 1951 Convention. Notwithstanding its importance, the principle of *non-refoulment* is of relatively recent usage within international treaty law. It was first explicitly mentioned in Article 3 of the 1933 Convention relating to the International Status of Refugees whereby the contracting parties undertook not to remove resident refugees or keep them from their territory 'by application of police measures, such as expulsions or non-admittance at the frontier ("refoulment")' unless necessary for the purpose of national security or public order. The principle of *non-refoulement* is provided in Article 33 of the 1951 Convention which provides as follows:

1. No Contracting State shall expel or return ('refouler') a refugee in any manner whatsoever to the frontiers of territories where his life or freedom would be threatened on account of his race, religion, nationality, membership of a particular social group or political opinion.
2. The benefit of the present provision may not, however, be claimed by a refugee whom there are reasonable grounds for regarding as a danger to the security of the country in which he is, or who, having been convicted by a final judgment of a particularly serious crime, constitutes a danger to the community of that country.

---

[169] 'Mexico Declaration and Plan of Action to Strengthen the International Protection of Refugees in Latin America', 17 *IJRL* (2005) 802 at p. 803.
[170] Ibid. p. 804.
[171] Ibid. p. 809.

The *non-refoulement* principle is applicable regardless of whether the individual has been granted a formal status of refugee by the receiving State and regardless of the illegality of the entry of the asylum-seeker. The construction of Article 33 has not been without controversy. A point in case is as to whether the Article only applies once an individual has entered a foreign State or could the principle form the basis of admission.[172] However, the consensus now seems to be that:

> States in their practice and in their recorded views, have recognized that *non-refoulement* applies at the moment at which asylum seekers present themselves for entry, either within a State or at its border. Certain factual elements may be necessary before the principle is triggered, but the concept now encompasses non-return and non-rejection.[173]

Indeed, a pragmatic view and one that is in accord with human rights law is to enforce the application of the principle for any individual to apply from the moment asylum-seekers present themselves for entry, either at the border or after having entered the State. This view is increasingly being reflected in State practices.[174]

After the Second World War the *non-refoulement* principle merged into the human rights protection of victims of persecution and is reflected in international human rights instruments. The principle of *non-refoulement* was adopted by the jurisprudence that developed around Article 3 of ECHR and Article 7 of the ICCPR. The principle finds an explicit expression in Article 3 of the United Nations Convention against Torture and Other Cruel, Inhuman or Degrading Treatment or Punishment which stipulates that '[n]o State Party shall expel, return ("refouler") or extradite a person to another State where there are substantial grounds for believing that he would be in danger of being subjected to torture'.[175] Furthermore, Article 3(2) goes on to provide that 'for the purpose of determining whether there are such grounds, the competent authorities shall take into account all relevant considerations including, where applicable, the existence in the State concerned of a consistent pattern of gross, flagrant or mass violations of human rights'.[176]

In the European Human Rights Court, considerable jurisprudence has accumulated around Article 3 of the ECHR. The European human rights case-law has established that an individual cannot be extradited, expelled or deported to a country where he or she faces a real risk of being subjected to torture, or to inhuman or degrading treatment or punishment. The prohibition on expulsion (unlike the case of the Convention against Torture) includes both a real risk of being subjected to torture, as well to inhuman or degrading

---

[172] According to Weis, the *non-refoulement* 'leads the way to the adoption of the principle that a State shall not refuse admission to a refugee, i.e. it shall grant him at least temporary asylum. If non-admission is tantamount to surrender to the country of persecution'. Weis, 'Legal Aspects of the Convention of 28 July 1951 relating to the status of refugees' 30 *BYIL* (1953) 478 at pp. 482–483.

[173] Goodwin-Gill and McAdam, above n.1, p. 208 (footnotes omitted).

[174] See Lord Bingham in *R. (European Roma Rights Centre and Others)* v. *Immigration Officer at Prague Airport (UNHCR Intervening)* [2004] UKHL 55, [2005] 2 AC 1, para 26. See also Lauterpacht and Bethlehem, 'The scope and content of the principle of *non-refoulement*' in Feller *et al.*, above n.1, pp. 87–181.

[175] Article 3(1) Convention against Torture.

[176] Article 3(2) Convention against Torture.

treatment or punishment.[177] That said, as we shall analyse shortly, the European Court of Human Rights is more prone to applying the principle of *non-refoulement* in cases where the risk of torture is involved.

The significant distinction which the European Court of Human Rights has established, is that the provisions of Article 3 are non-derogable and, therefore, no exceptions can be made to the aforementioned principle, even in instances where the individual's presence is likely to be a threat to national security, no matter how 'undesirable or dangerous' a threat an individual poses.[178] The European Union Qualification Directive 2004 prevents a member State from returning an individual, in circumstances where the individual faces the death penalty or execution, torture or inhuman or degrading treatment or punishment, to his or her native country, or to a 'serious and individual threat to a civilian's life or person by reason of indiscriminate violence in situations of international or internal armed conflicts'.[179]

There are, however, crucial distinctions in the application of *non-refoulement* principle within international human rights instruments. The European human rights institutions have drawn distinctions between torture on the one hand and 'inhuman, degrading treatment or punishment' on the other. However, in respect of *non-refoulement* it has yet to draw such a distinction, as Article 3 which incorporates both torture and inhuman and degrading treatment or punishment is non-derogable.[180] The provisions of Article 7 of ICCPR are also not restricted to torture alone and have been applied more broadly to acts of torture, as well cruel, inhuman and degrading treatment or punishment.[181] According to the Human Rights Committee, Article 7 contains a 'duty not to extradite, deport, expel or otherwise remove a person from the territory, where there are substantial grounds for believing that there is a real risk of irreparable harm, such as that contemplated by Article 6 and 7 of the Covenant, either in the country to which removal is to be effected or in any country to which the person may subsequently be removed'.[182] The 1949 Geneva Convention relative to the Protection of Civilian Persons in Time of War defines 'protected persons' as 'those who, at a given moment and in any manner whatsoever, find themselves, in case of a conflict or occupation, in the hands of a Party to the conflict or Occupying Power of which they are not nationals'.[183] Article 45 states *inter alia* that:

> [p]rotected persons shall not be transferred to a Power which is not a party to the Convention . . . In no circumstances shall a protected person be transferred to a country where he or she may have reason to fear persecution for his or her political opinions or religious beliefs.[184]

---

[177] See *D* v. *UK* (1997) 24 E.H.R.R. 423, where it was held by the Court that if the man – who was dying of AIDs-related complications – was deported to the Caribbean island of St Kitts, this would amount to 'inhuman treatment' and violate Article 3 of the Convention; also see Egan, 'Sanctuary in Strasbourg: The Implications of the European Convention on Human Rights on Irish Asylum Law and Policy' in Fraser and Harvey (eds), *Sanctuary in Ireland: Perspectives on Asylum Laws and Policy* (Institute of Public Administration, 2003) pp. 51–80.

[178] See Lambert, above n.98.

[179] Article 15, Council Directive 2004/83/EC of April 2004 on Minimum standards for the Qualification and Status of Third Country Nations or Stateless Persons as Refugees or as Persons OJ L304/12.

[180] See *Soering* v. *UK* (1989) 11 E.H.R.R. 439 *Chahal* v. *UK* (1996) 23 E.H.R.R. 413, *Ramzy* v. *The Netherlands* (Decision of 27 May 2008) Application No. 25424/05, for further discussion of this point.

[181] See above chapter 5.

[182] HRC, General Comment No. 31 (2004) on the Nature of Legal Obligations on States Parties to the Covenant, UN Doc. CCPR/C/21/Rev.1/Add.13 (2004), para 12.

[183] Article 4.

[184] Article 45.

The *non-refouelment* principle is also contained in regional instruments such as Article 2(3) of the 1969 OAU/AU Convention Governing the Specific Aspects of Refugee Problems in Africa, while Article 12(3) of the African Convention on Human and Peoples' Rights provides for a right to seek and obtain asylum. The 1969 American Convention on Human Rights also endorses the principle of *non-refoulement* in Article 22(8).

As noted earlier, the *refoulement* principle within the Refugee Convention is not an absolute principle – instead Article 33(2) of the Refugee Convention provides for two explicit exceptions. These relate firstly to 'national security' and secondly to 'public order'. An individual can be returned to the country of origin in cases of an individual posing a threat to the national security of the receiving State. However, these terms pose difficulties since the concepts of national security and public order are not defined by international law and their applicability remain at the discretion of the States. Lauterpacht and Bethlehem have argued that given the serious implication which the application of *refoulement* will have on an individual, States need to demonstrate both 'reasonable grounds' that the individual poses a risk to national security and that the threshold for establishing an exception to the *non-refoulement* principle ought to be very high.[185] It is not clear that a conviction of a serious offence on its own would provide sufficient evidence for Article 33(2) to be applicable (public order). In any event, it is a fundamental requirement that due process of law should be applied. A further issue relates to the extent to which the prohibition of returning a person to a State where they are likely to face torture, inhuman or degrading treatment or punishment overrides any qualifications contained in Article 33(2). Further issues arise as to what happens to an individual who notwithstanding coming under the ambit of Article 33(2) could not be removed due the wider application of the *non-refoulement* principle. As noted earlier, it is contended that while the individual concerned will lose this refugee status, they could still not be deported to the State where they face a serious risk of torture, etc.

Goodwin-Gill and McAdam argue that the *non-refoulment* principle as advanced in the 1951 Convention as well the wider *non-refoulment* principle as interpreted by human rights treaty bodies has now become a principle of customary international law. They make the point that:

> [b]oth article 33 of the 1951 Convention and article 3 of the 1984 Convention are of a 'fundamentally norm-creating character such as could be regarded as forming the basis of a general rule of law', as that phrase was used by the International Court of Justice in the *North Sea Continental Shelf* cases. The prohibition on *refoulement* to torture or cruel, inhuman or degrading treatment or punishment is absolute. The *refoulement* may be permitted under the 1951 Convention in exceptional circumstances does not deny this premise, but rather indicates the boundaries of discretion. So far as both provisions are formally addressed to the contracting parties, the universality of the principle of *non-refoulement* has nevertheless been a constant emphasis of other instruments including declarations, recommendations, and resolutions at both international and regional levels . . . The evidence relating to the meaning and scope of *non-refoulement* in its treaty sense amply supports the conclusion that today the principle forms part of general international law. There is substantial, if not conclusive, authority that the principle is binding on all States, independently of specific intent.[186]

---

[185] Lauterpacht and Bethlehem, 'The scope and content of the principle of non-refoulement: Opinion', UNHCR: 20 June 2001, www.unhcr.org/protect/PROTECTION/3b33574d1.pdf <last visited 15 October 2008>, para 169.

[186] Goodwin-Gill and McAdam, above n.1, at pp. 345–346.

Rights of refugees and internally displaced persons

Conditions in asylum detention in the host State can amount to violation of Article 3 of the European Convention. The Court has European Court of Human Rights has recognised that 'the State must ensure that a person is detained in conditions which are compatible with respect for his human dignity'.[187] Furthermore, the treatment received by asylum-seekers in the host State can by its nature lead to an independent violation of Article 3. Such an approach was adopted in the United Kingdom case *R. (on the applications of Adam, Tesema, and Limbuela) v. Secretary of State for the Home Department* (2004),[188] where it was held that the failure to provide shelter and assistance to destitute asylum-seekers amounted to a violation Article 3, European Convention on Human Rights. However, the jurisprudence of the European Court of Human Rights, has clearly established that such treatment should reach a minimum level of severity before constituting a violation of Article 3.

> [T]he Convention does not guarantee, as such, socio-economic rights, including the right to charge-free dwelling, the right to work, the right to free medical assistance, or the right to claim financial assistance from a State to maintain a certain level of living.
>
> To the extent that this part of the application related to Article 3 of the Convention, which prohibits torture or inhuman or degrading treatment, the Court observes, on the basis of the applicant's submissions, that her present living conditions do not attain a minimum level of severity.[189]

Whether refugees can constitute a minority in the receiving country and, thus, receive minority rights, has been a matter of some controversy. Article 27 of the International Covenant on Civil and Political Rights (ICCPR) states that:

> [i]n those States in which ethnic, religious or linguistic minorities exist, persons belonging to such minorities shall not be denied, in community with the other members of their group, to enjoy their own culture, to profess and practice their own religion, or to use their own language.

It is important as a starting point to note that the Article refers to 'persons' as opposed to 'nationals' or 'citizens', therefore ensuring that there is no proviso of nationality established by the provision itself. As examined in Chapter 13, Special Rapporteur Capotorti's definition of 'minorities' devised in the context of Article 27 of the ICCPR has been criticised *inter alia* because of his exclusion of non-nationals, including refugees, from the ambit of the protection accorded to minorities.[190] General Comments 15 and 23 of the ICCPR, further elaborate upon this. General Comment 15 on 'The Position of Aliens under the Covenant', specifically mentions the rights of aliens in the context of Article 27:

---

[187] See *Kalashnikov v. Russia*, ECtHR 2002, para 95.
[188] [2004] EWCA 540, [2004] QB 1440 All ER (D) 323, Judgments of 21 May 2004.
[189] *Pancenko v. Latvia*, Application No. 40772/98 (28 October 1999), para 2 http://cmiskp.echr.coe.int//// tkp197/viewhbkm.asp?action=open&table=F69A27FD8FB86142BF01C1166DEA398649&key=22148&sessio nId=20638395&skin=hudoc-en&attachment=true <last visited 15 March 2009>.
[190] See above chapter 14.

> In those cases where aliens constitute a minority within the meaning of article 27, they shall not be denied the right, in community with members of their group, to enjoy their own culture, to profess and practice their own religion and to use their own language.[191]

General Comment 23 on 'The Rights of Minorities', establishes that the aliens in question need not be permanent residents, specifically using migrant workers as an example of those aliens entitled to minority rights.[192] While General Comments are not binding, Article 27 of ICCPR is. Interpreting Article 27 in the light of General Comments 15 and 23, can only lead to the conclusion that refugees can constitute a minority. However, there is a considerable amount of discussion surrounding what constitutes a minority within the meaning of Article 27, and while it is possible for a group of refugees to be considered a minority, they nevertheless encounter the many hurdles within the definitional debates as were examined in our earlier examination.[193]

In 1993, as a consequence of a comprehensive note produced by the UNHCR, wide ranging guidelines and provisions were drafted for the protection of refugee women.[194] The UN General Assembly Declaration on the Elimination of Violence against Women recognises the violence against women in refugee camps and detention centres and condemns such actions.[195]

5 INTERNATIONAL LAW AND INTERNALLY DISPLACED PERSONS (IDPs)[196]

The internal displacement of persons presents a serious global challenge, more serious perhaps than the refugee crises. In terms of numbers and sheer impact, the internal displacement is more troubling – there are currently 51 million IDPs in over 40 States of the world. IDPs can be found in every continent though the problem is most noticeable in Africa and Asia. Africa contains nearly half of the worlds IDPs. From an international law perspective, IDPs remain the responsibility of the territorial State, however, in practice due to serious conflict the State in question may be unable or unwilling to accord any such protection. At the same time, State authorities are themselves often implicated in generating the exodus. As this chapter examines, generalised violence and lawlessness may not be covered under the ambit of international humanitarian law.[197] It is also the case that common Article 3 of the Geneva Conventions 1949, unlike human rights treaties, does not provide for any

---

[191] CCPR General Comment No. 15, The Position of Aliens under the Covenant (Twenty-seventh session, 1987) para 7.
[192] CCPR General Comment No. 23, The Rights of Minorities (Article 27) (Fiftieth session, 1994) para 5.2.
[193] See above chapter 13.
[194] See the Executive Committee Conclusion No. 73 (1993) on Refugee Protection and Sexual Violence Guidelines on preventing and responding to sexual violence have been formulated: 'Report of the Working Group on Refugee Women and Refugee Children' UN Doc. EC/SCP/85 (5 July 1994), para 42.
[195] UN Doc. A/RES/48/104, Goodwin-Gill and McAdam, above n.1 at p. 474; Deng, 'Dealing with the Displaced: A Challenge to the International Community' 1 *Global Governance* (1995) 45.
[196] Phuong, *The International Protection of Internally Displaced Persons* (Cambridge University Press, 2004); Geissler, 'The International Protection of Internally Displaced Persons' 11 *IJRL* (1999) 451.
[197] Goodwin-Gill and McAdam, above n.1, at p. 484.

enforcement mechanisms.[198] While the UNHCR has been actively involved in incidents of internal displacement since 1972, there has been a huge amount of uncertainty regarding who should be providing support for IDPs. As IDPs have not crossed international borders, they are not refugees and, indeed, fall outside of the ambit of UNHCR's work. This situation has been dogged by a number of issues, including the lack of a binding definition of an IDP and indeed a binding document addressing the issue, the lack of any single organisation willing to take responsibility for IDPs and in some cases even recognising that there is a problem, the encroachment into State sovereignty that international involvement would bring, and indeed making States accountable for their shortcomings when it comes to providing protection and basic support for IDPs.

One of the protracted issues in the establishment of a legal regime is that of formulating a legal definition. There is no universally agreed definition of IDPs. The lack of a definition, undoubtedly, does not help when it comes to apportioning responsibility to international agencies. In 1998, Francis Deng, the former Special Representative of the Secretary-General on human rights issues submitted a set of 'Guiding Principles on Internal Displacement' to the 54th Session of the Human Rights Commission providing a definition of IDPs. According to this definition, IDPs are:

> persons or groups of person who have been forced or obliged to flee or to leave their homes or places of habitual residence, in particular as a result of or in order to avoid the effects of armed conflict, situations of generalized violence, violations of human rights or natural or human-made disasters, and who have not crossed an internationally recognised State border.[199]

A further definition was devised by the ILA Committee on Internally Displaced Persons in 2000.[200] This definition omitted references to the root cause of natural or man-made disasters. There, thus, remains the controversy as to whether the regime of IDPs should cover 'natural or man-made disasters'. IDPs face a substantial difficulty in that their *de facto* legal situation remains unaltered. In order to invoke protection an assortment of principles from general international law are relied upon. These are largely principles of international human rights and international humanitarian law. In terms of international humanitarian law principles, common Article 3 of the Geneva Conventions is of great significance for the IDPs. Governments are keen to avoid recognising an internal armed conflict so as to avoid the applicability of common Article 3 and no objective definition of internal armed conflict has been forwarded. However, it is generally recognised that common Article 3 of the Geneva Convention is applicable in situations whenever an open armed conflict occurs within the territory of a State which are led by military units of a relatively organised structure and responsible command.[201] Protocol II to the 1949 Convention is also applicable to non-international armed conflict though it has a higher threshold as it requires substantial

---

[198] See below chapter 22.
[199] UN Doc. E/CN.4/1998/53/Add.2, Guiding Principles on Internal Displacement, Principle 2.
[200] International Law Association, 'The Declaration of International Law Principles on Internally Displaced Persons' 12 *IJRL* (2000) 672.
[201] See below chapter 21.

control of territory by a dissident armed force.[202] IDPs are generally protected by international human rights law. Fundamental rights, e.g. the right to life, the prohibition of torture and right to liberty, are all the rights that are needed most by people in distress and forcibly displaced. One important right regarding the plight of IDPs is the right to liberty to return to their homes. However, IDPs often find that the source of their problems is non-State actors, and while States are bound by international human rights law, this is not the case for non-State actors.[203] Article 16(3) of the Convention Concerning Indigenous and Tribal Peoples in Independent Countries (ILO) No. 169 is the only human rights treaty which provides for the right to return.[204] Another important right for the IDPs is that of *non-refoulement*, which is to be recognised on a basis which is similar to the refugees, save for the fact that IDPs invoke this right whilst within the territorial jurisdiction of the State.

Guiding Principles on Internal Displacement[205] and the ILA Declaration[206] provide for a detailed protection against forcible return.[207] They also provide for the right of family reunification. One of the major problems relates to the limitation of national sovereignty. During large-scale conflicts reliance can be placed on the work of IGOs, NGOs, UNHCR and ICRC. However, in the past the response of these organisations has been inconsistent with both huge protection gaps and significant overlap regarding the aid provided. The lack of a single organisation to take the lead and co-ordinate efforts has significantly hindered the situation. Furthermore, humanitarian assistance is dependent on the consent of the State.[208] One way to provide humanitarian assistance is through Chapter VII humanitarian intervention without the consent of the State. The interference with State sovereignty has been of concern to States when attempting to provide a solution to the problem.

It was certainly not the intention that UNHCR would deal with the situation of IDPs when it was given its mandate.[209] However, the fact that the situation of IDPs is of growing concern and their number is estimated to be significantly higher than that of refugees is without doubt an issue that requires attention from the international community. A frequent suggestion has been that owing to the similar plight of refugees and IDPs, UNHCR should be made responsible for IDPs. This is not to say the proposition is not

---

[202] Ibid.

[203] Goodwin-Gill and McAdam, above n.1, at p. 483.

[204] 72 ILO Bulletin 59 (1989); 28 I.L.M. 1382 (entry into force 5 September 1991).

[205] Guiding Principles on Internal Displacement, Contained in the annex of document E/CN.4/1998/53/Add.2 (11/02/1998) www.unhchr.ch/html/menu2/7/b/principles_lang.htm <last visited 2 November 2008>.

[206] International Law Association, Declaration of International Law Principles on Internally Displaced Persons, 29 July 2000.

[207] Article 5(1) of the ILA Declaration provides that 'All internally displaced persons have the right to return to their homes or places of habitual residence freely and in security and dignity, as soon as the conditions giving rise to their displacement have ceased'. Guiding Principles on Internal Displacement, E/CN.4/1998/53/Add.2 (11/02/1998) Principle 28(1) provides 'Competent authorities have the primary duty and responsibility to establish conditions, as well as provide the means, which allow internally displaced persons to return voluntarily, in safety and with dignity, to their homes or places of habitual residence, or to resettle voluntarily in another part of the country'. Such authorities shall endeavour to facilitate the reintegration of returned or resettled internally displaced persons. Principle 28(2) notes that 'Special efforts should be made to ensure the full participation of internally displaced persons in the planning and management of their return or resettlement and reintegration'.

[208] See above chapter 3 as regards the complications on interventions based on chapter VII (UN Charter).

[209] Ibid. p. 482.

controversial; indeed, a reading of UNHCR's statute indicates that the organisation lacks the legal competence to deal with IDPs, as they do not fall within the definition of a refugees as enumerated in Article 1 of the Refugee Convention.[210] Nevertheless, UNHCR in the past has relied upon a progressive reading of Article 9 of its Statute, in conjunction with General Assembly Resolutions, in order to extend its work to cover IDPs.[211] This extension of the mandate is dependent upon the consent of the UN General Assembly and the availability of funds in order to carry out the work. However, until recently the UNHCR's involvement with IDPs has been unpredictable[212] and selective.[213] 'UNHCR has been willing to become involved with internally displaced persons when such involvement contributes to the search for solutions to refugee problems.'[214]

Furthermore, UNHCR's involvement with IDP issues is controversial from the perspective that there is also a dispute as to whether they have the same needs as refugees. In some situations the overlap between refugees and IDPs has been significant, so that it has been impossible to extend protection and aid to one group without the other. 'Where UNHCR engaged in activities for refugees or returnees who lived alongside internally displaced persons, it was very often impractical not to extend these activities to the latter populations.'[215] Furthermore, in 2000 the Executive Committee further elaborated upon the overlap between UNHCR's work and IDPs. This includes when 'refugees and displaced persons are generated by the same causes and straddle the border', when 'effective reintegration of returnees requires assistance to be extended also to the internally displaced in the same locality or community' and when 'refugees have sought asylum across the border in areas where there are also internally displaced'.[216] Rafiqual Islam concludes that 'the distinction between IDPs and refugees for the purpose of their material aid and protection is artificial'.[217] However, this opinion is not widely held. Whereas there are situations where refugees and IDPs have the same needs, this is not always the case. There are also times when the needs of IDPs significantly overlap with the needs of ordinary civilians in the area. It would be somewhat unreasonable to then hope for UNHCR to extend its help to these populations as well, without the connection to its mandate of refugees. As Phuong rightly points out, '[a]ssigning responsibility to UNHCR for all internally displaced persons may lead UNHCR to become in fact the agency for populations in need'.[218] The needs of refugees and IDPs are also potentially different, meaning the UNHCR may not be in the best position to provide what is required. Regarding refugees, UNHCR's work mainly involves legal activities and assistance and protection activities, whereas regarding IDPs it may be of a more logistical nature.[219] So while the similarities between refugees and IDPs in theory may be numerous, with the main difference being that IDPs have not crossed a

[210] Ibid. pp. 485–486.
[211] Phuong, 'Improving the United Nations Response to Crises of Internal Displacement', 13 *IJRL* (2002) 491, p. 494, United Nations General Assembly Resolution 53/125 (1998).
[212] Ibid. p. 498.
[213] Informal Consultative Meeting, The Protection of Internally Displaced Persons and the Role of UNHCR 27.02.07, www.unhcr.org/excom/EXCOM/45dd5a712.pdf <last visited 3 June 2008>, para 3.
[214] Phuong, above n.211, p. 499.
[215] Ibid. p. 495.
[216] Executive Committee of the High Commissioner's Programme, EC/50/SC/INF.2, 'Internally Displaced Persons: The Role of the United Nations High Commissioner for Refugees'.
[217] Rafiqul Islam, 'The Sudanese Darfur Crisis and Internally Displaced Persons in International Law: The Least Protection for the Most Vulnerable', 18 *IJRL* (2006) 354 at p. 362.
[218] Phuong, above n.211, at p. 503.
[219] Ibid. p. 503.

State boundary, it is also reasonable to conclude that UNHCR may not always be the best organisation to deal with a situation. Often, the needs of IDPs are not the same as refugees and the nature of the work, as IDPs often live in unsafe environments, is vastly different. A whole range of other issues impact on UNHCR's ability to support IDPs, ranging from funding constraints to the impact that this work has on the right to asylum.

The plight of IDPs is obviously negatively affected by the lack of a single agency providing for their needs. However, there has been no international support for an IDP agency[220] and as a result it has been left to a variety of other agencies, UNHCR included, to cobble together support. This has been blighted with inconsistencies, while the number of IDPs has steadily increased. Only recently has there been any attempt at formulating a common IDP policy, which has unsurprisingly left UNHCR in a prominent role. In 2000 the Executive Committee of UNHCR elaborated on the agency's interest in IDPs and its growing role:

UNHCR has an interest in the protection and welfare of persons who have been displaced by persecution, situations of general violence, conflict or massive violations of human rights, because of their similarity to refugees in terms of the causes and consequences of their displacement and their humanitarian needs.

This interest, arising from the Office's humanitarian mandate and endorsed by successive General Assembly resolutions, places upon UNHCR a responsibility to:

■ advocate on behalf of the internally displaced;

■ mobilise support for them;

■ strengthen its capacity to respond to their problems; and

■ take the lead to protect and assist them in certain situations.

In view of the growing linkages between refugee problems and internal displacement, UNHCR is committed to greater engagement with the internally displaced within the parameters of its principles and prerequisites for operational involvement. The pros and cons of involvement will be assessed carefully in light of the need for effective international humanitarian action and the relevance of UNHCR's expertise, as well as the impact on UNHCR's humanitarian mandate and responsibility towards refugees.[221]

However, it has been repeatedly reiterated that UNHCR's involvement with IDPs should not come at a cost regarding its work with refugees and asylum-seekers and, furthermore, should not impact on the right to asylum.[222] The Guiding Principles of 1998 were a first step towards such an approach, in recognising the relevance of IDP issues and establishing a definition.

As a consequence of the protection gap, the Guiding Principles seek to identify 'the rights and guarantees relevant to protection of the internally displaced in all phases of displacement'.[223] While this document is not binding, this has allowed it to be more flexible and therefore gained more support than a binding document may have done. It has been described as 'the first step on a long journey in developing an international normative

---

[220] Ibid. p. 499.

[221] Executive Committee of the High Commissioner's Programme, above n.216 at pp. 1–2.

[222] Informal Consultative Meeting, above n.213, at paras 43–44; Phuong, above n.211, at p. 502.

[223] Guiding Principles, principle 2(1), Brownlie and Goodwin-Gill, *Basic Documents on Human Rights* (Oxford University Press, 2005) at p. 220; Kalin, 'The *Guiding Principles* on Internal Displacement – Introduction' 10 *IJRL* (1998) 557.

regime for IDPs'.[224] However, these standards have also been criticised for not ensuring compliance and reliance on political goodwill.[225] This progress was further added to by UNHCR when establishing its parameters and conditions of involvement with IDPs in 2000. These include: the impact on the non-political and humanitarian nature of UNHCR's mandate; 'impact on refugee protection and the institution of asylum'; 'impact on internal displacement; relevance of UNHCR's experience and expertise'; 'a specific request or authorisation from the UN Secretary General or other competent principal organ of the UN'; 'consent of the state concerned, and where relevant, other entities in a conflict; access to the affected population and adequate security for UNHCR and implementing partners to operate effectively'; 'clear lines of responsibility and accountability with the ability to intervene directly with all parties concerned, particularly on protection matters'; and 'adequate resources and capacity to carry out activities'.[226]

This in turn has led to even more significant progress in this field. In July 2004 the Inter-Agency International Displacement (IAID) and in 2005 the Intern-Agency Standing Committee (IASC), were set up under the UN Office for the Coordination of Humanitarian Affairs, in order to address the issue of internal displacement and to co-ordinate the efforts of different agencies. IAID has been criticised for failing 'to develop a consistent standard and predictable inter-agency approach, effective monitoring and accountability'.[227] However, IASC has more successfully allocated roles to different UN agencies. There are, nevertheless, a number of non-UN agencies that have a mandate that is relevant to IDPs including the ICRC and IOM. As different elements of IDP support and protection fall within their respective competencies, it was been necessary to formulate the 'cluster approach' in 2006. This gives a particular agency responsibility for certain areas of response, thus attempting to eradicate both gaps and overlap. UNHCR is the lead agency for protection, camp co-ordination and management and emergency shelter. 'The cluster approach is not in itself a mandate-giving mechanism. It is an arrangement through which the existing mandates of international organizations are brought together in a coordinated and predictable fashion.'[228] Despite its involvement in the 'cluster approach', it is also important to note that UNHCR continues to stress that regarding IDPs the primary responsibility still lies with the State in question.[229]

UNHCR considers that the Cluster Approach provides a valuable basis for the development of an enhanced inter-agency response to the protection of IDPs, while recognizing that this approach is still a 'work in progress' that will need to be reviewed and revised in the light of experience.[230]

There are still a number of issues with the 'cluster approach', including that a large number of UNHCR's activities with IDPs are not implemented under this approach.[231]

---

[224] Rafiqul Islam, above n.217, at p. 364.
[225] Ibid.
[226] Executive Committee of the High Commissioner's Programme, above n.216, at pp. 7–8.
[227] Rafiqul Islam, above n.217, at p. 375.
[228] Informal Consultative Meeting, above n.213, at para 13.
[229] Informal Consultative Meeting, Policy Framework and Corporate Strategy, UNHCR's Role in Support of an Enhanced Inter-Agency Response to the Protection of Internally Displaced Persons, 30.1.07, www.unhcr.org/excom/EXCOM/45c1ab432.pdf <last visited 3 June 2008>, para 19.
[230] Ibid. para 16.
[231] Informal Consultative Meeting, above n.213, at para 51.

'The provision of protection in emergency response situations' has also been highlighted as a major gap.[232] However, the 'cluster approach' has been utilised and in May 2007 UNHCR identified its use in seven pre-existing situations and 'six "major new emergencies" (Yogyakarta/Indonesia, Mozambique, the Philippines, Madagascar, Pakistan, and Lebanon)'.[233] The 'cluster approach' is still very much in its infancy and with the lack of both a binding document dealing with IDPs and an organisation with a specific mandate, this system, although far from perfect, again represents a major step forward in meeting the needs of IDPs. Organisations are able to work in their areas of expertise with IDPs without overstepping their mandate. While the system is still very much flawed, positive steps are being taken to plug protection gaps and it is a marked improvement on the previous system. The drafting by the African Union of the 'Convention for the Protection and Assistance of Internally Displaced Persons in Africa' highlights that IDP issues have finally been brought to the attention of the international community.[234]

6 CONCLUSIONS

The exceptional situation concerning IDPs is in many ways more critical than the situation of refugees. The lack of any satisfactory method of dealing with this phenomenon is particularly troubling. The present chapter has indicated that notwithstanding serious deficiencies in the framework for the protection of IDPs, there is, at least, an increased recognition of the problem and a growing political will to resolve the issues confronted by IDPs. There is a clear need to draft a Declaration and eventually a Convention regarding the situation of IDPs. This Declaration and Convention would need to articulate the rights of the IDPs and to develop a coherent international approach. The principles of international criminal law must be taken into account and there must be increased accountability for international crimes regarding both IDPs and refugees. Additionally, the development of the concept of 'safe areas' as a method of 'in country protection' needs to be refined.

From the perspective of international refugee law there are still a number of issues that need to be resolved. There is a need to define more clearly the scope of *non-refoulement* in order to prevent States from creating legal loopholes to by-pass their international obligations. Ensuring the respect for the *non-refoulment* principle is particularly important when many States have threatened deportations of suspected terrorists to territories where these individuals may face torture. The fact that States create such tactics indicates that they wish to be seen to comply with their obligations under international law, albeit somewhat ironically, confirming that they take the obligations enumerated in the Refugee Convention seriously. The system by which the UNHCR is funded is a significant weakness of the system; it would be preferable that a Treaty Body is created in order to ensure that the Convention is implemented effectively. There are also clear definitional issues in respect of 'social group' in Article 1A of the Convention, especially regarding gender-based persecution, as well as the terms employed in the exemption clauses.

---

[232] Informal Consultative Meeting, 'UNHCR's Role in Support of an Enhanced Humanitarian Response to Situations of Internal Displacement: Update on UNHCR's Leadership Role within the Cluster Approach and IDP Operational Workplans', 25.5.07, www.unhcr.org/excom/EXCOM/464dd68f2.pdf <last visited 3 June 2008>, para 64.

[233] Ibid. para 5.

[234] See ICRC, 'Internal Displacement of Populations in Armed Conflicts', 4 July 2008 www.icrc.org/Web/Eng/siteeng0.nsf/html/internal-displacement-africa-040708 <last visited 2 November 2008>.

19 Rights of migrant workers and their families[1]

Today we recognize the 200 million international migrants, 50 per cent of whom are women and men migrant workers, who have left their homes and communities to find work and better opportunities elsewhere in the world to support their families and communities. They make huge but often unrecognized contributions to growth and development of both their host countries and home communities . . . The current global financial and economic crises have serious implications for migrant workers worldwide. Past experience makes us painfully aware that migrant workers, especially women workers and those in irregular status, are among the hardest hit and most vulnerable during crisis situations . . . It is important that migrant workers do not become scapegoats for the current financial and economic crisis.[2]

1 INTRODUCTION

The rights of migrant workers and their families remains a major concern for international human rights law. Migration is a phenomenon as old as human history with theologians pointing to the removal of Adam and Eve from the Garden of Eden as the first instance of forced migration. Human migration has continued to take place throughout history although technological advancement and improvements in transportation have resulted in a considerable increase in the migration of people. Developments during the course of the 20th century have been disturbing insofar as the rights of migrant workers are concerned.[3] Migrants exist in every region, affecting every State, both in the developing and the developed world. It is estimated that globally there are well over 200 million migrants – a term

---

[1] Aleinikoff (ed.), *Migration and International Legal Norms* (Asser Press, 2003); Cholewinski, *Migrant Workers in International Human Rights Law: Their Protection in Countries of Employment* (Clarendon Press, 1997); Clark and Niessen, 'Equality Rights and Non-Citizens in Europe and North America: The Promise, the Practice and Some Remaining Issues' 14 *NQHR* (1996) 245; Berg, 'At the Border and Between the Cracks: The Precarious Position of Irregular Migrant Workers under International Human Rights Law' 8 *MJIL* (2007) 1; Hune, 'Migrant Women in the Context of the International Convention on the Protection of the Rights of All Migrant Workers and Members of their Families' 25 *International Migration Review* (1991) 800; Sohn and Buergenthal (eds), *The Movement of Persons Across Borders* (American Society of International Law, 1992); Jakubowski 'International Commerce and Undocumented Workers: Using Trade to Secure Labor Rights' 14 *Indiana Journal of Global Legal Studies* (2007) 509.

[2] Statement by Juan Somavia on International Migrants Day (18 December 2008) www.ilo.org/public/english/protection/migrant/ <last visited 20 May 2009>.

[3] For a historical analysis of migration see Cholewinski, above n.1, pp. 15–22.

broadly defined to include people who leave their countries of origin for a variety of reasons including economic migration and refugees.[4] Amongst these, tentative figures suggest over 125 million are migrant workers or members of their families. While 60 per cent of migrants live in the developed world, 40 per cent are resident in the developing world.[5] The primary reason for migration is poverty, and economic, social and political vulnerabilities. As has been discussed in the previous chapter there is also a fine line between economic migrants and those fleeing discrimination and persecution based on denials of fundamental rights.[6] Considerable migration takes place as a consequence of lawlessness, warfare and civil disturbances, or political instabilities.

The vulnerability of migrant workers is established by the fact that many millions do not have the requisite documentation or permission to work in the host countries: the illegality of their status renders them vulnerable to abuse and exploitation. Even those who reside legally and have permission to work face specific issues including recruitment, remittances, political participation, family reunification, naturalisation and repatriation.[7] Migrant workers continue to face various forms of discrimination, including exclusion from a variety of jobs and are in many instances excluded from social services provided by the host State. In the context of employment, different standards are frequently applied that distinguish nationals from migrant workers. Migrant workers lack job security and the risk of expulsion or removal from the employing State places the migrant workers and members of their families at a serious disadvantage. In order to address these issues the UN drafted the International Convention on the Protection of the Rights of All Migrant Workers and Members of their Families (ICRMW), which was adopted in 1990.[8]

2 MIGRANT WORKERS AND HUMAN RIGHTS MOVEMENT

International human rights law, by its very nature, is premised upon non-discrimination and equality for all 'without distinction of any kind, such as race, colour, sex, language, religion, political or other opinion, national or social origin, property, birth or other status'.[9]

---

[4] Statement by Juan Somavia on International Migrants Day, see above n.2. See also the Presentation by Ambassador Parsad Kariyawasam, Chairman of the UN Committee on Migrant Workers (30 November 2005) www.iom.ch/jahia/webdav/site/myjahiasite/shared/shared/mainsite/microsites/IDM/sessions/90th/docs/pdf/UN_Committee_90th.pdf <last visited 18 May 2009>.

[5] In the developed world one in every 10 people is a migrant. The highest concentration of migrant workers and members of their families can be found in North America with over 18 million, South America with 12 million, 30 million in Europe, 10 million in Middle Eastern Countries with the remaining dispersed in various other regions of the world. The largest exporters of migrant workers are the Philippines and Mexico. Historically, the States with the largest influxes of migrants includes the United States and the Russian Federation. However, in contemporary terms, the four countries with the highest concentration of migrants are all within the Middle-East. These are also States with a majority of population consisting of migrant workers. The Untied Arab Emirates has the highest number of migrants – 75 per cent of the total population. See Keane and McGeehan, 'Enforcing Migrant Workers' Rights in the United Arab Emirates' 15 *IJMGR* (2008) 81.

[6] See Foster, *International Refugee Law and Socio-Economic Rights* (Cambridge University Press, 2007) pp. 250–263; see further above chapter 18.

[7] Niessen, 'Migrant Workers' in Eide, Krause and Rosas (eds), *Economic, Social and Cultural Rights: A Textbook* (Martinus Nijhoff Publishers, 2001) pp. 389–405 at p. 390.

[8] The Convention was opened for signature on 18 December (1990), New York, UN Doc. A/RES/45/158. It entered into force on 1 July 2003. Various documents and instruments most prominently the report of the Special Rapporteur Ms. Halima Warzazi on the exploitation of Labour through illicit and clandestine trafficking proceeded this document.

[9] Universal Declaration of Human Rights, GA Res. 217A (III), UN Doc. A/810 at 71 (1948), Article 2. See also above chapter 4.

This perspective is evident in all human rights instruments, including the international bill of rights.[10] Having said that, the picture is more complex and complicated in that international law (as well as the State practice which determines the establishment of such law) consistently sanctions discrimination and distinctions on the basis of nationality. International human rights instruments, to that extent, also allow considerable elements of exclusion and distinctions based on nationality. Such exclusion is most clearly visible in the provision of employment and political rights which are granted on the basis of nationality.[11] Given these limitations, International human rights instruments have supported, albeit in an *ad hoc* and incoherent manner, migration rights and the rights of migrants workers. The right to freedom of movement has been recognised in the Universal Declaration on Human Rights, 1948 (UDHR).[12] Article 13(2) of the UDHR notes, '[e]veryone has the right to leave any country, including his own, and to return to his country'. The Declaration, however, does not grant a right to enter another country, or to enter another country in order to seek gainful employment.

Article 23 of the UDHR provides for right to work, which was followed and expanded in binding form by the ICESCR,[13] though these are provisions based on the acceptance of national immigration restrictions. Article 6 of the International Covenant of Economic, Social and Cultural Rights (1966) (ICESCR) provides for 'the right of everyone to the opportunity to gain his living by work'.[14] The plethora of standards enshrined in the instruments of another organisation, the International Labour Organization (ILO), also attempts to provide protection to migrant workers. Equal treatment for legal migrants commensurate to that of nationals is provided for in the ILO Migration for Employment Convention (Revised) No. 97 of 1949.[15] The Migrant Workers Convention (Supplementary Provisions) (No. 143) of 1975 also enshrines fundamental human rights values which includes taking steps to prevent smuggling and trafficking.[16]

Much like the ILO, the concern for the position of non-nationals and migrant workers within the United Nations has been long-standing.[17] The United Nations Economic and Social Council (ECOSOC) alarmed at the illegal transportation of labour to parts of the

---

[10] See Part II above.

[11] See International Convention on the Elimination of All Forms of Racial Discrimination, New York, 7 March 1966 United Nations, *Treaty Series*, vol. 660, p. 195; Article 1(2) provides: 'This Convention shall not apply to distinctions, exclusions, restrictions or preferences made by a State Party to this Convention between citizens and non-citizens'. For commentary see above chapter 12; Article 25 of the ICCPR restricts the provision of 'Political' rights to citizens. *International Covenant on Civil and Political Rights*, New York, 16 December 1966 United Nations, 999 U.N.T.S. 171; 6 I.L.M. (1967) 368. See above chapter 5.

[12] GA Res. 217A (III), UN Doc. A/810 at 71 (1948).

[13] New York, 16 December 1966, 993 U.N.T.S. 3; 6 I.L.M. (1967) 360.

[14] In its General Comment, the Committee on the Economic, Social and Cultural Rights, the Committee makes the following observations: 'The principle of non-discrimination as set out in Article 2.2 of the Covenant and in Article 7 of the International Convention on the Protection of the Rights of All Migrant Workers and Members of Their Families should apply in relation to employment opportunities for migrant workers and their families. In this regard the Committee underlines the need for national plans of action to be devised to respect and promote such principles by all appropriate measures, legislative or otherwise,' CESCR, *The Right to Work*, General Comment No. 18 Adopted on 24 November 2005 E/C.12/GC/18 6 (6 February 2006), para 18.

[15] ILO *Migration for Employment Convention (Revised)* No. 97 (1949), 120 U.N.T.S. 70, entered into force January 22 1952, www.ilo.org/ilolex/cgi-lex/convde.pl?C097 <last visited 10 May 2009>.

[16] ILO Migrant Workers Convention (Supplementary Provisions) (ILO No. 143) entered into force 9 December 1978 of 1975 Convention concerning Migrations in Abusive Conditions and the Promotion of Equality of Opportunity and Treatment of Migrant Workers www.ilo.org/ilolex/cgi-lex/convde.pl?C143 <last visited 10 May 2009> entered into force 9 December 1978.

[17] See the Office of the High Commissioner for Human Rights, *The Rights of Migrant Workers*, Fact Sheet No. 24 (2005).

European Continent passed a resolution in 1972.[18] In this resolution the ECOSOC condemned the exploitation of workers and their export from Africa which was 'akin to slavery and forced labour'.[19] In 1972, the UN General Assembly also condemned discrimination conducted against foreign workers and called upon governments to end such practices and to improve reception arrangements for foreign migrant labour.[20] The Resolution *inter alia* urged governments to ensure compliance with the provisions of the International Convention on the Elimination of All forms of Racial Discrimination (1966) and further encouraged governments to provide high priority towards the ratification of the Convention of the International Labour Organisation concerning Migration for Employment (Revised 1949) in order to prevent illicit trafficking of foreign labour.[21]

During the early part of 1970s, Mrs. Halima Warzazi, a former member of the UN Sub-Commission on the Prevention of Discrimination and Protection of Minorities, conducted a study on the exploitation of labour through illicit and clandestine trafficking.[22] Her final report and recommendations were examined by the Human Rights Commission.[23] A further study was completed by Baroness Elles, another member of the Sub-Commission in 1979.[24] Her study, which focused on human rights of non-citizens, recommended the adoption of a draft declaration on 'human rights of individuals who are not citizens of the country in which they live'.[25] In 1985, the ECOSOC adopted a resolution recognising the need for further efforts to improve the conditions of migrant workers.[26] While inviting States to establish and to improve the welfare programmes for migrant workers, the resolution reiterated the importance of the protection of migrant workers and members of their families.[27] Amidst this backdrop and growing concern for the position of migrant workers and their families, the first United Nations World Conference to Combat Racism and Racial Discrimination (1978)[28] recommended the drafting of a Convention and in 1980 a working group was established to draft this treaty.

The working group, which was reconstituted at successive sessions of the UN General Assembly, produced several drafts of the proposed Convention. After a considerable draft and a gestation period of 10 years the UN Convention on the Protection of the Rights of All Migrant Workers and their Families was adopted in 1990.[29] The present chapter aims to examine the strengths and weaknesses of the Convention as well as highlight the existing

---

[18] Economic and Social Council (ECOSOC) Resolution 1706 (LIII) 28 July 1972.

[19] Ibid. Preamble.

[20] General Assembly Resolution 2920 (XXVII) Exploitation of Labour through Illicit and Clandestine Trafficking (15 November 1972), para 1.

[21] Ibid. paras 2 and 5.

[22] UN Commission on Human Rights, Sub Commission on the Prevention of Discrimination and Protection of Minorities, 28th session, *Exploitation of Labour through Illicit and Clandestine Trafficking* (Final Report of Mrs. Halima E. Warzazi Special Rapporteur UN Doc. E/CN.4/Sub.2/L.629, 4 July 1975).

[23] *The Rights of Migrant Workers* (2005) above n.17, at p. 7.

[24] UN Commission on Human Rights, Sub-Commission on the Prevention of Discrimination and Protection of Minorities, study prepared by Baroness Elles, Special Rapporteur, *International Provisions Protecting the Human Rights of Non-Citizens* UN Doc. E/CN.4/Sub.2/392. Rev.I (1980).

[25] Ibid.

[26] Economic and Social Council (ECOSOC) Resolution 1985/24 'Welfare of migrant workers and their families' (1985).

[27] Ibid. para 1.

[28] See *Report of the World Conference to Combat Racism and Racial Discrimination, Geneva, 14–25 August 1978* (United Nations publication, Sales No: E.79.XIV.2).

[29] International Convention on the Protection of the Rights of All Migrant Workers and Members of their Families, New York, 18 December 1990, UN Doc. A/RES/45/158 www2.ohchr.org/english/law/cmw.htm <last visited 10 May 2009>.

deficiencies in the international protection of human rights of migrant workers and members of their families.

3 THE INTERNATIONAL CONVENTION ON THE PROTECTION OF THE RIGHTS OF ALL MIGRANT WORKERS AND MEMBERS OF THEIR FAMILIES

The relationship of the rights of migrant workers with the mainstream of human rights law is acknowledged by the provisions of the Convention: the preamble of the Convention makes reference to the International Bill of Rights as well as other major human rights treaties.[30] The Convention is one of the most detailed human rights treaties and represents a detailed elucidation of both the substantive rights of migrant workers and members of their families as well as the procedural mechanism for implementation. In view of the plethora of substantive rights and guarantees, the Convention can be regarded as the 'Magna Carta of migrant workers'. Having said that, and as this chapter explores, the Convention contains a number of weaknesses. While many of the provisions are limited in their reach, the Convention has been criticised for its weakness in protecting various groups and communities, in particular irregular migrants and members of their families.

(i) Defining migrant workers and members of their families

The UN International Convention on Migrant Workers – as stated in Article 1 – is applicable to all migrant workers and their families without any discrimination based on concepts 'such as sex, race, colour, language, religion or conviction, political or other opinion, national, ethnic or social origin, nationality, age, economic position, property, marital status, birth or other status'.[31] This extremely broad range of categories is reflected later on in the Convention in Article 7. This provision is consolidated by Article 88 which prohibits the exclusion of any category of migrants. The Convention establishes the principle that all migrant workers regardless of their legal status are entitled to certain fundamental rights in addition to those enshrined in core human rights instruments. The Convention provides for a comprehensive definition of migrant workers and members of their families.[32] The Convention is applicable to migrants working in the territory of the State party, regardless of whether the country of origin of the migrant worker has ratified the Convention or not.[33] According to Article 2 of the Convention a 'migrant worker' 'refers to a person who is to be engaged, is engaged or has been engaged in a remunerated activity in a State of

---

[30] Having regard to the standard as established by the ILO, the preamble specifically refers to ILO convention concerning *Migration for Employment* (ILO No. 97), the Convention concerning Migrations in Abusive Conditions and the Promotion of Equality of Opportunity and Treatment of Migrant Workers (ILO No. 143), Migration for Employment Recommendation (Revised) (ILO No. 86), 1949 adopted on 1 July 1949, the Migrant Workers Recommendation (ILO No. 151) adopted on 24 June 1975, the Forced Labour Convention (ILO No. 29), 39 U.N.T.S. 55, entered into force 1 May 1932 and the Abolition of Forced Labour Convention (ILO No. 105), 320 U.N.T.S. 291, entered into force 17 January 1959.

[31] Article 1(1) ICRMW.

[32] Articles 2 and 4.

[33] See Cholewinski, above n.1, p. 150.

which he or she is not a national'. There are, however, a range of migratory workers and further elaboration is provided by subsequent provision of Article 2. Article 2 provides definitions of 'frontier worker', 'seasonal worker', 'seafarer', 'worker on an offshore installation', 'itinerant worker', 'project tied worker', 'specified-employment worker' and 'self-employed worker'. Article 2(2) provides accordingly:

(a) The term 'frontier worker' refers to a migrant worker who retains his or her habitual residence in a neighbouring State to which he or she normally returns every day or at least once a week;

(b) The term 'seasonal worker' refers to a migrant worker whose work by its character is dependent on seasonal conditions and is performed only during part of the year;

(c) The term 'seafarer', which includes a fisherman, refers to a migrant worker employed on board a vessel registered in a State of which he or she is not a national;

(d) The term 'worker on an offshore installation' refers to a migrant worker employed on an offshore installation that is under the jurisdiction of a State of which he or she is not a national;

(e) The term 'itinerant worker' refers to a migrant worker who, having his or her habitual residence in one State, has to travel to another State or States for short periods, owing to the nature of his or her occupation;

(f) The term 'project-tied worker' refers to a migrant worker admitted to a State of employment for a defined period to work solely on a specific project being carried out in that State by his or her employer;

(g) The term 'specified-employment worker' refers to a migrant worker:

   (i) Who has been sent by his or her employer for a restricted and defined period of time to a State of employment to undertake a specific assignment or duty; or

   (ii) Who engages for a restricted and defined period of time in work that requires professional, commercial, technical or other highly specialized skill; or

   (iii) Who, upon the request of his or her employer in the State of employment, engages for a restricted and defined period of time in work whose nature is transitory or brief; and who is required to depart from the State of employment either at the expiration of his or her authorized period of stay, or earlier if he or she no longer undertakes that specific assignment or duty or engages in that work;

(h) The term 'self-employed worker' refers to a migrant worker who is engaged in a remunerated activity otherwise than under a contract of employment and who earns his or her living through this activity normally working alone or together with members of his or her family, and to any other migrant worker recognized as self-employed by applicable legislation of the State of employment or bilateral or multilateral agreements.

The Convention does not apply to those individuals who are either employed by international organisations or are representatives of their State (e.g. diplomats), or those State officials conducting developmental work and programmes.[34] Nor does it apply to investors, refugees, stateless persons or students or trainees.[35] Investors were excluded at the behest of the representatives of the developing world who were keen to focus on the protection of the

---

[34] Article 3 ICRMW.
[35] Ibid. Article 3. On refugees and internally displaced persons, see above chapter 18.

most vulnerable migrants.[36] Refugees and stateless persons were not included in the definition on the basis of available existing protection within international law and international treaties.[37] Article 4 of the International Convention on Migrant Workers (ICRMW) further defines the members of the family of the migrant workers. These are persons:

> married to migrant workers or having with them a relationship that, according to applicable law, produces effects equivalent to marriage, as well as their dependent children and other dependent persons who are recognized as members of the family by applicable legislation or applicable bilateral or multilateral agreements between the States concerned.

This provision does raise a number of difficult and problematic issues: presumably spouses from polygamous marriages would have the same entitlement as regards reunion and rights. For several jurisdictions, there would be concerns surrounding heterosexual couples outside of marriages as well as homosexual couples who are not married or where their union is recognised by the States of their origin but not by the State of employment.[38] Compliance with the official requirements to engage in a remunerated activity in the State of employment leads a migrant worker to be recognised as being in a regular and documented situation.[39] Those workers, who are unable to comply with the official requirements of the State, in respect of employment, are regarded as 'non-documented' or in an 'irregular' situation.[40]

Part II and Part III of ICRMW provide a number of human rights for migrant workers and their families. Article 7 contained in Part II provides for non-discrimination in respect of rights, thereby undertaking to apply the provisions of the Convention 'without distinction of any kind such as sex, race, colour, language, religion or conviction, political or other opinion, national, ethnic or social origin, nationality, age, economic position, property, marital status, birth or other status'. Notwithstanding its broad scope, and existing parallels with human rights provisions (e.g. UDHR and ECHR), Article 7 raises a number of complexities. The use of the term 'nationality' begs the question as to the extent to which States can legitimately discriminate amongst nationals of one State as opposed to others. Discrimination on the basis of nationality is a prerogative of State sovereignty and forms the essence of such regional economic agreements, as those concluded under the auspices of the European Union.[41] The answer to this is provided in Article 81, whereby domestic laws and practices as well as bilateral and multilateral treaties that grant more favourable rights to certain nationalities of migrant workers and members of their families do not breach the provisions of the ICRMW, if minimum standards are complied with insofar as other nationalities are concerned.[42]

Part III provides a detailed set of human rights for migrant workers and members of their families. These include the right to leave any State including their own,[43] alongside the

---

[36] see Cholewinski, above n.1, p. 153.
[37] See above chapter 18.
[38] On homosexual unions in the United Kingdom see Civil Partnership Act 2004; for the debate on sexuality within Muslim traditions see in particular above chapters 11 and 15.
[39] See Article 5(a) ICRMW.
[40] Ibid. Article 5(b).
[41] See above chapter 8.
[42] Article 81(1) ICRMW.
[43] Ibid. Article 8(1).

right to enter their State of origin.[44] These are interesting provisions in that whilst providing migrant workers and members of their families a right to leave any State, including their own, they do not provide for a right to enter another State. Article 9 provides for protection by law, whereas Article 10 prohibits torture, cruel, inhuman or degrading treatment or punishment.[45] If practically and effectively implemented, such protection would benefit greatly millions of migrant workers (especially in the countries of the Middle and Far East) facing unsatisfactory and inadequate mechanisms for regulation of labour standards. Freedom from slavery, servitude, forced or compulsory labour is also guaranteed.[46] Migrant workers and members of their families are accorded the right to freedom of thought, conscience and religion, which also includes the freedom to have or adopt a religion or belief of their choice and to manifest their religious beliefs either individually or in community with others in worship, observance, practice and teaching.[47] The right to freedom of thought, conscience and religion, as we have already examined, is a complicated right within international law.[48] Insofar as migrant workers and their families are concerned, there are likely to be difficulties in respect of the right to change religion, especially under repressive dictatorial repressive regimes or in those States which attach criminal sanctions to change of religion. There are also significant complexities in the public expression of religious belief within a number of States for religious minorities and migrant workers.[49] An ILO report makes the following observations about the situation of non-Muslim migrant workers in Saudi Arabia and Iran:

> [R]eligious discrimination is often worse in societies where no freedom of religion exists or where a state religion tends to disadvantage or exclude other religions. In Saudi Arabia, for instance, migrant workers who are not Muslim must refrain from public display of religious symbols such as Christian crosses or Hindu *tilaka*. Other forms of discrimination consist of job advertisements excluding applicants belonging to certain religious groups (Hindus in particular), or of preventing migrant workers from practising their religion openly. The situation of the Baha'i in the Islamic Republic of Iran has long been a subject of comment by both ILO and United Nations.[50]

---

[44] Ibid. Article 8(2).
[45] Ibid. Article 10; see below chapter 22.
[46] Ibid. Article 11.
[47] Ibid. Article 12.
[48] See above chapter 12.
[49] In her report, subsequent to a country visit to Maldives, the United Nations Special Rapportuer on Freedom of Religion or Belief makes the following comments as regards public expression of migrant workers in the Maldives. She notes '[I]n relation to non-Muslim foreigners, the Special Rapporteur notes that there are practical limitations on their right to manifest their religion publicly, and these limitations are supported by the vast majority of the population. As a matter of practice, they are not allowed to build places of worship or carry out prayers or religious rituals outside of their homes. They are allowed to congregate in their own homes to pray and carry out religious rituals, but they are not allowed to invite Maldivians to these gatherings. In the Maldives there is not a single official place of worship for religions other than Islam. Any suggestion of allowing foreign workers, teachers and other non-Muslim residents to worship openly is met with firm resistance. All foreigners are prohibited from propagating their religion or carrying out missionary work. Furthermore, the Special Rapporteur has been informed that expatriate school pupils who choose not to study Islam are unable to pass their end of year school exams. The Special Rapporteur is extremely concerned by the current limitations placed on the right of migrant workers and other foreigners to manifest their religion or belief. She notes that these limitations are implemented as a matter of practice, and not as a matter of law.' Report of the Special Rapporteur on Freedom of Religion or Belief, Asma Jahangir, A/HRC/4/21/Add.3, (7 February 2007) paras 47–48 and 68.
[50] International Labour Office, *Declaration on Fundamental Principle at Work, Discrimination at Work in the Middle East and North Africa* www.ilo.org/wcmsp5/groups/public/—ed_norm/—declaration/documents/publication/wcms_decl_fs_92_en.pdf <last visited 12 May 2009>.

Migrant workers and members of their families are also granted freedom to hold opinions without interference and the right to freedom of expression.[51] They also have additional rights including the right to family and the right not to be subjected to arbitrary interference with respect to aspects of their correspondence and private life. Similarly unlawful attacks on their honour and reputation are prohibited.[52] Arbitrary deprivation of property, belonging to migrant workers, is not permitted.[53] Furthermore, they are to be provided with liberty and security of person.[54] Migrant workers and their families are to be provided security by the host State against violence, harassment or physical injury by State officials or by private individuals.[55] They are also not to be subjected to arbitrary arrest and deprivation of liberty,[56] and those who are arrested on criminal charges are to have prompt recourse to the operative judicial mechanisms.[57] Migrant workers or members of their families, upon arrest or judicial custody pending trial, have the right to seek assistance through consular or diplomatic missions from their States of origin.[58] Whilst deprived of their liberty and in custody, migrant workers or members of their families are to have the same rights as those nationals of the host country, including visits from members of their families.[59]

Cultural identity is an important feature of the Convention and is to be protected even in instances where the migrant workers or members of their families are deprived of their liberty.[60] Migrant workers or members of their families that are accused of crimes, are to be separated and provided a different treatment from convicted persons.[61]

Equality before the law is further emphasised in Article 18 of the Convention.[62] The provisions provide for a fair trial and 'a public hearing by a competent, independent and impartial tribunal' when dealing with trials related to migrant workers or members of their families.[63] The presumption of innocence until proven guilty is emphasised and a set of minimal rights are provided to migrant workers or members of their families during criminal proceedings.[64] These minimal rights – based on Article 14 of the ICCPR and Article 6 of the ECHR – include the right to be informed promptly and in detail in a language understood by the migrant worker, the nature and cause of charge against them,[65] the right to have adequate time and facilities for the preparation of defence[66] and the right to communicate with the counsel of their own choosing,[67] to have trials without undue delay,[68] the right to be present during the course of proceedings against them including the right to being able to examine witnesses and to ensure the presence of witness on their behalf.[69]

[51] Article 13 ICRMW.
[52] Ibid. Article 14.
[53] Ibid. Article 15.
[54] Ibid. Article 16(1).
[55] Ibid. Article 16(2).
[56] Ibid. Article 16(4).
[57] Ibid. Article 16(6).
[58] Ibid. Article 16(7)(a).
[59] Ibid. Article 17(5).
[60] Ibid. Article 17(1).
[61] Ibid. Article 17(3).
[62] Ibid. Article 18(1).
[63] Ibid.
[64] Ibid. Article 18(2) and (3).
[65] Ibid. Article 18(3)(a).
[66] Ibid. Article 18(3)(b).
[67] Ibid.
[68] Ibid. Article 18(3)(c).
[69] Ibid. Article 18(3)(d) and (e).

Article 18 also provides for assistance of an interpreter, if so required by the migrant worker.[70] According to Article 18(3)(g), migrant workers or members of their families have the right not to be forced into self-incrimination or confessions. The provisions of the Article also draw a clear distinction between juveniles and adults, with trial proceedings required to take account of the age and capacity of the accused.[71] Migrant workers or members of their families have the right to appeal against their conviction or sentence and if this is overturned they should be entitled to compensation in accordance with law.[72] The Convention also affirms the rule against double-jeopardy.[73]

ICRMW provides for rules against non-retrospective criminality,[74] prohibits imprisonment for failure to fulfil contractual obligations,[75] prohibits collective expulsion,[76] and reaffirms the right to have recourse to the protection and assistance of the consular or diplomatic authorities of their State of origin.[77] Article 24 further reiterates the right to recognition before the law. Article 25 establishes that migrant workers are to enjoy treatment not less favourable than that which applies to nationals of the State of employment in respect of remuneration, which includes *inter alia* conditions of work (e.g. overtime, holidays with pay, safety, health, hours of work, weekly rest) and other terms of employment. Furthermore, host States are under an obligation to ensure that any irregularity in their status as migrant workers does not have a negative impact – particularly those relating to their contracts – on the rights that they would otherwise have under this Convention.[78] Whilst, in theoretical terms, these provisions appear attractive, their practical application particularly as regards irregular workers seems highly improbable. Insofar as 'regular' or 'documented' migrant workers are concerned, their conditions of employment are further consolidated by Article 54 and Article 55. These provide for protection against dismissal, access to unemployment benefits and access to public schemes intended to combat unemployment.

According to Article 26, 'States Parties recognize the right of migrant workers and members of their families: (a) To take part in meetings and activities of trade unions and other associations'. Furthermore, Article 27 entitles migrant workers and members of their families to social security benefits at the same level as the nationals. During the drafting stages a number of delegates were in favour of relocating the provisions of Article 27 to Part IV of the Convention, thereby confining these to migrant workers with a regular status. However, after considerable opposition the provision was retained in its original position.[79] The current location of Article 27 means that this represents the minimum standards to which both regular and irregular migrant workers are entitled. That said, Article 27 is restrictive in that the provisions are applicable 'in so far as they fulfil the requirements provided for by the applicable legislation of that State and the applicable bilateral and multilateral treaties'.[80] In instances, where a benefit is not provided by the host State, Article 27(2)

---

[70] See ibid. Article 18(3)(f).
[71] Ibid. Article 18(4).
[72] Ibid. Article 18(5) and (6).
[73] Ibid. Article 18(7).
[74] Ibid. Article 19.
[75] Ibid. Article 20.
[76] Ibid. Article 22.
[77] Ibid. Article 23.
[78] Ibid. Article 25(3).
[79] See Cholewinski, above n.1, p. 161.
[80] Article 27(1) ICRMW.

encourages the concerned State to examine the possibility of reimbursement for the amount of contributions made by them in relation to that benefit on the basis of treatment which is accorded to nationals of the State in similar circumstances.[81]

Migrant workers and their families have a 'right to receive any medical care that is urgently required for the preservation of their life or the avoidance of irreparable harm to their health on the basis of equality of treatment with nationals of the State concerned'.[82] While, the treatment cannot be refused as a consequence of any irregularity in relation to their stay or employment,[83] it needs to be noted that the right is only restricted to medical care in serious emergencies, 'for the preservation of their life or the avoidance of irreparable harm to their health'.[84]

ICRMW provides a number of rights to the children of migrant workers, rights which reinforce the overall regime of the protection of the rights of the child.[85] These include 'the right to a name, to registration of birth and to a nationality'.[86] Furthermore, the children of migrant workers also have a basic right of access to education on the basis of equality of treatment with nationals of the State concerned. ICRMW recognises the fundamental and essential nature of the right to education.[87] Article 30 of the Convention goes on to provide that access to pre-school education shall not be denied as a result of the irregular situation of the stay or employment of either parent or by reason of the irregularity of the child's stay in the State of employment.[88] Furthermore, the Convention in Article 31 places an obligation on States parties 'to ensure respect for the cultural identity of migrant workers and members of their families and [States parties] shall not prevent them from maintaining their cultural links with their State of origin'.[89]

In accordance with Article 32, migrant workers have the right to transfer their earnings and savings upon the termination of their employment, as well as their personal belongings and effects. Migrant workers also have the right to be informed of their rights under the Convention by their State of origin as well as the State of employment.[90]

(ii) Dichotomy between documented/regular migrant workers and undocumented/irregular migrant workers

Part IV of the Convention provides a number of additional rights to migrant workers and members of their families who are documented, or in a regular situation. They are entitled to be informed by the State of origin or the State of employment regarding the conditions of their stay and the terms of remuneration.[91] According to the provisions of Article 38, migrant workers and members of their families shall be allowed to be temporarily absent from the host State and, in authorising such leave, the States of employment are required

---

[81] Ibid. Article 27(2).
[82] Ibid. Article 28.
[83] Ibid.
[84] Cholewinski, above n.1, at p. 168.
[85] See above chapter 16.
[86] Article 29 ICRMW.
[87] For the right to education see further above chapter 6.
[88] Article 30 ICRMW.
[89] Ibid. Article 31(1).
[90] Ibid. Article 33(1).
[91] Ibid. Article 37.

to take account of the special needs and obligations of migrants workers and their families.[92] Article 39 provides that '[m]igrant workers and members of their families have the right to liberty of movement in the territory of the State of employment and freedom to choose their residence there'. There are a number of additional rights, including public participation and involvement in the public affairs of the State of employment.[93] These include the right of migrant workers and members of their families to form associations and trade unions,[94] and wider participation in public affairs.[95] The right of public participation, however, is a problematic one as it also sanctions the right to vote and be elected within the State of employment.[96] Domestic legislation governing voting rights and right to be elected to a public office is normally tied to nationality or a substantial term of residence and it remains unlikely that States parties would be agreeable to such a provision without the limitation that such public participation must be 'in accordance with its legislation'.[97] Article 42 provides that States parties are required to:

> consider the establishment of procedures or institutions through which account may be taken, both in States of origin and in States of employment of special needs, aspirations and obligations of migrant workers and members of their families and shall envisage, as appropriate, the possibility for migrant workers and members of their families to have their freely chosen representatives in those institutions.[98]

In addition to this, migrant workers should be consulted and permitted to participate in 'decisions concerning the life and administration of local communities'.[99] Nevertheless, States still have a broad discretion when complying with these rights. In recognising the *de facto* limitations placed on the migrant workers in according political rights, Article 42(3) of the Convention states that, '[m]igrant workers may enjoy political rights in the State of employment if that State, in the exercise of its sovereignty, grants them such rights'.

The provisions of Article 43 provide migrant workers with the right to:

> equality of treatment with nationals of the State of employment, in relation to:
>
> (a) Access to educational institutions and services . . . ;
>
> (b) Access to vocational guidance and placement services;
>
> (c) Access to vocational training and retraining facilities and institutions;
>
> (d) Access to housing, including social housing schemes, and protection against exploitation in respect of rents;
>
> (e) Access to social and health services . . . ;
>
> (f) Access to co-operatives and self-managed enterprises . . . ;
>
> (g) Access to and participation in cultural life.

---

[92] Ibid. Article 38(1).
[93] Ibid. Article 40 and 41.
[94] Ibid. Article 40.
[95] Ibid. Article 41(1).
[96] Ibid.
[97] Ibid. Article 41(1) and (2).
[98] Ibid. Article 42(1).
[99] Ibid. Article 42(2).

Article 44(1) provides that the Convention recognises that 'the family is the natural and fundamental group unit of society' and that in this capacity the family unit is entitled to protection from society. The State shall, therefore, take appropriate measures to ensure the protection of the unity of the families of migrant workers. Article 45 in expanding the scope of the Convention, echoes Article 43 and provides for equality of treatment in respect of access to educational institutions;[100] access to vocational guidance and training institutions and services;[101] access to social and health services;[102] and access to and participation in cultural life,[103] to the families of migrant workers.

According to Article 46, migrant workers and their families enjoy exemption from import and export duties in respect of personal and household effects, as well as the equipment deemed necessary for their employment, upon the departure from their State of origin, initial entry into the country of employment and final departure from country of employment to their country of origin. Migrant workers have the right to transfer their earnings.[104] According to Article 48, migrant workers are not to be made liable for taxes, duties or charges that place the migrant worker at a disadvantage in comparison to nationals.[105] In instances of the change of circumstances of migrant workers, either as a result of death or dissolution of marriages, the Convention invites the State of employment to favourably consider granting an authorisation to stay, taking into account the length of time they have already resided in that State.[106]

Part VI of the Convention provides for the '[p]romotion of sound, equitable, humane and lawful conditions in connection with international migration of workers and members of their families'. This shall be achieved through consultation and co-operation amongst States parties.[107] Furthermore, due regard is to 'be paid not only to labour needs and resources, but also to the social, economic, cultural and other needs of migrant workers and members of their families involved'.[108]

According to Article 65(1), States parties are required to 'maintain appropriate services to deal with questions concerning international migration of workers and members of their families'. Their functions include:

(a) The formulation and implementation of policies regarding such migration;

(b) An exchange of informational, consultation and co-operation with the competent authorities of other States Parties involved in such migration;

(c) The provision of appropriate information, particularly to employers, workers and their organizations on policies, laws and regulations relating to migration and employment, on agreements concluded with other States concerning migration and on other relevant matters;

[100] Ibid. Article 45(1)(a).
[101] Ibid. Article 45(1)(b).
[102] Ibid. Article 45(1)(c).
[103] Ibid. Article 45(1)(d).
[104] Ibid. Article 47(1).
[105] Ibid. Article 48(1)(a).
[106] Ibid. Article 50(1).
[107] Ibid. Article 64(1).
[108] Ibid. Article 64(2).

> (d) The provision of information and appropriate assistance to migrant workers and members of their families regarding requisite authorizations and formalities and arrangements for departure, travel, arrival, stay, remunerated activities, exit and return, as well as on conditions of work and life in the State of employment and on customs, currency, tax and other relevant laws and regulations.

States parties are also under an obligation to provide appropriate consular facilities and all other facilities 'necessary to meet the social, cultural and other needs of migrant workers'.[109]

Article 68 requires States parties, as well as States of transit, to collaborate with each other in order to prevent or eliminate the illegal or clandestine movements of irregular migrant workers. Article 68 also provides for measures which include, 'appropriate measures against the dissemination of misleading information relating to emigration and immigration'.[110] Furthermore, States parties undertake to take measures to eradicate the illegal movement of migrant workers and their families as well as 'to impose effective sanctions on persons, groups or entities which organize, operate or assist in organizing or operating such movements' or use violence, threats or intimidation against irregular migrants.[111] According to Article 68(2), States which employ the migrant workers are under an obligation to:

> take all adequate and effective measures to eliminate employment in their territory of migrant workers in an irregular situation, including, whenever appropriate, sanctions for employers of such workers. The rights of migrant workers vis-à-vis their employer arising from employment shall not be impaired by these measures.[112]

State parties are obliged to undertake all possible efforts to prevent the persistence of the irregular situation of migrant workers within their jurisdiction.[113] In instances where a State party is considering possibilities for the regularisation of the situation of persons who have previously been irregular migrants, the State party is required to take account of a range of circumstances, including the circumstances of their entry, duration of their stay in the country concerned, and in particular, the circumstances relating to the situation of the family.[114]

There is an obligation on States parties in respect of the working and living conditions of migrant workers and their family members. Thus, Article 70 provides that States parties shall ensure that measures are no less favourable when compared with their own nationals. These measures include maintaining recognised 'standards of fitness, safety, health and principles of human dignity'.[115] States parties are also required to facilitate 'the repatriation to the State of origin of the bodies of deceased migrant workers or members of their families'.[116] States parties are required to provide all possible assistance to relatives and

---

[109] Ibid. Article 65(2).
[110] Ibid. Article 68(1)(a).
[111] Ibid. Article 68(1)(b) and (c).
[112] Ibid. Article 68(2).
[113] Ibid. Article 69(1).
[114] Ibid. Article 69(2).
[115] Ibid. Article 70.
[116] Ibid. Article 71(1).

family members, in respect of the provision of compensation and settlement of all matters related to the death of a migrant worker or members of his or her family.[117]

(iii) Criticism and limitations of the substantive provisions of the convention

One of the major criticisms of the Convention is the dichotomy drawn between 'regular or documented' migrant workers as opposed to irregular or undocumented migrants. As noted above, in defining migrant workers and members of their families with documented or regular status, Article 5(a) regards these as those 'documented or in a regular situation if they are authorized to enter, to stay and to engage in a remunerated activity in the State of employment pursuant to the law of that State and to international agreements to which that State is a party'. Others failing to comply with the above provisions are considered as non-documented migrants or in an irregular situation.

These irregular or undocumented migrants include those individuals who entered a State with valid authorisation, but were employed contrary to their visa stipulations or once having lawfully entered on a valid work visa and either overstay or overstep the conditions of their residence. Often on the fringes of human existence, these undocumented and irregular migrants are abused and exploited. Their exploitation is evident in the lower wages and hazardous working conditions they have to encounter. They are open to ill-treatment and abuse by employers and frequent threats, harassment and torture by law-enforcing agencies.

Opinions amongst policymakers, community representatives and politicians vary as to the possible rights of these irregular migrants. There has been a growing trend to impose sanctions on those who engage in the practice of irregular migration. Strict and punitive controls are perceived as a formula to deter further irregular migration. International law and State practices which establish international law represent equivocacy; this has placed considerable strain on the position of irregular migrants and members of their families. General human rights law contains a number of guarantees available to all individuals regardless of their status within domestic law. Although, as discussed in this book, the international bill of human rights has been established on the basis of equality and non-discrimination for all individuals regardless of their national status, there are, nevertheless, critical distinctions between nationals and non-nationals. These distinctions in the application of rights are particularly striking in the context of irregular or undocumented migrant workers. The ICCPR provides for the right to non-discrimination to all individuals but restricts such rights as the right to liberty only to those lawfully in the State.[118] Article 13 of the ICCPR is also a restrictive provision in that it restricts procedural rights for those aliens lawfully present.[119] Article 25 of the ICCPR disallows aliens from enjoying political participation and a role in the governance of the State. The situation of irregular migrants,

---

[117] Ibid. Article 71(2).

[118] Article 12(1) provides that 'Everyone lawfully within the territory of a State shall, within that territory, have the right to liberty of movement and freedom to choose his residence' ICCPR; see above chapter 5.

[119] Article 13 of the ICCPR provides that 'An alien lawfully in the territory of a State Party to the present Covenant may be expelled therefrom only in pursuance of a decision reached in accordance with law and shall, except where compelling reasons of national security otherwise require, be allowed to submit the reasons against his expulsion and to have his case reviewed by, and be represented for the purpose before, the competent authority or a person or persons especially designated by the competent authority.' Ibid.

it would appear, is worse than refugees, since irregular migrants are not immune from penalties for being present on foreign territory without authorisation on account of their illegal presence. In the European, regional human rights context, the European Convention on Human Rights (ECHR) provides for procedural safeguards against expulsion: the freedom of movement applies strictly to lawfully resident aliens.[120] Article 5(1) of the ECHR, in placing further restrictions, notes that:

> [e]veryone has the right to liberty and security of person. No one shall be deprived of his liberty save in the following cases and in accordance with a procedure prescribed by law . . . (f) the lawful arrest or detention of a person to prevent his effecting an unauthorised entry into the country or of a person against whom action is being taken with a view to deportation or extradition.

A more significant limitation is provided in Article 16, which states that nothing in the provisions regarding freedom of peaceful assembly, to association with others, including the right to form and to join trade unions and non-discrimination shall be regarded as preventing States from imposing restrictions on the political activities of aliens.

Within the Migrant Workers Convention, unlike regular migrants, undocumented workers have no rights to liberty of movement, family reunion, to form associations and trade unions, protection from expulsion and within general international law there is no prohibition on discrimination on the basis of immigration status.

Under the Convention, there are no obligations to regularise the status of the undocumented migrant worker. In fact, the Convention obliges States parties to prevent and eliminate all forms of irregular movement or employment of workers. As previously discussed, Article 68(1) places a mandatory requirement on States parties as well as the transit States to sanction and prevent the illegal transfer and employment of people within their territorial jurisdiction. In order to attain such an objective, States parties are required to undertake appropriate measures against the dissemination of misleading information relating to emigration and to impose effective sanctions upon those agencies, individuals

---

[120] Protocol 7 Article 1(1) provides: 'An alien lawfully resident in the territory of a State shall not be expelled therefrom except in pursuance of a decision reached in accordance with law and shall be allowed: (a) to submit reasons against his expulsion (b) to have his case reviewed, and (c) to be represented for these purposes before the competent authority or a person or persons designated by that authority. An alien may be expelled before the exercise of his rights under paragraph 1(a), (b) and (c) of this Article, when such expulsion is necessary in the interests of public order or is grounded on reasons of national security.' Protocol No. 7 to the Convention for the Protection of Human Rights and Fundamental Freedoms (as amended by Protocol No. 11) ETS No. 117 http://conventions.coe.int/Treaty/EN/Treaties/Html/117.htm <last visited 12 May 2009>. Entered into force 1 November 1988 (as at 13 May 2009, 41 States parties). According to Protocol 4, Article 2 – Freedom of movement: (1) Everyone lawfully within the territory of a State shall, within that territory, have the right to liberty of movement and freedom to choose his residence. (2) Everyone shall be free to leave any country, including his own. (3) No restrictions shall be placed on the exercise of these rights other than such as are in accordance with law and are necessary in a democratic society in the interests of national security or public safety, for the maintenance of *ordre public*, for the prevention of crime, for the protection of health or morals, or for the protection of the rights and freedoms of others. (4) The rights set forth in paragraph 1 may also be subject, in particular areas, to restrictions imposed in accordance with law and justified by the public interest in a democratic society. Protocol No. 4 to the Convention for the Protection of Human Rights and Fundamental Freedoms, securing certain rights and freedoms other than those already included in the Convention and in the first Protocol thereto (as amended by Protocol No: 11) ETS No. 046 http://conventions.coe.int/Treaty/EN/Treaties/Html/046.htm <last visited 12 May 2009>. Entered into force 2 May 1968 (as at 13 May 2009, 42 States parties).

or groups who are involved in this action. Furthermore, there is an undertaking to impose sanctions on those gangs or individuals engaged in violence against irregular migrant workers or members of their families.

According to the provisions of Article 69(1), States parties are under a duty to take appropriate measures to ensure that a situation whereby illegal migrants are present within their territory does not persist. Furthermore, Article 69(2) provides that whenever States parties are considering the regularisation of the situation of such people they should take into account 'the circumstances of their entry, the duration of their stay in the States of employment and other relevant considerations, in particular those relating to their family situation'. There is thus, as the *travaux prepartories* of the Convention establishes, no general obligation to regularise the situation of illegal migrants, the only requirement being a discretion that certain matters be taken into consideration once a State decides to regularise or provide amnesties to illegal migrants.[121] The provisions in Article 69 are to be read in conjunction with Article 35, contained in Part III which provides that:

> Nothing in the present part of the Convention shall be interpreted as implying the regularization of the situation of migrant workers or members of their families who are non-documented or in an irregular situation or any right to such regularization of their situation, nor shall it prejudice the measures intended to ensure sound and equitable-conditions for international migration as provided in part VI of the present Convention.

In the light of these features, one commentator makes the point that:

> the lack of a clear obligation in the [ICRMW] to regularize the illegal status of migrant workers, particularly if they have resided in and contributed to the economy of the country of employment for some considerable time, or at least to move towards some gradual redefinition of their situation, further undermines their exercise of the [ICRMW] rights in the absence of provisions providing them with protection against detection if they attempt to avail themselves of these rights.[122]

At the heart of the Convention lies the tension between State sovereignty on the one hand and the rights of migrants who as individuals claim equality and fundamental human rights. Similar tensions persist with regional human rights instruments. As noted already, the ECHR reserves a number of rights including political rights for citizens.[123] Within the ECHR, there has been some ancillary recognition that immigration controls must be compatible with conventions rights, most notably Article 8.[124] In the recent case of *Da Silva and Hoogkamer* v. *The Netherlands*, the European Court of Human Rights found a violation of Article 8 by the Dutch authorities for their refusal to grant residency status.[125] A similar positive decision has been arrived at by the IACHR.[126]

---

[121] Cholewinski, above n.1, p. 191.

[122] Ibid. p. 191.

[123] ECHR, Article 16.

[124] The right to respect for private and family life (for further analysis see above chapter 7).

[125] (2007) 44 E.H.R.R. 34.

[126] *Juridical Condition and Rights of the Undocumented Migrants*, Advisory Opinion OC-18/03, 17 September 2003, Inter-Am. Ct. H.R. (Ser. A) No. 18 (2003).

(iv) Women as migrant workers

In the story of migration and migrant workers, the situation of women has frequently been sidelined. Contrary to common perceptions, women in fact form over 50 per cent of the total migrant worker population.[127] Major destinations for migrant workers include the Middle-East as well as North America. Insofar as women are concerned, their experiences are shaped by the type of work they perform. Men generally migrate for a variety of jobs, from low-skilled to highly-skilled. Women, on the other hand, labour on the bottom rungs of the economy. Women predominantly migrate for female-dominated jobs in the areas of domestic care, entertainment, service and the light manufacturing sectors. In host countries, women are often forced into accepting the lowest levels of employment, regardless of their training or education. Considerable inequalities are encountered by women migrant workers on the basis of pre-existing gender stereotypes.[128] Therefore, notwithstanding educational and professional qualifications, in many societies and States women as employees or workers have restricted career opportunities limited to certain spheres: these women are least likely to have access to promotional career opportunities.[129]

Women migrant workers also face widespread discrimination in the employment market. Whilst gender-based discrimination continues to persist in both the developing and the developed world, women migrant workers are extremely susceptible to such forms of discrimination. Women migrant workers are often perceived as the least likely to raise complaints about the nature of employment and levels of remuneration. Women migrant workers also suffer from lower levels of job security and fewer benefits as compared to their male counterparts. Furthermore, women migrant workers often end with jobs which have already been refused by nationals or by foreign men – these forms of employment have been described as the 3Ds (dirty, dangerous and degrading).[130] Women migrant workers, in particular, irregular migrants face considerable harassment both at their places of work and within their homes. Irregular women migrants are open to abuse and exploitation. Their irregular, undocumented status is often perceived by exploitative elements within the society (including employers and law-enforcement agencies) as a licence for sexual abuse and exploitation.

Although equality of treatment with nationals is integral to the Convention, the Migrant Workers Convention (ICRMW) does not explicitly provide protection from unequal wages between men and women, nor from gender-based, occupational segregation. However, Article 7 establishes non-discrimination on the grounds of sex in respect of the rights contained in the Convention. On the other hand, the Convention is blind to the specific needs of women and does not take into consideration the differing treatment of male and female workers.[131]

---

[127] Borak, 'Women Migrant workers: Embracing Empowerment over Victimization' Paper presented at 'When Women Gain, So Does the World' IWPR's Eighth International Women's Policy Research Conference (June 2005) at p. 5.

[128] Fitzpatrick and Kelly, 'Gendered Aspect of Migration: Law and the Female Migrant' 22 *Hastings International and Comparative Law Review* (1998) 47.

[129] Borak, above n.127, at pp. 6–8.

[130] Noeleen Heyzer, Executive Director UN Development Fund for Women (UNIFEM) *Combating Trafficking in Women and Children: A Gender and Human Rights Framework* (13–15 November 2002) www.hawaii.edu/global/projects_activities/Trafficking/Noeleen.pdf <last visited 12 May 2009>.

[131] Borak, above n.127, at pp. 17–18.

Although such treatment would be contrary to UN principles of non-discrimination, the issue of disparate treatment is not specifically addressed in the Convention on Migrant Workers. A further criticism of the ICRMW from a gender perspective is its failings to address 'the more practical question of work–family balance. The Convention does not address the fact that women are generally primary caregivers of their children. The Convention does not mention access to child care, or the need for women to move in and out of the labour force while raising their children'.[132]

(v) Reluctance on the part of States to ratify or to follow principles of the Convention

Notwithstanding that the Convention was adopted in 1990, there are only 41 States that have ratified it;[133] almost all of them from the developing world and largely exporters of migrant workers. None of those States ratifying are based in the developed world – including the European Union; North-America and the Middle-East. The argument for the non-ratification of the Convention by these States is self-contradictory: on the one hand, it is argued that there is no need for ratification as the human rights of migrant workers are already protected in the domestic/regional human rights framework; and, on the other hand, States have argued that ratification would result in requiring substantial changes in existing laws. An allied argument is that ratification (since it provides rights also to illegal migrant workers) would result in providing a magnet for undocumented, irregular workers.

(vi) Implementation of the Convention

Part VII of the Convention provides for an elaborated implementation mechanism of the Convention. Article 72 sets up a Committee, called the Committee on the Protection of the Rights of All Migrant Workers and Members of Their Families.[134] At the time of the entry into force of the Convention (in 2003) the Committee consisted of an initial 10 members.[135] Since the most recent increase in the State Party ratification to 41 – in accordance with Article 72(b) – the membership of the Committee is due to be increased to 14 experts.[136] In line with the other UN treaty-based bodies, this Committee also comprises of members with high moral standing, with complete impartiality and be recognised for their competence in the field.[137] According to Article 72(2)(a) members of the Committee are elected by secret ballot from a list of persons nominated by States parties with emphasis on equitable geographical distribution and the representation of the principal legal systems. Each State party is authorised to nominate only one person from amongst its own nationals,[138] with elected members to serve in their personal capacity.[139] Chapter VII also provides for the election of the Committee members – the initial elections were held within six months of the date of entry into force of Convention.[140] Subsequent elections have been

---

[132] Ibid. at p. 18.
[133] Figures correct as of 17 May 2009; for an analysis see Hune and Niessen, 'Ratifying the UN Migrant Workers Convention: Current Difficulties and Prospects' 12 *NQHR* (1994) 393.
[134] ICRMW Article 72(1).
[135] Ibid. Article 72(1)(b).
[136] Ibid.
[137] Ibid. Article 71(1)(b).
[138] Ibid. Article 72(2)(a).
[139] Ibid. Articles 72(1)(b).
[140] Ibid. Article 72(3).

held every second year.[141] In establishing further details, Article 72(3) notes that at least four months before the date of each election, the United Nations Secretary General is to address a letter to all States parties inviting them to submit their nominations within two months.[142] The Secretary General shall prepare a list in alphabetical order of all persons thus nominated, indicating the States parties that have nominated them, and shall submit it to the States parties not later than one month before the date of the corresponding election, together with the curricula vitae of the persons nominated.[143] Members of the Committee are elected at a meeting of States parties convened by the UN Secretary General.[144] At that meeting, a quorum of members is constituted with the presence of two-thirds of the States parties to the Convention.[145] According to Article 72(5)(a) members of the Committee serve a four-year term, although they are eligible for re-election if they are nominated. Death or resignation of a member allows the relevant State party to appoint another expert from amongst its nationals, with the new member being eligible for the remainder of the term.[146] Such an appointment is subject to approval of the Committee.[147] According to Article 72(7) the Secretary General of the United Nations is required 'to provide the necessary staff and facilities for the effective performance of the functions of the Committee'. Committee members are not entitled to a salary, but can claim emoluments from the UN resources.[148] Committee members are also entitled to the facilities, privileges and other immunities of experts, whilst they are on a UN mission.[149]

(a) Implementation mechanisms

The implementation mechanisms of the Convention are articulated in Article 73. According to Article 73(1) States parties undertake to submit a report to the United Nations Secretary-General for consideration by the Committee 'on the legislative, judicial, administrative and other measures they have taken to give effect to the provisions of the present Convention', within one year of the entry into the Convention and, thereafter, every five years.[150] The Convention requires that the reports contain information on all the factors including difficulties which affect the implementation of the Convention and information on the migratory flows so far as the State party is concerned.[151] The Committee was required to provide guidelines in relation the content of the report, which it did in the first year of its formation.[152] In the light of its established guidelines, the Committee is required

---

[141] Ibid.
[142] Ibid.
[143] Ibid.
[144] Ibid. Article 72(4).
[145] Ibid. Article 72(4).
[146] Ibid. Article 72(6).
[147] Ibid. Article 72(6).
[148] Ibid. Article 72(8).
[149] Ibid. Article 72(9).
[150] Ibid. Article 73(1).
[151] Ibid. Article 73(2).
[152] Provisional Guidelines regarding the form and contents of initial reports to be submitted by States parties under article 73 of the International Convention on the Protection of the Rights of All Migrant Workers and Members of their Families. HRI/GEN/2/Rev.2/Add.1 (6 May 2005). For Periodic Reports, see International Convention on the Protection of the Rights of All Migrant Workers and Members of Their Families, Guidelines for the Periodic Reports to be Submitted by States Parties under Article 73 of the Convention CMW/C/2008/1 (22 May 2008). For Rules of Procedure see Provisional Rules of Procedure: Committee on the Protection of the Rights off All Migrant Workers and Members of their Families HRI/GEN/3/Rev.1/Add.1 (7 May 2004).

to examine the State reports and to transmit to the State party appropriate comments.[153] The Committee is mandated to seek further additional or supplementary information.[154] The State party can respond to the Committee's comments through its observations.[155] According to Article 74(2) the United Nations Secretary-General, prior to the opening of each regular session, is required to transmit to the Director-General of the International Labour Office reports submitted by States parties concerned and information relevant to the consideration of these reports. This is meant to enable the ILO to provide all possible assistance to the Committee in relation to matters dealt with by it. The Committee is required to consider the issues in the light of comments and materials provided by the ILO. After having consulted members of the Committee, the United Nations Secretary-General also has the authority to transmit relevant documentation to specialised agencies as well as to inter-governmental organisations.[156] The Committee may in the light of information received request that these specialised agencies or other bodies submit for their views, written information that falls within their sphere of activities.[157] The ILO at the request of the Committee, or the Committee on its own initiative, may invite representatives of other specialist agencies and organs of the United Nations to be present and be able to participate in matters falling within their competence.[158]

The Committee is required to present an annual report on the implementation of the Convention, along with its own considerations and recommendations.[159] The United Nations Secretary-General is required to transmit the annual reports of the Committee to various entities including the States parties, as well as the Economic and Social Council, the Human Rights Council and the Director-General of the International Labour Office.[160] According to Article 75(1) of the Convention, the Committee adopts its own rules of procedure. It meets annually at the United Nations Headquarters,[161] with its officers being elected for a term of two years.[162]

The Convention follows the pattern of the ICCPR in that it allows for inter-State as well as an individual complaints mechanism. The inter-State mechanism is provided for in Article 76, according to which any State party may declare 'that it recognizes the competence of the Committee to receive and to consider communications to the effect that a State Party claims that another State Party is not fulfilling its obligations under the present Convention'.[163] Communications, however, are only to be received and considered if submitted by a State party that has made a declaration permitting the Committee to consider such communications in regard of itself.[164] No communication is to be received and considered by the Committee if it concerns a State party which has not made such a declaration.[165] Communications received under this Article are dealt with by the following procedure: State (A) that considers another State (B) is in breach of the provisions of the

---

[153] ICRMW Article 74(1).
[154] Ibid.
[155] Ibid.
[156] Ibid. Article 74(3).
[157] Ibid. Article 74(4).
[158] Ibid. Article 74(5) and (6).
[159] Ibid. Article 74(7).
[160] Ibid. Article 74(8).
[161] Ibid. Article 75(4).
[162] Ibid. Article 75(2).
[163] Ibid. Article 76(1).
[164] Ibid. Article 76(1).
[165] Ibid. Article 76(1).

Convention can bring that fact to the attention of the State Party (B). State (A) may also inform the Committee of this matter. State (B) must respond to the allegations within three months, providing a written explanation clarifying the matter with reference to domestic procedures and remedies taken, pending as well as those that are available.[166] If, however, within six months the matter has not been resolved since the receipt of the initial communication either State may bring the matter to the attention of the Committee through notice to the Committee and the other State.[167] The Committee must decide whether all local remedies have been exhausted before considering the case in closed sessions.[168] Furthermore, States parties are entitled to be represented and to make oral or written submissions.[169] The Committee's task is to make an attempt to resolve the dispute through its good offices.[170] The Committee could request that the States parties supply all relevant information pertaining to the case.[171] The Committee is obliged to produce a written report within 12 months of the date of receipt of notice of complaint.[172] If a solution is reached, then the Committee's report will be brief and confined to facts and the solution reached.[173] If a friendly solution has not been reached then the Committee is required to confine its report to a brief statement of facts.[174] The written submissions and a record of the oral submissions made by the States parties are to be attached to the report.[175] The inter-State procedure will commence only when 10 States have accepted this procedure.[176]

The Convention also contains an individual complaints mechanism, similar to the first Optional Protocol to the ICCPR.[177] According to these provisions, a State party may make a declaration under the Convention that it recognises the competence of the Committee to receive and consider communications made by or on behalf of individuals who are subject to its jurisdiction and claiming violation of their individual rights.[178] However, the Committee is unable to consider any communications in respect of those States that have not made the relevant declaration.[179] Similar to other international procedures, communications may not be considered by the Committee that are anonymous, an abuse of the right of submission or are deemed incompatible with the provisions of the Convention.[180] Furthermore, the procedure excludes those communications which have been or are being examined under another procedure of international investigation or settlement and those in which domestic remedies remain to be exhausted.[181] The rule of exhaustion of domestic remedies is inapplicable, where the remedy in question 'is unreasonably prolonged or is unlikely to bring any effective relief' to the individual concerned.[182] The Committee is

---

[166] ICRMW Article 76(1)(a).
[167] Ibid. Article 76(1)(b).
[168] Ibid. Article 76(1)(c) and (e).
[169] Ibid. Article 76(1)(g).
[170] Ibid. Article 76(1)(d).
[171] Ibid. Article 76(1)(f).
[172] Ibid. Article 76(1)(h).
[173] Ibid. Article 76(1)(h)(i).
[174] Ibid. Article 76(1)(h)(ii).
[175] Ibid. Article 76(1)(h)(ii).
[176] Ibid. Article 76(2).
[177] On the First Optional Protocol see above chapter 5.
[178] ICRMW Article 77(1).
[179] Ibid. Article 77(1).
[180] Ibid. Article 77(2).
[181] Ibid. Article 77(3).
[182] Ibid. Article 77(3)(b).

required to bring to the attention of the relevant State party the alleged violation.[183] Within six months, the receiving State undertakes to provide written explanations or statements which would clarify the matter and all possible remedial action.[184] The Committee then considers the communication in the light of all available information and examines the case in a closed meeting.[185] After its examination, the Committee forwards its views to the relevant State party and to the individual concerned.[186] As already noted, the Convention provides that the rights of migrant workers or members of their families cannot be renounced by the State party.[187] Nor is it permissible to place any form of pressure on migrant workers or their families to renounce their rights.[188] The Convention also provides guarantees of effective remedies, notwithstanding the fact that breaches of the provisions of the Convention have been conducted by persons whilst acting in their official capacity.[189] There is also an undertaking to adopt legislative and other mechanisms for the effective implementation of the Convention.[190]

The Committee held its first session in March 2004 and is currently composed of 10 independent experts. Since 2005, the Committee has held sessions twice a year, in April and November. As of May 2009, neither the inter-State complaints procedure nor the individual complaints procedure had entered into force. Thus, the work of the Committee is limited to the consideration of State reports regarding the implementation of the Convention by individual States parties. The Committee began to consider State reports in 2006, although this process has been drawn out, with only seven State reports having been considered during 2006–08.[191] Some progress has been made as during the Committee's 10th session (20 April 2009–1 May 2009) where a further four State reports were considered.[192]

4 THE ROLE OF THE INTERNATIONAL LABOUR ORGANIZATION IN PROTECTING THE RIGHTS OF MIGRANT WORKERS AND MEMBERS OF THEIR FAMILIES

The role of the International Labour Organization (ILO) in projecting the human rights of indigenous peoples and the organisation's efforts to 'establish universal and lasting peace' through means of social justice has already been considered elsewhere in this book.[193] The ILO has also played a particularly important role in protecting the rights of migrant workers and has adopted a range of international conventions for protecting the rights of workers including migrant workers. These instruments include Convention No. 97 concerning

---

[183] Ibid. Article 77(4).
[184] Ibid. Article 77(4).
[185] Ibid. Article 77(5)(6).
[186] Ibid. Article 77(7).
[187] Ibid. Article 82.
[188] Ibid. Article 82.
[189] Ibid. Article 83(a).
[190] Ibid. Article 84.
[191] These are Mali, Mexico, Egypt, Ecuador, Bolivia, Syrian Arab Republic and El Salvador.
[192] The State reports of Azerbaijan, Bosnia and Herzegovina, Colombia and the Philippines were considered in the (20 April–1 May 2009) session of the Committee.
[193] Preamble to the Constitution of the ILO, 62 Stat. 3485; 15 U.N.T.S. 35, entered into force 9 October 1946; Brownlie (ed.), *Basic Documents in International Law* (Clarendon Press, 1981) at p. 45; Wolf, 'Human Rights and the International Labour Organisation' in Meron (ed.), *Human Rights in International Law: Legal and Policy Issues* (Clarendon Press, 1984) pp. 273–305.

Migration for Employment (Revised) (C 97)[194] and Recommendation No. 86 of 1949 concerning Migration for Employment (Revised) (R86),[195] and Convention (No. 143) concerning Migrations in Abusive Conditions and the Promotion of Equality of Opportunity and Treatment of Migrant Workers (1975).[196] The Conventions are applicable to all migrant workers irrespective of their country of origin and regardless of whether or not the sending countries have ratified the relevant Convention. The State of employment has to have ratified the Convention in question in order for it to be applicable. At the time of writing Convention No. 97 had received 48 ratifications, while Convention No. 143 had only received 23. This limited number of ratifications hinders the application of uniform standards in respect of migrant workers. Additionally, a considerable number of States parties to these Conventions are more likely to be the sending States of migrant workers as opposed to States of employment.[197]

According to ILO Convention No. 97, States parties are required to apply treatment to migrant workers no less favourable than that which they apply to their own nationals, in respect of remuneration, family allowances, working hours, holidays, restrictions on home work, the work of young persons, membership of trade unions and enjoyment of the benefits of collective bargaining, accommodation, social security, employment taxes and dues or contributions payable in respect of the persons employed.[198]

Part I of Convention No. 143 focuses upon migration in abusive conditions. Article 1 of the Convention provides that States must respect the basic human rights of all migrant workers. The remainder of Part I focuses on the suppression of clandestine movements and employment of migrant workers, calling for the application of administrative, civil and penal sanctions (including imprisonment) in respect of illegal employment and organisation of clandestine movements.[199] The sanctions concern the employers and traffickers of clandestine workers and do not concern the workers themselves.

Part II of Convention No. 143 expands on Convention No. 97 in respect of equal treatment. States parties are obliged to declare and pursue a national policy with a view to promoting and guaranteeing equality of opportunity and treatment with respect to employment and occupation, social security and trade unions.[200] Cultural rights are included in addition to the individual and collective freedoms of migrant workers and their family members.[201] Article 11 defines a migrant worker as 'a person who migrates or who has

---

[194] Migration for Employment Convention (Revised) (ILO No. 97) (1949), 120 U.N.T.S. 70, entered into force 22 January 1952 www.ilo.org/ilolex/cgi-lex/convde.pl?C097 <last visited 10 May 2009>.
[195] Migration for Employment Recommendation (Revised) (ILO No. 86), 1949 adopted on 1 July 1949. www.oit.org/ilolex/cgi-lex/convde.pl?R086 <last visited 10 May 2009>.
[196] Convention concerning Migrations in Abusive Conditions and the Promotion of Equality of Opportunity and Treatment of Migrant Workers: Migrant Workers Convention (Supplementary Provisions) (ILO No. 143) entered into force 9 December 1978 www.ilo.org/ilolex/cgi-lex/convde.pl?C143 <last visited 10 May 2009>.
[197] Convention No. 97 is ratified by Albania, Algeria, Armenia, Bahamas, Barbados, Belize, Bosnia and Herzegovina, Cameroon, Cuba, Jamaica, Malawi, Republic of Moldova, Montenegro, Saint Lucia, Trinidad and Tobago and the United Kingdom amongst others. For full details of ratifications see www.ilo.org/ilolex/cgi-lex/ratifce.pl?C097 <last visited 15 May 2009>. Convention No. 143 is ratified by Albania, Armenia, Benin, Bosnia and Herzegovina, Burkina Faso, Cameroon and Philippines amongst others. For full details of ratifications see www.ilo.org/ilolex/cgi-lex/ratifce.pl?C143 <last visited 15 May 2009>.
[198] Article 6 ILO Convention No. 97.
[199] Articles 3–6 ILO Convention No. 143.
[200] Articles 10 ILO Convention No. 143.
[201] Article 10 ILO Convention No. 143.

migrated from one country to another with a view to being employed otherwise than on his own account and includes any person regularly admitted as a migrant worker'. States parties are to implement national laws in co-operation with organisations of employers and workers for the purpose of securing migrants' rights.[202] States parties are obliged to ensure that measures providing migrant workers with the right to preserve their national and ethnic identity, and their cultural ties with their country of origin are implemented.[203] Article 13 provides encouragement to States parties to undertake measures for facilitating the reunification of the family of the migrant workers, which includes the spouse, dependent children, father and mother.[204] Thus, in summary, both Convention No. 97 and No. 143 engage with questions of irregular migration and in so doing expressly incorporate references to fundamental human rights, as provided in the United Nations primary human rights treaties.[205] The ILO instruments remain restricted as a consequence of the limitation in the scope of the organisation and, therefore, cannot deal with such broader issues as immigration policies, political rights and the right to education or culture. The small numbers of ratifications and the lack of ratification by the majority of States of employment also significantly hinder the application of a common standard of rights to migrant workers under the banner of the ILO Conventions.

5 REGIONAL STANDARDS

(i) The Council of Europe

Regional instruments, not unlike international standards, are highly restrictive. The European human rights mechanisms are not generally supportive of migrant workers, in particular irregular or undocumented migrant workers. As already noted, the Council of Europe's ECHR does not contain specific rights on nationality and immigration or protection of aliens from expulsion.[206] Nor does the Convention or its Protocol's provide any right of political asylum to aliens,[207] although as has been considered at various part of this book, expulsion from a Member State may trigger Article 3 whereby there is substantial risk that the person concerned, if deported, faces a real risk of being subjected to torture, cruel or inhuman treatment or punishment in the receiving State. In such instances, Article 3 places an obligation not to deport that person to that country where he faces the threat.[208]

---

[202] Article 12(a) ILO Convention No. 143.

[203] Article 12(f) ILO Convention No. 143.

[204] Article 13(1)(2).

[205] ILO, Vulnerable Groups: Migrant Workers (April 2003) www.jcwi.org.uk/policy/uklaw/ilo_vulnerablegroups.pdf <last visited 20 March 2008>.

[206] Note, however, that violations of ECHR may nevertheless take place if State actions amount to 'degrading treatment', discrimination, or breaches of other substantive rights. See discussion of the European Commission in *East African Asians* v. *UK* (1995) 19 E.H.R.R. CD1; Harris, O'Boyle, Bates and Buckley, *Harris, O'Boyle and Warbrick Law of the European Convention on Human Rights* (Oxford University Press, 2009) pp. 800–801; also see Toner, *Partnership Rights, Free Movement, and EU Law* (Hart, 2004) at p. 88.

[207] *Vilvarajah and others* v. *UK* (1992) 14 E.H.R.R. 248, para 102, and *Ahmed* v. *Austria* (1997) 24 E.H.R.R. 278, para 38.

[208] See *Soering* v. *UK* (1989) 11 E.H.R.R. 439, paras 90–91; *Vilvarajah and others* v. *UK* (1992) 14 E.H.R.R. 248; *Ahmed* v. *Austria* (1997) 24 E.H.R.R. 278, paras 38–39; *HLR* v. *France* (1998) 26 E.H.R.R. 29, para 34; *Jabari* v. *Turkey*, 9 B.H.R.C. 1, [2001] I.N.L.R. 136, para 38; and *Sheekh* v. *The Netherlands* (2007) 45 E.H.R.R. 50, para 135; for further analysis see above chapter 7.

This Convention also does not address the issue of migration or migrant workers. A more significant limitation is provided in Article 16 which states that nothing in the provisions regarding freedom of peaceful assembly, to associate with others, including the right to form and to join trade union's, and non-discrimination shall be regarded as preventing States from imposing restrictions on the political activities of aliens. Procedural safeguards are provided in Article 1 of Protocol No. 7 to ECHR against the arbitrary expulsion of legally resident aliens.[209] Article 4 Protocol 4 also prohibits the collective expulsion of aliens. The Convention, notwithstanding its humanitarianism, retains a distinction between lawful aliens and those with an irregular status. We have already noted the restriction placed in Article 5(1)(f) of the ECHR. There are also further implicit restrictions on those not lawfully present in a State party under the provisions of Article 2(1) Protocol No. 4. As has been discussed in earlier chapters, within the ECHR, there has been some ancillary and incidental recognition that immigration controls must be compatible to convention rights. This has primarily been through provisions relating to the respect for private and family life as provided in Article 8, although other Articles have also been relied upon.[210]

Two additional instruments devised by the Council of Europe, the European Social Charter[211] and the European Convention on the Legal Status of Migrant Workers[212] have considerable relevance with migrant workers. ESC accords protection only to those individuals who are nationals of contracting States parties to the Convention.[213] Furthermore, any possible protection is of a restrictive nature since the ratification of instruments is confined to Council of Europe Member States. The application is limited to those migrant workers lawfully residing in the territory of States parties. As has been considered elsewhere in the book, within the ESC, ratifying States are not obliged to accept all the provisions of the Charter, so long as they accept six out of the nine 'core' Articles[214] and not less than 10 out of the other Articles or 45 numbered paragraphs.

ESC and its additional Protocol deal with Social and Economic Rights and aim to protect rights pertinent to workers – these include the rights related to better remuneration, suitable working conditions and social security. Specific rights within the ESC provide protection to migrant workers. Article 18 and Article 19 address the position of migrant workers. Article 18 provides for the right to engage in gainful occupation in the territory of other contracting parties and Article 19 provides for the right of migrant workers and their families to protection and assistance. Commenting on Article 18, the former Committee of Independent Experts (now the European Committee on Social Rights ECSR) has commended the provision as highly useful, allowing States to move towards the progressive improvement of the situation of migrant workers.[215] Article 19 is one of the 'core' articles within the ESC and provides for the rights of migrant workers including family reunion, co-operation between social services and aspects regarding the employment of migrant

[209] Protocol No. 7 to the Convention for the Protection of Human Rights and Fundamental Freedoms, ETS No. 117.

[210] See above chapter 7.

[211] European Social Charter, ETS No. 035, adopted at Turin 18 October, 1961 entered into force, 26 February 1965, and European Social Charter (revised), ETS No. 163. See above chapter 8.

[212] ETS No. 093, entered into force 1 May 1983. The Convention has only been ratified by 11 States: Albania, France, Italy, Moldova, the Netherlands, Norway, Portugal, Spain, Sweden, Turkey and Ukraine.

[213] See above chapter 8.

[214] The core Articles of the Revised European Social Charter are Articles 1, 5, 6, 7, 12, 13, 19 and 20.

[215] Conclusions II. 59, cited in *The European Social Charter* (University Press of Virginia, 1984) at p. 148.

workers. The ESC is restricted to nationals of contracting parties. Article 19 of the ESC engages with migrant workers' rights and the rights of the families of migrant workers. The implementing body, the ESCR, has provided a broad interpretation of Article 19 of the ESC.

The other relevant Council of Europe convention is the European Convention on the Legal Status of Migrant Workers (EMW), which provides an even narrower focus. In common with ESC, EMW is also operative on the basis of reciprocity and is confined to according protection to the nationals of ratifying States parties of the Council of Europe. The implementing body, the Consultative Committee, adopts recommendations, proposals from States parties and prepares periodic reports for the attention of Committee members, which contains information on the compliance with provisions of the EMW by the States parties.

Article 1(1) EMW Convention provides a definition of migrant worker as 'a national of a Contracting Party who has been authorized by another contracting Party to reside in its territory in order to take up paid employment'. The definition is restrictive as it explicitly excludes migrant workers in an irregular situation: it applies to those who are in paid employment thereby excluding those who are self-employed or not economically active.[216] Article 1(2) also excluded a number of migrants from the definition that have been explicitly provided for by the ICMW. These include frontier workers, seamen and seasonal workers.

(ii) The European Union

The *rasion d'être* of the European Union (EU) is the free movement of workers on the basis of equality and non-discrimination. Equality of treatment and non-discrimination has been guaranteed through the founding treaties of the Union. EU nationals can enter another Member State in order to seek employment without the need to acquire a work permit or permission. Whilst free movement of workers is ensured under EU law, certain exceptions remain. These exceptions relate to employment in public services,[217] those limitations justified on grounds of public policy, security or public health[218] and in certain cases on linguistic knowledge.[219] Insofar as EU citizens are concerned, the right to equal access to employment throughout the territory of a host country to a worker's spouse and children under 21 years of age or to his or her dependent children is guaranteed regardless of nationality.[220] EU law also ensures equality in respect of social security for migrant workers and their families within Member States. The nationals of the community have now also become entitled to a general right of residence in any of the other Member States, regardless of whether they are pursuing any economic activity or agenda. The TEU provides that 'every citizen of the Union shall have the right to move and reside freely within the territory of member States, subject to limitations and conditions laid down in the treaty and measures adopted to give it effect'.[221]

---

[216] Cholewinski, above n.1, at p. 228.
[217] Article 48(4) EC Treaty.
[218] Article 48(3) EC Treaty.
[219] Reg. 1612/68/EEC, Article 3(1).
[220] Evans, 'Third Country Nationals and the Treaty of European Union' 5 *EJIL* (1994) 199 at p. 205.
[221] Cholewinski, above n.1, at p. 392.

Such generosity has previously been limited to European Union citizens. The Treaty of Rome (1957) provided for free movement of workers and self-employed workers within the Community and subsequent Community policies have extended this fundamental principle. Under Community Law, EU citizens have the right to work in another State within the community and also have the right to seek employment. The Community also provides rights to family members and dependants of State nationals irrespective of their nationality. Free movement of workers within the Community also enshrines the principle of non-discrimination. This principle, therefore, establishes non-discrimination between workers in the area of employment, remuneration and other conditions of work and employment. It also entitles workers to equality of treatment, social and fiscal measures. There also needs to be non-discrimination and equality of treatment in such areas as housing conditions and entitlement to benefits. Immigration from outside the EU in the past has been regarded primarily a matter for individual member States. However, after the EU Council Meeting in Tampere in Finland in 1999, the EU has moved towards progressively adopting a common integration policy.[222] The Tampere Agenda established that the common integration policy be based on the ideas of:

- a comprehensive approach to the management of migratory flows so as to find a balance between humanitarian and economic admission;

- include fair treatment for third-country nationals aiming as far as possible to give them comparable rights and obligations to those of nationals of the Member State in which they live;

- a key element in management strategies must be the development of partnerships with countries of origin including policies of co-development.[223]

In respect of regular migrant workers, the Council Directive on family reunification[224] and long-term resident status[225] are particularly relevant. In respect of family reunification, the Directive outlines that this applies only to the nuclear family, 'that is to say the spouse and the minor children'.[226] The purpose of the Directive is to 'ensure fair treatment of third country national residing lawfully on the territory of the Member States and that a more vigorous integration policy should aim at granting them rights and obligations comparable to those of citizens of the European Union'.[227] As regards long-term resident status, Article 4 of the Directive establishes that this status must be granted to those 'third-country nationals who have resided legally and continuously within its territory for five years immediately prior to the submission of the relevant application'.[228] Additionally,

---

[222] TEU Article 18; Denmark has opted out of Title IV of the EC Treaty and therefore is not subject to EU immigration policy. The UK and Ireland decided on a case by case basis whether they will 'opt-in' to the policy in question.

[223] http://ec.europa.eu/justice_home/fsj/immigration/fsj_immigration_intro_en.htm <last visited 5 May 2009>.

[224] Council Directive 2003/86/EC.

[225] Council Directive 2003/109/EC.

[226] Council Directive 2003/86/EC, para 9.

[227] Ibid. para 3.

[228] Council Directive 2003/109/EC.

the EU has established standards in respect of the integration of third State nationals[229] and combating illegal immigration.[230]

(iii) The Organization of American States (OAS)

In addition to the protection afforded to migrant workers through the various European systems, the Organization of American States has established a Special Rapporteurship on Migrant Workers and Their Families. The position was created by the Inter-American Commission in response to two OAS resolutions.[231]

The principal objectives of the Rapporteurship include:

(a) To generate awareness of the states' duty to respect the human rights of migrant workers and their families;

(b) To make specific recommendations to the member states on areas related to the protection and promotion of the rights of migrant workers and their families, so that they adopt measures in their favor;

(c) To prepare reports and special studies on the situation of migrant workers and, more broadly, studies on issues pertaining to migration; and

(d) To act promptly on petitions or communications in which it is noted that the human rights of migrant workers and their families are violated in any member state of the OAS.[232]

The Rapporteur has carried out a number of thematic reports including the subjects of discrimination, racism and xenophobia; migration and human rights; due process; detention conditions; and guidance, smuggling of migrants and trafficking in persons. In respect of the work of the Rapporteur, it has been said that while 'it has been a productive and successful initiative, the Rapporteur operates with budgetary constraints that are unusually tight even in the generally under-resourced field of international human rights law'.[233]

The Inter-American Court and the Inter-American Commission have played an important role in the establishing of rights for migrant workers. These bodies have defined a

---

[229] Communication from the Commission to the Council, the European Parliament, the European Economic and Social Committee and the Committee of the Regions on immigration, integration and employment /* COM/2003/0336 final */, Communication from the Commission to the Council, the European Parliament, the European Economic and Social committee and the Committee of the Regions – A Common Agenda for Integration – Framework for the Integration of Third-Country Nationals in the European Union/* COM/2005/0389 final */, Handbook on Integration for Policy-Makers and Practitioners, 2nd edn, http://ec.europa.eu/justice_home/doc_centre/immigration/integration/doc/2007/handbook_2007_en.pdf <last visited 5 May 2009>. Council Conclusions on the strengthening of integration policies in the EU by promoting unity in diversity, www.consilium.europa.eu/ueDocs/cms_Data/docs/pressData/en/jha/94682.pdf#page=23 <last visited 5 May 2009>.

[230] See the Action Plan on Illegal Immigration, of 22 February 2002 and the Return action programme adopted on 28 November 2002.

[231] AG/RES 1404 XXVI-O/96 and AG/RES 1480 XXVII-O/97.

[232] www.cidh.org/Migrantes/migrants.functions.htm <last visited 5 May 2009>.

[233] Lyon and Paoletti, 'Inter-American Developments on Globalization's Refugees: New Rights for Migrant Workers and their Families', 3 *European Yearbook of Minority Issues* (2003/4) 63 at p. 86.

migrant worker as a 'person who is to be engaged, is engaged or has been engaged in remunerated activity in a State of which he or she is not a national'.[234] However, as Lyon and Paoletti correctly point out '[t]o date, the regional rights of migrant workers are based in equality and non-discrimination, and not in substantive economic, social and cultural rights'.[235] The Advisory Opinion of the Court on the Legal Status and Rights of Undocumented Migrants, however, ensured the individual rights of migrant workers through non-discrimination and equality, including undocumented migrant workers.[236]

Additionally, OAS adopted a Resolution on the Human Rights of All Migrant Workers and their Families in June 2000. This Resolution urges member States 'to give serious consideration to signing, ratifying, or acceding to the International Convention on the Protection of the Rights of All Migrant Workers and Members of Their Families'. The Inter-American system has a wide range of case-law elaborating upon the wide range of rights held by migrant workers, including: the right to education and nationality;[237] the right to equality and non-discrimination;[238] the right to residence and movement;[239] and the right to personal liberty and information on consular protection.[240] In conclusion, the argument seems acceptable that 'The Inter-American human rights system has acted effectively to establish progressive case law on the human rights of migrant workers, contributing both to the development of international law and to the dignity of migrant workers'.[241]

(iv) The Association of South East Asian Nations (ASEAN)

Despite being a non-binding document, the ASEAN Declaration on the Protection and Promotion of the Rights of Migrant Workers is particularly valuable in a region without a regional human rights treaty[242]. The Declaration outlines general principles, the obligations of the receiving and sending States, as well as the commitments of ASEAN. Only regular or documented migrants are protected by the Declaration, unless they 'through no fault of their own have subsequently become undocumented'.[243] Furthermore, paragraph 4 further establishes that '[n]othing in the present Declaration shall be interpreted as implying the regularisation of the situation of migrant workers who are undocumented'. Sending States are under an obligation to 'eliminate recruitment malpractice',[244] while receiving States must protect the human rights of migrant workers

---

[234] *Juridical Condition and Rights of the Undocumented Migrants*, Advisory Opinion OC-18/03, 17 September 2003, Inter-Am. Ct. H.R. (Ser. A) No. 18 (2003), para 69(h), Inter AmCommHR, Progress Report on the Situation of Migrant Workers and Their Families in the Hemisphere (1996 Annual Report), paras 10 and 11. Ibid. p. 66.

[235] Lyon and Paoletti, above n.233, at p. 69.

[236] Ibid. p. 75.

[237] *Dilcia Yean and Violeta Bosica* v. *Dominican Republic* (admissibility), Case 12.819, Report No. 28/01, Inter-Am. C.H.R., OEA/Ser.L/V/II.111 Doc. 20 rev. at 252 (2000).

[238] *Daniel David Tibi* v. *Ecuador*, Case 12.124, Report No. 90/00, OEA/Ser.L/V/II.111 Doc. 20 rev. at 262 (2000), *Margarita Cecilia Barberia Miranda* v. *Chile*, Case 292/03, Report No. 59/04, Inter-Am. C.H.R., OEA/Ser.L/V/II.122 Doc. 5 rev. 1 at 178 (2004).

[239] *Alberto Texier* v. *Chile*, Case 5713, Resolution No. 56/81 Inter-Am. C.H.R., 16 October 1981.

[240] *Jesús Enrique Valderrama Perea* v. *Ecuador*, Case 12.090, Report No. 12/02, Inter-Am. C.H.R., Doc. 5 rev. 1 at 258 (2002).

[241] Lyon and Paoletti, above n.233, at p. 87.

[242] Association of South East Asian Nations ASEAN Declaration on the Protection and Promotion of the Rights of Migrant Workers www.aseansec.org/19264.htm <last visited 12 May 2009>.

[243] ASEAN Declaration on the Protection and Promotion of the Rights of Migrant Workers, para 2.

[244] Ibid. para 14.

and provide adequate access to legal recourse in cases of 'discrimination, abuse, exploitation, [and] violence'.[245]

In July 2007 ASEAN established the ASEAN Committee on the Implementation of the ASEAN Declaration on the Protection and Promotion of the Rights of Migrant Workers.[246] The Committee shall:

1. Explore all avenues to achieve the objectives of the Declaration;

2. Facilitate sharing of best practices in the ASEAN region on matters concerning the promotion and protection of the rights of migrant workers;

3. Promote bilateral and regional cooperation and assistance on matters involving the rights of migrant workers;

4. Facilitate data sharing on matters related to migrant workers, for the purpose of enhancing policies and programmes to protect and promote the rights of migrant workers in both sending and receiving countries;

5. Encourage international organisations, ASEAN Dialogue Partners and other countries to respect the principles and extend support and assistance to the implementation of the measures contained in the Declaration;

6. Promote harmonisation of mechanisms between both sending and receiving countries that promote and protect the rights of migrant workers to implement the ASEAN commitment reflected in paragraph 17 of the Declaration;

7. Work closely with the ASEAN Secretariat in the preparation of the report of the Secretary-General of ASEAN to the ASEAN Summit; and

8. Work towards the development of an ASEAN instrument on the protection and promotion of the rights of migrant workers.[247]

The commitment of ASEAN to developing a bind legal instrument in order to reinforce the rights of migrant workers is demonstrated by the setting up of the Committee. However, the Committee could be hindered in its work by the 'national laws, regulations and policies' of the Member States, which the Committee is subject to.[248]

6 CONCLUSIONS

The essence of international human rights – as this study demonstrates – is the application of fundamental human rights law on the basis of non-discrimination. However, as this chapter has examined, the frequent instances of violations of rights of the migrant workers are condoned by national domestic systems. State as well as non-State actors consistently tend to adopt a discriminatory policy which result in exclusion, ostracisation and marginalisation of migrant workers and their families. As a UN document notes:

---

[245] Ibid. paras 5 and 9.
[246] Statement on the Establishment of the ASEAN Committee on the Implementation of the ASEAN Declaration on the Protection and Promotion of the Rights of Migrant Workers, www.aseansec.org/20768.htm <last visited 7 May 2009>.
[247] Ibid.
[248] Ibid.

A primary obstacle to full respect and enjoyment of the basic human rights of migrants is the absence, non-application or non-acceptance of the universal standards and norms in national law which explicitly recognize and extend to migrants basic human rights. Numerous countries have incorporated international human rights standards in their domestic legal systems, generally restricting their application to citizens or nationals. Even where they have been incorporated, universal human rights standards are not fully enjoyed by migrants, or are violated. Ignorance, non-awareness or disregard of relevant human rights norms by local authorities or individuals also negatively affect migrants. This phenomenon restricts the ability of the affected migrant community and potential supporters to advocate and act to defend their rights.[249]

The ILO and the United Nations have made noticeable contributions to develop norms for the protection of migrant works. After decades of struggle, the United Nations was able to draft a comprehensive Convention on the Protection of the Rights of All Migrant Workers and Members of Their Families (ICRMW). A number of positive features have been ascertained from ICRMW. It is the first comprehensive instrument dealing with the rights of migrant workers, providing a detailed definition of migrant workers and their families and analysing the position of both regular and irregular migrant workers. In terms of the substantive rights, the Convention extends and consolidates general human rights provisions to those specifically affecting migrant workers and members of their families. In its comprehensive reach the Convention establishes a number of rights for migrant workers. The Convention can in this sense become the standard-bearer for the rights of migrant workers at a global level. The Convention also contains a supervisory body and a range of implementation mechanisms. That said there are a number of limitations and weaknesses within the Convention. At the heart of these limitations is the tension between State sovereignty on the one hand and the protection of human rights on the other. This is reflected in the dichotomy between the provisions on regular and irregular migrants and their families. Furthermore, the rights to free choice of employment and family reunification are nothing more than recommendations; there are no rights to naturalisation or right of permanent residence under the Convention, which is a considerable restraint. It would be unlikely that States would be willing to give up sovereignty over such subjects as immigration control and citizenship, in order to ensure the right to remain for undocumented migrants. The Convention, in common with other UN human rights treaty-based obligations, does not provide for any binding enforcement mechanisms. Even in the presence of such attenuated implementation machinery, the disinterestedness on the part of the State towards this Convention is obvious. As noted earlier, less than a quarter of the UN Member States have become parties to ICRMW thus far. The limited work of the Committee has been confined to a consideration of a handful of reports – none of the other procedures including the individual complaints procedures have come into operation as yet.

---

[249] Commission on Human Rights, Working group of intergovernmental experts on the human rights of migrants, Third session, 23–27 November 1998, Fourth session, 8–12 February 1999, Item 14 (a) of the provisional agenda E/CN.4/1999/80 (9 March 1999), para 79.

Part V

Issues arising in international human rights law

20 International criminal law and international human rights law[1]

1 INTRODUCTION

There is a considerable relationship between international human rights law and international criminal law (ICL). However for a long time these topics were treated as discrete categories. ICL, as well as international human rights law, represents overlapping and interrelated branches of public international law,[2] and as this chapter examines, both international human rights law and ICL are very much interdependent upon each other. The demand for justice and the need for accountability in cases of gross human rights violations have provided the impetus for the establishment of national and international tribunals. In historical terms, while many of the efforts collapsed, there have nevertheless been some limited successes. International Military Tribunals in the form of the Nuremberg Tribunal and the International Military Tribunal for the Far East were established in the aftermath of the Second World War. In more recent times, *ad hoc* tribunals were established for the former Yugoslavia and Rwanda and, in 1998, the Statute of the International Criminal Court (ICC) was adopted. There has also been the adoption of the Statute of the Special Court for Sierra Leone, the Special Tribunal for Lebanon and Rules of the Extraordinary Chambers in the Courts of Cambodia and the Special Panels for Timor-Leste.

The development of ICL has matched the progress made in the field of the international standard-setting of human rights.[3] As we shall consider in this chapter, ICL has not only come to concern itself with issues like piracy, terrorism and drug trafficking, but has also more recently engaged itself with crimes which directly offend international human rights norms.[4] This interaction is reflected vividly through provisions of the Genocide Convention,[5] the Convention on the non-applicability of statutory limitations to war

---

[1] Bassiouni and Nanda (eds), *A Treatise on International Criminal Law* (Charles C. Thomas, 1973); Bantekas and Nash, *International Criminal Law* (Routledge Cavendish, 2007); Cassese, *International Criminal Law* (Oxford University Press, 2008); Cassese, 'International Criminal Law' in Evans (ed.), *International Law* (Oxford University Press, 2006) pp. 719–752; De Than and Shorts, *International Criminal Law and Human Rights* (Sweet & Maxwell, 2004); Steiner, Alston and Goodman (eds), *International Human Rights in Context: Law, Politics, Morals: Text and Materials* (Oxford University Press, 2008) pp. 1243–1384; Ratner, 'The Schizophrenias of International Criminal Law' 33 *Texas International Law Journal* (1998) 237.

[2] See Schwarzenberger, *International Law as Applied by International Courts and Tribunals* (Stephens, 1957), pp. 254–272.

[3] Bassiouni, 'International Criminal Law and Human Rights' 9 *Yale Journal of World Public Order* (1982) 193.

[4] See Bassiouni and Nanda (eds), above n.1.

[5] New York, 9 December 1948, United Nations, *Treaty Series*, vol. 78, at p. 277.

crimes and crimes against humanity,[6] the draft code of crimes against peace and security of mankind prepared by the International Law Commission,[7] the International Convention on the Suppression and Punishment of the crime of Apartheid,[8] the Convention against Torture, the jurisprudence of the *ad hoc* tribunals of the former Yugoslavia (ICTY) and Rwanda (ICTR) and more recently the International Criminal Court.[9] The jurisprudence of the ICTY and ICTR, in particular, highlights the reliance of the tribunals upon human rights instruments. In the *Furundžija* case,[10] for example, both parties as well as the Appeal Chamber made repeated references to the European Convention on Human Rights, particularly in relation to the right to a fair hearing as enunciated in Article 6.[11]

2 DEFINITION AND CHARACTERISTICS OF INTERNATIONAL CRIMINAL LAW

International criminal law (ICL) has been defined as a 'body of international rules designed both to proscribe international crimes and to impose upon States the obligation to prosecute and punish . . . those crimes. It also regulates international proceedings for prosecuting and trying persons accused of such crimes.'[12] According to Professor Cherif Bassiouni, 'international criminal law is a complex legal discipline consisting of overlapping and concurrent sources of law and emanating from international legal system and from national legal systems.'[13] As noted in an earlier chapter, the sources of international legal systems (international law) are enumerated in Article 38 of the Statute of the International Court of Justice.[14] They are (1) treaty law, (2) customary law, (3) general principles of law, and as a subsidiary means of determining the law, (4) judicial decisions and the writings of the most distinguished publicists. Yet, international crimes arise out of the international system through conventions, customs and general principles.

ICL can also be described as a hybrid branch of public international law and yet 'impregnated with notions, principles and legal constraints derived from national criminal law [International Humanitarian Law] as well as human rights law'.[15] Although principally a product of public international law, and while sharing the same sources as public international law, within ICL there are a number of specific sources which need to be highlighted. Amongst treaty law, particular importance is given to the London Agreement of 8 August

---

[6] New York, 26 November 1968, 754 U.N.T.S. 73; 8 I.L.M. 68; Miller, 'The Convention on the Non-Applicability of Statutory Limitations to War Crimes and Crimes Against Humanity' 65 *AJIL* (1971) 476.

[7] Draft Report of the International Law Commission on the work of its 43rd session UN Doc.A/CN.4/L.464 Add.4, 1991; also appended in Sunga, *Individual Responsibility in International Law for Serious Human Rights violations* (Martinus Nijhoff Publishers, 1992) at p. 169.

[8] New York, 30 November 1973, United Nations, *Treaty Series*, vol. 1015, p. 243; Brownlie (ed.), *Basic Documents on Human Rights* (Clarendon Press, 1981) at p. 164; see *Multilateral Treaties in respect of which the Secretary-General performs Depository functions* (1978) pp. 120–121.

[9] See below chapter 23.

[10] *The Prosecutor* v. *Anto Furundžija*, Case No. IT-95-17/1-T.

[11] See further *Prosecutor* v. *Jean-Paul Akayesu* Trial Chamber, Case No. ICTR-96-4-T; *Prosecutor* v. *Tadić* – Case No. IT-94-I-AR72; De Than and Shorts, above n.1, at p. 12.

[12] Cassese, 'International Criminal Law' in Evans (ed.), above n.1, at p. 719.

[13] Bassiouni, 'The Sources and Content of International Criminal Law: A Theoretical Framework, in Bassiouni (ed.), *International Criminal Law, Crimes* (Transnational Publishers, 1998) vol. 1, 3–126, at p. 4.

[14] See above chapter 2.

[15] Cassese, *International Criminal Law*, above n.1 at p. 7.

1945, which set up substantial and procedural law of the IMT of Nuremberg.[16] The 1998 Statute of the International Criminal Court is also a product of a multilateral treaty agreement.[17] Additional treaties of primary significance are the four Geneva Conventions (1949) and the three additional Protocols.[18] Customary international rules could be drawn from analysing State practices, case-law, as well as practical implementation of treaties. General principles of international criminal law play an instrumental role – some of these include, for example, presumption of innocence, equality of arms between parties and the principle of command responsibility. Similarly, in order to establish offences and legal principles, ICL has often had to rely upon major legal traditions of the world. Thus, in attempting to define rape, the trial chamber in the *Furundžija* case was unable to obtain an adequate definition either from treaty or customary law and thus found it 'necessary to look for principles of criminal law common to the major legal systems of the world'.[19] Similarly, procedural rules have also been devised from general principles or reliance upon national laws. That said, this borrowing from domestic legal systems has not always been unproblematic, given the different context within which international accountability mechanisms operate, and the application of the law to mass atrocities (as opposed to individual incidents as is more the norm within domestic legal systems).[20]

3 THE DEVELOPMENTAL PROCESS OF ICL

Notwithstanding the substantial modern relevance of ICL which incorporates various aspects of public international law, human rights law and international humanitarian law, the discipline itself is in a rudimentary and formative phase.[21] The first substantial attempt to establish international criminal institutions was conducted in the aftermath of the First World War. In 1919 the Commission on the Responsibility of the Authors of the War and on the Enforcement of Penalties[22] advanced the idea for the establishment of a 'high tribunal composed of Judges drawn from many nations, and included the possibility of trail before that tribunal of a former head of state with the consent of that state itself secured by

---

[16] For the text of the Charter of the International Military Tribunal and other related documents see the Avalon Project at Yale Law School www.yale.edu/lawweb/avalon/imt/proc/imtconst.htm <last visited 2 May 2009>.

[17] Rome Statute of the International Criminal Court, 2187 U.N.T.S. 90, entered into force 1 July 2002, www.icc-cpi.int/library/about/officialjournal/Rome_Statute_120704-EN.pdf <last visited 15 May 2009>.

[18] Convention (I) for the Amelioration of the Condition of the Wounded and Sick in Armed Forces in the Field. Geneva, 12 August 1949; Convention (II) for the Amelioration of the Condition of Wounded, Sick and Shipwrecked Members of Armed Forces at Sea. Geneva, 12 August 1949; Convention (III) Relative to the Treatment of Prisoners of War. Geneva, 12 August 1949; Convention (IV) Relative to the Protection of Civilian Persons in Time of War. Geneva, 12 August 1949; Protocol Additional to the Geneva Conventions of 12 August 1949, and relating to the Protection of Victims of International Armed Conflicts (Protocol I), 8 June 1977; Protocol Additional to the Geneva Conventions of 12 August 1949, and relating to the Protection of Victims of Non-International Armed Conflicts (Protocol II), 8 June 1977; Protocol additional to the Geneva Conventions of 12 August 1949, and relating to the Adoption of an Additional Distinctive Emblem (Protocol III), 8 December 2005.

[19] Note, however, that a definition of rape has already been adopted in the Akayesu judgment at the ICTR (*Prosecutor* v. *Jean-Paul Akayesu* Trial Chamber, Case No. ICTR-96-4-T), but the ICTY chose not to rely on this. See further *Prosecutor* v. *Anto Furundžija*, Case No. IT-95-17/1-T, 10 December 1998, para 177.

[20] See MacKinnon, 'The ICTR's Legacy on Sexual Violence' 14 *New Eng. J. Int'l & Comp. L.* (2008) 211.

[21] Cassese, 'International Criminal Law' in Evans (ed.), above n.1, 719–752, at p. 720.

[22] See *Report Presented to the Preliminary Peace Conference by the Commission on the Responsibilities of the Authors of War and on Enforcement of Penalties* (Carnegie Endowment for International Peace, Division of International Law Pamphlet No. 32, 1919), reprinted in 14 *AJIL* (1920) 95.

articles in, the Treaty of Peace'.[23] The provisions of the Treaty of Versailles also provided for the punishment of those engaged in war crimes committed before and during the First World War. Article 227 provided for the accountability of the German Emperor (Wilhelm II) for 'Supreme offence against international morality and sanctity of treaties'.[24] Within the treaty it was also envisioned to establish a 'special tribunal', composed of five Judges (consisting of the United States, Great Britain, France, Italy and Japan) who would have the responsibility of trying the German Emperor.[25] The trial never came to fruition for a variety of political reasons – there was concern as to the issue of fairness of such a trial, as well as the exact legality of the offences for which the Emperor would be tried. Thus, in the end, trials, as envisaged by Articles 228–230, of war criminals by an international criminal court did not take place. A few trials did take place before a German court 'the Imperial Court of Justice' although the effort to indict war criminals before an international criminal court ended in failure. In addition there were attempts to conduct trials against the Germans, at the end of the First World War, and efforts were made to try Turks involved in the genocide of the Armenians.[26] Unfortunately, these as well as other attempts made during the period between the two World Wars, did not bear fruit. Further efforts by the League of Nations to establish an international criminal court were frustrated through the turmoil and instability preceding the commencement of the Second World War.

The first serious and substantial landmark in the concretisation of ICL took place in the aftermath of the Second World War. The desire to punish and bring to justice those involved in acts of genocide and crimes against humanity, led to a number of efforts for the establishment of a permanent international criminal tribunal. During the summer of 1945, representatives from the victorious allied powers in the Second World War convened in London, where a decision was made to conduct trials and to punish high-ranking Nazi war criminals. On 8 August 1945, the London Agreement for the Prosecution and Punishment of Major War Criminals of the European Axis was concluded, attached to which is the Nuremberg Charter for the establishment of the International Military Tribunal.[27] Article 6 of the Charter of the International Military Tribunal annexed to the agreement signed by the Four-Powers in 1945 provided for the establishment of a tribunal to prosecute and punish war criminals, who were involved in the commission of any of the following offences:

(a) Crimes against Peace;
namely planning preparation, initiation or waging of a war of aggression, or a war in violation of international treaties, agreements or assurances, or participation in a common plan or conspiracy for the accomplishment of any of the foregoing;

---

[23] Ibid. at p. 116.
[24] 28 June 1919, L.N.T.S. No. 24; 112 B.F.S.P.1.
[25] Ibid.
[26] See Milanović, 'State Responsibility for Genocide' 17 *EJIL* (2006) 553 at p. 563; Kuper, 'The Turkish Genocide of Armenians, 1915–1917' in Hovannisian (ed.), *The Genocide in Perspective* (Transaction Publishers, 1986) pp. 43–59.
[27] *International Military Tribunal Charter, also known as the London Charter and the Nuremburg Charter, in Agreement for the Prosecution and Punishment of the Major War Criminals of the European Axis (London Agreement)*, 8 August 1945, 58 Stat. 1544, E.A.S. No. 472, 82 U.N.T.S. 280. For the text of the Charter of the International Military Tribunal see the Avalon Project at Yale Law School www.yale.edu/lawweb/avalon/imt/proc/imtconst.htm <last visited 2 May 2009>.

(b) War Crimes;

namely, violations of the laws or customs of war. Such violations shall include, but not be limited to murder, ill-treatment or deportation to slave labour or for any other purpose of civilian population of or in occupation of or in occupied territory, murder or ill treatment of prisoners of war or persons on the seas, killing of hostages, plunder of public or private property, wanton destruction of cities, towns or villages, or devastation of cities, towns or villages, or devastation not justified by military necessity;

(c) Crimes against Humanity;

murder, extermination, enslavement, deportation and other inhumane acts committed against any civilian population before or during the war, or persecution on political, racial or religious grounds in execution of or in connection with any crime within the jurisdiction of the tribunal, whether or not in violation of the domestic law of the country where perpetrated.[28]

Whilst war crimes and crimes against peace had been recognised as international criminal offences prior to the commencement of the Second World War, the acknowledgement of the presence of crimes against humanity as a distinct category of offence was a particularly controversial subject. As shall be examined in more detail, the concept of crimes against humanity, at the end of the Second World War, posed serious and substantial controversies.[29] Crimes against humanity had occupied a subsidiary position to war crimes, and did not emerge as a separate concept in international law until at least 1923,[30] meaning thereby that offences committed by governments against their own nationals were not within any of the recognised categories of international crime.[31] Fortuitously, the assortment of human rights violations during the Second World War presented a unique opportunity to accept crimes against humanity as a distinct category within international criminal law. Furthermore, the atrocities committed by the Nazis had produced a united front against those involved in serious crimes of international law and also opened up the possibility of the expansion of crimes against humanity to include the criminalisation of genocide.[32]

---

[28] International Military Tribunal Charter, also known as the London Charter and the Nuremburg Charter, in Agreement for the Prosecution and Punishment of the Major War Criminals of the European Axis (London Agreement), August 8, 1945, 58 Stat. 1544, E.A.S. No. 472, 82 U.N.T.S. 280.

[29] Schwelb, 'Crimes Against Humanity' 23 BYIL (1946) 178, at p. 178; Brand, 'Crimes against Humanity and Nuremberg Trials' 28 Oregon Law Review (1949) 93; Bassiouni, above n.3; Bassiouni, 'Crimes against Humanity: The Need for a Specialized Convention' 31 Col.JTL (1992) 457; Kuper, Genocide Its Political Use in the Twentieth Century (Yale University Press, 1982) at p. 21; On war crimes see Lauterpacht, 'The Law of Nations and the Punishment of War Crimes' 21 BYIL (1944) 58.

[30] Bassiouni, 'International law and the Holocaust' 9 California Western International Law Journal (1978) 202 at p. 211. In the peace treaties of Versailles (Art. 228–230) Saint-Germain-en-laye (Art. 173–76), Trianon (Art. 157–159), Neuilly-sur-seine (Art. 118–120), the term crimes against humanity does not appear. Although in the Treaty of Sèvres (1920) the substance of the concept does make an appearance, the treaty itself remained unratified and was replaced by another treaty, the treaty of Lausanne which allowed for a general amnesty. Treaty of Peace with Turkey Signed at Lausanne, 24 July 1923, from The Treaties of Peace 1919–1923, Vol. II (Carnegie Endowment for International Peace, 1924); see Schwelb, above n.29, p. 182.

[31] Thornberry, International Law and the Rights of Minorities (Clarendon Press, 1991) at p. 88.

[32] Genocide, as a concept was signified as a Crime against Humanity in the Nuremberg Charter. It became a separate offence after the Genocide Convention of 1948.

International criminal law and international human rights law

20

The International Military Tribunal met from 14 November 1945 until 1 October 1946.[33] Trials were conducted by the occupying powers within Germany of lower-ranking defendants under the auspices of Control Council Law No. 10. The Potsdam Declaration of 26 July 1945 also pronounced the Allied Powers intention to hold trials of Japanese officials involved in serious crimes.[34] The resulting manifestation – the Tokyo trials – was modelled on a similar basis to the Nuremberg tribunal. The Tokyo trials which started in May 1946 continued for nearly two and a half years.[35]

Following the unconditional surrender of Germany, the supreme legislative authority in that country was exercised by the Allied Control Council composed of the authorised representatives of the four powers. On 20 December 1945, that body enacted Control Council Law No. 10 (CCL No. 10) to regulate the apprehension, surrender and trial of war criminals throughout Germany.[36] According to this law each occupying authority within its own zone of occupation had the right to bring to trial before an appropriate tribunal all persons accused of committing any of the crimes provided for in Article II of CCL No. 10. During the period from 26 October, 1946 until 14 April 1949, 12 subsequent Nuremberg trials were held. These trials were undertaken by civilian judges who were selected and brought to Germany to try the secondary leaders of those same classes of crimes as had been tried by the IMT.[37]

The Tokyo and Nuremberg trials in particular, have been criticised in a variety of manners.[38] In some instances, the Nazi and Japanese war criminals were tried for the offences which the Allied Victorious Powers had themselves committed. There were also accusations of the failure to apply the legal principle of *nullum crimen, nulla poena sine praevia lege poenali* (no crime, no punishment without a previous penal law). The trials and convictions resulting from these trails were viewed by many as a reflection of 'victor's justice' which was one-sided and biased. Professor Bassiouni laments the fact that:

[33] Trials were conducted of 22 defendants, of whom 19 were found guilty of some charges. While 12 were sentenced to death, seven received a variety of prison sentences ranging from 10 years to life imprisonment. For further details see Austin, 'The Nuremberg Trial: The Defendants and Verdicts' http://frank.mtsu.edu/~baustin/trials3.html <last visited 12 January 2009>.

[34] See Text of the Constitution and Other Documents, *Potsdam Declaration Proclamation Defining Terms for Japanese Surrender*, Issued at Potsdam, 26 July 1945 www.ndl.go.jp/constitution/e/etc/c06.html <last visited 15 May 2009>. For a detailed and systematic analysis of the International Military Tribunal at Nuremberg see Taylor, *The Anatomy of the Nuremberg Trials: A Personal Memoir* (Alfred A. Knopf, 1992); Willis, *Prologue to Nuremberg: The Politics and Diplomacy of Punishing War Criminals of the First World War* (Greenwood, 1982); Conot, *Justice at Nuremberg* (Weidenfeld and Nicolson, 1983); Sprecher, *Inside the Nuremberg Trial: A Prosecutor's Comprehensive Account* (University Press of America, 1999); Smith, *Reaching Judgment at Nuremberg* (Basic Books, 1977); Smith, *The American Road to Nuremberg: The Documentary Record 1944–1945* (Hoover Institution Press, 1982).

[35] Of the 28 defendants, two died during the course of the trial and a third was held mentally incapable. Amongst the remaining 25, seven were sentenced to death, 16 were awarded life imprisonment, one was handed a seven-year sentence of imprisonment and another one of 22 years. See further Bass, *Stay the Hand of Vengeance: The Politics of War Crimes Tribunals* (Princeton University Press, 2000). The International Military Tribunal for the Far East was first contemplated by the Cairo Declaration of 1 December 1943. Further references were made in the Declaration of Potsdam of 26 July 1945, the Instrument of Surrender of 2 September 1945, and the Moscow Conference of 26 December 1945. There were 55 counts, dealing with crimes against peace and war crimes. There were no charges of membership in criminal organisations and no crimes against humanity except where borne directly upon war crimes. For more details on the IMTFE see Appleman, *Military Tribunals and International Crimes* (Bobbs-Merrill, 1954) pp. 237–264.

[36] Allied Control Council Law No. 10 Punishment of Persons Guilty of War Crimes, Crimes Against Peace and Against Humanity, 20 December 1945 (CCL No. 10), Official Gazette of the Control Council for Germany, No. 3, Berlin, 31 January 1946. See Badar, *The Concept of Mens Rea in International Criminal Law: The Case for a Unified Approach* (Hart Publishing, 2009).

[37] See Appleman, above n.35, at IX.

[38] Roberts, 'The Laws of War: Problems of Implementation in Contemporary Conflicts' 6 *Duke Journal of Comparative and International law* (1995–1996) 11 at p. 24.

[O]ne sided justice does reveal the still arbitrary, *adhoc* nature of the international legal system. Germany, during World War I and World War II, had records of Allied violations of the very laws and rules which the Allies charged Germany of violating. The German documentation of World War I Allies' violations against Germany even escaped public attention and no significant trace of world war II Allied violations against Germany and against Germans and other appears in the recollection of world public opinion. Some exceptions exist, however, such as the dreadful firebombing of Dresden, a city of strategic importance in December 1944, after the war had been won. This event that remains in the worlds conscience as a symbol of the terrible and unnecessary suffering inflicted upon German civilian population. It is also shocking that the wholesale violations of conventional and customary rules of war against German prisoners of war by the USSR, have escaped international public attention. An equal disregard applies to the Allies' violations against the Japanese, the worst example of which the world community's apparent approval of the use of two atomic bombs in 1945 against the cities of Hiroshima and Nagasaki, killing and injuring hundreds of thousands of civilians. Had Japan and Germany so bombed an Allied power, there is no doubt that its perpetrators, from the decision-makers to the crews of the planes that dropped the bombs, would have been tried and convicted of war crimes.[39]

Notwithstanding, the substantial defects and the criticism of the Nuremberg and Tokyo trials, these trials were not totally without merits.[40] Several positives emerged for the development of ICL. It was the first time that international criminal trials were conducted and convictions obtained. Secondly, ICL was expanded through the induction, recognition and affirmation of crimes against humanity as well as the crime of genocide. Thirdly, ICL also made distinct advances towards the development of the principle of individual criminal responsibility and the formulation of a scheme of accountability through criminal prosecutions. The defendants were unable to rely upon the defence of State immunity or the defence of superior order *per se* (although the Tribunal took into account this defence when awarding sentencing). Fourthly, the jurisprudence emerging from the Nuremberg and Tokyo trials advanced greatly the norms pertaining to international criminal justice, and also provided an inspirational force behind further developments of general international law.

(i) Cold War politics and the stalemate in efforts to establish a permanent International Criminal Court

The end of the Second World War witnessed considerable activity in the advancement of ICL. The Nuremberg and Tokyo trials proved a burgeoning source of jurisprudence on which to further consolidate the emergent principles of crimes against humanity and genocide. Genocide, as shall be discussed shortly, evolved as an independent crime within international law with the text of Genocide Convention providing for the establishment of an 'international penal tribunal' for trials of acts amounting to genocide.[41] These developments promised an era of universal human rights and accountability for serious crimes

---

[39] Bassiouni, *Crimes against Humanity in International Criminal Law* (Kluwer Law International, 1999) at pp. 552–553.
[40] See ibid. pp. 547–556.
[41] Article VI, Genocide Convention. For analysis see above chapter 13.

against humanity with anticipation that such an international criminal court could exercise jurisdiction over all individuals at a global level. With such an objective, the United Nations General Assembly requested the International Law Commission (ILC) to examine the possibility of establishing a permanent International Criminal court. The ILC responded positively by producing two draft statutes, one in 1951[42] and the other in 1953.[43] The era of hope and enthusiasm was, however, to prove short lived. The work towards the establishment of the Court stalled as a consequence of Cold War politics and little substantive progress was made in the years that followed.

The Cold War years were characterised by a lack of interest, either in the establishment of an international tribunal or holding those involved in serious crimes accountable. In the subsequent 40 years, a handful of trials were conducted, almost exclusively within domestic courts. These included the infamous Eichmann trial in Israel in (1961),[44] Paul Touvier trial in France (1994),[45] Klaus Barbie (1983) in France,[46] Finta (1994)[47] in Canada, and Erich Preibke (1996) in Italy,[48] *Demjanjuk* in the United States and Israel (1987–1993),[49] and Andrei Sawoniuk (1999) in the United Kingdom.[50] There were also attempts made to hold international war criminals, as evidenced in the case of the establishment of the War Crimes Tribunal for the genocide and crimes against humanity in the former East Pakistan.[51] Such attempts in the international arena were stalled principally due to Cold War politics and selfish interests of the permanent members of the Security Council.

(ii) The *ad hoc* International Criminal Tribunals

The thaw in the relationship between former adversaries of Western and Eastern Europe and the collapse of the Communist Soviet Union, provided a brief spell of international consensus on human rights issues. This was a period which witnessed an unprecedented

[42] See Report of the Committee on the International Criminal Jurisdiction 1–3 August 1951; UN GAOR, 7th Session, Supp. No. 11, Annex 1 at 21, UN Doc. A/2136 (1952).

[43] See Report of the 1953 Committee on the International Criminal Jurisdiction 27 July–20 August 1953; UN GAIR, 9th Session Supp. No. 12 UN Doc. A/2645 (1954).

[44] *Attorney-General of the Government of Israel* v. *Eichmann* 36 ILR 5 (Dist. Ct. Jerusalem, 1961) *Attorney-General of the Government of Israel* v. *Eichmann*, 36 I.L.R. 277 (Israel Supreme Court 1962); Silving, 'In Re Eichmann: A Dilemma of Law and Morality' (1961) 55 *AJIL*, 307.

[45] Judgment of 2 June 1993, Cour d'Appel de Versailles; See Tigar, Casey, Giordami and Mardemootoo, 'Touvier and Crimes against Humanity' 30 *Texas ILJ* (1995) 285; Wexler, 'Reflections on the Trial of Vichy Collaborator Paul Touvier for Crimes against Humanity in France' 20 *Law and Social Inquiry* (1995) 191.

[46] Judgment of 20 December, 1985. Cass. Crim., 1985 Bull. Crim. No. 407 at 1038 (Fr.).

[47] *R.* v. *Finta* [1994] 1 R.C.S. 701 (Canada).

[48] CNN, 'Ex-Nazi Cleared of Most Serious Massacre Charge' 1 August 1996, www.cnn.com/WORLD/9608/01/priebke/index.html <last visited 2 May 2009>.

[49] See *Demjanjuk* v. *Petrovsky* 776 F 2d 571 (6th Cir. 1985), 582.

[50] [2000] 2 Cr. App. Rep. 220. See Hirsh, 'The Trial of Andrei Sawoniuk: Holocaust Testimony under Cross-Examination' 10 *Social and Legal Studies* (2001) 529; Cryer, Witness Evidence Before International Criminal Tribunals' 3 *The Law and Practice of International Courts and Tribunals* (2003) 411.

[51] See The Bangladesh Gazette Extraordinary, International Crimes (Tribunal) Act 1973, Bangladesh, Act No. XIX of 1973. Under the provisions of this Act, a Tribunal (with a permanent seat in Dacca) was to be established to try War Crimes, Crimes Against Peace, Genocide and Violations of the Geneva Convention 1949 conducted by the Pakistan Armed forces during the Civil war wished had ensued from March–December 1971; reprinted in Rehman, *The Weaknesses in the International Protection of Minority Rights* (Kluwer Law International, 2000) Appendix D. Also see Paust and Blaustein, 'War Crimes Jurisdiction and Due Process: The Bangladesh Experience' 11 *Vand.JTL* (1978) 1; International Commission of Jurists, *The Events of East Pakistan, 1971: A Legal Study* (International Commission of Jurists, 1972).

agreement within the Security Council and revitalised hope for the prosecution of international crimes such as crimes against humanity and genocide.[52] However, the end of the Cold War period also unfortunately coincided with terrible human rights violations in many parts of the world. The Superpower rivalry, which during the Cold War period had managed to sustain a modicum of international political order and stability, dissipated with the collapse of the Soviet Empire. The demise of communism in Eastern Europe unleashed forces of chaos and anarchy, accompanied by, as was witnessed in the break-up of the Former Yugoslavia, considerable bloodshed and human rights abuses. The 100 days of genocide in Rwanda was one of the worst atrocities witnessed in the 20th century. Despite calls for accountability and due process, neither domestic courts nor international institutions had judicial mechanisms for providing appropriate remedies and criminal sanctions.[53]

A partial attempt to redress the existing lacuna in the judicial machinery was conducted by the Security Council when, acting under Chapter VII of the United Nations Charter, in its Resolution 827 (1993)[54] and 955 (1994),[55] it established the *ad hoc* tribunals for the former Yugoslavia and Rwanda. There are many commonalities between the two tribunals. The tribunals used to have the same prosecutor and both share an identical Appeals Chamber.[56] In 2000, the Statute for Rwanda Tribunal was amended which allowed for the appointment of two appellate judges sitting in The Hague, alongside five judges from the Yugoslav tribunal, these Judges constitute the Appeals Chamber for the two Tribunals.[57] Both the *ad hoc* tribunals have also shared the same prosecutor, although from September 2003 the United Nations Security Council appointed separate prosecutors for the two tribunals, following criticism from the Rwandan government.[58]

The tribunals were, nevertheless, criticised for a variety of shortcomings, weakness and limitations. The principal criticisms as regards the ICTY was that it was more a symbol of the United Nations' inability to find a swift and adequate resolution to the conflict within Yugoslavia, that the establishment of the tribunal was *ultra vires*, the powers of the UN Security Council, and in the light of its limited jurisdiction, the Tribunal was providing a limited and rather ineffectual justice.[59] The ICTY has jurisdiction to try offences including grave breaches of the Geneva Conventions, violations of the laws and customs of war, genocide and crimes against humanity allegedly perpetrated in the former Yugoslavia since 1 January 1991.

---

[52] On the role of the Security Council see above chapter 5.

[53] Roberts, 'The Laws of War. Problems of Implementation in Contemporary Conflicts' 6 *Duke Journal of Comparative and International law* (1995–1996) 11 at p. 57.

[54] See SC Res. 827, 48 UN SCOR 3217th mtg., UN Doc. S/RES/827 (1993) reprinted 32 I.L.M. 1203; for the jurisprudence and case-law of the tribunal see www.un.org/icty <last visited 15 May 2009>.

[55] See SC Res. 955, UN SCOR 3453th mtg., UN Doc. S/RES/955 (1994) reprinted 33 I.L.M. 1598; for the jurisprudence of the tribunal see www.un.org/ictr <last visited 15 May 2009>.

[56] Oosthuizen and Schaeffer, 'Complete Justice: Residual functions and potential residual mechanisms of the ICTY, ICTR and SCSL' 3(1) *Hague Justice Journal* (2008) 48 at p. 64.

[57] UN Doc. S/RES/1329.

[58] Steiner, Alston and Goodman above n.1 at p. 1273; as the former Attorney-General Gahima noted, 'How can a genocide that claimed a million people be a person's part-time job? And this person is based at The Hague, not close to Rwanda'. UN Wire, Gov't, UN Prosecutor Trade Barbs Over Lack Of Cooperation, 25 July 2002. www.unwire.org/unwire/20020725/27905_story.asp <last visited 15 May 2009>.

[59] See Robertson, *Crimes against Humanity: The Struggle for Global Justice* (New Press; Distributed by W.W. Norton, 2006) at pp. 382–384.

The Rwanda tribunal (ICTR) was faced with substantial problems of administrative management and the scale of the genocide. Article 1 of the Statute of the ICTR provides that the tribunal:

> shall have the power to prosecute persons responsible for serious violations of international humanitarian law committed in the territory of Rwanda and Rwandan citizens responsible for such violations committed in the territory of neighbouring States, between 1 January 1994 and 31 December 1994, in accordance with the provisions of the present Statute.

The ICTR has jurisdiction to try crimes of genocide, crimes against humanity, violations of Article 3 of the Geneva Conventions and the Second Additional Protocol perpetrated in Rwanda (or in 'the territory of neighbouring States in respect of serious violations of international humanitarian law committed by Rwandan citizens') during the period between 1 January and 31 December 1994.

At the time of writing, the ICTY has indicted 161 individuals for serious violations of international humanitarian law. Among those 161 indictees there are 48 accused on ongoing proceedings and 116 on concluded proceedings. As for the ongoing proceedings there are: nine before the Appeals Chamber; 28 currently at trial; two under a judgment that still can be appealed; one awaiting Trial Chamber Judgment; five at pre-trial stage and two at large, namely Goran Hadžić, and Ratko Mladić (commander of the Bosnian Serb Army). As for the concluded proceedings: 10 were acquitted; 55 were sentenced; 13 referred to national jurisdiction pursuant to Rule 11*bis*; and 36 had their indictments withdrawn or are deceased. Slobodan Milošević, former President of Serbia 1989–97 and former President of the Federal Republic of Yugoslavia 1997–2000, is among the six deceased after transfer to the Tribunal.

The Yugoslavia Tribunal was heavily criticised on the grounds that it failed to conduct an expeditious trial for Milošević.[60] According to one commentator, the Trial of Milošević 'began in February 2002, but the Prosecution case alone took three years. By 24 November 2005 this "whale of a trial" had produced 46,639 pages of transcript and 2256 separate written filings amounting to 63,775 pages. The prosecution had introduced 930 exhibits, amounting to 85,526 pages, as well as 117 videos. The material disclosed to Milošević amounted to over 1.2 million pages of documentation – material he would never have time to read, let alone absorb. In answer to all this, he initially submitted a list of 1631 witnesses. By the end of 2005, 75 per cent of the way through the time allocated for his defence, he had introduced 50 videos and 9000 pages of exhibits but had led only 40 witnesses and had barely touched on the indictment relating to Croatia and Bosnia.'[61]

At the beginning of 2009, ICTR trial chambers had completed proceedings in 34 cases, resulting in some 29 convictions and five acquittals. Furthermore, there were 29 cases in progress, in addition to one appeal and nine awaiting trial.[62] The judgments delivered so far involve one prime minister (Jean Kambanda) who pleaded guilty for the crime of genocide and was sentenced to life imprisonment, six Ministers, one Prefect, seven Bourgmestres and several others holding leadership positions during the conflict in 1994,

---

[60] See Boas, *The Milošević Trial: Lessons for the Conduct of Complex International Criminal Proceedings* (Cambridge University Press, 2007).
[61] Ibid. at xii–xiiii.
[62] See Status of Cases www.69.94.11.53/default.htm <last visited 18 November 2008>.

in which the estimated total number of victims varies from 500,000 to 1,000,000 or more.[63] In comparison to the mass atrocities and human rights violations that have occurred, the actual number of individuals brought to justice is miniscule. Furthermore, the Security Council has instructed the *ad hoc* tribunals to complete their undertaking by the end of 2010 (completion strategy) and both tribunals are working towards this end.[64] The overall contribution of the *ad hoc* tribunals towards enforcing international criminal law, within the limited jurisdictions remains a matter of contention. The establishment of the tribunals have, nevertheless, not been a matter of a pure formality – the decisions as well as the jurisprudence of the tribunals have added to international criminal laws.[65]

4 THE INTERNATIONAL CRIMINAL COURT (ICC)[66]

During the 1980s various factors combined to reinvigorate efforts to establish an international Permanent Court. As noted above, these factors included the thaw in East–West relations as well as a growing concern over serious crimes such as drug trafficking and international terrorism. This tumultuous period produced a significant amount of agreement amongst the major powers and yet bore witness to incredible amount of international and regional conflicts resulting in serious and egregious violations of human rights. The impetus towards the establishment of an international criminal court however was provided by a suggestion from Trinidad and Tobago in 1989, that a specialised court be established to deal with the offence of drug trafficking.

The proposals from Trinidad and Tobago were taken up by the General Assembly which instructed the International Law Commission (ILC) to 'address the question of establishing an international criminal court'.[67] The ILC's report (although not entirely focused on the subject of drug-trafficking) completed in 1990 was received favourably by the General Assembly and the ILC was encouraged to develop further the draft of the ICC. The ILC was able to produce a comprehensive draft in 1993, which was further modified in 1994.[68] During the same year, in order to examine the major substantive issues in the draft Statute, the General Assembly established an Ad Hoc committee on the establishment of an International Criminal Court. In 1995 the General Assembly established a preparatory committee for the

---

[63] *Prosecutor v. Jean-Paul Akayesu*, Case No. ICTR-96-4-T, Judgment, 2 September 1998, para 111.

[64] See S/RES/1503 (2003) and S/RES/1534 (2004).

[65] For a flavour of the jurisprudence from the tribunals see, e.g., the following *Prosecutor v. Kunarac et al., Case No.* IT-96-23-T & IT-96-23/1-T; *Prosecutor v. Mucić et al.*, Case No. IT-96-21-A (2001) (Čelebići Camp), 8 April 2003; *Akayesu* (ICTR) *Prosecutor v. Ferdinand Nahimana, Jean-Bosco Barayagwiza and Hassan Ngeze*–Case no. ICTR-99-52-T (The *Hate Media* case) (ICTR).

[66] See Marquardt, 'Law without Borders: The Constitutionality of an International Criminal Court' 33 *Col.JTL* (1995) 73; Ambos, 'Establishing an International Criminal Court and an International Criminal Code: Observations from an International Criminal Law Viewpoint' 7 *EJIL* (1996) 519; Gilmore, 'The Proposed International Criminal Court: Recent Developments' 5 *Transnational Law and Contemporary Problems* (1995) 263; Bassiouni and Blakesley, 'The Need for an International Criminal Court in the New World Order' 25 *Vand.JTL* (1992) 151; Dugard, 'Obstacles in the way of an International Criminal Court' 56 *Cambridge Law Journal* (1997) 329; Stevens, 'Towards a Permanent International Criminal Court' 6(3) *European Journal of Crime, Criminal Law and Criminal Justice* (1998) 236; Goldsmith, 'The Self-Defeating International Criminal Court' *University of Chicago Law Review* (2003) 89.

[67] GA Res. 44/39 (4 December 1989).

[68] Report of the International Law Commission, 46th session (2 May–22 July 1994) UN GAOR, 49th Session, Supp. No. 10, UN Doc. A/49/10 (1994); Cassese 'International Criminal Law' in Evans (ed.), above n.1, at p. 727.

establishment of an International Criminal Court (PrepCom).[69] There were significant differences in the nature of assignments provided for by the two committees. While the Ad Hoc committee's role was of a more general nature as regards the proposition of having a viable court, the focus of the preparatory committee was squarely upon the text of the Court's statute.[70] The PrepCom, which consisted of States representatives as well as representatives from non-governmental organisations and international organisations, thus, had the more ambitious assignment of drafting a comprehensive instrument which was practicable and yet acceptable to all relevant parties. The PrepCom had two to three-week sessions in 1996 and presented the General Assembly with substantial revisions to the draft ILC statute.[71] In December 1997, it was decided by the General Assembly that the PrepCom should convene in two three-week sessions and in its first session 1997–98 'complete the drafting of a widely acceptable consolidated text of a convention [and that] a diplomatic conference of plenipotentiaries shall be held in 1998, with a view to finalizing and adopting a Convention on the establishment of an International Criminal Court'.[72]

After a series of sessions during 1997–98, the Committee (PrepCom) was able to submit to a Diplomatic conference held in Rome in July 1998 a draft statute and draft final act comprising of 116 Articles which contained 173 pages of text but with some 1300 words in 'square brackets'. The 'square brackets' indicated those issues of disagreement which had as yet to be resolved. The diplomatic conference also known as the United Nations Conference on Plenipotentiaries on the Establishment of an ICC took place from 15 June–17 July 1998 in Rome, Italy with the participation of 160 States and over 200 non-governmental organisations. The political groups highlighted the complexities facing the future of the Court.[73] The first political group is broadly described as consisting of the 'like-minded States'. The 'like-minded States' numbering up to 60 were made up primarily of European and Commonwealth States, with the United Kingdom joining at a later stage.[74] The 'like-minded States' favoured the establishment of strong court with 'automatic jurisdiction' over core crimes of genocide, crimes against humanity, war crimes and aggression, removal of the 'veto' powers of the Security Council, with an independent prosecutor with the authority to institute proceedings *proprio motu* and argued in favour of a broad definition of war crimes including crimes committed abroad in and internal armed conflicts.

The second political grouping, the so-called 'P–5' was led by the United States. This group was opposed to the 'automatic jurisdiction' and to the prosecutor being granted the power to initiate proceedings. The United States also was vociferous in its efforts to ensure that extensive powers were granted to the Security Council both in its ability to refer matters to the ICC and also to prevent cases being brought before the Court: thus, the principal US argument was that the ICC prosecutions must be limited to cases referred to it by the Security Council.[75] The United States initially signed the text of the Statute on

---

[69] GA Res. 50/46 (11 December 1995).
[70] Arsanjani, 'The Rome Statute of the International Criminal Court' 93 *AJIL* (1999) 22.
[71] See 'Report of the Preparatory Committee on the Establishment of an International Criminal Court' UN Doc. A/51/22.
[72] GA Res. 51/207, 17 December 1996.
[73] For useful information on the conference including background information see www.un.org/icc/index.htm <last visited 15 May 2009>.
[74] Schabas, *An Introduction to International Criminal Court* (Cambridge University Press, 2001) p. 15 n.53 lists the countries.
[75] Goldsmith, above n.66, at p. 90.

31 December 2000, but subsequently withdrew its signature in May 2002.[76] It has, henceforth, adopted a hostile attitude towards the treaty as well as the Court. The caucuses of the third group, the Non-Aligned Movement, wanted the Court to have jurisdiction over crimes of aggression and a number of these countries also wanted a broader jurisdiction covering offences such as drug-trafficking. Other States, such as India, Sri Lanka, Algeria and Turkey, wanted the inclusion of terrorism to fall within the jurisdiction of the Court. As a part of these wider caucuses, the Arab and Islamic group campaigned for the prohibition of nuclear weapons and the retention of capital punishment in the Statute. Despite many compromises in the text of the Rome Statute (some of which weaken the effectiveness of the ICC), it was not possible to keep the United States and some others on board.

A number of compromises were offered. The statute was eventually adopted by 120 votes to seven against (including the United States, Israel and China) with 21 abstentions.[77] The ICC statute entered into force on 1 July 2002 and the first judges were elected in February 2003.[78] The Statute consists of a preamble, 13 parts, including 128 Articles.[79] The number of States parties is currently 108. The United States coerced several states into entering bi-lateral agreements made pursuant to Article 98(2) of the Statute. The article prevents the court from proceeding with a request to surrender an accused person, if such an action would lead to a violation of an existing international agreement. It was intended to avoid conflicts arising where they were pre-existing Status of Forces Agreements or Status of Mission Agreements in place. The bi-lateral agreements were, however, much broader providing a cover for all US nationals. The US further threatened to veto all Security Council Resolutions authorising peace-keeping and collective security operations until the Security Council provided explicit immunity for such missions from the Court's jurisdiction.[80]

(i) The role, functions and jurisdictional issues of the ICC

The ICC is a permanent judicial institution, a product of an internationally binding instrument. It is endowed with a separate and distinct international legal personality. Article 34 establishes the following organs of the Court: (a) a Presidency, (b) an Appeals Division, a Trial Division and a Pre-Trial Division, (c) the Office of the Prosecutor, and (d) The Registry. The Court comprises of 18 full-time judges which are to be elected for a fixed term of nine years by the Assembly of State Parties (ASP).[81] No two judges are allowed to be nationals of the same State.[82] In accordance with the provisions of Article 38, the President and the First and Second vice Presidents are elected by an absolute majority of the judges.[83] They each serve a term of three years or until the end of their respective terms of office as judges, whichever expires earlier. They are eligible for re-election once.[84]

[76] See Magliveras, and Sourantonis, 'Rescinding the signature of an International Treaty: the United States and the Rome Statute Establishing the International Criminal Court' 14 *Diplomacy & Statecraft* (2003) 21.

[77] See Aksar, *Implementing International Humanitarian Law: From the ad hoc Tribunals to a Permanent International Criminal Court* (Routledge, 2004) at p. 62; Lee, *The International Criminal Court: The Making of the Rome Statute – Issues, Negotiations and Results* (Kluwer Law International, 1999) at p. 26.

[78] International Criminal Court, Historical Introduction, www.icc-cpi.int/about/ataglance/history.html <last visited 15 May 2009>.

[79] Ibid.

[80] S/RES/1422 (2002) Adopted by the Security Council at its 4572nd meeting, on 12 July 2002.

[81] Articles 36(1) and (9)(a) Rome Statute.

[82] Ibid. Article 36(7).

[83] Ibid. Article 38(1).

[84] Ibid.

20

International criminal law and international human rights law

Under Articles 43(4) and (5), the judges shall elect a registrar and may elect a deputy-registrar, whose office is re-electable for a further term. The office of the prosecutor is a separate and independent office of the Court. It has the responsibility of receiving referrals and any information attached to such referrals. The prosecutor's office is headed by a prosecutor, with full authority to manage the office.[85] The prosecutor is assisted by one or more deputy prosecutors who are 'entitled to carry out any of the acts required of the Prosecutor' as stated in the statute.[86] The prosecutor and his deputies must have different nationalities and serve on a full-time basis.[87] They hold office for a term of nine years and are ineligible for re-election.[88] The Court consists of a number of chambers, namely the Pre-Trial Chamber, the Trial Chamber and Appeals Chamber. The Court is normally located in The Hague but maintains the capacity of functioning elsewhere where this is more convenient.[89]

The ICC has a restrictive jurisdiction over 'the most serious crimes of concern to the international community as a whole'.[90] According to Article 5(1), these are: genocide, crimes against humanity, war crimes and the crime of aggression. Aggression was introduced as an offence, although the definition of aggression is as yet to be agreed upon.[91] The ICC, like the ICTY and ICTR has jurisdiction over natural persons (as opposed to States or other legal entities, e.g. corporations).[92] For the current period the jurisdiction of the Court is restricted to genocide, war crimes and crimes against humanity.

Under the provisions of Article 16, the Security Council, through a Resolution adopted under Chapter VII, has the power to defer a potential or existing investigation or prosecution for period of up to 12 months. The mandate of the Security Council is limited to the powers enshrined within the constraints of Chapter VII: '[A]ny threat to the peace, breach of the peace, or act of aggression',[93] although, as we have seen, the discretion to determine violations of Chapter VII has also been bestowed upon the Council itself. The powers of the Security Council under this provision were further enhanced by Security Council's Resolution 1422 which provides that:

> if a case arises involving current or former officials or personnel from a contributing State not a Party to the Rome Statute over acts or omissions relating to a United Nations established or authorized operation, shall for a twelve-month period starting 1 July 2002 not commence or proceed with investigation or prosecution of any such case, unless the Security Council decides otherwise.[94]

---

[85] Ibid. Article 42(2).
[86] Ibid. Article 42(2).
[87] Ibid. Article 42(2).
[88] Ibid. Article 42(4).
[89] Ibid. Article 3.
[90] Ibid. Rome Statute, Preamble, para 4.
[91] Ibid. Article 5(2) Rome Statute. For further discussion on the definition of 'Crimes of Aggression' see www.icc-cpi.int/asp/aspaggression.html <last visited 14 May 2009>.
[92] Article 25 Rome Statute.
[93] Article 39, Chapter VII, UN Charter, 26 June 1945, 59 Stat. 1031, T.S. 993, 3 Bevans 1153.
[94] SC Res. 1422 (2002) 12 July 2002, para 1, UN Doc. S/RES/1422 (2002) available at www.un.org <last visited 13 May 2009>. See MacPherson, 'Authority of the Security Council to Exempt Peace Keepers from International Criminal Court Proceedings' *ASIL Insight* July 2002; Stahn 'The Ambiguities of Security Council Resolution 1422 (2002) 14 *EJIL* (2003) 85; in relation to Res. 1422 (2002), Stahn raises doubts about the connection between exemption of peacekeepers from ICC jurisdiction and the threat to peace and security which provides the trigger for Chapter VII Resolutions; see ibid. at p. 86. On Chapter VII Resolutions, see above chapter 3.

As a consequence of this provision, officials of non-State parties, for example the United States Army personnel or civilians on United Nations business, could be deferred from being investigated or prosecuted before the ICC for violations of crimes provided in Article 5 of the Rome Statute. Resolution 1422 further consolidates the deferment powers accorded to the Council in Article 16 of the Rome Statute and establishes that, although initially lasting for 12 months, the Council's Resolution may request the 'renewal' of deferment for as long as may be necessary. In practice, therefore, the practice of deferment could be indefinite. States that are currently not parties include Russia, China and the United States, and this Resolution could prove to be of special assistance to these militarily very powerful States with permanent vetoing powers in the United Nations Security Council. It is much more likely that these States, in particular the United States, could be free from prosecution in the ICC for an indeterminate period. Notwithstanding these concessions, the US maintained its objections to referrals by State parties and by the Prosecutor, arguing that this rendered members of the US armed forces participating in peace-keeping around the world open to prosecution by the ICC and that the United States might be faced with cases instituted through political hostility.

(ii) ICC's jurisdiction

The Court can only exercise jurisdiction from the entry into force of the Statute and may only exercise its jurisdiction with respect to crimes committed after the entry into force of the Statute of the Court.[95] Article 124 provides an exception, which allows a State party the possibility of declaring that it will not be bound by the jurisdiction of the Court for a period of seven years, for war crimes committed in its territory or by one of its nationals from the date of ratification by that State.[96] This declaration is, however, restricted to war crimes and also excludes all other offences in Article 6.[97] Yet the International Criminal Court differs from other international tribunals that were created primarily to deal with atrocities that took place prior to their establishment.[98] As remarkably observed by one commentator:

> The issue of jurisdiction *ratione temporis* [temporal jurisdiction] should not be confused with the question of retroactive crimes. International human rights law considers the prohibition of retroactive crimes and punishments to be one of its most fundamental principles. Known by the Latin expression *nullum crimen nulla poena sine lege*, this norm forbids prosecution of crimes that were not recognized as such at the time they were committed.[99]

Territoriality and active personality (nationality of the offender) are the two bases on which the ICC can exercise its jurisdiction. Thus the International Criminal Court has jurisdiction over crimes committed on the territory of a State party or over nationals of State party who are accused of a crime, pursuant to Article 12(2)(b), regardless of where the acts or crimes were committed. Article 12 establishes, what it describes as pre-condition to the

---

[95] Article 11(1) Rome Statute.
[96] Ibid. Article 124.
[97] De Than and Shorts, above n.1 at p. 324.
[98] See earlier discussion on Nuremberg Tribunal and Tokyo Tribunal and the *ad hoc* tribunals.
[99] Schabas, above n.74, at pp. 68–69.

exercise of jurisdiction. According to Article 12(1), a State that becomes party to the Statute accepts the jurisdiction of the Court in relation to the crimes referred to in Article 5 of the Statute.

Article 12(2) goes on to provide as follows:

> In the case of article 13, paragraph (a) or (c), the Court may exercise its jurisdiction if one or more of the following States are Parties to this Statute or have accepted the jurisdiction of the Court in accordance with paragraph 3:
>
> (a) The State on the territory of which the conduct in question occurred or, if the crime was committed on board a vessel or aircraft, the State of registration of that vessel or aircraft;
>
> (b) The State of which the person accused of the crime is a national.

Article 12(3) advances a further jurisdictional ground, according to which a 'State may, by declaration lodged with the Registrar, accept the exercise of jurisdiction by the Court' on an *ad hoc* basis. In establishing the grounds for exercising jurisdiction, Article 13 notes that the Court may exercise its jurisdiction with respect to crimes referred to in Article 5 if:

> (a) A situation in which one or more of such crimes appears to have been committed is referred to the Prosecutor by a State Party in accordance with article 14;
>
> (b) A situation in which one or more of such crimes appears to have been committed is referred to the Prosecutor by the Security Council acting under Chapter VII of the Charter of the United Nations; or
>
> (c) The Prosecutor has initiated an investigation in respect of such a crime in accordance with article 15.

It is important to highlight the reasoning behind the aforementioned jurisdictional grounds. A majority of delegates present at the Rome Conference were attempting to construct a Court which was free and yet, at the same time, impartial and influential. Impartiality and comprehensiveness would trigger a universal jurisdiction for the Court. A certain group of States, led by the United States, were, however, not only against the granting of universal jurisdiction to the Court but also objected to non-signatory States' liability in crimes committed in signatory States. The end product is, therefore, Article 12, according to which the Court is restricted when invoking jurisdiction in relation to crimes committed within the territory of signatory States, where a national of a signatory States is accused of committing a crime or in instances where a State, by declaration accepts the jurisdiction of the Court on an *ad hoc* basis. Such a compromise, although leading to the conclusion of the treaty, has unduly restricted the jurisdiction of the Court and created unfairness in the accountability process. Thus, the Court is barred from the invoking its jurisdiction over crimes committed in non-signatory States, and yet is able to try individuals accused of the same crimes committed in a signatory State.[100] Such a scenario allows dictatorial regimes to refuse to ratify the ICC Statute and escape the jurisdiction of the Court.

---

[100] Goldsmith, above n.66, at p. 91.

A further problem is related to the relationship of the ICC with the Security Council, the latter being an executive organ of the United Nations, with enforcement powers in relation to threats to international peace and security. In establishing the 'trigger' mechanisms, Article 13 provides that the ICC exercises jurisdiction over crimes falling within the scope of the Statute, only when a situation has been referred to the Prosecutor by: (a) a State party to the Statute;[101] (b) by the Security Council acting under Chapter VII of the UN Charter;[102] or (c) where the prosecutor him or herself initiates an investigation, in accordance with Article 15.[103] The United States sought the Security Council control of the ICC arguing that the ICC 'must operate in co-ordination not in conflict – with the Security Council'.[104] In examining the 'trigger' mechanism, it is not difficult to imagine ways in which the ICC jurisdiction may come into conflict with the Security Council. Article 14 provides that a State is entitled to refer to the prosecutor situations where a crime appears to have been committed with the request that the prosecutor conducts an investigation, with the objective of determining as to whether charges ought to be advanced.[105] The referral by a State party to the prosecutor and subsequent prosecutions runs the risk that such referrals are open to political prejudice and perception. The United States has expressed serious reservations at the possibility that some of its own nationals might be the object of a politically motivated referral. In order to overcome such concerns, attempts were made to ensure the independence of the office of the prosecutor and to arm this office with substantial safeguards.

According to Article 15(1), the prosecutor has the mandate to initiate investigations *proprio motu* on the basis of the available information on relevant crime or crimes. The prosecutor examines the seriousness of the nature of the information and assesses whether any additional information is required for him or her to proceed.[106] If the prosecutor takes the view that there is a reasonable basis on which to proceed with the investigation, he or she then makes a submission before the Pre-Trial Chamber to request the authorisation of an investigation alongside all supporting materials.[107] However, if after preliminary investigation the prosecutor takes the position that there is no *prima facie* case, such a stance would not preclude the prosecutor from considering further information submitted to him or her in the future and in the light of new facts and evidence.[108] If the Pre-Trail Chamber finds a reasonable case to investigate, it is required to authorise an investigation by the prosecutor.[109] The refusal of the Pre-Trial Chamber to provide authorisation does not preclude the presentation of a subsequent request by the prosecutor based on new facts or evidence regarding the same situation.[110] As part of this investigation, victims of the crimes are provided with the entitlement to make representations to the Pre-Trial Chamber along

---

[101] Articles 13(a) and 14(1) Rome Statute.
[102] Ibid. Article 13(b).
[103] Ibid. Articles 13(c) and 15(1).
[104] Statement made by Hon. Bill Richardson, the United States Ambassador to the United Nations (17 June 1989) UN Press Release L/ROM/11, 'United States Declares at Conference that UN Security Council Must Play Important Role in Proposed International Criminal Court' (17 June 1998). Cassese in 'International Criminal Law' in Evans above n.1, at p. 729.
[105] Article 14(1) Rome Statute.
[106] Ibid. Article 15(2).
[107] Ibid. Article 15(3).
[108] Ibid. Article 15(6).
[109] Ibid. Article 15(4).
[110] Ibid. Article 15(5).

with legally admissible supporting material.[111] The Pre-Trial Chamber plays an instrumental role, in not only defining the scope of the prosecution but also curtailing the role of the prosecutor. The functions of the Pre-Trial Chamber are established in Article 57 and include being permitted to rule on a number of issues contained in Articles 15, 18, 19, 54(2), 6(17) and 72. Under the aforementioned articles, a majority ruling from the judges of the Pre-Trial Chamber is required before any of their decisions may be implemented. Under Article 57(2)(b) 'in all other cases, a single judge of the Pre-Trial Chamber may exercise the functions provided for in this Statute, unless otherwise provided for in the Rules of Procedure and Evidence or by a majority of the Pre-Trial Chamber'.

As noted earlier, in order to allay the fears of the United States of facing malicious and spurious referrals, a further safeguard through Article 16 was built into the Statute of the Court. In providing for deferral of investigation or prosecution, Article 16 provides that 'No investigation or prosecution may be commenced or proceeded with under this Statute for a period of 12 months after the Security Council, in a resolution adopted under Chapter VII of the Charter of the United Nations, has requested the Court to that effect; that request may be renewed by the Council under the same conditions'. However as a Human Rights Watch document accurately notes, the authority of the Security Council under the provisions of Article 16, is not unlimited, since the Article 'establishes a mechanism for deferring investigations or prosecutions on a case-by-case basis, subject to time limitations and a formal renewal process . . . The phrase [within Article 16], "no investigation or prosecution may be commenced or proceeded with" presupposes the existence of a particular "investigation" or "prosecution" that relates to a specific incident or the potential culpability of an individual regarding specific conduct. Article 15 of the Rome Statute spells this out. The Pre-Trial Chamber must authorize the commencement of a specific "investigation" All prosecutor inquiries up to this point are not "investigations", but only "preliminary examinations" . . . an Article 16 deferral request is not meant to be a tool for Security Council preventive, indiscriminate action, but a response to specific ICC proceedings. Any such deferral must be temporary, subject to the 12-month limit stipulated in Article 16, so that the perpetrators of any atrocities would ultimately be brought to account for their crimes – either via national judicial systems or the ICC'.[112]

Furthermore, whilst the Security Council has been provided with the mandate to refer a case involving an ICC non-signatory under Chapter VII, such referrals are open to the political views and perceptions of the Security Council members. This complaint was raised by the Mr. Elfathih Mohamed Ahmed Erwa, Sudan's representative at the time when the Security Council passed a Resolution on Situation in Sudan which referred the matter of the situation in Darfur to the Prosecutor of the ICC.[113]

The jurisdiction of the Court extends to those persons responsible for ordering, soliciting, attempting, aiding and abetting, inducing the commission or attempted commission of a crime, or otherwise assisting in its commission or attempted commission by a group with a common purpose or inciting others to commit the crime.[114] Diplomatic immunity is unacceptable under the provisions of Article 27. Article 27 provides as follows:

---

[111] Ibid. Article 15(3).

[112] Human Rights Watch, 'The ICC and the Security Council: Resolution 1422 *Legal and Policy Analysis*' www.hrw.org/legacy/campaigns/icc/docs/1422legal.htm <last visited 21 August 2009>.

[113] Security Council Resolution on Situation in Sudan and Explanations of Vote, SC Res. 1593, 31 March 2005, para 1.

[114] Article 25(3)(a)–(f) Rome Statute.

1. This Statute shall apply equally to all persons without any distinction based on official capacity. In particular, official capacity as a Head of State or Government, a member of a Government or parliament, an elected representative or a government official shall in no case exempt a person from criminal responsibility under this Statute, nor shall it, in and of itself, constitute a ground for reduction of sentence.

2. Immunities or special procedural rules which may attach to the official capacity of a person, whether under national or international law, shall not bar the Court from exercising its jurisdiction over such a person.

There is similarly a responsibility of military or *de facto* commanders or civilian superiors for the actions of their forces or subordinates under their 'command and control or effective authority and control'.[115] The criminal liability applies in cases where:

(i) That military commander or the person either knew or, owing to the circumstances at the time, should have known that the forces were committing or about to commit such crimes; and

(ii) That military commander or person failed to take all necessary and reasonable measures within his or her power to prevent or repress their commission or to submit the matter to the competent authorities for investigation and prosecution.[116]

The ICC has jurisdiction based on the principle of complementarity with national criminal jurisdiction: it should be noted that this is a key difference from the *ad hoc* tribunals. Firstly, it is the responsibility of national courts to prosecute violators of the crimes provided in Article 5. Under Article 17(1)(a)–(d) it is up to the Court to decide whether to proceed with the trial and the Court:

shall determine that a case is inadmissible where:

(a) The case is being investigated or prosecuted by a State which has jurisdiction over it, unless the State is unwilling or unable genuinely to carry out the investigation or prosecution;

(b) The case has been investigated by a State which has jurisdiction over it and the State has decided not to prosecute the person concerned, unless the decision resulted from the unwillingness or inability of the State genuinely to prosecute;

(c) The person concerned has already been tried for conduct which is the subject of the complaint, and a trial by the Court is not permitted under Article 20, paragraph 3;

(d) The case is not of sufficient gravity to justify further action by the Court.

States parties therefore have the primary responsibility and the preferred forum for trial to prosecute the accused in their own courts. Under Articles 17(2)(a)–(c) and 17(3), the Court's jurisdiction may be re-established in circumstances where the national court has been unwilling or unable to prosecute an individual, namely shielding the individual through, for example, internal political pressure not to prosecute or granting amnesty to

[115] Ibid. Article 28(a).
[116] Ibid. Article 28(a)(i)(ii).

International criminal law and international human rights law

the individual from any further prosecution, the proceedings being conducted inconsistently with an intent to prosecute or due to a unjustified delay, a total or substantial collapse of the national judicial system, absence of independence or impartiality or another circumstance affecting the State's ability to carry out its proceedings. Under Article 17(3), the Court will also decide on a State's inability to prosecute by examining such factors as a State being 'unable to obtain the accused or the necessary evidence and testimony or otherwise unable to carry out its proceedings'.[117] There are likely to be disagreements, for example, where the State takes the view that there are insufficient grounds for a prosecution and a contrary view is taken by the ICC. There may also be issues not only in relation to the prosecution but also the conviction and sentencing. Thus, the convicted person may not be sentenced appropriately for the nature of the offences he has committed. In such a case of disagreement, the ICC has the final word.

As already noted, once a State party has requested that the Prosecutor investigate a situation and the Prosecutor has decided that there is a reasonable basis to commence such an investigation or to initiate an investigation *proprio motu*, he is under an obligation to inform all States parties and those States directly concerned of his decisions,[118] but he may in the interest of justice limit the information in his notification if he believes that this notification would lead to such situations as evidence being destroyed or the suspect fleeing or being intimidated. The State concerned may then within a month inform the Court that it is undertaking an investigation into the criminal conduct alleged.[119] Unless the Pre-Trial Chamber objects, the prosecutor will then leave it up to the domestic State to take appropriate action and provide information on the progress of the case.[120] However, within a period of six months or in certain circumstances of considerable change, if the prosecutor is dissatisfied with the investigating State's progress, he may apply to the Pre-Trial Chamber to take over the case.[121] If the prosecuting State or the prosecutor's office is unhappy at the decision of the Pre-Trial Chamber, then either party may appeal to the Appeal Chamber for a ruling.[122]

According to the provision of Article 19, it is up the Court to decide as to whether it has jurisdiction, and whether a case is admissible under the provisions of Article 17.[123] These decisions may be challenged by the accused, a suspect or a State which has jurisdiction.[124] These challenges can normally be mounted prior to the commencement of the trial, although in exceptional cases challenges can also be brought in after the start of the trial, with the leave of the Court.[125]

(iii) The rights of the accused individual under investigation and trial

The rights of the accused individual that is being investigated are also provided for in the Statute and contained in Articles 55. Article 55(1)(a) establishes that no one is to be

---

[117] Ibid. Article 17(3).
[118] Ibid. Article 18(1).
[119] Ibid. Article 18(2).
[120] Ibid. Article 18(2).
[121] Ibid. Article 18(3).
[122] Ibid. Article 18(4).
[123] Ibid. Article 19(1).
[124] Ibid. Article 19(2).
[125] Ibid. Article 19(4).

compelled to incriminate him or herself or make any confession regarding guilt. No one is to be coerced or placed under duress or threat, tortured or subject to any form of cruel, inhuman or degrading treatment or punishment.[126] Article 55(1)(c) provides that if a person is questioned in a language other than their own, the accused is to have, free of any cost, the assistance of a translator or interpreter in a manner which meets the requirements of fairness.

Furthermore, and in accordance with established norms of international human rights law, no one is to be subjected to arbitrary arrest or detentions and is not to be deprived of his liberty, save for procedures established in the Statute.[127] All individuals suspected of having committed a crime, must be informed prior to any questioning that there are grounds to believe that they have committed a crime that falls within the jurisdiction of the Court.[128] They must also be notified of their right to remain silent, without such silence being taken as a consideration in the determination of their guilt.[129] They are also to be notified of their right to have legal assistance of their own choosing.[130] If the accused individual does not have legal assistance, he or she is entitled to have legal assistance, and without any payment on his or her part, if the individual concerned does not have the means to pay for such assistance.[131] The accused person is to be questioned only in the presence of their 'counsel unless the person has voluntarily waived his or her right to counsel'.[132]

After the commencement of the trial, the Statute sets out various provisions which must be complied with in order to ensure a fair hearing. Article 66 retains the core of the criminal justice system through the provision of, firstly, the principle of the presumption of innocence until proven guilty in accordance with applicable law.[133] Secondly, it reiterates the criminal law principle that the onus to prove the guilt of the accused is on the Prosecutor,[134] and, thirdly, it confirms that in order to produce a guilty verdict, the Court must be convinced that the accused is guilty beyond the level of all reasonable doubt.[135]

A catalogue of rights of the accused during his or her trial is provided by Article 67. These compliment and confirm the right of fair trial as established by Article 14 of the ICCPR and Article 6 of ECHR. The accused, according to Article 67(1), is entitled to a public and fair hearing conducted impartially in full equality and containing the following as minimum guarantees:

(a) To be informed promptly and in detail of the nature, cause and content of the charge, in a language which the accused fully understands and speaks;

(b) To have adequate time and facilities for the preparation of the defence and to communicate freely with counsel of the accused's choosing in confidence;

(c) To be tried without undue delay;

---

126 Ibid. Article 55(1)(b).
127 Ibid. Article 551(d).
128 Ibid. Article 55(2)(a).
129 Ibid. Article 55(2)(b).
130 Ibid. Article 55(2)(c).
131 Ibid. Article 55(2)(c).
132 Ibid. Article 55(2)(d).
133 Ibid. Article 66(1).
134 Ibid. Article 66(2).
135 Ibid. Article 66(3).

(d) Subject to article 63, paragraph 2, to be present at the trial, to conduct the defence in person or through legal assistance of the accused's choosing, to be informed, if the accused does not have legal assistance, of this right and to have legal assistance assigned by the Court in any case where the interests of justice so require, and without payment if the accused lacks sufficient means to pay for it;

(e) To examine, or have examined, the witnesses against him or her and to obtain the attendance and examination of witnesses on his or her behalf under the same conditions as witnesses against him or her. The accused shall also be entitled to raise defences and to present other evidence admissible under this Statute;

(f) To have, free of any cost, the assistance of a competent interpreter and such translations as are necessary to meet the requirements of fairness, if any of the proceedings of or documents presented to the Court are not in a language which the accused fully understands and speaks;

(g) Not to be compelled to testify or to confess guilt and to remain silent, without such silence being a consideration in the determination of guilt or innocence;

(h) To make an unsworn oral or written statement in his or her defence; and

(i) Not to have imposed on him or her any reversal of the burden of proof or any onus of rebuttal.

Under the provisions of Article 67(2), the prosecutor is required to disclose to the defence any evidence which the prosecutor has in his 'possession or control which he believes shows or tends to show the innocence of the accused', or highlights evidence of mitigation of the guilt of the accused or which could potentially 'affect the credibility of prosecution evidence'.[136]

The Court should reach a unanimous verdict, failing which a majority decision would be acceptable.[137] A range of punishments are provided by the Article 77, which include a term of prison not exceeding 30 years or imprisonment for life if warranted, depending on the seriousness of the crime. Articles 86–102 relate to the co-operation between the ICC and the State or the States involved with reference to investigatory or prosecution matters. Articles 103–111 are concerned largely with the enforcement provisions as regards sentencing.

5 CATEGORIES OF INTERNATIONAL CRIMES

(i) War crimes

War crimes have been defined as '*serious violations* of customary or treaty rules belonging to the corpus of the international humanitarian law of armed conflict'.[138] In further articulating the meaning of war crimes, the Appeals Chamber of the ICTY noted in *Tadić*

---

[136] Ibid. Article 67(2).
[137] Ibid. Article 74(3).
[138] Cassese, *International Criminal Law*, above n.1, at p. 81 (emphasis provided).

(Interlocutory Appeal) that (i) war crimes must consist of 'a serious infringement' of an international rule which constitutes 'a breach of rule protecting important values and the breach much must involve grave consequences for the victim', (ii) the rule violated must either belong to the corpus of customary law or be part of an applicable treaty, (iii) 'the violation must entail, under customary or conventional law, the individual criminal responsibility of the person breaching the rule'.[139]

War crimes are recognised as the oldest form of international crimes and were the first ones to be prosecuted as crimes in international law; at the end of the First World War, German soldiers were convicted of war crimes. As noted already, war crimes formed part of the Nuremberg and Tokyo trials which took place in the aftermath of the Second World War. War crimes are also enshrined in the four Geneva Conventions of 1949. The concept of war crimes is much broader than crimes committed during international armed conflict, as confirmed by the 1977 Protocols to the Geneva Conventions. Article 8 of the Rome Statute, while confirming the extension of war crimes to international and internal armed conflicts, also provides recognition to certain crimes, not previously explicitly warranted as war crimes. This includes rape, other sexual offences including sexual slavery, enforced prostitution, forced pregnancy, enforced sterilisation or any other form of sexual violence.[140] It is also an offence to conscript or enlist children under the age of 15 into national armed forces,[141] reinforcing provisions of the Convention on the Rights of the Child and Additional Protocol 1 of the Geneva Conventions.[142]

As the jurisprudence of the International Tribunals establishes, there must be a nexus between the armed conflict and the crime itself in order for the latter to constitute a war crime.[143] That said, the armed conflict itself could be either of an international or internal nature.[144] Historically, it was believed that the war crimes covered only international armed conflict. This view, however, is being increasingly discarded, and particularly since the *Tadić* (Interlocutory Appeal) 1995, it is now established that war crimes can be conducted during internal armed conflicts and civil wars. Article 8(2)(c–f) of the Statute of the International Criminal Court affirms this position.

War crimes are serious violations of international humanitarian law. This includes the 'Law of the Hague' and the 'Law of Geneva', although as shall be examined in the next chapter traditional distinctions have become blurred. The 'Law of the Hague' derives from the Hague Conventions of 1899 and 1907 on international warfare. The 'Law of the Hague' establishes a number of categories of lawful combatants and attempts at regulation of acts during warfare (methods as well as means of warfare) as well as the treatment of persons not directly involved in hostilities (wounded or sick) and those unable to take part (such as prisoners of war). The 'Law of the Geneva Conventions' consists primarily of the Four Geneva Convention of 1949 and the three Additional Protocols to the Geneva Conventions (1977). Representing the core of international humanitarian law, the Geneva Conventions were conceived as essentially dealing with those persons who do not or can no longer take part in combat. The Third Geneva Convention (1949) deals with combatants who have

---

[139] Cited in Cassese, *International Criminal Law*, above n.1 at p. 81 (para 94).
[140] Article 8(2)(b)(xxii) Rome Statute.
[141] Ibid. Article 8(2)(b)(xxvi).
[142] Article 38 CRC, Article 77 Additional Protocol 1 Geneva Convention. See above chapter 16.
[143] *Prosecutor* v. *Tadić*. Case No. IT-94-I-AR72, 15 July 1999, para 83.
[144] Cassese, *International Criminal Law*, above n.1, at p. 81.

become prisoners of war,[145] and while updating the Hague laws, in the process blur the distinction between the two. War crimes are committed by 'combatants' under the Geneva Conventions, primarily against 'protected persons', which include 'persons taking no active part in the hostilities', including civilians, prisoners of war and *hors de combat*.[146] As noted above, criminal offences, as a part of war crimes, must have a link with international or internal armed conflict and in the absence of such a linkage, this may constitute an offence under national criminal law, without being a war crime.

War crimes include crimes that are committed against persons not engaged in armed hostilities or those no longer able to take part in armed conflict. The list of such persons includes, *inter alia*, prisoners of war, civilians, and could consist of serious violations, such as violence against women. If occurring during international armed conflict, these crimes are regarded as 'grave breaches' against one of the 'protected persons'.[147] Within the definition of 'grave breaches', which also carry 'universal jurisdiction', are wilful killing, torture or inhuman treatment and causing serious bodily injury. In the case of internal armed conflict, whilst the same offences are deemed war crimes, they are not, as such, termed as 'grave breaches'.[148] A further category of war crimes includes crimes against enemy combatants and civilians through means of warfare which are prohibited.[149] These prohibited methods of warfare include intentionally targeting civilians during an armed conflict; terrorising a civilian population during an armed conflict; indiscriminately and disproportionately attacking civilians during an armed conflict; attacking medical facilities during an armed attack; starvation as a means of warfare; and long-term or deliberate damage to the environment. Additionally, the deployment of prohibited weapons and

---

[145] Article 4 A of the Third Geneva Convention. 'Art 4. A. Prisoners of war, in the sense of the present Convention, are persons belonging to one of the following categories, who have fallen into the power of the enemy:

(1) Members of the armed forces of a Party to the conflict, as well as members of militias or volunteer corps forming part of such armed forces.

(2) Members of other militias and members of other volunteer corps, including those of organized resistance movements, belonging to a Party to the conflict and operating in or outside their own territory, even if this territory is occupied, provided that such militias or volunteer corps, including such organized resistance movements, fulfil the following conditions:

    (a) that of being commanded by a person responsible for his subordinates;

    (b) that of having a fixed distinctive sign recognizable at a distance;

    (c) that of carrying arms openly;

    (d) that of conducting their operations in accordance with the laws and customs of war.

(3) Members of regular armed forces who profess allegiance to a government or an authority not recognized by the Detaining Power.

(4) Persons who accompany the armed forces without actually being members thereof, such as civilian members of military aircraft crews, war correspondents, supply contractors, members of labour units or of services responsible for the welfare of the armed forces, provided that they have received authorization, from the armed forces which they accompany, who shall provide them for that purpose with an identity card similar to the annexed model.

(5) Members of crews, including masters, pilots and apprentices, of the merchant marine and the crews of civil aircraft of the Parties to the conflict, who do not benefit by more favourable treatment under any other provisions of international law.

(6) Inhabitants of a non-occupied territory, who on the approach of the enemy spontaneously take up arms to resist the invading forces, without having had time to form themselves into regular armed units, provided they carry arms openly and respect the laws and customs of war.'

[146] Common Article 3 of the Geneva Conventions.

[147] Article 50 First Geneva Convention. This includes the wounded, shipwrecked persons, prisoners of war and civilians on the territory of Detaining Power.

[148] Cassese, *International Criminal Law*, above n.1, at p. 56.

[149] Articles 35–42 Protocol I, Geneva Convention.

projectiles which cause serious injury and unnecessary suffering, the use of poisonous weapons or other poisonous gases, and the deployment of chemical weapons, are prohibited, as is the use of booby-traps and landmines.

The Statute of the ICC accords the Court with the jurisdiction to prosecute offenders suspected of having engaged in 'War Crimes'. Article 8 provides a considerably elaborated definition of 'War Crimes' according to which, this crime:

> means grave breaches of the Geneva Conventions of 12 August 1949, which include any of the following acts against persons or property protected under the provisions of the relevant Geneva Convention:
>
> (i)   Wilful killing;
>
> (ii)   Torture or inhuman treatment, including biological experiments;
>
> (iii) Wilfully causing great suffering, or serious injury to body or health;
>
> (iv)   Extensive destruction and appropriation of property, not justified by military necessity and carried out unlawfully and wantonly;
>
> (v)   Compelling a prisoner of war or other protected person to serve in the forces of a hostile Power;
>
> (vi)   Wilfully depriving a prisoner of war or other protected person of the rights of fair and regular trial;
>
> (vii) Unlawful deportation or transfer or unlawful confinement;
>
> (viii) Taking of hostages.

War crimes, also include other serious violations of the laws and customs applicable in international armed conflict including such acts as intentionally directing attacks against the civilian population, against civilians not taking part in hostilities or against personnel, installations, material, units or vehicles involved in a humanitarian assistance or peacekeeping mission in accordance with the Charter of the United Nations.[150] Intentionally launching disproportionate attacks which are likely to cause loss of life or injury to civilians or damage to civilian objects or the environment are also prohibited.[151] This category of war crimes, under Article 8(2)(b) of the Rome Statute, also includes bombardment or attacks on civilian dwellings which remain undefended with no military objectives; wounding or killing of combatants who have laid down their arms; making improper or deceitful usage of a flag of truce or military insignia; transfer by the occupying power of its civilian population or deportation or transfer of population of the occupied territory; subjecting individuals to mutilation or to medical or scientific experiments; killing or wounding treacherously individuals; pillage of towns; deploying poison or poisoned weapons; or employing poisonous gases or other poisonous materials in wars; deploying projectiles and methods of warfare which cause undue and unnecessary pain and suffering; deploying outrages upon personal dignity, particular humiliating and degrading treatment against persons; involvement in such activities as rape, enforced prostitution, forced pregnancies and sexual slavery; the intentional starvation of civilians as a method of warfare;

---

[150] Article 8(2)(b)(i)(ii)(iii) Rome Statute.
[151] Ibid. Article 8(2)(b)(iv).

conscripting or enlisting children under the age of 15 years into the national armed forces or their usage to participate actively in hostilities.[152]

According to the Statute of the Court, in cases of armed conflict which are not categorised as that of an international character, Article 3 common to the four Geneva Conventions of 12 August 1949 applies. This states that in respect of:

(1) Persons taking no active part in the hostilities, including members of armed forces who have laid down their arms and those placed hors de combat by sickness, wounds or detention or any other cause . . . the following acts are and shall remain prohibited at any time and in any place whatsoever with respect to the above mentioned persons:

    (a) violence to life and person, in particular murder of all kinds, mutilation, cruel treatment and torture;

    (b) taking of hostages;

    (c) outrages upon personal dignity, in particular humiliating and degrading treatment;

    (d) the passing of sentences and the carrying out of executions without previous judgement pronounced by a regularly constituted court, affording all judicial guarantees which are generally recognized as indispensable by civilized peoples.

Other serious violations of the laws and customs applicable in armed conflict are also impressible in such instances.

(ii) Crimes against humanity

Within international criminal law, crimes against humanity bear the strongest relationship with human rights law, principally consisting of the most serious offences against human dignity. Crimes against humanity constitute a very broad category of offences. Both from the historic origins as well as the nature of these crimes, it is well-established that crimes against humanity are primarily intended to protect certain fundamental human rights. Crimes against humanity represent a serious attack on human dignity and humanity and result in the degradation and humiliation of one or more human beings. Crimes against humanity are part of a systematic policy of violence against the civilian population. Such systematic policy is initiated or at least tolerated by the government, although non-State actors may also engage in crimes against humanity. While there has been considerable debate over the matter, as our discussion elucidates, it is now settled that crimes against humanity under customary international law can be committed during times of war or peace, and can be committed against both civilians or under customary international law, against armed forces (e.g. in instances where the latter do not take part in hostilities). Cassese makes the point that 'indeed while international criminal law concerning war crimes largely derives from, or is closely linked to, international humanitarian law, international criminal law concerning crimes against humanity is to a great extent predicated

---

[152] Lubanga was the first accused before the ICC to be charged with the war crime of enlisting and conscripting children under the age of 15 in armed conflict, see *Prosecutor* v. *Thomas Lubanga Dyilo*, Case No. ICC-01/04-01/06-803, Décision sur la confirmation des charges, (*Lubanga* Décision sur la confirmation des charges), 29 January 2007.

upon international human rights law'.[153] Notwithstanding the various historical abortive attempts, crimes against humanity were established as a distinct offence in the Charter of the International Military Tribunal. There was, nevertheless, a link drawn between war crimes or crimes against peace. Professor Meron makes the following useful observations:

> In reaction to the atrocities committed in and by Germany during the war, it established, for the first time, direct international criminal responsibility under international law for atrocities committed in one country, even as between its citizens. However, this achievement was qualified by linkage to other crimes within the Tribunal jurisdiction, which effectively reduced crimes against humanity to wartime atrocities.[154]

At the end of the Second World War it was evident that a number of crimes committed by the Nazis or their allied forces were committed not against enemy forces or enemy civilians but against their peoples, such as German Jewish or Polish minorities – there was thus the need to confirm and induct the provisions relating to 'crimes against humanity'. Article 6 of the Charter of International Military Tribunal, annexed to an agreement signed by the Four-Powers in 1945, provided for the establishment of a tribunal to prosecute and punish war criminals and in providing for 'crimes against humanity' restricted these offences to:

> (c) crimes against humanity;
>   murder, extermination, enslavement, deportation and other inhumane acts committed against any civilian population before or during the war, or persecution on political, racial or religious grounds *in execution of or in connection* with any crime with in the jurisdiction of the tribunal, whether or not in violation of the domestic law of the country where perpetrated.[155]

Thus, the Charter clearly limited the jurisdiction of the tribunal to those offences that were conducted 'in execution of or in connection' with war crimes and crimes against peace.[156] The General Assembly in its Resolution affirmed the 'Principles of International Law recognised by the Charter of the Nuremberg Tribunal and Judgement of the Tribunal' on 11 December, 1946.[157] However, with the expansion of International Criminal Law, the nexus between crimes against humanity and war crimes and crimes against peace has been eroded.[158] Conventional law, as established through such treaties as the Genocide

---

[153] Cassese, 'International Criminal Law' in Evans (ed.), above n.1, at p. 737.

[154] Meron, 'The Humanization of Humanitarian Law' 94 *AJIL* (2000) 239 at p. 263.

[155] (Emphasis added.) Text of the agreement for the establishment of IMT and Annexed Charter, UNTS, 5, 251; AJIL, 39 (1945), Supplement 257.

[156] Roberts, 'The Laws of War: Problems of Implementation in Contemporary Conflicts' 6 *Duke Journal of Comparative and International law* (1995–1996) 11 at p. 28.

[157] General Assembly Resolution 95(I) Affirmation of the Principles of International Law Recognised by the Charter of the Nuremberg Tribunal. http://daccessdds.un.org/doc/RESOLUTION/GEN/NR0/033/46/IMG/NR003346.pdf?OpenElement <last visited 8 August 2008>.

[158] For further developments see Report of the Special Working Group on the Crime of Aggression ICC-ASP/6/20/Add.1 www.icc-cpi.int/iccdocs/asp_docs/SWGCA/ICC-ASP-6-20-Add1-AnnexII-ENG.pdf <last visited 5 March 2009>.

Convention,[159] the Convention on the non-applicability of statutory limitations to war crimes and crimes against humanity,[160] and the International Convention on the Suppression and Punishment of the Crime of Apartheid,[161] has confirmed the removal of such a connection. The Genocide Convention provides that '[t]he Contracting Parties confirm that genocide, whether committed in time of peace or in time of war, is a crime under international law which they undertake to prevent and punish'.[162]

Crimes against humanity can be conducted both in times of war and in peace, a position confirmed by the Statute of the ICC. That said, a number of instruments have adopted a restrictive approach in relation to the applicability of crimes against humanity. The United Nations Security Council while establishing the Yugoslavia Tribunal, stated in its Resolution that crimes against humanity 'must be committed in armed conflict, whether international or internal in character'.[163] Although limited to the statutory nature of the tribunal and its jurisdiction, such limitations may '*indirectly contribute* to the restriction of the customary rules'.[164] The restrictive view taken of crimes against humanity was reiterated by the Appeals Chamber of ICTY in the *Tadić* case. The Chamber noted:

> The Trial Chamber correctly recognised that crimes which are unrelated to widespread or systematic attacks on a civilian population should not be prosecuted as crimes against humanity. Crimes against humanity are crimes of a special nature to which a greater degree of moral turpitude attaches than to an ordinary crime. Thus to convict an accused of crimes against humanity, it must be proved that the crimes were *related* to the attack on a civilian population (occurring during an armed conflict) and that the accused *knew* that his crimes were so related.[165]

However, such a reference is missing in the Statute of the Rwanda Tribunal and the jurisprudence emerging from the case-law of the tribunals.[166] Meron makes the useful point that:

[159] New York, 9 December 1948, United Nations, *Treaty Series*, vol. 78, p. 277.

[160] New York, 26 November 1968, 754 U.N.T.S. 73; 8 I.L.M. 68; R Miller, 'The Convention on the non-applicability of statutory limitation to War Crimes and Crimes Against Humanity' 65 *AJIL* (1971) 476–501.

[161] New York, 30 November 1973, United Nations, *Treaty Series*, vol. 1015, p. 243; see *Multilateral Treaties in respect of which the Secretary-General performs Depository functions* (1978) pp. 120–121.

[162] Article I, Genocide Convention.

[163] Article 5 of the ICTY in defining crimes against humanity includes those crimes within the Tribunal's jurisdiction which are 'committed in armed conflict, whether international or internal in character'. Statute of the International Tribunal for the Prosecution of Persons Responsible for Serious Violations of International Humanitarian Law Committed in the Territory of the Former Yugoslavia since 1991, UN Doc. S/25704 at 36, annex (1993) and S/25704/Add.1 (1993), adopted by Security Council on 25 May 1993, UN Doc. S/RES/827 (1993).

[164] Cassese, *International Criminal Law*, above n.1, at p. 108.

[165] *Prosecutor* v. *Tadić* Appeals Chamber, International Criminal Tribunal for the Former Yugoslavia Case No. IT-94-I-AR72, 15 July 1999, para 271. www.un.org/icty/tadic/appeal/judgement/index.htm <last visited 30 May 2009>.

[166] Professor Cassese makes the point that 'murder, extermination, torture, rape, political, racial or religious persecution and other inhumane acts reach the threshold of crimes against humanity only if they are part of a practice. Isolated inhumane acts of this nature may constitute grave infringements of human rights or, depending on the circumstances, war crimes, but fall short of meriting the stigma attaching to crimes against humanity. On the other hand, an individual may be guilty of crimes against humanity even if he perpetrates one or two of the offences mentioned above, or engages in one such offence against only a few civilians, provided those offences are part of a consistent pattern of misbehaviour by a number of persons linked to the offender (for example, because they engage in armed action on the same side, or because they are parties to a common plan, or for any other similar reason)'. Cassese, *International Criminal Law*, above n.1, at p. 101.

by making no allusion to the international or non-international character of the conflict the broad language of Article 3 of the Rwanda Statute (entitle 'crime against humanity') both strengthens the precedent set by the commentary to the Yugoslavia Statue and enhances the possibility of arguing in the future that crimes against humanity (in addition to genocide) can be committed even in peacetime.[167]

At the same time it needs to be noted that the Rwanda Statute has the requirement that proof is presented that the crimes against humanity were committed 'as part of a wide spread or systematic attack against any civilian population on national, political, ethnic, racial or religious grounds'.[168]

Crimes against humanity include, murder, torture, extermination, rape, political and religious persecution and other inhumane acts if they are part of a routine or systematic practice. Isolated acts, although infringing human rights, will not be considered crimes against humanity. A limited number of offences may become part of the pattern of crimes against humanity provided these offences represent a consistent pattern of criminal behaviour on the part of the individual or individuals concerned.

Article 7 of the Rome Statute defines Crimes against Humanity through a number of limitations. One is the requirement of 'wide-spread and systematic attack'. 'Attack' being further defined as 'a course of conduct'.[169] The attack has to be carried out against a civilian population and not against combatants or armed forces.[170] The attack is carried out 'pursuant to or in furtherance of a State or organisational policy to commit such attack'.[171] These limitations would render Article 7 narrower than the comparable provisions in customary international law. Another subject of quite considerable significance both within general international law and in the drafting of the ICC Statute was the extent to which acts of terrorism constitute crimes against humanity.[172]

In defining crimes against humanity, Article 7 provides as follows:

For the purpose of this Statute, 'crime against humanity' means any of the following acts when committed as part of a widespread or systematic attack directed against any civilian population, with knowledge of the attack:

(a) Murder;

(b) Extermination;

(c) Enslavement;

(d) Deportation or forcible transfer of population;

(e) Imprisonment or other severe deprivation of physical liberty in violation of fundamental rules of international law;

(f) Torture;

---

[167] Meron, 'International Criminalization of Internal Atrocities' 89 *AJIL* (1995) 554 at p. 557.
[168] Article 3, Statute.
[169] Article 7(2)(a) Rome Statute.
[170] Ibid. Article 7(2)(a).
[171] Ibid. Article 7(2)(a).
[172] See Steiner, Alston and Goodman, above n.1, 375–471 at p. 376.

(g) Rape, sexual slavery, enforced prostitution, forced pregnancy, enforced sterilization, or any other form of sexual violence of comparable gravity;

(h) Persecution against any identifiable group or collectivity on political, racial, national, ethnic, cultural, religious, gender as defined in paragraph 3, or other grounds that are universally recognized as impermissible under international law, in connection with any act referred to in this paragraph or any crime within the jurisdiction of the Court;

(i) Enforced disappearance of persons;

(j) The crime of apartheid;

(k) Other inhumane acts of a similar character intentionally causing great suffering, or serious injury to body or to mental or physical health.

2. For the purpose of paragraph 1:

(a) 'Attack directed against any civilian population' means a course of conduct involving the multiple commission of acts referred to in paragraph 1 against any civilian population, pursuant to or in furtherance of a State or organizational policy to commit such attack;

(b) 'Extermination' includes the intentional infliction of conditions of life, inter alia the deprivation of access to food and medicine, calculated to bring about the destruction of part of a population;

(c) 'Enslavement' means the exercise of any or all of the powers attaching to the right of ownership over a person and includes the exercise of such power in the course of trafficking in persons, in particular women and children;

(d) 'Deportation or forcible transfer of population' means forced displacement of the persons concerned by expulsion or other coercive acts from the area in which they are lawfully present, without grounds permitted under international law;

(e) 'Torture' means the intentional infliction of severe pain or suffering, whether physical or mental, upon a person in the custody or under the control of the accused; except that torture shall not include pain or suffering arising only from, inherent in or incidental to, lawful sanctions;

(f) 'Forced pregnancy' means the unlawful confinement of a woman forcibly made pregnant, with the intent of affecting the ethnic composition of any population or carrying out other grave violations of international law. This definition shall not in any way be interpreted as affecting national laws relating to pregnancy;

(g) 'Persecution' means the intentional and severe deprivation of fundamental rights contrary to international law by reason of the identity of the group or collectivity;

(h) 'The crime of apartheid' means inhumane acts of a character similar to those referred to in paragraph 1, committed in the context of an institutionalized regime of systematic oppression and domination by one racial group over any other racial group or groups and committed with the intention of maintaining that regime;

(i) 'Enforced disappearance of persons' means the arrest, detention or abduction of persons by, or with the authorization, support or acquiescence of, a State or a political organization, followed by a refusal to acknowledge that deprivation of freedom or to give information on the fate or whereabouts of those persons, with the intention of removing them from the protection of the law for a prolonged period of time.

It is significant to make a number of observations. Firstly, that the catalogue of crimes against humanity mirrors serious and grievous violations of international human rights law. Secondly, whilst there are some variations, it appears to be the position that in customary law crimes against humanity are not tied with the presence of international and national armed conflict. The ICC statute in describing and defining crimes against humanity is broader than the statutes of *ad hoc* tribunals. It does not require a nexus to armed conflict. Similarly, as a contrast to the Statute of ICTR and jurisprudence of ICTY tribunal, the ICC does not require the presence of a discriminatory motive, save for the crime of the persecution.[173] Thirdly, the expanded definition of crimes against humanity, to include expanded references to sexual violence, is an important legacy of the jurisprudence of the ICTY and the ICTR.

(iii) Genocide

In contemporary terms, the activity of intentional killing and physical extermination of groups, or destruction of individuals, is labelled as genocide.[174] Raphael Lemkin, a Polish jurist of Jewish origin is accredited with developing the modern principles relating to the crime of genocide and indeed for coining the term itself.[175] In 1933, he presented his ideas based on the protection of groups in a special report to the Fifth International Conference for the Unification of Penal Law.[176] He later elaborated these perceptions, in his work, *Axis Rule in Occupied Europe*, to develop the term genocide which was derived partly from the Greek word *genos* meaning race, tribe or nation, and partly from the Latin verb *caedere* which denotes the act of killing.[177] In his view:

> By 'genocide' we mean destruction of a nation or of an ethnic group . . . generally speaking, genocide does not necessarily mean the immediate destruction of a nation, or except when accomplished by mass killings of all members of a nation. It is intended rather to signify a co-ordinated plan of different actions aiming at the destruction of essential foundations of life of national groups . . . The objective of such a plan would be the disintegration of the political and social institutions of culture, language, national feelings, religion, and the economical existence of national groups, and the destruction of personal security, liberty, health, dignity, and even lives of the individuals belonging to such groups. Genocide is directed against the national group as an entity, and the actions involved are directed against individuals, not in their individual capacity, but as members of the national group.[178]

---

[173] Meron, above n.154, at p. 265.

[174] Special Rapporteur Whitaker aptly describes this activity as 'the ultimate crime and gravest violation of human rights it is possible to commit' Whitaker, *The Study of the Question of the Prevention and Punishment of the Crime of Genocide* (revised and updated) UN Doc E/CN.4.Sub.2/1985/6 at p. 5.

[175] Lemkin, *Axis Rule in Occupied Europe* (Carnegie Endowment for International Peace, 1944) p. 79; Porter 'Introduction: What is Genocide? Notes towards a Definition' in Porter (eds), *Genocide and Human Rights: A Global Anthology* (University Press of America, 1982) pp. 2–32, at p. 5.

[176] Lemkin, 'Genocide as a crime in international law' 41 *AJIL* (1947) pp. 145–151. Lemkin 'Terrorisme' Actes de la Ve Conference Internationale pour l'Unification du Droit Penal, Paris, 1935, pp. 48–56.

[177] 'New conceptions require new terms. By "genocide" we mean the destruction of a nation or of an ethnic group. This new word, coined by the author to denote an old practice in its modern development, is made from the ancient Greek word genos (race, tribe) and the Latin, cide (Killing), thus corresponding in its formation to such words as tyrannicide, homicide, infanticide etc.' Lemkin, above n.175, p. 79.

[178] Ibid. p. 79.

Lemkin's views on genocide were graphically illustrated through the actions of Nazis. During the course of the Second World War, physical destruction of groups took place precisely because of their belonging to a national, racial or religious group. The most obvious targets were the Jews and the Gypsies, though there were many others facing destruction and decimation. Notwithstanding the widespread deployment of the technique of genocide during the Second World War, the Charter of the International Military Tribunal, which was aimed at dispensing justice, did not specifically mention the term genocide.[179] Within international legal discourse the usage of the term 'genocide' appeared for the first time during the Nuremberg trials in a separate category. It was used in the indictment of 8 October 1945 which charged major German war criminals of having committed 'deliberate and systematic genocide, viz. the extermination of racial and national groups, against civilian populations of certain occupied territories in order to destroy particular races and classes of people and national and racial groups'.[180] The concept re-emerged in various trials of the Nazi war criminals conducted in the National Courts by the Allies.[181] As has been discussed, the atrocities committed during the Second World War produced a united front for the punishment of those who had been involved in serious crimes against human kind including genocide. It, therefore, became a top priority of the UN to develop specific instruments condemning and criminalising genocide.

In its very first session, the United Nations General Assembly included in its agenda a resolution entitled Resolution on the Crime of Genocide and adopted it as Resolution 96(I) on 11 December 1946.[182] Although, a General Assembly Resolution and *prima facie* deprived of the status of binding legal obligations,[183] the unanimity of the Assembly in declaring that 'Genocide is a Crime under international law which the civilized world condemns' and the substance and form of the Resolution leads to a conviction that it was, in fact, declaratory of customary international law.[184]

The Resolution played a major role in the recognition of genocide as a crime in international law, for not only did it form the basis of the Genocide Convention of 1948, but several of its themes were taken up in various other international instruments. There was essentially a recognition of the emergence of this concept of genocide, quite independent to that of 'crimes against humanity'.[185] To concretise and provide a legal recognition to this independent concept, the establishment of a convention on genocide was deemed necessary and a convention was in fact adopted within the space of two years. The Convention on the Prevention and Punishment of the Crime of Genocide 1948 was the first instrument in the armoury of the ICL, and concerned itself directly with the physical protection of minority groups. We have already examined the weaknesses and limitations of the Convention:[186] these include the necessity to establish specific intent to destroy in whole or

[179] See Power, *A Problem from Hell: America and the Age of Genocide* (Harper Perennial, 2007).

[180] *Trial of the Major War Criminals before the International Military Tribunal*, 1947, vol. I 43–44.

[181] *Law Reports of Trials of War Criminals*, 1947–1949, vol. vi, 48; vol. vii 7, 24; vol. xii, 2, 3, 6, 112, 114 and vol. xv, 123.

[182] GA Res. 96, UN GAOR, 1st Session 55 mtg., UN Doc A/RES/96 (1946); YBUN, 1946–1947, p. 255.

[183] Kunz, 'The United Nations Convention on Genocide' (1949) 43 *AJIL* 738 at p. 738.

[184] '[S]uch Resolutions . . . are authority for the content of customary law only if they claim to be declaration of existing law. A clear example is Resolution 96(I) of 11 December 1946'. Akehurst, 'Custom as a Source of International Law' (1974–5) 47 *BYIL* 1–53 at p. 6. On the meaning of customary international law see above chapter 2.

[185] Note the views of the various delegates during the preparatory stages of the Genocide Convention GAOR, 3rd session, Part 1, Sixth committee, 63 meeting, 30 September 1948, 6, para 7.

[186] See above chapter 13.

in part a national, ethnical, racial or religious group; the exclusion from the definition of political or other groups and the inability of the Convention to condemn 'cultural' genocide as 'genocide' have been considered serious shortcomings.

Furthermore, as has already been discussed, the Convention has proved nothing short of a complete failure in terms of enforcement. In reinforcing this point, Professor Cassese observes that:

> at the *enforcement* level the Convention has long proved a failure. Only once did a United Nations body pronounce on a specific instance of massacres, that it defined as genocide: this occurred in the case of *Sabra* and *Shatila*, when UN GA characterized the massacre perpetrated there by Christain falangist troops as 'an act of genocide' in its resolution 37/123 D of 16 December 1982 . . . Subsequently in 1993 for the first time a State brought a case of genocide before [the International Court of Justice: *Bosnia and Herzegovina* v. *Federal Republic of Yugoslavia (Serbia and Montenegro)*].[187]

There exists unanimity in respect of the criminalisation of genocide in municipal and international law, although the precise scope of this criminalisation begs a number of questions. In international law a number of international instruments, led by the Genocide Convention, testify to the validity of the prohibition and the criminalisation of genocide. A primary focus of our attention, and as already examined, has been of the provisions on the matter as represented by the Genocide Convention. However, treaty rules can, and certainly do in the present case, work in conjunction with customary rules although the scope and substance may vary. A treaty provision could possess the customary force if it fulfils the basic criterion of the establishment of custom – it could reflect customary law if its text declares or its *travaux préparatoires* state, along with the requisite *opinio juris*, that its substance is declaratory of existing law.[188] Despite the absolute prohibition of the crime of genocide in both convention and customary law, there are possible variations in the nature of the protection accorded. The Convention is taken to provide the absolute minimum of rights, with the implication that customary law has more to offer. To what extent is the expansive and wider vision of the prohibition plausible insofar as customary international law is concerned? In order to address this issue adequately, we need to analyse the developmental stages of genocide being recognised as a crime under international law. The declaratory nature of the provisions of the General Assembly Resolution 96(I) have already been referred to. The Resolution is based on an ambitious agenda; it has a wider constituency and appeals to humanity in general. Genocide is considered in general terms as 'a denial of the right of existence of entire human groups'.

This wider perspective, as present in the General Assembly Resolution, is a reflection of the abhorrence with which the international community viewed the crime. The Nazi atrocities, fresh in the minds of international politicians and the public alike, had demonstrated the various forms in which genocide could be committed; the Resolution, reflected a general revulsion, aimed to provide a prohibition. The constraints which were subsequently to characterise the provisions of a binding Convention are not present in this

---

[187] Cassese, *International Criminal Law*, above n.1, at p. 131.
[188] Akehurst, *A Modern Introduction to International Law* (Routledge, 1987) pp. 26–27; Baxter, 'Multilateral Treaties as Evidence of Customary International Law' (1965–66) 41 *BYIL* 275.

20

International criminal law and international human rights law

idealistic expression; 'political' or 'other groups' are placed in the same bracket as racial or religious groups, culture is deemed an integral part of the existence of human groups.

It is necessary, however, to note that the nature of binding customary norms requires a higher form of allegiance. The declaratory nature of the prohibition of genocide as enunciated in Resolution 96(I) does not mean that everything that is expressed in it carries an equal value.[189] The prohibition of genocide, its applicability and content meant different things to different people – a point which could be confirmed through an analysis of the provisions of the Resolution and the Convention as well as their *travaux préparatoires*. For instance, on the issue of 'political' genocide, political groups featured in the text of the Resolution, although during the preparatory stages of the Convention a number of disagreements resurfaced in relation to the possible normative value of the subject. The point was made by Mr. Morozov of the USSR, when he reminded the Sixth Committee of the essential distinction and difference in the nature of the General Assembly Resolution and a legally binding convention. He noted that the task:

> [w]as to draw up a Convention on genocide. If the Resolution of the General Assembly had sufficed for the purpose in view, and if all the problems had been solved beforehand then there would have been no need to spend two years in drawing up a convention. Without infringing Resolution 96(I) the task assigned to the Sixth Committee must be examined without heat; that task was to frame a convention on genocide and nothing else.[190]

More fundamentally, there were differences as to the substantive nature of the reference to political groups in the General Assembly Resolution itself. According to the representatives of Poland, the operative part of the Resolution did not deal with political groups, but related only to the grounds on which genocide could be committed.[191] Similarly, according to the representatives of Venezuela[192] and Belgium[193] the terms of reference in the Resolution were only to be measured as guidelines and not interpreted literally for the purpose of deciding its customary value.

The *travaux préparatoires* of the Convention also reflect disagreements on the issue of 'cultural' genocide. Several representatives presented the view that although 'cultural' genocide was an evil in its own right; it was more appropriately dealt with within the ambit of international human rights law, rather than in a convention of this nature.[194] This is probably what has happened. While genocide of a culture was excluded from the Convention and has remained outside the ambit of international criminal law, over a period of time international instruments have gradually started to take a more serious interest in the cultural aspects of minorities. For the present purposes it needs to be noted that while Article 27 of the ICCPR is aimed at protecting minorities, it has, nevertheless, been criticised for adopting a passive approach towards their claims to a distinct identity.

---

[189] See the position of the Polish Representative; GAOR, 3rd session Part 1, Sixth Committee 64th meeting, 1 October 1948, p. 19.
[190] GAOR, 3rd Session, Part 1, Sixth Committee, 74th meeting, 14 October 1948; Mr. Morozov (USSR) p. 104.
[191] Ibid. 175 meeting, pp. 110–111.
[192] Ibid. pp. 112–113.
[193] Ibid. 74th meeting.
[194] See e.g. the views of the Indian delegate ibid., 64th meeting, at pp. 15–16.

748

In contrast to Article 27 of the ICCPR, the United Nations Declaration on the Rights of Persons Belonging to National or Ethnic, Religious and Linguistic Minorities (1992) adopts a more direct and positive stance. Article 1(1) provides as follows: States shall protect the existence and the national or ethnic, cultural, religious and linguistic identity of minorities within their respective territories and shall encourage conditions for the promotion of that identity.

The positive and firm structuring of the Article and a linkage of 'existence' with 'identity' may well represent the emergence of a new norm whereby the notion of 'existence' takes on a wider meaning; 'existence' also includes a 'cultural existence'. Some jurists in providing commentaries on the Declaration have already readily advanced such a proposition. Asbjørn Eide, in his report, *Possible Ways and Means of Facilitating the Peaceful and Constructive Solution of Problems Involving Minorities*, notes that:

[t]he cultural and spiritual dimensions of existence are also fundamental to the Declaration. Therefore the identity of minorities is to be protected and conditions for its promotion encouraged. In the past, minority groups were sometimes denied 'existence' through policies of forced assimilation or ethnocide. It is now generally recognised . . . that each culture has a dignity and value which must be respected and preserved, to the extent compatible with universal human rights.[195]

Eide is also of the view that:

[e]xistence requires respect for and protection of basic subsistence rights. Depriving a group of the basic economic resources necessary to sustain its existence would violate the Declaration, which goes beyond prohibiting fundamental attacks on group life and obligates States to pursue a programme of active protection.[196]

According to Eide, the duty to protect the existence of minorities means a condemnation of policies of 'ethnic cleansing' and forced population transfers. He presents a wide categorisation of the right to existence. In addition to physical existence, minorities would have the right to cultural, linguistic, economic and developmental existence. They would also be entitled to claim a right to the environment and geography. 'Cultural', 'economic' and 'geographic' existence are wide-ranging concepts with the potential of immensely differing meanings. It is unlikely to find consistency in State practice and judging from the experience of a number of States in Asia, the Americas, Africa and Eastern Europe it appears difficult to accord a wholesale approval to Eide's expanded vision of the presence of the right to existence. It also needs to be emphasised that the thrust of Eide's observations derive from the provisions within the 1992 Declaration, which, notwithstanding its tremendous potential is, nevertheless, a General Assembly Resolution – a non-binding instrument.

---

[195] Eide, E/CN.4/Sub.2/1993/34 (1993) paras 201.
[196] Ibid. para 198.

Whereas there is uncertainty in existing State practice in relation to the exact scope of the right to existence, international law may have made some advances in so far as the punishment of the entities involved in violating this right is concerned. Individual responsibility for crimes against humanity, including genocide and the physical destruction of minorities, is firmly established, though State responsibility is not. The debate on the subject of the criminal responsibility of States has been lively although not conclusive.[197] According to the traditional approach, as represented by Professor Ian Brownlie:

> the concept [of criminal responsibility of States] has no legal value, cannot be justified in principle, and is contradicted by the majority of developments which have appeared in international law. Its only sphere is that of morals and propaganda. Some supporters of the theory of the criminal responsibility of the state in fact only prescribe punishment for the individuals comprising the government, in which case the only difference between their position and that of those who say that there can only be criminal responsibility of individuals is terminological. The 'sanctions' which are referred to as providing the penal responsibility of states have an artificial look.[198]

Professor Brownlie has continued to remain 'unconvinced of the practical utility of the concept of criminal responsibility of States'.[199] Brownlie's views are represented in the approach adopted by recent international statutes. The *ad hoc* ICTY and ICTR as well as the Statute of the ICC have jurisdiction to hold individuals responsible for international crimes.[200] On the other hand, the International Law Commission Draft Articles on State responsibility includes acts of genocide carrying State responsibility.[201] In its order on the admissibility and jurisdiction on the *Application of the Convention on Prevention and Punishment of the Crime of Genocide* (Bosnia and Herzegovina), 11 July 1996, the International Court of Justice made a brief reference to the subject of State responsibility in so far as it affected Article IX of the Convention. While the precise ambit of the Court's approach is far from clear, in rejecting Yugoslavia's fifth preliminary objection the Court appeared to take a wider approach on this issue of State responsibility. The Court has in recent times adopted a more assertive approach towards State responsibility. In an expanded interpretation of the Genocide Convention, the World Court has confirmed that both individual and State responsibility attaches to the crime of genocide.[202] The recent practice of the organs of the United Nations may also be taken to advance the argument. After all, the sanctions imposed by the Security Council on States such as Iraq, Sudan and the former Yugoslavia are reflective of the punishment for criminal activities including crimes against humanity and genocide.

---

[197] See Shaw, 'Genocide and International Law' in Dinstein and Tabory (eds), *International Law at a Time of Perplexity: Essays in Honour of Shabtai Rosenne* (Martinus Nijhoff Publishers, 1989) pp. 799–820 at p. 814; Weil, 'Towards Relative Normativity in International Law' (1983) 77 *AJIL* 413.

[198] Brownlie, *International Law and the Use of Force by States* (Clarendon Press, 1963) pp. 152–153.

[199] Brownlie, *System of the Law of Nations: State Responsibility* (Part 1) (Clarendon Press, 1983) p. 33.

[200] See Article 25(1) of the Rome Statute.

[201] 18 ILM, 1979, 1568, Article 19(3)(c); also see Special Rapporteur T. Van Boven, *Study Concerning the Rights to Restitution, Compensation and Rehabilitation for Victims of Gross Violations of Human Rights and Fundamental Freedoms* E/CN.4/Sub.2/1993/8, 16.

[202] *Application of the Convention on the Prevention and Punishment of the Crime of Genocide (Bosnia and Herzegovina v. Serbia and Montenegro)* Judgment 26 February 2007 www.icj-cij.org/docket/index.php?p1=3&p2=3&k=f4&case=91&code=bhy&p3=4 <last visited 18 May 2009>, paras 170–179.

International criminal law and international human rights law

genocide.[218] In the ICTY, the *Krstić* judgment established that genocide had taken place in Srebrenica.[219]

As noted in an earlier chapter, some of the weaknesses in definition of 'genocide' as established by the 1948 Convention have been overcome: recent international instruments have covered some grounds to condemn forced or mass expulsions, and the jurisprudence emerging from international criminal tribunals have at least in some cases regarded the forcible expulsion of ethnic, racial or religious groups as constituting genocide.[220] It is positive to note that the case-law appears to be adopting a position that 'killing' of a culture can provide evidence of an intent to bring about physical genocide.[221]

(iv) Aggression

Aggression constitutes a crime in international law, although as shall be considered below, there remains considerable ambiguity as to its content and scope. Aggression conducted by one State against another was one of the foremost prohibitions in international law. It was first officially enunciated in Pact of Paris in 1928,[222] and is clearly established in the provisions of the United Nations Charter (1945). The crime of aggression was first stipulated within the category of 'crimes against peace'. Article 6 of the Charter of International Military Tribunal (1945) provided for the establishment of a tribunal to prosecute and punish war criminals who were involved in crimes against peace. The category of crimes against peace was defined as 'planning preparation, initiation or waging of a war of aggression, or a war in violation of international treaties, agreements or assurances, or participation in a common plan or conspiracy for the accomplishment of any of the foregoing'. At Nuremberg, Nazi war criminals were indicted and convicted of the crime of aggression. The Tokyo Trials also resulted in convictions for the crime of aggression. The UN General Assembly unanimously adopted Resolution 95(I) on 11 December 1946, thereby affirming the principles as established by the Nuremberg Charter and the Judgment of the Tribunal.[223] The Assembly followed this by a further Resolution requiring the International Law Commission to formulate these principles in its own work.[224]

Insofar as consolidating the definition of the crime of aggression is concerned, progress has been slow. The UN Draft Code on Offences Against the Peace and Security of Mankind as prepared by the International Law Commission in 1954 dealt primarily with the principles enshrined in the Charter of the Nuremberg Tribunal and with the judgment of the Tribunal.[225] Article 2 of the Code provides that the following acts are offences against the peace and security of mankind:

---

[218] *Prosecutor v. Jean Kambanda*, Case No. ICTR-97-23, Judgment and Sentence 4 September 1998.

[219] *Prosecutor v. Krstić* Case No. IT-98-33-A, Judgment 19 April 2004, pp. 2–6.

[220] See Judge Riad express affirmation and recognition of 'ethnic cleansing' as a form of 'genocide', *Prosecutor v. Kradžić and Mladić*, Case No. IT-95-18-I, 16 November 1995.

[221] *Prosecutor v. Kunarac* et al., Case No. IT-96-23-T & IT-96-23/1-T, Judgement 22 February 2001, para 568; *Prosecutor v. Kvočka* et al., Case No. IT-98-30-T (Omarska, Keraterm and Trnopolje Camps) Judgment 2 November 2001, para 123.

[222] For the text of the Pact and other related documents see the Avalon Project at Yale Law School www.yale.edu/lawweb/avalon/imt/proc/imtconst.htm <last visited 2 May 2009>.

[223] GA Res. 95(I). Affirmation of the Principles of International Law Recognized by the Charter of the Nurnberg Tribunal 11 December 1946.

[224] GA Res. 177(II); 2 YBILC (1950) 374.

[225] See UN GAOR Supp. (No. 9) at 11–12; UN Doc. A/2693 (1972).

(1) Any act of aggression, including the employment by the authorities of a State of armed force against another State for any purpose other than national or collective self-defence or in pursuance of a decision or recommendation of a competent organ of the United Nations.

(2) Any threat by the authorities of a State to resort to an act of aggression against another State.

The disagreements over the definition, however, continued and further hampered the progress towards the completion of the code. The General Assembly then took charge of its attempts at the definition of aggression, an issue that was only resolved through the General Assembly Resolution on the Definition of Aggression (1974).[226] Article 3(g) of the Resolution includes in its explanation of acts of aggression:

The sending by or on behalf of a State of armed bands, groups, irregulars or mercenaries, which carry out acts of armed force against another State of such gravity as to amount to the acts listed . . . or its substantial involvement therein.

A more substantial criticism is made by Professor Cassese when he notes that the definition of aggression:

was deliberately incomplete, for Article 4 provided that the definition was not exhaustive and left to the [Security Council] a broad area of discretion, by stating that it was free to characterize other acts as aggression under the Charter. Furthermore, the resolution did not specify that aggression could entail both state responsibility and individual criminal liability: in Article 5(2) of the Definition it simply provided that war of aggression is a crime against international law, adding that it 'gives rise to international responsibility'.[227]

Within the General Assembly Resolution on the Definition of Aggression (1979) there was, however, a caveat which exempts national liberation movements in their struggle for self-determination.[228] Such an exemption, although a feature of this Resolution (and a number of subsequent UN General Assembly Resolutions), injected considerable uncertainty into the entire debate of the concept of aggression. The subsequent adoption of the definition of aggression by the ILC in its Draft Code of Crimes against Peace and Security of Mankind (1996) has also remained unhelpful. Article 16 of the 1996 draft code provides:

---

[226] GA Res. 3314 (XXIX) 14 December 1974. 'Definition of Aggression' G.A.O.R 29th Sess., Supp. 31, 142; 69 AJIL (1975) 480.

[227] Cassese, above n.1, at pp. 152–153 (fn. 5).

[228] Article 7 of the Resolution provides: 'Nothing in this Definition, and in particular Article 3, could in any way prejudice the right to self-determination, freedom and independence, as derived from the Charter, of peoples forcibly deprived of that right and referred to in the Declaration on Principles of International Law concerning Friendly Relations and co-operation among States in accordance with the Charter of the United Nations, particularly peoples under colonial and racist regimes or other forms of alien domination; nor the right of these peoples to struggle to that end and to seek and receive support, in accordance with the principles of the Charter and in conformity with the above-mentioned Declaration.'

'An individual who, as leader or organizer, actively participates in or orders the planning, preparation, initiation or waging of aggression committed by a State shall be responsible for a crime of aggression.'[229] In the context of the International Criminal Court, as already mentioned, there were divisions as to the definition and possible content of aggression. In the end, the best that could be offered was a compromise. Aggression is recognised as one of 'the most serious crimes of concern to the international community as a whole'.[230] However, no definition of 'aggression' was forthcoming. Therefore, Article 5(2) of the Rome Statute provides that:

> [t]he Court shall exercise jurisdiction over the crime of aggression once a provision is adopted in accordance with articles 121 and 123 defining the crime and setting out the conditions under which the Court shall exercise jurisdiction with respect to this crime. Such a provision shall be consistent with the relevant provisions of the Charter of the United Nations.

Aggression remains a highly politically charged offence, and a determination of aggression by one State against another necessarily seeks a determination from the United Nations Security Council. A complex debate relates to the relationship between the ICC and the Security Council. Can the ICC, act independently or even in opposition to the position adopted by the Security Council?[231] In the light of the prevalent dissensions it appears unlikely that a consensus definition of the crime of aggression would be readily available.[232]

6 SUBSTANTIVE PRINCIPLE OF ICL: INDIVIDUAL CRIMINAL RESPONSIBILITY, IMMUNITIES AND 'SUPERIOR ORDERS'

Individual criminal responsibility has been an ancient phenomenon having been engaged historically in the enforcement of crimes of piracy, slave trading and trafficking. As noted above, individual criminal responsibility was deployed in the Treaty of Versailles (1919), Article 227 of which established individual criminal responsibility of the ex-German Emperor, Kaiser Wilhelm II for 'the supreme offences against international morality and

---

[229] Text adopted by the International Law Commission at its 48th session, in 1996, and submitted to the General Assembly Draft Code of Crimes against the Peace and Security of Mankind (1996) *Yearbook of the International Law Commission, 1996*, vol. II (Pt Two).

[230] Article 5(1) Rome Statute.

[231] See Report of the Special Working Group on the Crime of Aggression ICC-ASP/6/20/Add.1 www.icc-cpi.int/iccdocs/asp_docs/SWGCA/ICC-ASP-6-20-Add1-AnnexII-ENG.pdf <last visited 5 March 2009>.

[232] In describing some of the proposals that have been advanced, Wedgewood makes the following points: 'the ICC prosecutor need not wait for Council action before bringing a criminal charge of aggression. The Council would be referred any allegation of aggression, but if the Council failed to act within six or twelve months, the ICC could begin a case anyway. In one proposal, the prosecutor and ICC could proceed immediately. In another, the General Assembly would first be asked to take the Council's place in finding or dismissing the allegation of aggression. If the General Assembly also failed to act, the ICC could make the extraordinary judgment of what constitutes aggression.' Wedgewood, 'The Irresolution of Rome' 64 *Law and Contemporary Problems* (2001) 193 at p. 213.

sanctity of treaties'.[233] Article 228 provided for the prosecution of German military personnel who committed war crimes. Individual criminal responsibility for acts against humanity was authorised by the Treaty of Sèvres (1920) in dealing with the defeated and subjugated Ottoman Empire.[234] However, the treaty itself remained unratified and was replaced by another treaty, the Treaty of Lausanne (1923) which allowed for a general amnesty. A further initiative in 1937 by the League of Nations to set up an International Criminal Court with individual criminal responsibility was frustrated through the commencement of the Second World War. At the end of the Second World War, the International Military Tribunal for Nuremberg and Tokyo confirmed the principle of individual criminal responsibility. As the Nuremberg Tribunal famously noted:

> Crimes against international law are committed by men, not by abstract entities, and only by punishing individuals who commit such crimes can the provisions of international law be enforced.[235]

The practice that emerged from the tribunals was that regardless of rank or position, individuals could be held responsible.[236] This principle is applicable as much as to military officers as to Heads of States and governments and now appears to be firmly established as part of international customary law.[237] Article 7 of the Charter of IMT at Nuremberg affirmed the rule. Article 7(2) of the Statute of ICTY provides that '[t]he official position of any accused person, whether as Head of State or Government or as a responsible Government official, shall not relieve such person of criminal responsibility nor mitigate punishment'. As regards the irrelevance of official position, Article 27 of the Rome Statute explicitly mentions that:

> (1) This Statute shall apply equally to all persons without any distinction based on official capacity. In particular, official capacity as a Head of State or Government, a member of a Government or parliament, an elected representative or a government official shall in no case exempt a person from criminal responsibility under this Statute, nor shall it, in and of itself, constitute a ground for reduction of sentence.
>
> (2) Immunities or special procedural rules which may attach to the official capacity of a person, whether under national or international law, shall not bar the Court from exercising its jurisdiction over such a person.

---

[233] Treaty of Versailles, 28 June 1919, L.N.T.S. No. 24; 112 B.F.S.P.1.

[234] Schabas, above n.74, at p. 4.

[235] Trial of the Major War Criminals Before the Nuremberg Military Tribunals 14 November 1945–1 October 1946 (Official Documents 1947), 223.

[236] In the context of the applicability of individual criminal responsibility for breaches of Common Article 3, see Meron, 'International Criminalization of Internal Atrocities' 89 *AJIL* (1995) 554 at p. 562.

[237] See the jurisprudence of the ICTY in particular *Prosecutor v. Karadžić and Mladić*, Case No. IT-95-18-I, para 24; *Prosecutor v. Anto Furundžija*, Case No. IT-95-17/1-T para 140 and *Prosecutor v. Milošević, Slobodan*, Case No. IT-02-54 (Kosovo, Croatia and Bosnia) (decision on preliminary motions) para 28. See also the views of Lord Millet (171–9) and Lord Phillips of Worth Matravers (186–190).

A significant aspect of international criminal law and international humanitarian law is the concept of command or superior responsibility. As noted by the *ad hoc* tribunals and the Statute of the International Criminal Court, superiors or commanders themselves are not relieved of responsibility if they knew or had reason to know that their subordinates had conducted or were about to commit international crimes.[238]

The position is now confirmed by Article 33 of the Rome Statute, which provides that:

1. The fact that a crime within the jurisdiction of the Court has been committed by a person pursuant to an order of a Government or of a superior, whether military or civilian, shall not relieve that person of criminal responsibility unless:
   (a) The person was under a legal obligation to obey orders of the Government or the superior in question;
   (b) The person did not know that the order was unlawful; and
   (c) The order was not manifestly unlawful.
2. For the purposes of this article, orders to commit genocide or crimes against humanity are manifestly unlawful.

It is also significant to note that neither the *ad hoc* tribunals nor the International Criminal Court grant immunities to heads of State or governments for international crimes. In order for a superior (either military or civilian) to be found criminally responsible under Articles 7(3)/6(3) of the statutes of the *ad hoc* tribunals, the following elements must be established beyond reasonable doubt:

(i) an act or omission incurring criminal responsibility within the subject matter jurisdiction of the Tribunals has been committed by other(s) than the accused ('principal crime');
(ii) there existed a superior-subordinate-relationship between the accused and the principal perpetrator(s) ('superior-subordinate-relationship');
(iii) the accused as a superior knew or had reason to know that the subordinate was about to commit such crimes or had done so ('knew or had reason to know'); and
(iv) the accused as a superior failed to take the necessary and reasonable measures to prevent such crimes or punish the perpetrator(s) thereof ('failure to prevent or punish').[239]

---

[238] Articles 7(3)/6(3) of the ICTY/ICTR Statutes establish indirect liability based upon the power which the superior holds to for controlling the actions of his subordinates. The position has been restated by the ICTY trail chamber in *Halilović* case. It notes that: 'The commander is responsible for the failure to perform an act required by international law. This omission is culpable because international law imposes an affirmative duty on superiors to prevent and punish crimes committed by their subordinates. Thus "for the acts of his subordinates" as generally referred to in the jurisprudence of the Tribunal does not mean that the commander shares the same responsibility as the subordinates who committed the crimes, but rather that because of the crimes committed by his the subordinates, the commander should bear responsibility for his failure to act,' *Prosecutor v. Halilović*, Case No. IT-01-48-T (Grabovice-Uzdol) (Judgment 16 November 2005), para 54.

[239] *Prosecutor v. Orić*, Case No. IT-03-68 Trial Judgment, para 294; *Prosecutor v. André Ntagerura* et al., Case No. ICTR-99-46-T, Trial Judgment, 25 February 2004 (Ntagerura Trial Judgment) para 627; *Prosecutor v. Laurent Semanza*, Case No. ICTR-97-20 Trial Judgment, para 400; *Prosecutor v. Blaškić*, Case No. IT-95-14 (Lašva Valley) Appeal Judgment, para 484; *Prosecutor v. Aleksovski*, Case No. IT-95-14/1 Appeal Judgment, para 72.

The Statute of ICC and ICTY and ICTR addresses the issue of superior responsibility. According to Article 28 of the ICC:

In addition to other grounds of criminal responsibility under this Statute for crimes within the jurisdiction of the Court:

(a) A military commander or person effectively acting as a military commander shall be criminally responsible for crimes within the jurisdiction of the Court committed by forces under his or her effective command and control, or effective authority and control as the case may be, as a result of his or her failure to exercise control properly over such forces, where:

   (i) That military commander or person either knew or, owing to the circumstances at the time, should have known that the forces were committing or about to commit such crimes; and

   (ii) That military commander or person failed to take all necessary and reasonable measures within his or her power to prevent or repress their commission or to submit the matter to the competent authorities for investigation and prosecution.

(b) With respect to superior and subordinate relationships not described in paragraph (a), a superior shall be criminally responsible for crimes within the jurisdiction of the Court committed by subordinates under his or her effective authority and control, as a result of his or her failure to exercise control properly over such subordinates, where:

   (i) The superior either knew, or consciously disregarded information which clearly indicated, that the subordinates were committing or about to commit such crimes;

   (ii) The crimes concerned activities that were within the effective responsibility and control of the superior; and

   (iii) The superior failed to take all necessary and reasonable measures within his or her power to prevent or repress their commission or to submit the matter to the competent authorities for investigation and prosecution.

7   RECENT DEVELOPMENTS AT THE INTERNATIONAL CRIMINAL COURT

Thus far, the ICC has only been activated in a limited number of cases. These include cases of the so-called 'self-referrals' by States themselves, in which alleged crimes falling within the Court's jurisdiction have occurred: and these being Uganda, the Democratic Republic of the Congo (DRC) and Central African Republic. The prosecutor has opened investigations into the 'situations' existing in Uganda, the DRC and the Central African Republic. In its Resolution 1593 (2005) of 31 March 2005 the UN Security Council upheld the recommendations made by the UN Commission of Inquiry on Darfur in its report of 25 January 2005 to refer to the situation in Darfur to the ICC Prosecutor.[240]

The ICC has very recently started to hear cases, and recent developments in respect of the DRC and Darfur are particularly important. In the current *Lubanga* case, the ICC was initially forced to implement a stay in the proceedings due to the fact that:

---

[240] UN Doc. S/2005/60, paras 583–589.

In the view of the Trial Chamber, there was no prospect that a fair trial could be held because the Prosecutor was unable to disclose a large number of documents containing potentially exculpatory information and information relevant to the preparation of the defence. The Prosecutor had obtained the documents in question from several information providers, in particular from the United Nations, on the condition of confidentiality, and these information providers had refused to consent to their disclosure to the defence and, in most instances, to the Trial Chamber.[241]

The Appeals Chamber, however, did reverse the decision of the Trial Chamber's in refusing to release Lubanga and referred the matter back to the Trial Chamber.[242] However, on 18 November 2008, the Trial Chamber decided that the case against Lubanga should proceed with an initial trial date scheduled for 26 January 2009, due to the reasons for ordering the stay in proceedings having 'fallen away'.[243] Although this is the first case being heard by the ICC, in the light of prevailing controversies the outcome is far from certain.[244]

Another important development took place on 14 July 2008 when an opportunity for the ICC to exercise its powers under Article 27(2) occurred, which states that:

[i]mmunities or special procedural rules which may attach to the official capacity of a person, whether under national or international law, shall not bar the Court from exercising its jurisdiction over such a person.

Previously, it has not been possible for international courts and tribunals to issue arrest warrants or, indeed, try persons with diplomatic immunity. The prosecutor applied for an arrest warrant for the current President of Sudan, Hassan Ahmad Al Bashir, for the perpetration of war crimes, crimes against humanity and genocide in Darfur. However, the Pre-Trial Chamber has requested additional supporting information 'in relation to some confidential aspects of the Prosecution's request for a warrant of arrest'.[245] In the most recent development an arrest warrant for a current head of State has been issued, although it would still be a serious challenge to bring about a conviction and ultimate sentence.[246]

---

242 The Appeals Chamber confirms the stay of proceedings and reverses decision on the release of Thomas Lubanga Dyilo, The Hague, 21 October 2008, www.icc-cpi.int/press/pressreleases/433.html <last visited 17 November 2008>.

243 Stay of proceedings in the Lubanga case is lifted – trial provisionally scheduled for 26 January 2009, The Hague, 18 November 2008, www.icc-cpi.int/press/pressreleases/445.html <last visited 17 November 2008>.

244 For further information and developments see www.icc-cpi.int/cases.html <last visited 1 August 2009>.

245 Pre-Trial Chamber I requests additional materials in relation to the request for a warrant of arrest for Sudanese President Omar Hassan Al Bashir, The Hague, 16 October 2008, www.icc-cpi.int/press/pressreleases/430.html <last visited 17 November 2008>.

246 'On 4 March 2009 the judges of Pre-Trial Chamber I issued an arrest warrant for Sudanese President Omar Hassan Ahmad al-Bashir named by the Prosecutor of the International Criminal Court (ICC) Luis Moreno-Ocampo in his July 2008 filing in the Darfur situation. The Chamber held that there are reasonable grounds to believe that President al-Bashir bears criminal responsibility for crimes against humanity and war crimes allegedly committed in Darfur in the past five years. Omar Hassan Ahmad al-Bashir has been the President of Sudan since 1993' www.iccnow.org/?mod=darfur <last visited 5 May 2009>.

20

International criminal law and international human rights law

8 MIXED INTERNATIONAL CRIMINAL TRIBUNALS

A more recent development on the part of the UN has been the consideration of a number of other situation and attempts to set up judicial bodies. These include Sierra Leone, East Timor, Kosovo (UNMIK) and Cambodia. In these cases, mixed courts have been established as opposed to *ad hoc* tribunals along the lines of ICTY or ICTR. These mixed tribunals have the characteristics both of national and international tribunals. For Sierra Leone, the Statute of the Special Court was drafted in October 2000 at the request of the UN Secretary-General, which was adopted and came into force in January 2002. In the case of Cambodia, an agreement was reached on 17 March 2003 which was adopted by the UN General Assembly in May 2003 and ratified by the Cambodian Parliament in October 2004.[247] This has led to the establishment of the Extraordinary Chambers in the Courts of Cambodia (ECCC).

These tribunals consist of a mixed body of international judges and judges that are nationals of the States where these trials are to take place. Such courts and tribunals may be organs of the relevant State, being part of its judiciary. This is the position of the courts in Kosovo and the 'Special Panel for Serious Crimes' in East Timor and is also the model under consideration for the proposed Cambodian Extraordinary Chambers. The Court may be of a totally international nature – it may be set up under an international agreement and not be a part of the national judiciary as is the case with the Special Court for Sierra Leone.

There are inherent difficulties in conducting trials in situations of substantial conflict and unrest. In such instances there may well have been the breakdown of the judicial system as in the cases of civil wars in East Timor and Sierra Leone or as in the case of Kosovo, an international conflict. Historical instability may hinder a sound judicial system from developing (e.g. in Cambodia) or there may remain a continuing hostility towards a certain community (e.g. in Kosovo). However, mixed trials do have the advantage of providing local expertise with the objectivity of neutral and impartial decision-makers.

The hybrid tribunal was first utilised in East Timor, with the hope that 'the hybrid model is cheaper to operate than the ad hoc tribunals. It is considered to be politically less divisive, more meaningful to victim populations, and more effective at rebuilding local judiciary'.[248] However, the tribunal has been subject to much criticism, in respect of its inefficiency, lack of public participation and its failure to uphold standards of due process.[249] Two main issues have been cited as the cause of these issues: '(a) the UN decision to transfer control of the judiciary, with jurisdiction over ordinary crimes, almost immediately to inexperienced East Timorese officials and (b) a severe lack of funding.'[250]

The Special Court for Sierra Leone is a mixed court and as such made up of judges elected both by the Government of Sierra Leone and the UN Secretary General. The Court has, thus far, delivered final judgments in respect of the AFRC (Armed Forces Revolutionary Council) and the CDF (Civil Defence Forces) Trials. In the CDF Trial guilty verdicts were declared in respect of murder as a crime against humanity, for aiding and

---

[247] A/RES/57/228 B Khmer Rouge Trials.
[248] Katzenstein, 'Hybrid Tribunals: Searching for Justice in East Timor', 16 *Harv. Hum. Rts. J.* (2003) 245 at p. 246.
[249] Ibid.
[250] Ibid. p. 248 (footnotes omitted).

abetting such acts, violence to life, health and physical well-being of persons, 'other in-humane acts', cruel treatment and pillage.[251] Notably the defendants were not found guilty of acts of terrorism or conscripted and enlisting children under the age of 15.[252] In respect of the AFRC Trial, the accused were found guilty of:

> acts of terrorism; collective punishments; extermination; murder; violence to life, health and physical or mental well-being of persons, in marticular murder and mutilation; outrages upon personal dignity; conscripting children under the age of 15 years into armed groups and/or using them to participate actively in hostilities; enslavement; pillage; and rape.[253]

In the RUF (Revolutionary United Front) trial, each of the three defendants were found guilty by the Court on 29 February 2009. Sentences were awarded on 8 April 2009. In addi-tion to this, Charles Taylor, the former Liberian President is being tried in The Hague for his part in the atrocities that occurred in Sierra Leone. One of the main advantages of the Special Court has been the 'gender sensitive strategies' adopted in order to punish those responsible for different forms of sexual violence.[254] The SCSL has also been particularly successful in its community outreach programme. The SCSL also co-exists alongside the TRC in Sierra Leone, which has led to some difficulties in determining the relationship between both accountability mechanisms.

The ECCC has made recent headway despite being surrounded by controversy. Between 1975 and 1979 it is estimated that the Khmer Rouge was responsible for the deaths of some 1.7 million Cambodians as a result of starvation, disease, exhaustion, execution or torture.[255] The Court, operational some 28 years after the rule of the Khmer Rouge, is not funded by the UN after questions were raised prior to its establishment over the impartial-ity of a national court, due to the influence of the government in addition to a lack of qualified judges and lawyers. It is claimed that 'Hun Sen [The Cambodian Co-Prime Minister] remained insistent that any tribunal be more national than international, out of a desire to maintain national autonomy and perhaps form a court over which he could wield significant control'.[256] Between July and November 2007 five former Khmer Rouge leaders were arrested and charged with crimes against humanity and war crimes, at the say so of the hybrid court. The suspects include Kaing Guek Ean, the former director of the main security prison and torture centre of the Khmer Rouge, Tuol Sleng. Nuon Chea, the founding member of the Khmer Rouge's predecessor the Kampuchean People's Revolutionary Party and influential member of the Khmer Rouge, it is believed, 'may have actually played a greater role than Pol Pot in the regime's executions'.[257] Furthermore, Ieng Sary, the former Foreign Minister and Deputy Prime Minister and his wife, Ieng Thirith, former Social Affairs Minister, as well as Khieu Samphan, Head of State during the Democratic Kampuchea, have also been charged with crimes under international criminal

---

[251] CDF Trial, SCSL-04-14-A, pp. 1163–1666.

[252] Ibid.

[253] SCSL-2004-16-A p. 1990.

[254] Nowrojee, 'Making the Invisible War Crime Visible: Post-Conflict Justice for Sierra Leone's Rape Victims' 18 *Harv. Hum. Rts. J.* (2005) 85 at p. 85.

[255] Glaspy, 'Justice Delayed? Recent Developments at the Extraordinary Chambers in the Courts of Cambodia' 21 *Harv. Hum. Rts. J.* (2008) 143 at p. 143.

[256] Ibid. at p. 146.

[257] Ibid. at p. 151.

law. Despite these arrests being a considerable step towards achieving a measure of justice for those murders at the hands of the Khmer Rouge, many challenges still face the ECCC. The voluntary funding scheme raises questions regarding the impartiality and future of the Court.[258] Interference from the Cambodian government and a potential lack of independence of the judge also remain considerable concerns.[259]

Domestic politics seems to be an overriding theme when it comes to hybrid or mixed tribunals. Allowing the national courts to play a significant role in these trials can lead to the judiciary coming under political pressure, in a way that would not occur if the Court was made up primarily of international judges. However, if violations of international criminal law can be efficiently and effectively prosecuted at a national level, this can only be seen as adding legitimacy to the process. The trial of Saddam Hussein at the Iraqi Special Tribunal highlights the potential pitfalls of such trials occurring at a national level, which was dogged with claims of the lack of impartiality of the judiciary.[260]

9 CONCLUSIONS

This chapter has traced the developments of international criminal law – from rudimentary and *ad hoc* structures to a recognisable system, with possible enforcement mechanisms. During its assessment, the chapter has also confirmed that the developmental process of ICL would have been severely retarded without the assistance of the expanding norms of international human rights law. Notwithstanding their defects and limitations, the Nuremberg and Tokyo Trails established important precedents. The affirmation and acceptance of genocide as an independent crime in international law by the Genocide Convention (1948) was also an important milestone, although as we have examined in various sections of this study, the value of Convention can largely be gauged in symbolic terms.[261] The past 60 years have witnessed unforgiveable and horrific violations of individual and group rights. International criminal law did come round to dealing with some of these serious violations through the establishment of *ad hoc* tribunals for the former Yugoslavia and Rwanda. These tribunals – a product of the United Nations Security Council's activism – are limited in their scope of application and jurisdiction. Despite their precedential value and burgeoning jurisprudence, the tribunals have only had few successes in judicial accountability for individuals responsible of serious crimes under international law. As this chapter has examined, in more recent times, the international community has set up a range of tribunals. These include the Statute of the Special Court for Sierra Leone, Special Tribunal for Lebanon and Rules of the Extraordinary Chambers in the Courts of Cambodia.

Without a doubt the most significant development for international criminal law was the adoption of the Statute of International Criminal haw in 1998 and the enforcement of the Statute in 2002. At this present juncture, preliminary inferences that might be drawn on the operation of the Court do not present an optimistic prognosis. The Court's inability to commence a single trial (until January 2009) could either be a result of the incompetence

---

[258] Ibid. at p. 154.
[259] Ibid. at p. 153.
[260] Peterson, 'Unpacking Show Trials: Situating the Trial of Saddam Hussein' 48 *Harv. Int. L.J.* (2007) 257.
[261] For the difficulties with the implementation mechanisms of the Genocide Convention see above chapter 13.

of its officer or the result of the institutional flaws built into the system.[262] The International Criminal Court is, as was predicted at the outset, hampered by various limitations and constraints. As a multi-lateral treaty operating in a field immersed by political considerations and by national self-interests, many of its limitations are self-explanatory. Perhaps the most visible obstacle in establishing an effective and transparent system of judicial institution is due to the refusal of (Russia, China and the United States) the three permanent members of the Security Council to accept the jurisdiction of the Court.[263] The United States has been particularly vociferous in its opposition to the Court. As noted already, the United States signed the text of the Statute on 31 December 2000, but rescinded from the signature in 2002. It is unfortunate that the most powerful and militarily strongest State is against the existence and continuation of the International Criminal Court. For the world's leading democracy which has consistently campaigned for rule of law and accountability for crimes under international law such opposition appears incredible.[264] Those opposing the United States' involvement with the Court argue that:

> the ICC as currently organized is, and will remain, unacceptable to the United States. This is important because the ICC depends on U.S. political, military, and economic support for its success. An ICC without U.S. support – and indeed, with probable U.S. opposition – will not only fail to live up to its expectations. It may well do actual harm by discouraging the United States from engaging in various human rights-protecting activities. And this, in turn, may increase rather than decrease the impunity of those who violate human rights.[265]

Critics of such a view claim that, in reality, the United States has military and strategic interests which do not coincide with an impartial, objective and judicially accountable court of law. Wherever the truth lies, there is no escaping the fact that without the support of militarily and politically influential States such as the United States, Russia and China, the Court is likely to remain ineffectual.

---

[262] Note the on-going fiasco with the *Lubanga* case discussed above; also see Rozenberg, 'Lubanga: The Case Continues' 21 November 2008 www.telegraph.co.uk/news/newstopics/lawreports/joshuarozenberg/3480086/Lubanga-the-case-continues.html <last visited 20 May 2009>.

[263] For Commentaries see Wedgwood, 'The International Criminal Court: a American View' 10 *EJIL* (1999) 93; Hafner, Boon, Rübesame and Huston, 'A Response to the American View as Presented by Ruth Wedgwood' 10 *EJIL* (1999) 113; Bolton, 'Courting Danger: What's Wrong With the International Criminal Court' 54 *The National Interest* (1998/1999) 60; Jia, 'China and the International Criminal Court: Current Situation' 10 *Singapore Year Book of International Law* (2006) 1; Tuzmukhamedov, 'The ICC and Russian Constitutional Problems' 3 *Journal of International Criminal Justice* (2005) 621.

[264] The US interpretation of the concept of rule of law, however, is quite varied, expanding on which Kahn notes: 'The character of the controversy over the Court is particularly difficult to understand because the central term of the debate – the rule of law – is itself deeply contested . . . In the American constitutional frame, popular sovereignty and the rule of law are a single phenomenon constitutive of the national political identity. The rule of law, which begins and ends in American life with the Constitution, is the self-expression of the popular sovereign. Americans believe they created themselves as a "nation under law." That law is not a set of moral constraints imposed on the political process from outside, whether from natural law, *jus cogens*, or customary international law. Rather, the law expresses the substantive decisions of a self-governing community. The American Constitution expresses the will of "we the People." The rule of law is binding on the American political community not because it is reasonable or morally correct. It is binding because it arises out of the constitutive act of self-creation by that community. Thus, the rule of law is not a moral norm; rather, it is an existential condition signifying the continuing existence of the popular sovereign.' Kahn, 'Why is the United States so Opposed' *Crimes of War Magazine* www.crimesofwar.org/icc_magazine/icc-kahn.html (2003) <last visited 18 May 2009>.

[265] Goldsmith, above n.66 at p. 89.

International criminal law and international human rights law

20

21 International human rights law and international humanitarian law[1]

The humanization of the law of war received its greatest impetus . . . from the international human rights instruments adopted in the post–UN Charter period and the creation of international processes of state accountability . . . the fact that the law of war and human rights stem from different historical and doctrinal roots has not prevented the principle of humanity from becoming the common denominator of both systems. Current trends point to even greater reliance on that principle.[2]

The essence of the whole corpus of international humanitarian law as well as human rights law lies in the protection of the human dignity of every person, regardless of his or her gender. The general principle of respect for human dignity is . . . the very *raison d'etre* of international humanitarian law and human rights law; indeed in modern times this principle has become of such paramount importance as to permeate the whole body of international law. This principle is intended to shield human being from outrages upon the personal dignity, whether such outrages are carried out by unlawfully attacking the body or humiliating and debasing the honour, self-respect or the mental well being of a person.[3]

[1] Best, *Humanity in Warfare* (Columbia University Press, 1980); Best, *Law and War since 1945* (Clarendon Press, 1994); Detter, *The Law of War* (Cambridge University Press, 2000); Dinstein, *The Conduct of Hostilities under the Law of International Armed Conflict* (Cambridge University Press, 2004); Draper, 'The Relationship Between the Human Rights Regime and Laws of Armed Conflict' 1 *Israel Yearbook on Human Rights* (1971) 191; Green, *The Contemporary Law of Armed Conflict* (Manchester University Press, 2000); Kalshoven and Zegveld, *Constraints on the Waging of War: An Introduction to International Humanitarian Law* (Red Cross, 2001); Lubell, 'Challenges in Applying Human Rights Law to Armed Conflicts' 87 *International Review of the Red Cross* (2005) 737; McCoubrey, *International Humanitarian Law: The Regulation of Armed Conflicts* (Dartmouth Publishing Co, 1990); Meron, *Human Rights and Humanitarian Norms as Customary Law* (Clarendon Press, 1989): Meron, 'The Humanization of Humanitarian Law' 94 *AJIL* (2000) 239; Pictet, *Humanitarian Law and the Protection of War Victims* (ICRC, 1982); Robert and Merrills, *Human Rights in the World* (Manchester University Press, 1996) pp. 299–324; Rogers, *Law on the Battlefield* (Manchester University Press, 1996); Shaw, *International Law* (Cambridge University Press, 2008) pp. 1167–1203; Provost, *International Human Rights and Humanitarian Law* (Cambridge University Press, 2002); Steiner, Alston and Goodman (eds), *International Human Rights in Context: Law, Politics, Morals* (Oxford University Press, 2008) pp. 1243–1345; and Wills, *Protecting Civilians: The Obligations of Troops in International Law* (Oxford University Press, 2009).
[2] Meron, 'Humanization', above n.1, at p. 245.
[3] *Prosecutor v. Furundzja*, No. IT-95-17/1-T, Judgment, Para 183 (10 December 1998).

1 INTRODUCTION

There are numerous definitions of international humanitarian law (IHL)[4] though in a study focused on international law human rights, it can broadly and legitimately be visualised as a set of laws aiming to protect human rights during international or non-international armed conflicts.[5] The protection of the rights of the individuals during an armed conflict bears a close relationship to the regime of international protection of human rights. In highlighting this relationship Professors Robertson and Merrills makes the valuable point that 'human rights law is the genus of which humanitarian law is a species. The basic texts relating to human rights, notably the Universal Declaration and the United Nations Covenants, lay down standards of general application to all human beings, by reason of their humanity. Those standards ideally should apply at all times and in all circumstances'.[6] The close nexus between human rights norms and IHL is underlined by their mutual complementarity and considerable convergence. Humanitarian norms have contributed to the development of human rights law in significant respects. The protection of victims of conflict forms a critical element of modern human rights law and the concern is reflected in the jurisprudence of all major human rights organisations. As we have examined, human rights law grew from the ashes of the Second World War. The human rights regime drew inspiration from the development of notions such as crimes against humanity, genocide, and the four Geneva Conventions on IHL. Conversely, as we shall examine in the course of this chapter, many provisions within IHL treaties underline and re-establish fundamental human rights values.

That said, protecting individual and collective rights in times of armed conflict presents the sternest of challenges to the regime of human rights law. It is in this context that a detailed examination of IHL requires a considered analysis within texts devoted to international human rights law. An examination of international humanitarian law is of great contemporary significance for human rights lawyers and activists. Many parts of the world are currently besieged by international or internal armed conflicts and violations in various forms regularly take place. Whilst IHL is a specialised discipline within international law, the escalation of armed and violent conflicts and the continuation of the 'war on terror' have necessitated an examination of the principles of IHL for human rights lawyers.[7]

---

[4] IHL is also described as 'laws of armed conflict' or 'the laws of war'. From an international law perspective, IHL has been defined as 'law [that] seeks to regulate the conduct of hostilities (*jus in bello*) Shaw, above n.1, at p. 1167; 'law which applies once the decision to resort to force has been taken and fighting has started' Greenwood 'The Law of War (International Humanitarian Law)' in Evans (ed.), *International Law* (Oxford University Press, 2006) pp. 783–815 at p. 783; IHL 'embraces principles and rules designed to regulate warfare both by restraining states in the conduct of armed hostilities and by protecting those persons who do not take part, or no longer take part (having fallen into the hands of the enemy), in combat.' Cassese, *International Criminal Law* (Oxford University Press, 2008) at p. 6.

[5] The argument advanced by Robert and Merrills, therefore remains valid when they note that 'humanitarian law is one branch of the law of human rights, and that human rights provide the basis and underlying rationale for humanitarian law' above n.1, at p. 310.

[6] Robertson and Merrills, above n.1, at p. 311.

[7] Rehman and Ghosh, 'International Law, US Foreign Policy and Post-9/11 Islamic Fundamentalism: The Legal Status of the "War on Terror"' 77 *Nordic JIL* (2008) 87; Sassoli, 'The Status of Persons held in Guantanamo Under International Law' 2 *Journal of International Criminal Justice* (2004) 96; Taft, 'The Law of Armed Conflict after 9/11: Some Salient Features' 28 *Yale Journal of International Law* (2003) 319; Fitzpatrick, 'Speaking Law to Power: the War against Terrorism and Human Rights' 14 *EJIL* (2003) 241; Paust, 'War and Enemy Status after 9/11: Attacks on the Laws of War' 28 *Yale Journal of International Law* (2003) 325; McDonald and Sullivan, 'Rational interpretation in Irrational Times: The Third Geneva Convention and the "War on Terror"' 44 *Harvard Int.L.J.* (2003) 301.

2 HISTORIC ANTECEDENTS

Recognition of the rights of victims of armed conflicts has been a historical phenomenon and is affirmed in ancient scriptures as well as in the laws of nations.[8] Although international humanitarian law has an antiquated history and pre-dates the formation of human rights law, the development of humanitarian law has been piecemeal and patchy. Conflicts designed to bring about mass destruction and human rights violations have formed an integral part of human history. It is, therefore, not surprising that the issue of the rights of the victims of armed conflicts have also featured prominently both through religious prescriptions and man-made laws.[9] In historical terms – contrary to the position in contemporary societies – violence and conflicts was a regular feature with peaceful co-existence more often an aberration. During these prolonged periods of conflicts, worst forms of atrocities were inflicted upon an enemy. The winner in the battlefield had the right to take away not only the loser's life but also all his belongings including women, children, slaves and personal property.

(i) Religious ordinances on the laws of war

Incidents of barbarity are documented in classical historical texts as well as in the holy books. While sanctioning wars and conflicts, ancient religious scriptures also contain strong injunctions against violations of human dignity, generating undue suffering and destruction during warfare. Elaborating on some of injunctions ordained by God in the Old Testament, Leslie Green makes the following observations:

> [I]n the Book of Kings, we are told, that when Elisha was asked by the king whether he should slay his prisoners, the prophet replied: Thou shalt not smite those whom thou has taken captive with thy sword and with thy bow? Set bread and water before them, that they may eat and drink and go to their master. And he prepared great provision for them: and when they had eaten and drunk, he sent them away and they went to their master.[10]

In the ancient Hindu scripture, Maharbharata, it is declared that 'a King should never do such an injury to his foe as would rankle the latter's heart'. It goes on to prohibit attacks on a sleeping enemy and in condemning desecration of corpses ordains 'with death our enmity has terminated'.[11] Islamic tradition has, from the outset, endeavoured to develop regulatory norms for the conduct of wars and conflicts.[12] Within the *Sharia* (Islamic law)

---

[8] Cockayne, 'Islam and International Humanitarian Law: From a Clash to a Conversation Between Civilizations' 84 *International Review of the Red Cross* (2002) 597; McCoubrey, *International Humanitarian Law: Modern Developments in the Limitation of Warfare* (Dartmouth Publishing Co, 1998) pp. 12–14; Bennoune, ' "As-Salamu Alaykum?": Humanitarian Law in Islamic Jurisprudence' Joint AALS, American Society of Comparative Law and Law and Society Association, 2004 (Annual Meeting) www.aals.org/am2004/islamiclaw/international.htm <last visited 23 February 2009>; Subedi, 'The Concept in Hinduism of 'Just War' 8 *Journal of Conflict and Security Law* (2003) 339; Ali and Rehman, 'The Concept of Jihad in Islamic International Law' 10 *Journal of Conflict and Security Law* (2005) 321.

[9] Levie, 'History of the Law of War' International Review of the Red Cross (No. 838) pp. 339–350 www.icrc.org/web/eng/siteeng0.nsf/htmlall/57jqhg?opendocument <last visited 30 April 2008>.

[10] Kings, VI, 22–23; cited in Green, above n.1, at p. 20.

[11] Kings, VI, 22–23; cited in Green, above n.1 at p. 21.

[12] An-Naim, who considers *jihad* as an inherently aggressive concept declares that: 'Historically, *jihad* was a positive phenomenon because it humanised the practice of warfare in the Middle Ages. First, *Sharia* prohibited the prevalent practice of using war for material gain or revenge. Second, the Prophet and his companions,

there exist clear rules relating *inter alia* to, notice of commencement of hostilities (unless it is a defensive war), effects of war, methods of warfare, organisation of the army and navy, modes of fighting, time of fighting, preparation, discipline and regulation of the army. The *Jihad* manifested in war is to be conducted under certain rules which, though originating in the seventh and eighth century, are still relevant today. Rules for the conduct of warfare created a category of protected persons. Within *Sharia* a distinction is made between combatants and enemy non-combatants. Those non-combatants who are unable to participate in hostilities are classed as protected persons and cannot be attacked, killed or otherwise molested.[13] Islamic jurists differ on many details concerning protected persons, though there is general agreement that they include children, women,[14] the very old, blind, crippled, disabled (mentally and physically disabled) and sick.[15] In addition to these, 'monks and hermits who retire to a life of solitude in monasteries or cloisters, and other priests who do not associate with other people' are also to be categorised as protected persons.[16] Mahmassani cites an incident where the Caliph Abu Bakr forbade his commander from harming any religious person.[17] These instructions are in line with rules regarding inviolability of places of worship stated in the *Quran* in the following terms:

> And had it not been for God's repelling some men by means of others, cloisters, churches, oratories and mosques, wherein God's Name is oft mentioned, would have been demolished.[18]

In addition to rules regarding protected persons during armed conflict, rules exist in the Islamic tradition aimed at humane conduct of warfare. Treachery and mutilation are prohibited within Islamic law, except in case of reprisals.[19] A saying of the Prophet Muhammad is cited: 'Do not steal from the spoils, do not commit treachery, and do not mutilate'.[20] Another *Hadith* declares that 'if anyone of you fights, let him avert the face'. It is also forbidden to burn enemy warriors alive.[21] On the basis of the various sources regarding the conduct of armed conflict, Kasani has laid down a general rule regarding protected persons in Islam. He is of the opinion that any person capable of fighting may be killed while a person unable to fight must not be killed unless he physically participates in the fighting.[22] Within Islamic law, wanton destruction of property is prohibited. Similarly, killing animals during warfare is only permitted when it is necessitated for reasons of survival or is deemed necessary in order to obtain essential military objectives, e.g. killing the horse of an enemy

---

acting in accordance with the *Qur'an* and *Sunna*, laid down very specific and strict rules for honorable combat'. An-Naim, 'Islamic Law, International Relations, and Human Rights: Challenge and Response' 20 *Cornell International Law Journal* (1987) 317 at p. 326.

[13] Mahmassani, 'The Principles of International Law in the Light of Islamic Doctrine' 117(1) *Recueil des Cours de l'Académie de Droit International* (1966) at p. 301.

[14] A woman leader, however, forfeits this right.

[15] Mahmassani, above n.13, at pp. 302–303 who states that Shafei and Ibn Hazm limited the exemption of protected persons to women and children.

[16] Ibid. at p. 301.

[17] Shaibani I, pp. 39–55 cited by Mahmassani, ibid.

[18] The *Quran*, Chapter XXII: Verse 40.

[19] Hidayah, II, at 117, cited by Mahmassani, above n.13, at p. 303.

[20] Ayni, XIII at 115 cited by Mahmassani, ibid.

[21] Ibid. citing Mughni, X at p. 502; Hidayah, II, at p. 117, and Nawawi, Xii at p. 43.

[22] Kasani, VII, at p. 101 cited by Mahmassani, ibid. at p. 304.

in battle. An excellent exposition on the subject was provided by the first Caliph, Abu Bakr in a celebrated address during the first Syrian expedition:

> Stop, O people, that I may give you ten rules to keep by heart! Do not commit treachery, nor depart from the right path. You must not mutilate, neither kill a child or aged man or woman. Do not destroy a palm-tree, nor burn it with fire and do not cut any fruitful tree. You must not slay any of the flock or the herds or the camels, save for your subsistence. You are likely to pass by people who have devoted their lives to monastic services; leave them to that to which they have devoted their lives. You are likely, likewise, to find people who will present to you meals of many kinds. You may eat; but do not forget to mention the name of Allah.[23]

(ii) Early efforts to develop humanitarian laws

Notwithstanding the induction of humanitarianism through religious scriptures as well as concerns for humanity in general, the conduct of warfare by and large remained unregulated. It was, as indicated by Professor Meron, possibly the seriousness of the human calamities which drove the advancement of humanitarian law in that 'the more offensive or painful the suffering, the greater the pressure for accommodating humanitarian restraints'.[24] The first recognisable effort in establishing a code of conduct during war was introduced by Professor Francis Lieber.[25] After revisions introduced by a board of officers, Professor Lieber's code was promulgated as General Orders No. 100 of the Union Army in 1863.[26] The code advanced laws regulating the conduct of war by government forces and provided a framework for punishments of these laws either by government troops or the opposition during the American Civil War.[27]

Section II of the Lieber Code contained Articles 31–47 and accorded 'Protection of persons and especially of women, of religion, the arts and sciences. Punishment of crimes against the inhabitants of hostile countries.' Furthermore, the code also contained provisions requiring the humane treatment of prisoners of war.[28] Excessive expectations with the Code are however misplaced since this was a national initiative and was not adopted by the international community of States.

The most lasting and influential modern effort in developing IHL was conducted by the Swiss philanthropist Henri Dunant who was a witness to the appalling suffering of 40,000 soldiers at the Battle of Solferino in 1859. Dunant rallied villagers and volunteers to provide whatever support could be provided insisting on impartiality in the conflict. Unfortunately, in the absence of mechanisms to retrieve the wounded at the battlefield, thousands who could have been saved perished because of injury or lack of care and treatment. The product of Dunant's experiences, a book entitled *A Memory of Solferino* (1862)

---

[23] Tabari, *Tarikh*, I, 1850 cited in Khadduri, *The Islamic Law of Nations: Shaybanis Siyar* (John Hopkins University Press, 1966) at p. 102.

[24] Meron, 'Humanization', above n.1, at p. 243.

[25] Reprinted in Schindler and Toman (eds), *The Laws of Armed Conflicts: A collection of conventions, resolutions and other documents* (Brill, 1988).

[26] Ibid.

[27] McCormack, 'From Sun Tzu to the Sixth Committee: The Evolution of an International Criminal Law Regime' in McCormack and Simpson (eds), *The Law of War Crimes: National and International Approaches* (Kluwer Law International, 1997) p. 31 at p. 42.

[28] Lieber Code, Section III, Articles 49–80.

called for the establishment of a civilian volunteer relief corps to take care of the wounded in battlefield without any discrimination as to race, nationality or religion.[29] In 1863 Dunant formed the 'Committee of Five', which was an investigatory commission of the Swiss Society for Public Welfare. This quickly became known as the International Committee of the Red Cross (ICRC). A diplomatic conference was held in Geneva in 1864 where the delegates representing 16 European States adopted the Convention for the Amelioration of the Condition of the Wounded in Armies in the Field. This Convention – the first Geneva Convention[30] – provided the first modern manifestation of international humanitarian law.[31] The Convention contained within it principles of universality and tolerance in relation to race and nationality as well as religion.[32] A red cross on a white field was recognised as the mark for military medical personnel. On their part, Islamic States adopted an emblem of a red crescent with a white background. From henceforth onwards installations as well as medical staff were to be regarded as neutral.[33]

The Red Cross was accorded international recognition in 1919 by Article 25 of the Covenant of the League of Nations.[34] This was followed by providing a constitutional structure for the ICRC at the 18th international conference of the organisation (at the Hague in 1928) which approved statutes establishing the ICRC in Geneva; the League of Red Cross Societies, the League of Red Cross in Muslim Countries and the Red Lion in Iran.[35]

A distinct strand of humanitarian law relates to the use of weapons deployed in warfare. The Hague Peace Conference of 1899, Declaration (IV, 2) concerning asphyxiating gases contained an undertaking 'to abstain from the use of projectiles the sole object of which is the diffusion of asphyxiating or deleterious gases'.[36] Additionally, the Hague Convention of 1907 contained the prohibition on the use of poison or poisonous weapons in land warfare.[37] The Geneva Protocol 1925 prohibited use in war of asphyxiating, poisonous or other gases and also extended the prohibition to the use of bacteriological methods of warfare.[38]

Amidst a human history that bears testimony to wars as tragic episodes of death, destruction and suffering, one of the worst tragedies confronting humanity was the Second World War – it is estimated that the Second World War resulted in 50 million deaths, with over 24 million civilians and 26 million combatants perishing in the process.[39] In reliving those horrific memories, one of the initial concerns for modern IHL related to dealing with sickness or injury during warfare or conflict. This disquiet was subsequently extended to

---

[29] See Dunant, *A Memory of Solferino* (Red Cross, 1986).

[30] This was subsequently revised and redrafted in 1906, 1929 and 1949.

[31] Convention for the Amelioration of the Condition of the Wounded in Armies in the Field, (ser. 1) 607, 129 Consol. T.S. 361, entered into force 22 June 1865. Geneva, 22 August 1864.

[32] Ibid. Article 7.

[33] Office of the High Commissioner for Human Rights, *International Humanitarian Law and Human Rights* (Fact Sheet No: 13) www.unhchr.ch/html/menu6/2/fs13.htm <last visited 23 February 2009>.

[34] According to the provisions of Article 25, 'The Members of the League agree to encourage and promote the establishment and co-operation of duly authorised voluntary national Red Cross organisations having as purposes the improvement of health, the prevention of disease and the mitigation of suffering throughout the world'.

[35] Rosenne, 'The Red Cross, Red Crescent, Red Lion and Sun and the Red Shield of David' 5 *Israel Yearbook of Human Rights* (1975) 9.

[36] Hague IV, Declaration II – Concerning the Prohibition of the Use of Projectiles Diffusing Asphyxiating Gases, 29 July 1899, 26 Martens Nouveau Recueil (ser. 2) 998, 187 Consol. T.S. 453, entered into force 4 September 1900.

[37] Article 23 Hague Convention IV – Laws and Customs of War on Land: 18 October 1907, 36 Stat. 2277, 1 Bevans 631, 205 Consol. T.S. 277, 3 Martens Nouveau Recueil (ser. 3) 461, entered into force 26 January 1910.

[38] Protocol for the Prohibition of the Use in War of Asphyxiating, Poisonous or Other Gases and of Bacteriological Methods of Warfare Geneva, 94 L.N.T.S. 65, entered into force 8 February 1928.

[39] Robertson and Merrills, above n.1, at p. 301.

the prisoners of war who were captured but were no longer able to fight in the conflict. Concerns were also extended to civilians, in particular children, women and the aged, who were not combatants but were affected by methods of warfare. These substantial concerns provided the impetus for the adoption of the 1949 Geneva Conventions and subsequently produced a number of additional protocols to these treaties. Civilians have also been accorded protection, in particular by the Fourth Geneva Convention.

3 THE CONTENT OF INTERNATIONAL HUMANITARIAN LAW

Modern humanitarian law is a product of a series of international treaties, which have historically been bifurcated as the 'Hague Law' and 'Geneva Law'. The 'Hague Law' is represented by the Hague Conventions of 1899 and 1907. The 'Hague Law' has primarily dealt with the permissible means and methods of war, whereas the 'Geneva Law' has the protection of the victims of conflict as its focus. The 'Geneva Law' is represented through the four Geneva Conventions of 1949 (also known as the Red Cross Conventions) and the three additional protocols to the 1949 Conventions. The Geneva Conventions, have a unique and unquestionably authoritative standing within international law and international humanitarian law. In 2007, they were the first treaties of modern to times to have attained ratification by every State of the world.[40] Additionally, many of the provisions within the Geneva Conventions are considered binding in customary international law. This binding quality arguably also applies to many provisions contained in Protocols I and II additional to the Geneva Convention, although as we shall examine, disagreements persist over the binding effect of these instruments within general international law.[41]

In summary, the four Geneva Conventions deal with the following:

Geneva Convention (I) for the Amelioration of the Condition of the Wounded and Sick in Armed Forces in the Field, Geneva, 12 August 1949.[42]

Geneva Convention (II) for the Amelioration of the Condition of Wounded, Sick and Shipwrecked Members of Armed Forces at Sea, Geneva, 12 August 1949.[43]

Geneva Convention (III) Relative to the Treatment of Prisoners of War, Geneva, 12 August 1949.[44]

Geneva Convention (IV) Relative to the Protection of Civilian Persons in Time of War, Geneva, 12 August 1949.[45]

---

[40] Steiner, Alston and Goodman, above n.1, at p. 395.
[41] Kalshoven and Zegveld, above n.1, at p. 83.
[42] Geneva Convention (I) for the Amelioration of the Condition of the Wounded and Sick in Armed Forces in the Field, Geneva, 12 August 1949, 75 U.N.T.S. 31, entered into force 21 October 1950.
[43] Geneva Convention (II) for the Amelioration of the Condition of Wounded, Sick and Shipwrecked Members of Armed Forces at Sea, Geneva, 12 August 1949, 75 U.N.T.S. 85, entered into force 21 October 1950.
[44] Geneva Convention (III) Relative to the Treatment of Prisoners of War Geneva, 12 August 1949, 75 U.N.T.S. 135, entered into force 21 October 1950.
[45] Geneva Convention (IV) Relative to the Protection of Civilian Persons in Time of War, Geneva, 12 August 1949, 75 U.N.T.S. 287, entered into force 21 October 1950.

After the adoption of the 1949 Conventions, new legal and political developments raised humanitarian concerns requiring additional agreements. Since 1949, three Protocols additional to the Geneva Conventions have been introduced. These are:

> Protocol I (1977) Protocol Additional to the Geneva Conventions of 12 August 1949, and relating to the Protection of Victims of International Armed Conflicts.[46]
>
> Protocol II (1977): Protocol Additional to the Geneva Conventions of 12 August 1949, and relating to the Protection of Victims of Non-International Armed Conflicts.[47]
>
> Protocol III (2005): Protocol Additional to the Geneva Conventions of 12 August 1949, and relating to the Adoption of an Additional Distinctive Emblem.[48]

One of the early attempts to include human rights in IHL comes from the Martens Clause, which states that in unforeseen circumstances 'the inhabitants and the belligerents remain under the protection and the rules of the principles of the laws of nations, as they result from the usages established among civilised peoples, from the laws of humanity, and the dictates of the public conscience'.[49] The Martens Clause arose from disagreement between powerful States and smaller States over whether to treat resistance fighters as *franc-tireurs* (those entitled to protection) or combatants. The significance of Martens Clause lies in the recognition that although treaty law may not cover all aspects of humanitarian law, there nevertheless remains certain baseline applicable standards of humanity. As Professor Meron notes, 'the clause argues for interpreting international humanitarian law, in case of doubt, consistently with the principles of humanity and dictates of public conscience'.[50] This theme has been continued, with Protocol I to the Geneva Conventions arising from a movement which aimed to converge human rights law with IHL. In tracing back a relationship with human rights law, Article 1(4) Protocol I defines the field of application of the Protocol which would incorporate an armed conflict in which peoples are fighting racist, colonial or alien domination in the exercise of their right to self-determination.

As shall be examined shortly, in providing protection to victims of international armed conflicts, Protocol I contains provisions according protection to the civilian population, with Chapter II dealing specifically with women and children. Protocol I articulates the norms concerning the role of protecting powers designated by each party to a conflict, to supervise the application of the Conventions and Protocols. The Protocol contains provisions designed to improve the condition of the wounded, sick and shipwrecked, and provides for the collection and provision of information concerning the missing and dead.

[46] Protocol I (1977) Protocol Additional to the Geneva Conventions of 12 August 1949, and relating to the Protection of Victims of International Armed Conflicts, 1125 U.N.T.S. 3, entered into force 7 December 1978. As of 1 August 2009, there are 168 States parties to the Protocol (five States are signatories).

[47] Protocol II (1977): Protocol Additional to the Geneva Conventions of 12 August 1949, and relating to the Protection of Victims of Non-International Armed Conflicts, 1125 U.N.T.S. 609, entered into force 7 December 1978. As of 1 August 2009, there are 164 States Parties to the Protocol (four States are signatories).

[48] Protocol III (1990): Protocol Additional to the Geneva Conventions of 12 August 1949, and relating to the Adoption of an Additional Distinctive Emblem, 1125 U.N.T.S. 3, entered into force 8 December 2005. As of 1 August 2009, there are 46 States Parties to the Protocol (34 States are signatories).

[49] Laws and Customs of War on Land (Hague IV) 1907, see also Convention with respect to the laws of war on land (Hague II) 1899.

[50] Meron, 'The Martens Clause, Principles of Humanity and Dictates of Public Conscience' 94 *AJIL* (2000) 78, at p. 87. Also see Pustogarov, 'The Martens Clause in International Law' 1 *Journal of History of International Law* (1999) 125.

21

Protocol I prohibits the deployment of methods and means of warfare that may cause superfluous injury, unnecessary suffering and widespread, long-term and severe damage to the environment.[51] In establishing such a prohibition, Protocol I has effectively brought an end to the two separate streams of humanitarian law the 'Law of Geneva' and the 'Law of The Hague'.

The focus of Protocol II is upon the victims of internal armed conflicts. It deals with armed conflicts between governmental forces and dissidents or other organised groups which control part of its territory. However, Protocol II does not deal with internal disturbances and tensions in the form of riots, or other isolated and sporadic acts of violence.[52] Protocol II provides for rules relating to the victims of non-international armed conflicts and in so doing complements the basic principles laid down in Common Article 3.

Both Protocols, furthermore, call for the humane treatment of all persons who do not, or no longer, take part in hostilities. These provisions contain an absolute prohibition of murder, torture, mutilation and corporal punishment.[53] There are provisions for the care of the sick, wounded and shipwrecked,[54] and for the protection of civilians against acts or threats of violence,[55] starvation as a method of combat[56] and forced movement.[57] Hostile acts against historic monuments, works of art or places of worship – or their use in support of military aims – are prohibited.[58]

Although the four Geneva Conventions and the Protocols to those Conventions have established international standards for humanitarian law, several other instruments have also played a notable role. These include the Protocol for the Prohibition of the Use in War of Asphyxiating, Poisonous or Other Gases and of Bacteriological Methods of Warfare (1925);[59] UNESCO Convention for the Protection of Cultural Property in the Event of Armed Conflict (1954);[60] and the Geneva Convention on Prohibitions or Restrictions on the Use of Certain Conventional Weapons Which May Be Deemed to Be Excessively Injurious or to Have Indiscriminate Effects (1981).[61]

(i) Application of international humanitarian law

A complicated debate within international law has concerned how to establish when an armed conflict commences, which would trigger the laws of war or the laws of armed conflict. Historically, as well as in contemporary terms, it has been a difficult task to determine the commencement of an armed conflict or a war. States, generally, do not engage in conflict with a prior announcement of the commencement of hostilities and, therefore, the failure to declare war could not be allowed to prevent the application of IHL. In order to address this issue, Common Article 2 of the Geneva Conventions (1949) provides that a

---

[51] Ibid. Articles 35–42.
[52] Article 1(2), Protocol II.
[53] Article 75(2), Protocol I and Article 4(2) Protocol II.
[54] Part II, Protocol I.
[55] Article 51, Protocol I.
[56] Article 14, Protocol II.
[57] Article 17, Protocol II.
[58] Article 16, Protocol II.
[59] Protocol for the Prohibition of the Use of Asphyxiating, Poisonous or Other Gases, and of Bacteriological Methods of Warfare. Geneva, 17 June 1925.
[60] UNESCO Convention for the Protection of Cultural Property in the Event of Armed Conflict, 249 U.N.T.S. 240, entered into force 7 August 1956.
[61] Convention on Prohibitions or Restrictions on the Use of Certain Conventional Weapons Which May be Deemed to be Excessively Injurious or to Have Indiscriminate Effects, 1342 U.N.T.S. 137, 19 I.L.M. 1524.

declaration of legal war is not necessary and the provisions of the Geneva Conventions shall apply to 'all cases of declared war or of any other armed conflict which may arise between two or more of the High Contracting Parties, even if the state of war is not recognized by one of them'.[62] These provisions are designed to prevent States from refusing to apply IHL during an armed conflict.[63] The low threshold in the applicability of IHL is established through Articles 5 of Geneva Convention I, 4 of Geneva Convention II, 5 of Geneva Convention III and 6 of Geneva Convention IV of the 1949 Geneva Conventions (1949), which apply from the very start of the conflict or from the date of capture of the concerned individuals or until the ending of the operation or the final repatriation of the protected persons. Furthermore, breaches of international law in the initiation of war or armed conflict cannot be justified as a pretext for contravening the IHL principles.[64]

When the Geneva Conventions were adopted the general assumption was that these would apply between States engaged in conflict. In the intervening years, several developments have raised complications in relation to the application of the law of armed conflict to non-State entities, such as international organisations, national liberation movements (NLMs) or terrorist groups. One fundamental question relates to the application of international humanitarian law to the United Nations. The extent to which UN military operations or forces are bound by the laws of war is not fully established.[65]

While the UN is not a party to the Geneva Conventions, these instruments bind the UN as much as they bind any other State or entity. A related phenomenon is the application of IHL to conflicts involving non-governmental organisations such as NLMs or other entities which in varying degrees could be described as insurgents, revolutionaries or terrorists.[66] During the de-colonisation period, a number of countries from the developing world took the view that the laws of war should apply to any confrontation between National Liberation Movements and colonial regimes.[67] Accordingly, Article 1(4) of the Additional Protocol I, 1977 is applicable to 'armed conflicts in which peoples are fighting against colonial domination and alien occupation against racist regimes in the exercise of their right of self-determination'.[68] In such situations the NLMs can make a declaration accepting

---

[62] Common Article 2 Geneva Conventions 1949.

[63] Professor Leslie Green makes a number of important observations and notes: 'Since 1945 the number of hostile relationships not amounting to "war" has greatly increased and it was not until 1989 that Iran formally declared war against Iraq with which it had been engaged in hostilities since 1981. Other conflicts such as the Korean operations under the auspices of the United Nations, have been described as "police actions", or have been treated as if they were civil wars in which an outside party might have become involved as in the case of Vietnam, or for the restoration of democracy as with the United States invasion of Grenada in 1983 or Panama in 1989. Even the conflict between the United Kingdom and Argentina resulting from the invasion of the Falkland's in 1982 was not regarded as "war" . . . [but] it is becoming increasingly clear that the terms war and armed conflict are being used as if they were synonyms.' Green, above n.1, at pp. 71–72.

[64] See Protocol I, Preamble. Also see Common Article 1 of the Geneva Conventions which explicitly binds States parties 'in all circumstances'. Also see Article 2 which states that '[a]lthough one of the Powers in conflict may not be a party to the present Convention the Powers thereto shall remain bound by it in their mutual relations', thereby prohibiting States parties from contravening IHL principles in the instance that the other State or party to the conflict is not bound.

[65] One fundamental question relates to the application of international humanitarian law to the United Nations military operations.

[66] For a critical examination on the NLMs and IHL see Pomerance, *Self-Determination in Law and Practice: the New Doctrine in the United Nations* (Brill, 1982) pp. 48–62.

[67] See Baxter, 'Humanitarian Law or Humanitarian Politics? The 1974 Diplomatic Conference on Humanitarian Law' 16 *Harvard Int.L.J.* (1975) 1.

[68] Article 1(4): Protocol I (1977) Protocol Additional to the Geneva Conventions of 12 August 1949, and relating to the Protection of Victims of International Armed Conflicts.

the obligations placed by the Protocol and the Geneva Convention to make the protection available to the parties in the conflict.[69]

The applicability of IHL to a conflict between States and terrorist organisations, as exemplified in the United States' and United Kingdom's confrontation with Al-Qaeda and the Taliban in Afghanistan raises complex issues. In its conflict with Al-Qaeda in Afghanistan, the United States claims that the laws of international armed conflict apply.[70] Notwithstanding the applicability of Geneva Convention III (POW), the United States has taken the position that the [detainees are not entitled to prisoner of war (POW) status.[71] Such a stance is in contravention to the provision of POW Convention Article 4(1) according to which POW are members of armed forces of a party to the conflict who have fallen in enemy hands.[72] The denial of POW status has been based on the US assertion that the Taliban forces in Afghanistan (as well as the captured members of Al-Qaeda) have failed to have fixed distinctive uniforms and have not conducted their operations in accordance with the laws and customs of war.[73] Contrary to the US assertions, these possible disqualifying features apply to militias and volunteer corps and not to regular armed forces.[74]

---

[69] Additional Protocol I, Article 96(3).

[70] Farer, *Confronting Global Terrorism and American Neo-Conservatism* (Oxford University Press, 2008) pp. 95–96.

[71] The actual position has been more confusing than this. In February 2002, the President of the United States, George W. Bush took the position that the third Geneva Convention applied to the Taliban but not to Al-Qaeda. However, the President's spokesman expressed the view that the Taliban fighters were not entitled to the Prisoner of War Status. The convoluted US position therefore appeared to be that while the third Geneva Convention applied to Taliban forces, the Taliban are not entitled to any of the protection accorded by the Convention. See Mundis, 'Agora: Military Commissions – The Use of Military Commissions to Prosecute Individuals Accused of Terrorist Acts' 96 *AJIL* (2002) 320 at, p. 325; Aldrich, 'The Taliban, Al-Qaeda and the Determination of Illegal Combatants' 96 *AJIL* (2002) 891 at p. 894; Rona, 'Interesting Times for International Humanitarian Law: Challenges from the War on Terror' 27 *Fletcher F. World Aff.* (2003) 55; Vierucci, 'Is the Geneva Convention on Prisoners of War Obsolete?: the Views of the Counsel to the US President on the Application of International to the Afghan Conflict' 2 *J Int.Crim. Just* (2004) 866 at p. 869. *Cf.* Farer, above n.70, p. 85; Steiner, Alston and Goodman note: The US government contended that all Taliban and Al Qaeda members were "unlawful combatants" who, therefore, failed to qualify as prisoners of war (POW) under the Third Geneva Convention. What was at stake? According detainees, POW status would require the government to guarantee specific trial rights not provided by the US military commissions. POW status would also provide combatant immunity for membership in an enemy armed force (though no immunity applied to the commission of acts of terrorism, perfidy or other war crimes). POW status would also oblige the United States to provide for certain conditions of detention, though these conditions are not clearly far superior to conditions of detention required under the Civilians (Fourth Geneva Conventions). Steiner, Alston and Goodman, above n.1, at p. 404. In *Hamdan* v. *Rumsfeld*, the US Supreme Court invalidated the military commissions as set up by the President on the basis that they were not properly authorised by the Congress. According to the Court, the commissions violated a Congressional statute requiring the President to comply with International Humanitarian Law. See *Hamdan* v. *Rumsfeld*, 126 S. Ct 2749 (2006). The US Congress subsequently authorised such commissions through the United States Military Commission Act (MCA) of 2006, Pub. L. No. 109–366, 120 Stat. 2600 (17 October 2006), enacting Chapter 47A of title 10 of the United States Code (as well as amending section 2241 of title 28).

[72] Article 4 (A).

[73] Steiner, Alston and Goodman make the point that: 'The US Government declared that the Geneva Conventions applied to the international armed conflict with Afghanistan. The United States, however, contended that the Taliban and Al Qaeda failed to satisfy the criteria of Article 4(a)(2); that the criteria of Article 4(a)(2) apply to 4(a)(1) groups that Al Qaeda as a non-state actor (and especially as a terrorist group) could not receive the protections of the Geneva Conventions in any case; and that no doubt about status existed and hence there was not need for a tribunal under Article 5 of the POW convention'. Steiner, Alston and Goodman, above n.1 at p. 405.

[74] Vierucci, takes the view that: '[p]ursuant to the letter of Article 4(A)(1) GCIII, and in line both with judicial decisions and the vast majority of the legal literature, members of the armed forces are not explicitly required to meet the four conditions (having a responsible command, bearing a distinctive sign, carrying arms openly and abiding by the laws and customs of war) which are set forth in Article 4(A)(2) and are required for organized armed groups. Members of the armed forces are *supposed* to meet those conditions, and hence, are *presumed* to enjoy POW status if captured.' See Vierucci, above n.71, at p. 868. (Italics provided, footnotes omitted.)

Even if these disqualifying features were applicable to regular Taliban forces, any doubts as to the status of an individual captured during an armed conflict is to be resolved through the convening of a 'competent tribunal',[75] and not to be decided unilaterally. The provision of POW status remains critical for the captured detainees. They are entitled to a series of rights including exemption for lawful acts of war, humane treatment and the right to have a fair trial.[76] Significantly, the United States is not party to Protocol I, which states under Article 45(1) that those who have taken part in the hostilities shall be presumed to be POWs. Furthermore, under Article 45(2):

> [i]f a person who has fallen into the power of an adverse Party is not held as a prisoner of war and is to be tried by that Party for an offence arising out of the hostilities, he shall have the right to assert his entitlement to prisoner-of-war status before a judicial tribunal and to have that question adjudicated.

Even if the individual in question is not entitled to POW status under Article 45(3), they are still entitled to protection under Article 75 of the Protocol. Article 75 contains fundamental guarantees, including the right to a fair trial, rights which, it is argued, are also part of customary international law, and are therefore applicable and binding upon the United States.[77]

A further difficulty in relation to the applicability of IHL concerns the identification and precise nature of the armed conflict: determination of a conflict as 'internal' or 'international armed conflict', as shall be examined, has serious repercussions in terms of applicability of IHL norms.[78] In such circumstances of factual analysis, it is frequently States (or non-State actors such as international organisations or non-governmental organisations) whose views would carry weight.[79]

(ii) Entitlement to take part in the conflict

A fundamental question of IHL is the distinction drawn between those regarded as lawful combatants and others as 'unlawful'. The Hague Regulations on Land Warfare Articles 1 and 2 and Article 4 of Geneva Convention POW 1949 establish different standards for lawful combatants and 'unlawful' combatants. Lawful combatants comprise of members of armed forces of a belligerent party, including those whose specific assignment does not include taking part in active hostilities. As stated by the 1949 Conventional provisions, those engaged in hostilities can only be regarded as lawful combatants provided they are members of an organised force or that force belongs to members of other militias and member of volunteer corps, including those of organised resistance movements.[80] In the

---

[75] Geneva Convention III, Article 5.

[76] Ibid.

[77] Rules 87–105 Henckaerts, *Study on customary international humanitarian law*, www.icrc.org/web/eng/siteeng0.nsf/htmlall/customary-law-rules-291008/$FILE/customary-law-rules.pdf <last visited 23 February 2009>.

[78] See Greenwood, 'International Humanitarian Law and the Tadic Case' 7 *EJIL* (1996) 265; Meron, 'Classification of Armed Conflict in the Former Yugoslavia: Nicaragua's Fallout' 92 *AJIL* (1998) 236.

[79] The UN General Assembly has adopted the practice of placing reliance on the recognition of NLMs by regional organisations such as the AU (formerly OAU) or the League of Arab of States for them to be granted an observer Status (see e.g. GA Res. 35/167 (15 December 1980); 37/104 (16 December 1982); 45/37 (28 November 1990); 47/29 (25 November 1992).

[80] Article 4 POW, Geneva Convention III relative to the Treatment of Prisoners of War (1949).

latter instance the force has to be under the command of a person responsible for his subordinates and the members of the force wear a fixed, distinctive sign, recognisable at a distance. Members of the force are also required to carry arms openly and conduct operations fully in accordance with the laws and customs of war.

Article 4 of Geneva Convention III specifies that members of organised resistance groups in occupied territories may qualify as lawful combatants. In practice this provision is almost entirely symbolic as they are, nevertheless, required to comply with the conditions that apply to armed forces.[81] These provisions are repeated in Article 13 of the Geneva Convention I and Geneva Convention II dealing with the sick and shipwrecked. From a practical point of view, most unlawful combatants fall outside the condition as set out by the Hague Regulations or the Geneva Conventions. However, the situation has been changed radically by Protocol I which attempts to assimilate regular and irregular forces. Article 44(2)–(4), which lays down basic requirements for lawful and unlawful combatants, provides:

> Article 44(2): While all combatants are obliged to comply with the rules of international law applicable in armed conflict, violations of these rules shall not deprive a combatant of his right to be a combatant or, if he falls into the power of an adverse Party, of his right to be a prisoner of war, except as provided in paragraphs 3 and 4.
>
> Article 44(3): In order to promote the protection of the civilian population from the effects of hostilities, combatants are obliged to distinguish themselves from the civilian population while they are engaged in an attack or in a military operation preparatory to an attack. Recognizing, however, that there are situations in armed conflicts where, owing to the nature of the hostilities an armed combatant cannot so distinguish himself, he shall retain his status as a combatant, provided that, in such situations, he carries his arms openly:
>
> (a) During each military engagement, and
>
> (b) During such time as he is visible to the adversary while he is engaged in a military deployment preceding the launching of an attack in which he is to participate.
>
> Acts which comply with the requirements of this paragraph shall not be considered as perfidious within the meaning of Article 37, paragraph 1(c).

Article 44(4) provides that:

> [A] combatant who falls into the power of an adverse Party while failing to meet the requirements set forth in the second sentence of paragraph 3 shall forfeit his right to be a prisoner of war, but he shall, nevertheless, be given protections equivalent in all respects to those accorded to prisoners of war by the Third Convention and by this Protocol. This protection includes protections equivalent to those accorded to prisoners of war by the Third Convention in the case where such a person is tried and punished for any offences he has committed.

Combatants failing to follow the provisions of Article 44(2)(3) exhibit the war crime of perfidy, although they remain entitled to POW status until the time of their conviction. The insertion of Article 44(4) has proved highly controversial with a number of Western States

---

[81] Geneva Convention III, Article 4(2).

led by the United States refusing to ratify the Protocol. Professor Dinstein regards these provisions as 'unfortunate' claiming that Protocol I has done away with the technical legal distinction between lawful and unlawful combatants.[82] Conversely, it has been argued that the rules contained in Article 44(3) have brought about a divergence in relation to the treatment of unlawful combatants in that those States which have refused to ratify Protocol I are only obliged to follow the Hague Rules and the Geneva Conventions.[83]

Lawful combatants are under an obligation to take part in hostilities and if captured the Geneva Conventions accord them with the status of POWs. Lawful combatants can withdraw from taking part in hostilities by becoming *hors de combat* either through choice (e.g. surrender) or though force of circumstances (e.g. being sick, wounded or shipwrecked, etc.). As noted above, once *hors de combat*, lawful combatants are to be detained as POWs for the duration of hostilities and are not to be persecuted solely for having taken part in hostilities. Civilians, unlike lawful combatants, must not take part in armed conflict and, if they do so, they receive the designation of unlawful combatants. Similarly, civilians cannot claim the title of POWs and can be punished for their belligerent actions. That said, notwithstanding the unlawfulness or illegality of their actions, unlawful combatants are provided minimal rights of 'being treated with humanity and in case of trial . . . are not to be deprived of the rights of fair and regular trial'.[84] Unlawful combatants are also accorded the guarantees as provided in Common Article 3 of Geneva Conventions and Article 75 Protocol I. Lawful combatants forfeit their status if they engage in conflict disguising themselves as civilians or they perform their military activities disguised as civilians.[85] However, as stated above in Article 44(3), there are exceptions to the general rule of distinction, as long as combatants bear arms openly.

(iii) Human rights and the amelioration of the condition of the sick and wounded at the field or at sea (GC1 and GC2)

We have already considered several 'common articles' which are applicable to the four Geneva Convention of 1949. In its application towards members of the armed personnel in the army in the field or at sea, the First and Second Geneva Conventions provide additional protection. Article 12 of the two conventions notes that the wounded or sick combatants:

> shall be treated humanely and cared for by the Parties to the conflict without any adverse distinction founded on sex, race, nationality, religion, political opinions, or any other similar criteria. Any attempts upon their lives, or violence to their persons, shall be strictly prohibited; in particular, they shall not be murdered or exterminated, subjected to torture or to biological experiments; they shall not willfully be left without medical assistance and care, nor shall conditions exposing them to contagion or infection be created . . . Only urgent medical reasons will authorize priority in the order of treatment to be administered . . . Women shall be treated with all consideration due to their sex.[86]

---

[82] Dinstein, above n.1, at p. 45.
[83] Greenwood, above n.4, at p. 790.
[84] Convention (IV) Relative to the Protection of Civilian Persons in Time of War, Article 5.
[85] See *Mohamed Ali* v. *Public Prosecutor* [1969] AC 430, 449 (where the Privy Council in confirming the death sentence of the applicant noted the fact that he had planted explosives whilst disguised in civilian clothing and thereby could not be regarded as POW).
[86] Article 12.

Article 14 of the First Geneva Convention and Article 16 of the Second Geneva Convention provides that those belligerents who fall into enemy hands shall be regarded as POWs and the provisions applicable to POWs shall apply to them.[87] Upon capture of the wounded, sick or dead combatants, the State parties are under an obligation to record all particulars which would be useful in identification.[88] These records includes designation of power, army regimental, personal or serial number, first name and surname, any particulars shown on an identity card, date and place of capture or death, and particulars concerning wounds, illness or cause of death. Chapter III of both these Conventions aims to provide protection to military hospitals and medical establishments with the underlying principle that under no circumstances could these be attacked or captured. Chapter IV of both Conventions deals with personnel. It provides for the protection of religious, medical and hospital personnel declaring that they must be respected and protected while serving.[89] If these personnel fall into enemy hands they will be treated as POWs.[90] Chapter VII of Geneva Convention I and Chapter VI of Geneva Convention II deal with the subject of distinctive emblems. The emblem of the Red Cross is to be displayed on the flags, armlets and on all equipment employed in the medical service.[91]

(iv) Rights of prisoners of war (POWs)

A significant contribution of IHL is the protection of the human rights of combatants who have been captured by the enemy during armed conflict. As already noted, according to the established principles of IHL these combatants are to be treated as POWs, with an entire catalogue of rights dedicated towards their protection. These rights are principally contained in Geneva Convention III (1949) and have been expanded upon in the Additional Protocols to the Geneva Conventions.

Common Article 3 details those provisions of the Convention which must be followed by all individuals within a signatory State during an armed conflict which is not of an international character (regardless of citizenship or lack thereof). According to these provisions non-combatants, those combatants who have laid down their arms, and combatants who are *hors de combat* (out of the fight) due to wounds, detention or any other cause are in all circumstances to be treated humanely. This humane treatment includes, but is not confined to, prohibition of outrages upon personal dignity, in particular humiliating and degrading treatment.[92] The passing of sentences have to be 'pronounced by a regularly constituted court, affording all the judicial guarantees which are recognized as indispensable by civilized peoples'.[93] Article 3's protection exists even where a person is not classified as a POW. Article 3 also states that parties to the internal conflict should endeavour to bring into force, by means of special agreements, all or part of the other provisions of Geneva

---

[87] Article 14 Geneva Convention I (1949) and Article 16 of the Geneva Convention II (1949).
[88] Article 16 Geneva Convention I; Article 19 Geneva Convention II.
[89] Article 24 Geneva Convention I; Article 36 Geneva Convention II.
[90] Article 29 Geneva Convention I.
[91] Article 39 Geneva Convention I and Article 41 of Geneva Conventions II.
[92] Common Article 3(1)(c) Geneva Conventions I–IV; see also Rodley, 'Prohibition of Torture: Absolute Means Absolute' 34 *DenJIP* (2006) 145 at p. 150.
[93] Article 3(1)(d) Geneva Conventions I–IV.

Convention III. Furthermore, Article 3, which in the words of Professor Meron stems 'from the influence of human rights law on humanitarian law'[94] remains binding on all parties regardless of treaty obligations or conduct of enemy combatants.[95] The provisions contained within Article 3 have been accorded standing in international customary law. The World Court in the *Nicaragua* case treated common Article 3 as reflecting 'elementary consideration of humanity' which was applicable to all armed conflicts.[96] In elaborating upon this position, the Court notes that:

> Article 3 which is common to all four Geneva Conventions of 12 August 1949 defines certain rules to be applied in the armed conflicts of a non-international character. There is no doubt that, in the event of international armed conflicts, these rules also constitute a minimum yardstick, in addition to the more elaborate rules which are also to apply to international conflicts; and they are rules which, in the Court's opinion, reflect what the Court in 1949 called 'elementary considerations of humanity' (*Corfu Channel, Merits, I.C.J. Reports 1949*, p. 22; paragraph 215 above).[97]

Article 3 has a much broader application, and unlike Protocol II (which also applies to non-international armed conflict) there is no requirement of State involvement, and has a much lower threshold covering, for example, instances of armed conflict reflected as internal strife in order to trigger applicability. It needs to be noted that although the threshold is not as high as Protocol II, there is nevertheless a threshold that must be met before the applicability requirements of Article 3 will be met, i.e. it must be armed conflict and thus mere internal unrest or rioting would be insufficient to trigger Article 3.

Additionally, unlike Protocol II, territorial control by the group is not a pre-requisite for applicability. In the light of the broad nature of applicability of Common Article 3 and its significantly lower threshold, it is not surprising that considerable dissensions persist as to the criteria for triggering the provisions of the Article.[98]

Article 4 of Geneva Convention III provides a definition of POWs, according to which:

---

[94] Meron, 'Humanization' (2000), above n.1, at p. 246.

[95] Provost, above n.1, at p. 156.

[96] *Military and Paramilitary Activities in and Against Nicaragua (Nicaragua v. USA) Merits, Judgment,* I.C.J. Reports 1986, p. 14.

[97] Ibid. para 218. Common Article 3, has since the adoption of the Geneva Conventions, been anticipated as ensuring fundamental human rights. See Gutteridge, 'The Geneva Conventions of 1949' *BYIL* (1949) 294 at p. 300; Aksar, *Implementing International Humanitarian Law: From the ad hoc Tribunals to a Permanent International Criminal Court* (Routledge, 2004) at p. 192.

[98] ICRC presented the following criterion as 'convenient criterion' in determining the existence of a non-international armed conflict in the context of Article 3. This criterion includes: recognition (implicitly or explicitly) of insurgency by the State or the UN; organisation of the insurgent forces under a responsible command exercising control over a determined area of national territory in which the group has the capability of enforcing the provisions of the convention; the belligerent group have some control over a population or territory; and the applicability of military force by the State to subdue insurgency. Discussed by Provost, above n.1, at pp. 265–266. This criterion has however, been criticised as excessively narrow in its applicability by Provost, ibid. at p. 266. See also Forsythe, 'Legal Management of Internal War: The 1977 Protocol on Non-International Armed Conflict' 72 *AJIL* (1978) 272; Murray, 'The Status of the ANC and SWAPO in International Humanitarian Law' 100 *South African Law Journal* (1983) 402.

A. Prisoners of war, in the sense of the present Convention, are persons belonging to one of the following categories, who have fallen into the power of the enemy:

(1) Members of the armed forces of a Party to the conflict, as well as members of militias or volunteer corps forming part of such armed forces.

(2) Members of other militias and members of other volunteer corps, including those of organized resistance movements, belonging to a Party to the conflict and operating in or outside their own territory, even if this territory is occupied, provided that such militias or volunteer corps, including such organized resistance movements, fulfil the following conditions: (a) that of being commanded by a person responsible for his subordinates; (b) that of having a fixed distinctive sign recognizable at a distance; (c) that of carrying arms openly; (d) that of conducting their operations in accordance with the laws and customs of war.

(3) Members of regular armed forces who profess allegiance to a government or an authority not recognized by the Detaining Power.

(4) Persons who accompany the armed forces without actually being members thereof, such as civilian members of military aircraft crews, war correspondents, supply contractors, members of labour units or of services responsible for the welfare of the armed forces, provided that they have received authorization, from the armed forces which they accompany, who shall provide them for that purpose with an identity card similar to the annexed model.

(5) Members of crews, including masters, pilots and apprentices, of the merchant marine and the crews of civil aircraft of the Parties to the conflict, who do not benefit by more favourable treatment under any other provisions of international law.

(6) Inhabitants of a non-occupied territory, who on the approach of the enemy spontaneously take up arms to resist the invading forces, without having had time to form themselves into regular armed units, provided they carry arms openly and respect the laws and customs of war.

According to Article 5, POWs are protected from the time of their capture until their final release and repatriation. It also specifies that when there is any doubt as to whether a combatant belongs to the categories in Article 4, they should be treated as such until their status has been determined by a 'competent tribunal'.[99] Although the tribunal need not be a court, the determination should nevertheless be made by a properly 'constituted tribunal'.[100] If the person in question is not held as a POW and is being tried for offences in relation to his conduct in hostilities, he is entitled to assert his rights as a POW during the trial. Unless the trial is held *in camera* due to security reasons by the holding State, representatives of the protecting power must be informed of the proceedings and they are entitled to attend those proceedings.[101]

The Convention provides a series of rights for POWs, and is articulated in Part II. According to Article 12, POWs are to be handed over to an enemy power but not to individuals or military units who captured them; the detaining power is responsible for their

[99] See Article 5 Geneva Convention III.
[100] See *Public Prosecutor* v. *Koi* [1968] AC 829. Note the considerable debate on the US position on captured members of Al-Qaeda and Taliban force, above n.50.
[101] Protocol I, Article 45. (The scope of POWs has been considerably enhanced by Protocol I of Geneva Convention 1977.)

treatment.[102] According to Article 13, POWs must at all times be treated humanely and must not be endangered or placed at risk of death, physical integrity or seriously endangering their health.[103] Reprisals against them are prohibited. According to Article 14, they are to be respected; in particular, due regard has to given to the integrity and honour of women.[104] Article 15 establishes that POWs are to receive free of charge maintenance and free medical attention[105] while Article 16 prohibits distinctions based on race, nationality, religious beliefs or political opinions in the treatment of POWs.[106] Part III, in Article 17, provides that POWs are only required to provide their surname, first names, rank and other essential details.[107] They are not to be tortured, physically or mentally, or coerced in any way. According to Article 18, all personal effects and articles of POWs are to remain in their possession, this included effects and articles that are related to clothing and feeding that are also regulation military equipment.[108] POWs must not be kept without identity documents, with the detaining power under an obligation to supply such documents.[109] POWs are to be evacuated as soon as possible after their capture, with the exception of those who are wounded or sick.[110] Article 20 provides that POWs shall be treated humanely, with sufficient provisions of food and water during evacuation.[111] While, according to Article 21, POWs may be subject to internment, the condition of humane treatment applies. According to Article 26 they must be provided with sufficient daily rations and drinking water,[112] with Article 27 imposing obligations on the detaining power to provide sufficient and adequate quantities of clothing and underwear. Chapter III of the Convention ensures the POWs have the essential hygiene and medical attention.[113]

Chapter V deals with the significant areas of protection of religious, intellectual and physical activities of POWs. According to Article 34, POWs are to enjoy 'latitude in the exercise of their religious duties', which includes attending religious services. POWs are to be provided with premises for offering religious services.[114] According to Article 38, while respecting individual preferences of every POW, detaining powers are obliged to encourage the practice of intellectual, educational and recreational pursuits, sports and physical exercise.[115] Article 44 confirms that POWs are to be treated with due regard to their rank and age.[116] Article 49 permits the usage of labour of POWs, with due consideration to their age, sex, rank and physical health, although POWs must not be unduly compelled to work.[117] The POWs should be provided with acceptable working conditions. Section IV (Articles 58–68) of the Convention deals with the financial resources of POWs, which also allows for the detaining power to grant POWs a monthly wage.[118] POWs are allowed to send

---

[102] Article 12 Geneva Convention III.
[103] Ibid. Article 13.
[104] Ibid. Article 14.
[105] Ibid. Article 15.
[106] Ibid. See Article 16.
[107] Ibid. Article 17.
[108] Ibid. Article 18.
[109] Ibid. Article 18.
[110] Ibid. Article 19.
[111] Ibid. Article 20.
[112] Ibid. Article 26.
[113] Ibid. Chapter III Article 29–33.
[114] Ibid. Article 24.
[115] Ibid. Article 38.
[116] Ibid. Article 44.
[117] Ibid. Article 49.
[118] Ibid. Article 60.

and receive letters and cards, although the detaining powers have the authority to limit the number of letters.[119] Section VI (Chapter I, Article 78) of GCIII allows POWs to make complaints in relation to the conditions of captivity.[120] The Convention also ensures fair trials and prohibits confessions as a means of admitting guilt, and POWs should be provided with all relevant information of the case against them.[121] POWs shall be entitled to legal advice and counsel in the defence of their case.[122] POWs are entitled to the right to appeal from any sentence pronounced against them.[123] Part IV of the Convention (Articles 109–121) details the conditions of the termination of captivity. An important provision in this regard is Article 118, which provides for POWs' release and repatriation without delay after the cessation of active hostilities. POWs have an unconditional right of release and repatriation without any pressure being placed on them by the detaining country to reject repatriation.[124]

(v) Protection of the civilian persons in times of war/armed conflict

Geneva Convention IV relative to the Protection of Civilian Persons in Time of War (1949) focuses upon the protection of civilians during the times of war, conflict or any occupation by a foreign power. They are, as such, not prisoners of war, a term used in Geneva Convention III. As examined already Article 3 remains applicable most directly to civilians and reaffirms that even where there is a conflict which is not of international character, the parties must, as a minimum, adhere to certain levels of minimal protection. The significance and value of Common Article 3 within customary law has already been examined and its utility for protecting civilians involved in non-international armed conflict cannot be underestimated. Article 4 provides the definition of a 'protected person', according to which '[p]ersons protected by the Convention are those who, at a given moment and in any manner whatsoever, find themselves, in case of a conflict or occupation, in the hands of a Party to the conflict or Occupying Power of which they are not nationals'. This restrictive policy based on nationality has been the object of serious criticism. Provost, in expressing historical examples, makes the point that:

> the exclusion on the basis of nationality of a significant portion of civilians during wartime thus covers essential protection concerning personal integrity, religious conviction, equality and the prohibition of torture, medical experiments, mass deportation, forced enlistment in the armed forces etc. For example, the general internment of American and Canadian Citizens of German and Japanese descent in the United States and Canada during the Second World War, including women and children, would not be contrary to the Fourth Geneva Convention. Even more graphically, the extermination policy of Nazi Germany concerning Jewish members of its own population and that of co-belligerents would not contravene the 1949 Fourth Geneva Convention . . .[125]

---

[119] Ibid. Article 71.
[120] Ibid. Chapter I, Article 78.
[121] Ibid. Article 99.
[122] Ibid. Article 105.
[123] Ibid. Article 106.
[124] Meron, 'The Humanization', above n.1, at p. 254. Professor Meron raises the most complex question of instances where the POW does not wish to be repatriated. The legal position as it currently stands is that the State of nationality can demand repatriation; an option providing the POW a choice in these circumstances was considered but rejected because of the fear of abuse by detaining powers and the difficulties in granting asylum. On asylum issues, see above chapter 18.
[125] Provost, above n.1, at pp. 38–39 (footnotes omitted).

This restrictive approach has however been relaxed by Part II of Geneva Convention IV and as noted already by common Article 3 which remains applicable to everybody not taking any part in active hostilities. Further dilution has taken place by the more recent jurisprudence of the International Criminal Tribunals. Thus, the Appeals Chamber of ICTY in the *Tadić* case held that murder and torture of Croats and Muslims in the so-called Republika Srpska constituted grave breaches even though the perpetrator of atrocities and the victims held the same nationality. The Appeals Chamber noted:

> Article 4 of Geneva Convention IV, if interpreted in the light of its object and purpose, is directed to the protection of civilians to the maximum extent possible. It therefore does not make its applicability dependent on formal bonds and purely legal relations. Its primary purpose is to ensure the safeguards afforded by the Convention to those civilians who do not enjoy the diplomatic protection, and correlatively are not subject to the allegiance and control, of the State in whose hands they may find themselves. In granting its protection, Article 4 intends to look to the substance of relations, not to their legal characterisation as such.
>
> Hence, even if in the circumstances of the case the perpetrators and the victims were to be regarded as possessing the same nationality, Article 4 would still be applicable. Indeed, the victims did not owe allegiance to (and did not receive the diplomatic protection of) the State (the FRY) on whose behalf the Bosnian Serb armed forces had been fighting.[126]

Additionally, the provisions of Article 4 explicitly exclude nationals of a State which is not bound by the Convention and the citizens of a neutral state or an allied state if that state has normal diplomatic relations within the State in whose hands they are in. The provisions of Article 4 exclude lawful combatants and POWs.[127] A section of the Geneva Convention IV, Part II (Articles 13–26) has a broader application in that it is applicable also to the belligerent's own population and nationals of co-belligerent states. This section of the Convention includes protection from sieges and blockages, evacuations of the wounded and sick civilians, and special care of children below the age of 15. Article 13 establishes that provisions of Part II cover the entirety of the population and is applicable without any distinction based on race, nationality, religion or political opinion.[128] According to Article 14,

---

[126] *Prosecutor v. Tadić*, Appeals Chamber, International Criminal Tribunal for the Former Yugoslavia Case No. IT-94-I-AR72, 15 July 1999, paras 168–169, www.un.org/icty/tadic/appeal/judgement/index.htm <last visited 1 January 2009>. Decision upheld by the Appeals Chamber in *Prosecutor v. Mucić* et al., Case No. IT-96-21-A (2001) (Čelebići Camp), 8 April 2003, www.un.org/icty/celebici/appeal/judgement/index.htm <last visited 15 March 2009>.

[127] These atrocities against own nationals of the States would of course be crimes against humanity and also constitute the crime of genocide. Provost goes on to mention the case of *Tadić* (see note above) where the ICTY provided a broad interpretation to 'Protected Persons' and held that lack of allegiance to the party of the conflict, as primary criterion as opposed the formal connection of nationality. It needs to be noted that no restriction based on the nationality of concerned individuals can be found either in the application of provisions of 1949 Geneva Conventions I and IV (Article 12/12) nor in common Article 3 relative to non-international armed conflict. (States own nationals are therefore accorded protection under these provisions.) Similarly, the two additional protocols shift away from the notion of nationality in that both Protocols are declared to be applicable to 'all those affected by' the international and non-international armed conflict (Article 9, Protocol I; Article 2, Protocol II). Article 75 of Protocol I provides protection to those left almost entirely excluded by Geneva Convention IV (i.e. State's own nationals and nationals of neutral and co-belligerent States which still maintain diplomatic relation with the State under whose power they find themselves). Provost, above n.1, at p. 40.

[128] Geneva Convention IV, Article 13.

parties to conflict may establish hospitals and safety zones to protect the wounded, sick and aged person, children under 15 and expectant mothers and mothers of children under seven. Under IHL, the protection granted to the individual is generally derived not from human nature, but from membership in a group, be it a resistance group or a nation entertaining a specific kind of relationship with the State under whose power the group finds itself. Within the frame of Article 75 of the additional Protocol I an exception is provided as the Article aims to separate humanitarian protection without the precondition of membership of a particular group of protected person. It is in this context that international humanitarian norms come closest to international human rights law.[129]

Further protection to the civilian population is provided by Protocol I, additional to the 1949 Conventions. Article 50(1) Additional Protocol I elaborates and enhances the scope of civilian population. It excludes combatants and POWs (as stated and defined in Article 4(1), (2), (3) and (6) of Geneva Convention III) as well as in Article 43 of the Additional Protocol I. However, the inclusionary nature is reflected by the provisions that the civilian population includes all those who are civilians and that in case of any doubts as to the status of a person, that person shall be regarded as a civilian person.[130]

According to Article 50(3), the presence of non-civilians amidst the civilian population is not a bar for the population to have a civilian character. Article 51 establishes certain fundamental principles for the protection of civilians. These are firstly that the civilian population and individual civilians are to enjoy protection against dangerous military operations.[131] Secondly, in order to achieve this result the civilian population is not to be made the object of attack.[132] Thirdly, there is a complete prohibition on acts or threat of violence with the purpose of terrorising a population.[133] Fourthly, the civilian population is to be protected (unless it takes part in hostilities) from indiscriminate attacks – including those attacks not directly targeting military objectives[134] or deploying means of combat that cannot be directed at specific military objectives[135] or that deploy a method or means that cannot be limited.[136] Fifthly, according to the provisions of Article 51(8) a belligerents' violation of the prohibition of using civilians to shield military targets under Article 51(7) 'shall not release the Parties to the conflict from their legal obligations with respect to the civilian population and civilians'.[137] Several articles from the Geneva Convention IV specify how protecting powers, the ICRC and other humanitarian organisations may aid protected persons. The protecting powers and the ICRC are invited to provide support through their good offices in order to facilitate the institution and recognition of these hospitals and safety zones.[138] Part II Geneva Convention IV deals with General Protection of Populations against Certain Consequences of War. Parties are authorised to establish neutralised zones under the provisions of Article 15 for providing shelter to the wounded, sick and non-combatants.[139] Article 16 further emphasises the special protection of the

---

[129] Provost, above n.1, at p. 42.
[130] Article 50(1) and (2) Protocol I.
[131] Ibid. Article 51(1).
[132] Ibid. Article 51(2).
[133] Ibid. Article 51(2).
[134] Ibid. Article 51(3) and (4)(a).
[135] Ibid. Article 51(4)(b).
[136] Ibid. Article 51(4)(c) .
[137] Ibid. Article 51(7) and (8).
[138] Article 14 Geneva Convention IV.

wounded, sick, infirm and expectant mothers. According to Article 18, civilian hospitals may not be the object of attack and are required to be marked by distinctive emblems. Civilian hospitals are protected unless they are used to commit 'acts harmful to the enemy'.[140] Protection may however cease only after due warning has been given and, notwithstanding the passage of a reasonable time, such warnings are unheeded.[141] According to the provisions of Article 21 and 22 convoys of vehicles or aircrafts deployed for the transfer of wounded and sick civilians will not be impeded and such transportation will be respected.[142] Furthermore, all States parties agree upon the free passage of all medical and hospital related consignments as well as 'essential foodstuffs, clothing and tonic intended for children under fifteen, expectant mothers and maternity cases'.[143] Orphaned or separated children below the ages of 15 should not be left to their own resources; and that educational facilities including exercise of their religion are provided to such children.[144] In dealing with the Status and Treatment of Protected Persons, Part III through Article 27 provides that protected person are entitled to respect for their honour, person and religious conviction and their manners and customs, and are to be treated humanely. Special protection is provided to women who are to be protected against any form of sexual violence, rape or enforced prostitution and these protections are to be deployed regardless of race, religion or political opinion.[145] The protected persons, according to Article 30, are to be allowed to seek assistance from international organisations such as the International Committee of the Red Cross. Protected persons are not to be subjected to moral or physical coercion;[146] they must not be subjected to physical or mental torture.[147] Reprisals against protected persons or against their properties are prohibited.[148] Article 34 prohibits the taking of hostages. Article 34 (alongside Common Article 3) represent highly significant provisions, since this prohibition on taking of hostages during armed conflicts formed the basis of a wider norm within international law on the criminalisation of hostage taking. The wholesale denunciation of hostage-taking as a crime in international law is, as we shall examine in Chapter 24, a product of the United Nations General Assembly's Convention against the Taking of Hostages.[149] According to Article 35, protected persons have the right to leave the territory at the beginning of the conflict or during the course of the conflict unless such departure is deemed to be contrary to the national interest of the State. Protected persons have the right to look for paid employment,[150] but must not be compelled to work,[151] and cannot be compelled to serve in the occupying powers' armed forces.[152]

---

[139] Ibid. Article 15.
[140] Ibid. Article 19.
[141] Ibid. Article 19.
[142] Ibid. Articles 21 and 22.
[143] Ibid. Article 23.
[144] Ibid. Article 24.
[145] Ibid. Article 27.
[146] Ibid. Article 31.
[147] Ibid. Article 32.
[148] Ibid. Article 33.
[149] International Convention Against the Taking of Hostages, GA Res. 146(XXXIV), U.N.GAOR, 34th Sess., Supp. No. 46, at 245, UN Doc. A/34/46 (1979), entered into force 3 June 1983. See below chapter 24.
[150] Article 39 Geneva Convention IV.
[151] Ibid. Article 40.
[152] Ibid. Article 51.

As regards individual or mass forcible transfers, Article 49 takes a resolute position. According to Article 49: 'Individual or mass forcible transfers, as well as deportations of protected persons from occupied territory to the territory of the Occupying Power or to that of any other country, occupied or not, are prohibited, regardless of their motive.' Deportations and mass transfers of civilian population constitute a crime against humanity under Article 7 of the Statute of the International Criminal Court, and has also been recognised as forming part of crimes against humanity within customary international law.[153] The second paragraph of Article 49 provides that persons displaced during armed conflict must be transferred back to their homes as soon as hostilities in the area in question have ceased. This right of displaced persons is often referred to as the 'right of return' and has been reaffirmed in later international treaties and within human rights law.[154] State practice also establishes this rule as a norm of customary international law.[155]

4 HUMAN RIGHTS AND HUMANITARIAN VALUES IN THE CONDUCT OF WARFARE

(i) Distinguishing civilian from military targets and the strict focus on achieving military objectives

In its Advisory Opinion on *Legality of the Threat or Use of Nuclear Weapons*, the ICJ set out 'cardinal principles contained in the texts constituting the fabric of humanitarian law'.[156] According to the ICJ, 'States must never make civilians the object of attack and must consequently never use weapons that are incapable of distinguishing between civilians and military targets.'[157] IHL has always insisted on a distinction between civilian and military targets. Armed attacks are to be confined solely for attaining 'military objectives'.[158] This principle has been consistently reiterated in the 1923 Hague Rules of Air Warfare,[159] the

---

[153] Article 7, Rome Statute of the International Criminal Court (1998) 2187 U.N.T.S. 90, entered into force 1 July 2002; de Zayas, 'The Right to One's Homeland, Ethnic Cleansing, and the International Criminal Tribunal for the Former Yugoslavia', 6 *Criminal Law Forum* (1995) 257; de Zayas, 'The Illegality of Population Transfers and the Application of Emerging International Norms in the Palestinian Context' 6 *Palestine Yearbook of International Law* (1990/1991) 17; Iyer, 'Mass Expulsion as Violation of Human Rights', 13 *Indian Journal of International Law* (1973) 169; see above chapter 21.

[154] See Article 13(2), UDHR 48; Article 12(4), ICCPR 66; Article 5(d)(ii), 1965 International Convention on the Elimination of all Forms of Racial Discrimination: 660 *IWTS* 195; Article VIII, American Declaration on the Rights and Duties of Man, OAS OR OEA/Ser.L/V/II.23, doc.21, rev.6 (1979); Article 22(5), 1969 American Convention on Human Rights: *OASTS* No. 36, at 1, OAS OR OEA/Ser.L/V/H.23, doc. 21, rev. 6 (1979); Article 12(2), 1981 African Charter on Human and Peoples Rights: OAU doc. CAB/LEG/67/3 Rev. 5, 21 *ILM* 58 (1982); Article 3(2), Protocol No. 4, European Convention for the Protection of Human Rights and Fundamental Freedoms, 16 September 1963: 213 6W75 221.

[155] On the 'Right to Return' see generally Radley, 'The Palestinian Refugees: The Right to Return in International Law' 72 *AJIL* (1978) 586; Zedalis, 'Right to Return: A Closer Look' 6 *Georgetown Immigration Law Journal* (1992) 499; Lawand, 'The Right to Return of Palestinians in International Law' 8 *International Journal of Refugee Law* (1996) 532.

[156] *Advisory Opinion on Law of Threat or Use of Nuclear Weapons* [1996] ICJ Rep 226, 257.

[157] Ibid.

[158] For discussion and analysis see Henckaerts, Doswald-Beck, Alvermann, Dormann and Rolle, *Customary International Humanitarian Law: Volume 1, Rules* (Cambridge University Press, 2005).

[159] The Hague Rule of Air Warfare 1923 Parliamentary Papers, Cmd. 2201, Miscellaneous No. 14 (1924) (Article 24(1)).

1949 Geneva Conventions,[160] the 1954 Hague Cultural Property Convention,[161] in particular the 1999, Second Protocol appended to the Hague Convention,[162] and the 1998 Rome Statute of the International Criminal Court.[163] In prescribing a definition of 'military objectives', Protocol I Additional to the Geneva Conventions states, that:

> [a]ttacks shall be limited strictly to military objectives. In so far as objects are concerned, military objectives are limited to those objects which by their nature, location, purpose or use make an effective contribution to military and whose total or partial destruction, capture or neutralization, in the circumstances ruling at the time, offers a definite military advantage.[164]

Article 52(3) of Additional Protocol 1 provides:

> In case of doubt whether an object which is normally dedicated to civilians purposes, such as a place of worship, a house or other dwelling or a school, is being used to make an effective contribution to military action, it shall be presumed not to be so used.

The definition contained in Article 52(2) has been restated in a number of other international instruments including Protocols II and III Annexed to the 1980 Conventional Weapons Convention;[165] the 1999 Second Protocol to the Hague Cultural Property Convention;[166] and the San Remo Manual of 1995 on International Law Applicable to Armed Conflict at Sea.[167] Although the provisions contained in Article 52(2) have attained a status, according to some commentator's representing customary international law,[168]

---

[160] See the Geneva Convention I for the Amelioration of the Condition of the Wounded and Sick in Armed Forces, (1949) (Article 19(2)); Geneva Convention IV relative to the Protection of Civilian Persons in Time of War (Article 18).

[161] UNESCO Convention for the Protection of Cultural Property in the Event of Armed Conflict, 249 U.N.T.S. 240, entered into force 7 August 1956 (Article 8(1)(a)).

[162] Second Protocol to the Hague Convention of 1954 for the Protection of Cultural Property in the Event of Armed Conflict, 26 March 1999, 38 I.L.M. 769 (1999) (Articles 6(a), 8, 13(1)(b)).

[163] Rome Statute of the International Criminal Court (1998) (Article 8(2)(b)(ii), (v), (ix)).

[164] Article 52(2), Protocol I.

[165] Convention on Prohibitions or Restrictions on the Use of Certain Conventional Weapons (1980); Protocol on Prohibitions or Restrictions on the Use of Mines, Booby-Traps and Other Devices (Protocol II), 1342 U.N.T.S. 168, 19 I.L.M. 1529, entered into force 2 December 1983; as amended 3 May 1996, 35 I.L.M. 1206, Article 2(4): Protocol on Prohibitions or Restrictions on the Use of Incendiary Weapons (Protocol III), 1342 U.N.T.S. 171, 19 I.L.M. 1534, entered into force 2 December 1983, Article 1(3).

[166] Second Protocol to the Hague Convention (1954) (Article 1 (f)).

[167] Doswald-Beck (ed.), *San Remo Manual of 1995 on International Law Applicable to Armed Conflict at Sea* (Cambridge University Press, 1995) p. 114.

[168] 'The definition of a military objective in Article 52(2) is generally regarded as declaratory of customary law', Greenwood, 'Customary International Law and the First Geneva Protocol of 1977 in the Gulf Conflict' in Rowe (ed.), *The Gulf War 1990–1991 in International and English Law* (Routledge, 1993) at p. 63; 'The definition of a military objective found in Protocol I seems to be recognized as representing customary international law', Hampson, 'Remarks in a Panel on Implementing Limitations on the Use of Force: The Doctrine of Proportionality and Necessity' *American Society of International Law Proc.* (1992) 39 at p. 50; 'the Protocol I definition of military objective is the definition generally accepted today' Fenrick, 'The Law Applicable to Targeting and Proportionality after Operation Allied Force: A View from the Outside' 3 *YBIHL* (2000) 53 at p. 57; Holland, 'Military Objective and Collateral Damage: Their Relationship and Dynamics' 7 *YBIHL* (2004) 35.

there is nevertheless a lack of clarity. It is frequently difficult to establish whether the identity of an object and its destruction because of 'nature, location, purpose or use' offers a legitimate military advantage. Military arsenal such as weapons, aircrafts and warships, military fortifications, military camps, military depots and military laboratories form an obvious legitimate target. However, there are certain objects, which although not normally deployed for military usage, could convert into a legitimate target. These would, for example, include civilian cars and transportation used for military purposes. There are other objects, such as bridges and roads, that potentially serve a dual purpose – their destruction, alongside the bombing of government offices have been the object of criticism. In analysing the legitimacy of attacks on dual use objects – those civilian installations (e.g. electricity grids) with military objectives, etc., the fundamental question relates to the extent to which collateral damage will result in bringing about civilian casualties. The situation is, however, often far from clear cut. In the recent conflicts in Iraq and Afghanistan the allied forces have faced challenges such as attacks being conducted from a school or from a mosque. The United Kingdom's understanding of the matter is that:

> The military advantage anticipated from an attack is intended to refer to the advantage anticipated from the attack considered as a whole and not only from isolated or particular parts of the attack.

It is doubtful whether the bombing of civilian TV stations and radio stations during an armed conflict could be justified as advancing a legitimate military objective. However, in March 2003, the United States bombed Iraqi TV Satellite arguing that this was a legitimate military target.

In this considerably unsettled situation, it has been stated persuasively that in practice there are 'no fixed borderlines between civilian objects and military objectives'.[169] The question, therefore, remains as to whether attacks on power stations constitute legitimate targets to attain a military objective. In the 1990–91 Kuwait conflict, the US-led coalition treated power stations as legitimate targets. In such a scenario, it is important that commanders should ask themselves as to whether an impartial observer would consider the military gains expected from the attack to be worth the likely civilian casualties and damage. A primary concern should always be the impact of an attack on the civilian population.

(ii) Prohibition on causing unnecessary suffering

A significant principle of convergence between IHL and international human rights law is the obligations upon all parties to ensure the prohibition of unnecessary suffering for all those affected by the conflict. The principle of prohibition of unnecessary suffering, as affirmed by the International Court of Justice in its Advisory Opinion on the *Legality of the Threat or Use of Nuclear Weapons*, dates back several centuries and has been a major

---

[169] Randelzhofer, 'Civilian Objects' in Bernhardt (ed.), 1 *Encyclopedia of Public International Law* (North Holland Publishing Co, 1992) pp. 603, 604.

concern in the developmental stages of IHL.[170] It was reinstated in the Preamble of the 1868 Saint Petersburg Declaration[171] and Article 23(e) of the Hague Convention with Respect to the Laws and Customs of War on Land (1899).[172] In the *Nuclear Weapons Case*, the ICJ notes as follows:

> The cardinal principles contained in the texts constituting the fabric of humanitarian law are the following. The first is aimed at the protection of the civilian population and civilian objects and establishes the distinction between combatants and non-combatants; States must never make civilians the object of attack and must consequently never use weapons that are incapable of distinguishing between civilian and military targets. According to the second principle, it is prohibited to cause unnecessary suffering to combatants: it is accordingly prohibited to use weapons causing them such harm or uselessly aggravating their suffering. In application of the second principle, States do not have unlimited freedom of choice of means in the weapons they use.[173]

Treaty law confirms the principle of international customary law, which the World Court described as representing the 'overriding consideration of humanity'.[174] In terms of the actual ruling on the prohibition of nuclear weapons the court's views are disappointing. After examining State practice, the court position was that nuclear weapons were neither prohibited expressly or specifically within international law. According to the court, nuclear weapons could not be prohibited through a strategy of drawing analogies with poisoned gases which are prohibited by the Second Hague Declaration of 1899, Article 23(a) of the Regulations respecting the Laws and Customs of War on Land annexed to the Hague Convention IV of 18 October 1907 and the Geneva Protocol of 1925.[175] Similarly, according to the court, the cumulative effect of such treaties as the Nuclear Test Ban Treaty (1963), the Outer Space Treaty (1967), etc. did not confirm the prohibition of nuclear weapons. The Court found existing State practices as providing insufficient evidence of an established *opino juris* which could lead to the formation of customary law.[176] Having regard to the existing and established legal principles, the court was unable to draw the conclusion that international humanitarian law, or the norms of neutrality or self-defence, prohibited the threat or usage of nuclear weapons.[177] Such a disappointing verdict, however, needs to be seen in the light of existing realities and international State practices. There is no doubt as to the devastating nature and enormous suffering resulting from the use of nuclear

---

[170] ICJ Reports, 1996, at 226.

[171] Declaration Renouncing the Use, in Time of War, of Explosive Projectiles under 400 Grammes Weight. Saint Petersburg, 29 November/11 December 1868, in Schindler and Toman, above n.25, at p. 102.

[172] Hague Convention (II) with Respect to the Laws and Customs of War on Land and its annex: Regulation concerning the Laws and Customs of War on Land: 29 July 1899, 32 Stat. 1803, 1 Bevans 247, 26 Martens Nouveau Recueil (ser. 2) 949, 187 Consol. T.S. 429, entered into force 4 September 1900.

[173] ICJ Reports, 1996, at p. 257, para 78.

[174] Ibid. at p. 262, para 95.

[175] Ibid. at p. 248, paras 54–58. Hague Convention IV – Laws and Customs of War on Land: 18 October 1907, 36 Stat. 2277, 1 Bevans 631, 205 Consol. T.S. 277, 3 Martens Nouveau Recueil (ser. 3) 461, entered into force 26 January 1910.

[176] See above n.173, 'the members of the international community are profoundly divided on the matter of whether non-recourse to nuclear weapons over the past 50 years constitutes the expression of an *opinio juris*. Under these circumstances the Court does not consider itself able to find that there is such an *opinion juris*'. Ibid. p. 254, para 67.

[177] Ibid. at pp. 262–263; paras 92–97.

International human rights law and international humanitarian law

weapons. At the same time, efforts to establish firm legal principles prohibiting the use of nuclear weapons have provoked controversy. In appreciating the court's point of view, the position remains that neither the possession of nuclear weapons nor their use *in extremis* (and in accordance with principles of proportionality) would be contrary to existing norms of international law.[178]

In highlighting a convergence between IHL and human rights law, Article 35(2) of Protocol I states that: 'It is prohibited to employ weapons, projectiles and material and methods of warfare of a nature to cause superfluous injury or unnecessary suffering'. The focus of a subsequent convention – the Convention on the Prohibition or Restrictions on the Use of Certain Conventional Weapons Which May be Deemed to Be Excessively Injurious or to Have Indiscriminate Effects[179] – is the effective implementation of this principle. This Convention has four protocols: the Protocol on Non-Detectable Fragments; the Protocol on Prohibitions or Restrictions on the Use of Mines, Booby-Traps and Other Devices; the Protocol on Prohibitions or Restrictions on the Use of Incendiary Weapons; and the Protocol on Blinding Laser Weapons. These were decided at the same conference and contain the substantive element of the rules on weapons, which is not provided by the Convention itself. It is difficult to set guidelines or identify with precision those weapons which would cause 'superfluous injury or unnecessary suffering'. There is, nevertheless, consensus on a number of issues, including the following. Firstly, that the use of weapons which cause suffering or injury which could otherwise be prevented are proscribed. Secondly, the prohibition extends to the use of those weapons which have a disproportionate effect in causing suffering or harm vis-à-vis the military objectives aimed to be achieved. Thirdly, and perhaps most significantly, the principle of proportionality means that civilians must not become targets while achieving military objectives. According to Article 3(a) of the Statute of the International Criminal Tribunal for the Former Yugoslavia (ICTY), the usage of 'employment of poisonous weapons or other weapons calculated to cause unnecessary suffering' is deemed a violation of the laws or customs of war giving rise to individual criminal responsibility.[180] Similarly Article 8(2)(b)(xx) of the 1998 Rome Statute in its list of war crimes notes:

> Employing weapons, projectiles and material and methods of warfare which are of a nature to cause superfluous injury or unnecessary suffering or which are inherently indiscriminate in violation of the international law of armed conflict.[181]

Conventional and customary law establishes the following as causing unnecessary suffering: poison through contamination of drinking water, food or usage of poisoned weapons; certain projectiles, which are either explosives or charged with fulminating or inflammable substances; booby-traps, landmines; incendiaries; and chemical weapons as well as biological and bacteriological weapons.

---

[178] 'Accordingly, in view of the present state of international law viewed as a whole, as examined above by the Court, and of the elements of fact at its disposal, the Court is led to observe that it cannot reach a definitive conclusion as to the legality or illegality of the use of nuclear weapons by a State in an extreme circumstance of self-defence, in which its very survival would be at stake', ibid. at p. 263, para 97; also see Shaw, above n.1, at p. 1189.

[179] The Convention on Prohibition or Restrictions on the Use of Certain Conventional Weapons Which May be Deemed to Be Excessively Injurious or to Have Indiscriminate Effects Geneva, 10 October 1980.

[180] (Updated) Statute of the International Tribunal for the Former Yugoslavia UN Doc. S/25704 at 36, annex (1993) and S/25704/Add.1 (1993), adopted by Security Council on 25 May 1993, UN Doc. S/RES/827 (1993).

[181] Rome Statute of the International Criminal Court, Article 8(2)(b)(xx).

(iii) The principle of proportionality and protection of civilians

Earlier sections have already analysed the significance of the protection of civilian population in an armed conflict. It is well established that during an armed conflict, the protection of civilians outweighs any collateral military objectives. As Judge Higgins noted in her dissenting opinion in the *Legality of the Threat or Use of Nuclear Weapons* case:

> the law of armed conflict has been articulated in terms of a broad prohibition – that civilians may not be the object of armed attack – and the question of numbers or suffering (provided always that this primary obligation is met) falls to be considered as part of the 'balancing' or 'equation' between the necessities of war and the requirements of humanity. Articles 23 *(g)*, 25 and 27 of the Annex to the Fourth Hague Convention have relevance here. The principle of proportionality, even if finding no specific mention, is reflected in many provisions of Additional Protocol I to the Geneva Conventions of 1949. Thus even a legitimate target may not be attacked if the collateral civilian casualties would be disproportionate to the specific military gain from the attack. One is inevitably led to the question of whether, if a target is legitimate and the use of a nuclear weapon is the only way of destroying that target, any need can ever be so necessary as to occasion massive collateral damage upon civilians.[182]

Source: The United Nations is the author of the original material.

The principle of proportionality is reflected in many provisions of Additional Protocol I to the Geneva Convention of 1949. Thus, even a legitimate target may not be attacked if the collateral civilian casualties would be disproportionate to the specific military gain from the attack.[183] Protocol I establishes further safeguards with Article 57, stating that:

1. In the conduct of military operations, constant care shall be taken to spare the civilian population, civilians and civilian objects.

2. With respect to attacks, the following precautions shall be taken:

   (a) Those who plan or decide upon an attack shall:

      (i) Do everything feasible to verify that the objectives to be attacked are neither civilians nor civilian objects and are not subject to special protection but are military objectives within the meaning of paragraph 2 of Article 52 and that it is not prohibited by the provisions of this Protocol to attack them,

      (ii) Take all feasible precautions in the choice of means and methods of attack with a view to avoiding, and in any event to minimizing, incidental loss of civilian life, injury to civilians and damage to civilian objects;

      (iii) Refrain from deciding to launch any attack which may be expected to cause incidental loss of civilian life, injury to civilians, damage to civilian objects, or a combination thereof, which would be excessive in relation to the concrete and direct military advantage anticipated;

---

[182] Advisory Opinion of 8 July 1996; Judge Higgins (Dissenting Opinion) at p. 587, para 20 www.icj-cij.org/docket/index.php?p1=3&p2=4&k=e1&case=95&code=unan&p3=4 <last visited 9 August 2008>.

[183] See Judge Higgins (Dissenting Opinion) at p. 587 www.icj-cij.org/docket/index.php?p1=3&p2=4&k=e1&case=95&code=unan&p3=4 <last visited 9 August 2008>; also see Holland, above n.168.

(b) An attack shall be cancelled or suspended if it becomes apparent that the objective is not a military one or is subject to special protection or that the attack may be expected to cause incidental loss of civilian life, injury to civilians, damage to civilian objects, or a combination thereof, which would be excessive in relation to the concrete and direct military advantage anticipated;

(c) Effective advance warning shall be given of attacks which may affect the civilian population, unless circumstances do not permit.

3. When a choice is possible between several military objectives for obtaining a similar military advantage, the objective to be selected shall be that the attack on which may be expected to cause the least danger to civilian lives and to civilian objects.

4. In the conduct of military operations at sea or in the air, each Party to the conflict shall, in conformity with its rights and duties under the rules of international law applicable in armed conflict, take all reasonable precautions to avoid losses of civilian lives and damage to civilian objects.

5. No provision of this Article may be construed as authorizing any attacks against the civilian population, civilians or civilian objects.

Military officers are under an obligation to take all possible actions to protect a civilian population. Protocol I, Article 58 establishes an undertaking on the part of the parties to 'endeavour to remove the civilian population, individual civilians and civilian objects under their control from the vicinity of military objectives'.[184] This requirement was breached by Iraq after its invasion of Kuwait in 1990. Not only did the Iraqi regime concentrate in the vicinity of militarily sensitive locations, it also refused to allow foreign nationals to depart – a further breach of international law. In addition to the duty of protecting civilians, Article 58 provides for a duty to 'avoid locating military objectives within or near densely populated areas'.[185]

There are, as already examined, provisions within the First, Second and Third Geneva Conventions and Article 8–31 of Protocol I, which prohibit attacks on medical facilities, personnel and transport of the population. In this regard it is worth noting that the Hague Convention on Cultural Property (1954) contains special provisions for the protection of historic monuments and items of religious and cultural importance.[186] Article 53 of Additional Protocol I to the Geneva Conventions contains several provisions for the protection of historic monuments and items of religious and cultural importance.[187] Article 54(1) of Additional Protocol I prohibits starvation of civilians as a method of warfare and Article 54 generally prohibits attacks on objects indispensable for the survival of the civilian population.[188] Article 55 protects the natural environment against the effects of attack.[189]

The law also places an obligation upon commanders to take action to protect the civilian population under their control from the effects of enemy attacks.[190] Certain facilities are to

---

[184] Article 58(a) Protocol I.
[185] Ibid. Article 58(b) Protocol I.
[186] The UNESCO Hague Convention on Cultural Property, 1954. http://portal.unesco.org/en/ev.php-URL_ID= 13637&URL_DO=DO_TOPIC&URL_SECTION=201.html <last visited 25 November 2008>.
[187] Article 54(1), Protocol I.
[188] Ibid. Article 54(2), Protocol I.
[189] Ibid. Article 55, Protocol I.
[190] Ibid. Article 58, Protocol I.

be protected: these include prohibition of attacks on medical facilities, personnel and transport. Article 56, Protocol I prohibits attacks on dams, dykes and nuclear electrical generating stations, even if they are military objectives, if such attacks are likely to cause the release of dangerous forces and consequent severe losses among the civilian population.[191]

(iv) IHL, the right of self-determination and national liberation movements[192]

Earlier chapters have analysed the complexities generated in the articulation of the right to self-determination. The present discussion aims to focus on the issues which the purported application of the right to self-determination has generated in the context of IHL. With the rapid strengthening of the decolonisation movement during the 1960 and 1970s the UN General Assembly further affirmed the rights of national liberation movements (NLMs) for their struggle against colonial, alien and racist regimes. The recognition of the struggles by liberation movements as NLMs entitled to the right to self-determination and the call in the applicability of the 1949 Geneva Conventions was conducted under the impetus of the developing world in association with the Soviet Block. In December 1973, General Assembly Resolution 3103 (XXVIII) adopted Basic Principles as regards the Legal Status of Combatants Engaged in National Liberation Struggles Against Colonial, Alien and Racist Regimes.[193] According to para 3 such conflicts 'are to be regarded as international armed conflicts in the sense of the 1949 Geneva Conventions'[194] with the aim being to remove these from the ambit of common Article 3 and incorporate these as international armed conflicts. Such an objective was achieved through Protocol I, Articles 1(3) and 1(4).

Article 1 provides:

> (3) This Protocol, which supplements the Geneva Conventions of 12 August 1949 for the protection of war victims, shall apply in the situations referred to in Article 2 common to those Conventions
>
> (4) The situation referred to in the preceding paragraph include armed conflicts in which peoples are fighting against colonial domination and alien occupation and against racist regimes in the exercise of their right of self-determination, as enshrined in the Charter of the United Nations and the Declaration on Principles of International Law concerning Friendly Relations and Co-operation among States in accordance with the Charter of the United Nations.

In order for a conflict to come within the ambit of the provisions of Articles 1(3) and 1(4), a number of requirements need to be satisfied. Firstly, there must be a conflict involving an NLM representing a people, who are involved in a struggle of self-determination against

---

[191] Ibid. Article 56.
[192] See Pomerance, above n.66, at pp. 48–62; Chadwick, *Self-Determination, Terrorism and the International Humanitarian Law of Armed Conflict* (Martinus Nijhoff Publishers, 1996); Rehman, *Islamic State Practices, International Law and the Threat from Terrorism: A Critique of the 'Clash of Civilizations' in the New World Order* (Hart Publishing, 2005) pp. 97–113.
[193] Basic Principles of the Legal Status of the Combatants Struggling Against Colonial and Alien Domination and Racist Regimes GA Res. 3103 (XXVIII), 12 December 1973.
[194] Ibid.

colonial domination, alien occupation or a racist regime. We have already assessed the difficulties encountered in the identification of a 'people' *vis-à-vis* the right to self-determination;[195] these difficulties are exacerbated in the context of IHL. Even if it is possible to locate a 'people', it appears well-established that not all peoples fighting for their right to self-determination are entitled to claim protection from the regime of IHL.[196] Secondly, and as provided by Protocol I, Article 96(3), in order for the legal regime applicable in times of international armed conflict to apply, the authority representing the 'people' in their struggle of the right to self-determination must make a declaration.[197] Uncertainty arises where is there is no recognised or established authority representing the 'people' or where several factions have emerged each claiming to be the representative authority of the 'people'. Furthermore, in relation to the authority making the declaration under Article 96(3), the authority must have the characteristics of an armed force as established in Article 43 of the Protocol. It must be an organised force under responsible command, equipped with an internal disciplinary system charged with *inter alia* enforcing compliance with humanitarian law.[198]

(v) IHL, non-international armed conflicts and the protection offered under Protocol II[199]

We have already, albeit briefly, considered the provisions and applicability of Common Article 3. Similarly, as noted above, Protocol I, Article 4 has blurred the distinction between international and non-international armed conflicts in the context of peoples 'fighting against colonial domination and alien occupation and against racist regimes in the exercise of their right of self-determination'.[200] Protocol II, which applies to non-international armed conflicts whilst overlapping with Common Article 3, extends the protection granted. With the proliferation of internal armed conflicts and civil war, and the necessity to protect human rights during such conflict, it remains important to note the significance as well as limitations of this Protocol. Article 1 of Protocol II provides as follows:

---

[195] See above chapters 13 and 14.

[196] See above chapter 14.

[197] Article 96(3), Protocol I.

[198] Article 43 provides as follows: 'Article 43(1) The armed forces of a Party to a conflict consist of all organized armed forces, groups and units which are under a command responsible to that Party for the conduct or its subordinates, even if that Party is represented by a government or an authority not recognized by an adverse Party. Such armed forces shall be subject to an internal disciplinary system which, inter alia, shall enforce compliance with the rules of international law applicable in armed conflict. Article 43(2) Members of the armed forces of a Party to a conflict (other than medical personnel and chaplains covered by Article 33 of the Third Convention) are combatants, that is to say, they have the right to participate directly in hostilities. Article 43(3) Whenever a Party to a conflict incorporates a paramilitary or armed law enforcement agency into its armed forces it shall so notify the other Parties to the conflict.'

[199] Moir, 'The Historical Development of the Application of Humanitarian Law in Non-International Armed Conflicts to 1949' 47 *ICLQ* (1998) 337; Moir, *The Law of Internal Armed Conflict* (Cambridge University Press, 2002); Meron, *Human Rights in Internal Strife* (Cambridge University Press, 1987); Forsythe, 'Human Rights and Internal Conflicts: Trends and Recent Developments' 12 *California Western Journal of International Law* (1982) 287; Forsythe, 'Legal Management of Internal War: The 1977 Protocol on Non-International Armed Conflict' 72 *AJIL* (1978) 272; Cassese, 'The Status of Rebels under the 1977 Geneva Protocol on Non-International Armed Conflicts' 30 *ICLQ* (1981) 416; Eide, Rosas and Meron, 'Combating Lawlessness in Gray Zone Conflicts Through Minimum Humanitarian Standards' 89 *AJIL* (1995) 215.

[200] Article 4, Protocol I.

Article 1 – Material field of application

1. This Protocol, which develops and supplements Article 3 common to the Geneva Conventions of 12 August 1949 without modifying its existing conditions or application, shall apply to all armed conflicts which are not covered by Article 1 of the Protocol Additional to the Geneva Conventions of 12 August 1949, and relating to the Protection of Victims of International Armed Conflicts (Protocol I) and which take place in the territory of a High Contracting Party between its armed forces and dissident armed forces or other organized armed groups which, under responsible command, exercise such control over a part of its territory as to enable them to carry out sustained and concerted military operations and to implement this Protocol.

2. This Protocol shall not apply to situations of internal disturbances and tensions, such as riots, isolated and sporadic acts of violence and other acts of a similar nature, as not being armed conflicts.

Three essential conditions can be delineated as a prerequisite to the applicability of Article 1. Firstly, there must be a conflict between a State involving its armed forces and dissident armed forces or other organised armed groups. Thus, armed insurgencies within the country not involving the State's official armed forces are not covered by the provisions of Article 1. Secondly, the dissident armed forces or other organised armed groups must have some degree of organisation and the presence of a responsible command. Thirdly, the group in question, having been in control over some part of the national territory must have the capability of undertaking concerted and sustained military operations as well as implementing the provisions of Protocol II. In the absence of a basic organisational structure, the group is unlikely to be in a position to carry out sustained or concerted military operations, have any control over territory or implement the provisions of the Protocol. The cumulative effect of the conditions imposed by Article 1 is to render the provisions of applicability highly restrictive. Provost makes the useful point that:

> [t]he global effect of these conditions is to curtail Protocol II's field of application severely. In defending the idea of state sovereignty in the context of non-international armed conflicts, governments in effect have required that the belligerent part posses all the characteristic of a state – organisation, population and territory – before accepting any role for international humanitarian law.[201]

Furthermore, Meron makes the point that a very high degree of threshold is required to trigger the application of Protocol II, with the situation nearing or at the level of full-scale war.[202] Notwithstanding its jurisdictional limitations, Protocol II provides significant protection and fundamental guarantees. In Part II of the Protocol entitled 'Humane Treatment', fundamental guarantees are accorded to all non-combatants.[203] All such persons should be accorded the respect of person, honour, convictions and religious practices.[204] They are to be treated humanely with no distinctions to be drawn on such factors as race,

---

[201] Provost, above n.1, at p. 264.
[202] Meron, 'Humanization', above n.1, at p. 261.
[203] Part II 'Humane Treatment' Protocol II.
[204] Article 4(1) Protocol II.

colour, language, religion, political or other opinion, national or social origin, wealth or birth.[205] Violence, torture or forms of corporal punishment, or acts of terrorism is prohibited, as is collective punishments and hostage-takings.[206] Similarly, the Article prohibits outrages upon dignity, acts of humiliation and degradation, rape or enforced prostitution, and slavery, as well as any threats to commit any of the aforementioned acts.[207] In providing special protection to children Article 4(3) notes that children are to receive education instruction including religious and moral education, that accords with their upbringing and incorporates the wishes of the parents or carers.[208] Efforts are to be made to reunite children with their families.[209] Recruitment of children into armed forces, as shall be examined shortly, remains a particular concern of international humanitarian and human rights law. Article 4(3) not only prohibits the recruitment of under-15s to armed forces but also bans their taking part in hostilities.[210] All possible efforts are to be made to remove children from areas of hostility to safer areas to ensure their well-being and safety.[211]

In the case of combatants or other persons deprived of their liberty, the Protocol affords certain minimum guarantees. When deprived of their liberty or otherwise captured during armed conflict, all persons are entitled to be treated on equal terms with the local population in the provision of food and drinking water, and are to be afforded safeguards in relation to hygiene and health matters.[212] They are to be treated humanely and justly and are to be allowed their religious practices, and if made to work have the benefit of having working conditions similar to those of the local population.[213] Those subjected to internment are entitled to communicate through letters with their families.[214] The detention of such persons would be located in safe zones and are not to be exposed to dangers arising from armed conflicts.[215]

Article 6 of the Protocol deals with penal prosecutions of offences committed by individuals related to armed conflict. The article establishes certain minimum guarantees which are based on fairness, impartiality and independence of trail and the transparency and fairness in a conviction obtained pronounced by a court.[216] The provisions in relation to trail and its outcome contain the same essential guarantees as contained in international law and reflected within Article 14 of the International Covenant of Civil and Political Rights. Amongst the fundamental human rights guarantees are the presumption of innocence until proven guilty by law,[217] having the right to be present during trail[218] and the privilege against self-incrimination.[219] The accused is to be informed promptly of the particulars of the offence alleged against him or her and is to be provided before and during the trail with

---

[205] Ibid.
[206] Ibid.
[207] Ibid.
[208] Ibid. Article 4(3)(a).
[209] Ibid. Article 4(3)(b).
[210] Ibid. Article 4(3)(c) .
[211] Ibid. Article 4(3)(d)(e).
[212] Ibid. Article 5(1)(b).
[213] Ibid. Article 5(1)(d)(e).
[214] Ibid. Article 5(2)(b).
[215] Ibid. Article 5(2)(e).
[216] Ibid. Article 6(2).
[217] Ibid. Article 6(2)(d).
[218] Ibid. Article 6(2)(e) .
[219] Ibid. Article 6(2)(f) .

all necessary means to present a defence.[220] The Article affirms the established international criminal law and international human rights law principles of individual criminal responsibility[221] and *nullum crimen sine lege* and *nulla poena sine lege*.[222] Article 6(4) borrows a further principle from the ICCPR, in that it prohibits the death penalty on persons below the ages of 18 when the offences were committed, nor is it permissible to carry out this sentence on pregnant women or mothers with young children.[223]

Part IV of the Protocol, dedicated to the protection of the civilian population, also accords a series of rights, including the protection of the civilian population from dangers arising from military operations.[224] Civilian populations are not to be attacked or made the subjects of harassment, violence or terrorism.[225] Starvation of civilians, as a means of combat, is prohibited and therefore any attacks on means on sustenance, such as agricultural or food products, crops, livestock and drinking water installations, are unlawful.[226] Article 15 provides that works or installations that contain dangerous forces, dams, dykes and nuclear electrical generating stations are not to be attacked if these attacks risk releasing dangerous forces and consequently injuring civilian populations.[227] This prohibition remains intact even when attacks on these installation constitute legitimate military objectives.[228] Article 16 establishes the protection of cultural objects and places of worship.[229] Article 17 reinforces and reiterates the principle that civilians are not to be compelled to leave their territories and that any displacement of civilian populations can only be conducted lawfully for their own safety or for imperative military necessity.[230]

(vi) Provisions for special protection

In underlining the nexus between IHL and international human rights law, the protection of various groups, including combatants and civilians, has been considered in earlier sections. In recognition of the fact that during an armed conflict it is the vulnerable elements of a community that suffer most, IHL has further established principles to protect groups such as the women and children. In the vocabulary of IHL, the protection of the environment is also increasingly becoming a major concern. Although references have been made to the protection of these vulnerable segments, they nevertheless deserve a more focused analysis in the context of a study on international human rights law.

---

[220] Ibid. Article 6(2)(a).

[221] Ibid. Article 6(2)(b): 'no one shall beconvicted of an offence except on the basis of individual penal responsibility.'

[222] Ibid. Article 6(2)(c): 'no one shall be held guilty of any criminal offence on account of any act or omission which did not constitute a criminal offence, under the law, at the time when it was committed; nor shall a heavier penalty be imposed than that which was applicable at the time when the criminal offence was committed; if, after the commission of the offence, provision is made by law for the imposition of a lighter penalty, the offender shall benefit thereby.'

[223] Article 6(4) Protocol II.

[224] Part IV (Articles 13–18).

[225] Article 13(2) Protocol II.

[226] Ibid. Article 14 Protocol II.

[227] Article 15 Protocol II.

[228] Ibid.

[229] Article 16 Protocol II.

[230] Article 17(1)(2) Protocol II.

(a) Women[231]

Discrimination, harassment and victimisation of women during times of peace have been explored elsewhere in this book.[232] However, women inevitably face the worst possible consequences in situations where law and order breaks down. Wars, armed conflicts and civil wars tend to associate themselves with horrific crimes against the honour and dignity of women. Women are confronted with acts of sexual violence, enforced pregnancies and rape.[233] In addition to the sexual abuse and degradation of women, armed conflicts increase the level of inequalities already prevalent in the society: women are often subjugated into poverty and converted into instruments of forced labour. Women also have specific health issues, with reproductive health being a major concern during armed conflicts.

Several provisions within the Geneva Conventions and the Additional Protocols to the Conventions aim to provide protection for women. Article 27 of Geneva Convention IV specially offers protection to women against any attack on their honour, particularly against rape, enforced prostitution or any form of indecent assault. The principle is expanded in Article 76(1) of Protocol I to include all civilian women as 'protected persons' regardless of the constraints of nationality as were hitherto placed by Geneva Convention IV. Rape, acts of sexual slavery or enforced prostitution constitute war crimes under Article 8(2)(b)(xxii) of the Rome Statute of International Criminal Court. The United Nations General Assembly adopted the Declaration on the Protection of Women and Children in Emergency and Armed Conflict (1974).[234] The interaction between women's rights and IHL is further highlighted by the concern expressed by modern international human rights instruments. Article 11 of Protocol to the African Charter on Human and Peoples Rights on the Rights of Women in Africa provides that:

1. States Parties undertake to respect and ensure respect for the rules of international humanitarian law applicable in armed conflict situations which affect the population, particularly women.

2. States Parties shall, in accordance with the obligations incumbent upon them under the international humanitarian law, protect civilians including women, irrespective of the population to which they belong, in the event of armed conflict.

---

[231] Gardam and Charlesworth, 'Protection of Women in Armed Conflict' 22 *HRQ* (2000) 148; *Report of the Special Rapporteur on Violence Against Women, Its Causes and Consequences, Ms. Radhika Coomaraswamy, Submitted in Accordance with Commission on Human Rights Resolution 1997/44*, UN ESCOR, Comm'n on Hum. Rts., 54th Sess., Agenda Item 9(a), UN Doc. E/CN.4/1998/54 (1998); *Preliminary Report of the Special Rapporteur on the Situation of Systematic Rape, Sexual Slavery and Slavery-like Practices During Periods of Armed Conflict, Ms. Linda Chavez*, UN ESCOR, Comm'n on Hum. Rts., 48th Sess., Agenda Item 15, UN Doc. E/CN.4/Sub.2/1996/26 (1996). See also Vienna Declaration and Programme of Action, UN GAOR, World Conf. on Hum. Rts., 48th Sess., 22d plen. mtg., part I, UN Doc. A/CONF.157/24 (1993), reprinted in 32 I.L.M. 1661 (1993); Declaration on the Elimination of Violence Against Women, adopted 20 December 1993, GA Res. 48/104, UN GAOR, 48th Sess., 85th plen. mtg., UN Doc. A/RES/48/104 (1993), reprinted in Degener and Koster-Dreese (eds), *Human Rights and Disabled Persons: Essays and Relevant Human Rights Instruments* (Kluwer, 1995) p. 416.

[232] See above chapter 15.

[233] Chinkin, 'Rape and Sexual Abuse of Women in International Law Issues', 5 *EJIL* (1994) 326; Gardam, 'Women and the Law of Armed Conflict: Why the Silence?' 46 *ICLQ* (1997) 55.

[234] *Declaration on the Protection of Women and Children in Emergency and Armed Conflict*, UN Doc. A/RES/3318 (XXIX) (1974).

3. States Parties undertake to protect asylum seeking women, refugees, returnees and internally displaced persons, against all forms of violence, rape and other forms of sexual exploitation, and to ensure that such acts are considered war crimes, genocide and/or crimes against humanity and that their perpetrators are brought to justice before a competent criminal jurisdiction.

4. States Parties shall take all necessary measures to ensure that no child, especially girls under 18 years of age, take a direct part in hostilities and that no child is recruited as a soldier.[235]

Whilst IHL and general international law has made significant advances in according greater protection to women during times of conflict, significant gaps remain. One key lacuna is the negligible role of women in decision making during times of conflict and their minimal involvement in peace deals and rebuilding processes. In a majority of conflicts, it is men who make all the significant decisions including those involving military operations and measures to protect non-combatants. Women's interests, including such issues as those pertaining to their health, safety and security, are unfortunately far too often overlooked. The subject of involvement is also often culturally or religiously sensitive. Nevertheless, the importance of women playing a significant role cannot be underestimated.

(b) Children[236]

The vulnerability of children during times of crises and conflict is a recognised fact. Aspects of these worrying features have already been analysed in the overall debate on the right of child within general international law.[237] The increasing concern over the treatment of children during armed conflict, prompted a number of provisions within the Fourth Geneva Convention on the Protection of Civilians (1949) aimed at protecting children and also providing general protection to those children living in occupied or unoccupied territories.[238] The General Assembly, as noted in relation to women, adopted the Declaration on the Protection of Women and Children in Emergency and Armed Conflict (1974).

According to Article 77 of Protocol I:

2. The Parties to the conflict shall take all feasible measures in order that children who have not attained the age of fifteen years do not take a direct part in hostilities and, in particular, they shall refrain from recruiting them into their armed forces. In recruiting among those persons who have attained the age of fifteen years but who have not attained the age of eighteen years the Parties to the conflict shall endeavour to give priority to those who are oldest.

---

[235] Protocol to the African Charter on Human and Peoples' Rights on the Rights of Women in Africa, Adopted by the 2nd Ordinary Session of the Assembly of the Union, Maputo, CAB/LEG/66.6 (13 September 2000); reprinted in 1 *Afr. Hum. Rts. L.J.* 40, entered into force 25 November 2005.

[236] Van Bueren, 'The International Legal Protection of Children in Armed Conflict' 43 *ICLQ* (1994) 809; Kuper, *International Law Concerning Child Civilians in Armed Conflict* (Clarendon Press, 1997); Mann, International law and the Child Soldier' 36 *ICLQ* (1987) 32; Happold, 'Child Soldiers in International Law: The Legal Regulation of Children's Participation in Hostilities' 47 *NILR* (2000) 27; O'Keefe, 'The Meaning of "Cultural Property" under the 1954 Hague Convention' 46 *NILR* (1999) 26.

[237] See above chapter 16.

[238] See Articles 14, 17, 23–25, 38, 50, 51, 68, 76, 81, 82, 89, 94 and 132 of the Geneva Convention IV.

3. If, in exceptional cases, despite the provisions of paragraph 2, children who have not attained the age of fifteen years take a direct part in hostilities and fall into the power of an adverse Party, they shall continue to benefit from the special protection accorded by this Article, whether or not they are prisoners of war.

4. If arrested, detained or interned for reasons related to the armed conflict, children shall be held in quarters separate from the quarters of adults, except where families are accommodated as family units as provided in Article 75, paragraph 5.

5. The death penalty for an offence related to the armed conflict shall not be executed on persons who had not attained the age of eighteen years at the time the offence was committed.

The Additional Protocol (II) to the Geneva Conventions, whilst operating in the context of internal armed conflicts, provides a number of assurances to children in Article 4(3) which are as follows:

Children shall be provided with the care and aid they require, and in particular:

(a) they shall receive an education, including religious and moral education, in keeping with the wishes of their parents, or in the absence of parents, of those responsible for their care;

(b) all appropriate steps shall be taken to facilitate the reunion of families temporarily separated;

(c) children who have not attained the age of fifteen years shall neither be recruited in the armed forces or groups nor allowed to take part in hostilities;

(d) the special protection provided by this Article to children who have not attained the age of fifteen years shall remain applicable to them if they take a direct part in hostilities despite the provisions of subparagraph (c) and are captured;

(e) measures shall be taken, if necessary, and whenever possible with the consent of their parents or persons who by law or custom are primarily responsible for their care, to remove children temporarily from the area in which hostilities are taking place to a safer area within the country and ensure that they are accompanied by persons responsible for their safety and well-being.

Article 6 of Protocol II which deals with penal prosecutions, provides that:

(4) The death penalty shall not be pronounced on persons who were under the age of eighteen years at the time of the offence and shall not be carried out on pregnant women or mothers of young children[239]

These provisions have been further consolidated by the Rome Statute of International Criminal Court which declares conscription or enlistment of children under the age of 15 as a war crime.[240] As examined already, the most recent addition of the rights to protect children in armed conflict are reflected through the provisions of the Optional Protocol

---

[239] Article 6(4).
[240] Article 8(2)(b)(xxvi) of the Rome Statute of the International Criminal Court.

on the Rights of the Child on the Involvement of Children in Armed Conflict.[241] According to Article 2 of the Protocol, persons below the age of 18 years are not to be compulsorily recruited into the armed forces of States parties.[242] The Protocol extracts an undertaking from State parties to undertake all 'feasible measures' that those members of their armed forces that have not attained the age of 18, do not take a direct part in hostilities.[243] The difficulties inherent in such a formula has been analysed in our earlier discussion.[244] Suffice it to note that the term 'feasible measures' within the Protocol represents a compromise to accommodate those States, including militarily powerful States such as the United States and the United Kingdom. These States continue with a policy of recruiting 17-year-olds and therefore in strict military terms could not guarantee that these persons would in all circumstances be prevented from taking a 'direct part' in armed conflict or hostilities.[245] Those States which continue to permit voluntary recruitment of under-18s in their armed forces are required to ensure firstly that such recruitment is genuinely voluntary,[246] secondly that it is carried out with the informed consent of the individual's parent or legal guardian,[247] thirdly that it is agreed upon with full proof of the age[248] and finally the State has provided complete information of the duties involved in the military service.[249] Furthermore, in accordance with Article 3(2) of the Protocol, parties undertake to make a binding declaration that establishes a minimum age at which they will permit voluntary recruitment into national armed forces.[250] Many parts of the world have witnessed the deployment of children by all warring factions. While such an undertaking is not always in the control of the States, States parties to the Protocol nevertheless commit themselves to taking all 'feasible measures' to prevent such recruitment by non-State actors.[251]

Within the regional context, the African Charter on the Rights and Welfare of the Child also sets 18 as the minimum age for the recruitment.[252] Notwithstanding the adoption of these international standards, there is nevertheless a question-mark as to compulsory recruitment of children within general international law. It is probably too ambitious to declare that a general prohibition of customary international law now exists in relation to the recruitment of children below the age of 18 though the dividing line may be somewhere between 15 and 18.

Despite these legal safeguards, children are not only conscripted as soldiers to fight at a very young age, they are frequently sexually abused and their physical integrity violated.[253]

---

[241] Optional Protocol to the Convention on the Rights of the Child on the involvement of children in armed conflict, New York, 25 May 2000 UN Doc. A/RES/54/263.
[242] Article 2.
[243] Article 1.
[244] See above chapter 16.
[245] Dennis, 'Newly Adopted Protocols to the Convention on the Rights of the Child' 94 *AJIL* (2000) 789 at p. 791.
[246] Article 3(3)(a).
[247] Article 3(3)(b).
[248] Article 3(3)(d).
[249] Article 3(3)(c).
[250] Article 3(2).
[251] Article 4.
[252] Article 22(2) read in conjunction with Article 2 of the African Charter on the Rights and Welfare of the Child; see above chapter 11.
[253] Gardam, 'The Law of Armed Conflict: A Feminist Perspective' in Mahoney and Mahoney (eds), *Human Rights in the Twenty-First Century: A Global Challenge* (Martinus Nijhoff, 1993) pp. 419–436; Elahi, 'The Rights of the Child Under Islamic Law: Prohibition of the Child Soldier' 19 *Columbia Human Rights Law Review* (1988) 259.

Children were abused in some of the most deadly armed conflicts such as the Iran–Iraq war (1980–88) and during the invasion of Kuwait by Iraq. It is reported that in many of the conflicts in countries such as Sri Lanka, Afghanistan and in parts of Africa, children as young as five are being forced to fight. Children are also being used as weapons by extremists in suicide bombings in several regions of the world.

(c) The environment[254]

The relationship as well as the significance of the environment for the development and progression of individual and collective rights has already been examined.[255] War, armed conflicts and civil disturbances pose particular threats to the environment, as it is the environment which frequently becomes a major casualty of wanton destruction.[256] Established principles of international environmental law, such as Principle 21 of the Stockholm Declaration[257] and Principle 2 of the Rio Declaration[258] have been advanced to suggest the protection of environmental rights by States.[259] Existing IHL contains regulations for the preservation and protection of the environment during an armed conflict.

Two treaties, supplemented by three texts provide an overall umbrella for the protection of the environment. According to Article I of the Environmental Modification Convention:[260]

> 1. Each State Party to this Convention undertakes not to engage in military or any other hostile use of environmental modification techniques having widespread, long-lasting or severe effects as the means of destruction, damage or injury to any other State Party.
>
> 2. Each State Party to this Convention undertakes not to assist, encourage or induce any State, group of States or international organization to engage in activities contrary to the provisions of paragraph 1 of this article.

Article II of the Convention goes on to provide that:

> As used in article 1, the term 'environmental modification techniques' refers to any technique for changing – through the deliberate manipulation of natural processes – the dynamics, composition or structure of the Earth, including its biota, lithosphere, hydrosphere and atmosphere, or of outer space.

---

[254] Almond, 'The Use of Environment as an Instrument of War' 2 *YIEL* (1991) 455; Baker, 'Legal Protection for the Environment in Times of Armed Conflict' 33 *VJIL* (1992–3) 351; Desgagne, 'The Prevention of Environmental Damage in Time of Armed Conflicts: Proportionality and Precautionary Measures' 3 *YIHL* (2000) 109; Leibler, 'Deliberate Wartime Environmental Damage: New Challenges for International Law' 23 *Cal.WILJ* (1992–3) 67; Tarasofsky, 'Legal Protection of the Environment during International Armed Conflict' 24 *NYIL* (1993) 17; Verwey, 'Protection of the Environment in Times of Armed Conflict' 8 *LJIL* (1995) 7 and Yuzon, 'Deliberate Environmental Modification through the Use of Chemical and Biological Weapons: "Greening" the International Laws of Armed Conflict to Establish an Environmentally Protective Regime' 11 *AUJILP* (1995–6) 793.

[255] See above chapters 13 and 14.

[256] Article 56, Protocol I.

[257] The Stockholm Declaration on the United Nations Conference on the Human Environment 1972, UN Doc. A/Conf.48/14/Rev. 1 (1973); 11 ILM 1416 (1972).

[258] The Rio Declaration on Environment and Development 1992, UN Doc. A/CONF.151/26 (vol. I); 31 ILM 874 (1992)

[259] Baker, above n.254, at p. 355.

[260] Convention on the Prohibition of Military or Any Other Hostile Use of Environmental Modification Techniques, 1977, 1108 U.N.T.S. 151, entered into force 5 October 1978.

The Convention prohibits States parties from engaging in deliberate, military or hostile modification of the environment. The action must not also result in 'widespread, long-lasting or severe effects'. The Convention is clearly limited in its prohibitions in that the environmental damage has to be widespread.

Protocol I, Geneva Convention 1977 in its Article 35(3) provides 'Basic Rules' and establishes that '[i]t is prohibited to employ methods or means of warfare which are intended, or may be expected, to cause widespread, long-term and severe damage to the natural environment'. Many of the provisions already noted in the Geneva Conventions 1949 could be taken to apply to the environment, with environmental protection reiterated and reaffirmed in Protocol I to the Conventions. Article 55 in providing protection of the natural environment notes that:

1. Care shall be taken in warfare to protect the natural environment against widespread, long-term and severe damage. This protection includes a prohibition of the use of methods or means of warfare which are intended or may be expected to cause such damage to the natural environment and thereby to prejudice the health or survival of the population.

2. Attacks against the natural environment by way of reprisals are prohibited.

Article 35(3) appears to be rather more carefully drafted and repeats the phraseology of the Convention – in that prohibition is for causing 'widespread, long-term and severe damage to natural environment', whereas 'health or survival of the population' in Article 55 is somewhat broader and may also lead to the prohibition on the destruction of the means of subsistence of the population. It has been pointed out that the provisions only apply to international armed conflict.[261] Additional protection for the environment was established through Protocol III to the UN Conventional Weapons Convention, on the use of incendiary weapons. Under Article 2(4):

[i]t is prohibited to make forests or other kinds of plant cover the object of attack by incendiary weapons except when such natural elements are used to cover, conceal or camouflage combatants or other military objectives, or are themselves military objectives.

In 1992, the UN General Assembly adopted without vote a Resolution entitled 'Protection of the Environment in Times of Armed Conflict' where the Assembly emphasised that the destruction of the environment, not justified by military necessity and carried out wantonly, is clearly contrary to existing international law.[262] During the Iran–Iraq war considerable loss to the environment occurred to both sides to the conflict. The Iraqi regime released huge quantities of oil in the Persian Gulf leading to the world's largest ever oil spill.[263] Considerable environmental damage was conducted by Saddam Hussein's regime after its invasion of Kuwait in 1991. As a war tactic, it set fire to over 600 Kuwait

---

[261] Dinstein, above n.1, at p. 189.
[262] UN General Assembly Resolution 47/37 (1992).
[263] Roberts, 'Environmental Issues in International Armed Conflict: The Experience of the 1991 Gulf War' 69 *ILS* 222.

oil wells causing smoke plumes and heavy atmospheric pollution in Kuwait.[264] Iraq was subsequently punished *inter alia* for its crimes against the environment. The United Nations Security Council in its Resolution 687 (1991) stated that Iraq:

> is liable under international law for any direct loss, damage – including environmental damage and the depletion of natural resources – or injury to foreign Governments, nationals and corporations as a result of Iraq's unlawful invasion and occupation of Kuwait.[265]

A Compensation Commission alongside a Compensation Fund were founded by the Security Council Resolution 692 (1991); the Compensation Fund was subsequently used to provide compensation and cost for extinguishing of the fires.[266] Inflicting damage to the environment is categorised as a war crime, and is stated as such by Article 8 of Statute of the International Criminal Court according to which war crimes include '[i]ntentionally launching an attack in the knowledge that such attack will cause . . . widespread, long-term and severe damage to the natural environment which would be clearly excessive in relation to concrete and direct overall military advantage anticipated'.[267] Article 8 provisions have however been criticised for being:

> [a] huge leap backwards by allowing the defence that 'widespread, long-term and sever damage to the natural environment' caused by the perpetrator – not just 'clearly excessive' (perhaps it was excessive, but not 'clearly excessive') in relation to the concrete and direct overall military advantage anticipated.[268]

5 ENFORCING INTERNATIONAL HUMANITARIAN LAW

> [T]he questions at issue in humanitarian law, no matter how varied and complicated, can be reduced to two fundamental problems: viz., the problem of balancing humanity against military necessity, and the obstacles in doing so posed by state sovereignty.[269]

In common with international human rights law, the enforcement of international humanitarian law raises serious difficulties. We have noted the creation of international and national criminal tribunals aimed at individual accountability for serious crimes of international humanitarian law. Such presence has in the experience of Professor Meron in

---

[264] Green, 'The Environment and the Laws of Conventional Warfare' 29 *CYIL* (1991) 222 at p. 233.
[265] SC Resolution 687 (1991), 30 ILM 848, 852 (1991), para 16.
[266] See Alford, 'Well Blowout Control Claim' 92 *AJIL* (1998) 287 at p. 288.
[267] See Article 8(2)(b)(iv) Rome Statute of the International Criminal Court.
[268] Green, above n.264, at p. 233.
[269] Kalshoven and Zegveld, above n.1, at p. 203.

reality 'engendered little demonstrable deterrence'.[270] Having regard to the nature of the violations and the circumstances in which such violations take place, any enforcement of humanitarian norms appears particularly challenging. In the light of these challenges, attempts have been made to establish some, albeit rudimentary, mechanism for enforcing international humanitarian law. States that are parties to the Geneva Conventions (and the Protocols additional to the Conventions) are obliged to follow the provisions of the treaties.[271] Furthermore, States parties are under an obligation to disseminate the knowledge pertaining to the provisions of the Convention.[272] A number of mechanisms have been established. A significant mechanism is through the establishment of 'Protecting Powers' which are to be appointed to oversee the interests of the nationals of any of the States engaged in conflict and under the control of the other, in conditions as POWs or under occupation as civilians. The role of the Protecting Powers includes *inter alia* ensuring compliance with the provisions of humanitarian law, acting as guarantors for the protected persons and acting as a channel of communication with the State to which the detainees belong. This system, however, has many drawbacks: the principal weakness exhibited is in the consensual nature of the arrangement. The Protecting Power, as well as the parties to the conflict, including those whose nationals are under occupation must provide consent.[273] The negotiating strength and capability of the Protected Power is also a very relevant factor. During the Second World War, Switzerland and Sweden acted as Protecting Powers, in many instances not very satisfactorily. In the post-Second World War conflicts further deficiencies have emerged in the system. China's refusal to consent to the appointment of the Protecting Power during its conflict with India (1962), Pakistan's international armed conflict with India and the resulting refusal of India to co-operate on issues of POWs (1971) represent important examples.[274]

Protocol I, additional to the Geneva Conventions, also provides for the establishment of an International Fact-Finding Commission for competence for enquiry into grave breaches of the Geneva Conventions and the Protocols.[275] The mandate of the fact-finding mission includes facilitation through good offices the 'restoration of an attitude of respect' for these treaties. It is also possible for the parties within a conflict to establish an *ad hoc* enquiry into alleged violations of international humanitarian law.[276] The relevance of the International Committee of the Red Cross (ICRC) has already been noted and its institutional position has been established within the Geneva Conventions. The ICRC continues to take a leading role in the implementation processes of international humanitarian law. Operational within internal and international armed conflict, the ICRC has been instrumental in providing support to detainees and civilians, as well as POWs. The role and involvement of the ICRC can be witnessed in many of the current conflicts including those in Iraq, Afghanistan and Sri Lanka.

---

[270] Meron, 'Humanization' (2000) above n.1, at p. 276.
[271] Common Article 1 Geneva Conventions 1949.
[272] See Article 127 and 144 of the Third and Fourth Geneva Conventions, Article 83 of Protocol 1 and Article 19 of Protocol II (1977).
[273] Shaw, above n.1, at p. 1199.
[274] Ibid.
[275] Article 90, Protocol I (1977).
[276] Articles 52, 53, 132, 149 of the Four Geneva Conventions.

6 CONCLUSIONS

A substantial argument which is increasingly becoming a matter of contention is the applicability of human rights norms during armed conflict.[277] The international human rights regime, as examined in earlier chapters, allows for derogation of certain rights in times of emergency and armed conflict. Yet, human rights law contains rights, most prominently contained in the International Covenant on Civil and Political Rights (ICCPR) which are non-derogable and therefore must be applied at all times. The applicability of economic, social and cultural rights also remains effective since the primary Covenant – the International Covenant on Economic, Social and Cultural Rights (ICESCR) – does not contain derogation provisions.[278] International organs, such as the International Court of Justice as well as the Human Rights Committee, have taken the view that human rights, including economic, social and cultural rights, cannot be entirely displaced but should be applicable during times of armed conflict and emergencies.[279] A historic limitation of human rights law is that many of the treaty-based bodies or other monitoring agencies are restricted to reviewing violations of the rights contained within the treaty itself. Thus, the European Court of Human Rights is limited to reviewing rights contained in the ECHR. Similarly, the Human Rights Committee and other treaty-based bodies such as the Committee on Torture are mandated to find violations contained within their respective treaties. In the case of *Isayeva and others*,[280] the European Court of Human Rights, while analysing the situation of a non-international armed conflict, confined its examination to violations of human rights and not IHL. *Ozkan* v. *Turkey* concerned detentions, deaths and

---

[277] Heintze, 'On the Relationship between Human Rights Law Protection and International Humanitarian Law' 86 *International Review of the Red Cross* (2004) 798; Dennis, 'Agora: ICJ Advisory Opinion on Construction of a Wall in the Occupied Palestinian Territory: Application of Human Rights Treaties Extraterritoriality in Times of Armed Conflict and Military Occupation' 99 *AJIL* (2005) 119; Byron, 'Blurring of the Boundaries: The Application of International Humanitarian Law by Human Rights Bodies,' 47 *VJIL* (2007) 839.

[278] ICESCR Committee criticised the Sri Lankan government for the housing and health and nutritional conditions for civilians displaced in the civil war. See Concluding Observation of the Committee on Economic, Social and Cultural Rights, Sri Lanka, E/C.12/1/Add.24 16 June 1998, para 7. The Committee has similarly been critical of economic suffering of the Palestinian by the State of Israel, and of Russia in conditions within Chechnya. See Concluding Observations of the Committee on Economic, Social and Cultural Rights, Israel, E/C.12/1/Add.90 26 June 2003, para 19 and Russia, E/C.12/1/Add.94, 12 December 2003, para 10. The UN Special Rapporteur on the Right to Food during 2002 reported that the use of food was a 'method of warfare against insurgents and civilian populations' by the Myanmar Government. The Special Rapporteur has similarly been critical of situations perpetuated in the Palestinian territory and Afghanistan. E/CN.4/2002/58 Report by the Special Rapporteur on the right to food, Mr. Jean Ziegler, submitted in accordance with Commission on Human Rights resolution 2001/25, 10 January 2002. See also E/CN.4/2004/10/Add.2 31 October 2003 Report by the Special Rapporteur, Jean Ziegler Addendum Mission to the Occupied Palestinian Territories. The Special Rapportuer on the Right to Health has similarly expressed concern on the health of civilians in the city of Falluja after the military operations by US military. E/CN.4/2005/51 2 February 2005, Report of the Special Rapporteur on the right of everyone to the enjoyment of the highest attainable standard of physical and mental health, Paul Hunt, Addendum, Summary of cases transmitted to Governments and replies receives, para 73.

[279] In the *Legal Consequences of the Construction of Wall in the Occupied Palestinian Territory*, the World Court makes the point that 'the Court is of the opinion that the construction of the wall and its associated regime impede the liberty of movement of the inhabitants of Occupied Palestinian Territories (with the exception of Israeli citizens and those assimilated thereto) as guaranteed under Article 12, paragraph 1, of the International Covenant on Political Rights. They also impede the exercise by the persons concerned of the right to work, to health, to education and to an adequate standard of living as proclaimed in the International Covenant on Economic, Social and Cultural Rights . . .' *Legal Consequences of the Construction of a Wall in the Occupied Palestinian Territory* (2004) ICJ Reports 136, para 134.

[280] *Isayeva and others* v. *Russia* (2005) 41 E.H.R.R. 38, 39.

burning of the houses during Turkey's military operation in South-East Turkey.[281] Although several aspects of the case were directly relevant to IHL, the consideration of the case was focused on international human rights law as the court lacked competence in respect of IHL. The Charter-based mechanisms are less restrictive in placing reliance on violations of IHL and international human rights law. Thus, the Special Rapporteurs on various human rights as well as the Charter-based mechanisms are able to complement violations of international human rights and IHL wherever relevant.[282] The UN High Commission for Refugees also uses IHL principles where appropriate. Furthermore, at a regional level the Inter-American Commission on Human Rights:

> has, in effect, gone one step further, explicitly evaluating incidents they have occurred in countries involved in armed conflict, both in terms of human rights and humanitarian law. It has had recourse to rules of humanitarian law both as a device for the interpretation of applicable human rights rules . . . as well as to add an extra basis for decisions that specific conduct has violated fundamental precepts of humanity.[283]

Notwithstanding a narrow approach recently advanced by the European Court of Human Rights, it is established that human rights and IHL obligations have an extra-territorial impact. States could be held liable for violations of human rights and IHL on an extra-territorial basis if they are in effective control of the territory. In its General Comment, the Human Rights Committee makes a note of protecting 'anyone within the power or effective control of that State Party, even if not situated within the territory of the State Party'.[284]

---

[281] *Özkan and others* v. *Turkey* Application no. 21689/93, (Decision of 6 April 2004).
[282] Kalshoven and Zegveld, above n.1, at p. 200.
[283] Kalshoven and Zegveld, above n.1, at p. 200.
[284] General Comment 31 [No. 80] *Nature of the General Legal Obligation Imposed on States Parties to the Covenant: 26/05/2004. CCPR/C/21/Rev.1/Add.13 (General Comments)* para 10.

Torture as a crime in international law and the rights of torture victims[1]

1 INTRODUCTION

One of the most atrocious violations against human dignity is the act of torture, the result of which destroys the dignity and impairs the capability of victims to continue their lives and their activities.[2]

Throughout the present study we have made references to offences of torture, inhuman and degrading treatment or punishment. The pervasive nature of the practices of torture, however, demand a more detailed and thorough investigation. Actions amounting to torture unfortunately are as ancient as human history itself, having been practised in all societies since time immemorial.[3] A historical legal analysis depicts a melancholy picture of the antiquity of this crime. During the 20th century, torture was conducted in various forms. The two World Wars provide tragic examples of torture being conducted during military operations as well as in non-armed conflicts against ordinary civilians. Since the

---

[1] Boulesbaa, *The UN Convention on Torture and Prospects for Enforcement* (Brill, 1999); Burgers and Danelius, *The United Nations Convention against Torture and other Cruel, Inhuman or Degrading Treatment or Punishment* (Brill, 1988); Ginbar, *Why not Torture Terrorists?: Moral, Practical and Legal Aspects of the 'Ticking Bomb' Justifications for Torture* (Oxford University Press, 2008); Harris, *Cases and Materials on International Law* (Sweet & Maxwell, 2004) pp. 758–785; Levinson (ed.), *Torture: A Collection* (Oxford University Press, 2006); Mukherjee, *Torture and the United Nations: Charter and Treaty Based Monitoring* (Cameron May, 2008); Nowak *et al.*, *The United Nations Convention against Torture: A Commentary* (Oxford University Press, 2008); Rodley, *The Treatment of Prisoners under International Law* (Clarendon Press, 1999); Roth, Worden and Bernstein (eds), *Torture: Does it Make us Safer? Is it Ever OK?: A Human Rights Perspective* (New Press, 2005); and Steiner, Alston and Goodman (eds), *International Human Rights in Context: Law, Politics, Morals* (Oxford University Press, 2008) pp. 224–262.

[2] *Vienna Declaration and Programme of Action* adopted by the World Conference on Human Rights, UN Doc. A/CONF.157/23 12, (July 1993) para 55 (pt II).

[3] In providing a historical analysis Nowak presents the following useful summary: 'Torture was practiced by many peoples and in various cultures during different historical periods. Particular brutal and well documented examples were the practices of torture against slaves and Christians during Roman times, against criminal suspects during the Middle Ages, against witches by the Roman Catholic inquisition in Europe, against African slaves in the American hemisphere and against peoples under colonial domination of European Powers in Africa, Asia and Latin America. Although torture, as slavery, was *legally abolished* in Europe and the American hemisphere during the 18th and 19th centuries as a result of the age of enlightenment, natural law, humanism and rationalism, it continued to exist or re-appeared in practice. Most notorious were the systematic and extremely cruel practices of torture under totalitarian regimes of Stalinism and National Socialism before and during the World War II.' Nowak *et al.*, above n.1, at p. 2; see also Rehman, *Weaknesses in the International Protection of Minority Rights* (Kluwer Law International, 2000) pp. 52–75.

end of the Second World War, there have been many instances of gruesome acts of torture. It is also a crime that is currently practised on a regular basis in many States of the world.[4]

Torture is an offence against human dignity, and is rightly regarded as a crime against humanity.[5] Since the establishment of the United Nations in 1945 significant efforts have been made to eradicate acts of torture. The catalogue of international provisions condemning torture is so extensive that it would be impossible to make a comprehensive list. There is currently an array of international documents prohibiting and condemning acts in the nature of torture. Amongst general human rights instruments torture, inhuman or degrading treatment or punishment is prohibited by UDHR,[6] the ICCPR[7] and by the regional human rights mechanisms.[8] The international machinery in the fight against those conducting torture has been supplemented through a variety of related instruments. The whole thrust of international humanitarian law is to attempt (as far as it is possible) to reduce pain, suffering and torture during international and non-international armed conflicts.[9] As has been examined already, forms of torture conducted during international armed conflict or internal conflicts constitute crimes against humanity.[10]

Specific human rights instruments dealing with, *inter alia*, genocide,[11] slavery and the slave trade,[12] racial discrimination,[13] apartheid,[14] children,[15] women[16] and refugees[17] have also condemned acts of torture and violence. We have already noted that the former

---

[4] Boulesbaa, above n.1, at p. 99.

[5] The Statute of the International Criminal Court incorporates torture as a 'crime against humanity'. See Article 7(1)(f). It defines torture as 'the intentional infliction of severe pain or suffering, whether physical or mental, upon a person in the custody or under the control of the accused; except that torture shall not include pain or suffering arising only from, inherent in or incidental to, lawful sanctions' Article 7(2)(e).

[6] Article 5 provides that 'No one shall be subjected to torture or to cruel, inhuman or degrading treatment or punishment'. See above chapter 4.

[7] According to Article 7, 'No one shall be subjected to torture or to cruel, inhuman or degrading treatment or punishment. In particular, no one shall be subjected without his free consent to medical or scientific experimentation'. The Human Rights Committee has established a substantial jurisprudence on this subject. See above chapter 6.

[8] Article 3 ECHR (1950), see above chapter 7; Article 5 ACHR (1969), see above chapter 9; Article 5 AFCHPR (1981), see above Part III

[9] See the Geneva Conventions and the Protocols to these Conventions. In particular note the Common Article 3 of the Conventions. See above chapters 20 and 21.

[10] However, in order to establish crimes against humanity, the underlying requirements for these crimes must be satisfied, i.e. torture must be part of a widespread or systematic practice or attack on a population and the persons conducting such acts must be aware that his actions were constitutive and part of the widespread or systematic practice or attack on a population. See Cassese, *International Criminal Law* (Oxford University Press, 2008) p. 150.

[11] Convention on the Prevention and Punishment of the Crime of Genocide, New York, 9 December 1948, United Nations, *Treaty Series*, vol. 78, p. 277. Considered above chapter 13.

[12] The Supplementary Convention on the Abolition of Slavery, Slave Trade, and Institutions of Slavery and Practices Similar to Slavery, Geneva, 7 September 1956, United Nations, *Treaty Series*, vol. 266, p. 3.

[13] International Convention on the Elimination of All Forms of Racial Discrimination, New York, 7 March 1966 United Nations, *Treaty Series*, vol. 660, p. 195. See above chapter 12.

[14] International Convention on the Suppression and Punishment of the Crime of Apartheid, New York, 30 November 1973, United Nations, *Treaty Series*, vol. 1015, p. 243.

[15] Convention on the Rights of the Child, New York, 20 November 1989 United Nations, *Treaty Series*, vol. 1577, p. 3, Article 37; see above chapter 16.

[16] UN Declaration on the Elimination of Violence against Women, General Assembly Resolution 48/104 of 20 December 1993; Inter-American Convention on the Prevention, Punishment and Eradication of Violence Against Women, 33 I.L.M. 1534 (1994), entered into force 5 March 1995. See above chapter 15.

[17] 1951 Convention Relating to the Status of Refugees 189 U.N.T.S. 150, entered into force 22 April 1954. 1967 Protocol Relating to the Status of Refugees, 606 U.N.T.S. 267, entered into force 4 October 1967.

UN Commission on Human Rights set up a working group on Enforced or Involuntary Disappearances in 1980,[18] which has led to the establishment of the International Convention for the Protection of All Persons from Enforced Disappearances. In 1982 a UN Special Rapporteur was appointed on Summary or Arbitrary Executions followed by the UN Special Rapporteur on Torture in 1985.[19]

In addition to the aforementioned instruments and mechanisms, the United Nations, as this chapter will consider in detail, has established a binding treaty which deals exclusively with the subject of torture, cruel, inhuman or degrading treatment or punishment. This United Nations Convention, known as the UN Convention Against Torture and Other Cruel, Inhuman or Degrading Treatment or Punishment, was adopted on 10 December 1984.[20] The adoption of the Treaty at the universal level provided the impetus for other regional treaties concentrating on torture. In December 1985, the General Assembly of the OAS adopted the Inter-American Convention to Prevent and Punish Torture,[21] and in 1987 the European Convention for the Prevention of Torture and Inhuman and Degrading Treatment or Punishment was approved by the Council of Europe.[22]

The existing prohibitions in treaty law on the subject are strengthened by international customary laws. In an earlier chapter we considered that treaties provide evidence of State practice. An overwhelming acceptance of a treaty may lead to the formation of customary international law, which would be binding on all States. In the case of torture, having regard to the substantial number of ratifications to the treaties concerned with prohibiting torture (combined with the fact that neither the ICCPR nor any of the regional human rights treaties allow any derogations from those articles that deal with the prohibition of torture) provide persuasive evidence that the norm is binding in international law. Furthermore it can also be asserted forcefully that the prohibition on torture is a norm of *jus cogens*, a norm from which no derogation is permissible.[23]

States are bound under international law not only from refraining from torturing their citizens and residents (including those residing on a temporary basis, e.g. visitors) but they are also required to punish those involved in committing this act. Having made this universally accepted statement on the prohibition on torture, there nevertheless remain a number of controversial issues. Firstly, while consensus exists on the prohibition of torture, there are disagreements over the meaning and scope of the term 'torture'.[24] Secondly, there

---

[18] See above chapter 3. See also chapter 23.

[19] See below discussion in this chapter.

[20] Convention against Torture and Other Cruel, Inhuman or Degrading Treatment or Punishment, New York, 10 December 1984 United Nations, *Treaty Series*, vol. 1465, p. 85.

[21] (A-51) O.A.S. *Treaty Series* No. 67, entered into force 28 February 1987, reprinted in Basic Documents Pertaining to Human Rights in the Inter-American System, OEA/Ser.L.V/II.82 doc. 6 rev.1 at 83, 25 I.L.M. 519 (1992). See Kaplan, 'Combating Political Torture in Latin America: An Analysis of the Organisation of Inter-American Convention to Prevent and Punish Torture' 25 *Brooklyn Journal of International Law* (1989) 399; Davidson, 'No More Broken Bodies or Minds: The Definition and Control of Torture in the Late Twentieth Century' 6 *Canterbury Law Review* (1995) 25.

[22] European Convention for the Prevention of Torture and inhuman or Degrading Treatment of Punishment ETS No. 126.

[23] Professor Nigel Rodley makes the valid point that 'it is safe to conclude that the prohibition is one of general international law, regardless of whether a particular state is party to a treaty expressly containing the prohibition. Indeed, it may well be that the same reasons, especially the fact of non-derogability of the prohibition in the human rights treaties, permit acceptance of the view that the prohibition is itself a norm of *jus cogens* or a "peremptory norm of general international law"'. Rodley, above n.1, at p. 74. On the meaning of *jus cogens* norms see above chapter 2.

[24] See Nowak, 'What Practices Constitute Torture?: US and UN Standards' 28 *HRQ* (2006) 809.

are difficulties in identifying the nature of the prohibitions involved in treatment or punishment that is cruel, inhuman or degrading. Societies as well as individuals differ in their perceptions. Thus, some societies view certain punishments as cruel, inhuman or degrading whereas others regard them as a fair and just means of retribution.[25] Issues of cultural relativism are directly relevant to this debate.[26] Thirdly, there are difficulties in implementing and enforcing the prohibition of torture. As this chapter elaborates, while the UN Convention against Torture provides for implementation mechanisms there are several limitations and weaknesses in the system which need to be explored.

2 THE CONVENTION AGAINST TORTURE (TORTURE CONVENTION)

The Convention against Torture is the product of a sustained campaign to respond to growing instances of torture and violence. Many occurrences of torture including those of the treatment of political opponents in the East Bengal civil war (1970), in Chile (1973) and under regimes of men like Idi Amin of Uganda (1971–79) and Francisco Macias Nguema of Equatorial Guinea (1968–79) highlighted the necessity for concerted international action. Like the Convention on the Elimination of All Forms of Discrimination against Women and the International Convention for the Elimination of All Forms of Racial Discrimination, the Torture Convention was preceded by a General Assembly Resolution.[27] In 1977 the now defunct Commission on Human Rights was requested by the General Assembly to draft a Convention against torture and other cruel, inhuman or degrading treatment. These negotiations in the Commission (and in later stages in the General Assembly) took place during 1977–84. Debate centred on a number of areas. These included the implementation of the Convention, and jurisdictional issues such as universal jurisdiction.[28] Agreement was particularly difficult to reach on the scope of the Convention, issues relating to implementation, the competence of the proposed Committee to issue comments, and actions in relation to State reports, as well as the nature of the inquiry procedure.[29] In March 1984, the drafts of the treaty were transmitted to the General Assembly to finalise the document. During much of 1984, the General Assembly worked towards the improvement of the text and agreement on the implementation of the Treaty. A final comprise in the implementation issues was the insertion of an 'opting-out clause' in Article 28 of the Treaty and generalised provisions on 'General Comments' on specific State reports in Article 19(3).[30] The Convention was adopted by the General Assembly on 10 December 1984 – on the 36th anniversary of the adoption of UDHR. The Convention came into operation in 1987 and has currently 146 State parties signed up to it. The Convention is divided into three parts. Substantive rights are contained in Part I (Articles 1–16); within

---

[25] See the Report of the 1982 Working Group, UN Doc. E/CN/1982/L/40 (1982). Text reproduced Addendum UN Doc. E/1982/12/Add.1 (1982) p. 3. On capital punishment see above chapters 5 and 6.

[26] See above chapter 1.

[27] See Declaration on the Protection of All Persons from Being Subjected to Torture and Other Cruel, Inhuman or Degrading Treatment or Punishment adopted by GA Res. 3452 (XXX) of 9 December 1975.

[28] Pennegård, 'Article 5' in Alfredsson and Eide (eds), *The Universal Declaration of Human Rights: A Common Standard of Achievement* (Kluwer Law International, 1999) pp. 121–146 at p. 130.

[29] See Nowak *et al.*, above n.1, at p. 5.

[30] Ibid., at p. 5.

Part II (Articles 17–24) implementation machinery is provided; and Part III, the final part (Articles 25–33) deals with clauses relating to ratification, amendments, etc. Expressing a commitment to making 'more effective the struggle against torture and other cruel, inhuman or degrading treatment or punishment throughout the world', the Preamble of the Convention also makes references to the United Nations Charter,[31] to Article 5 of UDHR and Article 7 of ICCPR. It also refers to the Declaration on the Protection of All Persons from Being Subjected to Torture and Other Cruel, Inhuman or Degrading Treatment or Punishment, adopted by the General Assembly.[32]

(i) Provisions contained in the Convention

Article 1	Definition of torture
Article 2	Obligation on States to take effective legislative, administrative, judicial or other measures to prevent acts of torture
Article 3	Obligation on States not to return or expel people to countries where they may be subjected to torture
Article 4	Obligation upon States to criminalise all acts (and attempted acts) of torture with appropriately severe punishments
Article 5	Obligation upon States to establish jurisdiction over the offences of torture
Article 6	Obligation to take alleged torturers into custody
Article 7	Obligation to extradite or submit case to competent authorities for prosecution
Article 8	Obligation to ensure that extradition is available for tortures
Article 9	Obligation for States parties to afford one another assistance in connection with criminal proceedings in respect of torture, including supply of evidence
Article 10	Obligation to ensure education and information regarding the prohibition against torture
Article 11	Obligation to keep under review interrogation rules and practices for the custody and treatment of persons subjected to any form of arrest, detention or imprisonment, to prevent torture
Article 12	Obligation to proceed to a prompt and impartial investigation in cases of torture
Article 13	Obligation to ensure that the rights of torture victims (including the right to complain and have case heard by competent authorities)
Article 14	Obligation to provide remedies
Article 15	Obligation to exclude evidence obtained through torture
Article 16	Obligation to prevent acts of cruel, inhuman or degrading treatment or punishment (not amounting to torture)

---

[31] Particularly Article 55.
[32] Adopted by General Assembly Resolution 3452 (XXX) of 9 December 1975.

(ii) Defining the concept of 'torture', 'cruel', 'inhuman' or 'degrading treatment' or 'punishment'

A preliminary issue relates to the meaning of the terms of 'torture', 'cruel', 'inhuman' or 'degrading treatment or punishment'. In our survey of the Torture Convention, at the very outset there appears to be a discrepancy; while the Convention defines 'torture', there is no detailed exposition of the terms 'cruel', 'inhuman' 'degrading treatment or punishment'. The Convention defines torture as:

> For the purposes of this Convention, the term 'torture' means any act by which severe pain or suffering, whether physical or mental, is intentionally inflicted on a person for such purposes as obtaining from him or a third person information or a confession, punishing him for an act he or a third person has committed or is suspected of having committed, or intimidating or coercing him or a third person, or for any reason based on discrimination of any kind, when such pain or suffering is inflicted by or at the instigation of or with the consent or acquiescence of a public official or other person acting in an official capacity. It does not include pain or suffering arising only from, inherent in or incidental to lawful sanctions.[33]

A number of issues emerge from this definition. Firstly, the Convention defines and envisages 'torture' as a product of an 'act'. Could an omission with equally serious consequences amount to torture? While the matter was debated during the drafting of the Convention, no clear position seems to have been established. It is submitted that omissions if *intentionally conducted* (e.g. denial of food to prisoners) amount to torture. There is evidence to support this argument from case-law emergent from human rights bodies.[34]

Similar to the debate on the scope of 'an act', controversy surrounds the meaning of 'severe'. During the drafting stages several proposals were made in order to delete the term from the definition.[35] It was, however, retained, with some States expressing the view that pain or suffering must attain a certain threshold before it could amount to torture.[36] There are other limitations in the definition of torture as well. Pain and suffering must be afflicted intentionally and for the purposes listed in Article 1(1) in order to constitute torture. The requirement of specific purpose also distinguishes it from other cruel, inhuman or degrading treatment.[37] Pain and suffering administered as a 'lawful sanction' does not come within the definition of torture, although it may lead to 'cruel, inhuman or degrading treatment or punishment'.[38]

---

[33] Article 1(1).

[34] In *Denmark, Norway, Sweden v. Greece*, Applications No. 3321/67, No. 3322/67, No. 3323/67, No. 3344/67, the European Commission on Human Rights held that 'the failure of the Government of Greece to provide food, water, heating in winter, proper washing facilities, clothing, medical and dental care to prisoners constitutes an "act" of torture in violation of article 3 of ECHR'. See the *Greek Case* Yearbook XII (1969) 1, at p. 461. Also see *Loizidou* v. *Turkey* (Preliminary Objections) (1995) 20 E.H.R.R. 99, para 62.

[35] See the *Report prepared by the Secretariat on the fifth UN Congress on the Prevention of Crime of Torture and the Treatment of Offenders* (1976) p. 38.

[36] See the summary prepared by the Secretary-General in accordance with the Commission Resolution 18 (XXXIV) containing the comments received from governments on the Draft Articles of the Convention on Torture, Commission on Human Rights, thirty-fifth session, UN Doc. E/CN/1314/Add.1 (1979) p. 2.

[37] See Nowak *et al.*, above n.1, at p. 74. There is, however, no need to establish 'systematic' infliction of pain and suffering. Thus as Nowak *et al.* suggest single and isolated acts may also constitute torture, at p. 39.

[38] See Harris, above n.1, at p. 763.

The ambit of torture is limited to those who conduct this activity 'by or at the instigation of or with the consent or acquiescence of a public official or other person acting in an official capacity'. This definition only covers torture conducted by public officials (e.g. police or other agencies established by the State).[39] The public officials also include paramilitary organisations, vigilantes or death-squads. Torture may also be inflicted by private individuals provided that they act on the instigation, consent or acquiescence of State officials. The definition is, however, restrictive in that it excludes acts of torture conducted by non-State actors and private individuals against other individuals or State officials. This appears an unfortunate limitation as many instances of torture can be found where torture is committed by non-State actors or private individuals. The Committee against Torture, however, has expanded the scope of this limitation by pronouncing that torture (or cruel, inhuman or degrading treatment or punishment) could take place in circumstances of the States' inaction and acquiescence in the face of torture (or cruel, inhuman or degrading treatment or punishment) contrary to Article 1 (or Article 16) of the Convention.[40] However,

[39] In *Dragan Dimitrijevic* v. *Serbia and Montenegro* Communication No. 207/2002, UN Doc. CAT/C/33/D/207/2002 (2004), a Serbian citizen of Romani origin was arrested in 1999 in connection with the investigation of a crime. The applicant was taken to a local police station in Kragujevac, where the applicant was seriously beaten by policemen, resulting in his being confined to bed for several days. When the State party failed to provide any information, the Committee accepted the applicant's applications. In deciding that the treatment dispensed to the applicant was akin to 'severe pain or suffering intentionally inflicted by public officials in the context of the investigation of a crime' leading to 'torture within the meaning of article 1 of the Convention', para 5.3. The Committee held that the facts disclosed led to a breach of Article 2(1) in connection with Article 1. In *Jovica Dimitro* v. *Serbia and Montenegro*, Communication No. 171/2000, UN Doc. CAT/C/34/D/171/2000 (2005) para 7.1, the applicant was arrested in 1996 from his home in the province of Vojvodina. No arrest warrant was presented and the applicant was taken to a police station and no reasons were provided for his being taken into custody. The applicant complained of severe beating with the doctor's medical report concluding that 'the patient should be referred to a neurologist and a laboratory for tests'. The applicant, while afraid of reprisals, did not register a complaint. In its decision of May 2005, the Committee took the view that actions conducted against the applicant amounted to torture since the treatment faced by the applicant resulted in severe pain or suffering intentionally inflicted by public officials in the context of investigation of a crime. The Committee found violation of Article 2(1) in connection with Article 1.
[40] *Danilo Dimitrijevic* v. *Serbia and Montenegro*, Communication No. 172/2000, UN Doc. CAT/C/35/D/172/2000 (2005). The complainant was arrested and detained in a police station where he was severely beaten by a man in civilian clothes. During beating sessions a police officer witnessed the activity though made no attempt to stop these beatings. For the next three days, he was subjected to continued detention, denial of food and water and refusal of access to medical attention. The Committee took the view that the facts disclosed violations of Article 2(1), in connection with Articles 1, 12, 13 and 14 of the Convention (para 7.4). The State officials had 'acquiesced' in the beatings and torture conducted by the man in civilian clothes. In order to establish 'acquiescence' evidence need to be provided of complicity or approval (tactic or implicit) in acts of torture and would not be established where the government itself is fighting the rebel group in question; furthermore 'acquiescence' does not equate to an incapacity to take action. In *G.R.B.* v. *Sweden*, Communication No. 83/1997, UN Doc. CAT/C/20/D/83/1997 (1998), the complainant had complained that were she to be deported to Peru there would be a risk of her being tortured by a rebel group based in Peru, and therefore her deportation would constitute a violation of Article 3 of the Convention. The Committee took the view that Article 3 was not triggered since acts of torture by Peruvian non-government rebel groups did not constitute torture within the definition set out in Article 1 of the Convention. The government of Peru could not be said to 'acquiesce' in the acts, or future acts, of a terrorist group that it was actively fighting against. Acts by groups exercising quasi-judicial authority could fall within Article 1 but not where a central government with control exists. See *Elmi* v. *Australia*, Communication No. 120/1998, UN Doc. CAT/C/22/D/120/1998 *(1999)*. (The question was whether if the complainant was forced to Somalia while under threat from the Hawiye clan is this constitutive of torture? The situation in *Elmi* was exceptional since Somalia did not have a recognised government at that time. The Committee responded in the affirmative and held a violation of Article 3 against Austria.) *Cf. H.M.H.I* v. *Australia*, Communication No. 177/2001, UN Doc. CAT/C/28/D/177/2001 (2002), the Committee reached a different conclusion, since in its view there was now an identifiable central government and thus local clan militias no longer classify as 'public officials' for the purposes of Article 1 of the Convention. The risk of torture by such clan militias will therefore no longer activate protection under the Convention unless the government was for some reason involved in such acts of torture.

without the State's acquiescence, it is to be expected that such behaviour by non-State actors would be punishable under national criminal law.

The definition provided in Article 1 also raises the issue of the scope of the crime. The obvious intention of the article is to protect the detainees, in the custody of law enforcement agencies or security forces, etc. The question has been raised as to the scope of torture outside of places of detention, e.g. in public schools or State mental institutions.[41] Andrew Byrnes in suggesting a broader approach notes the possible application of torture to institutions which are not *per se* regarded as places of detention e.g. State-run hospitals, offices and Schools.[42]

Having pointed to the complexities in the definition of torture, the next issue concerns distinguishing torture from other forms of ill-treatment. These distinctions have been scrutinised by some human rights bodies more closely than others (see e.g. ECHR as opposed to ICCPR). Under the Torture Convention, whilst States are under an obligation to prevent acts amounting to cruel, inhuman or degrading treatment or punishment, the distinction is of significance since certain provisions can only apply to torture (see e.g. Article 20). A number of important provisions are only applicable when the offences attain the threshold of torture. These provisions are contained in Articles 3–9, 14 and 15.

The absence of specific definitions of terms other than torture has already been alluded to; there is a similar dearth of analysis of these terms in the general corpus of international human rights law. One strategy adopted by some human rights treaty bodies is that of avoiding the issues of distinctions altogether. Thus, the Human Rights Committee, the European Committee for the Prevention of Torture and the Inter-American Commission has generally avoided distinguishing torture from cruel, inhuman or degrading treatment or punishment.[43] This is possibly a result of the varying notions of torture; a generalised treatment of violations of particular articles is often seen as less controversial. Andrew Byrnes makes the valid point that:

> while it is obviously desirable that international bodies concerned with the prevention and punishment of torture not work at cross purposes, it is also important to keep in mind that there is no one, standard definition of torture and other ill-treatment that applies in every context. What 'torture' means for the work of one body will depend on the text, purpose and history of its enabling instrument, as well as on its own practice and the relevant practice of States.[44]

In the light of these complexities inherent in defining torture, a broad approach is recommended. It would also be useful for CAT (the Committee which implements the Torture Convention) to develop its jurisprudence in the light of related cases from other treaty bodies. The case-law of the Human Rights Committee has been extensive, and provides

---

[41] Byrnes, 'The Committee Against Torture' in Alston (ed.), *The United Nations and Human Rights: A Critical Appraisal* (Clarendon Press, 1992) pp. 509–546 at p. 515.

[42] Ibid. p. 516.

[43] Davidson, 'The Civil and Political Rights Protected in the Inter-American Human Rights System' in Harris and Livingstone (eds), *The Inter-American System of Human Rights* (Clarendon Press, 1998) pp. 213–288 at p. 230.

[44] Byrnes, 'The Committee Against Torture' in Alston (ed.), above n.41, at p. 513.

useful guidelines. The Human Rights Committee has classified physical acts such as beat-ings, punching and kicking,[45] forcible standing for hours,[46] electrocution and shocks,[47] and enforcement of malnutrition and starvation[48] as torture. Other regional bodies have estab-lished that physical beatings,[49] the death penalty,[50] kidnapping,[51] prolonged periods of detention incommunicado,[52] rape,[53] putting hoods on so as to suffocate the victim,[54] mock burials and mock executions,[55] amount to torture. The jurisprudence emerging from the ICTY and the ICTR also confirms the broad definition of torture.[56] It is also firmly estab-lished that torture results not only through physical force, but is also manifested by mental torture and suffering.

Article 2(1) of the Convention creates an obligation on all parties to 'take effective legislative, administrative, judicial or other measures to prevent acts of torture in any territory under its jurisdiction'.[57] A recurring debate, particularly as a consequence of the 'war on terror', has been whether it is ever possible to have exceptions to the prohibitions on torture, cruel, inhumane or degrading treatment or punishment. Could torture ever be justified? Treaty law and customary international law provide an unequivocal answer: torture, as well as cruel, inhuman or degrading treatment could not be inflicted upon any person regardless of the circumstances.[58] Article 2(2) of the Torture Convention in confirming

---

[45] *Miguel Angel Estrella* v. *Uruguay*, Communication No. 74/1980 (17 July 1980), UN Doc. Supp. No. 40 (A/38/40) at 150 (1983); *Linton* v. *Jamaica*, Communication No. 255/1987, UN Doc. CCPR/C/46/D/255/1987 (1992).

[46] *Moriana Hernandez Valentini de Bazzano, Luis Maria Bazzano Ambrosini, Martha Valentini de Massera and Jose Luis Massera* v. *Uruguay*, Communication No. R.1/5 (15 February 1977), UN Doc. Supp. No. 40 (A/34/40) at 124 (1979).

[47] *Alberto Grille Motta* v. *Uruguay*, Communication No. 11/1977 (29 July 1980), UN Doc. CCPR/C/OP/1 at 54 (1984).

[48] *Raul Sendic Antonaccio* v. *Uruguay*, Communication No. R.14/63 (28 November 1979), UN Doc. Supp. No. 40 (A/37/40) at 114 (1982); *Roslik* et al. v. *Uruguay*, Case 9274, Res. No. 11/84, 3 October 1984, OAS/Ser.L/V/II.66, doc.10 rev 1, at 121.

[49] See *Denmark, Norway, Sweden* v. *Greece*, Applications No. 3321/67, No. 3322/67, No. 3323/67, No. 3344/67, 504; *Raul Sendic Antonaccio* v. *Uruguay*, Communication No. R.14/63 (28 November 1979), UN Doc. Supp. No. 40 (A/37/40) at 114 (1982), paras 16(2) and 20.

[50] In its 1993 Resolution on Peru (IACHR) Annual Report 1993, 478, it noted: 'For the Inter-American Commission on Human Rights, there is no premium that can be placed upon human life. The death penalty is a grievous affront to human dignity and its application constitutes cruel, inhuman and degrading treatment of the individual sentenced to death.'

[51] See *Lissardi and Rossi* v. *Guatemala*, Case 10.508, Report No. 25/94, Inter-Am.C.H.R., OEA/Ser.L/V/II.88 rev.1 Doc. 9 at 51 (1995) at 54.

[52] *Velasquez Rodriguez* Case, Judgment of 29 July 1988, Inter-Am.Ct.H.R. (Ser. C) No. 4 (1988).

[53] *Aydin* v. *Turkey* (1998) 25 E.H.R.R. 251, para 86; *Caracoles Community* v. *Bolivia*, Case 7481, Res. No. 30/82, March 8, 1982, Inter-Am. C.H.R., OAS/Ser.L/V/II.57, Doc. 6 Rev. 1, at 20 September 1982, at 36 (1994). and *Raquel Martí de Mejía* v. *Perú*, Case 10.970, Report No. 5/96, Inter-Am.C.H.R., OEA/Ser.L/V/II.91 Doc. 7 at 157 (1996) at 182–188.

[54] *Lovato* v. *El Salvador*, Case 10.574, Report No. 5/94, Inter-Am.C.H.R., OEA/Ser.L/V/II.85 Doc. 9 rev. at 174.

[55] Report on the Human Rights Situation in Chile, Chapter IV, The Right to Personal Integrity, Inter-Am C.H.R. OEA/Ser.L/V/II.66 Doc. 17 9 September 1985, para 38.

[56] See the case of *Furundžija* before the ICTY Trial Chamber *Furundžija*, ICTY, TC II, 10 December 1998 (case No. IT-95-17/1) discussed in Cassese, *International Criminal Law* (Oxford University Press, 2008) at p. 111. For a consideration of jurisprudence of *ad hoc* tribunals see Burchard, 'Torture in the Jurisprudence of the *ad hoc* Tribunals: A Critical Assessment' 6 *Journal of International Criminal Justice* (2008) 159.

[57] Thus a failure to honour the obligations contained in Article 2(1) was conducted when civil guards involved in acts of torture were pardoned by the State party's judicial and political institutions, *Guridi* v. *Spain*, Communication No. 212/2002, UN Doc. CAT/C/34/D/212/2002 (2005), held violations of Articles 2(1), 4 and 14.

[58] See Rodley, 'Prohibition of Torture: Absolute Means Absolute' 34 *DenJIP* (2006) 145.

this prohibition notes that: 'No exceptional circumstances whatsoever, whether a state of war or a threat or war, internal political instability or any other public emergency, may be invoked as a justification of torture.' The jurisprudence of the Committee Against Torture establishes that Article 2 ordains States parties to implement an absolute and unequivocal prohibition on torture; no derogation is permitted from this peremptory norm.[59] Commenting on the provisions, and reiterating the absolute prohibition of torture as provided in Article 2(2), the Committee makes the following stark statements. It establishes:

> Article 2, paragraph 2, provides that the prohibition against torture is absolute and non-derogable. It emphasizes that *no exceptional circumstances whatsoever* may be invoked by a State Party to justify acts of torture in any territory under its jurisdiction. The Convention identifies as among such circumstances a state of war or threat thereof, internal political instability or any other public emergency. This includes any threat of terrorist acts or violent crime as well as armed conflict, international or non-international. The Committee is deeply concerned at and rejects absolutely any efforts by States to justify torture and ill-treatment as a means to protect public safety or avert emergencies in these and all other situations. Similarly, it rejects any religious or traditional justification that would violate this absolute prohibition. The Committee considers that amnesties or other impediments which preclude or indicate unwillingness to provide prompt and fair prosecution and punishment of perpetrators of torture or ill-treatment violate the principle of non-derogability ... The Committee reminds all States parties to the Convention of the non-derogable nature of the obligations undertaken by them in ratifying the Convention. In the aftermath of the attacks of 11 September 2001, the Committee specified that the obligations in articles 2 (whereby 'no exceptional circumstances whatsoever ... may be invoked as a justification of torture'), 15 (prohibiting confessions extorted by torture being admitted in evidence, except against the torturer), and 16 (prohibiting cruel, inhuman or degrading treatment or punishment) are three such provisions that 'must be observed in all circumstances' (See the Committee's observations of 22 November 2001 A/57/54 paras 17–18). The Committee considers that articles 3 to 15 are likewise obligatory as applied to both torture and ill-treatment.[60]

Addressing the situation, whereby torture, or other forms of ill-treatment, is conducted in detention centres which are outside the territory of the State, the Committee in its General Comment makes the following points:

> Article 2, paragraph 1, requires that each State party shall take effective measures to prevent acts of torture not only in its sovereign territory but also 'in any territory under its jurisdiction.' The Committee has recognized that 'any territory' includes all areas where the State party exercises, directly or indirectly, in whole or in part, de jure or de facto effective control, in accordance with international law. The reference to 'any territory' in article 2, like that in articles 5, 11, 12, 13 and 16, refers to prohibited acts committed not only on board a ship or

➡

---

[59] See Nowak *et al.*, above n.1, at pp. 117–118.

[60] See Committee Against Torture, Convention Against Torture and Other Cruel, Inhuman or Degrading Treatment or Punishment, General Comment No. 2 Implementation of Article 2 by States Parties CAT/C/GC/2 (24 January 2008), paras 5 and 6. In 2002, the Committee has expressed concern at the United States report, considering that the United States had authorised interrogation techniques and regretted the implementation of 'confusing interrogation rules' leading to abuses of detainees, justified as 'war on terror' CAT/C7USA/CO/2, para 24. See further discussion below chapter 24.

aircraft registered by a State party, but also during military occupation or peacekeeping operations and in such places as embassies, military bases, detention facilities, or other areas over which a State exercises factual or effective control. The Committee notes that this interpretation reinforces article 5, paragraph 1(b), which requires that a State party must take measures to exercise jurisdiction 'when the alleged offender is a national of the State'. The Committee considers that the scope of 'territory' under article 2 must also include situations where a State party exercises, directly or indirectly, de facto or de jure control over persons in detention.[61]

Furthermore, in establishing this prohibition Article 2 does not permit such defences as Superior Orders.[62]

(iii) Non-expulsions and the Torture Convention

Article 2(1) of the Convention places an obligation on States parties to the Convention to 'take effective legislative, administrative, judicial or other measures to prevent acts of torture in any territory under its jurisdiction'. The obligation is immediate and the emphasis is upon *effective* measures to prevent acts of torture. While these provision are directed towards ensuring that State parties remain under an obligation to ensure effective prevention of torture within their own respective jurisdictions, complications have surfaced where a State decides to expel or extradite individuals to another State in the knowledge that upon their return (to their State of residence or nationality) they are likely to suffer from torture. Such expulsions of non-nationals have been the subject of intense debate in general international law. We have already considered a number of cases whereby the Human Rights Committee and the European Commission and European Court of Human Rights have been confronted with this issue.[63] Article 3 of the ECHR has in particular led to some striking and exceptional decisions where the claimants have successfully relied on the argument that if expelled or extradited they would suffer from torture, inhuman degrading treatment or punishment.[64] Article 3 of the Torture convention inspired by the case-law of the ECHR provides that:

(1) No State Party shall expel, return ('refouler') or extradite a person to another State where there are substantial grounds for believing that he would be in danger of being subjected to torture.

(2) For the purpose of determining whether there are such grounds, the competent authorities shall take into account all relevant considerations including, where applicable, the existence in the State concerned of a consistent pattern of gross, flagrant or mass violations of human rights.

[61] See Committee Against Torture, Convention Against Torture and Other Cruel, Inhuman or Degrading Treatment or Punishment, General Comment No. 2, para 16.
[62] On 'Superior Orders' also see above chapter 20.
[63] See above chapters 4 and 6.
[64] See *Soering* v. *UK* (1989) 11 E.H.R.R. 439; *Chahal* v. *UK* (1997) 23 E.H.R.R. 413.

Article 3 provisions, which are non-derogable in nature, emphasise the fundamental right of *non-refoulement,* which is now considered part of customary international law.[65] Similar provisions can be found in Article 33 of the 1951 Geneva Convention on the Status of the Refugees.[66] However, Article 3 provides a stronger guarantee in that, unlike Article 33 of the Convention on the Status of the Refugees, Article 3 permits no exceptions to the principle of *non-refoulement.*[67] The significance of Article 3 of the Torture Convention is confirmed firstly by the fact that it has been the subject of regular scrutiny by the Committee against Torture (CAT) in its consideration of State reports. Secondly, in recognition of the significance of the provisions contained therein, CAT produced its first 'General Comment' on this Article, and thirdly and most significantly a majority of cases dealt with by CAT relate to this particular Article.

An interesting example of the application of Article 3 is provided *by Alan* v. *Switzerland.*[68] In this case, the author of the communication, Ismail Alan, was a Turkish national who had been involved in political activities in Turkey for the outlawed Marxist-Leninist group KAWA. During 1981–83 he was detained a number of times during which he claimed to have been tortured by the Turkish authorities. He was sentenced in 1984 to two and a half years of imprisonment and was awarded a 10-month period of internal exile for his involvement with the militant organisation KAWA. During 1988 and 1989 he was re-arrested. The author claimed that during this period he was tortured and his house was searched by the Turkish police. In 1990, after having left Turkey on a forged passport, Ismail Alan sought asylum in Switzerland. Despite having produced medical evidence of scars on his body, the Swiss authorities turned down his application on the basis that there were too many inconsistencies in his claim for asylum. Ismail Alan, relying upon Article 3 of the Convention, then complained to the Committee against Torture (CAT). The Committee took account of all the relevant considerations as provided in Article 3(2) of the Convention.[69] It considered that the existing consistent and systematic pattern of serious violations of human rights in Turkey had been confirmed by its own findings in its enquiry under Article 22 of the Convention.[70] According to the Committee, the critical factor in assessing the validity of the claims based under Article 3 was a determination of whether the person in question would be in danger of being subjected to torture upon his return to the country. Specific grounds must exist establishing that the individual concerned would be at risk personally.[71] In upholding the author's claim, the Committee made the following observations:

---

[65] Kjærum, 'Article 14' in Alfredsson and Eide (eds), above n.28, pp. 279–295 at p. 285. However, note that by its nature Article 3 *non-refoulement* provisions are restricted to acts of torture – this is in contrast to Article 7 ICCPR, Article 3 ECHR and Article 5(2) ACHR which are not restricted to torture. See Goodwin-Gill and McAdam, *The Refugee in International Law* (Oxford University Press, 2007) p. 302.

[66] 1951 Convention Relating to the Status of Refugees 189 U.N.T.S. 150, entered into force 22 April 1954. See above chapter 18.

[67] Goodwin-Gill and McAdam, above n.65, at p. 301. The view taken by the Canadian Supreme Court in *Suresh* v. *Canada* [2002] 1 SCR 3, which attempted to balance individuals interests with those of the State's national security has been criticised by the Human Rights Committee 'Consideration of Reports: Concluding Observations on Canada'. UN Doc. CCPR/C/79/Add.105 (7 April 1999), para 13. Also note the position of the European Court of Human Rights in *Selmouni* v. *France* (1999) 29 E.H.R.R. 403, para 95.

[68] *Ismail Alan* v. *Switzerland,* Communication No. 21/1995, UN Doc. CAT/C/16/D/21/1995 (1996).

[69] Paras 11.2 and 11.5.

[70] Para 11.2; see below on Article 22 procedure.

[71] Ibid.

> [i]n the instant case, the Committee considers that the author's [Kurdish] ethnic background, his alleged political affliction, his history of detention, and his internal exile should all be taken into account when determining whether he would be in danger of being subjected to torture upon his return. The State party has pointed to contradictions and inconsistencies in the author's story, but the Committee considers that complete accuracy is seldom to be expected by victims of torture and that such inconsistencies as may exist in the author's presentation of the facts are not material and do not raise doubts about the general veracity of the author's claims.[72]

In its General Comment adopted in 1997, CAT set forth the following useful guidelines as useful in determining the validity of the applicant's claim under Article 3 of the Convention:

> (a) Is the State concerned one in which there is evidence of a consistent pattern of gross, flagrant or mass violations of human rights (see art. 3, para 2)?
>
> (b) Has the author been tortured or maltreated by or at the instigation of or with the consent of acquiescence of a public official or other person acting in an official capacity in the past? If so, was this the recent past?
>
> (c) Is there medical or other independent evidence to support a claim by the author that he/she has been tortured or maltreated in the past? Has the torture had after-effects?
>
> (d) Has the situation referred to in (a) above changed? Has the internal situation in respect of human rights altered?
>
> (e) Has the author engaged in political or other activity within or outside the State concerned which would appear to make him/her particularly vulnerable to the risk of being placed in danger of torture were he/she to be expelled, returned or extradited to the State in question?
>
> (f) Is there any evidence as to the credibility of the author?
>
> (g) Are there factual inconsistencies in the claim of the author? If so, are they relevant?[73]

In another more recent case, *A.S. v. Sweden*,[74] CAT relied on the aforementioned guidelines to decide in favour of an asylum claim brought by an Iranian national. The case concerned an Iranian widow, whose husband had died while performing services for the State. After her husband's death, although provided with greater material support, the complainant was subjected to a strict Islamic code and was forced into a marriage with one of the high ranking Ayatollahs. This marriage, the author complained, was enforced through threats of physical harm to her and her children. The author claimed that while not expected to live with the Ayatollah, she was used for sexual services whenever required. The author subsequently met a Christian man and in her attempts to elope with him was apprehended and allegedly severely beaten and tortured by the police. She was subsequently successful in leaving Iran and on arrival in Sweden submitted an application for asylum. She also submitted that since her departure from Iran she had been awarded the Islamic sentence

---

[72] Para 11.3.
[73] General Comment No. 01: Implementation of article 3 of the Convention in the context of article 22: 21/11/97 A/53/44, annex IX, CAT, para 8.
[74] *A.S. v. Sweden*, Communication No. 149/1999. CAT/C/25/D/149/1999 (1999).

for adultery (stoning to death) and was fearful of the execution of such sentence were she to be returned. The Swedish Immigration board turned down her application for asylum, based on what it perceived as inconsistencies in the author's claim. On her communication before CAT, the Committee in upholding the author's claim noted:

> [c]onsidering that the author's account of events is consistent with the Committee's knowledge about the present human rights situation in Iran, and that the author has given plausible explanations for her failure or inability to provide certain details which might have been of relevance to the case, the Committee is of the view that, in the prevailing circumstances, the State party has an obligation, in accordance with article 3 of the Convention, to refrain from forcibly returning the author to Iran or to any other country where she runs a risk of being expelled or returned to Iran.[75]

In many instances it appears the individual communications system under the Torture Convention is used as a Court of Appeal for unsuccessful asylum claims. In recent cases the Committee has held deportation not to lead to the violation of the Convention, in cases where there is insufficient evidence to prove that the author will be subjected to torture upon their return[76] or when the author has previously failed to seek the protection of the authorities in cases of torture by non-State actors.[77] However, in *Bachan Singh Sogi* v. *Canada*,[78] Canada deported the author prior to the Committee's decision that:

> [i]n the light of the foregoing, and taking account in particular of the fact that the complainant is allegedly a member of what is regarded as a terrorist organization, and that he was wanted in his country for attacks on several public figures in Punjab, the Committee considers that, by the time he was returned, the complainant had provided sufficient evidence to show that he personally ran a real and foreseeable risk of being subjected to torture were he to be returned to his country of origin.[79]

Consequently, Canada had not acted in good faith with regard to its obligations under Article 22 of the Convention by failing to comply with the Committee's requests for interim measures. The Committee, therefore, held that Canada had violated both Articles 3 and 22 of the Convention.[80]

(iv) Torture and the issues of sovereign immunity and universal jurisdiction

The criminalisation of torture is universally acknowledged and in this regard our earlier discussion needs to be recalled. Notwithstanding the prohibition and criminalisation of

---

[75] Ibid. para 9.
[76] *R.K. et al.* v. *Sweden*, Communication No. 309/2006, UN Doc. CAT/C/40/D/309/2006 (2008) para 8.5, *Z.K.* v. *Sweden*, Communication No. 301/2006, UN Doc. CAT/C/40/D/301/2006 (2008), *M.X.* v. *Switzerland*, Communication No. 311/2007, UN Doc. CAT/C/40/D/311/2007 (2008), para 9.6.
[77] *J.A.M.O* v. *Canada*, Communication No. 293/2006, UN Doc. CAT/C/40/D/293/2006 (2008), para 10.6.
[78] Communication No. 297/2006, UN Doc. CAT/C/39/D/297/2006 (2007).
[79] Ibid. para 10.10.
[80] Ibid. para 10.11.

torture, two issues of fundamental importance remain to be considered. Firstly, does there exist universal jurisdiction to try and punish those involved in crimes of torture? Secondly, to what extent can State or governmental officials rely upon their position to claim immunity from any challenges brought by their victims in domestic courts?

International law has struggled to provide definitive answers since both these questions affect the very core of the international legal system, which is based upon State sovereignty. Subsequent discussion aims to highlight the existing tensions through case-law, State practice and the treaty provisions of the UN Convention. A frequently invoked case on the subject is *Filártiga* v. *Peña-Irala*.[81] The case concerned a claim of torture brought in the United States by two Paraguayan refugees against a Paraguayan (former police officer) who was apprehended in the United States. The applicants instituted civil proceedings for damages against the defendant even though the alleged acts of torture took place outside the United States. The plaintiffs claimed that the US court had jurisdiction under the United States Judiciary Act 1789, which establishes original federal court jurisdiction over 'all causes where an alien sues for a tort . . . [committed] in violation of the law of nations.'[82] The United States Circuit Court of Appeal, in confirming the US Courts' jurisdiction to hear the case, noted:

> a threshold question on the jurisdictional issue is whether the conduct alleged violates the law of nations. In the light of the universal condemnation of torture in numerous international agreements, and the renunciation of torture as an instrument of official policy by virtually all of the nations of the world (in principle if not in practice) we find that an act of torture committed by a State official against one held in detention violates established norms of the international law of human rights and hence the law of nations.[83]

In the *Filártiga* case, although the defendant was a former police officer, any defences based on acts conducted in an official capacity were disregarded. The decision in *Filártiga*, in particular the recognition by the Court that torture is prohibited by customary international law, has been widely welcomed and publicised.[84] At the same time the views expressed by the Court must be considered with a hint of caution for two reasons. Firstly, because the Court was dealing with a civil liability (as opposed to criminal liability) action where the 'culprits' were required to compensate for those violations,[85] and secondly, because it does not address the subject of the universality of jurisdiction in the case of torture.[86]

---

[81] 630 F. 2d 876 (1980); 19 ILM 966. US. Circuit Court of Appeals, 2nd Circuit.

[82] 28 U.S.Ct 1350; See Kunstle, '*Kadic* v. *Karadzic*: Do Private Individuals Have Enforceable Rights and Obligations under the Alien Torts Claim Act?' 6 *Duke J. Comparative and International Law* (1996) 319.

[83] *Filártiga*, 630 F.2d 876 (June 30 1980), subsequently, 577 F.Supp. 860 (January 10 1984), and see U.S. amicus brief, 19 I.L.M. 585 (May 29 1980). United States Court of Appeals for the Second Circuit No. 79-6090, Per Circuit Judge, Kaufman, part II.

[84] See Blum and Steinhardt, 'Federal Jurisdiction over International Human Rights Claims: The Alien Tort Claims Act after *Filártiga* v. *Peña-Irala*' 22 *Harvard Int.L.J.* (1981) 53.

[85] Cassese, *International Criminal Law* (Oxford University Press, 2003) at p. 8.

[86] Rodley notes that the case: 'did not deal, however, with the intractable question of when an international law prohibition, even one that requires penal action by States to repress violations, becomes one that requires or permits universality of criminal jurisdiction' and that 'it must be remembered that *Filártiga* case was one of civil, not criminal law. There is no reason to conclude that criminal liability would not also be the case, but as yet there is no state practice to endorse the point. Indeed, the chances of establishing such a practice will be rare: evidence is hard to come by in torture cases, especially in cases heard outside the country where the torture took place; other rules of international law (such as the Geneva Conventions, . . . , or rules of diplomatic immunity) may inhibit the exercise of universal criminal jurisdiction.' Rodley, above n.1, at pp. 128–129 (footnotes omitted).

The enforcement of the Torture Convention appears to have addressed some of these uncertainties. The thrust of the Convention against Torture is directed towards any individual committing acts of torture. The holding of official or public positions is, therefore, not an excuse or justification for conducting torture. In other words, as Lord Browne-Wilkinson noted in the *Pinochet* case[87] 'the notion of a continued immunity for ex-heads of States is inconsistent with the provisions of the Torture Convention' and that torture, as established by the Convention, 'cannot be a State function'.[88]

The Convention also sets out jurisdictional principles. Article 5 in establishing a multi-jurisdictional system provides that:

> 1. Each State Party shall take such measures as may be necessary to establish its jurisdiction over the offences referred to in article 4 in the following cases:
>   (a) When the offences are committed in any territory under its jurisdiction or on board a ship or aircraft registered in that State;
>   (b) When the alleged offender is a national of that State;
>   (c) When the victim is a national of that State if that State considers it appropriate.

Under the provisions of Article 5(1), States parties are required to establish criminal jurisdiction in cases of torture where torture is conducted in its territory;[89] relying upon the nationality principle, when the offender is its national;[90] and relying upon the passive personality principle, where the victims have the State's nationality.[91] The provisions in Article 5(1) are reinforced by Article 5(2) according to which:

> [e]ach State Party shall likewise take such measures as may be necessary to establish its jurisdiction over such offences in cases where the alleged offender is present in any territory under its jurisdiction and it does not extradite him pursuant to article 8 to any of the States mentioned in paragraph I of this article.

Article 5(2) and Article 7 of the Convention place an obligation upon the State either to extradite the alleged torturers or to submit their case to the competent authorities to prosecute them.[92]

The existence of multi-State grounds of jurisdiction as provided in the Torture Convention has often been equated with 'universal jurisdiction'.[93] Such a view, however, remains questionable, since in the absence of attaining the status of customary international law

---

[87] *R. v. Bow Street Metropolitan Stipendiary Magistrate Ex p. Pinochet Ugarte (No. 3)*, (HL) 24 March 1999, [1999] 2 WLR 827.

[88] Ibid. at p. 847.

[89] Article 5(1)(a) CAT.

[90] Article 5(1)(b) CAT.

[91] Article 5(1)(c) CAT.

[92] Rodley, above n.1, at p. 129.

[93] See Burgers and Danelius, above n.1, at pp. 132–133; According to Professor Harris, '[s]ignificantly, the Convention grounds for criminal jurisdiction include universality jurisdiction; it is sufficient that "the alleged offender is present" in its territory for the Convention to apply Article 5(2)'. Harris, above n.1, at p. 763.

the jurisdictional provisions only bind States parties to the treaty.[94] Some commentators have suggested that under the Torture Convention, the multi-State jurisdiction 'would permit *all* States, including those not parties to the convention against torture to prosecute or extradite torturers found in their territory'.[95] Others however have questioned this approach. According to Boulesbaaa:

> [t]he term 'universal jurisdiction' . . . does not connote the same technical meaning as 'universal jurisdiction' over piracy in which any State may prosecute the pirate if it obtains personal jurisdiction over him regardless of whether it has any connection with the crime or the pirate. The multi-State jurisdiction in the Torture Convention merely connotes 'a multiplicity of jurisdictions' limited to the State parties of the Torture Convention which is intended to deny torturers any safe haven in such States. It does not include those States not party to the Torture Convention.[96]

He goes on to make the point that:

> the multi-State jurisdiction provided in Articles 5 and 7 of the Torture Convention is not identical with the Universal jurisdiction over piracy in which all States of the world have an equal interest so that any State can exercise its jurisdiction over the pirate if it has obtained personal jurisdiction over him, regardless of whether or not it has any connection with or with the crime. It is limited to State parties to the Torture Convention, although other States not parties can still exercise jurisdiction over the offenders of torture under their national laws, as in the *Filártiga* case where the U.S., at that time was not a party to the Torture Convention.[97]

This position appears to be affirmed by Professor Nowak in his recent exhaustive study on the Convention against Torture.[98] Nowak's and Boulesbaa's arguments appear persuasive in the light of the high profile case concerning General Pinochet. In its second substantive hearing in the House of Lords, although their Lordships relied upon a range of sources from general international law and came to deny blanket immunity to General Pinochet, they nevertheless limited the scope of the offence of torture and conspiracy to the committing of torture after 8 December 1988.[99] The majority of their Lordships recognised that

---

[94] On treaty provisions as binding in customary international law see above chapter 2.

[95] Rogers, 'Argentina's Obligations to Prosecute Military Officials for Torture' 20 *Columbia Human Rights Law Review* (1988–89) 259, pp. 289–290, n.154.

[96] Boulesbaa, above n.1, at p. 205.

[97] Ibid. p. 234.

[98] Nowak discusses a number of cases under the subject of universal jurisdiction, in which a significant majority includes those where States parties in fact refused to exercise the principle of 'universal jurisdiction'. See Nowak *et al.*, above n.1, at pp. 289–308.

[99] The Pinochet saga raised remarkable interest and provoked substantial legal questions concerning *inter alia* the immunity of a former head of State for perpetuating crimes against humanity and torture. General Augusto Pinochet who had remained in power in Chile until 1990, visited the United Kingdom on a private visit in September 1988. Whilst in the UK, Pinochet's extradition was sought by Spanish authorities to stand trial for alleged atrocities he had committed while in power in Chile. On 16 October 1988 an international arrest warrant was issued against Pinochet, with a magistrate in London issuing provisional warrant under the provisions of s.8 of the Extradition Act 1989. The Queen's Bench Division quashed the 16 October warrant as well as a subsequent arrest warrant on the basis of immunity of Heads of State. In the light of the significance of the case, leave of appeal to House of Lords was granted to the Crown Prosecution Service. In its first hearing, the House

jurisdiction in so far as UK courts were concerned, was established from the time of the incorporation of the Convention into UK law.[100] The Law Lords agreed on this position in reliance upon the principle of double-criminality. The principle requires an act to constitute a criminal offence both under Spanish and UK law at the time when it was committed. Since retrospective effect was impermissible, for a majority of their Lordships, the relevant date was 8 December 1988 – this was the date when all three countries involved (i.e. the United Kingdom, Spain and Chile) were bound by the provisions of the Torture Convention.[101] However, the issue also raised confusion. Thus, according to Lord Brown-Wilkinson:

> [t]he *jus cogens* nature of the international crime of torture justifies states in taking universal jurisdiction over torture wherever committed. International law provides that offences *jus cogens* may be punished by any state because the offenders are 'common enemies of all mankind and all nations have an equal interest in their apprehension and prosecution' . . . In the light of the authorities to which I have referred (and there are many others) I have no doubt that long before the Torture Convention of 1984 state torture was an international crime in the highest sense.[102]

Having made these substantial comments, he goes on to say that:

> [n]ot until there was some form of universal jurisdiction for the punishment of the crime of torture could it really be talked about as a fully constituted international crime. But in my judgment the Torture Convention did provide what was missing: a worldwide universal jurisdiction. Further, it required all member states to ban and outlaw torture.[103]

Lord Millet, who dissented on jurisdictional issues, claimed that torture had already been recognised as a crime under international law by 1973, when General Pinochet seized

of Lords by a majority of three votes to two held that Pinochet did not have immunity from trial in respect of prosecution of crimes under international law – see *R. v. Evans ex p. Pinochet Ugarte (No. 1)*, (HL) 25 November 1998, [1998] 3 WLR 1456. This judgment, however, was set aside on the basis of the improper constitution of the Appellate Committee of the House of Lords. The failure of Lord Hoffmann to declare his interest in Amnesty International led to setting aside of the judgment – see *R. v. Bow Street Stipendiary Magistrates and others ex parte Pinochet Ugarte (No. 2)* [1999] 2 WLR 272 (*Pinochet II*). The Appellate Committee of the House of Lords was reconstituted which delivered a final judgment – see *R. v. Bow Street Metropolitan Stipendiary Magistrate ex parte Pinochet Ugarte (No. 3)* [1999] 2 WLR 827. For a useful commentary on *Pinochet* cases see Chinkin, 'Regina v. Bow Street Stipendiary Magistrates, Ex Parte Pinochet Ugarte (No. 3) [1999] 2 WLR 827' 93 *AJIL* (1999) 703. For a subsequent successful conviction procured through the adoption of the universal jurisdiction (the first of its kind within the United Kingdom) see *R. v. Zardad*, High Court Judgment of 19 July 2005. The case is discussed by Nowak *et al.*, above n.1, at pp. 305–308.

[100] Incorporation of the treaty effected through s.134 of the Criminal Justice Act 1998. The minority view was that English courts had jurisdiction from 29 September 1988, the date when s.134 came into force. See Birnbaum, 'Pinochet and Double Criminality' *Criminal Law Review* (2000) 127 at p. 128. In its application of the double criminality principle, the House of Lords interpreted the Extradition Act 1989 as requiring the conduct alleged by requesting State to have been an offence within the UK law at the time of the Commission of the act – for criticism of such interpretation see Birnbaum, above.

[101] See Chinkin, above n.99, at p. 705; Bianchi, 'Immunity vs Human Rights: the Pinochet Case' 10 *EJIL* (1999) 237 at p. 243.

[102] *R. v. Bow Street Metropolitan Stipendiary Magistrate ex parte Pinochet Ugrate (No. 3)* [1999] 2 WLR 827, [2000] 1 AC 147, p. 198.

[103] Ibid. pp. 204–205.

power.[104] In his view, the *jus cogens* nature of the prohibition of torture and its recognition as a crime under international law, sanctioned individual States and, in this case, the United Kingdom to invoke universal jurisdiction. He notes:

> [t]he jurisdiction of English criminal courts is usually statutory, but is supplemented by the common law. Customary international law is part of common law and accordingly . . . the English courts have and always have had extraterritorial criminal jurisdiction in respect of crimes of universal jurisdiction and customary international law.[105]

A detailed consideration of the judgments delivered by their Lordships in the *Pinochet* cases highlight the existence of a lack of clarity, not only regarding issues of the jurisdiction of domestic courts, but also in relation to the subject of immunities as a whole. The Pinochet cases related to the immunity of a former Head of State – perhaps less of a controversial subject – though subsequent domestic UK and international courts have been confronted with the question of immunities of current office holders.

In *Al-Adsani* v. *Government of Kuwait*,[106] the plaintiff, who had been tortured by the members of the Kuwaiti Royal Family, brought a civil action for damages against the Government of Kuwait (the first defendant) and individual members of the Royal Family (as second, third and fourth defendants). In dismissing the appeal insofar as it related to the first defendant, the Court of Appeal relied upon the limitations of State immunity as provided by the State Immunity Act 1978. While leave to appeal to the House of Lords was refused, it was, however, advised that the plaintiff petition the European Court of Human Rights.[107] The European Court of Human Rights, in distinguishing *Al-Adsani* from the *Furundzija* and *Pinochet* cases, took the view that *Al-Adsani* did not concern the criminal liability of an individual for allegedly conducting acts of torture. This case was, instead, about State immunity in a civil suit for damages in relation to alleged acts of torture committed outside the jurisdiction of the State. While recognising the special character of the prohibition of torture within international law, the Court was nevertheless 'unable to discern in the international instruments, judicial authorities or other materials before it any firm basis for concluding that, as a matter of international law, a State no longer enjoys immunity from civil suit in the courts of another State where acts of torture are alleged'.[108] In upholding the English Court of Appeal's reliance on the State Immunity Act 1978, the Court made the following observations:

> while noting the growing recognition of the overriding importance of the prohibition of torture, [the Court] does not accordingly find it established that there is yet acceptance in international law of the proposition that States are not entitled to immunity in respect of civil claims for damages for alleged torture committed outside the forum State. The 1978 Act, which grants immunity to States in respect of personal injury claims unless the damage was caused within the United Kingdom, is not inconsistent with those limitations generally accepted by the community of nations as part of the doctrine of State immunity.[109]

---

[104] Ghandhi and Barker, 'The *Pinochet* Judgment: Analysis and Implications' 40 *Indian Journal of International Law* (2000) 657, at p. 678; Provost, *International Human Rights and Humanitarian Law* (2002) at p. 109.

[105] [2000] 1 AC 147 p. 276.

[106] *Al-Adsani* v. *Kuwait* (1996) 107 I.L.R. 536.

[107] Squires, 'English Courts and International Law: the Pinochet and Al-Adsani cases' *Cov. L.J.* (2002) 13 at p. 16.

[108] *Al-Adsani* v. *UK* (2002) 34 E.H.R.R. 11, Judgment para 61.

[109] Ibid. para 66.

The civil law versus criminal law dichotomy was further raised by the House of Lords in *Jones* v. *Saudi Arabia*.[110] In this case, the plaintiffs brought a claim against a number of defendants including the Head of the Ministry of Interior, a captain and a lieutenant in the Saudi Arabian police force, and a colonel in the Ministry of Interior and the deputy governor of a prison facility. The House of Lords decided that individual governmental officials equated to the acts of the Saudi State when adjudicating upon the issue of sovereign immunity. Sovereign immunity against alleged acts of torture, therefore, barred an action against the State or its governmental actions. Lord Bingham made the following observations:

> It is certainly true that in *Pinochet (No .1)* and *Pinochet (No .3)* certain members of the House held that acts of torture could not be functions of a head of state or governmental or official acts. I have some doubt about the value of the judgments in *Pinochet (No. 1)* as precedent, save to the extent that they were adopted in *Pinochet (No. 3)*, since the earlier judgment was set aside, but references may readily be found in *Pinochet (No. 3)*: see, for example, p. 205 (Lord Browne-Wilkinson), pp. 261–262 (Lord Hutton). I would not question the correctness of the decision reached by the majority in *Pinochet (No. 3)*. But the case was categorically different from the present, since it concerned criminal proceedings falling squarely within the universal criminal jurisdiction mandated by the Torture Convention and did not fall within Part 1 of the 1978 Act. The essential ratio of the decision, as I understand it, was that international law could not without absurdity require criminal jurisdiction to be assumed and exercised where the Torture Convention conditions were satisfied and, at the same time, require immunity to be granted to those properly charged. The Torture Convention was the mainspring of the decision, and certain members of the House expressly accepted that the grant of immunity in civil proceedings was unaffected: see p. 264 (Lord Hutton), p. 278 (Lord Millett) and pp. 280, 281, 287 (Lord Phillips of Worth Matravers). It is, I think, difficult to accept that torture cannot be a governmental or official act, since under Art. 1 of the Torture Convention torture must, to qualify as such, be inflicted by or with the connivance of a public official or other person acting in an official capacity. The claimants' argument encounters the difficulty that it is founded on the Torture Convention; but to bring themselves within the Torture Convention they must show that the torture was (to paraphrase the definition) official; yet they argue that the conduct was not official in order to defeat the claim to immunity.[111]

Al-Adsani, *Jones* and a number of similar decisions spell considerable disappointment.[112] The International Court of Justice has attempted to provide guidelines, which it has to be conceded – also appear disappointing.[113] In the *Case Concerning the Arrest Warrant of 11 April 2000 (Democratic Republic of Congo v. Belgium)* before the ICJ, a Belgian judge had issued an arrest warrant *in absentia* against the then incumbent Foreign Minister of the Democratic

---

[110] *Jones* v. *Ministry of Interior Al-Mamlaka Al-Arabyia AS Saudiya* [2006] UKHL 26. Ibid. para 19.

[111] Ibid. para 19.

[112] *Bouzari* v. *Islamic Republic of Iran* [2002] OJ No. 1624; see Novogrodsky, 'Immunity for Torture: Lessons from *Bouzari* v. *Iran*' 18 *EJIL* (2008) 939.

[113] *Arrest Warrant of 11 April 2000 (Democratic Republic of Congo v. Belgium)*, Judgment 14 February 2002, (2002) ICJ Reports 3. For commentaries on the case see Cassese 'When May Senior State Officials Be Tried for International Crimes? Some Comments on the *Congo* v. *Belgium* Case' 13 *EJIL* (2002) 853; Wouters 'The Judgment of the International Court of Justice in the Arrest Warrant Case: Some Critical Remarks' 16 *LJIL* (2003) 253; Rispin 'Implications of Democratic Republic of the *Congo* v. *Belgium* on the Pinochet Precedent: a Setback for International Human Rights Litigation?' 3 *Chicago Journal of International Law* (2002) 527.

Republic of Congo, Abdulaye Yerodia Ndombasi. In the warrant Mr. Ndombasi was charged with having committed war crimes and crimes against humanity, allegedly committed during 1998 while acting as the Principal Private Secretary of the late President, Laurent Kabila. At the time of the issuance of the arrest warrant, Mr. Ndombasi was not within Belgium territory, although Belgium purported to exercise universal jurisdiction *in absentia*.[114]

The Government of the Democratic Republic of Congo initiated proceedings against Belgium before the World Court, claiming that the issuance of the arrest warrant breached the principles of sovereign immunity and jurisdiction within international law. Belgium acknowledged that governmental minsters, whilst in office, enjoyed immunity from jurisdiction before foreign courts although the point was made that 'such immunity applies only to acts carried out in the course of their official functions, and cannot protect such persons in respect of private acts or when they are acting otherwise than in the performance of their official functions'.[115]

In recognising the principle of absolute immunity enjoyed by governmental officials the Court set out the following rather unhelpful criteria:

> 60. The Court emphasizes, however, that the *immunity* from jurisdiction enjoyed by incumbent Ministers for Foreign Affairs does not mean that they enjoy *impunity* in respect of any crimes they might have committed, irrespective of their gravity. Immunity from criminal jurisdiction and individual criminal responsibility are quite separate concepts. While jurisdictional immunity is procedural in nature, criminal responsibility is a question of substantive law. Jurisdictional immunity may well bar prosecution for a certain period or for certain offences; it cannot exonerate the person to whom it applies from all criminal responsibility.

> 61. Accordingly, the immunities enjoyed under international law by an incumbent or former Minister for Foreign Affairs do not represent a bar to criminal prosecution in certain circumstances. First, such persons enjoy no criminal immunity under international law in their own countries, and may thus be tried by those countries' courts in accordance with the relevant rules of domestic law. Secondly, they will cease to enjoy immunity from foreign jurisdiction if the State which they represent or have represented decides to waive that immunity. Thirdly, after a person ceases to hold the office of Minister for Foreign Affairs, he or she will no longer enjoy all of the immunities accorded by international law in other States. Provided that it has jurisdiction under international law, a court of one State may try a former Minister for Foreign Affairs of another State in respect of acts committed prior or subsequent to his or her period of office, as well as in respect of acts committed during that period of office in a private capacity. Fourthly, an incumbent or former Minister for Foreign Affairs may be subject to criminal proceedings before certain international criminal courts, where they have jurisdiction. Examples include the International Criminal Tribunal for the former Yugoslavia, and the International Criminal Tribunal for Rwanda, established pursuant to Security Council resolutions under Chapter VII of the United Nations Charter, and the future International Criminal Court created by the 1998 Rome Convention. The latter's Statute expressly provides, in Article 27, paragraph 2, that '[i]mmunities or special procedural rules which may attach to the official capacity of a person, whether under national or international law, shall not bar the Court from exercising its jurisdiction over such a person'.

---

[114] Nowak *et al.*, above n.1, at p. 302.
[115] See *Case Concerning the Arrest Warrant* para 49.

The court, in taking this position, was obviously influenced by – as it indeed mentions in its judgment – the Statutes of the International Criminal Tribunal for Yugoslavia (Article 7(2)) and the International Criminal Tribunal for Rwanda (Article 6(2)). The Court's approach could also be applied to the case involving Mr. Charles Taylor, the former President of Liberia. Charles Taylor was elected President of Liberia in 1997, though he was subsequently indicted for having supported rebels in war against humanity and war crimes and torture during armed conflict in Sierra Leone. The tribunal that indicted Mr. Taylor was of an exceptional nature, having been created by the UN Security Council Resolution 1315 (2000) of 14 August 2000 and based on an agreement between the United Nations and the State of Sierra Leone.[116] Article 6(2) of the Statute of the Tribunal – the Special Court for Sierra Leone (SCSL) – provides that '[t]he official position of any accused persons, whether as Head of State or Government or as a responsible government official, shall not relieve such person of criminal responsibility nor mitigate punishment'.[117] Before the SCSL, Mr. Taylor's counsel raised a purported defence of immunity based on the assertion that as an incumbent Head of State at the time of the commencement of proceedings against him, he enjoyed immunity. At the time of the appeal, Mr. Taylor was no longer President of Liberia and resident in Nigeria.[118] This defence of immunity from prosecution was rejected by the Appeals Chamber on the basis that SCSL was a product of an agreement between the United Nations and Sierra Leone, and was therefore an expression of the will of the international community.[119]

The exceptional nature of this agreement revoked any arguments based on immunity for former Heads of State for crimes against humanity, including the crime of torture.[120] After a UN Security Council Resolution and an order by the President of the Special Court which ordered a change in venue of the trial for security reasons, Charles Taylor was transferred to the Hague, where his trial started on 4 June 2007. The Trial Chamber had heard the testimony of over 80 prosecution witnesses.[121] On May 2009 a defence motion for Charles Taylor's acquittal was dismissed by the Trial Chamber. At the time of writing, his trial continues in the Hague.

The right to a remedy and reparation is granted only to the victims of torture and/or the dependants of these victims. This right of remedy is provided by Article 14(1) of CAT. Article 16, which deals with other forms of ill-treatment, while making reference to Articles 10, 11, 12 and 13, does not make an explicit reference to Articles 3, 14 and 15. However, the view of the commentators as well as the practice of the Committee suggest that such limitations are not precise.[122] Article 16 deploys the terminology 'in particular' thereby suggesting the coverage of a broader range of rights. In *Dzemajl et al. v. Yugoslavia*, the Committee relying upon the term 'prevent' cruel, inhuman or degrading treatment, as contained in Article 16(1), ruled that Article 14 was also applicable to Article 16 violations. The Committee noted:

---

[116] UN Security Council, *Security Council resolution 1315 (2000) [on establishment of a Special Court for Sierra Leone]*, 14 August 2000. S/RES/1315 (2000).

[117] For commentaries on SCSL see Shaw, *International Law* (Cambridge University Press, 2008) pp. 418–420; Cryer, 'A "Special Court" for Sierra Leone?' 50 *ICLQ* (2001) 435.

[118] *Prosecutor* v. *Charles Ghankay Taylor*, Appeals Chamber (31 May 2004) SCSL-2003-0I-059, para 1.

[119] *Prosecutor* v. *Charles Ghankay Taylor*, Appeals Chamber (31 May 2004) SCSL-2003-0I-059, para 38.

[120] Ibid. para 50.

[121] For up-to-date information see www.sc-sl.org/Taylor.html <last visited 8 January 2009>.

[122] For analysis see Nowak *et al.*, above n.1, at pp. 485–487.

that the scope of application of the said provision only refers to torture in the sense of article 1 of the Convention and does not cover other forms of ill-treatment. Moreover, article 16, paragraph 1, of the Convention while specifically referring to articles 10, 11, 12, and 13, does not mention article 14 of the Convention. Nevertheless, article 14 of the Convention does not mean that the State party is not obliged to grant redress and fair compensation to the victim of an act in breach of article 16 of the Convention. The positive obligations that flow from the first sentence of article 16 of the Convention include an obligation to grant redress and compensate the victims of an act in breach of that provision. The Committee is therefore of the view that the State party has failed to observe its obligations under article 16 of the Convention by failing to enable the complainants to obtain redress and to provide them with fair and adequate compensation.[123]

3 THE COMMITTEE AGAINST TORTURE (CAT)[124]

Part II (Articles 17–24) of the Convention deals with the implementation of the treaty. Article 17, establishes a Committee against Torture (CAT) which consists of 10 independent experts. CAT, alongside the Committee on the Rights of the Child, represents the smallest of the treaty-based bodies in the UN system. The small size of the CAT is arguably a consequence of its relatively specific mandate and increasing financial constraints. These members of CAT are of high moral standing and are well known for their knowledge and competence in human rights law.[125] They serve on the CAT in their personal capacity and are elected for a term of four years.[126] They are eligible for re-election if re-nominated.[127] The Committee members are elected by the States parties although consideration is provided to equitable geographical distribution and to the expertise (in particular legal experience) of the individuals.[128]

The Committee members are elected by secret ballot from a list of persons nominated by States parties.[129] Each State party is allowed to nominate one person from amongst its nationals.[130] In nominating individuals for membership to the Committee, States parties are required to consider the usefulness of persons who are also members of the Human Rights

---

[123] No. 161/2000, para 9.6.

[124] Dormenval, 'UN Committee against Torture: Practice and Perspectives' 8 *NQHR* (1990) 26; Byrnes, 'The Committee Against Torture' in Alston (ed.), above n.41, at pp. 509–545; O'Flaherty, *Human Rights and the UN: Practice before the Treaty Bodies* (Brill, 2002) at pp. 124–146.

[125] Article 17(1) Convention Against Torture.

[126] Ibid. Article 17(5).

[127] Ibid. Article 17(5). Article 17(3) of the Convention provides that 'Elections of the members of the Committee shall be held at biennial meetings of States Parties convened by the Secretary-General of the United Nations. At those meetings, for which two thirds of the States Parties shall constitute a quorum, the persons elected to the Committee shall be those who obtain the largest number of votes and an absolute majority of the votes of the representatives of States Parties present and voting'. The current committee members are: Belmir, Essadia (Morroco, term ending 2009); Gaye, Adboulaye (Senegal, 2011); Felice Gaer (US, 2011) Gallegos Chiriboga, Luis (Ecuador, 2011) Claudio Grossman (Chile, 2011); Alexandre Kovalev (Russian Federation, 2009); Fernando Mariño Menendez (Spain, 2009); Kleopas, Myrna Y (Cyprus, 2011); Sveaass, Nora (Norway, 2009); Wang, Xuexian (China, 2009).

[128] Article 17(1)(2) Convention Against Torture.

[129] Ibid. Article 17(2).

[130] Ibid.

Committee established under the ICCPR and who are willing to serve on the CAT.[131] There is, at present, no overlap of membership. Unlike most other treaty-based bodies, it is the State parties and not the United Nations who are responsible for the expenses related to the meetings of the Committee which includes staffing and other facilities. This feature was modelled on CERD, although in the latter case the costs of the Secretariat are provided for from the United Nations budget.[132] The financial liabilities on State parties potentially discourage them from ratifying the treaty. There is also the danger that States could in a way hold the Committee 'to ransom'. As States parties go into arrears, there also remains the uncertainty about the prospect of future sessions. Article 18 authorises the Committee, *inter alia*, to formulate its own rules of procedures, which according to the Article must establish a quorum of six members. The decisions of the Committee are to be made by a majority vote by the members present. Since May 1999, the Committee has had a three-week session in April/May of each year and a two-week session in November.[133] Recent years have seen the November session stretched to almost three weeks.

22

Torture as a crime in international law and the rights of torture victims

4 IMPLEMENTATION MECHANISMS

Four methods of monitoring implementation are provided in the Convention. These comprise: firstly, of the reporting procedure; secondly, of an inter-State complaints procedure; thirdly of an individual complaints procedure; and fourthly, through the initiation of enquiry and the reporting of acts of systematic torture. The reporting procedure is the only compulsory procedure, others being optional; the inquiry procedure cannot be rendered compulsory since there remains the possibility of States parties 'opting-out' under the provisions of Article 28. We shall be dealing with each of these mechanisms in greater detail in the remainder of this chapter. The implementation mechanisms and the monitoring functions of the Committee are further elaborated by the Rules of Procedure (RoP) which are adopted by the Committee in accordance with Article 18(2) of the Convention.

(i) Reporting procedures[134]

Article 19 of the Convention deals with the reporting system, a procedure largely modelled on Article 40 of the ICCPR.[135] According to Article 19(1), each State party is obliged to submit a report within one year after the entry into force of the Convention. These reports are to be submitted to the Committee via the UN Secretary-General.[136] States parties are

---

[131] Ibid.

[132] Byrnes, 'The Committee Against Torture' in Alston (ed.), above n.41, at p. 521.

[133] See UN Doc. A/54/44.

[134] See references above n.1; in addition see Bank, 'Country-Oriented Procedures under the Convention against Torture: Towards a New Dynamism' in Alston and Crawford (eds), *The Future of UN Human Rights Treaty Monitoring* (Cambridge University Press, 2000) at pp. 145–174; Shaw, *International Law* (Cambridge University Press, 2008) at pp. 326–330; Byrnes, 'The Committee against Torture' in Alston (ed.), above n.41, at p. 509; Dormenval, above n.24.

[135] See Nowak *et al.*, above n.1, at p. 625.

[136] Article 19(1) Convention against Torture.

required to report 'on the measures they have taken to give effect to their undertakings under this Convention'.[137] As noted above, periodic reports are to be submitted once every four years or at the request of the Committee. CAT is given, *inter alia*, the task of providing consideration to State reports. In its initial phase CAT held two regular sessions every year, each lasting for two weeks. During each of the sessions on average five to seven reports are considered.[138] However, and as noted above, since its 10th session in May 1998 the duration of the annual April–May session has been extended to three weeks, which has allowed to the Committee to consider up to 10 reports.[139] The November session has also recently been extended to nearly three weeks.[140]

As in the case of other treaty bodies there is an enormous amount of reluctance in submitting reports as it opens the way for public criticism of State compliance.[141] At the same time, CAT also faces a back-log of reports to examine that have been submitted and, in the case of reports that are examined, pressure of time often does not allow a thorough or adequate discussion. CAT, like other human right treaty bodies, has issued reporting guidelines to States parties. The guidelines for initial reports are of a very similar nature to that of the Human Rights Committee. In order to reduce complexity all the treaty-based bodies have issued consolidated guidelines for the introductory sections of both the initial and periodic State reports. States are invited to submit the same document as a core document for responding to all the reports. The guidelines and the form and content of initial and periodic reports can be found online.[142] Insofar as the initial guidelines are concerned, CAT requests that in the introductory part (Part A) reports should contain cross-references to the core document (e.g. general political nature, legal framework regarding human rights protection, etc.). In the second part (Part B), it is anticipated that States will provide information on an article-by-article basis as regards legislative, administrative and other measures which are in force, giving effect to the provisions of the Convention as well as providing details of the difficulties experienced by States parties in the implementation of the Convention. The guidelines for periodic reports require that the first part provide information on new developments in the period subsequent to the previous report, which relates to the implementation of the Convention as stated in Article 1–16. It is anticipated that Part II will contain information requested by CAT, which had not previously been provided to the Committee during its consideration of State reports. Finally, Part III, should contain information on measures taken by the State party to comply with the recommendations and conclusions of CAT at the end of its previous report (either initial or periodic). As indicated earlier, CAT faces many of the issues confronted by other treaty bodies (e.g. a growing backlog with overdue reports, inadequate reports or failure to provide additional information). The reports that have, thus far, been submitted (like reports submitted to other treaty bodies) have been variable in quality and relevance of information and length.

---

[137] Ibid.

[138] Bank, 'Country-Oriented Procedures under the Convention against Torture: Towards a New Dynamism' in Alston and Crawford (eds), above n.134, at p. 147.

[139] Ibid. p.149.

[140] Note e.g. the November 2008 session duration (3–21 November 2008) and the November 2007 session (5–23 November 2007).

[141] CAT has considered (without implementing) plans of discussing Convention's implementation in relation to the States that have not submitted reports. Ibid. p. 148.

[142] Initial reports (CAT/C/4/Rev.3, 18 July, 2005) and Periodic Reports (CAT/C/14/Rev. 1, 2 June 1998).

(ii) Procedure for the consideration of reports[143]

During each session, CAT selects the reports which will be considered and examined in the next session. The normal course is to select State reports based on the chronological order of submission. At the same time, CAT accords priority to initial reports *vis-à-vis* periodic reports. The procedure for the consideration of the State reports is similar to that adopted by other treaty bodies. It is the norm that one member of CAT acts as the Country Rapporteur and another as Co-Rapporteur (also known as alternate Country Rapporteur). The task of these members is to consider the reports in detail, to identify key issues, and to formulate a list of questions and comments to be put forward to the State representatives. In order to formulate his views the Country Rapporteur relies upon the State report itself, on any previous reports, on information received from the Special Rapporteur on Torture and from NGOs.[144]

As from 2002 – a practice initiated by CAT and now followed by all of the treaty bodies except for CERD – pre-sessional Working Groups are developed to formulate lists of questions.[145] These lists, which present a focus for further questioning, are sent to the government ahead of the review of the State report.[146] CAT considers State reports in public sessions. It is customary to devote two public meetings to the consideration of a State report.[147] An initial half day is followed by the afternoon of the following day being spent on this exercise. In the first initial meeting CAT invites a State representative to introduce the report.[148] The outline by the State representative is followed by questions put to him or her by the Committee members. These questions are usually initiated by the Country Rapporteur or Co-Rapporteur. Once Committee members have spoken, made comments or raised questions on the report, the State representative is provided with an opportunity to respond. The representative, if unable to answer the questions, appears before the Committee at the subsequent meeting to address the issues. At this subsequent meeting, CAT members may pose additional questions. The Committee then formulates what are termed as 'Conclusions and Recommendations' or 'Concluding Observations/Comments'.[149] These Conclusions and Recommendations, while synthesising the Committee's views of the report and the overall situation pertaining to torture, consist of an introduction, positive aspects of the report, factors and difficulties impeding the application of the provisions of

[143] See O'Flaherty, above n.124, at pp. 124–146; Bayefsky, *Report: The UN Human Rights Treaty System: Universality at the Crossroads* (2001); Committee Against Torture, *Working Methods. Overview of the working methods of the Committee Against Torture* www2.ohchr.org/english/bodies/cat/workingmethods.htm#a2 <last visited 30 December 2008>.

[144] O'Flaherty, above n.124, at p. 132.

[145] Working Methods of the Committee Against Torture. III. A. Pre-Sessional Working Group, www2.ohchr.org/english/bodies/cat/workingmethods.htm#a3a <last visited 6 December 2008>; Farrior, 'International Reporting Procedures' in Hannum (ed.), *Guide to International Human Rights Practice* (Transnational Publishers, 2004) pp. 189–215, at p. 199. CERD continues with its practices of appointing one of its members to act as Rapporteur for each country that is being reviewed, ibid. 199.

[146] Ibid.

[147] Working Methods of the Committee Against Torture. III. B. Constructive Dialogue, www2.ohchr.org/english/bodies/cat/workingmethods.htm#a3a <last visited 6 December 2008>.

[148] CAT RoP allow the Committee to consider a report in the absence of representation of the relevant State party. This however takes place where there is a failure of the State representative to present him or herself without providing any adequate/satisfactory reasons. RoP, Rule 66(2).

[149] Working Methods of the Committee Against Torture. III. C. Concluding Observations/Comments, www2.ohchr.org/english/bodies/cat/workingmethods.htm#a3a <last visited 6 December 2008>.

Torture as a crime in international law and the rights of torture victims

22

the Convention, subjects of concern and recommendations.[150] In order to provide strength to its concluding observations, in 2002, CAT amended its Rules of Procedure to provide authorisation to itself to appoint one or more Rapporteurs to follow up on a reporting State's 'compliance with the Committee's conclusions and recommendations'.[151] As a consequence of this authorisation, during 2002, CAT nominated two of its members as Rapporteurs with the decision that:

> these rapporteurs would seek information as to a State party's implementation of and compliance with the Committee's conclusions and recommendations upon the former's initial, periodic or other reports, and/or would urge the State party to take appropriate measures to that end. The rapporteurs would report to the Committee on the activities they have undertaken pursuant to this mandate.[152]

In 2003, during the Committee's 30th session, it was decided to set up a Working Group on overdue reports. The Working Group invites representatives of permanent missions in Geneva and seeks to assist in the drafting of the Report. In the course of such meetings, State representatives are also warned of the possibility that the Committee might consider the situation pertaining to torture in the Country even in the absence of a submission – a decision which is the product of the revised Rules of Procedure, Rule 65(3). According to Rule 65(3), the Committee is able to inform a State of its intention to examine the measures which have been undertaken by the State as regards the subject matter of torture and make general comments even in the absence of a submitted report.[153]

Like the Human Rights Committee and other treaty bodies, CAT is authorised to make 'General Comments'.[154] The authority for formulating these 'General Comments' is based on the same premise as the one provided for other treaties. CAT has, thus far, utilised its authority in this regard very cautiously adopting two General Comments: one on Article 3 and the more recent one on the implementation of Article 2 of the Convention.[155] Under its Rules of Procedure, Rule 62, CAT invites NGOs to submit information that is relevant to the Convention. This information is usually produced in writing. As already noted, such information can prove instrumental to CAT members in their review of State reports. NGO delegations are also authorised to brief CAT members orally during the course of the sessions. Such briefings are arranged outside of the formal process of meetings of the Committee and are also limited to CAT members only. CAT has also adopted the practice of informing national human rights institutions of the relevant country as regards consideration of their country's report and has invited written submissions from national human rights institutions.

---

[150] Rule 68, Rules of Procedure, UN Doc. HRI/GEN/3/Rev.3 28 May 2008. For recent examples see Conclusions and Recommendations of the Committee against Torture: China (21/11/2008) CAT/C/CHN/CO/4. Kazakhstan (21/11/2008) CAT/C/KAZ/CO/2. Kenya (21/11/2008) CAT/C/KEN/CO/1.

[151] Report of the Committee Against Torture, 1 November 2002, A/57/44 at Annex X (Amended Rule of Procedure 68(1)); See O'Flaherty, 'The Concluding Observations of United Nations Human Rights Treaty Bodies' 6 *Human Rights Law Review* (2006) 27 at p. 47.

[152] Report of the Committee Against Torture, 1 November 2002, A/57/44 at Annex X (Amended Rule of Procedure 68(1), para 15.

[153] CAT/C/SR.260, para 14; CAT/C/SR.521, paras 33–37; CAT/C/SR.525, paras 12–15. See Nowak *et al.*, above n.1, at p. 642.

[154] See Article 19(3) Convention against Torture.

[155] The Committee Against Torture, *General Comment No. 1. – Implementation of article 3 of the Convention in the context of article 22* A/53/44 (21 November 1997) *General Comment No. 2 – Implementation of Article 2 by States Parties* CAT/C/GC/2 (24 January 2008).

(iii) Inter-State procedure

Article 21 provides for an inter-State complaints procedure, and has distinct similarities to the provisions of Article 41 of ICCPR. Although part of the same convention, the procedure is optional with States interested in using this mechanism being required to make an additional declaration.[156] For the procedure to be operative, the complainant State and the State against whom the complaint is made must have made a declaration under Article 21.[157]

To pursue this procedure a State (A) that considers another State (B) is violating the Convention can bring that fact to the attention of the State party concerned (i.e. State B). State B must respond to the allegations within three months.[158] If, however, within six months the matter has not been resolved since the receipt of the initial communication either State may bring the matter to the attention of the Committee.[159] The Committee must decide whether all local remedies have been exhausted (unless they are unreasonably prolonged or are unlikely to bring effective relief to the victim) before considering the case in closed sessions.[160] The Committee's task is to make an attempt to resolve the dispute through its good offices.[161] In order to pursue its functions of conciliation the Committee may appoint an *ad hoc* Conciliation Commission. The provision relating to the establishment of the Commission is similar to the one provided in Article 41 of ICCPR. However, unlike ICCPR, the procedures or mechanisms of the Conciliation Commission are not addressed in this Convention. The Committee is obliged to produce a written report within 12 months of the date of receipt of notice of the complaint.[162] If a solution is reached then the Committee's report will be brief and confined to facts and the solution reached.[163] If a friendly solution has not been reached then the Committee is required to confine its report to a brief statement of facts. The written submissions and a record of the oral submissions made by the States parties are to be attached to the report.[164] In our study we have considered that inter-State mechanisms have been put in place in several human rights instruments.[165] While occasional usage has been made of the inter-State procedures (see e.g. the ECHR), by and large, States remain reluctant to use these procedures. This reluctance derives largely from a concern of straining diplomatic and political relations. Nor do States wish to establish a precedent, which may ultimately be used against themselves.[166] It is, therefore, not surprising to notice that CAT has not received an inter-State complaint. The inter-State procedure under Article 21 has been recently reconfirmed as 'the weakest' amongst the various monitoring mechanisms under the Convention.[167]

---

[156] Article 21(1) Convention against Torture.
[157] Ibid.
[158] Ibid. Article 21(1)(a).
[159] Ibid. Article 21(1)(b).
[160] Ibid. Article 21(1)(c)(d).
[161] Ibid. Article 21(1)(e).
[162] Ibid. Article 21(1)(h).
[163] Ibid. Article 21(1)(h)(i).
[164] Ibid. Article 21(1)(h)(ii).
[165] See e.g. the ICCPR; Race Convention and the three Regional treaties (European, Inter-American and African).
[166] See Leckie, 'The Inter-State Complaint Procedure in International Human Rights Law: Hopeful Prospects or Wishful Thinking?' 10 *HRQ* (1988) 249.
[167] Nowak *et al.*, above n.1, p. 701.

(iv) Individual complaints procedure

Article 22 provides for the individual complaints procedure. According to Article 22(1):

> A State Party to this Convention may at any time declare under this article that it recognizes the competence of the Committee to receive and consider communications from or on behalf of individuals subject to its jurisdiction who claim to be victims of a violation by a State Party of the provisions of the Convention. No communication shall be received by the Committee if it concerns a State Party which has not made such a declaration.

The individual complaints procedure is optional and requires that States parties make an additional declaration to recognise the competence of the Committee to receive and consider communications. As of 31 March 2009, 64 States had made declaration under Article 22.[168] Like the inter-State procedure described above, the individual complaints procedure is also modelled very closely on the First Optional Protocol to ICCPR, and the Rules of Procedure adopted by CAT largely mirror those adopted by the Human Rights Committee. There are a number of distinctions between the Optional Protocol and Article 22 which need to be highlighted. Firstly, under Article 22(1) the Communication can be made either by or on behalf of the individual, provided there is evidence of authorisation on the part of the victim him or herself.[169] By contrast, the wording of the First Optional Protocol is restrictive in that it only allows the Human Rights Committee to consider communications from 'individuals'.[170] In practice, however, as we have considered in an earlier chapter, the Human Rights Committee has allowed others to petition on behalf of the victim in circumstances where the victim himself is unable to petition (e.g. the victim is being held incommunicado, there is strict mail censorship, or there is an incapacitating illness of the victim consequent to his detention or the victim's death has occurred as a result of a State's actions or omissions).[171]

It is also noticeable that while the provisions of Article 22(1) of the Torture Convention authorise communications to be made on behalf of the victims, the position regarding submissions by NGOs remains uncertain.[172] Thus far, there appears to be only two communications which have been submitted by an NGO,[173] although there are over a dozen

---

[168] The Committee had 366 communications, including 72 living cases, 59 inadmissible cases, 89 discontinued, 47 cases containing no violation and 109 cases disclosing violations. www2.ohchr.org/english/bodies/cat/stat3.htm <last visited 6 April 2009>.

[169] See CAT Rules of Procedure 107(a); ICCPR, First Optional Protocol procedure as discussed above chapter 6.

[170] Ibid.

[171] See *Herrera Rubio* v. *Colombia*, Communication No. 161/1983, UN Doc. Supp. No. 40 (A/43/40) at 190 (1988); *Miango* v. *Zaire*, Communication No. 194/1985, UN Doc. Supp. No. 40 (A/43/40) at 218 (1988). See Ghandhi, *The Human Rights Committee and the Right of Individual Communication: Law and Practice* (Dartmouth Publishing Co, 1998) at p. 85.

[172] According to one source, NGOs may be entitled to take cases where they can 'justify their acting on the victim's behalf'. See UN Centre for Human Rights, Fact Sheet No. 17, *The Convention against Torture*.

[173] *X (name deleted)* v. *Spain*, Communication No. 23/1995, UN Doc. CAT/C/15/D/23/1995 (1995). In a communication submitted by Spanish Refugee Aid Commission in the absence of the alleged victim, the communication was held inadmissible but not because it did not fall within the ambit of the Convention. In respect of the Spanish Refugee Aid Commission representing the alleged victim the case was held to be admissible, para 7.2. In other cases NGOs have represented the alleged victims but not *in absentia*. See for example: *Mr. Bouabdallah Ltaief* v. *Tunisia*, Communication No. 189/2001, UN Doc. CAT/C/31/D/189/2001 (2003). *Jovica Dimitrov* v. *Serbia and Montenegro*, Communication No. 171/2000, UN Doc. CAT/C/34/D/171/2000 (2005). *Radivoje Ristic* v. *Yugoslavia*, Communication No. 113/1998, UN Doc. CAT/C/26/D/113/1998 (2001). The Committee found violations of Articles 12 and 13 in respect of Milan Ristic (deceased).

cases in which the victim has been explicitly stated to have been represented by an NGO as counsel.[174]

Like the Human Rights Committee acting under the Optional Protocol to the ICCPR, CAT has also not allowed *actio popularis* submissions to be made.[175] In *B.M'B* v. *Tunisia*,[176] a communication on behalf of a dead victim was held inadmissible since the author of the communication was not able to establish sufficient evidence of authority to act on behalf of the deceased victim.[177] Secondly, according to the provisions of Article 22, the same matter must also not have been (and must not currently be being) considered under another international procedure.[178] Thus, CAT is ineligible to hear cases already examined by, for example, the European Court of Human Rights or the Human Rights Committee. However it does not affect those situations considered under the current Human Rights Council procedures or those situations under the consideration of the Special Rapporteur on Torture. Similarly it would not be affected by a consideration of such bodies as the UN Expert Mechanism on the Rights of Indigenous Peoples or the Independent Expert on Minority Issue.[179] In affirming the limited remit of this provision, in at least two cases the concerned State parties have failed to plead that cases have been inadmissible as a consequence of a general situation already under consideration by the Special Rapporteurs or the former Commission on Human Rights.[180] Finally, unlike the First Optional Protocol procedure whereby the Human Rights Committee is restricted to taking account of 'written' information, CAT can consider all the information made available to it by or on behalf of the individual and the State party.[181]

Article 22 also provides the admissibility requirements, which are similar to those of the other treaty bodies. Thus, the communications must not be anonymous.[182] Nor should

---

[174] N. D. *(name deleted)* v. *France*, Communication No. 32/1995, UN Doc. CAT/C/15/D/32/1995 (1995); *D* v. *France*, Communication No. 45/1996, UN Doc. CAT/C/19/D/45/1996 (1997); *E.H.* v. *Hungary*, Communication No. 62/1996, UN Doc. CAT/C/22/D/062/1996 (1999); *I. A. O.* v. *Sweden*, Communication No. 65/1997, UN Doc. CAT/C/20/D/65/1997 (1998); *Z.T. (name withheld)* v. *Norway*, Communication No. 127/1999, UN Doc. CAT/C/23/D/127/1999 (2000); *S. C. (name withheld)* v. *Denmark*, Communication No. 143/1999, UN Doc. CAT/C/24/D/143/1999 (2000); *E.T.B.* v. *Denmark*, Communication No. 146/1999, UN Doc. A/57/44 at 117 (2002); *Hajrizi Dzemajl* et al. v. *Yugoslavia*, Communication No. 161/2000, UN Doc. CAT/C/29/D/161/ 2000 (2002); *Bouabdallah Ltaief* v. *Tunisia*, Communication No. 189/2001, UN Doc. CAT/C/31/D/189/2001 (2003); *Imed AbdellI* v. *Tunisia*, Communication No. 188/2001, UN Doc. CAT/C/31/D/188/2001 (2003); *Dhaou Belgacem Thabti* v. *Tunisia*, Communication No. 187/2001, UN Doc. CAT/C/31/D/187/2001 (2003); *Hanan Ahmed Fouad Abd El Khalek Attia* v. *Sweden*, Communication No. 199/2002, UN Doc. CAT/C/ 31/D/199/2002 (2003); for further discussion and analysis see Lindblom, *Non-Governmental Organisations in International Law* (Cambridge University Press, 2006) at pp. 234–235.
[175] Joseph, Mitchell, Gyorki and Benninger-Budel, *Seeking Remedies for Torture Victims: A Handbook on the Individual Complaints Procedure of the UN Treaty Bodies* (OMCT Handbook Series vol. 4, 2006), at p. 54 www.omct.org/pdf/UNTB/2006/handbook_series/vol4/eng/handbook4_full_eng.pdf?PHPSESSID=84a328cf b055df39fb8894c7ee573174 <last visited 21 May 2009>.
[176] *Faïsal Barakat and Family.* v. *Tunisia*, Communication No. 14/1994, UN Doc. A/50/44 at 70 (1995).
[177] *Radivoje Ristic* v. *Yugoslavia*, Communication No. 113/1998, UN Doc. CAT/C/26/D/113/1998 (2001). The Committee found violations of Articles 12 and 13 in respect of Milan Ristic (deceased). However, in *Michael Osaretin Akhimien* v. *Canada*, Communication No. 67/1997, UN Doc. CAT/C/21/D/67/1997 (1998), the Communication was held inadmissible due to the failure to exhaust domestic remedies (and not due to the inability to establish sufficient evidence to act on the deceased victim's behalf).
[178] Article 22(5) Convention against Torture.
[179] Flaherty, above n.124, (2002), at p. 143.
[180] *Z.Z.* v. *Canada*, Communication No. 123/1998, UN Doc. CAT/C/26/D/123/1998 (2001); *Mutombo* v. *Switzerland*, Communication No. 13/1993, UN Doc. CAT/C/12/D/13/1993 (1994).
[181] Article 22(4) CAT.
[182] Article 22(2) CAT.

they be an abuse of the right of submission of such communications[183] or in any manner incompatible with the provisions of this Convention.[184] The individual, before making a communication, must also have exhausted all domestic remedies unless they are ineffective or unreasonably prolonged.[185] The Committee has taken the view that a delay of 15 months in investigating alleged torture is unreasonably prolonged.[186] As regards the burden of proof, CAT has refused to accept sweeping generalisations by authors as insufficient evidence of exhausting domestic remedies;[187] it has required the authors of the communication to establish a *prima facie* evidence of having exhausted domestic remedies. Those communications, which are held inadmissible because of the non-exhaustion of domestic remedies, can be re-submitted once domestic remedies have been exhausted.[188] At the same time a genuine (although ill-directed) effort to invoke domestic remedies has been held as satisfying the admissibility requirement.[189] Even in cases where a communication is deemed inadmissible for its failure to exhaust domestic remedies, there remains the possibility that it subsequently be held admissible if the exhaustion of domestic remedies can be established.[190]

The procedure for handling communications is very similar to that operated by the Human Rights Committee. The Communication should provide all the material information. In its 28th session, the Committee revised the Rules of Procedure to establish the Rapporteur for new complaints and interim measures. On receipt of the Communication, the Rapporteur, the Committee or the Secretary General of the United Nations registers the complaint, but:

2. No complaint shall be registered by the Secretary-General if:

(a) It concerns a State which has not made the declaration provided for in article 22, paragraph 1, of the Convention; or

(b) It is anonymous; or

(c) It is not submitted in writing by the alleged victim or by close relatives of the alleged victim on his/her behalf or by a representative with appropriate written authorization.[191]

---

[183] Ibid.

[184] Ibid.

[185] Article 22(5)(b) Convention against Torture. According to the revised Rule 107(f) of CAT Rules of Procedure 'the time elapsed since the exhaustion of domestic remedies in not so unreasonably prolonged as to render consideration of the claims unduly difficult by the Committee or the State party'. CAT/C3/Rev.4

[186] *Halimi-Nedzibi* v. *Austria*, Communication No. 8/1991, UN Doc. A/49/44 at 40 (1994), para 6.2.

[187] See *R.E.G* v. *Turkey*, Communication No. 4/1990 reported in UN Doc. A/46/46 (In this case the alleged victim had taken no action to seek redress at the domestic level and had presented the argument that he had no hope of receiving justice in Turkey, the Committee held the communication inadmissible for failure to exhaust domestic remedies).

[188] *N. D. (name deleted)* v. *France*, Communication No. 32/1995, UN Doc. CAT/C/15/D/32/1995 (1995), paras 5–6.

[189] See *Henri Unai Parot* v. *Spain*, Communication No. 6/1990, UN Doc. A/50/44 at 62 (1995). See also *I.U.P* v. *Spain*, Communication No. 6/1990 reported in UN Doc. A/48/44 Annex VI.

[190] *N. D. (name deleted)* v. *France*, Communication No. 32/1995, UN Doc. CAT/C/15/D/32/1995 (1995), paras 5–6.

[191] Rule 98 Rules of Procedure.

After being screened the complaint is allocated to a member of CAT who is known as the Special Rapporteur.[192] In practice the Special Rapporteur seeks the information on both the admissibility and merits of the case.[193] When the Special Rapporteur has collated all the relevant information, the case is put before the Committee. The Committee brings the matter to the attention of the concerned State. The concerned State is required to respond within six months by submitting written explanations or statements clarifying the matter and any remedies that have been undertaken.[194] The Committee then considers communications received under this article in the light of all information that is made available to it by or on behalf of the individual and by the State party concerned.[195] There is an opportunity for the author of the communication and the State party to further their case or to defend it at both the admissibility and merit stages.[196] Depending on the nature of the issues raised, the Special Rapporteur, as well as the Committee, can request the relevant State take appropriate action – such as interim measures – to protect the alleged victim.[197] Urgent requests for interim measures are advanced in instances where there is a threat of deportation to a State where the complainant risks torture or other serious and irreversible threat.[198] The Committee regards compliance with the provisional measures as 'essential in order to protect the person in question from irreparable harm, which could, moreover, nullify the end result of the proceedings before the Committee'.[199]

To initiate the procedure under Article 22, complaints need to be sent in writing to the Secretariat. In accordance with the Rules of Procedure, Rule 98 complaints can be entertained by the Committee, by the Secretariat or by the Rapporteur for New Communications. Interim measures, in practice, are usually registered by the Rapporteur in accordance with the Secretariat's recommendation. On registration, the Secretariat briefs complainants on further procedures.[200] The conditions of registration are provided in Article 98 in the Rules of Procedure and Article 22.[201] At the admissibility stage, the author of the Communication is given four weeks on issues regarding admissibility and six weeks at the merit stage to comment and to provide further evidence to substantiate his or her case. CAT may also seek relevant information from other international agencies and UN specialised agencies.[202]

The Committee may make a decision to combine the decision on admissibility and merit.[203] CAT goes on to consider the case on its merits in the light of all available information.[204] The Committee makes decisions in closed meetings during its examination of the questions, and after consideration forwards its 'views' – which are in fact described as decisions – to the relevant State party and the individual.[205] There are no sanctions attached

---

[192] Rules 98, 106(3) Rules of Procedure.
[193] Rule 107 Rules of Procedure.
[194] Article 22(3) Convention against Torture and Rule 109(1) Rules of Procedure.
[195] Rule 112(1) Rules of Procedure.
[196] Rules 109(10) and 111(4) Rules of Procedure.
[197] Rule 108 Rules of Procedure.
[198] Rule 108 Rules of Procedure.
[199] *T.P.S.* v. *Canada*, Communication No. 99/1997, UN Doc. CAT/C/24/D/99/1997 (2000), para 16.1.
[200] Rule 99(5) Rules of Procedure.
[201] Lewis-Anthony and Scheinin, 'Treaty-Based Procedures for Making Human Rights Complaints within the UN System' in Hannum (ed.), above n.145, at pp. 43–63 at p. 58.
[202] Rule 112(2) Rules of Procedure.
[203] Rule 112 Rules of Procedure.
[204] Rule 112(1) Rules of Procedure.
[205] Rule 112(4) and (5) Rules of Procedure.

to the failure of the concerned State for not respecting the views of CAT or indeed interim measures. The Committee reaches its decisions by consensus, although members are free to append individual opinions.[206] Once the Committee has reached a decision, the views are forwarded both to the State party and the individual concerned. According to the Rules of Procedure, the State party is invited to inform the Committee of actions it has undertaken to act in conformity with the Committee's views 'within a specified time'. CAT has developed a follow-up procedure in its attempts to encourage compliance of its views by State parties.

The Rules of Procedure, Rule 114, provide for the following follow-up procedure:

(1) The Committee may designate one or more rapporteur(s) for follow-up on decisions adopted under article 22 of the Convention, for the purpose of ascertaining the measures taken by States parties to give effect to the Committee's findings.

(2) The Rapporteur(s) may make such contacts and take such action as appropriate for the due performance of the follow-up mandate and report accordingly to the Committee. The Rapporteur(s) may make such recommendations for further action by the Committee as may be necessary for follow-up.

(3) The Rapporteur(s) shall regularly report to the Committee on follow-up activities.

(4) The Rapporteur(s), in discharge of the follow-up mandate, may, with the approval of the Committee, engage in necessary visits to the State party concerned.

Continued failure on the part of the States results in the matter being taken up by the Committee in its subsequent reporting session and through a possible reference in the Committee's annual report to the General Assembly.[207] Under the provisions of Article 24, the Committee is required to submit an annual report on its activities and to the General Assembly of the United Nations. From a brief history of CAT, it is apparent that the individual complaints procedure has not been used readily; the contrast with the procedures under the ICCPR and ECHR is striking. A number of reasons can be advanced for this, including the fact that:

[t]he overwhelming majority of countries accepting the optional article 22 individual complaints procedure are also subject to one or more analogues procedures under the Optional Protocol to the International Covenant on Civil and Political Rights or the European or American Conventions on Human Rights, which potential applicants may feel provide more authoritative remedies . . . there is little knowledge of the Convention and its protection system even among lawyers. It may well be that the procedure will only be of substantial use in respect of countries to which no other international procedure is applicable or as regards Convention provisions which are more convention-specific. In this connection it should be noted that the Committee has set up an expedited procedure for dealing with threatened expulsion cases.[208]

---

[206] Rule 113 Rules of Procedure.
[207] Rule 115(3).
[208] Rodley, above n.1, at p. 157.

(v) Investigation on its own initiative (Article 20)

At the time of its inception CAT was unique amongst other international treaty-based bodies in that it was authorised to initiate investigations on its own initiative.[209] The inquiry procedure has proved to be an inspirational feature of subsequent human rights instruments. We have already examined the reinstatement of similar provisions reflected in Article 8 and 9 of the Optional Protocol of CEDAW and Article 6 of the Optional Protocol to CRPD.[210]

An essential prerequisite for the initiation of this process is for the Committee to receive 'reliable information which appears to it to contain well-founded indications that torture is being systematically practised in the territory of a State Party'.[211] While the trigger must be 'reliable information', such information many emanate from any source including the media or NGOs. In practice, CAT receives such information from NGOs, national organisations and intergovernmental organisations. CAT has provided an interpretation of 'systematic practice' according to which:

> [t]orture is practised systematically when it is apparent that the torture cases reported have not occurred fortuitously in a particular place or at a particular time, but are seen to be habitual, widespread and deliberate in at least a considerable part of the territory of the country in question. Torture may in fact be of a systematic character without resulting from the direct intention of a Government. It may be the consequence of factors which the Government has difficulty in controlling, and its existence may indicate a discrepancy between policy as determined by the central government and its implementation by the local administration. Inadequate legislation which in practice allows room for the use of torture may also add to the systematic nature of this practice.[212]

As noted above, Article 20 is applicable only to 'well-founded indications that torture is being systematically practiced', which thus excludes cruel, inhuman or degrading treatment as well as isolated acts of torture. After having formulated a view that it has received reliable information of systematic practises of torture, the Committee invites the State party concerned to co-operate through the submission of observations on the alleged practices of torture.[213] It requests that the concerned State appoint a representative to meet with the members designated to conduct the inquiry so as to provide them with the relevant

---

[209] Lewis-Anthony and Scheinin, 'Treaty-Based Procedures for Making Human Rights Complaints within the UN System' in Hannum (ed.), above n.145, at p. 56; commenting on its potential Sir Nigel Rodley remarks 'there is no model for a procedure such as that provided by Article 20 in a United Nations human rights treaty. The innovative character of the procedure is particularly suited to the special elements of the systematic practice of torture. The uniformly clandestine circumstances in which torture occurs make it necessary for information to be compiled from a range of sources including families of victims and national and international Organizations'. Rodley, above n.1, at p. 160.

[210] Both Article 8 of the OP to Women's Convention as well as Article 7 of the OP to CRDP provide for procedure of enquiry similar to Article 20 of CAT. Additionally Articles 9 and Article 7 of the optional protocol to Women's Convention and CRDP establish follow-up systems to the inquiry procedure which has not been contained in Convention against Torture. For further examination see Nowak *et al.*, above n.1, at pp. 660–661.

[211] Article 20(1) Convention against Torture.

[212] See Doc. A/48/44/Add.1, para 39.

[213] Ibid. Rule 76(1) Rules of Procedure.

information.[214] The inquiry on the part of Committee members may also include, with the consent of the State party, a visit to its territory by the designated members, who may gather evidence and proceed with hearings from witnesses.[215]

In the light of all the available information, and if the Committee considers that there is sufficient evidence to proceed, it appoints one or more of its members to conduct further investigations and report to the Committee as a matter of urgency.[216] After an inquiry has been conducted by its members, the Committee is required to submit its finding to the concerned State party along with its views, comments and suggestions.[217]

This innovative procedure is potentially of great significance for highlighting practices of torture.[218] Its broad nature and possible sources of information present similarities with the former ECOSOC Resolution 1503 procedure. However, unlike ECOSOC Resolution 1503, exhaustion of domestic remedies or other limitations do not apply.[219] The only crucial test is that the information provided contains well-founded indications that 'torture is being systematically practised in the territory of a State Party'.[220] Furthermore, the procedure can be deployed against any State party regardless of whether the State has made a declaration under Article 22. The possible sources of information include not only individuals but also NGOs and occasionally States parties themselves.

Despite the potentially broad nature of this procedure, there are a number of limitations that need to be noted. Firstly, as noted above, the procedure is confined to situations of torture, and is inapplicable to cruel, inhuman or degrading treatment or punishment. Secondly, the procedure is confidential in nature.[221] Thirdly, and most significantly, it can be conducted only with the co-operation of the State. States parties are given a further option to 'opt-out' of the procedure by making a declaration under Article 28(1). This 'opt-out' facility is available upon signature, accession or ratification but not once the procedure has been accepted. At the time of writing, only 11 States have maintained a reservation to Article 20. Notwithstanding the enormous significance and potential of Article 20, the procedure has only been used sparingly. CAT has completed seven of nine enquiries, thus far conducted under the Article 20 procedure; the remaining two are ongoing. The seven completed procedures have been against Turkey,[222] Egypt,[223] Peru,[224] Sri Lanka,[225] Mexico,[226] Serbia and Montenegro,[227] and Brazil.[228] Finally, and following on with the

---

[214] Rule 79(a) Rules of Procedure.
[215] Rule 80 Rules of Procedure.
[216] Ibid. Rule 78(1) Rules of Procedure.
[217] Article 20(4) Convention against Torture.
[218] See Harris, above n.1, at p. 764.
[219] See above chapter 2.
[220] Article 20(1) CAT.
[221] Article 20(5) CAT.
[222] See Activities of the Committee against Torture pursuant to Article 20 of the Convention against Torture and other Cruel, Inhuman or Degrading Treatment or Punishment: Turkey, UN GAOR., 48th Sess., UN Doc. A/48/44/Add.1 (1993). See Rodley, 'United Nations Human Rights Treaty Bodies and Special Procedures of the Commission on Human Rights – Complementarity or Competition' 25 *HRQ* (2003) 882, at p. 888.
[223] Report of the Committee against Torture, UN GAOR, 51st Sess., Supp. No. 44, paras 180–222, UN Doc. A/51/44 (1996).
[224] Report of the Committee against Torture, UN GAOR, 56th Sess., Supp. No. 44, paras 144–93, UN Doc. A/56/44 (2001).
[225] UN Doc. A/57/44, paras 123–195.
[226] UN Doc. CAT/C/75.
[227] UN Doc. A/59/44, paras 156–240.
[228] UN Doc. A/63/44, paras 64–72.

consent principle, whenever a visit is considered necessary, the formal approval and consent of the State concerned is required.[229] Such a request is made by the Committee through the Office of the Secretary-General. Implicit in agreeing to allow Committee members to conduct a visit, is the agreement that members are able to visit any place or institution, including prisons and detention centres, and interview in confidence alleged victims of torture. In all the cases save for Egypt (where the Egyptian government refused permission) it has been possible to conduct a visit to the State.[230]

The completion of the inquiry culminates with a report of the full Committee, which is transmitted to the government concerned.[231] The State party is then invited to make comments, suggestions and undertake actions in response to the Committee's report. On the completion of this confidential inquiry under Article 20, CAT may at its discretion produce only 'summary accounts' of the result in its annual report, which are published.[232] No other sanctions are attached to the Committee's findings under Article 20. Under the Committee's jurisprudence, for systematic torture to take place, such practices do not have to take place all across the country; it would suffice that the practice of torture takes place in any one part of the country.[233] Save for the case of Sri Lanka, the Committee has found torture being systematically practised in all the inquiries which have thus far been completed. In relation to Peru, the view taken by the Committee was that long periods of detention in Peruvian places of detention, combined with, for example, spending nights in interrogation rooms handcuffed, amounted to torture as defined by Article 1 of the Convention.[234] Mexico was the first country which allowed the Committee to publish the inquiry report in its entirety. For Mexico, the Committee found such practices, *inter alia*, as water containing irritants of carbonic acid and chilli powder poured over the mouth and nose of the detained, tying detainees with hands behind their backs and pulling their arms backwards, tying them to their feet and blindfolding them, and suffering generated through plastic bags being tied around their necks – as amounting to torture.[235] As regards Turkey, the Committee found detentions in the so-called 'coffins' amounted to practices of torture. Individuals were detained in miniature cells, known as 'coffins', limiting the detainees to standing and without access to light or fresh air.[236] In finding systematic torture under the inquiry procedure, on a practical level, the Committee has made a number of recommendations including the recommendation of creation of independent investigating mechanisms;[237] limiting the power of military and national security courts;[238] and establishing the practice of central registers for detainees all over the country.[239]

22

Torture as a crime in international law and the rights of torture victims

---

[229] Tomuschat, *Human Rights: Between Idealism and Realism* (Oxford University Press, 2003) at p. 188.
[230] See A/48/44/Add.1 para 12; A/56/44, para 10; A/57/44, para 129; CAT/C/75, para 15; A/59/44, para 157. See A/51/44, paras 196 and 200 for the lack of consent from Egypt. See also Bank, 'Country-Oriented Procedures under the Convention against Torture: Towards a New Dynamism' in Alston and Crawford (eds), above n.134, at p. 167; Tomuschat, above n.229, at p. 188.
[231] Rule 83 Rules of Procedure.
[232] Article 20(1); also Article 20(5) CAT. Summary Account of proceedings can be published in an annual report notwithstanding serious opposition from the State party concerned (as in the case of Egypt).
[233] See Nowak *et al.*, above n.1, at p. 695.
[234] UN Doc. A/56/44, para 178.
[235] UN Doc. CAT/C/75.
[236] UN GAOR., 48th Sess., UN Doc. A/48/44/Add.1 (1993) para 52.
[237] A/51/44, para 221.
[238] A/56/44, para 47(b); CAT/C/75, para 220 (g).
[239] A/57/44, para 136(b).

Egypt refused to allow the visit of Committee members and, hence, deprived the Committee of formulating its views on the basis of a fact-finding visit.[240] In the case of Sri Lanka, the inquiry had been triggered at the behest of five London-based NGOs.[241] In its report regarding Brazil, the Committee noted that notwithstanding the co-operation from the government of Brazil with the Committee during its visit to the country, and the desire of the government to improve the situation, it found that 'tens of thousands of persons were still held in delgacias and elsewhere in the penitentiary system where torture and similar ill-treatment continued to be meted out on a widespread and systematic basis'.[242] As regards Serbia, the Committee found that under the previous regime of President Slobadon Milosevic torture had been widely practised. While the Committee found a reduction of torture in the post-Milosevic era, it provided the State with a list of 20 recommendations to meet its obligations under the Torture Convention. Subsequent information received by the Committee from NGOs of the region and the Committee's assessment is contained in its annual report of 2004.[243]

5 THE UN SPECIAL RAPPORTEUR, THE QUESTION OF TORTURE AND OTHER INITIATIVES TAKEN BY THE UN

(i) The UN Special Rapporteur on torture and other cruel, inhuman or degrading treatment or punishment

A significant element in furthering human rights norms has been the usage of the institution of Rapporteurs, focusing on a thematic, geographical or territorial basis. The present study has taken advantage of the works conducted by several Rapporteurs – these include Capotorti, Deschênes, Ruhashyankiko, Abdelfattah Amor, Whitaker, Eide, Krishnaswami, Benito and Jahangir. Of particular significance in the campaign against torture has been the role of the UN Special Rapporteur on torture and other cruel, inhuman or degrading treatment or punishment. The initial appointment of the Rapporteur was authorised by the Commission on Human Rights in its Resolution 1985/33.[244] This appointment was to last for a period of one year, and in 1986 the mandate was renewed for a further year. The Commission has since that time extended the mandate of the Special Rapporteur.[245] The first Special Rapporteur was Professor Kooijmans from the Netherlands (1985–93), who was succeeded by Professor (Sir) Nigel Rodley from the United Kingdom (1993–2001). Sir Rodley gave up his position during 2001 in order to become a member of the Human Rights Committee. Theo Van Boven held the office between 2001–04. The current Special Rapporteur is Manfred Nowak from Austria who succeeded Professor Van Boven in 2004.

---

[240] See Rodley, above n.222, at p. 888.
[241] The inquiry lasted for three years (April 1999–May 2002) details can be found in the 2002 Report of the CAT UN Doc. A/57/44, 59–71. See also UN Doc. A/56/54 (2001) para 164.
[242] Report of the Committee against Torture, Thirty–Ninth Session (5–23 November 2007); Fortieth Session (28 April–16 May 2008) GAOR 63 Session Supp. No. 5 A/63/44, November 2008, para 70.
[243] See the Annual Report of the Committee against Torture UN Doc. A/59/44 (2004).
[244] Commission on Human Rights Resolution 1985/33 (para 1).
[245] The latest renewal (for a period of three years) was conducted by the Human Rights Council, Resolution 8/8 (2008).

The role of the Special Rapporteur has been of great significance in *inter alia* 'examin[ing] questions relevant to torture'[246] and reporting 'on the occurrence and extent of its practice'.[247] He has been able to gain a valuable insight into the nature of torture and its modern usage. Since his appointment the Special Rapporteur has submitted yearly and interim reports, which are extremely instructive not only in highlighting incidents of torture but also in providing constructive solutions and making valuable recommendations. The work of the Special Rapporteur is characterised by a number of activities – these include seeking information on torture from governments, specialised agencies and intergovernmental organisations and NGOs, responding effectively to the information he receives, sending communications to various States and analysing their responses in the light of the prevalent human rights standards.[248] The Communications also include urgent appeals where a particular individual or a group is under imminent threat. Another significant feature of Special Rapporteur work is *in situ* visits (with the consent of the State party concerned) and their follow-ups, which are valuable for gathering both opinions and comments on all alleged incidents of torture. The previous Special Rapporteur made a number of significant visits to several countries, including such afflicted spots as Rwanda (1994),[249] Pakistan (1996)[250] and Columbia (1994).[251] The current Special Rapporteur has also made a number of notable visits to various countries including Nigeria (2007),[252] Togo (2007)[253] Denmark (including Greenland) (2008)[254] and Moldova (2008).[255]

A further significant task of the Special Rapporteur has been his joint visits or joint communications with other Rapporteurs. Thus from 4–11 July 2008, the Special Rapporteur on torture, together with the Special Rapporteur on violence against women, its causes and consequences, visited Moldova, including the Transnistrian region, from 4 to 11 July 2008.[256] The Special Rapporteurs in their report noted with alarm the considerable violence against women as well as torture of individuals whilst in police custody.[257] Other examples of joint statements and initiatives include the statement of 10 April 2008: jointly with other mandate holders, the Special Rapporteur issued a statement calling for restraint and transparency as mass arrests were reported in the Tibetan Autonomous Region of China and surrounding areas.[258] Another highly useful example of collective communications is reflected through a joint communiqué provided by the Special Rapporteur on Torture, alongside the UN Special Rapporteurs on the right of everyone to the highest attainable standard of physical and mental health, the independence of judges and lawyers, and

---

[246] Commission on Human Rights Resolution 1985/33 (para 1).
[247] Ibid. (para 7).
[248] In his interim report, the Special Rapporteur notes that during the period from 15 December 2007 to 25 July 2008, the Special Rapporteur sent 42 letters of allegations of torture to 34 governments, and 107 urgent appeals on behalf of persons who might be at risk of torture or other forms of ill-treatment to 42 governments. See *Interim report of the Special Rapporteur on torture and other cruel, inhuman or degrading treatment or punishment* A/63/175 28 July 2008, para 6.
[249] See UN Doc. E.CN.4/1995/34, para 7.
[250] See UN Doc. E.CN.4/1997/7/ Add.2.
[251] See UN Doc. E.CN.4/1995/111.
[252] See A/62/221.
[253] See A/62/221.
[254] See A/63/175, para 8.
[255] See A/63/175, para 9.
[256] See *Interim report of the Special Rapporteur on torture and other cruel, inhuman or degrading treatment or punishment* A/63/175 28 July 2008, para 8.
[257] Ibid. para 9.
[258] Ibid. paras 37–69.

frccdom of religion or belief, and the Chairperson of the Working Group on Arbitrary Detention calling for the immediate closure of Guantánamo Bay. Notwithstanding the fact that the US administration under President George W. Bush failed to comply with the collective voice of the United Nations human rights expert, such an expression confirmed the unlawfulness and illegality inherent in such detention centres.[259]

A highly useful initiative adopted by the Special Rapporteur is to use the umbrella of his mandate to elaborate upon the crime of torture or inhuman or degrading treatment or punishment that is visited on specific groups such as religious minorities or disabled persons. In his recent work, the Special Rapporteur has condemned practices of torture against disabled persons.[260] He notes:

> Persons with disabilities are often segregated from society in institutions, including prisons, social care centres, orphanages and mental health institutions. They are deprived of their liberty for long periods of time including what may amount to a lifelong experience, either against their will or without their free and informed consent. Inside these institutions, persons with disabilities are frequently subjected to unspeakable indignities, neglect, severe forms of restraint and seclusion, as well as physical, mental and sexual violence. The lack of reasonable accommodation in detention facilities may increase the risk of exposure to neglect, violence, abuse, torture and ill-treatment . . . In the private sphere, persons with disabilities are especially vulnerable to violence and abuse, including sexual abuse, inside the home, at the hands of family members, caregivers, health professionals and members of the community.[261]

While it is true that the findings and recommendations of the Special Rapporteur do not have any binding effect and cannot be enforced, they have nevertheless had an impact in raising awareness of the subject, and have been helpful in providing solutions to the problem of torture. Commenting on the value of a Special Rapporteur's contributions, Sir Nigel Rodley notes:

> [h]is work confirms that a person who is tortured or threatened with torture is no longer outside the concern of the main organizations of the world's states; on the contrary, the organization now seeks to hold its members to account for the fate of that individual.[262]

A question that has often been raised relates to the overlap (and possible conflict) with the work of CAT and the Special Rapporteur. Although CAT and the Special Rapporteur are pursuing the same goals (the prevention of torture and punishment of those involved in torturing individuals), the ambit of the Special Rapporteur's mandate is in many respects much broader. Firstly, unlike CAT, in his work he is not restricted to investigating State parties to the Convention against Torture; the Special Rapporteur's mandate in this respect

---

[259] United Nations, United Nations Human Rights Experts Request Urgent Closure of Guantánamo Detention Centre, Press Release, www.unhchr.ch/huricane/huricane.nsf/view01/D916F2EB424D1588C1257188004 EDB76?opendocument <last visited 31 March 2009>.
[260] *Interim Report of the Special Rapporteur*, above n.256, Ibid. para 11.
[261] Ibid. paras 38–39.
[262] Rodley, above n.1, at p. 150.

is global. Nor is he inhibited by the limited definition of torture as is provided in the Torture Convention. Secondly, the Special Rapporteur can respond to a call of torture almost immediately. He is not bound by the procedures that are set out in the Torture Convention (e.g. the exhaustion of domestic remedies, etc.) under Article 22. The Special Rapporteur, unlike CAT under Article 22, looks at situations rather than individual cases. In relation to the examination of investigations under Article 20, the situation has to reach a particular threshold before it is possible for CAT to examine it; no such limitations apply to the work of the Special Rapporteur.

22

(ii) The United Nations Voluntary Fund

In addition to the appointment and continued retention of the Special Rapporteur, the United Nations has also established a special fund called the United Nations Voluntary Fund for Victims of Torture. The fund was established by virtue of the General Assembly through its Resolution 36/151 of 16 December, 1981.[263] The fund is aimed at providing aid to 'individuals whose human rights have been severely violated as a result of torture and to relatives of such victims'.[264] The fund is administered by a board of trustees. Although there are, as such, no geographical limitations as to the origin of the beneficiaries, GA Resolution 36/151 provides that priority needs to be given to aid 'victims of violation by States in which the human rights situation has been the subject of resolutions or decisions adopted by either the Assembly, the Economic and Social Council or the [Human Rights Council]'.[265] At the time of writing for 2007–08 the fund had received donations amounting to a total of US$1,731,668 and pledges amounting to $1,116,543.[266]

(iii) Optional Protocol to the Convention Against Torture and Other Cruel, Inhuman or Degrading Treatment or Punishments[267]

After considerable efforts an Optional Protocol to the Convention was adopted by the General Assembly on 18 December 2002. It was adopted by a vote of 127 votes in favour, 42 abstentions with four votes against.[268] The Protocol provides for an international mechanism for carrying out visits to places of detention.[269] It came into force on 22 June 2006 (30 days after the ratification of the 20th ratification instrument), and currently has 40 State parties. The Protocol is separated into seven parts, including: Part I, General Principles; Part II, Subcommittee on Prevention; Part III, the Mandate of the Subcommittee on Prevention; and Part IV, National Preventative Mechanisms.

---

[263] GA Res. 36/151 (16 December 1981).
[264] GA Res. 36/151 operative para 1(a).
[265] Ibid. operative para 1(a).
[266] UN Voluntary Fund for Victims of Torture, Report of the Secretary-General, Sixty-third session, UN Doc. A/63/20 pp. 4–5.
[267] New York, 18 December 2002 GA Res. A/RES/57/199 of 9 January 2003. For useful background information see Association for the Protection of Torture (APT) www.apt.ch/content/view/33/58/lang,en/ <last visited 31 December 2008>. Also see OPCAT Project www.bristol.ac.uk/law/research/centres-themes/opcat/index.html <last visited 31 December 2008>. Evans, 'Getting to Grips with Torture' 51 *ICLQ* (2002) 365; Evans and Haenni-Dale, 'Preventing Torture? The Development of the Optional Protocol to the UN Convention Against Torture' 4 *Human Rights Law Review* (2004) 19.
[268] Press Release GA/10124 18/12/2002.
[269] See Doc. A/56/54 (2001).

The Preamble to the Optional Protocol places emphasis on the relationship with the Convention against torture, and the obligations of State parties to the Convention to undertake effective steps to preventing acts of torture and other cruel, inhuman or degrading treatment or punishment in territories under their jurisdiction. It makes reference to the significance of non-judicial mechanisms of a preventative nature, based on a mechanism of visits to places of detentions. The objective of the Optional Protocol, as noted in Article 1 of the Protocol, is 'to establish a system of regular visits undertaken by independent international and national bodies to places where people are deprived of their liberty, in order to prevent torture and other cruel, inhuman or degrading treatment or punishment'. The aim, therefore, is to protect detainees by establishing a process of preventive visits to all places of detention.[270] The rationale being that since torture frequently takes place behind closed doors and in secrecy, scrutiny through a scheme of visits would help prevent such torture.[271] The prospect of an unannounced visit by an international investigatory team may carry the desired deterrent effect and, therefore, continues the obligations of Article 2 and 16 of the Convention against Torture to take effective steps to prevent acts of torture and other forms of ill-treatment. The Protocol establishes a two-tier system, which allows for visits to be carried out both through international and national mechanisms. Article 2 of the Optional Protocol establishes a Sub-committee on Prevention of Torture and Other Cruel, Inhuman or Degrading Treatment or Punishment. The members of the Sub-committee are elected by States parties to the Optional Protocol and not by the members of the Committee against Torture, thereby allowing for the autonomy of the Sub-committee. According to Article 3, States parties undertake to establish within their jurisdiction 'visiting bodies' for the purpose of preventing torture or other forms of ill-treatment. This mechanism is also called the 'national preventative mechanism (NPM)'. Part IV further elaborates upon the States parties' obligations in respect of NPMs. States parties are obliged to ensure the functional independence of NPMs and ensure that they have appropriate staff and resources.[272] Under Article 19:

The national preventive mechanisms shall be granted at a minimum the power:

(a) To regularly examine the treatment of the persons deprived of their liberty in places of detention as defined in article 4, with a view to strengthening, if necessary, their protection against torture and other cruel, inhuman or degrading treatment or punishment;

(b) To make recommendations to the relevant authorities with the aim of improving the treatment and the conditions of the persons deprived of their liberty and to prevent torture and other cruel, inhuman or degrading treatment or punishment, taking into consideration the relevant norms of the United Nations;

(c) To submit proposals and observations concerning existing or draft legislation.

Importantly, under Article 21(1) there shall be no sanctions for communicating with the NPM and a confidentiality clause is established by Article 21(2). The States parties are obliged to assist NPMs by granting them access to all pertinent information and places of detention.[273] Article 4 confirms the obligations on the part of States parties to allow visits

---

[270] Nowak *et al.*, above n.1, at p. 890.
[271] Ibid., at p. 890.
[272] Article 18 Optional Protocol.
[273] Ibid. Article 20.

from both the UN Sub-committee on Prevention as well as the NPMs. With the establishment of these processes, governmental consent is no longer required as the parties waive their rights of prior approval of the Sub-committee's missions to their territories.[274] There is, nevertheless, a proviso contained in Article 24, through which States parties, upon ratification of the Protocol may make a declaration to postpone their obligations, in respect of establishing a NPM within one year and allowing visits by both mechanisms, for a maximum period of three years. Furthermore, the Torture Committee may extend that period for an additional period of two years.[275]

Part II establishes the composition of the Sub-committee whereas Part III establishes its mandate. Article 11 establishes that:

1. The Subcommittee on Prevention shall:

   (a) Visit the places referred to in article 4 and make recommendations to States Parties concerning the protection of persons deprived of their liberty against torture and other cruel, inhuman or degrading treatment or punishment;

   (b) In regard to the national preventive mechanisms:

      (i) Advise and assist States Parties, when necessary, in their establishment;

      (ii) Maintain direct, and if necessary confidential, contact with the national preventive mechanisms and offer them training and technical assistance with a view to strengthening their capacities;

      (iii) Advise and assist them in the evaluation of the needs and the means necessary to strengthen the protection of persons deprived of their liberty against torture and other cruel, inhuman or degrading treatment or punishment;

      (iv) Make recommendations and observations to the States Parties with a view to strengthening the capacity and the mandate of the national preventive mechanisms for the prevention of torture and other cruel, inhuman or degrading treatment or punishment;

   (c) Cooperate, for the prevention of torture in general, with the relevant United Nations organs and mechanisms as well as with the international, regional and national institutions or organizations working towards the strengthening of the protection of all persons against torture and other cruel, inhuman or degrading treatment or punishment.

In order to fulfil its mandate as established in Article 11, the Sub-committee is to complete visits to States parties[276] and the States parties themselves are obliged to assist the Sub-committee with the fulfilment of this.[277] In the event of the State failing to comply, the Sub-committee may request the Committee make a public statement on the matter or make the Sub-committee's report public.[278] The report of the Sub-committee and the State party's response to this report may only be made public upon the request of the State party in question.[279] Non-governmental agencies could play a critical role in bringing to the

---

[274] Ibid. Article 12(a).
[275] Ibid. Article 24 .
[276] Ibid. Article 13(1).
[277] Ibid. Article 12.
[278] Ibid. Article 16(4).
[279] Ibid. Article 16(2).

Torture as a crime in international law and the rights of torture victims

Sub-committee's attention matters of concern and informing the detainees and the relevant authorities about the provisions.[280] The Sub-committee's reports are useful for providing information on the violation of the rights of detained people and have become an instrumental factor in reform, either through political pressure or through legal action.

The Sub-committee, which is made up of 10 independent experts,[281] held its first session in February 2007. It convenes three times a year for a session of one week in Geneva. During its Second Session the Sub-committee decided upon the first set of States it would visit, these were Mauritius, Sweden, the Maldives and Paraguay, and were to be conducted in late 2007 or early 2008.[282] Trips to Benin and Mexico were added in the Third Session. In 2008 the Sub-committee concluded its missions to Mexico, Benin and Sweden, with the mission to Paraguay, at the time of writing, still outstanding.[283] Although the impact of the Optional Protocol as well as the effectiveness of its institutional mechanisms is yet to be fully established, the instrument nevertheless has tremendous potential for offering 'complementary protection' to all those in detention including refugees, asylum-seekers and other vulnerable groups.[284]

6 REGIONAL INITIATIVES

(i) The European Convention for the Prevention of Torture and Inhuman and Degrading Treatment or Punishment[285]

The attempt to condemn and to prohibit torture and inhuman and degrading treatment or punishment is also reflected at the regional level. Within the European context, the COE has adopted the European Convention for the Prevention of Torture and Inhuman and Degrading Treatment or Punishment.[286] In accordance with Article 1 of the Convention, a Committee is established – the Committee for the Prevention of Torture (CPT) – which consists of the same amount of independent experts as States parties,[287] with a mandate to 'by means of visits, examine the treatment of persons deprived of their liberty with a view of strengthening, if necessary, the protection of such persons' from torture, inhuman or

---

[280] Article 11(c) Optional Protocol.

[281] Article 5(1) Optional Protocol (The membership of the Sub-Committee would be increased to 25 after the 50th ratification or accession).

[282] UN Press Release, www.unhchr.ch/huricane/huricane.nsf/view01/E84C9A2EAA3F1310C125731400700CD5? opendocument <last visited 17 April 2009>.

[283] See for further information www2.ohchr.org/english/bodies/cat/opcat/index.htm#membership <last visited 7 April 2009>.

[284] Edwards, 'The Optional Protocol to the Convention against Torture and the Detention of Refugees' 57 *ICLQ* (2008) 789, at p. 791.

[285] Evans and Morgan (eds), *Protecting Prisoners: The Standards of the European Committee for the Prevention of Torture in Context* (Oxford University Press, 1999); Evans and Morgan, *Combating Torture in Europe: The Work and Standards of the European Committee for the Prevention of Torture* (Stationery Office Books, 2001); Murdoch, 'The Work of the Council of Europe's Torture Committee' 5 *EJIL* (1994) 220; Evans and Morgan 'The European Torture Committee: Membership Issues' 5 *EJIL* (1994) 249; Evans and Morgan, 'The European Convention on the Prevention of Torture: Operational Practice' 41 *ICLQ* (1992) 590 and Cassese, 'A New Approach to Human Rights: The European Convention for the Prevention of Torture' 83 *AJIL* (1989) 128.

[286] CETS No. 126. This entered into force on 1/2/1989 and currently has 47 ratifications.

[287] Article 4(1) European Convention. Under Article 4(3) 'No two members of the Committee may be nationals of the same State', therefore, every State party is represented on the Committee.

degrading treatment.[288] The broad ambit of the Convention allows the Committee to visit 'any place . . . where persons are deprived of their liberty by a public authority'.[289] Such places include *inter alia* prisons, police cells, psychiatric hospitals and detention centres for asylum-seekers.[290] The State concerned is informed about the periodic visits (usually once every two years) although, exceptionally, *ad hoc* unannounced visits may also take place.[291] During these visits the Committee is mandated to speak to detainees and others involved in such detentions and produce a confidential report, which is presented to the State, along with relevant recommendations.[292] If a State fails to co-operate with the Committee or fails to implement the recommendations, the Committee may make a public statement on the subject.[293] The inspiration for the approach taken by the CPT comes from the work of the International Committee of the Red Cross, which also uses the idea of protecting detained persons through visits.[294]

Unlike the UN Convention against Torture, the European Convention for the Prevention of Torture and Inhuman and Degrading Treatment or Punishment does not contain substantive rights; nor does the European Convention contain any reporting obligations or individual complaints mechanisms. It is more analogous to the Optional Protocol to the UN Convention against Torture, as discussed above, which establishes the Subcommittee and NPMs, which also visit the detention facilities of States and make recommendations in this respect. However, the procedure under the Optional Protocol of Convention against Torture is extremely new, whereas the European Convention entered into force in 1989. At the time of writing the CPT had carried out 285 visits, including 160 periodic visits and 98 *ad hoc* visits. In addition to this, the CPT had published 209 reports.[295] In order to fulfil its mandate the CPT has produced a set of standards.[296] These refer to a number of situations where torture may occur including: police custody; health care services in prisons; foreign nationals detained under aliens legislation; and involuntary placement in psychiatric establishments. Issues such as the training of law enforcement personnel and combating impunity are also addressed.

(ii) Other regional initiatives

The African Union does not have a separate Convention dealing with torture, with the main protection from such treatment being contained within Article 5 of the African Charter on Human and Peoples' Rights, which states that:

> Every individual shall have the right to the respect of the dignity inherent in a human being and to the recognition of his legal status. All forms of exploitation and degradation of man particularly slavery, slave trade, torture, cruel, inhuman or degrading punishment and treatment shall be prohibited.[297]

---

[288] Article 1 European Convention.
[289] Ibid. Article 2.
[290] The CPT in Brief, CPT/Inf/E (2002) 2 – Rev. 2006, p. 2.
[291] Article 7(1) European Convention.
[292] Ibid. Articles 8, 10(1) and 11(1).
[293] Ibid. Article 10(2).
[294] Preventing ill-treatments, an introduction to the CPT CPT/Inf/E (2002) 3.
[295] www.cpt.coe.int/en/about.htm <last visited on 7 April 2009>.
[296] The CPT Standards CPT/Inf/E (2002) 1, Rev. 2006.
[297] For further discussion of the AFCHPR see above chapter 10.

In contrast to the African Union, the Organization of American States has adopted a specific convention focused on the prevention and punishment of torture. The Inter-American Convention to Prevent and Punish Torture, entered into force on 28 February 1987.[298] There are currently 17 States parties to this Convention, although notably not the United States. The Convention has a narrow scope, limited only to torture in the majority of instances, however, Articles 6 and 7, extend the scope in respect of the prevention and punishment of cruel, inhuman or degrading treatment as well as torture. Article 2 establishes that:

> [f]or the purposes of this Convention, torture shall be understood to be any act intentionally performed whereby physical or mental pain or suffering is inflicted on a person for purposes of criminal investigation, as a means of intimidation, as personal punishment, as a preventive measure, as a penalty, or for any other purpose. Torture shall also be understood to be the use of methods upon a person intended to obliterate the personality of the victim or to diminish his physical or mental capacities, even if they do not cause physical pain or mental anguish.
>
> The concept of torture shall not include physical or mental pain or suffering that is inherent in or solely the consequence of lawful measures, provided that they do not include the performance of the acts or use of the methods referred to in this article.

Article 3 goes on to state that torture can be committed by either a public servant or employee or a private individual at the instigation of a public servant or employee. The Convention goes on to establish that the crime of torture is not permitted in any circumstances.[299] Furthermore, no exemptions can be provided for having acted under the orders of a superior.[300] States are under an obligation to undertake effective measures to prevent and punish acts of torture.[301] The Convention provides for the right to an impartial examination of the case in instances of alleged torture.[302] It also incorporates the right to compensation for torture victims.[303] The Convention places an obligation on States parties to take all necessary steps to extradite those accused of torture – the Convention retains the *aut dedere aut judicare* principle as established within international law.[304] There is also an obligation built in Article 12 on the part of States parties to take measures to establish the necessary jurisdiction over instances of torture.[305] The Inter-American Commission supervises the application of the Convention under Article 17. Importantly, the provisions of the Convention cannot be read to limit the right to asylum or the provisions of other international instruments, particularly the American Convention on Human Rights.[306]

---

[298] (A-51) O.A.S. Treaty Series No. 67, entered into force 28 February 1987, reprinted in *Basic Documents Pertaining to Human Rights in the Inter-American System*, OEA/Ser.L.V/II.82 doc. 6 rev.1 at 83, 25 I.L.M. 519 (1992).
[299] Article 5 Inter-American Convention.
[300] Ibid. Article 4.
[301] Ibid. Article 6.
[302] Ibid. Article 8.
[303] Ibid. Article 9.
[304] Ibid. Articles 11 and 12.
[305] Ibid. Article 12.
[306] Ibid. Articles 15 and 16.

7 CONCLUSIONS

A persistent point of reference in our study has been the international community's concerns over acts of torture, cruel, inhuman and degrading treatment or punishment. We have already noted that all international human rights instruments condemn and prohibit torture and other forms of ill-treatment. A number of treaty bodies have established substantial jurisprudence on the subject. In the fight against torture and gross violations of human rights, the enforcement of the Torture Convention represents a significant step forward. The chapter has been critical of the narrow definition that has been given to the offence of torture by this Convention. It is recommended that wherever possible CAT should take account of the jurisprudence emergent from related articles of other human rights instruments.

As this chapter has explored, the Convention against Torture contains a number of useful mechanisms to protect the rights of the individual. While examining State reports, CAT has performed a commendable task in highlighting the positive, and more importantly the worrying features, within the legislative and administrative practices of the parties. Its imaginative procedures, such as seeking information from NGOs and national human rights institutions, as well as pronouncing interim measures to prevent irreparable harm, and the follow-up procedures to monitor compliance with its recommendations, are worthy of appreciation. Having said that, CAT is not immune from criticism and it has limitations. In relation to its review of State reporting the work of CAT has been criticised on a number of grounds. These include a failure to investigate the most pertinent questions, a superficiality and vagueness in the consideration of reports and posing of questions, and inconsistencies in approaching issues amongst members of the Committee. These shortcomings remain, although the Committee members have over time gained more experience and the Committee has, on the whole, been receiving greater recognition from the world community.

A particularly innovative procedure is provided by Article 20 whereby CAT may investigate a State on its own initiative after having received reliable information that torture is being systematically practised. Article 20 is subject to an opt-out clause although it is fortunate that only a small minority of States has opted out of this procedure. CAT has, thus far, been unable to utilise the procedure to its full potential and a greater use of Article 20 is recommended for the future.

On the whole, however, CAT (since commencing its work) has conducted an impressive job. The funding and resource problem which CAT faces needs to be addressed. As we have noted in this chapter, CAT is funded largely by States parties. However, the purpose of CAT would be much better served if it were funded out of the United Nations budget.[307] Improvements are also required in the provision of resources to this Committee. The present Secretariat comprises of one part-time member, which is inadequate to deal with the substantial work-load. While in the early years of the Convention, NGO involvement was limited, various organisation have gradually shown an increasing amount of interest in the proceedings of CAT, which has led to informed discussion of State reports and decisions

---

[307] The attempts by the United Nations General Assembly through its resolution to finance the Committee to take measures to finance the Committee from United Nations funds is yet to bear fruition. See GA Res. 47/111. Discussed by Nowak *et al.*, above n.1, at p. 594.

on individual complaints. The role of the Special Rapporteur on Torture now seems necessary. Despite the limitations within which the UN system operates, the Special Rapporteur has examined the subject with great maturity and highlighted various instances of torture. His work has also been constructive for many governments in developing procedures and strategies to combat acts of torture. The UN voluntary fund for the victims of torture also represents a valuable initiative, although its overall impact has thus far been limited.

This chapter has also, albeit briefly, examined the regional mechanisms aimed at preventing and punishing torture, cruel, inhuman and degrading treatment or punishments. In this survey, clearly the European Convention deserves particular attention, recognition and commendation. The success of the European Convention as well as the work of the CPT has aptly demonstrated the justification of having such a mechanism and the useful role it can play in preventing torture at the regional, European level.[308] It is unfortunate that regions such as Africa, Asia and the Middle East, which are particularly prone to State-institutionalised torture or cruel and inhuman treatment, have still not been able to adopt specific binding regional standards.

[308] See Evans, 'Getting to Grips with Torture', above n.267, at p. 366.

International human rights law and enforced disappearances[1]

The phenomenon of disappearances is a complex form of human rights violation that must be understood and confronted in an integral fashion.[2]

1 INTRODUCTION

Enforced disappearances constitute 'a multiple human rights violation'[3] and, therefore, are a matter of serious concern within international human rights law. Enforced disappearances represents a violation of the right to life, the prohibition on torture and cruel, inhuman and degrading treatment, the right to liberty and security of the person, and the right to a fair and public trial. Enforced disappearances obviously violate the rights and dignity of individuals concerned, though their impact on the family, relatives and friends of the victims can be particularly devastating.[4] The shock and prolonged anguish represents a substantial mental torture. Enforced disappearances also establish fear and a sense of vulnerability amidst the society at large. Legal mechanisms are rendered ineffective with the realisation of any individual being swept off the street and being brutalised without any apparent reason. As a historical and global phenomenon, enforced disappearances have been of major concern for human rights law. Although enforced disappearances have blighted all

---

[1] Anderson, 'How Effective is the International Convention for the Protection of All Persons from Enforced Disappearances Likely to be in Holding Individuals Criminally Responsible for Acts of Enforced Disappearance' 7 *Melb. J. Int'l L.* (2006) 245; Lippman, 'Disappearances: Towards a Declaration on the Prevention and Punishment of the Crime of Enforced or Involuntary Disappearances' 4 *Conn. J. Int'l L.* (1988–1989) 121; McCrory, 'The International Convention for the Protection of all Persons from Enforced Disappearance' 7 *HRLR* (2007), 545; Berman and Clark, 'State Terrorism: Disappearances' 13 *Rutgers Law Journal* (1982) 531; Nyamuya Maogoto, 'Now You See, Now You Don't: The State's Duty to Punish Disappearances and Extra-Judicial Executions' (2002) *Australian International Law Journal* 176; Shestack, 'The Case of the Disappeared' 4 *Human Rights* (1980) 24; Rodley, 'United Nations Action Procedures against "Disappearances," Summary or Arbitrary Executions, and Torture' 8 *HRQ* (1986) 700; Reoch, ' "Disappearances" and the International Protection of Human Rights' 36 *Y.B. World Aff.* (1982) 166.
[2] *Velásquez Rodríguez* Case, Judgment of 29 July 1988, Inter-Am.Ct.H.R. (Ser. C) No. 4 (1988) para 150.
[3] See Ibid. para 155; Human Rights Watch, International Convention for the Protection of All Persons from Enforced Disappearance, Joint Written Statement to the First Session of the Human Rights Council, 26 June 2006 www.hrw.org/en/news/2006/06/26/international-convention-protection-all-persons-enforced-disappearance <last visited 16 May 2009>.
[4] Lippman, above n.1, at p. 128.

regions of the world, it would be accurate to suggest that some regions of the world have suffered more from such acts than others.[5] Considerable violations in the form of enforced disappearances have taken place in South America, Asia, Africa, Central and Eastern Europe. The scourge of enforced disappearances has continued to accompany human existence. With the advancement of technology, it is unfortunate that the practice has taken on a variety of forms.

During the era of the United Nations, considerable efforts have been made to combat the curse of enforced disappearances. The distressing nature of enforced disappearances and the anguish involved for the families of the disappeared persons prompted the Human Rights Commission to establish a working group on Enforced and Involuntary Disappearances (WGEID) in 1980.[6] The establishment of the working group, was one of the earliest activities in respect of the United Nations Special Procedures and indeed the first of the thematic mechanisms with a global mandate.[7] Further attention to this serious challenge to human rights values was provided, *inter alia*, through the UN General Assembly,[8] the Economic and Social Council[9] and the former Sub-commission for the Prevention of Discrimination and Protection of Minorities.[10]

In common with other human rights treaties, the precursor to the International Convention on Enforced Disappearances is a United Nations General Assembly Resolution – the United Nations General Assembly Resolution 47/133 adopted on 18 December 1992. The first specifically focused and legally binding treaty was however adopted at a regional level. In 1994, the General Assembly of the Organization of American States (OAS) adopted the Inter-American Convention on Forced Disappearances of Persons (1994).[11]

The subject of enforced disappearances led to the first contentious case brought before the Inter-American Court of Human Rights. The *Velásquez Rodríguez* case arose out of the arrest and subsequent disappearance of Angel Manfredo Velásquez Rodríguez.[12] The details of the case will be examined in due course, though it needs to be stated that while finding Honduras in violation of the various provisions of the American Convention on Human Rights, including the right to liberty, the Court made a number of stark observations in relation to enforced disappearances. The Court observed that:

> [d]isappearances are not new in the history of human rights violations. However, their systematic and repeated nature and their use not only for causing certain individuals to disappear, either briefly or permanently, but also as a means of creating a general state of anguish, insecurity or fear, is a recent phenomenon.[13]

---

[5] See Lafontaine, 'No Amnesty or Statute of Limitation for Enforced Disappearances: The Sandoval Case before the Supreme Court of Chile' 3 *Journal of International Criminal Justice* (2005) 469.

[6] Commission on Human Rights, Question of Missing and Disappeared Persons, Resolution 20 (XXXVI) 29 February 1980, Adopted at 1563rd meeting, on 29 February 1980, without a vote. See Rodley, *The Treatment of Prisoners in International Law* (Clarendon Press, 1999) pp. 270–276.

[7] See Gutter, 'Special Procedures and the Human Rights Council: Achievements and Challenges Ahead' 7 *HRLR* (2007) 93; Harris, *Cases and Materials on International Law* (Sweet & Maxwell, 2004) at pp. 659–660.

[8] Resolution 33/173 of December 20, 1978.

[9] Economic and Social Council Resolution 1979/38 of 10 May 1979.

[10] Sub-commission for the Prevention of Discrimination and Protection of Minorities Resolution 5B (XXXII) of 5 September 1979.

[11] Inter-American Convention on Forced Disappearance of Persons (A-60) 33 I.L.M.1429 (1994), entered into force 28 March 1996.

[12] *Velásquez Rodríguez* Case, above n.2.

[13] Ibid. at para 149.

The crime of enforced disappearances has increasingly been recognised by international instruments engaged with international criminal law and international human rights law. The Statute of the International Criminal Court (ICC) regards the enforced disappearances of persons as a crime against humanity.[14] In elaborating upon the crime of enforced disappears it defines the offence as:

> (i) the arrest, detention or abduction of persons by, or with the authorization, support or acquiescence of, a State or a political organization, followed by a refusal to acknowledge that deprivation of freedom or to give information on the fate or whereabouts of those persons, with the intention of removing them from the protection of the law for a prolonged period of time.[15]

Enforced disappearances in the form of arbitrary deprivation of liberty also equate to torture.[16] Such description of enforced disappearances was established by the Committee against Torture which, as has been examined in the previous chapter, operates under the Convention against Torture.[17] The Committee, in its response to the report from the United States on the Convention against Torture, regretted the US administration's approach that enforced disappearance did not constitute torture.[18]

2 BACKDROP TO THE INTERNATIONAL CONVENTION

(i) The Working Group on Enforced and Involuntary Disappearances (1980) (WGEID)

As noted earlier, the escalation and serious nature of the crime of enforced disappearance led the UN General Assembly as well as the former United Nations Human Rights Commission to undertake concerted action in condemning and establishing legal norms prohibiting this practice. In its Resolution 33/173 (1978) entitled 'Disappeared Persons', the UN General Assembly expressed its grave concern over practices or enforced and involuntary disappearances and the failings on the part of relevant State authorities to acknowledge that persons have been held in custody or to otherwise account for the missing persons.[19] The General Assembly urged all governments, in the event of enforced disappearances, to devote resources to searching for such persons and to undertake speedy, effective and impartial investigations.[20] The Assembly also requested the Human Rights Commission to

---

[14] Article 7(1)(i) Rome Statute of the ICC.

[15] Ibid. Article 7(2)(i) of the Rome Statute of the ICC.

[16] See Conclusions and recommendations of the Committee against Torture, United States of America, CAT/C7USA/CO/2, (25 July 2006) para 18.

[17] See above chapter 22.

[18] 'The Committee is concerned by reports of the involvement of the State party in enforced disappearances. The Committee considers the State party's view that such acts do not constitute a form of torture to be regrettable (arts. 2 and 16). The State party should adopt all necessary measures to prohibit and prevent enforced disappearance in any territory under its jurisdiction, and prosecute and punish perpetrators, as this practice constitutes, *per se*, a violation of the Convention.' Conclusions and Recommendations of the Committee against Torture, United States of America, CAT/C7USA/CO/2, (25 July 2006) para CAT/C/USA/C0/2 para 18.

[19] GA Res. 33/173, 33 UN GAOR Supp. (No. 45) at 158. UN Doc. A/33/45 (1978).

[20] Ibid. para 1(a).

'consider the question of disappeared persons with a view to making appropriate recommendations'.[21] In response during its 1980 session, the Human Rights Commission approved Resolution 20 (XXXVI) without a vote, which established the Working Group on Enforced and Involuntary Disappearances.[22] In pursuit of this Resolution the Commission established 'a working group consisting of five of its members, to serve as experts in their individual capacities, to examine questions relevant to enforced or involuntary disappearances of persons'.[23] The establishment of WGEID had the distinction of being the first thematic mechanism set up in the framework of the Special Procedures dealing with specific violations of human rights.[24] The mandate of the Working Group (WGEID) has from that time been renewed, initially by the Human Rights Commission and since 2006, the Human Rights Council. The most recent extension to the mandate of WGIED was authorised by the Human Rights Council up until 2011.[25]

The Working Group is mandated to examine questions concerning enforced or involuntary disappearances. Its primary role is to provide assistance to families of the disappeared and detained persons to ascertain the fate of their family members.[26] The Working Group receives and examines reports presented by the family of the disappeared person or by non-governmental organisations. Once having established substance and merit in these reports, the Working Group transmits these to the relevant governments with requests for investigations. The Working Group has global jurisdiction in the sense that it can request to investigate any State regardless of whether the State is a party to any international legal instruments – hence in this sense ratification of international human rights treaties is not an a prerequisite for the Working Group to approach a government.

The Working Group works on individual cases, country reports and the general phenomenon of disappearances, including the question of impunity. The Working Group holds, in private, three sessions during the course of the year. Activities within these sessions includes a review of all newly-submitted cases and further review of information and updates on accepted cases. During its sessions, the Working Group dedicates a number of days (the first three days of every session) in its meetings with family members or NGOs concerned with disappeared persons as well as representative from governments. At the conclusion of its sessions the Working Group formally writes to the governments as to the view it has established as regards a particular disappearance. As part of its mandate the WGEID is obliged to report on an annual basis to the Human Rights Council on its activities. This report includes information on its communications with governments and NGOs, and its visits and activities in relation to cases of disappearance received during the course of the year.

---

[21] Ibid. para 2.
[22] Commission on Human Rights, Question of Missing and Disappeared Persons, Resolution 20 (XXXVI) 29 February 1980, Adopted at 1563rd meeting, on 29 February 1980, without a vote. See Rodley, above n.6, pp. 270–276; Kramer and Weissbrodt, 'The 1980 UN Commission on Human Rights and the Disappeared' 3 *HRQ* (1981) 18.
[23] Commission on Human Rights, Question of Missing and Disappeared Persons, Resolution 20 (XXXVI) 29 February 1980, para 1.
[24] On Special Procedures and thematic mechanisms see above chapter 3.
[25] UN Doc. A/HRC/7/L.30. The Current members of the WGEID are: Mr. Santiago Corcuera, Chairperson (Mexico, appointed in 2004); Mr. Olivier de Frouville (France, appointed in 2008); Mr. Jeremy J. Sarkin (South Africa, appointed in 2008); Mr. Saied Rajaie Khorasani (Islamic Republic of Iran, appointed in 2003); Mr. Darko Göttlicher (Croatia, appointed in 2004).
[26] See United Nations, *Enforced or Involuntary Disappearances: Fact Sheet No. 6* (Rev. 2), pp. 5–6.

Since its establishment, the Working Group has considered 50,000 cases from over 70 countries.[27] Between 2002–08, the Working Group clarified the fate or whereabouts of nearly 3000 disappeared persons.[28] Members of the group have also conducted visits to various countries including Guatemala, Honduras, El Salvador, Nepal, Democratic Republic of the Congo, Sri Lanka and Turkey.[29] The most recent visit conducted by WGEID was in Argentina during July 2008. The Working Group has called for the investigation, prosecution and punishment of those responsible for disappearances. During 2007, WGEID transmitted 629 new cases of enforced disappearances to governments of 28 countries, 65 of these cases were sent under the urgent action procedure.[30] During this period, the WGEID also clarified 224 cases in 16 countries. In addition, WGEID during 2007 transmitted two communications to two governments, as regards the apparent harassment and threats delivered upon human rights defenders supporting people who have disappeared.[31] In its most recently concluded session, the 86th session from 26 November–4 December 2008, WGEID examined 21 reported cases under its urgent action procedure. At the same time WGEID was able to review 505 newly reported cases of enforced disappearances and dealt with information from 35 States in relation to previously accepted cases.[32]

After the adoption of the UN General Assembly Declaration on the Protection of All Persons from Enforced Disappearance, WGEID was also provided with the additional mandate of monitoring and reviewing the implementation of the Declaration on the part of States.[33] During its operations in 2007–08, WGEID also transmitted general allegations to governments, based on information received from NGOs in relation to the lacunae in the implementation of the UN General Assembly Declaration on the Protection of All Persons from Enforced Disappearance within their countries. In order to further enhance its work, WGEID revised it Methods of Work on 30 November 2007, with further alterations taking place in the 86th session during November–December 2008.[34] The Methods of Work define:

[27] Ibid.
[28] See Human Rights Council, Working Group on Enforced or Involuntary Disappearances, Inter-active Dialogue with the Council, Statement of the Chair-Rapporteur during the period covered by the Report, Santiago Corcuera Cabezut, 10 March 2008, para 2.
[29] See Guatemala, UN Doc. A/HRC/4/41/Add.1 (February 2007), Honduras, UN Doc. A/HRC/72/Add.1 (October 2007), El Salvador UN Doc. A/HRC/7.2.Add.2 (October 2007), Nepal UN Doc. E/CN 4/2005/65/Add.1 (December 2004), Democratic Republic of Congo UN Doc. E/CN.4/2003/44, Sri Lanka UN Doc. E/CN.4/2000/64/Add.1 (October 1999), Turkey UN Doc. E/CN.4/1999/62/Add.2 (September 1998). See Rodley, above n.5, at p. 274.
[30] See Human Rights Council, Working Group on Enforced or Involuntary Disappearances, Inter-active Dialogue with the Council, Statement of the Chair-Rapporteur during the period covered by the Report, Santiago Corcuera Cabezut, 10 March 2008, para 3.
[31] See Human Rights Council, Working Group on Enforced or Involuntary Disappearances, Inter-active Dialogue with the Council, Statement of the Chair-Rapporteur during the period covered by the Report, Santiago Corcuera Cabezut, 10 March 2008, para 4.
[32] United Nations, UN Working Group on Disappearances concluded its 86th Session and adopted Annual Report, 5 December 2008 www.unhchr.ch/huricane/huricane.nsf/view01/A99B286F7F62A7D5C12575160038970 F?opendocument <last visited 8 May 2009>.
[33] See WGEID, www2.ohchr.org/english/issues/disappear/index.htm <last visited 7 May 2009>.
[34] United Nations, UN Working Group on Disappearances concluded its 86th Session and adopted Annual Report, 5 December 2008 www.unhchr.ch/huricane/huricane.nsf/view01/A99B286F7F62A7D5C12575160038970F? opendocument <last visited 8 May 2009>.

> enforced disappearances occur when persons are arrested, detained or abducted against their will or otherwise deprived of their liberty by officials of different branches or levels of Government or by organized groups or private individuals acting on behalf of, or with the support, direct or indirect, consent or acquiescence of the Government, followed by a refusal to disclose the fate or whereabouts of the persons concerned or a refusal to acknowledge the deprivation of their liberty, which places such persons outside the protection of the law.[35]

The Methods of Work elaborate upon the mandate of the Working Group. In addition to monitoring compliance with the Declaration on the Protection of All Persons from Enforced Disappearance,[36] the Working Group 'endeavours to establish a channel of communication between the families and the Governments concerned, with a view . . . to clarifying the fate or whereabouts of the disappeared persons'.[37] The admissibility criteria for reports on violations of the Declaration are significantly elaborated upon as well as well as the procedure for the consideration of such reports. Importantly the Methods also state that:

> cases of intimidation, persecution or reprisal against relatives of missing persons, witnesses to disappearances or their families, members of organizations of relatives and other non-governmental organizations, human rights defenders or individuals concerned with disappearances are transmitted to the pertinent Governments, with the appeal that they take steps to protect all the fundamental rights of the persons affected. Cases of that nature, which require prompt intervention, are transmitted directly to the Ministers for Foreign Affairs by the most direct and rapid means.[38]

The Working Group has published a number of General Comments on the interpretation of the Declaration.[39] Significantly, this has included a General Comment on the definition of enforced disappearance. In addition to elaborating upon Article 4 of the Declaration, the General Comment refers to Article 3 of the International Convention. In cases where the dead body of the 'disappeared person' has been located, the case is not admissible under the individual communications procedure, however, crucially, this does not mean the there has not been an enforced disappearance.[40] Furthermore, a legitimate detention may be followed by an extra-judicial detention, in which circumstances the case falls within the mandate of the Working Group.[41]

---

[35] Working Group on Enforced or Involuntary Disappearances Revised methods of work of the Working Group (Adopted 4 December 2008) at p. 1.
[36] Ibid. p. 1.
[37] Ibid.
[38] Ibid. p. 7.
[39] Working Group on Enforced or Involuntary Disappearances, Compilation of General Comments on the Declaration on the Protection of all Persons from Enforced Disappearance www2.ohchr.org/english/issues/disappear/docs/GeneralCommentsCompilationMay06.pdf <last visited 9 May 2009>.
[40] General Comment on the Definition of Enforced Disappearance, para 6. www2.ohchr.org/english/issues/disappear/docs/disappearance_gc.doc <last visited 9 May 2009>.
[41] General Comment on the Definition of Enforced Disappearance, paras 9 and 10.

The contribution of the Working Group on Enforced and Involuntary Disappearances to the protection of persons subject to the practice cannot be underestimated. In addition to considering individual communications, the Working Group has also drawn the attention of the world to the consistent violation of the prohibition by States. Its wide mandate and the humanitarian nature of the work, aimed at assisting the families of the disappeared,[42] have arguably improved the effectiveness of the Working Group.

The contributions and role of the Working Group encouraged the General Assembly to adopt the Declaration on the Protection of All Persons from Enforced Disappearances on 18 December 1992.[43] The Declaration expanded the Working Group's mandate to monitor compliance with duties under the Declaration, including the obligation to establish civil liability as well as criminal responsibility for disappearances.

In the Vienna Declaration and Programme of Action (1993), the World Conference on Human Rights, while welcoming the adoption by the General Assembly of the Declaration on the Protection of All Persons from Enforced Disappearance, called upon all States to take effective legislative, administrative, judicial or other measures to prevent, terminate and punish acts of enforced disappearances. The Conference on Human Rights reaffirmed that it was the duty of all States to carry out investigations whenever there is reason to believe that an enforced disappearance has taken place on a territory under their jurisdiction and, if allegations are confirmed, to prosecute its perpetrators.[44]

3 INTERNATIONAL CONVENTION FOR THE PROTECTION OF ALL PERSONS FROM ENFORCED DISAPPEARANCE

On 20 December 2006, the United Nations General Assembly adopted the International Convention for the Protection of All Persons from Enforced Disappearance.[45] The text of the Convention was opened for signature on 6 February 2007. Such a feat was remarkable since the adoption took place less than four years after the first meeting of the Human Rights Commission's Working Group convened to negotiate the draft text.[46] The draft of the Convention had been prepared by a Working Group which was established pursuant to the former Commission on Human Rights under Resolution 2001/46.[47]

In advancing towards the decision to authorise the drafting of the treaty, the Human Rights Commission was assisted considerably by Professor Manfred Nowak in his capacity as independent expert. Whilst identifying significant gaps in international law, Professor Nowak made the recommendation that the formulation of an international Convention on enforced disappearances should 'be most appropriate for drawing the attention of States to the extreme seriousness of this human rights violation and for enumerating the

---

[42] Working Group on Enforced or Involuntary Disappearances Revised methods of work of the Working Group (Adopted on 30 November 2007), para 3.
[43] Adopted 16 December, 1992, GA Res. 133, UN GAOR, 47 Sess., Supp. 49 at 207; UN Doc. A/Res/47/133. 32 I.L.M. (1993) 903.
[44] A/CONF.157/23 (12 July 1993) B. Equality, Dignity and Tolerance: 6(62), para 62. www.unhchr.ch/huridocda/huridoca.nsf/(Symbol)/A.CONF.157.23.En <last visited 27 March 2008>.
[45] International Convention for the Protection of All Persons from Enforced Disappearance, New York, 20 December 2006, UN Doc. A/61/488.
[46] McCrory, above n.1, at p. 547.
[47] Commission on Human Rights Resolution 2001/46.

various detailed state obligations relating to criminal action, preventative measures, remedies and reparations'.[48]

The Working Group, that was established in order to produce the draft Convention, was able to agree on a finalised version of the Convention in its fifth session during September 2005. The draft was subsequently adopted by consensus by the newly formed Human Rights Council in its very first session in June 2006. After its adoption by the Human Rights Council, the treaty was referred to the General Assembly for adoption by United Nations members. As the first internationally binding instruments with an exclusive focus on enforced disappearances, the treaty represents a landmark achievement. However, it has yet to come into force despite being opened for signature since February 2007. The Convention is to enter into force in accordance with Article 39, which states that:

> [t]his Convention shall enter into force on the thirtieth day after the date of deposit with the Secretary-General of the United Nations of the twentieth instrument of ratification or accession.

At the beginning of August 2009, the Convention had only received 13 ratifications, from Albania, Argentina, Bolivia, Cuba, France, Honduras, Kazakhstan, Mexico, Senegal, Japan, Mali, Nigeria and Uruguay. The speed with which the Convention was drafted and approved presents a marked contrast to the likely period before the Convention becomes operative. States appear reluctant to bind themselves to international obligations in respect of enforced disappearances. The absence of ratification by Latin American States that are already bound by the Inter-American Convention on Forced Disappearance of Persons is particularly significant, as is the notable absence of the States of South-Asia (e.g. Sri Lanka and Nepal) with high instances of enforced disappearances.[49] Having said that, the Convention represents an important tool in the fight against impunity for those engaged in the crime of enforced disappearances, kidnappings and extortions. It overcame the considerable lacuna within international criminal law – namely the absence of an explicit right not to be subjected to enforced disappearance.[50] It also heralds an era which vindicates truth and justice and possible reparations for victims and their families. The core provisions of the treaty – the right not be subjected to enforced disappearance – is based on customary international law and is also arguably a norm of *jus cogens*.[51] The customary international law nature of the central elements of the Treaty bind States regardless of their ratification status. It is also significant to note this Treaty is the first binding instrument at the global level which defines enforced disappearance as a human rights violation. The Convention prohibits secret detention and also bans the deprivation of liberty in non-officially recognised and supervised places. The Convention recognises the right of *habeas corpus* as a non-derogable right. The Convention also recognises enforced disappearance as a crime against humanity

---

[48] Report submitted by Mr. Manfred Nowak, independent expert charged with examining the existing international criminal and human rights framework for the protection of persons from enforced or involuntary disappearances pursuant to paragraph 11 of Commission resolution 2001/46, 8 January 2002, E/CN.4/2002/71, para 99.
[49] Uprety, 'Against Enforced Disappearance: the Political Detainees' Case before the Nepal Supreme Court' 7 *Chinese Journal of International Law* (2008) 429.
[50] McCrory, above n.1, at p. 547.
[51] On the meaning of *jus cogens* see above chapter 2.

which can be subject to international criminal prosecution. In accordance with Article 26, the implementation of the Convention is to be conducted by the Committee on Enforced Disappearances, which will be established upon the Convention entering into force. In addition to functions of monitoring and consideration of individual and inter-State complaints, the Committee on Enforced Disappearances is granted a procedure for urgent action,[52] the power to undertake visits to the State in question[53] and the ability to urgently bring to the attention of the UN General Assembly situations of widespread and systematic enforced disappearances.[54] The Convention is modelled and structured on existing human rights treaties although there is a significant resemblance to the Convention against Torture.[55] The Convention is divided into three parts. Part I articulates the key substantive rights and sets out requirements that need to be addressed by ratifying States. Part II, as noted above, establishes a Committee and defines its role and procedure, whereas Part III deals with such requirements as ratification and accession.

(i) Analysing the provisions of the Convention

The Preamble of the Convention make reference to the UN Charter,[56] the Universal Declaration of Human Rights[57] and the International Covenants,[58] and relates to all other relevant human rights, humanitarian law and international criminal law instruments.[59] It recalls the UN General Assembly Declaration on the Protection of All Persons from Enforced Disappearance adopted by the General Assembly of the United Nations in its resolution 47/133 of 18 December 1992.[60] As well as highlighting the 'extreme seriousness' of enforced disappearances the Preamble regards it as a crime within national and international law. The Preamble to the Convention provides a reminder that enforced disappearances can constitute a crime against humanity and that the victims and their families have the right to know the truth about enforced disappearances. It reiterates the rights of persons not to be subjected to enforced disappearance and to just compensation or reparation for such persons.[61] Article 1, contained in Part I of the Convention, prohibits all forms of enforced disappearances[62] and affirms the non-derogable nature of the prohibition even in 'a state of war or under the threat of a war, internal political instability or any other public emergency'.[63] The firm language of Article 1 that 'no one shall be subject to enforced disappearances' carries a meaning which is beyond symbolism and is a declaratory statement of customary international law. Article 2 of the Convention defines the crime of enforced disappearances as:

---

[52] Article 30 International Convention for the Protection of All Persons from Enforced Disappearance.
[53] Article 33.
[54] Ibid. Article 34.
[55] See above chapter 22.
[56] Charter of the United Nations, 26 June 1945, 59 Stat. 1031, T.S. 993, 3 Bevans 1153; see above chapter 3.
[57] GA Res. 217A (III), UN Doc. A/810 at 71 (1948). See above chapter 4.
[58] International Covenant on Civil and Political Rights, New York, 16 December 1966 United Nations, 999 U.N.T.S. 171; 6 I.L.M. (1967) 368; *International Covenant on Economic, Social and Cultural Rights*, New York, 16 December 1966, 993 U.N.T.S. 3; 6 I.L.M. (1967) 360. See above chapters 5 and 6 respectively.
[59] See above chapter 22.
[60] GA Res. 47/133 of 18 December 1992.
[61] See Preamble to the Convention.
[62] Article 1(1).
[63] Article 1(2).

> the arrest, detention, abduction or any other form of deprivation of liberty committed by agents of the State or by persons or groups of persons acting with the authorization, support or acquiescence of the State, followed by a refusal to acknowledge the deprivation of liberty or by concealment of the fate or whereabouts of the disappeared person, which place such a person outside the protection of the law.

The definition places a four-fold requirement in order to establish the crime of enforced disappearances. Firstly, there must be detention/deprivation of liberty. Secondly, it must be carried out with the authorisation, support or acquiescence of the State or by its agents; such detention/deprivation of liberty must be followed by a refusal to acknowledge the detention or a concealment of the fate of the disappeared person. Finally, there must be the placement of the disappeared person outside the protection of law. There are similarities between the aforementioned Convention and other offences related to enforced disappearances. In common with the Torture Convention, this Convention restricts itself to deprivation of liberty committed by State agents or groups acting with the authorisation or support of the State. The restriction of enforced disappearances to State actors does not resolve the massive problems of such disappearances taking place at the behest of private non-State actors.[64] There are various obvious and clear similarities with Article II of the Inter-American Convention[65] and, as noted above, it also bears a resemblance to the crime of 'enforced disappearance of persons' articulated by Articles 7(1)(i) and Article 7(2)(i) of the Rome Statute of the International Criminal Court.

Article 3 represents a considerably onerous provision in that every State party undertakes to take all appropriate measures to investigate acts of enforced disappearances as stated in this Convention where these are 'committed by persons or groups of persons acting without the authorization, support or acquiescence of the State'. Whilst these actions would not constitute enforced disappearances as defined by Article 2, there is, nevertheless, an obligation on the part of the State to investigate such actions and bring the perpetrators to justice. The reasoning behind these provisions appears to be to expand the scope of enforced disappearance to incorporate disappearance conducted by private actors and bring this within the field of national criminal law. In accordance with the provisions of Article 4, every State party undertakes to ensure that enforced disappearance is declared a criminal offence under its domestic law. There is no obligation on State parties to incorporate the Convention although legislative mechanisms appear to be the most appropriate method to ensuring enforcement.[66] In this regard, the provisions bear a resemblance to the provisions of the Torture Convention.[67] Article 5 provides a reaffirmation that the widespread or systematic practice of enforced disappearance constitutes a crime against humanity and, therefore, shall attract the punishments that are applicable to crimes against humanity in

---

[64] See above chapter 22.

[65] Article II of the Inter-American Convention on Forced Disappearance of Persons states '[f]or the purposes of this Convention, forced disappearance is considered to be the act of depriving a person or persons of his or their freedom, in whatever way, perpetrated by agents of the state or by persons or groups of persons acting with the authorization, support, or acquiescence of the state, followed by an absence of information or a refusal to acknowledge that deprivation of freedom or to give information on the whereabouts of that person, thereby impeding his or her recourse to the applicable legal remedies and procedural guarantees.' I.L.M.1429 (1994), entered into force 28 March 1996.

[66] McCrory, above n.1, at p. 550.

[67] Article 2(1) Convention Against Torture; McCrory, above n.1, at p. 550.

international law.[68] According to Article 6, each State is to take necessary steps to hold all those individuals who commit, order, solicit or induce the commission of, attempt to commit, or are an accomplice in the crime of enforced disappearances, criminally responsible.[69] Furthermore, any superior who '[k]new, or consciously disregarded information which clearly indicated, that subordinates under his or her effective authority and control were committing or about to commit a crime of enforced disappearance' has criminal responsibility.[70] Criminal responsibility is also attached to any superior who fails 'to take all necessary and reasonable measures within his or her power to prevent or repress the commission of an enforced disappearance' or failed to submit the matter to competent authorities for investigation and prosecution.[71] Furthermore, Article 6(2) establishes that no order or instructions from any public authority can be invoked to justify the commission of this offence. According to Article 7, parties undertake to provide appropriate penalties for enforced disappearances in the light of the extremely seriousness nature of the offence, although there are provisions for allowing mitigating circumstances in instances where an individual takes action to produce or have someone released. Any statutory terms of limitation have to be of 'long duration and [be] proportionate to the extreme seriousness of this offence'[72] and are to commence from the time when the offence of enforced disappearance ceases, having regard to its continuous nature.[73] States parties also guarantee the right to victims of an effective remedy during the term of limitation.[74]

(ii) Jurisdiction, investigation, extradition, assistance and co-operation between States parties

Article 9 represents a commitment on the part of States parties to take necessary measures to establish jurisdiction over the offence of enforced disappearance in circumstances when the offence is committed in any territory under its jurisdiction, on aircraft or board a ship registered in that State;[75] relying upon the nationality principle, when the alleged offender is one of its nationals;[76] and relying upon the passive personality principle, where the disappeared person has the State's nationality.[77] These provisions are strengthened by Article 9(2) whereby:

> [e]ach State Party shall likewise take such measures as may be necessary to establish its competence to exercise jurisdiction over the offence of enforced disappearance when the alleged offender is present in any territory under its jurisdiction, unless it extradites or surrenders him or her to another State in accordance with its international obligations or surrenders him or her to an international criminal tribunal whose jurisdiction it has recognized.

---

[68] See above chapter 20.
[69] International Convention for the Protection of All Persons from Enforced Disappearance, Article 6(1)(a).
[70] Ibid. Article 6(1)(b)(i).
[71] Ibid. Article 6(1)(b)(iii).
[72] Ibid. Article 8(1)(a).
[73] Ibid. Article 8(1)(b).
[74] Ibid. Article 8(2).
[75] Ibid. Article 9(1)(a).
[76] Ibid. Article 9(1)(b).
[77] Ibid. Article 9(1)(c).

Article 9 is very closely modelled on Article 5 of the Torture Convention and, therefore, raises similar issues as to whether it establishes a multi-State or, indeed, 'universal' jurisdiction.[78] Similar to the provisions of the Torture Convention, Article 10 provides that once a State receives satisfactory information regarding the presence of a person alleged to have committed the offence of enforced disappearance in its territory and is subject to its jurisdiction, the State is required to take the person into its custody which should continue only for such a period as necessary so as to ensure that it is possible to bring them to trial or extradition proceedings.[79] Upon the arrest and custody of the individual concerned, the State party is under an obligation to conduct a preliminary inquiry to establish all the facts of the case.[80] A person arrested and taken into custody is entitled to contact their own State representative, or if they are a stateless person the representative of the State where they usually reside.[81] Article 10(1) preserves the *aut dedre aut judicare* principle, in that Article 11(1) provides that:

> [a] State party in the territory under whose jurisdiction a person alleged to have committed an offence of enforced disappearance is found shall, if it does not extradite that person or surrender him or her to another State in accordance with its international obligations or surrender him or her to an international criminal tribunal whose jurisdiction it has recognized, submit the case to its competent authorities for the purpose of prosecution.

The States parties are required to take their decision having regarding to the seriousness of the offence in question and at the same time recognising the right to a fair trial of the accused and the establishment of an impartial tribunal.[82]

States parties undertake to conduct proper investigations of the complaints of enforced disappearances, including allowing individuals who allege to be victims of the offence to report the commission of the offence.[83] States parties also undertake to protect the complainant, the witnesses and the relatives of the victims from ill-treatment, revenge or intimidation by perpetrators of this offence.[84] This represents a highly significant provision – failure of making a formal complaint could be a product of various reasons including fear, due to threats and intimidation of the complainants. The provisions place the responsibility squarely on the State authorities to conduct investigations and they cannot hide behind an excuse of non-submission of a formal complaint. Furthermore, Article 12 provides that in instances where there is reasonable evidence to suggest that an enforced disappearance has taken place, the authorities may conduct an investigation even in the absence of a formal complaint.[85] States parties undertake to invest necessary powers and resources to conduct the investigation effectively, including access to documentation and other information relevant to the investigation and to have access to the place where there

---

[78] See above chapter 22.
[79] International Convention for the Protection of All Persons from Enforced Disappearance Article 10(1).
[80] Ibid. Article 10(2).
[81] Ibid. Article 10(3).
[82] Ibid. Article 11(2) and (3).
[83] Ibid. Article 12(1).
[84] Ibid. Article 12(1).
[85] Ibid. Article 12(2).

are reasonable grounds for believing that the disappeared person may be present. There is also an undertaking to take all necessary measures to prevent any hindrance to the conduct and course of investigations.[86] Nor should any State party allow those suspected of having committed enforced disappearance to influence the progress of investigations by any means including threats, intimidation and/or other forms of pressure.[87] In common with the Torture Convention, the offence of enforced disappearance is not to be regarded as a political offence or any offence that is related to a political offence or inspired by political motives.[88] Thus, Article 13 clearly establishes that a request cannot be turned down on the grounds that such an offence is of a political nature, and the offence shall be regarded as an extraditable offence in any extradition treaty between States parties.[89] In instances where there is no extradition treaty in place, this Convention is regarded as the legal basis for providing extradition.[90] According to Article 13(6) extradition is to be made subject to the conditions provided for by the law of the requested State or by applicable extradition treaties which include conditions relating to the minimum requirement for extradition and the grounds upon which the requested State party may refuse extradition or make it subject to conditions.[91] The final provision within Article 13 also contains an exclusionary proposition which allows States parties to refuse extradition in circumstances where there are substantial grounds for believing that an accused person is being prosecuted on the basis of his sex, race, religion, national, ethnic origin, membership of a particular social group or political opinions.[92]

According to Article 14, States parties undertake to provide mutual legal assistance in criminal proceedings of cases on enforced disappearance including the supply of all the evidence,[93] although such mutual assistance is subject to conditions as laid down within domestic law or within legal commitments undertaken through binding treaties.[94] Article 15 invokes assurances on the part of States parties to provide maximum cooperation to each other for assisting victims of enforced disappearances and their families 'in searching for, locating and releasing disappeared person, and in the event of death, in exhuming and identifying them and returning their remains'.[95] The provisions of Article 16 are of great relevance and reaffirm the general international law principle of *non-refoulement*.[96] In the context of the present Convention, States parties are obliged not to return, extradite or surrender a person where, having regard to all the available information, there are reasonable grounds to believe that the person in question faces the risk of being subjected to enforced disappearance.[97] As an aid to such determination, States parties are required to take into account all relevant considerations including a consistent pattern of violations of human rights and international humanitarian law.[98] Once the Convention becomes

---

[86] Ibid. Article 12(4).
[87] Ibid. Article 12(4).
[88] Ibid. Article 13(1).
[89] Ibid. Article 13(1), (2) and (3).
[90] Ibid. Article 13(4).
[91] Ibid. Article 13(6).
[92] Ibid. Article 13(7).
[93] Ibid. Article 14(1).
[94] Ibid. Article 14(2).
[95] Ibid. Article 15.
[96] See chapter 18 above.
[97] International Convention for the Protection of All Persons from Enforced Disappearance Article 16(1).
[98] Ibid. Article 16(2).

operative, as in the case of the Convention against Torture, this provision is likely to be heavily invoked.[99]

Article 17 provides for a re-enforcement of the right of liberty. It prohibits secret detentions and re-emphasises the value of the right to liberty.[100] States parties are required to establish strict, regulatory conditions under which the deprivation of liberty may be permissible.[101] State parties are also required to indicate and identify authorities having the power to order the deprivation of liberty;[102] to provide guarantees that persons deprived of liberty are to be held solely in officially recognised and supervised places of detention;[103] to ensure that those detained are guaranteed fundamental rights such as communication with counsel and visits with family members; and in the case of foreigners to communicate with the consular authorities of their own State.[104] The States parties are also required to guarantee access to persons held in custody and to ensure their access to courts in order to challenge the lawfulness or validity of the deprivation of liberty.[105] States parties also undertake to retain a register of record of persons deprived of their liberty, which is to be made available promptly to any judicial or other relevant competent authority.[106] The information contained in the register should as a minimum include, '[t]he identity of the person deprived of liberty',[107] the date, time and location of such a deprivation,[108] the authority which made the decision to deprive the individual of their liberty and the reasons upon which the decision was based,[109] the authority which is responsible for supervising the detention of the individual, the details of the place of detention which would include the address, date and time of admission to the place of detention. There is also a compulsory undertaking as regards the obligation to provide information on the state of the physical integrity of the person deprived of liberty,[110] and in the event of death during detention, complete and full information as regards the circumstances of the death and the location of the remains.[111] Information also needs to be retained if the individual concerned was released or transferred.[112]

Articles 18–20 deal with the subject of access to information. Article 18 commits States parties to providing all relevant information to the relatives or others with a legitimate interest in the person deprived of their liberty.[113] These rights, as Article 20 elaborates, can only be restricted in exceptional circumstances, such as when there is a risk of hindrance to the criminal investigation or the undermining of the privacy or safety of the person.[114] Article 19, however, ensures that sensitive personal information such as medical and genetic data is not made available to anyone or for any other purpose, save for the search

---

[99] Convention against Torture and Other Cruel, Inhuman or Degrading Treatment or Punishment, New York, 10 December 1984 United Nations, Treaty Series, vol. 1465, p. 85. For the Convention against Torture, see above chapter 22.
[100] International Convention for the Protection of All Persons from Enforced Disappearance, Article 17.
[101] Ibid. Article 17(2)(a).
[102] Ibid. Article 17(2)(b).
[103] Ibid. Article 17(2)(c).
[104] Ibid. Article 17(2)(d).
[105] Ibid. Article 17(2)(f).
[106] Ibid. Article 17(3).
[107] Ibid. Article 17(3)(a).
[108] Ibid. Article 17(3)(b).
[109] Ibid. Article 17(3)(c).
[110] Ibid. Article 17(3)(f).
[111] Ibid. Article 17(3)(g).
[112] Ibid. Article 17(3)(h).
[113] Ibid. Article 18(1).
[114] Ibid. Article 20(1).

for the disappeared person.[115] Furthermore, the personal data that has been collected from the individual concerned must not be acquired in breach of fundamental human rights or in violation of human dignity.[116] States parties accord the person deprived of his liberty the right to 'prompt and effective judicial remedies' as a means of obtaining, without delay, the information that is referred to in Article 18.[117] This right to a remedy is non-derogable.[118] Article 21 attempts to ensure that, once released, official verification is provided for those who have been released from detention. The Convention retains a special emphasis on the training of those individuals who are likely to deal closely with persons deprived of liberty.[119] These include law enforcement personnel, civil and military police, medical personnel and public officials.[120] Such training incorporates information and education, *inter alia* on the prevention of the involvement of these officials in activities pertaining to enforced disappearances,[121] placing emphasis on the importance of the prevention and investigation of cases of enforced disappearances,[122] and a need to ensure that orders or instructions for enforced disappearances are banned.[123]

Article 22 reiterates the obligation on States parties to prevent and impose sanctions for delays or obstruction of the remedies to the deprivation of liberty; the failure to accurately record deprivation of liberty; or the refusal to provide accurate information on the deprivation of liberty of a person. States parties also agree to take all necessary measures to ensure that persons who have reason to believe that an enforced disappearance has occurred or is planned are in a position to report the matter to their superiors and, where necessary, to the appropriate authorities or organs vested with reviewing or remedial powers.[124]

(iii) Victims of enforced disappearance and enforced disappearances of children

Article 24 of the Convention provides a meaning of the term 'victim' within the context of this Convention. According to this Convention it means either the disappeared person or any other individual who has suffered harm as a consequence of an enforced disappearance.[125] Article 24 goes on to articulate the rights of the victim which include 'the right to know the truth as regards the circumstances of the enforced disappearance',[126] the progress and results of the investigation and the outcome of any such investigations and the fate of the disappeared person.[127] States parties are under an obligation to conduct appropriate and proper searches.[128] Each State party also undertakes to take all appropriate measures to

---

115 Ibid. Article 19(1).
116 Ibid. Article 19(2).
117 Ibid. Article 20(2).
118 Ibid. Article 20(2).
119 Ibid. Article 23.
120 Ibid. Article 23(1).
121 Ibid. Article 23(1)(a).
122 Ibid. Article 23(1)(b).
123 Ibid. Article 23(2).
124 Ibid. Article 23(3).
125 Ibid. Article 24(1).
126 Ibid. Article 24(2).
127 Ibid. Article 24(3).
128 Ibid. Article 24(3).

locate and release the disappeared person and in the event of the death of the person to return the remains.[129] There is an undertaking on the part of States parties to ensure the right of the victims to obtain justice in the form of prompt and fair compensation or reparations.[130]

> The right to obtain reparation referred to in paragraph 4 of this article covers material and moral damages and, where appropriate, other forms of reparation such as:
>
> (a) Restitution;
>
> (b) Rehabilitation;
>
> (c) Satisfaction, including restoration of dignity and reputation;
>
> (d) Guarantees of non-repetition.[131]

Article 25 establishes a significant provision, not only in the context of the present Convention but also in relation to the protection of children within general international law.[132] Children are subject to the phenomenon of enforced disappearance not only as specific targets but are also victimised due to the enforced disappearances of their parents, including in circumstances where they are born during the captivity of their mothers.[133] Article 25(1) commits States parties to undertaking all necessary measures to prevent and punish under their domestic criminal jurisdiction, the wrongful removal and enforced disappearance of children themselves, the wrongful removal of those children whose parents or legal guardians have been subjected to enforced disappearance, and the removal of those children who are born during the course of the captivity of a mother who has been subjected to enforced disappearance.[134] There is also an undertaking to make the falsification, concealment or destruction of documents which attest to the correct identity of the children or children whose parents or legal guardians have been subjected to enforced disappearance, criminal offences.[135] States parties are under an obligation to identify children who have been wrongfully removed and have been subjected to enforced disappearance and to return them to their families.[136] There is also a commitment to the identification and search for children subject to removal and enforced disappearance and a commitment on the part of States parties to support one another in such searches.[137] The Convention reaffirms the fundamental principles of upholding the best interests of the child as mentioned in the Convention on the Rights of the Child, and to that effect Article 25 establishes an undertaking on the part of States parties to 'preserve, or to have re-established, their identity, including nationality, name and family relations as recognized by law'.[138] The Article provides that those States which have systems of adoption or related forms of placement of

---

[129] Ibid. Article 24(3).
[130] Ibid. Article 24(4).
[131] Ibid. Article 24(5).
[132] See above chapter 16.
[133] McCrory, above n.1, at p. 566.
[134] International Convention for the Protection of All Persons from Enforced Disappearance, Article 25(1)(a).
[135] Ibid. Article 25(2).
[136] Ibid. Article 25(2).
[137] Ibid. Article 25(3).
[138] Ibid. Article 25(4).

children shall allow in their legal procedures for the review of the adoption or placement of children subjected to enforced disappearances.[139] Article 25 reiterates the principle of the best interests of the child as a primary consideration and the views of the child are required to be given due consideration in the light of his age or maturity.[140]

(iv) Implementation of the Convention

Similar to other human rights treaties, the Convention establishes a committee, which will be known as the 'Committee on Enforced Disappearances'.[141] The Committee members will consist of 10 individuals of high moral integrity and characters and are recognised in the field of human rights.[142] These members are to act in their personal capacity and perform their functions independently and impartially.[143] The members are to be elected by States parties having regard to geographical balance.[144] The elections of the members are to be conducted through a 'secret ballot from a list of persons nominated by States Parties from amongst their nationals, at biennial meetings of States Parties convened by the Secretary-General of the United Nations for this purpose'.[145] During these meetings, two-thirds of States parties are required to be present in order to constitute a quorum, with those persons elected that obtain the highest number of votes.[146] The initial election of the Committee members will be conducted within six months of the entry into force of the Convention.[147] Members of the Committee will be elected for a term of four years, although they will be eligible for re-election once.[148] However, the provisions of Article 26 note that 'the term of five of the members elected at the first election shall expire at the end of two years: immediately after the first election, the names of these five members shall be chosen by lot by the chairman of the meeting'.[149] Article 26 also contains provisions regarding members of the Committee that die or resign.[150] In the case of the death or resignation of a member, the State party which nominated the member has the authority to appoint another candidate from amongst its own nationals to serve out the remainder of the term. This condition is subject to approval of majority of States.[151] The Committee has the mandate to establish its own rules of procedure.[152] There is an undertaking on the part of the UN Secretary General to provide staff and facilities for the effective performance of the functions of the Committee.[153] Similarly, the members of the Committee are entitled to the privileges, facilities and immunities of experts on missions of the United Nations as have

---

[139] Ibid. Article 25(4).
[140] Ibid. Article 25(5).
[141] As at 31 July 2009, the Convention had yet to enter into force the Commitee has not been established.
[142] International Convention for the Protection of All Persons from Enforced Disappearance, Article 26(1).
[143] Ibid. Article 26(1).
[144] Ibid. Article 26(1).
[145] Ibid. Article 26(2).
[146] Ibid. Article 26(2).
[147] Ibid. Article 26(3).
[148] Ibid. Article 26(4).
[149] Ibid. Article 26(4).
[150] Ibid. Article 26(5).
[151] Ibid. Article 26(5).
[152] Ibid. Article 26(6).
[153] Ibid. Article 26(8).

been laid down in the regulations of the Convention on the Privileges and Immunities of the United Nations.[154]

In establishing a positive and innovative step, Article 27 states that upon the expiry of four years (and at latest six years) of the Convention having been in operation, a conference involving all States parties will evaluate the functioning of the Committee. The conference will also decide whether to retain the system or to transfer the monitoring of this convention to another body.[155] The Committee will be required to co-operate with relevant organs, offices and specialised agencies and funds of the United Nations and with regional intergovernmental agencies and organisations as well as State institutions or offices working for the protection of persons against enforced disappearances.[156] The Committee will also be required to consult and communicate with other relevant human rights bodies, most prominently the Human Rights Committee.[157] The stated objective is to ensure 'the consistency of their respective observations and recommendations'.[158]

The Convention contains a number of implementation mechanisms. These are as follows.

(a) State reporting

According to the provisions of Article 29, every State party is required to submit to the Committee, a report on the measures that it has undertaken to give effect to its obligations under this Convention.[159] The initial State report is to be submitted within two years after the entry into force of this Convention for the State party concerned.[160] The Secretary-General is required to make the report available to all States parties.[161] The reports are then to be individually considered by the Committee. After having provided due consideration, and in a procedure likely to be similar to those of other treaty-based bodies, the Committee is mandated to provide its comments, recommendations and conclusions.[162] These comments, observations and recommendations are to be communicated to the State party concerned with a view to receiving their response, either on its own initiative or at the Committee's request.[163] The Committee is also authorised to request States parties to provide additional information as regards the implementation of the Convention.[164]

(b) Request for urgent action

Article 30 establishes a system which allows the relatives of the disappeared persons, their legal representatives or anyone with a legitimate interest in that person to request to the Committee that a disappeared person should be sought and found as a matter of urgency. If the Committee considers that such a request for urgent action is not manifestly ill-founded, does not constitute an abuse of the right of application, the complaint has already

---

[154] Ibid. Article 26(8).
[155] Ibid. Article 27.
[156] Ibid. Article 28(1).
[157] Ibid. Article 28(2).
[158] Ibid.
[159] Ibid. Article 29(1).
[160] Ibid.
[161] Ibid. Article 29(2).
[162] Ibid. Article 29(3).
[163] Ibid. Article 29(3).
[164] Ibid. Article 29(4).

been presented to competent bodies which are authorised to undertake investigations and is not incompatible with the provision of the Convention, and the same matter is not under examination through another procedure or investigation of the same nature, the Committee is required to request the State party to provide it with information on the situation of the relevant persons within the time limit set by the Committee.

(c) Individual complaints procedure

The Convention contains an individual complaints procedure which is very similar to the ICCPR procedure. Article 31 provides that any State party to the Convention may, after its ratification of the treaty, make a declaration 'that it recognizes the competence of the Committee to receive and to consider communications from or on behalf of individuals', who while subject to the State's jurisdiction complain of having been made victims of the violations of the rights as provided for in this Convention.[165] However (in common with other human rights treaties), no communication is to be received and considered against a State party which has not made such a declaration.[166] The procedure as noted above, bears strong similarities with the First Optional Protocol of the ICCPR as well as Article 22 of the Convention Against Torture. In each instance, States parties are required to make an explicit declaration recognising the competence of the relevant Committee to receive and consider communications. The communications are to be declared inadmissible in circumstances where they are anonymous,[167] the communication constitutes an abuse of the right of submission of such communications[168] or is otherwise incompatible with the provisions of this Convention.[169] A communication is also inadmissible in circumstances where the same matter is being examined under another procedure of international investigation or settlement, or where all effective and available domestic remedies have not been exhausted.[170] In common with other international procedures the applicability of the rule of exhaustion of domestic remedies is subject to the proviso that it must not be subject to unreasonable delay.[171] According to the provisions of Article 31(3), if the Committee takes the view that the communication is admissible, it is required to submit the communication to the relevant State party with a request to provide observations and comments within a time limit set by the Committee.[172]

Furthermore, any time after having received the communication and before making a determination on the merits of the case, 'the Committee may transmit to the State Party concerned for its urgent consideration a request that the State Party . . . take such interim measures as may be necessary to avoid possible irreparable damage to the victims of the alleged violation'.[173] In instances '[w]here the Committee exercises its discretion, this does not imply a determination on admissibility or on the merits of the communication'.[174] The Committee is also required to hold closed meetings when examining communications

---

[165] Ibid. Article 31(1).
[166] Ibid. Article 31(1).
[167] Ibid. Article 31(2)(a).
[168] Ibid. Article 31(2)(b).
[169] Ibid. Article 31(2)(c).
[170] Ibid. Article 31(2)(d).
[171] Ibid. Article 31(2)(d).
[172] Ibid. Article 31(3).
[173] Ibid. Article 31(4).
[174] Ibid. Article 31(4).

under the Article 31.[175] The Committee is additionally required to inform the author of the Communication of the provided responses of the State party concerned.[176] Once the Committee decides to finalise the procedure, it is required to communicate its views to the State party and to the author of the Communication.[177]

In the light of information provided by the State party, the Committee is required to formulate its recommendations and transmit these to the State party. The recommendations could include a request to undertake all necessary measures including interim measures to locate and protect the persons and accordingly inform the Committee within a specified time. The Committee would be under an obligation to transmit its recommendations to the person making the initial request. The Committee would be obliged to continue its efforts with the State party until a time when the person is identified and the individuals requesting the inquiry are to be kept informed of the progress made.

(d) Inter-State complaints mechanism

The Convention contains an inter-State complaints procedure. Article 32 provides that:

> [a] State party to this Convention may at any time declare that it recognizes the competence of the Committee to receive and consider communications in which a State Party claims that another State Party is not fulfilling its obligations under this Convention. The Committee shall not receive communications concerning a State Party which has not made such a declaration, nor communications from a State Party which has not made such a declaration.

(e) Initiating visits

According to the provisions of Article 33, the Committee may initiate a visit to the State if it receives reliable information indicating grave violations by that particular State party of the Convention. However, this may only take place after consultation with the State party concerned.[178] The Committee is required to 'notify the State Party concerned, in writing, of its intention to organise a visit, indicating the composition of the delegation and the purpose of the visit', with the State party being required to answer the Committee within a reasonable time.[179] As a consequence of 'a substantiated request by the State party, the Committee may decide to postpone or cancel its visit.'[180] In the event that the State party agrees to the visit, then it shall work together with the Committee in order to agree upon the details of such a visit including the facilities required by the Committee.[181] After its visit, the Committee is required to communicate to the State party concerned its observations and recommendations.[182] According to Article 34:

---

[175] Ibid. Article 31(5).
[176] Ibid. Article 31(5).
[177] Ibid. Article 31(5).
[178] Ibid. Article 33(1).
[179] Ibid. Article 33(2).
[180] Ibid. Article 33(3).
[181] Ibid. Article 33(4).
[182] Ibid. Article 33(5).

[i]f the Committee receives information which appears to it to contain well-founded indications that enforced disappearance is being practised on a widespread or systematic basis in the territory under the jurisdiction of a State Party, it may, after seeking from the State Party concerned all relevant information on the situation, urgently bring the matter to the attention of the General Assembly of the United Nations, through the Secretary-General of the United Nations.[183]

(f) Action upon receiving information which appears to contain well-founded indications that enforced disappearance is being practised on a widespread or systematic basis

Article 35 provides that the Committee has competence only in respect of those enforced disappearances which began after the entry into force of the Convention. States parties are only bound in respect of those disappearances which commenced after the ratification of the State in question. The Committee is required to submit an annual report to both State parties and the UN General Assembly on its activities under the Convention.[184] Article 36(2) provides that:

[b]efore an observation on a State party is published in the annual report, the State party concerned shall be informed in advance and shall be given reasonable time to answer. This State party may request the publication of its comments or observations in the report.[185]

Article 43 provides that:

[t]his Convention is without prejudice to the provisions of international humanitarian law, including the obligations of the High Contracting Parties to the four Geneva Conventions of 12 August 1949 and the two Additional Protocols thereto of 8 June 1977, or to the opportunity available to any State Party to authorize the International Committee of the Red Cross to visit places of detention in situations not covered by international humanitarian law.[186]

A significant question relates to the relationship of the Committee with the Working Group on Enforced and Involuntary Disappearance (WGEID) established by the Human Rights Commission in 1980. Once the Committee is established both would be working in the same field and there remains the likelihood of tensions and conflict. However, as in the cases of other subject-areas, differences of operations remain in the work of UN Charter-based bodies and treaty bodies. WGEID has a broad mandate and is not subject to the limitations of treaty provisions and State ratifications. The Working Group is entitled to receive and seek information from a variety of sources such as governments, inter-governmental organisations, humanitarian organisations and other reliable sources. Furthermore, the scope of the Working Group is broader and is not limited to receiving communications from States parties. Since, the popularity of the Convention is still to be

---

[183] Ibid. Article 34.
[184] Ibid. Article 36(1).
[185] Ibid. Article 36(2).
[186] Ibid. Article 43.

established – and it may be a considerable time before the Convention receives a substantial amount of ratifications – the value of WGEID will continue to remain of great value for international human rights law.

4 REGIONAL INSTRUMENTS ON FORCED DISAPPEARANCES

South America and Latin America have a longstanding issue of enforced disappearances.[187] Disturbed at the instances of disappearances, the General Assembly of the OAS during 1982 and 1983 declared enforced disappearances as a crime against humanity.[188] In order to concretely deal with this problem, in 1994, in Brazil, the General Assembly of the OAS opened the Inter-American Convention on Forced Disappearance of Persons for signature. This is the only regional instrument dealing explicitly with forced disappearances and entered into force in 1996. There are currently 13 States parties to the Convention, including Honduras and Mexico which are also party to the UN Convention.[189] Within the Preamble, Member States note that 'the systematic practice of the forced disappearance of persons constitutes a crime against humanity'. Article II of the Convention defines forced disappearances as:

> the act of depriving a person or persons of his or their freedom, in whatever way, perpetrated by agents of the state or by persons or groups of person acting with the authorization, support, or acquiescence of the state, followed by an absence of information or a refusal to acknowledge that deprivation of freedom or to give information on the whereabouts of the person, thereby impeding his or her recourse to the applicable legal remedies and procedural guarantees.

The Convention undertakes a commitment on the part of States parties neither to practise nor to permit forced disappearances.[190] States parties also undertake to implement legislation to punish those involved in these crimes.[191] The provisions of the treaty also consider various jurisdictional issues including extradition.[192] According to Article VIII, the defence of superior orders or instructions is inapplicable.

The *Velásquez Rodríguez* case[193] was brought before the Inter-American Court of Human Rights in 1988, prior to the drafting of the Inter-American Convention on Forced

---

[187] See Brody and González, 'Nunca Mas: An Analysis of International Instruments on Disappearances' 19 *HRQ* (1997) 365; Pasqualucci, 'The Whole Truth and Nothing But the Truth: Truth Commissions, Impunity and the Inter-American Human Rights System' 12 *Boston University International Law Journal* (1994) 321.

[188] Resolution concerning 1982/83 Annual Report of the Inter-American Commission on Human Rights OAS Doc. AG/Res. 666 (XIII-0/83), para 4; Resolution concerning 1983/84 Annual Report of the Inter-American Commission on Human Rights OAS Doc. AG/Res. 742 (XIV-0/84), para 4.

[189] At the time of writing the other States parties were Argentina, Bolivia, Colombia, Costa Rica, Ecuador, Guatemala, Panama, Paraguay, Peru, Uruguay and Venezuela.

[190] Article I(a) Inter-American Convention.

[191] Article I(d), III and IV Inter-American Convention.

[192] Article V and VI Inter-American Convention.

[193] Judgment of 29 July 1988, Inter-Am.Ct.H.R. (Ser. C) No. 4 (1988); See Méndez and Miguel Vivanco, 'Disappearances and the Inter-American Court: Reflections on a Litigation Experience' 13 *Hamline Law Review* (1990) 507; Grossman, 'Disappearances in Honduras: The Need for Direct Victim Representation in Human Rights Litigation' 15 *Hastings International and Comparative Law Review* (1992) 363.

Disappearance of Persons. However, with the dearth of instruments within general international law, as well as in other regional systems explicitly dealing with the practice of enforced disappearance, the reasoning of the Court in this case is particularly pertinent. *Velásquez* was a student, considered by the government of Honduras to be a threat to national security.[194] The Court decided that the facts before it established:

> (1) a practice of disappearances carried out or tolerated by Honduran officials existed between 1981 and 1984; (2) Manfredo Velásquez disappeared at the hands of or with the acquiescence of those officials within the framework of that practice; and (3) the Government of Honduras failed to guarantee the human rights affected by that practice.[195]

The Court additionally discussed that the practice of enforced disappearances, as practiced by Honduras from 1981 to 1984, 'is a multiple and continuous violation of many rights under the Convention that the States Parties are obligated to respect and guarantee'.[196] These human rights include: the right to personal liberty and security;[197] the right to be taken before a judge;[198] the right of recourse to a competent court;[199] the right to physical, mental and moral integrity;[200] the prohibition of torture;[201] and the right to life.[202] Consequently the Court held that Honduras had, in the case before it, violated Articles 4, 5 and 7 of the American Convention on Human Rights.[203]

The approach taken by the Inter-American Court in the *Velásquez Rodríguez* Case has been echoed in the jurisprudence of the European Court of Human Rights on the subject of enforced disappearances. This issue of enforced disappearances has been a particular concern in respect of suspected PKK members in Turkey. In the case of *Kurt* v. *Turkey*[204] the applicant's son disappeared after being held by soldiers during a clash between the PKK and the security forces.[205] During its consideration of the case before it the Court considered both the Inter-American Convention and case-law including, *Velásquez Rodríguez* v. *Honduras, Godínez Cruz* v. *Honduras*[206] and *Cabellero Delgado and Santana* v. *Colombia*.[207] The European Court decided that it was not necessary to consider the case in the light of Article 2, the right to life, of the European Convention on Human Rights. However, the Court did hold that there had been a violation of Article 5, the right to liberty and security of the person, concluding:

---

[194] *Velásquez Rodríguez* Case, Judgment of 29 July 1988, Inter-Am.Ct.H.R. (Ser. C) No. 4 (1988) Ibid. para 147(g)(i).
[195] Ibid. para 148.
[196] Ibid. para 155.
[197] Ibid.
[198] Ibid.
[199] Ibid.
[200] Ibid. para 156.
[201] Ibid.
[202] Ibid. para 157.
[203] Ibid. para 194.
[204] *Kurt* v. *Turkey* (1999) 27 E.H.R.R. 373.
[205] Ibid. para 48.
[206] Judgment of 21 January 1989, Inter-Am.Ct.H.R. (Ser. C) No. 5 (1989).
[207] Judgment of 8 December 1995 Inter-Am. Ct. H.R. (Ser. C) No. 22 (1995).

that the authorities have failed to offer any credible and substantiated explanation for the whereabouts and fate of the applicant's son after he was detained in the village and that no meaningful investigation was conducted into the applicant's insistence that he was in detention and that she was concerned for his life. They have failed to discharge their responsibility to account for him and it must be accepted that he has been held in un-acknowledged detention in the complete absence of the safeguards contained in Article 5.[208]

The absence of an effective investigation additionally amounted to a violation of Article 13. Furthermore, the Court held that there had been a violation of Article 3 of the European Convention in respect of the applicant herself, stating that:

[h]aving regard to the circumstances described above as well as to the fact that the complainant was the mother of the victim of a human rights violation and herself the victim of the authorities' complacency in the face of her anguish and distress, the Court finds that the respondent State is in breach of Article 3 in respect of the applicant.[209]

In the case of *Aydin* v. *Turkey*,[210] the European Court considered the Declaration on the Protection of all Persons from Enforced Disappearance,[211] in addition to its own jurisprudence in *Kurt* v. *Turkey*,[212] when finding violations of Articles 2, 3 and 13.

5 CONCLUSIONS

At the time of the adoption of the new Convention, the representative from Honduras welcomed the treaty as the 'dawn of a new age and a day of hope for all'.[213] As the Convention has yet to come into force it remains to be seen how far this promise will be realised. The UN Working Group on Enforced and Involuntary Disappearances has proven to be an effective method of monitoring States' compliance with their obligations under the Declaration on the Protection of All Persons from Enforced Disappearances as well as other related rights such as the prohibition on torture, the right to liberty and security and the right to life. As has been seen in the European Court of Human Rights and the Inter-American Court of Human Rights, prior to the adoption of the International Convention for the Protection of All Persons from Enforced Disappearance, it has been possible to consider this practice of enforced disappearance by States without having an explicit prohibition of the practice. However, there is little doubt that the International Convention on this Protection of All Persons from Enforced Disappearance is an important step forward in establishing protection for the victims of such an unacceptable and disgusting practice. There is a clear risk that the work of the Committee will overlap with the work of the Working Group when and, indeed, if the Convention comes into force. However, the Working Group will continue to retain the added advantage of a wider mandate not limited to States parties to the Convention and not limited to the rights contained in the Convention itself. It is yet to be seen how the two bodies will coexist and interact.

[208] (1999) 27 E.H.R.R. 373. para 128.
[209] Ibid. para 134.
[210] *Aydin* v. *Turkey* (1998) 25 E.H.R.R. 251.
[211] Ibid. para 153.
[212] Ibid. para 152.
[213] See UN Press Release, Concluding Considerations of the third Committee Report, General Assembly Adopts Convention on Enforced Disappearance, 20 December 2006, GA/10563.

24 Terrorism as a crime in international law[1]

We are all determined to fight terrorism and to do our utmost to banish it from the face of the earth. But the force we use to fight it should always be proportional, and focused on the actual terrorists. We cannot and must not fight them by using their own methods – by inflicting indiscriminate violence and terror on innocent civilians, including children.[2]

1 INTRODUCTION

The consideration of international terrorism in the present chapter provides a befitting conclusion to a volume dedicated to the study of international human rights law. As events since 11 September 2001 have established, in the new millennium, terrorism poses the most serious threat to international order and global human rights. The crime of international terrorism also represents the culmination of many other human rights violations. Whatever definition is accorded to terrorism, it violates fundamental human rights as enshrined in the International Bill of Rights.[3] Terrorism also constitutes a violation of specific human rights treaties such as the Convention on the Prevention and Punishment of the Crime of

---

[1] See Alexander (ed.), *International Terrorism: National, Regional and Global Perspectives* (Praeger, 1976); Alexander (ed.), *International Terrorism: Political and Legal Documents* (Oxford University Press, 1992); Bassiouni (ed.), *Legal Responses to Terrorism* (Martinus Nijhoff, 1988); Byers, 'Terrorism, the Use of Force and International Law after 11 September' 51 *ICLQ* (2002) 401; Delbrück, 'The Fight Against Global Terrorism: Self-Defense or Collective Security as International Police Action?' 44 *GYIL* (2001) 9; Freedman, *Terrorism and International Order* (Routledge, 1986), Gearty, 'Terrorism and Morality' (2003) 4 *EHRLR* 377; Higgins and Flory (eds), *Terrorism and International law* (Routledge, 1997); Lambert, *Terrorism and Hostages in International Law: A Commentary on the Hostages Convention 1979* (Cambridge University Press, 1990); Laqueur, 'Postmodern Terrorism' 75 *Foreign Affairs* (1996) 24; Lodge (ed.), *Terrorism: A Challenge to the State* (Wiley Blackwell, 1981); Moeckli, *Human Rights and Non-Discrimination in the 'War on Terror'* (Oxford University Press, 2008); Paust, 'Use of Armed Force against Terrorists in Afghanistan, Iraq, and Beyond' (2002) 35 *Cornell International Law Journal* 533; Paust, 'Human Rights, Terrorism and Efforts to Combat Terrorism' in Mertus and Helsing (eds), *Human Rights And Conflict: Exploring the Links between Rights, Law, and Peacebuilding* (US Institute of Peace Press, 2006) pp. 239–266; Steiner, Alston and Goodman, *International Human Rights in Context* (Oxford University Press, 2008) pp. 375–471.

[2] Kofi Annan, Former United Nations Secretary-General addressing the United Nations General Assembly (18 November 1999).

[3] See e.g. *United States Diplomatic and Consular Staff in Tehran (United States of America v. Iran)*, Judgment 24 May 1980, (1980) ICJ Reports 3, where the International Court of Justice notes 'Wrongfully to deprive human beings of their freedom and to subject them to physical constraint in conditions of hardship is in itself manifestly incompatible with the principles of the Charter . . . as well as with the fundamental principles enunciated in the Universal Declaration of Human Rights', para 91. See above chapter 5.

Genocide,[4] the UN Convention against Torture and Other Cruel, Inhuman or Degrading Treatment or Punishment, the Convention against Torture,[5] the Convention on the Elimination of All Forms of Discrimination against Women[6] and the Convention on the Rights of the Child.[7] While terrorism provides the breeding-ground for gross violations of human dignity, as this chapter elaborates, there is no established definition as to the precise meaning and scope of terrorism. The ambiguity in definition has produced unfortunate results. On the one hand, these ambiguities are exploited by some States to deny their peoples legitimate rights such as freedom of expression and religion, and collective group rights, particularly the right to self-determination.[8] On the other hand, violence and extremism have increasingly featured as a trademark of non-State actors and radical organisations. The lack of agreement on a definition of terrorism is not merely academic or theoretical but, as Saul describes, has serious 'operative legal significance' in respect of the implementation machinery of Security Council Resolutions such as the Resolution 1373, as 'Resolutions have also implicitly referred to self-defence against terrorism, so lack of definition allows States to unilaterally target "terrorists" in military operations'.[9]

The present chapter advances the view that international law remains a difficult medium to address the subject of terrorism. There is, firstly, the difficulty in defining terrorism; perceptions vary in terms of differentiating a terrorist from a freedom fighter. Should terrorism be confined to acts of violence against persons or should attacks on property also come within the ambit of terrorism?[10] Secondly, there is the complex issue of defining the meaning and scope of so-called 'political offences': should individuals who have committed acts of violence be exempt from prosecution or extradition because their actions are purportedly based on political motivations?[11] Thirdly, there is the difficulty of identifying perpetrators of the crime of terrorism: should the focus of international concern be individuals and other non-State organisations or should attention to be directed towards State-sponsored terrorism? If States are implicated in terrorism, how can international laws be made more effective? Finally, there is the subject of remedies for victims of terrorism. In a fragmented and incoherent system that deals with international terrorism, victims of

---

[4] See above chapter 13.

[5] See above chapter 22.

[6] See above chapter 15.

[7] See above chapter 16.

[8] Saul makes the useful point that 'Some States have deployed the international legitimacy conferred by Council authorization to define terrorism to repress or de-legitimize political opponents . . . Thus China bluntly characterizes Uighur separatists in Xinjiang as terrorists; Russia asserts that Chechen rebels are terrorists, even though many are fighting in an internal conflict; and India seldom distinguishes militants from terrorists in Kashmir. In Indonesia, insurgencies in Aceh and West Papua have been described and combated as terrorism, as have a Maoist insurgency in Nepal and an Islamist movement in Morocco'. (footnotes omitted) Saul, 'Definition of "Terrorism" in the UN Security Council: 1985–2004' 4 *CJIL* (2005) 141, at p. 160; see Pomerance, *Self-determination in Law and Practice* (Brill, 1982); Rigo Sureda, *The Evolution of the Right of Self-Determination: A Study of United Nations Practice* (Kluwer Law International, 1973); Kirgis Jr., 'The Degrees of Self-Determination in the United Nations Era' 88 *AJIL* (1994) 304; Thornberry, 'Self-Determination, Minorities, Human Rights: A Review of International Instruments' 38 *ICLQ* (1989) 867; Hannum, *Autonomy, Sovereignty and Self-Determination* (University of Pennsylvania Press, 1990) p. 33; Blum, 'Reflections on the Changing Concept of Self-Determination' 10 *Israel Law Review* (1975) 509; Emerson, 'Self-Determination' 65 *AJIL* (1971) 459; Koskenniemi, 'National Self-Determination Today: Problems of Legal Theory and Practice' 43 *ICLQ* (1994) 241.

[9] Saul, above n.8, pp. 159–160.

[10] Shaw, *International Law* (Cambridge University Press, 2008) at p. 1159.

[11] See Blakesley, 'Terrorism, Law and Our Constitutional Order' 60 *University of Colorado Law Review* (1989) 471 at p. 514; Green, 'Terrorism, the Extradition of Terrorists and the "Political Offence" Defence' 31 *GYIL* (1988) 337.

this crime have frequently been denied access to national and international tribunals to claim their rights.[12]

This chapter has been divided into six sections. After these introductory comments, the next section analyses the difficulties in defining international terrorism. Section 3 presents an overview of the historical developments, whereas section 4 considers international efforts to formulate legal principles in dealing with this crime. Section 5 looks at the subject in the light of the political events of 11 September. Section 6 provides a number of concluding observations.

2 THE DEFINITIONAL ISSUES[13]

In his celebrated essay Professor Baxter expresses his doubts about energising efforts to define terrorism. He notes, '[w]e have cause to regret that a legal concept of "terrorism" was ever inflicted upon us. The term is imprecise; it is ambiguous; and above all, it serves no operative legal purpose'.[14]

As we have noted throughout our study, definitional issues have generated substantial complications in formulating international human rights standards.[15] The term 'terrorism' is probably the most difficult to define because of varied perceptions over the characterisation of terrorist acts, purpose and motivation behind such acts, and the variable identity of the perpetrator. Indeed, the issue has been so controversial that divisions have emerged not only in the proposed definitions but more fundamentally as to whether it is worthwhile attempting to define such an elusive concept.[16] Any attempt to reach a consensus on definitional issues is immediately confronted with significant complications.[17] An immediate and intractable question relates to the identification of 'terrorists'. In any ideological and political conflict, is it possible to objectively distinguish between a terrorist from a freedom fighter? In contemporary politics, our perceptions of acts of violence conducted by such groups as the Palestinians, the Kashmiris, the Northern Irish Catholics or the Tamil Tigers

---

[12] Professor Dinstein correctly points out that 'the principal obstacle on the path of efforts to suppress international terrorism is that too many countries display a double standard in their approach to the problem. While concerned about acts of terrorism directly affecting their own interests (or those of their close allies) they demonstrate a marked degree of *insouciance* to the predicament of others. In the aggregate, the international community seems to lack the political will to take concerted action against terrorists of all stripes. As a result, terrorists frequently manage to get away with murder in the literal meaning of the phrase'. Dinstein, 'Terrorism as an International Crime' 19 *IYDIIR* (1989) 55 at p. 56.

[13] See Green, 'Terrorism and Armed Conflict: The Plea and the Verdict' 19 *IYBHR* (1989) 131; Levitt, 'Is "Terrorism" Worth Defining?' 13 *Ohio Northern University Law Review* (1986) 97; Murphy, 'Defining International Terrorism: A Way Out of the Quagmire' 19 *IYBHR* (1989) 13; Murphy 'The Future of Multilateralism and Efforts to Combat International Terrorism' 25 *ColJTL* (1986) 35; Saul, *Defining Terrorism in International Law* (Oxford University Press, 2006); Saul, above n.8.

[14] Baxter, 'A Sceptical Look at the Concept of Terrorism' 7 *Akron Law Review* (1974) 380 at p. 380.

[15] On the issue of minorities see above chapter 13 and on indigenous peoples see above chapter 14.

[16] As Professor Bassiouni makes the point that 'there is . . . no internationally agreed upon methodology for the identification and appraisal of what is commonly referred to as "terrorism"; including: causes, strategies, goals and outcomes of the conduct in question and those who perpetuate it. There is also no international consensus as to the appropriate reactive strategies of States and the international community, their values, goals and outcomes. All of this makes it difficult to identify what is sought to be prevented and controlled, why and how. As a result the pervasive and indiscriminate use of the often politically convenient label of "terrorism" continues to mislead this field of inquiry'. Bassiouni, 'A Policy – Oriented Inquiry into the Different Forms and Manifestations of "International Terrorism"' in Bassiouni (ed.), above n.1, at p. xvi.

[17] Higgins, 'The General International Law of Terrorism' in Higgins and Flory (eds), above n.1, 13–29 at p. 14.

is variable. There is a great measure of truth in the well known cliché that 'one man's terrorist is another man's freedom fighter'.

Furthermore, there is the difficulty in agreeing on the entities which could conceivably perpetrate the crime of terrorism. In this regard, there has remained a major ideological conflict between the developing States (predominantly African, Arab and Islamic States) on the one hand and the developed world on the other. While developing States have placed emphasis on State terrorism largely in the context of racial oppression and colonial regimes, the developed world has concerned itself with individual acts of terrorism.[18] From a human rights perspective, key question is whether it is arguable that every form of the taking of life, assassination, killings, bombings, hostage-taking and hijacking, may be categorised as a terrorist activity.[19] The motive, characteristics and underlying causes of any such actions ought not to provide a justification. On the other hand, depending on one's moral and political views many of these actions have been justified or condoned.[20] State-sponsored terrorism in the form of colonialism is far more devastating in its impact than individual acts of terrorism. This is particularly the case where State-terrorism is generated by militarily powerful States. According to one estimate, the 20th century witnessed 70 million casualties of State sponsored terrorism as opposed to 100,000 deaths which were caused by individual non-governmental acts of terrorism.[21] Since the US led invasion of Iraq in March 2003, on average 500 people have been killed in the country on a daily basis.

The controversies generated by the definitional debate have exercised the minds of many draftsmen and academics; a leading authority has noted that between 1936–81, no less than 109 definitions of terrorism were put forward.[22] Within this timeframe, one of the earliest and most prominent definitions was advanced through the 1937 Convention for the Prevention and Punishment of Terrorism.[23] According to Article 1(2) of the Convention:

> In the present Convention, the expression 'acts of terrorism' means criminal acts directed against a State intended or calculated to create a state of terror in the minds of particular persons, or a group of persons or the general public.

To be subject to the provisions of this Convention, an act had to come within the ambit of the aforementioned definition. It had to be directed against a State party and the concerned activity had to involve one of the enumerated actions in Articles 2 and 3 of the Convention namely 'any wilful act causing death or grievous bodily harm or loss of liberty' to specified

---

[18] As Levitt correctly points out 'governments that have a strong political stake in the promotion of "national liberation movements" are loath to subscribe to a definition of terrorism that would criminalize broad areas of conduct habitually resorted to by such groups; and on the other end of the spectrum, governments against which these groups' violent activities are directed are obviously reluctant to subscribe to a definition that would criminalize their own use of force in response to such activities or otherwise'. Levitt, above n.13, at p. 109.

[19] Higgins, 'The General International Law of Terrorism' in Higgins and Flory (eds), above n.1, 13–29 at pp. 14–15.

[20] Examples are also put forward about possible justifications of the (hypothetical) killings of international criminals and gross violators of human rights such as Adolf Hitler. See Blakesley, above n.11, at p. 474.

[21] Bassiouni, *International Terrorism: Multilateral Conventions (1937–2001)* (Transnational Publishers, 2001) at p. 46.

[22] Laqueur, 'Reflections on Terrorism' 65 *Foreign Affairs* (1986–87) 86 at p. 88; Saul 'Attempts to Define "Terrorism" in International Law' *NILR* (2005) 57.

[23] The Convention for the Prevention and Punishment of Terrorism, 16 November 1937, 19 League of Nations Official Journal (1938) 23 reprinted 27 UN GAOR, Annex I, Agenda Item No. 92, UN Doc. A/C.6/418 (1972).

category of public officials, 'wilful destruction of, or damage to, public property' or 'any wilful act calculated to endanger the lives of members of the public'.

However, the aforementioned definition of terrorism along with the 1937 Convention failed to be adopted. Despite this abortive attempt, renewed efforts were made in the 1950s and 1960s to formulate a consensus definition of international terrorism. In 1972 the United States presented a Draft Convention for the Prevention and Punishment of Certain Acts of International Terrorism.[24] Within this draft, offences of 'international significance' include offences committed with intent to damage the interests of or obtain concessions from a State or an international organisation under certain enumerated transnational circumstances, consisting of unlawfully killing, causing serious bodily harm or kidnapping another person (including attempts and complicity in such acts).[25] These actions should have been 'committed neither by nor against a member of the armed forces of a State in the course of military hostilities'.[26]

The 1972 US Draft Convention, like the 1937 Convention, failed to gain the approval of the international community. Instead, the United Nations General Assembly established an Ad Hoc Committee on International Terrorism to 'consider the observations of States [and] submit its report with recommendations for possible co-operation for the speedy elimination of the problem . . . to the General Assembly'.[27] A Subcommittee of the Ad Hoc Committee was established and within the deliberations of the Subcommittee the following definition of 'international terrorism' was advanced:

(1) Acts of violence and other repressive acts by colonial, racist and alien regimes against peoples struggling for their liberation . . .

(2) Tolerating or assisting by a State the organization of the remnants of fascist or mercenary groups whose terrorist activity is directed against other sovereign countries;

(3) Acts of violence committed by individuals or groups of individuals which endanger or take innocent human lives or jeopardise fundamental freedoms. This should not affect the inalienable right to self-determination and independence of all peoples under colonial and racist regimes and other forms of alien domination and the legitimacy of their struggle . . . ;

(4) Acts of violence committed by individuals or groups of individuals for private gain, the effects of which are not confined to one State.[28]

The contrast between this definition and the 1972 and 1937 definitions considered earlier is striking. The concern for the Subcommittee is primarily about racist and alien regimes. There also appears to be some form of exception accorded to those activities which are conducted in pursuance of the inalienable right to self-determination. Within the definition,

---

[24] United States Draft Convention for the Prevention of Certain Acts of International Terrorism, UN Doc. A/C.6/L.850 (1972) reprinted in 67 Dep't State Bull. 431 (1972).

[25] Article 1.

[26] Ibid.

[27] 'Measures to Prevent International Terrorism which Endangers or Takes Innocent Human Lives or Jeopardizes Fundamental Freedoms, and Study of the Underlying Causes of those Forms of Terrorism and Acts of Violence which lie in Misery, Frustration, Grievance and Despair and which Cause Some People to Sacrifice Human Lives, Including Their Own, in an Attempt to Effect Radical Changes' GA. Res. 3034, 27 UN GAOR Supp. (No. 30) at 119, UN Doc. A/RES/3034, paras 9, 10.

[28] 28 UN GAOR Supp. (1973).

the issue of intent according to one commentator 'has been turned on its head';[29] private gain rather than political motives present the key determining factor.

Ideological divisions regarding the definition have hampered further efforts to draft a treaty dealing with international terrorism. As a consequence of these differences, the most effective way for the international community to proceed has been the consideration of specific aspects of the subject.[30] Thus, binding instruments have been adopted in areas of, *inter alia*, aircraft hijacking,[31] unlawful acts against the safety of civil aviation,[32] marine terrorism,[33] hostage-taking[34] and theft of nuclear materials.[35]

(i) Recent developments on definitional issues

As subsequent sections shall analyse, since the end of the Cold War, a greater consensus has emerged over the necessity to prevent all form of political violence and terrorism. The General Assembly as well as the Security Council has addressed the issue of terrorism on several occasions.[36] In its Resolution 51/210, the General Assembly established an Ad Hoc Committee:

> to elaborate an international convention for the suppression of terrorist bombings and, subsequently, an international convention for the suppression of acts of nuclear terrorism, to supplement related existing international instruments, and thereafter to address means of further developing a comprehensive legal framework of conventions dealing with international terrorism.[37]

The mandate for the Ad Hoc Committee has been renewed annually by the General Assembly. Under the terms of the current mandate as provided by General Assembly Resolution 63/129[38] the Committee is required to continue its work towards *inter alia* drafting a convention on terrorism.[39] The mandate for drafting the Convention was renewed in 2008.[40] The General Assembly in its Resolution 63/129 adopted on 11 December 2008 further

---

[29] Levitt, above n.13, at p. 100.
[30] Cassese, *International Criminal Law* (Oxford University Press, 2003) at p. 123.
[31] See the Convention on Offences and Certain Other Acts Committed on Board Aircraft (1963) 704 U.N.T.S. 219; the Convention for the Suppression of Unlawful Seizure of Aircraft, (1970) 860 U.N.T.S. 105.
[32] See Convention for the suppression of Unlawful Acts against the Safety of Civil Aviation (1971) 974 U.N.T.S. 177; 10 I.L.M. (1971) 1151.
[33] See the Convention for the Suppression of Unlawful Acts against the Safety of Maritime Navigation 27 I.L.M. 668 (1988); the Protocol for the Suppression of Unlawful Acts against the Safety of Fixed Platforms Located on the Continental Shelf, 1988, 27 (1988) I.L.M. 685.
[34] See the Convention on the Prevention and Punishment of Crimes against Internationally Protected Persons, including Diplomatic Agents, (1973) 1035 U.N.T.S. 167; International Convention against the Taking of Hostages 34 UN GAOR Supp. (No. 39) at 23, UN Doc. A/34/39 (1979) 18 I.L.M. (1979) 1456.
[35] See Convention on the Physical Protection of Nuclear Materials (1980) 18 I.L.M. (1979) 1419.
[36] Levitt, n.13 above, at p. 100; see Saul, above n.22; Saul, above n.8.
[37] See 'Measures to Eliminate International Terrorism' General Assembly Resolution No. 51/210 of 17 December 1996, UN Doc. A/RES/51/210, at para 9; Halberstam, 'The Evolution of the United Nations Position on Terrorism' (2003) 41 *ColJTL* 573, at p. 579.
[38] Adopted on 11 December 2008.
[39] UN GA Res. 58/81, (2004), paras 14–19.
[40] See Ad Hoc Committee Established by the General Assembly Resolution 51/210 of 17 December 1996, www.un.org/law/terrorism/index.html <last visited 4 December 2008>.

required the Ad Hoc Committee to expeditiously elaborate the draft comprehensive convention on international terrorism.[41]

A working-group of the Committee, in 2000, considered a draft convention proposed by India.[42] However, in actual practice not much headway has been made in producing the substantive provisions of the treaty. The Committee has struggled with the definitional, substantive and procedural issues. According to a previous draft, the Convention would, *inter alia*, define terrorism, require states to criminalise terrorism, establish jurisdictional principles and affirm the principle of *aut dedere aut judicare*.[43] During its 56th session, the working-group produced the following definition of terrorism:

Article 2

(1) Any person commits an offence within the meaning of this Convention if that person, by any means, unlawfully and intentionally, causes:

   (a) Death or serious bodily injury to any person, or:

   (b) Serious damage to public or private property, including a place of public use, a State or government facility, a public transportation system, an infrastructure facility or the environment; or

   (c) Damage to property, places, facilities or systems referred to in paragraph 1(b) of this article, resulting or likely to result in major economic loss, when the purpose of the conduct, by its nature or context, is to intimidate a population, or to compel a Government or an international organization to do or abstain from doing any act.[44]

The definition renders it a criminal offence to make serious and credible threats to commit offences (as stated in Article 1), organise or direct others to commit such offences or contribute to these offences.[45] The draft bans a wide range of criminal behaviour and prohibits any exceptions regardless of 'political, philosophical, ideological, racial, ethnic [or] religious considerations'[46] that may have been the motivating factor. There is also an explicit rejection of the application of 'political offence exception' for the purposes of extradition.[47] Notwithstanding the commendable features in the draft Convention, it still exists in draft formation. A recipe for future disagreements has already been evident with the Malaysian proposal (submitted on behalf of the Organisation of the Islamic Conferences) seeking exemptions for 'Peoples' struggling against armed occupation, and foreign aggression.[48] While

[41] See the General Assembly Resolution 63/129, www.un.org/law/terrorism/index.html <last visited 4 April 2009>.

[42] See General Assembly, *Draft Comprehensive Convention on International Terrorism: Working Document Submitted by India* (28 August 2000) UN Doc. A/C.6/55/1.

[43] See Report of the Ad Hoc Committee established by General Assembly Resolution 51/210 17 December 1996, Sixth Session (28 January–1 February 2002) UN Doc. A/57/37.

[44] Measures to Eliminate Terrorism: Report of the Working Group Fifty-Sixth Session, 29 October 2001, UN Doc. A/C.6/56/L.9, annex I.9. Text available at: http://ods-dds-ny.un.org/doc/UNDOC/GEN/N02/248/17/PDF/N0224817.pdf?OpenElement <last visited 15 March 2008>; also see Report by the International Bar Association's Task Force on International Terrorism, *International Terrorism: Legal Challenges and Responses* (2003) at pp. 2–3.

[45] Ibid. Article 2(2)(3)(4).

[46] Ibid. Article 5.

[47] Ibid. Article 14.

[48] See Subedi, 'The UN Response to International Terrorism in the Aftermath of the Terrorist Attacks in America and the Problem of the Definition of Terrorism in International Law' (2002) 4 *International Law Forum du droit International* 159, at p. 163. Another OIC Member State attempted to formally launch a reservation to exclude the application of the convention to situations of self-determination struggles to which several (primarily western) States objected; see Saul, above n.22, at p. 78.

the Committee continues its efforts, the prospects for a fully acceptable definition as well as achieving consensus in the main body of any such treaty are remote.[49]

In the aftermath of the tragic events of 11 September 2001, the Security Council adopted a landmark resolution, Resolution 1373. The Resolution deliberately avoided the thorny issue of defining 'terrorism'.[50] Instead of faltering over the subject of definition, the text of the Resolution addresses key areas for the prevention and punishment of terrorists and sets up a compulsory implementation mechanism through State reporting; the reports to be monitored by the newly established United Nations Counter Terrorism Committee. Another significant development was the adoption of Security Council Resolution 1566, also passed under Chapter VII of the UN Charter in August 2004. In breaking new ground, the Council recalled:

> that criminal acts including, against civilians, committed with the intent to cause death or serious bodily injury, or taking of hostages, with the purpose to provoke a state of terror in the general public or in a group of persons or particular persons, intimidate a population or compel a government or an international organization to do or to abstain from doing any act, which constitute offences within the scope of and as defined in the international conventions and protocols relating to terrorism, are under no circumstances justifiable by considerations of a political, philosophical, ideological, racial, ethnic, religious or other similar nature.[51]

Resolution 1566 does not provide, and indeed does not proclaim to provide, a comprehensive or universally agreed upon definition of terrorism. This deliberate avoidance of the issue of definition of terrorism has been a continued feature of modern international law. As the chapter examines, while a number of documents and binding instruments have been adopted, they deal only with specific aspects of the crime of terrorism – thus, international treaties have been formulated in areas of, *inter alia*, aircraft hijacking,[52] unlawful acts against the safety of civil aviation,[53] marine terrorism,[54] hostage-taking[55] and theft of nuclear materials.[56]

---

[49] See Trahan, 'Terrorism Conventions: Existing Gaps and Different Approaches' 8 *New England Journal of International and Comparative Law Annual* (2002) 215 at p. 232.

[50] Zagaris, 'Financial Aspects of the War on Terror: The Merging of the Counter-Terrorism and Anti-Money Laundering Regimes' 34 *Law and Policy in International Business* (2002) 45 at p. 76.

[51] SC Resolution 1566 (2004), para 3. www.un.org/News/Press/docs/2004/sc8214.doc.htm <last visited 5 November 2008>.

[52] See the Convention on Offences and Certain Other Acts Committed on Board Aircraft 1963 (adopted on 14 September 1963, entered into force 4 December 1969) 704 U.N.T.S. 219; the Convention for the Suppression of Unlawful Seizure of Aircraft, 1970 (adopted on 16 December 1970, entered into force 14 October 1971) 860 U.N.T.S. 105.

[53] See Convention for the suppression of Unlawful Acts against the Safety of Civil Aviation 1971 (adopted on 23 September 1971, entered into force 26 January 1973) 974 UNTS 177; 10 ILM (1971) 1151.

[54] See the Convention for the Suppression of Unlawful Acts against the Safety of Maritime Navigation 1988 (adopted on 10 March 1988, entered into force 1 March 1992) 27 I.L.M. 668 (1988); the Protocol for the Suppression of Unlawful Acts against the Safety of Fixed Platforms Located on the Continental Shelf 1988 (adopted on 10 March 1988, entered into force 1 March 1992) 27 I.L.M. 685.

[55] See the Convention on the Prevention and Punishment of Crimes against Internationally Protected Persons, including Diplomatic Agents, 1973 (adopted on 14 December 1973, entered into force 20 February 1977) 1035 U.N.T.S. 167; International Convention against the Taking of Hostages 34 UN GAOR Supp (No. 39) at 23, UN Doc. A/34/39 1979 (adopted on 17 December 1979, entered into force 3 June 1980) 18 I.L.M. (1979) 1456.

[56] See Convention on the Physical Protection of Nuclear Materials 1979 (adopted on 26 October 1979, entered into force 8 February 1987) 18 I.L.M. 1419.

(ii) Review of comparative regional perspectives on defining and conceptualising terrorism

A survey of the regional instruments provides an array of definitions of terrorism. These definitions vary, depending upon ideological, social and geo-political views. The Arab Convention on the Suppression of Terrorism (1998)[57] has established a Convention on terrorism. In elaborating upon the concept, 'terrorism' is regarded as:

> Any act or threat of violence, whatever its motives or purposes, that occurs in the advancement of an individual or collective criminal agenda and seeking to sow panic among people, causing fear by harming them, or placing their lives, liberty or security in danger, or seeking to cause damage to the environment or to public or private installations or property or to occupying or seizing them, or seeking to jeopardize a national resources.[58]

The premier Council of Europe treaty dealing with terrorism, the European Convention on Prevention of Terrorism (adopted on 16 May 2005, Warsaw) does not contain a definition of terrorism.[59] Article 1 provides as follows:

> 1. For the purposes of this Convention, 'terrorist offence' means any of the offences within the scope of and as defined in one of the treaties listed in the Appendix.
>
> 2. On depositing its instrument of ratification, acceptance, approval or accession, a State or the European Community which is not a party to a treaty listed in the Appendix may declare that, in the application of this Convention to the Party concerned, that treaty shall be deemed not to be included in the Appendix. This declaration shall cease to have effect as soon as the treaty enters into force for the Party having made such a declaration, which shall notify the Secretary General of the Council of Europe of this entry into force.

The Appendix of the Convention goes on to list 10 Conventions. These offences concern aerial terrorism, as expressed in the Hague Convention (1970) and the Montreal Convention (1971), offences against internationally protected persons, hostage taking and terrorist bombings.[60]

---

[57] Arab Convention on the Suppression of Terrorism, signed at a meeting held at the General Secretariat of the League of Arab States in Cairo on 22 April 1998, reprinted in United Nations, International Instruments Related to the Prevention and Suppression of International Terrorism 152, UN Sales No. E.01.V.3 (2001). Deposited with the Secretary-General of the League of Arab States. (Unofficial translation from Arabic by the United Nations English translation service) text available at www.al-bab.com/arab/docs/league/terrorism98.htm <last visited 15 April 2009>.

[58] Ibid. Article 1(2).

[59] See the European Convention on Terrorism Council of Europe Treaty Series 196. http://conventions.coe.int/Treaty/EN/Treaties/Word/196.doc <last visited 15 April 2009>.

[60] See Article 1(1–5).

The Convention also highlights the relationship of terrorism with human rights. Article 3(1) provides:

> Each Party shall take appropriate measures, particularly in the field of training of law enforcement authorities and other bodies, and in the fields of education, culture, information, media and public awareness raising, with a view to preventing terrorist offences and their negative effects while respecting human rights obligations as set forth in, where applicable to that Party, the Convention for the Protection of Human Rights and Fundamental Freedoms, the International Covenant on Civil and Political Rights, and other obligations under international law.

In providing conditions and safeguards, Article 12(1) notes:

> Each Party shall ensure that the establishment, implementation and application of the criminalisation under Articles 5 to 7 and 9 of this Convention are carried out while respecting human rights obligations, in particular the right to freedom of expression, freedom of association and freedom of religion, as set forth in, where applicable to that Party, the Convention for the Protection of Human Rights and Fundamental Freedoms, the International Covenant on Civil and Political Rights, and other obligations under international law.

Unlike the Council of Europe, the European Union does not have a specific treaty targeting international or regional terrorism. However in June 2002, the EU adopted a Framework Decision on Terrorism, which includes a common definition of terrorist offences and serious criminal sanctions, and aims at promoting extradition and information-exchanging procedures across Europe.[61] Article 1, defines 'terrorist offences' as:

> [. . .] intentional acts referred to as below in points (a) to (i) as defined as offences under national law, which, given their nature or context, may seriously damage a country or an international organisation where committed with the aim of:
>
> – seriously intimidating a population, or
> – unduly compelling a government or international organizations to perform or abstain from performing any act, or
> – seriously destabilising or destroying the fundamental political, constitutional, economic or social structures of a country or an international organization, shall be deemed to be terrorist offences:
>
> (a) attacks upon a person's life which may cause death;
> (b) attacks upon the physical integrity of a person;
> (c) kidnapping or hostage taking;
> (d) causing extensive destruction to a Government or public facility, a transport system, an infrastructure facility, including an information system, a fixed platform located on the continental shelf, a public place or private property likely to endanger human life or result in major economic loss;

---

[61] Council Framework Decision of 13 June 2002 on Combating Terrorism Official Journal L 164, 22/06/2002 P.0003–0007; text available at www.juris.u-szeged.hu/tanszekek/bunteto/egyeb/pdf/2002475jha.pdf <last visited 4 March 2009>.

(e) seizure of aircraft, ship or other means of public or goods transport;
(f) manufacture, possession, acquisition, transport, supply or use of weapons, explosives or of nuclear, biological or chemical weapons, as well as research into and development of, biological and chemical weapons;
(g) release of dangerous substances, or causing fires, floods or explosions the effect of which is to endanger human life;
(h) interfering with or disrupting the supply of water, power or any other fundamental natural resources the effect of which is to endanger human life;
(i) threatening to commit any of the acts listed in (a) to (h).[62]

The Organization of African Unity (now the African Union) adopted the Convention on the Prevention and Combating of Terrorism at its 35th Ordinary Session of the Assembly of Heads of State and Government in 1999, in Algiers.[63] The Convention provides a detailed definition of a 'terrorist act'. According to Article 1(3):

(a) any act which is a violation of the criminal laws of a State Party and which may endanger the life, physical integrity or freedom of, or cause serious injury or death to, any person, any number or group of persons or causes or may cause damage to public or private property, natural resources, environmental or cultural heritage and is calculated or intended to:

(i) intimidate, put in fear, force, coerce or induce any government, body, institution, the general public or any segment thereof, to do or abstain from doing any act, or to adopt or abandon a particular standpoint, or to act according to certain principles; or
(ii) disrupt any public service, the delivery of any essential service to the public or to create a public emergency; or
(iii) create general insurrection in a State;

(b) any promotion, sponsoring, contribution to, command, aid, incitement, encouragement, attempt, threat, conspiracy, organizing, or procurement of any person, with the intent to commit any acts referred to in paragraph (a)(i) to (iii).

Article 3, however, has the caveat that:

[n]otwithstanding the provisions of Article 1, the struggle waged by peoples in accordance with the principles of international law for their liberation or self-determination, including armed struggle against colonialism occupation, aggression and domination by foreign forces shall not be considered as terrorist acts.

---

[62] Ibid. Article 1.
[63] OAU Convention on the Prevention and Combating of Terrorism adopted at Algiers on 14 (1999) OAU Doc. *AHG/Dec. 132 (XXXV)* 1999. Despite the adoption of the Convention, the African States still have to overcome handicaps, generated by lack of means and capabilities to combat terrorism; few African States have these means at their disposal. See *Press Note Meeting of African Union Member States on the Prevention and Combating of Terrorism* (New York, Mission of Algeria to UN, 26 August 2002).

Another significant provision is Article 22 which states that '[n]othing in this Convention shall be interpreted as derogating from the general principles of international law, in particular the principles of international humanitarian law, as well as the African Charter on Human and Peoples' Rights'. It is, nevertheless, unfortunate that the standards and principles of human rights are not further articulated within the Convention. The OAU, which is now represented in the form of the African Union (AU), also decided to set up an African Centre for the Study and Research on Terrorism and in September 2002 adopted a Plan of Action on the Prevention and Combating of Terrorism.[64] We have already noted in chapter 11 the OIC Convention on Terrorism.

The South Asian Association for Regional Cooperation (SAARC) has also addressed the subject of international and regional terrorism. The SAARC Regional Convention on the Suppression of Terrorism has a broad approach towards definitional issues.[65] Article I lists a number of international treaties and offences which are deemed terrorist acts. The treaties listed include: the Convention for the Suppression of Unlawful Seizure of Aircraft (1970); the Convention of the Suppression of Unlawful acts Against the Safety of Civil Aviation (1971); and the Convention on the Prevention and Punishment of Crimes Against International Protected Persons, including Diplomatic Agents (1973). Furthermore, according to the provisions of Article I(d) a terrorist offence includes '[a]n offence within the scope of any Convention to which SAARC Member States concerned are parties and which obliges the parties to prosecute or grant extradition'.

The wide ambit of the definition of terrorism is exemplified by the incorporation of violations of public order, leading to violence against individuals and property. The offences include murder, manslaughter, serious bodily harm, kidnapping, hostage-taking and offences relating to firearms, weapons, explosives and dangerous substances when used as a means to perpetuate indiscriminate violence resulting in death or serious damage to human lives or property. There is further discretion provided to Member States to expand the scope of terrorist acts, by recognising other serious violent offences and deny these the stature of political offences.[66]

This overview of definitions from comparative regional instruments provides interesting perspectives on the debate. A critical review of these instruments, however, reveals the breadth and expansive approaches to the subject. This breadth of the scope allows for the incorporation of a range of terrorist actions. Having said that, there are provisions which provide Member States undue discretion in curbing dissent and political opposition. This feature is evident in the AU and the Arab League Conventions. The AU Convention includes within its ambit 'acts . . . calculated or intended to create general insurrection in a State'. Similarly the Arab League Convention regards, *inter alia*, those aiming to 'sow panic among people, causing fear by harming . . . cause damage to the environment or to public or private installations or property or to occupying or seizing them, or seeks to jeopardize a national resources'. These definitions are echoed in the domestic legislation of

---

[64] See Decision on Terrorism in Africa, Assembly/AU/Dec.15(II); Plan of Action of the African Union High Level Inter-Governmental Meeting on the Prevention and Combating of Terrorism in Africa, Mtg/HLIG/Conv.Terror/Plan (I); Murray, *Human Rights in Africa: From the OAU to the African Union* (Cambridge University Press, 2004) at p. 132.

[65] SAARC Regional Convention on Suppression of Terrorism 1987 (signed at Kathmandu on 4 November 1987, entered into force 22 August 1988). The treaty is deposited with the Secretary-General of the South Asian Association for Regional Cooperation. http://untreaty.un.org/English/Terrorism.asp. <last visited 14 August 2008>.

[66] See Article II.

Member States.[67] It is this element of discretion and authorisation to deploy a subjective assessment to the situation which is dangerous for both civil liberties and the protection of individual and group rights.

3 TERRORISM AND INTERNATIONAL LAW – HISTORICAL DEVELOPMENTS

A historical analysis establishes an unfortunate picture of the antiquity of the crime of terrorism.[68] The phenomenon of terrorism is as old as human history; since time immemorial there have been sad tales of terrorism and violence against the weak and the inarticulate. Many examples can be found where terrorism was accompanied by gross violations of human rights including torture and genocide. Amongst these one could mention the horrifying massacres resulting from the Assyrian warfare during the seventh and eight centuries BC and the Roman obliteration of the city of Carthage and all its inhabitants.[69] Certain religious ideologies, and the wars that were conducted to further those ideologies, had a large element of terrorism and intolerance.[70]

In more recent times the term 'terror' was associated with the Jacobin 'Reign of Terror' in the aftermath of the French Revolution.[71] The Jacobin 'Reign of Terror' led to 17,000 official executions, with several thousand deaths and disappearances.[72] The First World War was the product of an international act of terrorism – the assassination of Archduke Francis Ferdinand on 28 June 1914 by the Serbians.[73] In the course of the next 50 years, the expression was broadened to include 'anyone who attempts to further his views by a system of coercive intimidation; especially applied to members of one of the extreme revolutionary societies in Russia'.[74] Throughout the 20th century, the rise of nationalism, totalitarian ideologies such as Nazism and Stalinism, and the upsurge of racial, religious and linguistic extremism have been accompanied by terrorism. It is also the case that the essence of colonialism was terrorism in the form of violence and intimidation of indigenous peoples.[75] In the aftermath of the Second World War, State-sponsored terrorism was

Terrorism as a crime in international law

[67] The Algerian penal code, for example, includes within its definition of terrorism 'harm[ing] the environment, means of communication or means of transport'. Article 1 of Decree No. 93-03, reproduced in article 87 bis of Ordinance No 95.11 of 25 February 1995 amending and supplementing Ordinance No 66.156 of 8 June 1966 enacting the Penal Code. Text provided in the Report submitted by Algeria to the Security Council Committee established pursuant to resolution 1373 (2001) S/2002/972 at 6.

[68] See Laqueur and Alexander (eds), *The Terrorism Reader: A Historical Anthology* (Routledge, 1987); Rehman, *The Weaknesses in the International Protection of Minority Rights* (Kluwer Law International, 2000) pp. 51–75.

[69] Kuper, *Genocide: Its Political Use in the Twentieth Century* (Yale University Press, 1983) pp. 11–18; Porter (ed.), *Genocide and Human Rights: A Global Anthology* (University Press of America, 1982); Kuper, *The Prevention of Genocide* (Yale University Press, 1985); Kuper, *International Action Against Genocide* (Minorty Rights Group, 1984); Fein (ed.), *Genocide Watch* (Yale University Press, 1992).

[70] Kuper, above n.69, pp. 12–14; see Special Rapporteur B. Whitaker, *Revised and Updated Report on the Question of the Prevention and Punishment of the Crime of Genocide* UN Doc. E/CN.4/Sub.2/1985/6B, pp. 6–7; also see Brownlie, *International Law and the Use of Force by States* (Clarendon Press, 1963).

[71] See Murphy, above n.13, at p. 14.

[72] Lambert, above n.1, at p. 15.

[73] Dinstein, above n.12, at p. 56.

[74] Cited in Green, above n.11, at p. 337.

[75] See Qureshi, 'Political Violence in the South Asian Subcontinent' in Alexander (ed.), above n.1, at pp. 151–193; see also the Reports of the sessions of the Working Group on Indigenous Populations and the Working Group on Minorities; Porter, above n.69, at p. 16; Kuper, above n.69, at p. 15.

deployed to resist granting the right of self-determination to many of the oppressed nations and peoples.[76] The terrorism of colonialism produced a backlash. Terrorism was often met with counter-terrorism; the colonisers used terror as an instrument to maintain their hold over their overseas territories, whereas the indigenous peoples and their national liberation movements resorted to terrorism and political violence as a means to gain emancipation and independence.[77] In their effort to rid themselves of what they perceived as alien, foreign and unlawful domination resistance movements were formed. Many of the so-called 'national liberation movements' such as the Algerian Liberation Movement (FLN)[78] African National Congress (South Africa),[79] Irish Republican Army (Ireland),[80] Indian National Congress and Muslim League (British India) have all, at one point, been deemed terrorist organisations.[81]

At the height of the decolonisation movement, the issue of terrorism became a matter of serious contention between States with overseas colonies on the one hand and the newly independent and communist States on the other. Even at the end of the decolonisation period, the legacies of colonial times render the subject often an unpalatable one. There is a substantial relationship with the right to self-determination for such groups or peoples as the Palestinians.[82] In this context it needs to be noted that Osama Bin Laden, the prime suspect for the attack on the World Trade Center on 11 September 2001 has consistently placed an emphasis on the right of self-determination for the Palestinian peoples as a prerequisite to world peace and security. Another particularly controversial area is the right of the Kashmiri Muslims to self-determination; the conflict between India and Pakistan on the territory of Kashmir already having produced three wars.[83]

(i) International efforts to formulate legal principles prohibiting all forms of terrorism

(a) Inter-War years 1919–39

The absence of established judicial bodies, executive agencies and effective enforcement powers has led to particular difficulties in devising international legal norms to combat terrorism. Such lacunae have also resulted in serious difficulties in the detection and punishment of terrorists. International terrorism was debated by the third (Brussels) International Conference for the Unification of Penal law held on 26–30 June 1930.[84] Parallel efforts were made by the League of Nations to formulate a binding instrument on

---

[76] Elagab, *International Law Documents Relating to Terrorism* (Cavendish, 1995) p. iv.

[77] For a useful analysis see Minority Rights Group (ed.), *World Directory of Minorities* (Minority Rights Group, 1997).

[78] See Kuper, *The Pity of it All: Polarisation of Racial and Ethnic Relations* (Gerald Duckworth & Co, 1977).

[79] See Dubow, *The African National Congress* (Sutton Publishing Ltd, 2000); Beinart and Dubow, *Segregation And Apartheid in Twentieth-Century South Africa* (Routledge, 1995).

[80] See Patterson, *The Politics of Illusion: A Political History of the IRA* (Serif, 1997); Smith, *Fighting for Ireland?: The Military Strategy of the Irish Republican Movement* (Routledge, 1995).

[81] Hardy, *The Muslims of British India* (Cambridge University Press, 1972); Tomlinson, *The Indian National Congress and the Raj, 1929–1942: The Penultimate Phase* (Maclean-Hunter Press, 1976); Jalal, *The Sole Spokesman: Jinnah, the Muslim League, and the Demand for Pakistan* (Cambridge University Press, 1985).

[82] On the complication generated by the definition of 'peoples' and 'indigenous peoples' see above chapter 14.

[83] For further consideration see Rehman, 'Re-Assessing the Right to Self-Determination: Lessons from the Indian Experience' 29 *AALR* (2000) 454.

[84] Labayle, 'Droit International et Lutte Contre Le Terrorisme' 32 *Annuaire Français de droit International* (1986) 105, at p. 114.

international terrorism. Following the assassination of King Alexander of Yugoslavia and Mr. Louis Barthou, Foreign Minister of the French Republic in Marseilles in October 1934, the League of Nations drafted a Convention for the Prevention and Punishment of Terrorism.[85] The treaty contained a number of positive elements. In addition to containing a definition, it obliged States parties to prevent and punish acts of terrorism. It imposed criminal sanctions for such acts as attacks on the lives and physical integrity of heads of States and other public officials, destruction of public property and acts calculated to endanger the lives of members of the public.[86] Despite its many positive aspects, the Convention failed to become operative. A prominent feature (which discouraged further ratifications) was the broad definition accorded to terrorism. The Convention remained ineffective, having received one ratification, that from British India. In any event the forces of aggression and terrorism emerged in Europe; the Second World War heralded the demise of the League of Nations, along with its Convention on Terrorism.

(b) Post-1945 developments

At the end of the Second World War, there were renewed efforts to produce a consolidated instrument dealing with terrorism. However, the first two decades of the United Nations period were taken up by a range of issues within which the subject of terrorism only formed an incidental part. The Draft Code on Offences against the Peace and Security of Mankind as prepared by the International Law Commission in 1954 dealt primarily with the principles enshrined in the Charter of the Nuremberg Tribunal and with the judgment of the Tribunal.[87] Article 2(6), however, defines an offence against the peace and security of mankind as:

> the undertaking or encouragement by the authorities of a State of terrorist activities in another State, or the toleration by the authorities in another State, or the toleration by the authorities of a State of organized activities calculated to carry out terrorist acts in another State.

Further progress on the completion of the code was hampered, *inter alia,* by disagreements over the definition of aggression. The General Assembly then turned its attention to the subject of the definition of aggression, an issue that was only resolved through the General Assembly Resolution on the Definition of Aggression (1974).[88] Article 3(g) of the Resolution includes in its explanation of acts of aggression:

> The sending by or on behalf of a State of armed bands, groups, irregulars or mercenaries, which carry out acts of armed force against another State of such gravity as to amount to the acts listed above, or its substantial involvement therein.

---

[85] The Convention for the Prevention and Punishment of Terrorism, 16 November 1937, 19 League of Nations Official Journal (1938) 23 reprinted 27 UN GAOR, Annex I, Agenda Item No. 92, UN Doc. A/C.6/418 (1972); Saul, above n.22, at p. 61.

[86] Article 2.

[87] See UN GAOR Supp. (No. 9) at 11–12; UN Doc. A/2693 (1972).

[88] GA Res. 3314 (XXIX) Annex 14 December 1974. G.A.O.R 29th Sess., Supp. 31, 142; 69 AJIL (1975) 480.

There was, however, a caveat which exempts national liberation movements in their struggle for self-determination.[89] Such an exemption, although a feature of this Resolution (and a number of subsequent UN General Assembly Resolutions), has added considerable uncertainty as regards the condemnation of terrorist activities. In 1979 the General Assembly passed its Resolution 34/145 which condemned all acts of terrorism. At the same time, the Resolution also condemned 'the continuation of repressive and terrorist acts by colonial, racist and alien régimes in denying people their legitimate right to self-determination and independence and other human rights and fundamental freedoms'.[90] The title and the text of the Resolution also confirms that the focus of the Resolution is upon the 'underlying causes of those forms of terrorism and acts of violence which lie in misery, frustration, grievance and despair and which cause some people to sacrifice human lives, including their own, in an attempt to effect radical changes'.[91] The same emphasis on the underlying causes of terrorism is placed in General Assembly Resolutions 36/109 (1981)[92] and General Assembly Resolution 40/61 (1985).[93]

The debates within the United Nations General Assembly have represented fundamental divisions between the developing and the developed world. The developed world has insisted on the absolute prohibition of terrorism, regardless of the motives and underlying causes. The developing world, on the other hand, has remained suspicious of this approach, claiming that underlying causes of terrorism need to provide the determining factors and national liberation movements must be allowed to resort to every conceivable means to rid themselves from colonial or racist regimes. This conflict has been so severe as to seriously jeopardise any progress in devising international mechanisms to deal with terrorism.

(c) Ending of the Cold War and shift in policies

The end of the Cold War and a thaw in East–West relations has brought about a significant change in the policies of the former Communist States. Many of these States have embraced the global human rights regime and have also renounced sponsorship of terrorist activities.[94] Over the years, the developing States themselves have shown signs of changing their position. This changing position can be attributed to a variety of reasons. Firstly, with the independence of a vast majority of former European colonies the basis of supporting the national liberation movements has diminished. The case for liberation movements is confined to the struggle of States such as Israel. Secondly, and perhaps more significantly, the new States which emerged from the rubble of decolonisation have themselves been challenged by secessionist movements represented by various groups. Amongst these

---

[89] Article 7 of the Resolution provides: 'Nothing in this Definition, and in particular Article 3, could in any way prejudice the right to self-determination, freedom and independence, as derived from the Charter, of peoples forcibly deprived of that right and referred to in the Declaration on Principles of International Law concerning Friendly Relations and co-operation among States in accordance with the Charter of the United Nations, particularly peoples under colonial and racist regimes or other forms of alien domination; nor the right of these peoples to struggle to that end and to seek and receive support, in accordance with the principles of the Charter and in conformity with the above-mentioned Declaration.'

[90] UN GA Res. 34/145 (1979), para 4.

[91] UN GA Res. 34/145 (1979).

[92] UN GA Res. 36/109 (1981).

[93] UN GA Res. 40/61 (1985).

[94] For the ratification of human rights treaties of the former Communist States see the UN website.

groups one could cite the Tamil Tigers, the Sudanese Peoples Liberation Army and the Kashmiri Mujaheedaen.[95] These groups adopted similar tactics hitherto used against the nationalists seeking independent statehood from European colonisers. Many of the new States, while emphasising the principle of territorial integrity, have treated these secessionist organisations as terrorist groups. Increasingly, these organisations have targeted diplomatic personnel and there have been instances of hijacking of national aircrafts owned by developing States. The emergence of common concerns has led to fluidity in the position of many of the countries of Asia and Africa.

Signs of a common concern in respect of terrorism were already emerging in the 1970s. According to the Declaration on Principles of International Law Concerning Friendly Relations and Co-operation Amongst States in Accordance with the Charter of the United Nations (1970):[96]

> Every State has the duty to refrain from organizing, instigating, assisting or participating in acts of civil strife or terrorist acts in another State or acquiescing in organized activities within its territory directed towards the commission of such acts, when the acts referred to in the present paragraph involve a threat or use of force.

In 1979, the Ad Hoc Committee on Terrorism, a committee formed pursuant to General Assembly Resolution 3034[97] recommended, *inter alia*, that the General Assembly: condemn attacks of terrorists; take note of the underlying causes contained in the Committee's reports; work towards the elimination of terrorism in compliance with their obligations under international law; refrain from organising, instigating, assisting or participating in terrorist acts in other States and allowing their territory to be used for such acts; and take all possible measures to co-operate with each other to combat international terrorism.

The General Assembly adopted these recommendations, although as noted in the earlier section these recommendations were tempered by the terminology of 'underlying causes' and the 'right to self-determination'. Further progress was made in 1985 when the UN General Assembly adopted a Resolution in which it urged States to take measures 'with a view to the speedy and final elimination of the problem of international terrorism'.[98] The Assembly also took the position that it:

> [u]nequivocally condemns, as criminal, all acts, methods and practices of terrorism wherever and by whomever committed, including those which jeopardize friendly relations among States and their security [and] . . . Deeply deplores the loss of innocent human lives which results from such acts of terrorism.[99]

A distinctive feature of the Resolution is that, after a protracted debate of 15 years, for the first time in the United Nations, this Resolution associates the term 'criminal' with

---

[95] For consideration of these and other cases see Minority Rights Group (ed.), above n.77.
[96] GA Res. 2625 (XXV) (1970).
[97] See Report of the Sixth Committee, UN GAOR A/8969 (1972) at p. 5.
[98] GA Res. 40/61 (1985), para 5.
[99] GA Res. 40/61 (1985), paras 1 and 2.

terrorism.[100] Another Resolution (based along the lines of the 1985 Resolution) condemning terrorism was adopted by the General Assembly in 1987.[101] In 1994, the General Assembly adopted a Resolution entitled 'The Declaration on Measures to Eliminate International Terrorism'.[102] Peace, security and restraint of the use of force represent the basis of the Declaration. In condemning terrorism the Declaration also calls upon States to refrain from organising, instigating, assisting or participating in terrorist activities and from acquiescing in or encouraging activities within their territories directed towards the commission of any such acts. The Ad Hoc Committee that was formed in 1996 (GA Res. 210) was instrumental in drafting of the Convention for the Suppression of Terrorist Bombing 1997, Financing of Terrorism 1999 and the Convention on Nuclear Terrorism. The Ad Hoc Committee, as discussed earlier, has also been active in the drafting of a comprehensive treaty on international terrorism.[103] It is noticeable that since the end of the Cold War, the General Assembly has been active in its condemnation of global terrorism. Such activism and unified views on the subject represent a positive development. At the same time it is important to recognise the fact that a significant reason for such activism is that General Assembly Resolutions are not legally binding *per se*; ambiguous terminology can be deployed to represent a show of unanimity in condemning terrorism.[104] The situation would be radically different if States were required to subscribe to any internationally binding agreement on global terrorism. The old differences and suspicions are certain to resurface.

(d) Dealing with specific terrorist activities

As we have noted above, in the light of substantial disagreements over the definition, nature and scope of terrorism, the international community has been unable to formulate a single consolidated instrument dealing with terrorism. Progress has, however, been made in a number of related areas. A range of treaties have been entered under the auspices of the United Nations and regional organisations. In addition, the International Civil Aviation Organization (ICAO) and the International Maritime Organization (IMO) have also been successful in sponsoring conventions dealing with aerial and maritime terrorism respectively. There are currently more than 12 Conventions and Protocols that deal with the various aspects of terrorism. These include: the Convention on the Prevention and Punishment of Crimes against Internationally Protected Persons, Including Diplomatic Agents, adopted by the General Assembly of the United Nations (1973);[105] the International Convention against the Taking of Hostages, adopted by the General Assembly of the United Nations (1979);[106] the International Convention for the Suppression of Terrorist Bombings, adopted by the General Assembly of the United Nations on 15 December 1997;[107] the

---

[100] Van den Wyngaert, 'The Political Offence Exception to Extradition: How to Plug the "Terrorists' Loophole" without Departing from Fundamental Human Rights' 19 *IYBHR* (1989) 297 at p. 297.

[101] GA Res. 42/159 7 Dec 1987. Writing in 1989, Lambert made the following useful points: 'The change in language in the most recent General Assembly Resolutions must be seen some progress towards a universal consensus that acts of terrorism are not to be tolerated regardless of the cause. It must also be recognised, however, that the General Assembly continues to send out somewhat mixed signals regarding the issue of national liberation movements.' Lambert, above n.1, at p. 44.

[102] GA Res. A/Res/49/60.

[103] See Report of the Sixth Committee, 2003 A/56/593; also see GA Res. 63/129 (11 December 2008).

[104] On the value of General Assembly Resolutions, see above chapter 2.

[105] 1035 U.N.T.S. 167; 13 I.L.M. 41 (1974).

[106] 1316 U.N.T.S. 205; 18 I.L.M. 1460 (1979).

[107] Doc. A/Res/52/164; depository notification C.N.801.2001.TREATIES-9 of 12 October 2001.

International Convention for the Suppression of the Financing of Terrorism, adopted by the General Assembly of the United Nations on 9 December 1999;[108] the Convention on Offences and Certain Other Acts Committed on Board Aircraft (1963);[109] the Convention for the Suppression of Unlawful Seizure of Aircraft, signed at the Hague on (1970);[110] the Convention for the Suppression of Unlawful Acts against the Safety of Civil Aviation (1971);[111] the Convention on the Physical Protection of Nuclear Material (1980);[112] the Protocol on the Suppression of Unlawful Acts of Violence at Airports Serving International Civil Aviation, supplementary to the Convention for the Suppression of Unlawful Acts Against the Safety of Civil Aviation, signed at Montreal on 24 February 1988;[113] the Convention for the Suppression of Unlawful Acts against the Safety of Maritime Navigation (1988);[114] the Protocol for the Suppression of Unlawful Acts against the Safety of Fixed Platforms Located on the Continental Shelf (March 1988);[115] and the Convention on the Marking of Plastic Explosives for the Purpose of Detection, (1991).[116] As noted above, there are also a number of regional conventions on terrorism. These include: the Arab Convention on the Suppression of Terrorism (1998);[117] the Convention of the Organisation of the Islamic Conference on Combating International Terrorism (1999);[118] the Council of Europe's Convention on the Prevention of Terrorism concluded in Warsaw on 16 May 2005;[119] the OAS Convention to Prevent and Punish Acts of Terrorism Taking the Form of Crimes against Persons and Related Extortion that are of International Significance (1971);[120] the OAU Convention on the Prevention and Combating of Terrorism, adopted at Algiers (1999);[121] the SAARC Regional Convention on Suppression of Terrorism, (1987);[122] and the Treaty on Co-operation among States Members of the Commonwealth of Independent States in Combating Terrorism (1999).[123] Furthermore, a range of non-binding international instruments have been adopted. The following sections consider some of the international instruments that have been adopted at the international and regional levels to combat terrorism; the relevance *vis-à-vis* human rights obligations is of great significance.

24

Terrorism as a crime in international law

---

[108] Resolution A/Res/54/109; depository notifications C.N.327.2000.TREATIES-12 of 30 May 2000. This Convention within its texts 'includes the first general definition of terrorism'; see Steiner, Alston and Goodman, above n.1, at p. 376.

[109] 2 I.L.M. 1042 (1963).

[110] 10 I.L.M. 133 (1971).

[111] 10 I.L.M. 1151 (1971).

[112] Text available at www.untreaty.un.org/English/Terrorism.asp <last visited 31 March 2009>.

[113] 27 I.L.M. 627 (1988).

[114] 27 I.L.M.668 (1988).

[115] 27 I.L.M 685 (1988).

[116] 30 I.L.M. 726 (1991).

[117] Arab Convention on the Suppression of Terrorism, signed at a meeting held at the General Secretariat of the League of Arab States in Cairo on 22 April 1998. (Deposited with the Secretary-General of the League of Arab States), reprinted in United Nations, International Instruments Related to the Prevention and Suppression of International Terrorism 152, UN Sales No. E.01.V.3 (2001).

[118] Text available at www.untreaty.un.org/English/Terrorism.asp <last visited 31 March 2009>.

[119] 2005. ETS No. 196.

[120] 10 I.L.M. 255 (1971).

[121] OAU Convention on the Prevention and Combating of Terrorism, adopted at Algiers on 14 July 1999. OAU Doc. *AHG/Dec. 132 (XXXV)* 1999.

[122] Text available at www.untreaty.un.org/English/Terrorism.asp <last visited 31 March 2009>.

[123] Treaty on Co-operation among States Members of the Commonwealth of Independent States in Combating Terrorism, done at Minsk on 4 June 1999. (Deposited with the Secretariat of the Commonwealth of Independent States). http://untreaty.un.org/English/Terrorism/csi_e.pdf <last visited 3 March 2009>.

4 ACTS OF TERRORISM AND HUMAN RIGHTS VIOLATIONS

Acts of terrorism constitute a serious assault on human dignity. Terrorist actions lead to gross violations of fundamental human rights, such as the right to life, integrity, personal liberties and freedoms. The international community has acted with great vigour to adopt international instruments and standards in the aftermath of major terrorist incidents. Amongst these instruments, one could take the example of key treaties such as those dealing with the prohibition of hostage taking, the protection of internationally protected persons as well as the criminalisation of maritime and aerial terrorism. The taking of hostages is synonymous with arbitrary deprivation of liberty although the crime of taking hostages was originally only confined to armed conflict. A number of indictments were brought forward in the Nuremberg Trials for acts of hostage taking.[124] As noted in an earlier chapter, the prohibition on hostage taking during armed conflict is incorporated in Article 3 and 34 of the Fourth Geneva Conventions (1949).[125] Hostage taking was denounced as a terrorist offence and a crime in international law by the International Convention Against the Taking of Hostages, adopted by the General Assembly of the United Nations (1979).[126] The conclusion of the Convention was surrounded by a range of incidents including the Munich killings of 1972;[127] the kidnappings of German businessmen in and outside of the Federal Republic of Germany;[128] the Entebbe raid;[129] and the American hostage taking in Iran.[130]

The Hostage-Taking treaty – itself a product of laborious compromise – is laced with references to human rights, appealing to humanitarian norms and laws. The preamble recognises that 'everyone has the right to life, liberty and security of person, as set out in the Universal Declaration of Human Rights and the International Covenant on Civil and Political Rights'.[131] Hostage taking is an 'offence of grave concern' to the international community, and it is a matter of immediate urgency to prevent, prosecute and punish all acts of taking of hostages.[132] The text of the treaty regards hostage taking, *inter alia*, as seizure, detention and threats to kill or harm individuals with an objective of compelling third parties to undertake or abstain from particular actions.[133] In this definition of hostage taking, the human rights dimension of preserving individual liberty and the right not to be exploited is well articulated. The humanitarian frame of reference is reflected in the obligations of the State party in possession of the hostages. The undertaking is to engage in all appropriate measures, *inter alia*, to secure their release and facilitate their departure.[134] In instances

---

[124] See Elagab, above n.76, at p. 577.
[125] 75 U.N.T.S. 287 (1950); see above chapter 21.
[126] 1316 U.N.T.S. 205; 18 I.L.M. 1460 (1979).
[127] See Rosenstock, 'International Convention Against the Taking of Hostages: Another International Community Step Against Terrorism' 9 *Journal of International Law and Policy* 169, at p. 173.
[128] Ibid. at p. 169.
[129] For further consideration see Green, 'Rescue at Entebbe–Legal Aspects' (1976) 6 *IHYBR* 312; Shaw, 'Some Legal Aspects of the Entebbe Incident' (1978) 1 *Jewish Law Annual* 232; Harris, *Cases and Materials on International Law* (Sweet & Maxwell, 2004) pp. 933–937.
[130] *United States Diplomatic and Consular Staff in Tehran Case (United States of America v. Iran)* [1980] ICJ Reports 3; Harris, above n.129, at pp. 371–375; Gross, 'The Case Concerning United States Diplomatic and Consular Staff in Tehran: Phase of Provisional Measures' 74 *AJIL* (1980) 395; Grzybowski, 'The Regime of Diplomacy and the Tehran Hostages' 30 *ICLQ* (1981) 42.
[131] Preamble to the International Convention Against the Taking of Hostages.
[132] Ibid.
[133] Article 1 the International Convention Against the Taking of Hostages.
[134] Ibid. Article 3(1).

where an object comes into the custody of a State party, there is an obligation on the State party to restore it either to the hostage or to an appropriate third party as the case may be.[135]

Crimes against internationally protected persons, itself a crime within general international law, also constitutes a serious violation of the rights of the individuals concerned: these individuals are targeted and victimised as a consequence of their official positions. These crimes against internationally protected persons continue to be one of serious global concern. According to one study, during 1946–80, there were no less than 186 attacks either against the diplomatic missions or against the missions themselves; 44 deaths occurred in the process.[136] A proliferation of incidents led the international community to adopt binding instruments condemning and criminalising hostage taking in all its forms. One unfortunate example of the violation of the rights of internationally protected persons was the murder of the ambassador of Yugoslavia in Stockholm in April 1971.[137] An additional, more publicised incident was the hostage taking in Vienna during 1975 whereby terrorist seized 60 OPEC ministers.[138]

Amidst this cycle of violence the United Nations was involved in taking legislative measures to counter attacks on internationally protected persons. In April 1971, the representative of the Netherlands had requested a binding instrument to overcome existing gaps in international law from the President of the United Nations Security Council. The proposal of the Netherlands representative was transmitted to the ILC.[139] The ILC placed the question of the protection of the inviolability of diplomats on its agenda for the 1972 session and proceeded to draft articles pertaining to this matter. Simultaneously a working group was established which drew up and presented 12 draft articles to the ILC during the same session.[140] The drafts were discussed and amendments having been made were submitted by the ILC to the General Assembly's Sixth (Legal) Committee. While there were concerns over some issues, the draft on the whole was well received.

In 1973, the General Assembly adopted, by consensus, Resolution 3166 (XXVIII) attached to which is the Convention on the Prevention and Punishment of Crimes against Internationally Protected Persons, Including Diplomatic Agents (1973).[141] This Convention (also known as the New York Convention) represents the most far-reaching global instrument dealing with crimes committed against internationally protected persons. It has, in the words of Dembinski, three primary functions:

(a) to make sure that every person committing or participating in a crime covered by the Convention will be tried or extradited and will not remain unpunished; (b) to dissuade in this way possible offenders from committing these crimes and finally, (c) to secure a minimum of international co operation in preventing them.[142]

---

[135] Ibid. Article 3(2).
[136] Dembinski, *The Modern Law of Diplomacy: External Missions of States and International Organizations* (Brill, 1988) at p. 167.
[137] See the Pavelic Papers, 'Miro Baresic's Deportation from Sweden' (December 1987) www.pavelicpapers. com/documents/baresic/mb0002.ht <last visited 10 September 2008>.
[138] Organization of the Petroleum Exporting Countries. See 'Suspect in OPEC Hostage-taking Arrested' 15 October 1999 www.ict.org.il/spotlight/det.cfm?id=340 <last visited 15 March 2009>, 'Repentant German Terrorist Given Nine-year Sentence' 15 February 2001 www.ict.org.il/spotlight/det.cfm?id=566 <last visited 20 April 2008>; Davies, *Terrorism: Inside a World Phenomenon* (Virgin Books, 2003) pp. 103–106.
[139] Dembinski, above n.136, at p. 13.
[140] Ibid. at p. 13.
[141] Adopted 14 December 1973, entered into force 20 February 1977 1035 UNTS 167; (1974) 13 ILM 41.
[142] Dembinski, above n.136 at pp. 167–168.

The New York Convention protects certain categories of persons from the offences of murder, kidnapping or other attacks upon their official premises, private accommodation and means of transportation. Attempts to commit any such acts are also categorised as offences.[143] Similarly, according to Article 2, actions of accomplices and participants are also deemed criminal offences.[144] In detailing the category of internationally protected persons, Article 1 provides:

[f]or the purposes of this Convention:

1. 'Internationally Protected Person' means:

   (a) A Head of State, including any member of a collegial body performing the function of a Head of State under the constitution of the State concerned, a Head of Government or a Minister for Foreign Affairs, whenever any such person is in a foreign State, as well as members of his family who accompany him;

   (b) Any representative or official of a State or any official or other agent of an international organization of an intergovernmental character who, at the time when and in the place where a crime against him, his official premises, his private accommodation or his means of transport is committed, is entitled pursuant to international law to special protection from any attack on his person, freedom or dignity, as well as members of his family forming part of his household.

States are required to co-operate with one another in the prevention of crimes against internationally protected persons. Efforts to prevent the crimes of violence against internationally protected persons entail the 'exchanging of information and coordinating the taking of administrative and other [appropriate] measures'[145] as well as taking 'all practicable measure to prevent preparations in their respective territories for the commission of those crimes within or outside their territories'.[146] The jurisdiction of the State is established when crimes are committed against internationally protected persons either in its territory, on board a ship or aircraft registered in that State or when the offender is one of its nationals.[147] The State is under an obligation to take all necessary steps to establish its jurisdiction, if it fails to extradite the individual to another State, thereby confirming the principle *aut dedere aut judicare*.[148] Aspects of this principle are further elaborated through Articles 6 and Articles 7. According to Article 6, States parties are required to take the appropriate measures to ensure the presence of the alleged offender either to stand trial or to be extradited. In addition to hostage taking and crimes against internationally protected persons, maritime and aerial terrorism represents a major international concern.

The act of maritime terrorism, as conducted in the hijacking of the *Achille Lauro* and involving the unfortunate murder of a disabled Jewish man Leo Klinghoffer on board the

---

[143] Article 2(1)(d) the Convention on the Prevention and Punishment of Crimes against Internationally Protected Persons, including Diplomatic Agents.
[144] Ibid. Article 2(1)(e).
[145] Ibid. Article 4(b).
[146] Ibid. Article 4(a).
[147] Ibid. Article 3(1).
[148] Ibid. Article 3(2).

Achille Lauro[149] galvanised the international community to review international standards on maritime terrorism. The Convention for the Suppression of Unlawful Acts Against the Safety of Maritime Navigation was adopted in Rome during March 1988. In order to shorten the otherwise complex process, the Council of the International Maritime Organization established an *ad hoc* Preparatory Committee which was to be open to all States with the 'mandate to prepare, on a priority basis, a draft Convention for the Suppression of Unlawful Acts Against the Safety of Maritime Navigation'. The meetings of the Preparatory Committee took place in March and May 1987 in London and Rome respectively. A final text was approved in a conference held in Rome in March 1988. In defining, the terrorist offences, the Convention also contains the inclusion of murder as a separate crime – clearly a confirmation of the impact of the murder of Leo Klinghoffer.[150]

As the acts of 11 September 2001 confirm, aerial terrorism can lead to substantial violations of human rights and indeed trigger serious international conflicts. The events of 11 September 2001 which triggered the so-called 'war on terror' have important implications for human rights and shall be examined in more detail later in the chapter. The international community has moved swiftly towards an emphasis on freezing of assets of those involved in terrorist actions in order to prevent them receiving vital financial support. The International Convention for the Suppression of the Financing of Terrorism (1999), as its title suggests, aims to suppress all forms of funding and financing of terrorism. States are under an obligation to deny a safe haven to those who finance terrorists and to bring to justice all those who have been engaged in the financing of terrorism. With both State and non-State actors involved in committing offences, terrorism can be supported by the financial dealings of private agents, banks and other monetary institutions. The scrutiny of funds raised through donations, charities,[151] charitable trusts[152] and money laundering[153] present considerable challenges to the domestic, as well as to international financial institutions.[154] Individual States have attempted to curb the international financing of terrorism through sanctions or other coercive measures, although often with limited success.[155] As we shall examine shortly, after the 11 September 2001 terrorist acts, the United Nations

---

[149] For detailed consideration of the incident see McCredie, 'Contemporary Uses of Force against Terrorism: The United States Response to Achille Lauro: Question of Jurisdiction and its Exercise' 16 *Georgia Journal of Comparative and International Law* (1986) 435; Larsen, 'The Achille Lauro Incident and the Permissible Use of Force' 9 *Loyola of Los Angeles Journal of International and Comparative Law* (1987) 481; Halberstam, 'Terrorism on the High Seas: The Achille Lauro, Piracy and the IMO Convention on Maritime Safety' 82 *AJIL* (1988) 269; Paust, 'Extradition and United States Prosecution of the Achille Lauro Hostage-Takers: Navigating the Hazards' 20 *Vanderbilt Journal of Transnational Law* (1987) 235; Gooding, 'Fighting Terrorism in the 1980's: The Interception of the Achille Lauro Hijackers' 12 *Yale Journal of International Law* (1987) 158; Pancracio 'L'affaire de L'Achille Lauro et Le Droit International' 31 *Annuarie Français de Droit International* (1985) 219.

[150] Halberstam, 'Terrorist Acts Against and on Board Ships' 19 *IYBHR* (1989) 331 at p. 333.

[151] See GA Res. 51/210 adopted 17 December 1996, para 3(f).

[152] See UK Charities Commission, Iran Aid (10 December 2001) available at www.charity-commission.gov.uk/investigations/inquiryreports/iran.asap. <last visited 20 March 2004>. In accordance with ss.15 and 16 of the Terrorism Act 2000, the UK authorities are required to criminalise fund-raising and use and possession of funds directed for terrorist purposes; Walker, *Blackstone's Guide to the Anti-Terrorism Legislation* (Oxford University Press, 2002) pp. 68–74.

[153] See Financial Action Task Force [FATF] Report on Money Laundering Typologies (2000–2001), Doc. FATF-XII, at 19–20 (1 February 2001).

[154] Bantekas, 'The International Law of Terrorist Financing' 97 *AJIL* (2003) 315, at p. 316.

[155] On the background of international economic sanctions see Carter, *International Economic Sanctions: Improving the Haphazard US Legal Regime* (Cambridge University Press, 1988); Hufbauer, *et al.*, *Economic Sanctions Reconsidered: History and Current Policy* (Institute for International Economics, 1985).

Security Council embarked upon a strict scrutiny of financial transactions aimed to suppress all forms of financing of terrorism. The Security Council's actions have led to the freezing of assets of individuals and organisations, some of these actions arguably based on arbitrary and vindictive judgments made within the Council.[156]

This chapter is limited by its scope of highlighting the interaction between terrorism and human rights law. Nevertheless, a brief analysis of regional instruments is required since such an exercise would underline the contrasting strategies adopted by various regional players in dealing with terrorism and yet at the same time attempting to uphold human rights values. As considered earlier, a number of regional instruments have been adopted to combat terrorism. The Council of Europe has passed a series of Resolutions and Declarations.[157] It has also adopted the European Convention on Prevention of Terrorism (adopted on 16 May 2005, Warsaw) and the Agreement on the Application of the European Convention for the Suppression of Terrorism (the Dublin Agreement).[158]

The Council of Europe Convention on the Prevention of Terrorism,[159] several provisions similar to other terrorism conventions including that on jurisdiction;[160] the duty to investigate;[161] extradite or prosecute;[162] extradition;[163] and the exclusion of the political exception clause.[164] There is a clear focus on the importance of human rights when combating terrorism, due to the Convention being updated by a Protocol after the terrorist attacks of 11 September 2001, to be discussed later in this chapter. The Preamble places emphasis on:

> the need to strengthen the fight against terrorism and reaffirming that all measures taken to prevent or suppress terrorist offences have to respect the rule of law and democratic values, human rights and fundamental freedoms as well as other provisions of international law, including, where applicable, international humanitarian law.

[156] The Report by the International Bar Association's Task force makes the following observations: 'The effect on the right of individuals whose assets are frozen either through specific legislation or inclusion on a list is profound. Therefore it is of particular concern that neither the relevant Security Council resolutions nor the guidelines published by the CTC establish a minimum legal framework regulating the process of asset freezing. In effect, states that introduce these measures often protect the secrecy of the information they possess. The opportunity to challenge the state's action is therefore restricted as persons affected by freezing orders and the like simply have no information as to the basis of the order, and are thus disadvantaged in any challenge they make to the orders affecting them. Whilst it is accepted that there may be security reasons for failing to provide certain information, this must be balanced by the need of the individuals to protect themselves from such draconian measures . . . The freezing of assets has the potential to irreparably damage financial interests, as well as to stigmatise a person's name and reputation.' Report by the International Bar Association's Task Force on International Terrorism, above n.44, at pp. 126–127.

[157] These include Recommendation 684 (1972) on International Terrorism; Recommendation 703 (1973) on International Terrorism; Declaration on Terrorism; Recommendation 852 (1979) on Terrorism in Europe; Recommendation 916 (1981) on the Conference on 'Defence of Democracy against Terrorism in Europe – Tasks and Problems'; Recommendation No. R (82) of the Committee of Ministers to Member States Concerning International Co-operation in the Prosecution and Punishment of Acts of Terrorism; Recommendation 941 (1982) on the Defence of Democracy against Terrorism in Europe; Recommendation of the Committee of Ministers to Member States on Measures to be Taken in Cases of Kidnapping followed by a Ransom Demand (1982); Recommendation 982 (1984) on the Defence of Democracy against Terrorism in Europe; Council of Europe Pledge to Step up Fight against Terrorism (1986); European Conference of Ministers Responsible for Combating Terrorism (1980).

[158] 19 I.L.M. 325 (1982).

[159] Signed Warsaw, 16.v.2005, ETS No. 196.

[160] Article 14 Convention on the Prevention of Terrorism.

[161] Ibid. Article 15.

[162] Ibid. Article 18.

[163] Ibid. Article 19.

[164] Ibid. Article 20.

Furthermore, Article 3 states that:

1. Each Party shall take appropriate measures, particularly in the field of training of law enforcement authorities and other bodies, and in the fields of education, culture, information, media and public awareness raising, with a view to preventing terrorist offences and their negative effects while respecting human rights obligations as set forth in, where applicable to that Party, the Convention for the Protection of Human Rights and Fundamental Freedoms, the International Covenant on Civil and Political Rights, and other obligations under international law . . .

3. Each Party shall promote tolerance by encouraging inter-religious and cross-cultural dialogue involving, where appropriate, non-governmental organisations and other elements of civil society with a view to preventing tensions that might contribute to the commission of terrorist offences.

The emphasis on inter-religious and cross-cultural dialogue is a particularly interesting addition to the 'War on Terror' and highlights the commitment of the Council of Europe not only to prevent terrorism but also 'its negative effects on the full enjoyment of human rights and in particular the right to life, both by measures to be taken at national level and through international co-operation'.[165] Rather than dealing just with the crime of terrorism and its consequences, the Convention attempts to deal with the cause of terrorism and imputes that society should take responsibility in reducing the risk. 'This is a crucial aspect of the Convention, given that it deals with issues which are on the border between the legitimate exercise of freedoms, such as freedom of expression, association or religion, and criminal behaviour'.[166] Offences such as public provocation to commit a terrorist offence,[167] recruitment for terrorism[168] and training for terrorism[169] are also defined by the Convention. Training for terrorism includes 'instruction in the making or use of explosives, firearms or other weapons or noxious or hazardous substances'. It is irrelevant whether or not the terrorist act is actually committed in order for it to constitute an offence under Articles 5 to 7.[170] Article 9 covers ancillary offences, whereas Article 10 covers legal entities.

The Council of Europe has placed particular emphasis on the respecting of human rights while combating terrorism as evidenced by Recommendation 1550 of the Parliamentary Assembly and its Opinion No. 242;[171] the Guidelines of the Committee of the Ministers on protecting freedom of expression and information in times of crisis;[172] and Parliamentary Assembly Resolution 1507 (2006) on 'Alleged secret detentions and unlawful inter-state transfers of detainees involving Council of Europe member states'.

---

[165] Explanatory Report to the Council of Europe Convention on the Prevention of Terrorism, para 24, http://conventions.coe.int/Treaty/EN/Reports/Html/196.htm <last visited 9 March 2009>.

[166] Ibid., para 30, http://conventions.coe.int/Treaty/EN/Reports/Html/196.htm <last visited 9 November 2008>.

[167] Article 5 Convention on the Prevention of Terrorism.

[168] Ibid. Article 6.

[169] Ibid. Article 7.

[170] Ibid. Article 8.

[171] Council of Europe Parliamentary Assembly Recommendation 1550 (2002) on combating terrorism and respect for human rights, Parliamentary Assembly Opinion No. 242 (2003).

[172] Guidelines of the Committee of Ministers of the Council of Europe on protecting freedom of expression and information in times of crisis (Adopted by the Committee of Ministers on 26 September 2007 at the 1005th meeting of the Ministers' Deputies).

The European Union (EU) has also passed numerous Declarations and Resolutions, and entered into treaty arrangements in order to deal with the problem of terrorism and terrorist activities.[173] The Organization of American States (OAS), which has frequently encountered this problem, has also adopted numerous specialist instruments dealing with terrorism. These include the Convention to Prevent and Punish the Act of Terrorism Taking the Form of Crimes Against Persons and Related Extortion that are of International Significance (1971);[174] the OAS General Assembly Resolution on Acts of Terrorism (1970);[175] and the Inter-American Convention Against Terrorism (2002).[176] The OAS Convention to Prevent and Punish the Act of Terrorism (1971)[177] is of special significance in that it does not allow for the political offence exception. The Convention establishes a duty for States parties to co-operate in the prevention and punishment of 'acts of terrorism'. According to Article 2 of the Convention:

> kidnapping, murder, and other assaults on life or personal integrity of those persons to whom the State has the duty to give special protection according to international law, as well as extortion in connection with those crimes, shall be considered common crimes of international significance, regardless of motive.

Furthermore, the Inter-American Convention against Terrorism (2002) establishes under its Article 11 that:

> [f]or the purposes of extradition or mutual legal assistance, none of the offenses established in the international instruments listed in Article 2 shall be regarded as a political offense or an offense connected with a political offense or an offense inspired by political motives. Accordingly, a request for extradition or mutual legal assistance may not be refused on the sole ground that it concerns a political offense or an offense connected with a political offense or an offense inspired by political motives.

These provisions are of particular interest whilst having regard to the fact that Latin American countries have a history of providing political asylum, including asylum to 'free-

---

[173] See the European Union Counter-Terrorism Strategy 14469/4/05 REV.4, available at http://register.consilium. eu.int/pdf/en/05/st14/st14469-re04.en05.pdf <last visited 7 April 2009>. Communication to the European Parliament and the Council of 6 November 2007 – Stepping up the fights against terrorism COM(2007)649 final. Council Framework Decision 2002/475/JHA of 13 June 2002 on Combating Terrorism. See also the Declaration by the European Council on International Terrorism (1976); Resolution on Acts of Terrorism in the Community (1977); European Communities: Agreement Concerning the Application of the European Convention on the Suppression of Terrorism among the Member States (1979); European Parliament Resolution on Problems Relating to Combating Terrorism (1989); also see the Treaty of European Union 1992 (Provisions on Co-operation in the Spheres of Justice and Home Affairs–Article A). 2007/124/EC, Euratom: Council Decision of 12 February 2007 establishing for the period 2007 to 2013, as part of General Programme on Security and Safeguarding Liberties, the Specific Programme 'Prevention, Preparedness and Consequence Management of Terrorism and other Security related risks'. The Hague Programme: Ten priorities for the next five years. The Partnership for European renewal in the field of Freedom, Security and Justice. COM(2005) 184 final.

[174] 10 I.L.M. (1971) 255.

[175] 9 I.L.M. (1970) 1084.

[176] AG/RES.1840 (XXXII-O/02).

[177] www.oas.org/juridico/English/treaties/a-49.html <last visited 27 December 2008>.

dom fighters'. In the light of the previously mentioned cliché, that 'one man's freedom fighter is another man's terrorist', this practice must come to an end.[178]

The OAS Convention to Prevent and Punish the Act of Terrorism (1971) is based on the principle of *aut dedere aut judicare* and has provisions regarding extradition.[179] Article 6 provides for the right of asylum and a number of obligations are contained in Article 8 for the purpose of ensuring a general duty of co-operation in the prevention and punishment of the crimes covered. According to Article 9, the Convention is open to participation of States other than members of the OAS.

In the contemporary debate on terrorism, a number of misconceptions have arisen concerning Islam, Islamic law and the State practices of Islamic States. Our earlier analysis has already elaborated on the OIC Convention on Terrorism although in the context of regional treaties it would be important to make a brief reference to this convention. As noted in an earlier chapter, the OIC was formed in Rabat, the Kingdom of Morocco, in September 1969. It has currently a membership of 56 States. In view of the growing concerns emergent from terrorism, the OIC adopted the Convention of the Organisation of the Islamic Conference on Combating International Terrorism (1999).[180] The Convention represents a strong condemnation of terrorist activities. It defines terrorism in a very clear and precise manner. Thus, according to Article 1(2) of the Convention:

> 'Terrorism' means any act of violence or threat thereof notwithstanding its motives or intentions perpetrated to carry out an individual or collective criminal plan with the aim of terrorizing people or threatening to harm them or imperilling their lives, honor, freedoms, security or rights or exposing the environment or any facility or public or private property to hazards or occupying or seizing them, or endangering a national resource, or international facilities, or threatening the stability, territorial integrity, political unity or sovereignty of independent States.

While suggesting an exception in cases of self-determination,[181] the Convention ensures that OIC members accept the established norms which prohibit and condemn international terrorism.[182] The Convention lists major treaties on the subject and requires States parties to follow the principles established in these treaties.[183] According to the Convention, special preventive measures are to be introduced by State parties and members undertake to co-operate in combating international terrorism.[184] The OIC also retains a special focus on peoples' right to self-determination and this Convention also presents a strong affirmation of the right of self-determination. Accordingly, therefore, peoples' struggle against foreign aggression and colonial or racist regimes is not to be considered a terrorist crime.[185]

---

[178] On the right to self-determination see above chapter 14.
[179] Articles 3, 5, and 7 OAS Convention to Prevent and Punish the Act of Terrorism.
[180] Text available at http://untreaty.un.org/English/Terrorism.asp <last visited 31 January 2008>.
[181] Article 2(a) Convention of the Organisation of the Islamic Conference on Combating International Terrorism (1999).
[182] Ibid. Article 2.
[183] Ibid. Article 1(4).
[184] Ibid. Article 3.
[185] Ibid. Article 2(a).

5 INTERNATIONAL LEGAL DEVELOPMENTS SINCE 11 SEPTEMBER 2001

On Tuesday 11 September 2001, four commercial planes were hijacked by terrorists. One hijacked passenger jet leaving Boston, Massachusetts crashed into the north tower of the World Trade Center at 8.45am setting the tower on fire. Eighteen minutes later, a second hijacked airliner, United Airlines Flight 175 from Boston, crashed into the south tower of the World Trade Center and exploded. Both airliners caused massive structural damage to the towers. Later that morning both the north and south tower collapsed, plummeting into the streets below. At 9.43am, a third hijacked airliner (American Airlines Flight 77) crashed into the Pentagon sending a huge plume of smoke. A portion of the building later collapsed. At 10.10am a fourth hijacked airliner (United Airlines Flight 93) crashed in Somerset county, Pennsylvania, south-east of Pittsburgh.[186] The crashing of these hijacked airliners into buildings and on land were the worst terrorist attack in the history of the United States. This led to the loss of nearly 3000 innocent lives and damaged property running into billions of dollars.

The terrorist attacks not only served as a chilling reminder of the dangers inherent in international terrorism, but also sent shock waves all around the world. The attacks were unequivocally condemned by all States and by all international organisations. On 12 September 2001, the United Nations General Assembly passed a resolution condemning the heinous acts which had resulted in loss of lives and enormous destruction.[187] While showing solidarity with the people of the United States, it called for international co-operation to bring to justice the perpetrators, organisers and sponsors of the crimes committed on 11 September. On 12 September, the United Nations Security Council also condemned the terrorist acts expressing them as a threat to international peace and security.[188] The Council called upon all States to work together urgently to bring to justice the perpetrators of the crime, organisers and sponsors of the terrorist attacks.[189] A further resolution, Resolution 1373 was adopted on 28 September 2001, requiring States to undertake a series of actions. Since the Security Council was acting under Chapter VII, all of its decisions were binding upon States.[190] Under this Resolution, the Security Council required States to adopt and implement the existing international legal instruments on terrorism, and to prevent and suppress the financing and the freezing of funds and financial matters. It also required that States allow one another assistance for criminal investigations and proceedings related to the financing or support of terrorist acts.[191] According to the Resolution, States are also to prevent the movement of terrorists or their groups by effective border controls. The Security Council also determined that States shall intensify and accelerate the exchange

---

[186] Information taken from CNN. 11 September 2001: Chronology of terror http://edition.cnn.com/2001/US/09/11/chronology.attack/ <last visited 5 March 2009>.

[187] GA Res. 56/1 (12 September 2001) www.un.org/documents/ga/docs/56/agresolution.htm <last visited 20 December 2008>.

[188] S/RES/1368 Adopted by the Security Council at its 4370th meeting.

[189] Ibid. para 3.

[190] For legal implications of Security Council Resolutions passed under Chapter VII of the UN Charter see above chapter 3.

[191] Security Council SC/7158 (4385th Meeting) 28 September 2001. Security Council unanimously adopts wide-ranging Anti-Terrorism Resolution calls for Suppressing, Financing, Improving International Co-operation. Resolution 1373 (2001) Also created the Committee to Monitor Implementation.

of information regarding terrorist actions or movements; forged or falsified documents; traffic in arms and sensitive material; use of communications and technologies by terrorist groups; and the threat posed by the possession of weapons of mass destruction. In addition, States are required to exchange information and co-operate to prevent and suppress terrorist acts and to take action against the perpetrators of such acts. The Security Council in pursuance of Chapter VII of the UN Charter established the Counter-Terrorism Committee. All States were required to submit reports on the steps they had undertaken to implement the provisions of the Resolution to the Committee within 90 days of the Resolution being adopted (28 September 2001). The reporting procedure, as set out in this Resolution, have, on the whole, proved to be a success. Since 2005, the Counter-Terrorism Committee has also been conducting visits to States. Furthermore, the information emerging out of these reports submitted to the Committee has been particularly revealing in ascertaining State practices dealing with terrorism.[192] Subsequent resolutions of the Security Council have affirmed both the substantive principles as well as the implementation mechanism installed in Resolution 1373.[193] Thus the Counter-Terrorism Committee was consolidated through the establishment of the Executive Directorate in 2004, the Directorate consisting of various experts and administrative support staff.[194] The mandate of the Counter-Terrorism Committee Executive Directorate (CTED) has been extended by the Security Council until 31 December 2010. The Security Council has, through its Resolution 1540 (2004), established another committee assigned with the task of examining the implementation of Resolution 1540, which requires all States to establish domestic controls in order to prevent access by non-State actors to nuclear, chemical and biological weapons.[195] The Resolution also requires effective measures to be adopted for preventing proliferation of these materials. States were, under this Resolution, required to present a first report on the measures undertaken within six months of the adoption of Resolution 1540. Security Council Resolution 1810 of 25 April 2008 further extended the mandate of the 1540 Committee for a further three years until 25 April 2011.[196]

(i) The United Nations, international community and the aftermath of 9/11: international human rights versus international terrorism

One of the most complex problems since 11 September 2009 has been that of the attempts on the part of the international community to provide an adequate balance between prevention and punishment of terrorism on the one hand and protection of the rights of the suspected communities on the other. In highlighting this intricate relationship between the concerns of terrorism and protection of civil liberties, the United Nations Policy Working Group on the United Nations and Terrorism makes the following profound observations:

---

[192] See S/2008/379 Survey of the implementation of Security Council Resolution 1373(2001) Report of the Counter-Terrorism Committee. For a review of the work of the Committee (the Counter Terrorism Committee) see www.un.org/sc/ctc <last visited 7 November 2008>; see Shaw, above n.10, at pp. 1162–1163.
[193] See S/RES/1390 (2002) 16 January 2002; S/RES/1452 (2002) 20 December 2002.
[194] See S/RES/1535 (2004) Adopted by the Security Council at its 4936th meeting on 26 March 2004.
[195] See S/RES/1540 (2004) Adopted by the Security Council at its 4956th meeting on 28 April 2004.
[196] See S/RES/1810 (2004) Adopted by the Security Council at its 5877th meeting on 25 April 2008.

The protection and promotion of human rights under the rule of law is essential in the prevention of terrorism. First, terrorism often thrives in environments in which human rights are violated. Terrorists may exploit human rights violations to gain support for their cause. Second, it must be understood clearly that terrorism itself is a violation of human rights. Terrorist acts that take life violate the right to life set forth in article 6 of the International Covenant on Civil and Political Rights. Third, it must also be understood that international law requires observance of basic human rights standards in the struggle against terrorism. The struggle against international terrorism will be further enhanced if the most serious crimes committed by terrorists are tried before the International Criminal Court and prosecuted under its Statute (provided that the relevant national court cannot or will not prosecute). Since the Statute covers the category of crimes against humanity, which includes murder and extermination committed as part of a widespread or systematic attack on any civilian population, certain terrorist acts might therefore be tried under the Statute.[197]

In the aftermath of the terrorist acts on 11 September 2001, notwithstanding the substantial political pressure exerted by powerful members such as the United States and the United Kingdom, the United Nations made strenuous effort to uphold principles of human rights. Thus it is not surprising that within the United Nations bodies, restraint, caution and respect for fundamental human rights have been the key phrases when addressing the 'war on terror'. In his report of the work of the United Nations, the former Secretary General cautions that: 'While States must take measures to protect their citizens against terror, they must also recognize that security cannot be achieved at the expense of human rights. On the contrary, stronger protection of and respect for human rights, democracy and social justice are integral to the promotion of security.'[198] Soon after the terrorist atrocities of 9/11, it became obvious that the United States intended to use all means possible against individuals implicated in terrorism, including torture, cruel and inhuman and degrading punishments or treatment. In response to this the UN Committee Against Torture, in a Statement issued on 22 November 2001, reminded all States parties to the Convention against Torture of the non-derogable nature of the provisions contained in the Convention.[199] The Committee against Torture emphasised that regardless of the exceptional circumstances, no justification could be provided to permit the authorisation of torture, or cruel, inhuman or degrading treatment or punishment. Furthermore, it is prohibited to admit as evidence in a court of law, confessions obtained through torture, except as evidence against the torturer.[200] The Committee against Torture has been critical of the policies of many States, in particular the United States and the United Kingdom which have deviated from the aforementioned principles.[201] Similarly, the Committee on

[197] Report of the Policy Working Group on the United Nations and Terrorism A/57/273 (S/2002/875), para 26.
[198] Report of the Secretary-General on the work of the organisation A/57/1, 2002, para 148; Statement of CERD (8 March 2002) A/57/18 pp. 106–107, and the statement by CAT 22 November 2001 CAT/C/XXVII/Misc.7; Gearty, above n.1, at pp. 377–383.
[199] The statement by CAT 22 November 2001 CAT/C/XXVII/Misc.7.
[200] The statement by CAT 22 November 2001 CAT/C/XXVII/Misc.7.
[201] 'The Committee remains concerned at the absence of clear legal provisions ensuring that the Convention's prohibition against torture is not derogated from under any circumstances, in particular since 11 September 2001 (arts. 2, 11 and 12) para 19; the Committee, noting that detaining persons indefinitely without charge constitutes per se a violation of the Convention, is concerned that detainees are held for protracted periods at

the Elimination of All Forms of Racial Discrimination has reiterated that racial non-discrimination constitutes a non-derogable norm of international law and that 'measures to combat terrorism must be in accordance with the Charter of the United Nations and that they are only legitimate if they respect the fundamental principles and the universally recognized standards of international law, in particular, international human rights law and international humanitarian law'.[202] The Special Rapporteur on Contemporary Forms of Racism, Racial Discrimination, Xenophobia and Related Intolerance also expressed considerable anguish that followers of the Muslim faith and their religious observance in many parts of the world were erroneously identified with terrorism.[203]

Notwithstanding their politicised nature, the United Nations organs have consistently urged member States to uphold fundamental human rights even when facing the threat of terrorism. The United Nations Security Council Resolution 1456, adopted on 20 January 2003, emphasises that:

> States must ensure that any measure taken to combat terrorism comply with all their obligations under international law, and should adopt such measures in accordance with international law, in particular international human rights, refugee, and humanitarian law.[204]

Guantánamo Bay, without sufficient legal safeguards and without judicial assessment of the justification for their detention (arts. 2, 3 and 16) (para 22); the Committee is concerned that in 2002 the State party authorised the use of certain interrogation techniques that have resulted in the death of some detainees during interrogation. The Committee also regrets that "confusing interrogation rules" and techniques defined in vague and general terms, such as 'stress positions', have led to serious abuses of detainees (arts. 11, 1, 2 and 16) (para 24); the Committee is concerned by reliable reports of acts of torture or cruel, inhuman and degrading treatment or punishment committed by certain members of the State party's military or civilian personnel in Afghanistan and Iraq. It is also concerned that the investigation and prosecution of many of these cases, including some resulting in the death of detainees, have led to lenient sentences, including of an administrative nature or less than one year's imprisonment (art. 12) (para 26).' See Committee against Torture, *Conclusions and Recommendations of the Committee against Torture*, Thirty-sixth session 1–19 May 2006 CAT/C/USA/CO/2 25 July 2006. Committee Against Torture, *Conclusions and Recommendations: United Kingdom of Great Britain and Northern Ireland* 10/12/2004 CAT/C/CR/33/3 (Concluding Observations/Comments) whereby the Committee expressed its concern *inter alia* at 'article 15 of the Convention prohibits the use of evidence gained by torture wherever and by whomever obtained; notwithstanding the State party's assurance set out in paragraph 3(g), *supra*, the State party's law has been interpreted to exclude the use of evidence extracted by torture only where the State party's officials were complicit' para 4(a)(1). Also see Committee Against Torture, Convention Against Torture and Other Cruel, Inhuman or Degrading Treatment or Punishment, General Comment No. 2 Implementation of Article 2 by States Parties CAT/C/GC/2 24 January 2008, paras 5 and 6.

[202] Statement of CERD (8 March 2002) A/57/18. Report of the Committee on Racial Discrimination, GAOR, Fifty-Seventh Session Supplement No. 18, pp. 106–107. In its Concluding observations of the Committee on the Elimination of Racial Discrimination: United States of America CERD/C/USA/CO/6 whereby the Committee draws the attention of the United States administration 'to its general recommendation No. 30 (2004) on discrimination against non-citizens, according to which measures taken in the fight against terrorism must not discriminate, in purpose or effect the grounds of race, colour, descent, or national or ethnic origin, and urges the State party, in accordance with article 2 paragraph 1(c), of the Convention, to put an end to the National Entry and Exit Registration System (NEERS) and to eliminate other forms of racial profiling against Arabs, Muslims and South Asians', para 14. Also see Concluding observations of the Committee on the Elimination of Racial Discrimination: United Kingdom of Great Britain and Northern Ireland. 10/12/2003 CERD/C/63/CO/11. (Concluding Observations/Comments), para 17.

[203] See E/CN.4/2006/17, paras 2 and 23.

[204] UN Doc. S/RES/1456(2003), para 6.

This position was again stressed in Resolution 1624 which established a new mandate for the Counter-Terrorism Committee.[205] Security Council Resolution 1822 and General Assembly Resolution 62/272 established the implementation of the Global Strategy which also refers to the responsibility of both States and the United Nations to comply with international law, including international human rights law, refugee law and international humanitarian law.

In view of the growing threat to human rights from States operating under the veneer of the 'War on Terror' the United Nations Human Rights Commission on 21 April 2005 also established a Special Rapporteur on the Promotion and Protection of Human Rights and Fundamental Freedoms While Countering Terrorism.[206] Having been assumed by the newly formed Human Rights Council, the mandate of the Special Rapporteur has recently been extended in 2007 for a further three years.[207]

The mandate of the UN Special Rapporteur on the Promotion and Protection of Human Rights and Fundamental Freedoms while Countering Terrorism highlights the importance of the protection of human rights at all times by Member States. During his work, the Special Rapporteur, Martin Scheinin has visited Guantánamo Bay in order to observe Military Commission hearings. He concluded that:

> the visit confirmed my misgivings concerning the operation of the Military Commissions and I find it highly unlikely that they would be able to provide a trial that meet the standards of international human rights law concerning the right to a fair trial.[208]

Other missions carried out by the Special Rapporteur, include to Turkey, South Africa and Israel.[209] During his work, the Rapporteur has placed particular emphasis on the right to a fair trial in terrorism cases;[210] and the impact of economic, social and cultural rights when fighting terrorism, and the impact of counter-terrorism measures on the enjoyment of these rights.[211]

While huge human rights violations are still committed in the name of counter-terrorism measures, this has gradually become less acceptable especially from the perspective of the international community. The increasing number of measures taken by the United Nations and the emphasis placed on human rights while combating terrorism is encouraging and it is clear that there is a growing consensus regarding this. At this stage, however, it is unclear

[205] UN Doc. S/RES/1624(2005), para 4. The Security Council '[s]tresses that States must ensure that any measures taken to implement paragraphs 1, 2 and 3 of this resolution comply with *all* of their obligations under international law, *in particular international human rights law*, refugee law, and humanitarian law' (emphasis added).

[206] Human Rights Commission, Protection of Human Rights and Fundamental Freedoms while Countering Terrorism, Human Rights Resolution 2005/80 (adopted without a vote, 21 April 2005) http://ap.ohchr.org/documents/E/CHR/resolutions/E-CN_4-RES-2005-80.doc <last visited 28 March 2009>.

[207] Human Rights Council Resolution 6/28 www2.ohchr.org/english/issues/terrorism/rapporteur/srchr.htm <last visited 28 March 2009>.

[208] Special Rapporteur on the Promotion and Protection of Human Rights and Fundamental Freedoms while Countering Terrorism, Statement by Professor Martin Scheinin to the Counter-Terrorism Committee of the Security Council, 20 October 2008, New York, p. 3.

[209] For further information see www2.ohchr.org/English/issues/terrorism/rapporteur/visits/htm <last visited 9 March 2009>.

[210] UN Doc. A/63/223 Report of the Special Rapporteur on the promotion and protection of human rights and fundamental freedoms while countering terrorism (6 August 2008).

[211] UN Doc. A/HRC/6/17 Report of the Special Rapporteur on the promotion and protection of human rights and fundamental freedoms while countering terrorism (21 November 2007).

whether this approach will have any affect on those currently held in Guantánamo Bay and other detention facilities, who are being denied their basic human rights.

(ii) The 'War on Terror' and the repercussions for international human rights law

The position adopted by the international community as a whole needs to be contrasted with the stance which the United States took in response to the terrorist atrocities of 11 September 2001. Such an approach was manifest in the Presidential address of George W. Bush to a Joint Session of Congress and the American People, where he defined the scope of the 'War on Terror':

> Our war on terror begins with al Qaeda, but it does not end there. It will not end until every terrorist group of global reach has been found, stopped and defeated. . . . This war will not be like the war against Iraq a decade ago, with a decisive liberation of territory and a swift conclusion. It will not look like the air war above Kosovo two years ago, where no ground troops were used and not a single American was lost in combat. Our response involves far more than instant retaliation and isolated strikes. Americans should not expect one battle, but a lengthy campaign, unlike any other we have ever seen. It may include dramatic strikes, visible on TV, and covert operations, secret even in success. We will starve terrorists of funding, turn them one against another, drive them from place to place, until there is no refuge or no rest. And we will pursue nations that provide aid or safe haven to terrorism. Every nation, in every region, now has a decision to make. Either you are with us, or you are with the terrorists.[212]

The United States, United Kingdom and their partners proceeded with the bombings of Afghanistan on 7 October 2001, less than four weeks after the 11 September atrocities. The aerial campaign was justified under international law, and specifically through the UN Charter and customary international law based on the right of self-defence.[213] In reality, however, without authorisation from the Security Council, the veneer of legitimacy through reliance upon a right to self-defence remains 'highly problematic'.[214] An assertion

[212] 'Address to a Joint Session of Congress and the American People'. Speech delivered by George W. Bush to the United States Congress, 20 September 2001. Transcript by White House Office of the Press Secretary www.whitehouse.gov/news/releases/2001/09/20010920-8.html <last visited 15 March 2009>.

[213] See Article 51 UN Charter, signed 26 June 1945, 59 Stat. 1031, T.S. No. 993, 3 Bevans 1153 (entered into force 24 October 1945); Byers, above n.1, at p. 405.

[214] Paust, 'Use of Armed Force against Terrorists in Afghanistan, Iraq, and Beyond', 35 *Cornell International Law Journal* (2002) 533, at p. 557. Military force was deployed despite the attempted mediation of individual Islamic states and the OIC to obtain the custody of Osama Bin Laden from the Taliban. See An-Nai'm, 'Upholding International Legality Against Islamic and American Jihad' in Booth and Dunne, *Worlds in Collision: Terror and the Future of Global Order* (Palgrave MacMillan, 2002) p. 162 at p. 169. Even in the presence of overwhelming and unequivocal evidence against Al-Qaida, there would still remain the issue of the imputablity of terrorist acts upon the Afghan state and the Taliban government. Substantial doubts have been raised as regards the role of Afghanistan and the Taliban in authorising the terrorist acts of 11 September 2001; it appears to be the established legal position that in the absence of firm evidence against the Taliban for aiding and supporting the attacks on the United States, the bombing of Afghanistan was unlawful under general international law. On this particular issue, the International Bar Association's task force observe that '[a] strict interpretation of the UN Charter suggests that whilst it might be permissible for a state to take defensive action against groups mounting ongoing attacks, taking military action against another state which is not directly participating in attacks perpetuated by terrorist based within its borders would be impermissible.' Report by the International Bar Association's Task Force on International Terrorism, above n.44.

that the use of force had been sanctioned by the Security Council in order to preserve the individual and collective right to self-defence of the United States and its allies against Afghanistan appears flawed for a number of reasons: these include, firstly, a failure of any mention of this right in the *operative* parts (as opposed to the preambles) of the two relevant Security Council Resolutions; secondly, the deliberate avoidance of any reference to an armed attack by the Security Council which triggers this right in international law; thirdly, the absence of attribution by the Security Council of the 11 September attacks to either the Taliban or, indeed, Afghanistan; fourthly, that the claim of the use of force in self-defence ceased once in accordance with Article 51 'the Security Council [had] taken the measures necessary to maintain international peace and security'; and fifthly, a failure on the part of the United States and the United Kingdom to establish that the bombing campaign was a genuine act of self-defence as opposed to acts of reprisal.[215] Even if the exercise of the right of self-defence could be justified in principle, the disproportionate nature of the continuous and unrelenting bombing rendered the action unlawful under international law.[216]

The allied aerial campaign which was accompanied by evidence of the indiscriminate bombardment and civilian casualties, presented an unfortunate development for residents of Afghanistan and the Tribal belt bordering Pakistan and Afghanistan.[217] The United Kingdom took the lead in bombing Afghanistan and was involved in missile attacks from the very inception of the campaign on 7 October.[218] An unrelenting military campaign with an open-ended agenda on the amorphous though lethal War on Terrorism devastated the families and surroundings of many of the local communities. As the 'War on Terror' gained momentum, religious communities were targeted not only in Afghanistan, but also in other countries such as Pakistan, Saudi Arabia, the United Kingdom and the United States. While the scale of the United States led policies of kidnapping, detentions, torture and renditions is yet to become fully apparent,[219] the abuse of the principles of international humanitarian law was evident with the commencement of the bombardment of Afghanistan in October 2001.

---

[215] For a substantiation of these arguments see Stahn, The Attack on the World Trade Center: Legal Responses' Security Council Resolutions 1368 and 1373 (2001): What They Say and What They Do Not Say, EJIL, Discussion Forum, available at www.ejil.org/forum_WTC/ny-stahn.pdf; Myjer and White, 'The Twin Towers Attack: An Unlimited Right to Self-Defense?', 7 *Journal of Conflict and Security Law* (2002) 5; Kirgis, *Addendum: Security Council Adopts Resolution on Combating International Terrorism*, ASIL Insights (1 October 2001), available at www.asil.org/insights/insigh77.htm#addendum7; Charney, 'The Use of Force against Terrorism and International Law', 95 *AJIL* (2001) 835; Quigley, 'The Afghanistan War and Self-Defense', 37 *Valparaiso Univ. L.Rev* (2002–2003) 541. Many Western academics, while attempting to justify use of force on the basis of 'self-defense' fail to appropriately addressed these issues. Byers, above n.1, at p. 409, legitimises the 'armed attack' argument against Taliban on the basis of the Taliban 'apparently endorsing the terrorist attacks'. Gray adopts an even broader approach that '[i]t seems that the massive State support for the legality of the US claim of self-defence could constitute instant customary international law and an authoritative re-interpretation of the UN Charter, however radical the alteration from many States' prior conception of the right to self-defense.' Gray, *The Use of Force and International Legal Order*, in Evans (ed.), *International Law* (Oxford University Press, 2006) p. 602.
[216] Quigley, supra n.215, at p. 551; Bassiouni, 'Legal Control of International Terrorism: A Policy-Oriented Assessment' 43 *Harvard Int. L.J.* (2002) 83, at p. 87.
[217] See Frank and Rehman, 'Assessing the Legality of the Attacks by the International Coalition against Terrorism (I.C.A.T) against Al-Qaeda and Taliban in Afghanistan: An Inquiry into the Self-Defense Argument under Article 51 of the United Nations Charter' 67 *Journal of Criminal Law* (2003) 415; Herold, *Counting the Dead: Attempts to Hide the Number of Afghan Civilians Killed by US Bombs are an Affront to Justice*, Guardian Unlimited, 8 August 2002, available at www.guardian.co.uk/afghanistan/comment/story/0,11447,770999,00.html <last visited 15 March 2009>.
[218] Gray, above n.215, at p. 602.
[219] See Rapporteur Dick Marty, Switzerland, AS/Jur (2006) 16 Part II (June 2006) available at http://assembly.coe.int/Main.asp?Link=/CommitteeDocs/2006/20060606_Ejdoc162006PartII-FINAL.htm <last visited 5 March 2009>; BBC News 'Inquiry Call Over Torture Claim' 4 August 2009.

A further, more disturbing element emerging from the 'War on Terror' was the decision of the United States to transfer captured individuals from Afghanistan to Camp X-ray (subsequently Camp Delta), a detention camp at the US naval base at Guantánamo Bay, Cuba.[220] Since January 2002, over 660 captives (including a number of British nationals or subjects) have been sent to this base.[221] *Incommunicado* detentions, torture and inhuman and degrading treatment have been visited upon these individuals. Captivity in conditions described by Amnesty International as 'falling below minimum standards for humane behaviour' has generated substantial criticism from international human rights agencies.[222] In February 2006, the United Nations, through its Special Rapporteur on Torture, Professor Manfred Nowak, heavily criticised the activities in the camp and called for its immediate closure.[223]

Amidst the labyrinth of legal challenges within the United States, the US Supreme Court has accorded the Guantánamo Bay detainees jurisdiction to challenge the legality of their detentions[224] and has provided US citizens captured in Afghanistan the right to challenge the status of their detention.[225] The most devastating blow to the United States government came during the Supreme Court decision of *Hamdan* v. *Rumsfeld*.[226] In a judgment delivered on 29 June 2006, the Court declared the Military Commissions established to try the Guantánamo Bay detainees as illegal. In elaborating upon its decision, a 5–3 majority of the Court took the view that the Federal government lacked the authority to set up the Special Military Commissions; the constitutional and procedural basis of the commission was rendered illegal under US military law (the Uniform Code of Military Justice) and was in contravention of United Nations Geneva Conventions on the Laws of War.[227] More recently the US Supreme Court, on 12 June 2008, held the Military Commissions Act to be unconstitutional due to the denial of prisoners' right to *habeas corpus*, by a majority of 5–4.[228] Through the detentions at Guantánamo and elsewhere, the United States, in collusion with other partners in the 'War on Terror', has shown disdain not only of accepted norms of international human rights law and international humanitarian laws but also of the religious values of Muslims.[229] Examples of such humiliating exercises include in the apparent desecration of the *Qur'an*, forcing Muslim detainees to shave-off their beards and perform sexual activities contrary to their religious beliefs.[230] The former Law Lord, Lord

---

[220] Katselli and Shah, 'September 11 and the UK Response' 52 *ICLQ* (2003) 245 at p. 250.

[221] Steyn, 'Guantanamo Bay: The Legal Black Hole' 53 *ICLQ* (2004) 1 at p. 7.

[222] Cited in Thomas, 'September 11th and Good Governance' 53 *Northern Ireland Legal Q.* (2002) 366 at p. 379.

[223] See United Nations, *Situation of Detainees at Guantánamo Bay* UN Doc. E/CN.4/2006/120 (15 February 2006) http://news.bbc.co.uk/1/shared/bsp/hi/pdfs/16_02_06_un_guantanamo.pdf <last visited 5 March 2009>.

[224] *Rasul* v. *Bush* 124 S. Ct 2686 (2004) No. 03-334, argued 20 April 2004, decided 28 June 2004. Judgment available at http://caselaw.lp.findlaw.com/scripts/getcase.pl?court=US&vol=000&invol=03-334 <last visited 5 March 2009>.

[225] *Hamdi* v. *Rumsfeld* 124 U.S. 2633 (2004) No. 03-6696, argued 28 April 2004, decided 28 June 2004, Judgment available at www.jenner.com/files/tbl_s69NewsDocumentOrder/FileUpload500/379/03-6696_decision_hamdi.pdf <last visited 5 March 2009>.

[226] *Hamdan* v. *Rumsfeld, Secretary of Defense* et al. 548 U.S. (2006) No. 05-184, argued 28 March 2006, decided 29 June 2006, available at www.supremecourtus.gov/opinions/05pdf/05-184.pdf <last visited 5 March 2009>.

[227] See the majority opinion of J. Stevens, ibid. at 49–72.

[228] *Boumediene* et al. v. *Bush, President of the United States*, et al., 533 U.S. (2008) No. 06-1195, argued 5 December 2007, decided 12 June 2008. See the majority opinion of Justice Kennedy.

[229] Katselli and Shah, above n.220, at p. 250.

[230] *Newsweek* Magazine had initially reported news of the desecration of the Holy Book (9 May 2005). Subsequently there were attempts to retract from this report. The damage to Muslim–West relations was nevertheless visible in international rioting and violence (resulting in at least 15 deaths in Afghanistan and other countries) see *Newsweek Backs off Quran Desecration Story*, CNN.COM, 15 May 2005, available at http://edition.cnn.com/2005/WORLD/asiapcf/05/15/newsweek.quran/ <last visited 5 March 2009>.

Steyn in describing the practices at the detention centre 'as a monstrous failure of justice'[231] and warned that 'the type of justice meted out at Guantánamo Bay is likely to make martyrs of the prisoners in the moderate Muslim world with whom the West must work to ensure world peace and stability.'[232] Most governments have failed to publicly criticise the Guantánamo detentions and violations of international humanitarian law. Nor was there been any tangible evidence that the world community is exerting any influence on the United States for the release of the British Muslim residents at the detention facility. British detainees were eventually released, although no liability has been accepted by either the British or the United States government for torture, humiliation and inhuman and degrading treatment suffered by these men and their families.[233] The former detained men and human rights organisations regard the Guantánamo captivities as evidence of the United States and United Kingdom pursuing an Islamophobic agenda.[234]

The fusion of the 'War on Terror' with the threat to international peace and security allowed the United States to prepare a case for invading Iraq in March 2003.[235] It was alleged that the threat from Iraq's weapons of mass destruction was so substantial and real that the international community had to take immediate military action. According to the US administration there was unequivocal evidence that the Iraqi President Saddam Hussein had an arsenal of weapons of mass destruction, which he intended to use against his neighbours and other States. The Bush administration consistently made cross-references to terrorist threats from Al-Qaeda, the threat from Saddam's weaponry and the inherent right to use force as provided by Article 51 of the United Nations Charter.[236] The build-up to the invasion of Iraq also saw a human rights argument advanced by the United States and the United Kingdom. President Saddam Hussein's dictatorial regime and Iraq's repression of its ethnic and religious communities were put forward as additional grounds for justifying invasion and the removal of the regime. This argument was fallacious since for years Saddam Hussein conducted such action with the knowledge and support of the United States.[237] Furthermore, the promotion and projection of human rights has only been a factor when its suits the political ambitions of powerful States; the worst violators of human rights in the region of Iraq continue to be the closest allies and friends of the

---

[231] Johan Steyn, *In the Dock of Guantánamo Bay, 27th F.A. Mann Lecture*, Times, 30 November 2003. Available at www.cageprisoners.com/print.php?id=173.

[232] Steyn, above n.221 at p. 14.

[233] See Branigan, 'I am Just Amazed: He is Finally Coming Home', *Guardian* 20 February 2004; on the futility of legal challenges see *R. (on the Application of Feroz Ali Abbasi and another) v. Secretary of State for Foreign and Commonwealth Office and Secretary of State for Home Department* [2002] EWCA Civ 1316.

[234] See Begg, 'Is Torture Ever Justified': in Graham Turnbull Essay Competition (2006) at p. 13; Press Release, Islamic Human Rights Commission, 'Failure to Repatriate Britons Masks Islamophobic Policy' (11 August 2003).

[235] See McGoldrick, *From '9-11' to the 'Iraq War 2003': International Law in an Age of Complexity* (Hart, 2004) at pp. 11–20.

[236] *Plans For Iraq Attack Began On 9/11*, CBS NEWS, Washington, 4 September 2002, available at www.cbsnews.com/stories/2002/09/04/september11/main520830.shtml <last visited 17 February 2009>; Clarke, *Against All Enemies: Inside America's War on Terror* (Free Press, 2004); Corn, *The Lies of George W. Bush: Mastering the Politics of Deception* (Crown Publishers, 2003); Prados, *Hoodwinked: The Documents that Reveal How Bush Sold Us a War* (The New Press, 2004); Rampton and Stauber, *Weapons of Mass Deception: The Uses of Propaganda in Bush's War on Iraq* (Robinson Publishing, 2003); Franck, 'What Happens Now? The United Nations after Iraq' 97 AJIL (2003) 607.

[237] See Mahajan, *Full Spectrum Dominances: U.S. Power in Iraq and Beyond* (Seven Stories Press, 2003); Zunes, *Tinderbox: U.S. Middle East Policy and the Roots of Terrorism* (Common Courage Press, 2003).

United States.[238] Indeed, this so-called 'War on Terror' has provided an excuse to dictatorial and autocratic regimes all over the world to repress, torture and violate fundamental human rights – the international community is determined to remain tight-lipped so long as these regimes continue to purport allegiance to the ambitions of United States foreign policy.[239] Duplicity, double standards and selectivity have not only troubled the Muslim communities but also others who retain an objective vision of law and politics.[240]

The global opposition to war also included a campaign for the usage of all necessary measures to be taken under the auspices of the United Nations Security Council. Military action would only be permissible after all means of negotiations had been exhausted. In the absence of securing a United Nations Security Council Resolution authorising the use of force, it became almost impossible to construct a valid and rational legal argument to invade Iraq.[241] The United States was isolated in its claims of (pre-emptive) self-defence.[242] Furthermore, the United States and United Kingdom placed reliance upon a misleading and 'ultimately unsustainable'[243] interpretation of the previous United Nations Security Council Resolutions, 678, 687 and 1441 – an interpretation which provided legal cover for the use of force in invading Iraq.[244] It is difficult to find any persuasive legal basis to justify the invasion and occupation of Iraq; as Professor Vaughan Lowe has put it succinctly 'the invasion lacked any legal justification.'[245] Kofi Annan, the then United Nations Secretary-General, declared the intervention unlawful, with many senior international lawyers condemning this action as a substantial breach of law.[246] The role and position of the United

---

[238] Note the criticisms of violations of human rights conducted by the US Middle-Eastern allies such as Saudi Arabia and Kuwait. See Amnesty International Report, Saudi Arabia (2006), available at www.amnesty.org/report2006/sau-summary-eng; Amnesty International Report, Kuwait (2006), available at www.amnesty.org/report2006/kwt-summary-eng.

[239] See Gearty, 'Terrorism and Morality', 4 *EHRLR* (2003) 377 at p. 382; an Amnesty International Report reinforces this point when it notes: 'The impact of the so called "war on terror" [hereinafter "war on terror"] on human rights in the Gulf and the Arabian Peninsula has been profound and far reaching. Governments in the region and the US government have treated nationals and residents of the area with a disturbing disregard for the rule of law and fundamental human rights standards. The results have been mass arrests, prolonged detention without charge or trial, incommunicado detention, torture and ill treatment, strict secrecy surrounding the fate and whereabouts of some detainees, and apparent extra-judicial killings. These human rights violations have had profound effects not only on individual victims but also on their relatives and the general human rights situation in the region,' See Amnesty International, 'The Gulf and the Arabian Peninsula: Human Rights Fall Victim to the "War on Terror"' (22 June 2004) AI Index: MDE 04/002/2004, available at www.amnesty.org/library/Index/ENGMDE040022004?open&of=ENG-USA <last visited 17 February 2009>.

[240] See Brownlie, *Principles of Public International Law* (Oxford University Press, 2008) at p. 557.

[241] Franck, above n.236, at p. 611; Gray, above n.215, at p. 609.

[242] Wedgwood, 'The Fall of Saddam Hussein: Security Council Mandates and Preemptive Self-Defence' 97 *AJIL* (2003) 576; Gray, above n.215, at p. 609.

[243] Franck, above n.216, at p. 611 *cf.* McGoldrick, above n.235, at p. 66, who regards 'the legal argument based on SC resolutions [as] admittedly sophisticated, but . . . legally tenable and defensible'.

[244] Myjer and White, 'The Use of Force Against Iraq', 8 *Journal of Conflict and Security Law* (2003) 1; Lowe, 'The Iraq Crisis: What Now' 52 *ICLQ* (2003) 859; Gray, above n.215, at pp. 609–10; Franck, above n.236; Ratner, The United Nations Charter and the Use of Force Against Iraq (2002) available at www.lcnp.org/global/Iraqstatemt.3.pdf <last visited 5 November 2008>.

[245] Lowe, above n.244, at p. 866.

[246] The verdict of Kofi Annan, the former United Nations Secretary-General represents the position insofar as the United Nations and the Charter is concerned. He notes 'I have indicated it [i.e. the invasion of Iraq] was not in conformity with the UN charter, from the charter point of view, it was illegal'. *Iraq War Illegal, Says Annan: The United Nations Secretary-General Kofi Annan has told the BBC the US-led invasion of Iraq was an illegal act that contravened the UN Charter*, BBC News UK edn., 16 September 2004, available at http://news.bbc.co.uk/1/hi/world/middle_east/3661134.stm <last visited 17 Febrarury 2009>. According to the former Chief UN Weapons Inspector in Iraq, Hans Blix, by withholding an authorisation desired if not formally requested, the Council disassociated the UN from an armed action that most Member States thought was not justified. Blix,

Kingdom in its capacity as the leading ally of the United States has come under heavy criticism. In the words of Lord Steyn, in order to present justifications for the invasion of Iraq, the British government was 'scraping the bottom of the legal barrel'.[247] Furthermore, there is a considerable body of international lawyers and legal practitioners who take the position that not only was the invasion of Iraq and occupation unlawful but it also constitutes a war crime. According to Ronald Kramer and Raymond Michalowski 'existing international law alone establishes the United States and the United Kingdom as guilty of state crimes linked to the invasion and occupation of Iraq.'[248]

The failure to recover weapons of mass destruction and the continuing violations of human rights in Iraq has generated a huge global backlash.[249] In the build-up to the invasion of Iraq, the US and the UK governments not only exaggerated the threat from Saddam Hussein's regime, they also avoided a proper debate on the future of Iraq post-Saddam Hussein. The US-led invasion has resulted in enormous suffering for the Iraqi people – human rights communities have felt aggrieved at the violations committed by US and UK officers in detention centres such as Abu Ghraib and others in Southern Iraq. In their capacities as the occupation powers, the United States and the United Kingdom have been responsible for substantial violations of human rights law, humanitarian law and environmental damage.[250] Domestically, the United States and its allies in the 'War on Terror' have introduced several pieces of draconian legislation and administrative practices, which have led to orders of indefinite detention, internment without trial and detention orders that have allowed various exercises of so-called 'extraordinary rendition' and the admissibility of evidence obtained through torture.

The British response to the events of 9/11 was to further consolidate its laws through the adoption of the Anti-Terrorism, Crime and Security Act 2001 (ATCSA).[251] The 2001 Act, as a substantial piece of legislation, authorised considerable draconian measures, including incarceration and detentions without trial. Amongst the most contentious aspects of the legislation was its Part IV entitled Immigration and Asylum: Suspected International Terrorists, which authorised the Home Secretary to issue a certificate against any non-UK national if it was his reasonable belief that the individual's presence in the United Kingdom was a threat to national security and that this individual was a suspected terrorist. The certificate by the Home Secretary authorised the continued detention of the individuals concerned who could not be deported because such deportations would expose them to treatment contrary to Article 3 of the European Convention on Human Rights (ECHR). The legislation presented substantial difficulties in the light of existing international and

---

Disarming Iraq (Bloomsbury, 2004); Normand *et al.*, *Tearing Up the Rules; The Illegality of Invading Iraq* (2003) www.embargos.de/irak/irakkrieg2/vr/tearing_up_the_rules_cesr.htm <last visited 21 May 2009>.

[247] Gibb, 'Law Lord Damn's "Half-Baked Reforms and Ill-legal Iraq War"', *The Times*, 19 October 2005, available at www.timesonline.co.uk/article/0,,2-1832270,00.html <last visited 5 November 2008>.

[248] Kramer and Michalowski, 'War, Aggression and State Crime' 45 *British Journal of Criminology* (2005) 446 at p. 448.

[249] The Iraq invasion also proved embarrassing and in some cases disastrous. There were tragic consequences for several hundred families of servicemen and servicewomen who have been killed in the battlefield. There were also tragic consequences for the families of David Kelly and Ken Bigly. Antony Barnett, *David Kelly Death–Paramedics Query Verdict*, Centre for Research on Globalisation (12 December 2004), available at http://globalresearch.ca/articles/BAR412A.html <last visited 17 February 2009>.

[250] See Buncombe, 'U.S. Admits it Used Napalm Bombs in Iraq', The *Independent*, 10 August 2003; Ridha, Presentation on the Use of Incendiary Weapons, *World Tribunal on Iraq*, New York, 8 May 2004.

[251] Anti-Terrorism, Crime and Security Act, Ch. 24 (2001), available at www.legislation.gov.uk/acts/acts2001/20010024.htm <last visited 17 February 2009>.

European human rights jurisprudence. The ECHR (most provisions of which were incorporated through the Human Rights Act 1998) allows States parties to deport foreigners when their presence presents risks to national security. However, as indicated above, Article 3 provisions have been accorded extra-jurisdictional scope by the European Court of Human Rights. Thus, under the *Soering*[252] principle, extradition of an individual from States parties to ECHR, to another State, remains impermissible where there is a real prospect of the individual concerned being subjected to torture, inhuman and degrading treatment, or punishment. In the *Chahal* case,[253] the European Court of Human Rights had gone further and decided that since the right of individuals not to be tortured was absolute, it could not be trumped by considerations of national security. This principle has recently been reaffirmed by the European Court of Human Rights in *Saadi* v. *Italy*.[254]

In the post-11 September environment, the British government claimed that allowing dangerous individuals suspected of international terrorism to remain at large in the United Kingdom was no longer acceptable. The government therefore felt it necessary to make derogations to Article 5(1) of the ECHR and Article 9 of the ICCPR:[255] provisions that accord individuals the right to liberty and prohibit detentions without trial.[256] The government established a Human Rights Act (Designated Derogation Order 2001) in order to derogate from Article 5(1) of the ECHR.[257] It was extraordinary that the United Kingdom was the only Member State of the Council of Europe to have entered such a derogation provision as a consequence of the events of 11 September 2001. In the first of the high-profile cases decided by the House of Lords on 16 December 2004, in an unprecedented sitting of nine judges, the Appellate Committee of the House of Lords declared Section 23 – the offending provision in Part IV of the 2001 Act – incompatible with ECHR.[258]

While a majority of their Lordships were inclined to favour the government's position that there was a public emergency threatening the life of the nation, thereby validating the derogation under Article 15 of ECHR, they were not prepared (as a matter of judicial deference) to accept that the detention provisions contained in the 2001 Act were necessary, proportionate and rational, or, as stated in the terms of Article 15, 'strictly required by the exigencies of the situation'. The House of Lords resoundingly declared the detentions as disproportionate and unnecessary and therefore incompatible with the grounds as provided in Article 15 of ECHR.[259] Their Lordships also found violations of the Convention rights of the principle of non-discrimination on the basis of nationality, when read in

---

[252] *Soering* v. *UK* (1989) 11 E.H.R.R. 439.

[253] *Chahal* v. *UK* (1997) 23 E.H.R.R. 413.

[254] The case of *Saadi* v. *Italy* (Application No. 37201/06) 28 February 2008, paras 122, 123.

[255] See Dickson, 'Law Versus Terrorism: Can Law Win?' 9 *EHRLR* (2005) 11; Justice, Response to the Joint Committee on Human Rights: Inquiry into UK Derogations from Convention Rights (May 2002), available at www.justice.org.uk/images/pdfs/derogations.pdf <last visited 17 February 2009>.

[256] See Michaelsen, 'Derogating from International Human Rights Obligations in the War Against Terrorism?: A British–Australian Perspective' 17 *Terrorism and Political Violence* (2005) 131.

[257] Human Rights Act 1998 (Designated Derogation), Order 2001 (SI 2001/3644), (11 November 2001), available at www.opsi.gov.uk/si/si2001/20013644.htm

[258] See *A. and others* v. *Secretary of State for the Home Department* [2004] UKHL 56, at para 155 (2004). For commentaries on the case see Dickson, above n.254, 11; Walker, 'Prisoners of "War all the Time"' *EHRLR* (2005) 50; Shah, 'The UK's Anti-Terror Legislation and the House of Lords: The First Skirmish', 5 *HRLR* (2005) 403; Arden, 'Human Rights in the Age of Terrorism', 121 *LQR* (2005) 604; Elliott, 'United Kingdom: Detention without Trial and the "War on Terror"' 4 *IJCL* (2006) 553.

[259] [2004] UKHL 56, above n.179, paras 33–43 (Lord Bingham), para 76 (Lord Nicholls), paras 127–32 (Lord Hope), para 140 (Lord Scott), para 189 (Lord Roger), para 228–31 (Baroness Hale), para 240 (Lord Carswell), paras 209–18 (Lord Walker).

conjunction with Article 5.[260] Another historical judgment delivered by the House of Lords established the absolute impermissibility of the utilisation of evidence in the United Kingdom obtained through torture, albeit obtained in foreign jurisdictions and by foreign agents.[261] In this case the Law Lords, while undermining the government's position on intelligence gathering in the War on Terror, brought English law in line with international human rights law.

In the more recent case of *R. (Al Skeini and others)* v. *Secretary of State for Defence*,[262] the House of Lords considered its competence to examine cases of human rights violations committed by British troops abroad. Five of the six cases concerned the shooting of Iraqi civilians by British soldiers in their homes or on the street, whereas the sixth – Baha Mousa – concerned the death in custody of an Iraqi civilian, again at the hands of British soldiers, allegedly as a result of torture. The families of the victims wished an independent inquiry into the killings to take place. The main issue that has been raised by these cases is whether the British courts have jurisdiction to hear the cases as the human rights violations occurred outside the territory of the United Kingdom, in addition to whether the Human Rights Act has extra-territorial effect.[263] The House of Lords in *Al Skeini* held that the Human Rights Act, in principle, applies to British Forces serving abroad.[264] However, it could only establish jurisdiction in cases concerning detention centres and, therefore, only Baha Mousa's case could be dealt with by the British courts.[265] In respect of the other five cases, the House of Lords left it to the European Court of Human Rights to clarify the law regarding jurisdiction after its earlier *Banković* decision.[266]

6 CONCLUSIONS

11 September 2001 has gone down as one of the most tragic days in the history of mankind. The hijacking of American Airline aircraft, their crash into the World Trade Center and the collapse of the Twin Towers continues to haunt not only the survivors of the tragedy but all those who believe in the inherent dignity and worth of mankind. The terrorist attacks of 11 September led the way for the bombing and devastation of Afghanistan. The continuing attack on Afghanistan has led to the unfortunate deaths of thousands of Afghani men, women and children. 11 September terrorist attacks were, unfortunately and highly mistakenly, used as a platform for the invasion of Iraq in 2003. Although these events represent a tragedy of the enormous magnitude, they also provide a number of lessons. Firstly, they reconfirm the view that international terrorism is a crime against humanity, and that the international community of States should treat it as such. In this context it is

---

[260] Ibid. paras 234–239 (Baroness Hale), paras 45–70 (Lord Bingham), paras 76–84 (Lord Nicholls), para 138 (Lord Hope), paras 158–159 (Lord Scott), para 189 (Lord Roger) para 240 (Lord Carswell), *cf.* Lord Walker (209–218).

[261] *A and others* v. *Secretary of State for the Home Department (No. 2)* [2005] UKHL 71, [2006] AC 221.

[262] [2007] UKHL 26.

[263] [2007] UKHL 26, paras 3–5.

[264] [2007] UKHL 26, paras 58–59.

[265] [2007] UKHL 26, para 61.

[266] [2007] UKHL 26, paras 66–69. *Banković* v. *Belgium*, Application No. 52207/99 (Decision of 12 December 2001), where the European Court held the case, against NATO states, inadmissible as it could not establish a jurisdictional link between the victims of a NATO bombing in Belgrade and the respondent States.

interesting to note that during the drafting stages of the Statute of the International Criminal Court, attempts were made to provide the new court with a specific jurisdiction to try terrorist offences.[267] However, such efforts proved unsuccessful because of the opposition of many countries, including the United States. In hindsight such an approach can only be regarded as unfortunate. Despite the absence of a specific incorporation of the crime of terrorism, there is sufficient breadth in the definition of crimes against humanity to try crimes of terrorism. An international criminal court should provide a useful, impartial and internationally acceptable forum for trials of individuals indicted with the crime of international terrorism. Secondly, the events of 11 September reinforce the need for an internationally binding agreement which condemns terrorism and provides for severe penalties for those involved in committing this crime. This chapter has considered the enormous ideological and political differences in defining and conceptualising international terrorism. At the same time, a great measure of consensus exists on the absolute criminalisation of certain forms of activities, such as the hostage taking of civilians and internationally protected persons, as well as the banning of aerial and maritime terrorism. This chapter has established that notwithstanding considerable threat from international terrorism, the United Nations and the international community has made efforts to uphold human rights values, including affording protection to those who are suspected of having been engaged in terrorist offences. Initiatives such as the establishment of the Special Rapporteur on the Promotion of Human Rights and Fundamental Freedoms while Countering Terrorism, and an insistence on the Prohibition of Torture and arbitrary detentions, confirm this approach. The foreign and domestic legislative policies of the United States, the United Kingdom and many other allied States in this tumultuous phase of the 'War on Terror' have proved disappointing. The substantial assaults on international human rights law and international humanitarian law during the 'War on Terror' needs to provide a sobering reflection. At the writing of this book in the early part of 2009, it is yet unclear as to whether the 'war-on-terrorism' has officially been brought to an end by the incoming administration of President Barak Obama. There is some cause for optimism in that President Obama has expressed enthusiasm and a compelling desire towards ensuring US compliance with established norms of international human rights and international humanitarian law.

---

[267] For further consider of the Statute of the International Criminal Court see above chapter 20.

Appendix: Studying and research in the international law of human rights

Internet sources (as at May 2009)

International organisations and related human rights

The United Nations
www.un.org/en/

United Nations Human Rights Council
www2.ohchr.org/english/bodies/hrcouncil/

United Nations Treaty Bodies
www.unhchr.ch/tbs/doc.nsf

United Nations Special Procedures
www2.ohchr.org/english/bodies/chr/
special/index.htm

United Nations Security Council
www.un.org/Docs/sc/

United Nations Economic and Social
Council
www.un.org/ecosoc/

International Labour Organization (ILO),
Geneva, Switzerland
www.ilo.org/global/lang–en/index.htm

World Health Organization
www.who.int/en/

UN Children's fund (UNICEF)
www.unicef.org/

UN Environment Programme (UNEP)
www.unep.org/

Office of the High Commissioner for
Human Rights
www.ohchr.org/EN/Pages/
WelcomePage.aspx

United Nations Commission for the Status
of Women
www.un.org/womenwatch/daw/csw/

UN High Commissioner for Refugees,
Geneva, Switzerland
www.unhcr.ch/

UN Development Programme
www.undp.org/

UN Division for the Advanced for Women
www.un.org/womenwatch/daw/index.html

Regional human rights

Council of Europe
www.coe.int/

European Union
http://europa.eu/

Organization for Security and
Co-operation in Europe
www.osce.org/

NATO
www.nato.int/cps/en/natolive/indcx.htm

European Committee for the Prevention of
Torture
www.cpt.coe.int/en/

European Centre for Minority Issues
www.ecmi.de/

African Union
www.africa-union.org/

Decisions of African Commission
www1.umn.edu/humanrts/africa/
comcases/allcases.html

African Commission on Human and
Peoples' Rights
www.achpr.org/

Organization of American States
www.oas.org/

Inter-American Commission on Human Rights
www.cidh.oas.org/DefaultE.htm

Association of Southeast Asian Nations
www.aseansec.org/

League of Arab States
www.arableagueonline.org/las/index.jsp

Organisation of the Islamic Conference
www.oic-oci.org/

South Asian Association for Regional Cooperation
www.saarc-sec.org/

International and regional courts

International Court of Justice, the Hague, the Netherlands
www.icj-cij.org/

European Court of Human Rights
www.echr.coe.int/echr/

European Court of Justice
http://curia.europa.eu/jcms/jcms/Jo1_6308/ecran-d-accueil

Inter-American Court of Human Rights
www.corteidh.or.cr/index.cfm?CFID=689975&CFTOKEN=56819828

African Court of Justice
www.africa-union.org/root/au/organs/Court_of_Justice_en.htm

International Criminal Tribunal for the Former Yugoslavia
www.icty.org/

International Criminal Tribunal for Rwanda
www.ictr.org/

Non-governmental organisations

Save the Children
www.savethechildren.org/

Amnesty International
www.amnesty.org/

Human Rights Watch
www.hrw.org/

International Committee of the Red Cross
www.icrc.org/

Index on Censorship
www.indexonline.org/

Human Rights Internet
www.hri.ca/

Minority Rights Group, International
www.minorityrights.org/

World Organisation against Torture
www.omct.org/

Educational and research websites in international human rights law

UN University, Tokyo, Japan (UNU)
www.unu.edu/

Human and Constitutional Rights
www.hrcr.org/

University of Minnesota, Human Rights Library
www1.umn.edu/humanrts/

University of Essex, Library
http://libwww.essex.ac.uk/Human_Rights/treaties.htm

US Department of State
www.state.gov/

The United Nations Human Rights Treaties
www.bayefsky.com/

International Human Rights Lexicon
www.internationalhumanrightslexicon.org/

Netherlands Institute of Human Rights
http://sim.law.uu.nl/SIM/Dochome.nsf?Open

The Avalon Project
http://avalon.law.yale.edu/default.asp

Universal Human Rights Index of United Nations Documents
www.universalhumanrightsindex.org/

Index